The SAP Fiori Handbook

A Step-By-Step Guide to SAP Fiori Essentials

Manpreet S. Brara
Subba Rao M. V. Parvathaneni

Apress®

The SAP Fiori Handbook: A Step-By-Step Guide to SAP Fiori Essentials

Manpreet S. Brara
Northville, MI, USA

Subba Rao M. V. Parvathaneni
Naperville, IL, USA

ISBN-13 (pbk): 979-8-8688-1611-6
https://doi.org/10.1007/979-8-8688-1612-3

ISBN-13 (electronic): 979-8-8688-1612-3

Copyright © 2025 by Manpreet S. Brara, Subba Rao M. V. Parvathaneni

This work is subject to copyright. All rights are reserved by the Publisher, whether the whole or part of the material is concerned, specifically the rights of translation, reprinting, reuse of illustrations, recitation, broadcasting, reproduction on microfilms or in any other physical way, and transmission or information storage and retrieval, electronic adaptation, computer software, or by similar or dissimilar methodology now known or hereafter developed.

Trademarked names, logos, and images may appear in this book. Rather than use a trademark symbol with every occurrence of a trademarked name, logo, or image we use the names, logos, and images only in an editorial fashion and to the benefit of the trademark owner, with no intention of infringement of the trademark.

The use in this publication of trade names, trademarks, service marks, and similar terms, even if they are not identified as such, is not to be taken as an expression of opinion as to whether or not they are subject to proprietary rights.

While the advice and information in this book are believed to be true and accurate at the date of publication, neither the authors nor the editors nor the publisher can accept any legal responsibility for any errors or omissions that may be made. The publisher makes no warranty, express or implied, with respect to the material contained herein.

Managing Director, Apress Media LLC: Welmoed Spahr
Acquisitions Editors: James Robinson-Prior and Divya Modi
Editorial Assistant: Jacob Shmulewitz

Cover designed by eStudioCalamar

Cover image designed by Freepik (www.freepik.com)

Distributed to the book trade worldwide by Springer Science+Business Media New York, 1 New York Plaza, New York, NY 10004. Phone 1-800-SPRINGER, fax (201) 348-4505, e-mail orders-ny@springer-sbm.com, or visit www.springeronline.com. Apress Media, LLC is a Delaware LLC and the sole member (owner) is Springer Science + Business Media Finance Inc (SSBM Finance Inc). SSBM Finance Inc is a **Delaware** corporation.

For information on translations, please e-mail booktranslations@springernature.com; for reprint, paperback, or audio rights, please e-mail bookpermissions@springernature.com.

Apress titles may be purchased in bulk for academic, corporate, or promotional use. eBook versions and licenses are also available for most titles. For more information, reference our Print and eBook Bulk Sales web page at http://www.apress.com/bulk-sales.

Any source code or other supplementary material referenced by the author in this book is available to readers on GitHub. For more detailed information, please visit https://www.apress.com/gp/services/source-code.

If disposing of this product, please recycle the paper

I dedicate this book to all the Sikh Gurus for inspiring my zeal and guidance. I also dedicate this book to my late father, Lt. Colonel Darshan S. Brara (Retd), a remarkable man who always encouraged me to work hard to succeed, and my late mother, Mrs. Darshan K. Brara, who pushed me to pursue higher studies and whose support helped me reach where I am today. I would also like to thank my wife, Harveen Kaur, who reviewed many of my manuscripts. Besides this, I would also like to thank many of my relatives and friends who encouraged me to write this book.

—*Manpreet S. Brara*

I dedicate this book to my mother, Smt. Parvathaneni RajyaLaxmi, and to my late father, Sri Parvathaneni Satya Narayana, who was always there for me, supporting me, keeping me grounded, and encouraging me to stay connected to my roots. I would also like to express my heartfelt gratitude to my wife, Latha, and my son, Samanyu, for their patience and support, even during the countless hours, family commitments, and weekends that were taken away from them while I devoted my time working on this book. I would like to express my heartfelt gratitude to my sister Jyoti and my brother-in-law Dharma Dumpala (DD). They played a crucial role in helping me enter the SAP field and provided unwavering support during my most challenging times as I worked to establish my career.

—*Subba Rao M. V. Parvathaneni*

Table of Contents

About the Authors xxiii

About the Technical Reviewer xxv

Acknowledgments xxvii

Introduction xxix

Chapter 1: Introduction to SAP Fiori 1

    1.1 Introduction 1

        1.1.1 SAP Fiori Design Principle 2

        1.1.2 Additional SAP Fiori Features 4

        1.1.3 Deployment Option for SAP S/4HANA 7

        1.1.4 Deployment Options with SAP Business Suite 8

        1.1.5 Main Features of S/4HANA 8

        1.1.6 SAP Fiori Apps Reference Library 10

        1.1.7 SAP Fiori App Recommendations 11

        1.1.8 SAP Readiness Check 2.0 11

        1.1.9 SAP Fiori Lighthouse Scenarios 11

        1.1.10 Prerequisites for Setting Up Fiori 11

        1.1.11 RFC and Trusted RFC 13

        1.1.12 SAP Fiori Launchpad 14

        1.1.13 Personalization 16

        1.1.14 SAP Fiori Clients 18

        1.1.15 SAP Fiori App Types: Overview 19

        1.1.16 More Examples of SAP Fiori Apps 22

    1.2 SAP Fiori Various Objects Definition 22

        1.2.1 Fiori Catalogs 22

        1.2.2 Technical Catalog (TC) 23

TABLE OF CONTENTS

    1.2.3 Business Catalog (BC) 23

    1.2.4 Fiori Catalog Groups (BCG) 23

    1.2.5 Fiori Spaces (SP) 24

    1.2.6 Fiori Pages (PG) 24

    1.2.7 SAP Fiori Business Roles (BR) 24

    1.2.8 Fiori Tiles and Target Mapping 25

    1.2.9 SAP Fiori Tiles (T) 25

    1.2.10 SAP Target Mapping (TM) 26

    1.2.11 SAP Fiori OData Service 26

    1.2.12 SAP Fiori SICF Service 26

1.3 Summary 26

1.4 References 27

Chapter 2: SAP Fiori Apps Reference Library 29

2.1 Introduction 29

    2.1.1 Concept and Library Details 30

    2.1.2 Accessing the Fiori Apps Reference Library 32

    2.1.3 How to Use the Fiori Apps Reference Library 32

    2.1.4 Fiori Library Exploration 33

    2.1.5 Basic Information Related to the App 37

    2.1.6 Verifying App Details in the System 43

    2.1.7 SAP Object Symbols 44

    2.1.8 Other Features of the Fiori Library 44

    2.1.9 Download the Entire Fiori Library 51

2.2 SAP Tools Within the Library 59

    2.2.1 Get SAP Fiori App Recommendations 59

    2.2.2 Run SAP Fiori Upgrade Impact Analysis 60

2.3 Summary 60

Chapter 3: SAP Fiori Apps Recommendation Report 61

3.1 Introduction 61

3.2 App Recommendations Report Process 63

    3.2.1 Explore 63

3.2.2 Plan 64

3.2.3 Set Up and Configure 64

3.2.4 Operate and Update 65

3.3 Prerequisites 65

3.4 Preparing Data and System Files 66

3.4.1 Usage Profile 66

3.4.2 Front-End and Back-End System Profiles 81

3.4.3 Native HANA DB System Profile 85

3.5 Log Into the Fiori Reference Library 86

3.5.1 Step 1: Select the Type of Analysis 87

3.5.2 Step 2: Upload the Usage Profile 89

3.5.3 Step 3: Update System Profiles 94

3.5.4 Step 4: Defining Analysis 101

3.5.5 Step 5: Results and Analysis 104

3.6 Different Types of Views (Detail and List Views) 106

3.7 System Readiness Status 108

3.8 Relevance Score 109

3.8.1 Relevance Score: Level 3 Rating 109

3.8.2 Relevance Score: Level 2 Rating 110

3.8.3 Relevance Score: Level 1 Rating 110

3.9 Working with the Analysis Results 111

3.10 Summary 118

Chapter 4: SAP Fiori Implementation and Deployment 119

4.1 Introduction 119

4.2 Greenfield Implementation 119

4.2.1 Approach 120

4.2.2 Key Characteristics 120

4.2.3 When to Consider Greenfield 120

4.2.4 Steps Involved in Greenfield Implementation 121

4.2.5 Benefits of Greenfield Implementation 122

4.2.6 Challenges of Greenfield Implementation 122

TABLE OF CONTENTS

- 4.2.7 Additional Considerations 122
- 4.2.8 Conclusion 123
- 4.2.9 Summary 123
- 4.3 Brownfield Implementation 123
  - 4.3.1 Approach 123
  - 4.3.2 Key Characteristics 124
  - 4.3.3 When to Consider Brownfield 124
  - 4.3.4 Steps Involved in a Brownfield Implementation 124
  - 4.3.5 Benefits of Brownfield Implementation 125
  - 4.3.6 Challenges of Brownfield Implementation 126
  - 4.3.7 Additional Considerations 126
  - 4.3.8 Conclusion 126
  - 4.3.9 Summary 127
- 4.4 Bluefield Implementation 127
  - 4.4.1 What Is Bluefield Implementation? 127
  - 4.4.2 Key Characteristics 128
  - 4.4.3 When to Consider Bluefield 128
  - 4.4.4 Steps Involved 128
  - 4.4.5 Benefits of Bluefield Implementation 129
  - 4.4.6 Challenges of Bluefield Implementation 130
  - 4.4.7 Additional Considerations 130
  - 4.4.8 Conclusion 130
  - 4.4.9 Summary 131
- 4.5 Implementation Pros and Cons 131
- 4.6 SAP Fiori Deployment Architecture 132
- 4.7 Embedded Deployment 132
  - 4.7.1 Other Features of an Embedded System 134
  - 4.7.2 Components Required for Embedded Deployment 135
  - 4.7.3 Schematic of an Embedded System 135
  - 4.7.4 Pros and Cons of Embedded Deployments 136

TABLE OF CONTENTS

4.8 Central Hub Deployment 137
    4.8.1 Advantages of Central Hub Deployment of SAP Gateway 138
    4.8.2 Components Required for Central Hub Deployment 139
    4.8.3 Schematic of a Central Hub Deployment 140
    4.8.4 Pros and Cons of Central Hub Deployments 140

4.9 Summary of Deployment Options 142
    4.9.1 Embedded Deployment 142
    4.9.2 Central Hub Deployment 142

4.10 SAP NetWeaver Gateway: Overview and Deployment 142
    4.10.1 Key Features 143

4.11 Deployment Options of SAP Gateway 144
    4.11.1 Embedded Deployment 144
    4.11.2 Central Hub Deployment 145

4.12 Activate SAP Gateway 146
    4.12.1 Task List 146
    4.12.2 Transaction Code: SPRO 147
    4.12.3 Transaction Code: /IWFND/IWF_ACTIVATE 149
    4.12.4 Summary 150

4.13 Central Hub Deployment 150
    4.13.1 Advantages 151
    4.13.2 Disadvantages 151
    4.13.3 Deployment Pros and Cons 152
    4.13.4 Deployment Options: S/4HANA Schematic 153
    4.13.5 Conclusion 153

4.14 System Alias 154
    4.14.1 System Alias 154
    4.14.2 System Alias in Embedded Deployment 154
    4.14.3 System Alias in Central Hub Deployment 154

4.15 Configuration Steps for Embedded Deployment 155

4.16 System Alias in Central Hub Deployment 156
    4.16.1 Configuration Steps for Central Hub Deployment 156

ix

TABLE OF CONTENTS

- 4.16.2 Best Practices for System Alias Configuration 157
- 4.16.3 Transaction Codes for Creating a System Alias 158
- 4.16.4 Tables Available to View for System Aliases 159
- 4.16.5 Conclusion 163
- 4.17 Summary 163

Chapter 5: SAP Fiori Configuration 165

- 5.1 Introduction 165
  - 5.1.1 Prerequisites 166
- 5.2 Rapid Activation Task Lists for Embedded Deployment 168
- 5.3 Execute Task Lists Manually 168
  - 5.3.1 Prerequisites for Manual Configuration 169
  - 5.3.2 Fiori Deployments 170
  - 5.3.3 List of Task Lists to Be Configured 172
  - 5.3.4 Terminologies Used Within the Task Lists 173
  - 5.3.5 Overview of Steps for Executing Task Lists 174
- 5.4 Task List 1: SAP_GW_FIORI_ERP_ONE_CLNT_SETUP 176
  - 5.4.1 Introduction 176
  - 5.4.2 Steps to Execute the Task List 178
  - 5.4.3 Executing the Task List 187
  - 5.4.4 Task List Verification 191
  - 5.4.5 Summary 194
- 5.5 Task List 2: SAP_ESH_INITIAL_SETUP_WRK_CLIENT 195
  - 5.5.1 Introduction 195
  - 5.5.2 Steps to Activate the Task List 196
  - 5.5.3 Final Status of the Task List with Subtasks Configured 204
  - 5.5.4 Execute the Job in Background Mode 205
  - 5.5.5 Background Job Completed 207
  - 5.5.6 Consistency Check 208
  - 5.5.7 Summary 209
- 5.6 Task List 3: /UIF/SCHEDULE_LREP_JOB 209
  - 5.6.1 Introduction 209

5.6.2 Steps to Activate the Task List	210
5.6.3 Executed Task List	211
5.6.4 Summary	213
5.7 Task List 4: SAP_FIORI_FOUNDATION_S4	**213**
5.7.1 Introduction	213
5.7.2 Steps to Activate the Task List	215
5.7.3 Completed Task and Subtask List	228
5.7.4 Execute the Task List in Background Mode	229
5.7.5 Background Job Completed	233
5.7.6 Review Task List Activation Status	234
5.7.7 Validate Foundation Roles Created	235
5.7.8 Validate URL Working	237
5.7.9 Validate Spaces and Pages Activated	237
5.7.10 Validate App Support Activated	238
5.7.11 Summary	238
5.8 Task List 5: /UI2/FLP_HEALTH_CHECKS	**238**
5.8.1 Introduction	238
5.8.2 Steps to Activate the Task List	239
5.8.3 Review the Task and Subtask List	240
5.8.4 Execute the Task List in Foreground Mode	241
5.8.5 Summary	241
5.9 Task List 6: SAP_GATEWAY_ACTIVATE_ODATA_SERV	**242**
5.9.1 Introduction	242
5.9.2 Prerequisites	242
5.9.3 Execute the Task List	242
5.9.4 Summary	248
5.10 Task List 7: SAP_FIORI_CONTENT_ACTIVATION	**248**
5.10.1 Introduction	248
5.10.2 Prerequisite	250
5.10.3 Business Role	250
5.10.4 Review and Verify the Business Role Contents	253

TABLE OF CONTENTS

    5.10.5 Steps to Activate the Business Role via the Task List... 260

    5.10.6 Completed Task List... 266

    5.10.7 Execute the Task List in Foreground Mode... 267

    5.10.8 Verify the Business Role Generated... 269

    5.10.9 Validate Test User Details.. 272

    5.10.10 Verify Output in the Launchpad 272

    5.10.11 Additional Resources... 278

    5.10.12 Summary... 279

  5.11 Task List 8: SAP_FIORI_FCM_CONTENT_ACTIVATION 279

    5.11.1 Introduction.. 279

    5.11.2 Execute the Task List.. 281

    5.11.3 Validate the Role Created 287

    5.11.4 Generate the Role... 288

    5.11.5 Validate Test User Access 288

    5.11.6 Testing Access 289

    5.11.7 Summary.. 290

  5.12 Configuring the SAP Fiori Logon and Logoff Screens 291

    5.12.1 Configuring the Logoff Screen.. 292

    5.12.2 Summary.. 299

  5.13 Customizing the Logon Screen with a Company Logo... 300

    5.13.1 Introduction 300

    5.13.2 Setup Process... 301

  5.14 Summary... 306

Chapter 6: Introduction to Fiori Apps **307**

  6.1 Introduction.. 307

    6.1.1 Characteristics of SAP Fiori Apps 307

    6.1.2 The Architecture of Fiori Apps 308

    6.1.3 Implementing SAP Fiori Apps 308

  6.2 Fiori Apps 309

  6.3 SAP Transactional Apps... 309

    6.3.1 Main Features.. 310

TABLE OF CONTENTS

    6.3.2 Product Features 311

    6.3.3 Implementation Information 311

    6.3.4 Summary: Transactional Apps 319

  6.4 Analytical Apps 319

    6.4.1 Introduction 319

    6.4.2 Main Features 321

    6.4.3 Summary: Analytical Apps 322

  6.5 SAP Factsheet Apps 322

    6.5.1 Introduction 322

    6.5.2 Main Features 322

    6.5.3 Summary: Factsheet Apps 327

  6.6 SAP GUI Apps 328

    6.6.1 Introduction 328

    6.6.2 Main Features 328

    6.6.3 Summary: GUI Apps 330

  6.7 SAP Custom Apps 330

    6.7.1 Introduction 330

    6.7.2 Main Features 330

  6.8 Comparison of Various Apps 331

  6.9 Pros and Cons of SAP Fiori Apps 333

  6.10 Summary 333

Chapter 7: Introduction to SAP Fiori Catalogs 335

  7.1 Introduction 335

    7.1.1 SAP GUI 337

    7.1.2 SAP Fiori Launchpad 337

  7.2 Catalogs 339

  7.3 Technical Catalogs 339

  7.4 Business Catalogs 340

  7.5 Business Catalog Group 341

  7.6 Business Roles (SAP_BR*) 341

TABLE OF CONTENTS

7.7 SAP Fiori Objects Used in Catalogs 342
    7.7.1 Tile 342
    7.7.2 Target Mapping 342

7.8 Understanding Intents 345

7.9 SAP Best Practice Recommendations 346

7.10 Summary 346

Chapter 8: SAP Fiori Launchpad App Manager 347

8.1 Introduction 347
    8.1.1 Deep Copy 348
    8.1.2 Soft Copy 350

8.2 Technical Catalogs 352
    8.2.1 Prerequisite 352
    8.2.2 Transaction Code: MM_APP 352
    8.2.3 Transaction Code: /UI2/FLPAM 353
    8.2.4 Switch to Facet Filter 364
    8.2.5 Switch to Adaptation Mode 374

8.3 Create a Technical Catalog 375
    8.3.1 Technical Catalog Naming Convention 375
    8.3.2 Apps to Be Deployed Within a Technical Catalog 376
    8.3.3 Process of Creating a Technical Catalog 377

8.4 Update the Technical Catalog 390

8.5 Remove Apps from the Technical Catalog 393

8.6 Delete the Technical Catalog 395

8.7 Validate the Technical Catalog 398

8.8 Verification of the Technical Catalog in the Launchpad Content Manager 399

8.9 Summary 402

Chapter 9: SAP Fiori Launchpad Content Manager 403

9.1 Introduction 403
    9.1.1 Key Features 404

9.2 FLP Content Manager Details 405
    9.2.1 Catalogs 407

TABLE OF CONTENTS

- 9.2.2 Tiles/Target Mappings 410
- 9.2.3 Roles 412
- 9.2.4 Technical Catalog Reference Details and Copy 413
- 9.3 Creating a Custom Business Catalog 416
  - 9.3.1 Search Apps Based on a Technical Catalog 420
  - 9.3.2 Search Apps Based on an App/Tile 421
  - 9.3.3 Create a Business Role (PFCG) 426
- 9.4 Validation, Testing, and Verification 432
- 9.5 Updating a Custom Business Catalog 434
- 9.6 FLP Content Manager Other Functionality 443
  - 9.6.1 Catalogs Tab Options 443
  - 9.6.2 Tiles/Target Mappings Tab Options 453
  - 9.6.3 Roles Tab Options 454
- 9.7 Recommendation 455
  - 9.7.1 SAP-Delivered Catalogs 455
  - 9.7.2 Spaces and Pages 456
  - 9.7.3 Business Group 457
- 9.8 Summary 457

Chapter 10: Introduction to SAP Fiori Spaces and Pages 459

- 10.1 Introduction 459
  - 10.1.1 Challenges/Drawbacks with the Groups Concept 460
- 10.2 Definition of Spaces, Pages, Sections, and Tiles 462
  - 10.2.1 Spaces and Pages 462
  - 10.2.2 Sections 470
  - 10.2.3 Links 471
- 10.3 Schematic of Spaces and Pages 474
- 10.4 Prerequisites to Implement Spaces and Pages 475
  - 10.4.1 Mandatory OData Service Activation 475
- 10.5 Setup of the Spaces Setting in the User Menu 477
- 10.6 Creating New Roles 480
- 10.7 Business Objects to Be Created 480

xv

TABLE OF CONTENTS

10.8 Create Spaces and Pages 481
    10.8.1 Create a Space 482
    10.8.2 Create a Page 495
    10.8.3 Create Sections 505
    10.8.4 Testing and Validation 514
    10.8.5 Create an Additional Page 517
    10.8.6 Testing and Validation 525
10.9 Create a Space with a Page 525
    10.9.1 Create a New Space 526
    10.9.2 Create and Add Another Page 533
    10.9.3 List of Spaces and Pages Created 535
    10.9.4 Assign Test User ID to the Roles 537
    10.9.5 Testing and Validation 537
    10.9.6 Sorting Spaces Order 539
    10.9.7 Merge Spaces 544
10.10 Switching Between Spaces and Groups 546
10.11 My Home 550
    10.11.1 Home 551
    10.11.2 Pages 551
    10.11.3 Apps 555
    10.11.4 Insights 556
10.12 High-Level Steps: Create Spaces and Pages 556
10.13 Report /1BCDWB/DB/UI2/STPGA 561
10.14 Summary 561

Chapter 11: Converting SAP Fiori Groups to Pages 563

11.1 Introduction 563
    11.1.1 Background 564
    11.1.2 Prerequisite 567
    11.1.3 Process to Convert Existing Groups to Pages 567
    11.1.4 Launching the SAP Fiori Launchpad 568
    11.1.5 Create Launchpad Pages from Groups 568

11.1.6 Create a Space	576
11.1.7 Assign a Role to a Space	578
11.1.8 Create Sections	579
11.1.9 Validation of Group-to-Page Conversion	582
11.2 Summary	584

Chapter 12: Configure Custom SAP Fiori Apps 585

12.1 Introduction	585
12.2 Create a Custom App for Any SAP Transaction Using /UI2/FLPAM	586
12.2.1 Demo 1: Transaction SU53 – Convert to an App	587
12.2.2 Demo 2: Tile for a Custom Transaction Code	609
12.2.3 Demo 3: Dynamic Tile for a SAPUI5 App	613
12.3 Create a Custom App for Any SAP Transaction Using /UI2/FLPD_CUST	622
12.3.1 Demo 4: Custom Transaction ZPARAM_REP – Convert to an App	622
12.3.2 Demo 5: Custom App F0763A – Convert to a Dynamic App	639
12.4 Summary	649

Chapter 13: SAP Fiori App Support and Troubleshooting 651

13.1 Configuring App Support	652
13.1.1 Introduction	652
13.1.2 Prerequisites	655
13.1.3 Steps Required to Activate App Support Automatically	657
13.1.4 Steps Required to Activate App Support Manually	657
13.1.5 Create/Configure the Plugin in Customizing	665
13.1.6 Authorization Errors	671
13.1.7 Analyze the Authorization Error File	679
13.1.8 Transaction SU53	683
13.1.9 STAUTHTRACE	684
13.1.10 STUSERTRACE	687
13.2 Missing Target Mapping	690
13.3 Services Missing	692
13.4 Missing Business Catalog	695

13.5 Clearing Cache 696

13.6 Reference Lost 697

13.7 OData Services Are Not Active 697

13.8 500 Error: Request Failed 698

13.9 Summary 698

Chapter 14: SAP Fiori Upgrade Impact Analysis 699

14.1 Introduction 699

    14.1.1 Impact Analysis During Upgrade 699

    14.1.2 Key Features 700

    14.1.3 Benefits 701

    14.1.4 How to Use the Tool 701

14.2 Prerequisite 702

    14.2.1 Prepare Your System 702

    14.2.2 Run the Impact Analysis Tool 702

    14.2.3 Analyze Results 702

    14.2.4 Review Recommendations 703

    14.2.5 Plan the Upgrade 703

    14.2.6 Execute and Monitor 703

    14.2.7 Document and Communicate 703

    14.2.8 Outcome 703

    14.2.9 Check and Verify 704

14.3 Upgrade Process Steps 704

    14.3.1 Preparation 704

    14.3.2 Configure the Tool 704

    14.3.3 Run the Impact Analysis 704

    14.3.4 Analyze and Plan Remediation 705

    14.3.5 Execute the Upgrade 705

    14.3.6 Post-upgrade Testing 705

    14.3.7 Documentation and Communication 705

14.4 Execute the Upgrade Process 705

    14.4.1 Generate an Input Data File 706

14.4.2 Run the Impact Analysis Tool 707
14.4.3 Results 710
14.4.4 Analyze Results 711
14.5 Summary 716
14.6 References 716

Chapter 15: SAP Fiori Adapt UI 717

15.1 Introduction 717
15.1.1 Main Features 718
15.1.2 UI Adaptation Features 718
15.1.3 Advantages of App Variants 719
15.1.4 Steps to Create an App Variant 719
15.1.5 Use Adapt UI 720
15.2 Set Up Adapt UI 721
15.2.1 Creation of an App Variant Using Adapt UI 723
15.2.2 Create a New Business Catalog 749
15.2.3 Create a Business Role and Assign the Catalog 750
15.2.4 Testing and Validation 751
15.2.5 Transport 752
15.2.6 Conclusion 752
15.3 Summary 752

Chapter 16: SAP Fiori Reports 753

16.1 Introduction 753
16.2 Transaction: /UI2/FLPCA 754
16.2.1 Introduction 754
16.2.2 Prerequisite 755
16.2.3 Using Transaction /UI2/FLPCA 755
16.2.4 Execute the Transaction 757
16.2.5 Summary 776
16.3 Transaction Code: /UI2/RSP_LIST 776
16.3.1 Introduction 776
16.3.2 Main Features and Use 776

16.3.3 Demo Examples 777

16.3.4 Summary 778

16.4 Transaction: /UI2/FLIA 778

    16.4.1 Introduction 778

    16.4.2 Main Features and Use 778

    16.4.3 Demo Examples 779

    16.4.4 Summary 784

16.5 Transaction: /UI2/FLT 785

    16.5.1 Introduction 785

    16.5.2 Main Features and Use 785

    16.5.3 Demo Examples 786

    16.5.4 Summary 791

16.6 Transaction: /UI2/FLC 791

    16.6.1 Introduction 791

    16.6.2 Main Features and Use 792

    16.6.3 Demo Examples 793

    16.6.4 Summary 796

16.7 Transaction: /UI2/CUST 796

    16.7.1 Introduction 796

    16.7.2 Main Features and Use 797

    16.7.3 Demo Examples 798

    16.7.4 Summary 798

16.8 Transaction: SUIM 798

    16.8.1 Introduction 798

    16.8.2 Main Features and Use 799

    16.8.3 Demo Examples 800

    16.8.4 Search for Single Roles with Authorization Data 802

    16.8.5 Search for Applications in Role Menu 807

    16.8.6 Search for Startable Application in Roles 815

    16.8.7 Summary 817

TABLE OF CONTENTS

16.9 Report /UI2/FLP_ADMIN_UI ... 818
- 16.9.1 Introduction ... 818
- 16.9.2 Main Features and Use ... 818
- 16.9.3 Demo Examples ... 818

16.10 Report RSUSR_START_APPL ... 820
- 16.10.1 Main Features and Use ... 821
- 16.10.2 Demo Examples ... 821
- 16.10.3 Summary ... 824

16.11 Table USOBHASH ... 825
- 16.11.1 Introduction ... 825
- 16.11.2 Demo Examples ... 825
- 16.11.3 Summary ... 828

16.12 Finding OData Services from Hash Keys in a Role ... 828
- 16.12.1 Main Features and Use ... 829
- 16.12.2 Demo Examples ... 829
- 16.12.3 Summary ... 832

16.13 Report /1BCDWB/DB/UI2/STPGAC ... 832
- 16.13.1 Introduction ... 832
- 16.13.2 Main Features and Use ... 833
- 16.13.3 Demo Examples ... 833
- 16.13.4 Summary ... 834

Index ... 835

About the Authors

Manpreet S. Brara has a BS in Aerospace Engineering from India and an MS in Mechanical Engineering from the United States. He has more than 45 years of experience in both fields and has been an IT professional for the last 25 years, working as a systems analyst, programmer, developer, and SAP security consultant.

He is a highly accomplished senior solution architect specializing in SAP security. With extensive global experience in designing and implementing robust SAP security solutions, he has established a proven track record of delivering effective security strategies tailored to complex environments. He has worked across various industries, including energy, aerospace, automotive, appliances, retail, life sciences, manufacturing, and mining. His expertise encompasses different areas of SAP security, including ECC, S/4HANA, Fiori, and GRC (Governance, Risk, and Compliance), with a particular focus on access control and process control. Additionally, he has authored several blogs on Fiori security.

In addition to his technical skills, he is adept at developing comprehensive security frameworks that ensure seamless integration and compliance across various systems. He excels in creating detailed documentation and delivering engaging training sessions, which empower support teams to perform at their best. His commitment to excellence and continual improvement has equipped organizations to navigate the challenges of SAP security effectively.

ABOUT THE AUTHORS

Subba Rao M. V. Parvathaneni is an IT professional with more than 33 years of experience. He has worked in various IT-related areas, including systems programming, training, and teaching.

Subba Rao began his SAP career in 1998 and has extensive expertise in architecting and implementing SAP application security across various solutions, including ECC, BI, BOBJ, CRM, S/4HANA, Fiori, Native HANA DB security, SAP BTP, IAG, upgrades, and automation. He has worked on projects and implementations in a diverse range of industries, such as airlines and aerospace defense, pharmaceuticals, insurance, industrial distribution, consumer packaging, the public sector, defense, telecommunications, manufacturing, logistics, and shipping.

Subba Rao is a content creator on YouTube, where he runs his own popular channel: https://www.youtube.com/@s3s. On this channel, he creates and shares content focused on SAP security. Additionally, he has written blogs covering topics related to SAP GRC and HANA DB security.

Subba Rao has also published courses on SAP HANA DB security and SAP Fiori on the Udemy platform, contributing to the broader learning community. From 1999 to 2009, Subba Rao hosted a highly popular website where he shared various documents and learning materials that he created.

About the Technical Reviewer

With over two decades in the field, **Bhaskar Kommareddy** is a seasoned senior technical architect specializing in SAP solutions for public and private sector organizations. He is recognized for his expert knowledge of ABAP, SAP HANA, OData, SAP Fiori, SAP Mobile technologies, and SAP BTP. In his consulting capacity, Bhaskar has architected impactful solutions for numerous client implementations.

Acknowledgments

We would like to extend our heartfelt thanks to Divya Modi for her belief in the concept of this book and for her invaluable guidance and advice throughout the writing process. Her insights and suggestions played a crucial role in our decision-making regarding the topics to be included.

We would like to express our gratitude to Bhaskar Kommareddy for agreeing to assist with the technical review of this book. He identified some technical inaccuracies and helped us correct them. Additionally, he provided valuable suggestions that enhanced the content of the book.

We would like to sincerely thank SSA Imran Shahid for providing us with system access throughout the entire book-writing process. His outstanding support in promptly troubleshooting and resolving system issues was invaluable in helping us complete the book on time.

We would like to express our sincere gratitude to Deepa Shirley Tryphosa Chellappa, James Robinson-Prior, and the entire editorial and publishing team at Apress. We appreciate their trust in our book concept and for giving us the opportunity to write it.

Introduction

The SAP Fiori Handbook: A Step-By-Step Guide to SAP Fiori Essentials is a comprehensive guide that simplifies SAP Fiori concepts in an easy-to-understand manner. This book is a valuable resource for both beginners entering the SAP Fiori space and experienced professionals looking to enhance their skillset.

The main purpose of this book is to be a comprehensive guide to SAP Fiori. It aims to provide an accessible and engaging resource for our readers. The book is designed to simplify complex concepts, making them easy for any reader to understand and apply, whether they are learning about Fiori for the first time or experienced users looking to enhance their skills. It will provide detailed, step-by-step instructions to facilitate learning and mastery of Fiori. The book will be a valuable reference guide for users involved in the implementation, configuration, and administrative support of SAP Fiori.

The book provides an overview of Fiori fundamentals and guides readers through configuring Fiori, managing technical and business catalogs, and implementing Fiori apps. It also covers troubleshooting methods, including the App Support tool, and offers insights into the SAP Fiori library and recommendation reports. By the end of the book, readers will be equipped to configure and manage content in the SAP Fiori Launchpad (FLP), understand various Fiori concepts, and learn how to implement spaces and pages and convert existing groups to pages.

Each chapter has been customized to provide a concise theory and a detailed, step-by-step process. The flow of the chapters is structured in a manner that will make it easy to understand and systematically learn SAP Fiori.

How to Read This Book

The book is based on S/4HANA 2023 FPS02 and is organized into four main sections, with each chapter offering a brief theory overview and a step-by-step explanation of the concepts. This structure promotes a clear and systematic understanding of SAP Fiori.

The first section contains three chapters that explain the basics of SAP Fiori, discussing essential topics such as the SAP Fiori Apps Reference Library and the SAP Fiori App Recommendations Report.

Introduction

The second section explains how to configure the SAP Fiori environment. It contains two chapters detailing the SAP Fiori deployment options and providing task lists for its configuration.

After you learn to configure the SAP Fiori environment, the next two chapters in the third section will cover topics such as SAP Fiori apps and catalogs.

The first three sections lay the essential groundwork for implementing SAP Fiori apps. In the fourth section, the book offers a systematic, step-by-step explanation of the technical aspects involved in their implementation. This includes topics such as creating and managing technical catalogs, business catalogs, spaces, and pages, as well as troubleshooting, analyzing the impact of SAP Fiori upgrades, and converting SAP Fiori groups into pages.

Additionally, the Appendix section covers topics such as the SAP Fiori Launchpad Designer for creating and managing catalogs and groups.

Organization of This Book

This book is structured to serve the various individuals who work on SAP Fiori Launchpad content development. Each chapter illustrates a specific area of knowledge and builds on the skills gained in previous sections. The chapters are as follows:

Chapter 1: Introduction to SAP Fiori
The book starts with an introduction to SAP Fiori, its architecture, various elements, and terminologies in Chapter 1. Readers will get an overview of SAP Fiori and its components.

Chapter 2: SAP Fiori Apps Reference Library
After introducing SAP Fiori to readers, in Chapter 2, the book discusses the SAP Fiori Apps Reference Library, one of the key areas that the readers and Fiori users need to have a clear understanding and knowledge of. Various types of Fiori apps are also introduced in this chapter.

Chapter 3: SAP Fiori Apps Recommendation Report
Discussion on the SAP Fiori Apps Reference Library is followed by a detailed explanation of the SAP Fiori Apps Recommendation Report, an indispensable tool that is available in the SAP Fiori Apps Reference Library, in Chapter 3. This report is an extremely

useful tool that could be used as a baseline by customers seeking to migrate from SAP ECC to SAP S/4HANA or incorporate SAP Fiori into Greenfield projects. This report offers precise recommendations on SAP Fiori apps tailored to the customer's SAP configuration and setup.

Chapter 4: SAP Fiori Deployment Methodology
In Chapter 4, readers will learn about SAP Fiori deployment options such as embedded and central hub. We will also discuss the pros and cons of both options.

Chapter 5: SAP Fiori Configuration
After all the necessary background on SAP Fiori is discussed, in Chapter 5, users will learn how to configure the SAP Fiori environment. The chapter discusses in detail all the task lists and their underlying steps that need to be executed to configure SAP Fiori for the embedded deployment scenario. Task lists required for central hub deployment options are covered in brief.

Chapter 6: Introduction to SAP Fiori Apps
After configuring SAP Fiori, the system is now ready to implement various SAP Fiori apps. Chapter 6 will introduce different SAP Fiori apps available for implementation and how to deploy them.

Chapter 7: Introduction to SAP Fiori Catalogs
Catalogs are repositories of SAP Fiori apps and are used to deploy them. Catalogs are one of the two types of containers that contain SAP Fiori apps. In Chapter 7, we discuss the concepts of technical catalogs and business catalogs and how and when they are used.

Chapter 8: SAP Fiori Launchpad App Manager
In Chapter 8, readers will learn how to create and manage technical catalogs using the SAP Fiori Launchpad App Manager. The chapter goes through the steps for creating the catalog and how to add tiles for Fiori apps in it.

Chapter 9: SAP Fiori Launchpad Content Manager
After technical catalogs, we will learn about business catalogs. These are the catalogs that are assigned to users. Business catalogs are created and managed by using the SAP Fiori Launchpad Content Manager. Chapter 9 covers all the steps in detail.

INTRODUCTION

Chapter 10: SAP Fiori Spaces and Pages
After the SAP Fiori apps are added to the catalogs, the next step is to assign them to the users so that they can access them in their Fiori Launchpad. With S/4HANA 2020, SAP introduced a concept called spaces and pages. In Chapter 10, readers will learn how to configure and implement spaces and pages in detail.

Chapter 11: Converting SAP Fiori Groups to Pages
Before S/4HANA 2020, Fiori apps were accessed in the Fiori Launchpad using the concept of groups. With S/4HANA 2020, SAP introduced spaces and pages as a new way of presenting apps in the Fiori Launchpad. It also announced that groups will be deprecated soon. For customers who had already implemented SAP Fiori and were using groups, with S/4HANA 2021, SAP introduced a functionality to convert groups into pages. In Chapter 11, we will tackle and go through the steps to convert groups into pages.

Chapter 12: Configure a Custom SAP Fiori App
In the SAP Fiori Apps Reference Library, we may not have apps for all transaction codes (T-codes) or functionalities. In such situations, customers may create custom applications or transaction codes. Readers will learn how to create a custom Fiori app for Launchpad access in Chapter 12.

Chapter 13: SAP Fiori App Support and Troubleshooting
In Chapter 13, we will delve into a key aspect of SAP Fiori, focusing on different tools and techniques for troubleshooting SAP Fiori-related issues, including a new App Support tool introduced by SAP with S/4HANA 2020. Readers will learn detailed steps on how to configure and use App Support, as well as other available troubleshooting tools.

Chapter 14: SAP Fiori Upgrade Impact Analysis
SAP releases a new version of S/4HANA every year with improved apps and discontinues some apps. To assist customers wanting to upgrade to the latest version of S/4HANA, SAP has provided an SAP Fiori Upgrade Impact Analysis report in the SAP Fiori Apps Reference Library. In Chapter 14, readers will learn how to generate and understand this report.

Chapter 15: SAP Fiori Adapt UI
Chapter 15 discusses the steps to customize the SAP Fiori Launchpad screen of an app, enabling the disabling or enhancement of features as needed using SAP Fiori Adapt UI functionality.

Chapter 16: SAP Fiori Reports

In Chapter 16, we explore various useful reports in SAP Fiori for generating different levels of information that can be used to analyze issues, roles, etc.

Appendixes

With every SAP S/4HANA release, SAP continues to enhance the user experience by simplifying the development of Launchpad content. However, even after upgrading to higher releases, customers still rely on older concepts such as groups.

In Appendix A, readers will learn how to register and activate OData (Open Data Protocol) services and SICF (Service Information and Configuration Framework) services required for the SAP Fiori apps to function.

In Appendix B, readers will find instructions on creating and managing catalogs and groups using the SAP Fiori Launchpad Designer.

Appendixes C and D will cover important transaction codes and background jobs related to SAP Fiori.

Appendixes E, F, G, and H will list the features and functionalities introduced in each S/4HANA release from 2020 onward.

Please find the Appendixes available on the book's GitHub repository: `https://github.com/Apress/The-SAP-Fiori-Handbook`.

CHAPTER 1

Introduction to SAP Fiori

This chapter gives a simple overview of SAP Fiori. It lists the main components and explains their functions.

1.1 Introduction

SAP S/4HANA is an enterprise resource planning (**ERP**) system designed for large businesses. SAP introduced a new web-based interface called Fiori, which was launched in 2014. Instead of logging into the traditional ERP system via SAP GUI (Graphical User Interface), you use Fiori. It is the successor of SAP R/3 and SAP ERP and is optimized for SAP's in-memory database, SAP HANA. This is also called SAP 4th Generation. SAP Fiori is a collection of apps created based on SAP user experience (UX) rules. SAP Fiori is built using SAPUI5, which is based on HTML, and using this, Fiori apps are developed. SAP Fiori is installed on top of the **SAP NetWeaver Application Server ABAP**. SAP Fiori is the front-end server (**FES**), and S/4HANA is the back-end server or system (**BES**). Business applications are called BES, and they include S/4HANA, ECC, BW, etc. Note that data conversion is possible in S/4HANA. Data can be migrated from ECC to S/4HANA by the BASIS team.

In other words, SAP S/4HANA is an enterprise resource planning (ERP) suite built on the SAP HANA in-memory database. SAP Fiori is a user experience (UX) design approach and a collection of applications that provide simplified, role-based user experience across various devices. When embedded in S/4HANA, Fiori enhances usability by offering intuitive, easy-to-use interfaces that improve productivity and user satisfaction. It provides finance, supply chain, manufacturing, and sales capabilities, leveraging real-time data processing and advanced analytics. Fiori is the front-end server (**FES**), and S/4HANA is the back-end server (**BES**). The first release of Fiori was with 25 transactional apps, and SAP steadily started increasing periodically with every new release. Currently, it has 14,704 apps, which include the following:

CHAPTER 1   INTRODUCTION TO SAP FIORI

- **UI5** (SAP Fiori app)
- **GUI** (GUI transaction)
- **WDA** (ABAP Web Dynpro application)
- **WCF** (Web Client UI Framework)
- **URL** (URL)

SAP Fiori is not just a user experience (UX) framework design system for SAP software and applications; it is a gateway to a modern and intuitive world of business apps. It is a system that enables the creation of business apps with a contemporary look and feel, offering state-of-the-art, role-based applications for various business functions that can be personalized across all lines of business, tasks, and devices. The collection of apps is available online in the SAP Fiori Apps Reference Library for various releases, offering a modern (Windows-like), intuitive, personalized user experience for SAP applications. Here are some critical points about SAP Fiori.

1.1.1 SAP Fiori Design Principle

SAP Fiori is based on five core **design principles** that simplify the system and break down transactions into task-based use interface (UI) applications. The five core principles are

- Role-based
- Adaptive
- Simple
- Coherent
- Delightful

These principles ensure user-friendly and practical applications. Furthermore, SAP Fiori ensures uniform user experience on various devices (desktops, tablets, and smartphones) and platforms, providing relevant information and insight. Note that the user experience is tailored to individual roles within an organization.

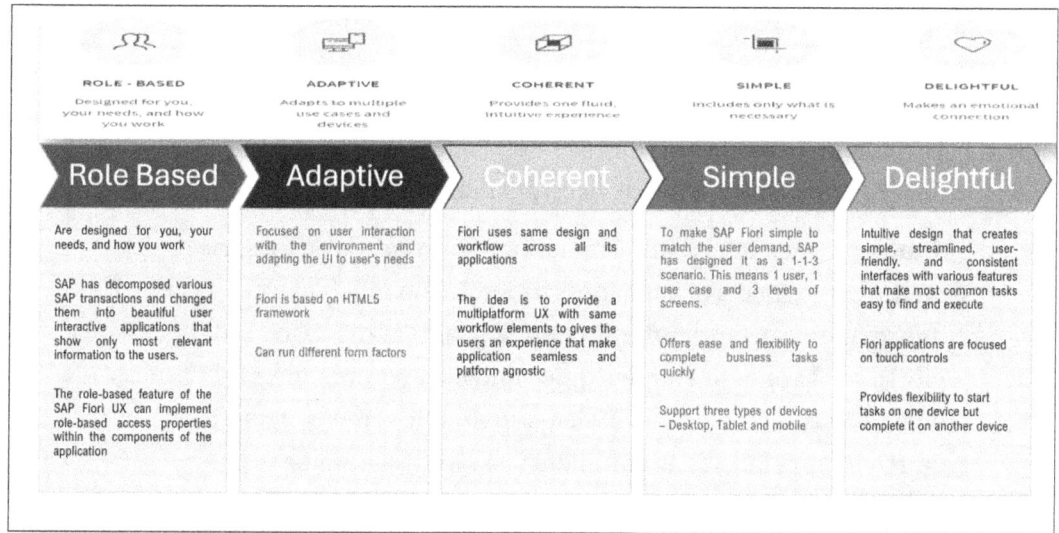

Figure 1-1. SAP Fiori core design principles

Role-Based: Fiori applications are not just designed for users. They are designed for you based on your role. This ensures you only see what is relevant to your job or task, improving efficiency and reducing complexity. It is a system that understands and caters to your specific organizational role.

SAP has delivered over 600 predefined business roles for SAP S/4HANA on-premise and over 700 business roles for S/4HANA public cloud for various business functions like finance, human resources, procurement, and sales. These templates include apps and classic UIs that correspond to specific business roles based on functionality and can be used in sandbox or development environments. For example, a sales manager might have a role-based app that provides quick access to sales order processing, customer data, and related tasks.

Adaptive: SAP Fiori's adaptive design principle ensures that applications provide a seamless user experience across various devices and screen sizes. This principle is rooted in creating interfaces that dynamically adjust to the user's context, whether using a desktop, tablet, or mobile device. Since SAP Fiori applications are built on the HTML5 framework, they can run on various devices, offering multiple interaction modes. This allows users to expect a consistent experience regardless of their device. The adaptive design also ensures applications perform efficiently on all devices, leveraging device-specific capabilities.

Simple: A great UX is simple to tailor to user needs and focuses on the core aspects of a business process. Too much extra information can clutter the UX, making tasks take longer. SAP Fiori's 1:1:3 approach targets quick and easy completion of business tasks on desktop, tablet, and mobile screens. Thus, SAP Fiori lets you effortlessly complete tasks and customize your experience to focus on relevant activities.

Coherent: A coherent design system is fundamental in creating a standardized multiplatform UX. This system encompasses core workflow elements that streamline user interactions while maintaining the right balance of flexibility and automation. The primary objective is to provide an intuitive, consistent experience across different platforms without stifling innovation and creativity.

Delightful: Besides enabling increased productivity, SAP Fiori enhances your work experience by allowing you to complete your tasks quickly. SAP Fiori ensures that applications are efficient, functional, and delightful. This approach improves user satisfaction, fosters a positive emotional connection with the application, and encourages continued engagement.

1.1.2 Additional SAP Fiori Features

Integration with S/4HANA: SAP Fiori applications are tightly integrated with S/4HANA processes, delivering a smooth user experience that combines transactional and analytical capabilities.

Native HANA DB: It is advisable to install S/4HANA on HANA DB to utilize all the functionality of Fiori applications, especially the analytical and factsheet apps.

Technology: SAP Fiori continually evolves, integrating features like intelligent home pages, conversational user experiences, and active handling of business situations. It provides a fresh, modern look and feel for users.

Mobility: The SAP Fiori UX also provides mobile deployment capabilities, increasing users' usability and accessibility.

Delightful: Besides enabling increased productivity, SAP Fiori enhances your work experience by allowing you to complete your tasks quickly. Fiori provides a clean and simple UI design that focuses on essential functions, reduces complexity, and enhances usability. It also provides a uniform look and feel across all applications, ensuring users have a consistent experience regardless of the device or task.

Simplified Interfaces: The user interfaces are simple and easy to use, reducing the learning curve and helping users perform tasks more efficiently.

Personalization: Users can customize their Fiori Launchpad according to their preferences – rearranging tiles; creating groups, spaces, and pages; and setting default values for fields. They can also create shortcuts for frequently used apps. The Launchpad allows users to set preferences for language, theme, and other settings to tailor their experience.

Responsive Design: SAP Fiori applications are built to be responsive, ensuring a seamless experience across different devices (desktop, tablet, and mobile). The application automatically adjusts the layout and controls based on the screen size and orientation. It allows users to perform tasks anywhere, anytime and is very user-friendly, intuitive, and highly responsive.

Task-Centric Apps: Each Fiori app is designed to accomplish specific tasks or processes, such as approving purchase orders or managing timesheets. It presents actionable information at the right time, reducing the need for navigation and search.

Accessibility: Fiori supports keyboard navigation and screen readers for improved accessibility. It adheres to accessibility standards, ensuring that applications are usable by people with disabilities.

Insightful Analytics: Fiori's embedded analytics provides real-time insights and analytics within business processes, helping users make informed decisions quickly. It also offers handy reports for viewing and analyzing, including visual reports, which include interactive charts, graphs, and reports for better data visualization and analysis.

UI Technologies: SAP has developed Fiori apps based on the user interface SAPUI5, a JavaScript framework, and the iOS and Android software development kits (SDKs) for native mobile SAP Fiori apps for creating user interfaces, combined with HTML5 and CSS3 to ensure great user experience.

Launchpad: The SAP Fiori Launchpad is the primary access point for all Fiori applications. It offers a personalized, role-based home page with tiles representing various applications, notifications, and tasks. The Fiori Launchpad shows tiles tailored to the user's role. Users are presented with apps and content pertinent to their assigned business role upon logging in. The Launchpad also simplifies navigation between related apps and classic UIs.

Integration: Fiori seamlessly integrates with SAP back-end systems such as SAP S/4HANA, SAP's ERP suite, and other third-party applications, enhancing the overall SAP experience with a modern UI layer. It uses the OData protocol for data integration and interaction with SAP and non-SAP systems.

Notifications and Approvals: Users can receive real-time notifications and approve tasks directly from the Fiori Launchpad, streamlining workflows and reducing delays.

Smart Business Cockpits: These role-based dashboards offer a complete view of key performance indicators (KPIs) and metrics, enabling users to monitor and manage their areas of responsibility effectively.

Customization and Extensibility: SAP Fiori enables customization and extension of standard applications to meet specific business needs without affecting the core functionality.

Unified Development: Provides development frameworks (e.g., SAP Fiori elements and SAPUI5) to streamline the creation of Fiori applications.

Real-Time Collaboration: Integrates with collaboration tools and platforms, enabling users to communicate and collaborate within the context of their work in real time.

Consistent Experience: It ensures a uniform user experience across all business functions, irrespective of the user's task.

Enhanced Productivity: Enables quick execution of everyday tasks directly from the home page or notification bar.

Security and Performance: Fiori applications are developed with strong security measures and optimized for performance to ensure a secure and efficient user experience.

Thus, SAP Fiori signifies SAP's transition to a more user-centered approach, improving productivity and satisfaction for SAP users through a modern, intuitive, and efficient user interface.

1.1.3 Deployment Option for SAP S/4HANA

SAP S/4HANA Cloud

An integrated ERP solution (software as a service (**SaaS**)) that contains the built-in SAP Fiori Launchpad and FES.

SAP Fiori for SAP S/4HANA Embedded (Recommended)

This deployment method deploys the FES on the same server as the SAP back end, enabling rapid activation of SAP Fiori using task lists. This helps maintain both the front-end and the back-end authorizations in a single role.

SAP Fiori for SAP S/4HANA on Standalone FES

The front-end server (**FES**) is deployed separately for each SAP S/4HANA system, while the back-end server (**BES**) is standard for all SAP applications that consume business data. This deployment requires configuring distinct roles for each system to ensure they are always coordinated.

1.1.4 Deployment Options with SAP Business Suite

SAP FES Embedded (Recommended)

In this deployment type, the business logic and classic UIs are deployed in the SAP BES, while other components, such as the SAP Fiori Launchpad and SAP Gateway, are deployed in the central FES.

SAP FES Central Hub Deployment

In this deployment model, SAP Fiori apps are deployed in separate systems. The SAP Fiori front-end server (FES) is a central hub, providing UIs and OData access for multiple SAP back-end systems. The BESs and FESs are connected via remote function calls (**RFCs**) and require specific authorization objects, such as **S_RFC** and **S_RFCACL**.

A detailed description of the deployment options will be discussed in **Chapter 4**.

1.1.5 Main Features of S/4HANA

ECC can run on multiple databases, such as Oracle, DB2, etc., but is not very efficient in displaying reports and data. In an ERP system, the data is stored in multiple tables, whereas in S/4HANA, many tables are combined into one table for faster processing. S/4HANA's key features are as follows:

- S/4HANA can only run on HANA DB.

- S/4HANA can run either on the cloud or on-premise.

- SAP Fiori apps are available in S/4HANA for performing activities and generating real-time reports.

- HANA database tables are column-based in S/4HANA, resulting in speed from fewer distinct values and parallel processing.

- In S/4HANA, there are no summary tables or index tables; instead, line-item tables are used.

- In S/4HANA, many tables have been combined into one table for faster processing.

- S/4HANA employs a single line-item table, ACDOCA (Universal Journal, combining GL, AP, AR, FI, AA, CO, and ML tables).

- In S/4HANA, inventory management is reduced from 26 tables to a single table MATDOC (Material Document Line-Item).

- A material ledger is mandatory and helps valuation in two additional currencies in S/4HANA.

- In S/4HANA, a parallel ledger is a prerequisite for accounting of new assets.

- Cost elements are merged into GL accounts in S/4HANA, so there is no need for reconciliation from CO to FI.

- In the S/4HANA pricing table, KNOV is replaced by a new table called PRCD_ELEMENTS.

- S/4HANA includes a migration cockpit.

- In S/4HANA, material numbers have been increased to 40 characters.

- In S/4HANA, customers and vendors are integrated as business partners. A new business partner transaction code, BP, was introduced to replace the 53 transaction codes.

- In S/4HANA, many transaction codes have been **blacklisted (program: ABLM_BLACKLIST)**, and SAP has provided a **simplified list for S/4HANA** for all releases.

- In S/4HANA, some transaction codes have been merged (program: PRGN_CORR2).

- In S/4HANA, some new objects have been introduced, like S_PROGNAM, S_BTCH_NAI, etc.

1.1.6 SAP Fiori Apps Reference Library

The SAP Fiori Apps Reference Library (ondemand.com) is a comprehensive metadata repository of SAP Fiori apps. It offers detailed information about app installation, configuration, extensibility, and support. The library includes search filters and grouping options to help users explore technical information related to the planning and implementation of various SAP Fiori apps and classic applications based on SAP GUI. Additionally, SAP Fiori provides a beginner's user guide (SAP Fiori Apps Reference Library – User Guide | SAP Help Portal) that offers guidance on the various features and how to use them effectively to access accurate information.

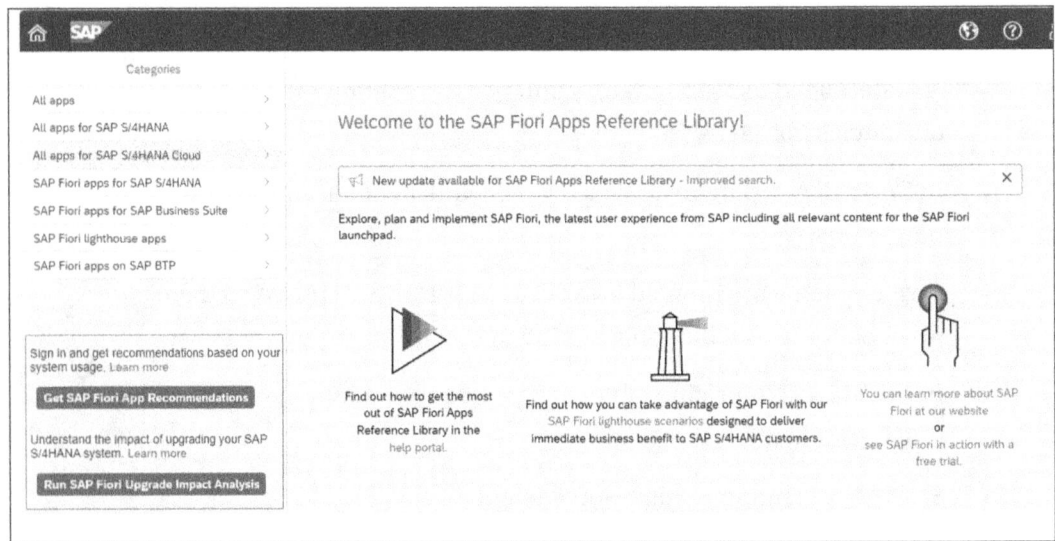

Figure 1-2. Initial screen of the SAP Fiori Apps Reference Library

In the **SAP Fiori Apps Reference Library**, as shown in Figure 1-2, the **left panel** options help categorize apps based on systems and deployments. **"All apps"** lists every available app. **"All apps for SAP S/4HANA (Private Cloud and On-Premise)"** focuses on apps for private cloud or on-premise S/4HANA. **"All apps for SAP S/4HANA Public Cloud"** covers apps for the public cloud version. **"SAP Fiori apps for SAP Business Suite"** includes apps for older SAP systems like ECC. **"SAP Fiori lighthouse apps"** highlights innovative, best-practice apps, and **"SAP Fiori apps on SAP BTP"** showcases apps using the SAP Business Technology Platform (BTP) for advanced cloud capabilities. These categories help users quickly identify apps based on their system, deployment, and innovation needs.

1.1.7 SAP Fiori App Recommendations

The **SAP Fiori App Recommendations** tool generates a detailed report from the SAP Fiori Apps Reference Library. The report lists recommended SAP Fiori apps based on your business processes and system landscape. You can upload your profiles to generate a report that categorizes the apps based on various criteria and provides system readiness details.

1.1.8 SAP Readiness Check 2.0

SAP Readiness Check 2.0 helps customers prepare for conversion when switching from SAP ERP to SAP S/4HANA by providing details on business functions, custom code analysis, data management, add-on compatibility, and recommended SAP Fiori apps. It is used with various SAP Notes, with older notes needing to be de-implemented before applying the latest ones.

1.1.9 SAP Fiori Lighthouse Scenarios

These SAP Fiori apps offer immediate business benefits to users of SAP S/4HANA, SAP S/4HANA Cloud, and SAP BTP with SAP Business Suite. They provide rich and enhanced user experience and the latest features that simplify processes and tasks associated with the SAP Fiori apps. **Note:** The newest lighthouse SAP Fiori apps, such as finance, treasury, sales, logistics, and master data, cover 24 functional areas.

1.1.10 Prerequisites for Setting Up Fiori

Implementing SAP Fiori requires specific prerequisites to ensure the correct setup of the system landscape and components. You need SAP Fiori front-end server 5.0 (NW 7.52 or above), containing the necessary components and versions. It includes the following components with the respective versions:

SAP NetWeaver Version:

- You need the appropriate version of SAP NetWeaver that supports SAP Fiori.
- The SAP NetWeaver component should be 7.31 or higher.

CHAPTER 1   INTRODUCTION TO SAP FIORI

SAP Gateway:

SAP Gateway, a key component, must be installed and configured. In an embedded deployment, the gateway is part of the same system and should be activated as the back end, whereas in a central hub deployment, it is a separate system.

The main component is **SAP_GWFND**; SAP NetWeaver Gateway Foundation 7.50 or higher is required.

This component provides the framework for exposing data as OData services.

SAPUI5:

- The SAPUI5 library must be installed on the front-end server.
- The main component is **SAP_UI**; user interface technology should be 7.50 or higher.
- This component contains the SAP Fiori Launchpad and SAPUI5 runtime libraries.

SAP BASIS Component:

The main component is **SAP_BASIS**; an SAP BASIS component of 7.5 or higher is required.

SAP Fiori Front-End Server (FES):

- The Fiori front-end server must be installed, including the UI components and the Fiori Launchpad.
- The main component is **SAP_UI**.

SAP Back-End System:

- Ensure the back-end system is compatible and contains the necessary business suite applications.
- Component: Varies based on the specific business suite application (e.g., ECC, S/4HANA).

Roles and Authorizations:

- Ensure users have the necessary roles and authorizations to access and use Fiori applications.
- SAP usually provides role templates and can be customized as needed.

CHAPTER 1 INTRODUCTION TO SAP FIORI

Browser Compatibility:

- Ensure that the end user devices have compatible web browsers installed (e.g., the latest versions of Chrome, Firefox, or Microsoft Edge).

- UI for BASIS Applications (software component version UI FOR BASIS APPLICATIONS 200) – containing SAP NetWeaver Fiori apps.

1.1.11 RFC and Trusted RFC

In SAP Fiori, remote function calls (RFCs) are often used to facilitate communication between the front-end Fiori applications and the back-end SAP system. When deploying SAP Fiori, the RFC (remote function call) configuration differs based on whether you use an embedded or central hub deployment.

In an embedded deployment, SAP Gateway (front-end server) and SAP ERP (back-end system) are on the same system. This simplifies the configuration since no cross-system communication and a trusted RFC are required.

In a central hub deployment, SAP Gateway (front-end server) and SAP ERP (back-end system) are on separate systems. This setup requires more configuration to establish communication between the two systems, and a trusted RFC is needed.

Note In a **normal RFC**, you use an RFC ID (communication or system type) or batch user ID. In a **trusted RFC**, you use your ID, which serves as a dialogue ID for communication, and a batch user ID is not required. In the case of a trusted RFC, the user needs authorization for two objects: **S_RC** and **S_RFCACL**. When configuring Fiori, there is no need for a batch user ID; you should create a trusted RFC and use your **ID** for communication. Thus, setting up RFCs appropriately for both embedded and central hub deployments of SAP Fiori ensures effective communication and functionality of the SAP Fiori applications. Transaction code **SM59** is used to create various RFCs.

1.1.12 SAP Fiori Launchpad

The SAP Fiori Launchpad (FLP) is the central entry point for accessing SAP Fiori apps. It provides a unified, role-based, and personalized user experience, enabling users to navigate tasks and workflows efficiently. The FLP offers several features to help end users perform their functions efficiently.

- FLP's centralized and intuitive interface reduces the time and effort required to find and use applications, boosting user productivity. Its consistent and personalized user experience across devices enhances user satisfaction and adoption.

- Depending on the user's role, certain app groups or spaces and pages are displayed. Users see only the apps and information relevant to their roles, enhancing efficiency and reducing clutter. This role-based approach ensures that users can access the necessary tools without being overwhelmed by unnecessary options.

- Users can customize and personalize their Launchpad by rearranging tiles, creating groups, and adding or removing tiles based on their preferences and frequently used apps. The ability to customize the Launchpad to individual preferences allows users to tailor their workspace to their needs.

- The Launchpad uses a tile-based layout where each tile represents an application or a function. Tiles can display real-time information and updates, providing users with instant insights.

- The Launchpad is designed to be responsive, ensuring seamless user experience across different devices, including desktops, tablets, and smartphones.

- An integrated search function allows users to quickly locate apps, documents, and business objects. Navigation is intuitive, enabling users to access detailed views and related information easily.

- Users receive real-time notifications and can handle approvals directly from the Launchpad, streamlining workflows and reducing delays.

CHAPTER 1 INTRODUCTION TO SAP FIORI

- Tiles can offer summarized information about the data available for the user in the app.

- Embedded analytics within the Launchpad provides users with real-time data and insights, enabling informed decision-making without switching between different tools.

- This information can be visualized using a simple number, color coding based on key performance indicators (KPIs), and even charts showing comparisons, trends, or contributions

- The Launchpad supports single sign-on (SSO), allowing users to access all their applications with single credentials, improving security and user convenience.

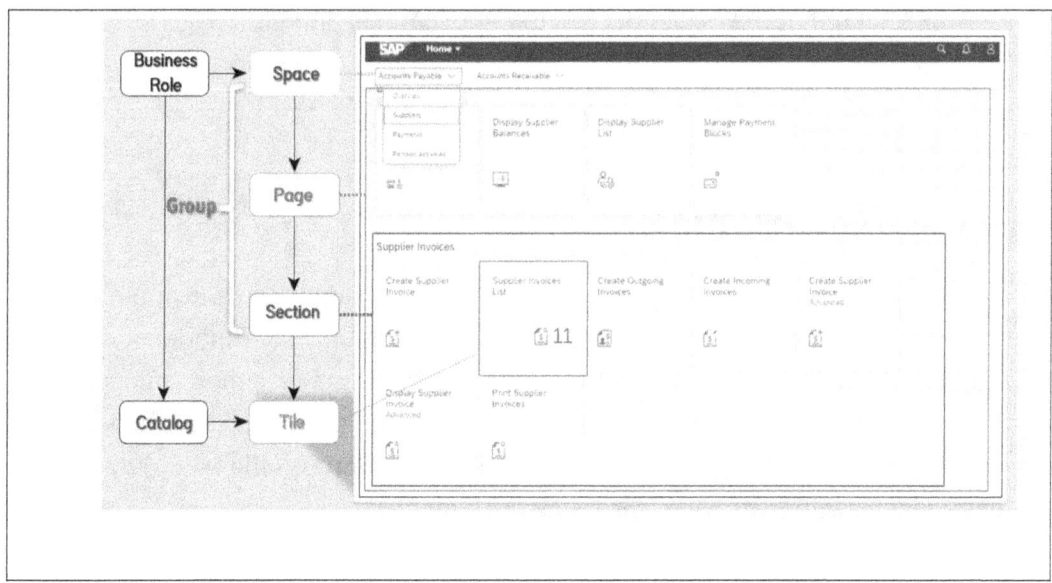

Figure 1-3. SAP Fiori Launchpad user initial login screen

CHAPTER 1 INTRODUCTION TO SAP FIORI

Note The Fiori Launchpad setup and configuration require careful planning to meet the organization's and users' needs.

- The FLP should be integrated with the back-end systems (S/4HANA, ERP, etc.) to ensure the necessary data and applications are accessible.

- Always customize the Launchpad based on user needs, including layout, tiles, groups, spaces, and pages.

- The number displayed on the tile comes from the analytical app, for example, Promise to Pay – today and has 1.15k entries.

- Test the Launchpad to make sure it works properly. This includes checking that users can access the applications and data they need.

1.1.13 Personalization

SAP Fiori personalization allows users to customize their Launchpad and applications to suit their preferences and work habits better, enhancing the user experience. By utilizing SAP Fiori personalization features, individuals can create a more efficient and customized workspace, which enhances their overall productivity and satisfaction with the system. This feature can be accessed from the **User Menu** (Profile Menu) by selecting **Settings**. Personalization provides the following benefits:

- **Personalized Home Page:**

    - The users can rearrange, add, or remove tiles on their Fiori Launchpad home page.

    - This allows users to prioritize and access frequently used applications more quickly.

- **Tile Customization:**
  - The users can create their tiles with specific filters, allowing quick access to customized views of application data. For example, users can create a tile showing only their open purchase orders.

- **App Personalization:**
  - The users can personalize settings such as table layouts, column visibility, and sorting preferences within individual Fiori applications.
  - These settings are often saved automatically and retained across sessions.

- **Theme Designer and Personalization:**
  - The users can change the theme of the Fiori Launchpad to suit their visual preferences.
  - This includes adjusting colors, fonts, and overall UI themes.
  - Choose from available themes like SAP Morning Horizon, Quartz Light, Quartz Dark, accessibility themes High-Contrast Black (HCB) and High-Contrast White (HCW), etc.
  - The user can also create a new custom theme.

- **User Settings:**
  - Users can set their default language, time zone, and other personal settings that affect how data is displayed and managed within Fiori applications.

- **User Defaults:**
  - The user can adjust default values for language, time zone, and other personal preferences.

- **Improved User Efficiency:**
  - Personalized settings help users navigate and use the system more efficiently by focusing on what is most relevant.

- **Enhanced User Satisfaction:**
    - Allowing users to tailor their interface leads to higher satisfaction and better user adoption.

1.1.14 SAP Fiori Clients

SAP Fiori clients provide a runtime environment for SAP Fiori apps, enabling users to access these apps on various devices such as desktops, tablets, and smartphones. These clients ensure consistent user experience across different platforms and devices. Users can access their applications and data from anywhere, at any time, improving flexibility and efficiency. Integrating Fiori clients with existing SAP systems allows for a smooth transition and reduces the learning curve for users. Thus, organizations can use SAP Fiori clients to ensure their users have a consistent, secure, and efficient way to access SAP Fiori applications regardless of their devices. There are a couple of ways to access Fiori, and they are as follows:

SAP Fiori Launchpad (FLP):

- This is the main entry point for accessing SAP Fiori apps, providing unified, role-based access to applications.
- This is a central access point where personalization, search, and navigation activities can be performed.
- It utilizes a **web browser** to access. Any HTML5-ready browser can be used, or you can invoke the URL with the transaction code **/UI2/FLP**.
- You can start the **FLP** by using the URL **https://<host>:<port>/sap/bc/ ui5_ui5/ui2/ushell/shells/abap/FioriLaunchpad.html** in an HTML5-ready browser.
- Another option to start the **FLP** is using the URL **Error! Hyperlink reference not valid.** in an HTML5-ready browser.

SAP Business Client:

- The SAP Fiori Launchpad system connections can be created for SAP Business Client 6.0, a desktop application that combines the SAP Fiori Launchpad with traditional SAP GUI transactions and can be installed on Windows desktops.

- This feature provides a unified user interface for Fiori apps and classic SAP GUI transactions, integrating them into a single desktop environment.

- Once the SAP Business Client is installed on your Windows desktop, it must be configured. Then, SAP Fiori apps and traditional SAP GUI transactions can be accessed from a single interface.

Note

- The BASIS team creates the URLs for logging into the SAP Fiori Launchpad. There are two ways to do this.

- The transaction code **/UI2/FLP** starts the **FLP** via **HTTP** by default. An entry in the database table **HTTPURLLOC** can be used to call a reverse proxy like SAP Web Dispatcher via **HTTPS**.

1.1.15 SAP Fiori App Types: Overview

SAP Fiori apps are a collection of role-based applications that provide simple and intuitive user experience for interacting with SAP systems. These apps are designed to work seamlessly across various devices, offering consistent user experience whether accessed from a desktop, tablet, or smartphone. All SAP Fiori apps utilize the SAPUI5 and SAP Gateway technologies. There are **five** types of SAP Fiori apps available. They are different in terms of their usage and technologies:

- Transactional apps
- Analytical apps
- Factsheet apps
- SAP GUI apps/Web Dynpro apps
- Custom apps

CHAPTER 1   INTRODUCTION TO SAP FIORI

The relevant OData and SICF services available from the SAP Fiori Apps Reference Library must be activated for all the above apps to work efficiently. Instead of manually activating OData services individually for each app, you can activate the OData services for several apps at once by using a task list: **SAP_GATEWAY_ACTIVATE_ODATA_SERV**.

Transactional Apps

These apps are designed to perform specific tasks, such as creating or updating records. They allow users to execute transactions such as making sales orders, approving purchase requisitions, or entering timesheet data. These apps allow users to run simple SAP transactions on mobile devices and desktops or laptops, such as leave requests, travel requests, purchase orders, etc. These apps can be run on any database, but HANA DB is preferred, for example:

- **Manage Sales Orders (VA01)**
  - **App ID**: F1873
  - This app enables users to create sales orders, manage order details, and submit them for processing.

Analytical Apps

Analytical apps provide real-time insights into business data. They help users monitor key performance indicators (KPIs), analyze trends, and make informed decisions. SAP Fiori analytical apps run on the SAP HANA database and use virtual data models. They integrate the power of SAP HANA with SAP Business Suite and provide real-time information from a large volume of data in a front-end web browser. Examples include sales analysis, inventory management, and financial reporting, for example:

- **Sales Volume – Detailed Analysis**
  - **App ID**: F2235
  - This app comprehensively analyzes sales volumes with customizable drill-down options for various dimensions and time periods.

Factsheet Apps

Factsheets offer a 360-degree view of key business objects, providing detailed information and navigation to related entities. Users can drill into specific details and navigate associated documents and transactions. Factsheets run only on an SAP HANA database and require an ABAP stack, and they cannot be ported to SAP HANA Live tier-2 architecture. Examples include customer factsheets, product factsheets, and supplier factsheets, for example:

- **Customer Factsheet**
    - **App ID**: F2187 (Customer – 360° View)
    - This app provides an overview of a specific customer by reviewing aggregated sales data from both the past and present.

SAP GUI Apps

SAP Fiori GUI apps represent a modernized approach to the traditional SAP GUI transactions by incorporating them into the Fiori Launchpad. These apps aim to provide a more intuitive and user-friendly experience while retaining the functionality of classic SAP transactions. Fiori GUI apps give a cleaner, more modern interface than traditional SAP GUI screens. The interface is designed to be intuitive and easier to navigate. Fiori GUI apps are integrated into the Fiori Launchpad, allowing users to access traditional and modernized apps from a single entry point. Like traditional SAP GUI transactions, Fiori GUI apps provide real-time access to SAP data, enabling users to perform transactions and view information instantly, for example:

- **Display Sales Order – VA03**
    - **App ID**: VA03
    - This app allows the display of specific types of sales documents.

Custom Apps

SAP Fiori custom apps are tailored applications developed to meet specific business needs that are not covered by standard Fiori apps. These custom apps leverage the SAP Fiori design principles and SAPUI5 framework to provide consistent and intuitive user experience. Custom apps can be built to enhance existing processes, integrate with other systems, or provide unique functionalities required by the organization. Any SAP transaction code with no matching app in the SAP Fiori Apps Reference Library can be converted into a Fiori app with all its functionality, for example:

- **Transaction Codes**
    - SU53, SMX, SP02, SU3, LAST_SHORTDUMP, SUIM, etc.

1.1.16 More Examples of SAP Fiori Apps

My Inbox: Allows users to manage their workflow tasks and approvals. Users can view, approve, or reject requests and navigate to detailed information about each task.

Create Sales Orders: This enables sales representatives to create new orders quickly and efficiently with an intuitive interface that guides them through the process.

Approve Purchase Requisitions: This function allows managers to review and approve purchase requisitions, ensuring timely procurement and operational efficiency.

Track Sales Orders: This feature provides real-time visibility into the status of sales orders, allowing users to monitor progress and address issues promptly.

Manage Product Master Data: This feature enables users to create and update product master data, ensuring accurate and up-to-date information across the organization.

Cash Flow Analyzer: This tool provides insights into cash flow status and trends, helping financial managers make informed decisions about cash management.

1.2 SAP Fiori Various Objects Definition

In the SAP Fiori Launchpad, catalogs, groups, spaces, and pages organize and present applications in a user-friendly way that aligns with the business's needs. These elements help manage and structure the content users interact with, ensuring they can access the applications and information they need.

1.2.1 Fiori Catalogs

Catalogs consist of collections of Fiori apps grouped based on business roles or functions. They determine the availability of apps to users and their assignment to roles in the SAP system. Users are assigned specific catalogs based on their roles to ensure they can only access relevant apps for their job functions. Administrators can manage which apps are included in each catalog and update them as needed. They can add any tiles (transactional, analytical, factsheet, etc. to a catalog). Multiple catalogs can be created and assigned to roles, allowing for flexibility in how apps are distributed among users. Administrators can control access to different apps by assigning catalogs to roles and enhancing security. There are two types of catalogs available: technical and business catalogs.

1.2.2 Technical Catalog (TC)

A technical catalog in SAP Fiori is a collection of apps, UI components, and target mappings necessary to support the functionality of business catalogs. Administrators use technical catalogs to manage and deploy the underlying components of business roles and catalogs. These catalogs should never be assigned to the end users. A technical catalog can be created using transaction code **/UI2/FLPAM**. The SAP-delivered technical catalog in the SAP Fiori Apps Reference Library has the prefix **SAP_TC_***.

1.2.3 Business Catalog (BC)

A business catalog in SAP Fiori is a collection of related Fiori apps and UIs (user interfaces) grouped based on specific business roles or tasks. Business catalogs organize related Fiori apps for specific business roles or tasks. These catalogs help streamline users' access to relevant applications, enhancing their efficiency by providing a customized and role-specific view of available apps. A business catalog can be created using transaction code **/UI2/FLPCM_CUST**. The SAP-delivered business catalog in the SAP Fiori Apps Reference Library has the prefix **SAP*_BC_***.

1.2.4 Fiori Catalog Groups (BCG)

Groups are used to organize tiles on the Fiori Launchpad, making it easier for users to find and access the apps needed. Each group can contain tiles from one or more catalogs. Groups help users navigate the SAP Fiori Launchpad by categorizing apps into logical sections. Users can personalize their groups by adding or removing tiles or rearranging them according to their preferences. Administrators can define default groups for users, but users can also create their own groups. Groups are displayed on the

Launchpad home page for quick access to frequently used apps by users. Users can tailor their Launchpad by organizing tiles into custom groups. The SAP-delivered business catalog group in the SAP Fiori Apps Reference Library has the prefix **SAP_*_BCG_***.

1.2.5 Fiori Spaces (SP)

Spaces are a new concept. They are a way to further enhance the organization of the Fiori Launchpad by providing a structured layout that groups related content and applications into distinct areas. They replace Fiori groups, which SAP has deprecated. Spaces allow for a hierarchical organization where related pages are grouped under a single space and help users navigate through associated applications and content. Like catalogs and groups, spaces are assigned to user roles, ensuring users see spaces relevant to their functions. Spaces provide an additional layer of organization, making it easier for users to find and use related applications. Spaces can be designed around specific tasks or business processes, improving efficiency. The SAP-delivered spaces in the SAP Fiori Apps Reference Library have the prefix SAP_*_SP_*, for example, SAP_SD_SP_SALES_MANAGER.

1.2.6 Fiori Pages (PG)

Fiori pages are the building blocks within spaces containing the actual content and tiles users interact with. Each page can have a different layout and can include multiple sections and tiles. Pages offer flexible layouts that can be customized to display several types of content and applications. Pages organize tiles and links in a way that supports user tasks and workflows. Pages can provide contextual information and navigation to related applications, enhancing the user experience. Administrators can create custom page layouts to match business requirements and user needs. The SAP-delivered pages in the SAP Fiori Apps Reference Library have the prefix **SAP_*_PG_**, for example, SAP_SD_PG_SALES_MGR_OVR.

1.2.7 SAP Fiori Business Roles (BR)

SAP Fiori business roles with the prefix **SAP_BR*** are predefined roles provided by SAP to simplify the assignment of roles to users in SAP S/4HANA, for example, SAP_BR_MANAGER, SAP_BR_PURCHASER, etc. These roles are designed to match typical job functions within an organization and include all the necessary authorizations and Fiori applications relevant to those functions. These roles are designed based on best practices and typical business processes in various industries instead of creating roles from scratch; organizations can use these predefined roles to quickly assign the necessary authorizations to users based on their job functions. Each business role includes a set of Fiori applications (tiles) relevant to the job function. Authorizations for both front end (UI) and back end (data access) are included, ensuring users can access all necessary functionalities. While SAP_BR* roles are predefined, they can be customized to better fit specific organizational needs. These roles should only be used for evaluating in the sandbox or development environment. This approach reduces the complexity and time involved in role design and assignment. The SAP-delivered business role in the SAP Fiori Apps Reference Library has the prefix **SAP_BR_***.

1.2.8 Fiori Tiles and Target Mapping

In SAP Fiori, tiles are the entry points for applications on the Fiori Launchpad. They are interactive visual elements representing different apps, providing a user-friendly way for users to access and launch their applications. Target mapping is the configuration that defines what happens when a user clicks a tile, such as launching a specific Fiori app, SAP GUI transaction, or Web Dynpro application. The combination of tile (**T**) and target mapping (**TM**) is called **intent**.

1.2.9 SAP Fiori Tiles (T)

Tiles are visual elements on the Fiori Launchpad that users click to launch applications. They provide essential information and quick access to apps, making navigation intuitive and efficient. There are two types of tiles – static and dynamic:

- **Static Tiles:**
    - Display fixed content such as a title, subtitle, and icon.
    - Do not change dynamically; they are purely for navigation.
- **Dynamic Tiles:**
    - Display real-time information that updates periodically.
    - Can show data such as numbers, statuses, or trends directly on the tile (e.g., number of open tasks).

1.2.10 SAP Target Mapping (TM)

Target mapping defines the navigation behavior for tiles on the Fiori Launchpad. It specifies the target application or action to be executed when a tile is clicked, including parameters and context information required for the app. It is a combination of semantic objects, actions, parameters, and target applications. Thus, the target mapping configuration defines the navigation behavior when clicking a tile, including the target application and any necessary parameters.

1.2.11 SAP Fiori OData Service

OData (Open Data Protocol) is a standard protocol for creating and consuming RESTful APIs. In SAP Fiori, OData services enable communication between the front end (Fiori apps) and the back end (SAP systems like S/4HANA). These services allow Fiori applications to interact with the data stored in SAP systems by performing operations such as querying, updating, and deleting data. OData services can be activated using transaction code **/UI2/MAINT_SERVICE**. Once activated, the relevant SICF is also activated automatically.

1.2.12 SAP Fiori SICF Service

In SAP Fiori, the Internet Communication Framework (**ICF**) services must be activated for Fiori applications and OData services to function correctly. **SICF** (Service Information and Configuration Framework) is used to configure and manage **HTTP** services in the SAP NetWeaver Application Server. Enabling SAP Fiori apps is crucial, as many of these apps rely on web-based services to communicate with the back-end system. The transaction code **SICF** is used to manage these ICF services.

1.3 Summary

SAP Fiori transforms how users interact with SAP applications by providing a modern, role-based, intuitive user experience. Its main features, such as role-based design, responsive and adaptive interfaces, personalization options, embedded analytics, and seamless integration capabilities, make it a powerful tool for enhancing productivity and user satisfaction across various business functions and industries. By leveraging these features, organizations can ensure that their SAP applications are user-friendly, efficient, and aligned with modern UX standards.

This chapter introduced the reader to some of SAP Fiori's basic concepts. We briefly covered SAP Fiori and S/4HANA's main features and deployment options. We also discussed the various Fiori apps available for end users and explored various Fiori objects.

1.4 References

SAP Fiori Apps Reference Library (`https://fioriappslibrary.hana.ondemand.com/sap/fix/externalViewer/`)

CHAPTER 2

SAP Fiori Apps Reference Library

The SAP Fiori Apps Reference Library helps users find and explore Fiori apps based on their business roles, processes, or technical needs. Users can filter apps by industry, product version, and deployment options, making it easier to discover the right apps. This library is vital for planning implementations, checking compatibility, and maximizing Fiori's features.

2.1 Introduction

The **SAP Fiori Apps Reference Library** is a comprehensive resource for exploring, planning, and implementing SAP Fiori apps. It offers an overview of all available Fiori apps and essential details like technical requirements, configuration settings, and extensibility options. This valuable tool empowers businesses to identify relevant apps, understand their integration prerequisites, and make informed decisions about their Fiori implementation strategy. By leveraging the Apps Reference Library, organizations can streamline their Fiori adoption, enhance user experience, and drive better business value through streamlined processes and improved productivity.

SAP announced a new browser-based user interface, Fiori, in 2013 and released it in 2014. Instead of logging into the traditional ERP system via SAP GUI, you use Fiori. The first release of Fiori was with 25 transactional apps, and SAP steadily started increasing periodically with every new release. Currently, it has 14,704 apps, which include the following:

- **UI5** (SAP Fiori app)
- **GUI** (GUI transaction)

CHAPTER 2   SAP FIORI APPS REFERENCE LIBRARY

- **WDA** (ABAP Web Dynpro application)
- **WCF** (Web Client UI Framework)
- **URL** (URL)

SAP Fiori is a collection of apps representing SAP's new user experience and the face of SAP S/4HANA. SAP Fiori apps can be categorized by line of business, industry, most crucial user role, and technical foundation.

2.1.1 Concept and Library Details

All available apps can be explored using the SAP Fiori Apps Reference Library, which can be accessed by using the following link:

https://www.sap.com/fiori-apps-library

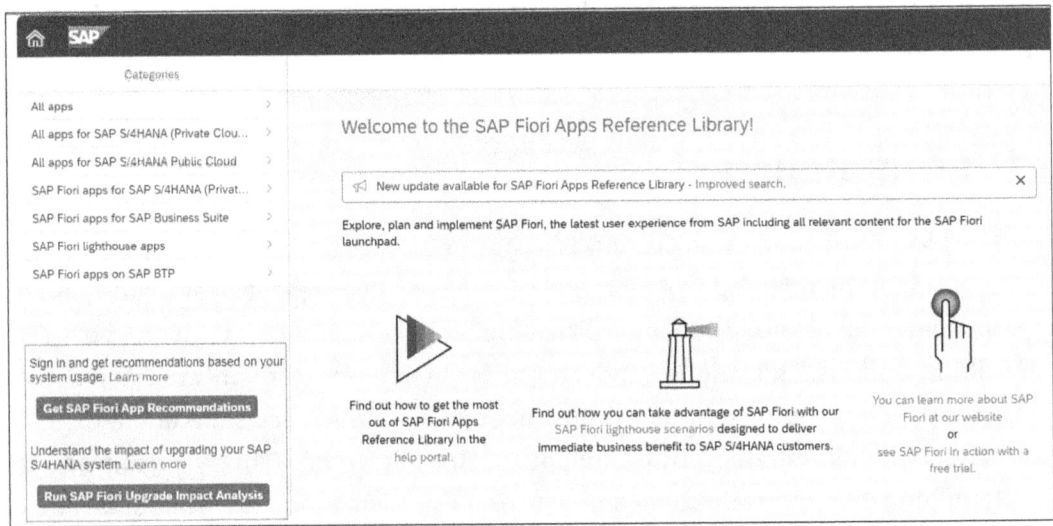

Figure 2-1. Initial screen of the SAP Fiori Apps Reference Library

Library Details

The SAP Fiori Apps Reference Library details are as follows:

- A **central repository** for information on all SAP Fiori apps and some classic applications
- Serves as a **self-service tool** for exploring, planning, and implementing Fiori apps

- Provides **detailed information** about each app, including

  - **Technical Data:** Product versions, software components, configuration settings, and extensibility options.

  - **Business Context:** Each app is relevant for business roles, processes, and industries.

  - **Implementation Prerequisites:** Back-end components and configurations required to run the app.

  - **Links to Additional Resources:** App documentation, user guides, and related SAP Notes.

Key Features and Benefits

- **App Discovery:**

  - Browse and search for Fiori apps by name, keywords, business role, or industry.

  - Filter apps based on your SAP product version and back-end components.

  - View screenshots, descriptions, and critical features of each app.

- **Implementation Planning:**

  - Access detailed technical information for each app, including required back-end components and configurations.

  - Understand the dependencies and integration points between Fiori apps and your existing systems.

  - Plan your Fiori implementation roadmap based on business priorities and technical feasibility.

- **Configuration and Extensibility:**

  - Find configuration options for customizing Fiori apps to your specific requirements.

  - Explore extensibility points for adapting or enhancing app functionality.

  - Access development guides and tools for building custom Fiori apps or extensions.

- **Relevance and Readiness Analysis:**
  - Identify relevant Fiori apps based on your business processes and industry.
  - Assess your system's readiness to adopt specific apps based on installed components and configurations.
  - Get recommendations for apps that fit your business needs and technical landscape.
- **Aggregated Information:**
  - View combined installation and configuration details for multiple apps.
  - Download app lists and technical information in various formats (e.g., Excel, PDF).

2.1.2 Accessing the Fiori Apps Reference Library

The Fiori library can be accessed in two ways:

> **Online:** Access the library directly through your web browser at the SAP Fiori Apps Reference Library website.
>
> **Embedded:** The library is also integrated into the SAP Fiori Launchpad, providing easy access within your Fiori environment.

2.1.3 How to Use the Fiori Apps Reference Library

This section describes the steps to use the SAP Fiori Apps Reference Library:

> **Define Your Scope:** Identify the business processes, roles, or industries for which you want to explore Fiori apps.
>
> **Search and Filter:** Use the search and filter options to narrow down the list of apps.
>
> **Explore App Details:** Click an app to view its detailed information, including technical data, business context, and implementation prerequisites.

CHAPTER 2   SAP FIORI APPS REFERENCE LIBRARY

Assess Relevance and Readiness: Use the analysis tools to identify relevant apps and assess your system's readiness for adoption.

Plan Your Implementation: Use the gathered information to create an implementation roadmap and prioritize app deployments.

2.1.4 Fiori Library Exploration

Under the **Categories** option, select **All apps**. This will list all the apps available within the **SAP Fiori Apps Reference Library**, as shown in the figure below.

Note   SAP keeps adding and removing apps in the SAP Fiori Apps Reference Library, so the number could be different when you check the reference library.

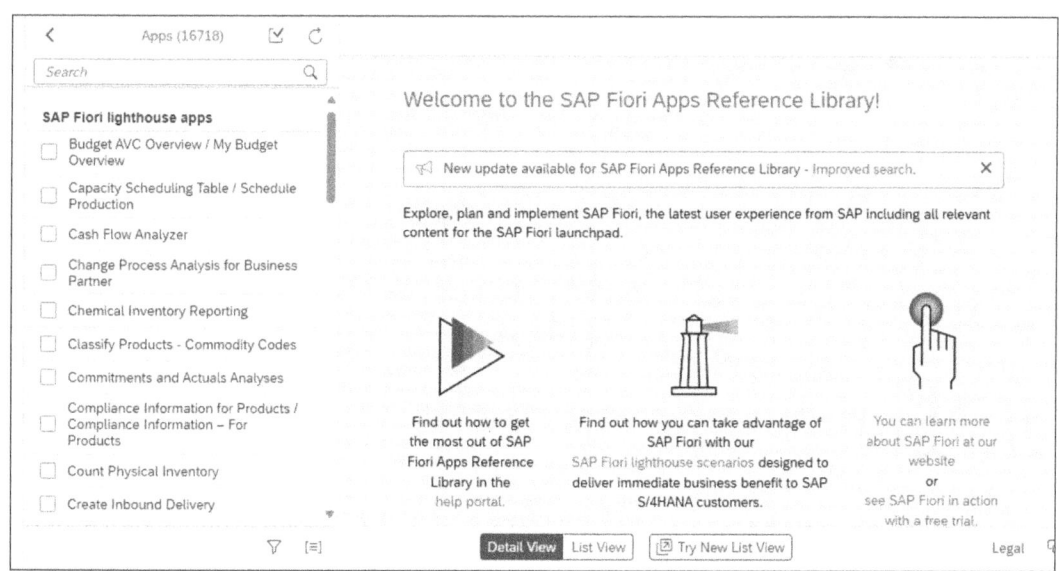

Figure 2-2. *List of all apps available within the SAP library*

33

CHAPTER 2   SAP FIORI APPS REFERENCE LIBRARY

The above figure shows that SAP provides 16,718 apps for various business processes, like finance, sales, logistics, etc. The above screen has the following attributes:

- **Symbol** ☑ : Select all
- **Symbol** ↻ : Clear selection
- **Symbol** ▽ : Filter
- **Symbol** [≡] : Group
- **Detail View**: Gives detailed information about a single app/title
- **List View**: Gives information about a single app, having a limited range of fields for quick scanning
- **Try New List View**: Another option for quickly finding apps

We can search for any app based on any transaction code or transactional app. To search for an app available, enter a transaction code, for example, VA01 (Create Sales Order), as shown in the figure below.

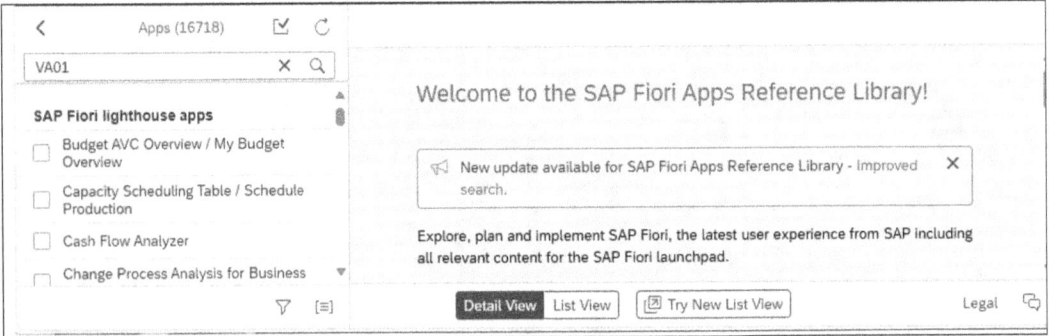

Figure 2-3. *Searching for an app related to transaction code VA01 within the library*

Now, click the **search** icon 🔍 . The system will return the matching apps available within the SAP Fiori Apps Reference Library, as shown in the figure below.

CHAPTER 2 SAP FIORI APPS REFERENCE LIBRARY

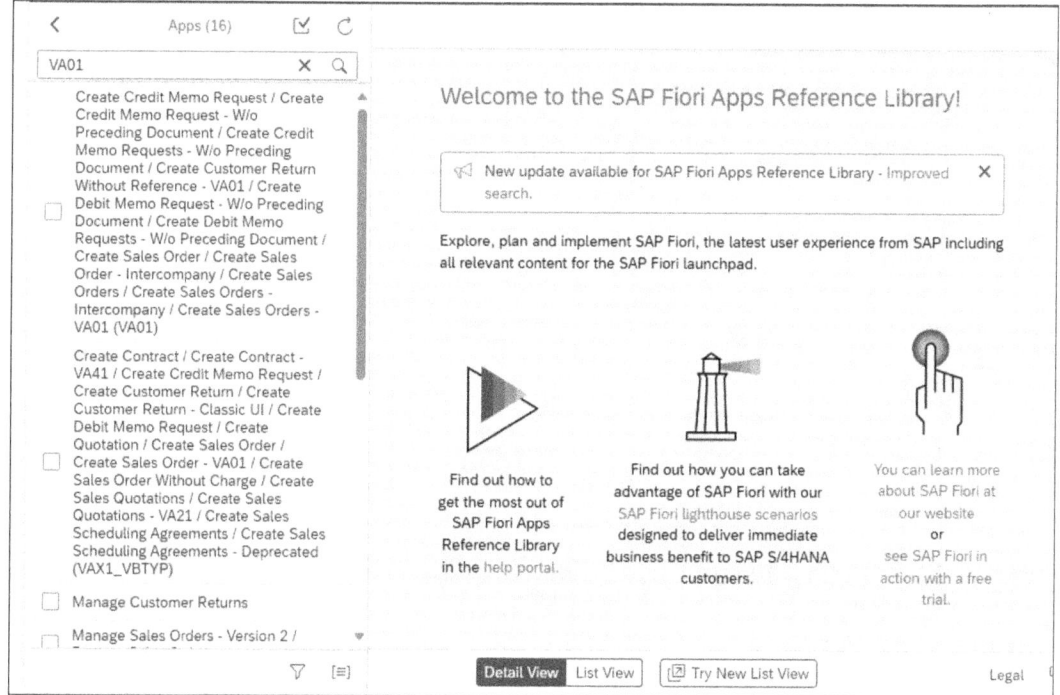

Figure 2-4. *Listing of apps available within the library for transaction code VA01*

Select Manage Sales Orders – Version 2 / Process Sales Orders on the left side. Double-click to open the app, which will give details of the app and the release version, as shown below.

Note Version 2 means it is the latest version of the app.

CHAPTER 2   SAP FIORI APPS REFERENCE LIBRARY

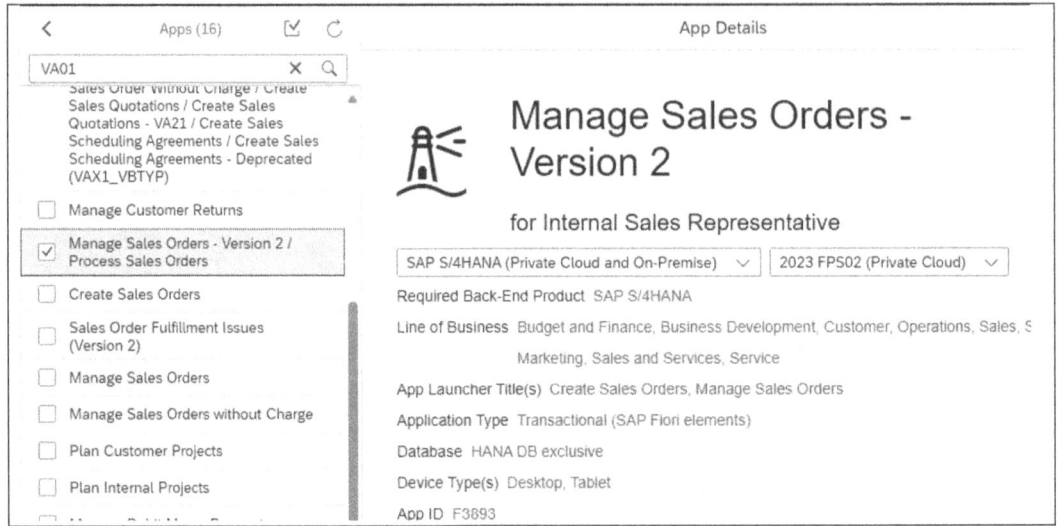

Figure 2-5. *Transaction code VA01 replaced with SAP Fiori app F3893*

SAP has now replaced transaction VA01 with the transactional app **F3893**. Here, you can select the version of S/4HANA installed in your system: SAP S/4HANA 2023 FPS02 (On-Premise). If you have an earlier version of S/4HANA, you can search for it as shown in the figure below.

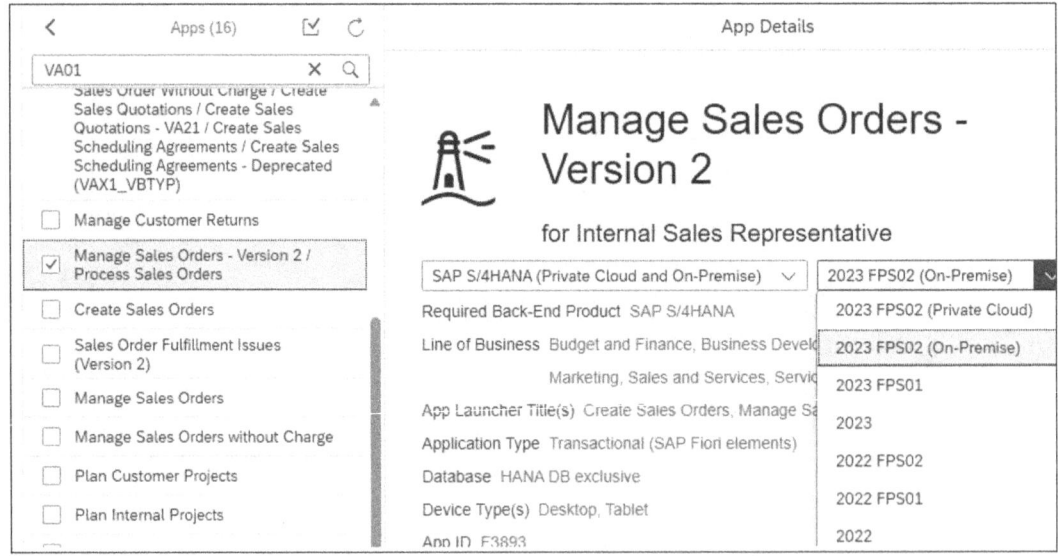

Figure 2-6. *Various variants of VA01 apps are available within the library*

CHAPTER 2   SAP FIORI APPS REFERENCE LIBRARY

The SAP Apps Reference Library gets updated when selecting the correct system, as shown in the figure below.

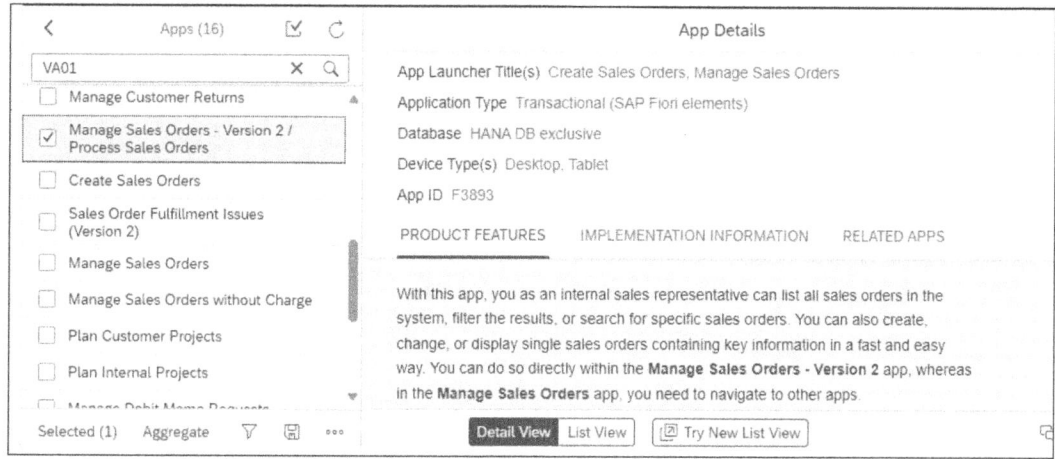

Figure 2-7. Fiori app F3893 for on-premise details

2.1.5 Basic Information Related to the App

SAP provides comprehensive details of the application for implementation. The details are as follows:

CHAPTER 2 SAP FIORI APPS REFERENCE LIBRARY

Details	Description
Required Back-End Product:	SAP S/4HANA
Line of Business:	Budget and Finance, Business Development, Customer, Operations, Sales, Sales and Marketing, Sales and Services, Services
App Launcher Title(s):	Create Sales Orders, Manage Sales Orders
Application Type:	Transactional (SAP Fiori Elements)
Database:	HANA DB exclusive
Device Type(s):	Desktop, Tablet
App ID:	F3893

Figure 2-8. Basic information related to the Fiori app in tabular format

PRODUCT FEATURES

Under the tab **PRODUCT FEATURES**, it displays the functionality of the app. With this app, an internal sales representative can list all sales orders in the system, filter the results, or search for specific sales orders. The agent can also create, change, or display single sales orders containing critical information quickly and easily. You can do this directly within the Manage Sales Orders – Version 2 app; you need to navigate to other apps in the Manage Sales Orders app. It also lists the **key features** of the **Sales Orders app**, which can be viewed in the SAP Fiori Apps Reference Library, as shown in the figure below.

CHAPTER 2   SAP FIORI APPS REFERENCE LIBRARY

> **Key Features**
>
> You can use this app to do the following:
>
> - List sales orders
>
>   You can search for single sales orders or filter the results (for example, by sold-to party), personalize the columns displayed in the table, or export the results list to a spreadsheet or a PDF file. The list is exported as displayed, that is, your column settings and sorting are kept.
>
> - Make changes to one or more sales orders directly in the list
>
>   You can set and remove billing blocks and delivery blocks.
>
> - Create sales orders

Figure 2-9. Product and key features – Fiori app ID F3893

IMPLEMENTATION INFORMATION

Similarly, we can find the following details about the app under the tab **IMPLEMENTATION INFORMATION**. The information is displayed under various categories.

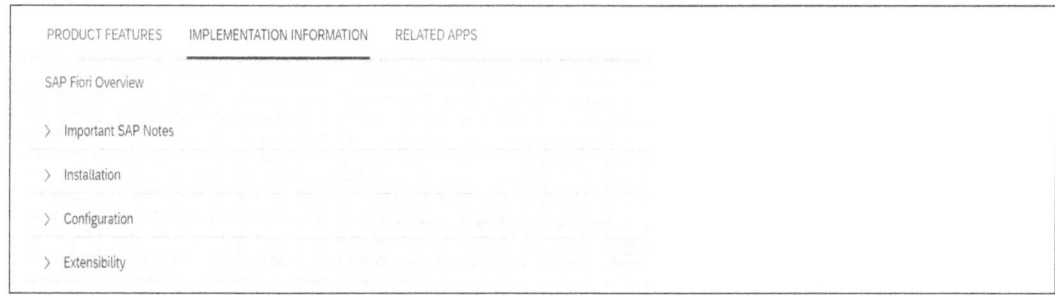

Figure 2-10. Implementation information – Fiori app ID F3893

Installation

The section **Installation** details the components that must be installed in the **front-end** and **back-end** systems for the app to work successfully, as shown in the figure below.

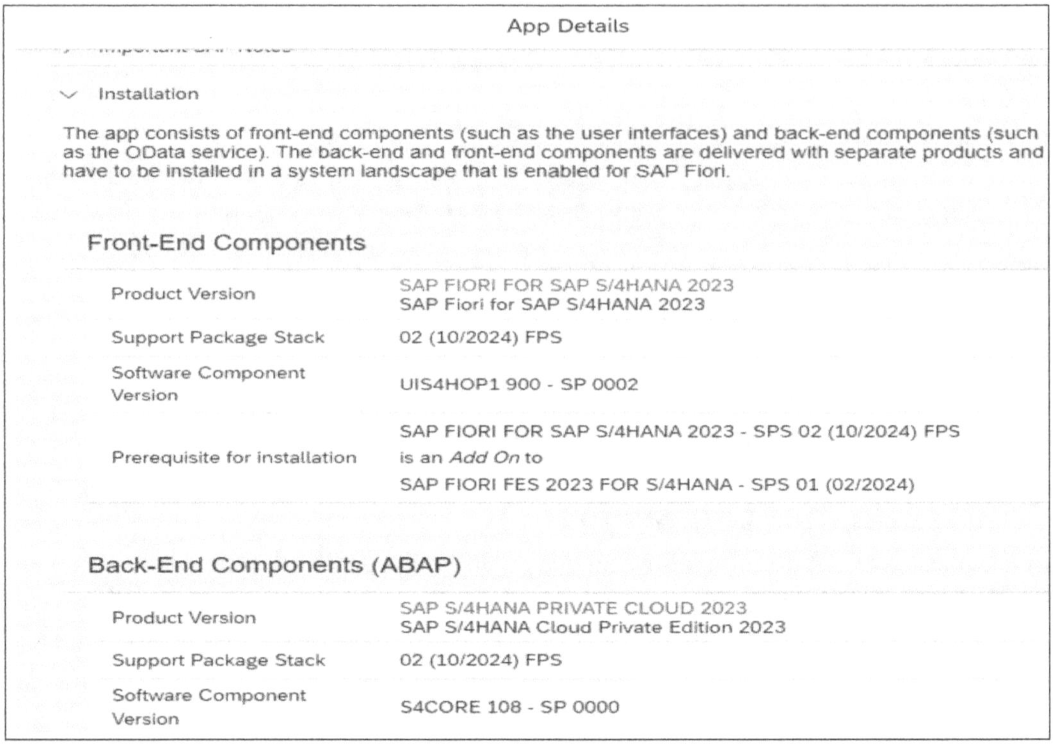

CHAPTER 2   SAP FIORI APPS REFERENCE LIBRARY

Figure 2-11. *Installation details – Fiori app ID F3893*

Configuration

The **Configuration** section includes important information needed to set up the app. They are listed as below. It gives all the information necessary to configure the app:

- SAPUI5 Application
- OData V4 Service Groups
- SAP Fiori Launchpad
- Technical Configuration
- App Launchers
- Target Mappings
- Technical Catalogs
- Business Catalogs

CHAPTER 2 SAP FIORI APPS REFERENCE LIBRARY

- Pages
- Spaces
- Business Roles

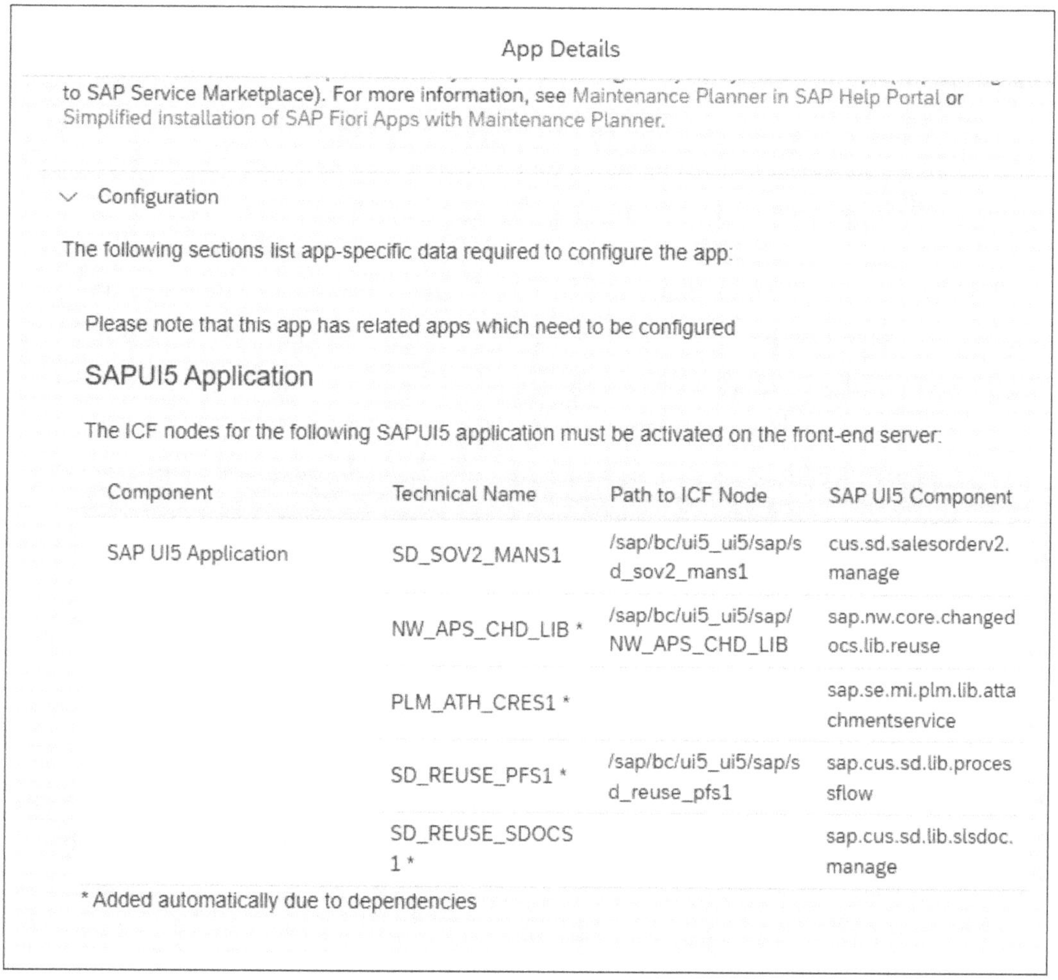

```
App Details

to SAP Service Marketplace). For more information, see Maintenance Planner in SAP Help Portal or
Simplified installation of SAP Fiori Apps with Maintenance Planner.

∨ Configuration

The following sections list app-specific data required to configure the app:

Please note that this app has related apps which need to be configured

SAPUI5 Application

The ICF nodes for the following SAPUI5 application must be activated on the front-end server:
```

Component	Technical Name	Path to ICF Node	SAP UI5 Component
SAP UI5 Application	SD_SOV2_MANS1	/sap/bc/ui5_ui5/sap/sd_sov2_mans1	cus.sd.salesorderv2.manage
	NW_APS_CHD_LIB *	/sap/bc/ui5_ui5/sap/NW_APS_CHD_LIB	sap.nw.core.changedocs.lib.reuse
	PLM_ATH_CRES1 *		sap.se.mi.plm.lib.attachmentservice
	SD_REUSE_PFS1 *	/sap/bc/ui5_ui5/sap/sd_reuse_pfs1	sap.cus.sd.lib.processflow
	SD_REUSE_SDOCS1 *		sap.cus.sd.lib.slsdoc.manage

* Added automatically due to dependencies

Figure 2-12. *Configuration details – Fiori app ID F3893*

The SAP Fiori Apps Reference Library provides detailed information on all the mentioned components and where to install them.

Extended Apps Selection

In July 2018, the SAP Fiori Apps Reference Library introduced a new feature that enables users to combine selected apps with related apps for a more comprehensive user experience. This feature is handy in SAP S/4HANA, where many individual SAP

CHAPTER 2 SAP FIORI APPS REFERENCE LIBRARY

Fiori apps are designed to work together to provide a complete user experience. When deploying a specific Fiori app, you may want to activate related apps simultaneously. The necessary information can be found in the **RELATED APPS** tab. For instance, you can select the associated business catalog for a given app, as shown in the figure below.

Business Catalog(s)		Extend Apps Selection
✓	Business Catalog	Business Catalog Description
✓	SAP_SD_BC_SO_PROC_OP	Sales - Sales Order Processing

Figure 2-13. *Business catalog(s) having Fiori app ID F3893*

The business catalog **SAP_SD_BC_SO_PROC_OP** contains a list of apps, which can be viewed by selecting the catalog and clicking the option Extend Apps Selection. The list of apps is shown in the figure below.

Selected Apps in Business Catalog(s)	
Search	
Selected: 1	
App Name	App ID
☐ Change Billing Document - VF02	VF02
☐ Change Credit Memo Request, Change Debit Memo Request, Change Sales Order Without Charge, Change Sales Orders, Change Sales Orders - VA02	VA02
☐ Change Item Condition	VAX2_CUSTEXPDPRIC
☐ Change Outbound Delivery	VL02N
☐ Complete Missing Data	VAX2_INCLOG

Figure 2-14. *Business catalog(s) Extend Apps Selection – Fiori app ID F3893*

RELATED APPS

The associated apps are shown in the figure below.

CHAPTER 2   SAP FIORI APPS REFERENCE LIBRARY

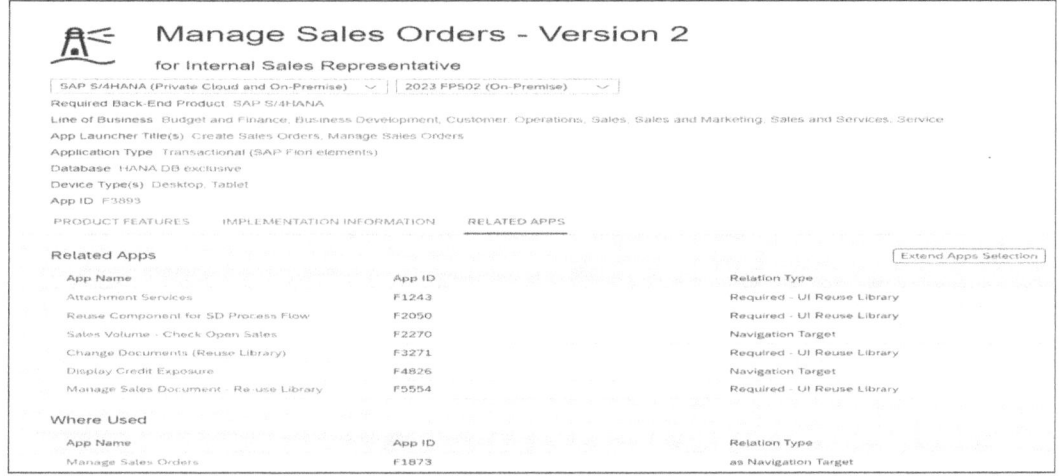

Figure 2-15. *Related apps – Fiori app ID F3893*

2.1.6 Verifying App Details in the System

Administrators or security personnel must verify the components before proceeding by checking the catalog details using the transaction code **PFCG** or **/UI2/FLCPM_CUST**.

Note Subsequent chapters will cover the transaction code **/UI2/FLCPM_CUST**.

Knowing the various component symbols within a specific role is essential, such as when checking the **SAP_BR_INTERNAL_SALES_REP** role. The execution transaction code is **PFCG.**

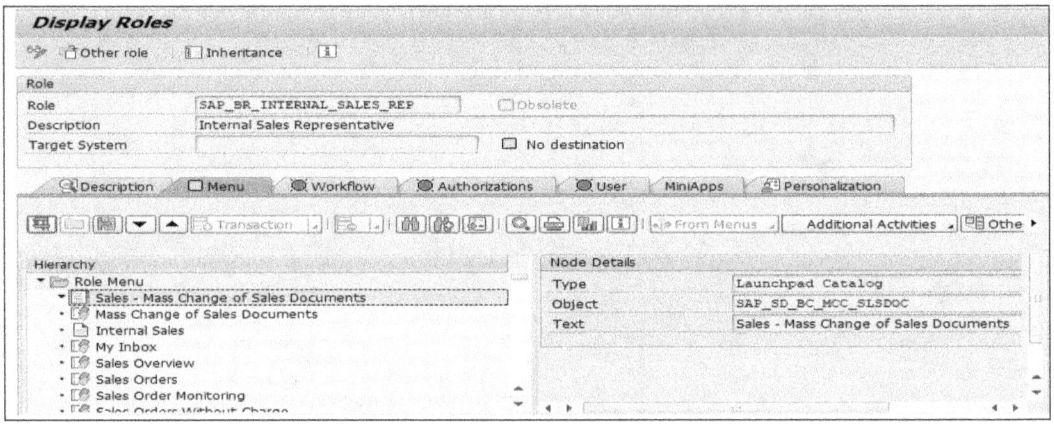

CHAPTER 2   SAP FIORI APPS REFERENCE LIBRARY

Figure 2-16.   Business role containing Fiori app ID F3893

2.1.7 SAP Object Symbols

The **symbols** for various components within the roles are

- **Launchpad Catalog**:
- **Launchpad Group**:
- **Spaces**:

2.1.8 Other Features of the Fiori Library

You can utilize the SAP Fiori Apps Reference Library to find relevant information based on different criteria. For example, select **All apps for SAP S/4HANA (Private Cloud or On-Premise)**.

CHAPTER 2   SAP FIORI APPS REFERENCE LIBRARY

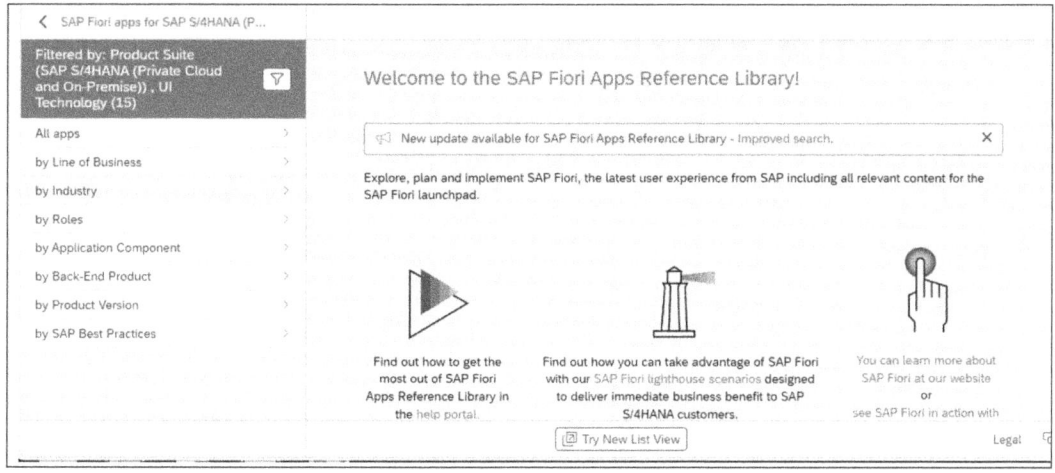

Figure 2-17. *Options available to search apps based on various categories*

The above figure lists multiple options for finding relevant apps, which are as follows:

- All apps
- by Line of Business
- by Industry
- by Roles
- by Application Component
- by Back-End Product
- by Product Version
- by SAP Best Practices

Select the option **by Line of Business**, and the list will appear as shown in the figure below.

45

CHAPTER 2   SAP FIORI APPS REFERENCE LIBRARY

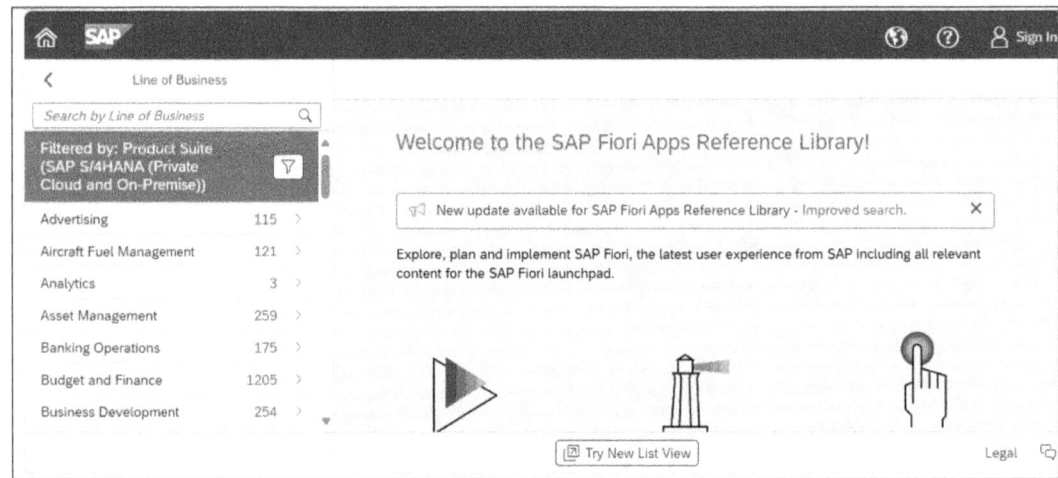

Figure 2-18. *Fiori apps available based on the criteria of the line of business*

The left-hand side of the figure above shows a list of various categories with associated apps under the option by Line of Business. For example, the category **Budget and Finance** has **1,205 apps**. We are expanding the same list of all apps available under the category, as shown in the figure below.

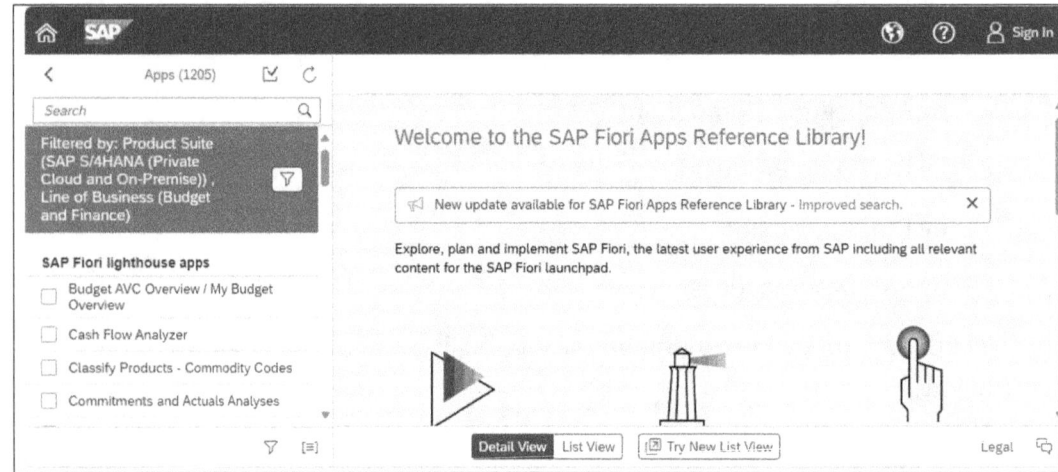

Figure 2-19. *Fiori apps available under the category Budget and Finance*

Similarly, selecting the option **by Roles** gives a list of roles, as shown in the figure below.

CHAPTER 2　SAP FIORI APPS REFERENCE LIBRARY

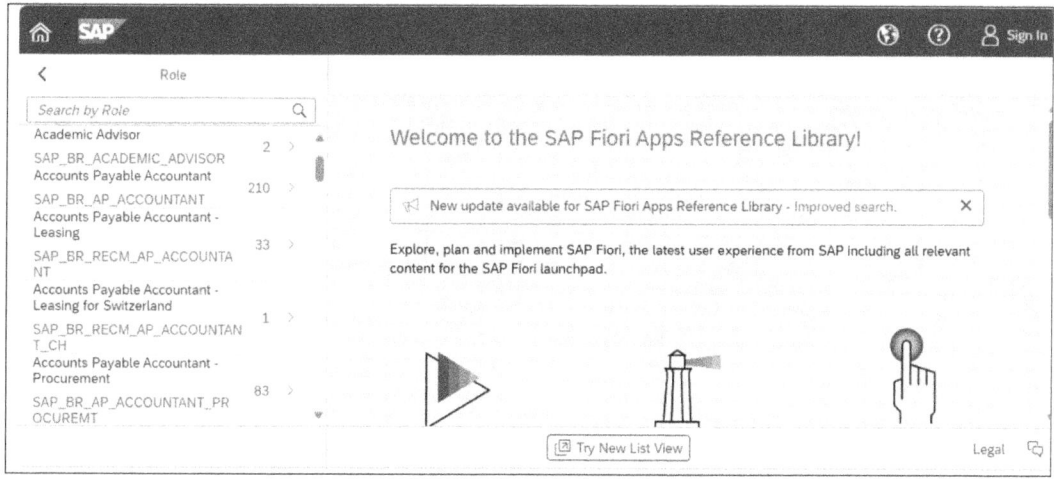

Figure 2-20. *Display of Fiori apps available under the business role*

The above figure displays the role of **SAP_BR_AP_ACCOUNTANT**, which has **210 apps**. Open any app as shown in the figure below.

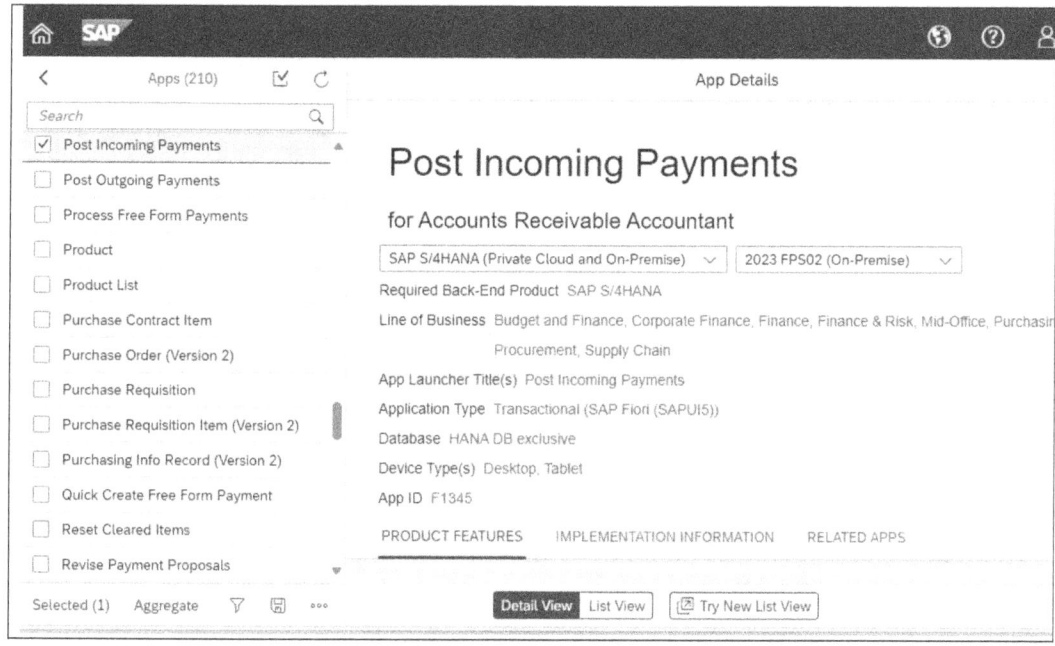

Figure 2-21. *App Post Incoming Payments*

47

CHAPTER 2　SAP FIORI APPS REFERENCE LIBRARY

In the figure above, two boxes at the bottom of the screen provide different viewing options as follows:

- Detail View
- List View

View Properties	Detail View	List View
Scope	Detailed information about a single app/Title.	Apps have a limited range of fields for quick scanning. However, the **List View** may exhibit redundant information, as the data for each app is listed separately. To tackle this issue, utilize the Aggregate function to generate a view without
Adaptation Options	No adaptation options are available.	The list view is highly adaptable, where columns can be displayed or hidden.
Possible Actions	View additional apps from the same business catalog or business role and include them in the current selection.	The File can be exported into an Excel **.csv** file with all available information. Use the Aggregate function, which helps you create and download configuration information for mass configuration. However, downloading the list view information may be incomplete, so it's not recommended. Also, the current view should be tested against the app's recommendations for analysis.

Figure 2-22. *Difference between Detail View and List View*

List View

The **List View** in SAP Fiori provides a tabular representation of all relevant apps or data entries. Users can tailor their view by adjusting the displayed columns using the **column display settings** (accessed via the "gear" button). This feature allows users to show or hide specific columns, enabling a personalized and streamlined interface that caters to individual requirements.

Click the option `List View` at the bottom of the above figure.

CHAPTER 2   SAP FIORI APPS REFERENCE LIBRARY

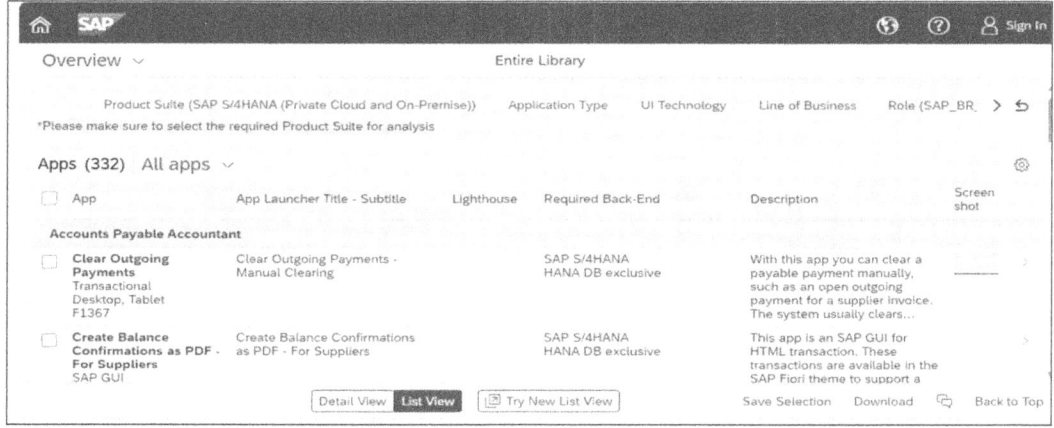

Figure 2-23. *Various views available within the library to review app details*

The above figure brings in three new options at the bottom right of the screen, which are as follows:

- Save Selection
- Download
- Back to Top

You can save the selection or download the file in **Excel** format. You can also select what to download using the symbol ⚙ for column display settings.

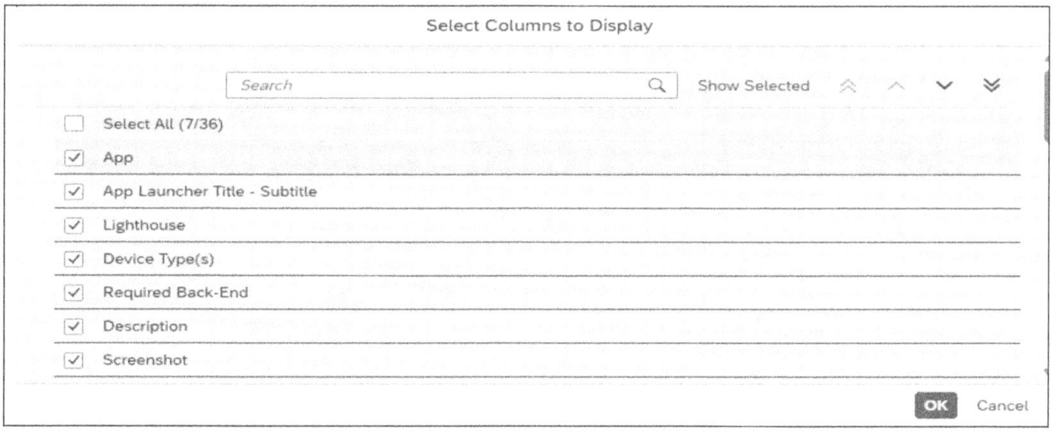

Figure 2-24. *List View categories available to select*

In the above figure, we can filter the list as shown, rearrange the desired output using arrows, and then select the option Show Selected.

49

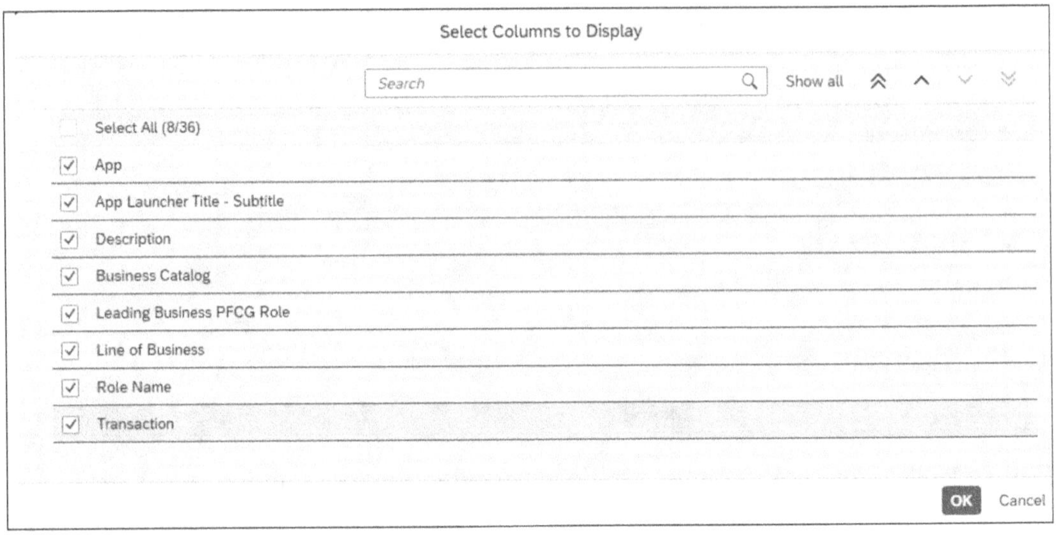

CHAPTER 2   SAP FIORI APPS REFERENCE LIBRARY

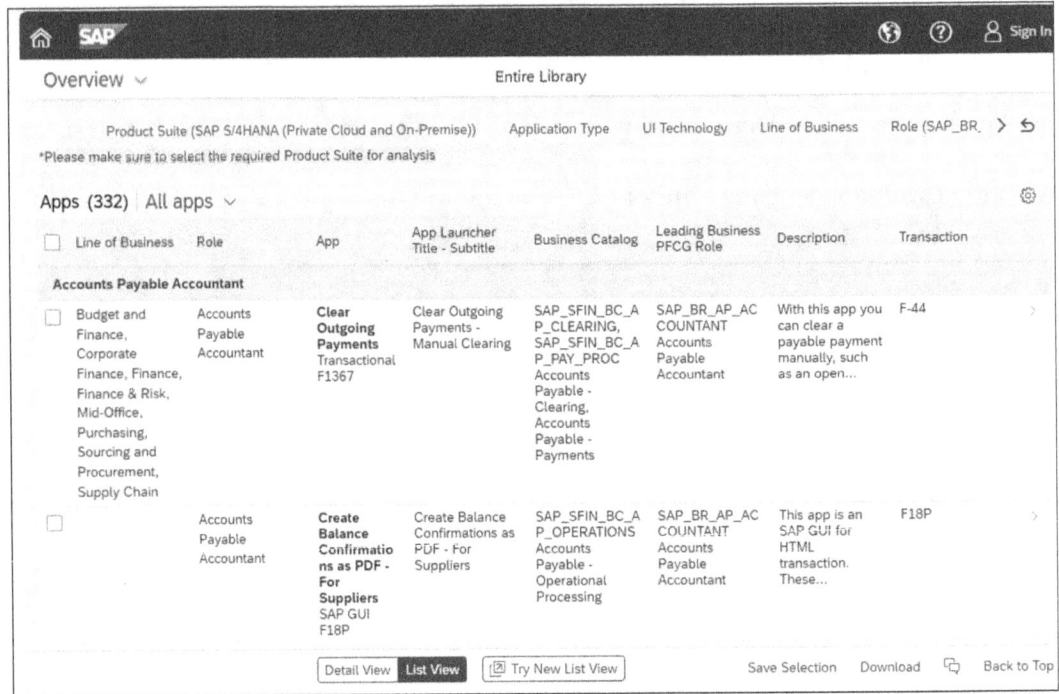

Figure 2-25. Desired output for List View selected

A new Overview window opens, displaying the categories of data.

Figure 2-26. Overview window's details

50

Once the desired information is finalized, click **OK**. Now click the option Download , and it will save data into a ***.csv** file in the **Downloads folder**. Open the Excel file.

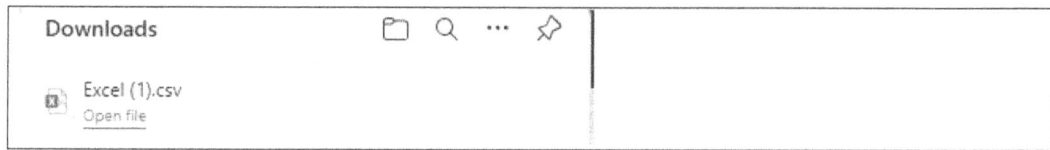

Figure 2-27. *Downloaded List View details into a *.csv file*

The data will be populated when opening the Excel file, as shown in the formatted figure below.

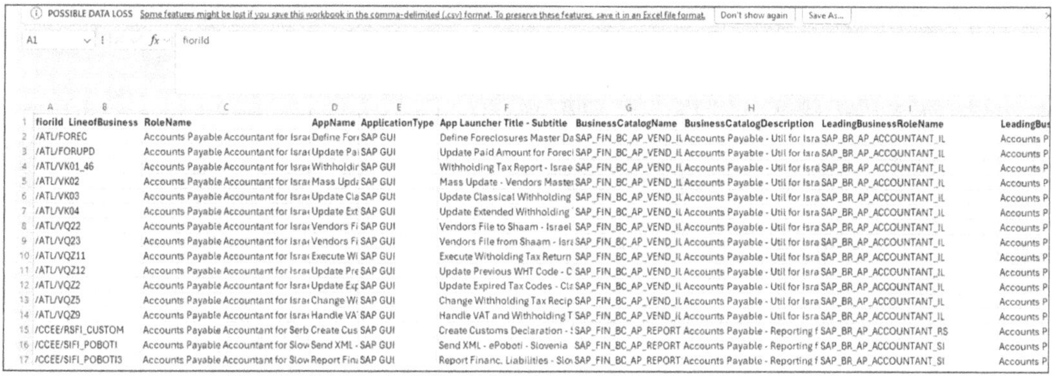

	A	B	C	D	E	F	G	H	I	
1	fiorild	LineofBusiness	RoleName	AppName	ApplicationType	App Launcher Title - Subtitle	BusinessCatalogName	BusinessCatalogDescription	LeadingBusinessRoleName	LeadingBu
2	/ATL/FOREC		Accounts Payable Accountant for Israe	Define For	SAP GUI	Define Foreclosures Master Da	SAP_FIN_BC_AP_VEND_IL	Accounts Payable - Util for Isra	SAP_BR_AP_ACCOUNTANT_IL	Accounts P
3	/ATL/FORUPD		Accounts Payable Accountant for Israe	Update Pa	SAP GUI	Update Paid Amount for Forecl	SAP_FIN_BC_AP_VEND_IL	Accounts Payable - Util for Isra	SAP_BR_AP_ACCOUNTANT_IL	Accounts P
4	/ATL/VK01_46		Accounts Payable Accountant for Israe	Withholdir	SAP GUI	Withholding Tax Report - Israe	SAP_FIN_BC_AP_VEND_IL	Accounts Payable - Util for Isra	SAP_BR_AP_ACCOUNTANT_IL	Accounts P
5	/ATL/VK02		Accounts Payable Accountant for Israe	Mass Upd	SAP GUI	Mass Update - Vendors Master	SAP_FIN_BC_AP_VEND_IL	Accounts Payable - Util for Isra	SAP_BR_AP_ACCOUNTANT_IL	Accounts P
6	/ATL/VK03		Accounts Payable Accountant for Israe	Update Cla	SAP GUI	Update Classical Withholding	SAP_FIN_BC_AP_VEND_IL	Accounts Payable - Util for Isra	SAP_BR_AP_ACCOUNTANT_IL	Accounts P
7	/ATL/VK04		Accounts Payable Accountant for Israe	Update Ext	SAP GUI	Update Extended Withholding	SAP_FIN_BC_AP_VEND_IL	Accounts Payable - Util for Isra	SAP_BR_AP_ACCOUNTANT_IL	Accounts P
8	/ATL/VQ22		Accounts Payable Accountant for Israe	Vendors Fi	SAP GUI	Vendors File to Shaam - Israel	SAP_FIN_BC_AP_VEND_IL	Accounts Payable - Util for Isra	SAP_BR_AP_ACCOUNTANT_IL	Accounts P
9	/ATL/VQ23		Accounts Payable Accountant for Israe	Vendors Fi	SAP GUI	Vendors File from Shaam - Isra	SAP_FIN_BC_AP_VEND_IL	Accounts Payable - Util for Isra	SAP_BR_AP_ACCOUNTANT_IL	Accounts P
10	/ATL/VQZ11		Accounts Payable Accountant for Israe	Execute Wi	SAP GUI	Execute Witholding Tax Return	SAP_FIN_BC_AP_VEND_IL	Accounts Payable - Util for Isra	SAP_BR_AP_ACCOUNTANT_IL	Accounts P
11	/ATL/VQZ12		Accounts Payable Accountant for Israe	Update Pre	SAP GUI	Update Previous WHT Code - C	SAP_FIN_BC_AP_VEND_IL	Accounts Payable - Util for Isra	SAP_BR_AP_ACCOUNTANT_IL	Accounts P
12	/ATL/VQZ2		Accounts Payable Accountant for Israe	Update Exp	SAP GUI	Update Expired Tax Codes - Cla	SAP_FIN_BC_AP_VEND_IL	Accounts Payable - Util for Isra	SAP_BR_AP_ACCOUNTANT_IL	Accounts P
13	/ATL/VQZ5		Accounts Payable Accountant for Israe	Change Wi	SAP GUI	Change Withholding Tax Recip	SAP_FIN_BC_AP_VEND_IL	Accounts Payable - Util for Isra	SAP_BR_AP_ACCOUNTANT_IL	Accounts P
14	/ATL/VQZ9		Accounts Payable Accountant for Israe	Handle VA	SAP GUI	Handle VAT and Withholding T	SAP_FIN_BC_AP_VEND_IL	Accounts Payable - Util for Isra	SAP_BR_AP_ACCOUNTANT_IL	Accounts P
15	/CCEE/RSFI_CUSTOM		Accounts Payable Accountant for Serb	Create Cus	SAP GUI	Create Customs Declaration - S	SAP_FIN_BC_AP_REPORT	Accounts Payable - Reporting f	SAP_BR_AP_ACCOUNTANT_RS	Accounts P
16	/CCEE/SIFI_POBOTI		Accounts Payable Accountant for Slov	Send XML -	SAP GUI	Send XML - ePoboti - Slovenia	SAP_FIN_BC_AP_REPORT	Accounts Payable - Reporting f	SAP_BR_AP_ACCOUNTANT_SI	Accounts P
17	/CCEE/SIFI_POBOTI3		Accounts Payable Accountant for Slov	Report Fin	SAP GUI	Report Financ. Liabilities - Slo	SAP_FIN_BC_AP_REPORT	Accounts Payable - Reporting f	SAP_BR_AP_ACCOUNTANT_SI	Accounts P

Figure 2-28. *Downloaded file details*

The entire SAP Fiori Apps Reference Library can be downloaded in Excel for future reference.

2.1.9 Download the Entire Fiori Library

Note SAP keeps adding and removing apps in the SAP Fiori Apps Reference Library. So when you check the reference library, the number could be different.

CHAPTER 2   SAP FIORI APPS REFERENCE LIBRARY

You can also download the entire Fiori library for your respective version – in our case, S/4HANA 2023 FPS02. Return to the Fiori library, select **All apps for SAP S/4HANA (Private Cloud and On-Premise)**, and then select **All apps** as shown in the figure below.

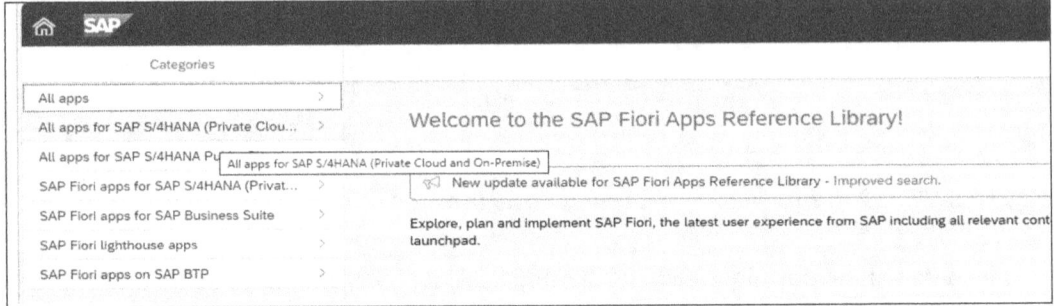

Figure 2-29. *Selection screen for downloading all apps from the SAP Fiori Apps References Library*

The next screen that pops up is as follows.

Figure 2-30. *Screen to select All apps*

CHAPTER 2   SAP FIORI APPS REFERENCE LIBRARY

Now select the option **All apps** in the figure above.

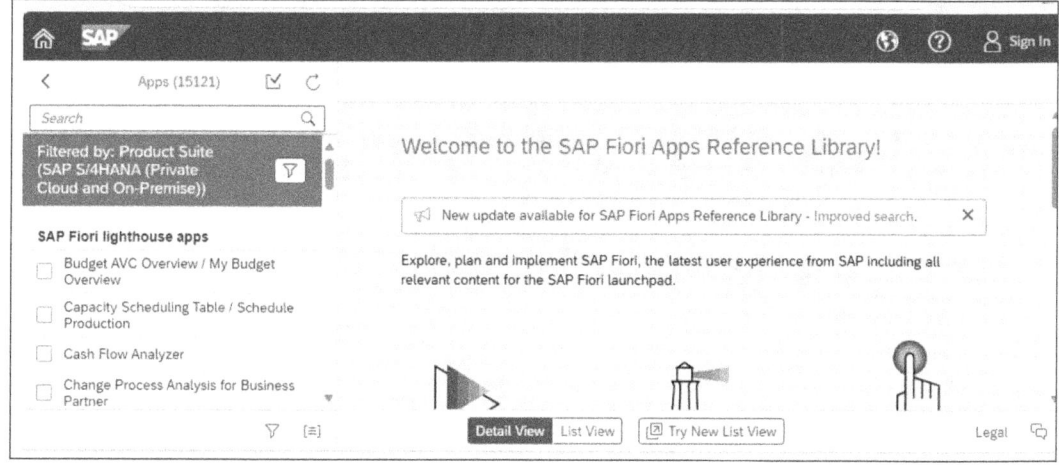

Figure 2-31.   *Listing a total of 15,121 Fiori apps*

It shows that 15,121 apps are available. Selecting the symbol ☑ will select all the apps, as shown in the figure below.

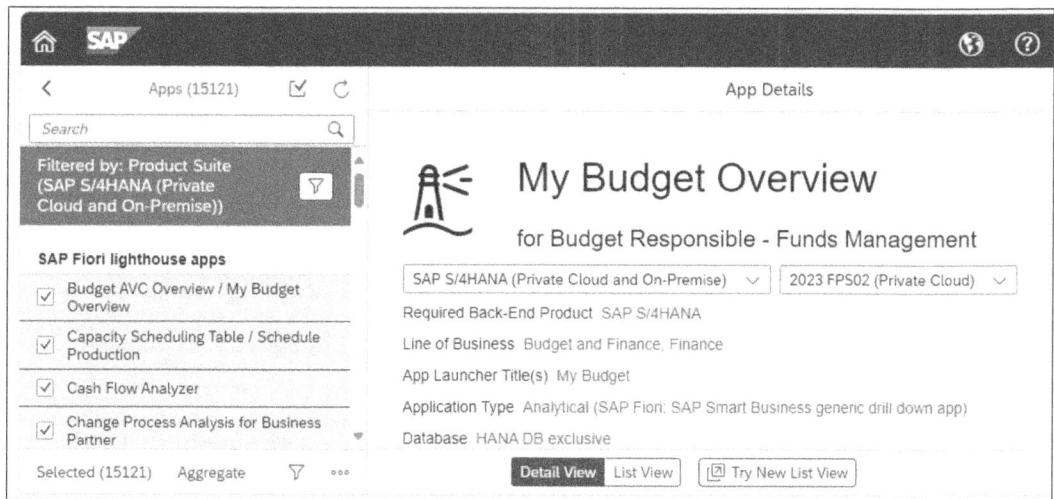

Figure 2-32.   *Screen showing all apps selected and to be downloaded*

CHAPTER 2   SAP FIORI APPS REFERENCE LIBRARY

Select the **Aggregate** option at the bottom-left panel of the above figure, which will provide aggregated information on all the Fiori apps to view and download. This will list all apps available in SAP S/4HANA 2023 FPS02 (**14,681**) and those unavailable (**440**), as shown in the figure below.

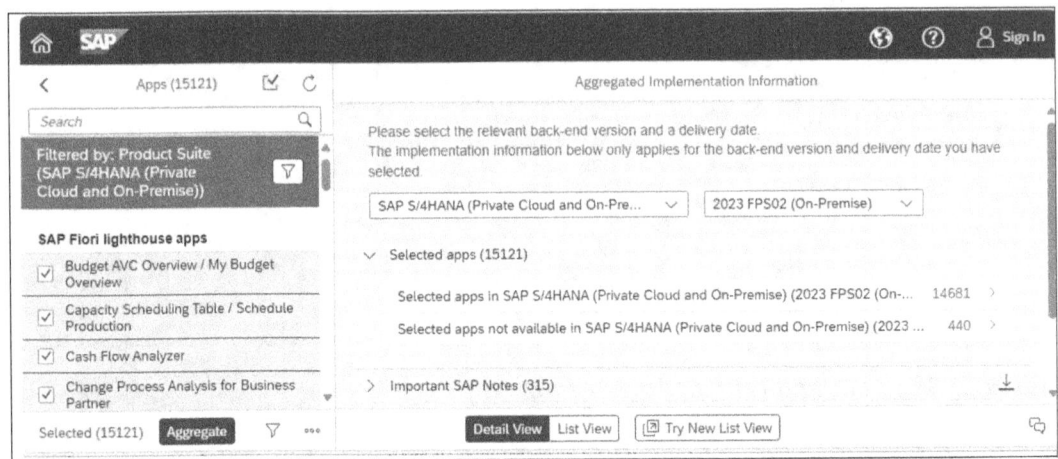

Figure 2-33. *Screen displaying aggregate of apps available to download*

Note   As shown in the figure above, ensure the correct SAP S/4HANA 2023 FPS02 version is selected. You can choose the required version based on your system.

Expand the unavailable apps, and this will list the apps not available in **red**. The figure below also shows the alternative app ID.

CHAPTER 2 SAP FIORI APPS REFERENCE LIBRARY

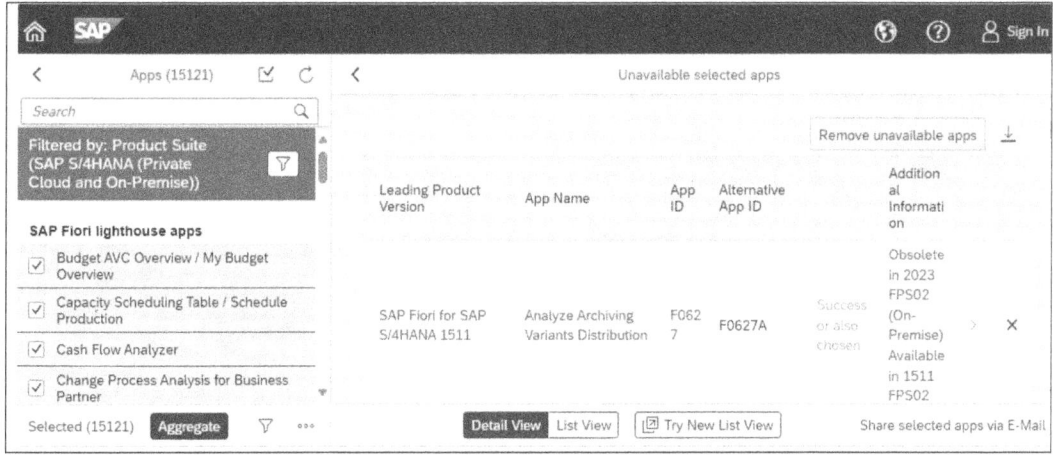

Figure 2-34. *Screen showing unavailable apps for the current version*

Now remove the app by selecting the option Remove unavailable apps.

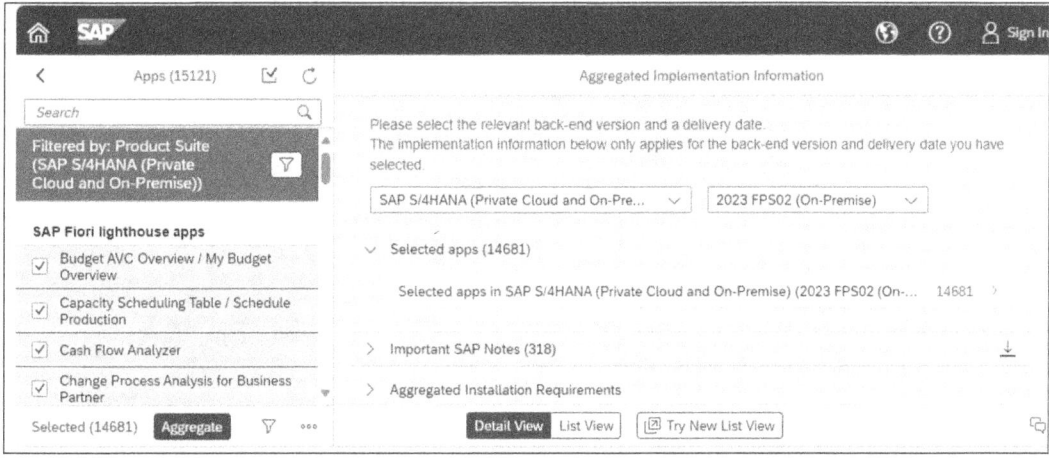

Figure 2-35. *Screen displaying unavailable apps removed for downloading*

The figure above shows that the unavailable apps have been removed. Now click the option List View at the bottom of the screen to download the apps after selecting the desired fields, as shown in the figure below.

55

CHAPTER 2 SAP FIORI APPS REFERENCE LIBRARY

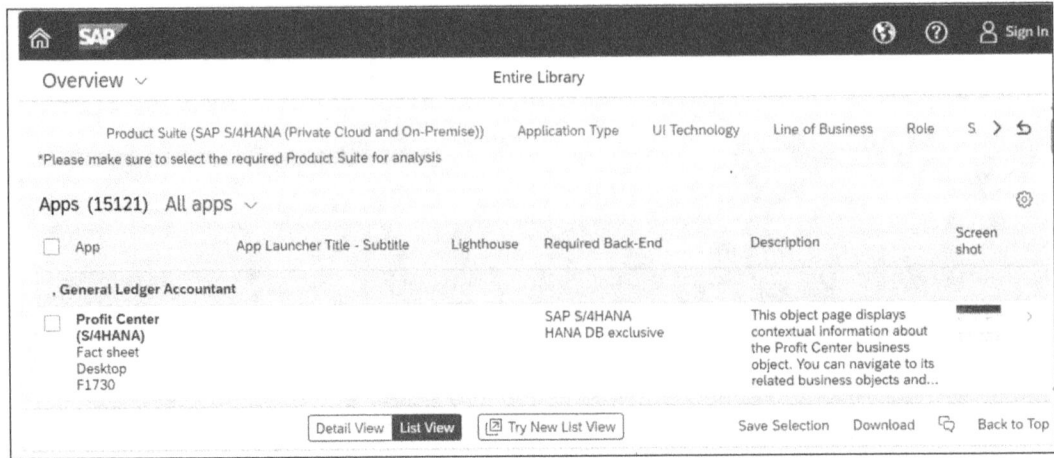

Figure 2-36. *Screen displaying corrected apps available to download*

Now go to ⚙ for column display settings, where we can select components as desired so that the same can be viewed in tabular format, the data displayed in column format. Select the output needed and rearrange. Once the desired output is selected in the order, click the tab option **Show Selected**.

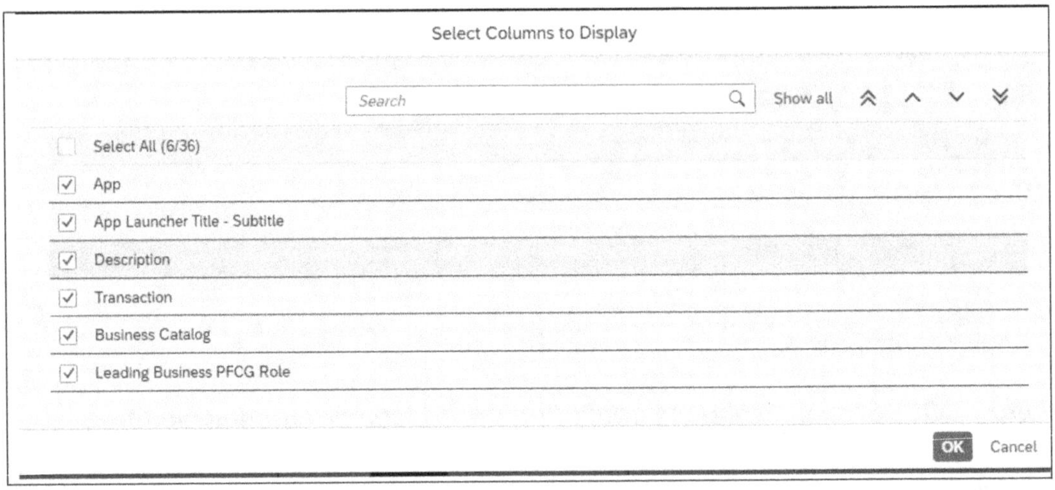

Figure 2-37. *SAP Fiori required app details selected*

Select **OK** and then Download.

CHAPTER 2 SAP FIORI APPS REFERENCE LIBRARY

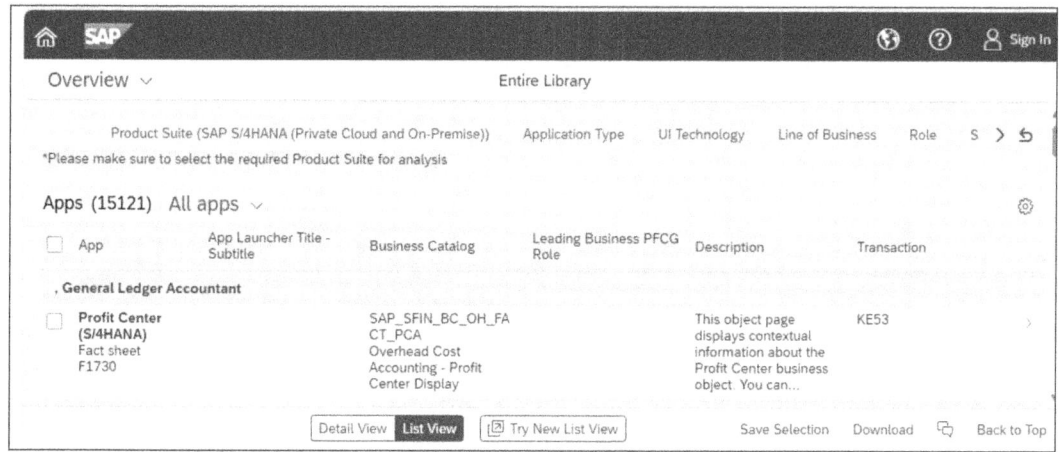

Figure 2-38. *Overview window – selection displayed for downloading*

The above figure displays the data in the desired column. Click the Download option to save the data in a ***.csv** file format. Rename the file to SAP Fiori App Library Data S4HANA 2023 FPS02, and then open it.

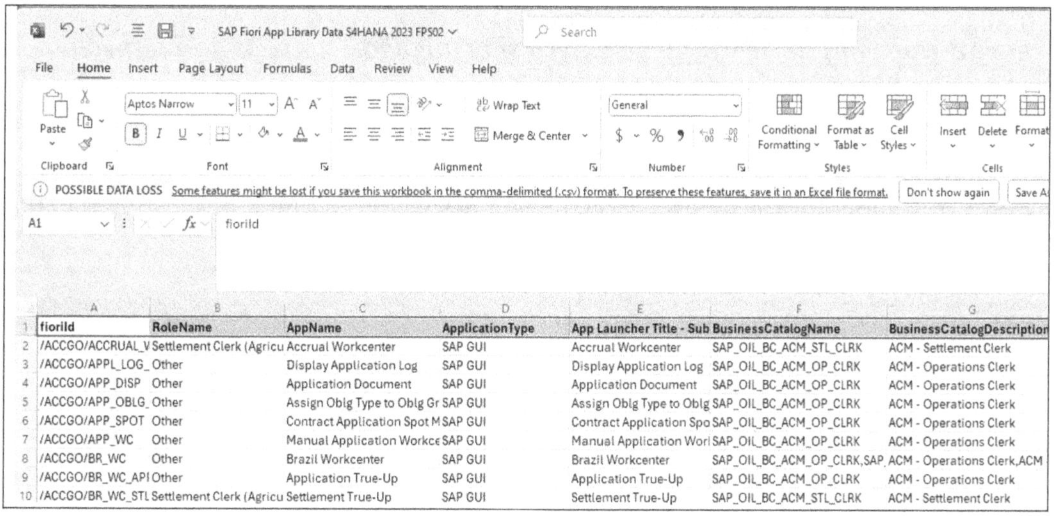

Figure 2-39. *Entire Fiori library downloaded details*

Note The data displayed is in random order and not as selected.

57

You can arrange the data as required. After rearranging the data, the final output needed to perform further analysis is shown in the figure below.

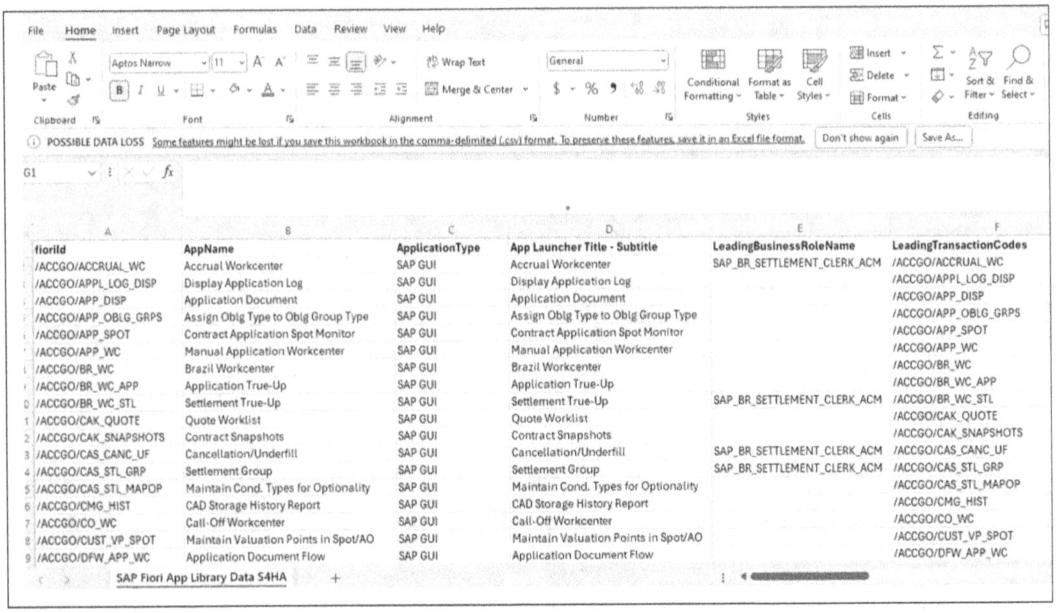

fioriId	AppName	ApplicationType	App Launcher Title - Subtitle	LeadingBusinessRoleName	LeadingTransactionCodes
/ACCGO/ACCRUAL_WC	Accrual Workcenter	SAP GUI	Accrual Workcenter	SAP_BR_SETTLEMENT_CLERK_ACM	/ACCGO/ACCRUAL_WC
/ACCGO/APPL_LOG_DISP	Display Application Log	SAP GUI	Display Application Log		/ACCGO/APPL_LOG_DISP
/ACCGO/APP_DISP	Application Document	SAP GUI	Application Document		/ACCGO/APP_DISP
/ACCGO/APP_OBLG_GRPS	Assign Oblg Type to Oblg Group Type	SAP GUI	Assign Oblg Type to Oblg Group Type		/ACCGO/APP_OBLG_GRPS
/ACCGO/APP_SPOT	Contract Application Spot Monitor	SAP GUI	Contract Application Spot Monitor		/ACCGO/APP_SPOT
/ACCGO/APP_WC	Manual Application Workcenter	SAP GUI	Manual Application Workcenter		/ACCGO/APP_WC
/ACCGO/BR_WC	Brazil Workcenter	SAP GUI	Brazil Workcenter		/ACCGO/BR_WC
/ACCGO/BR_WC_APP	Application True-Up	SAP GUI	Application True-Up		/ACCGO/BR_WC_APP
/ACCGO/BR_WC_STL	Settlement True-Up	SAP GUI	Settlement True-Up	SAP_BR_SETTLEMENT_CLERK_ACM	/ACCGO/BR_WC_STL
/ACCGO/CAK_QUOTE	Quote Worklist	SAP GUI	Quote Worklist		/ACCGO/CAK_QUOTE
/ACCGO/CAK_SNAPSHOTS	Contract Snapshots	SAP GUI	Contract Snapshots		/ACCGO/CAK_SNAPSHOTS
/ACCGO/CAS_CANC_UF	Cancellation/Underfill	SAP GUI	Cancellation/Underfill	SAP_BR_SETTLEMENT_CLERK_ACM	/ACCGO/CAS_CANC_UF
/ACCGO/CAS_STL_GRP	Settlement Group	SAP GUI	Settlement Group	SAP_BR_SETTLEMENT_CLERK_ACM	/ACCGO/CAS_STL_GRP
/ACCGO/CAS_STL_MAPOP	Maintain Cond. Types for Optionality	SAP GUI	Maintain Cond. Types for Optionality		/ACCGO/CAS_STL_MAPOP
/ACCGO/CMG_HIST	CAD Storage History Report	SAP GUI	CAD Storage History Report		/ACCGO/CMG_HIST
/ACCGO/CO_WC	Call-Off Workcenter	SAP GUI	Call-Off Workcenter		/ACCGO/CO_WC
/ACCGO/CUST_VP_SPOT	Maintain Valuation Points in Spot/AO	SAP GUI	Maintain Valuation Points in Spot/AO		/ACCGO/CUST_VP_SPOT
/ACCGO/DFW_APP_WC	Application Document Flow	SAP GUI	Application Document Flow		/ACCGO/DFW_APP_WC

Figure 2-40. *Fiori library data displayed showing Fiori app IDs and respective transaction codes*

Selecting **Transaction Codes** can filter the data shown in the figure above. This is achieved by modifying the dataset and concealing specific columns, as illustrated in the figure below.

CHAPTER 2   SAP FIORI APPS REFERENCE LIBRARY

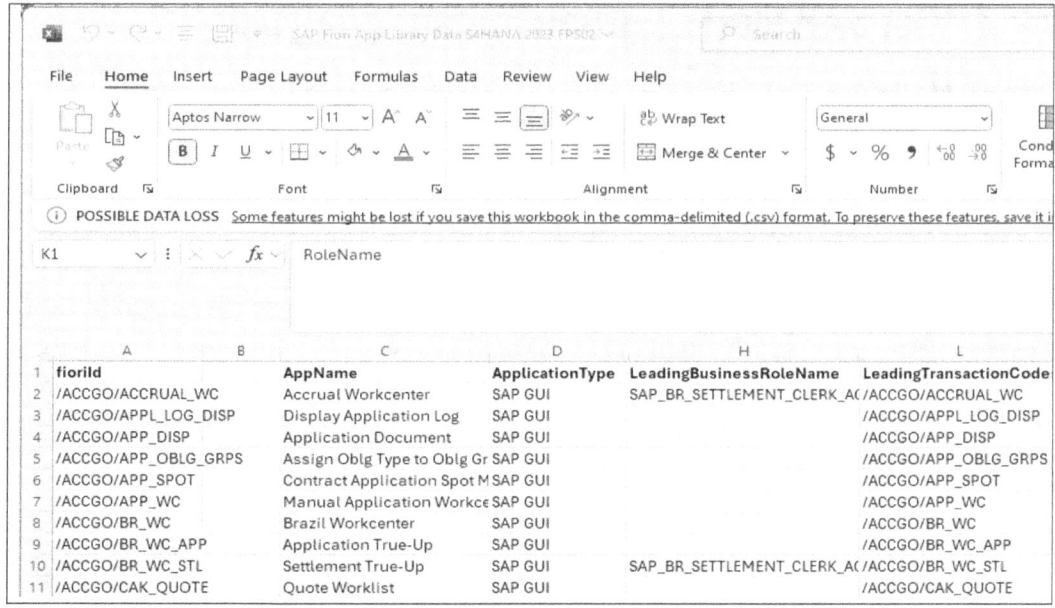

Figure 2-41. Filtered data displayed

2.2 SAP Tools Within the Library

SAP Fiori also provides two tools for analysis:

- Get SAP Fiori App Recommendations.
- Run SAP Fiori Upgrade Impact Analysis.

2.2.1 Get SAP Fiori App Recommendations

Get the **SAP Fiori App Recommendations** tool provided by SAP and generate a detailed report from the SAP Fiori Apps Reference Library. This report lists recommended SAP Fiori apps based on your business processes and system landscape. You can view a sample analysis file or upload your profiles (system details and transaction codes list) to generate a report that categorizes the apps based on various criteria such as product, application type, line of business, role, relevance, and UI technology. It also provides system readiness details. This report will be discussed in detail in Chapter 3.

59

2.2.2 Run SAP Fiori Upgrade Impact Analysis

The **SAP Fiori Upgrade Impact Analysis** tool is a valuable resource for assessing the effects of a planned SAP upgrade on your current Fiori app landscape. It streamlines identifying potential issues like deprecated or incompatible apps, allowing for proactive planning and mitigation. By providing detailed analysis, this tool helps you optimize your upgrade strategy, minimize disruptions, and ensure a smooth transition to the new SAP version, preserving the functionality and user experience of your Fiori applications. This report presentation is beyond the scope of this book.

2.3 Summary

The SAP Fiori Apps Reference Library is a valuable resource for organizations looking to adopt and implement Fiori apps. It contains detailed information to help plan and execute your Fiori strategy, ensuring a successful transition to a modern and user-friendly SAP experience. The library provides descriptions, technical specifications, configuration details, and deployment options for various SAP Fiori applications. It is essential to understand available Fiori apps, their functionalities, integration into your SAP environment, and finding apps for a given transaction code.

CHAPTER 3

SAP Fiori Apps Recommendation Report

The SAP Fiori App Recommendations Analysis Report finds the best Fiori apps for you based on how you use the system and your business roles. It helps you choose apps more efficiently, boosting productivity and improving user experience. This report supports a smooth transition to SAP Fiori that fits your business needs.

3.1 Introduction

The SAP Fiori Apps Reference Library is a powerful **self-service tool** that empowers you to explore, plan, and implement SAP Fiori apps and classic applications based on SAP GUI and Web Dynpro. It is an extensive online repository of available apps with vital technical details such as SAP Notes, prerequisites, support package levels, add-ons, and configuration information to get the apps up and working seamlessly. Furthermore, the library offers comprehensive information on product versions, software components, configuration settings, and extensibility points, enabling you to understand the implementation prerequisites for your SAP S/4HANA apps.

In the SAP Fiori Apps Reference Library, you can find apps that suit and fit your needs. The tool recommends apps based on relevance and readiness. Relevance refers to apps suitable for your business processes, while readiness indicates how prepared your system is to use SAP Fiori apps. In general, the SAP Fiori Apps Reference Library provides the following information:

> **Process-Specific Apps:** The library provides information on Fiori apps tailored to your business processes.
>
> **Preinstalled Apps:** The library provides information on SAP Fiori apps that are already installed and usable without system updates.

Upgrade Apps: The library provides information on SAP Fiori apps that can be used following a software update or database migration.

Technical Insights: The library provides comprehensive information on SAP Fiori apps, including vital technical data such as installation and configuration, empowering you with the needed knowledge.

Integration Configuration: The library provides information on the configuration required to integrate classic SAP GUI and Web Dynpro applications into the SAP Fiori Launchpad.

Version Specific: The library provides information on various SAP Fiori apps across various data versions, including current and previous versions.

Deployment Information: The library provides aggregated installation and configuration information for a selection of apps.

Reference Resources: The library provides information on SAP Fiori apps and links to related resources such as app documentation, the Product Availability Matrix, and the Maintenance Planner.

Plugin Requirements: The library provides information on the installations required (plugins) to use certain SAP Fiori apps.

The tool **SAP Fiori App Recommendations** analysis is based on the **SAP Fiori Apps Reference Library**. With this tool or report, you can identify the SAP Fiori apps that best suit your business process needs. This tool requires transaction codes as an input file, a mandatory step in running the analysis.

This tool or this report bases its recommendations on two factors: the **relevance of the apps** in your environment based on transaction usage and the **readiness of your systems** to implement Fiori apps. The significance of the apps is determined by their importance to your business processes, and your system's readiness is determined by the components installed.

The **App Recommendations Analysis Report** is a comprehensive analysis that provides valuable information regarding the relevant Fiori apps for your business processes. It highlights the installed Fiori apps that can be used without any system

CHAPTER 3 SAP FIORI APPS RECOMMENDATION REPORT

update. It identifies SAP Fiori apps that can be used after a software update or data migration. Moreover, it provides information about the installations, including plugins and add-ons, that may be required to use certain Fiori apps. This report recommends the corresponding Fiori apps based on the transaction codes, depending on the components installed in your systems.

3.2 App Recommendations Report Process

This section analyzes the equivalent Fiori apps for specific transaction codes using the option Get SAP Fiori App Recommendations . We will use the appropriate option to examine the prerequisites and information required to generate this report. The process for determining relevance and Fiori apps is outlined in the diagram below, along with a detailed explanation.

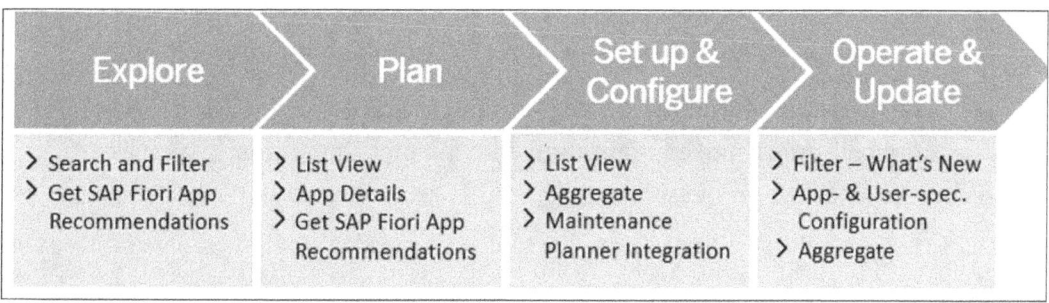

Figure 3-1. Schematic of steps to determine apps

3.2.1 Explore

The Explore phase of the process involves assessing whether functions and apps in SAP Fiori support your crucial business processes. This can be accomplished in the following ways.

- Utilize the **search** and **filter** functions to discover apps that align with your business and system needs. Each app includes essential information to assist you in assessing its technical requirements and the business context.

- Use the **SAP Fiori App Recommendations** function to obtain a list of SAP Fiori app recommendations based on your business processes (**relevance**) and the software components and versions in your system landscape (**readiness**).

3.2.2 Plan

In the Plan phase, you need an overview of the required updates and installations to set up your system landscape for the selected apps.

- Use the **List View** to get an overview of critical information for your app selection. This view creates a data table with one line per app containing essential information. You can filter and configure your choice and then download it to an **Excel (.csv)** file.

- Use the **Detail View (app details)** to access comprehensive information about each app's features and implementation.

- The **Aggregate function** provides your app with a validated and duplicate-free list of configuration data for specific purposes, such as a list of OData services.

3.2.3 Set Up and Configure

In the process's execution phase, you have chosen the apps to implement.

- You can use the **Aggregate function** to display implementation and configuration details for selected apps and their dependencies, including product versions and prerequisites. This view allows direct access to the Maintenance Planner to make necessary changes to your system landscape. You can also share this information via **email**.

- From the section on aggregated configuration requirements, you can export a list of ICF nodes and OData services and activate multiple ICF nodes and OData services using predefined task lists for automatic configuration.

3.2.4 Operate and Update

In the Operate and Update phase, look for new and updated app versions that require configuration or system landscape adjustments.

- Use the **What's New filter** to see new and updated apps from the last quarter, regardless of the product.

- Use the **Aggregate function** and the Maintenance Planner can help you make the required configuration and landscape updates.

3.3 Prerequisites

This report is designed to provide a comprehensive list of Fiori apps that are aligned with your business processes. It uses a list of transaction codes loaded into the Fiori Apps Reference Library and generates a tailored output with the Fiori App Recommendations analysis tool. You can download this report for future reference. As an additional feature, the report checks the readiness of your system environment by providing a detailed list of installed software component versions. It also identifies whether all required components are installed in your landscape and highlights the missing product versions necessary for installing a particular Fiori app.

To use this report, there are **five** prerequisites as listed below:

1. **S User ID:** To generate a recommendation report, you must log in with your SAP Marketplace S user **ID** into the Fiori Apps Reference Library.

2. **Transaction Code Input File:** Additionally, you must create a **list of transaction codes** (from BPO) used in your environment for Fiori app determination. Suppose you're implementing a new system from scratch. In that case, during the Greenfield business requirement gathering, you need to manually create a list of transaction usage based on business processes and associated transaction codes identified (roles and metrics defined). To identify datasets, permanently save the file in ***CSV** format with **header information (mandatory)**.

3. **System Component Installed Input File:** The security team needs to ask the BASIS team to provide a list of components installed in your system. You can download this list from the System Status option, listing elements, plugins, and add-ons installed. Save the file in **CSV format** with header information to identify datasets.

4. **Analysis Name:** Naming and running the analysis.

5. **Result and Analysis:** Review the result and analyze the output generated.

> **Note** All generated **CSV** files should contain header information to identify the datasets.

Furthermore, when migrating from an ECC system to an S/4HANA system and planning to implement Fiori through a Brownfield implementation, it is crucial to remember that there is a history of prior transaction codes in use. There are several ways of determining this earlier history, and given that the systems are already in place, it is possible to identify which components have been installed.

3.4 Preparing Data and System Files

Before using the tool, the data files for input into the SAP Fiori App Recommendations tool must be generated. The files needed are listed below:

- Usage profile
- Front-end/back-end system profile
- Native HANA DB system profile

3.4.1 Usage Profile

Here, we need the **usage profile**, a list of transaction codes used in your environment. This list can be obtained in three different ways, as listed below.

CHAPTER 3   SAP FIORI APPS RECOMMENDATION REPORT

Using Transaction Code ST03/ST03N

You can get the list by using transaction code **ST03** or **ST03N**. BASIS team members or business administrators can provide this list or report for a specific period, like six months or one year, as required. To generate the Excel file, follow the steps below:

Start the **Workload Monitor transaction ST03N** in the embedded S/4HANA system.

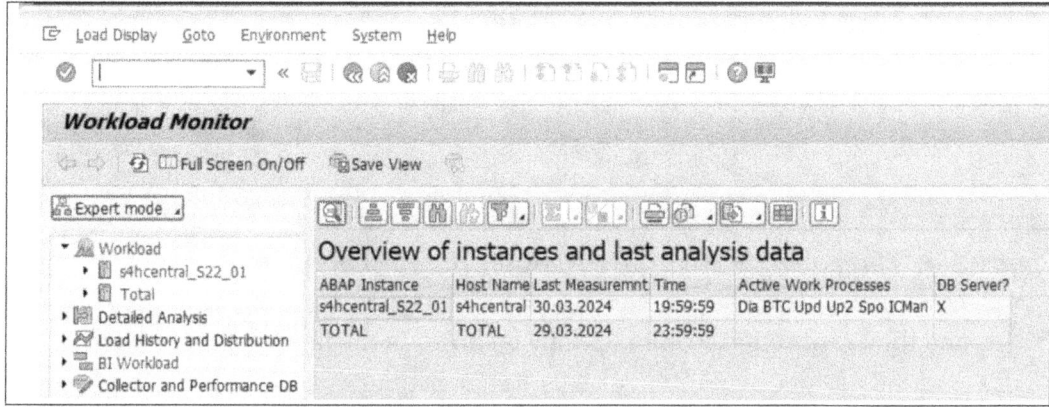

Figure 3-2. *Workload Monitor ST03N transaction code input screen*

As shown in the figure below, select the **Workload** option, expand the **Total** option, and then select the **Month** option.

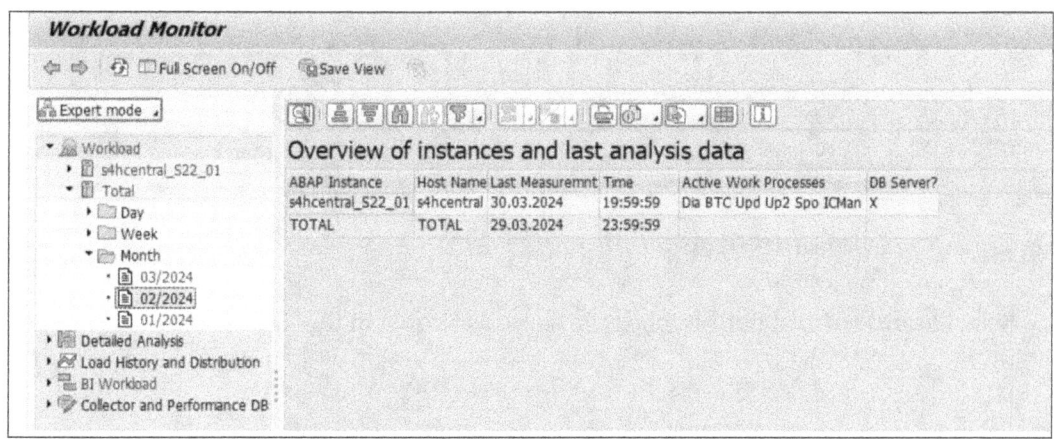

Figure 3-3. *Review ST03N for a given month as an example*

In the above figure, expand the option **Month**; select the appropriate month, for example, **02/2024**; and double-click it.

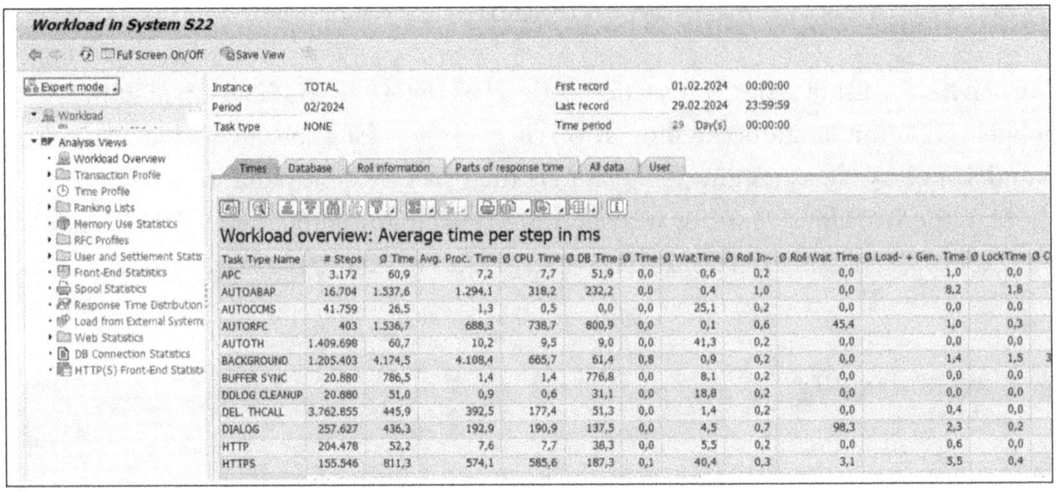

CHAPTER 3 SAP FIORI APPS RECOMMENDATION REPORT

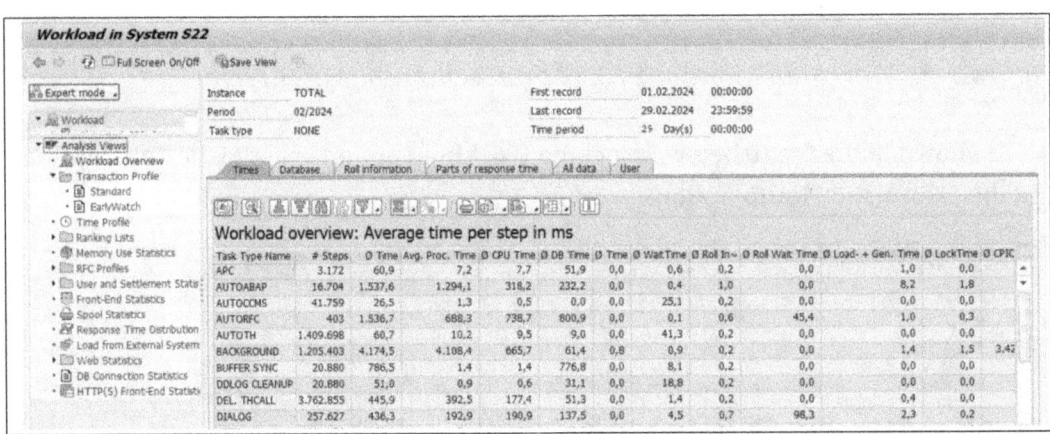

Figure 3-4. *Data available within ST03N for the given month*

Expand the **Transaction Profile** option, as shown in the figure below.

Figure 3-5. *Expanding Transaction Profile data*

Select **Standard** and double-click the same as shown in the figure below.

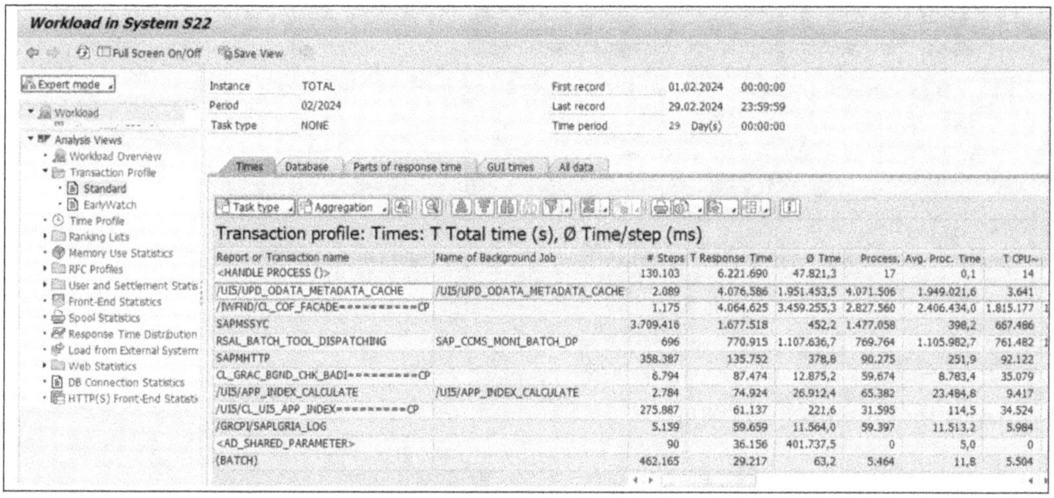

CHAPTER 3 SAP FIORI APPS RECOMMENDATION REPORT

Figure 3-6. *Selection of the Standard profile*

The figure above lists the transaction codes used in **02/2024**. Download the same by clicking the option Spreadsheet, and a window will open, as shown in the figure below.

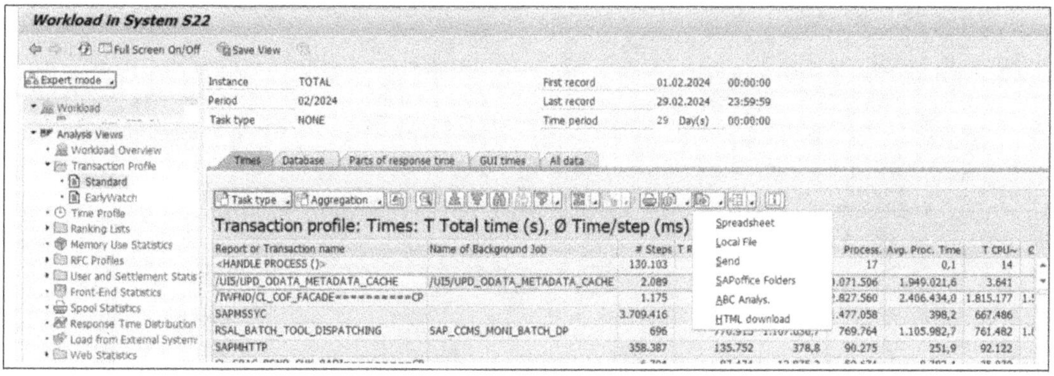

Figure 3-7. *Selecting Spreadsheet as an option to download*

You can download it by clicking the option **Spreadsheet**. A window titled **Select Spreadsheet** will open, as shown in the figure below.

69

CHAPTER 3   SAP FIORI APPS RECOMMENDATION REPORT

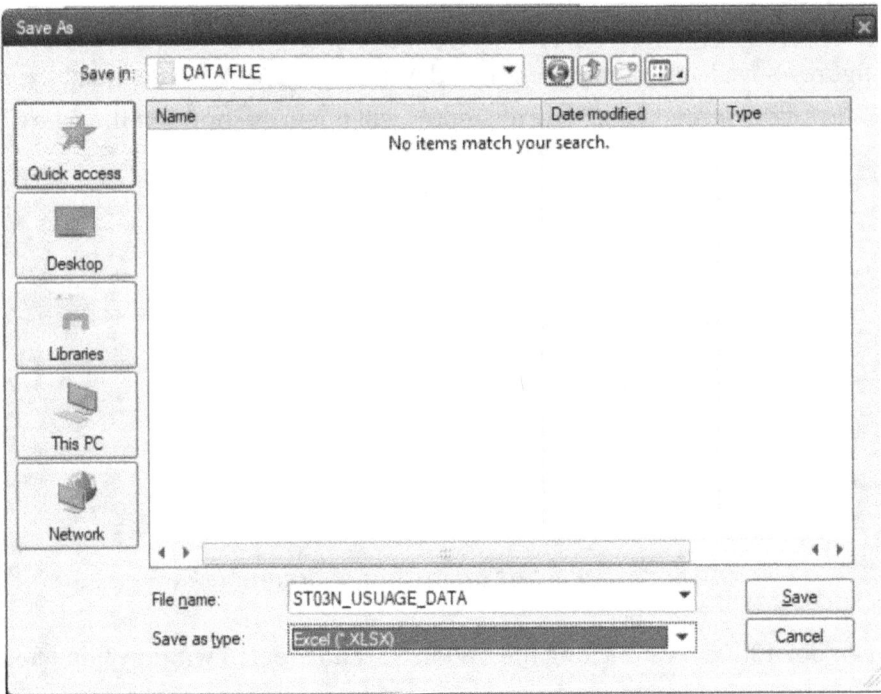

Figure 3-8.   Download option

To proceed further, click the continue icon.

Figure 3-9.   Saving ST03N usage data

In the above figure, give the name of the file as **ST03N_USUAGE_DATA.csv**, and for the option **Save as type**, use **CSV UTF-8 (Comma delimited) (*.csv)**, and then save the file by using the option Save. Once saved, open the file, and it will show data as shown in the figure below.

70

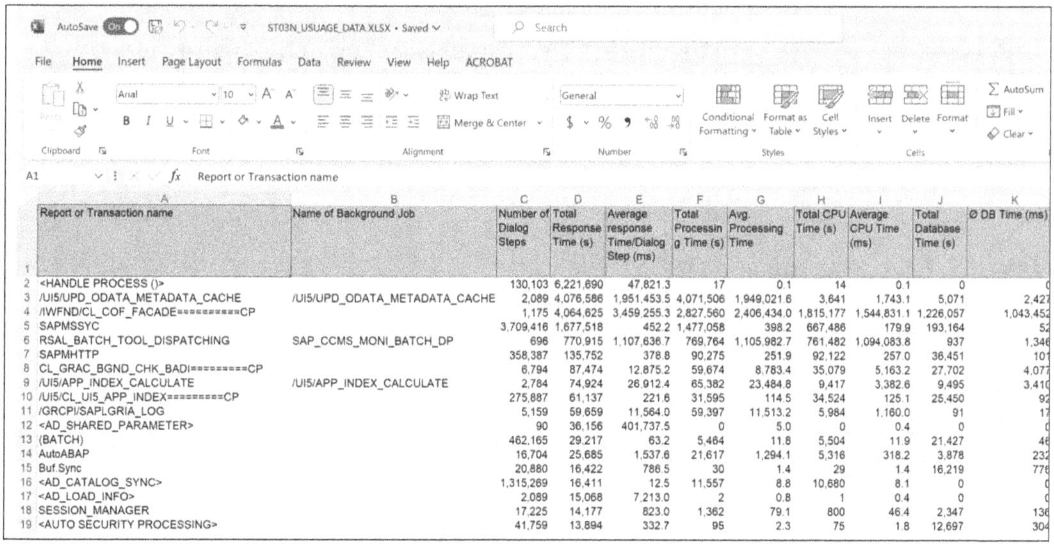

CHAPTER 3   SAP FIORI APPS RECOMMENDATION REPORT

Figure 3-10.   Downloaded transaction code ST03N data information

The next step involves extracting transaction codes from a generated list, removing duplicates, and adding a transparent header like **TransactionCodes**. The codes should be sorted in ascending order and saved in the desired format *.csv. The filtered data is displayed in the figure below.

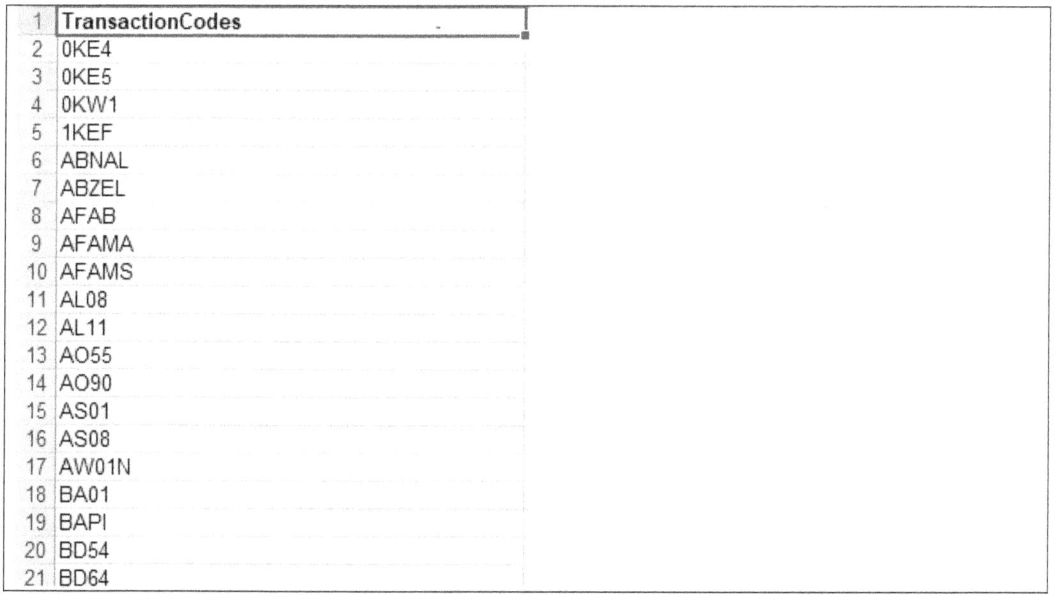

#	TransactionCodes
2	0KE4
3	0KE5
4	0KW1
5	1KEF
6	ABNAL
7	ABZEL
8	AFAB
9	AFAMA
10	AFAMS
11	AL08
12	AL11
13	AO55
14	AO90
15	AS01
16	AS08
17	AW01N
18	BA01
19	BAPI
20	BD54
21	BD64

Figure 3-11.   Filtered data showing only transaction code data from ST03N

71

CHAPTER 3   SAP FIORI APPS RECOMMENDATION REPORT

Re-save ( Save) the file in CSV format as shown in the figure below.

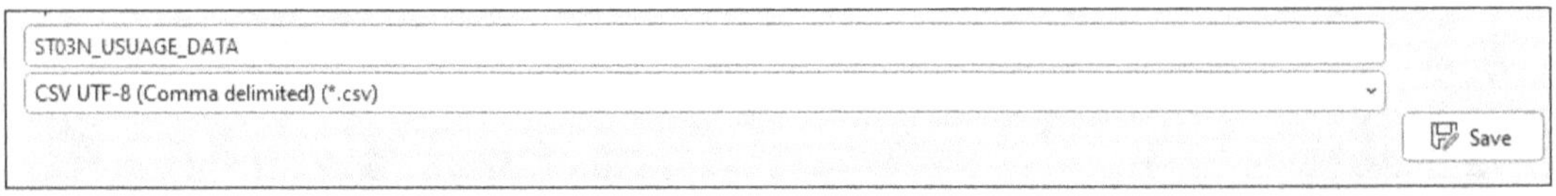

Figure 3-12. Data saved as a CSV file

The data input file has now been saved, as illustrated below. The newly generated list contains 753 transaction codes for which matching apps are required.

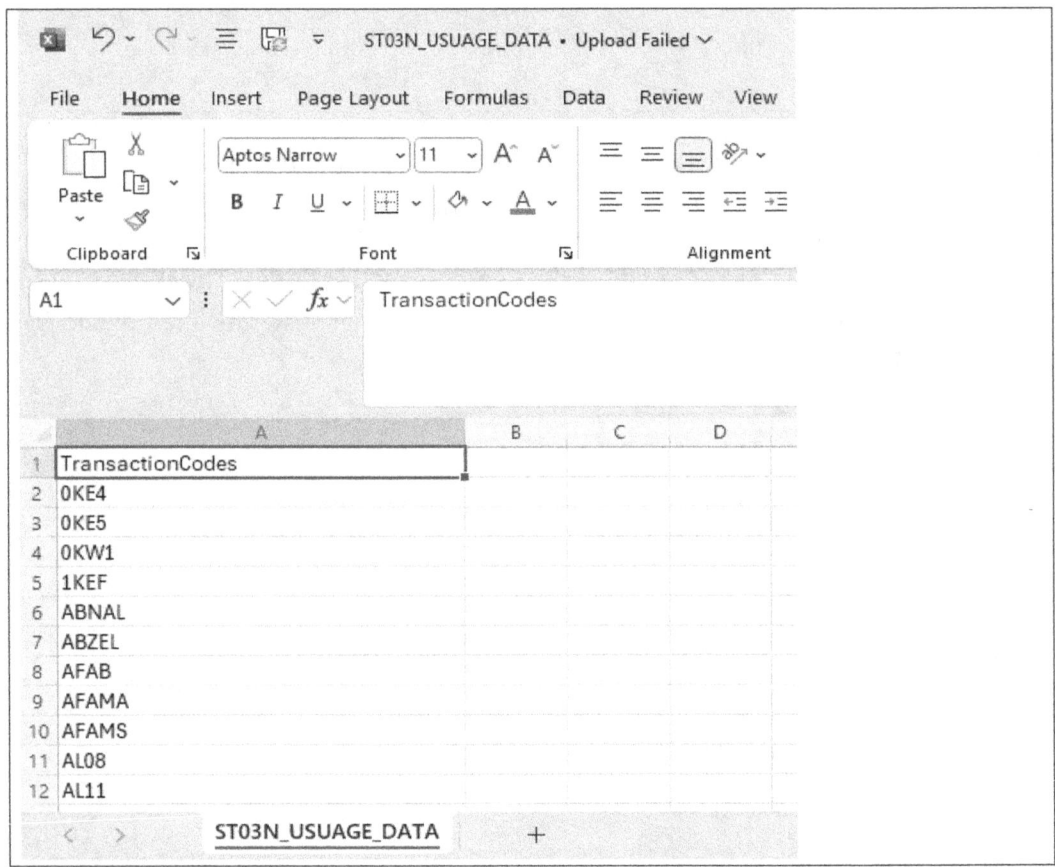

Figure 3-13. Filtered data generated file of transaction code ST03N

Once saved, this file can be used as input for analysis and becomes a component of the **usage profile**.

CHAPTER 3 SAP FIORI APPS RECOMMENDATION REPORT

Note Add the ST03NReport or TransactionCodes in the Excel file in the first row as a header.

Using SE16 and AGR_TCODES

In this scenario, we will access the production system using transaction **SE16** and table **AGR_TCODES**. From there, we will download data for all active and currently used roles, as illustrated in the figure below.

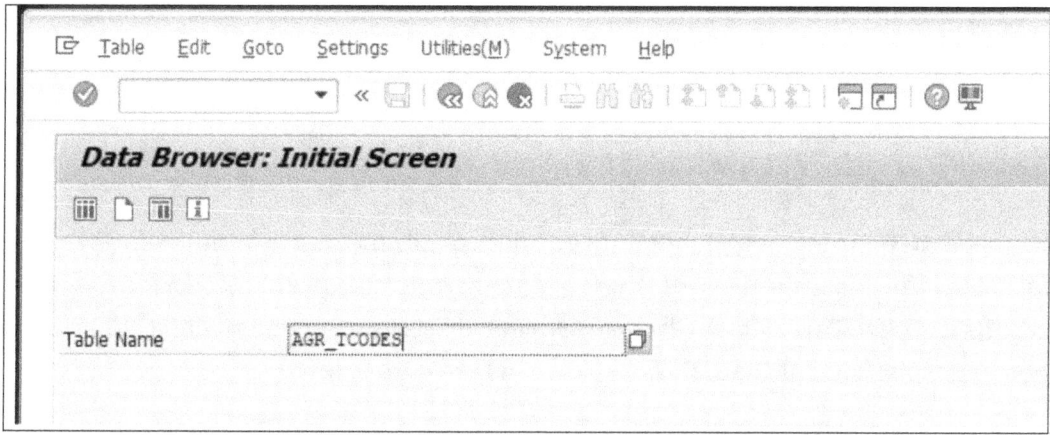

Figure 3-14. Using table AGR_TCODES within transaction code SE16

To proceed, click the execute icon or press the **Enter key**.

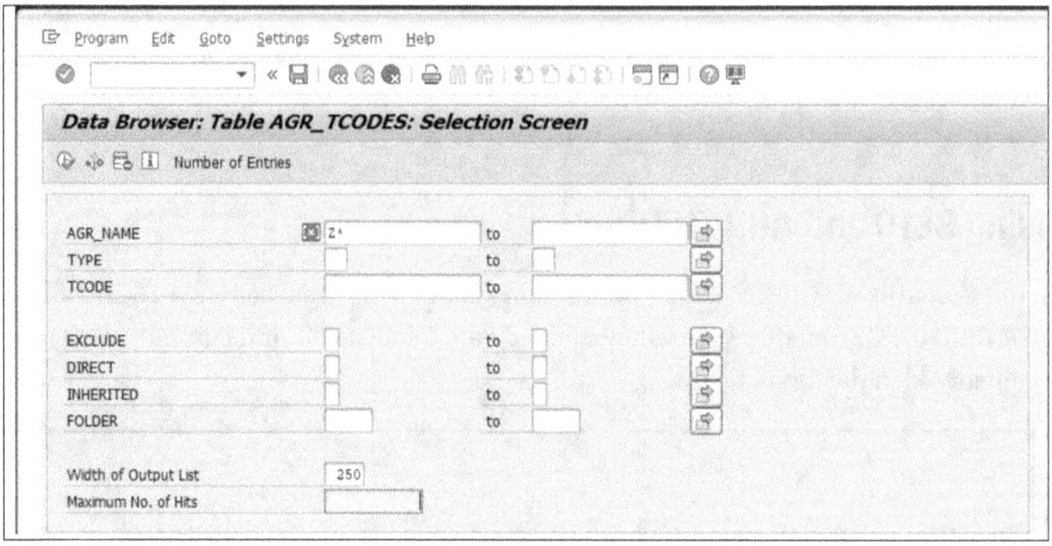

CHAPTER 3   SAP FIORI APPS RECOMMENDATION REPORT

Figure 3-15. AGR_TCODES table input screen

In the **AGR_NAME** field, input **Z*** to encompass all custom roles within the system. Ensure that the **Maximum No. of Hits** tab remains **empty**. Proceed by clicking the **execute** icon. This action will create a detailed list showing transaction codes next to their corresponding role names, as depicted in the figure below.

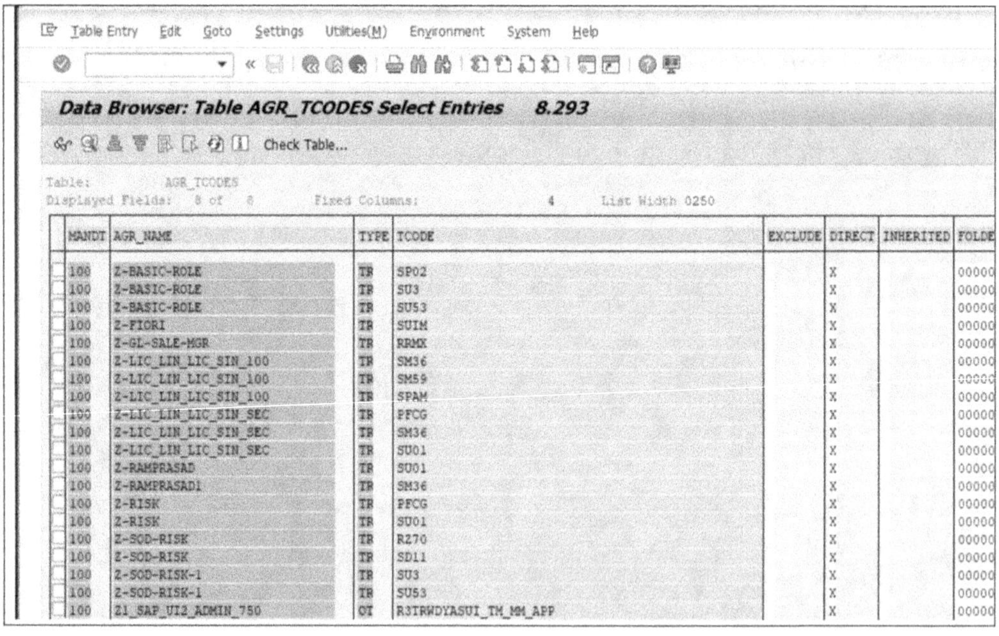

Figure 3-16. AGR_TCODES output screen listing all transactions in roles

CHAPTER 3   SAP FIORI APPS RECOMMENDATION REPORT

Refine the list to display solely the **TCODE** column, showcasing only the **transaction codes**. Save this filtered data in a ***.CSV** file format, ensuring the inclusion of **header information**. This generated file will serve as an **input** during analysis and become an integral part of the **usage profile**.

Using the Manual Option

In this scenario, we will manually create a ***.CSV** file containing the **transaction codes** for which Fiori apps are required. Start by setting up the **header** and then listing all the necessary transaction codes below it, as shown in the figure below.

Figure 3-17. Generate the transaction codes list manually

This generated file can be used as an input file during analysis and becomes part of the **usage profile**. The file name with the Transactions or Reports header is **S4HANA_TCODES_USUAGE_PROFILE.csv**, as shown in the figure below.

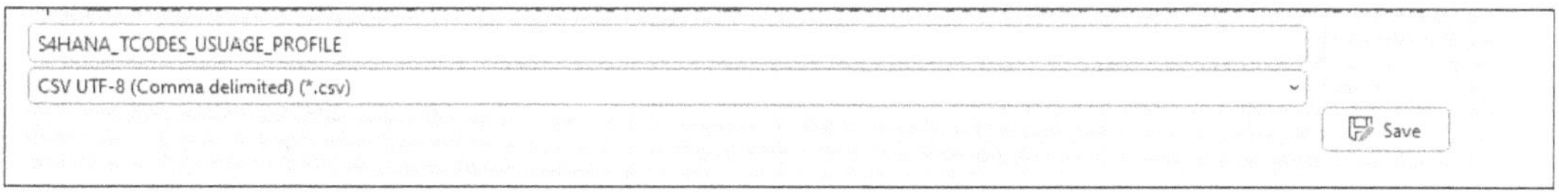

Figure 3-18. Usage profile data saved with a file name

75

CHAPTER 3 SAP FIORI APPS RECOMMENDATION REPORT

Retrieve Action Usage Data from GRC

There are two ways to receive data from GRC for input in the Fiori App Recommendations tool for the SAP system:

1. GRC Action Usage Table GRACACTUSAGE
2. GRC NWBC Role Mining Action Usage

GRC Action Usage Table GRACACTUSAGE

The GRACACTUSAGE table in SAP GRC tracks action usage and user transactions for access control. The generated list can be input into the SAP Fiori App Recommendations tool.

Go to the system GRC and enter transaction **SE16** and the table name **GRACACTUSAGE** as shown in the figure below.

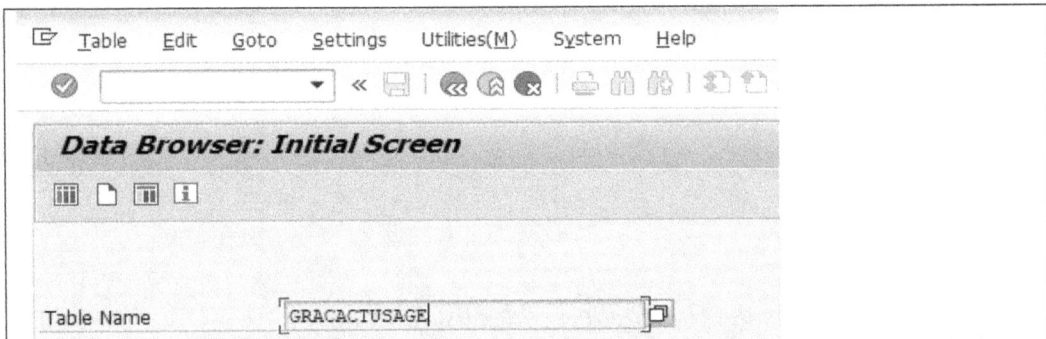

Figure 3-19. *Transaction SM30 input screen with table GRACACTUSAGE*

Execute the same by clicking the table content icon (**F7**) .

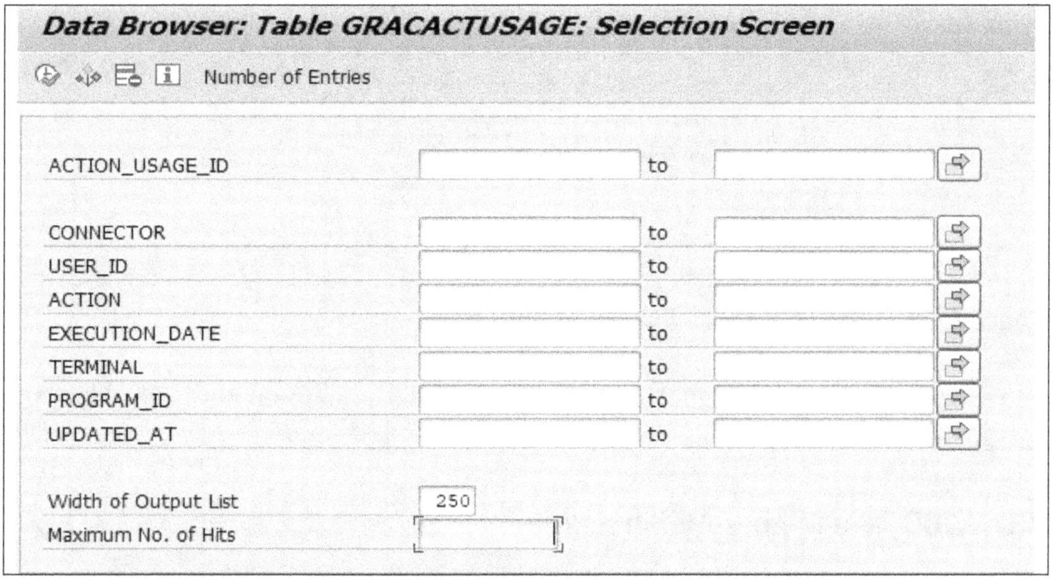

Figure 3-20. *Table GRACACTUSAGE input fields*

The key fields in the GRACACTUSAGE table, as shown in the figure above, are described as follows:

- **USER_ID**: The ID of the user performing the action.

- **ACTION**: The specific action (e.g., transaction code). **USAGE_COUNT**: It tracks the number of times the action has been used.

- **TIMESTAMP**: It records the date and time of the action's usage.

- **ROLE_ID**: The role associated with the user's access can be stored optionally.

- **SYSTEM_ID**: Identifies the system in which the action was performed.

- **APPLICATION**: Indicates the application or module where the action was carried out.

Keep everything blank and execute the same by clicking  . The result is displayed in the figure below.

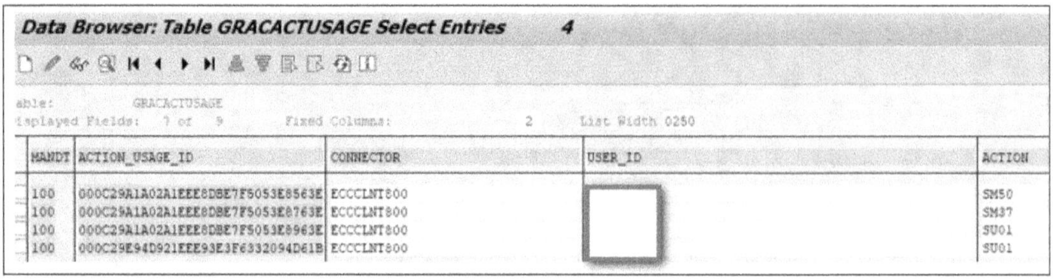

CHAPTER 3 SAP FIORI APPS RECOMMENDATION REPORT

Figure 3-21. Table GRACACTUSAGE output

This data can be downloaded as a **CSV** file and used as an input file for the Fiori App Recommendations tool.

GRC NWBC Role Mining Action Usage

The Action Usage option in SAP GRC NWBC Role Mining shows how often users access transactions, programs, or apps within roles. This option helps you understand how roles and their actions (like **transactions**, programs, or Fiori apps) are used. Before using this option, a **repository sync** and **action usage sync** must be performed within the GRC system under transaction SPRO.

Within **GRC**, go to **NWBC ➤ Access Management ➤ Role Mining**.

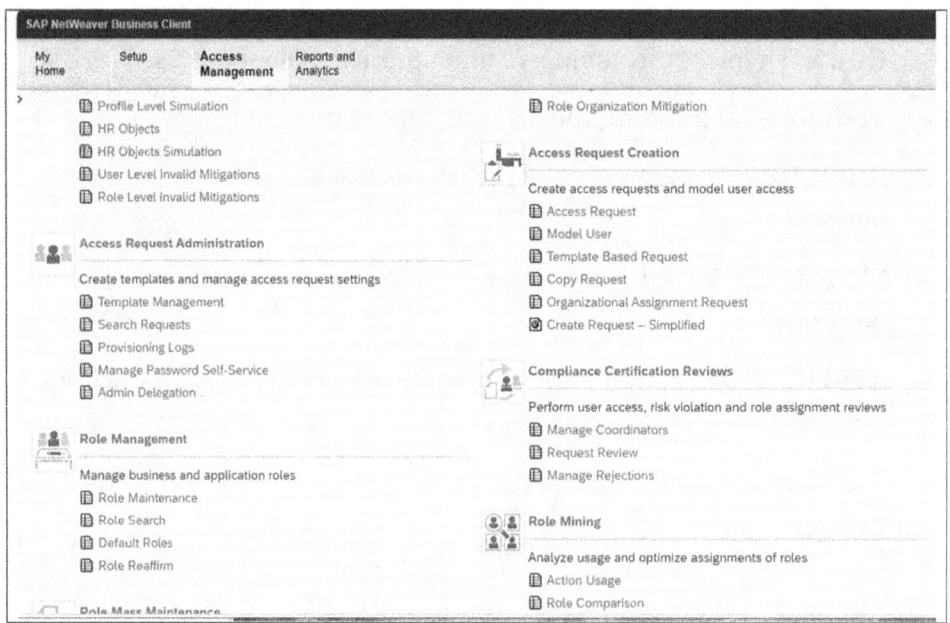

Figure 3-22. GRC NWBC screen

78

CHAPTER 3   SAP FIORI APPS RECOMMENDATION REPORT

Click the option Action Usage 📄 Action Usage .

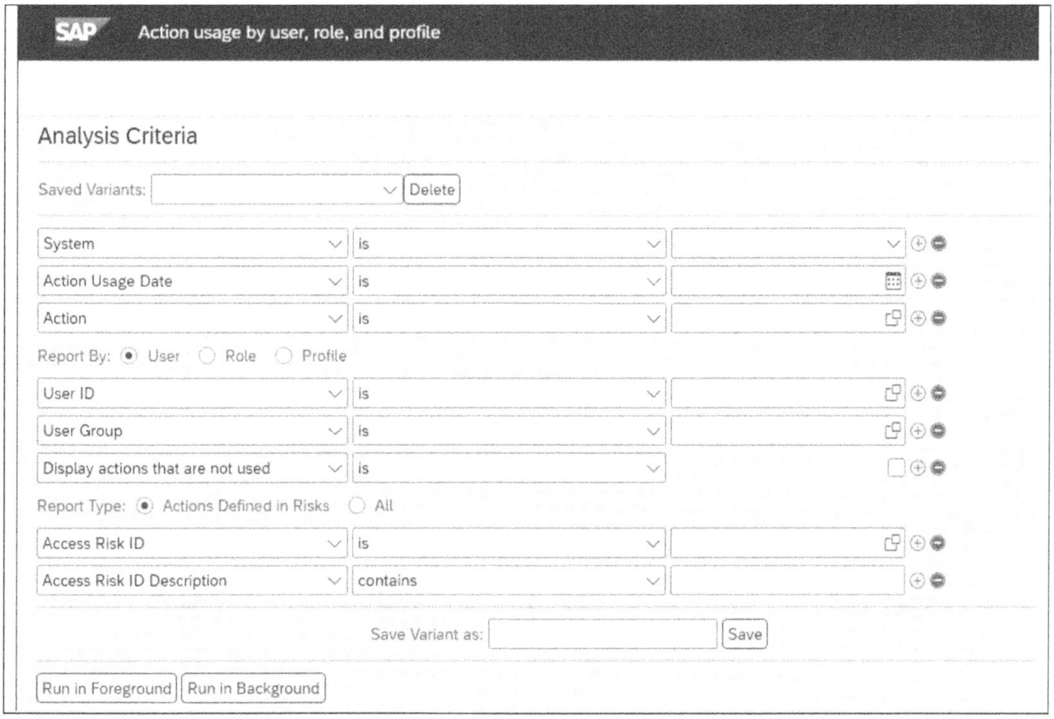

Figure 3-23. *Action Usage option initial input screen*

Enter data as shown in the figure below and select a date range for the last year.

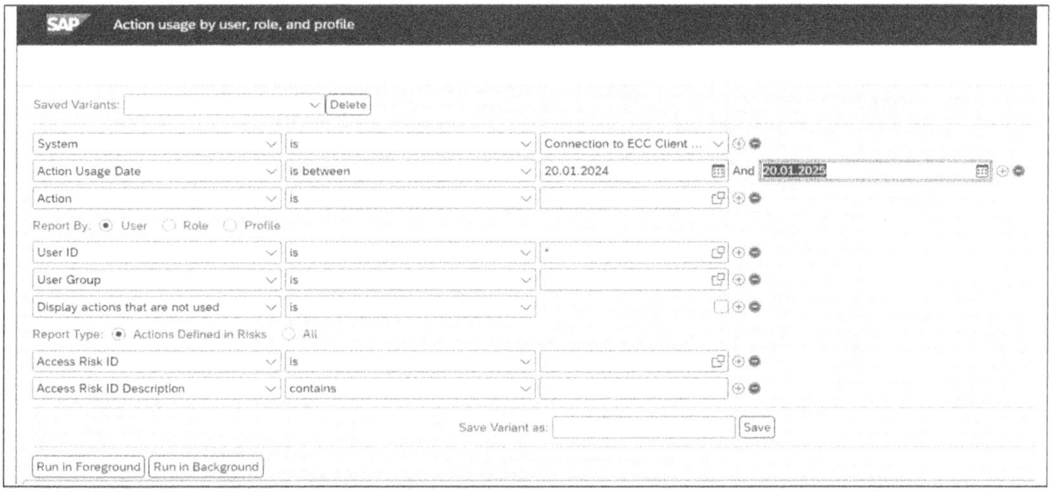

Figure 3-24. *Action Usage with filled fields*

79

CHAPTER 3 SAP FIORI APPS RECOMMENDATION REPORT

This report can be executed in two ways:

- Run in foreground
- Run in background

Once executed, the output is displayed in the figure below.

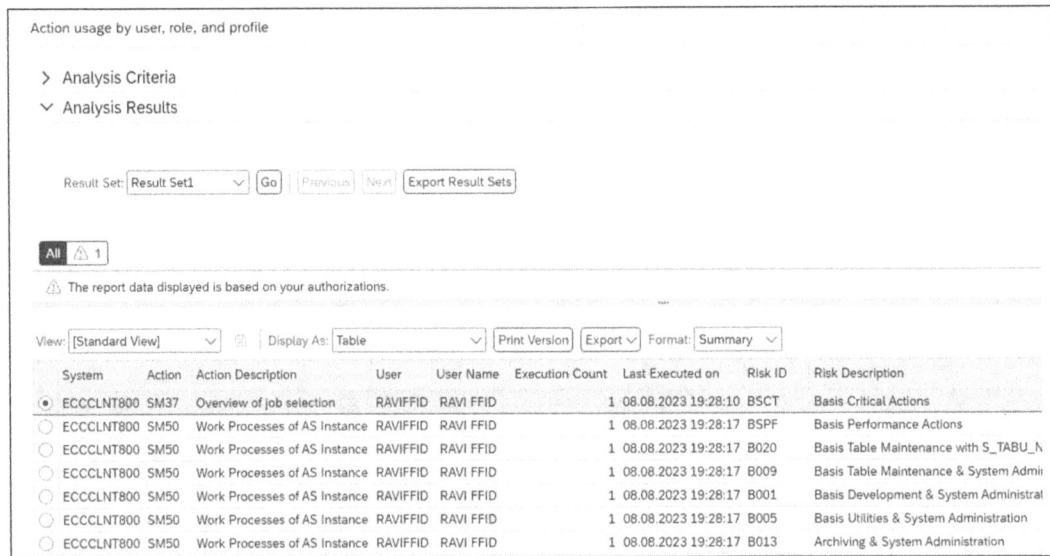

Figure 3-25. *Action Usage output details*

This data can be exported by clicking the tab Export → Export to Microsoft Excel.

Figure 3-26. *Action Usage output downloaded*

3.4.2 Front-End and Back-End System Profiles

To generate the list of **front-end/back-end system profiles**, log on to your front-end system (S/4HANA) and go to the **System** menu, as shown in the figure below.

To generate a list of **front-end/back-end system profiles**, log into your **S/4HANA front-end system** and navigate to the **System** menu, as illustrated in the image below.

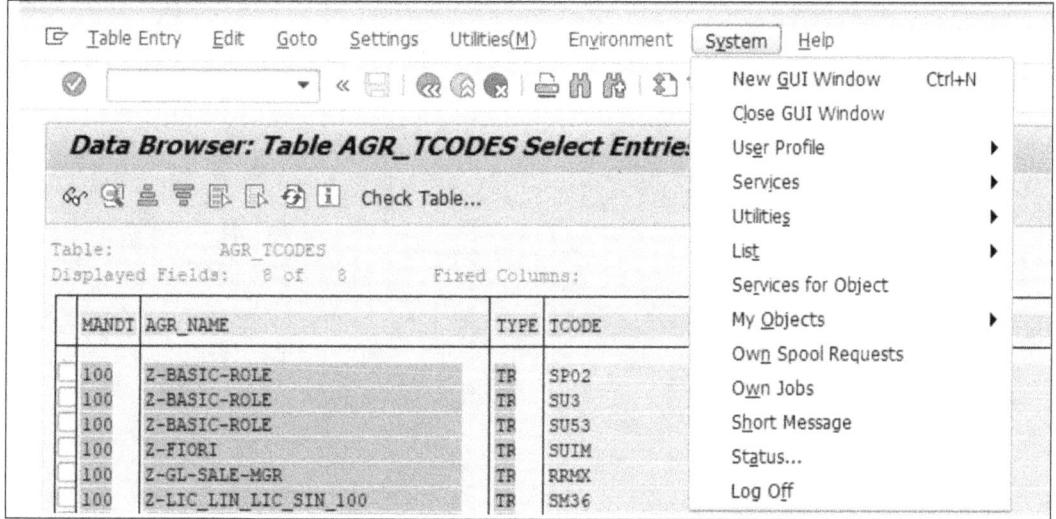

Figure 3-27. *Embedded system initial screen for finding Status*

Next, click the **Status** option from the **System menu**, and the screen below will appear.

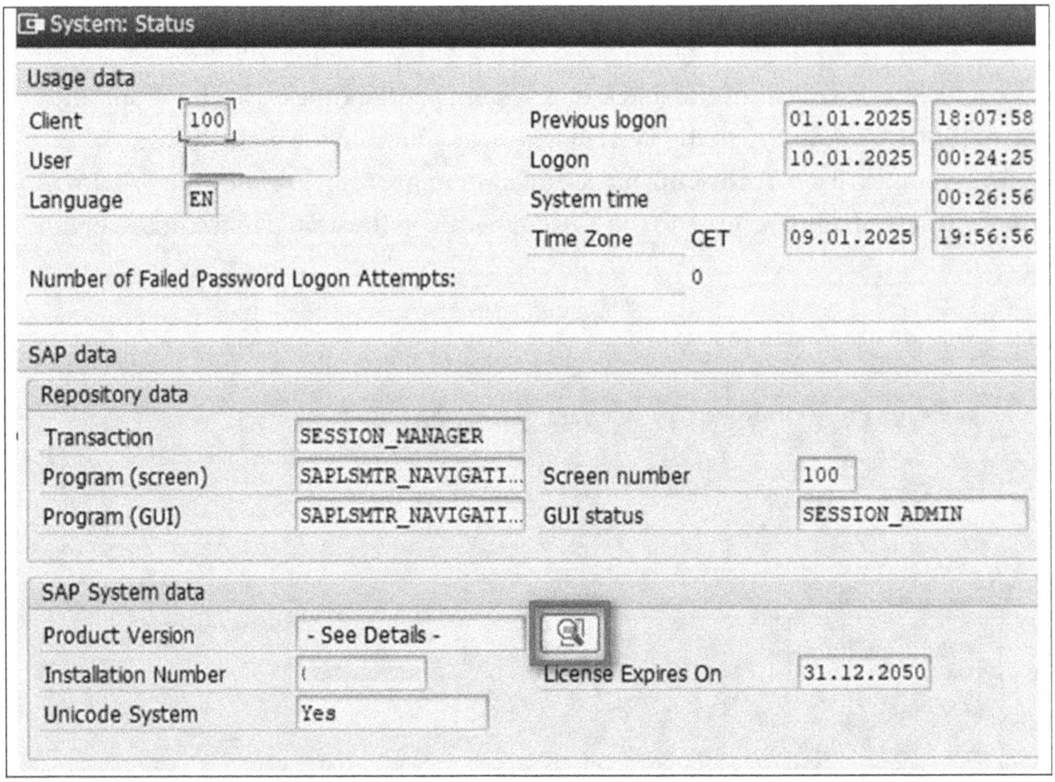

CHAPTER 3   SAP FIORI APPS RECOMMENDATION REPORT

Figure 3-28. *Embedded system Status screen*

In the image above, locate the **SAP System data** section and click the **details** icon. Subsequently, click the icon situated on the left of **Product Version** . This action will open a new window titled **Installed Software**, as illustrated in the figure below.

CHAPTER 3　SAP FIORI APPS RECOMMENDATION REPORT

Component	Release	SP-Le...	Support Package	Short Description of Component
SAP_BASIS	758	0001	SAPK-75801INSAPBASIS	SAP Basis Component
SAP_ABA	751	0001	SAPK-75I01INSAPABA	Cross-Application Component
SAP_GWFND	758	0001	SAPK-75801INSAPGWFND	SAP Gateway Foundation
SAP_UI	758	0001	SAPK-75801INSAPUI	User Interface Technology
ST-PI	740	0025	SAPK-74025INSTPI	SAP Solution Tools Plug-In
BI_CONT	757	0034	SAPK-75734INBICONT	Business Intelligence Content
BI_CONT_XT	757	0034	SAPK-75734INBICONTXT	Business Intelligence Content for Bobj I
SAP_BW	758	0001	SAPK-75801INSAPBW	SAP Business Warehouse
UIBAS001	758	0001	SAPK-75801INUIBAS001	UI for Basis Applications
GRCPINW	V1200_750	0023	SAPK-V1223INGRCPINW	SAP GRC NetWeaver Plug-In
MDG_FND	808	0001	SAPK-80801INMDGFND	S/4HANA MDG Foundation
S4FND	108	0001	SAPK-10801INS4FND	S/4HANA Foundation
MDG_APPL	808	0001	SAPK-80801INMDGAPPL	S/4HANA MDG Applications
S4CEXT	108	0001	SAPK-10801INS4CEXT	S/4HANA Applications EXT
S4CORE	108	0001	SAPK-10801INS4CORE	S/4HANA Core Applications 1
S4HCM	101	0002	SAPK-10102INS4HCM	Human Resources

Figure 3-29. *Details of system and products installed*

The following data points from the screen above are essential for the **system usage profile** data. They are

- Component
- Release
- SP-Level (super pack level)

Now, select the first three columns of data by highlighting them. Right-click and choose **Copy Text**. Then, paste this copied data into your **Excel spreadsheet**.

83

CHAPTER 3   SAP FIORI APPS RECOMMENDATION REPORT

Component	Release	SP-Level	Support Package	Short Description of Component
SAP_BASIS	758	0001	SAPK-75801INSAPBASIS	SAP Basis Component
SAP_ABA	751	0001	SAPK-75101INSAPABA	Cross-Application Component
SAP_GWF...			NSAPGWFND	SAP Gateway Foundation
SAP_UI			01INSAPUI	User Interface Technology
ST-PI			25INSTPI	SAP Solution Tools Plug-In
BI_CONT			4INBICONT	Business Intelligence Content
BI_CONT...			INBICONTXT	Business Intelligence Content for Bobj I
SAP_BW			1INSAPBW	SAP Business Warehouse
UIBAS001			INUIBAS001	UI for Basis Applications
GRCPINW	V12		INGRCPINW	SAP GRC NetWeaver Plug-In
MDG_FND			INMDGFND	S/4HANA MDG Foundation
S4FND	108	0001	SAPK-10801INS4FND	S/4HANA Foundation
MDG_APPL	808	0001	SAPK-80801INMDGAPPL	S/4HANA MDG Applications
S4CEXT	108	0001	SAPK-10801INS4CEXT	S/4HANA Applications EXT
S4CORE	108	0001	SAPK-10801INS4CORE	S/4HANA Core Applications 1
S4HCM	101	0002	SAPK-10102INS4HCM	Human Resources

Context menu overlay: Copy Text; Insert with Overwrite; Details; Optimize Width; Unfreeze Columns; Find...; Find Next; Set Filter...

Figure 3-30. *Select the three columns to download system details*

Open a blank spreadsheet and paste the copied data. Make sure the header is populated as shown in the figure below.

	Component	Release	SP-Level
1	Component	Release	SP-Level
2	SAP_BASIS	758	1
3	SAP_ABA	751	1
4	SAP_GWFND	758	1
5	SAP_UI	758	1
6	ST-PI	740	25
7	BI_CONT	757	34
8	BI_CONT_XT	757	34
9	SAP_BW	758	1
10	UIBAS001	758	1
11	GRCPINW	V1200_750	23
12	MDG_FND	808	1
13	S4FND	108	1
14	MDG_APPL	808	1
15	S4CEXT	108	1
16	S4CORE	108	1

Figure 3-31. *Details of embedded system and components installed*

CHAPTER 3 SAP FIORI APPS RECOMMENDATION REPORT

Note This tool does not require the columns Support Package and Short Description of Component.

Save the file as shown in the figure below.

Figure 3-32. *Data saved as Fiori front-end system details*

Now click the save option [Save]. The file FIORI_FRONTEND_SYSTEM_2023 is saved. Similarly, the back-end system profile called FIORI_BACKEND_SYSTEM_2023 should be created.

With these steps completed, the front-end and back-end system profiles have been successfully created and generated.

Note Even though this system is embedded, and the front-end and back-end components are the same, it is highly recommended that the respective files be named **distinct**. This practice promotes clarity and simplifies maintenance, making distinguishing between the two profiles easier, even though they represent the same underlying system.

3.4.3 Native HANA DB System Profile

This optional step entails adding **HANA DB system profiles**. Generating these profiles involves the following steps:

- Run the SQL query in the HANA SQL console: select * from "_SYS_REPO" . "DELIVERY_UNITS" where vendor = 'sap.com' ;

- To execute this query, select privilege on the DELIVERY_UNITS table in the _SYS_REPO. Execute this query with the SYSTEM user.

CHAPTER 3   SAP FIORI APPS RECOMMENDATION REPORT

- On the data preview screen, click the results window and select Export Results.
- Save the result as a CSV file.

3.5 Log Into the Fiori Reference Library

To utilize the SAP Fiori App Recommendations tool, an integral part of the Fiori Apps Reference Library, access it through your web browser by navigating to the following link:

https://fioriappslibrary.hana.ondemand.com/sap/fix/externalViewer/

A new web page opens, as shown in the figure below.

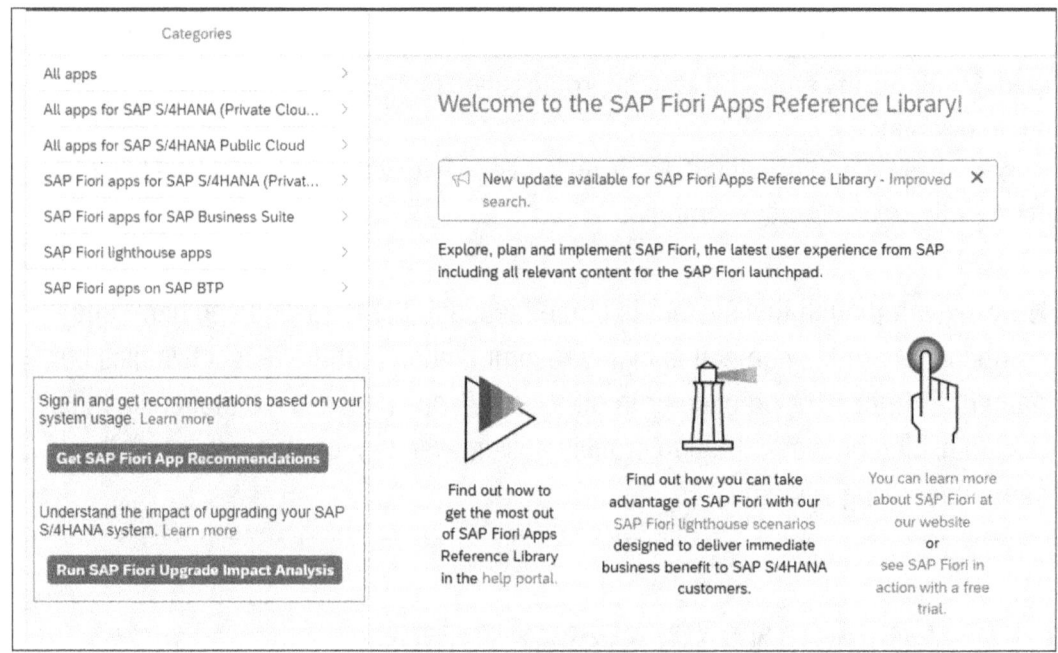

Figure 3-33. SAP Fiori Apps Reference Library initial screen

Next, we are going to look at the option **Get SAP Fiori App Recommendations**. Log into the library by clicking the button, and the below screen follows.

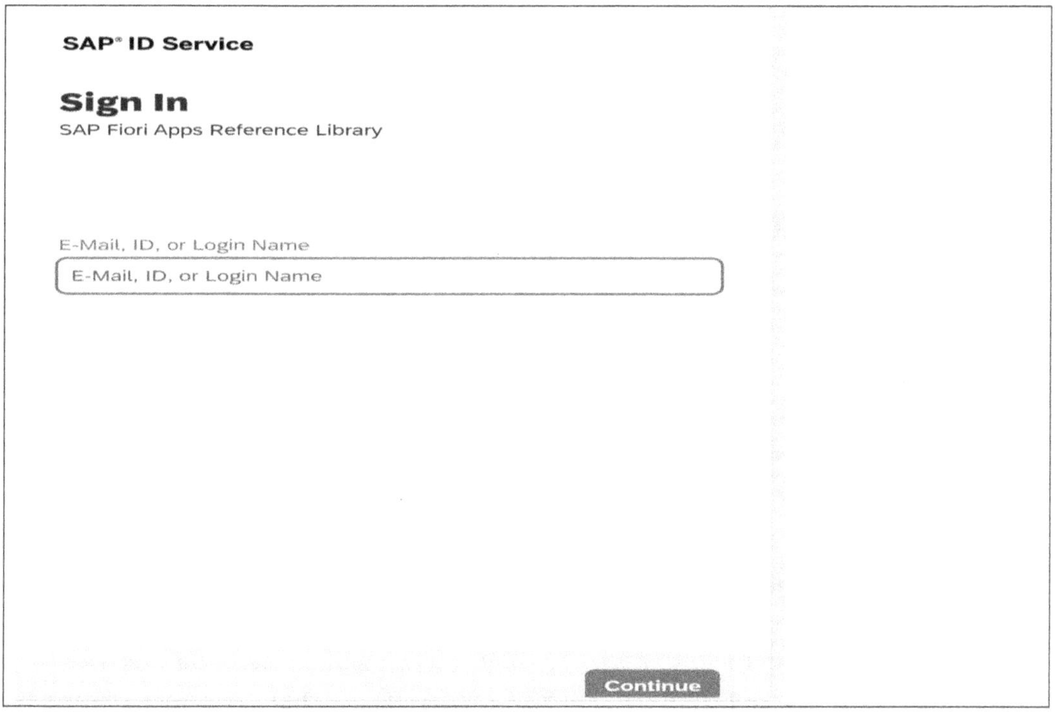

CHAPTER 3 SAP FIORI APPS RECOMMENDATION REPORT

Figure 3-34. Signing in to the recommendation report

To initiate a fresh analysis, input your registered **S user ID** and **password**, and then proceed by clicking the designated button Continue. This action will direct you to the screen displayed in the subsequent image. Creating a **new analysis** involves a structured five-step process.

3.5.1 Step 1: Select the Type of Analysis

To initiate the creation of an analysis, leverage the SAP-provided **wizard** option.

CHAPTER 3   SAP FIORI APPS RECOMMENDATION REPORT

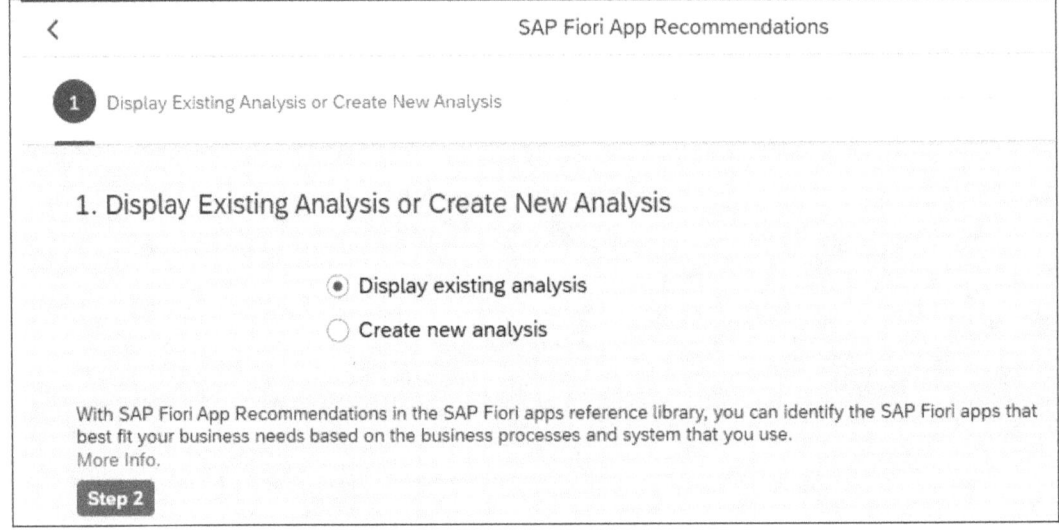

Figure 3-35. Type of analysis selection screen

The wizard simplifies the process by guiding you through the essential steps for conducting a relevance and readiness analysis to identify suitable Fiori apps. Within the wizard, you will encounter two distinct analysis options:

- **Display existing analysis:**
    - This display lists all the analyses already performed for the reviewing process.
    - You can use this report as many times as you want.

Note   You can use this option whenever you want to view an analysis from a particular data run.

- **Create new analysis:**
    - This option creates a brand-new analysis.

To proceed further, select the option **Create new analysis** (⦿ Create new analysis) as shown below.

CHAPTER 3   SAP FIORI APPS RECOMMENDATION REPORT

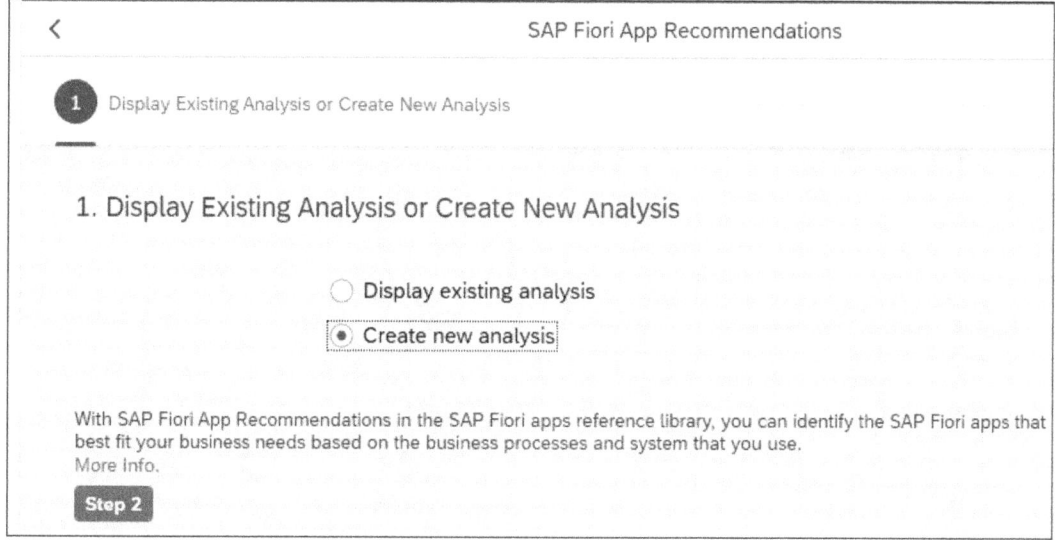

Figure 3-36. *Create new analysis screen*

Now, select the option [Step 2] to proceed to the next step of the analysis.

3.5.2 Step 2: Upload the Usage Profile

The next step is where we load the **usage profile** containing transaction codes. The wizard pops a new window, as shown in the figure below.

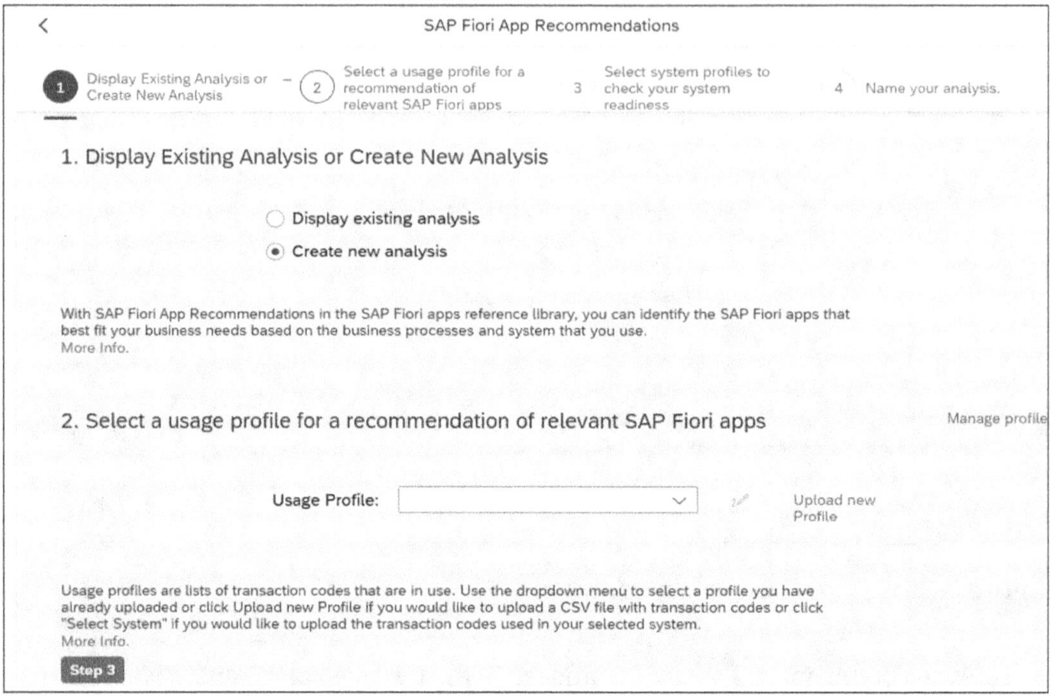

CHAPTER 3   SAP FIORI APPS RECOMMENDATION REPORT

Figure 3-37. Upload usage profile screen

Here, load the usage profile file already created by clicking Upload new Profile **Upload new Profile).** The following window, Usage Profile, opens.

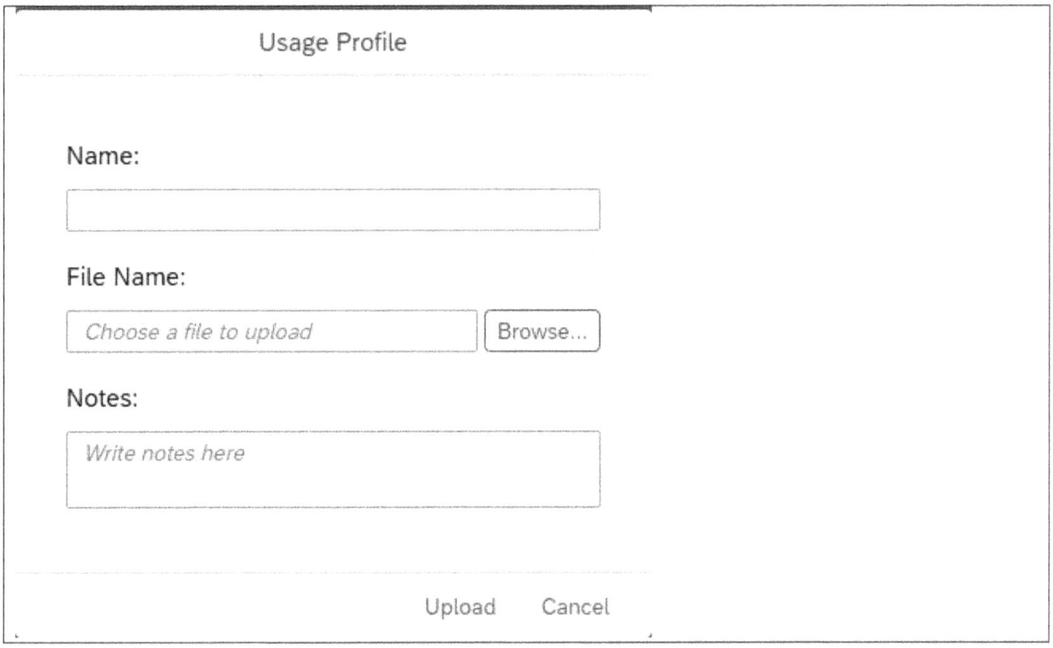

CHAPTER 3   SAP FIORI APPS RECOMMENDATION REPORT

```
┌─────────────────────────────────────────────────────────────┐
│                       Usage Profile                         │
│                                                             │
│  Name:                                                      │
│  ┌──────────────────────────────────────┐                   │
│  │                                      │                   │
│  └──────────────────────────────────────┘                   │
│  File Name:                                                 │
│  ┌──────────────────────────────┐ ┌─────────┐               │
│  │ Choose a file to upload      │ │ Browse… │               │
│  └──────────────────────────────┘ └─────────┘               │
│  Notes:                                                     │
│  ┌──────────────────────────────────────┐                   │
│  │ Write notes here                     │                   │
│  │                                      │                   │
│  └──────────────────────────────────────┘                   │
│                                                             │
│                              Upload   Cancel                │
└─────────────────────────────────────────────────────────────┘
```

Figure 3-38. *Initial screen to upload the usage profile file*

Proceed to enter the required details into the provided screen. It is crucial to ensure that the chosen profile name does not include any **spaces**, as this will result in an error, as illustrated in the subsequent image. To avoid this issue, utilize **underscores** (_) as separators within the profile name.

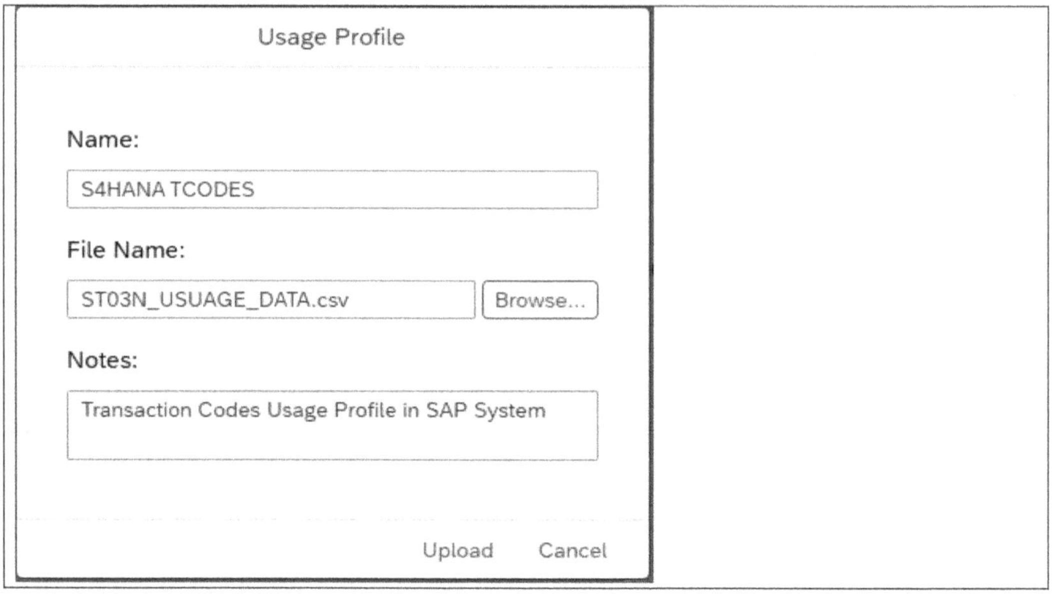

CHAPTER 3   SAP FIORI APPS RECOMMENDATION REPORT

```
                    Usage Profile

    Name:
    S4HANA TCODES

    File Name:
    ST03N_USUAGE_DATA.csv           Browse...

    Notes:
    Transaction Codes Usage Profile in SAP System


                                Upload   Cancel
```

Figure 3-39.   Uploaded usage profile file

Click the option Upload.

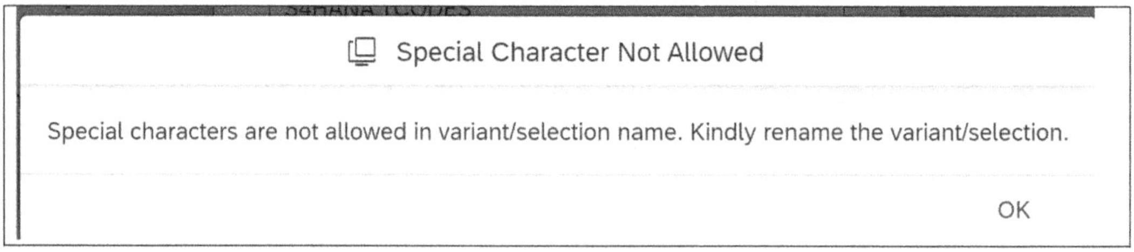

```
                     S4HANA TCODES
                  🖵  Special Character Not Allowed

    Special characters are not allowed in variant/selection name. Kindly rename the variant/selection.

                                                          OK
```

Figure 3-40.   Uploaded file error screen

This gives an error due to a gap in the usage profile Name field, as shown in the above figure.

Enter for the usage profile the following:

- **Name:** S4HANA_TCODES_USUAGE_PROFILE
- **File Name:** S4HANA_USUAGE_DATA.csv
- **Notes:** Transaction Codes Usage Profile in SAP System

After carefully populating all the required details, the final output screen should mirror the one shown in the figure below.

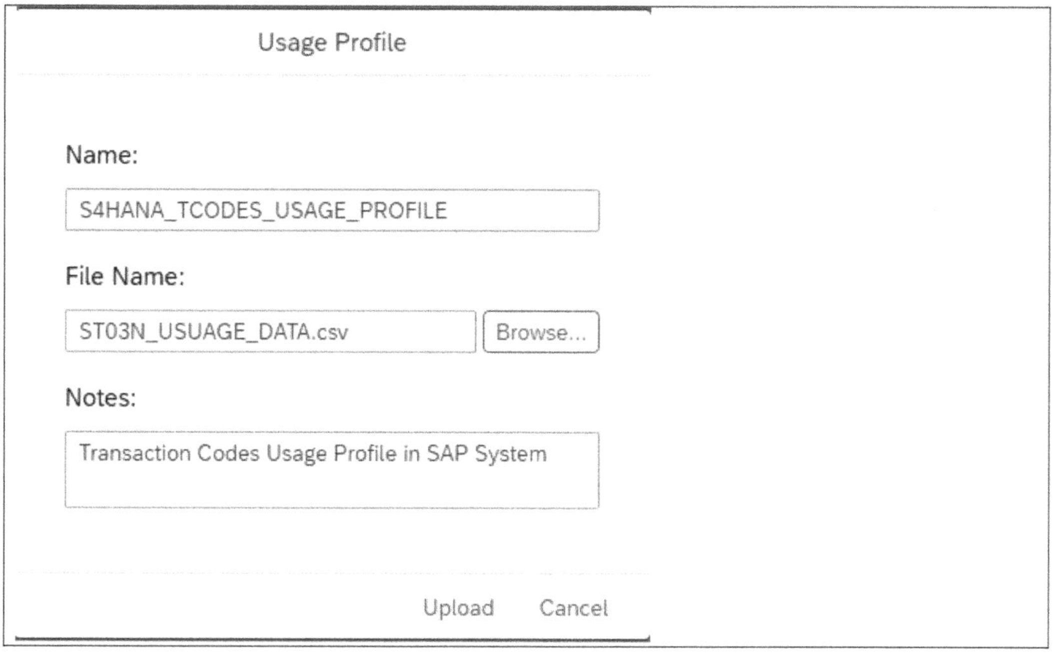

CHAPTER 3 SAP FIORI APPS RECOMMENDATION REPORT

```
┌─────────────────────────────────────────────────────────────┐
│                        Usage Profile                         │
├─────────────────────────────────────────────────────────────┤
│                                                              │
│  Name:                                                       │
│  ┌─────────────────────────────────┐                         │
│  │ S4HANA_TCODES_USAGE_PROFILE     │                         │
│  └─────────────────────────────────┘                         │
│  File Name:                                                  │
│  ┌─────────────────────────────────┐  ┌────────┐             │
│  │ ST03N_USUAGE_DATA.csv           │  │ Browse…│             │
│  └─────────────────────────────────┘  └────────┘             │
│  Notes:                                                      │
│  ┌─────────────────────────────────┐                         │
│  │ Transaction Codes Usage Profile in SAP System │           │
│  │                                 │                         │
│  └─────────────────────────────────┘                         │
│                                                              │
│                                      Upload    Cancel        │
└─────────────────────────────────────────────────────────────┘
```

Figure 3-41. *Usage Profile screen*

- Select the CSV file where your transaction codes list is stored and click Upload. This filtering process will effectively eliminate any invalid transaction codes that are either obsolete or blacklisted within the S/4HANA system, ensuring a cleaner and more relevant dataset for subsequent analysis. The specific transaction codes filtered out are listed in the image below for your reference.

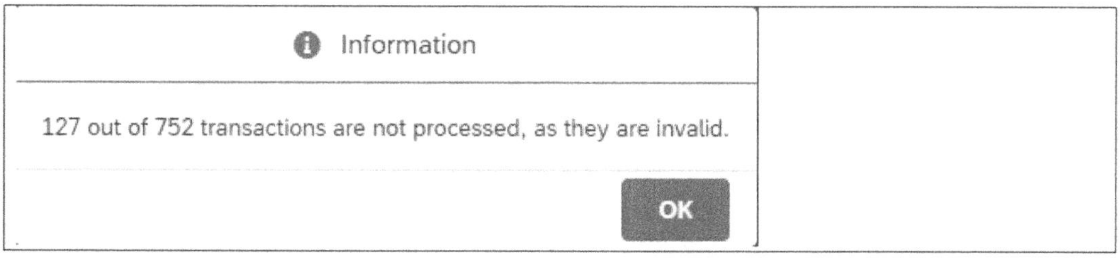

```
┌──────────────────────────────────────────────────────┐
│                   ⓘ  Information                      │
├──────────────────────────────────────────────────────┤
│ 127 out of 752 transactions are not processed, as they are invalid. │
│                                                       │
│                                          ┌────┐       │
│                                          │ OK │       │
│                                          └────┘       │
└──────────────────────────────────────────────────────┘
```

Figure 3-42. *Displays the number of transaction codes not processed*

CHAPTER 3   SAP FIORI APPS RECOMMENDATION REPORT

The above figure shows that 127 out of 752 transactions were not processed as **invalid or obsolete** within the S/4HANA system. Click **OK** to upload your usage profile.

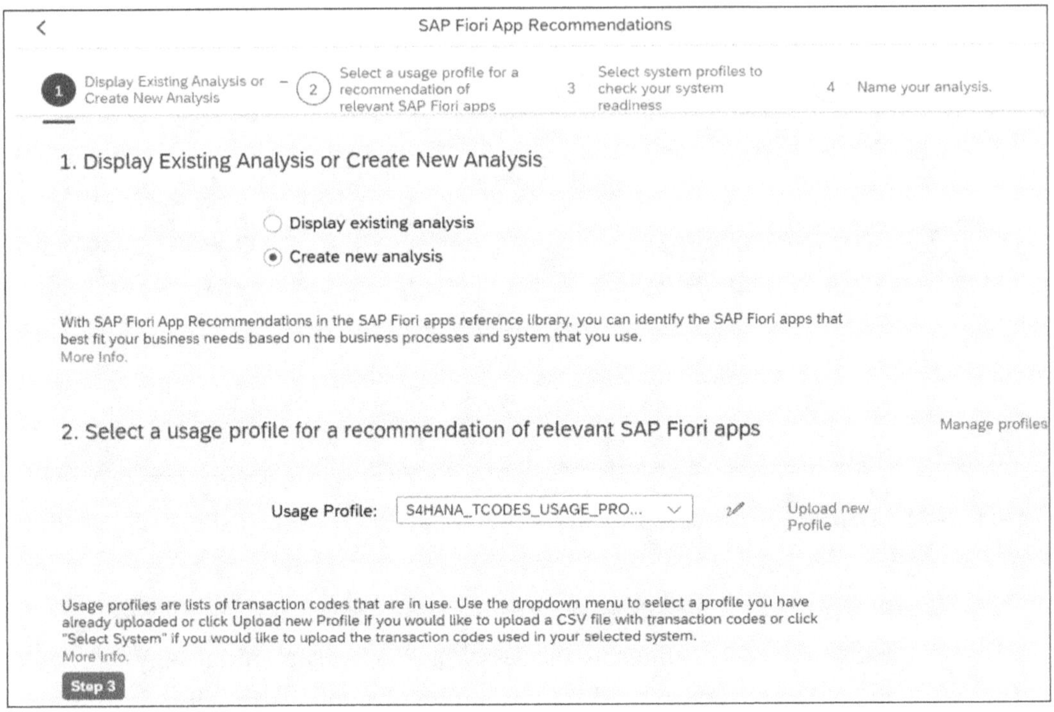

Figure 3-43. *Next step in the wizard*

The usage profile has been loaded successfully, as seen in the figure above. To proceed further, go to the wizard's next step by clicking **Step 3**.

3.5.3 Step 3: Update System Profiles

Click Step 3 to specify and enter the system details of the front-end and back-end systems. The step involving the **Native HANA DB** system profile is optional and can be left blank.

CHAPTER 3 SAP FIORI APPS RECOMMENDATION REPORT

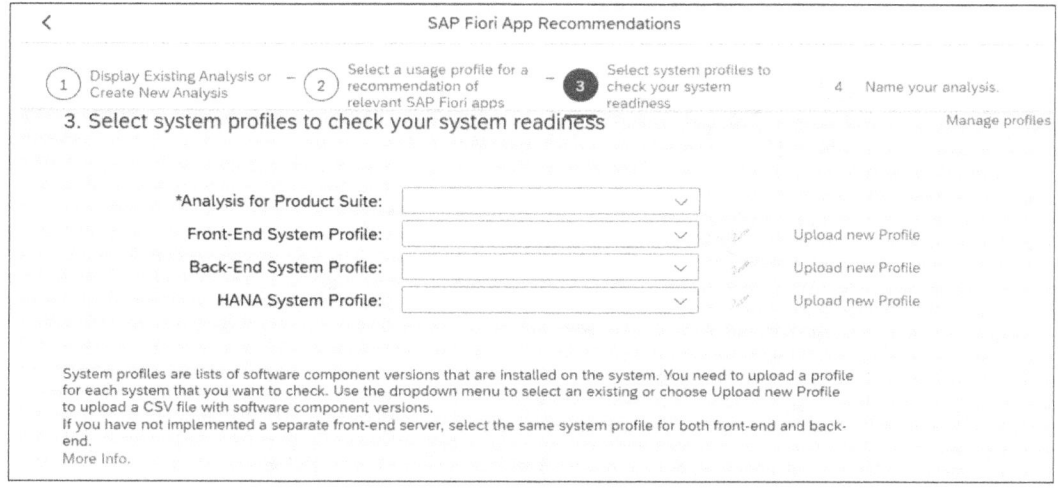

Figure 3-44. Screen to upload system profiles

In the above screen, the wizard has provided **four** options, mainly:

- Analysis for Product Suite
- Front-End System Profile
- Back-End System Profile
- HANA System Profile

Analysis for Product Suite

Furthermore, under **Analysis for Product Suite**, five options are provided:

- SAP S/4HANA (Private Cloud and On-Premise)
- SAP S/4HANA Public Cloud
- SAP Business Suite
- SAP Business Suite – lower back-end version
- Apps on BTP

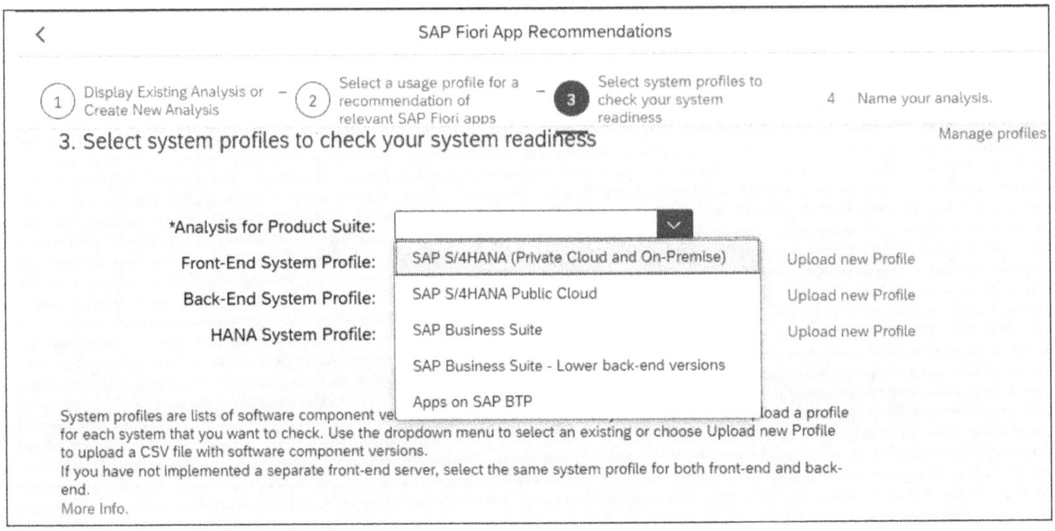

CHAPTER 3   SAP FIORI APPS RECOMMENDATION REPORT

Figure 3-45. *Input screen for Analysis for Product Suite*

Here, ensure that you select the product suite you are analyzing. In our case, the option **SAP S/4HANA** (Private Cloud and On-Premise) has been chosen, as shown in the figure below.

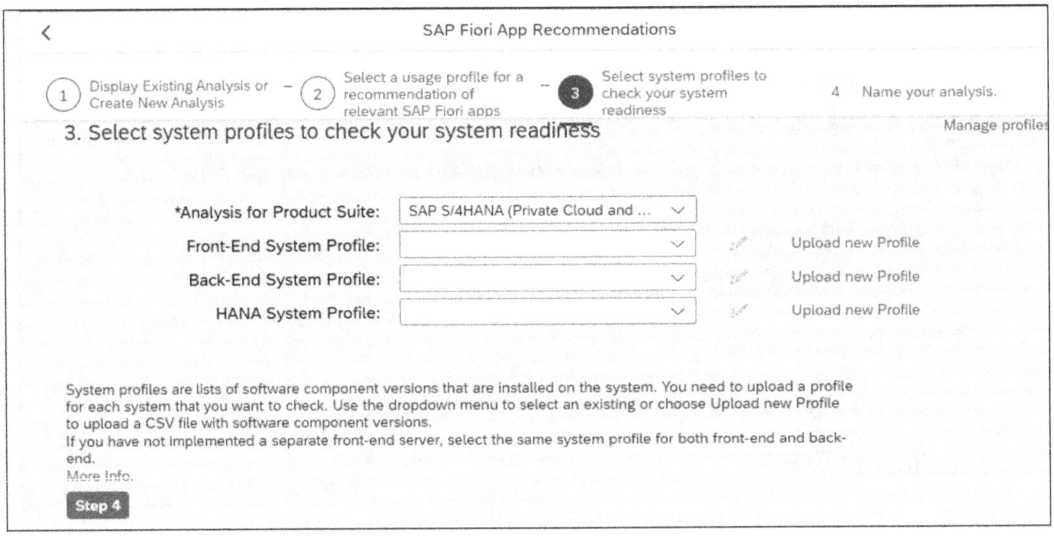

Figure 3-46. *Correct system selected for analysis*

CHAPTER 3   SAP FIORI APPS RECOMMENDATION REPORT

Front-End System Profile

Now, click the **edit** icon followed by **Upload new Profile** Upload new Profile , and it opens a new window called **Upload New System Profile**, as shown in the figure below.

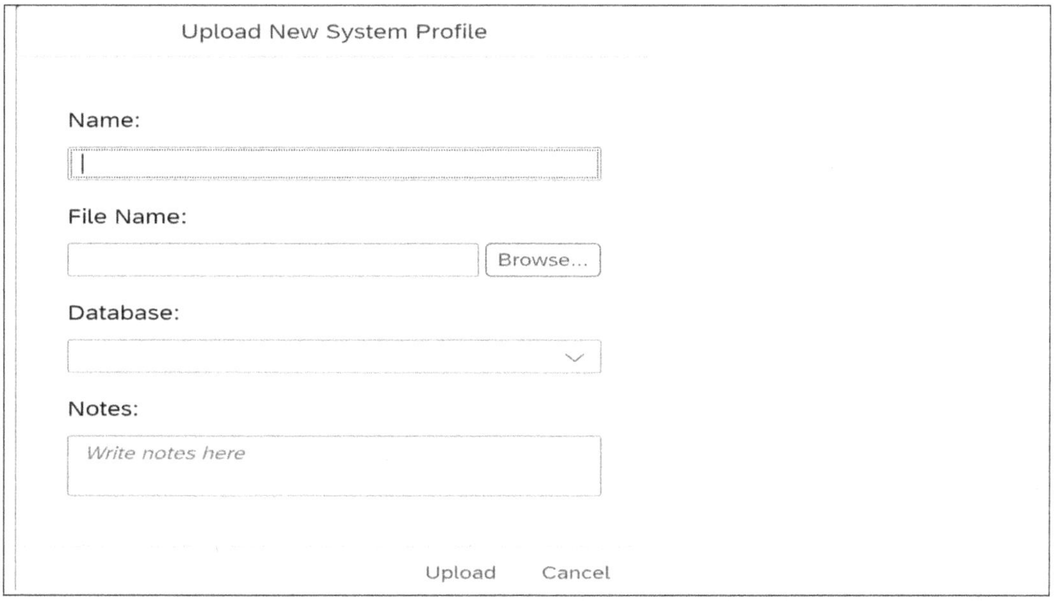

Figure 3-47. *Front-End System Profile input screen*

Enter the front-end system profile details as listed below:

- **Name:** FIORI_FRONTEND_SYSTEM_PROFILE_2023
- **File Name:** FIORI_FRONTEND_SYSTEM_2023.csv
- **Database:** HANA DB
- **Notes:** Fiori Front-End System Profile

CHAPTER 3   SAP FIORI APPS RECOMMENDATION REPORT

Figure 3-48. Front-end system profile loaded

Note   Database: This has two options:

- HANA DB
- Any DB

In our case, we chose HANA DB as the database for which S/4HANA is installed.

Figure 3-49. Front-end system profile loaded successfully

The above figure displays that the front-end system file has been uploaded successfully. Click the continue icon  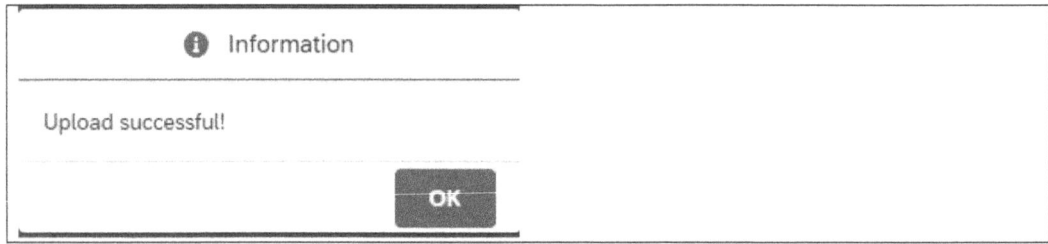.

CHAPTER 3   SAP FIORI APPS RECOMMENDATION REPORT

Figure 3-50. *Display of the Front-End System Profile details*

Back-End System Profile

Similarly, load the back-end system profile details as listed below:

- **Name:** S4HANA_BACKEND_SYSTEM_PROFILE_2023

- **File Name:** S4HANA_BACKEND_SYSTEM_2023.csv

- **Database:** HANA DB

- **Notes:** S/4 HANA Back-End System Profile

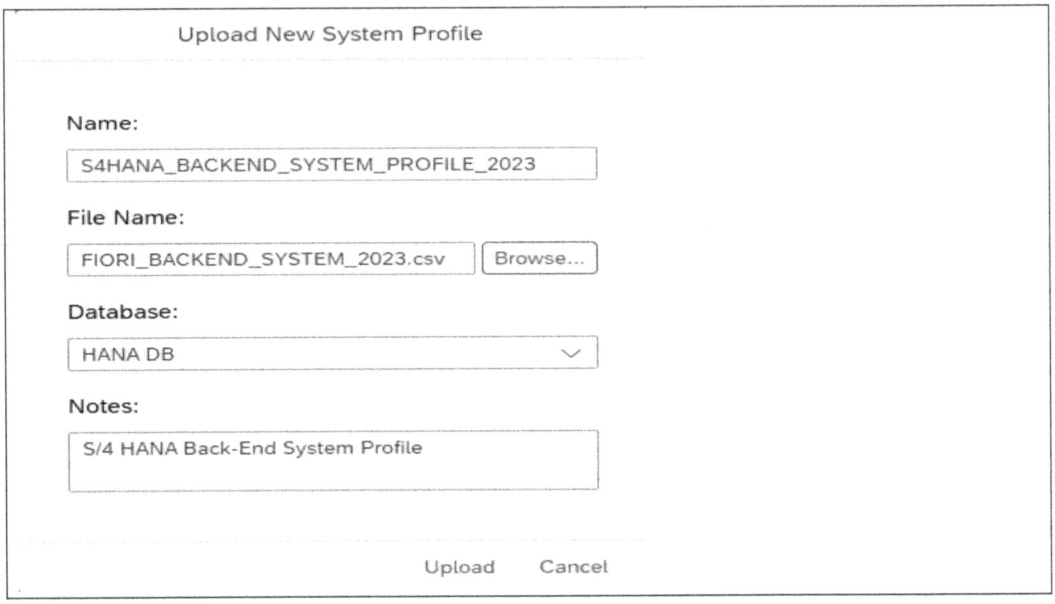

CHAPTER 3 SAP FIORI APPS RECOMMENDATION REPORT

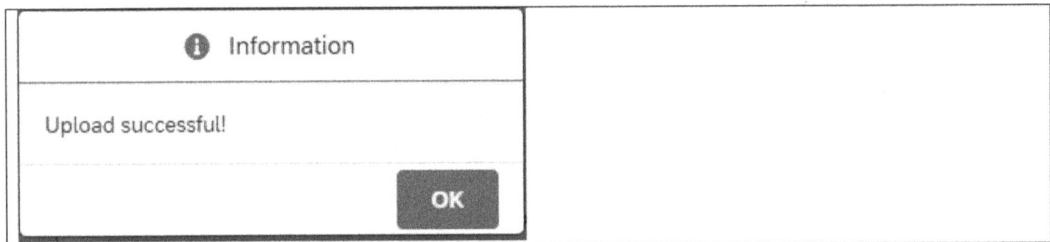

Figure 3-51. Back-end system profile uploaded

Upload the above information by clicking the option Upload. Then click OK If everything is loaded correctly.

Figure 3-52. Back-end system profile loaded successfully

The back-end system profile was successfully loaded. Now click OK. All the system-related files have been successfully loaded.

CHAPTER 3 SAP FIORI APPS RECOMMENDATION REPORT

Figure 3-53. All system profiles loaded

HANA System Profile

The HANA System Profile option is not mandatory for our analysis, so you do not need to include it. Hence, you can leave it empty or blank. Proceed to the next step by clicking **Step 4**.

3.5.4 Step 4: Defining Analysis

In this step, we define the analysis name and description.

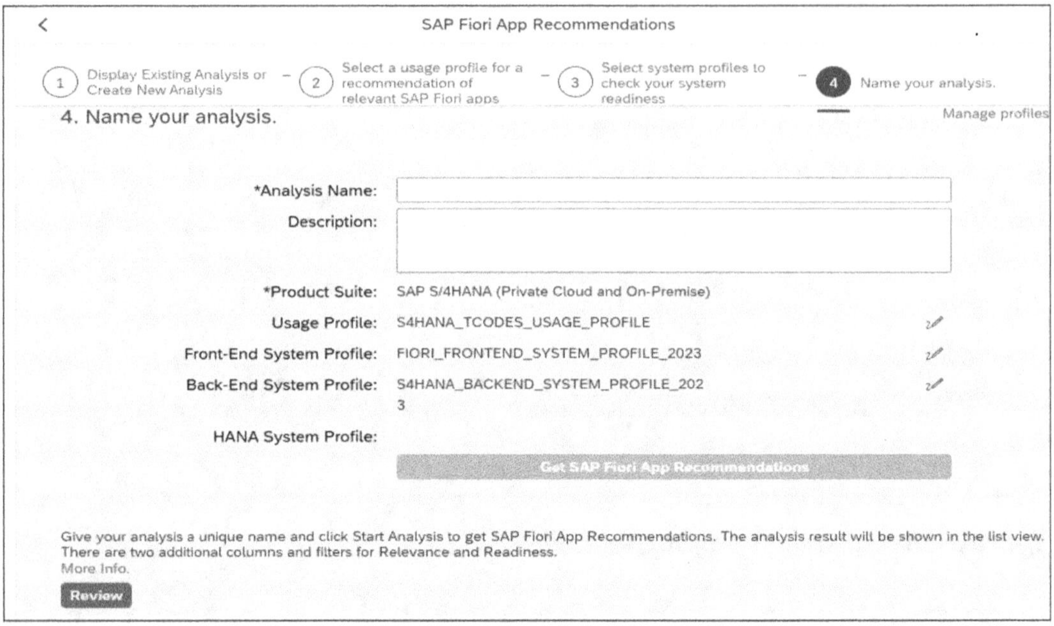

CHAPTER 3   SAP FIORI APPS RECOMMENDATION REPORT

Figure 3-54. Input screen for defining the type of analysis

Enter the following details:

- **Analysis Name:** FIORI APPS RECOMMENDATION REPORT
- **Description:** FIORI APPS RECOMMENDATION REPORT DETAILS

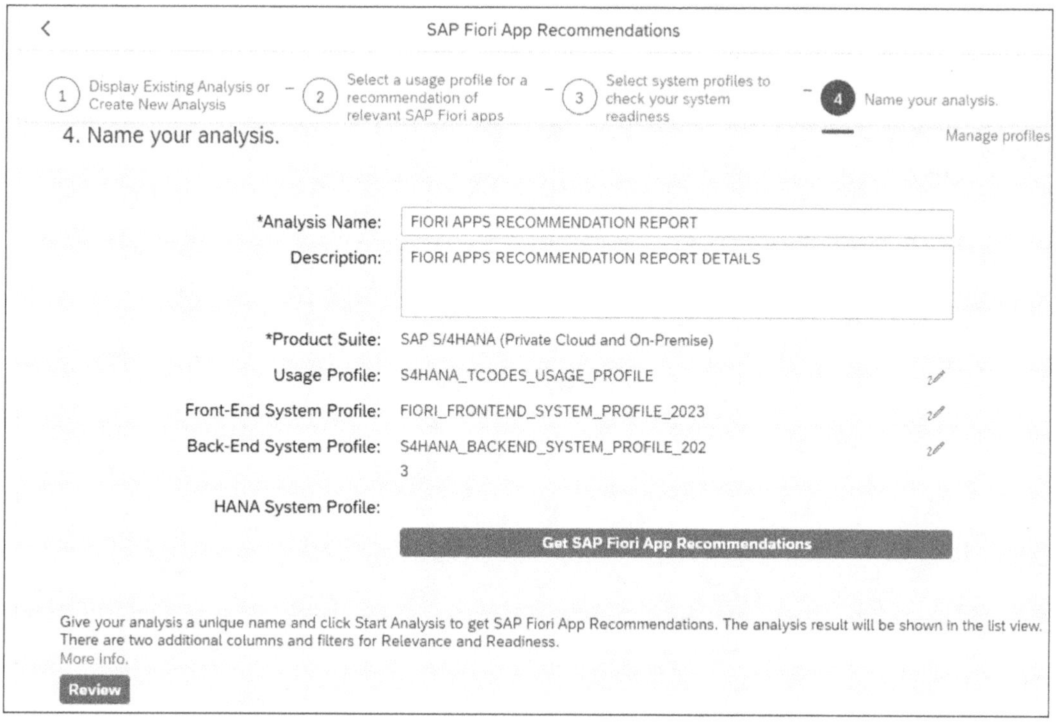

CHAPTER 3   SAP FIORI APPS RECOMMENDATION REPORT

Figure 3-55. Define and give the analysis name and description

The image above displays the uploaded profiles and the defined analysis. You can examine them in detail by clicking the "**Review**" button. Once you have completed the review and confirmed everything is accurate, proceed to the subsequent step by clicking the button **Get SAP Fiori App Recommendations**. This action will generate a list of Fiori apps corresponding to the transaction codes in the uploaded list. Note: This process may take some time to populate the results, as shown in the following image.

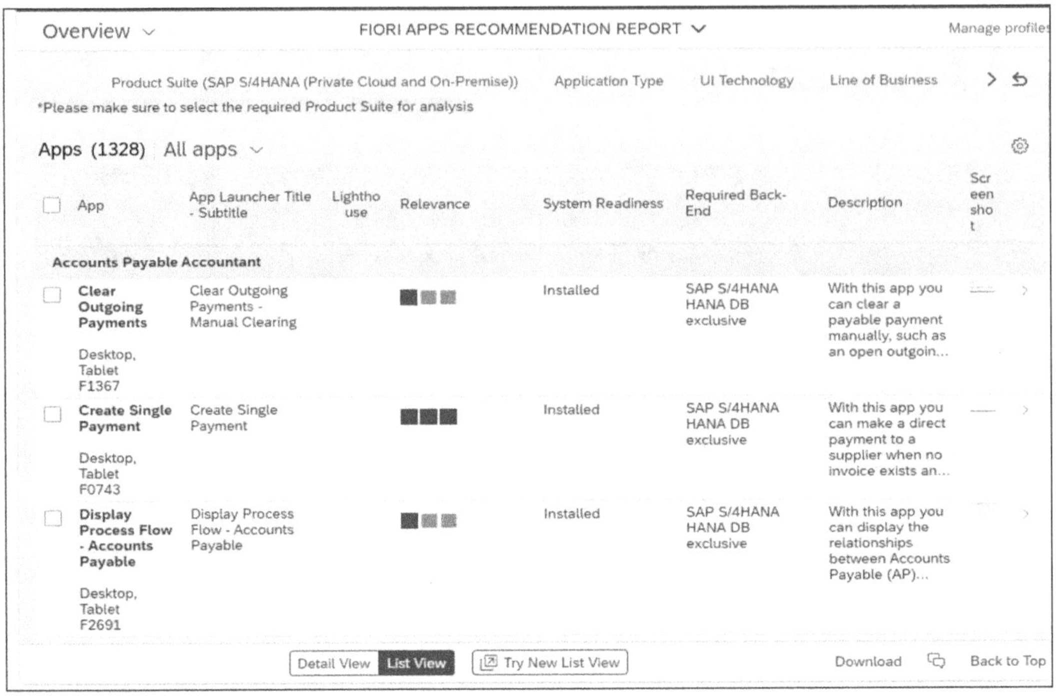

Figure 3-56. *App Recommendations output report*

3.5.5 Step 5: Results and Analysis

The figure above presents the analysis outcome, showcasing apps aligning with the specified transaction codes and their corresponding **relevance** and **readiness** levels. The **system readiness status** report offers a concise overview of whether the necessary software components are present in your system landscape based on the selected system profiles for your HANA product suite (front-end, back-end, or HANA system). It further indicates the installation status of these components, categorizing them as fully installed, partially installed, or not installed, as visually depicted in the subsequent figure.

CHAPTER 3 SAP FIORI APPS RECOMMENDATION REPORT

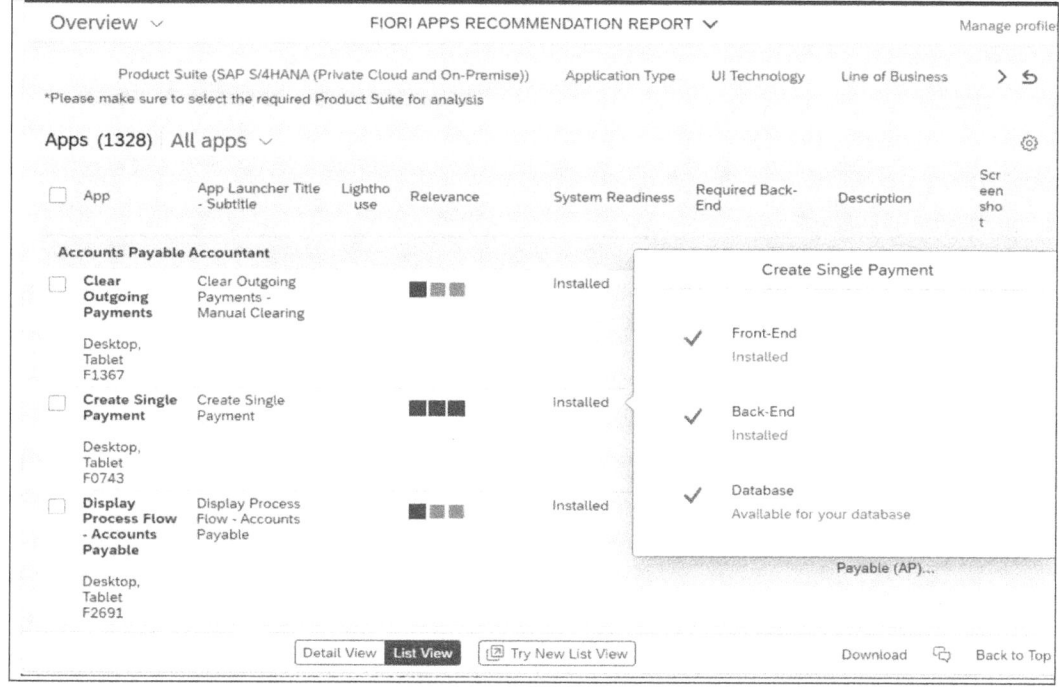

Figure 3-57.* System readiness details*

Check the system relevance details by right-clicking three bars (■■■).

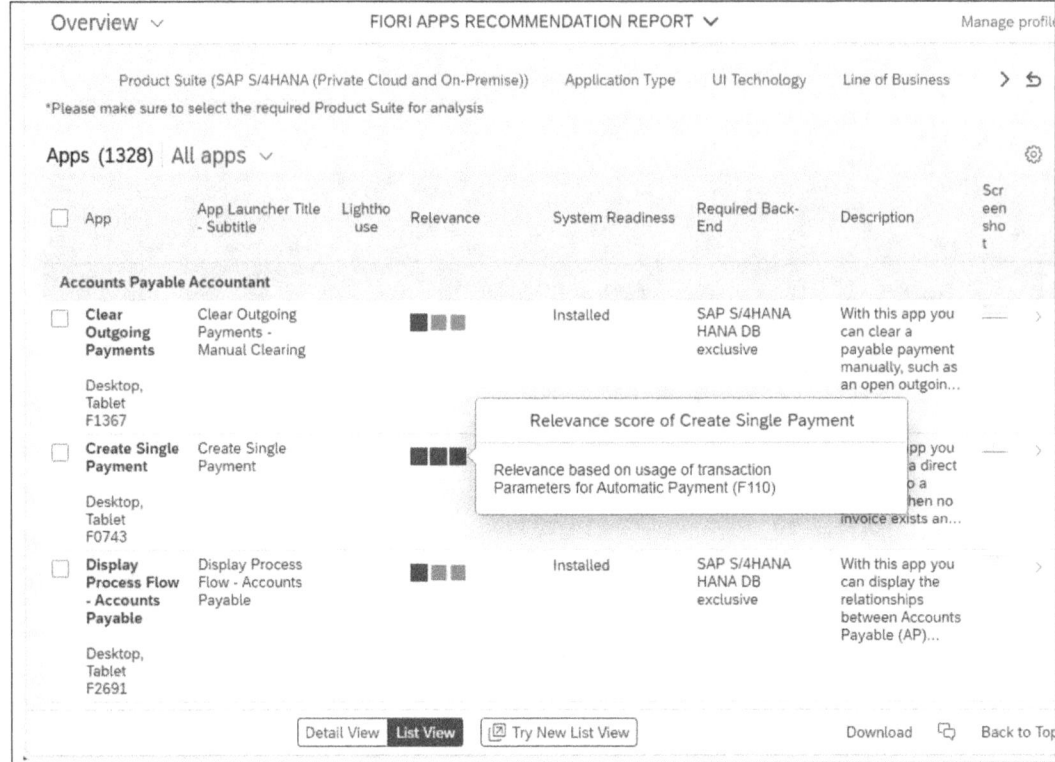

Figure 3-58. *App relevance details*

3.6 Different Types of Views (Detail and List Views)

Two tabs, **Detail View** and **List View**, appear at the bottom of the screen, as shown in the figure above. Both views help you decide whether certain apps you are considering for implementation meet your requirements regarding business processes and system landscape.

The **Detail View** shows you all the available information about one app. The **List View** gives you an overview of various apps and the types of information you are currently interested in. You can easily toggle between the two views, as shown at the bottom of your screen.

Figure 3-59. *Types of views available*

Detail View:

Once you have navigated to a group of relevant apps using the **search** and **filter** functions, you can select individual apps to view detailed information about their properties and implementation requirements. This helps you judge the suitability of an app you're considering for implementation.

The Product Features tab briefly describes the app's features, link to its documentation, screenshots, and lists of related and successor apps:

- A short description of the app's functions and key features
- A link to the app documentation
- Screenshots of the app, if available
- A list of more recent successor apps, if available
- A list of related apps

You can find related apps at the bottom of the view. Use the dropdown icon to switch between lists. They may contain apps assigned to the same leading product version or role as the one you are currently viewing. The Implementation Information tab gives you all the technical details necessary for planning the implementation of an app. By default, this information is for the app's most recent version of the chosen product suite. If the app is available in multiple versions, you can switch between them using the option from the dropdown menu.

Note When you change the app version in the Implementation Information tab, it will also update the information in the Product Features tab. The Implementation Information tab contains essential data such as SAP Notes, installation and configuration requirements, relevant business catalogs, business groups, business roles, details on extensibility and support, and a list of dependent apps. For instance, you can find the app F0743 (Create Single Payment) in the list of dependent apps.

List View:

The List View is a feature that presents brief information about different apps in a list format. It helps you quickly review numerous apps to determine which suits your business needs. You can switch between apps using the dropdown menu or filters. The List View continuously filters by a specific product suite, which you can modify. It provides information about the features and technical data of apps, focusing on types of information for an overview across various apps. You can tailor the List View to display only the information needed.

3.7 System Readiness Status

Based on the selected system profiles, the system readiness status provides an overview of whether all the necessary software components are installed for your product suite, front end, back end, and SAP HANA system.

The system readiness analysis provides the installation status for each SAP Fiori app and details the system status. You can view the installation information by hovering over the installation status or switching to the Detail View. Note that installation status is broken into three categories:

- Installed
- Partly installed
- Not installed

Note The system readiness check only verifies the software components, including the SAP Fiori app and your system profile. It does not verify the overall system's completeness and consistency. For a thorough check, you can utilize the SAP Maintenance Planner.

CHAPTER 3 SAP FIORI APPS RECOMMENDATION REPORT

3.8 Relevance Score

The list of SAP Fiori apps is filtered based on your usage profile to show only relevant ones. Each app has a relevance score displayed in the table. The score is calculated based on usage and considers transaction codes and application components. Hovering over the score provides a detailed description of the apps. Here, we interpret the relevance score, and various ratings **from 1 to 3** are described below.

3.8.1 Relevance Score: Level 3 Rating

This rating of **3** means that the SAP Fiori app is **highly relevant** to your requirement because it directly corresponds to a transaction code you already use. For example, if you frequently use the transaction code **F110** for the **Change Sales Order** transaction, then the SAP Fiori app **Manage Sales Item Proposals** will be given a relevance score of 3 because it directly matches the transaction **F110**. This rating of **3** also indicates the importance of apps based on the loaded usage profile file. When hovering the mouse over the option ■■■ under the Relevance column, we get the following.

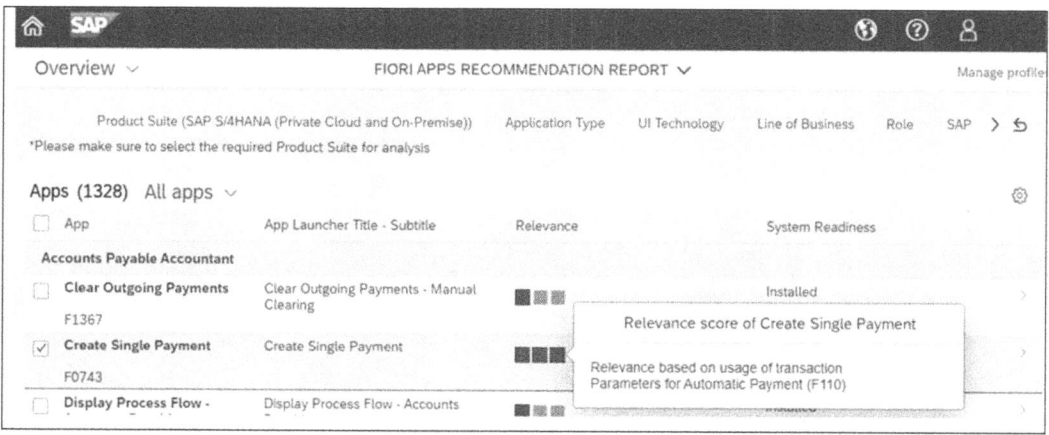

Figure 3-60. *Relevance score – level 3 rating*

The Relevance column showing the option ■■■ means that the app directly matches the transaction code F110 from the listed codes from the input file. In contrast, relevance rating of 1 or 2 indicates an exact matching Fiori app was not found.

109

CHAPTER 3   SAP FIORI APPS RECOMMENDATION REPORT

Note   A high relevance score does not mean the matching SAP Fiori app fully replaces or covers the SAP GUI transaction. The BPO team should be informed of this and verified to ensure it meets their requirements.

3.8.2   Relevance Score: Level 2 Rating

The relevance rating of **2** means an exact matching Fiori app was not found. This rating of **2** implies that the SAP Fiori app is relevant to you because you are using transactions from the application area to which the SAP Fiori app belongs. For example, the transactional SAP Fiori app Setting for Release Strategy (S/4HANA) is rated with a relevance score of **2** because your usage profile includes a transaction that belongs to the application area Purchasing (MM-PUR). Still, the analysis could not find a direct match for the transaction code.

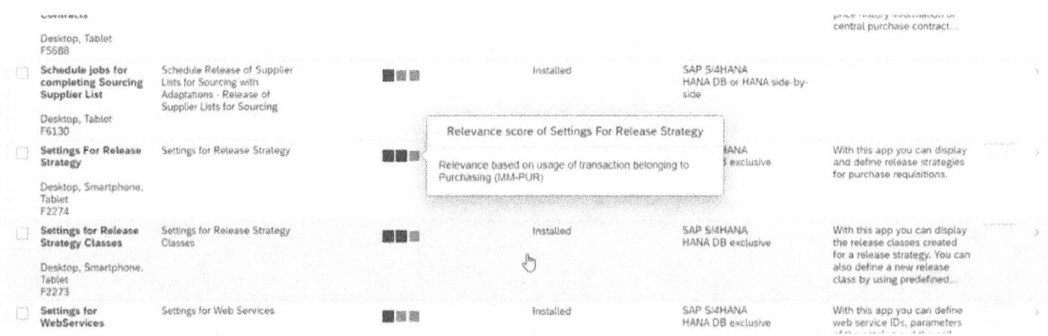

Figure 3-61. *Relevance score – level 2 rating*

3.8.3   Relevance Score: Level 1 Rating

The relevance rating of **1** means an exact matching Fiori app was not found. This level of rating depends on how close the transaction is to the application area in the application component hierarchy.

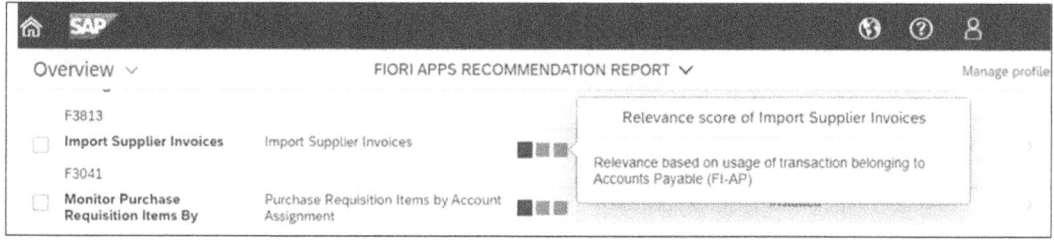

Figure 3-62. *Relevance score – level 1 rating*

The above figure gives the relevance score of the Monitor Purchase request item, which was determined based on transaction code usage. Here, the relevance is based on using transactions belonging to Purchasing (MM-PUR).

3.9 Working with the Analysis Results

The SAP Fiori App Recommendations analysis is fully integrated with the SAP Fiori Apps Reference Library. It adds two filters: relevance and system readiness. When you select a usage profile in the wizard, the analysis result displays only relevant apps by default. After running the analysis, you can use the following features:

- Use additional filters to narrow down your results.
- Configure fields to customize the data shown.
- Download and save the analysis results as an Excel document.
- Share a link to results for selected SAP Fiori apps via email.
- Save selected SAP Fiori apps.
- Utilize the Profiles Manager to conveniently access usage, system, and analysis profiles and save SAP Fiori app selections.

Results View:

After your analysis, the List View will display relevant apps based on your usage profile. The apps are sorted by business area and come with a short description and screenshot. The installation status in the Detail View provides information on system requirements, product versions, and required SAP Notes. You can drill down your results using filters and customize the display fields. The Detail View presents all available information about a specific app, while the List View offers an overview of multiple apps. You can switch between the views using the tabs at the bottom of your screen.

CHAPTER 3 SAP FIORI APPS RECOMMENDATION REPORT

Filter Result:

You can use filters such as product suite, line of business, role, inquiry, and required back-end product to narrow down your results. You can combine filters to display a specific set of SAP Fiori apps relevant to your needs. Some filters are already visible at the top of the results view. To add more filters, click the arrow at the upper right-hand side of the screen until you see the filter icon with a plus. Use this icon to choose the filters that best suit your needs.

Configuring the Display Fields:

You can customize the results list to display only the necessary data. To do this, click the gear icon ⚙ at the top right of the results list to configure display columns.

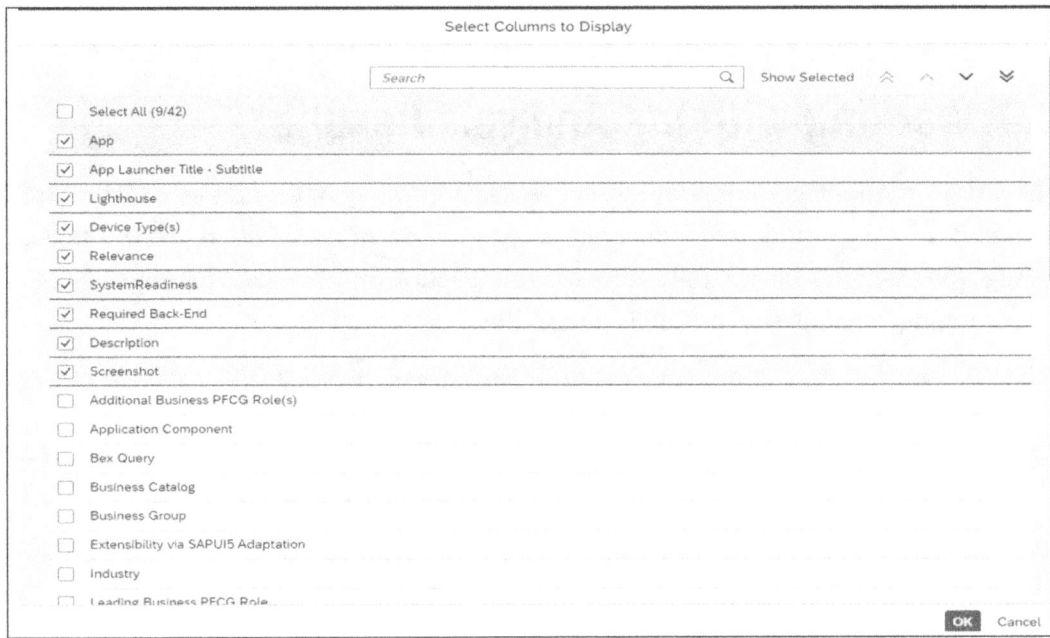

Figure 3-63. *Data selection screen*

In the above figure, we can select what we want to display by clicking **Show Selected** Show Selected .

CHAPTER 3   SAP FIORI APPS RECOMMENDATION REPORT

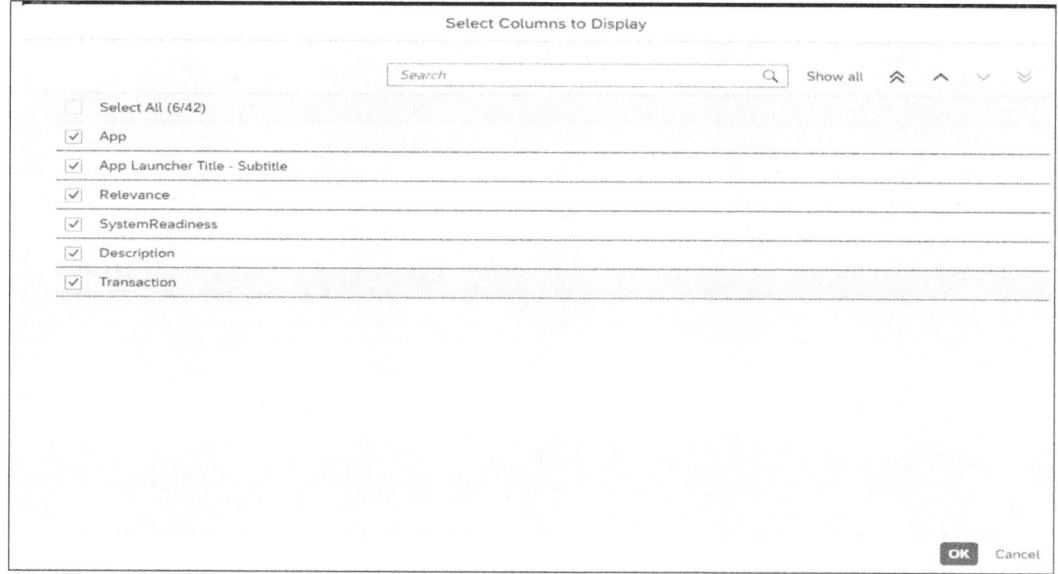

Figure 3-64. *Output categories of data selected*

Click **OK** at the bottom of the screen.

Figure 3-65. *Output data details*

The above result can be saved into an Excel file by clicking Download at the bottom of the screen, and the ***.csv** file is saved in the Downloads folder. Open the file.

	fioriId	RoleName	AppName	AppType	App Launc	Relevance	Relevance	SystemRe	ACH_L2	ACH_WO_	LeadingTransactionC	GTMAppD	Link
2	F0029	Internal S	Sales Ord	Transactional		Relevance	***	Not Instal	SD-HBA	SD-HBA	VA02, VA06, VA05	This app	https://fioriappslibrary.hana.ondemand.com/sap/fix/externalViewer/?appId=F002
3	F0029A	Internal S	Sales Ord	Transactional, Analy		Relevance	***	Installed	SD-HBA	SD-HBA	VA02, VA05N, VL02N, \	This app	https://fioriappslibrary.hana.ondemand.com/sap/fix/externalViewer/?appId=F002
4	F0046A	Internal S	Customer	Fact sheet		Relevance	***	Installed	LO-MD	LO-MD-Ch	XD03	With this	https://fioriappslibrary.hana.ondemand.com/sap/fix/externalViewer/?appId=F004
5	F0217	Manager -	Track Sup	Transacti	Track Sup	Relevance	**	Installed	FI-AP	FI-AP-TRA		With the tr	https://fioriappslibrary.hana.ondemand.com/sap/fix/externalViewer/?appId=F021
6	F0232A	Inventory	Inbound D	Fact sheet		Relevance	**	Installed	LE-SHP	LE-SHP-OBP		You can a	https://fioriappslibrary.hana.ondemand.com/sap/fix/externalViewer/?appId=F023
7	F0233A	Internal S	Outbound	Fact sheet		Relevance	**	Installed	LE-SHP	LE-SHP-OBP		You can a	https://fioriappslibrary.hana.ondemand.com/sap/fix/externalViewer/?appId=F023
8	F0234A	Internal S	Returns D	Fact sheet		Relevance	**	Installed	LE-SHP	LE-SHP-OBP		You can a	https://fioriappslibrary.hana.ondemand.com/sap/fix/externalViewer/?appId=F023
9	F0246	Productio	Monitor E	Transacti	Monitor E	Relevance	***	Installed	PP-MRP	PP-MRP	MD04	With this	https://fioriappslibrary.hana.ondemand.com/sap/fix/externalViewer/?appId=F024
10	F0247	Material P	Monitor M	Transactional		Relevance	***	Not Instal	PP-MRP	PP-MRP	MD06, MD04	With this	https://fioriappslibrary.hana.ondemand.com/sap/fix/externalViewer/?appId=F024
11	F0247A	Productio	Monitor M	Transacti	Monitor M	Relevance	***	Installed	PP-MRP	PP-MRP	MD06, MD04	With this	https://fioriappslibrary.hana.ondemand.com/sap/fix/externalViewer/?appId=F024
12	F0250	Productio	Manage E	Transactional		Relevance	***	Installed	PP-MRP	PP-MRP	MD06, MD04	With this	https://fioriappslibrary.hana.ondemand.com/sap/fix/externalViewer/?appId=F025
13	F0251	Productio	Manage M	Transacti	Check Ma	Relevance	*	Installed	PP-MRP	PP-MRP		With this	https://fioriappslibrary.hana.ondemand.com/sap/fix/externalViewer/?appId=F025
14	F0251A	Productio	Manage M	Transacti	Manage M	Relevance	***	Installed	PP-MRP	PP-MRP	MD04	With this	https://fioriappslibrary.hana.ondemand.com/sap/fix/externalViewer/?appId=F025
15	F0263	Productio	Monitor Ir	Transacti	Monitor Ir	Relevance	*	Installed	PP-MRP	PP-MRP		With this	https://fioriappslibrary.hana.ondemand.com/sap/fix/externalViewer/?appId=F026
16	F0266	Productio	Monitor P	Transacti	Monitor P	Relevance	***	Not Instal	PP-MRP	PP-MRP	MD04, MD05	With this	https://fioriappslibrary.hana.ondemand.com/sap/fix/externalViewer/?appId=F026
17	F0266A	Productio	Monitor P	Transacti	Monitor P	Relevance	***	Installed	PP-MRP	PP-MRP	MD04, MD05	With this	https://fioriappslibrary.hana.ondemand.com/sap/fix/externalViewer/?appId=F026
18	F0270	Productio	Manage Ir	Transactional		Relevance	***	Installed	PP-MRP	PP-MRP	MD04, MD05	With this	https://fioriappslibrary.hana.ondemand.com/sap/fix/externalViewer/?appId=F027

Figure 3-66. *Data output saved to a CSV file*

Rearranging the columns in the above figure will result in a new output screen appearing, as shown in the figure below.

	fioriId	AppName	AppType	Relevance Score	SystemReadiness	LeadingTransactionCodes
2	F0029	Sales Order Fulfillment Issues	Transactional	***	Not Installed	VA02, VA06, VA05
3	F0029A	Sales Order Fulfillment Issues (Version 2)	Transactional, Analytical	***	Installed	VA02, VA05N, VL02N, VA06, VA05
4	F0046A	Customer Master FactSheets	Fact sheet	***	Installed	XD03
5	F0217	Track Supplier Invoices	Transactional	**	Installed	
6	F0232A	Inbound Delivery (S/4HANA)	Fact sheet	**	Installed	
7	F0233A	Outbound Delivery (S/4HANA)	Fact sheet	**	Installed	
8	F0234A	Returns Delivery (S/4HANA)	Fact sheet	**	Installed	
9	F0246	Monitor External Requirements	Transactional	***	Installed	MD04
10	F0247	Monitor Material Coverage - Net Segments	Transactional	***	Not Installed	MD06, MD04
11	F0247A	Monitor Material Coverage (Version 2)	Transactional	***	Installed	MD06, MD04
12	F0250	Manage External Requirements	Transactional	***	Installed	MD06, MD04
13	F0251	Manage Material Coverage	Transactional	*	Installed	
14	F0251A	Manage Material Coverage (Version 2)	Transactional	***	Installed	MD04
15	F0263	Monitor Internal Requirements	Transactional	*	Installed	
16	F0266	Monitor Production Orders or Process Orders	Transactional	***	Not Installed	MD04, MD05
17	F0266A	Monitor Production Orders or Process Orders (Version 2)	Transactional	***	Installed	MD04, MD05
18	F0270	Manage Internal Requirements	Transactional	***	Installed	MD04, MD05
19	F0273	Manage Production Orders or Process Orders	Transactional	***	Installed	MD04, MD05
20	F0338A	Material Master	Transactional, Fact sheet	***	Not Installed	MM03
21	F0343	Overdue Purchase Order Items	Analytical	**	Installed	
22	F0346A	Supplier Invoice (S/4HANA)	Transactional	***	Not Installed	MIR4

Figure 3-67. *Output data rearranged*

Save the file as an Excel file called **Fiori App Recommendation Report – ST03N.**

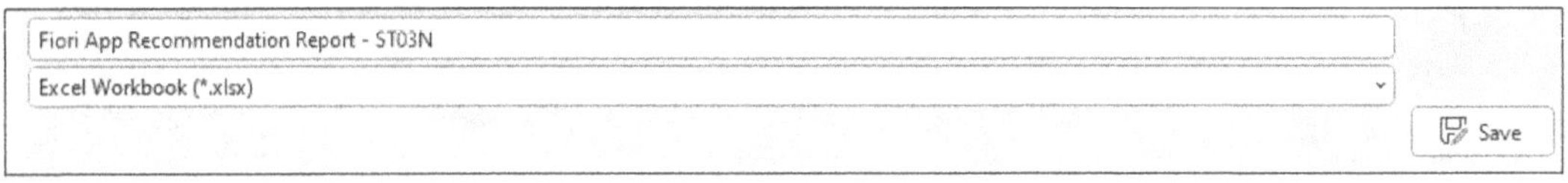

Figure 3-68. *App Recommendations Report details saved*

CHAPTER 3   SAP FIORI APPS RECOMMENDATION REPORT

Display existing analysis:

This option is used to review analyses that have been executed before.

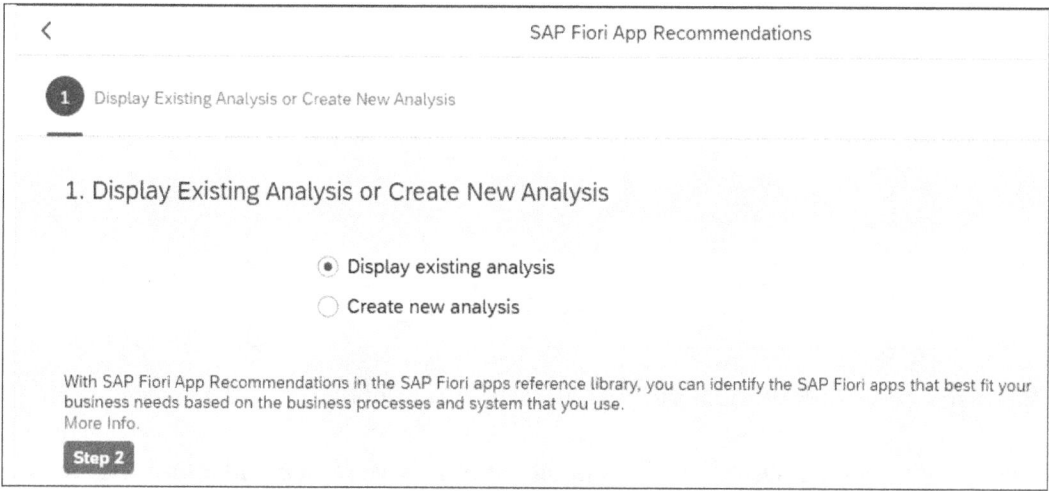

Figure 3-69. *Review the previously executed analyses.*

Select the option Step 2 .

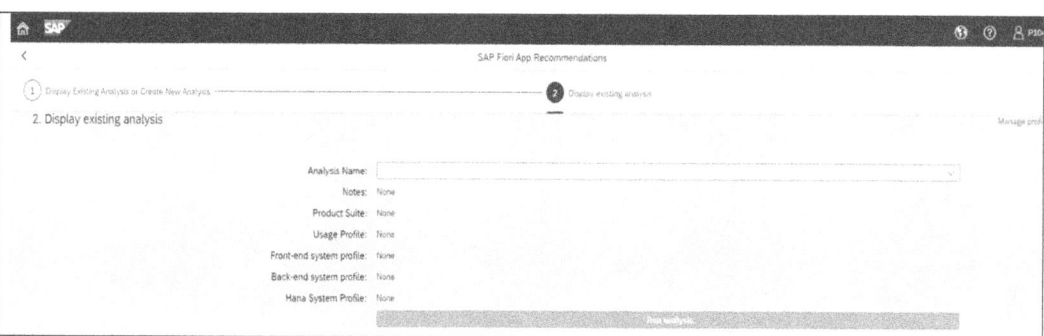

Figure 3-70. *Analysis selection screen*

You can click the dropdown button in the **Analysis Name** option to view previously completed analyses.

115

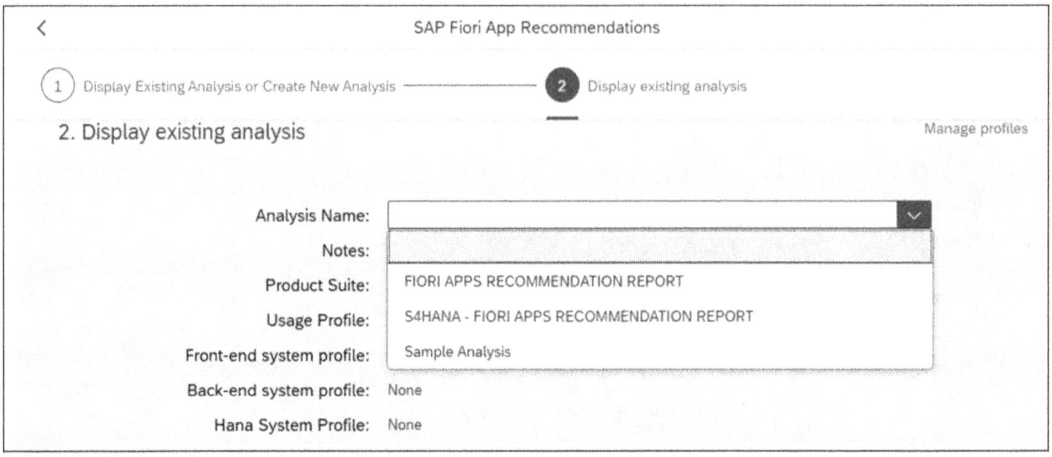

CHAPTER 3   SAP FIORI APPS RECOMMENDATION REPORT

Figure 3-71.   List of analysis options available to review

You can select the desired analysis name on the above screen and follow the steps listed above. Furthermore, you can also use another option, **Manage profiles**. This will provide you with a list of all the analyses that have been conducted.

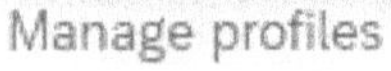

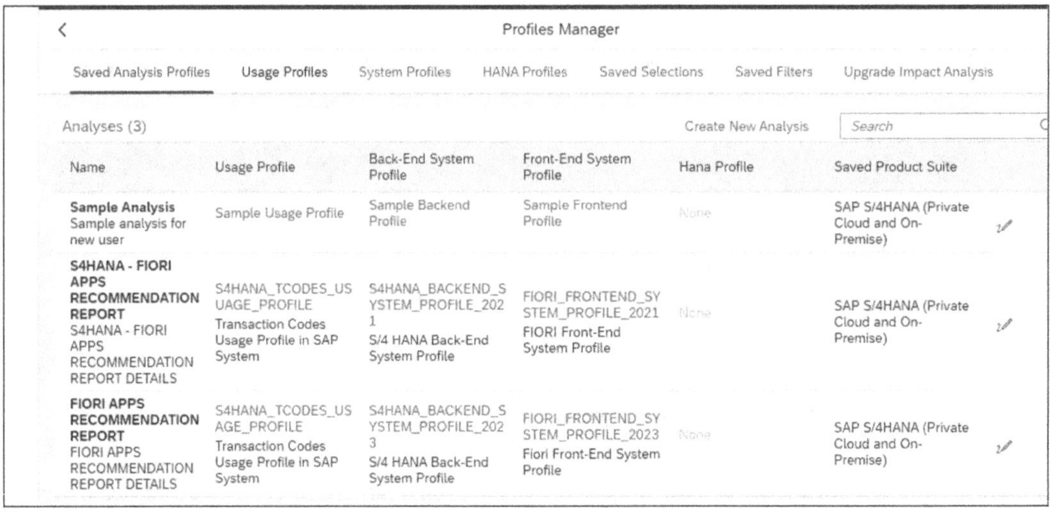

Figure 3-72.   Display analyses performed previously

Go back to **Step 2**, which gives the list of reports available for selection, and select the analysis as shown in the figure below.

CHAPTER 3 SAP FIORI APPS RECOMMENDATION REPORT

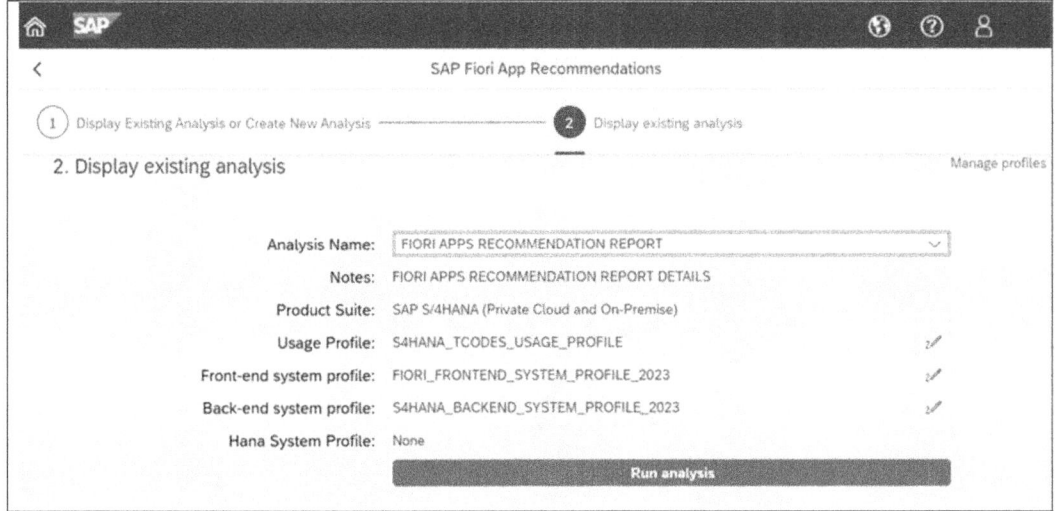

Figure 3-73. *Various analyses performed before are listed*

Note The system automatically populates all the relevant data related to the analysis selected, as shown in the figure above.

Now click **Run analysis**; this gives the same result as above, as shown in the figure below.

117

CHAPTER 3　SAP FIORI APPS RECOMMENDATION REPORT

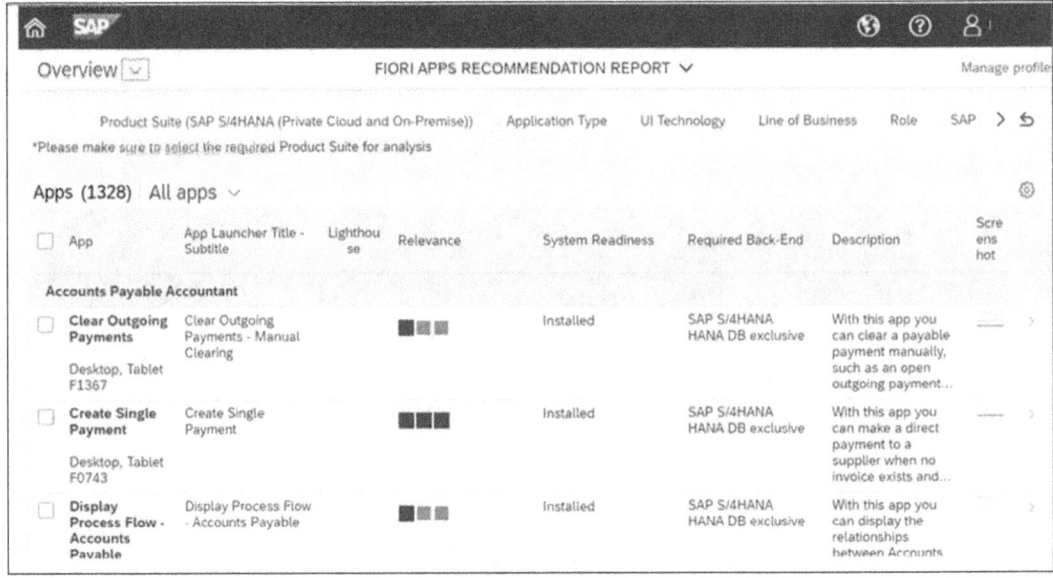

Figure 3-74. *Displays the report of the analysis*

The above gives the same report as listed in Figure 3-65.

3.10 Summary

This chapter discussed utilizing the SAP-delivered tool in the SAP Fiori Apps Reference Library. The SAP Fiori App Recommendations feature lists relevant SAP Fiori apps for business processes, such as finance, HR, and logistics. It also includes information about installed apps, those requiring updates, and any necessary installations for specific apps. This chapter also discusses various options to generate the input usage file needed for analysis.

CHAPTER 4

SAP Fiori Implementation and Deployment

Implementing SAP Fiori means creating an easy-to-use interface for business processes with role-based apps. Depending on your system's needs and complexity, you can deploy it using embedded or central hub architecture. This setup improves user experience, increases efficiency, and allows for smooth integration with SAP systems.

4.1 Introduction

SAP Fiori implementation can follow different approaches depending on the existing IT landscape, business requirements, and the level of transformation desired. The three main implementation strategies are Greenfield, Brownfield, and Bluefield. Each approach has its advantages and considerations. Here is a detailed explanation of each.

4.2 Greenfield Implementation

SAP recommends this implementation approach and follows the best practices. This implementation involves building a new system from scratch, such as creating a brand-new instance of the system in the context of SAP S/4HANA. Many companies nowadays choose this approach when they want to revamp their existing infrastructure and applications; it is like starting everything new. This implementation allows customers to streamline business processes, prioritize innovations, and integrate new cloud-based solutions. The main advantage of Greenfield implementation is the opportunity for more significant innovation potential. However, it also carries higher implementation risk because everything needs to be built on a new system.

4.2.1 Approach

In the context of SAP Fiori and S/4HANA, Greenfield implementation refers to a fresh, new system installation without migrating data or processes from a legacy system. It is like starting with a blank slate, allowing you to build a brand-new SAP landscape from the ground up.

4.2.2 Key Characteristics

Fresh Start: A completely new SAP S/4HANA system is set up.

No Legacy Data: No data or configurations are carried over from previous systems.

Process Re-engineering: Businesses can redesign and optimize their processes to leverage S/4HANA's capabilities.

Fiori Adoption: Fiori apps have become the primary user interface, offering a modern and intuitive user experience.

4.2.3 When to Consider Greenfield

New Implementations: When a company is implementing SAP for the first time.

Major Business Transformations: If a company is undergoing a significant transformation and wants to redesign its processes from scratch.

Heavily Customized Legacy Systems: A system conversion would be complex or risky in cases where the existing ERP system is heavily customized.

4.2.4 Steps Involved in Greenfield Implementation

- **Project Preparation:**
  - Define project scope, goals, and timelines.
  - Assemble the project team and identify key stakeholders.
  - Secure necessary resources and budget.

- **Blueprinting:**
  - Analyze business requirements and design future processes.
  - Define the system landscape and architecture.
  - Select and configure Fiori apps.

- **Realization:**
  - Configure the S/4HANA system based on the blueprint.
  - Develop any necessary customizations or extensions.
  - Set up the Fiori Launchpad and configure user roles.

- **Testing:**
  - Perform rigorous testing, including unit testing, integration testing, and user acceptance testing.
  - Address any identified issues or defects.

- **Data Migration (If Applicable):**
  - If any data needs to be migrated from external sources, perform data extraction, transformation, and loading (ETL).

- **Deployment:**
  - Go live with the new S/4HANA system and Fiori apps.
  - Provide training and support to end users.

- **Post-Go-Live Support:**
  - Monitor system performance and address any issues.
  - Continuously improve and optimize processes.

4.2.5 Benefits of Greenfield Implementation

Clean Slate: Start fresh with a streamlined system and optimized processes.

Innovation: Leverage the latest S/4HANA capabilities and Fiori user experience.

Flexibility: Design processes to meet specific business needs without the constraints of legacy systems.

Reduced Technical Debt: Avoid carrying over technical debt from older systems.

4.2.6 Challenges of Greenfield Implementation

Time and Resource Intensive: Requires significant time, effort, and resources.

Change Management: Involves substantial change for users, requiring comprehensive training and change management efforts.

Data Migration: This can be complex if data needs to be migrated from external sources.

4.2.7 Additional Considerations

SAP Activate Methodology: Follow SAP Activate, SAP's recommended implementation methodology, to guide the project through its various phases.

Expert Guidance: Engage experienced SAP consultants to assist with project planning, execution, and change management.

User Adoption: Focus on user adoption through training, communication, and ongoing support.

4.2.8 Conclusion

Overall, Greenfield offers the opportunity to build a modern, efficient, and user-friendly SAP environment. However, successful outcomes require careful planning, execution, and change management.

4.2.9 Summary

By following these guidelines and considering these factors, you can successfully execute a Greenfield implementation of SAP Fiori and S/4HANA, laying the foundation for digital transformation and improved business outcomes.

4.3 Brownfield Implementation

A Brownfield implementation in SAP S/4HANA involves migrating existing systems (usually SAP ECC) to the S/4HANA platform while maintaining pre-existing data, processes, and software customizations. This implementation is designed to improve performance, ensuring that your IT landscape stays the same, but you benefit from enhanced efficiency and real-time decision support.

4.3.1 Approach

System Conversion: In the context of SAP Fiori and S/4HANA, Brownfield implementation primarily involves a technical conversion of your existing SAP ERP system to S/4HANA.

Carryover of Data and Processes: This approach retains most, if not all, of your existing data, configurations, and customizations while transitioning to the new S/4HANA platform.

Fiori Layer on Top: The implementation focuses on introducing Fiori user experience (UX) on top of the converted system, often with minimal changes to underlying business processes.

4.3.2 Key Characteristics

Leverages the Existing System: The existing SAP ERP system is the foundation for migration.

Minimal Disruption: The goal is to minimize disruption to ongoing business operations during the transition.

Faster Time to Value: Compared with Greenfield implementations, Brownfield can be quicker as it does not require building everything from scratch.

Fiori as the New UX: The primary focus is adopting the Fiori user interface to improve user experience and productivity.

4.3.3 When to Consider Brownfield

Stable Systems: Suitable for organizations with stable and well-functioning ERP systems.

Limited Customization: It is ideal when the existing system has minimal customizations that can be easily adapted to S/4HANA.

Faster Adoption: When a rapid transition to S/4HANA is desired, especially if significant process changes are not required.

4.3.4 Steps Involved in a Brownfield Implementation

- **Preparation:**
  - Conduct a thorough system assessment to identify compatibility issues or required adjustments.
  - Prepare the existing system for conversion, including data cleansing and archiving.
  - Decide on the Fiori apps to be implemented and their integration points.

- **System Conversion:**
  - Use SAP's Software Update Manager (SUM) or a specialized migration tool to convert the ERP system to S/4HANA technically.
  - This includes database migration, code adaptation, and configuration adjustments.

- **Fiori Implementation:**
  - Activate and configure the necessary Fiori apps.
  - Set up the Fiori Launchpad and customize it according to user roles and requirements.
  - Integrate Fiori apps with the converted S/4HANA back end.

- **Testing:**
  - Perform extensive testing to ensure all functionalities, including custom code and interfaces, work correctly in the new S/4HANA environment with Fiori.

- **Deployment:**
  - Go live with the converted S/4HANA system and the new Fiori user interface.
  - Provide comprehensive training and support to users to facilitate adoption.

4.3.5 Benefits of Brownfield Implementation

Faster Implementation: Less time-consuming than Greenfield as it leverages the existing system.

Lower Risk: Preserves existing data and processes, reducing the risk of disruption.

Cost-Effective: It can be more cost-effective than Greenfield due to less re-implementation effort.

Improved UX: Introduces a modern Fiori user experience, enhancing usability and productivity.

4.3.6 Challenges of Brownfield Implementation

Limited Process Improvement: This does not provide the same opportunity for process re-engineering as Greenfield.

Technical Debt: Technical debt from the legacy system may be carried over if not addressed during the conversion.

Compatibility Issues: Potential compatibility issues with customizations or third-party add-ons.

User Adoption: Requires change management efforts to ensure a smooth user transition to the new Fiori interface.

4.3.7 Additional Considerations

SAP Readiness Check: Use the SAP Readiness Check tool to assess your system's compatibility with S/4HANA and identify any necessary adjustments.

Custom Code Remediation: If significant customizations exist, plan for code remediation to ensure compatibility with S/4HANA.

Fiori App Selection: Choose Fiori apps that align with your business needs and user roles.

4.3.8 Conclusion

Even in the Brownfield scenario, reviewing and optimizing processes can lead to more significant benefits from the S/4HANA migration. Leveraging existing systems and data offers a faster, less disruptive path to S/4HANA adoption. However, it requires careful planning, potential code remediation, and change management to ensure a successful transition without carrying over technical debt.

4.3.9 Summary

Overall, Brownfield implementation is a practical approach for organizations seeking a quicker path to S/4HANA adoption while preserving their existing investments in data and processes. However, to ensure a successful transition, it is crucial to carefully assess the system, address technical debt, and manage change effectively.

4.4 Bluefield Implementation

Bluefield implementation is a migration approach that respects your existing setup, combining Brownfield and Greenfield strategies. It can also be termed a hybrid implementation approach. The Bluefield approach enables organizations to transition to SAP S/4HANA with minimal business disruption and data loss. It also entails creating a new SAP S/4HANA system while retaining the existing SAP system. Critical data and processes are selectively moved to the new system, ensuring a smooth transition. This minimizes data loss, reduces migration time, and streamlines the new system. In general, this implementation balances preserving existing systems and embracing the benefits of SAP S/4HANA.

4.4.1 What Is Bluefield Implementation?

Hybrid Approach: Bluefield is a hybrid approach for SAP S/4HANA migration, combining elements of both Greenfield (new implementation) and Brownfield (system conversion) approaches.

Selective Transition: This involves setting up a new S/4HANA system alongside the existing ERP system and selectively migrating specific processes and data as needed.

Clean Core: Bluefield aims to achieve a "clean core" S/4HANA environment by re-evaluating and optimizing business processes during the transition.

4.4.2 Key Characteristics

New S/4HANA System: A fresh S/4HANA instance is created, separate from the existing ERP system.

Selective Migration: Only necessary data and processes are migrated, leaving legacy or obsolete processes behind.

Process Re-engineering: This is an opportunity to re-engineer and optimize business processes using S/4HANA capabilities.

Fiori Adoption: Fiori apps are implemented in the new S/4HANA system, providing a modern user experience.

Phased Approach: Migration can be done in phases, minimizing disruption to ongoing operations.

4.4.3 When to Consider Bluefield

Complex Landscapes: This is for organizations with complex and heavily customized ERP systems where an entire system conversion (Brownfield) might be challenging.

Selective Modernization: Modernizing specific business areas or processes while keeping other legacy system parts.

Clean Core Goal: To achieve a clean and optimized S/4HANA environment free from legacy data and processes.

Phased Transition: If you prefer a gradual transition to S/4HANA, minimizing risk and disruption.

4.4.4 Steps Involved

- **Preparation:**
  - Evaluate existing business processes and identify areas for improvement or simplification.

- Define the scope of the migration, including which processes and data to migrate.
- Set up the new S/4HANA system.

- **Data Migration:**
  - Extract, transform, and load (ETL) relevant data from the legacy system to the new S/4HANA system.
  - Cleanse and harmonize data during the migration process.

- **Process Re-engineering:**
  - Redesign and optimize business processes to take advantage of S/4HANA capabilities.
  - Implement Fiori apps to support the new processes.

- **Testing and Validation:**
  - Thoroughly test the migrated processes and data in the new S/4HANA system.
  - Validate that the new system meets business requirements.

- **Deployment:**
  - Deploy the new S/4HANA system and Fiori apps to users.
  - Provide training and support to ensure a smooth transition.

4.4.5 Benefits of Bluefield Implementation

Reduced Risk: Allows for a phased approach, minimizing disruption and risk compared with a complete system conversion.

Clean Core: Achieves a clean and optimized S/4HANA environment.

Process Improvement: Enables process re-engineering and optimization.

Modern User Experience: Introduces Fiori apps for a much better user experience.

Flexibility: Provides flexibility to migrate specific processes and data based on business priorities.

4.4.6 Challenges of Bluefield Implementation

Complexity: This approach can be more complex than a Greenfield or Brownfield approach due to the need for data and process harmonization between the two systems.

Data Consistency: Data consistency between legacy and new systems requires careful management during the transition period.

Change Management: Effective change management is needed to address user adoption and training challenges associated with new processes and Fiori apps.

4.4.7 Additional Considerations

Tool Support: Consider using tools like SAP Landscape Transformation (SLT) or SNP Bluefield to facilitate the data migration and process transformation.

Expert Guidance: Engage experienced SAP consultants to help with the planning, execution, and change management aspects of the Bluefield implementation.

4.4.8 Conclusion

Overall, the Bluefield approach offers a flexible and controlled path to S/4HANA adoption, particularly for organizations with complex landscapes or those seeking a clean core implementation. By carefully planning and executing migration, businesses can leverage the benefits of S/4HANA and Fiori while minimizing disruption and risk.

CHAPTER 4 SAP FIORI IMPLEMENTATION AND DEPLOYMENT

4.4.9 Summary

Bluefield implementation is a hybrid approach to SAP S/4HANA migration, combining elements of Greenfield and Brownfield. It involves setting up a new S/4HANA system alongside the existing one and selectively migrating data and processes, allowing for a phased transition and process optimization.

4.5 Implementation Pros and Cons

Implementation	Description	Pros	Cons
Greenfield	Starting from scratch with a new SAP Fiori implementation.	Clean slate with no legacy issues.	High initial cost due to complete redesign.
		Opportunity to re-engineer and optimize business processes.	Longer implementation time.
		Adoption of latest technologies and best practices.	Requires significant change management and user training.
		Flexibility in design and architecture.	Potential resistance from users accustomed to legacy systems.
Brownfield	Migrating existing SAP applications and customizations to SAP Fiori without major changes.	Lower cost compared to Greenfield since existing processes and data are reused.	May inherit inefficiencies and issues from legacy systems.
		D8Faster implementation as it leverages existing systems.	Limited ability to re-engineer and optimize processes.
		Reduced change management effort as users continue with familiar processes.	Potential compatibility issues with existing customizations and extensions.
		Minimal disruption to ongoing operations.	Less flexibility in design and architecture.
Bluefield	A hybrid approach combining elements of both Greenfield and Brownfield.	Balance between reusing existing processes and introducing new improvements.	Complex project management due to hybrid nature.
		Opportunity to re-engineer critical processes while retaining stable parts of the existing system.	Requires careful planning to determine what to keep and what to redesign.
		Faster than Greenfield and more flexible than Brownfield.	Potential integration challenges between old and new components.
		Can leverage existing data and processes where beneficial, while adopting new technologies and practices.	Higher cost and effort compared to pure Brownfield.

Figure 4-1. *Implementation pros and cons*

4.6 SAP Fiori Deployment Architecture

S/4HANA can be deployed via two different scenarios, and the schematic is as shown in the figure below:

- Embedded deployment
- Central hub deployment

Note Here are the components involved:

- **IW_PGW:** Provides the Fiori My Inbox app functionalities.
- **IW_BEP:** Enables the back-end system to expose business data as OData services.
- **SRA001:** Example component for the Fiori apps for transactional applications.
- **Fiori Apps (Various):** Each app requires specific components installed on the back-end and front-end systems. For example, Fiori transactional, factsheet, and analytical apps have different prerequisites and components.

4.7 Embedded Deployment

Embedded deployment typically means integrating a system or component directly into another rather than running it as a separate, standalone system. When deploying SAP Fiori for SAP S/4HANA, the recommended approach is to use **embedded deployment**, where the FES and BES are on the same server. With embedded deployment, you manage Fiori and S/4HANA in a single system landscape and avoid needing separate front-end servers or systems, reducing complexity and infrastructure costs. This simplifies administration, reduces maintenance efforts, and streamlines updates. Fiori apps are tightly integrated with the S/4HANA back-end system in an embedded deployment. This integration ensures seamless data exchange and consistent user experiences. Embedded Fiori leverages the exact security mechanisms as S/4HANA. User authentication, authorization, and role-based access control are unified,

CHAPTER 4   SAP FIORI IMPLEMENTATION AND DEPLOYMENT

enhancing security. Since Fiori apps run directly on the S/4HANA system, there's minimal latency. This improves app performance and responsiveness. Users access the transactional and analytical apps through the same Fiori Launchpad, ensuring a consistent and intuitive interface. Implementing embedded deployments can be complex and requires careful planning and expertise. In an embedded deployment, end users need authorizations for both the front-end server (SAP Fiori Launchpad, cards, etc.) and the back-end server (OData services). In this scenario, you can combine the front-end and back-end authorizations into a single PFCG business role. Furthermore, depending on the specific needs and growth of the organization, embedded deployments may require adjustments or scaling efforts. The few components that are installed with embedded deployment are

> **Embedded Fiori:** SAP Fiori is an approach to user experience (UX) design and a set of applications that offer simplified, role-based user experience across different devices. When integrated with S/4HANA, Fiori improves usability by providing intuitive, easy-to-use interfaces that enhance productivity and user satisfaction.
>
> **Embedded Analytics:** Embedded analytics in S/4HANA integrates analytical capabilities directly into the transactional system, allowing users to access real-time insights and perform data analysis without the need to extract, transform, and load data into a separate data warehouse. Integrating SAP Fiori within embedded analytics leverages the SAP Fiori user experience, offering intuitive, role-based access to reports and dashboards, improving user productivity and satisfaction.
>
> **Embedded EWM (Extended Warehouse Management):** Embedded Extended Warehouse Management (EWM) in S/4HANA integrates warehouse management capabilities directly within the S/4HANA ERP system, allowing for seamless management of complex warehouse operations.
>
> **Embedded TM (Transportation Management):** Embedded Transportation Management (TM) in S/4HANA integrates

transportation management functionalities directly within the S/4HANA ERP system. This integration allows for seamless management of transportation processes, from planning and execution to monitoring and settlement, within a unified environment.

4.7.1 Other Features of an Embedded System

Based on a newer release of SAP GUI (7.40 or 7.50), SAP S/4HAHA supports additional authentication options (Kerberos, SAML browser protocol, OAuth). In this scenario, the ABAP component SAP_GWFND (Gateway Foundation) is included in the SAP NetWeaver 7.4 and above instance that supports the SAP Business Suite system. SAP Fiori applications are directly deployed on the SAP Business Suite system. If multiple SAP Business Suite systems are used, SAP Gateway must be configured for remote back-end system(s) at various times. This needs less runtime as one remote call is required with one RFC.

The embedded deployment approach in the SAP Business Suite system has the following advantages:

- Direct local access to metadata and business data, meaning easy data reuse.
- Less runtime overhead as one remote call is reduced.
- No content merge for different applications is required.
- No additional, separate SAP Gateway system is required.
- Lower than the total cost of ownership as there is one less system to maintain.

CHAPTER 4 SAP FIORI IMPLEMENTATION AND DEPLOYMENT

4.7.2 Components Required for Embedded Deployment

Systems	SAP Netweaver < 7.4	SAP Netweaver >= 7.4
SAP BES	GW_CORE	SAP_GWFND
	IW_BEP	
	IW_FND	
SAPUI5	1.28 or Higher	1.28 or Higher

Figure 4-2. *Component requirement for embedded deployment*

4.7.3 Schematic of an Embedded System

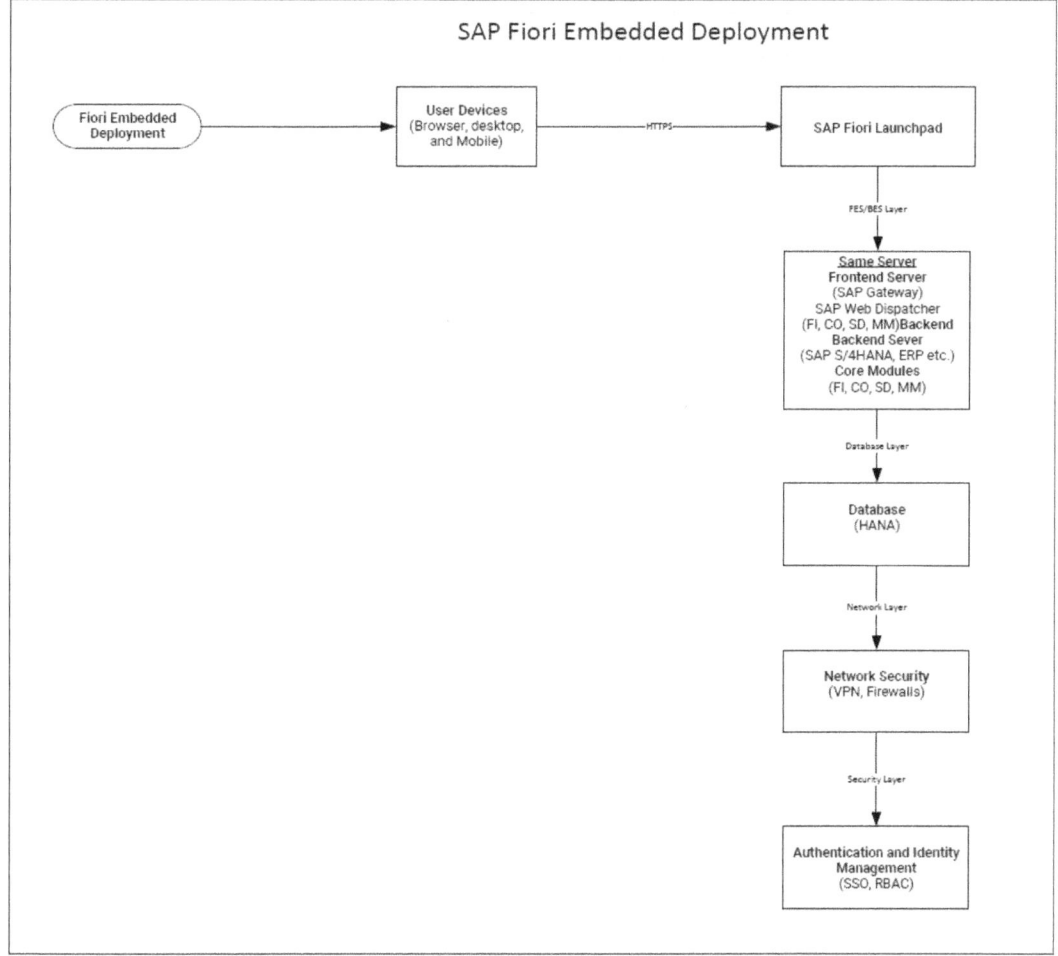

Figure 4-3. *Schematic of an embedded system*

4.7.4 Pros and Cons of Embedded Deployments

Embedded deployments offer distinct advantages and disadvantages depending on an organization's specific needs and context. A detailed comparison is listed below.

Embedded Deployment: Pros

Simplified Architecture: Fewer components and servers to manage, leading to a more straightforward IT landscape. It is easier to set up and maintain since everything is integrated within the S/4HANA system.

Reduced Latency: Direct communication between the Fiori front end and the back end reduces latency, improving performance.

Cost Efficiency: Lower infrastructure and maintenance costs as there is no need for additional servers or systems.

Streamlined Updates: More effortless synchronization of updates and patches as all components reside within a single system.

Enhanced Security: There are fewer points of potential failure or security breaches since the setup is less complex.

Embedded Deployment: Cons

Scalability Issues: Scaling in large environments can be challenging due to the load on a single system. Performance issues may arise with numerous users or transactions.

Upgrade Challenges: Upgrading the Fiori components may require simultaneously upgrading the S/4HANA system, which can be complex and disruptive.

Limited Flexibility: There is less flexibility in managing the user interface independently from the back end.

Resource Competition: Both transactional processing and user interface management share the same resources, potentially impacting performance.

4.8 Central Hub Deployment

The central hub deployment for SAP Fiori is a configuration where Fiori apps are managed and deployed separately from the SAP S/4HANA system. Fiori and S/4HANA are on different servers. This setup allows for more flexibility and scalability, particularly in larger or more complex environments. Multiple servers are needed for different systems as per the landscape.

A central hub system can be based on a newer release (7.40 or 7.50) that supports additional authentication options (Kerberos, SAML browser protocol, OAuth). This also supports SAPUI5 apps as a front-end server for SAP Fiori. The back-end server is based on 7.50 and higher.

- **Fiori** is deployed on the **front-end server** (FES), where the Fiori apps are deployed and managed. It handles the user interface layer, including the Fiori Launchpad, and communicates with the back-end systems to retrieve and process data.

- S/4HANA or other SAP systems are deployed on the **back-end server** (BES). This is where the core transactional and analytical data resides. The Fiori front-end server interacts with this system to fetch data and execute transactions.

- The SAP Gateway component SAP_GWFND is installed on the **FES** as a standalone **ABAP instance**. This component acts as a bridge between the Fiori front-end server and the back-end system. It handles OData services and other communication protocols required for data exchange. It comes with add-ons like IW_BEP, GW_CORE, IW_FND, and IW_HDB. The SAP Fiori applications are deployed on the FES, and gateway services are accessed on the BES. This is the preferred deployment scenario for production systems for the SAP Business Suite system.

The SAP front-end server hub deployment is the **recommended setup for multi-system SAP Business Suite scenarios**. The Fiori UI components, the SAP Fiori Launchpad content, and the SAP Gateway server are bundled on a central front-end server. At the same time, the classical UIs and the business logic remain on the back-end system. This setup allows one central entry point (SAP Fiori Launchpad) to business applications from multiple systems.

In this deployment, the Fiori Launchpad is the central entry point for users to access Fiori apps. Users log into the FES via a URL. It provides unified and personalized user experience, allowing users to navigate tasks and workflows. Also, in this deployment, Fiori apps and configurations are managed centrally on the front-end server, making it easier to maintain and update the user experience without affecting the back-end system.

This more flexible deployment allows for deploying Fiori apps in various environments, including cloud or on-premise setups. It also provides flexibility in how the user interface is managed and updated. Separating the user interface from the back end also improves performance, as the front-end server can be optimized specifically for handling user interactions.

Administrators can manage Fiori apps, roles, and configurations from a single point, streamlining administration and reducing complexity. In this deployment, the server is more accessible for upgrades and maintenance. Fiori app updates and changes can be made on the front-end server without impacting the backend system, simplifying maintenance and upgrades. Users experience a consistent and personalized interface across different back-end systems, enhancing usability and satisfaction.

Implementing a central hub deployment requires additional infrastructure for the front-end server and SAP Gateway, which can increase costs, which is a big drawback. Also, managing a central hub deployment can be more complex than an embedded setup, particularly ensuring synchronization between the front-end and back-end systems.

4.8.1 Advantages of Central Hub Deployment of SAP Gateway

The **central hub deployment** of SAP Gateway has the following advantages:

- Routing and composition of multiple systems is supported.
- Dedicated SAP Gateway content is available.
- Content can be deployed without touching the SAP Business Suite system.
- Decoupled lifecycle of consumer applications from the SAP Business Suite system.

- Central management of routing and connectivity with SAP Business Suite systems.

- SAP Gateway capabilities need to be deployed only once within the landscape.

- Better security, as a request, is validated in the dedicated box.

- The SAP Gateway system will not automatically affect the SAP Business Suite system.

- Independent innovation speed of SAP Gateway and the connected SAP Business Suite systems.

4.8.2 Components Required for Central Hub Deployment

Systems	SAP Netweaver < 7.4	SAP Netweaver >= 7.4
Netweaver Gateway - FES	GW_CORE	SAP_GWFND
	IW_FND	
SAP BES	IW_BEP	SAP_GWFND
SAPUI5	1.28 or Higher	1.28 or Higher

Figure 4-4. Components required for central hub deployment

4.8.3 Schematic of a Central Hub Deployment

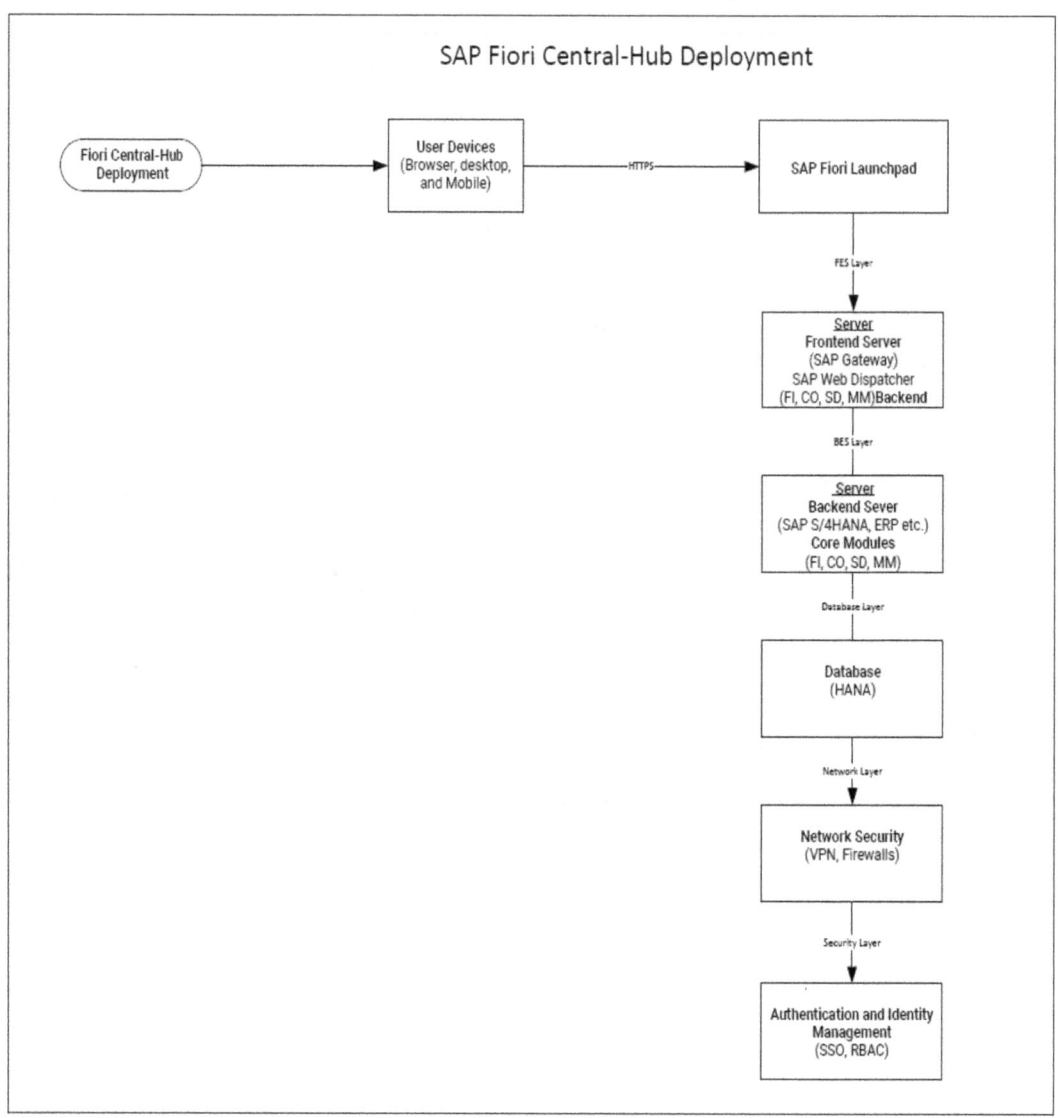

Figure 4-5. Schematic of a central hub deployment

4.8.4 Pros and Cons of Central Hub Deployments

Central hub deployments offer distinct advantages and disadvantages depending on an organization's specific needs and context. A detailed comparison is listed below.

Central Hub Deployment: Pros

Scalability: You can easily add more front-end servers to support more users without changing the back-end system. This setup can manage complex environments effectively.

Separation of Concerns: Separating the user interface from the back end makes it easier to update and manage performance for each part.

Centralized Management: Centralized control of Fiori apps and roles makes it easier to manage them. It allows for deployment across multiple back-end systems, creating a consistent user experience.

Improved Flexibility: You can manage and customize the user interface more easily, without affecting back-end operations.

Enhanced Security: You can improve security by using a central front-end server to control user access and data flow.

Central Hub Deployment: Cons

Increased Complexity: Complex architecture with extra parts needs careful planning to ensure it runs smoothly.

Higher Infrastructure Costs: Adding more servers and equipment costs money and makes it harder to take care of everything.

Potential Latency: Communicating between the front-end and back-end systems can cause delays, which may lower performance.

Implementation Effort: Integrating the front-end server with the back-end system takes a lot of effort. It can be hard to keep updates in sync and ensure everything works well together.

User Creation: Both the FES and BES need to have the same end user ID, which must exist in both the systems.

4.9 Summary of Deployment Options

4.9.1 Embedded Deployment

- This option is best for smaller and simpler setups where cost savings are important.
- It works well for organizations with fewer users and lower transaction volumes.

4.9.2 Central Hub Deployment

- This option is better for larger and more complex environments that need to grow and adapt.
- This solution is ideal for organizations that have many back-end systems or handle many users and transactions.
- Choosing between embedded and central hub deployment depends on your organization's size, performance and scalability needs, and available resources for infrastructure and maintenance.

4.10 SAP NetWeaver Gateway: Overview and Deployment

To run SAP Fiori apps effectively, it is recommended that an embedded deployment of SAP Gateway be used. This means installing SAP Gateway on the same server.

SAP NetWeaver Gateway is a technology that enables seamless integration between SAP systems and external applications, devices, and platforms using the Open Data Protocol (OData). It acts as a bridge, facilitating communication and data exchange between the SAP environment and the external world. SAP Gateway is essential for enabling modern, user-friendly interfaces such as SAP Fiori applications and integrating SAP systems with non-SAP systems.

4.10.1 Key Features

Some of the key features of SAP Gateway are listed below:

OData Services: This allows you to access SAP data and processes using the OData protocol. It makes SAP business data and processes available as OData services, so external applications can easily use them.

Integration Abilities and Capabilities: It helps connect SAP with other systems, whether they are SAP or non-SAP. It works with different programming languages and platforms. Additionally, it supports various types of applications, including mobile, web, and desktop.

Secure and Protected Communication: It allows you to log in using methods like SAML, OAuth, and X.509 certificates. It also protects your data by using encryption protocols like SSL and TLS.

Straightforward Development: It provides development tools and frameworks such as SAP Gateway Service Builder for creating and managing OData services. It uses reusable components and templates to streamline the development process.

Flexibility: It allows for two types of communication: synchronous and asynchronous. You can also add custom features to standard OData services. Additionally, it helps you include SAP business logic in the services you expose.

Performance Enhancement and Optimization: This system is designed to handle and process data efficiently for better performance. It also includes features like caching and load balancing to speed up responses and manage large amounts of data.

Security: This system features secure ways to send data and control who can access it.

4.11 Deployment Options of SAP Gateway

SAP NetWeaver Gateway can be deployed in two main ways: **embedded** and **central hub deployment. The choice between these deployments depends on various factors**, including organizational size, complexity, performance requirements, and budget.

4.11.1 Embedded Deployment

The gateway components are installed directly within the SAP Business Suite environment, sharing the same resources and instance. **Embedded deployment** is more suitable for smaller organizations with more straightforward requirements and a focus on cost efficiency and ease of implementation.

Description

In an embedded deployment, SAP NetWeaver Gateway is installed on the same system as the SAP Business Suite, like SAP ECC or SAP S/4HANA. This means that the gateway is part of the same setup as the back-end SAP applications. This option is best for small- to medium-sized businesses that have simpler system setups and fewer integration needs.

Advantages

- **Low Latency:** Access SAP data directly without any network delays.
- **Simplified Architecture:** Fewer parts and components to manage makes things simpler and easy.
- **Cost-Effective:** You do not need extra hardware or separate servers.

Disadvantages

- **Resource Contention:** Using the gateway and SAP Business Suite together can slow things down.
- **Limited Scalability:** Scaling the gateway may require scaling the entire SAP system, which can be both expensive and complicated.
- **Maintenance and Update Impact:** Working on the SAP system can make it hard to use the gateway.

4.11.2 Central Hub Deployment

In a central hub deployment for SAP Gateway, the gateway components are installed on a separate server, distinct from the SAP back-end system (e.g., ECC or S/4HANA). This setup is great for companies with complicated systems. It allows different systems to connect through one main spot called a gateway. This makes it easier to manage everything. However, it can make things a bit slower, cost more money for extra equipment, and be more complicated to handle.

Description

In a central hub setup, organizations install SAP NetWeaver Gateway on a different server from SAP Business Suite, such as SAP ECC or SAP S/4HANA. This keeps the gateway components separate from the main SAP applications. By doing this, organizations can manage OData services and integrations from a single location. This setup is effective for companies with complex systems, multiple integrations, or those that want to keep gateway services distinct from their back-end systems.

Advantages

- **Independent Architecture:** It keeps gateway services separate from back-end systems. This separation helps prevent performance issues that could affect SAP Business Suite operations.

- **Scalability:** The gateway system can grow on its own to handle greater demands without disrupting back-end systems.

- **Centralized Control:** This system makes it easier to connect with different back-end systems. It simplifies the management of OData services in a distributed environment.

- **Minimized Maintenance Impact:** Upgrades or maintenance on SAP Business Suite does not affect gateway services directly.

Disadvantages

- **Delayed Response:** Communication between the gateway and back-end systems may cause slight delays in the network.
- **Increased Cost:** Requires additional hardware, servers, or resources for the separate gateway instance.
- **Complexity:** The system becomes more complex, which means it takes more effort to set up, monitor, and maintain.
- **Integration Effort:** You need to set up proper system aliases and ensure connectivity for easy integration with back-end systems.

4.12 Activate SAP Gateway

Before using SAP Gateway functionality, you must activate it globally in your FES system. You can activate and deactivate SAP Gateway. When you deactivate it, all SAP Gateway services stop running, no consumer servers can communicate with it, and an error message is sent to any system that calls for the services. There are multiple options available to activate SAP Gateway in an SAP system, and they are mainly

1. Task list
2. Transaction code **SPRO**
3. Transaction code **/IWFND/IWF_ACTIVATE**

4.12.1 Task List

You can use the task list **SAP_GATEWAY_BASIC_CONFIG** to perform basic SAP Gateway settings, including activating using transaction code STC01.

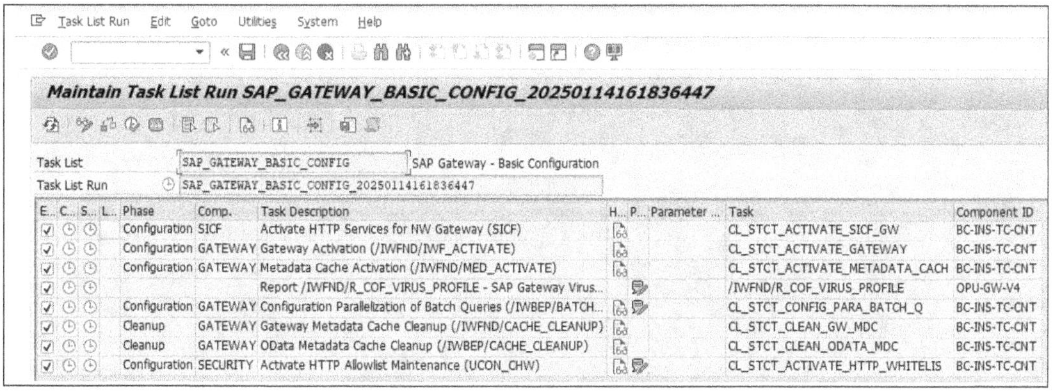

CHAPTER 4   SAP FIORI IMPLEMENTATION AND DEPLOYMENT

Figure 4-6. Task list SAP_GATEWAY_BASIC_CONFIG initial screen

4.12.2 Transaction Code: SPRO

There are two methods within SPRO to activate SAP Gateway.

Method 1: SPRO

Under SAP Customizing Implementation Guide (transaction code: **SPRO**), choose SAP **Reference IMG ➤ ABAP Platform ➤ UI Technologies ➤ SAP Fiori ➤ Initial Setup ➤ Manual Setup without Task Lists ➤ Connection Settings (Front-End Server to ABAP Back-End Server) ➤ Activate SAP Gateway**.

CHAPTER 4   SAP FIORI IMPLEMENTATION AND DEPLOYMENT

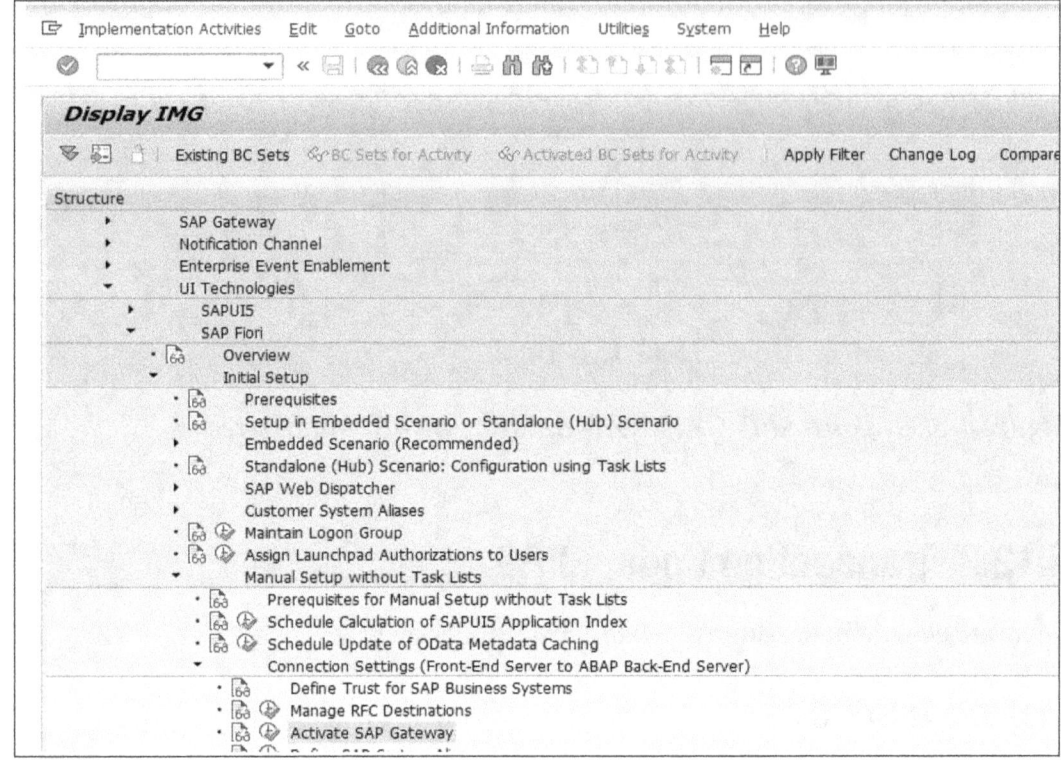

Figure 4-7. Method 1 – SPRO screen to activate SAP Gateway

Method 2: SPRO

Under SAP Customizing Implementation Guide (transaction code: **SPRO**), choose SAP **Reference IMG ➤ ABAP Platform ➤ SAP Gateway ➤ OData Channel ➤ Configuration ➤ Activate or Deactivate SAP Gateway**.

CHAPTER 4 SAP FIORI IMPLEMENTATION AND DEPLOYMENT

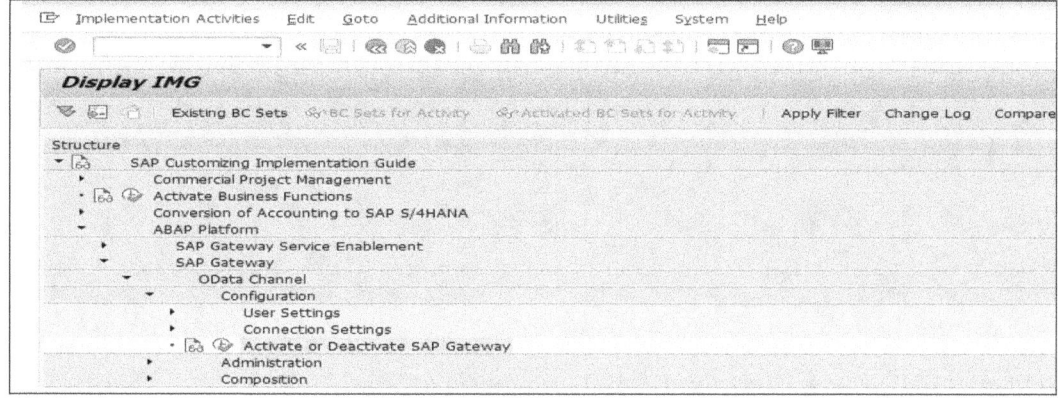

Figure 4-8. Method 2 – SPRO screen to activate SAP Gateway

4.12.3 Transaction Code: /IWFND/IWF_ACTIVATE

Start or execute the transaction **/IWFND/IWF_ACTIVATE**. This transaction can also activate SAP Gateway, as shown in the figure below.

Note If the gateway is activated, you will get the screen as shown in the figure below, by executing any of the above options mentioned.

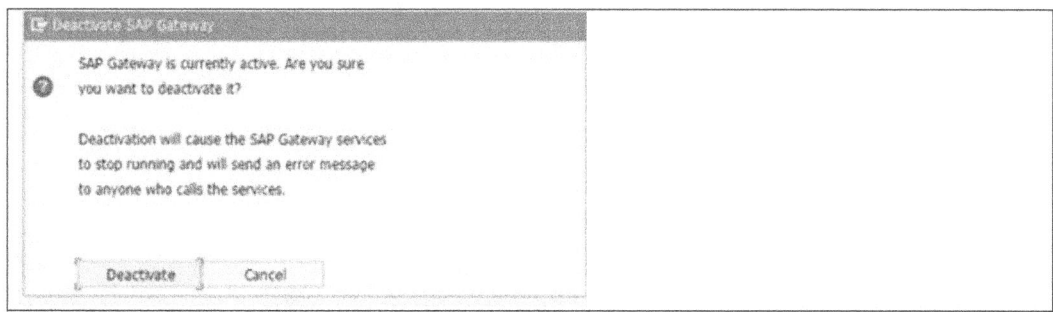

Figure 4-9. SAP Gateway active window

Click the option **Cancel**.

149

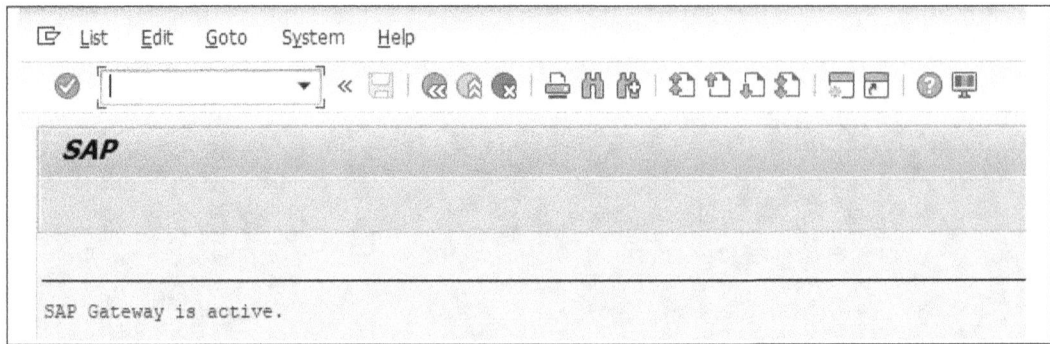

Figure 4-10. System displaying SAP Gateway is active

4.12.4 Summary

The embedded deployment of SAP NetWeaver Gateway provides a simple and cost-effective approach for small- to medium-sized enterprises with limited integration needs and less complex system landscapes. It enables direct access to business data, reducing delays and simplifying the architecture. However, it is essential to manage resources carefully to prevent performance issues.

4.13 Central Hub Deployment

In earlier versions of SAP, central hub deployment was preferred. Since Gateway is installed on an FES, it provides better scalability, no impact on back-end maintenance, centralized access, greater flexibility, enhanced security, easier downtime management, and dedicated performance monitoring. Some features of this deployment are as follows:

- In a central hub deployment, SAP NetWeaver Gateway is deployed on a separate server, distinct from the SAP Business Suite back-end systems.

- This configuration creates a dedicated gateway hub, a middleware layer between the SAP back end and external applications.

- Ideal for large enterprises with multiple SAP systems and significant integration requirements.

- **Installation in Central Hub Deployment**:

CHAPTER 4   SAP FIORI IMPLEMENTATION AND DEPLOYMENT

- The gateway components are installed on a separate server that handles gateway operations. This server communicates with multiple back-end SAP systems over the network.

4.13.1 Advantages

Isolated Resources: Gateway operations do not affect the performance of SAP Business Suite.

Scalability: Independent scaling of the gateway server based on load requirements.

Centralized Access: A single gateway hub can serve multiple SAP systems, simplifying integrations.

4.13.2 Disadvantages

Network Latency: Communication between Gateway and SAP systems can introduce delays over the network.

Complexity: More components and servers to manage, leading to a more complex infrastructure.

Higher Costs: Additional hardware and maintenance costs.

4.13.3 Deployment Pros and Cons

Aspect	Embedded Deployment	Central Hub Deployment (Co-Deployment)
Description	SAP Gateway is installed on the same instance as the SAP Business Suite backend system.	SAP Gateway is installed on a separate server, independent of the SAP Business Suite backend systems.
Latency	**Pros:** Lower latency due to direct access to business data without network overhead.	**Cons:** Potential network latency between the Gateway and backend systems.
Architecture Complexity	**Pros:** Simplified architecture with fewer components to manage.	**Cons:** More complex architecture with additional components to manage.
Cost	**Pros:** Reduced cost since no additional hardware or separate servers are required.	**Cons:** Higher costs due to additional hardware and maintenance.
Resource Management	**Cons:** Shared resources can lead to performance bottlenecks, especially under heavy loads.	**Pros:** Isolated resources ensure that Gateway operations do not affect backend system performance.
Scalability	**Cons:** Limited scalability as it requires scaling the entire SAP system, which can be costly and	**Pros:** Better scalability as the Gateway server can be scaled independently based on load requirements.
Maintenance Impact	**Cons:** Maintenance activities on the SAP Business Suite can impact Gateway availability, potentially leading to downtime for both components.	**Pros:** Maintenance activities on the Gateway do not impact the SAP Business Suite, and vice versa.
Implementation Speed	**Pros:** Faster implementation due to fewer components and simplified architecture.	**Cons:** Slightly longer implementation time due to additional configuration and setup.
Integration	**Pros:** Easier integration within the same system, simplifying internal communication.	**Pros:** Centralized access can serve multiple backend systems, simplifying integration with external applications.
Flexibility	**Cons:** Less flexibility in scaling and managing resources independently.	**Pros:** Greater flexibility in managing and scaling resources independently.
Security	**Cons:** Potentially higher risk as both Gateway and backend systems share the same security context and infrastructure.	**Pros:** Enhanced security through isolation; easier to implement robust security measures for Gateway and backend systems independently.
Downtime Management	**Cons:** Difficult to manage downtime as it affects both Gateway and backend systems simultaneously.	**Pros:** Easier to manage downtime as it can be scheduled independently for Gateway and backend systems.
Performance Monitoring	**Cons:** Shared performance monitoring and potential for resource contention.	**Pros:** Dedicated performance monitoring and management for the Gateway server, reducing the risk of resource contention.
Complexity for Users	**Pros:** Users experience a more integrated system with fewer points of failure.	**Cons:** Users may need to interact with multiple systems, increasing complexity.

Figure 4-11. Deployment pros and cons

4.13.4 Deployment Options: S/4HANA Schematic

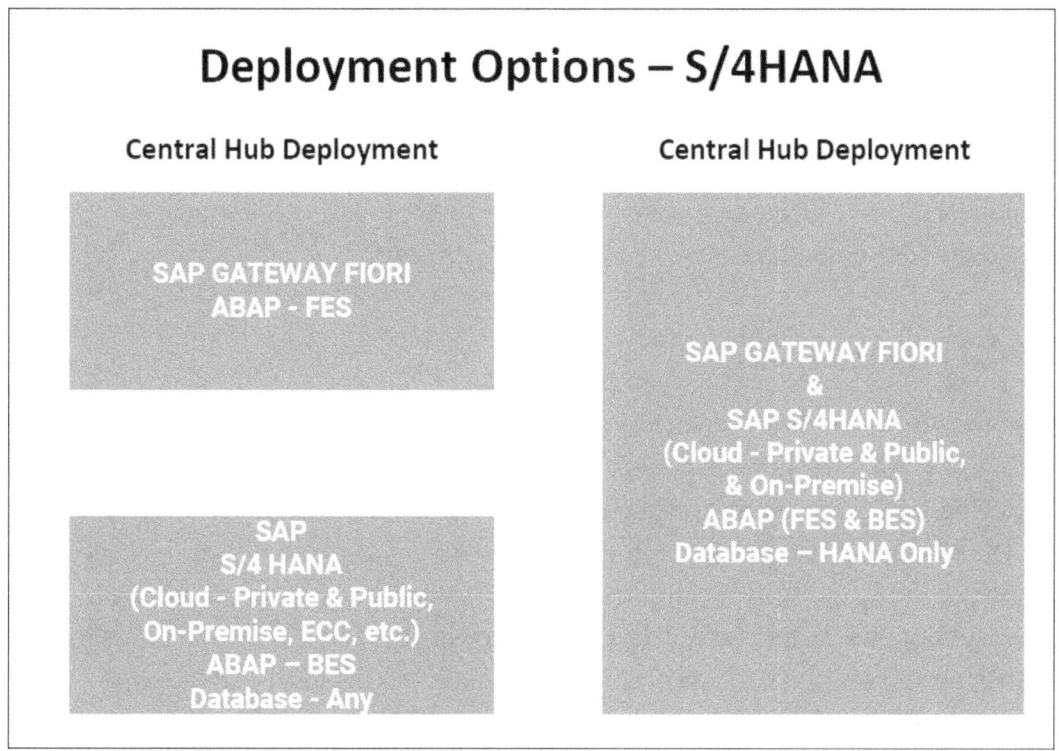

Figure 4-12. Deployment options – S/4HANA schematic

4.13.5 Conclusion

SAP NetWeaver Gateway is a powerful tool for integrating SAP systems with external applications using OData services.

Embedded deployment involves installing the gateway on the same instance as SAP Business Suite, offering simplicity and low latency but limited scalability.

Central hub deployment installs Gateway on a separate FES, providing better scalability and resource isolation at the cost of increased complexity and potential network latency.

The choice of deployment depends on the specific needs, size, and complexity of the organization's SAP landscape and integration requirements.

4.14 System Alias

As we know, SAP Fiori is designed to provide seamless and intuitive user experience for SAP applications. One of the critical components of SAP Fiori configuration is the system alias. The system alias is crucial in both embedded and central hub deployments, ensuring that SAP Fiori applications can correctly communicate with the back-end systems. Here, we will discuss the system alias in detail, focusing on its role and configuration in embedded and central hub deployments.

4.14.1 System Alias

A system alias in SAP Fiori is a logical name used to identify a back-end system that hosts the OData services required by SAP Fiori applications. It bridges the SAP Fiori front-end server and the back-end SAP system, ensuring that requests are routed correctly.

The system alias results from routing an inbound request on SAP Gateway. It can be a remote or a local system. Suppose the system alias is flagged as a Local GW (Local Gateway) instance. In that case, it means that the system responsible for processing (managing and storing) the data of an inbound request is the local SAP Gateway instance itself.

4.14.2 System Alias in Embedded Deployment

The front-end and back-end components are on the same system in an embedded deployment. This setup simplifies the configuration of the system alias because the Fiori front-end server directly communicates with the back-end system without making network calls to a separate server.

4.14.3 System Alias in Central Hub Deployment

A system alias connects the Fiori front-end server to the back-end system, where business data is stored in a central hub setup for SAP Fiori. This connection allows the front-end server to use essential services like OData to make applications work.

You can set up system aliases in the Fiori front-end server using transaction codes like **/IWFND/MAINT_SERVICE** or **/UI2/V_SYSALIAS**. These codes help link each service to its back-end system. This arrangement allows multiple back-end systems to work smoothly with the Fiori front end, ensuring consistent data access and better app performance.

4.15 Configuration Steps for Embedded Deployment

For embedded deployment, you do not need to create a system alias called **Local**, which is produced by default. If you need to create a system alias, follow the steps below:

Define a System Alias:

- Go to the transaction code /UI2/GW_SYS_ALIAS.
- Click "New Entries" and create a new system alias.
- Provide a name for the system alias and select the local system as the RFC destination.
  - It is usually called **Local and is created**.

Assign OData Services to the System Alias:

- Within the Service Builder, assign the created system alias to the required OData services.
- Ensure that the services are activated and correctly assigned to the alias.

Check Service Activation:

- Use the transaction code /IWFND/MAINT_SERVICE to verify that the OData services are active.
- Check that the system alias is correctly assigned to each service.

Testing:

- Test the configuration by accessing the SAP Fiori Launchpad and verifying that the applications load correctly.
- Ensure that the data from the back end is being retrieved correctly.

4.16 System Alias in Central Hub Deployment

In a central hub deployment, the SAP Fiori front-end server and the back-end SAP system are installed on separate systems. This separation requires additional configuration to ensure the front-end server can correctly communicate with the back-end system.

4.16.1 Configuration Steps for Central Hub Deployment

Define the RFC Destination:

- On the front-end server, create an RFC destination pointing to the back-end system (transaction code: SM59).
- Use the type "**3**" for ABAP connections and provide the necessary connection details.

Define a System Alias:

- Go to the transaction code /UI2/GW_SYS_ALIAS.
- Click "New Entries" and create a new system alias.
- Ensure that the system alias has the same name on both the front-end and back-end systems.

Assign OData Services to the System Alias:

- Assign the system alias to the required OData services in the Service Builder.
- Activate the services and ensure they are correctly assigned.

Activate OData Services on the Back End:

- On the back-end system, use transaction code /IWFND/MAINT_SERVICE to activate the OData services.
- Ensure that the system alias created on the front-end server is known to the back-end system.

Maintain System Aliases in the Launchpad:

- In the SAP Fiori Launchpad Designer, maintain the system alias for the catalogs and tiles.

- Ensure that the tiles and target mappings correctly reference the system alias.

Testing:

- Access the SAP Fiori Launchpad from the front-end server and test the applications.

- Verify that the applications can correctly communicate with the back-end system and retrieve data.

4.16.2 Best Practices for System Alias Configuration

Here are the best practices for configuring SAP system aliases:

Consistent Naming: To avoid confusion, use consistent naming conventions for system aliases across front and back systems.

Documentation: Maintain detailed documentation of system alias configurations, including RFC destinations and OData service assignments.

Regular Monitoring: Regularly monitor the performance and connectivity of system aliases to ensure there are no service disruptions.

Security: Ensure that secure connections (e.g., HTTPS) are used for communication between front-end and back-end systems, especially in central hub deployment.

Testing: Regularly test the configurations in a development or quality assurance environment before deploying changes to production.

CHAPTER 4   SAP FIORI IMPLEMENTATION AND DEPLOYMENT

4.16.3 Transaction Codes for Creating a System Alias

You have multiple options for maintaining system aliases in an SAP system:

- **Transaction Code /UI2/GW_SYS_ALIAS**: This sets up and manages system aliases for SAP Gateway. It ensures that SAP Fiori apps connect to the correct back-end data sources.

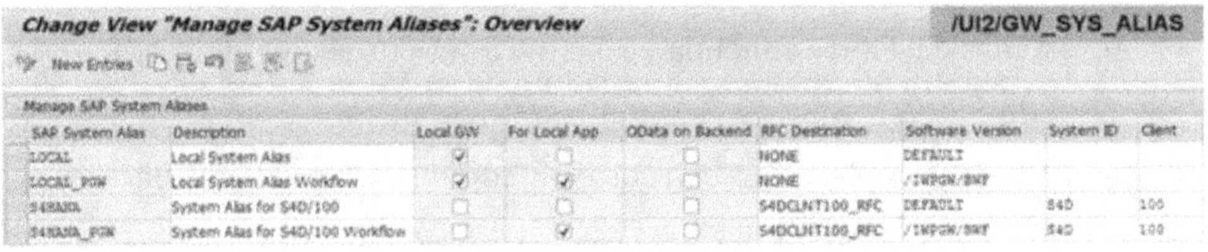

Figure 4-13. Output of transaction code /UI2/GW_SYS_ALIAS

- **Transaction Code /IWFND/ROUTING**: This tool tests and analyzes the routing setup for Fiori applications. It helps troubleshoot and verify how navigation and URL routing work in the Fiori Launchpad and embedded apps.

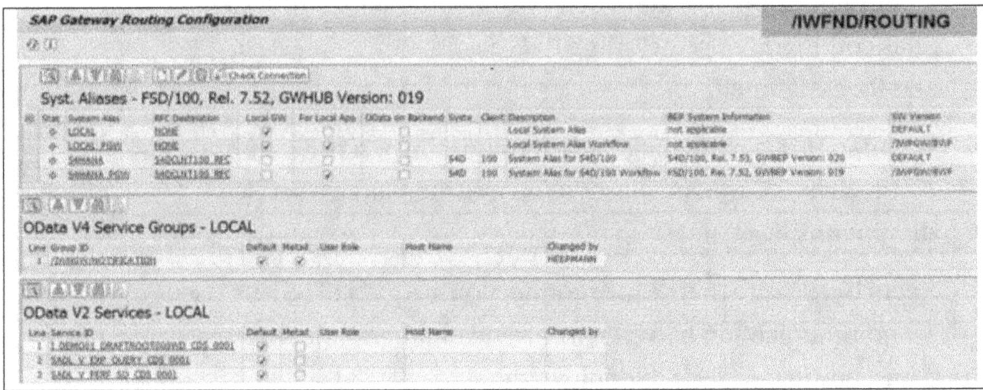

Figure 4-14. Output of transaction code /UI2/ROUTING

Note   This tool helps SAP Fiori administrators and developers ensure smooth app navigation and fix routing errors quickly.

CHAPTER 4 SAP FIORI IMPLEMENTATION AND DEPLOYMENT

4.16.4 Tables Available to View for System Aliases

The transaction code **SM30** allows you to view the SAP Fiori tables. Some of them are listed below:

> **Table /IWFND/V_DFSYAL:** The table **/IWFND/V_DFSYAL** in SAP Fiori holds the default settings for OData service system aliases. It indicates which back-end system an OData service should use, allowing easy communication between the Fiori front-end server and the back-end system. This table is essential for routing services. It is updated during the setup and troubleshooting of OData services.

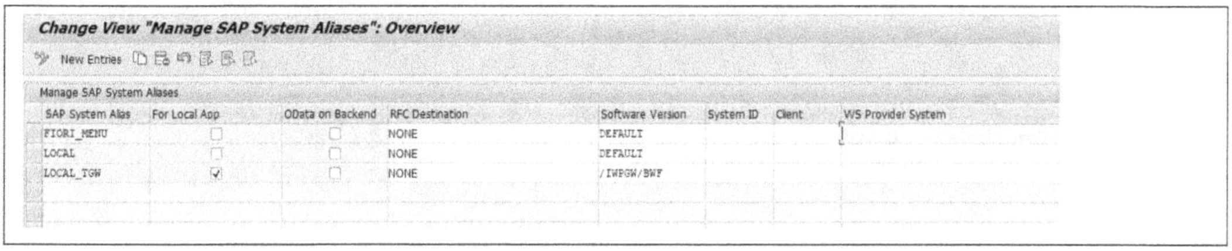

Figure 4-15. Table output of /IWFND/V_DFSYAL

> **Table /UI2/V_SYSALIAS**: The table **/UI2/V_SYSALIAS** in SAP Fiori helps manage system alias settings for SAP Gateway. It defines how the Fiori front-end server connects to the back-end server. Necessary details include the system alias name, client, RFC destination, and connection type (e.g., HTTP or HTTPS). This table is key for linking OData services to back-end systems, which allows Fiori apps to communicate and function smoothly. It is usually updated during setup and troubleshooting to ensure easy system integration.

CHAPTER 4　SAP FIORI IMPLEMENTATION AND DEPLOYMENT

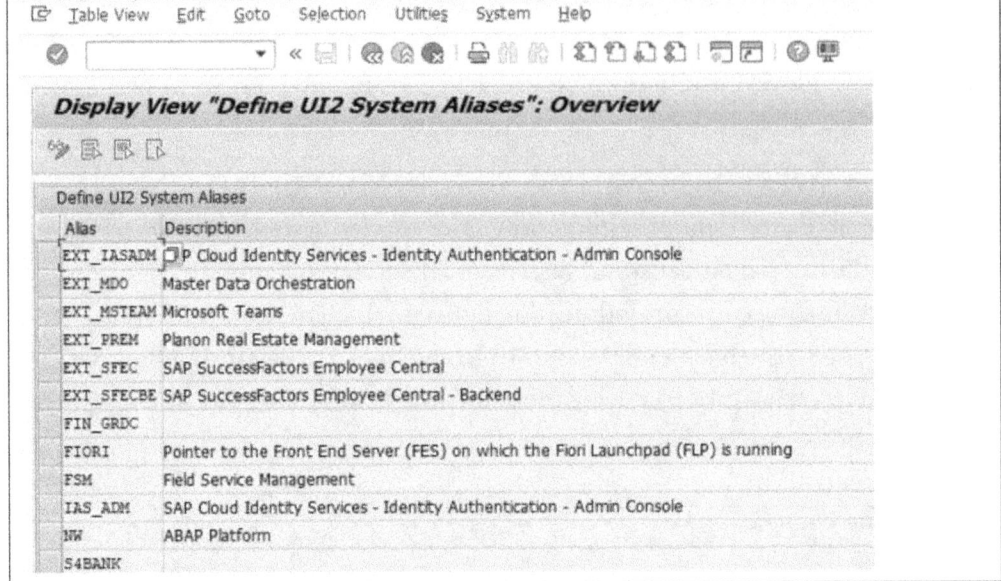

Figure 4-16. Table output of /UI2/V_SYSALIAS

Table /UI2/V_ALIASMAP: The table **/UI2/V_ALIASMAP** in SAP Fiori links multiple system aliases to one OData service. This setup allows the OData service to connect to different back-end systems based on specific settings, helping ensure that Fiori apps work smoothly with multiple systems.

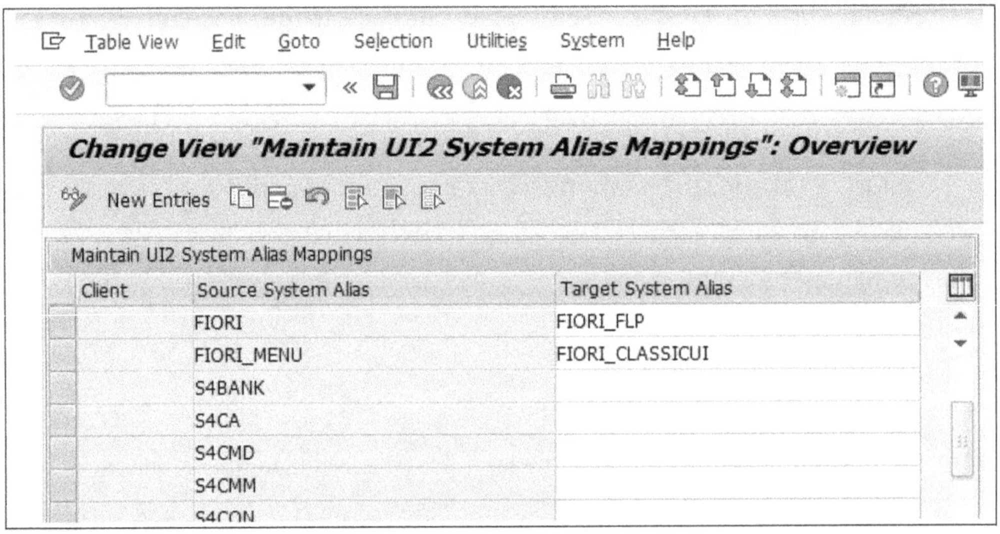

Figure 4-17. Table output of /UI2/V_ALIASMAP

CHAPTER 4   SAP FIORI IMPLEMENTATION AND DEPLOYMENT

Table /UI2/V_ALIASCAT: The table **/UI2/V_ALIASCAT** in SAP Fiori categorizes system aliases for better organization and management. It helps group and define categories for system aliases, making it easier to manage connections between the Fiori front-end server and multiple back-end systems. This is particularly useful in complex landscapes with numerous system aliases.

Technical Catalog ID	Alias of So...	Technical Catalog Title
SAP_NW_BE_APPS	NW	SAP ABAP Platform: Classic Apps
SAP_SFIN_TC_JVA_CLOUD	S4FIN	SAP Finance - Joint Venture Accounting - Cloud
SAP_TC_BANK_BCA_BE_APPS	S4BANK	SAP Deposits Management for Banking: Classic Apps
SAP_TC_BANK_CML_BE_APPS	S4BANK	SAP Loans Management for Banking: Classic Apps
SAP_TC_BANK_CMS_BE_APPS	S4BANK	SAP Collateral Management for Banking: Classic Apps
SAP_TC_BWF_AM_BE_APPS	NW	
SAP_TC_CA_AIF_BE_APPS	NW	
SAP_TC_CA_BP_BE_APPS	S4CMD	SAP CMD Business Partner: Classic Apps
SAP_TC_CA_COMMON_BE_APPS	S4CA	SAP Cross Application Common: Classic Apps
SAP_TC_CA_DAT_REP_BE_APPS	S4CA	SAP DRF Cross Application: Classic Apps
SAP_TC_CA_FND_BE_APPS	S4CA	SAP FND Cross Application: Classic Apps
SAP_TC_CA_HCM_BE_APPS	S4CA	SAP HCM Cross Application: Classic Apps
SAP_TC_CA_MD_DP_BE_APPS	S4CA	SAP MD Data Privacy Cross Applications: Classic Apps

Figure 4-18.   Table output of /UI2/V_ALIASCAT

Use the task list **SAP_GATEWAY_ADD_SYSTEM_ALIAS** to add a system alias or task list **SAP_GATEWAY_ADD_SYSTEM** to add a back-end system, including maintaining a system alias.

Transaction /UI2/APPDESC_GET: The transaction /UI2/APPDESC_GET extracts business catalogs to the front-end systems. This transaction is strongly recommended for SAP content replication via the business catalog, which will attempt to replicate all catalogs in the table **/UI2/V_ALIASCAT**.

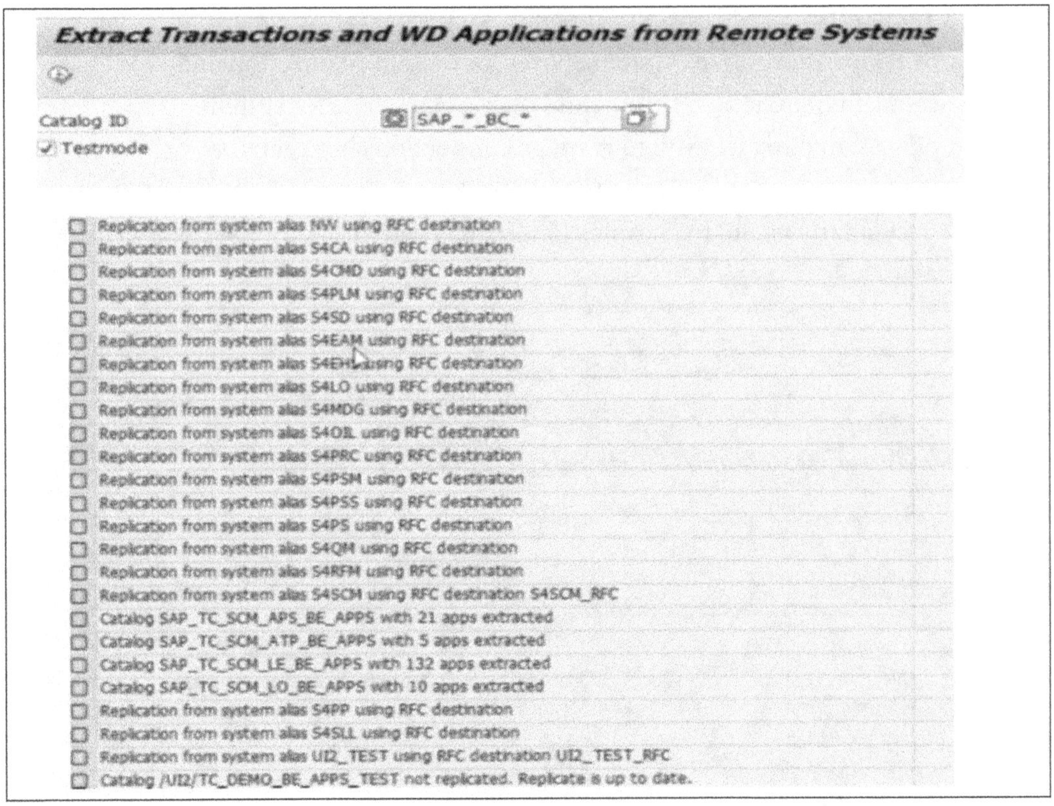

Figure 4-19. Transaction code /UI2/APPDESC_GET output

Note For the SAP Fiori system landscape, you need one system alias pointing to the front end with the indicator Local **GW** selected. If you use workflows in a front end, you need an additional system alias for task processing within the workflows used in this front end (name ending with PGW). Also, to develop apps, you must use Service Builder (transaction code: **SEGW**) to register OData services. An SAP Gateway alias must have at least one entry for the SAP Gateway hub front-end.

You have at least one system alias with the software version DEFAULT for each back-end you want to use. If you use workflows in a back-end, you need an additional system alias for task processing within the workflows used in this back end (name ending with PGW).

4.16.5 Conclusion

System alias configuration is critical to SAP Fiori deployments in an embedded or central hub setup. Proper configuration ensures that SAP Fiori applications communicate effectively with back-end systems, providing seamless access to data and functionality. Organizations can ensure robust and secure SAP Fiori implementations by following best practices and thorough configuration steps.

4.17 Summary

In this chapter, we discussed various options for Fiori implementation. Additionally, we covered the two deployment methods: embedded and central hub. We also discussed the pros and cons of the deployment. SAP Gateway functionality and configuration were also discussed.

CHAPTER 5

SAP Fiori Configuration

Using task lists for SAP configuration makes setting up and managing the system easier. Task lists provide a clear and precise sequence of steps for activities like the initial configuration of S/4HANA. They help ensure consistency by guiding users through preparation, configuration, and validation. This approach improves efficiency and reduces the risk of errors in system operations.

5.1 Introduction

SAP Fiori configuration helps set up the system to meet the business's and its users' needs. It starts with the Fiori Launchpad, the main access point for users. The setup includes connecting back-end systems, like SAP S/4HANA, with the Fiori front end. This process involves creating catalogs, groups, and roles and assigning tiles and apps to users. Good configuration makes it easy for users to navigate, work efficiently, and have a personalized experience while accessing real-time data from back-end systems. SAP provides tailored user experience options and task lists to help with this setup. This includes

Installing and Configuring Necessary Components: Both the front-end components, such as UI5, Launchpad, and Gateway, and the back-end components, including ERP and S/4HANA, must be installed and linked correctly.

Activating and Configuring OData/ICF Services: These services link and connect SAP Fiori apps to the back-end data they require to activate.

Deploying Fiori Apps: Selecting and choosing the right apps from the SAP Fiori Apps Library and making them available to users.

Customizing the Launchpad: You can customize the Launchpad's appearance and user experience by using themes, tiles, groups, spaces, and pages.

Setting Up User Authorizations: Ensure users can access the correct apps and data.

Proper Fiori configuration is crucial for delivering a seamless and personalized user experience, improving productivity, and driving business value. It requires a well-planned approach and close collaboration between technical and functional teams.

In this book, the SAP Fiori configuration is performed on the S/4HANA 2023 FPS02, an embedded system with **Fiori** and **S/4HANA** installed on the same server. SAP now recommends using embedded deployment as a preferred option. The details of the products installed on the server are as follows.

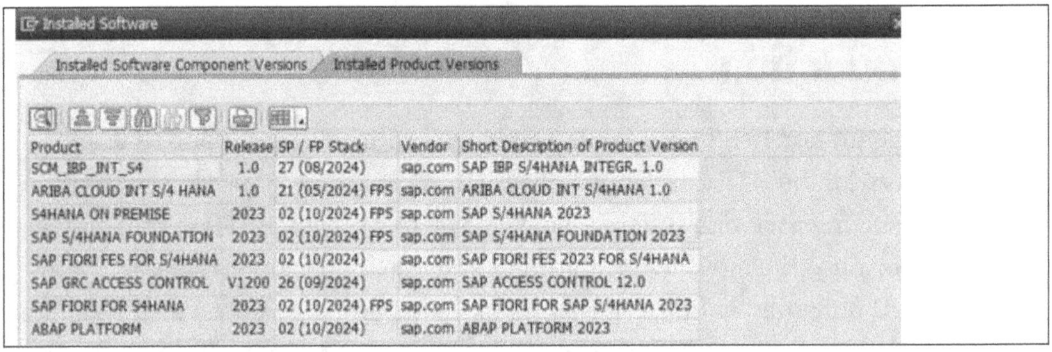

Installed Software

Installed Software Component Versions | Installed Product Versions

Product	Release	SP / FP Stack	Vendor	Short Description of Product Version
SCM_IBP_INT_S4	1.0	27 (08/2024)	sap.com	SAP IBP S/4HANA INTEGR. 1.0
ARIBA CLOUD INT S/4 HANA	1.0	21 (05/2024) FPS	sap.com	ARIBA CLOUD INT S/4HANA 1.0
S4HANA ON PREMISE	2023	02 (10/2024) FPS	sap.com	SAP S/4HANA 2023
SAP S/4HANA FOUNDATION	2023	02 (10/2024) FPS	sap.com	SAP S/4HANA FOUNDATION 2023
SAP FIORI FES FOR S/4HANA	2023	02 (10/2024)	sap.com	SAP FIORI FES 2023 FOR S/4HANA
SAP GRC ACCESS CONTROL	V1200	26 (09/2024)	sap.com	SAP ACCESS CONTROL 12.0
SAP FIORI FOR S4HANA	2023	02 (10/2024) FPS	sap.com	SAP FIORI FOR SAP S/4HANA 2023
ABAP PLATFORM	2023	02 (10/2024)	sap.com	ABAP PLATFORM 2023

Figure 5-1. *SAP products installed in an embedded deployment*

5.1.1 Prerequisites

We would require an SAP package (e.g., **ZFIORI_PKG**) **to transport** the configurations.

While it is not mandatory, **Workbench and Customizing request transport** could also be created to capture configurations that require Workbench transport and Customizing transport. If these transports are not created, the system will generate one as required as part of task list execution.

You can verify if any task lists have been executed earlier with transaction code **STC02**.

This chapter will use a newly installed system that has not yet been configured. This can be verified in transaction **STC02**, which, when executed, displays the initial screen shown in the figure below.

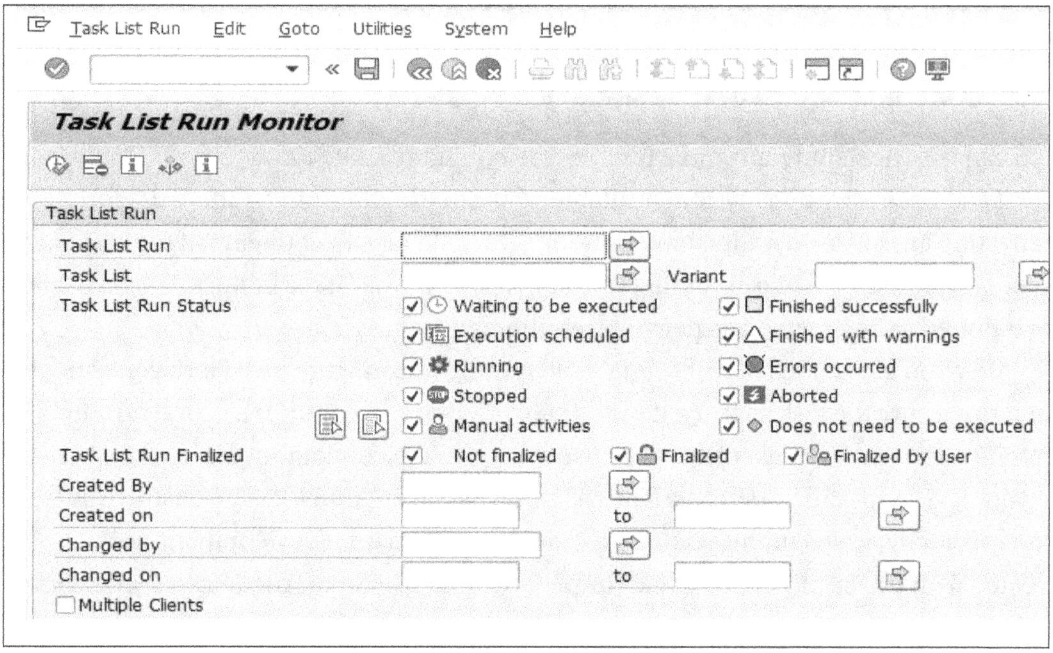

CHAPTER 5 SAP FIORI CONFIGURATION

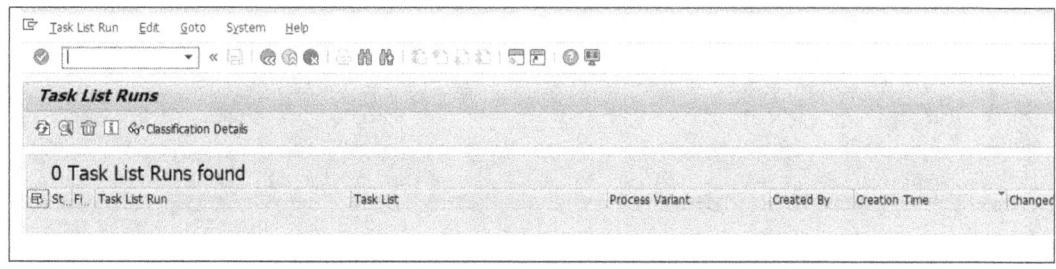

Figure 5-2. Initial screen of transaction STC02

Click the **execute** icon  , and the system will display the task lists executed previously, as shown in the figure below.

Figure 5-3. List of task lists executed previously

The figure above shows no prior executed task list, signifying that the system is **unconfigured** and SAP Fiori has not been set up.

5.2 Rapid Activation Task Lists for Embedded Deployment

You can use the Rapid Activation Task Lists to configure SAP Fiori.

If you have a sandbox system available, you can explore running the SAP Fiori Rapid Activation Task Lists to understand how long it would take to configure, if there are any issues encountered while executing the task lists, and what steps in the task lists would be required to be executed as per your requirements.

After you get an idea of what you would require to configure SAP Fiori, you can plan to execute the task lists in a development system and capture the configurations in transports. These transports will be used to move the configuration across systems in your SAP landscape to subsequent systems, such as QA and PRD. To ensure this is done correctly, we recommend using a transportable custom development package created with transaction SE80 while running the task lists so that activated content can be moved easily.

5.3 Execute Task Lists Manually

For **manual configuration**, use the transaction code **SPRO**. The steps and path to follow are **SPRO** ➤ **SAP Reference IMG** ➤ **ABAP Platform** ➤ **UI Technologies** ➤ **SAP Fiori** ➤ **Initial Setup** ➤ **Manual Setup without Task Lists**.

CHAPTER 5 SAP FIORI CONFIGURATION

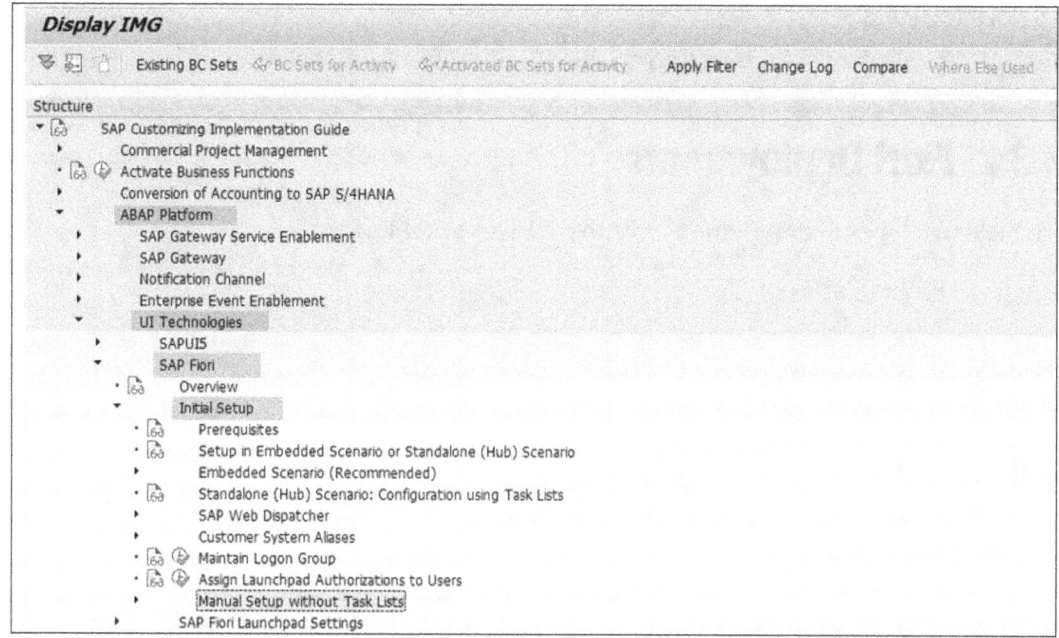

Figure 5-4. *Transaction SPRO – Manual Setup without Task Lists*

Refer to the nodes to set up a manual configuration titled Manual Setup without Task Lists, as shown in the figure above. It is advisable to always read the documentation and follow as illustrated below.

5.3.1 Prerequisites for Manual Configuration

Internet Communication Manager (ICM)

To ensure the SAP Fiori Launchpad functions properly, it's essential to establish a working HTTP(S) connection from the client (browser) to the current application server ABAP. You can verify the HTTP(S) settings, including the host name and port number, using transaction SMICM. Additionally, enter the complete domain name in the profile parameter "icm/host_name_full," which can be checked and modified in transaction RZ11.

Single Sign-On

To enable single sign-on, the front-end server needs to issue a single sign-on ticket. First, set the profile parameter **login/create_sso2_ticket** to **2**. Then, set the profile parameter **login/accept_sso2_ticket** to **1**. You can check these parameters in transaction RZ11.

SAP Gateway

SAP Gateway must be installed on the SAP Fiori front-end server.

5.3.2 Fiori Deployments

We have two types of deployment within S/HANA and Fiori, which are

- Embedded
- Central hub

Note Always thoroughly check the installation information in the Fiori Apps Reference Library before deploying any app. **Chapter 4** detailed the Fiori deployment options.

Embedded System Deployment

In an embedded SAP Fiori deployment, all front-end and back-end components are installed on the same SAP S/4HANA system. This means that you install SAP Gateway and consumer technologies on the same S/4HANA back-end system. This simplifies administration and reduces latency by eliminating multiple RFC connections in central hub deployments. It uses a predefined **NONE** destination, allowing UI and OData services to run locally. A local system alias (usually Local) must be set up in transaction /IWFND/MAINT_SERVICE to ensure OData services work correctly. While this setup reduces complexity, it may limit scalability and isolation compared with hub deployments.

CHAPTER 5 SAP FIORI CONFIGURATION

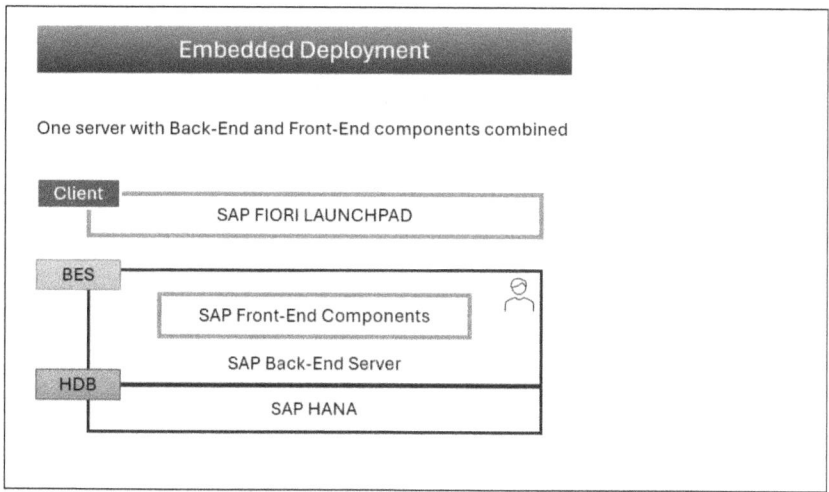

Figure 5-5. Embedded deployment

Central Hub Deployment

The front-end (Fiori applications) and back-end (S/4HANA) systems are separate in an SAP Fiori central hub deployment. You need to create an RFC destination (type 3) from the front end to the back end and establish at least one system alias (e.g., S4H_100) in transaction /IWFND/MAINT_SERVICE to link the OData services. If you use multiple back-end systems, you must create additional system aliases. Additionally, you require three RFC connections for this setup; however, discussing these connections in detail is beyond the scope of this book.

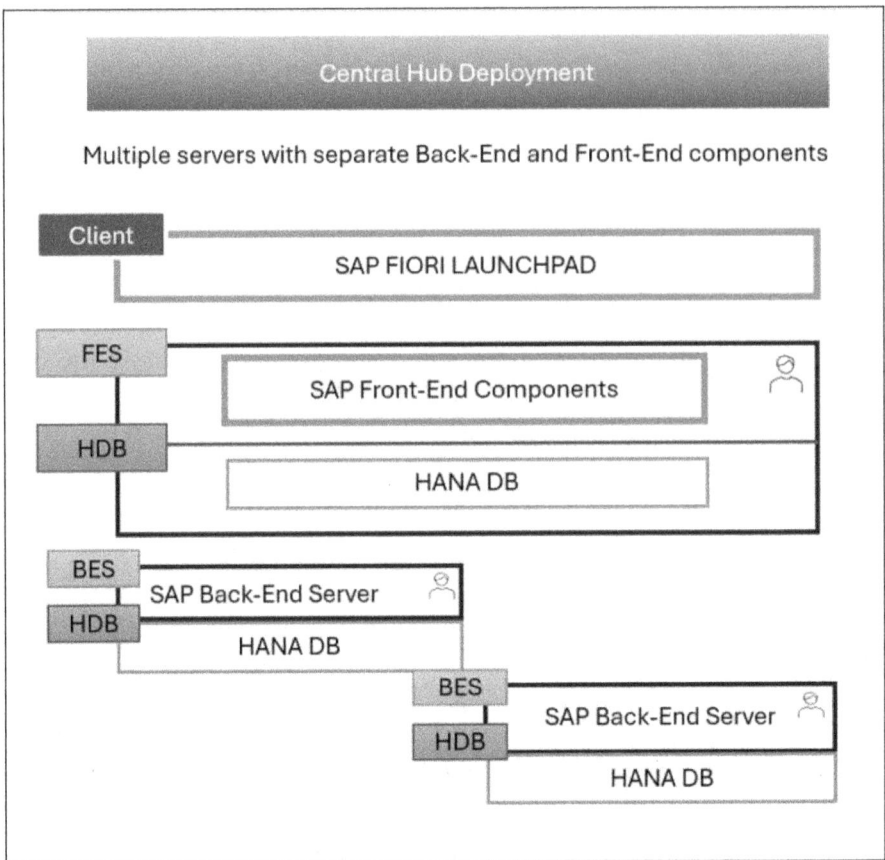

Figure 5-6. *Central hub deployment*

5.3.3 List of Task Lists to Be Configured

The task lists used to configure the SAP Fiori infrastructure in embedded mode are as follows. They can be activated using transaction code **STC01**:

1. SAP_GW_FIORI_ERP_ONE_CLNT_SETUP

2. SAP_ESH_INITIAL_SETUP_WRK_CLIENT

3. /UIF/SCHEDULE_LREP_JOB

4. SAP_FIORI_FOUNDATION_S4

5. /UI2/FLP_HEALTH_CHECKS

6. SAP_GATEWAY_ACTIVATE_ODATA_SERV

7. SAP_FIORI_CONTENT_ACTIVATION

8. SAP_FIORI_FCM_CONTENT_ACTIVATION

We recommend that you use the help option available for every step in the task lists, read the purpose of the step, and decide whether to select it.

5.3.4 Terminologies Used Within the Task Lists

Some of the terminologies encountered while executing the task lists are as follows.

SAP Fiori OData V2 Services

SAP Fiori OData V2 services are SAP Gateway services/tools that help SAP Fiori applications communicate with back-end SAP systems. They utilize the **OData** (Open Data Protocol) V2 standard, which enables **CRUD** (create, read, update, and delete) operations on business data through RESTful APIs. These services expose metadata, allow filtering, support batch processing, and integrate security. They are often used in SAPUI5 to facilitate the efficient retrieval and management of data.

SAP Fiori OData V4 Services

SAP Fiori OData V4 services are faster and easier to use than V2. They share smaller amounts of data, work more efficiently when handling multiple tasks simultaneously, and transmit information in a simple JSON format. V4 helps you easily access data, such as adding new items or finding things. While many SAP Fiori apps are migrating to V4, some continue to use V2.

SAP Fiori ICF Services

SAP Fiori **ICF** (Internet Communication Framework) services in SAP facilitate external access to SAP applications through HTTP(S). These services enable SAP Fiori, OData, Web Dynpro, and other web-based applications. They can be activated using the SICF transaction. ICF services support various authentication methods and enhance communication within SAP systems via HTTPS. These services get automatically activated once the relevant OData is activated.

5.3.5 Overview of Steps for Executing Task Lists

The initial transaction code, **STC01**, executes the task lists to configure the Fiori system. The screen will appear as shown below.

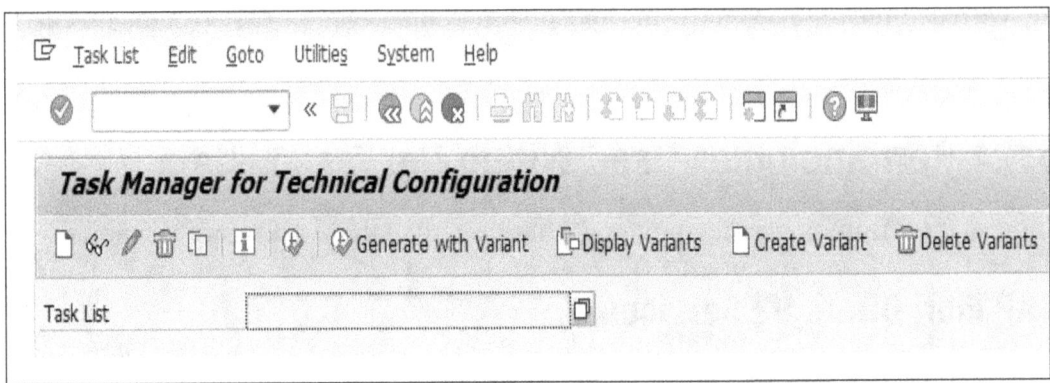

Figure 5-7. *Initial screen of transaction STC01 for executing task lists*

The following steps for configuring the system are common for all task lists:

Step 1: Enter the task list name in transaction **STC01**.

Step 2: Some tasks are automatically selected; leave it as it is. You can select and deselect any task list you desire. If you do not want to execute any subset of the task list, then under the tab **Execute, deselect/select the checkbox**. This step will be skipped or executed, and a message will be displayed at the bottom of the screen.

Note Before running the task list, reading the documentation provided by SAP is always helpful, as is clicking the **help** option icon .

Step 3: Find and fill in the parameter values for the suitable task in your configuration. Additionally, the parameters for every task cannot be changed, as the system sometimes does not allow it.

CHAPTER 5   SAP FIORI CONFIGURATION

Step 4: Press **F8** or click the **execute** icon in **dialog** mode .

Step 5: Press **F9** or click the **execute** icon in **background** mode .

Step 6: A note/message is displayed at the bottom of the screen when the task list is executed successfully.

Step 7: Monitor the activation in a different section using transaction code **STC02**, where you can check the details and results of task list runs.

Step 8: Check the logs generated once the task is completed by clicking the **display log** icon .

Step 9: Once the task is completed, a new message appears at the bottom of the screen, indicating the job's status: whether it was successful, encountered errors, or raised a warning.

Note

- Pre-create your package along with the Workbench transport request and customize transports before executing any task list. Furthermore, you can use system-generated transport or transport requests created earlier.

- You can execute a task list as many times as you want before it is completed.

- If you encounter a breakpoint issue, this task can be restarted by clicking, in the top menu, Utilities ➤ Breakpoints ➤ Delete all Breakpoints.

5.4 Task List 1: SAP_GW_FIORI_ERP_ONE_CLNT_SETUP

The Fiori task list **SAP_GW_FIORI_ERP_ONE_CLNT_SETUP** is a standard SAP task list that facilitates the setup of the Fiori system in a single-client environment. This is part of the standard SAP process for an embedded deployment.

5.4.1 Introduction

The **SAP_GW_FIORI_ERP_ONE_CLNT_SETUP** is designed explicitly for **embedded deployments**, where you configure SAP Gateway and SAP Fiori on the same client/server and where your business logic resides. This task list efficiently configures **SAP Gateway** and **SAP Fiori components** within a single client in an **embedded deployment scenario**. This streamlines the setup process, which is particularly useful when setting up Fiori in embedded deployments or scenarios with more straightforward landscapes, such as small- or medium-sized enterprises. This task list automates essential settings, including **SAP Gateway**, **OData services**, **Fiori Launchpad configuration**, **and user roles**, ensuring the system is ready for Fiori applications. This task list simplifies system setup, reduces manual configuration, and provides all required services to be activated for a seamless Fiori experience.

Main Features

- **SAP Gateway Services:** It activates all the OData services in the transaction /IWFND/MAINT_SERVICE and activates SAP Gateway.
- **Configures a System Alias:** This also configures system alias settings to facilitate server communication.
- **ICF Service Activation**: This task list enables and activates OData and ICF (Internet Communication Framework) services that Fiori apps require to function correctly. It enables and activates **SICF** nodes under DEFAULT_HOST (such as /sap/bc/ui5_ui5, /sap/bc/bsp/sap, and /sap/public/bc/ui2).
- **SAP Fiori Launchpad:** It sets up and activates the SAP Fiori Launchpad **(FLP)** services.

- **SAP Business Client:** It sets up SAP Business Client.

- **Configuration of Roles:** This task assigns standard SAP roles, like SAP_FIORI_LAUNCHPAD, to help users access the Fiori Launchpad and related apps.

- **Services:** Enables Fiori UI services, including tiles, groups, catalogs, and pages.

- **Logging and Error**: It sets up logging and error tracing.

- **RFC Destination:** It sets up and configures the RFC destination between SAP Gateway and the server.

- **Workflow and Notification Services:** It sets up and activates the SAP Workflow and My Inbox services.

- **Themes:** It sets up and configures theme design services.

- **Transport Request:** This task list includes steps to manage transport requests for any changes made during the setup process.

Note This task list helps easily set up **Fiori basic configuration** in a single-client environment. It serves as a comprehensive tool for automating the initial Fiori setup.

The task list includes steps from the following task lists, which means you do not have to execute them separately:

- **SAP_GATEWAY_BASIC_CONFIG:** Activates SAP Gateway – basic configuration

- **SAP_FIORI_LAUNCHPAD_INIT_SETUP:** SAP Fiori Launchpad initial setup

- **/UI5/SCHEDULE_JOB_UPDATE_CACHE:** Scheduling update of OData metadata caching

CHAPTER 5 SAP FIORI CONFIGURATION

- **SAP_GATEWAY_ACTIVATE_ODATA_SERV:** Activating all OData services for Fiori apps

- **SAP_BASIS_ACTIVATE_ICF_NODES:** SAP BASIS – activates HTTP services (SICF)

5.4.2 Steps to Execute the Task List

Execute Transaction Code STC01

Open transaction **STC01** and enter the task list name in the input field, as shown in the figure below.

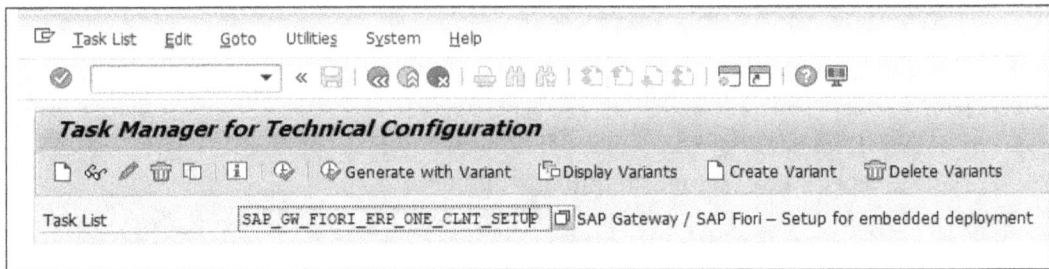

Figure 5-8. Initial screen for transaction STC01

Note You can use the **F4** help key in the task list to view the available task lists in the system.

To proceed, click the **execute** icon . A new window shows the subtask list, as shown in the figure below.

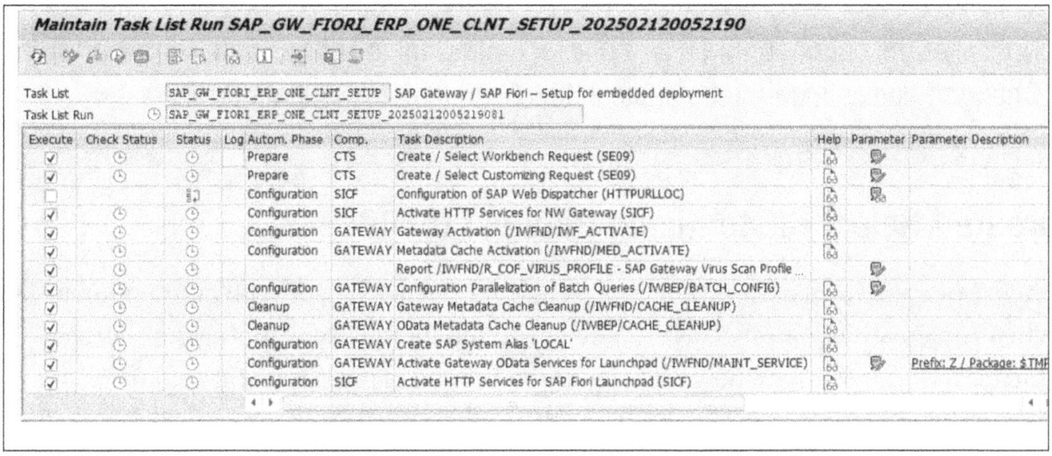

CHAPTER 5 SAP FIORI CONFIGURATION

Figure 5-9. Subtask list details within the STC01 for the task list

In the screen displayed above, we need to provide the required information.

Below are some of the **subtask descriptions** within the task list that should be viewed and the parameters updated in the above figure.

Create / Select Workbench Request (SE09/SE10)

To record changes made through automation tasks, create or select a Workbench request, which automatically generates a task. This task verifies if cross-client changes are permitted by checking the settings in transaction SCC4. Since user input is required for specific parameters , open the subtask and update the required information, which is package and transport details created earlier, and save the same by clicking the **save** icon . The task list is updated as shown in the figure below.

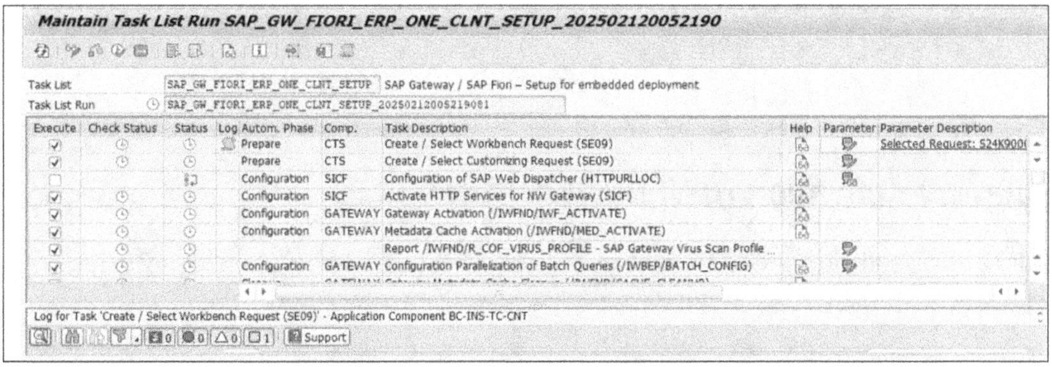

Figure 5-10. Workbench transport request updated

179

> **Note** At the bottom of the figure above, a message displays, **Task Configuration Changed**, indicating that the subtask has been updated without errors.

Create / Select Customizing Request (SE09)

Choose or create a customization request to track changes made with automation tasks. When you create a request, a task will be generated for the user running the task list. Once saved, you will see a new message at the bottom of the screen that confirms the task has been saved.

Configuration of SAP Web Dispatcher (HTTPURLLOC)

To create an entry for SAP Web Dispatcher in the HTTPURLLOC table for your current client, use the data browser with the transaction code SE16. Selecting this subtask is not mandatory, as it is not selected by default

> **Note** The symbol means **shall not be executed**.

Activate HTTP Services for NW Gateway (SICF)

This subtask activates the following HTTP services for NW Gateway configuration according to transaction **SICF**:

- /SAP/OPU/ODATA/*
- /SAP/PUBLIC/ICMAN
- /SAP/PUBLIC/ICF_INFO/*

Gateway Activation (/IWFND/IWF_ACTIVATE)

This subtask activates the SAP Gateway system. This can also be activated by using transaction /IWFND/WF_ACTIVATE.

Metadata Cache Activation (/IWFND/MED_ACTIVATE)

With this task, you can turn the metadata cache on or off, just like with the transaction **/IWFND/MED_ACTIVATE**. For production systems, keep the cache turned on. For development systems, you should turn the cache off. SAP advises that all development systems have the cache disabled.

Configuration Parallelization of Batch Queries (/IWBEP/BATCH_CONFIG)

Use this task to set up how to run batch queries simultaneously using transaction /IWBEP/BATCH_CONFIG.

Gateway Metadata Cache Cleanup (/IWFND/CACHE_CLEANUP)

This subtask list helps clean up the SAP Gateway OData metadata cache. This can also be done by executing the transaction /IWBEP/CACHE_CLEANUP.

OData Metadata Cache Cleanup (/IWBEP/CACHE_CLEANUP)

This subtask helps clean up the SAP Gateway OData metadata cache. This can also be done by executing the transaction /IWBEP/CACHE_CLEANUP.

Create SAP System Alias 'LOCAL'

This subtask creates the SAP system alias **Local** with the RFC destination **NONE**, marked **Local GW**. Use transaction **SM30** for object **/IWFND/V_DFSYAL** to ensure proper mapping. If **Local** already exists, the system skips this step.

Activate Gateway OData Services for Launchpad (/IWFND/MAINT_SERVICE)

This subtask activates the Gateway OData services for the Fiori Launchpad configuration, using transaction **/IWFND/MAINT_SERVICE**. Set the processing mode to **co-deploy only**, as we use **embedded deployment**.

- Once the task list is activated, review the following OData services that have been updated and are active:
    - /UI2/INTEROP

- /UI2/PAGE_BUILDER_PERS
- /UI2/PAGE_BUILDER_CONF
- /UI2/PAGE_BUILDER_CUST
- /UI2/TRANSPORT

When a transportable package is entered, service activation will be recorded for the "Create / Select Workbench Request (SE09)" and "Create / Select Customizing Request (SE09)."

The services listed above must be activated for SAP Fiori apps to function correctly.

Note Use the transaction **/IWFND/MAINT_SERVICES** to activate the above services separately and use **Local** as the alias system.

Activate HTTP Services for SAP Fiori Launchpad (SICF)

This subtask activates the HTTP services for the SAP Fiori Launchpad using transaction SICF. Check the table ICFINSTACT for the group names /UI2/FIORI and /UI2/FIORI_OP (if they exist, depending on the release) to find the required services:

- /sap/bc/ui2/smi/rest_tunnel
- /sap/bc/ui2/nwbc
- /sap/bc/ui2/start_up
- /sap/bc/ui5_ui5/sap/ar_srvc_launch
- /sap/bc/ui5_ui5/sap/ar_srvc_news
- /sap/bc/ui5_ui5/sap/arsrvc_upb_admn
- /sap/bc/ui5_ui5/ui2/ushell
- /sap/public/bc/ui2
- /sap/public/bc/ui5_ui5
- /sap/bc/ui2/flp
- /sap/bc/ui2/app_index
- /sap/bc/lrep

- /sap/bc/ra
- /sap/bc/ra/flp
- /sap/bc/ra/repo
- /sap/bc/ui2/c2g
- /sap/bc/rest/themes
- /sap/public/bc/ur
- /sap/public/bc/icf/logoff

Activate HTTP Services for UI5 (SICF)

This subtask activates the following **HTTP** services for UI5 configuration using transaction SICF:

- /sap/bc/ui5_ui5/ui2
- /sap/public/bc/ui5_ui5

Set Profile Parameter HTTPS (RZ10)

This setting is already set by default. You can use this task to change multiple profile settings at once. You can set each profile parameter for all application servers, specific servers, or the system's default profile. Keep everything the same here. Restart the ICM for profile parameter HTTPS (SMICM).

Follow these steps to restart the Internet Communication Manager (ICM) automatically. First, remember that all ICM restarts are recorded in the SAP system log. Then, the transactions **SMICM** and **SM21** will be used to restart the **ICM**.

Customize Launchpad URL for Cache Buster

This subtask is used to create an external alias for the default Launchpad URL using cache buster (transaction SICF); the URL "/sap/bc/ui5_ui5/ui2/ushell/shells/abap" should point to the target element "/sap/bc/ui2/flp." If the external alias already exists, skip this step.

Create SAPUI5 App. Index (full calculation)

This subtask will create a background job using transaction SM36 to run the report /UI5/APP_INDEX_CALCULATE in full calculation mode. It will take several minutes to complete.

Schedule job for calculation of SAPUI5 Application Index

This subtask sets up a scheduled job to run the report /UI5/APP_INDEX_CALCULATE in transaction SM36, which calculates the index for all SAPUI5 repositories. Use CCMS Background Monitoring to check the job and monitor results using your methods. Keep the other settings unchanged. Schedule a job to update the caching of data metadata.

This subtask will set up a recurring background job using transaction SM36 for the report /UI5/UPD_ODATA_METADATA_CACHE. Enter the default interval for running the job, which is **1 hour** and is set as the default. For Synchronize Page cache, this subtask will set up and create a background job to execute the report /UI2/PAGE_CACHE_SYNCHRONIZE using the transaction /UI2/SYNC_PBC. This report updates the differences between catalogs/groups' primary persistence and the page cache.

Set SAP System Alias for Fiori Launchpad

This subtask will set up a local HTTPS destination called **FIORI_FLP_HTTPS** and create aliases using transactions SM59 and SM30.

- **Customer System Alias**: /UI2/VC_SYSALIAS
- **System Alias Mapping**: /UI2/V_ALIASMAP

You need a system alias and a connection to the local HTTPS destination for SAP Fiori Launchpad callbacks.

Activate HTTP Allowlist Maintenance (UCON_CHW).

This subtask will help us maintain the updated list of allowed HTTP addresses per the transaction UCON_CHW.

Fiori URL to HTTP Allowlist (UCON_CHW)

This subtask adds new entries to the HTTP allowlist using transaction UCON_CHW. First, get the Fiori URL from the Set SAP System Alias for Fiori Launchpad task. If that task is unavailable, look for entries in the http_whitelist table (SE16) and manually add them to

CHAPTER 5 SAP FIORI CONFIGURATION

the new allowlist using UCON_CHW. Keep the other settings as shown in the figure above. After you save, a new message will appear at the bottom of the screen indicating that the variant is saved.

Add Launchpad / Launchpad Designer Transactions to Favorites for current user

This subtask will add the Fiori Launchpad/Launchpad Designer URLs (transactions /UI2/FLP and or /UI2/FLPD_CUST) to the current user's Favorites in the SAP Menu.

Add Fiori Content Manager Transaction to Favorites for current user

This subtask will add the Fiori Content Manager (transaction /UI2/FLPCM_CUST) to the current user's Favorites in the SAP Menu.

Set allowed catalog type for Launchpad App Manager

To set the catalog types permitted for the Launchpad App Manager, navigate to **SPRO** in the SAP system. Follow this path: ABAP Platform ➤ UI Technologies ➤ SAP Fiori ➤ Setting Up Launchpad Content ➤ Setting Up Technical Catalogs. Then, open the Maintain Allowed Catalog Types for Launchpad App Manager activity.

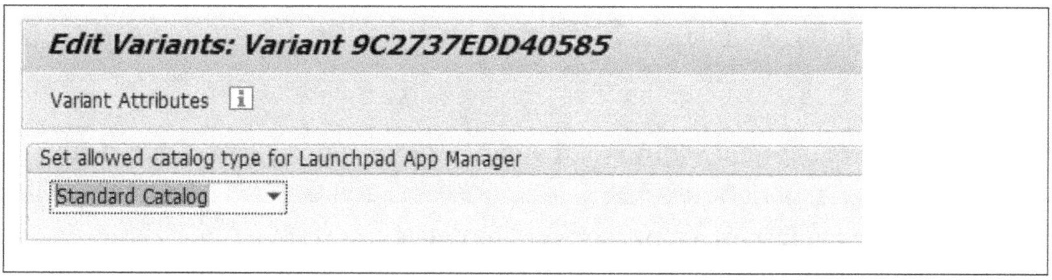

Figure 5-11. Set allowed catalog types for the Launchpad App Manager

Delete Workbench Request (if newly created and empty)

This subtask will delete any new and empty Workbench requests created before this task. If you have selected an existing request, it will not be affected. Only new and empty requests will be removed.

Delete Customizing Request (if newly created and empty)

This subtask will delete any new and empty Customizing requests created before this task. If you have selected an existing request, it will not be affected. Only new and empty requests will be removed.

Set transport options for to be activated OData Services

Set the transport options for the OData services to be activated.

Define OData Services for Activation

This subtask will prepare for the activation of the OData services.

Select Processing Mode / System Alias for Activation

This subtask chooses the processing mode or system alias for activating OData services. You can choose not to make any changes to the default setting.

Confirm OData Services for Activation

This subtask will activate OData services. You can choose not to make any changes to the default setting.

Delete Requests for OData Services Activation (if newly created and empty)

This task will delete new and empty Workbench/Customizing requests created with the task Set transport options for to be activated OData Services. Existing requests will remain untouched; only new, empty ones will be deleted.

Activate HTTP Services (SICF)

Use this task to activate specific HTTP services and use transaction SICF. You can choose the path of the ICF service node (URL) and make multiple selections. You can also set a service name with **DEFAULT_HOST** and use the expand flag to activate related nodes in the ICF service tree, if needed. Leave the remaining settings within the task list unchanged, as shown in the figure above. The task list is ready for execution by clicking

CHAPTER 5   SAP FIORI CONFIGURATION

the save icon 💾, and a message is displayed at the bottom of the screen that the task list has been saved. The task list is now ready to be executed, and the final screen appears as shown in the figure below.

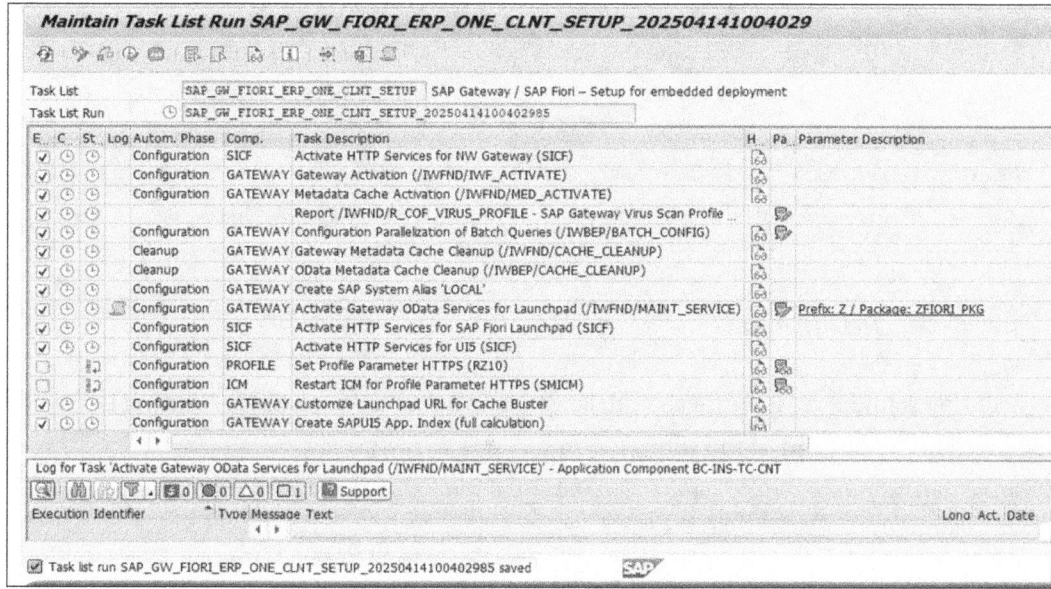

Figure 5-12. *Task list saved along with mandatory parameters*

5.4.3 Executing the Task List

Execute the task list using the **Start/Resume Task List Run in Dialog (F8) icon**.

CHAPTER 5   SAP FIORI CONFIGURATION

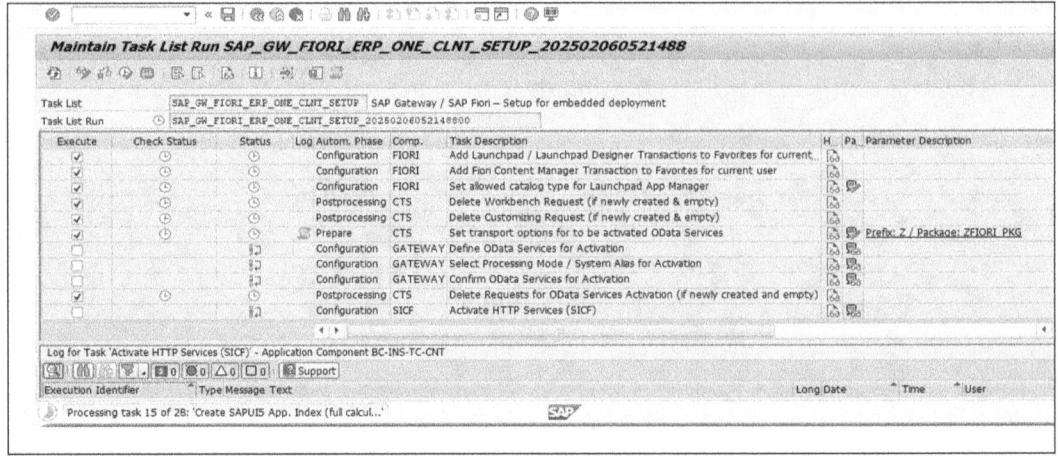

Figure 5-13. *Task listing is running*

As shown in the figure above, a message stating that the task list is running is displayed at the bottom of the screen.

Figure 5-14. *The task list is getting updated*

The task list is still running, and you can check the job status using transaction **STC02**.

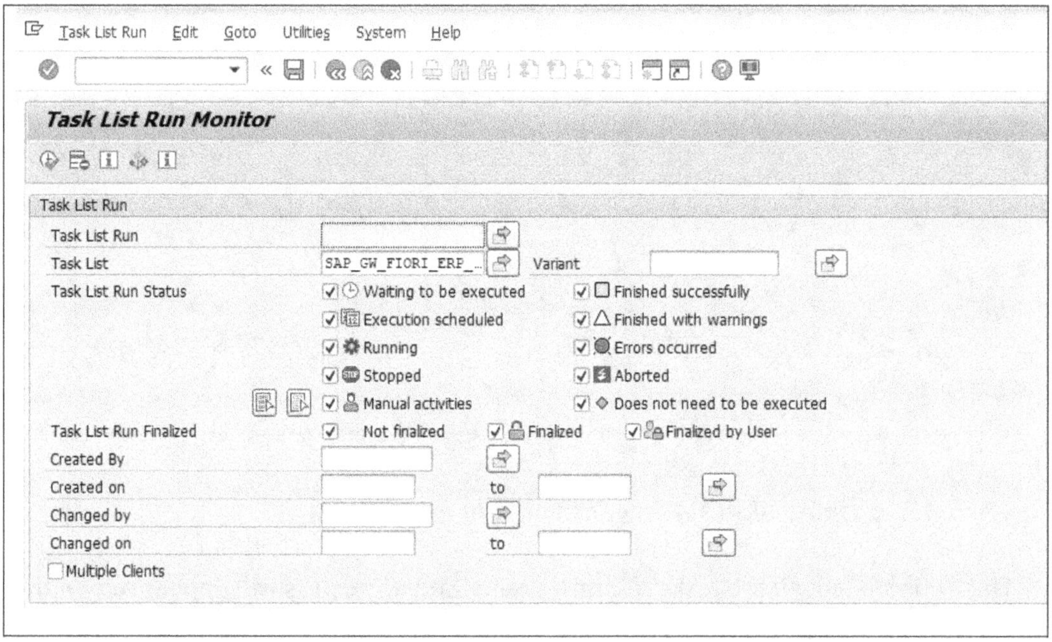

CHAPTER 5 SAP FIORI CONFIGURATION

Figure 5-15. Transaction STC02 displaying the task list to monitor

Click the execute icon , and it lists the currently running tasks.

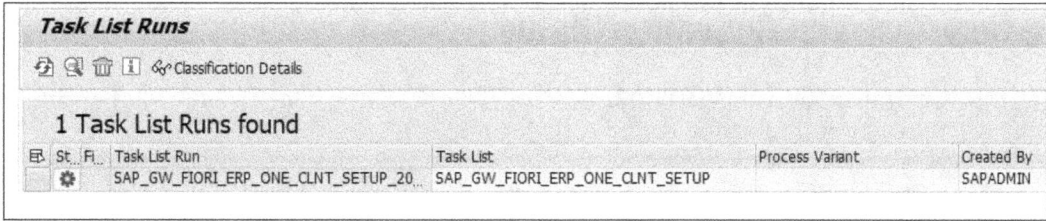

Figure 5-16. List of the tasks in the queue

Open the task list within the transaction STC02 by double-clicking the task list name.

189

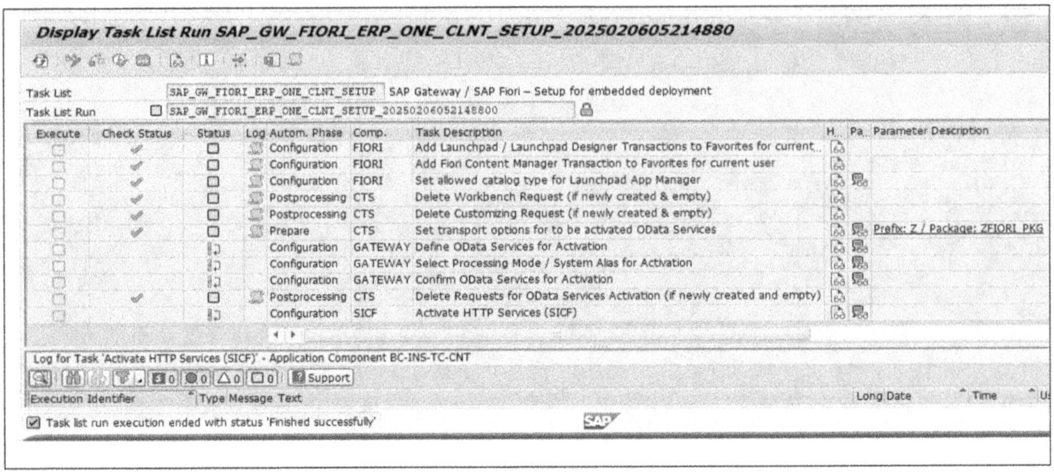

CHAPTER 5   SAP FIORI CONFIGURATION

Figure 5-17. Display of subtasks completed in green

Once completed, all the tasks will turn **green**, and any errors will appear **red** on the bottom screen. For any errors or mistakes, you can re-execute the task list again or restart from where it failed. **Warning errors** are acceptable. The task list has been completed as shown in the figure above, and a message is displayed at the bottom of the screen, **Task list run execution ended with status 'Finished successfully'**.

Review Task List Activation Status

Verify this in transaction code **STC02**.

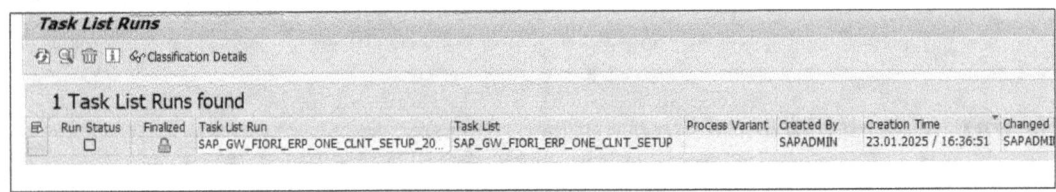

Figure 5-18. Showing run status is green, indicating the task completed successfully

The task list has been completed, as indicated by the green run status. Select the task list and press the **F2 key** to view the run details, as shown in the figure below.

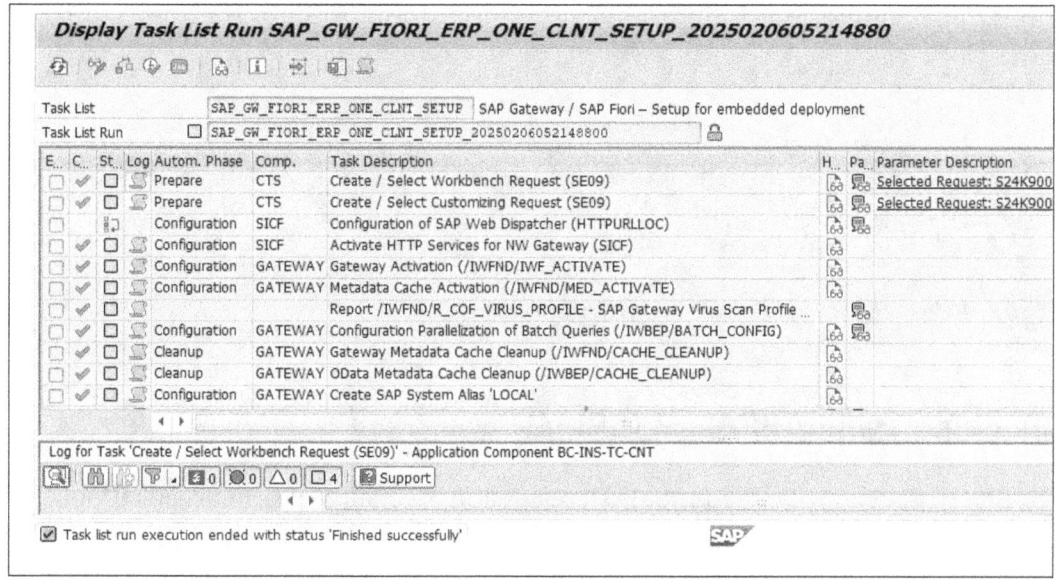

Figure 5-19. Task list final screen where everything is green

All the subtasks within the task list **SAP_GW_FIORI_ERP_ONE_CLNT_SETUP** are green, indicating that the task list has been successfully executed.

5.4.4 Task List Verification

Verify whether the task list has successfully created system aliases by utilizing transaction SM30 to ensure proper functionality. This process will help confirm that all necessary aliases are in place.

Checking Table /UI2/VC_SYSALIAS

The **/UI2/VC_SYSALIAS** table in SAP Fiori manages system aliases that connect the front-end server to back-end systems. It stores essential details like protocol (HTTP/HTTPS), host, port, and client, ensuring OData service requests from Fiori apps reach the correct back-end system. This table is key for smooth communication between the Fiori front end and back end, ensuring Fiori apps function correctly, even in landscapes with multiple back-end systems. The system generated the aliases **FIORI** and **FIORI_MENU**, as shown in the figure below.

CHAPTER 5   SAP FIORI CONFIGURATION

Display View "Define UI2 System Aliases (Customer)": Overview			
Define UI2 System Aliases (Customer)			
Alias	Time stamp	User Name	Description
FIORI	☐.241.025.163.652		
FIORI_MENU	20.250.126.014.838	SAPADMIN	

Figure 5-20. Table /UI2/VC_SYALIAS output

Checking Table /UI2/V_ALIASMAP

The SAP Fiori table /UI2/V_ALIASMAP creates and maintains links between OData service names and system aliases. This mapping ensures that OData requests from Fiori applications go to the correct back-end systems for data retrieval or processing. It defines how these services relate to each other.

- **Service Names**: The OData service that the Fiori app consumes
- **System Aliases**: The back-end system where the service runs

By setting up entries in /UI2/V_ALIASMAP, you create a path that directs OData calls from the Fiori front end to the correct back-end system. This setup allows the Fiori app to work correctly. Check the table output in **SM30**, as shown in the figure below.

Display View "Maintain UI2 System Alias Mappings": Overview		
Maintain UI2 System Alias Mappings		
Client	Source System Alias	Target System Alias
	FIORI	FIORI_FLP
	FIORI_MENU	FIORI_CLASSICUI
	NW	
	S4BANK	
	S4CA	
	S4CMD	

Figure 5-21. Output of the table /UI2/V_ALIASMAP

CHAPTER 5 SAP FIORI CONFIGURATION

The system generated the following:

- **Source System Alias:** FIORI
- **Target System Alias:** FIORI_FLP

Activation of Gateway Verification

The gateway is activated using the transaction code **SPRO**. The steps and path to follow are **SPRO** ➤ **SAP Reference IMG** ➤ **ABAP Platform** ➤ **SAP Gateway** ➤ **OData Channel** ➤ **Configuration** ➤ **Connection Settings** ➤ **Activate or Deactivate SAP Gateway**.

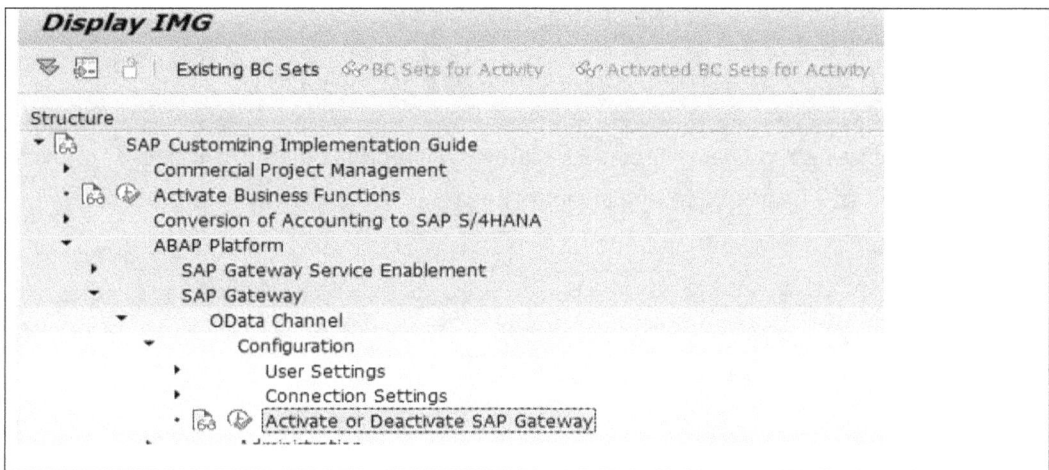

Figure 5-22. Display IMG

Execute ⋅ 🗐 ⊕ Activate or Deactivate SAP Gateway.

193

CHAPTER 5   SAP FIORI CONFIGURATION

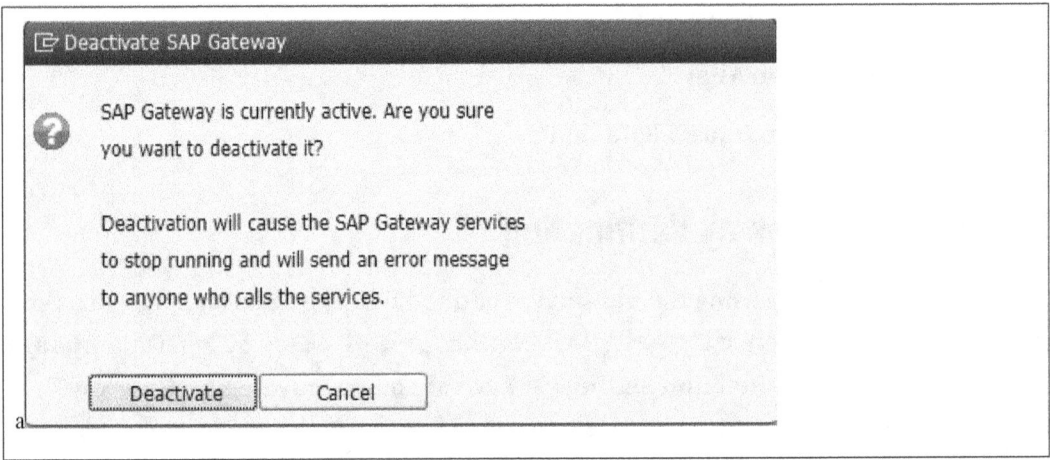

Figure 5-23. *The task list has already activated SAP Gateway*

The task list has already activated SAP Gateway, which is currently active, as shown in the figure below. The above image appears because SAP Gateway is already active in the system.

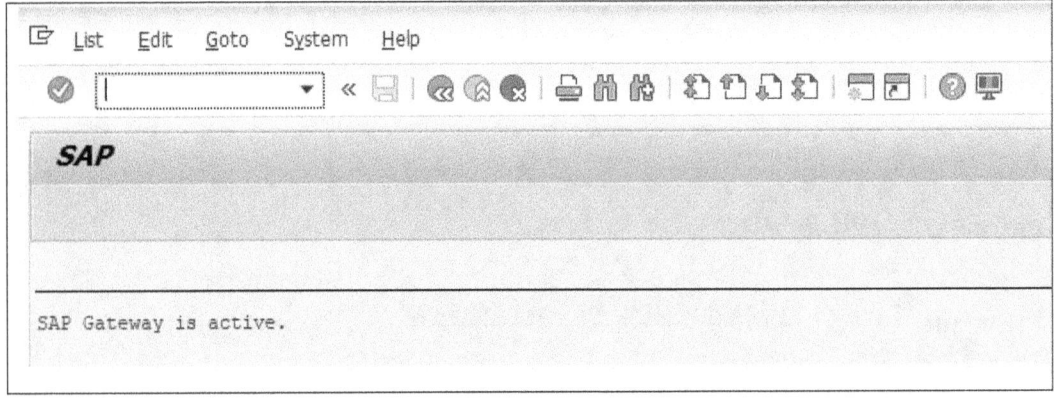

Figure 5-24. *SAP Gateway is active*

5.4.5 Summary

The task list SAP_GW_FIORI_ERP_ONE_CLNT_SETUP helps set up the main SAP Fiori apps in a system with just one client. It links the front-end and back-end parts, activates necessary services, and sets up roles so that the standard Fiori apps can operate correctly. This makes it easier to start using Fiori apps without requiring manual setup.

5.5 Task List 2: SAP_ESH_INITIAL_SETUP_WRK_CLIENT

5.5.1 Introduction

The **SAP_ESH_INITIAL_SETUP_WRK_CLIENT** task list outlines the necessary steps to set up **search** in the working client, and it is mandatory to be activated. It should run in the background because completing it takes a long time. The **SAP_ESH_INITIAL_SETUP_WRK_CLIENT** task list configures and starts **Enterprise Search (ESH)** for SAP Fiori and SAP S/4HANA in a working client. It helps automate the setup of search connectors, activates search models, and sets up Embedded Search. This ensures that business users can quickly search both structured and unstructured data. The task list simplifies setup by running background jobs, indexing search data, and activating TREX or HANA-based search features. This reduces the manual work needed to configure Enterprise Search.

In other words, the Fiori task list **SAP_ESH_INITIAL_SETUP_WRK_CLIENT** facilitates the initial setup of **Enterprise Search** in an **embedded deployment** by configuring **search models**, activating necessary services, and ensuring proper data indexing for practical search functionality within SAP Fiori. This task list is crucial to ensure that the search feature in SAP Fiori functions appropriately. It includes the key steps listed below.

Main Features

- **Activation of ICF Services**: This turns on and activates the necessary Internet Communication Framework (ICF) services for Enterprise Search.

- **Search Model Preparation**: This involves setting up and creating the search models needed for the search functions, ensuring they match the specific data in the system.

- **Authorization Checks**: This check ensures that users have the correct permissions to access and use the search features.

- **Indexing Data**: This process creates and maintains search indexes in a timely manner. It ensures that essential system data is organized and easily found during searches.

- **Technical Configuration**: This setup involves technical components, such as connectors and back-end settings, to ensure Enterprise Search works smoothly with other system components.

- **Validation and Testing**: This verifies and confirms that the search services are set up correctly and function properly. It also allows users to test the setup and identify any issues.

This task list is essential for organizations using SAP Fiori in an **embedded setup**. It helps prepare the system for a fully functional and user-friendly search experience.

5.5.2 Steps to Activate the Task List

You must perform several mandatory configuration steps to implement Enterprise Search in the working client. It is highly recommended that a task list for all search model activations be run during the initial setup of all sheet-related apps. The task list ensures that Enterprise Search is appropriately set up for your clients. This task list executes the required preparation steps for implementing Enterprise Search. Running this task list can take a long time, so SAP recommends starting it in the background. Once this task is completed, it is crucial to execute **SAP_ESH_CONSISTENCY_CHECK** to ensure system consistency. This task list completes the setup of SAP Fiori search. Setting up Enterprise Search is vital for efficient information retrieval within your SAP Fiori system landscape.

Note This task list must be executed in the S/4HAHA server, which is BES, for the central hub environment.

Execute the Task List

Execute the task list in transaction **STC01**, as shown in the figure below.

CHAPTER 5 SAP FIORI CONFIGURATION

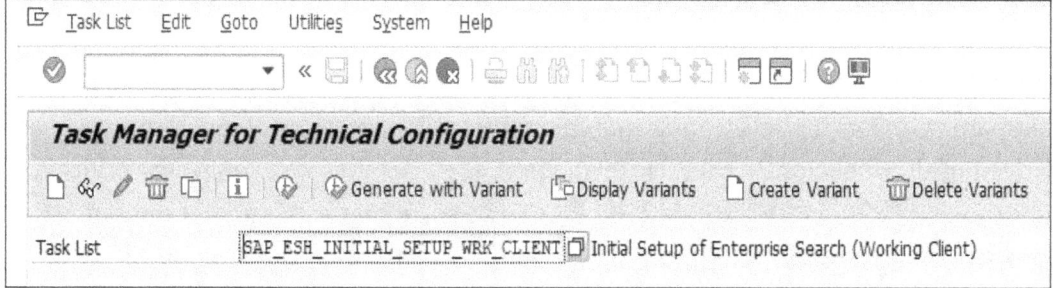

Figure 5-25. *Task list SAP_ESH_INITIAL_SETUP_WRK_CLIENT*

Once executed, the subtask list window opens, as shown in the figure below.

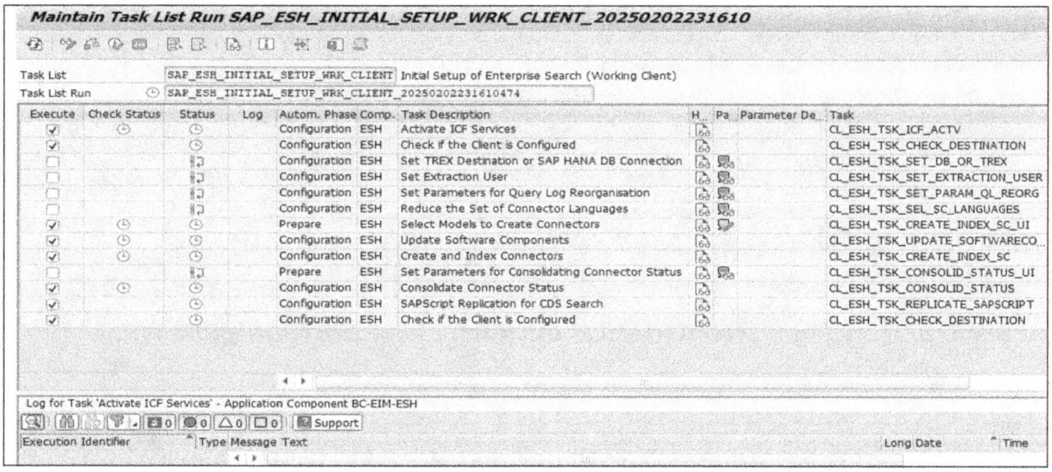

Figure 5-26. *SAP_ESH_INITIAL_SETUP_WRK_CLIENT with a subtask list*

In the figure above, we only input the mandatory field as required.

Activate ICF Services

This task activates and starts all the ICF services needed to run Enterprise Search for the embedded deployment. This subtask leaves everything unchanged.

Check if the Client is Configured

This subtask verifies whether the client is set up for Enterprise Search in the embedded deployment.

197

CHAPTER 5   SAP FIORI CONFIGURATION

Select Models to Create Connectors

This is the **most critical subtask** for setting up the current task list. Select a software component and its models to create connectors in this subtask. SAP recommends activating all connectors in the case of an **embedded deployment**. Select the critical task description `Select Models to Create Connectors`. To do so, open the parameter option , as shown in the figure below.

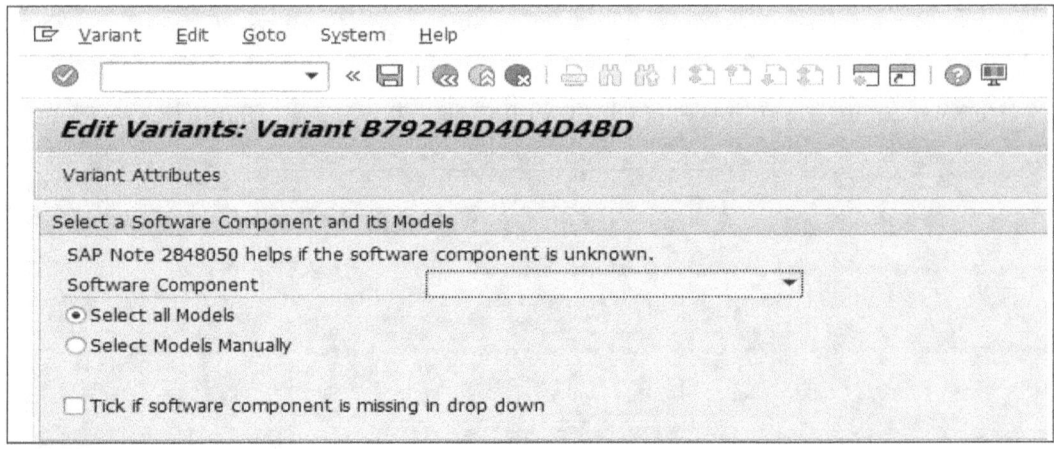

Figure 5-27. *Selection screen to select the model to create connectors*

Note   Select this subtask first before updating the other subtasks and parameters.

You can find the **search connectors** from the SAP Fiori Apps Reference Library under **Software Component** and select **SAPAPPLH**. These connectors are used for **factsheet apps**. Here we have two options:

- **Select all Models**: Will activate all models under the same.
- **Select Models Manually**: Here, you select individual models.

Use the search option to find and select the desired model, as illustrated in the figure below.

CHAPTER 5 SAP FIORI CONFIGURATION

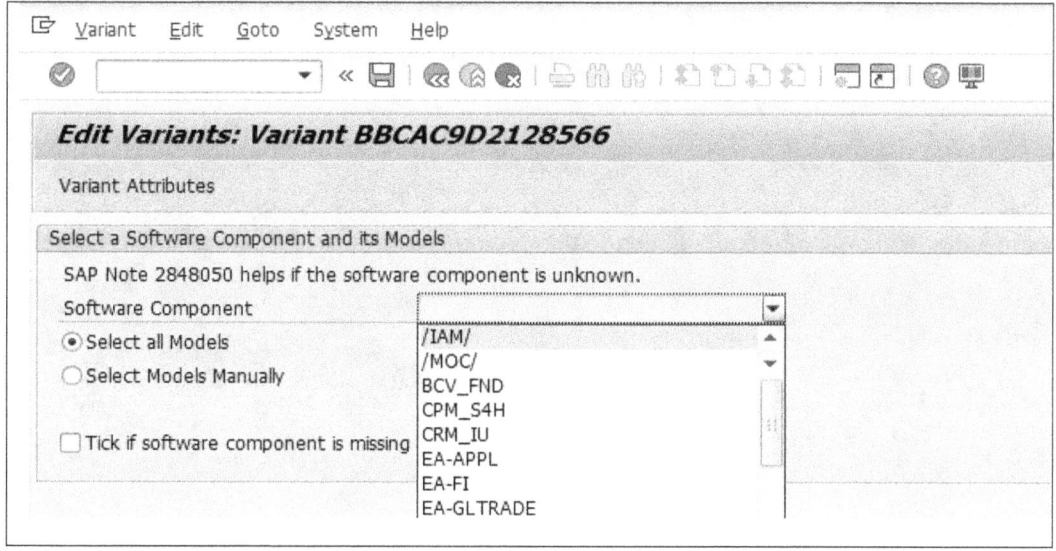

Figure 5-28. List of models available to select

If the search model is not visible, check if the software component version is installed. Scroll down and select the model **SAPAPPLH**, as shown in the figure below.

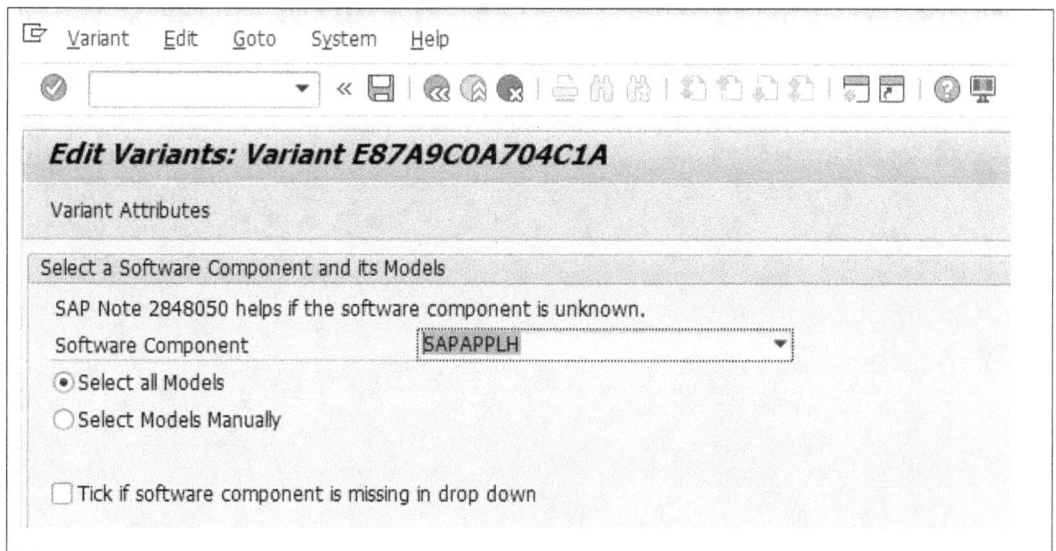

Figure 5-29. Model SAPAPPLH selected

Selecting the **Select Models Manually** radio button can also set an individual model.

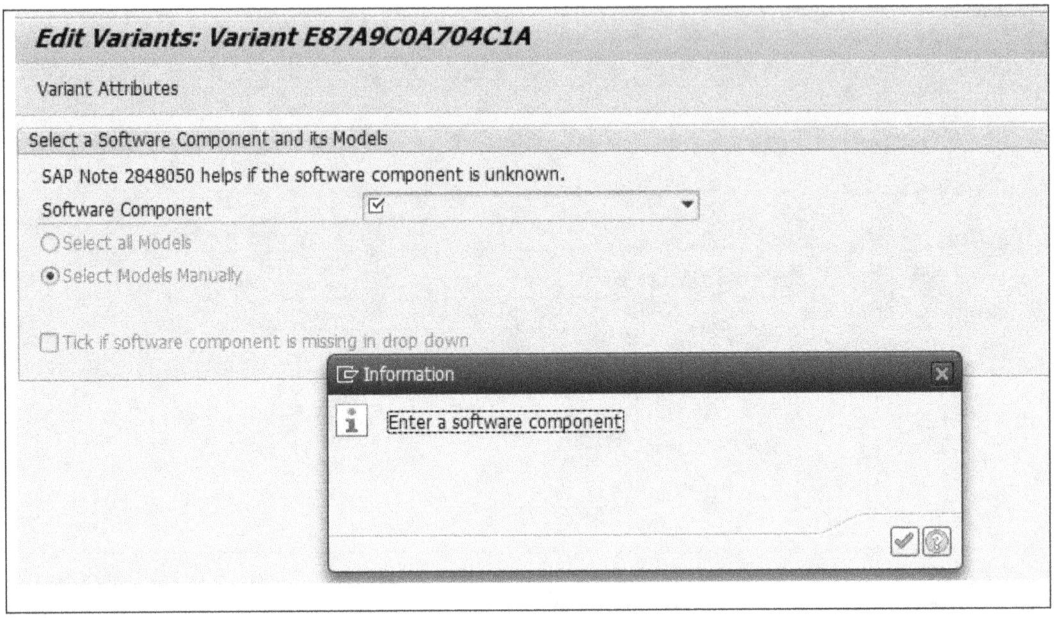

CHAPTER 5   SAP FIORI CONFIGURATION

Figure 5-30. *Radio button Select Models Manually*

Under the radio button **Select Models Manually** and then under the tab **Models**, select the search option. A new window called **Multiple Selection for Models** will open, as shown in the figure below.

CHAPTER 5   SAP FIORI CONFIGURATION

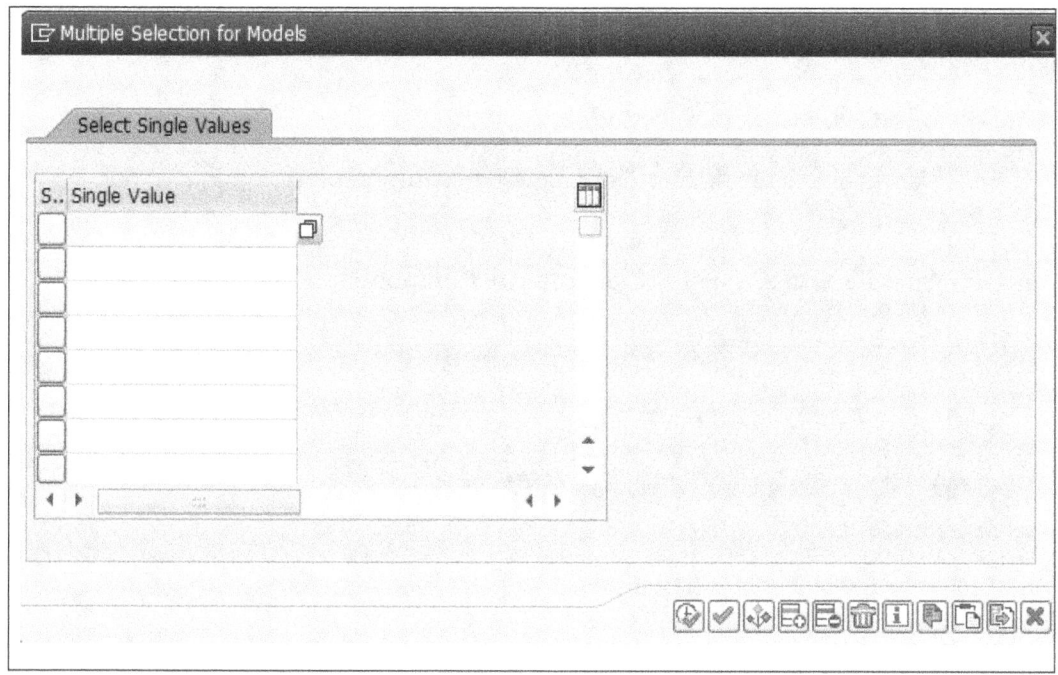

Figure 5-31.   Option to select models manually

Press the function key **F4**, and a list will appear for various models to select, as shown in the figure below.

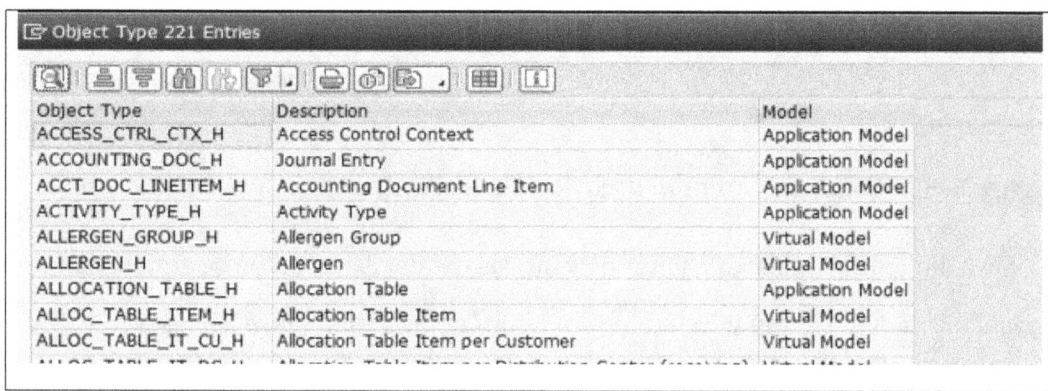

Figure 5-32.   List of models available to select

The above screen lists all applications and virtual models available for selection. In our case, we will use the radio button **Select all Models**.

CHAPTER 5   SAP FIORI CONFIGURATION

In our case, we will do the following for the software model as shown in the figure below:

- We will choose Select all Models.
- We will check the box for Tick if software component is missing in the drop down.
- We will select **SAPAPPLH** for Software Component.

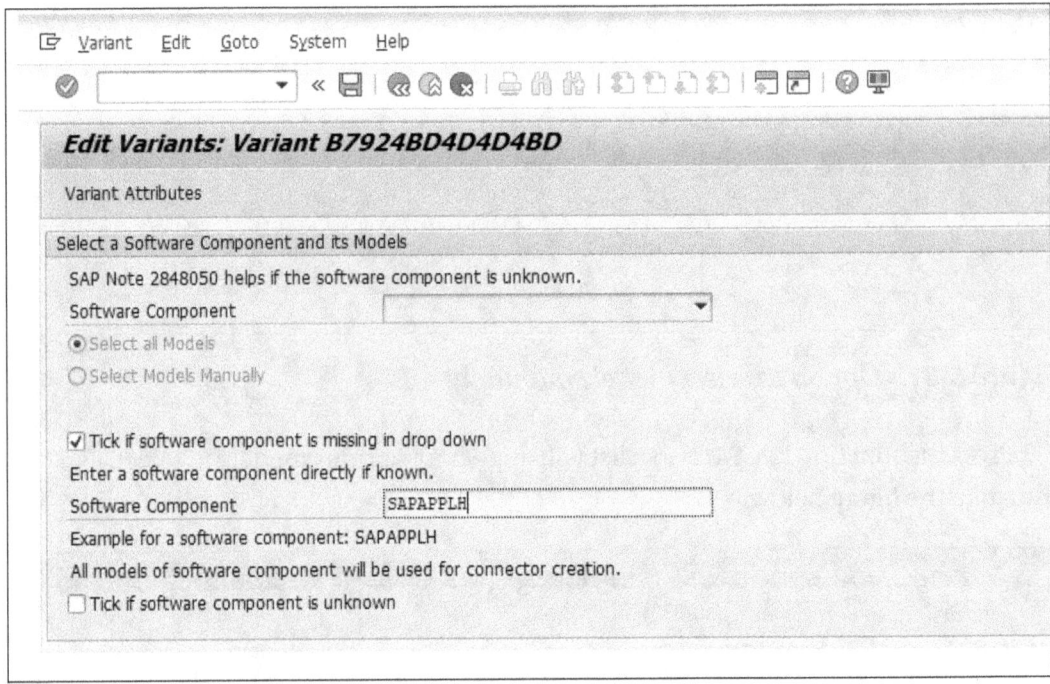

Figure 5-33. Software component SAPAPPLH selected

Save the setting by clicking 💾. A new message is displayed at the bottom of the screen, indicating that the selected **model** values of the variant have been saved ✓ Values of variant B7924BD4D4D4BD saved. Click the **go-back option** ⬅. The task list gets updated, as shown in the figure below.

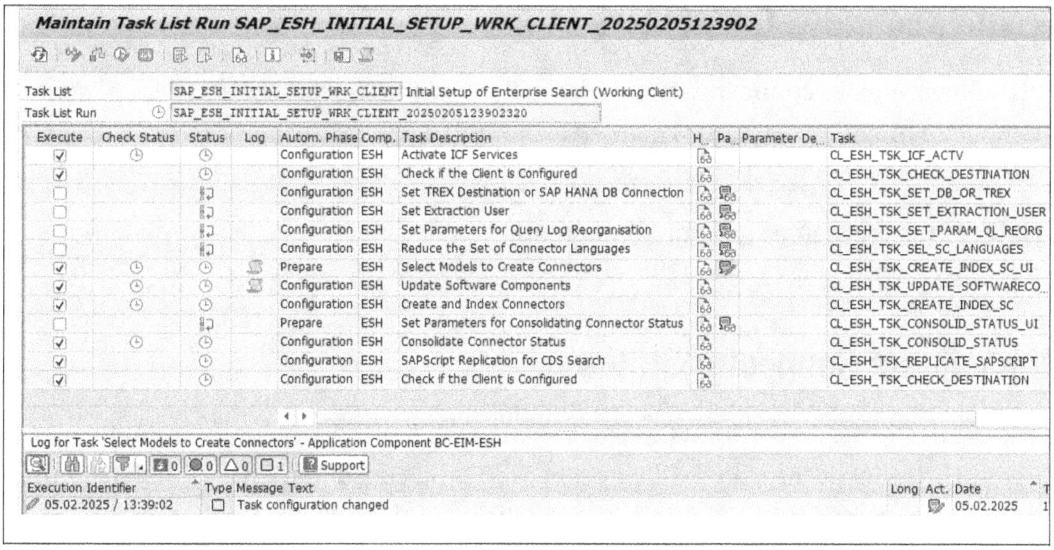

CHAPTER 5 SAP FIORI CONFIGURATION

Figure 5-34. Task list updated

> **Note** The system automatically puts a checkmark in the box. This subtask must be executed multiple times to activate the software and the connectors. Here, we executed only one software component.

The task list updates automatically as a checkmark appears. Under the column header Log, a **Show Task Log** icon appears. This means the system will also generate a log.

Update Software Components

This task automatically updates all software components in the current Enterprise Search client within the embedded deployment. Deselect this option for this task list.

> **Note** This parameter will not be updated.

Create and Index Connectors

This subtask creates connectors and indexes them within the embedded deployment. If a connector already exists and is marked as modified, the task will update it.

Note This parameter will not be updated.

Consolidate Connector Status

If the connector status consolidation task is ongoing, it will pause for five minutes. After the brief delay, the status will be rechecked until consolidation is complete or the maximum wait time of 24 hours is reached. In this step, no action is required.

SAPScript Replication for CDS Search

This task starts the first replication of SAPScript text in the background. After this, you can use the SAPScript text for CDS search. Updates to the SAPScript text will occur in real time after the initial replication. Remember that the background job runs only once and is not set to run again automatically.

Note This subtask is selected by default when executing the task list. We leave the option as it is here.

Check if the Client is Configured

This checklist verifies whether the client is set up for Enterprise Search.

5.5.3 Final Status of the Task List with Subtasks Configured

The task list **SAP_ESH_INITIAL_SETUP_WRK_CLIENT** is now ready for execution, as shown in the figure below.

CHAPTER 5 SAP FIORI CONFIGURATION

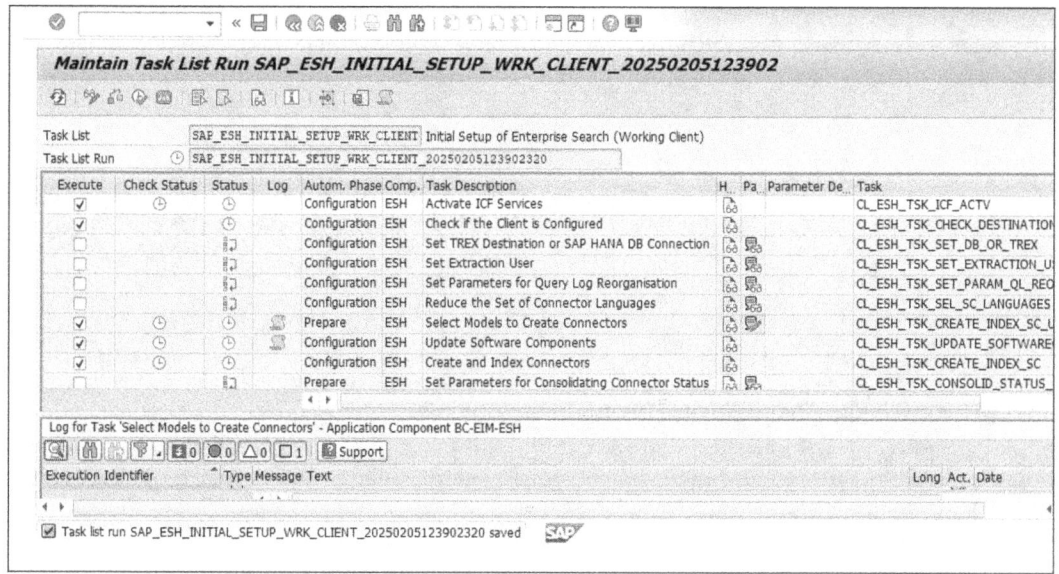

Figure 5-35. *Final task list as completed*

Click to save the task list. A new message will appear at the bottom of the screen indicating that the task list run SAP_ESH_INITIAL_SETUP_WRK_CLIENT has been saved.

5.5.4 Execute the Job in Background Mode

This job takes a long time to run; hence, it is executed in **background mode** by clicking the Job icon in the menu .

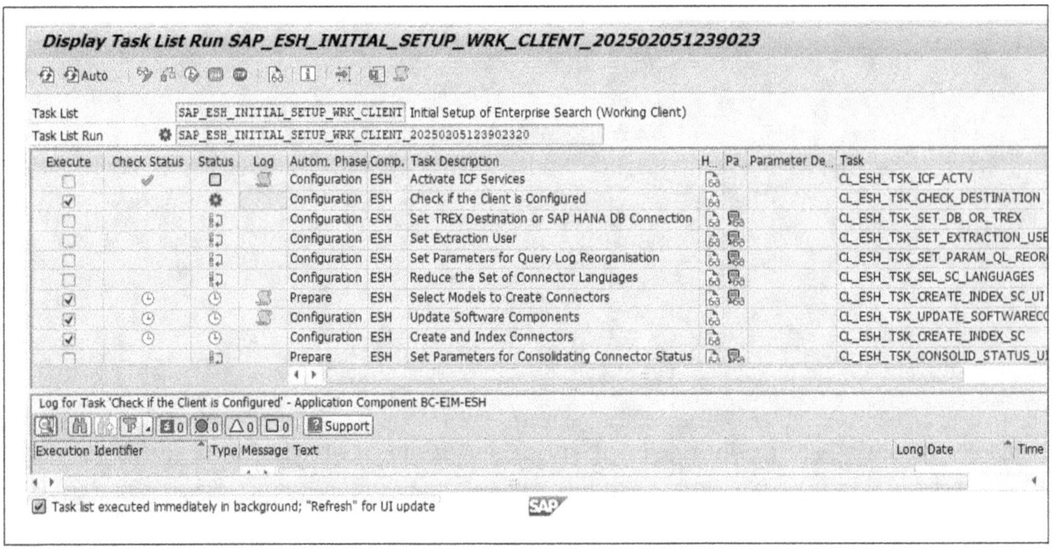

CHAPTER 5   SAP FIORI CONFIGURATION

Figure 5-36. *Job executed in background mode*

A new message is displayed at the bottom of the screen, **Task list executed immediately in background; "Refresh" for UI update**.

Using the refresh icon , the screen gets updated, as shown in the figure below.

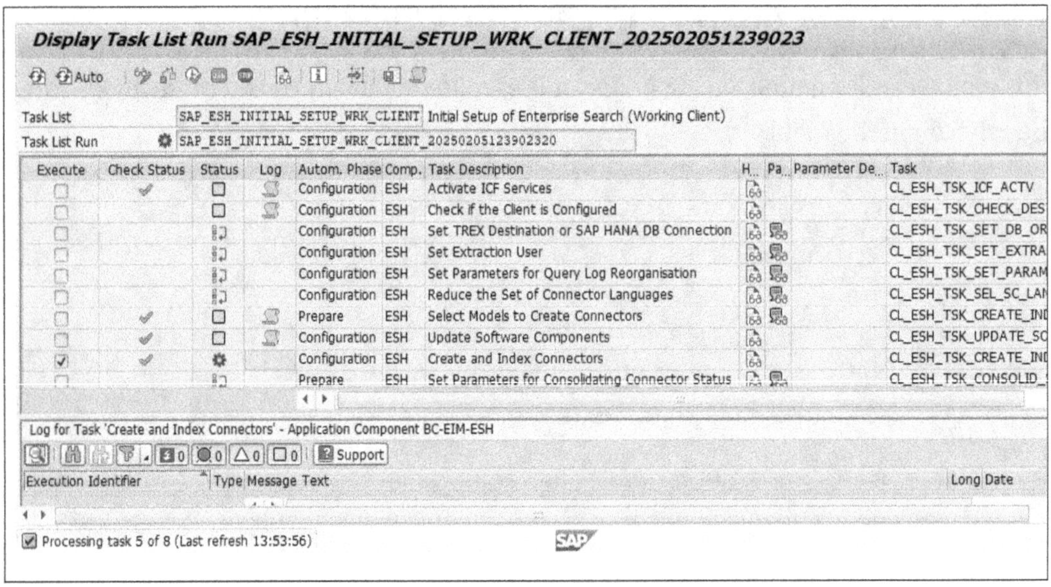

Figure 5-37. *The task list status is running*

206

CHAPTER 5 SAP FIORI CONFIGURATION

Note If you encounter any error, run the **SAP_ESH_ADJUST_AFTER_CLIENT_COPY** task list using the transaction **STC01**. Run the task list as it is, as shown in the figure below.

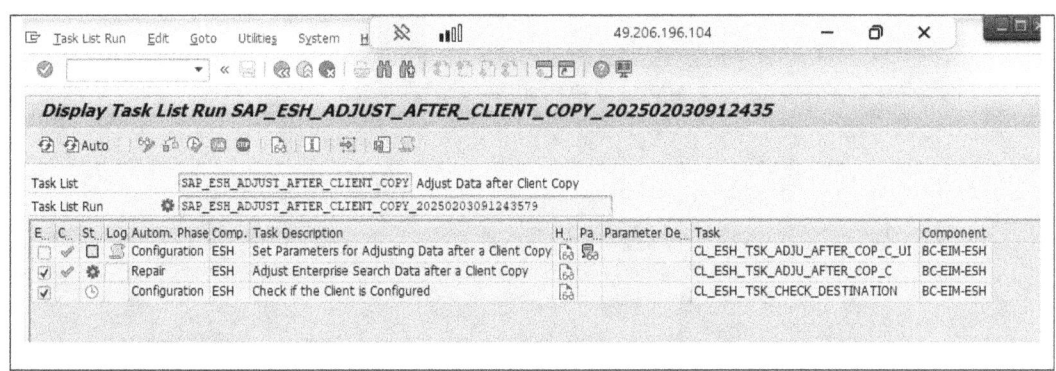

Figure 5-38. *Task list SAP_ESH_ADJUST_AFTER_CLIENT_COPY*

5.5.5 Background Job Completed

The background job has been completed.

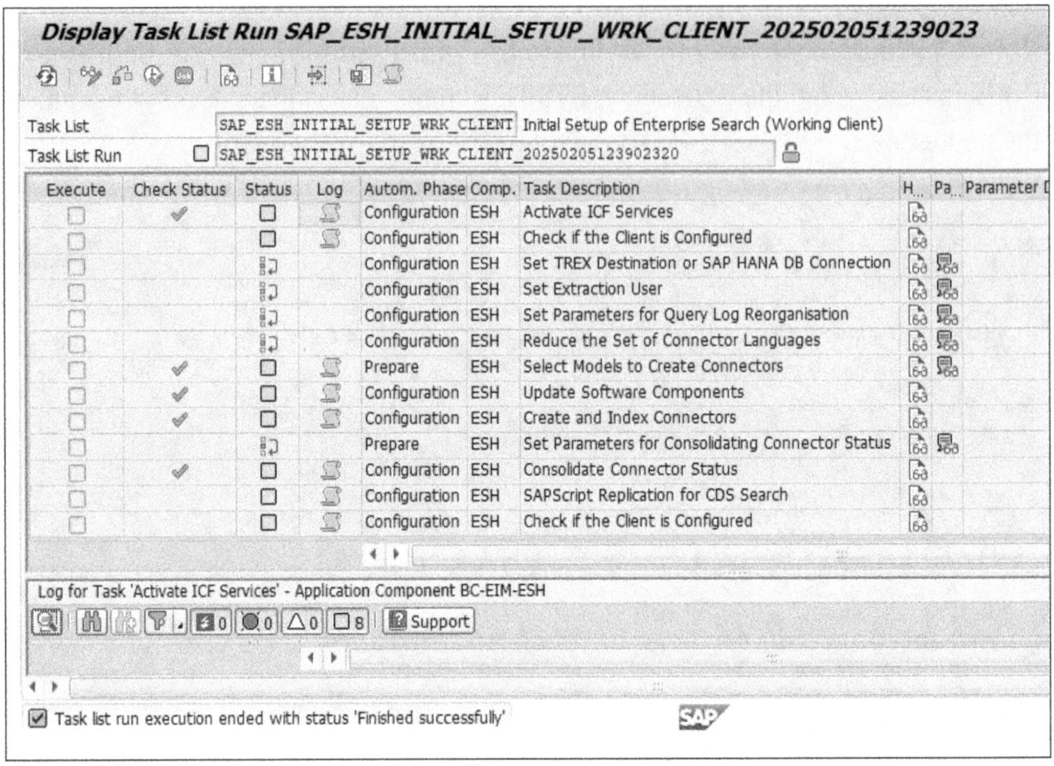

CHAPTER 5   SAP FIORI CONFIGURATION

Figure 5-39. Task list executed successfully

5.5.6 Consistency Check

To ensure that Enterprise Search and SAP Fiori search are set up correctly, use the automatic task list **SAP_ESH_CONSISTENCY_CHECK**. This will help you find any issues related to the setup. To resolve any warnings that appear, use the task list SAP_ESH_UPDATE_SC.

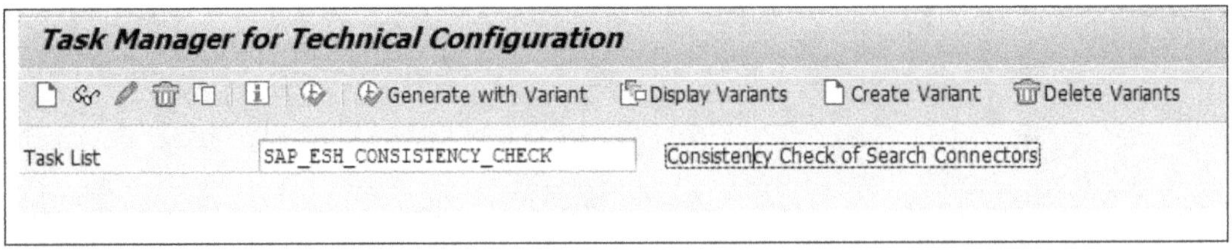

Figure 5-40. Task list SAP_ESH_CONSISTENCY_CHECK

CHAPTER 5 SAP FIORI CONFIGURATION

This task list takes considerable time and is executed in the background, as shown in the figure below.

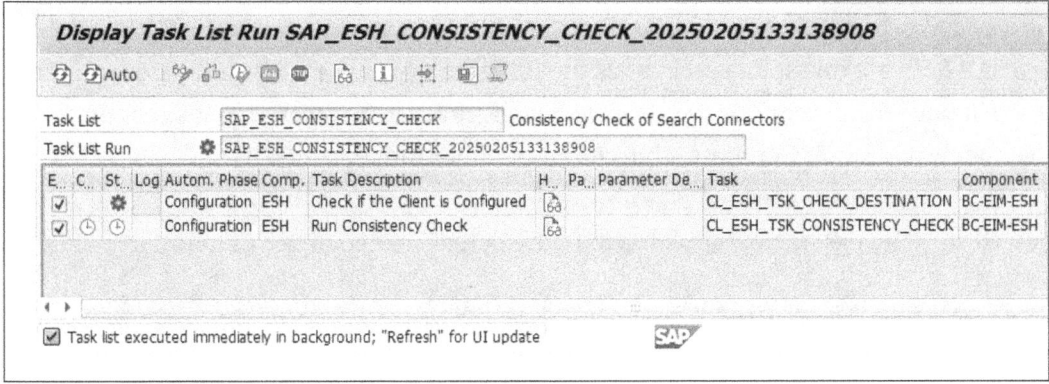

Figure 5-41. *Task list SAP_ESH_CONSISTENCY_CHECK executed*

5.5.7 Summary

The task list SAP_ESH_INITIAL_SETUP_WRK_CLIENT is essential for configuring Embedded Search (ESH) in an SAP Fiori system's working client. It prepares the necessary settings for search functionality, including connectors, models, and indexing, allowing users to efficiently find apps, business objects, and data through the Fiori search bar. The task list helps ensure that search functions smoothly and provides accurate results by streamlining behind-the-scenes processes.

5.6 Task List 3: /UIF/SCHEDULE_LREP_JOB

5.6.1 Introduction

The task list **/UIF/SCHEDULE_LREP_JOB** helps schedule jobs to manage the SAP Fiori Launchpad Repository in a special version of SAP called S/4HANA embedded deployment. It organizes items such as catalogs, tiles, and roles.

5.6.2 Steps to Activate the Task List

The **/UIF/SCHEDULE_LREP_JOB** task list is crucial for setting up and maintaining SAP Fiori systems, particularly for embedded deployment scenarios where SAP Gateway and SAP Fiori are on the same client as the ERP system. This job is scheduled for every client. It periodically checks and regenerates the load in the layered repository on an SAP Gateway system. Generate a background job for the report **/UIF/CHECK_LOAD_4_CONS_BG**. Below are some of the subtask descriptions within the task list that should be viewed, and the parameters updated in figure below are explained as follows.

Execute the Task List

Use the transaction **STC01** to run the task list, as shown in the figure below.

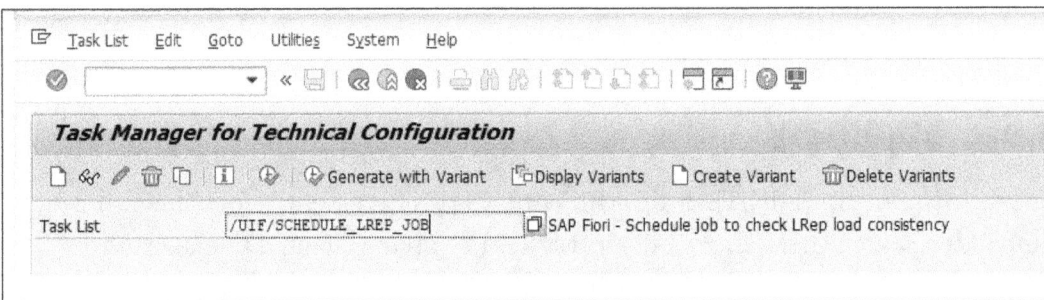

Figure 5-42. Task list /UIF/SCHEDULE_LREP_JOB

Execute the task list by selecting the execute icon.

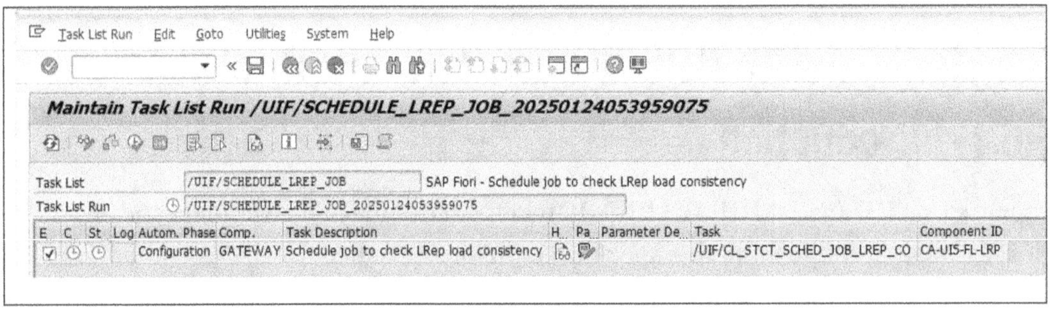

Figure 5-43. Subtask list within the task list

Click the parameter icon. As shown in the figure below, a window opens to set up the scheduled backup time.

CHAPTER 5   SAP FIORI CONFIGURATION

Figure 5-44. *Background job Minutes selection screen*

This job is scheduled to run every **60 minutes**; however, the frequency can be adjusted according to business needs. Click Save, and a new message will appear at the bottom of the screen, ☑ Values of variant E9B59C0917500B saved. Go back to the main screen. The final screen is as shown in the figure below.

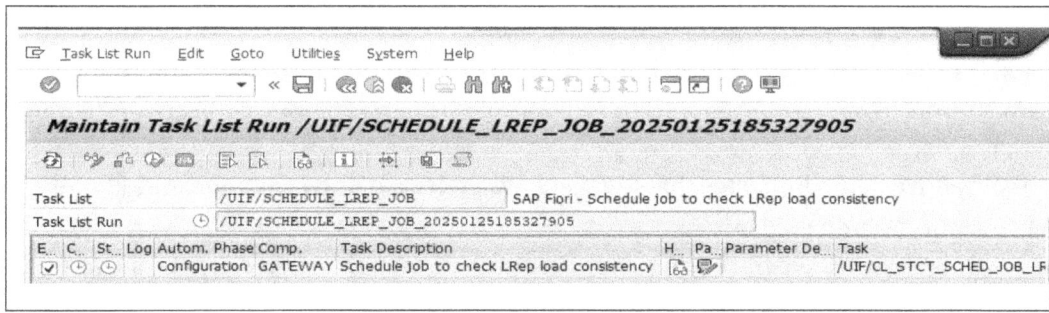

Figure 5-45. *Task list /UIF/SCHEDULE_LREP_JOB pre-execution screen*

5.6.3 Executed Task List

Execute the task in the background mode.

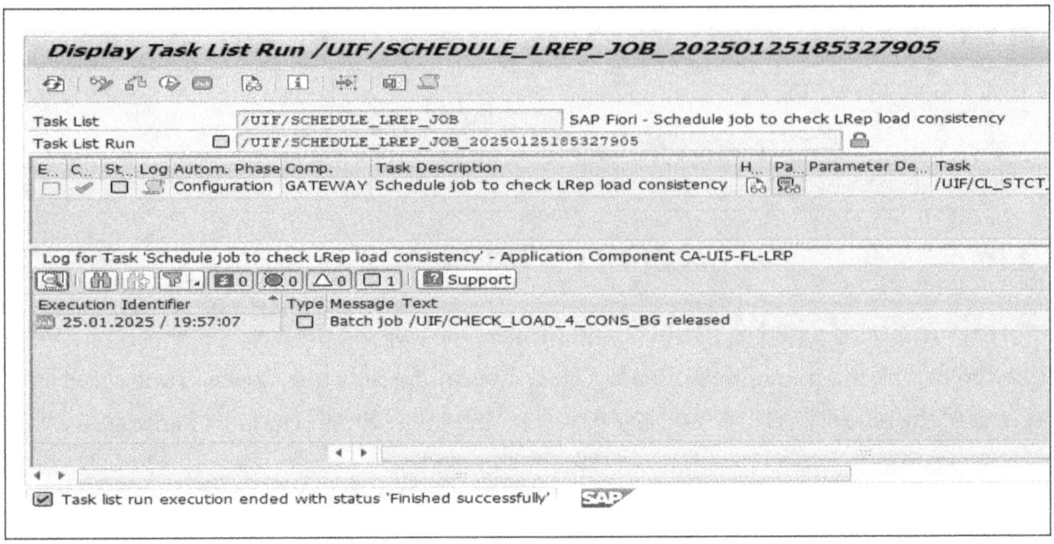

CHAPTER 5   SAP FIORI CONFIGURATION

Figure 5-46.   Task list /UIF/SCHEDULE_LREP_JOB execution in background mode

The above figure indicates that the batch was released and execution ended successfully, as indicated by the message ☑ Task list run execution ended with status 'Finished successfully'. **Note:** Everything within the checkbox is green. Check the status in transaction **STC02**.

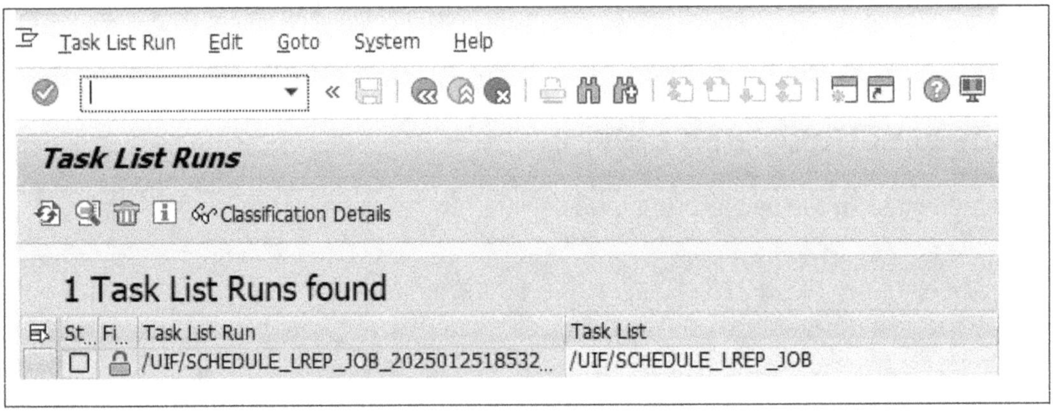

Figure 5-47.   Task list /UIF/SCHEDULE_LREP_JOB completed within STC02 transaction

The **SM37** transaction output display shows that the job was released and finished, as shown in the figure below.

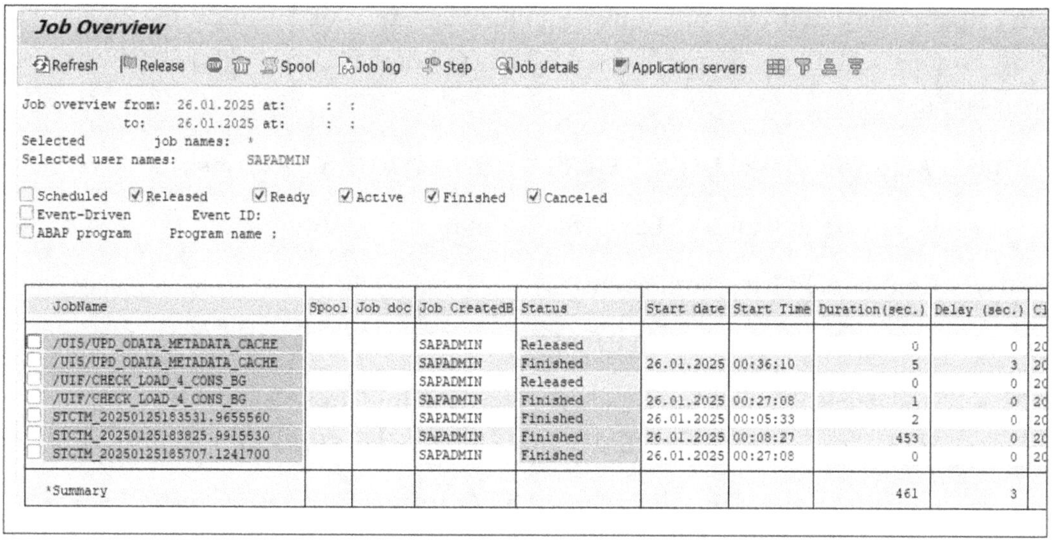

CHAPTER 5 SAP FIORI CONFIGURATION

Figure 5-48. SM37 output for the background job completed

5.6.4 Summary

The task list **/UIF/SCHEDULE_LREP_JOB** is essential for scheduling background jobs that refresh the content in Fiori apps. This includes updating catalogs and tiles displayed in the Launchpad. By regularly updating these elements, the task list ensures that users can always access the most current app changes without any delays. This process is crucial for maintaining an efficient and smooth-running Launchpad, enabling users to have the best experience navigating their applications.

5.7 Task List 4: SAP_FIORI_FOUNDATION_S4
5.7.1 Introduction

The SAP Fiori Foundation task list **SAP_FIORI_FOUNDATION_S4** is crucial for configuring and activating the SAP Fiori Launchpad for applications within SAP S/4HANA. This task list automates several steps to ensure the Fiori Launchpad is ready for use, particularly for **embedded deployments**. It is used to perform the initial setup of SAP Fiori applications and to generate generic roles for the SAP Fiori administrator and SAP Fiori user. These roles are essential for managing and accessing the SAP Fiori

CHAPTER 5   SAP FIORI CONFIGURATION

Launchpad. This task list is a prerequisite for further activating business roles and the corresponding SAP Fiori content via the SAP Fiori Content Activation for SAP Business Roles task list.

Rapid Activation Task List **SAP_FIORI_FOUNDATION_S4** also offers options to

- Configure FLP for SAP Easy Access Menu
- Configure FLP for Notifications
- Activate and Configure FLP for Spaces and Pages
- Activate ICF nodes and OData services required for SAP GUI for HTML and other generic SAP Fiori Launchpad features
- Initialize classic UI technologies (SAP GUI for HTML and Web Dynpro ABAP applications)
- Generate working SAP Fiori Launchpad roles for user and administrator

Note   Another requirement is for the SAP Fiori front-end server to be used with the embedded deployment option.

- The task list does not support the central hub deployment option, where there is a separate Fiori front-end server (FES) system for Fiori.
- After running the task list, you can access the SAP Fiori Launchpad via transaction **/UI2/FLP** or use the URL <HTTP/HTTPS>://<SERVER>:<PORT>/sap/bc/ui5_ui5/ui2/ushell/shells/abap/FioriLaunchpad.html.
- This task list is a prerequisite for running other task lists, as shown below.

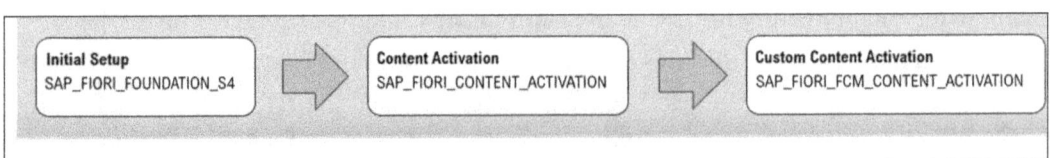

Figure 5-49. Pictorial display of the dependency of other task lists

214

CHAPTER 5   SAP FIORI CONFIGURATION

5.7.2 Steps to Activate the Task List

Below are some of the subtask descriptions within the task list that should be viewed, and the parameters updated in figure below are explained as follows.

Note   This task list is quite long, so you should periodically save entries to avoid re-entering information due to any errors.

Execute Transaction Code STC01

Select the transaction **STC01** to run the task list, as shown in the figure below.

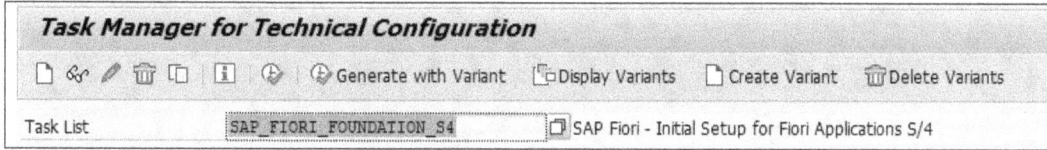

Figure 5-50. *Transaction STC01 input for task list SAP_FIORI_FOUNDATION_S4*

Click the execute icon . A new window opens where the subsequent subtask list must be maintained. The subtasks within the task list are shown in the figure below.

215

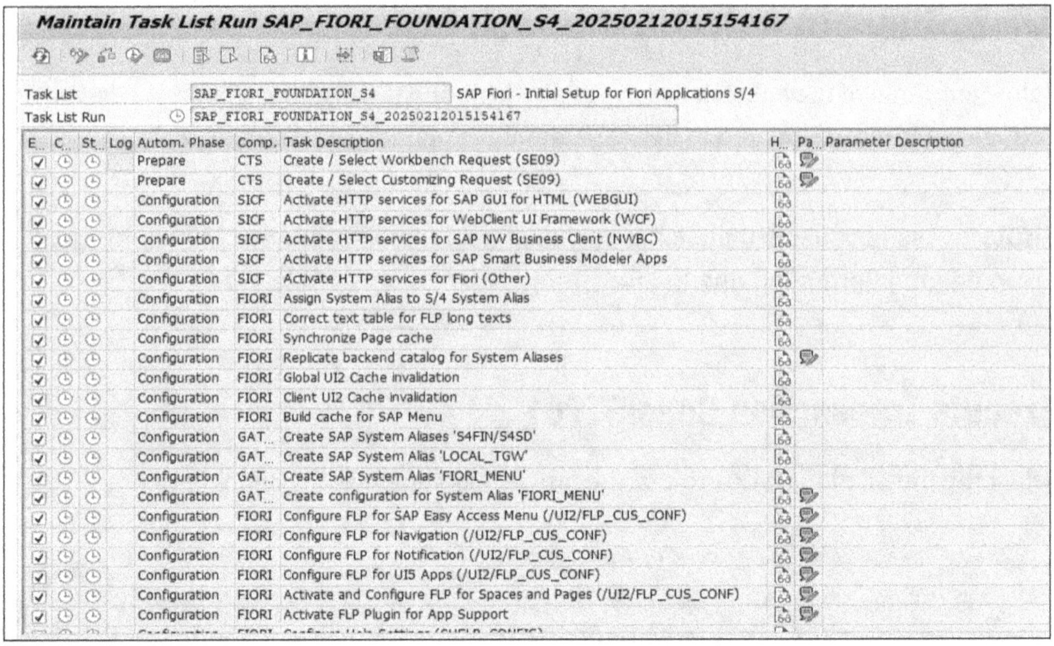

CHAPTER 5   SAP FIORI CONFIGURATION

Figure 5-51. Task List SAP_FIORI_FOUNDATION_S4 with its subtask list

Below are some of the subtask descriptions within the task list as shown in the above figure.

Create / Select Workbench Request (SE09)

Enter the details by selecting the parameter icon. Use the Workbench transport request created earlier in this chapter.

Create / Select Customizing Request (SE09)

Use the Customizing transport request created earlier in this chapter.

Activate Various HTTP Services

This subtask list automatically activates the following HTTP services:

- Activate HTTP services for SAP GUI for HTML (WEBGUI)
- Activate HTTP services for WebClient UI Framework (WCF)

216

CHAPTER 5   SAP FIORI CONFIGURATION

- Activate HTTP services for SAP NW Business Client (NWBC)
- Activate HTTP services for SAP Smart Business Modeler Apps
- Activate HTTP services for Fiori (Other)

The **SICF** services activated in the subtask list are as follows:

- /sap/public/bc/ur
- /sap/public/bc/icons
- /sap/public/bc/icons_rtl
- /sap/public/bc/webicons
- /sap/public/bc/pictograms
- /sap/public/bc/webdynpro/*
- /sap/bc/gui/sap/its/webgui
- /sap/bc/gui/sap/its/typeahead
- /sap/public/bc/its/mimes
- /sap/bc/apc/sap/webgui_services
- /sap/public/myssocntl
- /sap/bc/bsp/sap/bsp_dlc_frcmp
- /sap/bc/bsp/sap/bsp_wd_base
- /sap/bc/bsp/sap/bspwd_basics
- /sap/bc/bsp/sap/crm_ui_frame
- /sap/bc/bsp/sap/crm_ui_start
- /sap/bc/bsp/sap/crm_ui_sysmsg
- /sap/bc/bsp/sap/crm_thtmlb_util
- /sap/bc/bsp/sap/thtmlb_styles
- /sap/bc/bsp/sap/thtmlb_scripts
- /sap/bc/bsp/sap/wcf_jquery

- /sap/webcuif/uif_callback
- /sap/webcuif/uif_export_tab
- /sap/bc/nwbc/*
- /sap/bc/ui2/nwbc/nwbc_api
- /sap/bc/<path>/sap/sbrt_appssl
- /sap/bc/<path>/sap/sb_apps_assocsl
- /sap/bc/<path>/sap/sb_apps_ddsl
- /sap/bc/<path>/sap/sb_apps_evalsl
- /sap/bc/<path>/sap/sb_apps_kpisl
- /sap/bc/<path>/sap/sb_apps_libsl
- /sap/bc/<path>/sap/sb_apps_tilesl
- /sap/bc/<path>/sap/sb_apps_wssl
- /sap/bc/<path>/sap/ssbtileslibsl
- /sap/bc/<path>/sap/ssbtilessl
- /sap/bc/<path>/sap/analyticsdtsl
- <path>: bsp / ui5_ui5 (This will activate the path bsp and ui5-ui5)
- /sap/bc/webdynpro/sap/SUI_TM_MM_APP
- /sap/bw/ina
- /sap/bw/ina/GetServerInfo
- /sap/bw/ina/GetResponse
- /sap/bw/Mime
- /sap/bc/bsp/sap/sakp_genui_a_sl
- /sap/public/bc/uics/whitelist
- /sap/public/bc/icf/systemloginjs

Assign System Alias to S/4 System Alias

This subtask creates system aliases in the system using transaction **SM30**. The task picks entries that start with **S4*** and NW from the table UI2/V_SYSALIAS and adds them to the mapping table **UI2/V_ALIASMAP**. The **target system alias** is left blank to link to the local system.

Correct text table for FLP long texts

This subtask creates a background job using transaction **SM36** to execute the report **APB_LPD_CORRECT_TEXTTABLES**, which is used to correct long texts in the Fiori Launchpad.

Synchronize Page cache

This subtask creates a background job through transaction **/UI2/SYNC_PBC** to execute the report **/UI2/PAGE_CACHE_SYNCHRONIZE**, which updates the page cache with changes from primary catalogs/groups.

Replicate backend catalog for System Aliases

This subtask enables the display of back-end catalogs in the Launchpad and design-time tools, as well as their replication to the front-end server. A background job via transaction **SM36** needs to be created to execute the report **/UI2/GET_APP_DESCR_REMOTE_ALL**, which replicates back-end catalogs for system aliases. There are two available replication modes:

- **Full Replication:** All catalogs are replicated.
- **Delta Replication:** Only changes since the last replication are replicated.

Leave everything unchanged.

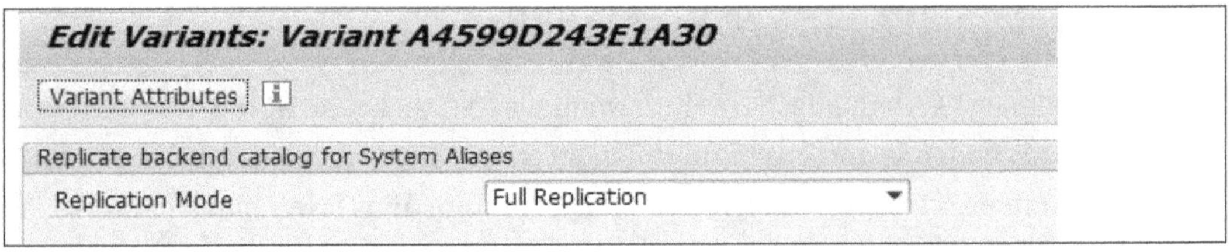

CHAPTER 5   SAP FIORI CONFIGURATION

Figure 5-52. Background job for catalog replication mode

Global UI2 Cache invalidation

This subtask creates a background job via transaction **SM36** to execute the report /UI2/INVALIDATE_GLOBAL_CACHES, invalidating all global UI2 caches.

Client UI2 Cache invalidation

This subtask creates a background job via transaction **SM36** to execute the report /UI2/INVALIDATE_CLIENT_CACHES, which is used to invalidate client UI2 caches.

Build cache for SAP Menu

This subtask creates a background job via transaction **SM36** to execute report **/UI2/EAM_BUILD_CACHE**. This report helps SAP Menu apps load quickly in the App Finder.

Create SAP System Aliases 'S4FIN/S4SD'

This subtask creates SAP system aliases **S4FIN** and **S4SD**, which are required for Design Studio apps. The aliases are then assigned to RFC destination **NONE** and flagged as **Local GW**. This is set up by using transaction **SM30** for the object /IWFND/V_DFSYAL. If the system alias already exists, the system will not recreate it; rather, it will skip the step.

Create SAP System Alias 'LOCAL_TGW'

This subtask creates SAP system alias **LOCAL_TGW** using transaction **SM30** and the object **/IWFND/V_DFSYAL** with the following parameter settings:

- **Local GW**: X
- **For Local App**: X

- **RFC Destination**: None
- **Software Version**: /IWPGW/BWF

This alias will activate the OData service **TASKPROCESSING** in later steps. If **LOCAL_TGW** already exists, the step will be skipped.

Create SAP System Alias 'FIORI_MENU'

This subtask creates SAP system alias **FIORI_MENU** using transaction **SM30** and the object **/IWFND/V_DFSYAL** with the following parameter settings:

- **Local GW**: X
- **RFC Destination**: None
- **Software Version**: DEFAULT

The alias enables the OData services **/UI2/EASY_ACCESS_MENU** and **/UI2/USER_MENU** in the next steps of the configuration. If the SAP system alias FIORI_MENU already exists, this step will be skipped.

Create configuration for System Alias FIORI_MENU

This subtask sets up a local HTTPS destination named **FIORI_CLASSICUI_HTTPS** and creates corresponding aliases for this system using transactions SM59 and SM30.

- **Customer System Alias**: /UI2/VC_SYSALIAS
- **System Alias Mapping**: /UI2/V_ALIASMAP

The **SAP Easy Access transactions** require the system alias and mapping to the local HTTPS destination.

Configure FLP for SAP Easy Access Menu (/UI2/FLP_CUS_CONF)

This subtask sets the **FLP** properties for the current client based on the transaction **/UI2/FLP_CUS_CONF**:

- **APPFINDER_EASYACCESSMENU_SAPMENU**: Enable and activate the SAP Menu tab within the App Finder SAP Easy Access menu.

- **APPFINDER_EASYACCESSMENU_USERMENU**: This setting enables the User Menu tab in the **SAP Easy Access menu** in the **App Finder**.

- **FLP_EAM_ALIASES = FIORI_MENU** (no overwrite of value, added to existing alias): This alias allows easy access to the Easy Access menu.

If the **FLP property value** differs, the system will ask you to confirm whether you want to overwrite it in the parameter interface.

Configure FLP for Navigation (/UI2/FLP_CUS_CONF)

This subtask sets the **FLP** properties for the current client based on the transaction /**UI2/FLP_CUS_CONF**:

- **NAVIGATION_GUI_INPLACE:** Open SAP GUI for HTML applications in-place.

- **NAVIGATION_GUI_STATEFUL_CONTAINER:** Use a stateful application container for SAP GUI for HTML apps.

- **NAVIGATION_WDA_INPLACE:** Open Web Dynpro applications in-place.

- **NAVIGATION_HOMETARGET:** Set the home navigation link to be the company logo. This feature is only available in spaces mode.

If the **FLP** property already exists with a different value, the system will prompt confirmation to overwrite the parameter UI setting.

Configure FLP for Notification (/UI2/FLP_CUS_CONF)

This subtask sets the **FLP** properties for the current client according to /**UI2/FLP_CUS_CONF**:

- **NOTIFICATION:** Enable and activate the Notifications shell service, and then allow push notifications in the Launchpad.

- **NOTIFICATION_UI:** Activate and enable out-of-the-box UI modules for notifications in the Launchpad.

Configure FLP for UI5 Apps (/UI2/FLP_CUS_CONF)

This subtask sets the following **FLP** property for the current client according to the transaction **/UI2/FLP_CUS_CONF**:

- **TIME_ZONE_FROM_SERVER_IN_UI5:** Use the server time zone for UI5 apps instead of the browser's time zone.

If the FLP property already exists with a different value, the system prompts confirmation before overwriting the setting in the parameter UI.

Activate and Configure FLP for Spaces and Pages (/UI2/FLP_CUS_CONF)

This subtask for configuration involves configuring **Fiori Launchpad spaces and pages**. It includes determining the OData and ICF services for business catalog SAP_BASIS_BC_UI_FLD to be activated. These services will then be passed to tasks Activate Gateway OData Services Foundation (/IWFND/MAINT_SERVICE) and Activate HTTP services for Fiori for activation. The current client will also set specific FLP properties to enable the functionality. If the FLP property has a different value, it will be confirmed to overwrite the setting in the parameter UI. To enable the functionality, the following **FLP** properties for the current client, according to transaction **/UI2/FLP_CUS_CONF**, are set as follows:

- **SPACES:** Enable SAP Fiori Launchpad spaces (*).
- **SPACES_ENABLE_USER:** Allow users to switch between SAP Fiori Launchpad spaces mode and the classic home page.
- **SPACES_MYHOME:** Allow users to access My Home.
- **SPACES_CUSTOM_HOME:** Turn on the custom home feature.
- **SPACES_CUSTOM_HOME_COMPONENT_ID:** Specify ID of the custom home component.

Activate FLP Plugin for App Support

To activate the Fiori Launchpad (FLP) Plugin for App Support, set **APP_SUPPORT** to be **Active** in transaction **/UI2/FLP_CUS_CONF**. If the FLP plugin has a different setting, confirm it is overwritten. This will activate HTTP services and the following:

CHAPTER 5 SAP FIORI CONFIGURATION

- OData service SUI_FLP_APP_SUP_SRV
- /sap/bc/bsp/sap/sui_flp_app_sup
- /sap/bc/ui5_ui5/sap/sui_flp_app_sup

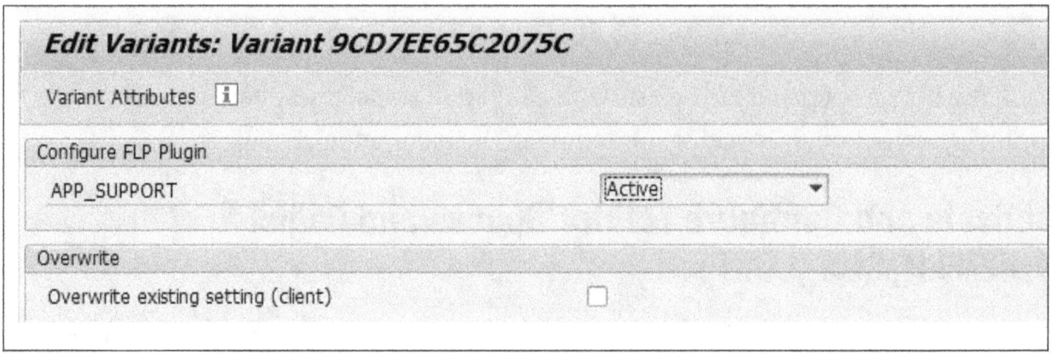

Figure 5-53. *Activate FLP Plugin for App Support*

Keep the remaining settings as they are shown in the figure above and save the settings. A message will appear at the bottom of the screen indicating that the variant has been saved.

Configure Help Settings (SHELP_CONFIG)

This subtask executes the report associated with transaction **SHELP_CONFIG** using its default settings to configure help settings for Fiori apps.

Note The task will not be executable if the transaction **SHELP_CONFIG** is unavailable.

Set transport options for to be activated OData Services

Here, we enter the package and transport details created earlier.

CHAPTER 5　SAP FIORI CONFIGURATION

Activate Gateway OData Services Foundation (/IWFND/MAINT_SERVICE)

This subtask is for activating Gateway OData services using transaction **/IWFND/MAINT_SERVICE**. An OData service will not be created again if it is already available. The processing mode, prefix, and package assignment will remain unchanged.

- **Processing mode co-deployed only (*):**
    - SMART_BUSINESS_RUNTIME_SRV
    - SMART_BUSINESS_DESIGNTIME_SRV
    - ESH_SEARCH_SRV
    - RSAO_ODATA_SRV
- **In case the task Activate and Configure FLP for Spaces and Pages is available and selected within the task list, the following OData services will also be activated:**
    - /UI2/FDM_PAGE_REPOSITORY_CUST_SRV
    - /UI2/FDM_PAGE_RUNTIME_SRV
    - /UI2/FDM_TRANSPORT_SRV
    - /UI2/FDM_SPACE_REPOSITORY_CUST_SRV
- **In case the task Activate FLP Plugin for App Support is available and selected, the following OData service will also be activated:**
    - SUI_FLP_APP_SUP_SRV
- **Processing mode routing-based with system alias FIORI_MENU:**
    - /UI2/EASY_ACCESS_MENU
    - /UI2/USER_MENU

Note　You will not encounter an error if the OData service is configured with the system alias Local. This is because the setup is working correctly. The log message will say, "Different processing mode, but alias **Local** found."

225

Publish Service Groups Foundation (/IWFND/V4_ADMIN)

This subtask publishes the following service groups according to transaction **/IWFND/V4_ADMIN**:

- /IWNGW/NOTIFICATION (Notification)
- /UI2/INSIGHTS_SRV (Insight Cards)
- S_APS_SB_DOC_HLP (SAP Help)

When you publish a service group, you will follow and execute these steps:

- Publish the service group, in case it is not already published.
- Activate ICF node /sap/opu/odata4.

Activate HTTP services Foundation

This subtask is used to activate HTTP services based on transaction SICF, which are determined by the tasks "Activate and Configure FLP for Spaces and Pages" (/UI2/FLP_CUS_CONF) and "Activate FLP Plugin for App Support" (/UI2/FLP_CUS_CONF).

Delete Requests for OData Services Activation (if newly created and empty)

This subtask deletes new and empty Workbench/Customizing requests created with the task Set transport options for to be activated OData Services. Existing requests will remain untouched.

Generate Fiori Foundation Roles

This subtask creates composite roles and generates authorizations for standard Fiori functionalities. It includes copying the roles SAP_FLP_ADMIN and SAP_FLP_USER to your namespace with a defined prefix. The copied roles will be enhanced with authorizations and menus for standard Fiori functionalities. For Enterprise Search, the authority object S_ESH_CONN will be customized to display only relevant search results. The copied roles will then be used to create composite roles using the PFCG transaction as follows:

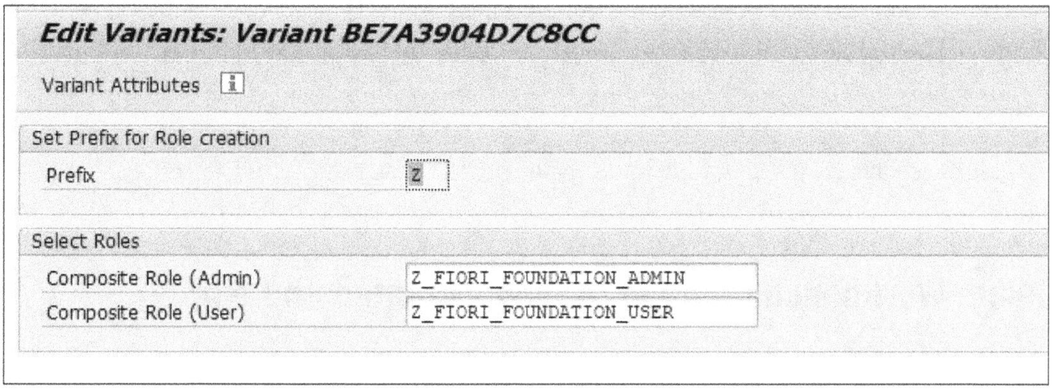

CHAPTER 5 SAP FIORI CONFIGURATION

Figure 5-54. Generate foundation roles

- **Composite Role**: Z_FIORI_FOUNDATION_ADMIN
- **Composite Role**: Z_FIORI_FOUNDATION_USER

In our case, as shown in the figure below, we will be using the following:

- **Prefix**: ZCU
- **Composite Role**: ZCU:FLP_ADMIN_USERS
- **Composite Role**: ZCU:FLP_END_USER

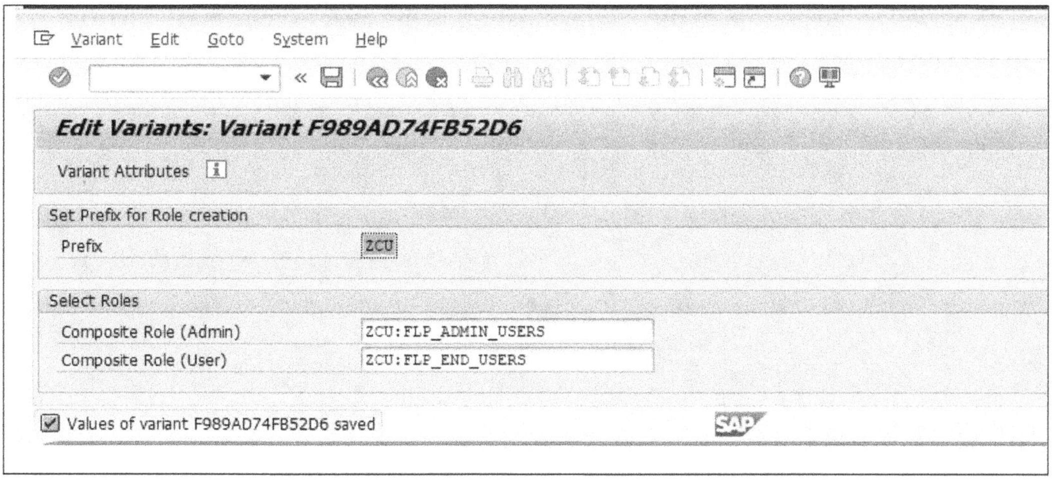

Figure 5-55. Generate Fiori Foundation Roles

227

CHAPTER 5   SAP FIORI CONFIGURATION

> **Note**   These roles can also be created manually by searching in PFCG.

Click the save icon 💾. A new message appears at the bottom of the screen, indicating that the variant and its values have been saved.

Delete Workbench Request (if newly created and empty)

Use this subtask to delete any new and empty Workbench requests created before this task. If you have selected an existing request, it will not be deleted; only new and empty requests will be removed.

Delete Customizing Request (if newly created and empty)

If needed, use this subtask to delete new and empty Customizing requests created before the task. If an existing request is selected, it will not be modified. Only new and empty requests will be deleted.

5.7.3 Completed Task and Subtask List

Save the completed task list as shown in the figure below. The saved message is also displayed at the bottom of the figure, illustrating the **task list run SAP_FIORI_FOUNDATION_S4 has been saved.**

CHAPTER 5 SAP FIORI CONFIGURATION

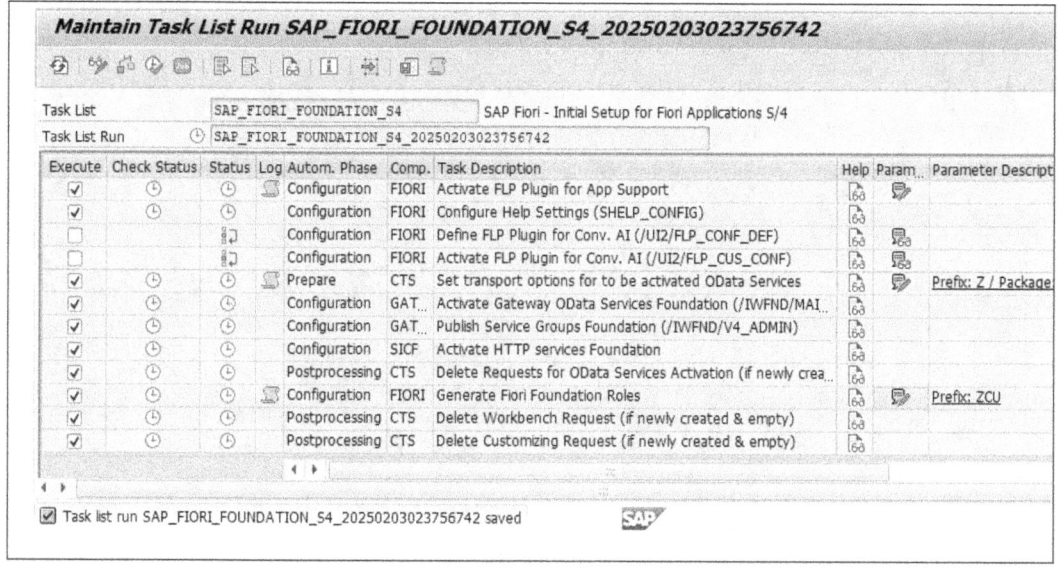

Figure 5-56. Completed task list

5.7.4 Execute the Task List in Background Mode

Execute the task list in background mode using the **Start/Resume Task List Run in Background (F9)** icon .

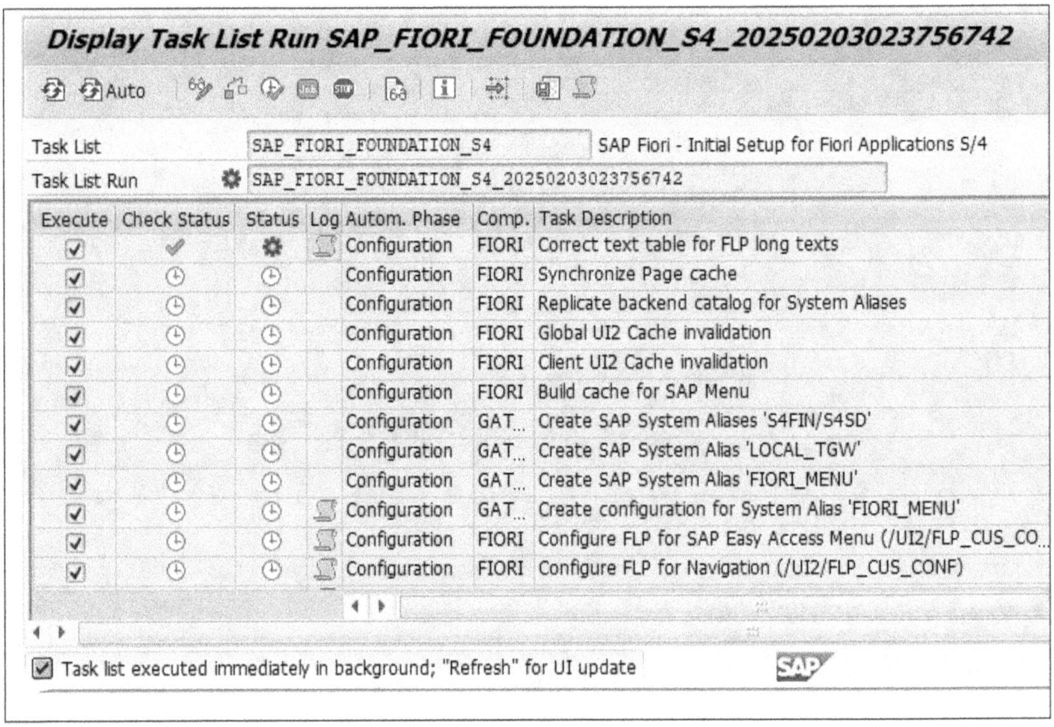

CHAPTER 5   SAP FIORI CONFIGURATION

Figure 5-57. Task list executed in background mode

CHAPTER 5 SAP FIORI CONFIGURATION

Refresh the task list by clicking the icon.

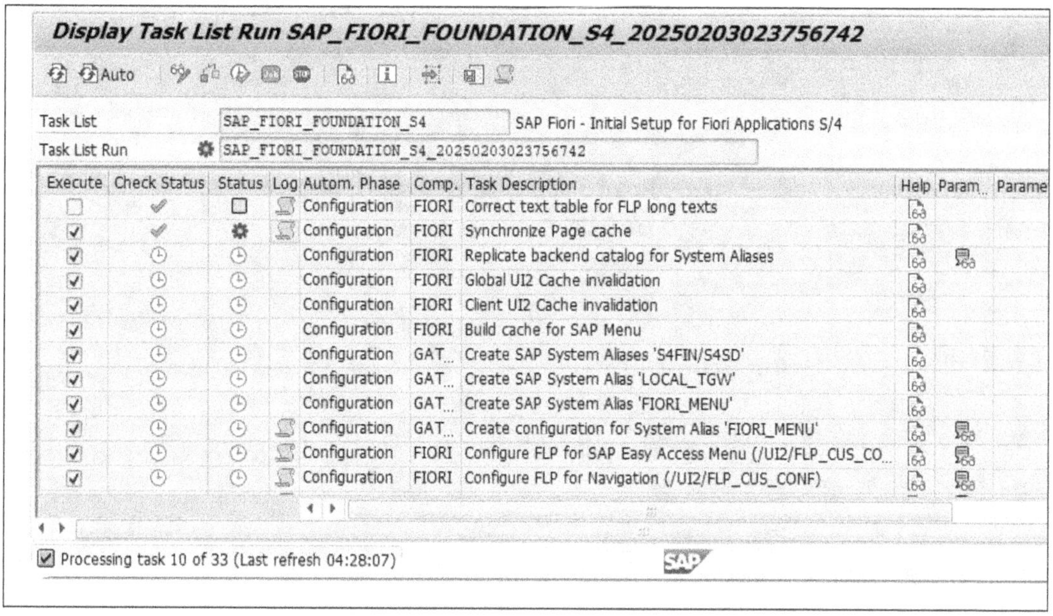

Figure 5-58. The task list in run status mode

We can also set the default Auto refresh by selecting the icon ⟳Auto, which is every 60 seconds. In our case, the execution encountered an issue, as illustrated in the figure below. It displays that the task list execution is suspended with a status of Stopped.

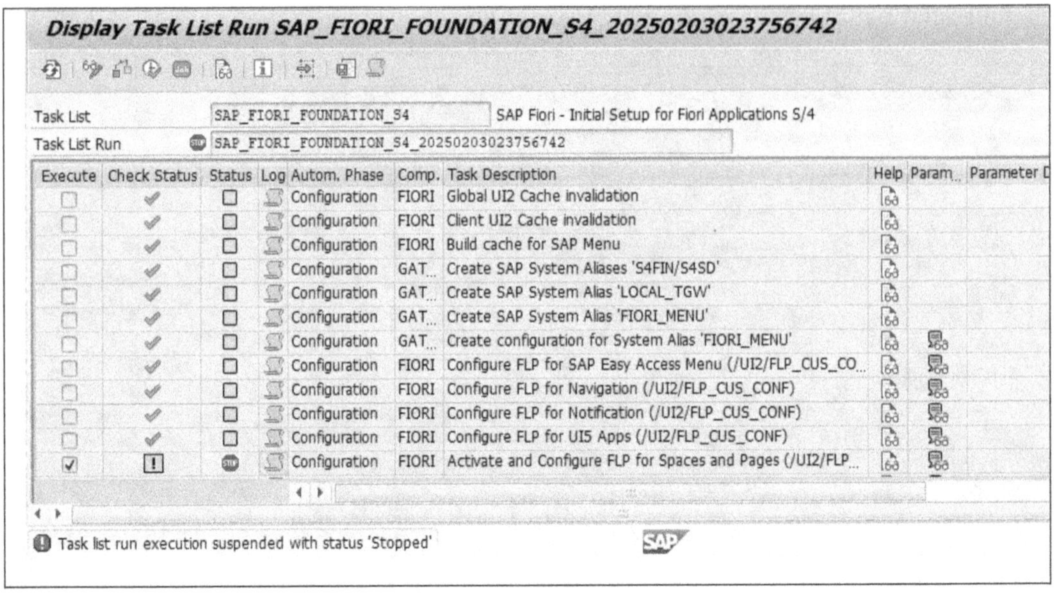

CHAPTER 5   SAP FIORI CONFIGURATION

Figure 5-59. Task list stopped with an error encountered

Double-click the status icon, and at the bottom of the screen, you will see that the system encountered a **breakpoint** in a certain subtask.

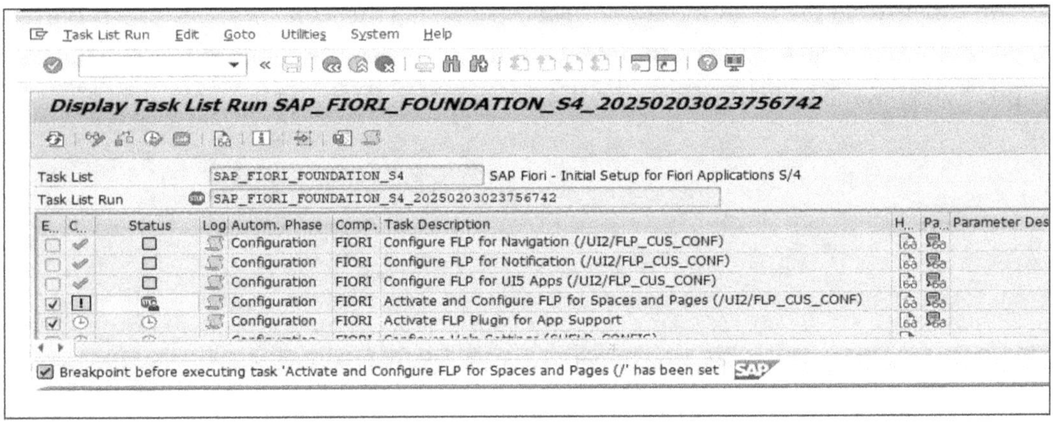

Figure 5-60. Breakpoint error

The task list can be restarted by going to top menu bar and clicking **Utilities ➤ Breakpoints ➤ Delete all Breakpoints**.

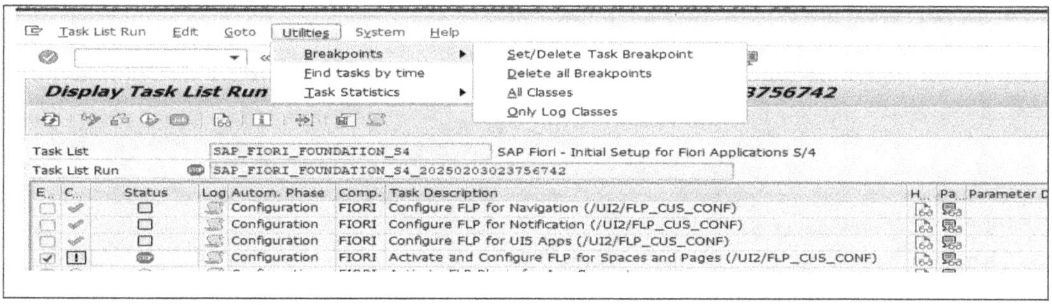

CHAPTER 5   SAP FIORI CONFIGURATION

Figure 5-61. Delete all Breakpoints option

The task list process will restart by clicking the execute icon.

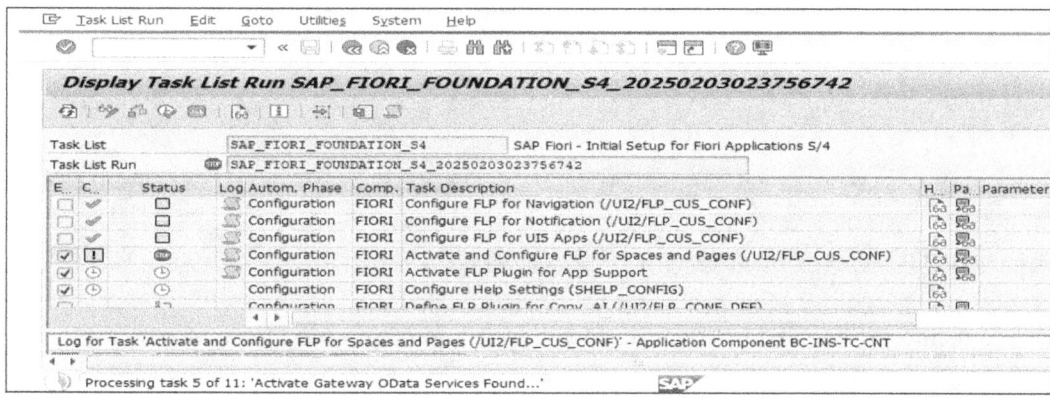

Figure 5-62. Task list executed again

After a few moments, the task list finished executing all the subtasks with a warning message.

5.7.5 Background Job Completed

The background job ran successfully, as shown in the figure below.

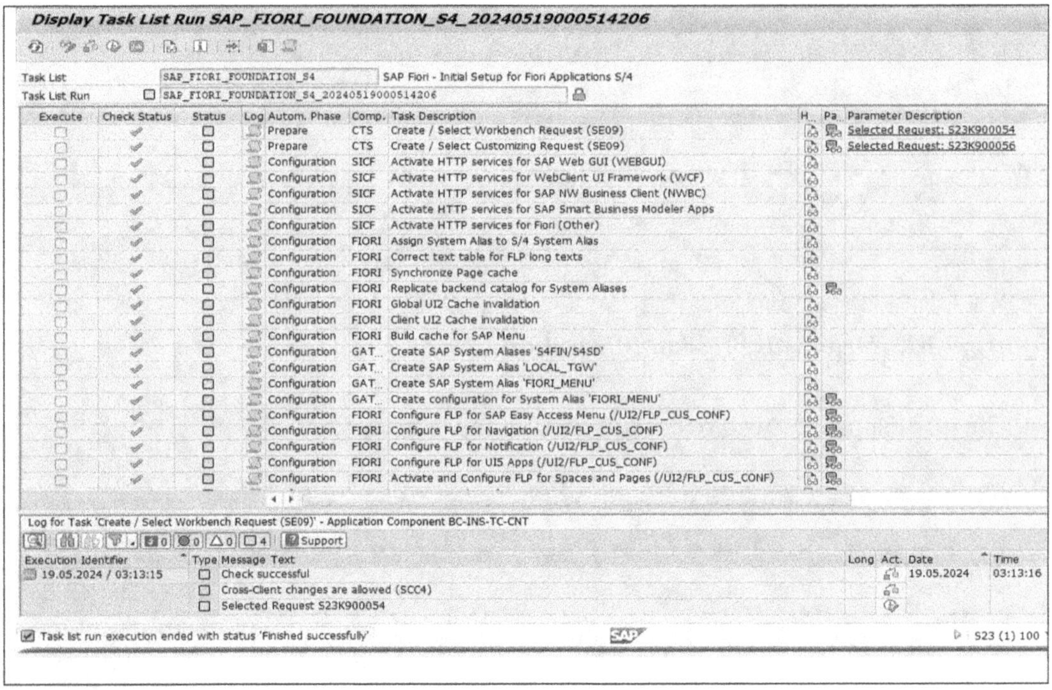

CHAPTER 5   SAP FIORI CONFIGURATION

Figure 5-63. Background job for the task list completed

Once the task and subtask list are completed, a new message appears at the bottom of the screen, indicating that the task list run execution ended with the status Finished successfully ☑ Task list run execution ended with status 'Finished successfully' .

5.7.6 Review Task List Activation Status

The status of the task and subtask list can be checked and monitored using the transaction STC02, as shown in the figure below.

CHAPTER 5 SAP FIORI CONFIGURATION

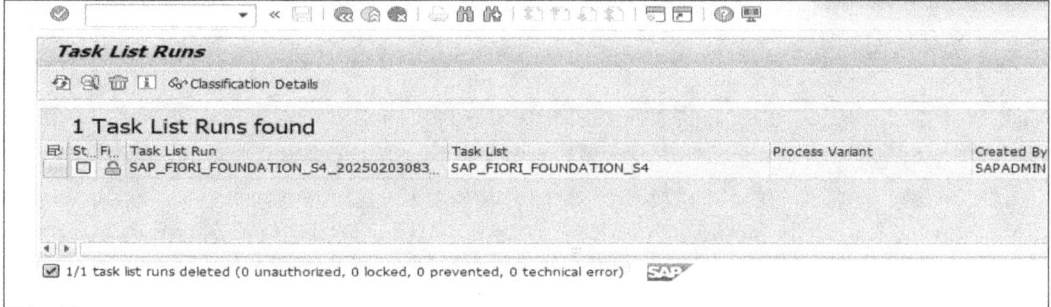

Figure 5-64. *Transaction STC02 displays the task list executed successfully*

The task list was executed successfully, as shown in the figure above.

5.7.7 Validate Foundation Roles Created

Check for the composite Fiori roles created as part of the subtask in transaction code **PFCG**.

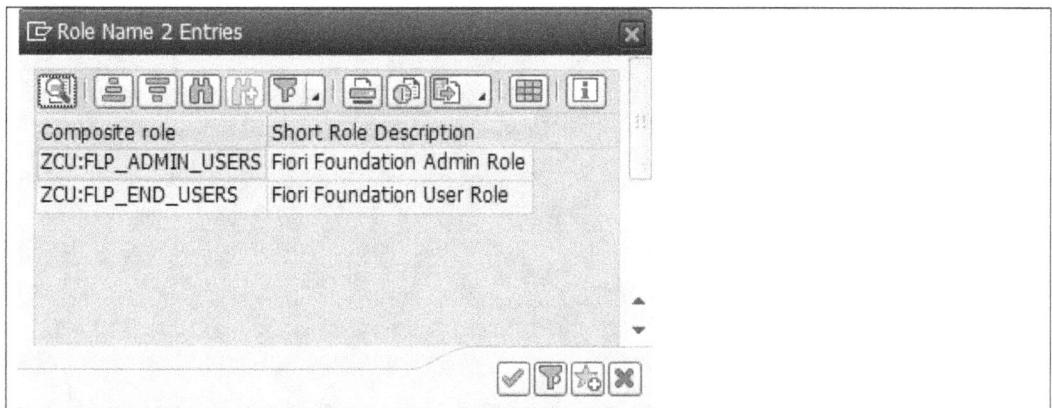

Figure 5-65. *Foundation roles for admin and end users created*

The above figure displays the task list generated composite roles for admin and end users. The users assigned the above role can access the main Launchpad and content layout tools, including the Launchpad App Manager, Launchpad Content Manager (cross-client), Manage Launchpad Spaces, and Manage Launchpad Pages.

235

CHAPTER 5 SAP FIORI CONFIGURATION

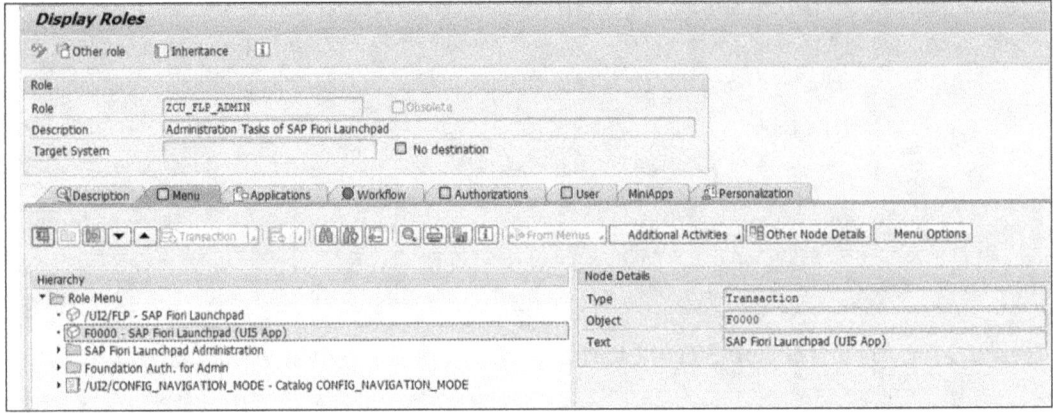

Figure 5-66. Admin role contents

The above figure displays the content of the admin role.

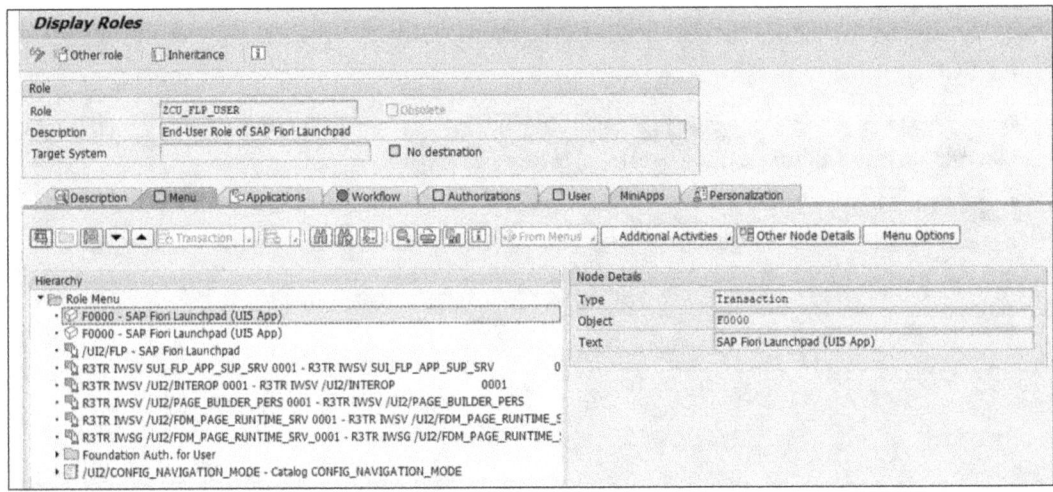

Figure 5-67. Common end user role content

Note The single role **ZCU_FLP_USER** is a common role that is a part of the composite role **ZCU:FLP_END_USER**, which is given to all business end users to log onto the SAP Fiori Launchpad home page.

CHAPTER 5 SAP FIORI CONFIGURATION

5.7.8 Validate URL Working

Log into the SAP Fiori Portal using the transaction **/UI2/FLP** to view the SAP Fiori Launchpad home page.

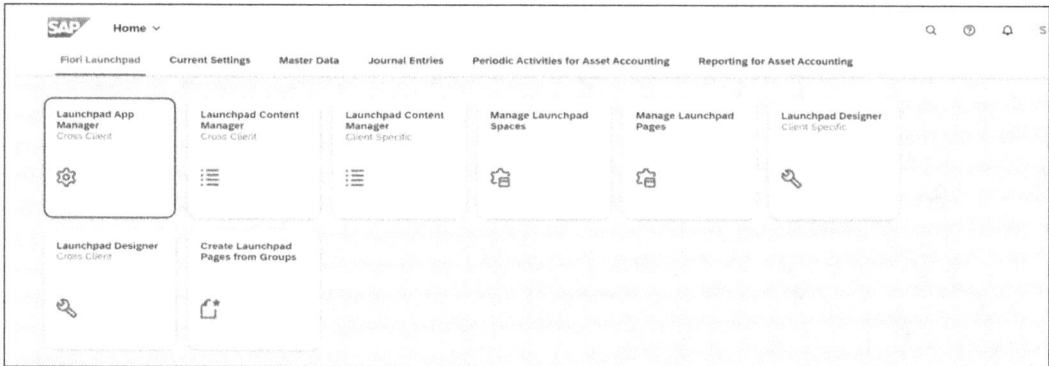

Figure 5-68. *The transaction /UI2/FLP launched successfully by displaying the SAP Fiori Launchpad home page*

The log process was successful, as shown in the figure above.

5.7.9 Validate Spaces and Pages Activated

Check activation of spaces and pages using transaction **/UI2/FLP_SYS_CONF**.

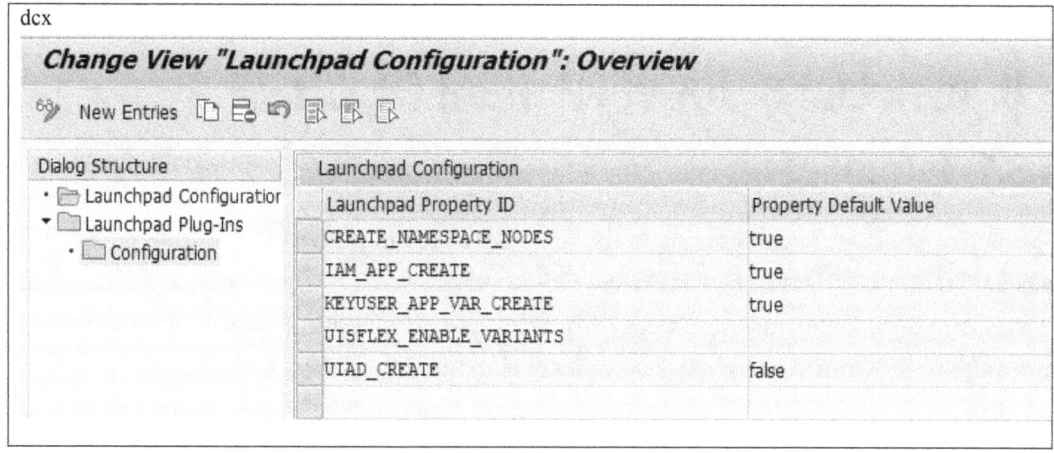

Figure 5-69. *Validate spaces and pages activated*

237

5.7.10 Validate App Support Activated

When you click the option Launchpad Plug-Ins, you will see app support is active, as shown in the figure below.

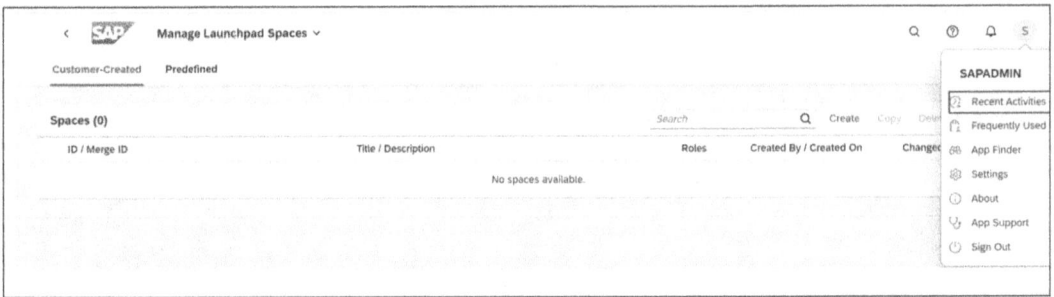

Figure 5-70. App support is working

5.7.11 Summary

The task list SAP_FIORI_FOUNDATION_S4 is designed to prepare a system for using SAP Fiori apps within S/4HANA. It includes important steps to activate the necessary tools, services, and user roles for the Fiori Launchpad to work properly. Completing this task list ensures that your system is set up correctly, making it easier to use and manage Fiori apps effectively.

5.8 Task List 5: /UI2/FLP_HEALTH_CHECKS

5.8.1 Introduction

To ensure the smooth functioning of the SAP Fiori Launchpad, it is essential to use the task list **/UI2/FLP_HEALTH_CHECKS**. This task list serves a crucial purpose in the SAP Fiori ecosystem. It allows you to verify whether the system configuration necessary for running the SAP Fiori Launchpad is in place. Here are the essential tasks it automatically performs:

- **OData and ICF Services Check**: These checks ensure that the essential OData and ICF services required for the Launchpad are active.

- **System Alias Consistency Check**: The task list examines the consistency of system aliases configured for the Launchpad.

Executing this task list will ensure your SAP Fiori Launchpad is set up correctly and ready for use. Any issues arising during the health check will be flagged for further investigation.

5.8.2 Steps to Activate the Task List

Below are some of the subtask descriptions within the task list that should be viewed, and the parameters updated in figure below are explained as follows.

Execute the Task List Using Transaction Code STC01

Execute the task list using transaction code STC01.

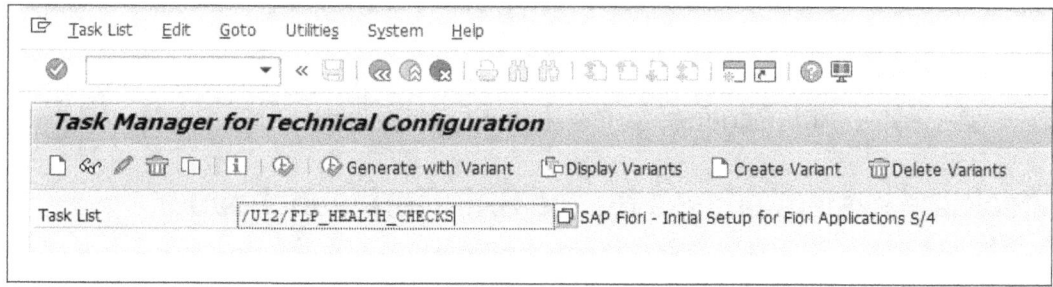

Figure 5-71. Task list executed by transaction STC01

Click the **execute** icon and review the subtask list, as shown in the figure below.

CHAPTER 5 SAP FIORI CONFIGURATION

5.8.3 Review the Task and Subtask List

This section will review and verify a few items from the subtask list.

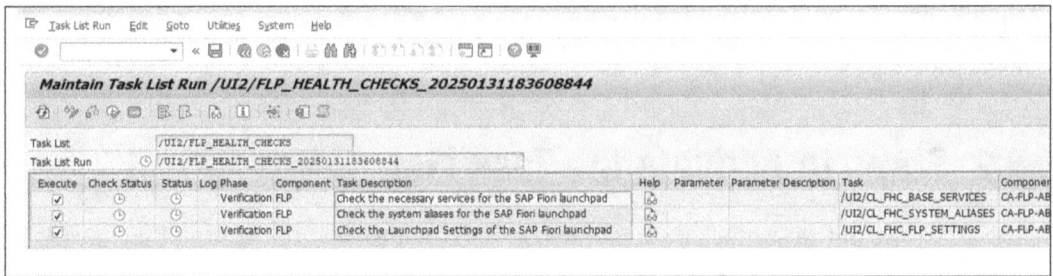

Figure 5-72. *Subtask list displayed*

Check the necessary services for the SAP Fiori launchpad

This check ensures that the services required by the SAP Fiori Launchpad are properly configured. It covers starting the SAP Fiori Launchpad, accessing its content in various areas, personalizing it, and utilizing different interoperability services.

Check the system aliases for the SAP Fiori launchpad

There is a new task to check the following aliases:

- **/UI2/SYSTEMALIAS - UI2**: System Alias Definition
- **/UI2/C_SYSALIAS - UI2**: System Alias Definition (Customer only)

Check the Launchpad Settings of the SAP Fiori launchpad

This task checks each set value from the Launchpad settings based on the data type or, if a value help exists, the value specified in the value help. Additionally, several specific checks are implemented to verify settings with prerequisites or only accept particular values.

Save the Task List

A new message appears at the bottom of the screen after saving the task list.

CHAPTER 5 SAP FIORI CONFIGURATION

5.8.4 Execute the Task List in Foreground Mode

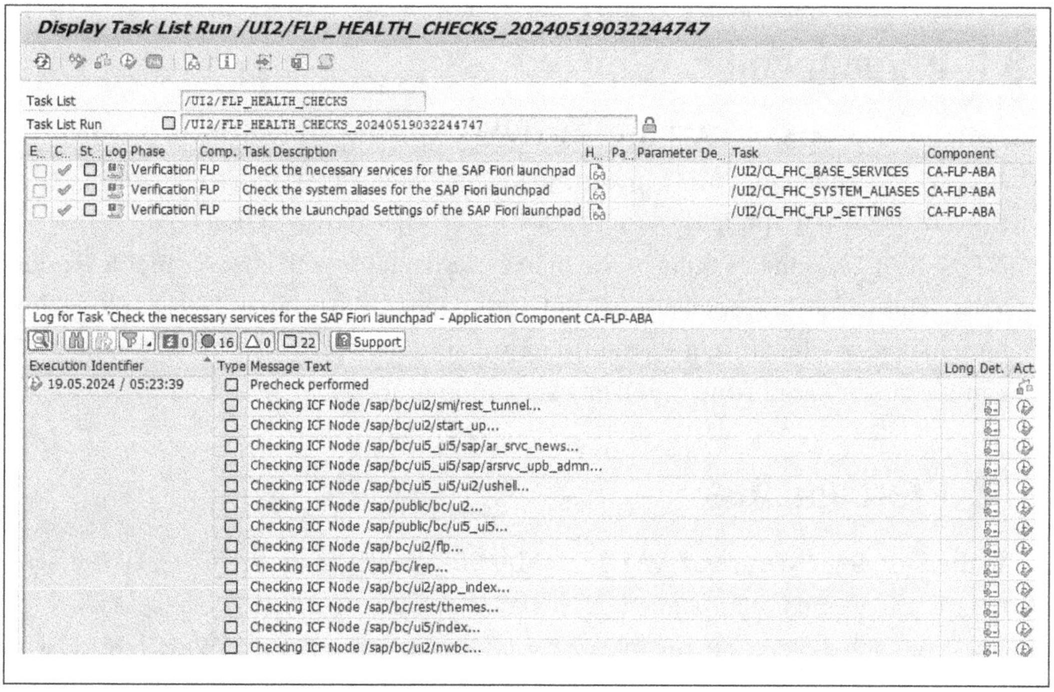

Figure 5-73. Task list executed in foreground mode

Th task list was executed successfully as all nodes in the above figure are green.

5.8.5 Summary

The SAP Fiori task list /UI2/FLP_HEALTH_CHECKS is a tool used to conduct a thorough health check of the SAP Fiori Launchpad environment. It analyzes system configurations, services, and connections to identify potential issues that could impact performance or functionality. By reviewing key components like ICF nodes, OData services, and system aliases, this task list helps administrators proactively detect and resolve setup errors, ensuring a smooth and stable user experience in the Fiori Launchpad.

CHAPTER 5   SAP FIORI CONFIGURATION

5.9 Task List 6: SAP_GATEWAY_ACTIVATE_ODATA_SERV

5.9.1 Introduction

The SAP Fiori task list **SAP_GATEWAY_ACTIVATE_ODATA_SERV** helps activate the OData services needed for SAP Fiori apps in the SAP Gateway system so that apps function correctly. It automates the activation of services in transaction /IWFND/MAINT_SERVICE, connects them to the right system aliases, and ensures that ICF nodes are active. This task list is especially helpful during the initial setup of Fiori apps, during system updates, or when installing multiple apps simultaneously. It reduces manual work and errors by simplifying the OData activation process.

5.9.2 Prerequisites

To run the SAP_GATEWAY_ACTIVATE_ODATA_SERV task list, ensure that SAP Gateway is properly configured for embedded deployment and that you have the necessary permissions, such as access to the relevant services and transaction **/IWFND/MAINT_SERVICE**. The OData services you wish to activate should already be installed, and a valid system alias – Local – must be set up. Additionally, the client's settings should allow for configuration changes.

It is also advisable to have the OData service if you want to be active in Excel format. This task list will automatically update the associated SICF services.

5.9.3 Execute the Task List

This activity is typically handled by the BASIS team, not the security team. Using this task list, you can activate the OData services you need. Transaction code STC01 executes the task list as illustrated in the figure below.

CHAPTER 5   SAP FIORI CONFIGURATION

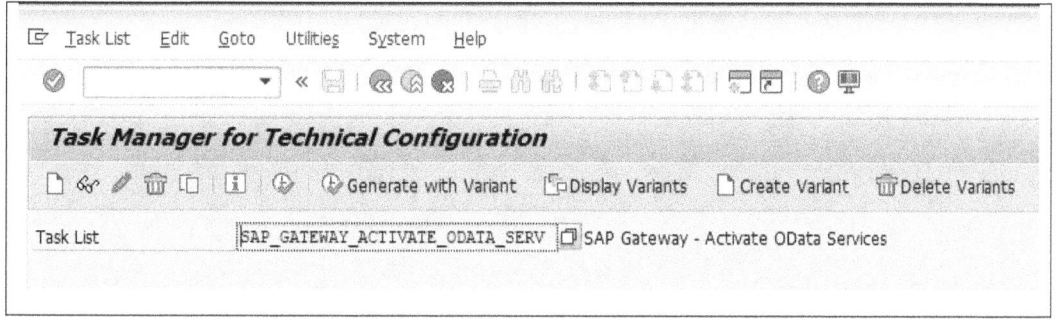

Figure 5-74. Task list SAP_GATEWAY_ACTIVATE_ODATA_SERV

Executing the task list opens a new window, as shown in the figure below.

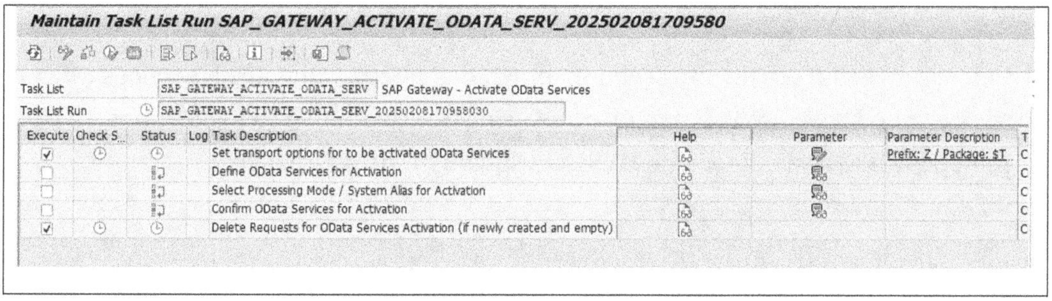

Figure 5-75. Input screen for task list SAP_GATEWAY_ACTIVATE_ODATA_SERV

To begin, enter the package along with its associated transport details. Then, under Task Description and **Select Processing / System Alias for Activation**, place a **checkmark** and ensure the **Co-deployed only** option is enabled for the embedded system, as illustrated in the figure below.

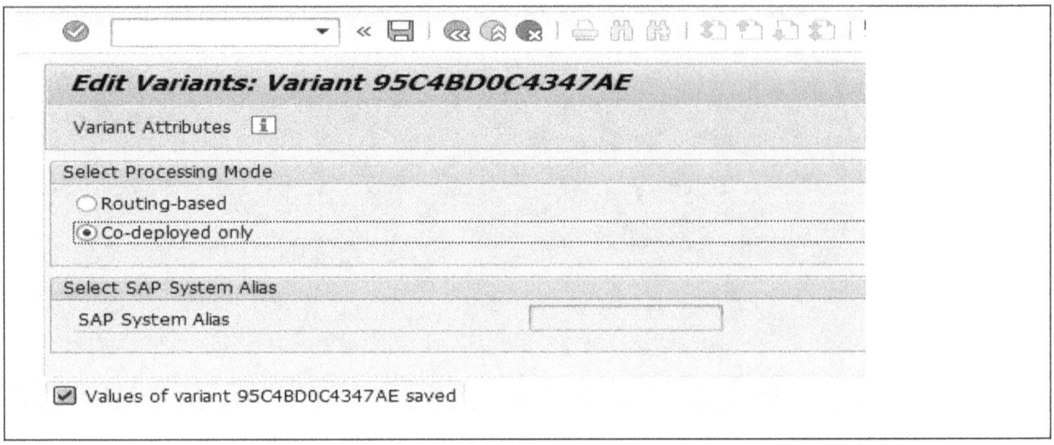

CHAPTER 5 SAP FIORI CONFIGURATION

Figure 5-76. Co-deployed only option selected for embedded deployment

Before proceeding to the next section, download all relevant OData services we need to activate in an Excel file. This can be done using transaction **SE16**, table name **TADIR**, program ID **R3TR**, and object type **IWSG**, as shown in the figure below.

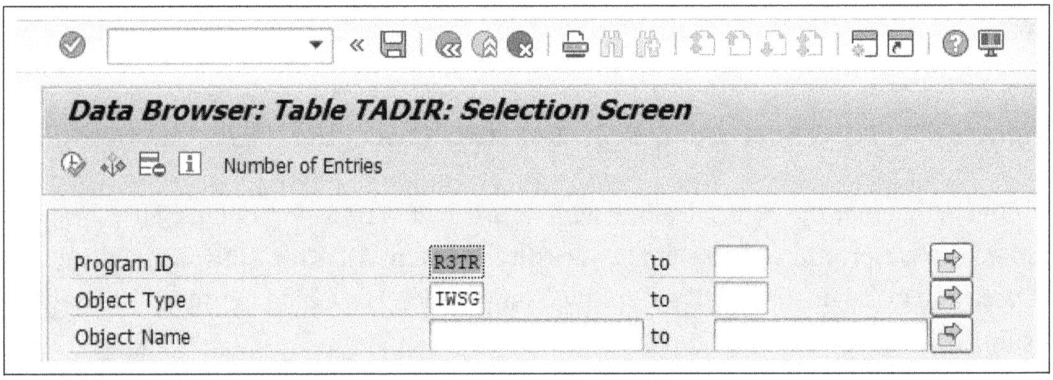

Figure 5-77. Table TADIR

Now click the execute icon and save the file as **IWSG ODATA SERVICE**, which will be used to activate the services, as shown in the figure above. It indicates there are 1,968 entries, as shown in the figure below.

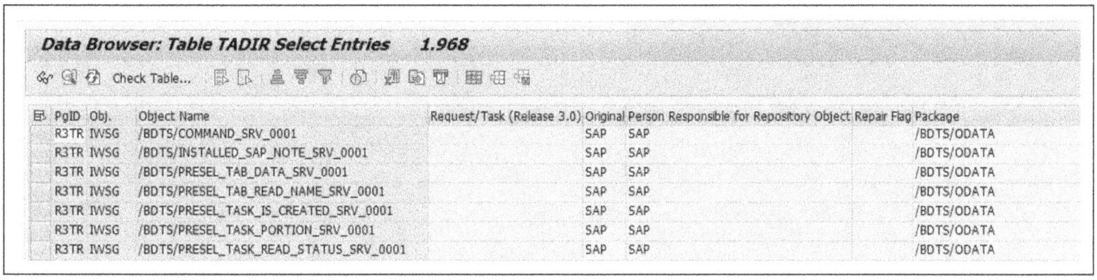

CHAPTER 5　SAP FIORI CONFIGURATION

Figure 5-78. Table TADIR output

Note Keep the maximum number of hits as blank.

Then, **define the OData services for activation**. Enter the OData services you want to activate, as shown in the figure below, and click the continue icon. In this case, we have selected only a limited number of services to activate.

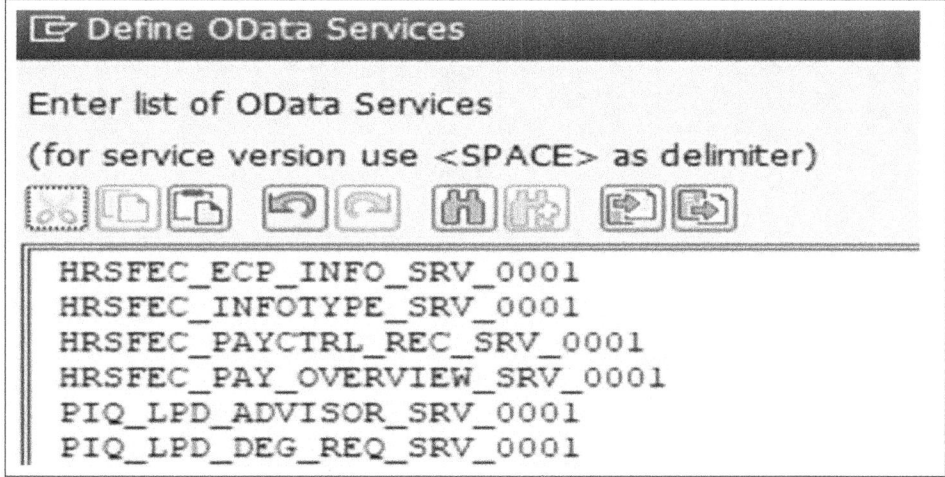

Figure 5-79. OData services to be activated

Similarly, **confirm the OData services for activation**. The system automatically fills in the services to be activated, as shown in the figure below.

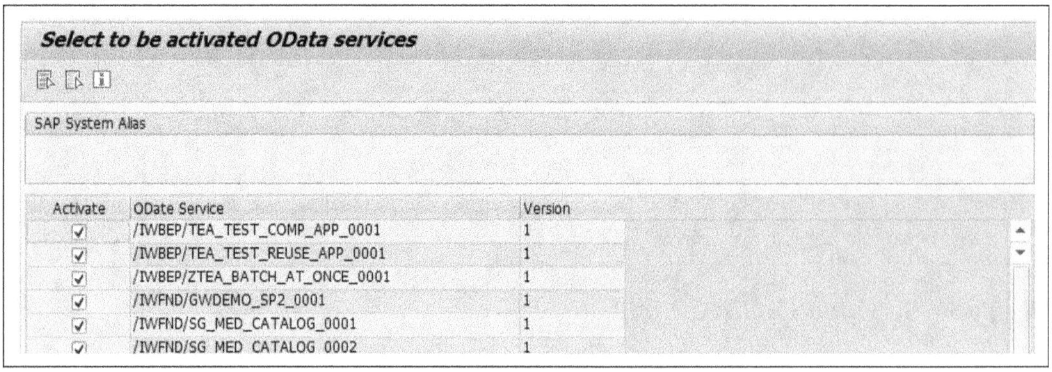

CHAPTER 5 SAP FIORI CONFIGURATION

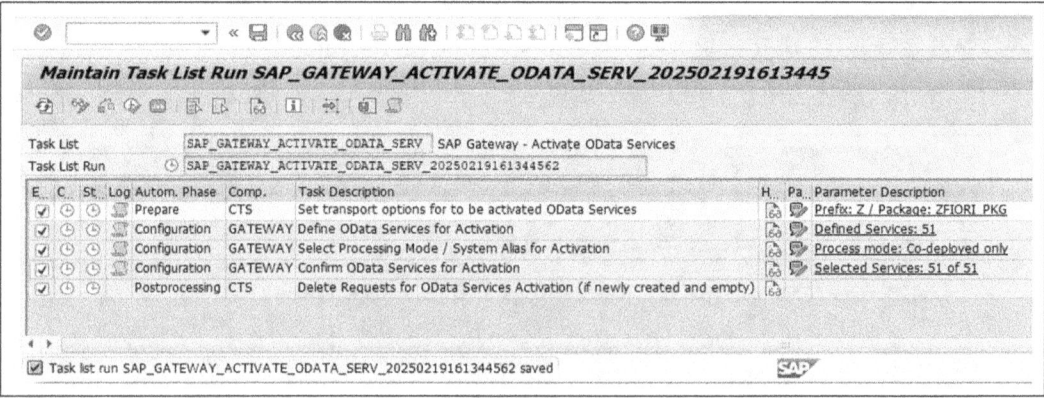

Figure 5-80. OData services selected to be activated

The final screenshot of the task list is shown in the figure below.

Figure 5-81. Final screen for SAP_GATEWAY_ACTIVATE_ODATA_SERV task list

Once saved, a new message appears at the bottom of the screen, indicating that the task list has been saved. Execute the task list **SAP_GATEWAY_ODATA_SERV** in foreground mode. The task list ran successfully, as shown in the figure below.

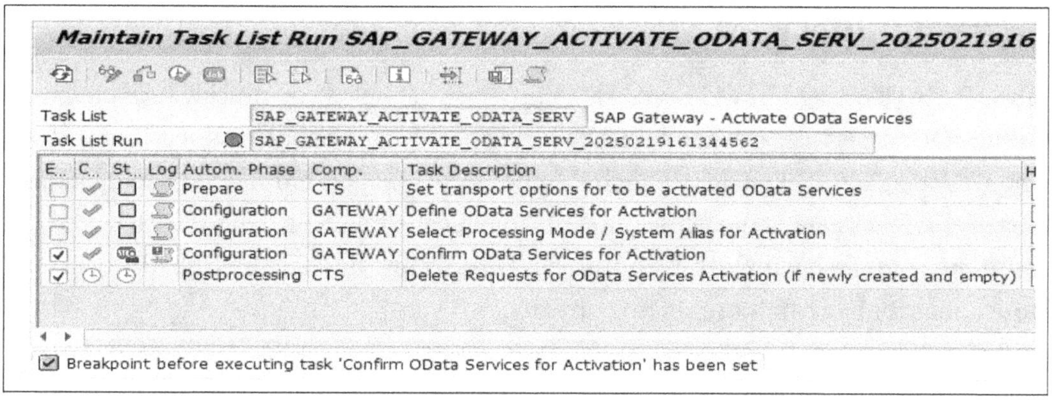

CHAPTER 5 SAP FIORI CONFIGURATION

Figure 5-82. Task list SAP_GATEWAY_ACTIVATE_ODATA_SERV executed

Note Some **breakpoint** was triggered while running, and the task list was re-executed.

Rechecking confirms that all **OData** and **ICF services** are **green**.

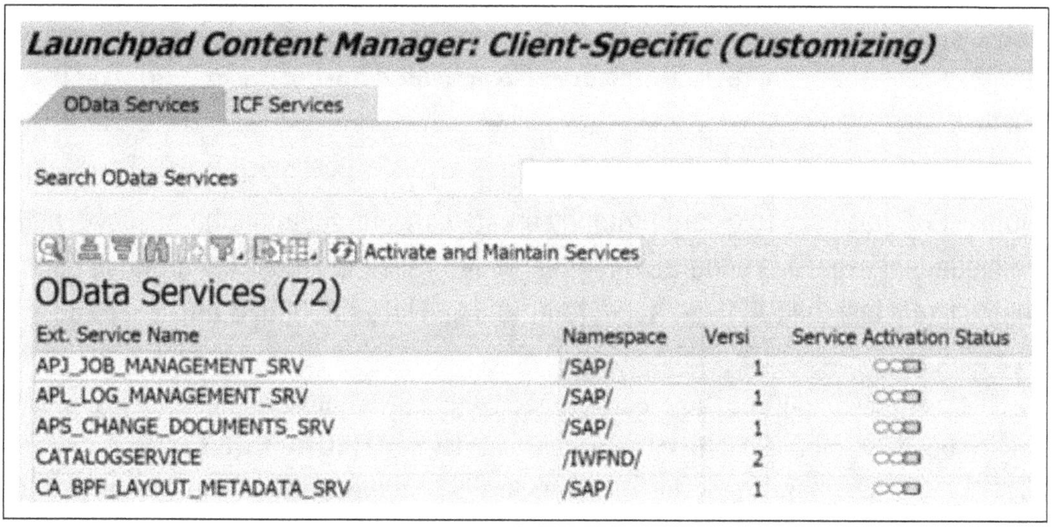

Figure 5-83. All OData services activated

247

5.9.4 Summary

The SAP_GATEWAY_ACTIVATE_ODATA_SERV task list helps you quickly turn on multiple OData services needed for SAP Fiori apps. You just choose the services and assign a system alias, like **Local**, which is optional, as we have embedded deployment. The task list takes care of the activation and enables the related ICF nodes. This method saves time compared with turning on services one by one and ensures that the back-end connections for Fiori apps are set up correctly.

5.10 Task List 7: SAP_FIORI_CONTENT_ACTIVATION

5.10.1 Introduction

The task list refers to a task list used in the SAP environment to activate SAP Fiori content for business roles. This process involves specifying one or more business roles (**SAP_BR***) delivered by SAP and automatically generating and activating these SAP business roles for tests in the sandbox system. It is part of the **rapid activation** process to enable SAP Fiori apps, classic UIs, app-to-app navigations, and more, aiming to provide roles ready for exploration. It determines and pulls all related services, such as **OData and SICF services**, within the roles, **which are also activated during the execution of the task list**.

> **Note** SAP business roles are promptly created in your customer namespace, and a unique test user ID is generated for every role. These test user IDs are then used to efficiently test the SAP Fiori apps; refer to **SAP Notes 2902673 and 2686456**.

This section will outline the process for activating SAP-delivered best practice business roles (**SAP_BR***) using the task list **SAP_FIORI_CONTENT_ACTIVATION**. These business roles serve as **shells** containing links to **spaces**, **pages**, **groups**, and **catalogs**. The task will create a copy of the business role and its related components, such as **IWSG/IWSV**. For example, we will provide a step-by-step approach to activate the **SAP_BR_AA_ACCOUNTANT** role aimed at benefiting an organization's BASIS and security teams.

CHAPTER 5   SAP FIORI CONFIGURATION

As shown in the figure below, SAP has delivered pre-configured roles (SAP_BR*), enabling companies to tailor them to their sandbox and development systems. The process involves copying the delivered role into the **Z** or **Y** naming standard, activating associated **OData** and **ICF services**, and automatically generating the role, with an option to create a **test user** for **validation**. This method helps avoid common development issues such as **missing authorizations or OData services**.

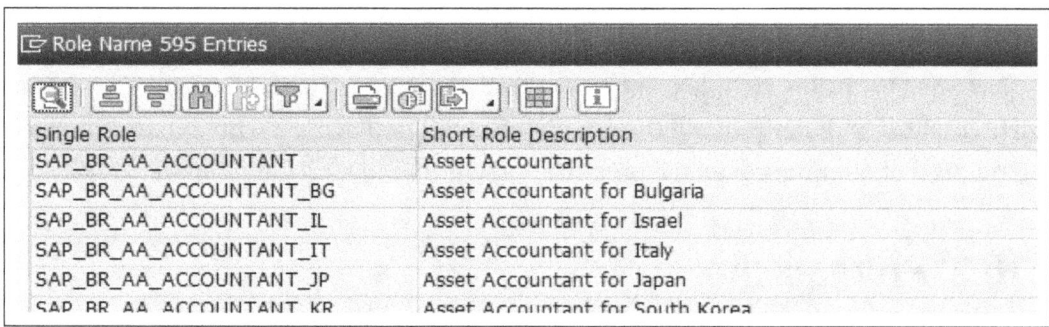

Figure 5-84. *Transaction PFCG listing SAP_BR* roles available within the system*

Activating the Fiori task list **SAP_FIORI_CONTENT_ACTIVATION** is crucial for setting up and configuring SAP Fiori content. This task list simplifies and automates the activation of Fiori applications, roles, catalogs, spaces, pages, and groups. The section covers a high-level overview of this efficient activation process.

Note   This task list allows you to activate one or more business roles. Group functional business roles, such as RTR and PTP teams, come together to simplify maintenance. This saves time and reduces mistakes. The task list can activate all the apps listed below:

- **UI5** (SAP Fiori app)
- **GUI** (GUI transaction)
- **WDA** (ABAP Web Dynpro application)
- **WCF** (Web Client UI Framework)
- **URL** (URL)

CHAPTER 5 SAP FIORI CONFIGURATION

You can run the task list multiple times until all items are activated and the status turns green. If there is an error, you must rerun the task list until everything is green. During initial development in the **sandbox or development system**, the task list **SAP_FIORI_CONTENT_ACTIVATION** is beneficial. It activates all related authorization objects from SU24 and fills the org hierarchy with * values. This task list also automatically activates all related OData and ICF services, generates roles as needed, and creates a unique test user ID for testing purposes. Remember, this task list only works with **SAP_BR*** business roles and not **custom roles**.

The **SAP_BR*** roles include **groups**, **spaces**, and **pages**. However, with the release of S/4HANA 2020, SAP **deprecated the groups concept**, replacing it with enhanced **spaces and pages** that offer improved tile organization within the Fiori Launchpad.

5.10.2 Prerequisite

The **SAP_FIORI_FOUNDATION_S4** task list sets up the essential components of SAP Fiori in S/4HANA. The BASIS team must execute the same before running the task list **SAP_FIORI_CONTENT_ACTIVATION**. Ensure you run this task list only after completing the necessary preliminary steps and entering the mandatory subtask list data. In this example, we will use the ZFIORI_PKG package and its transport, which was created earlier.

5.10.3 Business Role

The SAP-delivered business role **SAP_BR_AA_ACCOUNTANT** will be activated using this task list as an example. This **shell** role includes related tiles, apps, groups, spaces, and pages without authorizations. You can access the role through the transaction code **PFCG**, as shown in the figure below.

CHAPTER 5   SAP FIORI CONFIGURATION

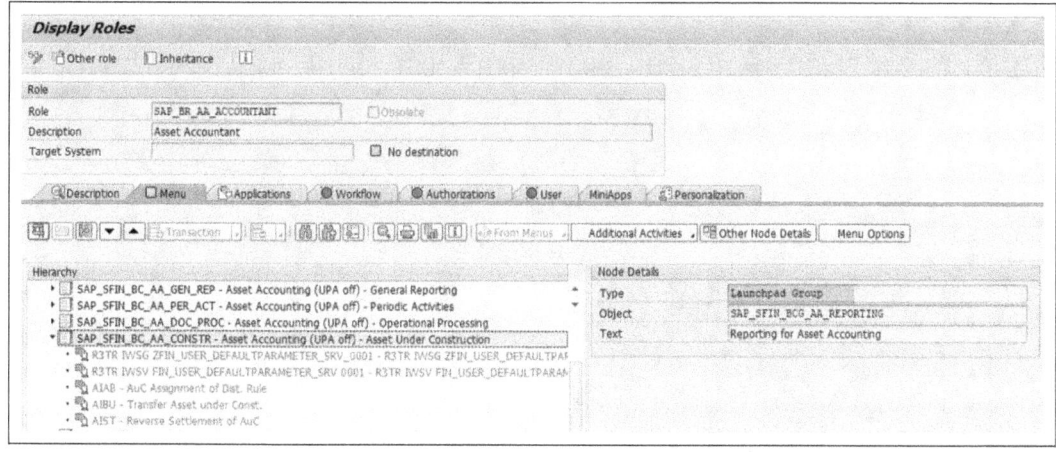

Figure 5-85. SAP business role SAP_BR_AA_ACCOUNTANT and associated business catalogs

The above figure displays various **business catalogs** that are part of the **SAP-BR_AA_ACCOUNTANT** role. Expanding the selected **business catalog**, the SAP_SFIN_BC_BA_CHAIN, displays the associated Fiori apps with their **IWSG/IWSV** components and GUI apps within the role. This, again, means that this is the shell role. This role contains the associated **Launchpad Space**, as shown in the figure below.

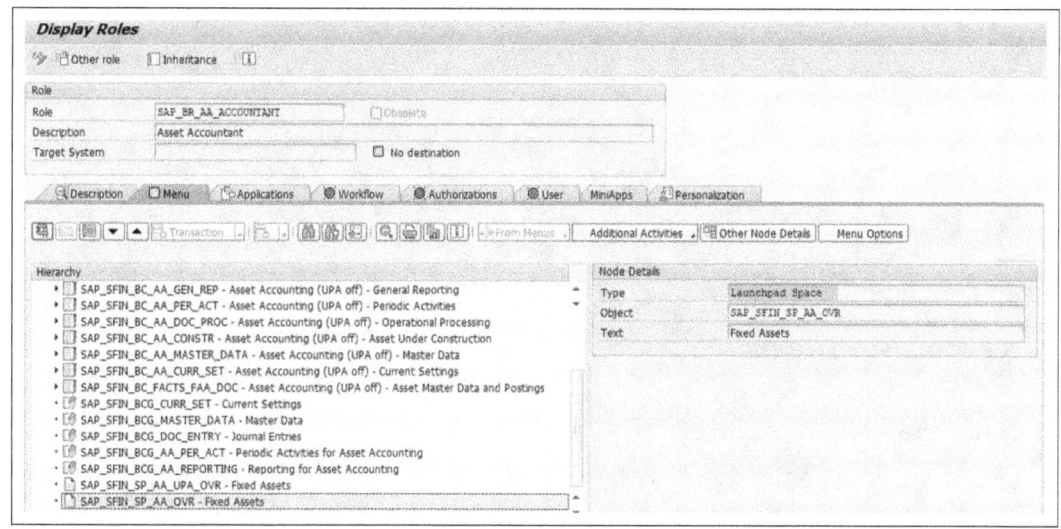

Figure 5-86. Business role with associated Launchpad Space

This version of roles (SAP_BR*) contains **groups**, **spaces**, and **pages**. The below figure displays the business role and the associated **Launchpad Group**.

251

CHAPTER 5 SAP FIORI CONFIGURATION

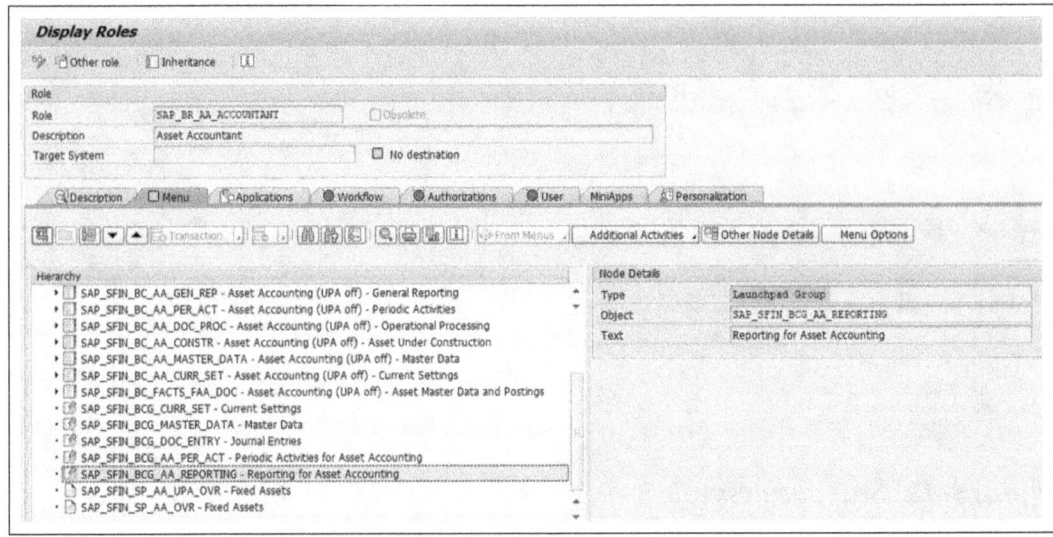

Figure 5-87. *Business role with associated Launchpad Group*

The **Authorizations** ⬤ Authorizations tab is red, meaning it has no maintained profile because the **profile name** is **blank**, as shown in the figure below.

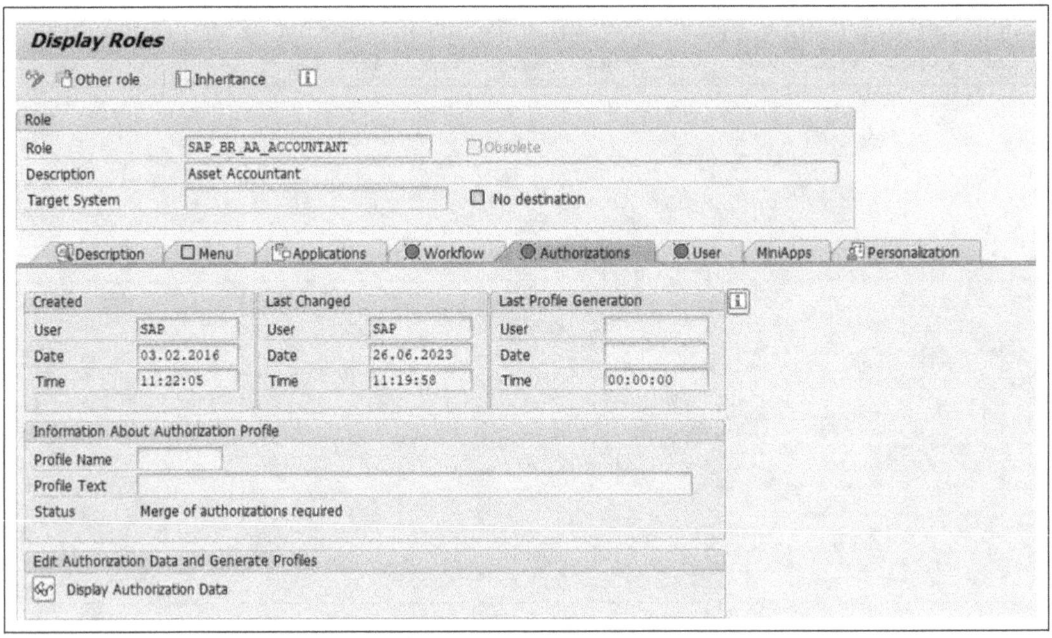

Figure 5-88. *Authorizations tab is red as no profiles are maintained*

252

CHAPTER 5 SAP FIORI CONFIGURATION

Checking the **Display Authorization Data** shows no authorizations are maintained, as shown below.

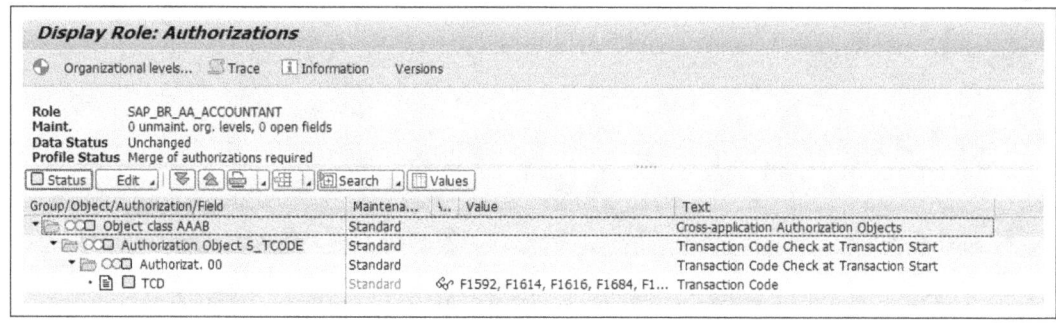

Figure 5-89. PFCG Authorizations tab for the business role with no underlying data

Furthermore, it is highly recommended that you activate the required **OData** and **ICF** before utilizing the task list. Doing so will help you avoid any potential issues and streamline your workflow. The BASIS team would have activated all the services as part of the configuration setup. You can check the services using the T-code **/UI2/FLPCM_CUST**.

5.10.4 Review and Verify the Business Role Contents

Verifying and validating the business role content using transaction code **/UI2/FLPCM_CUST** is crucial, as illustrated in the figure below. Go to the tab Roles. Then under **Search Roles**, enter the desired role name and click **Go** to proceed.

253

CHAPTER 5   SAP FIORI CONFIGURATION

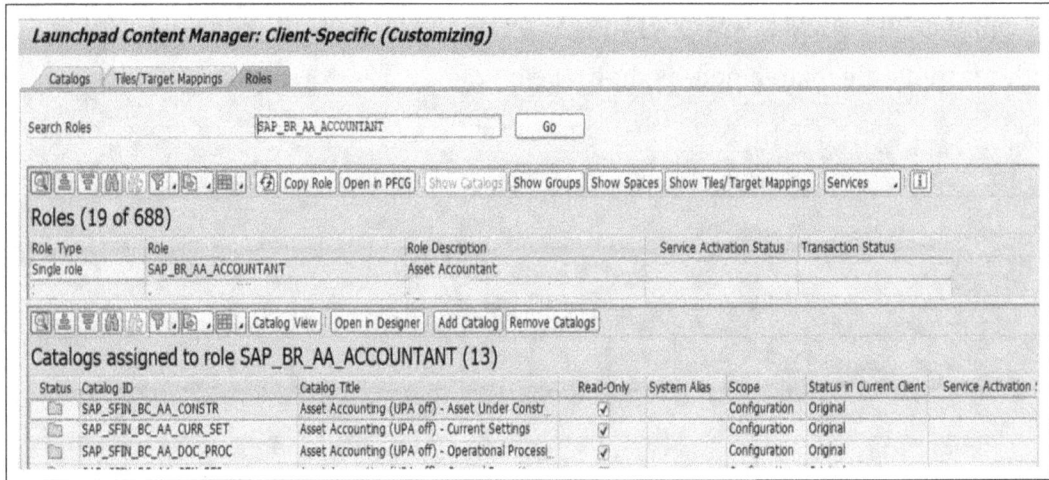

Figure 5-90. *Review business role content*

The above figure displays the business role SAP_BR_AA_ACCOUNTANT along with its business catalogs. Furthermore, the business role displays the number of business catalogs assigned to SAP business roles. This transaction lets you check whether the **OData** and **ICF services** are activated, as discussed in the section below.

Check Relevant Services

The BASIS team should have activated the necessary OData and ICF services. Verifying that all services are **marked green is essential**, as this will help prevent potential issues and ensure a smooth workflow. These services should already be activated as part of the configuration setup. To confirm, navigate to the **Services** tab and review the activation status, as shown in the figure below.

CHAPTER 5   SAP FIORI CONFIGURATION

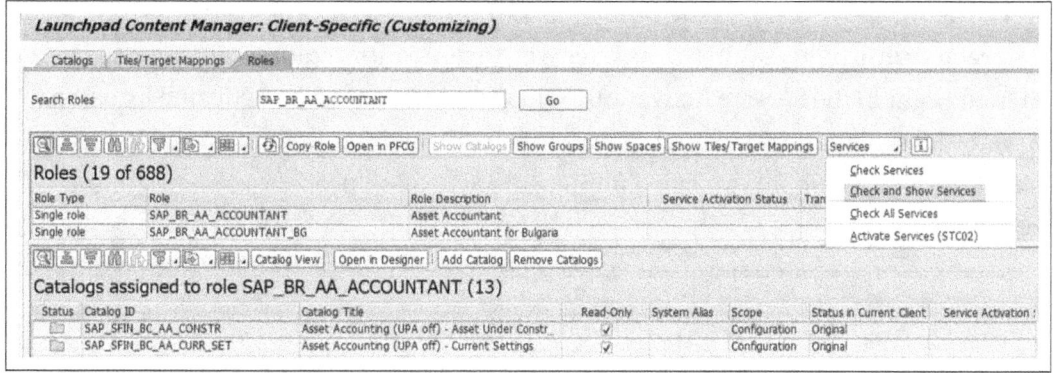

Figure 5-91. *Checking business role services*

Select the option **Check and Show Services** from the pull-down menu of the tab **Services** Services. It will take you to the **OData V2 Service** OData V2 Services tab, as shown in the figure below.

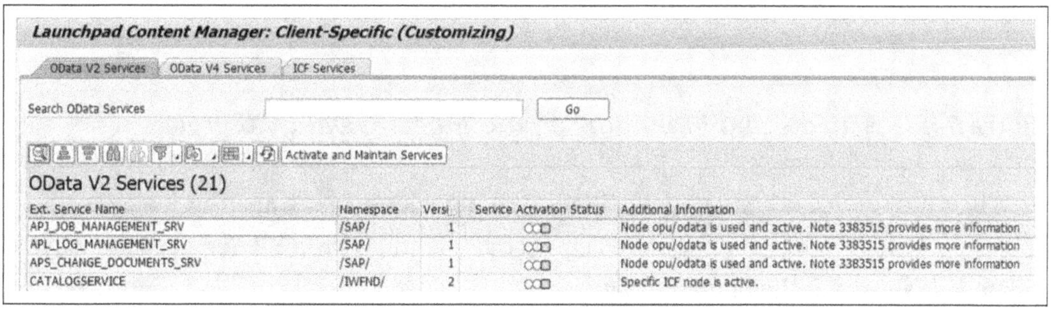

Figure 5-92. *OData V2 services within the business role*

OData V2 Services: Verification

In SAP Fiori, the **Activate and Maintain Services** tab (transaction **/IWFND/MAINT_SERVICE**) is used to activate and manage OData services, which are required for Fiori apps to function correctly. This process registers the service on SAP Gateway, connecting the front-end and back-end systems. Administrators can use this transaction to activate inactive services, manage service catalog entries, and fix service-related issues. Fiori apps cannot access or show data from the SAP system if the required services are not activated.

255

CHAPTER 5   SAP FIORI CONFIGURATION

The figure above displays the number of **OData V2 services** activated, as indicated by a **green traffic light**⚪⚪⚫ in **the Service Activation Status** column. If a service has a red traffic light in the Service Activation Status column, it must be activated by using the Activate and Maintain Services tab. This action will open transaction code **/IWFND/ MAINT_SERVICE**, where you can complete the activation process, as shown in the figure below.

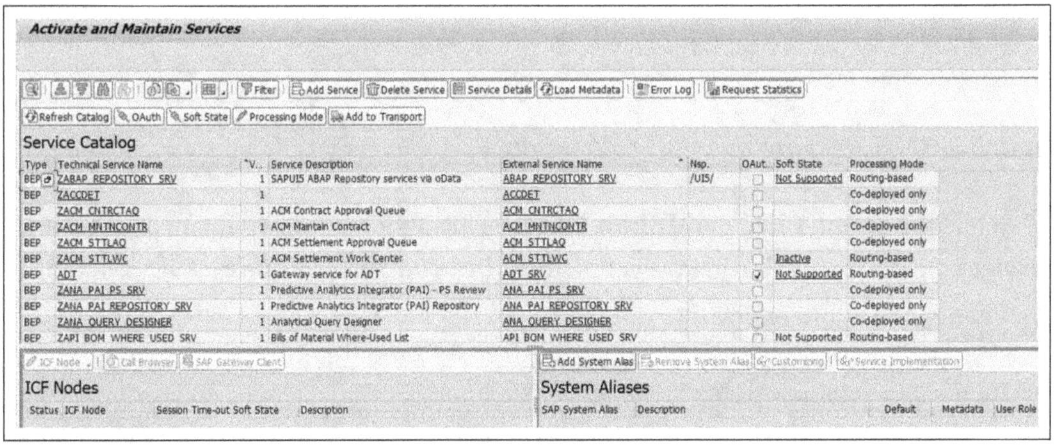

Figure 5-93. Activate and Maintain Services tab for OData V2 services

When the service is activated, it will request a **package** and transport it across the landscape. Once all the services have been activated, the **OData V2 Services** tab will be updated, as shown in the figure below.

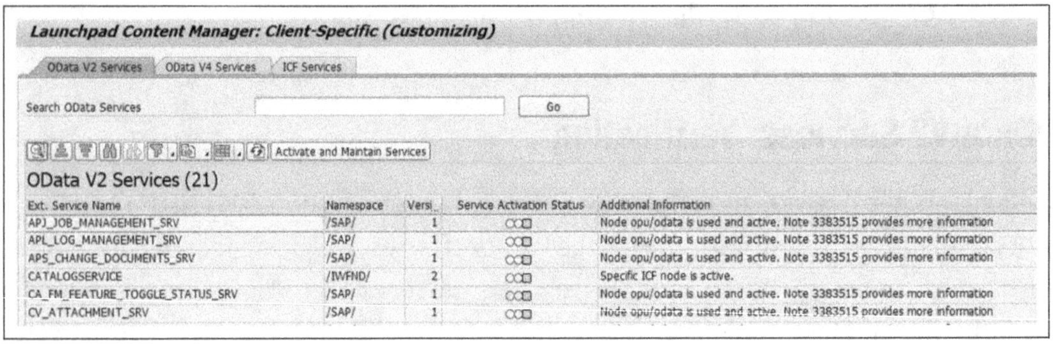

Figure 5-94. All OData V2 services are activated with status in green

CHAPTER 5 SAP FIORI CONFIGURATION

OData V4 Services: Verification

In SAP Fiori, **OData V4 services** enable front-end applications to communicate efficiently with back-end systems using the Open Data Protocol (OData) version 4. OData V4 introduces enhancements such as improved handling of data information, support for complex types, and the capability to make requests without waiting for responses. These features help accelerate the process of gathering and managing data. As a result, SAP Fiori applications can provide a more responsive and rich user experience. Utilizing OData V4 services ensures seamless integration and compatibility across various systems, thereby enhancing the overall efficiency of enterprise applications. No services appear, as shown in the figure below.

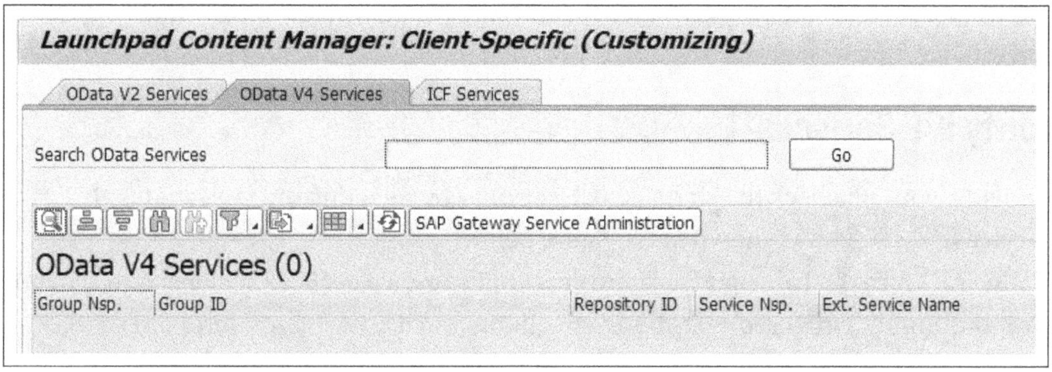

Figure 5-95. *No OData V4 services appear within the business role*

If the services have a **red traffic light** status, to activate these **OData V4 services** in SAP Fiori, click the **SAP Gateway Service Administration** tab to open the transaction **/IWFND/V4_ADMIN** and activate the services. This allows you to manage OData services, facilitating communication between front-end and back-end systems. Key tasks include registering services for user access, handling version control for updates, and maintaining documentation for each service. Monitoring tools also track service usage and performance, helping administrators quickly identify and resolve issues. Effective administration ensures the smooth operation of Fiori applications by enabling seamless data exchange between system components. Selecting **SAP Gateway Service Administration** displays the window to maintain the services, as shown in the figure below.

CHAPTER 5 SAP FIORI CONFIGURATION

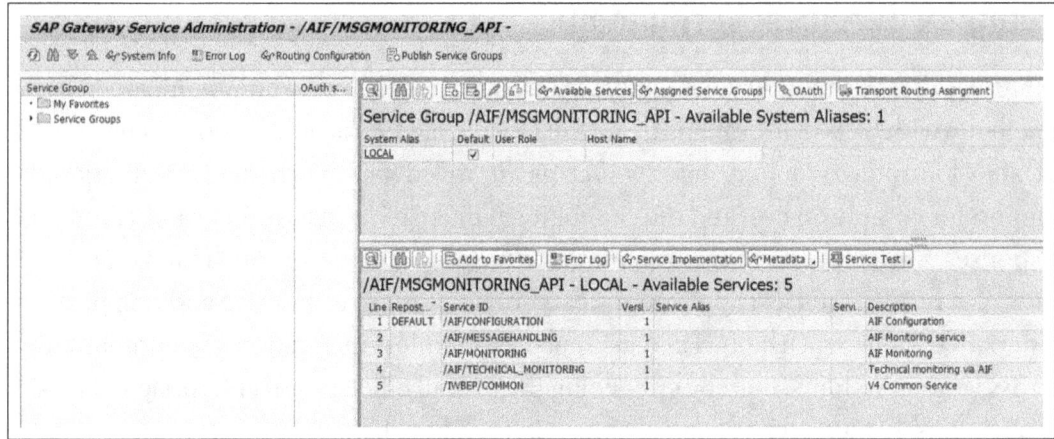

Figure 5-96. SAP Gateway Service Administration window to maintain services

Verify ICF Services

Similarly, you can check the status of **ICF services** by selecting the relevant tab, **ICF Services** ICF Services, as shown in the figure below.

In SAP Fiori, **the Internet Communication Framework (ICF) services are crucial for handling HTTP(S) requests between clients**, such as web browsers, and the SAP system. ICF connects the Internet Communication Manager (ICM) with HTTP-enabled ABAP applications, enabling smooth communication using standard protocols such as HTTP and HTTPS. Administrators manage these services through the transaction SICF, where services are organized hierarchically. It is crucial to activate only the necessary ICF services for security reasons, as active services can be accessed via the internet, which may expose the system to unauthorized access.

The ICF Services tab indicates that services are all activated, as denoted by the **green traffic light** in the figure below.

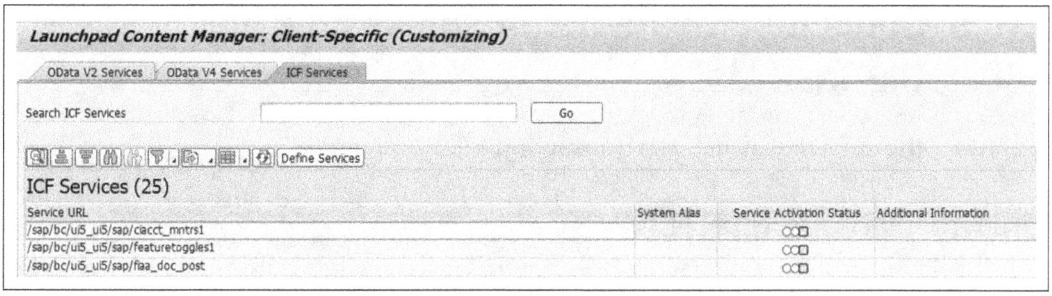

CHAPTER 5   SAP FIORI CONFIGURATION

Figure 5-97. Business role associated with ICF services

If some ICF services show red traffic lights, they must be set up and activated. To activate a service, click the **Define Services** Define Services tab. This will take you to the SICF transaction, where you can activate the service that needs attention, as shown in the figure below.

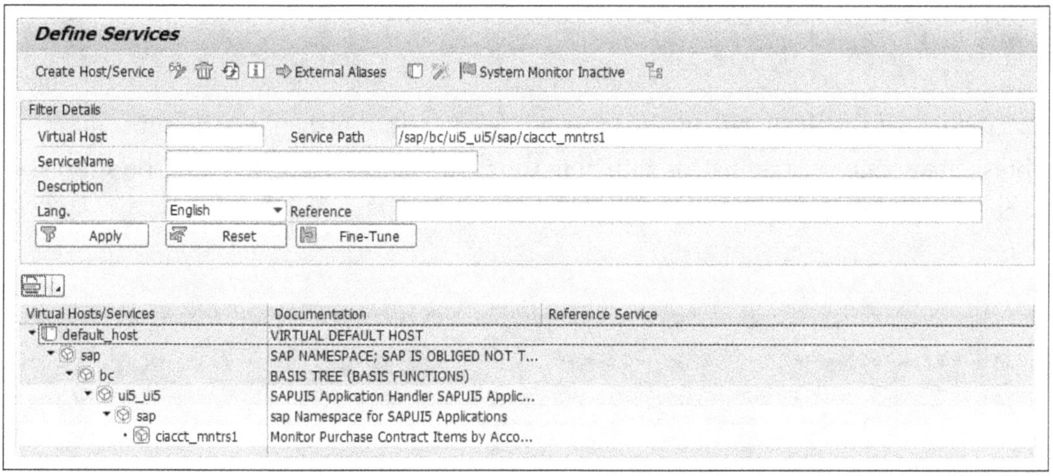

Figure 5-98. Define Services window, which is the same as transaction SICF

Note   To ensure a smooth role activation process, you should activate all associated **OData services** beforehand. The next step illustrates how to streamline this task using the task list **SAP_FIORI_CONTENT_ACTIVATION**. This task list will also activate the relevant ICF services associated with the OData.

259

CHAPTER 5 SAP FIORI CONFIGURATION

5.10.5 Steps to Activate the Business Role via the Task List

To activate the current task list, use transaction STC01.

Execute Transaction STC01

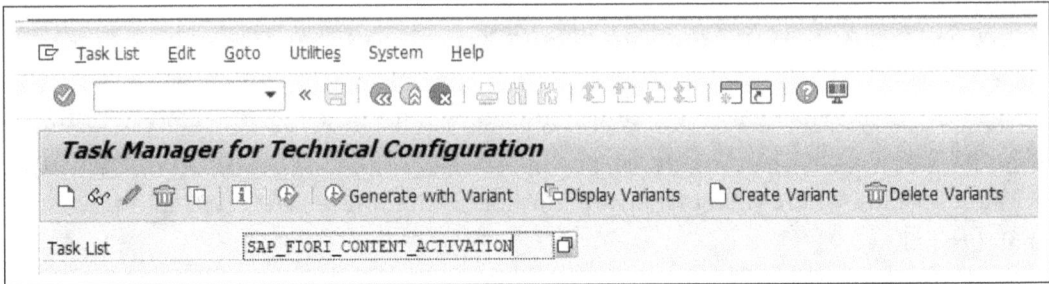

Figure 5-99. Task list to be executed

Execute the task list by using the icon . A new window displays the subsequent subtask list within the task list, as shown in the figure below. Here, a few of the subtasks are self-explanatory and will not be covered.

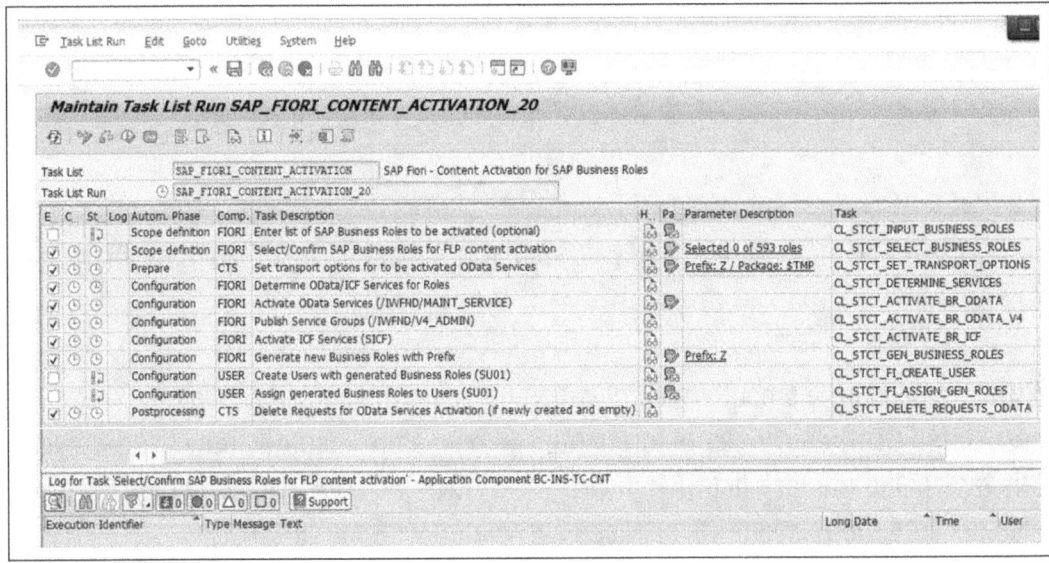

Figure 5-100. Executed task list displaying its subtask list

CHAPTER 5 SAP FIORI CONFIGURATION

The figure above displays the task and subtask list that require updates. It shows that SAP has **593 business roles** available for activation. This task list allows you to activate single or multiple business roles simultaneously.

Enter list of SAP Business Roles to be activated (optional)

This step is used when activating a given set of business roles. This step will be covered later in this section. You can enter defined business roles to be activated on the screen below.

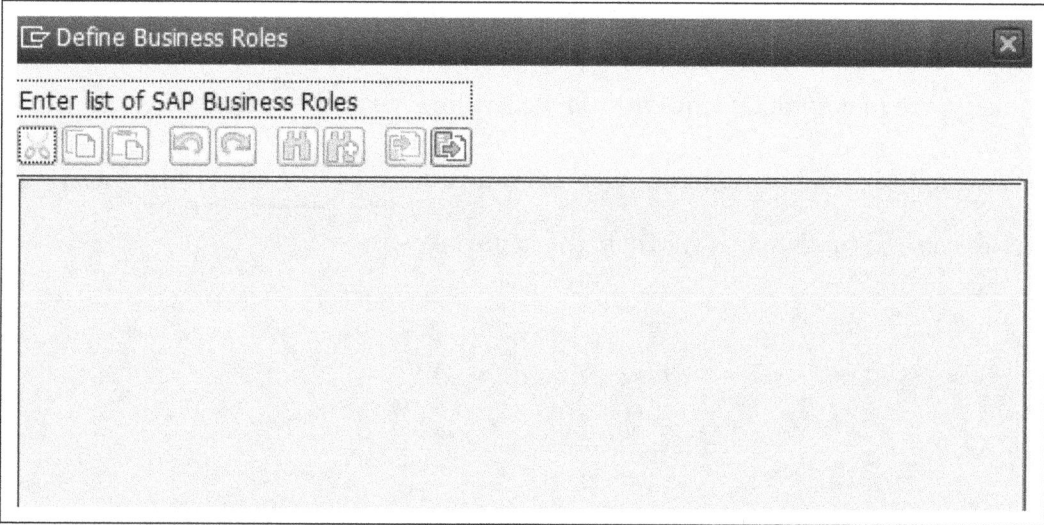

Figure 5-101. In this screen, you can enter the list of business roles to be activated

Select/Confirm SAP Business Roles for FLP content activation

This subtask selects SAP business roles (**SAP_BR***) for **activating FLP content**. For example, we will activate the SAP-delivered business role **SAP_BR_GL_ACCOUNT**. Select the parameter option, which will list all business roles. Enter the business role name in the field **Filter** and click the **filter icon**, and it will find the role as shown in the figure below.

261

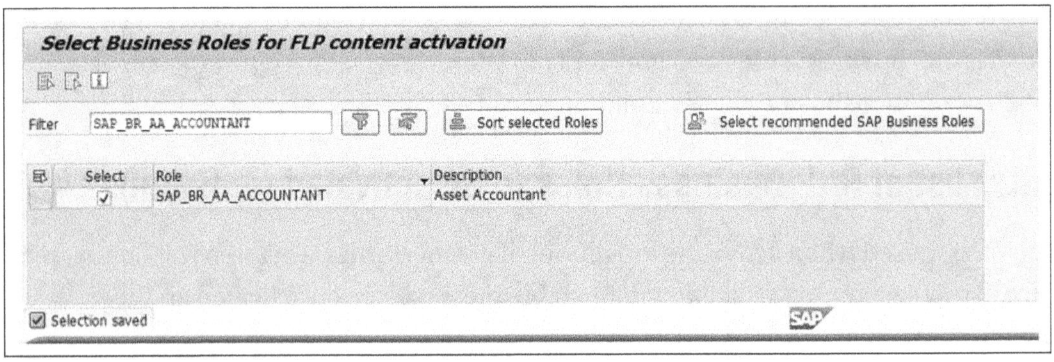

CHAPTER 5   SAP FIORI CONFIGURATION

Figure 5-102. SAP-delivered role selected for activation

Select the role, complete the entry, and click the **save** icon . A new message appears at the bottom of the screen, **Selection saved** . **Go back**, and the subtask list is updated, as shown in the figure below.

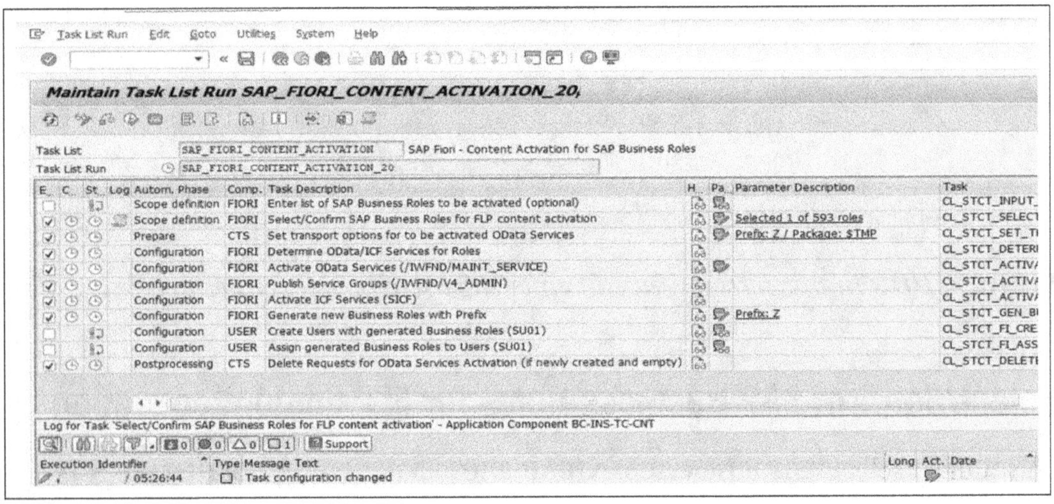

Figure 5-103. One business role selected

Set transport options for to be activated OData Services

This subtask defines and sets transport options for activating OData services. We will use **ZFIORI_PKG** and the associated transports created earlier.

CHAPTER 5 SAP FIORI CONFIGURATION

Generate new Business Roles with Prefix

The next step involves entering details for creating new roles with the proper naming conventions. Therefore, under the **Task Description** header and **Generate new Business Roles with Prefix**, click the parameter icon and select the **prefix** for the role defined by SAP **Z** or **Y**, as shown in the figure below.

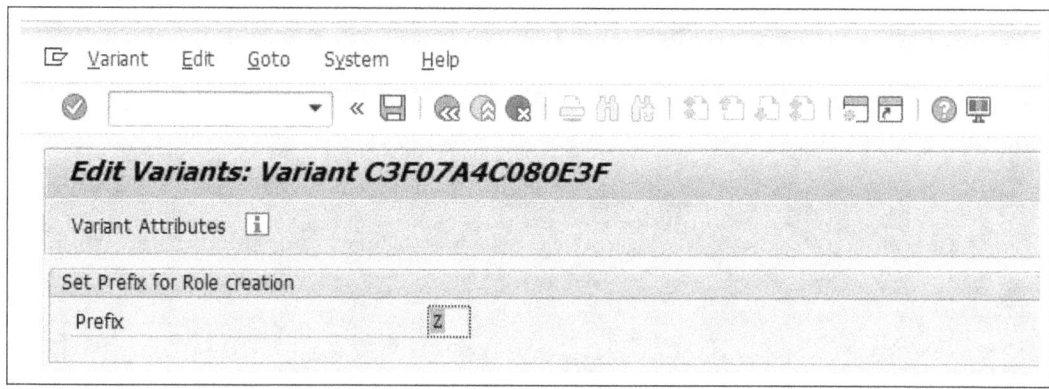

Figure 5-104. Role prefix screen

ZMU is a three-character prefix that means as follows:

- **Z:** Custom name space
- **M:** Master role
- **U:** Update

Figure 5-105. Prefix ZMU added

Now click the save icon . A message will appear at the bottom of the screen, indicating that the **values of the variant have been saved**. Now click the **go-back icon** , and the prefix **ZMU** is displayed in the task list, as shown in the figure below. The new role will start with **ZMU**.

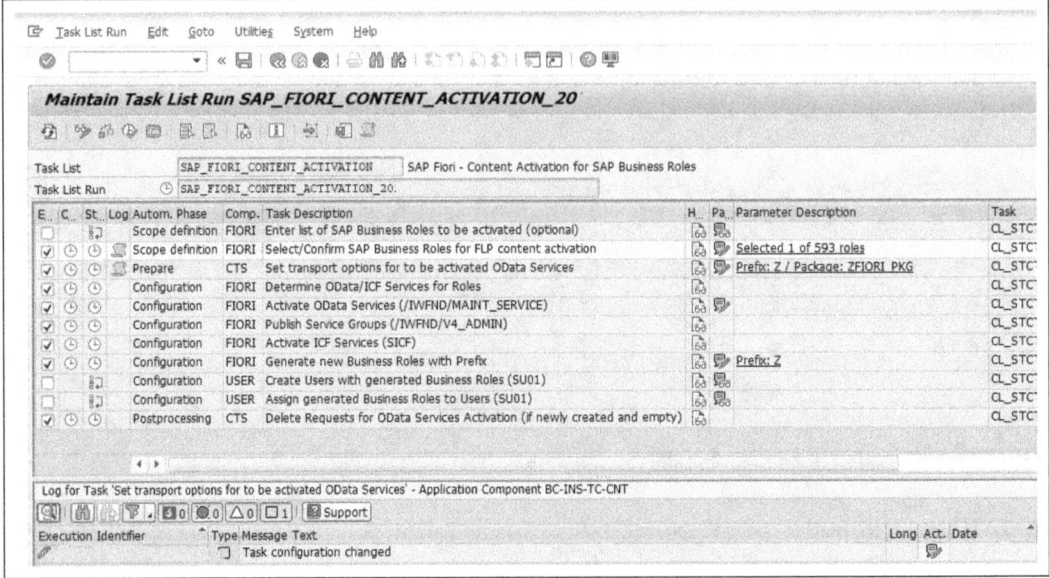

Figure 5-106. *Task list showing the prefix added*

Create Users with generated Business Roles (SU01)

The subtask will create a **test user ID** with the assigned activated business role. Now select the option Create Users with generated Business Roles (SU01).

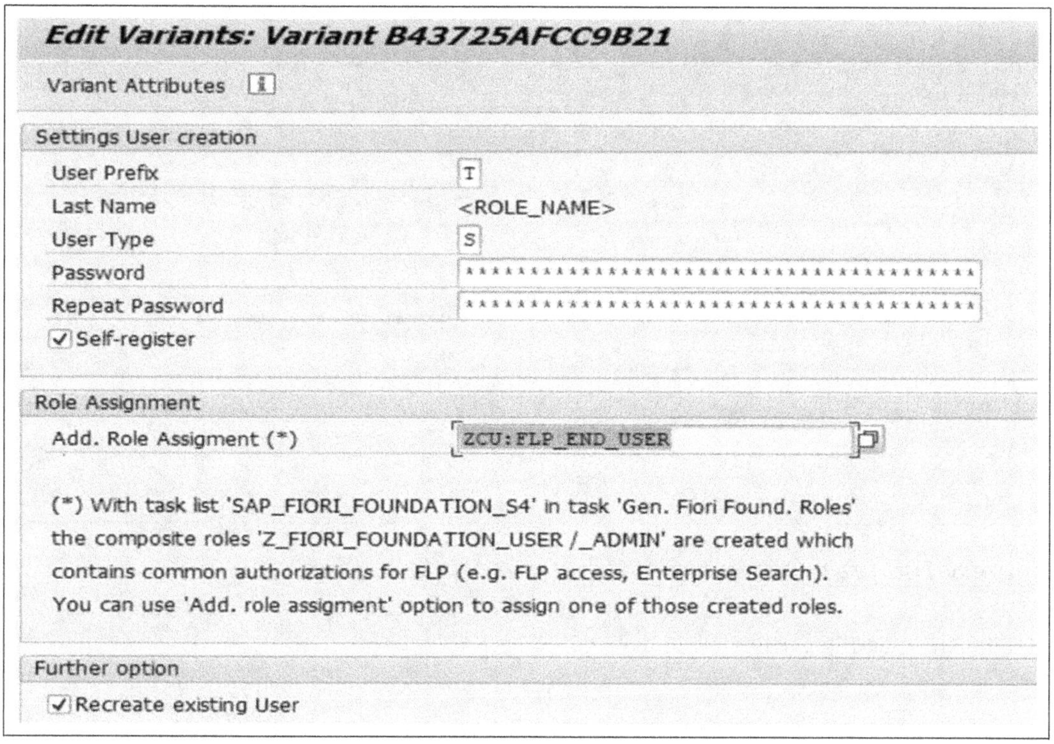

CHAPTER 5 SAP FIORI CONFIGURATION

Figure 5-107. Define a test user ID

Here, we can maintain the **User Type, Password**, and **Add Role Assignment**. The typical end user role should be added here. Click **Save**, and a message will appear at the bottom of the screen, displaying the values of the variant are saved. Click the go-back icon to save changes.

CHAPTER 5 SAP FIORI CONFIGURATION

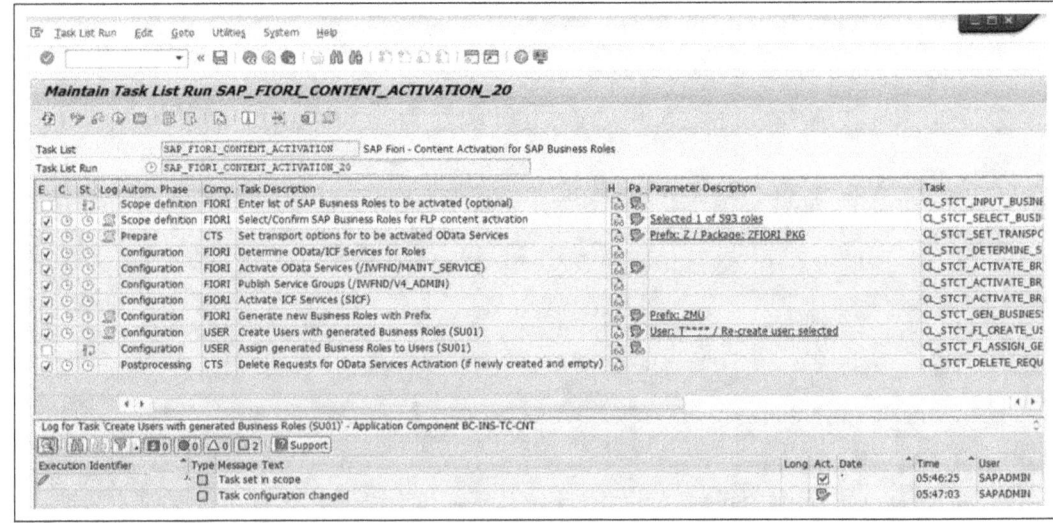

Figure 5-108. *Task list updated with test user information*

Click to save the setting.

5.10.6 Completed Task List

The updated final task list is ready for execution as shown in the figure below.

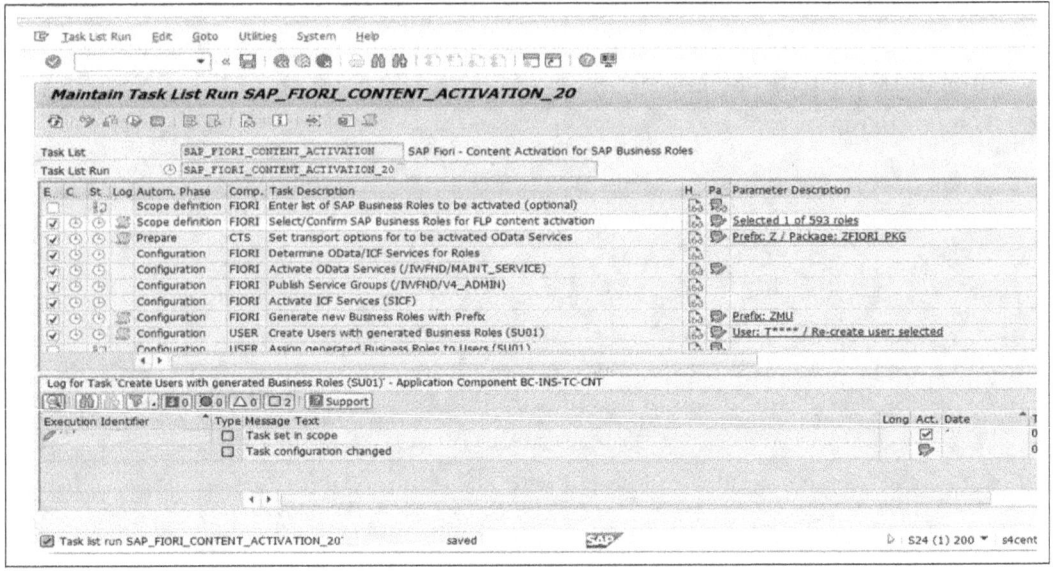

Figure 5-109. *Task list ready for execution*

CHAPTER 5   SAP FIORI CONFIGURATION

Once the task list is saved, a message at the bottom of the screen will state that the **task list run is saved**.

5.10.7 Execute the Task List in Foreground Mode

After entering the configuration input, click the execute icon ⊕ to run the task list. You can run the task list in dialog or background mode for one role and schedule a background job for multiple roles. Once the task list is completed, the output is shown with **green status boxes**, as illustrated in the figure below. It also confirms that user **T1_AAAC** was created as a test user.

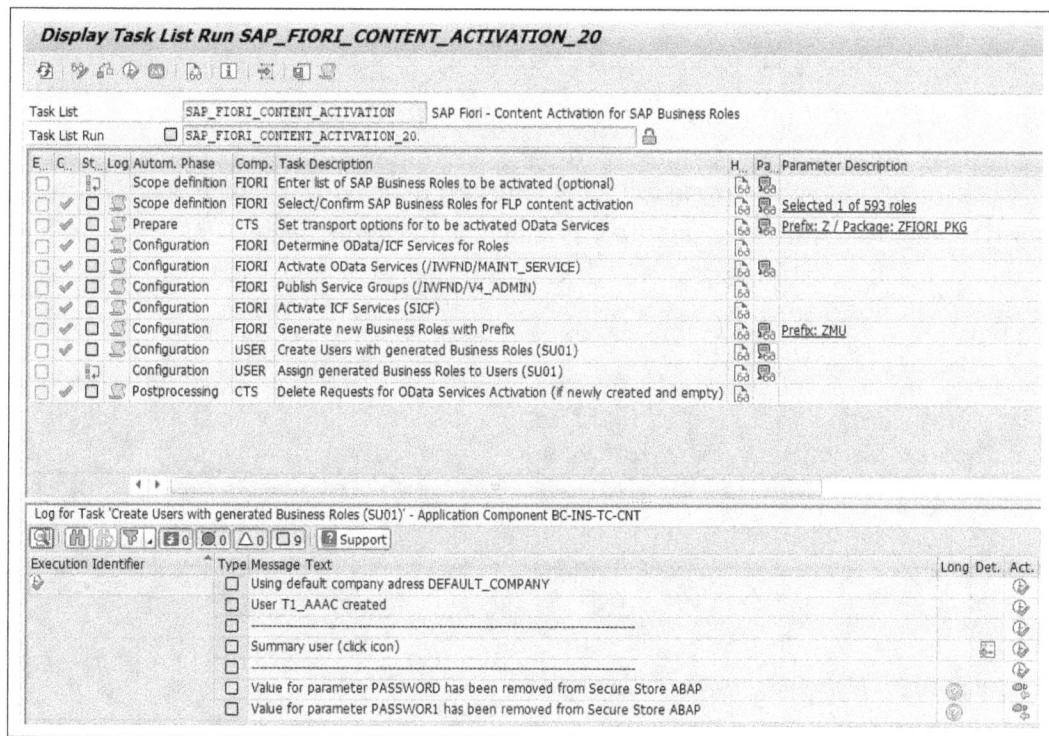

Figure 5-110. The task list was executed successfully

Note   It is always a good practice to review the logs 🗒 for errors or warnings that might provide insights into potential issues. In this case, everything is normal, as shown in the figure below.

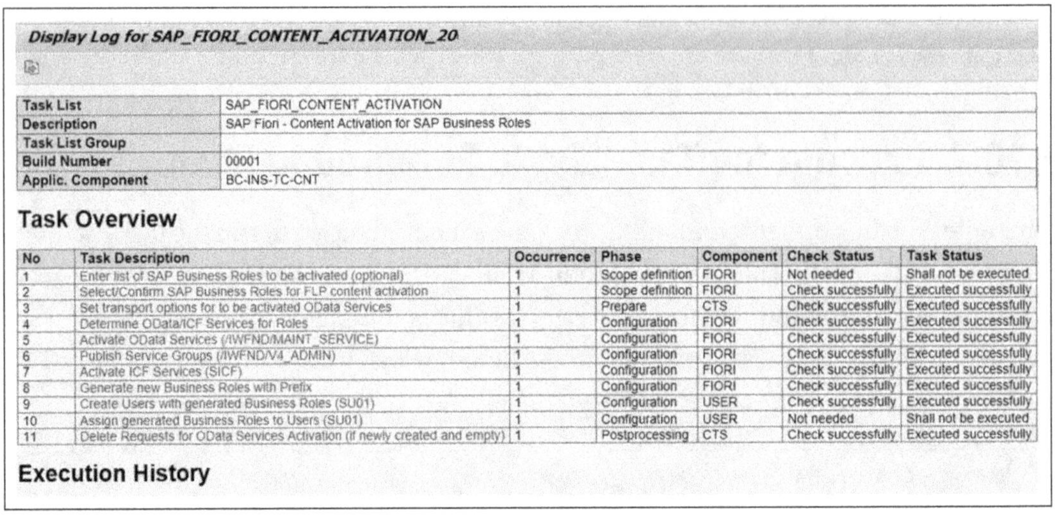

CHAPTER 5   SAP FIORI CONFIGURATION

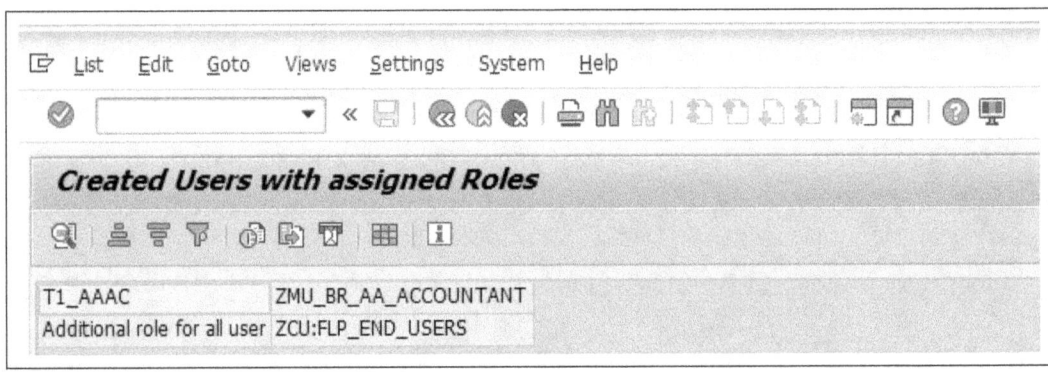

Figure 5-111. Display the logs of the task list executed

Click the option **Summary user (Click icon)** from the output, which displays the **user ID** created and the **roles** assigned, as shown in the figure below.

Figure 5-112. User assignment displayed

Note   The new role created is ZMU_BR_AA_ACCOUNTANT, as shown in the figure above. Within the role, SAP was replaced by **ZMU**; the prefix was given in the subtask list.

CHAPTER 5 SAP FIORI CONFIGURATION

5.10.8 Verify the Business Role Generated

The subsequent step entails checking and validating the business role created within the transaction **PFCG**. This will confirm whether the expected **IWSG/IWSV** components are present as specified in the SAP Fiori Apps Reference Library.

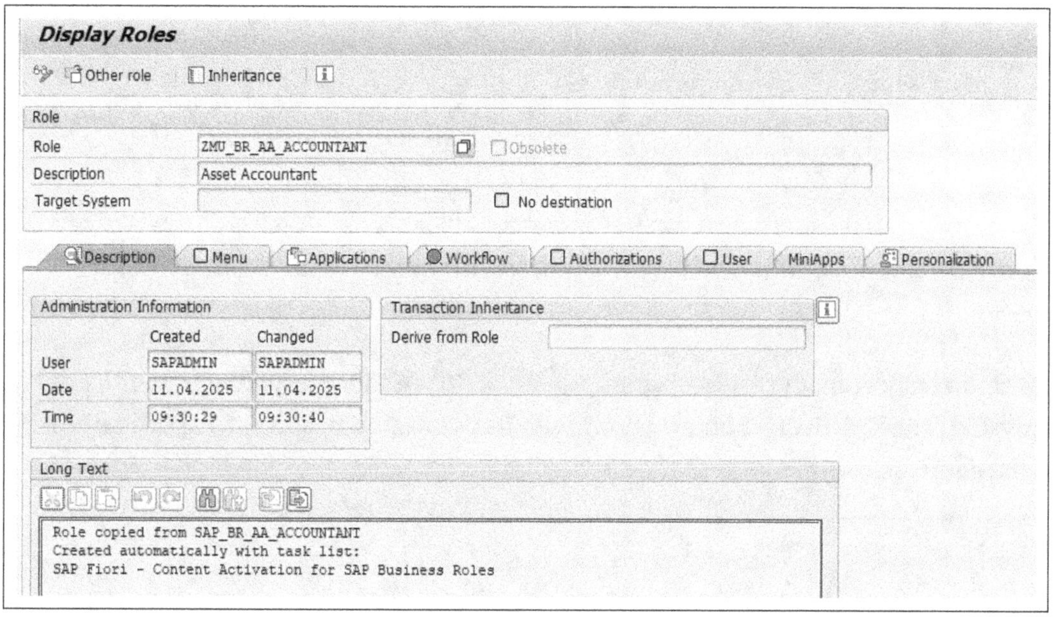

Figure 5-113. PFCG screenshot of the new business role created by using the task list

The role description clearly outlines the role information, and all tabs are displayed in **green**. The Authorizations and Menu tabs are green, which means the authorization was generated and was assigned to the user.

Expanding the tab ☐ Menu shows the activated **catalogs** along with the **IWSG/IWSV** components that are needed for **tiles/apps** to function correctly, as shown in the figure below.

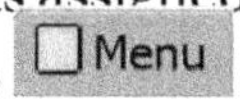

269

CHAPTER 5   SAP FIORI CONFIGURATION

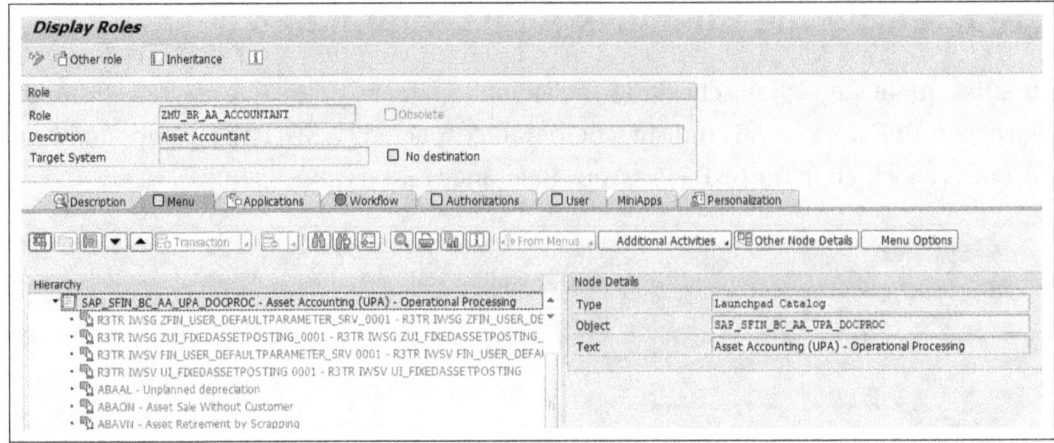

Figure 5-114. *Catalogs and IWSG/IWSV components in the Menu structure of the role*

Upon inspecting the Authorizations ☐ Authorizations tab, everything is in order and activated. The **S_SERVICE** object, along with its associated **hash** values, is also displayed in the figure below.

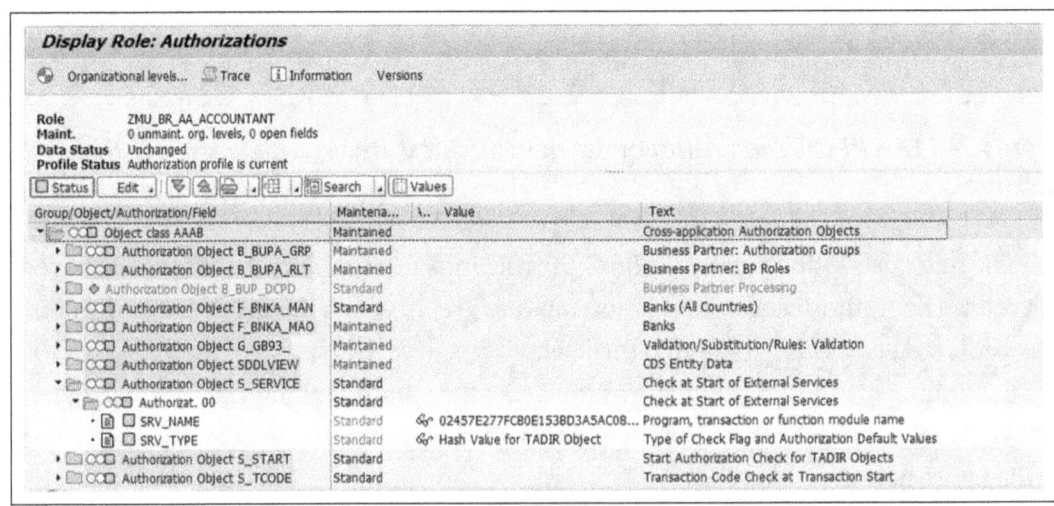

Figure 5-115. *Authorizations tab data with authorization objects displayed for S_SERVICE*

The object **S_TCODE** content is displayed in the figure below.

270

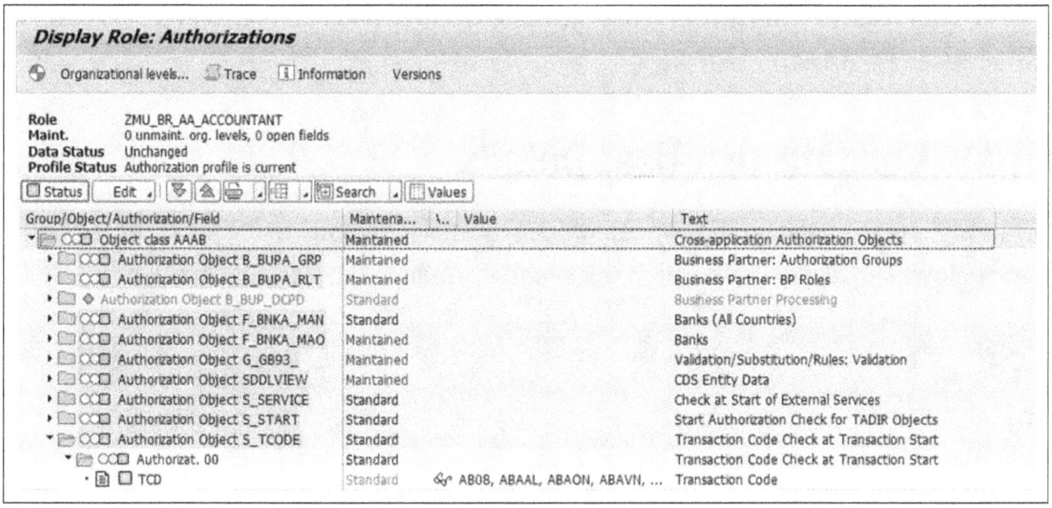

CHAPTER 5 SAP FIORI CONFIGURATION

Figure 5-116. Authorizations tab data with authorization objects displayed for S_TCODE

In the above figure, all open values for any object are maintained with a * value, all **org values** are kept as *, and the role is generated. Selecting Organizational levels... opens a window titled **Define Organizational Level**, which was maintained as * by the task list as shown in the figure below. Now check for the user **T1_AAAC** in the tab ☐User and the business role is assigned, as shown in the figure below.

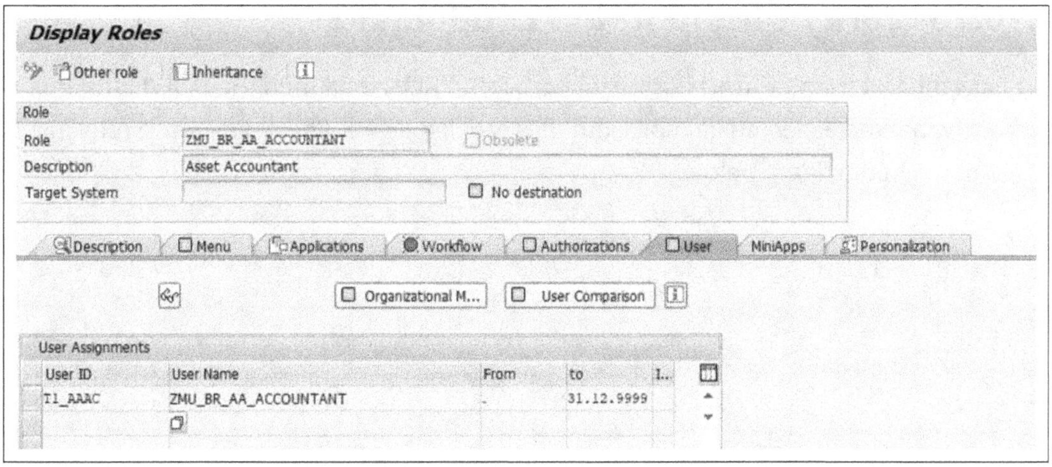

Figure 5-117. Test user ID was created

271

The figure above confirms that the business role has been activated and assigned to the new user **T1_AAAC**.

5.10.9 Validate Test User Details

The newly created user can be validated using transaction code **SU01**, as depicted in the figure below. The test user has three roles in the profile, as also shown in the figure.

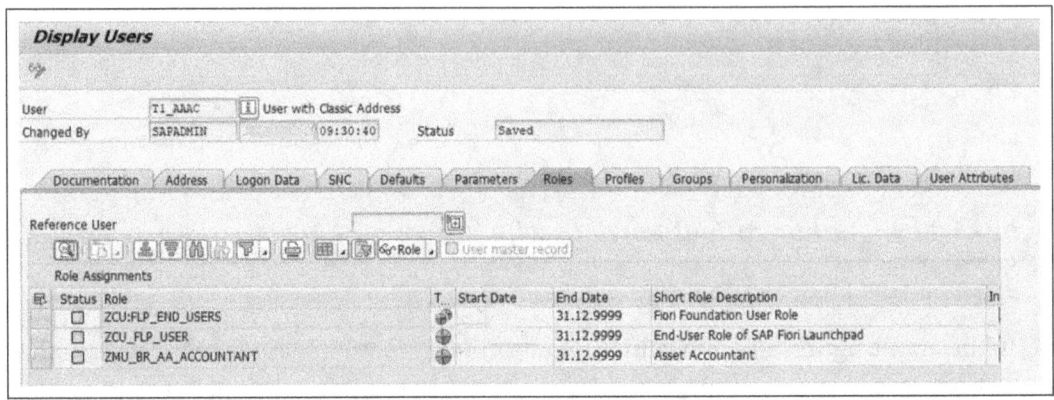

Figure 5-118. *Roles assigned to the test user*

5.10.10 Verify Output in the Launchpad

Log in as the test user **T1_AAAC** (transaction: /UI2/FLP) to launch the Fiori Launchpad and verify that the expected catalogs and tiles are displayed. The user successfully logged in, as shown in the figure below.

CHAPTER 5   SAP FIORI CONFIGURATION

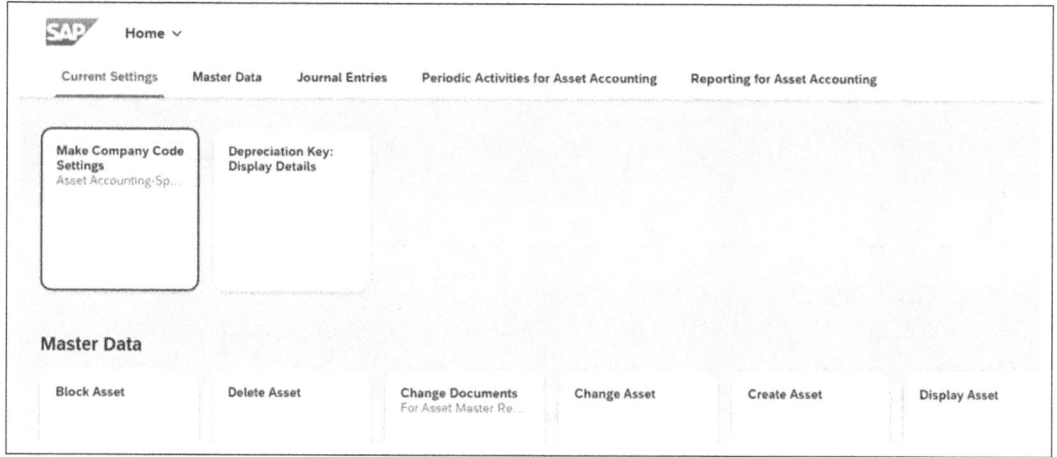

Figure 5-119. *Test user logged in successfully into the Fiori Launchpad, and groups are displayed with tiles*

To enable **spaces**, go to the **User Menu**, select **Settings**, then select the tab **Spaces and Pages**, and choose the **Use Spaces** option. This will update the SAP Fiori Launchpad home page to display **Spaces and Pages**, as illustrated in the figure below.

Figure 5-120. *Launchpad displaying Spaces and Pages*

The tile **Asset Accounting Overview** is launched successfully, as shown in the figure below.

273

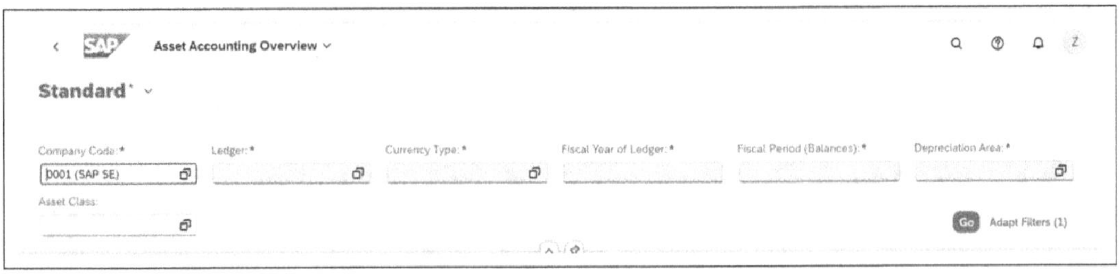

CHAPTER 5 SAP FIORI CONFIGURATION

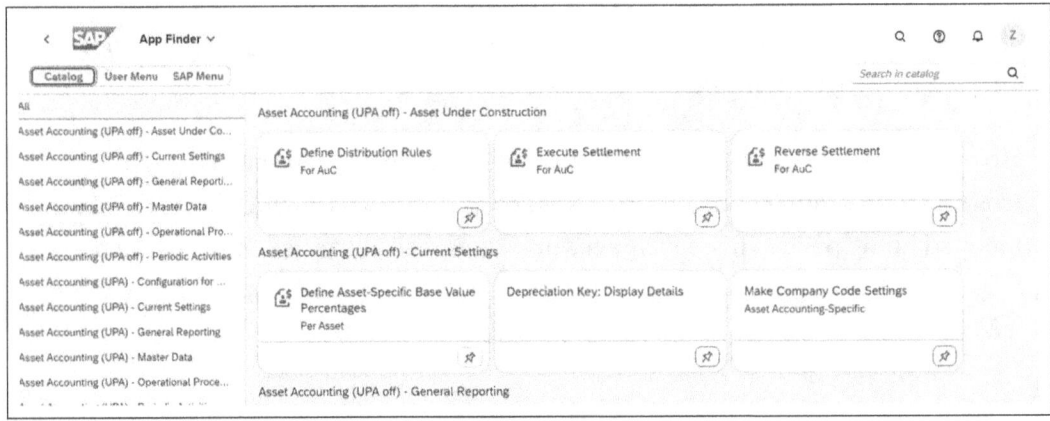

Figure 5-121. *Tile executed successfully*

Users can view related catalogs under the tab Catalog `Catalog` and associated tiles and apps by selecting the tab, as shown in the figure below.

Figure 5-122. *App Finder showing catalogs and apps*

In the SAP Fiori App Finder, the **User Menu** `User Menu` tab displays apps and transactions tailored to the user's roles, like the old **SAP GUI** menu. It reflects what the user is authorized to access. Meanwhile, the SAP Menu `SAP Menu` tab displays the entire system menu, listing all standard transactions and applications regardless of individual roles, though access is still subject to authorizations.

CHAPTER 5 SAP FIORI CONFIGURATION

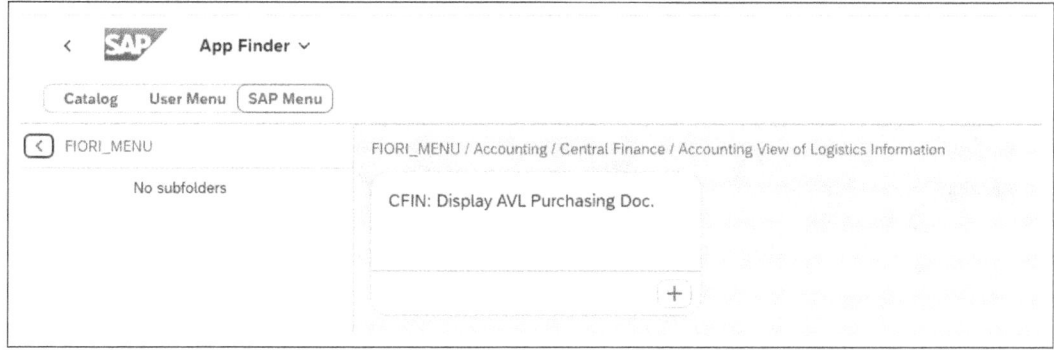

Figure 5-123. *Within the App Finder, SAP Menu tab with tiles displayed*

You can use the transaction code **/UI2/FLPCA** to view the contents of the activated role.

Similarly, the **User Menu** screen appears as in the figure below.

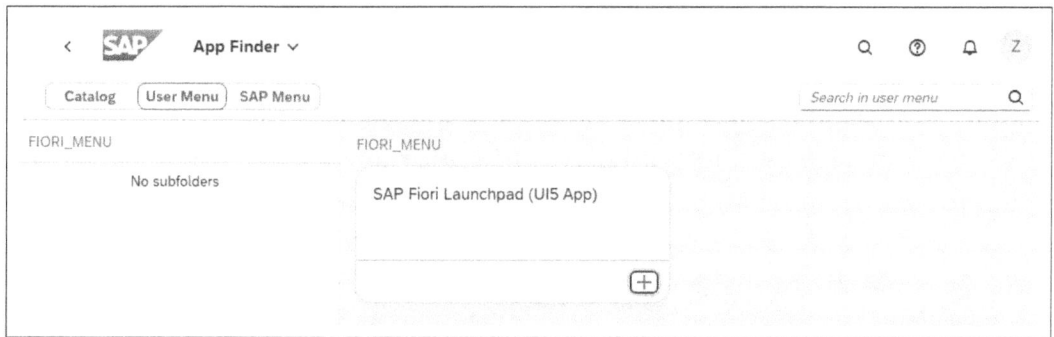

Figure 5-124. *Within the App Finder, User Menu tab*

The **My Home** tab is displayed, as shown in the figure below.

275

CHAPTER 5   SAP FIORI CONFIGURATION

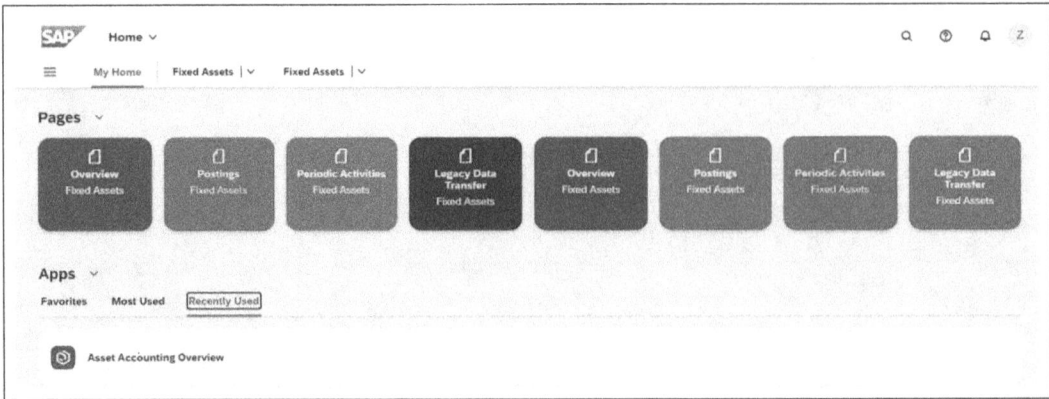

Figure 5-125. My Home with a recently added space

Activate Multiple Business Roles

The task list offers the capability to activate multiple business roles simultaneously. To do so, select the option FIORI Enter list of SAP Business Roles to be activated (optional), and a window titled **Define Business Roles** opens to enter multiple roles. You can conveniently import a list of roles from a file using the **Upload from Clipboard** icon as shown in the figure below. You can also type each role if desired.

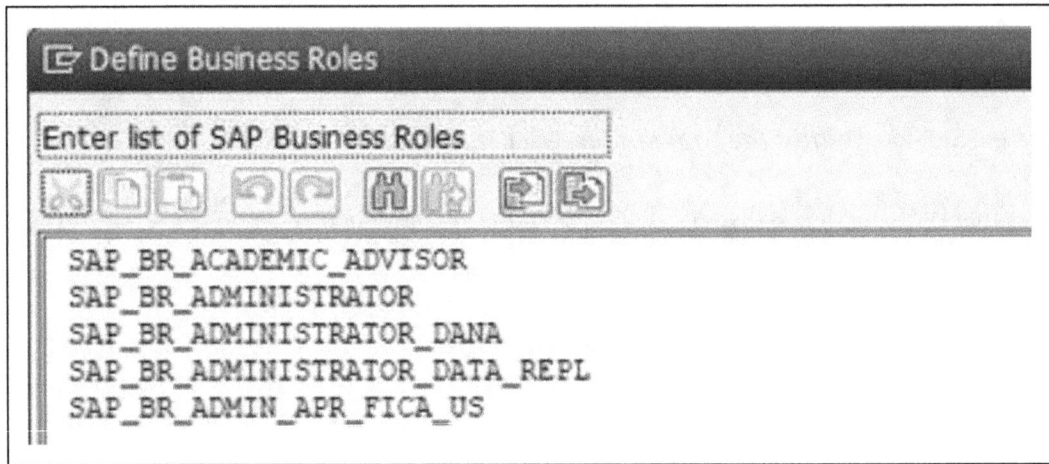

Figure 5-126. Inserting multiple roles into the task list

The final screen for the task list will look as shown in the figure below.

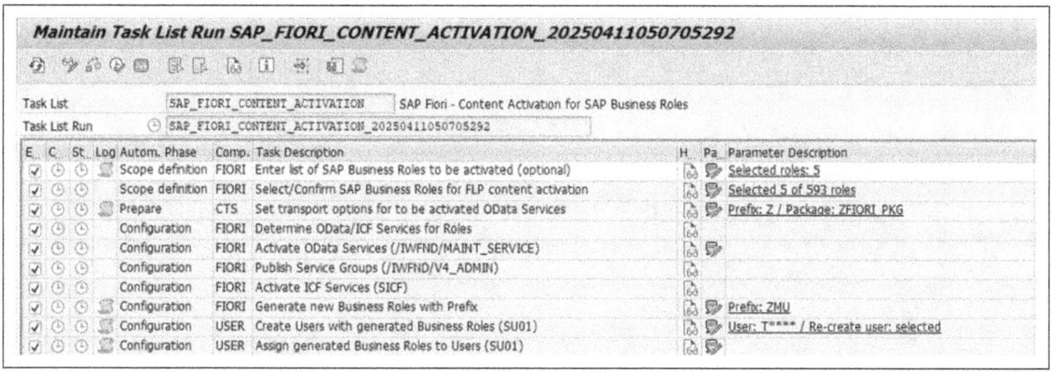

CHAPTER 5　SAP FIORI CONFIGURATION

Figure 5-127. Multiple roles selected for activation

Note Five roles were entered, and the task list will create five test users with a single role assignment and a common end user role.

Assign Generated Business Roles to Users (SU01)

This new option allows the newly created business role to be assigned to a group of users for testing, as illustrated in the following figure.

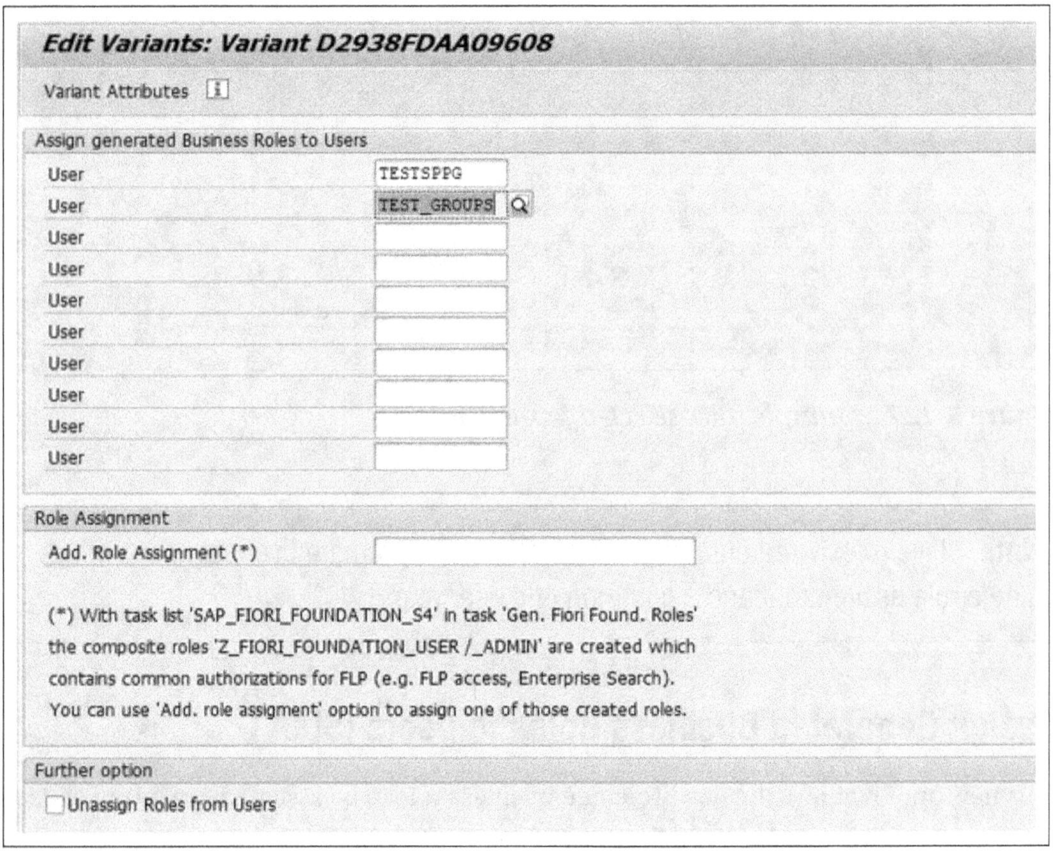

CHAPTER 5   SAP FIORI CONFIGURATION

Figure 5-128. Insert user IDs for the activated business role

5.10.11 Additional Resources

The SAP Help Portal provides detailed documentation on Fiori task lists and their configurations. You should also review the relevant SAP Notes, which provide additional guidance and troubleshooting tips for the activation process. You can also utilize the SAP community forums and discussion boards to ask questions and share experiences with other SAP professionals.

5.10.12 Summary

This section outlines the steps necessary to activate SAP-delivered best practice business roles, beginning with the SA_BR* nomenclature and utilizing the SAP task list **SAP_FIORI_CONTENT_ACTIVATION**. Following these steps and recommendations, you can effectively activate the task list and streamline your organization's deployment of SAP Fiori content.

5.11 Task List 8: SAP_FIORI_FCM_CONTENT_ACTIVATION

5.11.1 Introduction

This section outlines the process of activating SAP-delivered best practice business roles (SAP_BR*) using the task list **SAP_FIORI_FCM_CONTENT_ACTIVATION** to create custom business roles (CBRs) (Z*), following a specific role-naming convention. This approach is based on the SAP Fiori Content Activation task list. SAP_BR* roles are shell roles containing links to spaces, pages, groups, and catalogs. By copying these roles into custom business roles and activating them through the task list, you automatically include all related components within the development systems. This method enables the selective activation of content for production environments and generates transports for that content. The generated roles can be customized using transaction PFCG, and the Mass Transport option facilitates moving roles across the landscape. This section provides a step-by-step guide to activating the SAP_BR_GL_ACCOUNTANT role in development systems, offering practical insights for BASIS and security teams.

Create a **GUI script** to copy **SAP_BR*** roles into custom roles (**Z***) and update them using the task list. The task list can be executed multiple times in the development system, allowing you to activate the required apps based on your project scope. This flexibility enables the generation of various transports or the use of a dedicated transport to capture services activated during the role update. You can move the roles across the landscape using the Mass Transport option.

CHAPTER 5 SAP FIORI CONFIGURATION

Prerequisite

Assuming the task list **SAP_FIORI_FOUNDATION_S4** has been implemented, copy the **SAP_BR_AA_ACCOUNTANT** into a new role, for example:

- ZMU:BR_AA_ACCOUNTANT_TEST:XXXX

The above role is a master role with the following nomenclature:

- **Z:** Custom name space
- **M:** Master role
- **U:** Update
- **XXXX:** Company code, plant, sales organization, etc.

The copied role is as displayed in the figure below.

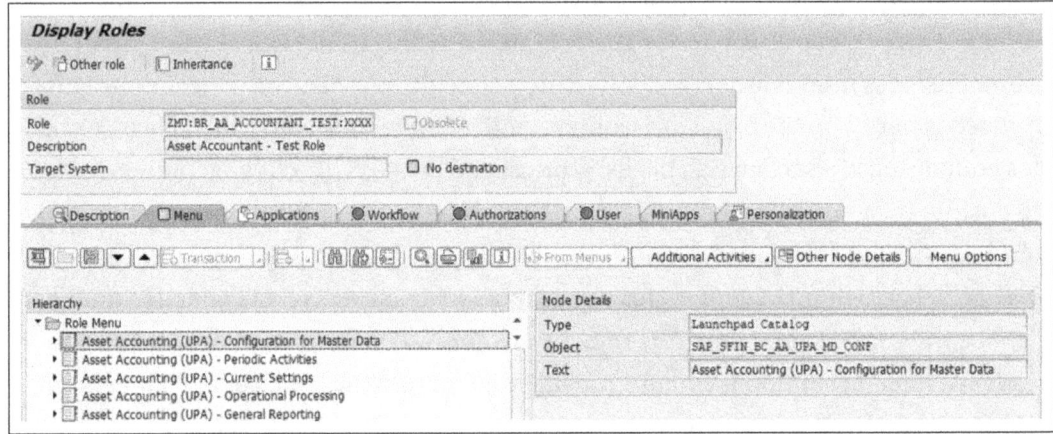

Figure 5-129. Custom role created for activation using the current task list

Furthermore, the role maintains no authorization as the Authorizations tab is red, as shown in the figure below.

CHAPTER 5   SAP FIORI CONFIGURATION

Figure 5-130. *Custom role with no authorization maintained*

You can activate one or more business roles from this task list. The business role with the new naming convention should already exist in the desired format (naming convention), a **mandatory step**. The system automatically retrieves all authorizations maintained in **SU24**. Upon execution, the task list **SAP_FIORI_FCM_CONTENT_ACTIVATION** seamlessly integrates **SU24** data into the **PFCG roles**. It incorporates the relevant Fiori components (IWSG/IWSV), associated authorization objects, and details of the organizational hierarchy.

Furthermore, the task list enables security team members to maintain open fields manually in both cases. The **organizational hierarchy** can also be managed. However, when dealing with **a master role**, we will leave all **org values blank** or give an **asterisk** * to all.

5.11.2 Execute the Task List

The **task list SAP_FIORI_FCM_CONTENT_ACTIVATION** can be activated using the transaction code **STC01**, as shown in the figure below.

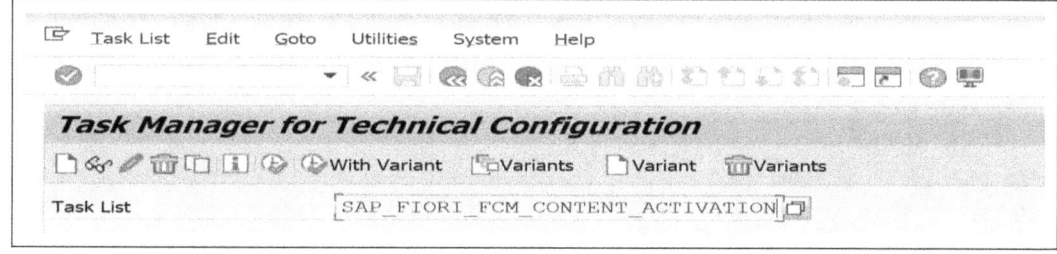

Figure 5-131. *Transaction STC01 initial screen with the task list*

CHAPTER 5   SAP FIORI CONFIGURATION

When executed, the initial screen appears, which needs to be maintained. Here, we can activate single or multiple roles at a given instance, like the other task lists that were activated earlier.

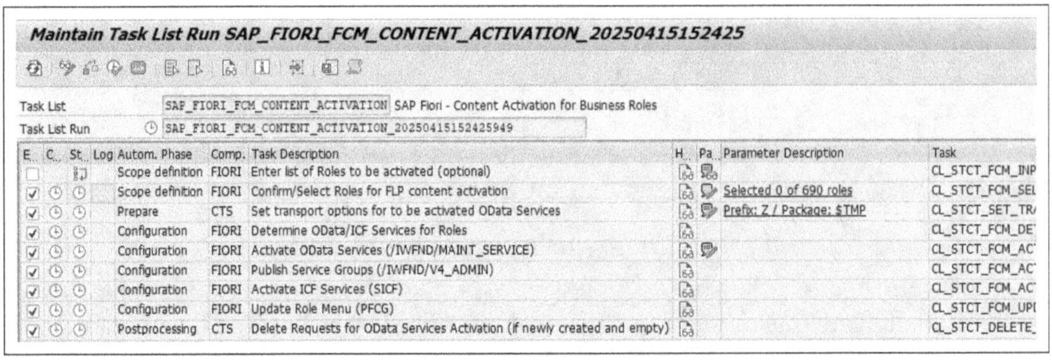

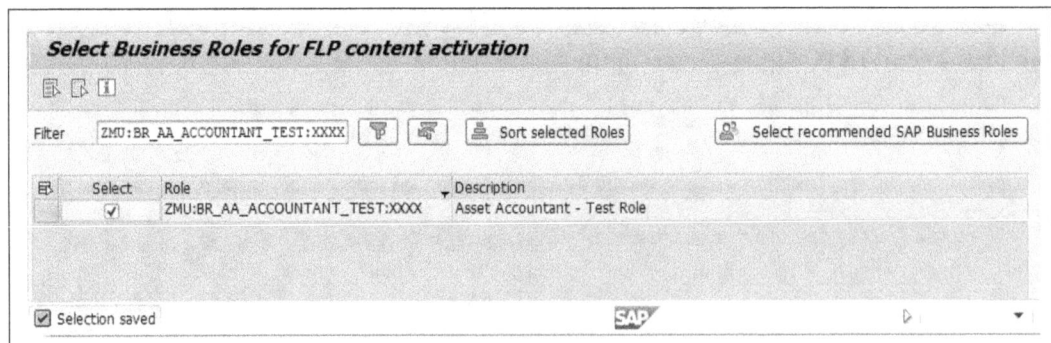

Figure 5-132. Input screen for task list SAP_FIORI_FCM_CONTENT_ ACTIVATION

Confirm/Select Roles for FLP content activation

Here, we can select our roles for activation under **FIORI Confirm/Select Roles for FLP content activation**. Click the **parameter** icon , enter the role name, and use the filter option as shown in the figure below.

Note   We can select multiple roles here; for this example, we use single roles.

Figure 5-133. Screen for selecting a custom business role

CHAPTER 5 SAP FIORI CONFIGURATION

Multiple roles can be selected at this stage; however, we are working with single roles. Once the roles are selected, click the **save icon**. This ensures that your changes are made and ready for further processing. Then click the **go-back** option.

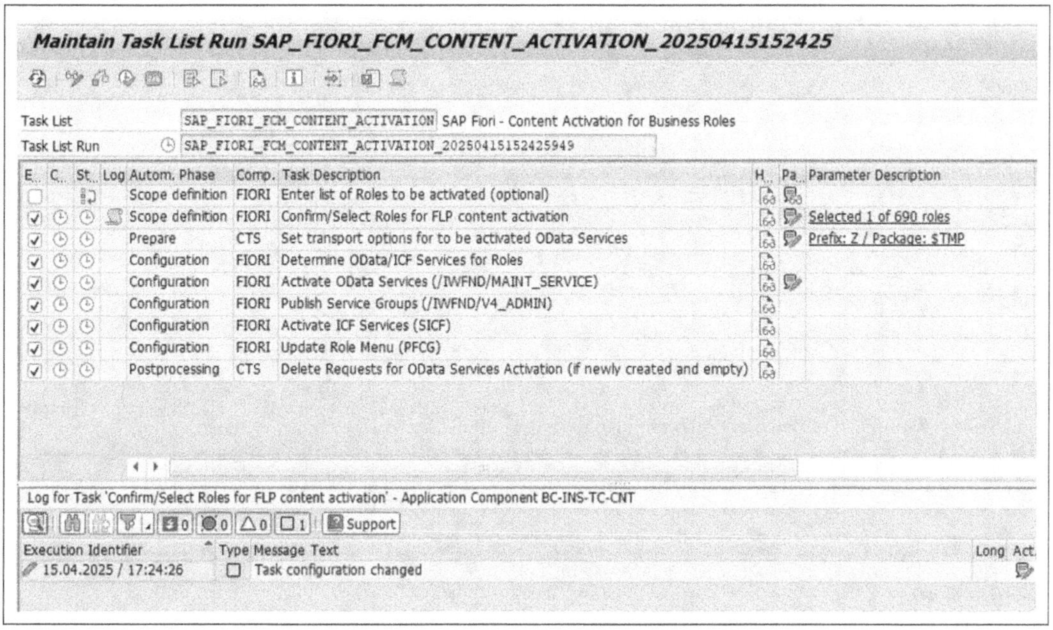

Figure 5-134. Single role saved with the task list for activation

In the above figure, leave the settings unchanged. Since the associated services for this role have already been activated, you can deselect the option for **Set transport options for to be activated OData Services**. This will ensure that no redundant services are activated again. Also, update the package and transport information.

Update Role Menu (PFCG)

Always ensure the **Update Role Menu (PFCG)** is selected when updating the Fiori tile catalog in the PFCG role menu. This option is selected by default within the task list. Once the task list is generated and successfully executed, it is essential to manually maintain authorizations and generate profiles in the Role Maintenance (**PFCG**) transaction. Additionally, the task log provides a link to the Roles: Mass Generation of Profiles (**SUPC**) transaction for managing authorizations and profile generation for the selected roles.

CHAPTER 5　SAP FIORI CONFIGURATION

Execute the Task List

Once saved, the updated final task list is as shown in the figure below.

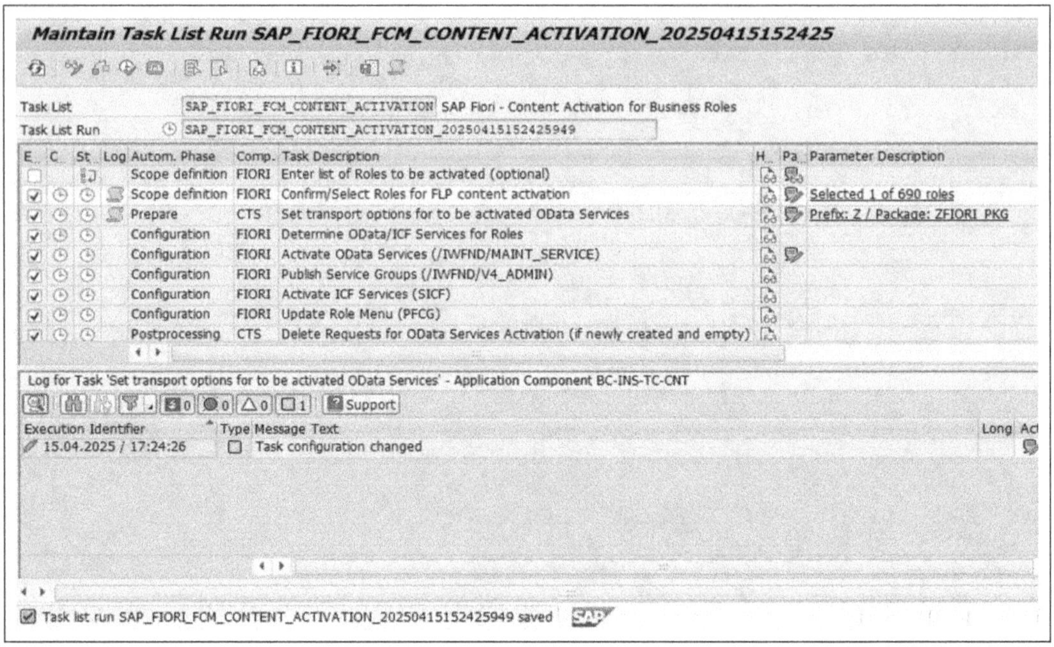

Figure 5-135. Task list ready for execution

The task list has now been configured. To activate it, click the execution icon. If you have multiple roles, you can activate them in the background mode. However, we will use the dialog mode since we only have one role.

During the process of executing, it displays messages at the bottom of the screen about the status of the run. The task list is currently running and is working on the subtask "Update Role Menu (PFCG)," as shown in the figure below.

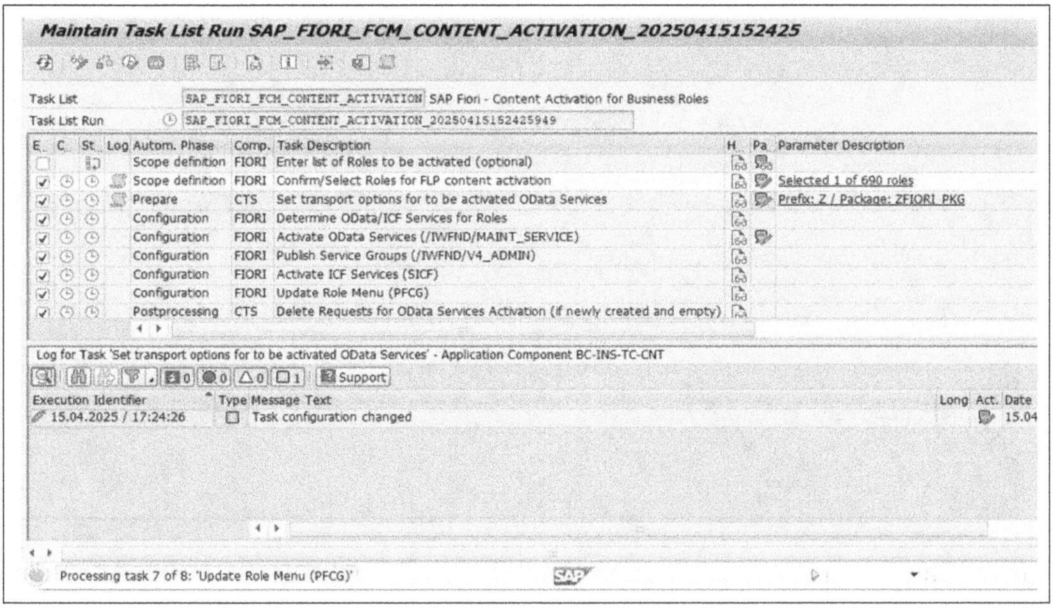

CHAPTER 5 SAP FIORI CONFIGURATION

Figure 5-136. *Task list updating the role menu in PFCG*

Once the task list is executed successfully, a message at the bottom of the screen states, **Task list run execution ended with status 'Finished Successfully'**, as shown in the below figure.

285

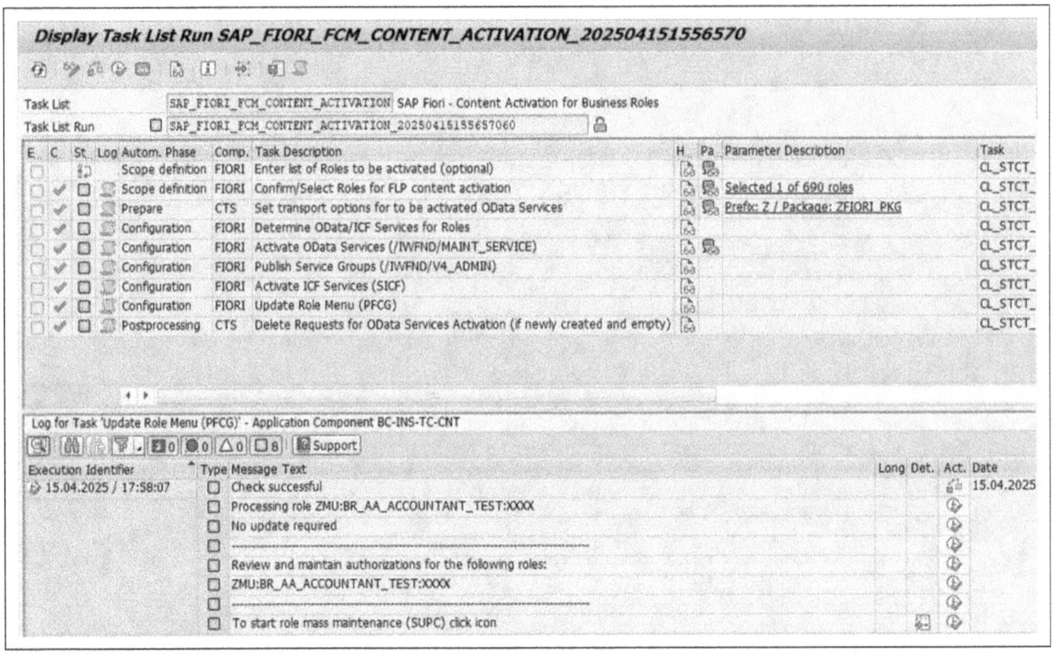

CHAPTER 5   SAP FIORI CONFIGURATION

Figure 5-137. Task list execution completed successfully

Note The above screen allows you to maintain the role authorization at the bottom of the output screen, which states, **To start role mass maintenance (SUPC) click icon**. Clicking the icon will direct you to the **SUPC** screen, as shown in the figure below.

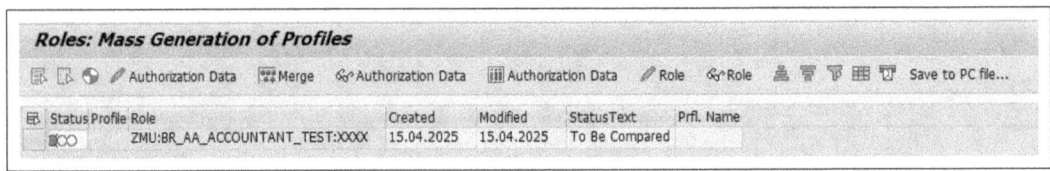

Figure 5-138. Role can be generated using transaction SUPC

Verifying the generated logs is always a good practice. You can check the logs by clicking the icon, and the output is displayed, as shown in the figure below.

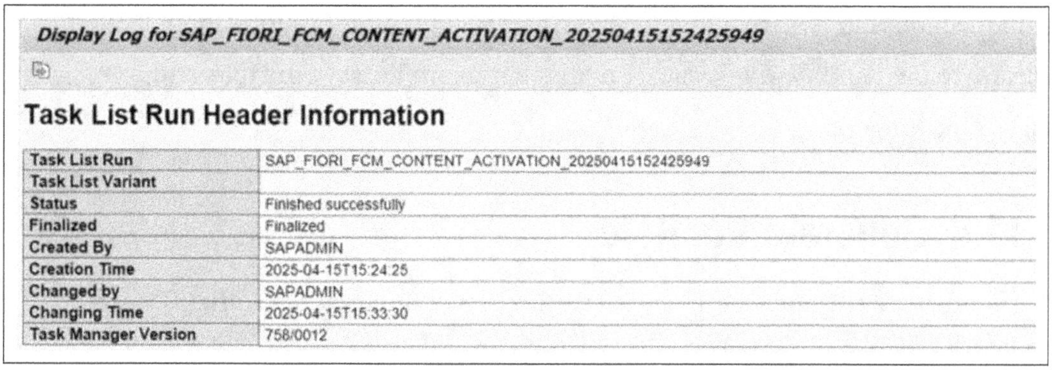

CHAPTER 5   SAP FIORI CONFIGURATION

Figure 5-139. *Log output generated while executing the task list*

5.11.3 Validate the Role Created

It is crucial to check the updated custom business roles in PFCG. Doing so will ensure that the roles are aligned with the latest changes and that your business operations run smoothly.

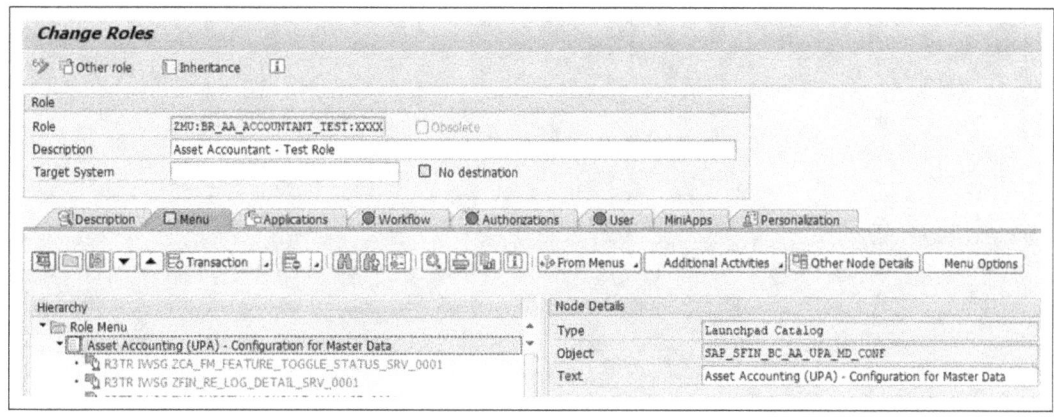

Figure 5-140. *PFCG screenshot of the new business role created by using the task list with IWSG/WSV components*

The **green color** of the Menu tab indicates that all catalog data has been successfully updated and activated with the necessary IWSG/IWSV components required for the proper functioning of the tile/app. You can see this on the screen above. However, the

CHAPTER 5 SAP FIORI CONFIGURATION

Authorizations tab is **red**, meaning we must maintain the authorization within the role. Go to the tab Authorizations, maintain the profile, save the role, and click Authorizations.

5.11.4 Generate the Role

The figure below displays a message at the bottom of the screen: **Profile(s) were updated**.

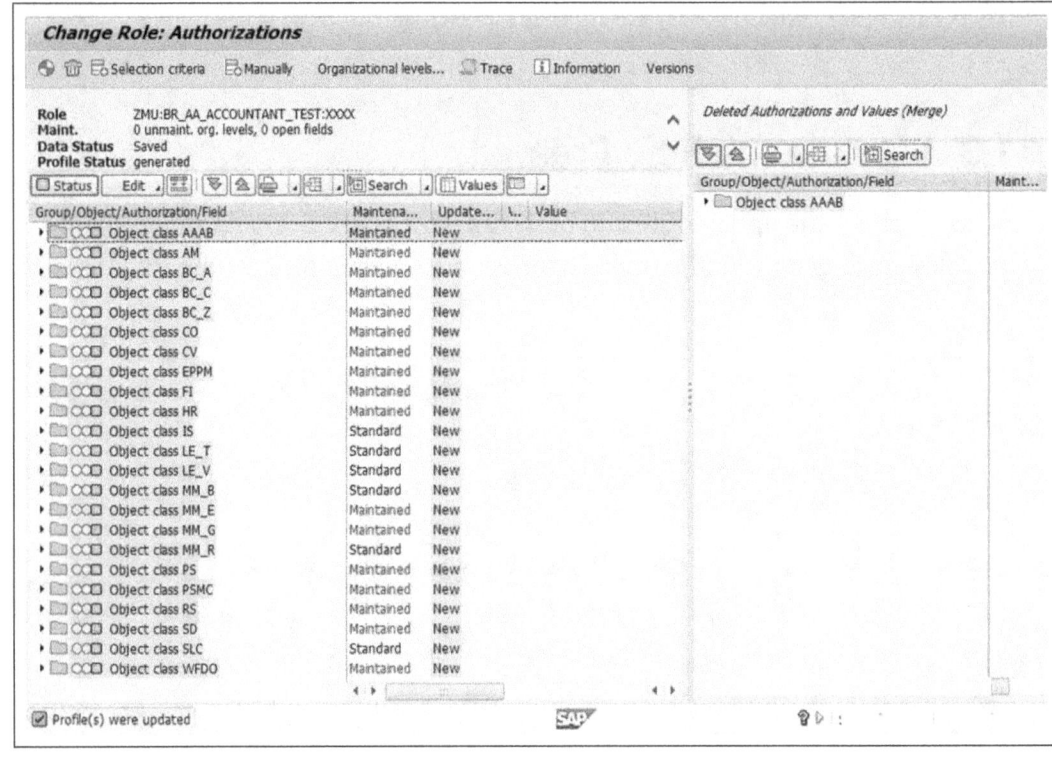

Figure 5-141. Business role generated

5.11.5 Validate Test User Access

Now, assign the custom business role to the test user **T2_AAAC**.

288

CHAPTER 5 SAP FIORI CONFIGURATION

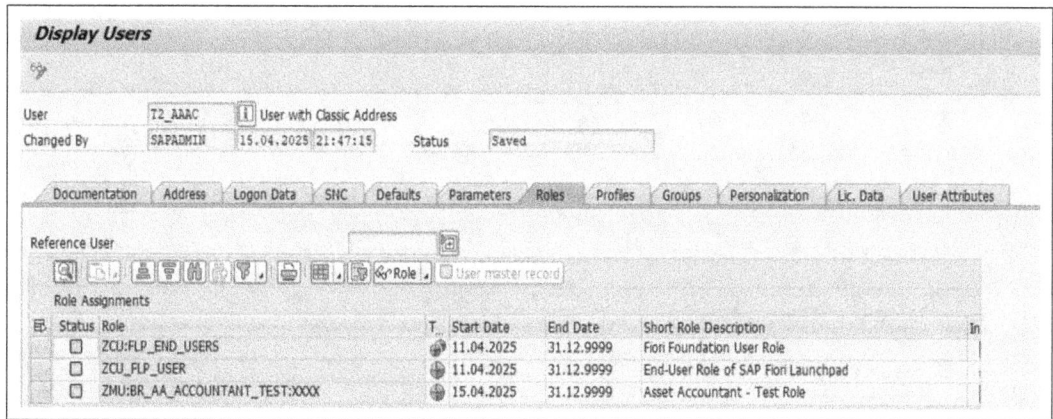

Figure 5-142. *Test user assigned the new role generated*

5.11.6 Testing Access

The test user **T2_AAAC** can successfully log into the development system, and the SAP Fiori Launchpad home page displays relevant apps, as shown in the figure below.

CHAPTER 5   SAP FIORI CONFIGURATION

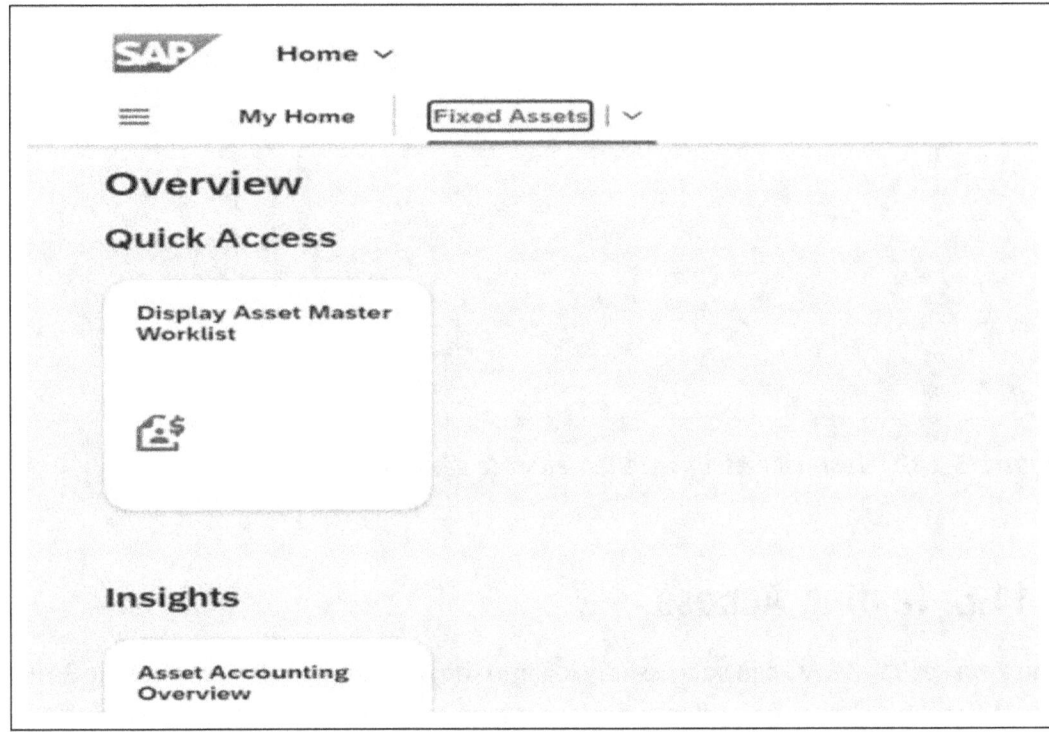

Figure 5-143. *The test user was successfully logged into the development system*

5.11.7 Summary

This section demonstrated the steps necessary to activate SAP best practice business roles using the SA_BR* nomenclature, employing the task list SAP_FIORI_FCM_CONTENT_ACTIVATION. The authorization fields and org values are updated based on what is maintained in **SU24**. Later, the security team can update the values of objects according to the business requirements. The SAP-delivered business role is then duplicated as a custom business role, using the appropriate naming convention. The business team is provided with **AGR_1251** data for updating values and **TOBJ** table data for describing authorization objects.

5.12 Configuring the SAP Fiori Logon and Logoff Screens

Setting up the SAP Fiori **logon** and **logoff screens** enhances user experience and reinforces branding while maintaining security. A personalized logon screen can show brand logos and messages, and the logoff screen can direct users to company resources or feedback forms. Both screens can include security alerts or legal notices. Overall, these changes make the system more user-friendly.

From a security point of view, when the end user logs off the SAP session by selecting the **User Menu** T and then the **Sign Out** option, a box titled **Sign Out** opens within the SAP home page for confirmation to quit, as shown in the figure below.

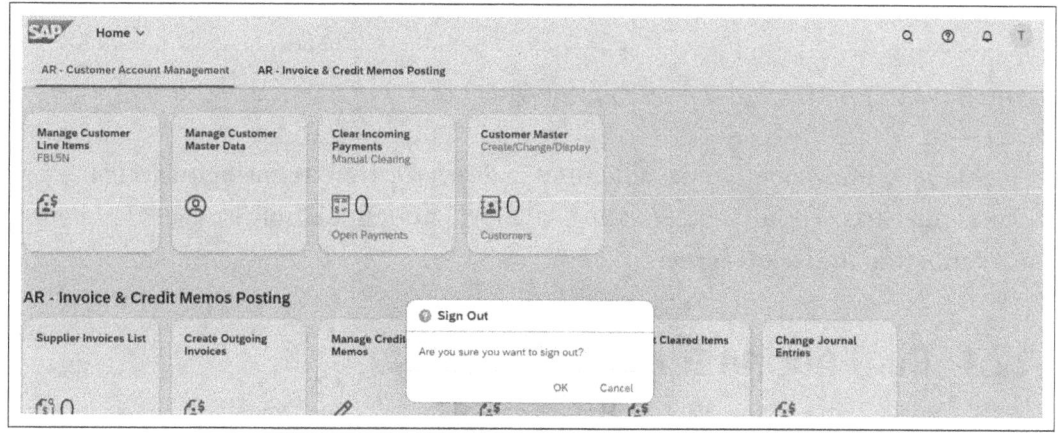

Figure 5-144. *End user trying to quit the SAP Launchpad home page*

To proceed, select **OK**, and the SAP Fiori Launchpad quits the home page and displays the message **Goodbye – You have been logged off**, as shown in the figure below.

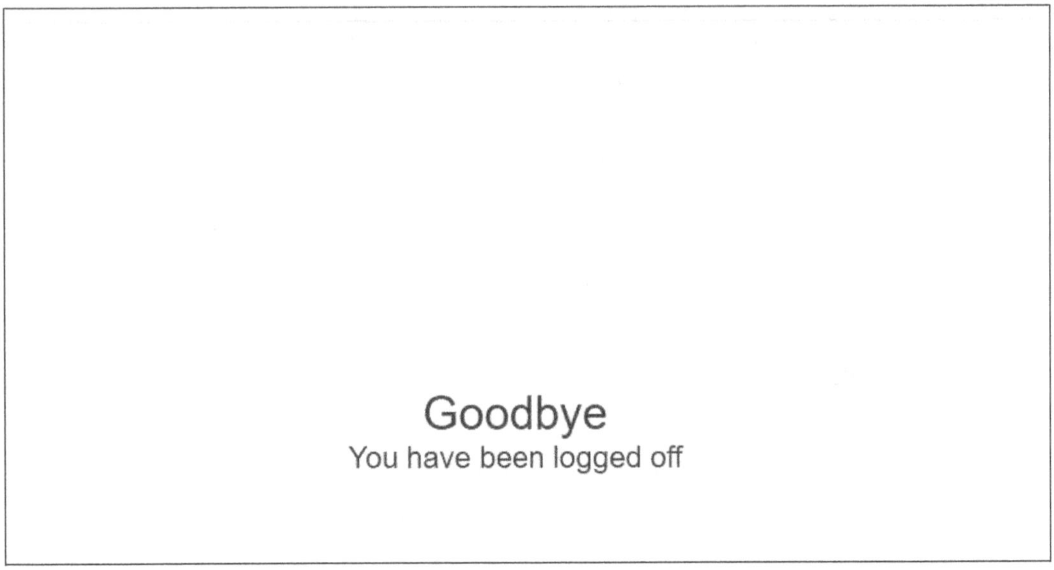

CHAPTER 5   SAP FIORI CONFIGURATION

> Goodbye
> You have been logged off

Figure 5-145. *End user logoff screen message*

In this case, the system is not configured to direct the user to the **logon screen**. The end user must log on again to access the **SAP Fiori Launchpad home page**. The section below configures the **logoff screen**.

5.12.1 Configuring the Logoff Screen

This requires activating an ICF service **/default_host/sap/public/bc/icf/logoff** by executing the transaction **SICF** and **searching for the service**, as shown in the figure below.

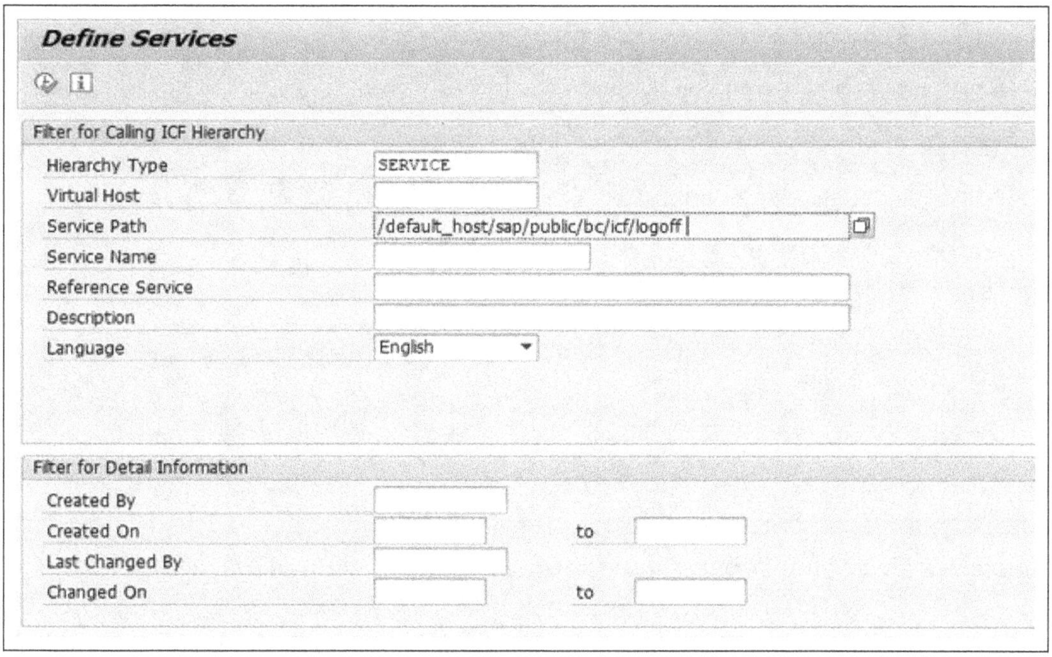

CHAPTER 5 ■ SAP FIORI CONFIGURATION

Figure 5-146. Logoff screen ICF service added

Note Alternatively, service path **/sap/public/bc/icf/logof** could be used.

Click the **execute** icon, and the **Define Services** window opens. The path to be expanded is shown in the figure below.

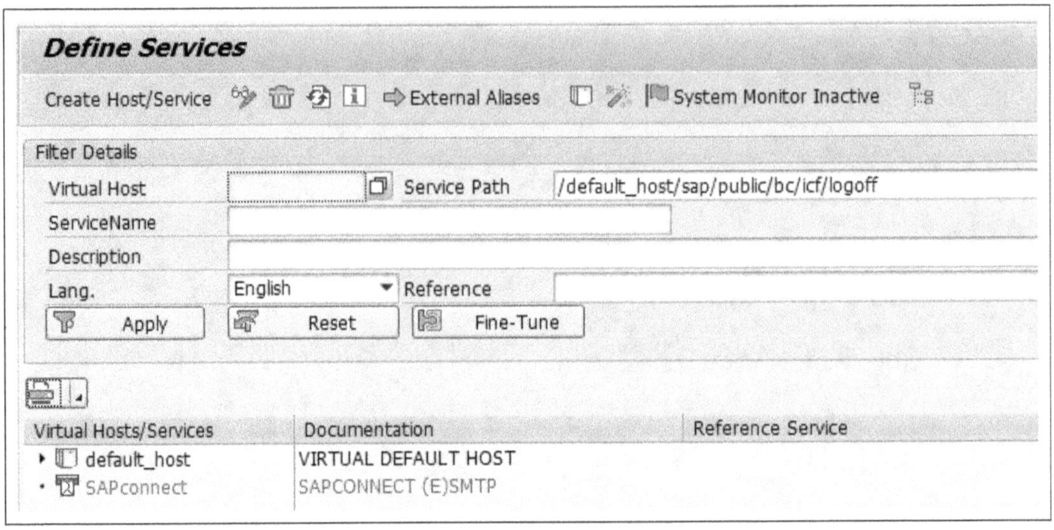

CHAPTER 5　SAP FIORI CONFIGURATION

Figure 5-147. Define Services window displaying the path of the default host

The above figure displays the path of the **default host**, which needs to be expanded. The expansion must follow chronological order: **default_host ➤ sap ➤ public ➤ bc ➤ icf ➤ logoff. This is depicted in the figure below.**

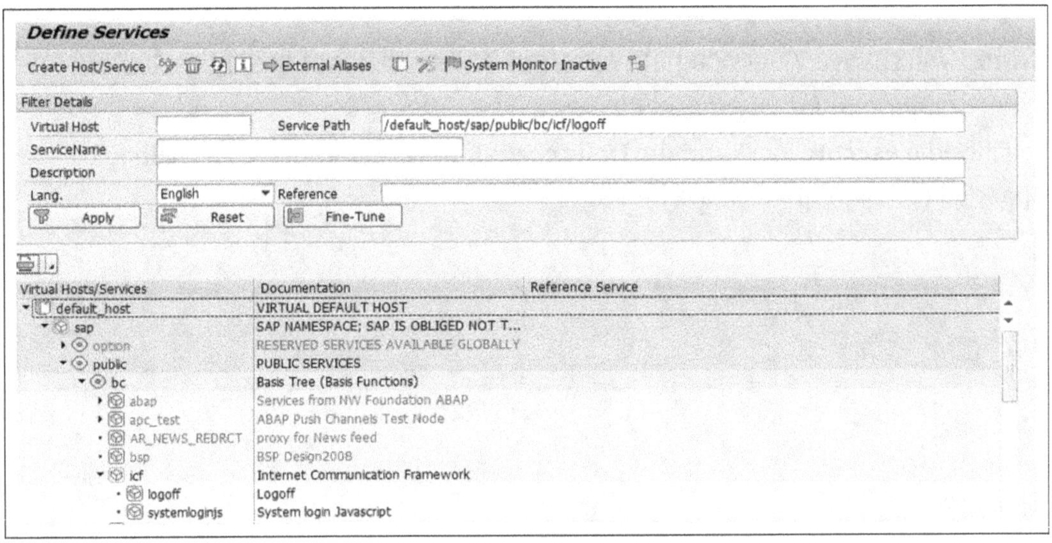

Figure 5-148. Showing path to the Logoff option for the ICF service

CHAPTER 5 SAP FIORI CONFIGURATION

Double-click the Logoff option in the above, and a new window, **Create/Change a Service**, opens. Then go to the tab **Error Pages**, followed by **Logoff Page**, as shown in the figure below.

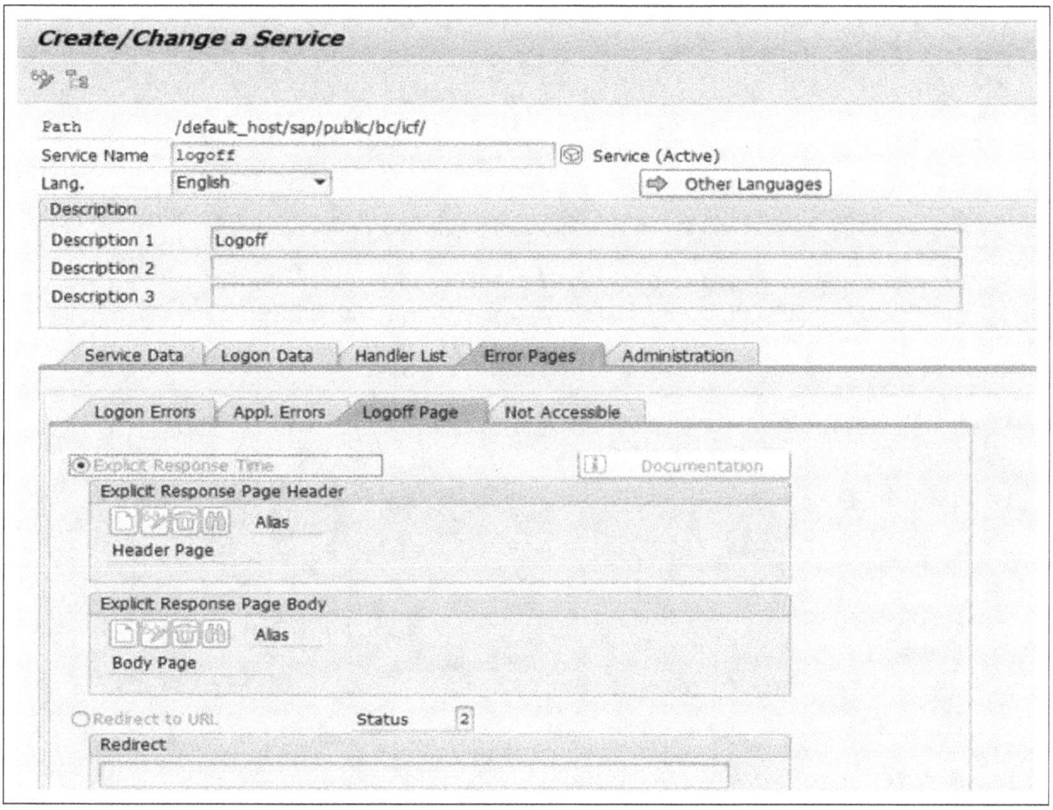

Figure 5-149. Logoff Page tab to configure

Here, we must select **Redirect to URL**, which is grayed out as we are in display mode. Click [ ] Change Authorization Data to enter **change mode**, select **Redirect to URL**, and enter the **URL** details, as shown in the figure below.

URL: /sap/bc/ui5_ui5/ui2/ushell/shells/abap/fiorilaunchpad.html

295

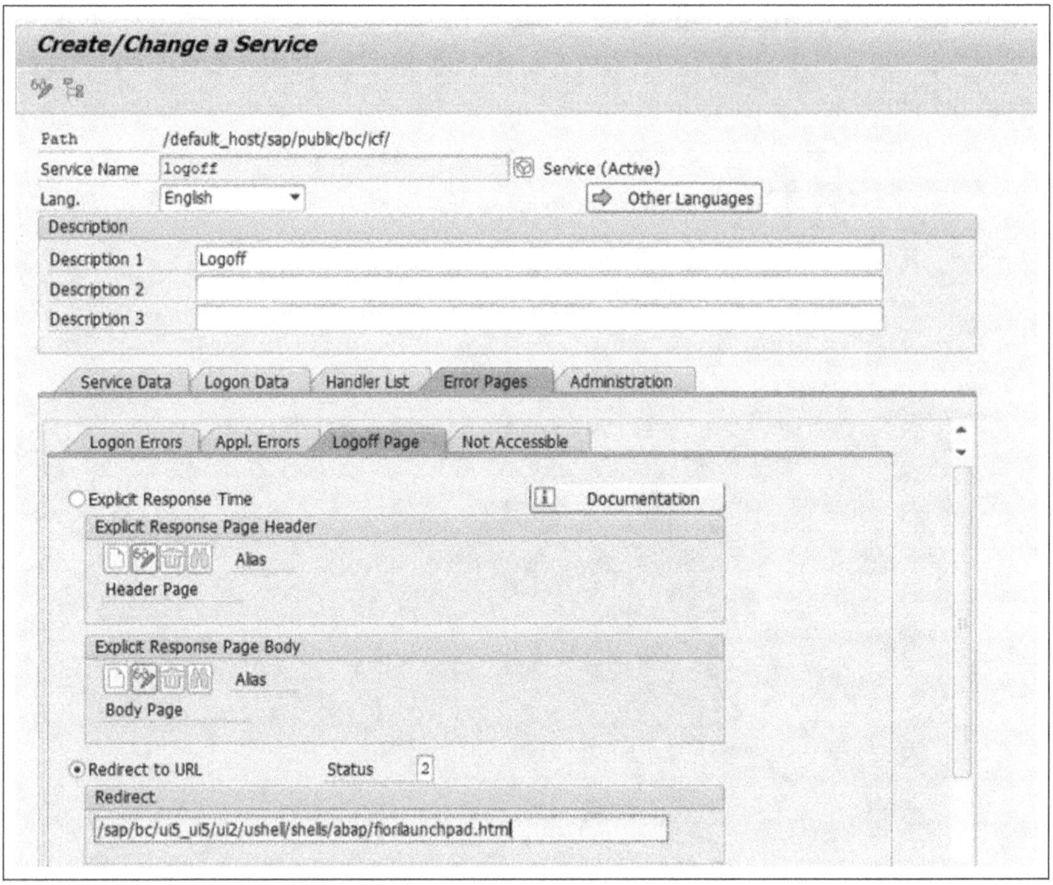

CHAPTER 5 SAP FIORI CONFIGURATION

Figure 5-150. Logoff screen URL entered

Click Save to save the setting. A box titled **Information** opens to **confirm repairs**, as shown in the figure below.

Figure 5-151. *Logoff screen configuration confirmation box*

Click the **continue** icon, and the system will prompt us to assign it to the **Workbench request transport**.

To proceed, click the **continue** icon and then save the settings. A message at the bottom of the screen states that the service has been **saved**, as shown in the figure below.

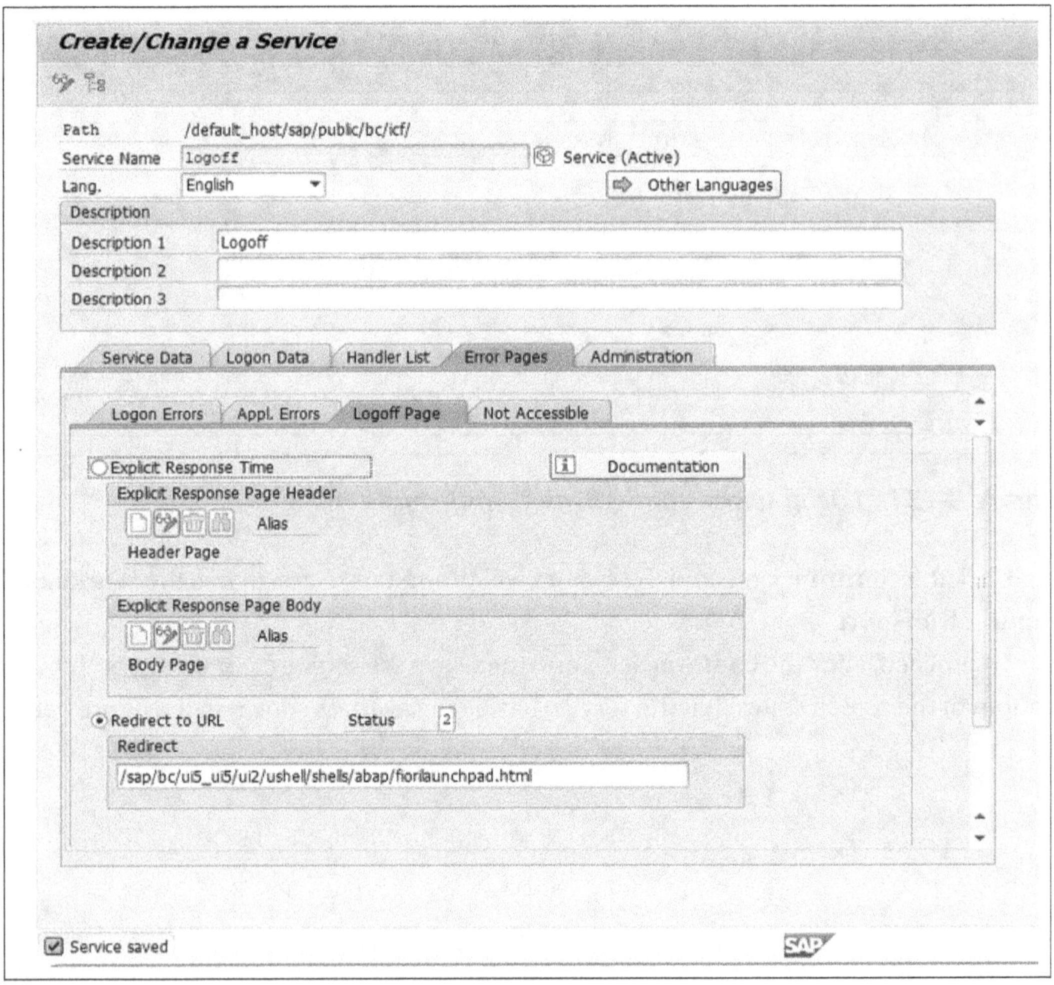

CHAPTER 5 SAP FIORI CONFIGURATION

Figure 5-152. *Logoff screen configuration changes saved*

When the end user **logs off** from the **SAP Fiori Launchpad** home page, the system **redirects** the user to the **Launchpad logon screen** instead of allowing them to relog on through the **URL**, as shown in the figure below.

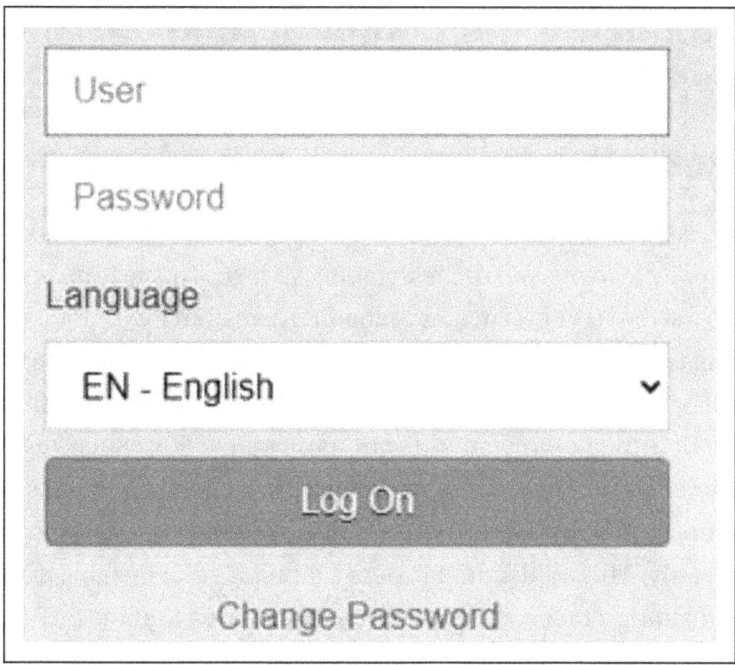

Figure 5-153. *User redirected to the logon screen*

5.12.2 Summary

Customizing the SAP Fiori logon and logoff screens is a great way to enhance the user experience and create a professional appearance for your application. You can personalize the logon page by adding your company logo, choosing a background image, and including a welcoming message for users. Additionally, when users log off, you can present them with a custom message or redirect them to a specific page. This makes the Fiori Launchpad feel more tailored to your organization and helps users feel more connected to the brand. Overall, these customizations contribute to a more engaging and visually appealing environment.

5.13 Customizing the Logon Screen with a Company Logo

5.13.1 Introduction

SAP Fiori allows administrators to **customize** the **Fiori Launchpad logon screen**, including a company logo instead of the default SAP logo. This feature enables various modifications to the logon page, such as uploading a custom logo, changing background images, adjusting text, and altering color themes. This process falls under the broader category of **Fiori branding** and **theming**, which can be achieved using the SAP Theme Designer or through direct modifications of system files. Such customization is particularly beneficial in environments with multiple clients or tenants, including development, **quality assurance**, and **production systems**, as it helps to **differentiate between them easily**. This adjustment fosters a familiar and engaging experience for employees by providing a tailored logon interface, ensuring that the SAP user interface aligns closely with the corporate identity.

When an **end user logs** onto the **SAP Fiori Launchpad**, it initially appears as shown in the figure below.

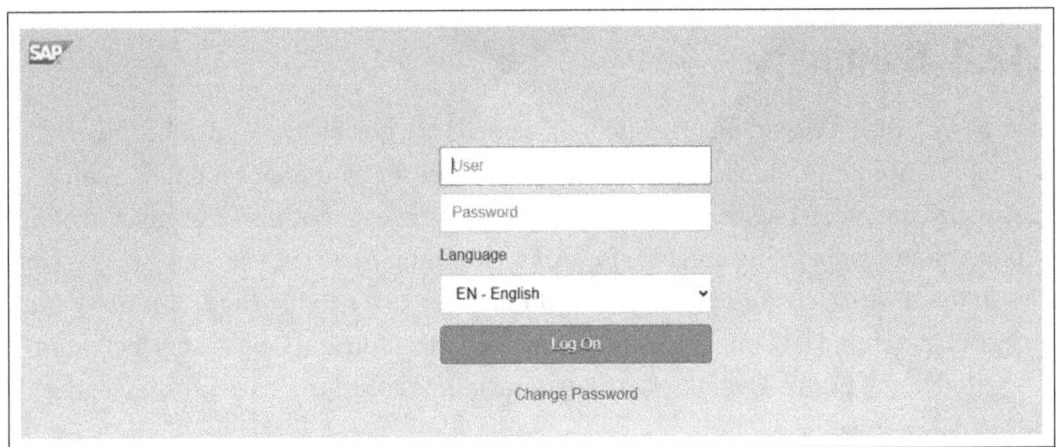

Figure 5-154. User initial logon screen with SAP logon logo displayed on the left side

The image above shows the user logon interface, featuring the **SAP logo** on the left side. This logo can be replaced with a company logo. The setup process is explained below.

CHAPTER 5 SAP FIORI CONFIGURATION

5.13.2 Setup Process

Before proceeding to update the logo, it is recommended to back up all the files available in the folder using the transaction **SE80 ➤ MIME Repository ➤ SAP ➤ PUBLIC**, as shown in the figure below.

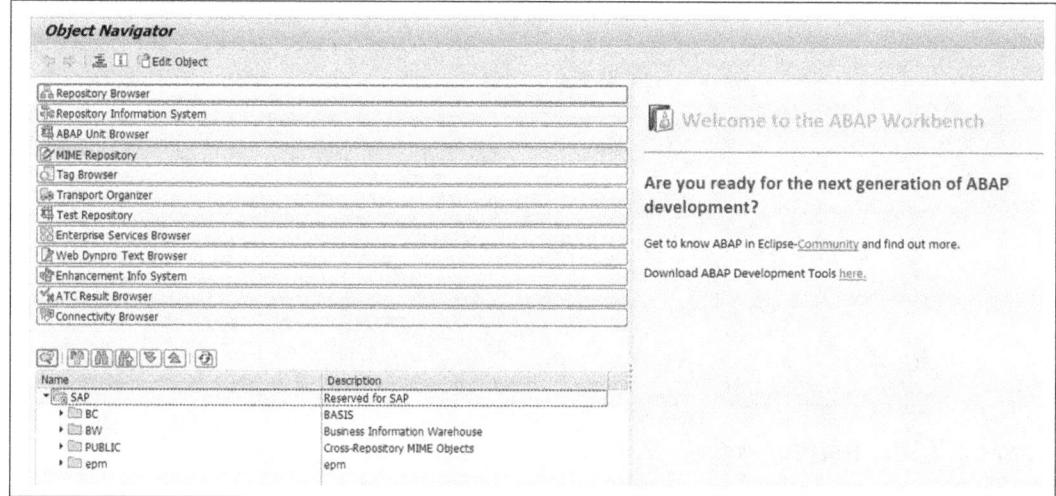

Figure 5-155. *Transaction SE80 with MIME Repository*

In the above figure, expand **SAP ➤ PUBLIC ➤ BC ➤ UI2 ➤ logon ➤ img**. This will display all the ***.JPG** image files that SAP uses as images, as shown in the figure below.

CHAPTER 5   SAP FIORI CONFIGURATION

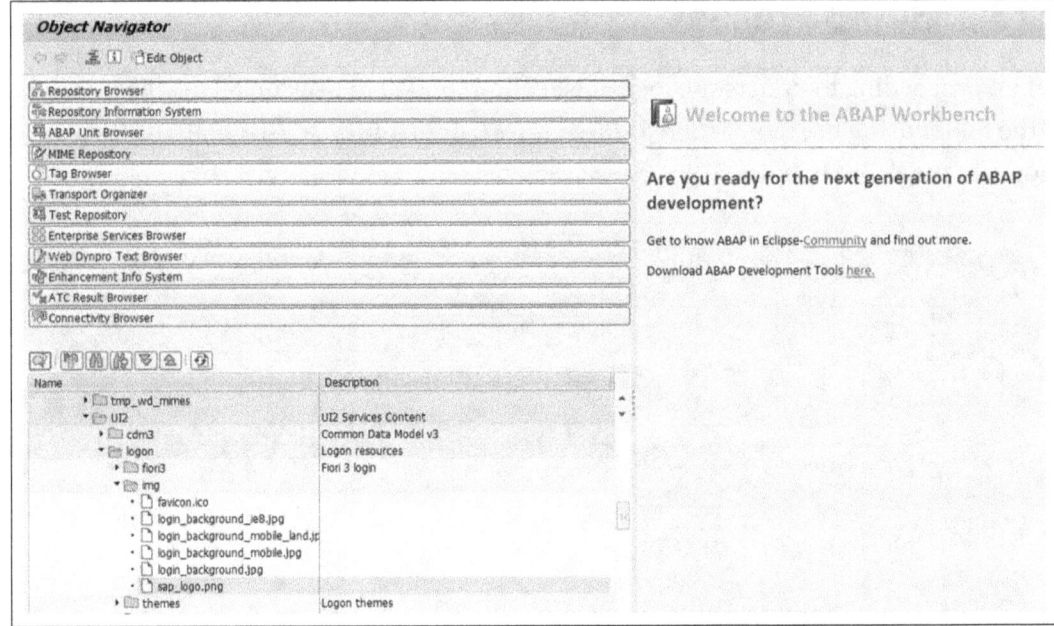

Figure 5-156. *All images used by SAP are stored in an img folder*

All these images must be downloaded as a backup before proceeding to upload these with the company logos by right-clicking the image **sap_logo.png** and choosing **Upload/Download ► Download**, as shown in the figure below.

CHAPTER 5 SAP FIORI CONFIGURATION

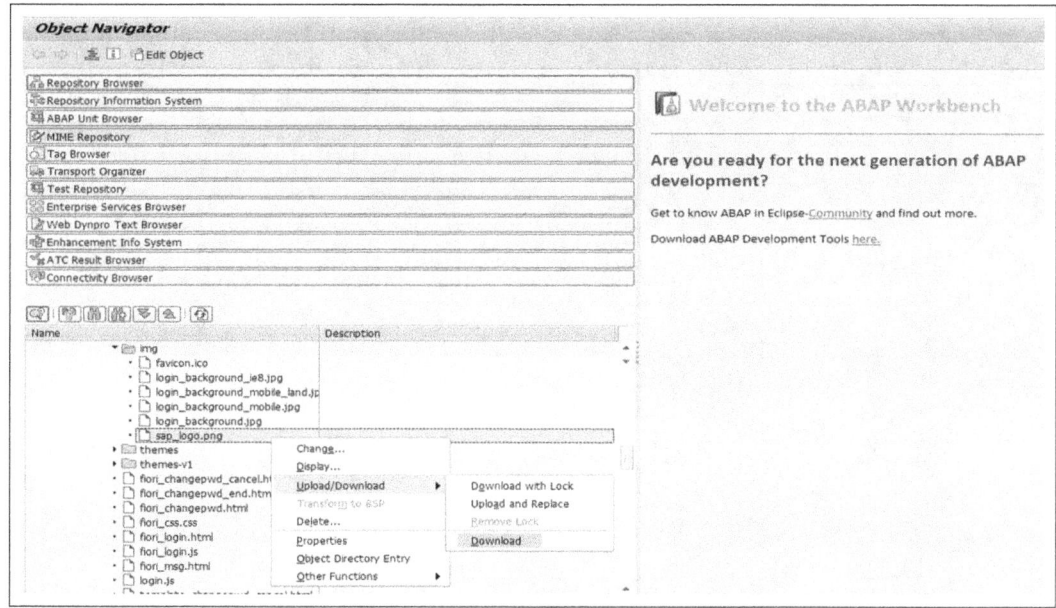

Figure 5-157. *Downloading SAP logo files as backup*

In the above figure, **save** the image to a backup folder. Once all the files are downloaded, the **backup folder** will contain all the images, as shown in the figure below.

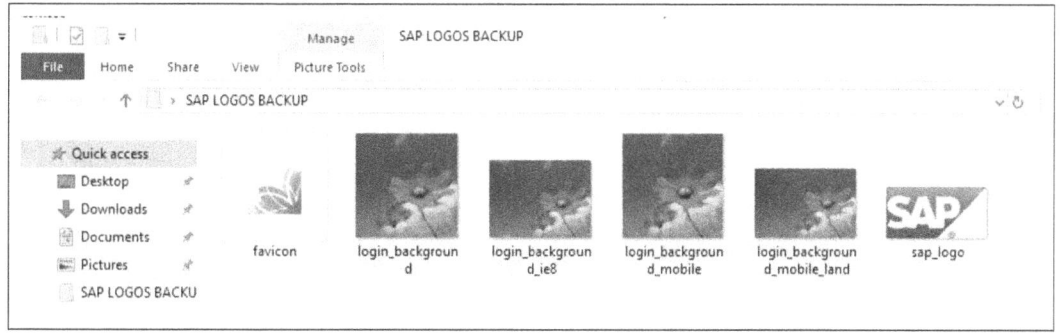

Figure 5-158. *Backup folder of SAP logos*

To upload a new company or custom logo, right-click the image **sap_logo.png** and choose **Upload/Download ➤ Upload and Replace**, as shown in the figure below.

303

CHAPTER 5   SAP FIORI CONFIGURATION

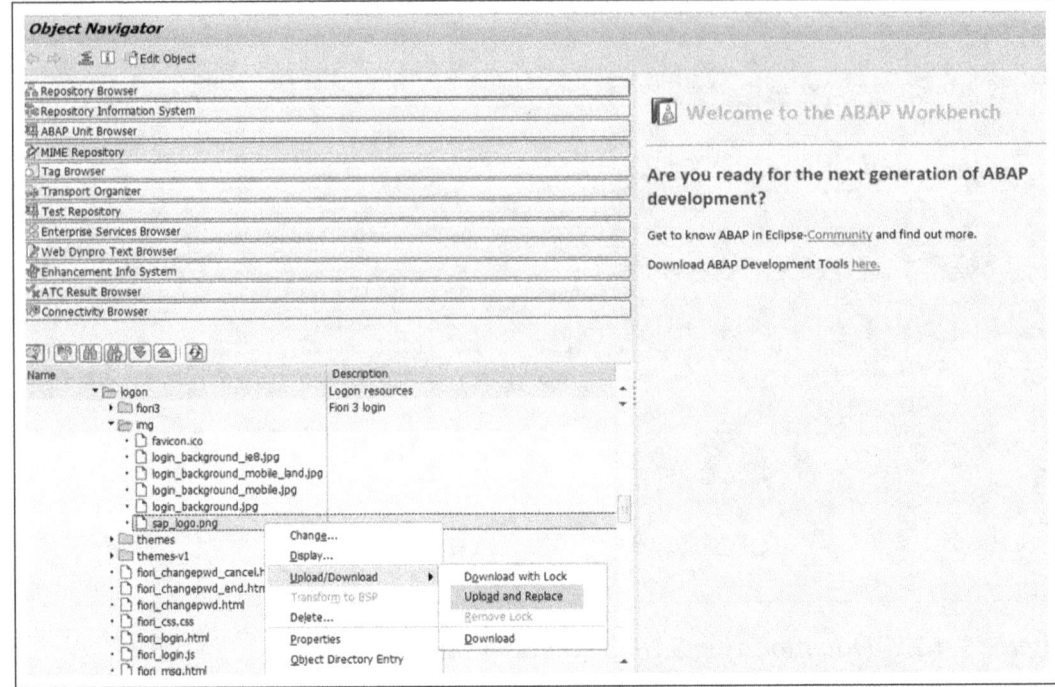

Figure 5-159.   Custom logo image option

Selecting the **Upload and Replace** option opens a window to enter the file name, as shown in the figure below.

CHAPTER 5 SAP FIORI CONFIGURATION

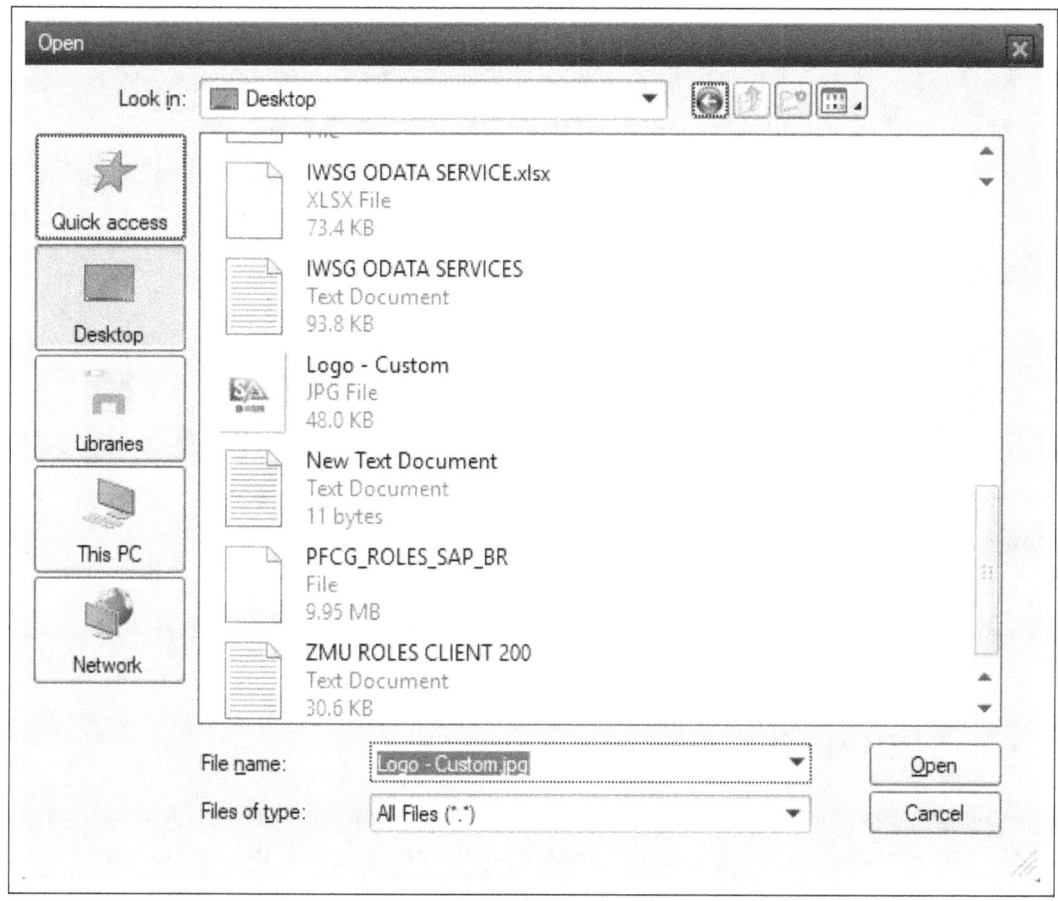

Figure 5-160. *Replacement image selection*

Once you open the file, the system will prompt for a transport. Enter the respective Workbench transport created earlier. The end user SAP Fiori Launchpad logon screen gets updated with a custom logo, as shown in the figure below.

CHAPTER 5 SAP FIORI CONFIGURATION

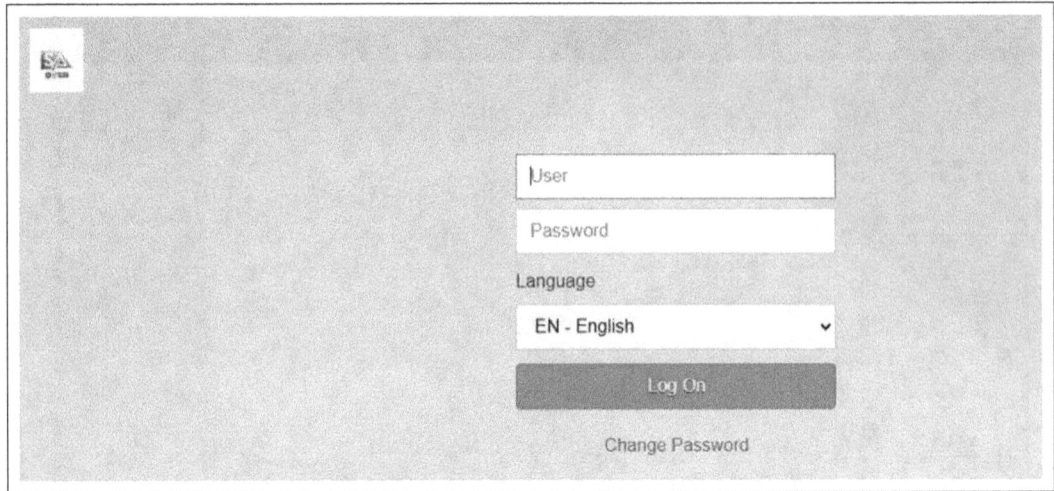

Figure 5-161. SAP logo replaced by custom logo

The above figure shows that a custom logo has replaced the SAP logo.

5.14 Summary

This chapter presents a straightforward method for configuring SAP Fiori within an SAP S/4HANA embedded system, with an emphasis on activating task lists using transaction STC01. It includes critical steps such as installing both front-end and back-end components, enabling OData services, deploying Fiori applications, customizing the Launchpad, and managing user permissions. Essential prerequisites involve having an SAP package for configuration transport and the capability to validate task list executions with STC02. The guide recommends using Rapid Activation Task Lists for easy configuration, as well as manual configurations using transaction SPRO, and establishing a connection for Launchpad access. It also covers the setup of login and logout screens, as well as interface branding, highlighting the importance of documenting configurations and conducting validations.

CHAPTER 6

Introduction to Fiori Apps

SAP Fiori is a design system that enhances the user experience for SAP applications with a modern and easy-to-use interface across various devices. It replaces the traditional SAP GUI with simple and personalized options. Fiori includes different types of apps: transactional, analytical, factsheet, GUI, and custom apps, all designed to support business tasks and provide real-time insights. Built on SAPUI5, these apps run on the SAP Business Technology Platform (BTP) or SAP S/4HANA, using OData services for data communication, which improves user efficiency and efficiency in enterprise operations.

6.1 Introduction

SAP Fiori represents a significant shift in the user experience for SAP applications, offering a more intuitive, role-based, and modern interface. In this chapter, we will discuss various types of Fiori apps provided by SAP, designed to work seamlessly across devices and provide users with consistent experience on a desktop, tablet, or smartphone.

SAP Fiori is a collection of web-based applications that provide a simplified and cohesive user experience across various business functions. Fiori apps are built using SAPUI5, a JavaScript-based framework, and leverage the OData protocol for data communication with SAP back-end systems.

6.1.1 Characteristics of SAP Fiori Apps

Listed below are some of the features within the SAP Fiori apps:

Role-Based: Fiori apps are created for specific user roles and business processes. They help users access the functions they need to work efficiently.

Responsive Design: The apps adjust to different screen sizes and orientations, providing a uniform experience using a desktop, tablet, or smartphone.

Simple and Intuitive: Fiori apps focus on simplicity. They provide a clean and easy-to-use interface that makes it simpler for users to learn how to navigate.

Seamless Experience: Fiori apps connect easily with SAP back-end systems, allowing users to access real-time data and perform transactions easily.

6.1.2 The Architecture of Fiori Apps

The architecture of SAP Fiori apps consists of several key components:

SAP Fiori Launchpad: The Launchpad is your portal for accessing Fiori apps. It provides users with a personalized home page featuring tiles that display the available apps. You can customize the appearance of these tiles and arrange them according to your preferences.

Front-End Components: Fiori apps are created using SAPUI5, which provides tools to build modern web applications. You can design the user interface with HTML5, CSS, and JavaScript.

Back-End Components: Fiori apps connect to SAP back-end systems through OData services, which provide access to essential business data and processes.

SAP Gateway: SAP Gateway allows Fiori apps to communicate with back-end systems like SAP ERP or S/4HANA.

6.1.3 Implementing SAP Fiori Apps

The main steps for implementing SAP Fiori apps are as follows:

Installation and Configuration: Use SAP Gateway to set up the SAP Fiori Launchpad and OData services, ensuring that the SAP NetWeaver and SAPUI5 components are installed and configured.

Role and Authorization Management: Utilize transaction code PFCG to create and assign roles for Fiori app access while managing authorizations for secure data access.

Customization and Extension: Use SAP Web IDE to improve Fiori apps and meet your business needs. You can add new features or connect to different data sources.

6.2 Fiori Apps

SAP Fiori apps are categorized into three main types based on their purpose and functionality: **transactional**, **analytical**, and **factsheet** apps. In addition, there are **GUI** and **custom** apps. The following sections will explore the **five types of SAP Fiori apps** in detail with examples. The five types of apps are

- Transactional apps
- Analytical apps
- Factsheet apps
- GUI apps
- Custom apps

6.3 SAP Transactional Apps

Transactional apps are designed for specific business tasks like creating sales orders and approving workflows, utilizing SAP's transactional processing capabilities. SAP Fiori's transactional apps enable efficient execution of tasks such as leave and travel requests. While optimized for the SAP HANA database, they also perform well on other databases. These apps allow users to complete simple SAP transactions on mobile devices, desktops, or laptops, including leave requests, travel requests, purchase orders, and purchase requisition processing.

6.3.1 Main Features

User-Centric Design: Transactional apps focus on the user. They have a simple and easy-to-use interface, which helps users complete tasks without much training.

Real-Time Data Access: Transactional apps let users work with real-time data, helping ensure that business processes run based on the latest information.

Role-Based: Transactional apps are designed for specific roles within an organization. For example, there are different apps for sales representatives, procurement managers, and HR personnel.

Mobile and Web Accessibility: You can access SAP Fiori transactional apps using web browsers and mobile devices. This allows users to perform tasks easily while on the go.

Integration with SAP Back-End Systems: These applications connect directly with SAP back-end systems, like ERP or S/4HANA. This connection allows users to easily perform tasks such as creating sales orders, approving purchase requests, and managing inventory.

Consistency and Standardization: SAP Fiori apps use a straightforward design that creates a uniform user experience. This consistency is essential for different applications and business processes.

Customization and Extensibility: SAP Fiori transactional apps are designed to be simple but can be customized or extended to meet specific business requirements.

Case Study of Implementing Fiori Apps

A team member has requested that you deploy an app. They will provide you with either an app ID or a description of the app, as well as business requirements from the SAP Fiori Apps Reference Library. This resource contains all the necessary features, including SICF nodes, OData details, technical and business catalogs, and more. The OData

CHAPTER 6 INTRODUCTION TO FIORI APPS

service is like a transaction code containing the authorization checks and functionality. In our specific case, we seek the transactional app F4700, which can be found by selecting All apps within the SAP Fiori Apps Reference Library.

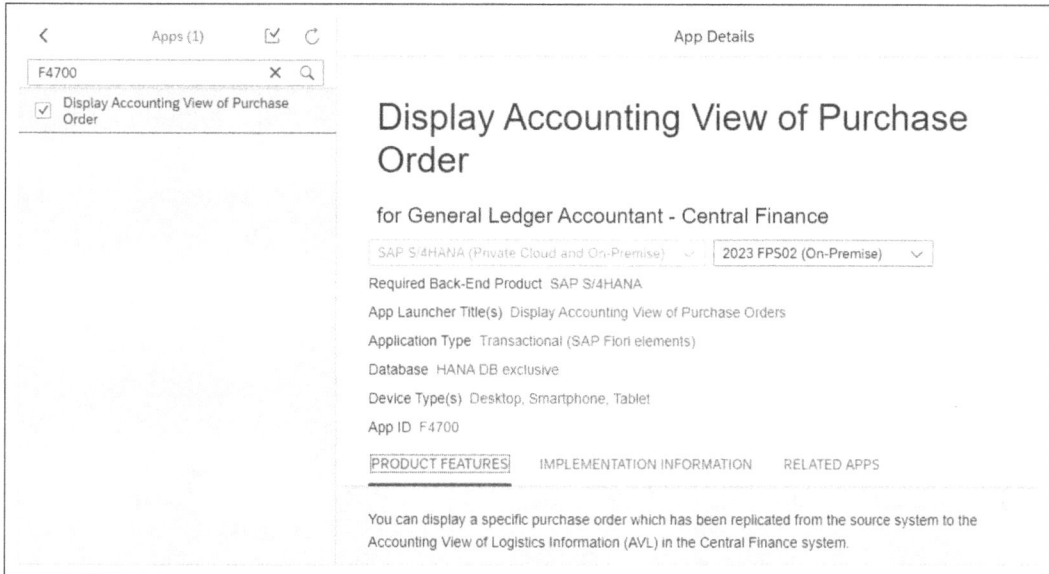

Figure 6-1. Transactional app F4700

6.3.2 Product Features

The **PRODUCT FEATURES** section provides key details about the functionality and business purpose of a specific SAP Fiori app. It helps users understand what the app does and how it fits into business processes. For example, the F4700 app allows you to display a specific purchase order replicated from the source system to the central finance system's Accounting View of Logistics Information (AVL).

6.3.3 Implementation Information

The **IMPLEMENTATION INFORMATION** section provides essential details for deploying the app, including prerequisites, system requirements (software components and versions), and steps for successful implementation in the SAP environment. The information is further divided into four categories, mainly:

- Important SAP Notes

CHAPTER 6   INTRODUCTION TO FIORI APPS

- Installation
- Configuration
- Extensibility

Important SAP Notes

The **Important SAP Notes** offer crucial links for implementing and operating the application, including configuration, updates, and troubleshooting guidance. They also provide information on the FES and BES. Reviewing these notes helps teams address challenges early and adhere to best practices.

System	Note Number	Description
Front-End Server	3336823	Release & Information Note: SAP Fiori for SAP S/4HANA 2023 - SPS 02 (10/2024) FPS
Back-End Server	3426239	Release & Information Note: SAP S/4HANA 2023 - SPS 02 (10/2024) FPS

Show additional notes in SAP Support Portal

Figure 6-2. *Important SAP Notes*

Installation

The **Installation** section outlines the required software components for the app, including SAP back-end versions and the front-end server. It covers deployment options, additional components, and steps for activation and configuration, ensuring technical teams install them efficiently.

Installation for the **FES (Fiori)** for the given app is shown in the figure below.

CHAPTER 6 INTRODUCTION TO FIORI APPS

Front-End Components	
Product Version	SAP FIORI FOR SAP S/4HANA 2023 SAP Fiori for SAP S/4HANA 2023
Support Package Stack	02 (10/2024) FPS
Software Component Version	UIAPFI70 902 - SP 0002
Prerequisite for installation	SAP FIORI FOR SAP S/4HANA 2023 - SPS 02 (10/2024) FPS is an *Add On* to SAP FIORI FES 2023 FOR S/4HANA - SPS 01 (02/2024)

Figure 6-3. *FES components – Fiori*

Installation for the **BES – S/4HANA (ABAP) –** for the given app is shown in the figure below.

Back-End Components (ABAP)	
Product Version	SAP S/4HANA 2023 SAP S/4HANA 2023
Support Package Stack	02 (10/2024) FPS
Software Component Version	S4CORE 108 - SP 0002

Figure 6-4. *BES components – S/4HANA (ABAP)*

Configuration

The **Configuration** section in the SAP Fiori Apps Reference Library guides setting up the app, including activating OData services, enabling business functions, and assigning roles. It also covers back-end configurations, such as maintaining business data. For complex setups, references to SAP Notes are included, ensuring the app is customized for organizational needs and integrates smoothly into the SAP environment. For the given app, the app-specific data is as follows.

CHAPTER 6 INTRODUCTION TO FIORI APPS

Configuration Data for the SAPUI5 Application

SAPUI5 Application			
The ICF nodes for the following SAPUI5 application must be activated on the front-end server:			
Component	Technical Name	Path to ICF Node	SAP UI5 Component
SAP UI5 Application	FIN_CFAVPO	/sap/bc/ui5_ui5/sap/fin_cfavpo	fin.cfin.avpo

Figure 6-5. *Configuration data for the SAPUI5 application*

Configuration Data for OData Services(s)

OData Service(s)			
The following OData services must be activated on the front-end server. Users require PFCG authorization for the front-end and back-end systems.			
OData Service	Version	Software Component Version	Back-End Authorization Role (PFCG)
UI_CFINRPLDPURCHASEORDER	0001	S4CORE 108	

Figure 6-6. *Configuration data for OData services(s)*

SAP Fiori Launchpad

You need the following information to grant users access to the app in the SAP Fiori Launchpad.

Configuration Data for Technical Configuration

Technical Configuration	
SAPUI5 Application	FIN_CFAVPO

Figure 6-7. *Configuration data for technical configuration*

CHAPTER 6 INTRODUCTION TO FIORI APPS

Details of App Launcher(s)

App Launcher(s)		
Title - Subtitle	Information	Parameter-Value
Display Accounting View of Purchase Orders		

Figure 6-8. *Details of App Launcher(s)*

Configuration Data for Target Mapping(s)

Target Mapping(s)		
Semantic Object	Semantic Action	Parameter-Value
CFinReplicatedPurchaseOrder	display	(GLAccount = %%UserDefault.extended.GLAccount%%)& (sap-keep-alive = restricted)& (sap-fiori-id = F4700)& (WBSElement = %%UserDefault.extended.WBSElement%%=>WBSElementExternalID)& (InternalOrder = %%UserDefault.extended.InternalOrder%%=>OrderID)& (ProfitCenter = %%UserDefault.extended.ProfitCenter%%)& (CompanyCode =

Figure 6-9. *Configuration data for target mapping(s)*

> **Note** Target mapping contains semantic objects and semantic action.

315

CHAPTER 6   INTRODUCTION TO FIORI APPS

Details of Technical Catalog(s)

Technical Catalog(s)	
Technical Catalog	Technical Catalog Description
SAP_TC_FIN_CFIN_COMMON	SAP Central Finance: Fiori Apps

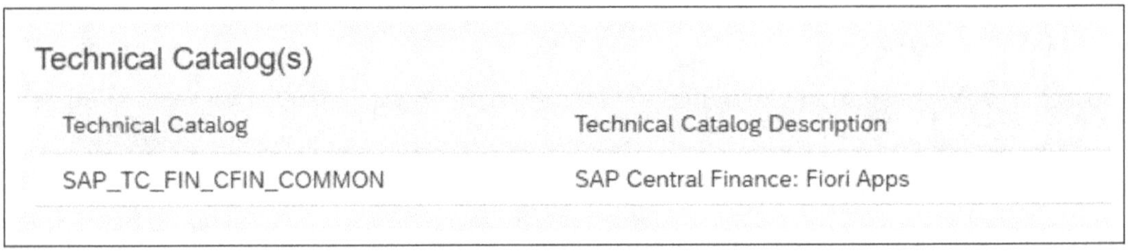

Figure 6-10. *Details of technical catalog(s)*

Details of Business Catalog(s)

Business Catalog(s)	Extend Apps Selection
Business Catalog	Business Catalog Description
☑ SAP_SFIN_BC_AVL_PO	Accounting View of Purchase Order - Display

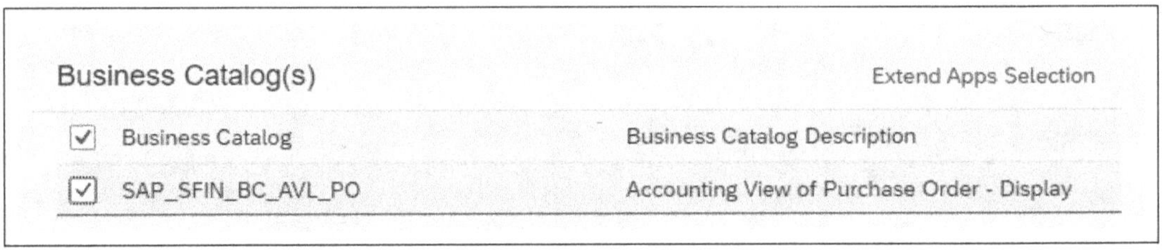

Figure 6-11. *Details of business catalog(s)*

Details of Business Catalog(s) with Extend Apps Selection

Click the option Extend Apps Selection to access the single app in the business catalog.

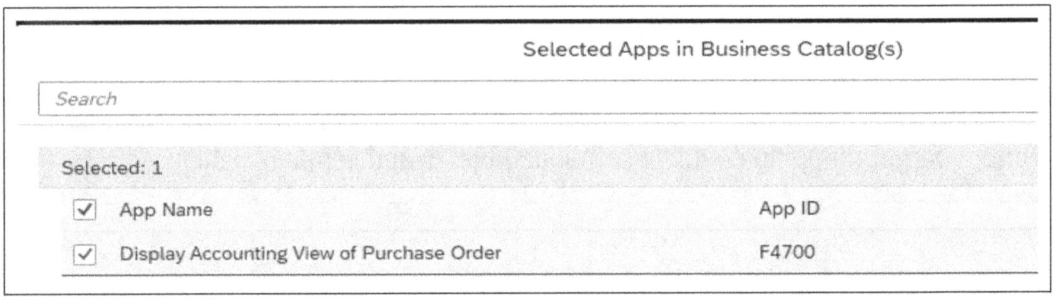

Selected Apps in Business Catalog(s)	
Search	
Selected: 1	
App Name	App ID
☑ Display Accounting View of Purchase Order	F4700

Figure 6-12. *Details of business catalog(s) with Extend Apps Selection*

CHAPTER 6 INTRODUCTION TO FIORI APPS

Details of Available Business Group(s)

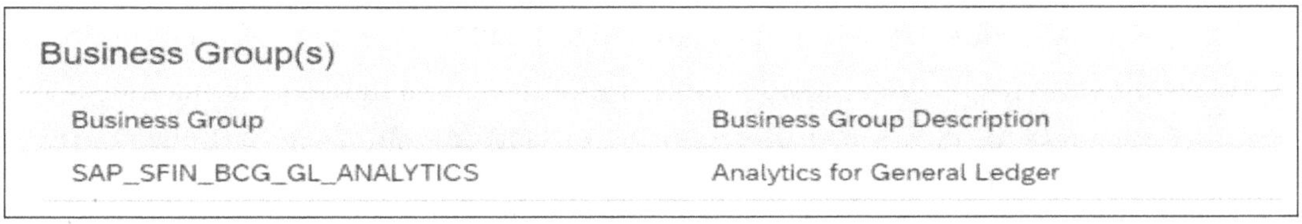

Business Group(s)	
Business Group	Business Group Description
SAP_SFIN_BCG_GL_ANALYTICS	Analytics for General Ledger

Figure 6-13. *Details of business group(s)*

Details of Available Business Role(s)

Business Role(s)	Extend Apps Selection
Business Role	Business Role Description
✓ SAP_BR_GL_ACCOUNTANT_CFIN	General Ledger Accountant - Central Finance

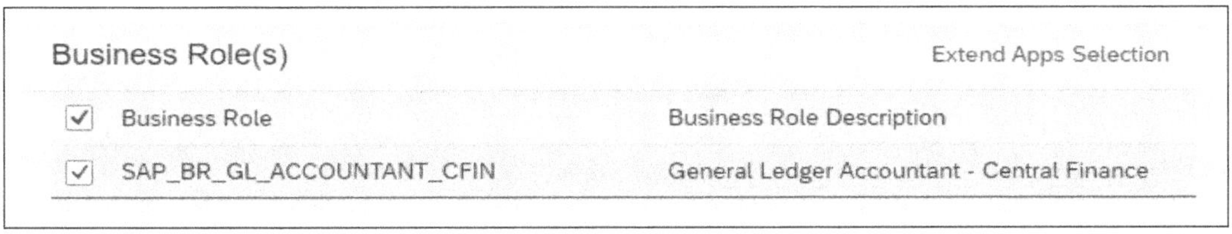

Figure 6-14. *Details of available business role(s)*

Details of Available Business Role(s) with Extend Apps Selection

Click the option Extend Apps Selection within business role(s).

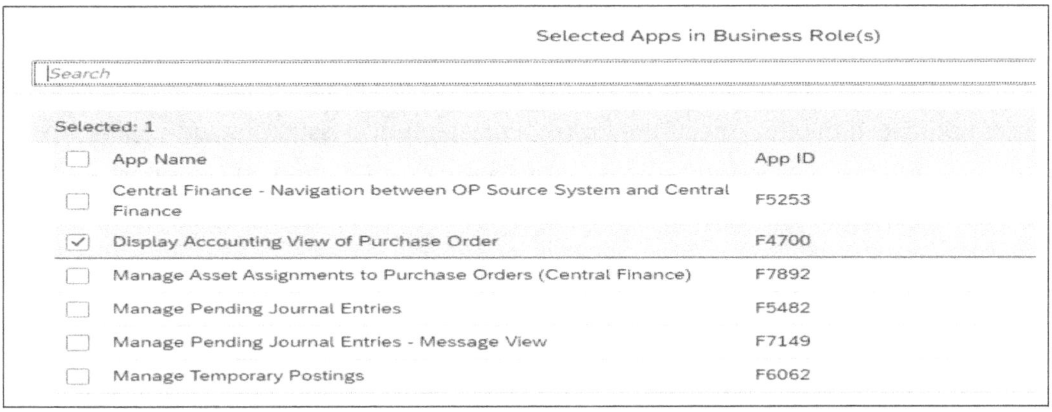

Selected Apps in Business Role(s)	
Search	
Selected: 1	
App Name	App ID
☐ Central Finance - Navigation between OP Source System and Central Finance	F5253
✓ Display Accounting View of Purchase Order	F4700
☐ Manage Asset Assignments to Purchase Orders (Central Finance)	F7892
☐ Manage Pending Journal Entries	F5482
☐ Manage Pending Journal Entries - Message View	F7149
☐ Manage Temporary Postings	F6062

Figure 6-15. *Details of available business role(s) with Extend Apps Selection*

Note The associated business role has the apps assigned to it, as shown in the figure above.

317

Extensibility

The **Extensibility** option for customizing an app to meet business needs includes user interface adjustments, business logic modifications, and data model enhancements using SAP Business Application Studio or SAP Web IDE. It includes features like custom fields and guidelines for maintaining app integrity during updates.

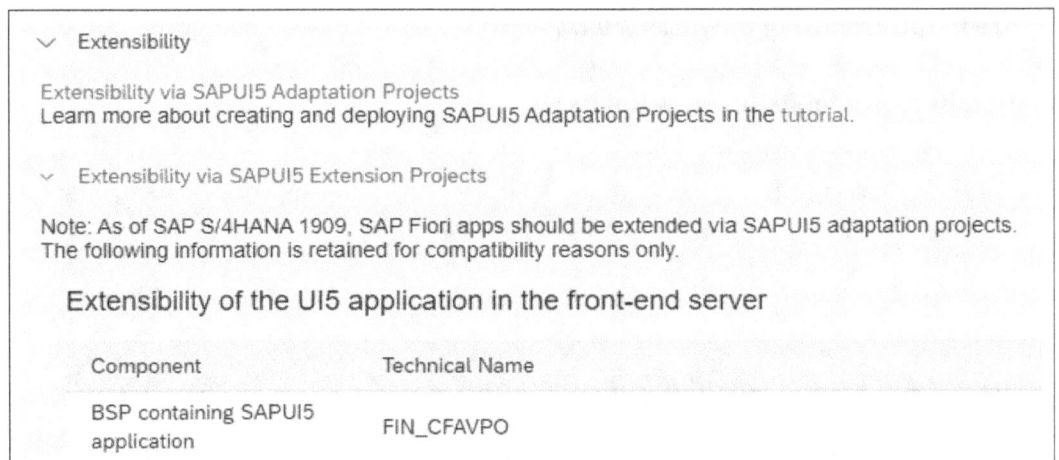

Figure 6-16. Extensibility option

Support

The Support section offers resources for resolving technical issues, including links to SAP Notes and troubleshooting guides, information on contacting SAP support, and maintenance recommendations.

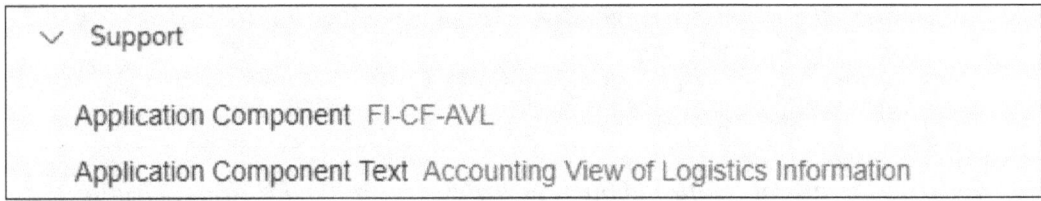

Figure 6-17. Support option

CHAPTER 6 INTRODUCTION TO FIORI APPS

Here are a couple of pointers to remember:

- **Note:** Remember that when you assign the tile or deploy an app, you must also assign target mapping. Otherwise, when the user clicks the tile in the Fiori Launchpad, it will give an **error**.

- **Note:** The associated SICF services will be activated automatically when you activate the OData service.

When deploying apps based on business requirements, it is advisable to create your own Excel file matrix with relevant data, as shown below, covering security and GRC.

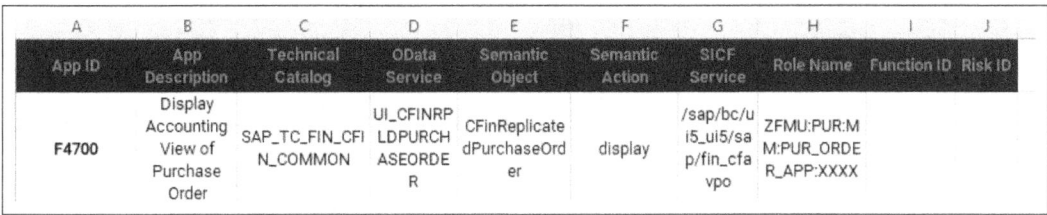

Figure 6-18. *App details in an Excel file*

6.3.4 Summary: Transactional Apps

SAP Fiori transactional apps are crucial in modernizing and simplifying the user experience for SAP users. They make business processes more efficient and accessible across devices. Furthermore, these apps make engaging with SAP systems easier, leading to faster, more informed decision-making and streamlined business processes.

6.4 Analytical Apps

6.4.1 Introduction

Analytical apps offer real-time insights into business data through visual dashboards, reports, and key performance indicators (KPIs). Operating exclusively on the HANA database, they combine SAP HANA's capabilities with SAP Business Suite to provide immediate access to large volumes of data via a web browser. These apps quickly process and analyze large volumes of data. Users can monitor KPIs to evaluate performance and conduct complex calculations, enabling quick responses to market changes. Analytical apps are typically used by business analysts, managers, and decision-makers who need to monitor key performance indicators (KPIs) and other business metrics. Analytical apps are of two types:

- Smart Business
- Virtual data models

To ensure smooth operation, specific prerequisites must be met before implementing analytical apps, as shown in the figure below. These include activating specific SICF services for KPI models and OData services. Failing to meet these requirements can hinder the apps' functionality.

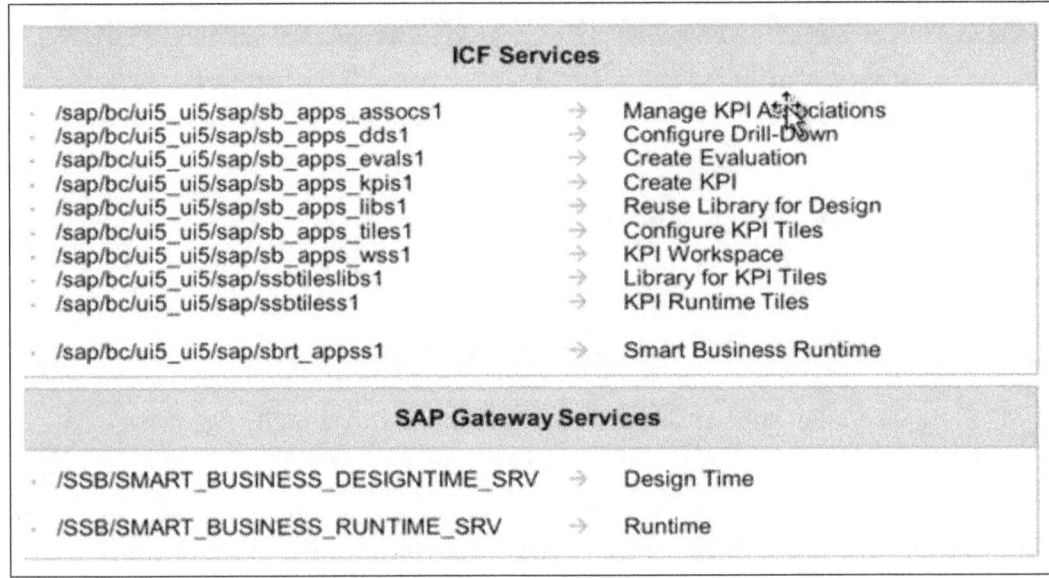

Figure 6-19. Services to be activated for analytical apps to work

With the 1,909 apps of S4HANA, SAP has provided a central app for implementing analytical apps and managing KPIs and reports (F2814). This comprehensive app is designed to streamline your operations and enhance your experience. The configuration of these apps is readily available and easily accessible in the SAP Fiori Apps Reference Library, ensuring a smooth and confident implementation process.

6.4.2 Main Features

Real-Time Data Analysis: SAP Fiori analytical apps leverage the power of SAP HANA to provide real-time data analysis. This enables users to access the most current information and make decisions based on up-to-date insights.

Interactive Dashboards: These apps offer interactive dashboards that allow users to explore data visually. Users can drill down into data, filter results, and view detailed reports directly from the dashboard.

Role-Based Access: Analytical applications are tailored to specific organizational roles, such as sales managers, financial analysts, or supply chain managers. This ensures that users can access the most pertinent data for their role.

Integration with Business Processes: SAP Fiori analytical apps integrate with business processes, enabling users to act based on insights. For example, a sales manager can identify underperforming products and initiate corrective actions.

Customizable KPIs: Users can customize the KPIs displayed in analytical apps to match their specific needs. This flexibility allows organizations to focus on the metrics that matter most to their business.

Accessibility Across Devices: Like other SAP Fiori apps, analytical apps are accessible via web browsers and mobile devices, providing flexibility and mobility for users who need to access data on the go.

Visual Data Representation: These apps provide various visualization options, such as charts, graphs, and maps, to help users quickly understand complex data. Visual representation of data makes it easier to identify trends and patterns.

6.4.3 Summary: Analytical Apps

SAP Fiori analytical apps are crucial in empowering decision-makers with the real-time insights they need to drive business success. By offering interactive dashboards, customizable KPIs, and seamless integration with SAP HANA, these apps help organizations monitor performance, identify trends, and take action based on data-driven insights. Whether accessed from a desktop or a mobile device, SAP Fiori analytical apps make it easier for users to stay informed and make strategic decisions that benefit the business.

6.5 SAP Factsheet Apps

6.5.1 Introduction

SAP Fiori factsheet apps give you quick access to detailed information about specific business objects, like customers or products. They also include links to related documents for more in-depth exploration. Factsheet apps are primarily informational, unlike transactional, action-oriented, or analytical apps, which focus on data analysis. These apps improve user experience by focusing on specific business needs while keeping the interface simple and easy to use.

The factsheet and analytical apps work only with the HANA database, while the transactional apps also support Oracle. They require an ABAP stack and are incompatible with SAP HANA Live tier-2 architecture. **A factsheet app lacks a tile but includes OData and SICF services**. Factsheet apps **enable enterprises** to search for specific data types based on set criteria.

In general, SAP Fiori factsheet apps provide detailed information about specific business objects like customers and products by consolidating relevant data from the SAP system. They are intuitive and focus on essential business insights.

6.5.2 Main Features

The main features of factsheet apps are as follows:

> **Comprehensive View:** Factsheet apps provide a 360-degree view of a specific business object, consolidating information from multiple sources within the SAP system. This includes master data, transactional data, and even related documents.

Real-Time Data Access: The information presented in factsheet apps is typically real time or near real time, ensuring that users have access to the most current data.

Search and Navigation: SAP Fiori's powerful search capabilities allow users to find specific business objects. Once a factsheet is opened, users can easily navigate to related objects or drill down into more detailed information.

Integration with Other Apps: Factsheet apps are often integrated with SAP Fiori transactional and analytical apps, allowing users to act on or analyze data based on the information provided in the factsheet.

Role-Based Access: Like other SAP Fiori apps, factsheet apps are role-based and tailored to provide the most relevant information for the user's role within the organization.

Interactive and Linked Data: Factsheet apps often include hyperlinks to related data or other apps, enabling users to explore related business objects or perform associated tasks directly from the factsheet.

Responsive Design: These apps are designed to be accessible across different devices, including desktops, tablets, and smartphones, ensuring users can access the information they need anytime and anywhere.

Navigation: You can navigate from one factsheet to its related **factsheets**. From a factsheet, we can drill down into its details. For example, you can navigate from a document to the related business partner or the master data.

- **Start Transactions**
    - From factsheets, you can start transactions by navigating to transactional apps or accessing the back-end system directly.
    - For example, from a document factsheet, you can access the back-end system to display details or edit the document in SAP GUI or Web Dynpro.

CHAPTER 6   INTRODUCTION TO FIORI APPS

- **Services**
    - Like transactional apps, each factsheet has an ICF node for the SAPUI5 application, which needs to be activated on the FES, and an SAP Gateway service in the BES, which needs to be registered on the FES. In addition, a **search connector needs to be created for the search model**.

The main difference between these three apps, apart from the purpose (different for each app), is that analytical apps and transactional apps have an App Launcher tile and associated target mapping. In contrast, a **factsheet app does not have an App Launcher tile**. However, all three of them will have an OData service associated with them. Add IWSG and IWSV components for all three apps when building end users' roles. These three apps work on the following databases:

> **Transactional App**: Any database (Oracle and SAP HANA database)
>
> **Analytical App:** SAP HANA database (exclusively)
>
> **Factsheet App:** SAP HANA database (exclusively)

Deployment of Factsheet Apps

For deploying a factsheet app, we need to activate the following:

- OData service
- ICG services
- Search components
- Search model

All the above for a given factsheet app can be found in the SAP Fiori Apps Reference Library.

CHAPTER 6   INTRODUCTION TO FIORI APPS

Note

- Each search connector may have multiple search models.

- For central hub deployment, the search connector components and model must be activated on the back-end S/4HANA system and not on the Fiori front-end system. In contrast, the Fiori front-end system activates OData and SICF services.

- For embedded system deployment, connectors and other services are activated on the same system.

- Factsheet apps do not have tile App Launcher associated with them.

- IWSG and IWSV components need to be added in the role for factsheet apps to work. Furthermore, the connector can be activated using two methods, mainly:

  - Manual method
  - Task list method via transaction code STC01

Manual Method to Activate Connectors

For manual activation, use transaction code SICF and activate the seven services given below along with the path:

- Under the path **/default_host/sap/bc/webdynpro/sap**

  - esh_eng_modeling
  - esh_eng_wizard
  - esh_search_results_ui
  - wdhc_help_center

- Under the path /default_host/sap/es/

  - Cockpit
  - Saplink
  - Search

325

CHAPTER 6   INTRODUCTION TO FIORI APPS

For activation, the following transactions can be used:

- Transaction code **ESH_IMG** for the **setup**
- Transaction code **ESH_COCKPIT** for the **search connector**

Task List Method to Activate Connectors

In this case, for the factsheet to work, the search model must be activated by executing the task list called **SAP_ESH_INITIAL_SETUP_WRK_CLIENT**, which is a **mandatory step** using transaction code **STC01**. This list was also activated as a part of the initial Fiori configuration and qualifies as a prerequisite step. This task list takes a long time to complete, as it should be executed in background mode. In the case of a new implementation, you can perform a blanket activation, which is **full activation** without harming the system for all such **connectors** and **search models** in one go rather than doing **app by app**. For the central hub system, this task list is executed in the S/4HANA back-end system. The task list will also use the manual method to activate all the SICF services.

> **Note**   If not already performed in the SAP_ESH_INITIAL_SETUP_WRK_CLIENT task list, the **SAP_ESH_CREATE_INDEX_SC** task list can be used to create the search connectors of multiple apps. The last step is then registering the SAP Gateway services for transactional apps. The screen below depicts the task list graphically.

CHAPTER 6 INTRODUCTION TO FIORI APPS

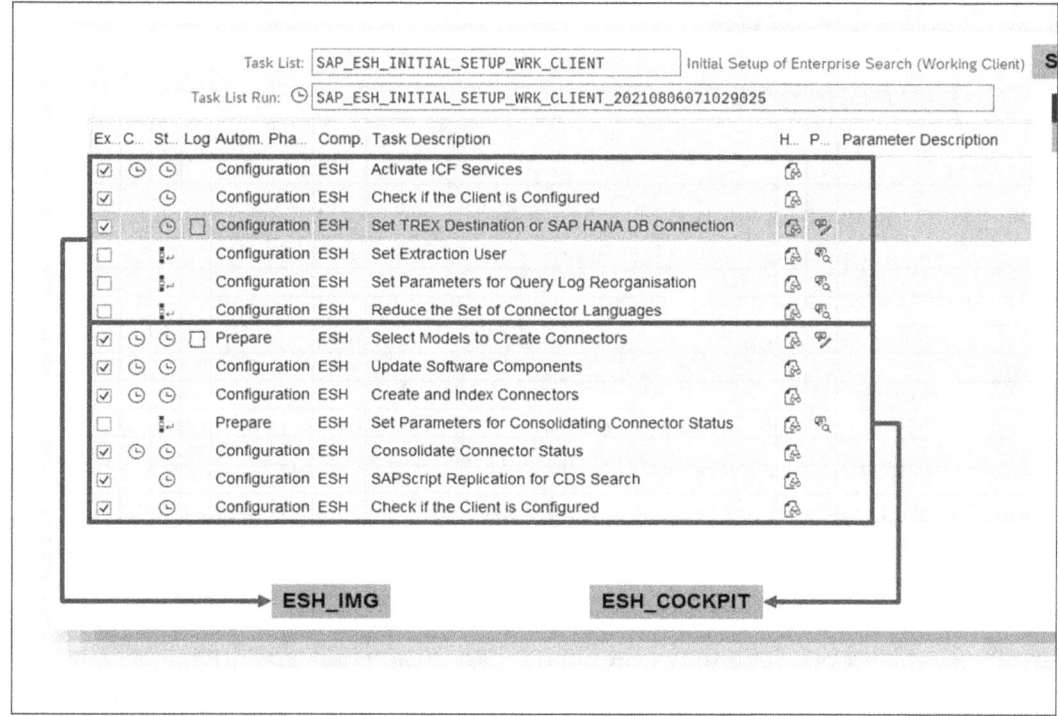

Figure 6-20. Task list SAP_ESH_INITIAL_SETUP_WRK_CLNT initial screen

6.5.3 Summary: Factsheet Apps

SAP Fiori factsheet apps are essential for users who need quick access to detailed information about specific business objects. By providing a comprehensive view of data from various sources within the SAP system, these apps help users understand the full context of a business object, enabling better decision-making and more informed actions. Whether used on a desktop or mobile device, SAP Fiori factsheet apps make it easier for users to find, view, and explore the information they need in a streamlined and efficient manner.

6.6 SAP GUI Apps

6.6.1 Introduction

SAP Fiori **GUI** (Graphical User Interface) **apps** integrate traditional SAP GUI transactions into the Fiori Launchpad, allowing users to access classic and modern applications together. These apps are valuable for scenarios where existing SAP GUI functions are essential and not yet replaceable by Fiori. These apps are launched via SAP GUI for HTML. They provide a web-based experience while maintaining familiar functionality, facilitating a gradual transition to SAP Fiori for organizations.

The SAP GUI application is a client interface that enables users to interact with SAP systems. It provides a graphical interface for data entry, database queries, report generation, and transaction execution. As the front end for SAP's enterprise software suite, it includes finance, human resources, and supply chain management modules.

Note SAP Fiori GUI apps may lack the modern design and user-friendliness of Fiori apps, but they are crucial for power users handling detailed, transaction-heavy tasks.

6.6.2 Main Features

Some of the main features of SAP Fiori GUI apps are

> **Comprehensive Functionality:** SAP GUI apps let you use all the tools in SAP. They help you handle complicated business tasks efficiently.
>
> **Transactional Processing**: These applications manage SAP transactions efficiently, such as VA01 for sales orders and ME21N for purchase orders. They are great for back-office tasks.
>
> **User Interface:** SAP GUI provides a user-friendly interface, enabling users to interact with the SAP system using graphical elements like windows, icons, and menus.

Versions: SAP GUI has several versions, including SAP GUI for Windows, SAP GUI for Java, and SAP GUI for HTML. Each version is designed to run on different operating systems and environments.

Connectivity: SAP GUI connects to the SAP Application Server, allowing users to perform tasks and retrieve or update data stored in the SAP system.

Customizability: Users and administrators can customize the interface to suit specific needs, such as creating shortcuts, personalizing the layout, and configuring settings for better usability.

Security: SAP GUI supports various security measures, including single sign-on (SSO), secure network communication, and user authentication, to ensure the safety of data and transactions.

Functionality: It provides access to various SAP functions, including transactions (transaction codes), reports, dashboards, and analytical tools.

Integration: SAP allows users to access traditional SAP GUI transactions directly within the Fiori Launchpad. This feature is helpful for those who still need to use complex SAP functions that Fiori apps have not yet replaced.

Cross-Module Functionality: Users can perform transactions that involve several SAP modules, such as MM, SD, and FI, all from one interface.

Access to Advanced Features: Many advanced and specialized features, such as configuration tools (e.g., SPRO) and system monitoring transactions (e.g., SM50, SM66), are only accessible via SAP GUI.

SAP Scripting and Automation: SAP GUI enables automation with SAP GUI scripting tools and third-party RPA tools, improving efficiency in repetitive tasks.

6.6.3 Summary: GUI Apps

There are no specific "SAP Fiori GUI apps," but traditional SAP GUI can be integrated into the Fiori environment. This integration acts as a bridge between older and newer SAP interfaces. With more functions transitioning to Fiori, the reliance on SAP GUI is decreasing. However, it still plays a significant role in the SAP landscapes of many organizations.

6.7 SAP Custom Apps

6.7.1 Introduction

SAP Fiori custom apps are specially designed applications built on the SAP Fiori framework to meet specific business needs not covered by standard apps. They use the UI5 framework and OData services for smooth integration with SAP back-end systems, offering a consistent and user-friendly experience. These custom apps provide flexibility to expand Fiori's capabilities and deliver tailored solutions for unique requirements. Fiori developers build these apps.

With SAP Fiori custom apps, companies can personalize workflows and functionalities, ensuring that employees have access to the tools they need in a way that aligns with their day-to-day tasks. This flexibility aids businesses in driving innovation and maintaining a competitive edge in the digital landscape.

6.7.2 Main Features

The main features of custom apps are as follows:

> **Tailored User Experience**: Custom Fiori apps are designed to meet specific business needs, with an optimized user interface that aligns with the SAP Fiori design principle.
>
> **Role-Based Access**: Custom apps give users access to the specific tools and information they need based on their roles. This approach helps improve efficiency and keeps data secure.

Integration with SAP Back End: These apps connect easily with SAP systems like S/4HANA and ECC using OData services. This setup allows users to interact with data in real time.

Enhanced Workflows: Custom apps simplify workflows by combining features from different standard apps or adding new functions that meet the business's specific needs.

Responsive Design: Custom apps built on the SAPUI5 framework work well on various devices, like desktops, tablets, and smartphones. They are designed to be responsive and easy to access.

Custom Analytics and Dashboards: Custom apps may include dynamic analytics, key performance indicators (KPIs), and dashboards that provide valuable user insights.

Improved Efficiency: Custom apps expedite processes like approvals, reporting, and data entry by removing redundant steps and offering real-time notifications.

Flexible UI Adaptations: Custom apps let businesses customize their look with themes, layouts, and filters. This helps match their brand and meet user preferences.

Seamless Launchpad Integration: Custom Fiori apps work well with the SAP Fiori Launchpad, which provides a uniform navigation experience like other standard applications.

Custom Notifications and Alerts: Custom apps can send push notifications for important updates and actions, informing users in real time.

6.8 Comparison of Various Apps

Various apps provided by SAP Fiori are compared below in a tabular format.

CHAPTER 6 INTRODUCTION TO FIORI APPS

Feature/Aspect	Transactional Apps	Analytical Apps	Factsheet Apps	GUI Apps
Purpose	To perform business transactions	To provide insights and analytics	To provide detailed information	To provide a graphical user interface
Functionality	Data entry, process transactions	Data analysis, reporting, dashboards	Detailed view of a single object	Access to SAP system and its modules
User Interaction	Interactive, action-oriented	Interactive, exploration, visualization	Read-only, detailed data presentation	Interactive, various user actions
Data Source	Operational data from SAP systems	Aggregated data, often from BW or HANA	Detailed object data, often real-time	Operational data from SAP systems
Typical Users	Operational users, clerks, managers	Analysts, managers, decision-makers	Managers, supervisors, users needing details	All SAP users
Examples	Sales order entry, purchase requisition	Sales performance dashboard, financial reports	Customer factsheet, material factsheet	SAP GUI for Windows, SAP GUI for Java
Technology Stack	SAP Fiori, ABAP, UI5	SAP Fiori, SAP HANA, BI tools	SAP Fiori, OData services	SAP GUI (various versions)
Customization	Highly customizable	Customizable to fit business needs	Limited customization	Customizable through GUI settings
Performance	Real-time or near real-time	Near real-time, batch processing	Real-time	Real-time
Access	Via web browser (Fiori Launchpad)	Via web browser (Fiori Launchpad)	Via web browser (Fiori Launchpad)	Desktop application
Security	Role-based access control	Role-based access control	Role-based access control	Role-based access control

Figure 6-21. *Comparison of various SAP Fiori apps*

6.9 Pros and Cons of SAP Fiori Apps

Aspect	Transactional Apps	Analytical Apps	Factsheet Apps	GUI Apps
Pros				
Efficiency	Streamline business processes	Provide deep insights for decision-making	Quick access to detailed information	Comprehensive access to SAP functionalities
Usability	User-friendly, task-specific interfaces	Intuitive data visualization and dashboards	Easy to navigate and understand	Familiar interface for SAP users
Real-time Data	Access to real-time operational data	Near real-time data analysis	Real-time detailed data	Real-time interaction with SAP system
Customization	Highly customizable to specific needs	Flexible and adaptable to business needs	Tailored views of object data	Customizable user settings and shortcuts
Integration	Seamless integration with SAP business processes	Integration with various data sources	Integrated with other SAP Fiori apps	Integration with all SAP modules
Accessibility	Accessible via web browsers and mobile devices	Accessible via web browsers and mobile devices	Accessible via web browsers and mobile devices	Desktop and some mobile interfaces
Cons				
Complexity	May require training for complex transactions	Can be complex to set up and maintain	Limited to specific object information	Can be overwhelming for new users
Performance	Dependent on network and system performance	Performance can be impacted by data volume	Limited to single object view	Performance varies based on system and network
Customization Cost	Customization can be time-consuming and costly	Customization may require significant effort	Limited customization options	High customization can lead to complexity
Scalability	Scalability may require significant effort	Scalability can be complex with large datasets	Limited scalability due to focused scope	Scalable but can be resource-intensive
Data Source Dependency	Dependent on operational data accuracy	Quality of insights depends on data accuracy	Limited by the detail and accuracy of object data	Dependent on the quality of backend systems
Security	Needs robust security measures	Requires strong data governance and security	Needs robust security measures	Requires comprehensive security protocols
User Roles	Primarily operational users	Primarily analysts and decision makers	Primarily managers and detailed reviewers	Wide range of users with varying

Figure 6-22. Pros and cons of various SAP Fiori apps

6.10 Summary

This chapter explored how SAP Fiori apps transform user experience with a modern, role-based interface that enhances device usability. Their responsive design and seamless integration with SAP back-end systems enable users to perform tasks more efficiently. We categorized Fiori apps into transactional, analytical, factsheet, and GUI apps, each serving distinct purposes: **Transactional apps** streamline processes like order creation and invoice posting. **Analytical apps** deliver real-time insights through data visualization for effective KPI monitoring. **By consolidating data from multiple sources, factsheet apps provide a 360-degree view of business objects, such as customers or materials**, and traditional **SAP GUI** apps manage complex tasks such as user management and system configuration. Overall, these apps significantly enhance productivity, facilitate informed decision-making, and optimize business operations, making understanding their architecture and implementation crucial for maximizing the benefits of SAP Fiori.

CHAPTER 7

Introduction to SAP Fiori Catalogs

*SAP Fiori catalogs are groups of Fiori apps organized by business roles. They help users find the applications they need in the **SAP Fiori Launchpad**. While catalogs show which apps users can access, they do not control how these apps are displayed – that's handled by **spaces and pages**. Catalogs can include tiles, target mappings, and links to different SAP applications, such as classic SAP GUI transactions, Web Dynpro apps, and Fiori apps. Administrators create and assign these catalogs using the SAP Fiori Launchpad Designer or SAP Fiori Launchpad Content Manager. This process ensures that users see only the applications that match their roles and business needs. Good catalog management enhances the user experience, boosts security, and increases system efficiency by making it easier to access the right tools.*

7.1 Introduction

SAP Fiori catalogs, a cornerstone of the SAP Fiori user experience, are meticulously designed with the user in mind. They are a structured collection of related apps, tiles, and links that users can access based on their roles. These catalogs, assigned to users through roles, ensure they can access only the apps and functions relevant to their job responsibilities. This user-centric approach enhances the user experience by providing a personalized and streamlined interface and helps maintain security and governance within the SAP environment.

SAP Fiori catalogs are not just a feature but an essential tool in managing and deploying SAP Fiori applications within an organization. They act as containers that group related apps, UI elements, and services, which are then made available to users based on their roles and responsibilities. Each catalog typically includes tiles representing specific Fiori apps and links to other resources, such as SAP GUI transactions, Web Dynpro applications, or external web links.

The primary function of a catalog is to empower users by simplifying access control and app distribution. It organizes apps into logical categories that align with business processes or user roles. For instance, a procurement manager might access a catalog that includes apps related to purchase order management, supplier evaluation, and inventory tracking. In contrast, an HR manager might have a different catalog with apps for employee records, leave approvals, and performance reviews. This system puts the control in the hands of the users, ensuring they have access to the tools they need and making them feel in control and efficient.

Catalogs are closely linked with SAP spaces and pages and with SAP Fiori groups, which contain collections of tiles users see on their Fiori Launchpad. While catalogs determine which apps a user can access, groups decide which apps are displayed on the user's Launchpad, providing a tailored view that meets the user's daily needs.

In addition to enhancing user experience through tailored access, SAP Fiori catalogs play a crucial role in maintaining security and compliance. By controlling access at the catalog level, administrators can ensure that users only have access to the specific apps and data they need, reducing the risk of unauthorized access and helping to maintain compliance with organizational policies and regulations. This robust system provides reassurance and confidence in the security of the SAP environment.

With the current addition of SAP S/4HANA, the SAP Fiori catalogs, spaces, and pages form the backbone of a personalized and intuitive user experience in the SAP Fiori environment. In this book, we will cover how to create various types of catalogs using three transaction codes:

- **SAP Fiori Launchpad App Manager: /UI2/FLPAM**
- **Launchpad Content Manager: /UI2/FLPCM_CUST**
- **Fiori Launchpad Designer: /UI2/FLPD_CUST**

Before proceeding further, we need to understand how you can create Fiori objects and assign them to the user to perform the task. The administrator personnel can create these Fiori objects. SAP allows two ways with which these objects can be developed:

- **SAP GUI**: Transaction code approach
- **SAP Fiori Launchpad**: /UI2/FLP and using SAP-delivered apps

7.1.1 SAP GUI

SAP GUI (Graphical User Interface) is the traditional client interface that interacts with SAP systems. It provides users with a graphical interface to perform various business transactions and tasks within SAP. SAP GUI is designed to connect users to SAP environments like SAP ERP, SAP S/4HANA, and other SAP applications, presenting a structured layout of screens, menus, fields, and buttons. Users can access functionalities such as data entry, reporting, and system administration through this interface. For example, a financial accountant might use SAP GUI to enter invoices, post journal entries, and run financial reports. SAP GUI can be installed on different platforms, including Windows and Java-based systems, and as a web-based version, making it flexible for different technical environments. Despite the growing adoption of the more modern SAP Fiori interface, SAP GUI remains widely used, especially in scenarios that require complex data entry and legacy transaction processing.

7.1.2 SAP Fiori Launchpad

The SAP Fiori Launchpad is a web-based starting point for SAP Fiori applications. It offers a personalized, role-based experience across different devices. Users can access their SAP Fiori apps, which are organized into tiles, groups, or spaces based on their roles and tasks. The Launchpad has a modern, easy-to-use interface that works well on desktops, tablets, and mobile devices. Users can quickly find their most common apps, search for new ones, and receive notifications, all from the Launchpad. It connects smoothly with SAP's systems, helping users complete their business processes efficiently. Users can customize their experience by adding tiles or rearranging groups. This makes the SAP Fiori Launchpad a valuable tool for easy access to enterprise applications.

Access a system via the Launchpad, for example, a sales manager might use the SAP Fiori Launchpad to monitor sales performance through a dashboard tile. In contrast, an HR manager might access tiles for employee data management or leave approval. The Launchpad's responsive design ensures that users can efficiently navigate their SAP environment regardless of their device.

CHAPTER 7 INTRODUCTION TO SAP FIORI CATALOGS

When the admin user logs into the Fiori Launchpad, they can access eight apps, as shown in the figure below. Users can manage catalogs, and a new option called "Create Launchpad Pages from Groups" has been introduced, as the business groups concept will soon be deprecated. The breakdown of these apps are as follows:

- Launchpad App Manager
- Launchpad Content Manager – Cross Client
- Launchpad Content Manager – Client Specific
- Manage Launchpad Spaces
- Manage Launchpad Pages
- Launchpad Designer – Client Specific
- Launchpad Designer – Cross Client
- Create Launchpad Pages from Groups

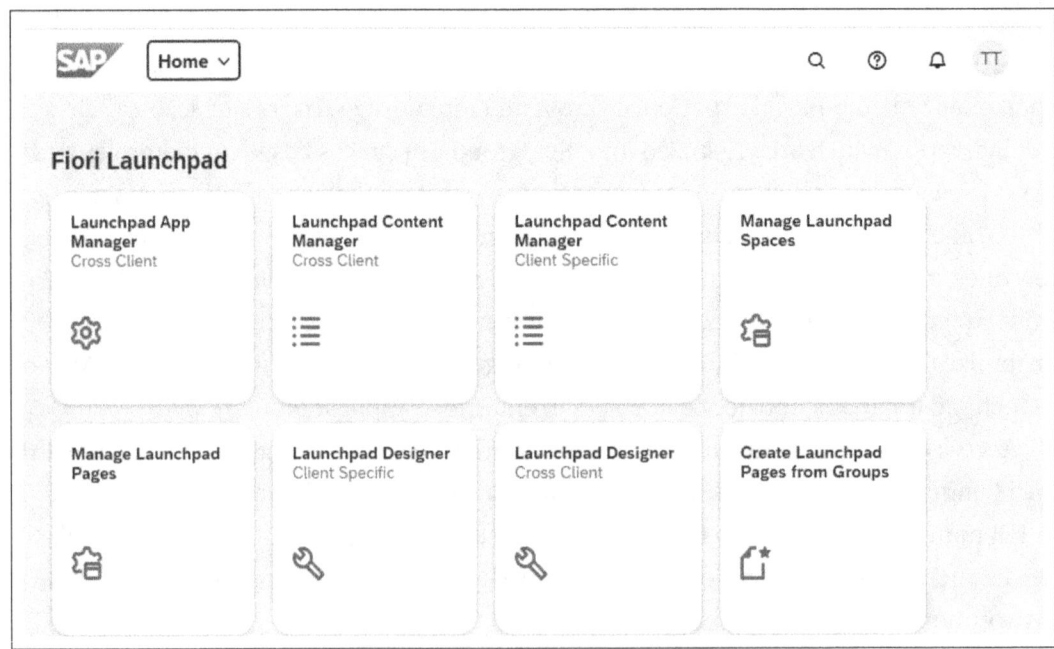

Figure 7-1. *SAP Fiori Launchpad for the security administrator*

7.2 Catalogs

Catalogs are the fundamental components that define apps for user selection and authorization. Users find apps in authorized catalogs using the App Finder or SAP Fiori search. Security administrators assign authorizations to a security role using catalogs to access all listed apps. In other words, catalogs are collections of all the tiles; each tile represents precisely one application. We create a catalog to package all tiles according to team, functional area, application component, functionality, and area of responsibility. Catalogs collect apps regardless of the technology type. For example, a single catalog can contain a mix of SAP Fiori apps, Web Dynpro ABAP applications, SAP GUI transactions, or WebClient applications. Depending on the role and the catalogs assigned to the role, users can browse the catalogs and choose the apps they want to display on the entry page of the SAP Fiori Launchpad.

Thus, SAP Fiori is a powerful product with pre-built catalogs, groups, spaces, pages, and roles, making it easy for users and security consultants to adapt and activate solutions quickly. SAP standard apps are designed to be more standard, so manual tiles are unnecessary, saving time and effort and reducing implementation costs. This provides **out-of-the-box SAP Fiori content** that businesses can use confidently. The SAP-delivered content within the SAP Fiori Launchpad is as follows:

- Technical catalog (TC)
- Business catalog (BC)
- Business catalog group (BCG)
- Business roles (BR)
- Spaces and pages

7.3 Technical Catalogs

An SAP Fiori technical catalog is a comprehensive collection of all available apps, UI elements, and services within the SAP Fiori environment, focused on the technical aspects of app management. Administrators primarily use these catalogs to organize and bundle the necessary components, such as roles, tiles, and target mappings, that enable the apps to function. Technical catalogs differ from business catalogs as they are not tailored to specific roles or processes. Instead, they provide a comprehensive repository of technical resources for various scenarios within the organization. This foundational role is vital for setting up and maintaining the SAP Fiori environment, ensuring access to all necessary technical components for different business contexts.

SAP technical catalogs store all SAP-delivered apps, including target mappings and App Launcher tiles. They are essential for managing apps in the SAP Fiori Launchpad and defining the structure and content of the Launchpad. These catalogs also contain original tiles and mappings used as references within the business catalogs. They are not directly assigned to users but provide the building blocks for other catalogs. **Technical catalogs** are essential for organizing and managing apps within the **SAP Fiori Launchpad**. They define the structure and content of the Launchpad, including how apps are grouped and accessed. SAP provides standard catalogs that could be used to reference apps in custom business catalogs. These standard catalogs can be searched by using the search criteria **SAP_TC_*<......>**. An example of a technical catalog is **SAP_TC_CEC_SD_COMMON**.

SAP recommends using technical catalogs, with the naming convention <...>_TC_<...>.

There are two ways to create a technical catalog:

- **Transaction Code MM_APP**: Applicable before S/4HANA 2020
- **Transaction Code /UI2/FLPAM**: Manage Launchpad Apps (Cross Client)

7.4 Business Catalogs

An SAP Fiori **business catalog** is a tailored collection of apps and services designed for specific business user roles. Unlike technical catalogs, which encompass all available apps, business catalogs provide only the necessary tools for users' job functions, enhancing productivity by reducing complexity. By aligning apps with business processes, they streamline workflows and make it easier for users to perform daily tasks. A business catalog can group related apps by purpose, such as factsheets for a particular line of business or an overview page with its target apps. Business catalogs can be shared across different roles.

Business catalogs reference tiles and target mappings in the technical catalog, meeting specific user requirements (e.g., sales representatives, purchasers, sales managers). They are assigned to business roles. This ensures consistency, with any changes in the technical catalogs being propagated to the business catalog. These standard business catalogs can be searched by using the search criteria **SAP_*_BC_*<......>**. An example of a business catalog is **SAP_SD_BC_SDOC_WIAPRV**.

SAP recommends using business catalogs, with the naming convention <...>_BC_<...>.

There are two ways to create business catalogs:

- **Transaction Code /UI2/FLPD_CUST**: Fiori Launchpad Designer – Client Specific

- **Transaction Code /UI2/FLP/FLPCM_CUST**: Fiori Launchpad Content Manager – Client Specific

7.5 Business Catalog Group

It is essential to categorize apps based on business requirements to allow users to find and access them easily. However, it is necessary to note that SAP introduced the concept of spaces and pages in S/4HANA 2020 and has announced that the concept of Fiori groups will be deprecated in future S/4HANA releases. A business group is a collection of apps from one or more catalogs, and the tiles displayed on a user's entry page depend on the groups assigned to the user's role. Users can personalize their entry page by adding or removing apps to or from pre-delivered or self-defined groups. While SAP does not mandate migration, it is highly recommended to do so. The SAP Fiori groups concept displays all apps assigned to users on one Launchpad page. Though it may seem to be a convenient approach to giving access to users, a large volume of apps assigned to users could result in performance issues and bad user experience. SAP has provided a technical naming convention for the technical business catalog group, **SAP_BCG -<...>**, for example, **SAP_SD_BCG_SALES_ORDER_PROCESSING**.

7.6 Business Roles (SAP_BR*)

A business role (SAP_BR*) is a template that gives all business catalog and group content access through a single point. As of SAP S/4HANA 2023, SP02 has more than 500 business roles, forming the foundation for rapid Fiori activation. You can find role names and search apps in the FLP reference library. During the fit-to-standard workshop, mapping roles to users is essential. An Excel file should be maintained. An example of an SAP business role is **SAP_BR_GL_ACCOUNTANT**.

7.7 SAP Fiori Objects Used in Catalogs

In SAP Fiori, "tile" and "target mapping" are fundamental concepts that define how users interact with applications within the SAP Fiori Launchpad. Together, tiles and target mappings form the backbone of the SAP Fiori Launchpad, enabling a user-friendly, efficient, and role-based navigation experience.

7.7.1 Tile

A tile in SAP Fiori is a visual element on the Launchpad that users can click to access an application. Tiles are designed to provide a quick overview or entry point to various functions and data. They can display real-time information, such as key performance indicators (KPIs), numbers, or status updates, and are organized into groups based on user roles or business functions. For example, a tile might show the number of open purchase orders, and clicking it would give the user a detailed view of those orders.

Tiles are customizable, allowing users or administrators to configure the displayed information and its appearance, which enhances the user experience. Therefore, a tile serves as a square box that provides an entry point or visual representation for an app on the Launchpad home page, consisting of two parts:

- **Tile**
  - **Tile Properties**: Title, subtitle, icon
- **Target Mapping**
  - Maps the intent with the actual Fiori app, WebGUI, T-codes, and Web Dynpro app

7.7.2 Target Mapping

Target mapping is the configuration that links a tile to a specific application or function. It defines what happens when a user clicks a tile, such as which application or transaction is launched, along with any parameters that should be passed to that application. Target mapping ensures the correct application is opened with the appropriate context, making it a critical component for navigating the SAP Fiori environment. For example, if a tile represents a report, the target mapping would define which specific report application is launched and what data is displayed when the user clicks the tile. This linkage between the tile and the application allows a seamless user experience, ensuring users are directed to the right tools and information with just one click.

Semantic Object

- The **semantic object** represents a business entity or object (e.g., "Customer," "Order," "Invoice"). It is a conceptual identifier used to categorize the type of application or action the tile will initiate. Semantic objects help standardize navigation across different applications.

Semantic Action

- The **action** is associated with the semantic object and defines what operation will be performed when the tile is clicked. Everyday actions include "display," "edit," "create," or "manage." For instance, with the semantic object "Customer," the action might be "display" to show customer details.

Note A target mapping consists of semantic object-semantic action, for example, SalesOrder-manage or OutboundDelivery-track. Semantic action is always in lowercase.

Target Application Type

- This defines the type of application that will be launched. The target could be a SAPUI5 application, Web Dynpro ABAP, SAP transaction, or an external URL. It specifies the technology and type of interface the user will interact with.

Target Parameters

- **Parameters** are optional elements that can be passed to the application to provide context or specific data. For example, when navigating to an "Order Display" application, parameters could include the order number or customer ID, ensuring the application opens with pre-populated relevant information.

Target Mapping ID

- The **target mapping ID** is a unique identifier within the system that helps reference and manage different target mappings.

Intent-Based Navigation

- **Intent-based navigation** combines the semantic object and action into a navigation intent. This intent is what links the tile to the specific application or functionality. It abstracts the underlying technical details, allowing users to navigate across different applications seamlessly. For example, tile Display Sales Order target mapping is SalesOrder-display. **Note:** Every application in the entire system has a unique intent.

Device-Specific Settings

- Target mapping can also include settings that dictate how the application should behave on different devices, such as desktops, tablets, or smartphones. This ensures a consistent user experience across all platforms.

Authorization and Role Mapping

- Target mapping also considers user roles and authorizations to ensure that only users with the appropriate permissions can access specific applications. This security layer protects sensitive data and functionality.

Note Target mapping maps the **intent** with the actual **Fiori app**, **WeBGUI**, **T-codes**, and **Web Dynpro app**.

Conclusion

Target mapping in SAP Fiori is a detailed configuration that ensures a tile on the Fiori Launchpad correctly launches the intended application with the appropriate context. It is a fundamental part of the user navigation experience in SAP Fiori.

7.8 Understanding Intents

Intents are part of the intent-based navigation that controls app-to-app navigation and navigation from tiles or links to apps. They are the logical connection that controls navigation between any SAP Fiori app and any other SAP Fiori app, classic UI, or URL.

An intent consists of two components:

- **Semantic Object**: The business object involved in the activity. Area of interest, for example, PurchaseRequisition, AccountingDocument, SalesOrder, PurchaseOrder, OutboundDelivery, Customer, Vendor, Sales.

- **Semantic Action**: Defines the purpose of our Fiori application. Indicative of the activity that we want to perform on the business object, for example, create, change, manage, edit, approve, import, track, maintain, execute, analyze.

The tile definition and the target mapping include the semantic object and semantic action in their definition.

When a business user selects a tile or link at runtime, the system uses the chosen action, device type, and other details to decide which app or interface to open. This is done through a URL pattern that includes the semantic object, action, and the parameters' values. The correct target mapping is then launched based on the mapping's semantic object, action, device type, and other specifics. The semantic object is key in how users move between apps, especially in dynamically generated navigation lists found in Fiori search results, lists of links, dialogs, and related apps.

Most importantly, these dynamic navigation use cases are why using the given SAP semantic object ID that best fits your use case when creating custom content is critical, that is, so your custom-created navigations are dynamically proposed alongside SAP-delivered navigations.

Note You should only create custom semantic objects if no SAP equivalent is available. For example, when you make a custom application for business entities specific to your organization and with no SAP equivalent, for security team SU53, SU01D, and SPRO, custom semantic objects should be in the customer namespace, that is, by convention, start with **Z** or **Y**.

7.9 SAP Best Practice Recommendations

SAP provides technical and business content for the catalogs, groups, and roles related to apps that use an App Launcher tile. The business content includes business catalogs and roles, which can be used as examples for designing your roles, catalogs, and groups.

When you create your catalogs, groups, and roles for these apps, SAP recommends using the technical content as a starting point. The technical content includes TCs containing apps for a particular product area. You can identify TCs by looking for SAP_TC_* in their technical name.

7.10 Summary

In SAP Fiori, catalogs are essential for defining and organizing the apps and services accessible to users, with two main types: technical and business catalogs. Technical catalogs focus on the technical aspects of app management, containing all apps, UI elements, and services that can be utilized within the SAP Fiori environment. These catalogs are not tailored to specific users but serve as a repository of all potential apps for various business scenarios administrators manage. In contrast, business catalogs are user-centric and designed around specific business roles and processes. They include a filtered subset of the technical catalogs, offering a more tailored experience that aligns with the needs of users or roles. This focused approach ensures users have streamlined access to relevant apps and services, enhancing productivity and reducing complexity. In essence, while technical catalogs provide a broad view of all technical elements, business catalogs offer a more focused, role-specific selection of tools and services.

CHAPTER 8

SAP Fiori Launchpad App Manager

The SAP Fiori Launchpad App Manager (/UI2/FLPAM) is an important tool in the SAP Fiori environment. It helps administrators and developers create and manage technical catalogs easily. This tool provides a simple interface to organize Fiori applications, making them easy to find and keep updated. It helps streamline the organization and management of application settings, improves overall efficiency, and creates a better digital workspace.

8.1 Introduction

This chapter will discuss how to create SAP Fiori technical catalogs. We have discussed the technical catalog concept in Chapter 7. Creating an SAP Fiori technical catalog involves organizing and bundling the technical components needed to support SAP Fiori apps. The process begins within the SAP Fiori Launchpad Designer, where an administrator defines a new technical catalog by specifying its name and ID. Once the catalog is created, the administrator adds various technical objects, such as tiles, target mappings, and **app descriptors**, which define the behavior and appearance of the apps within the Fiori Launchpad. These technical objects are linked to specific SAPUI5 applications or other Fiori elements that users will interact with. The administrator also assigns roles and authorizations to ensure that the right users have access to the relevant apps in the catalog. After the catalog is configured, it is tested to ensure that all components work as intended and that users can access the apps without issues. The final catalog can then be transported across the SAP landscape, making it available in

CHAPTER 8 SAP FIORI LAUNCHPAD APP MANAGER

different environments (e.g., development, testing, production). Generally, the Fiori Launchpad App Manager, also known as the **Mass Maintenance tool**, has the following features:

- A single tool for managing all Fiori technical catalogs
- Allows users to explore the existing SAP standard technical catalogs
- Provides excellent search functionality
- Enables exploration of all content, including tiles and target mappings, within the catalog
- Also enables the maintenance of the **Fiori LPD App Descriptor** item

Note SAP has introduced a new feature in the App Manager tool (**App Descriptor**) that involves target mapping based on the app type for one or more tiles. A technical catalog can include several Launchpad App Descriptor items. This tool makes it easy to manage content without navigating through many steps.

This structured approach ensures that all necessary technical elements are correctly organized and accessible, facilitating smooth app deployment and management within the SAP Fiori environment. There are two ways to create a technical catalog:

- Transaction code **MM_APP**
- Transaction code **/UI2/FLPAM – Manage Launchpad Apps (Cross Client)**

Before proceeding to create a technical catalog, it is essential to understand the concept of copying such a catalog. A custom technical catalog can be developed using deep and soft copy, as discussed below.

8.1.1 Deep Copy

In SAP Fiori, the term **deep copy** of a technical catalog refers to creating a complete, independent duplicate of an existing technical catalog, including all its associated objects, such as tiles, target mappings, and app descriptors. This differs from a regular copy, where only references to the original objects might be created, rather than complete, independent copies.

Features of Deep Copy

- **Full Duplication:** When performing a deep copy, the entire structure of the technical catalog is duplicated. This includes all the tiles, target mappings, and other related elements. Each component is copied as a new object, not just as a reference to the original.

- **Independence from Original:** The new catalog and its components are entirely independent of the original catalog. Any changes to the deep-copied catalog do not affect the original catalog and vice versa.

- **Customization:** Deep copying is beneficial when you create a new catalog based on an existing one, but it requires the flexibility to modify it without impacting the original. For example, if you need to adapt a standard SAP-delivered technical catalog to fit specific organizational needs, deep copying allows you to make those changes safely.

- **Use Case:** This approach is often used when customizing the Fiori environment to align with different business processes or roles. It allows organizations to maintain their version of a catalog while still preserving the original version for other uses or as a backup.

Examples of Deep Copy

- **Create a New Technical Catalog:** Use the Fiori Launchpad Designer or the /UI2/FLPAM transaction to create a new, empty technical catalog.

- **Manually Add App Descriptors:**
  - Open the original technical catalog and identify the app descriptors you want to copy.
  - In the new catalog, use the "Add New Launchpad App Descriptor Item" function to recreate each app descriptor manually from the original catalog.
  - Ensure you provide unique IDs for the new app descriptors to avoid conflicts.

CHAPTER 8   SAP FIORI LAUNCHPAD APP MANAGER

- **Configure Target Mappings:** If the original catalog had target mappings associated with its app descriptors, you must recreate them in the new catalog.

- **Assign to Business Catalogs (Optional):** If the original technical catalog was assigned to any business catalogs, you will need to assign the new technical catalog to the relevant business catalogs to make the copied apps available to users.

- **Key Points:**

  - This approach creates a new technical catalog with its app descriptors independent of the original catalog.

  - Changes to the app descriptors in one catalog will not affect the other.

  - This process can be time-consuming if the original catalog contains many app descriptors.

  - Consider using this approach when creating a genuinely isolated copy of a technical catalog for customization or experimentation purposes.

Note Always exercise caution when modifying or copying technical catalogs, as incorrect configurations can impact the availability and functionality of Fiori apps for users.

Thus, deep copying a technical catalog in SAP Fiori creates an entirely independent duplicate of an existing catalog, allowing for safe customization and modification without altering the original catalog.

8.1.2 Soft Copy

In the context of SAP Fiori, **soft copy** usually refers to a digital or electronic copy of an object or document within the system. This can include

- **Copied Business Objects:** When you use the "Copy" function within a Fiori app, you're creating a soft copy of an existing business object

CHAPTER 8 SAP FIORI LAUNCHPAD APP MANAGER

(e.g., a sales order, purchase requisition, or material master). This copy is a new, independent object that inherits data from the original but can be modified and saved separately.

- **Print Previews and Reports:** In some cases, "soft copy" might also refer to the digital output generated by a print preview or report within a Fiori app. This output can often be saved or shared electronically in formats like PDF or CSV.

Features of Soft Copy

- **Nonphysical:** A soft copy is intangible and exists only in digital form within the SAP system or as an exported file.

- **Editable:** Soft copies of business objects are typically editable, allowing you to make changes and save them as new objects.

- **Shareable:** Soft copies can be easily shared electronically via email, file-sharing platforms, or other digital means.

- **Environmentally Friendly:** Soft copies contribute to a more sustainable and eco-friendly approach by reducing the need for paper-based copies.

Examples of Soft Copy

- **Copying a Sales Order:** You create a new sales order by copying an existing one and modifying the copied version before saving it as a new order.

- **Generating a Purchase Requisition Report:** You run a report in a Fiori app that lists all open purchase requisitions. You then save the report output as a PDF file to share with colleagues.

- **Printing a Material Master Record:** You preview the print output of a material master record in a Fiori app and then save it as a PDF instead of printing a physical copy.

CHAPTER 8   SAP FIORI LAUNCHPAD APP MANAGER

Overall, the soft copy concept in SAP Fiori emphasizes the digital nature of information and processes within the system. It facilitates efficient data handling, collaboration, and sustainability by enabling the creation, modification, and sharing of electronic copies of various objects and documents.

8.2 Technical Catalogs

These can be created by using the following transactions:

- Transaction code MM_APP
- Transaction code /UI2/FLPAM

Transactions **MM_APP** and **/UI2/FLPAM** are identical and contain similar features. They are tools within SAP Fiori Administration that help manage Fiori apps, including catalog and role assignments.

8.2.1 Prerequisite

It is essential to maintain the catalog type based on the system setup. This helps the App Manager tool understand what Fiori administrators can change or create in the current system. For the deployment type, we need to maintain the following:

- **Embedded Deployment:**
  - Maintain the **technical catalog** as the **standard catalog**.
- **Central Hub Deployment:**
  - **Front-End System:** Maintain the **technical catalog** as the **standard catalog**.
  - **Back-End System:** Maintain the **technical catalog** as **empty**.

8.2.2 Transaction Code: MM_APP

The transaction code **MM_APP** can be used to create a technical catalog. This transaction code will be retiring soon and deprecated sometime in the future release. When executed, it will take you to the SAP Fiori Portal screen, as shown in the figure below.

CHAPTER 8   SAP FIORI LAUNCHPAD APP MANAGER

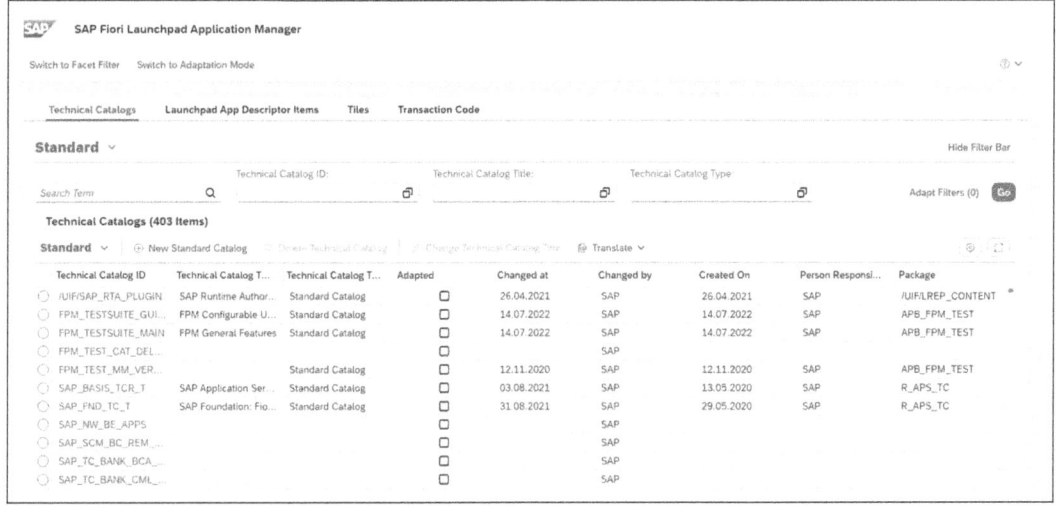

Figure 8-1. Transaction MM_APP initial screen

The above figure displays two options in the top menu, as listed below:

- Switch to Facet Filter
- Switch to Adaptation Mode

Note In this chapter, we will not discuss the functionality of the transaction **MM_APP** as it is identical to the new transaction/UI2/FLPAM, which will be covered in the next section.

8.2.3 Transaction Code: /UI2/FLPAM

The transaction code **/UI2/FLPAM** allows users to create a technical catalog. When executed, it opens a new portal page window and provides access to the **Fiori Launchpad App Manager**, as shown in the figure below.

353

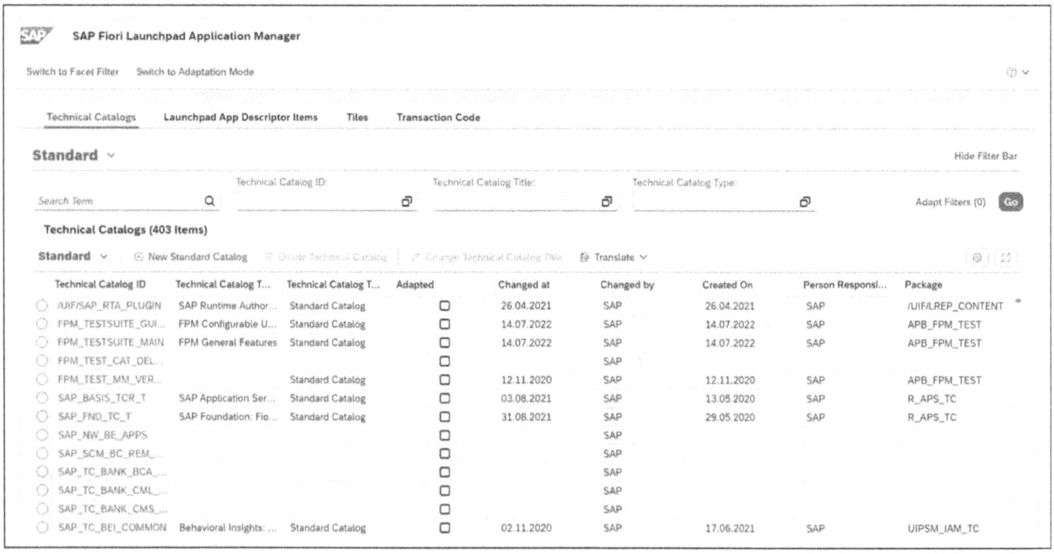

CHAPTER 8   SAP FIORI LAUNCHPAD APP MANAGER

Figure 8-2. Transaction /UI2/FLPAM initial screen

Note   The display screen for the transaction **MM_APP** has an identical layout to **/UI2/FLPAM**, as shown in the figure above.

This tool is essential for administrators managing the SAP Fiori environment, as it allows them to create, configure, and manage the apps that appear on the Fiori Launchpad. Through the Fiori Launchpad App Manager, administrators can organize apps into catalogs and groups, define target mappings, and assign roles and authorizations to ensure users access the correct apps. It also provides functionalities for maintaining tiles, adjusting app configurations, and managing app resources. This transaction code is handy for customizing the Fiori Launchpad to meet an organization's specific needs, ensuring users have a tailored and efficient interface to interact with their required applications.

The technical catalog created using this tool **/UI2/FLPAM** is stored in a **separate table**. The system will not display data created using the old transaction **MM_APP**, as it is unavailable in the new version. Starting SAP S/4HANA 2020, the old technical catalog created would have to be **migrated manually**. Currently, no automatic conversion of the old data into the latest data is available.

CHAPTER 8   SAP FIORI LAUNCHPAD APP MANAGER

The app or the transaction **/UI2/FLPAM** can be used to create a technical catalog. Such a catalog can consist of **custom apps**, **GUI apps**, **links**, and **Web Dynpro** and can later be used to develop a referenced BC. Thus, the relation between both transaction codes is as follows:

- Transaction code **MM_APP** replaced by transaction code **/UI2/FLPAM**.

- This new tool can maintain as many tiles as we want in one go, which is very handy and provides easy maintenance. When you copy the catalog, it is **referenced** to either the technical catalog or business catalog, not a **deep copy**. In the earlier version, the system created **static tiles** by default. Now, the new tool allows the creation of both **static** and **dynamic** tiles.

- Following the consistent naming convention for creating catalogs is advisable for better understanding.

- Technical catalog **name** length should not exceed **30 characters**.

- Technical catalog **description** length should not exceed **40 characters**.

- It is essential to keep precise records for each catalog. This record should explain the catalog's purpose, list its contents, and note any dependencies.

- Regularly update the technical catalogs to incorporate new apps and changes in existing apps.

- Thoroughly test the technical catalogs in a sandbox environment before deploying to production.

Furthermore, transaction code **/UI2/FLPAM** is the same as the app **Manage Launchpad Apps (Cross Client).** The app appears on the SAP Fiori Launchpad when the administrator logs into the system, as shown in the figure below.

CHAPTER 8   SAP FIORI LAUNCHPAD APP MANAGER

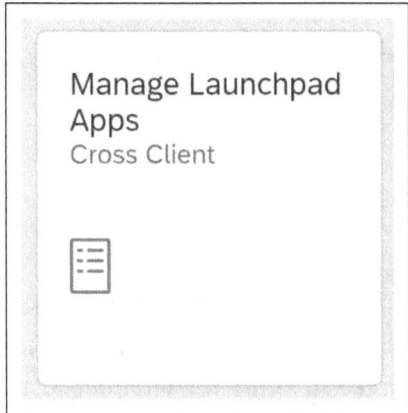

Figure 8-3. *Manage Launchpad Apps tile*

The SAP Fiori Launchpad Application Manager app was introduced in **S/4HANA 2020**. Executing it opens the web page to create a technical catalog. **The above app or the transaction code allows us to create, change, and maintain technical catalogs and app descriptors.**

It offers the option to view Search, Facet Filter, and Catalog Entry, which can be switched to any item via the buttons in the header. The primary view is **Search**, which offers all everyday tasks in technical catalogs.

The SAP Fiori Launchpad Application Manager gives you four options to search for data under **Switch to Facet Filter**, and those are as follows:

- Technical Catalogs
- Launchpad App Descriptor Items
- Tiles
- Transaction Code

356

CHAPTER 8   SAP FIORI LAUNCHPAD APP MANAGER

Technical Catalogs

The original Technical Catalogs window is displayed in the figure below.

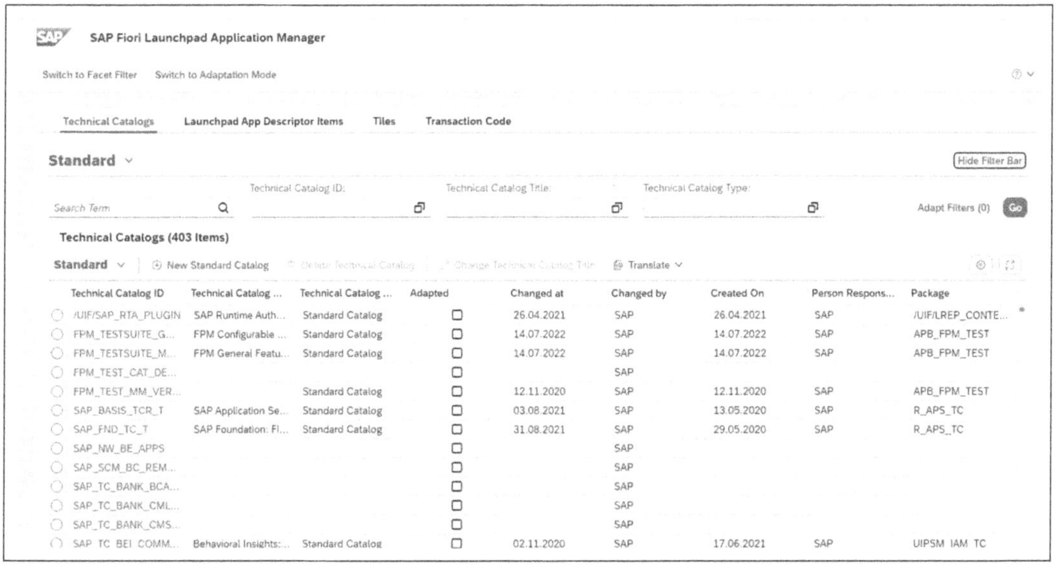

Figure 8-4. *Listing of apps within the SAP Fiori Launchpad Application Manager – /UI2/FLPAM*

Users can choose what type of data to view by selecting the **settings** icon, located on the right-hand side of the screen, which opens a new window for selection, as shown in the figure below.

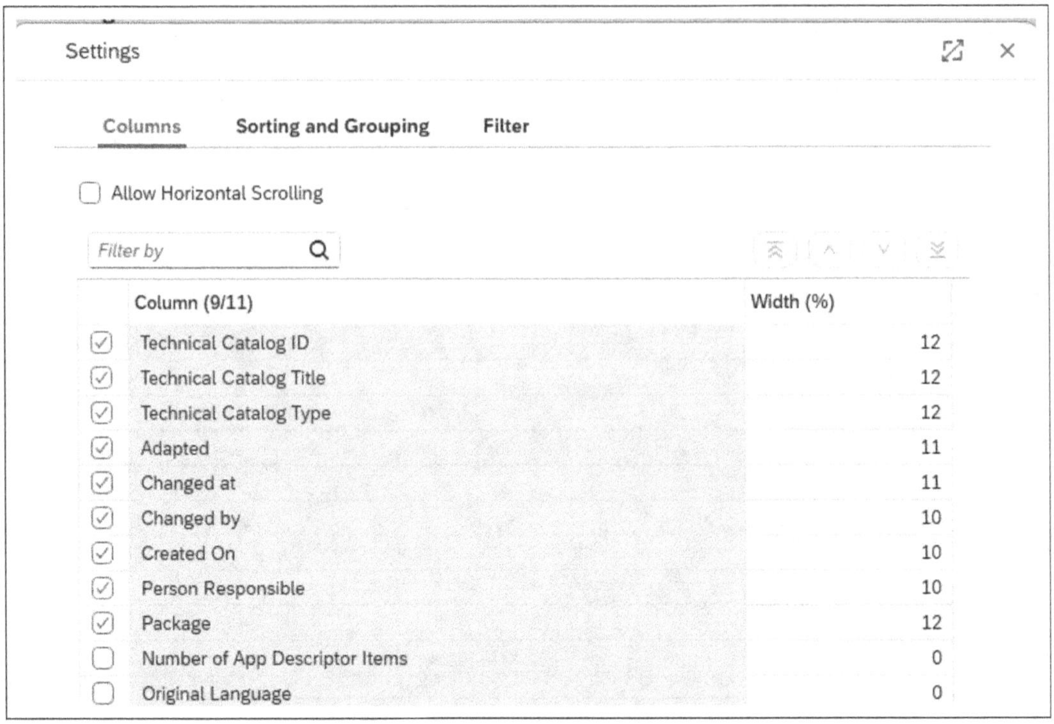

CHAPTER 8   SAP FIORI LAUNCHPAD APP MANAGER

Figure 8-5. Columns option in Settings to view data

Columns

The default displayed category **Columns**, as shown in the figure above, lets users choose subcategories, and most attributes are self-explanatory.

Sorting and Grouping

Select the category **Sorting and Grouping**, and a new Settings window will open with various options to select the data to view, as shown in the figure below.

CHAPTER 8 SAP FIORI LAUNCHPAD APP MANAGER

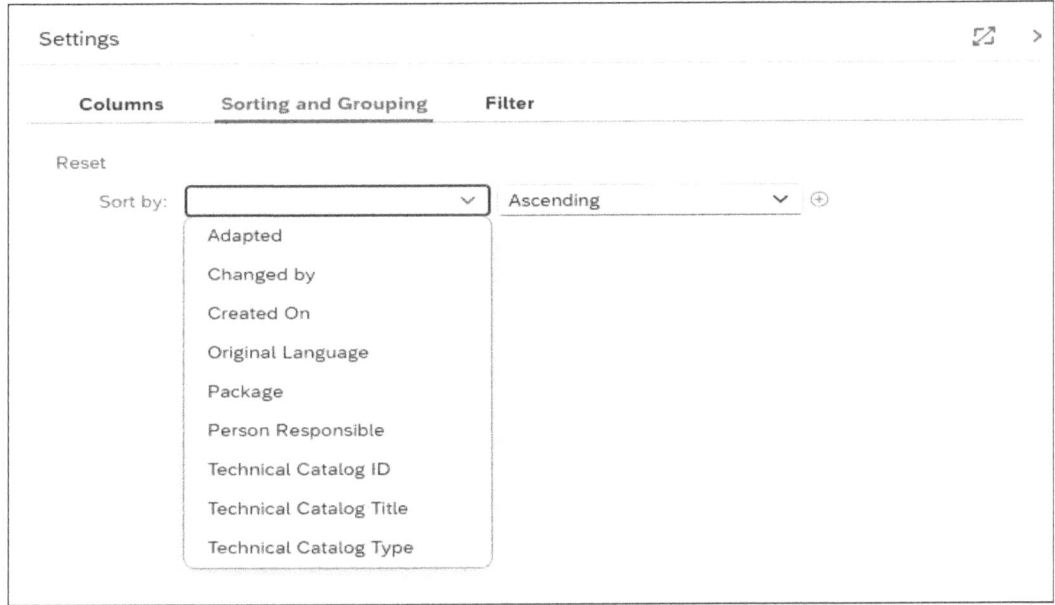

Figure 8-6. *Sorting and Grouping option in Settings to view data*

The user can sort the page content by using the option **Sort by** as per preference.

Filter

Select the category **Filter**, and a new Settings window will open with various options to select the data to view, as shown in the figure below.

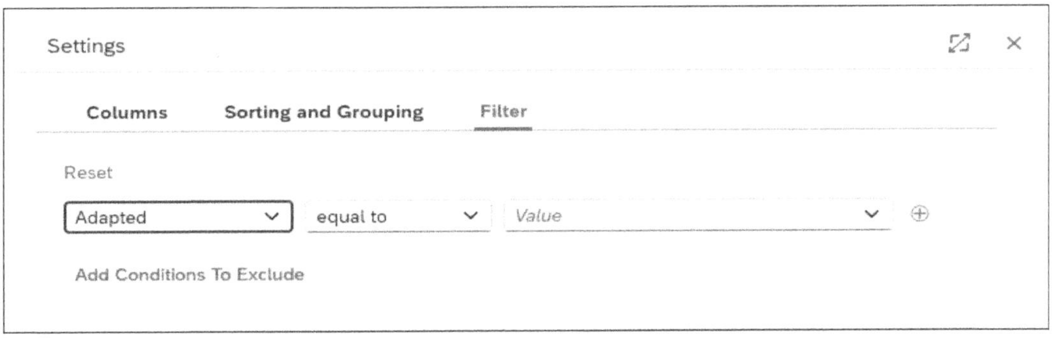

Figure 8-7. *Filter option in Settings to view data*

The user has a list of options available to filter data, as shown in the figure below.

359

CHAPTER 8   SAP FIORI LAUNCHPAD APP MANAGER

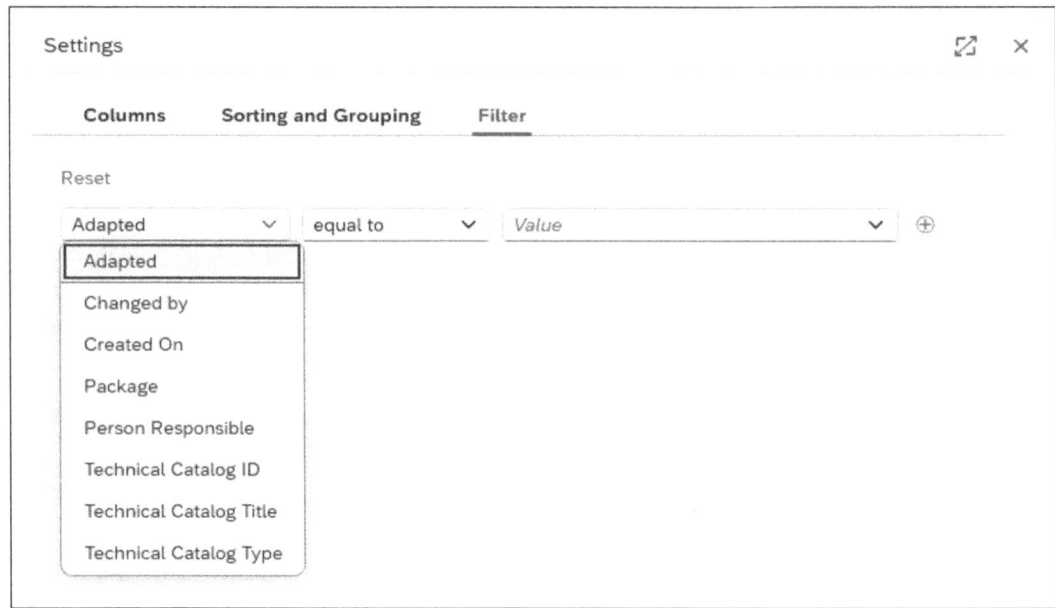

Figure 8-8.   Various options available to view data

Another option available is **Add Conditions To Exclude**. It adds a condition to exclude data when selected, as shown in the figure below.

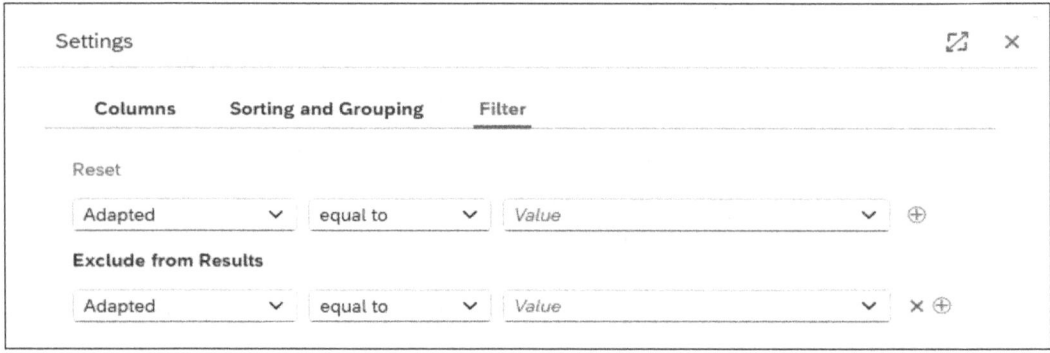

Figure 8-9.   Option to exclude data for selection on the technical catalog

360

CHAPTER 8　SAP FIORI LAUNCHPAD APP MANAGER

Launchpad App Descriptor Items

Select the category **Launchpad App Descriptor Items**; a new window will appear, as illustrated in the figure below.

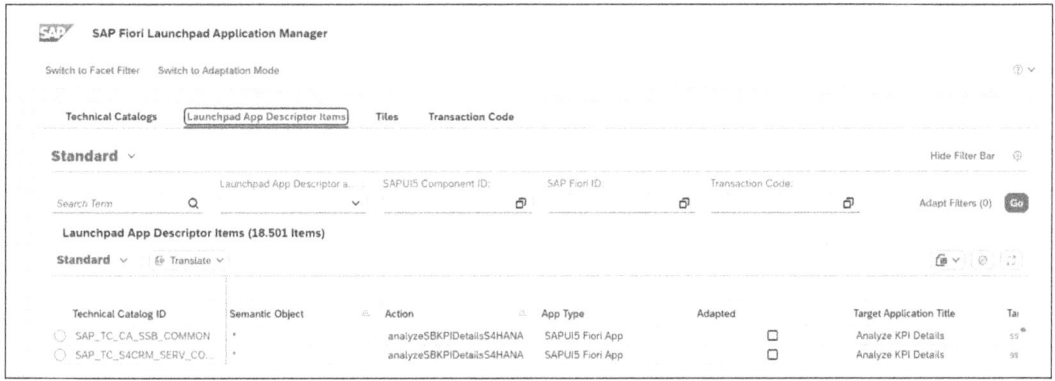

Figure 8-10. *Launchpad App Descriptor Items screen*

The above figure provides the user with various options to search for data, such as

- Search Term
- Launchpad App Descriptor adapted
- SAPUI5 Component ID
- SAP Fiori ID
- Transaction Code

In the above Launchpad App Descriptor Items screen, we will search for transaction code **VA03** by clicking the icon Go . The results appear as shown in the figure below, displaying the data.

361

CHAPTER 8 SAP FIORI LAUNCHPAD APP MANAGER

Figure 8-11. Data displayed for transaction code VA03

The above figure displays various **semantic objects** and **semantic actions** for transaction **VA03** and all the technical catalogs that contain it. It also indicates that there are **16 Launchpad App Descriptor items** associated with the transaction.

You can double-click any catalog to check the apps that the catalog contains. For example, double-click the selected row under the header **Technical Catalog ID** with the value **SAP_TC_LO_VC_COMMON**. A new window will appear, listing all apps within the selected catalog and displaying all attributes, as shown in the figure below. It also displays complete details for transaction **VA03**.

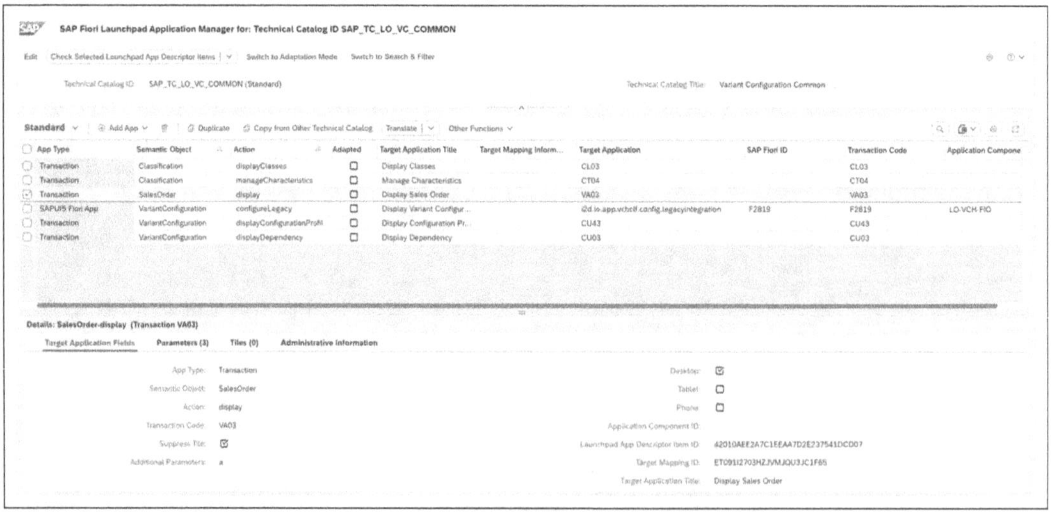

Figure 8-12. Transaction VA03 within the technical catalog

CHAPTER 8 SAP FIORI LAUNCHPAD APP MANAGER

Furthermore, the Launchpad App Descriptor Items window also allows you to do the following:

- Export.
- Configure settings.

Tiles

Select the category **Tiles**, and a new window will open, as shown in the figure below, which shows the tiles available in the systems.

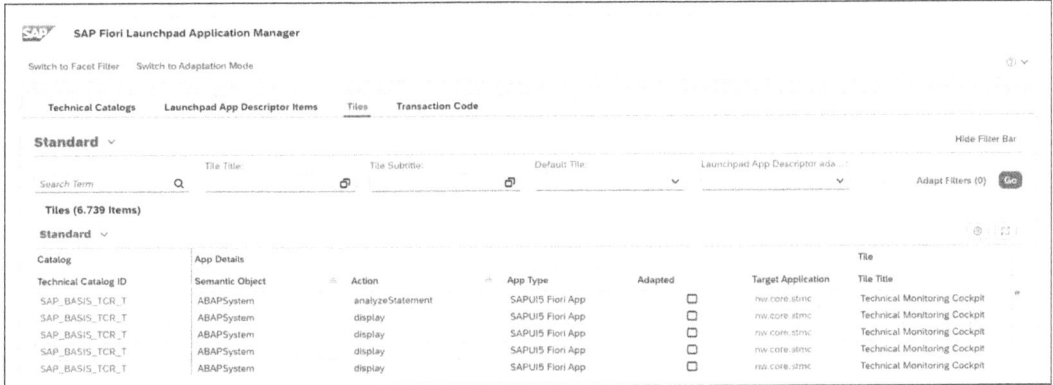

Figure 8-13. *View data based on tiles*

Transaction Code

Selecting the category **Transaction Code** will open a new window, as shown in the figure below.

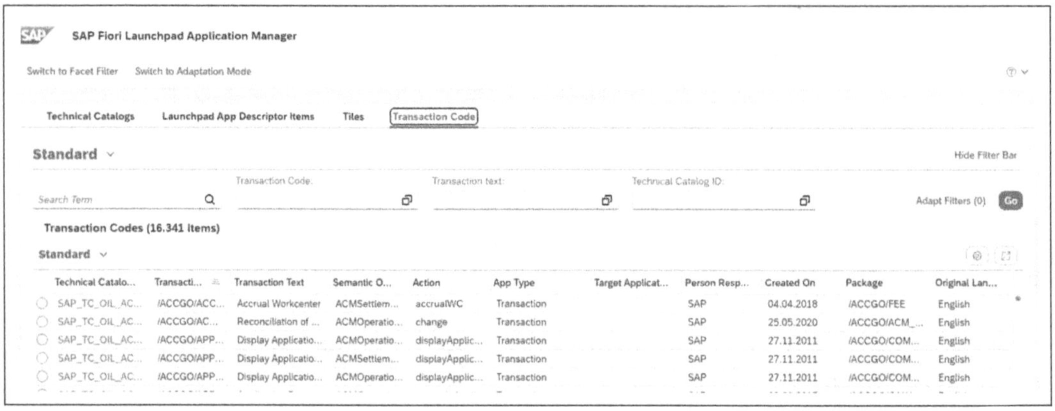

Figure 8-14. *View data based on transaction codes*

The above figure shows the list of transaction codes and associated information such as technical catalog, semantic object, sematic action, etc. When searching for transaction VA03, the output is as shown in the figure below. The output displays that the transaction VA03 is available in 16 technical catalogs.

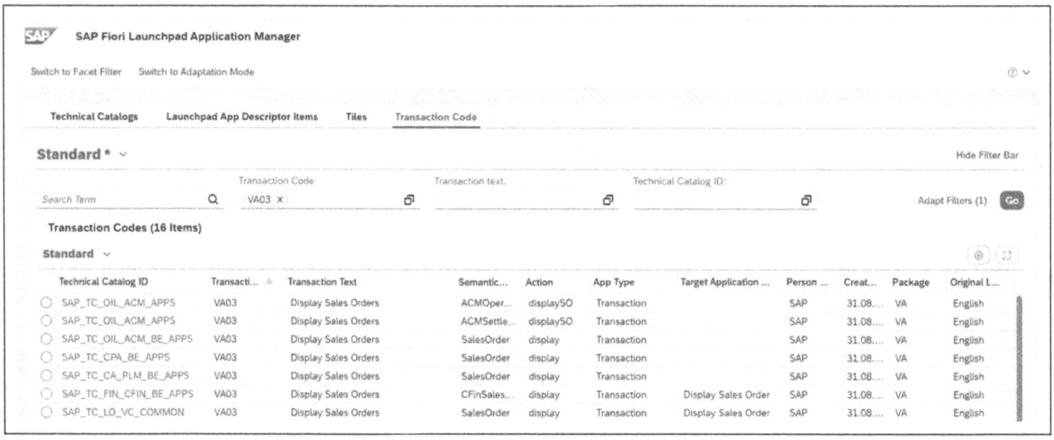

Figure 8-15. *Shows details of technical catalogs when searching for transaction code VA03*

8.2.4 Switch to Facet Filter

In the SAP Fiori **Launchpad App Manager** (/UI2/FLPAM), using Switch to Facet Filter, displayed as default when creating a technical catalog in SAP Fiori, makes it easier for users to search for applications. This feature allows users to filter apps based on criteria

CHAPTER 8 SAP FIORI LAUNCHPAD APP MANAGER

like business role, application type, or usage. Unlike a basic search, facet filters enable users to filter by multiple criteria simultaneously, which helps manage large catalogs more effectively. This way, administrators and developers can quickly find and organize apps, ensuring users can access the right applications in their business context.

Note Within **Switch to Facet Filter**, the user can perform the following actions related to creating a technical catalog:

- New Standard Catalog
- Delete Technical Catalog
- Translate

Selecting **Switch to Facet Filter** Switch to Facet Filter opens a new window, the **Launchpad Application Descriptor Item – Facet Filter**, as shown in the figure below. It enables users to search catalogs, Launchpad descriptors, or tiles by providing fields and functions for specifying user searches.

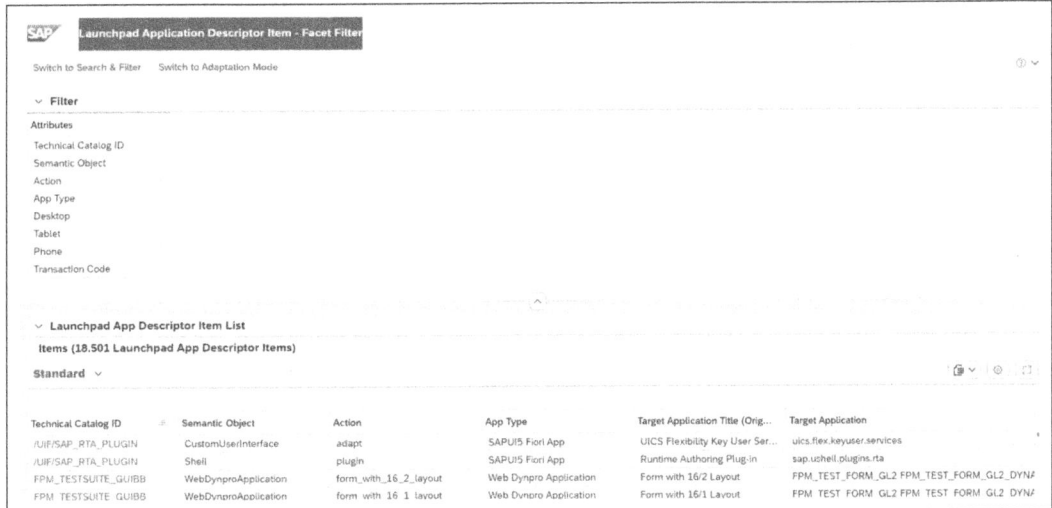

Figure 8-16. Switch to Facet Filter screen

CHAPTER 8   SAP FIORI LAUNCHPAD APP MANAGER

Switching to the **Switch to Facet Filter** feature provides a more interactive and organized way to filter the search. Using this filter, you can narrow down and find apps rapidly instead of scrolling up and down. You can filter data based on predefined categories to find apps based on 15 attributes. Some of the main attributes are listed below:

- Technical Catalog ID
- Semantic Object
- Action
- App Type
- Transaction Code

Note This filter lets users view data by displaying only relevant choices. It can be accessed as a dropdown on the left side of the window. The filter shows data based on the selected categories.

Technical Catalog ID

Selecting the **Technical Catalog ID** option presents the details illustrated in the figure below.

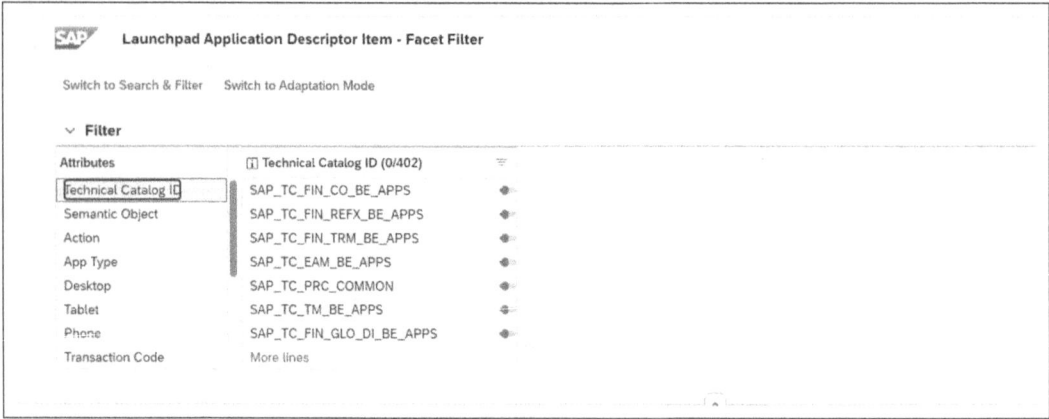

Figure 8-17. Display of technical catalog IDs within the system when the Technical Catalog ID attribute is selected

App Type

Selecting the App Type option presents the details illustrated in the figure below.

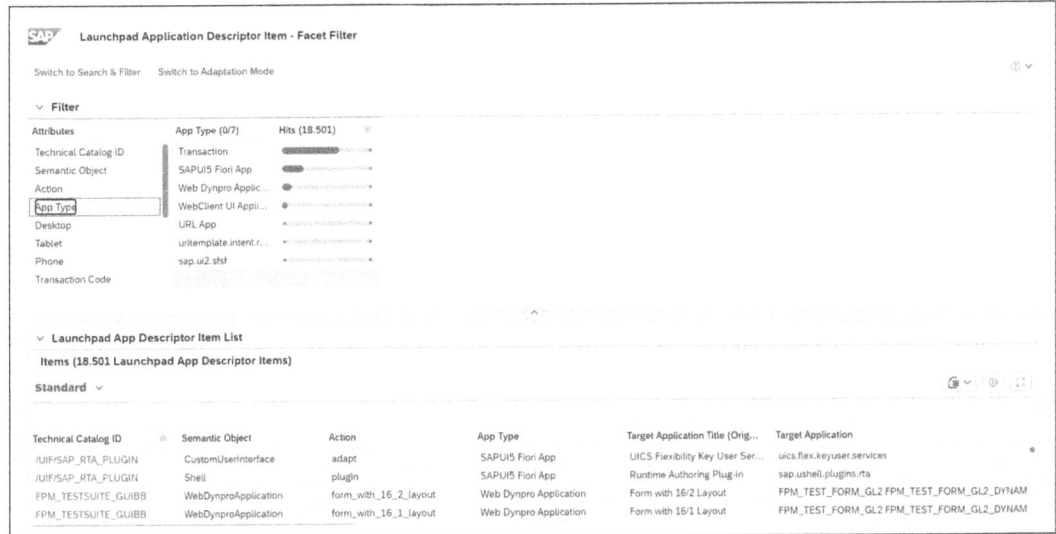

Figure 8-18. *Display of app types available within the system when the App Type attribute is selected*

The above figure displays the following:

- App Type (0/7)
- Hits (18,501)

Furthermore, some of the app types available in the system are

- Transaction
- SAPUI5 Fiori App
- Web Dynpro Application
- URL App

The filter also allows you to select multiple attributes, as shown in the figure below.

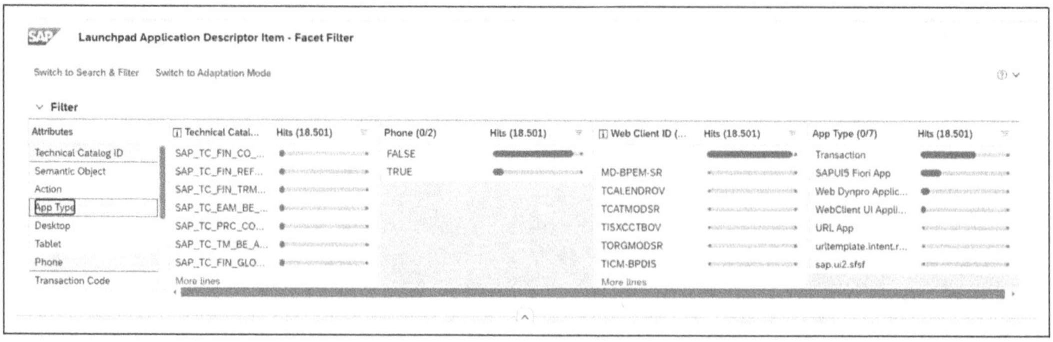

CHAPTER 8   SAP FIORI LAUNCHPAD APP MANAGER

Figure 8-19. Showing multiple attributes of data available

When you select the SAPUI5 Component ID option, the system will filter all the applications to show only Fiori apps, as shown in the figure below.

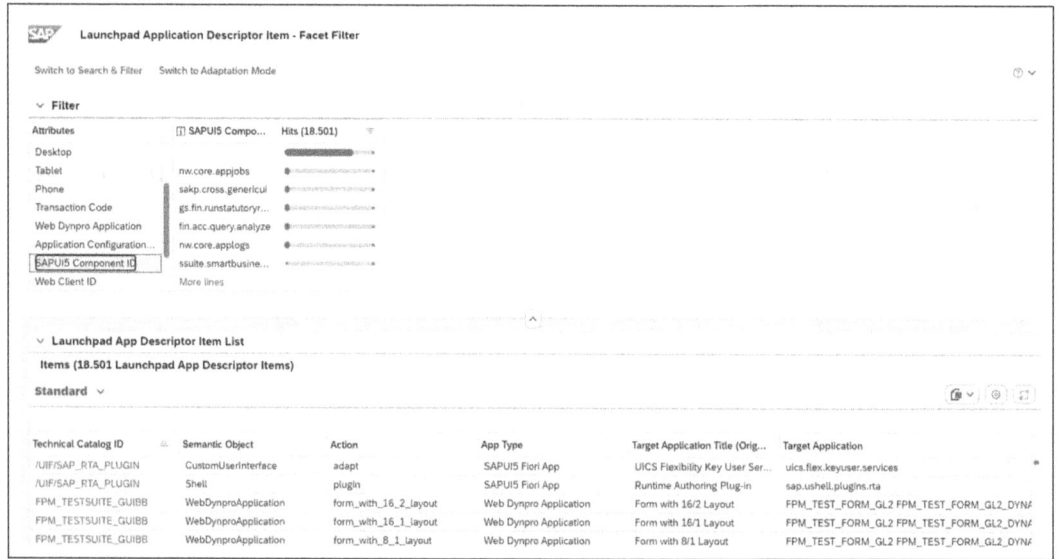

Figure 8-20. Listing of only SAPUI5 Fiori apps

CHAPTER 8   SAP FIORI LAUNCHPAD APP MANAGER

Note

- Under the App Type column in the above figure, it shows SAPUI5 Fiori App only.

- All categories of data can be downloaded using the icon. It lets you export data.

- The settings icon provides various options for how the user wants to view data, as shown in the figure below.

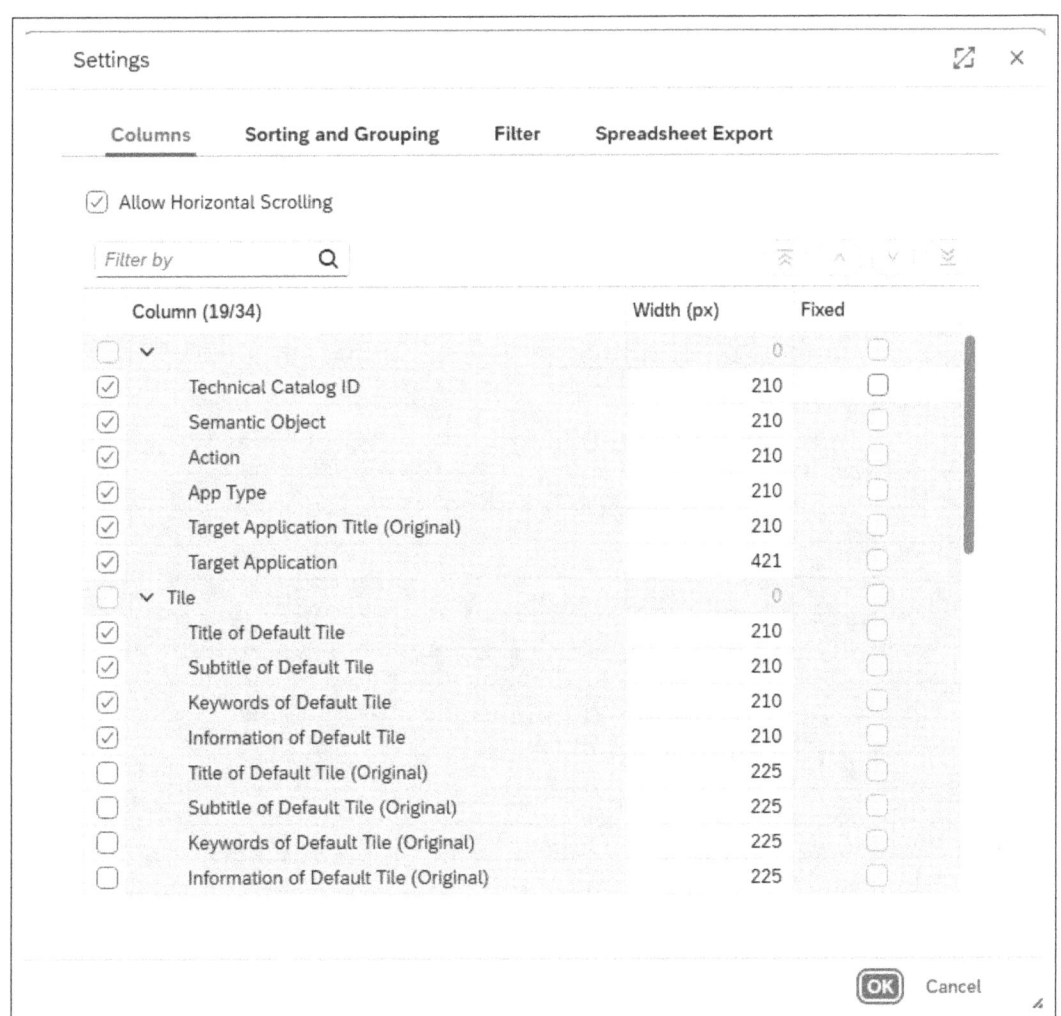

Figure 8-21. Settings option

CHAPTER 8 SAP FIORI LAUNCHPAD APP MANAGER

Furthermore, when the settings option is selected, the data can be segregated further based on the following attributes:

- Columns
- Sorting and Grouping
- Filter
- Spreadsheet Export

Columns

For example, within the **Columns** option, we want to display data based on our selections (Transaction Code and Fiori ID), as shown in the figure below.

Figure 8-22. *Columns Selection to Display*

CHAPTER 8 SAP FIORI LAUNCHPAD APP MANAGER

Note As a best practice, you should always select the checkbox **Allow Horizontal Scrolling**.

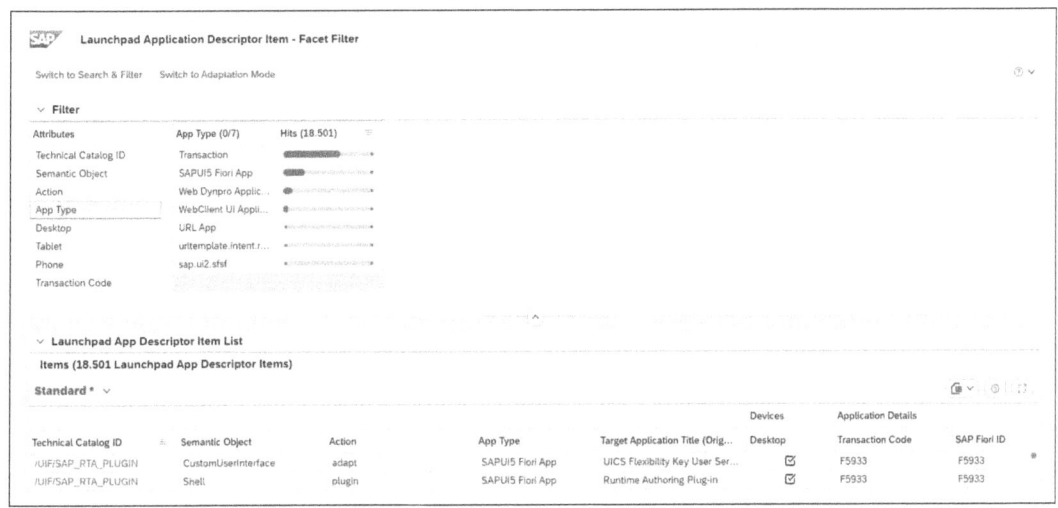

Figure 8-23. *Launchpad Application Descriptor Item - Facet Filter view*

Sorting and Grouping

The option **Sorting and Grouping** will display data based on selection as shown in the figure below.

371

CHAPTER 8   SAP FIORI LAUNCHPAD APP MANAGER

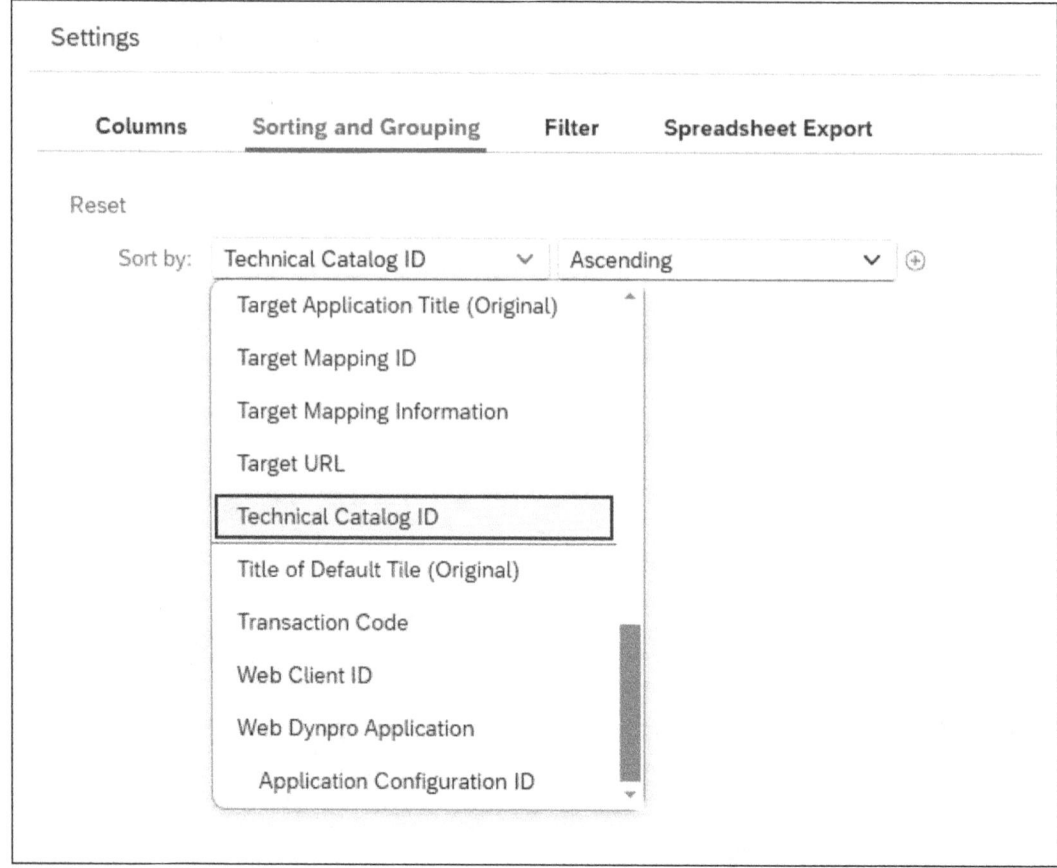

Figure 8-24. Setting options available for Sorting and Grouping

Filter

The option **Filter** will display data based on selection as shown in the figure below.

CHAPTER 8   SAP FIORI LAUNCHPAD APP MANAGER

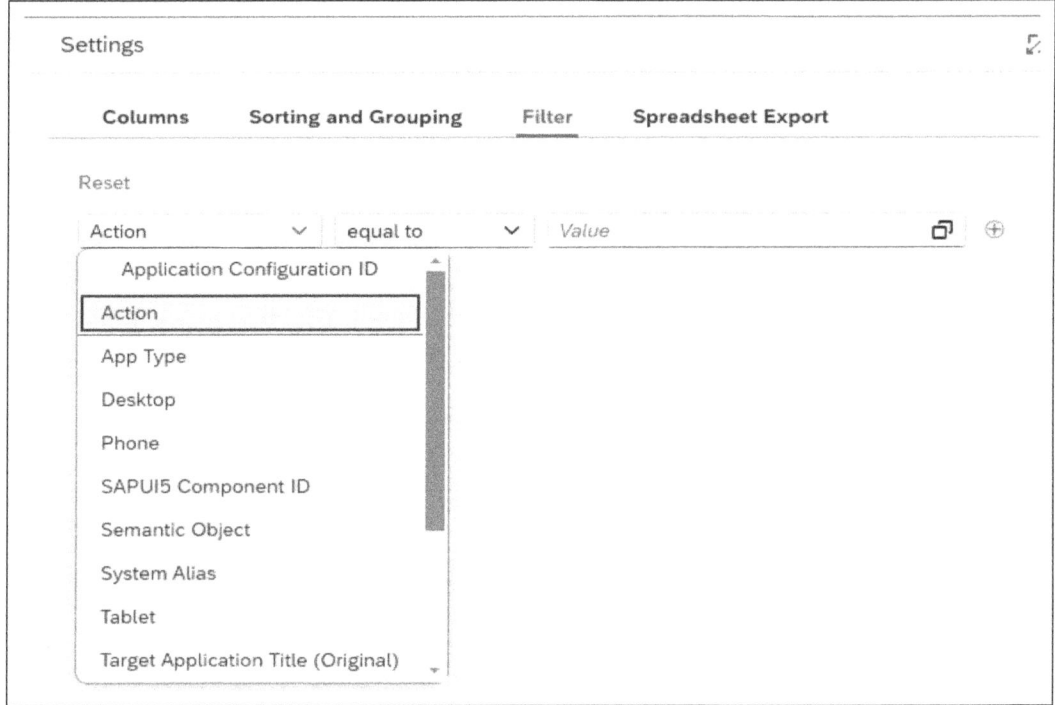

Figure 8-25. Filter option

Spreadsheet Export

The option **Spreadsheet Export** will display data based on selection as shown in the figure below.

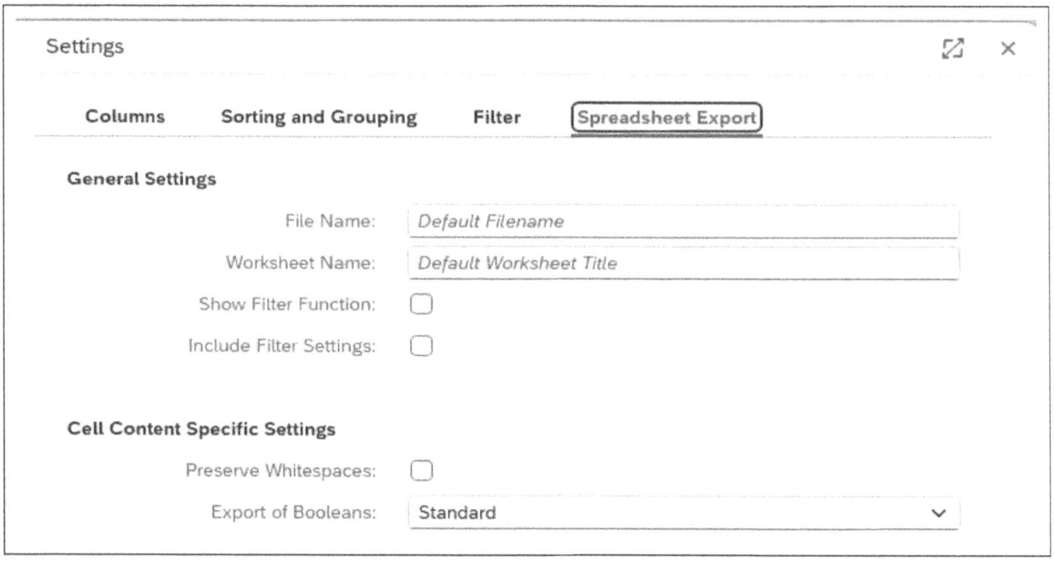

Figure 8-26. Spreadsheet Export option

8.2.5 Switch to Adaptation Mode

Using **Switch to Adaptation Mode** while creating a **technical catalog** in SAP Fiori empowers administrators to customize standard SAP-delivered catalogs without altering the original content. This mode is particularly beneficial for tailoring business roles, applications, and navigational targets to meet specific organizational needs. It allows users to add custom tiles, modify target mappings, adjust semantic objects, and enhance application parameters while preserving the main structure and ensuring that SAP updates remain intact. By enabling adjustments without direct modifications to SAP standard catalogs, Switch to Adaptation Mode offers flexibility, reduces the risk of conflicts during system upgrades, and simplifies system maintenance, ultimately ensuring a smoother and more efficient update process.

Note The technical catalog contains app-specific details and configurations like

- Semantic object and action (used in intent-based navigation)
- Target mapping details (navigation parameters)
- App type (transactional, analytical, factsheet)
- OData services and UI5 component information

Note In **Switch to Adaptation Mode**, any changes made to technical catalogs apply to all users and all clients.

8.3 Create a Technical Catalog

Before we create a technical catalog, we need to determine the naming convention for it and the required apps within it.

8.3.1 Technical Catalog Naming Convention

A sample naming convention will be used as listed below.

CHAPTER 8 SAP FIORI LAUNCHPAD APP MANAGER

Position	Values	Characters Length	Description
1	Z	1	Custom Catalogs
2	F & H	1	F - Fiori H - S/4HANA
3	_	1	Delimiter (Underscore)
4 - 7	TCLG/BCLG	4	TCLG Technical Catalog BCLG - Business Catalog
8	_	1	Delimiter (Underscore)
9 - 11	RTR, FIN, etc.	3	Functional area (3 Characters)
12	_	1	Delimiter (Underscore)
13, 14	AP, AR, FI, etc.	2	SAP Modules Abbreviation
15	_	1	Delimiter (Underscore)
16 - 30	Free text	15	Catalog Description

Figure 8-27. *Technical catalog naming convention used*

Example of a Technical Catalog

Here is an example of a technical catalog. We will create the technical catalog listed below:

- **Technical Catalog**: ZF_TCLG_FIN_AP_GUI_FIORI_APPS
- **Description**: TCLG:ADD:ON: GUI FIORI APPS AND LINKS

8.3.2 Apps to Be Deployed Within a Technical Catalog

The technical catalog will have the objects shown in the table below. We will use this information to create the technical catalog.

CHAPTER 8   SAP FIORI LAUNCHPAD APP MANAGER

Apps	Title - Subtitle	Semantic Object	Semantic Action	Technical Catalog(s)
F-03	Clear G/L Accounts	GLAccount	clear	SAP_TC_FIN_GL_BE_APPS
F0763A	Manage Chart of Accounts	ChartOfAccounts	manage	SAP_TC_FIN_ACC_COMMON
F0731A	Manage G/L Account Master Data	GLAccount	manage	SAP_TC_FIN_ACC_COMMON
FBV3	Display Parked Journal Entries	ParkedJournalEntry	displayParkedJournalEntry	SAP_TC_FIN_ACC_BE_APPS

Figure 8-28. *SAP GUI and Fiori apps used for the creation of the technical catalog*

8.3.3 Process of Creating a Technical Catalog

Select **New Standard Catalog** ⊕ New Standard Catalog to create a new technical catalog (creating an empty technical catalog only). As shown in the figure below, a new window called **New Standard Catalog** appears.

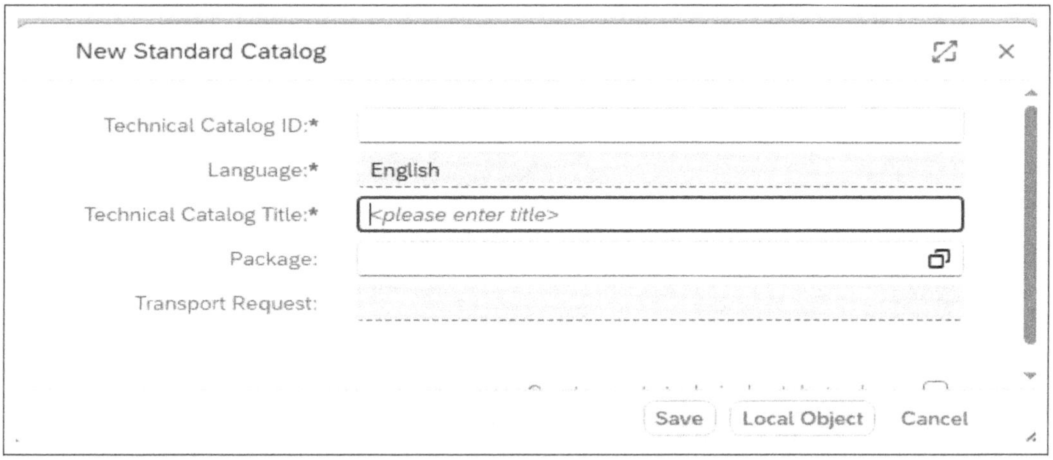

Figure 8-29. *Creation of a technical catalog initial screen*

In the new window, we need to provide the basic information. The information required is as follows:

- **Technical Catalog ID**: ZF_TCLG_FIN_AP_GUI_FIORI_APPS
- **Language**: English
- **Technical Catalog Tile**: TCLG - GUI FIORI APPS AND LINKS
- **Package**: ZFIORI_PKG
- **Transport Request**: S24K900010

CHAPTER 8   SAP FIORI LAUNCHPAD APP MANAGER

Enter the Technical Catalog ID and Technical Catalog Tile description details, as shown in the figure below.

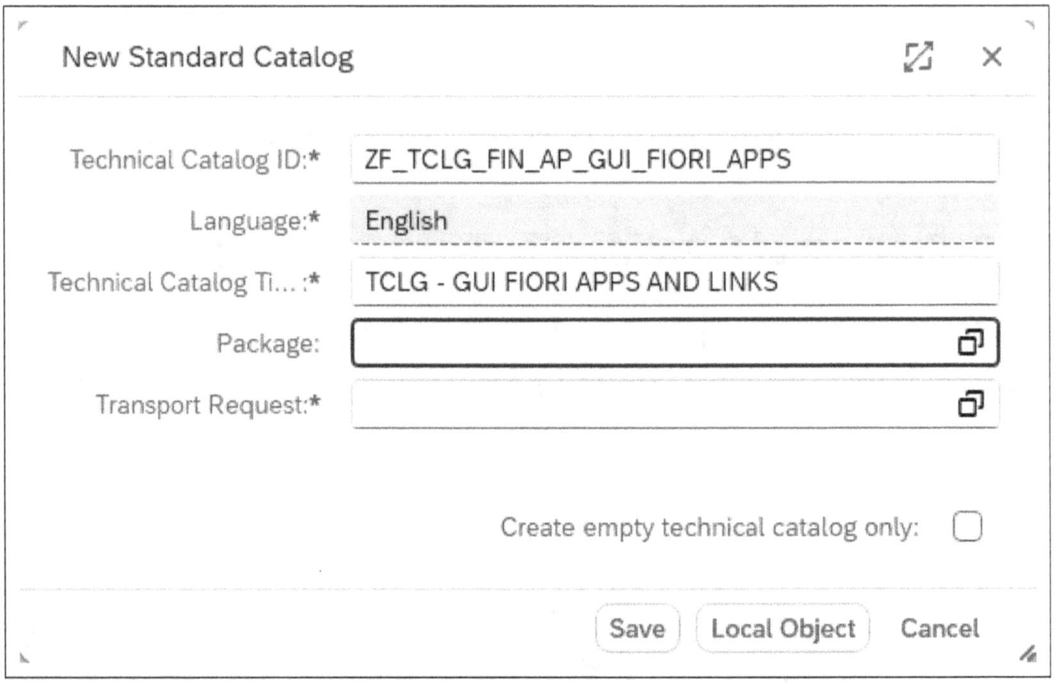

New Standard Catalog

Technical Catalog ID:*   ZF_TCLG_FIN_AP_GUI_FIORI_APPS
Language:*   English
Technical Catalog Ti... :*   TCLG - GUI FIORI APPS AND LINKS
Package:
Transport Request:*

Create empty technical catalog only: ☐

Save | Local Object | Cancel

Figure 8-30. *Technical Catalog ID and Technical Catalog Tile description details added*

Always use the **search icon** on the **Package field** for the **package** details. Select a package and transport. We will use the same package and transport we created earlier.

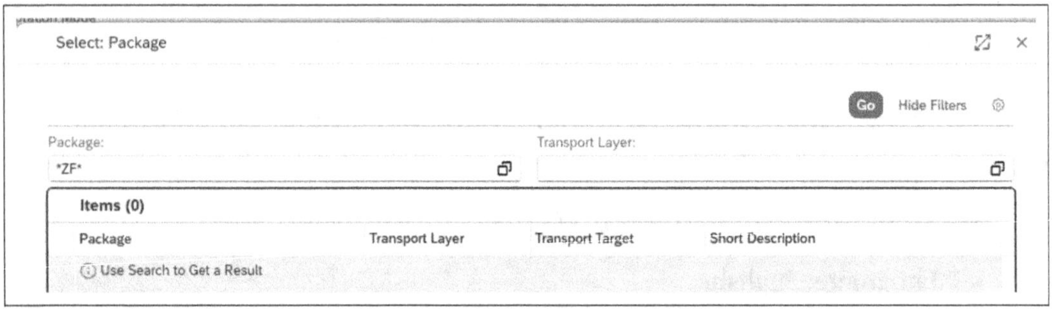

Select: Package

Package: *ZF*
Transport Layer:

Items (0)

Package	Transport Layer	Transport Target	Short Description
ⓘ Use Search to Get a Result			

Figure 8-31. *Screen to search for a package to assign to the technical catalog*

CHAPTER 8 SAP FIORI LAUNCHPAD APP MANAGER

In the figure above, enter under the header Package *ZF* and select the icon Go **Go**. Related packages will be displayed in the lower half of the screen, as shown in the figure below.

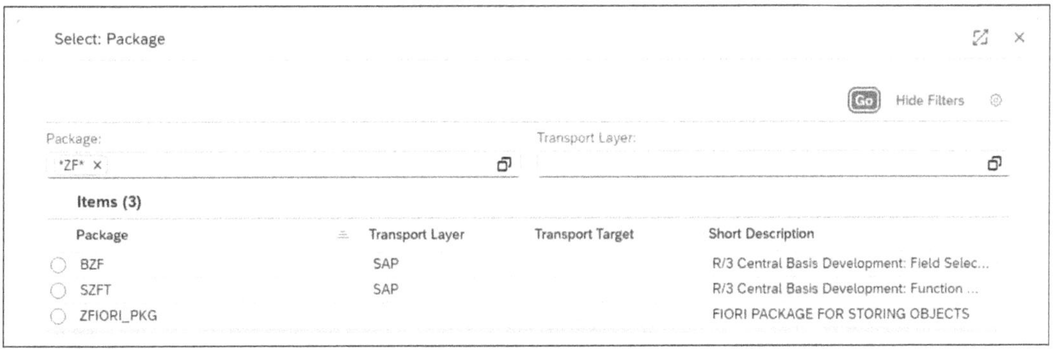

Figure 8-32. Packages available for selection

Select the package ZFIORI_PKG, and the catalog definition is updated automatically, as shown in the figure below.

Figure 8-33. Package added to New Standard Catalog

379

CHAPTER 8   SAP FIORI LAUNCHPAD APP MANAGER

Select the next item, **Transport Request**, and enter the Workbench request number created earlier. The final updated **New Standard Catalog** window with all essential information entered is as shown in the figure below.

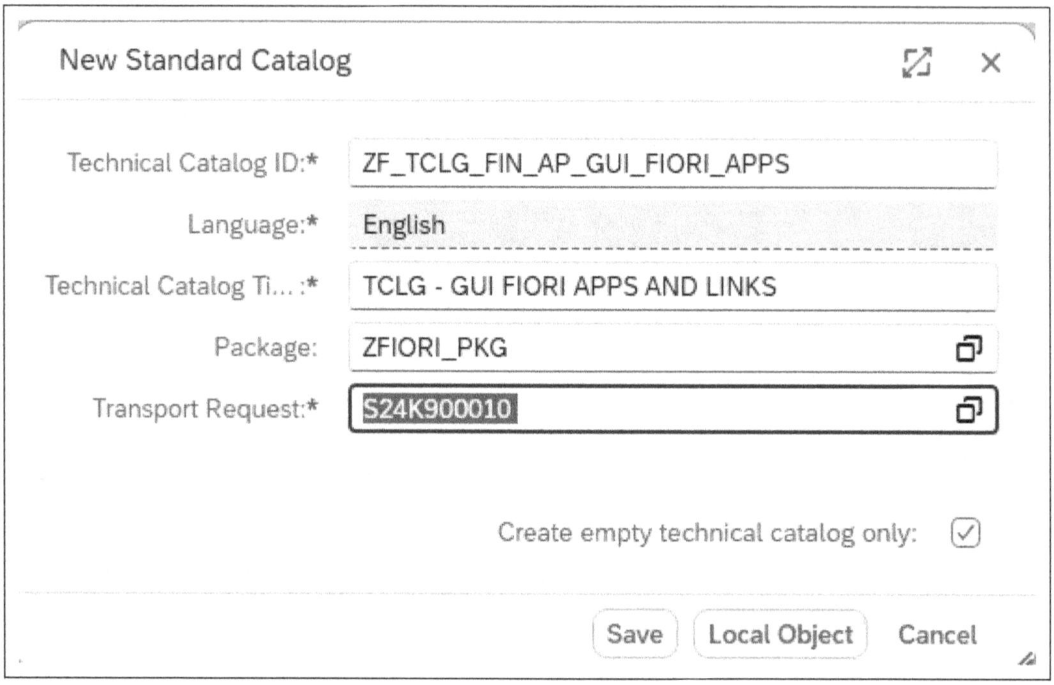

Figure 8-34. Complete details of the standard technical catalog to be created

---

Note   Check the box **Create empty technical catalog only**, as shown in the figure above.

You can save your changes by clicking the Save icon Save . You need to search for the technical catalog created by entering the technical catalog ID ZF_TCLG* under the corresponding header, as shown in the figure below.

CHAPTER 8 SAP FIORI LAUNCHPAD APP MANAGER

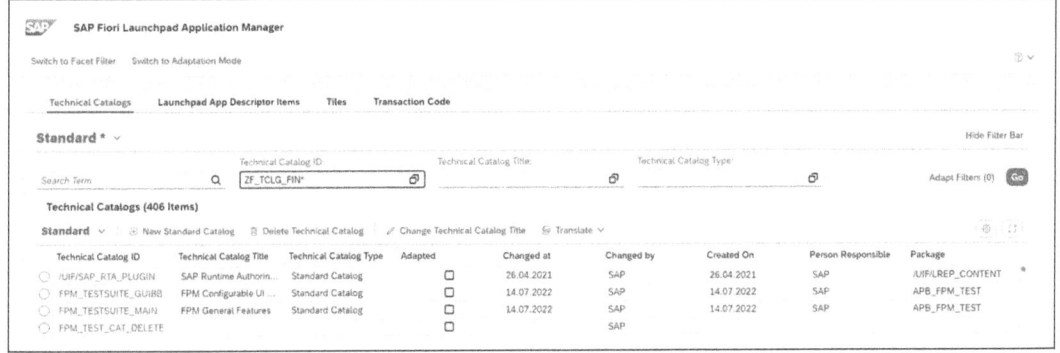

Figure 8-35. Search for the technical catalog created

Click the Go icon 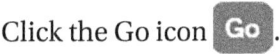.

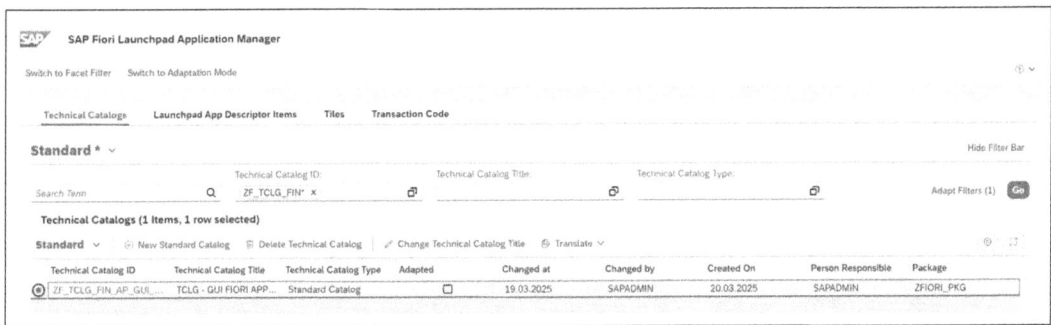

Figure 8-36. Standard technical catalog created

To open the technical catalog, select the complete line and double-click, as shown in the figure above. This will open a new window allowing you to enter apps within the technical catalog as required.

381

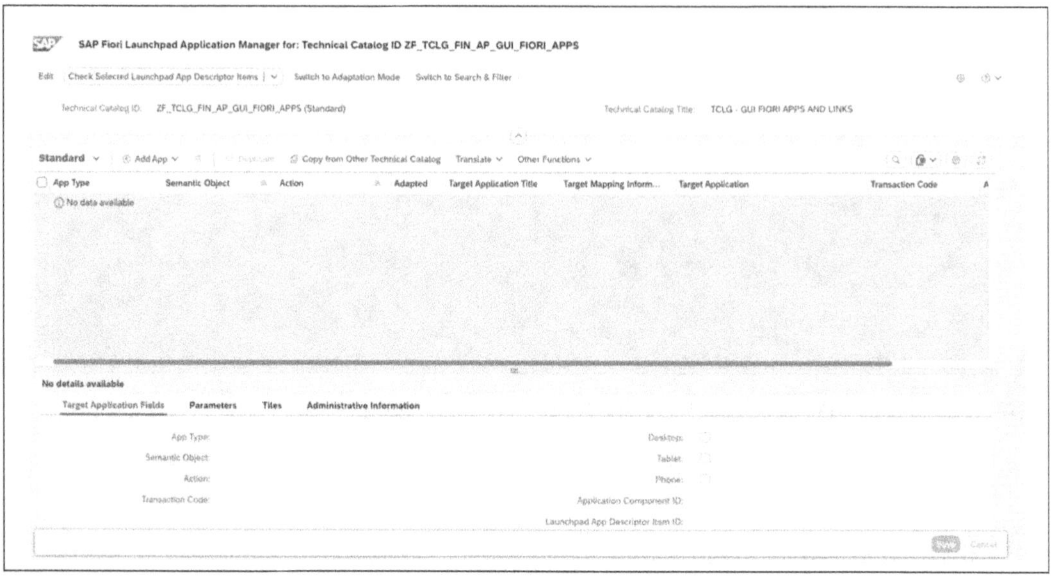

CHAPTER 8   SAP FIORI LAUNCHPAD APP MANAGER

Figure 8-37. Technical catalog input screen to add apps

The above figure gives an acceptable warning. As needed in the figure above, we can add custom semantic objects, Fiori apps, GUI apps, etc. To add an app, click the icon **Add App** ⊕ Add App ∨. Clicking the icon lets you select the type of app you are adding, as shown in the figure below.

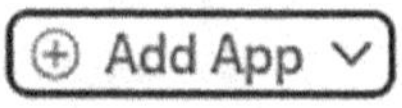

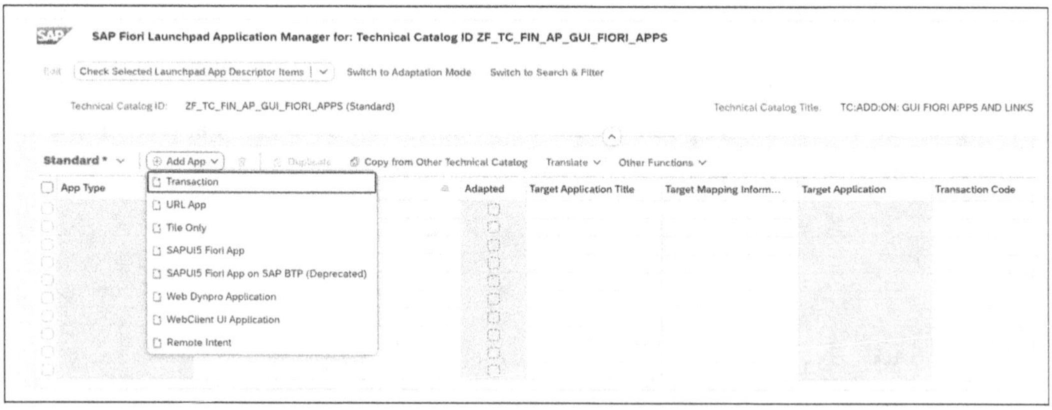

Figure 8-38. Add App option

CHAPTER 8 SAP FIORI LAUNCHPAD APP MANAGER

The app types available are

- Transaction
- URL App
- Tile Only
- SAPUI5 Fiori App
- SAPUI5 Fiori App on SAP BTP (Deprecated)
- Web Dynpro Application
- WebClient UI Application
- Remote Intent

Note The above option is used when you are creating custom apps.

To add **GUI apps F-03**, select **Copy from Other Technical Catalog** 📋 Copy from Other Technical Catalog, and a new window box will appear asking for package and transport information, as shown in the figure below.

Figure 8-39. Technical catalog package and transport information for adding apps

Click OK. A new window will appear – **Copy from Other Technical Catalog** – as displayed in the figure below.

383

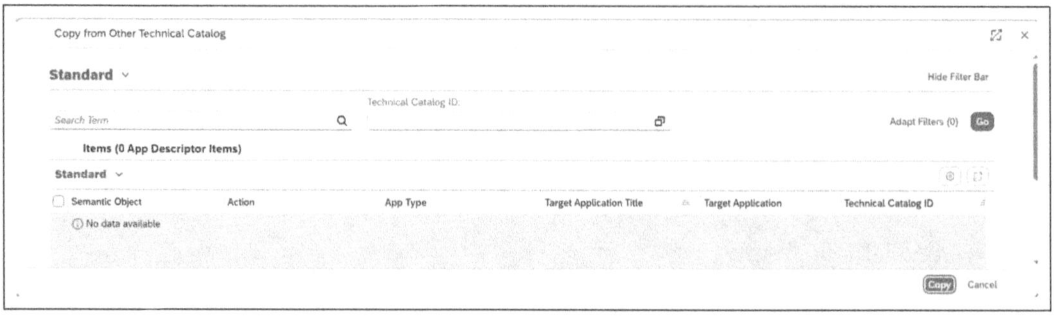

CHAPTER 8 SAP FIORI LAUNCHPAD APP MANAGER

Figure 8-40. Initial screen for Copy from Other Technical Catalog

Enter the GUI app transaction *****F-03***** to search, as shown in the figure below.

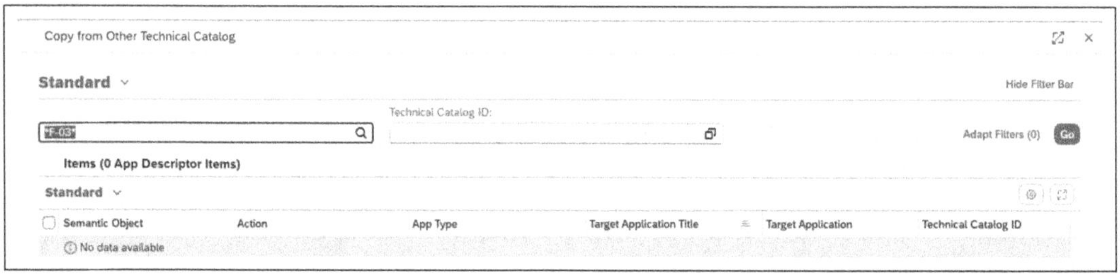

*Figure 8-41. Enter search term *F-03***

Click Go  and the system finds the GUI for the transaction **F-03**, as shown in the figure below.

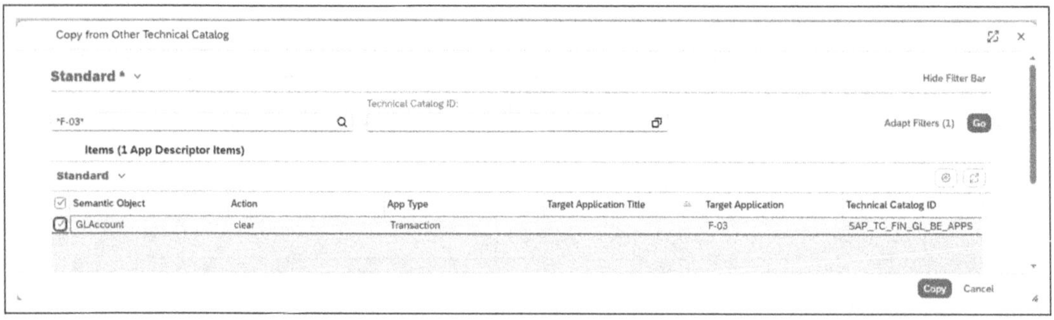

Figure 8-42. GUI app information found

Select the GUI found in the figure above and then select **Copy** Copy . The information will be updated on the technical catalog screen, as shown in the figure below.

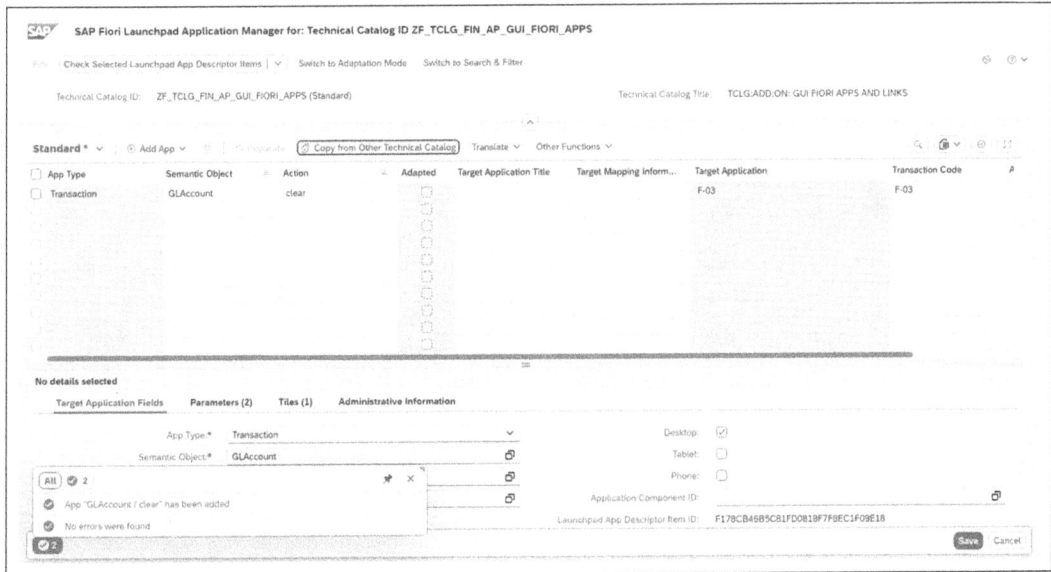

Figure 8-43. *GUI app information added*

Note The system may take some time to populate the **mandatory fields** automatically.

There are two messages displayed at the bottom of the screen:

- **App "GLAccountant / clear" has been added**
- **No errors were found**

Note The **Transaction** option was added automatically at the top of the figure, under the header **App Type**.

When the messages from the figure above are canceled, the GUI app information is displayed in detail, as shown in the figure below.

385

CHAPTER 8   SAP FIORI LAUNCHPAD APP MANAGER

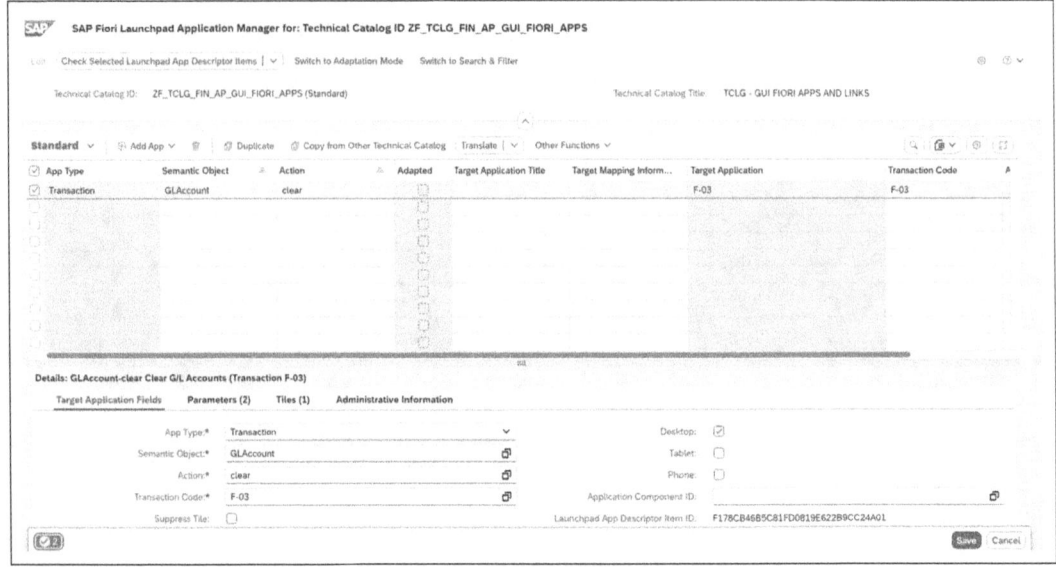

Figure 8-44. *GUI app with details displayed*

Save the GUI app information by clicking the **Save** button at the bottom of the screen.

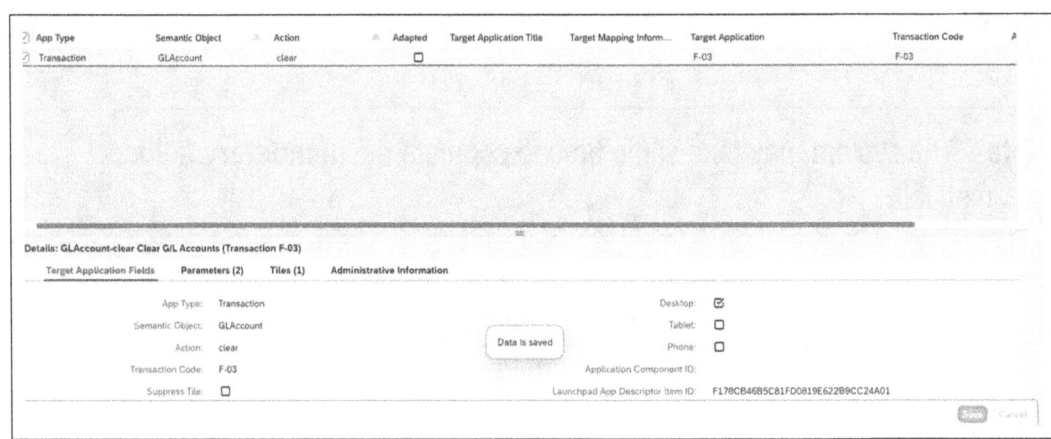

Figure 8-45. *GUI app data being saved*

While saving, it displays a box stating **Data is saved**, as shown in the figure above.

CHAPTER 8   SAP FIORI LAUNCHPAD APP MANAGER

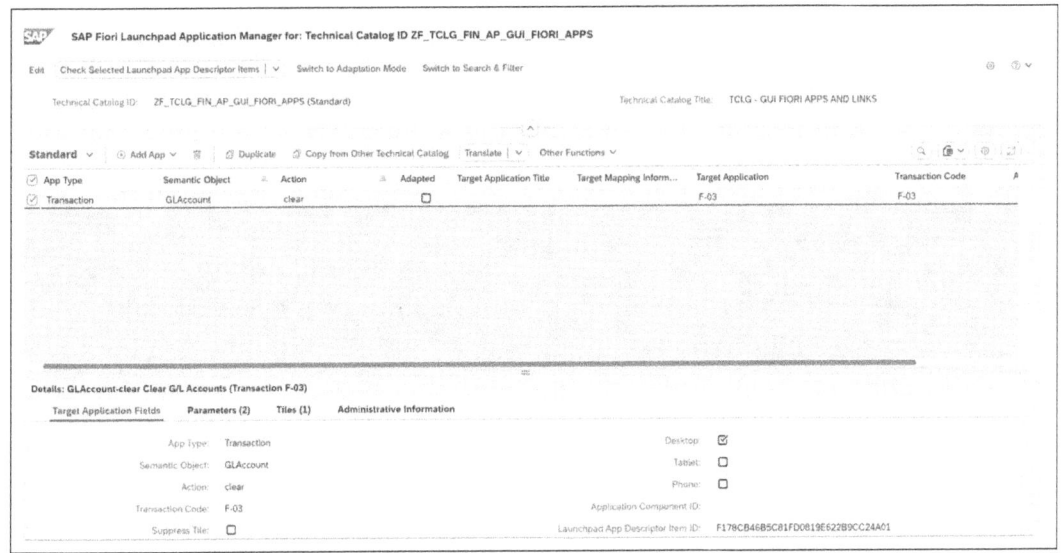

Figure 8-46. GUI app added

Now let us also add a native Fiori app called **F0731A**. Search for the app *F0731A* as shown below and select the row showing the Fiori app and the technical catalog associated with the app by clicking **Copy from Other Technical Catalog** 🗇 Copy from Other Technical Catalog .

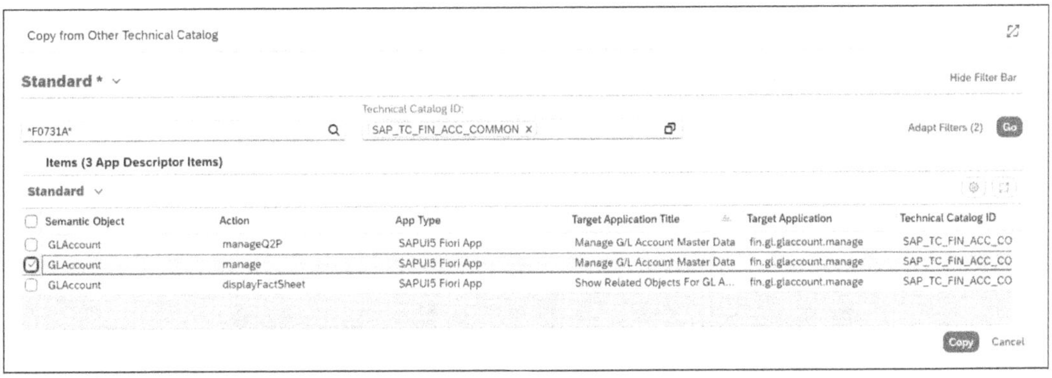

Figure 8-47. Fiori app F0731A selected with the correct semantic object and semantic action

387

CHAPTER 8   SAP FIORI LAUNCHPAD APP MANAGER

As shown in the figure above, three different apps (with different semantic objects and semantic actions) were found for the Fiori app F0731A. Select the app with the correct semantic object and action as per your requirement and click the icon Copy **Copy** as shown in the figure below.

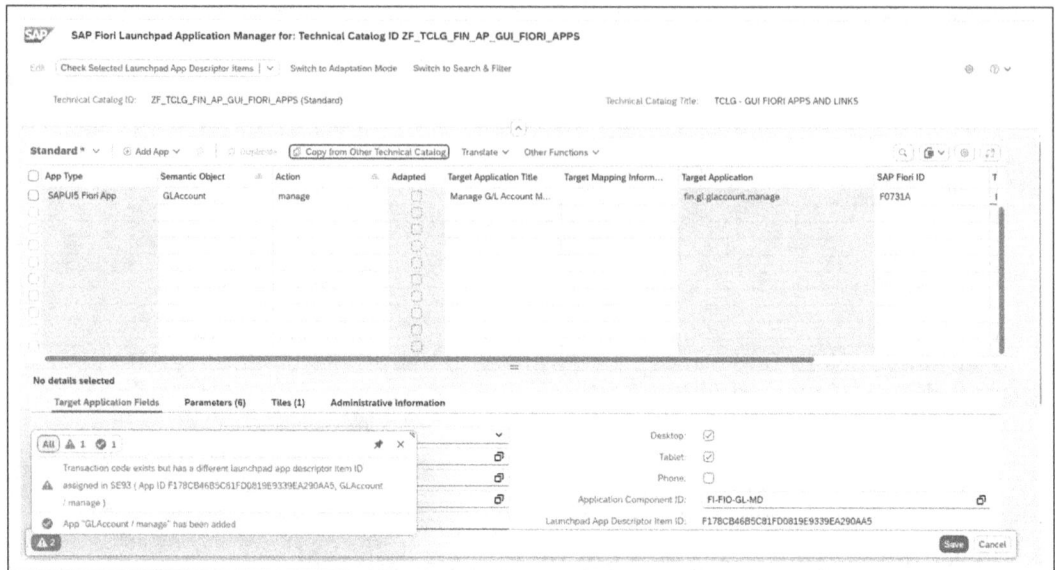

Figure 8-48. *Fiori app added with a warning message*

When the Fiori app is added, it displays two messages at the bottom of the screen in the figure **above**. It displays a warning message, which is acceptable. It also shows the message **App "GLAccount / manage" has been added**. Click **Save**.

CHAPTER 8   SAP FIORI LAUNCHPAD APP MANAGER

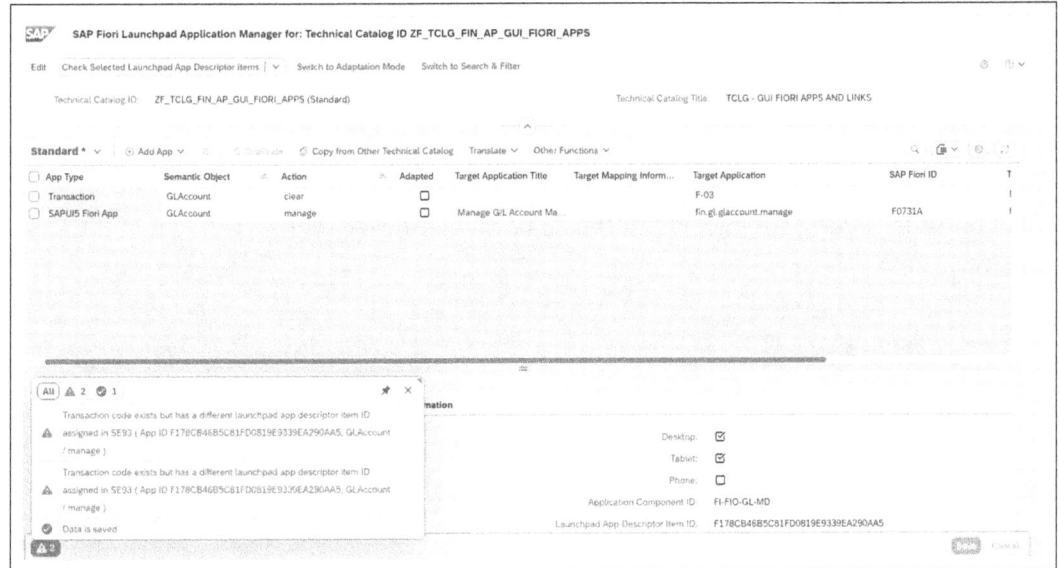

Figure 8-49. *Fiori app added successfully*

The figure above shows that the Fiori app was successfully added and displays a message **Data is saved**.

Clear the message screen, and the final screen appears as in the figure below.

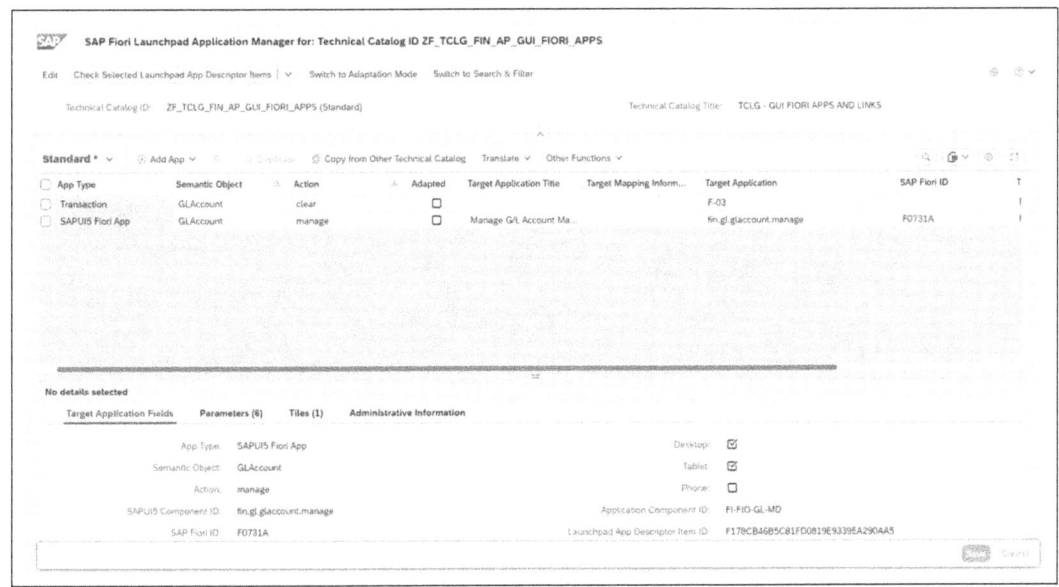

Figure 8-50. *Displays both apps added*

389

CHAPTER 8   SAP FIORI LAUNCHPAD APP MANAGER

Note   The **SAPUI5 Fiori App** option was automatically added at the top of the figure, under the header **App Type**.

Select Switch to Facet Filter to go back to the SAP Fiori Launchpad Application Manager initial screen and search for the custom technical catalog as shown in the figure below.

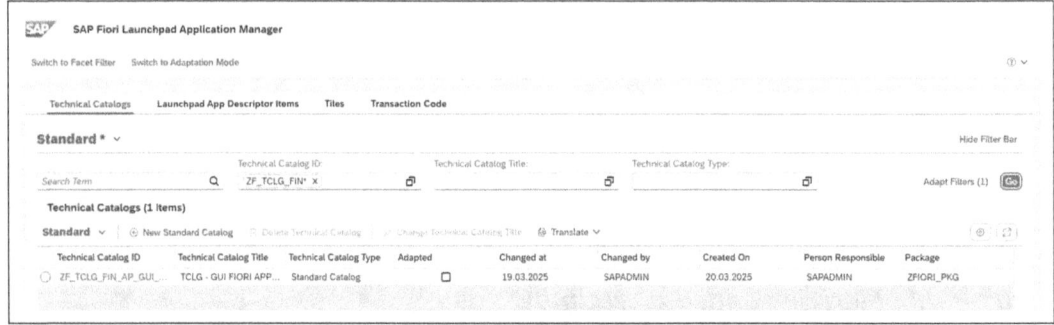

Figure 8-51. *Technical catalog displayed after selecting Switch to Facet Filter*

8.4 Update the Technical Catalog

To update the catalog, open the catalog and follow the same steps to add a new app. In this case, click ⊕ Add App ⌄ to add the app for FBV3.

CHAPTER 8   SAP FIORI LAUNCHPAD APP MANAGER

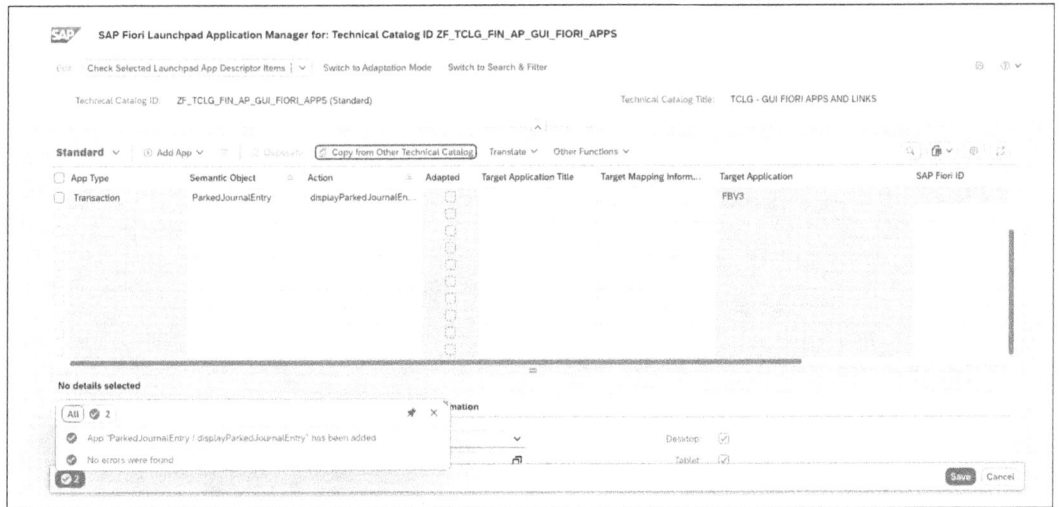

Figure 8-52. *The app FBV3 added successfully with no error*

New messages appear at the bottom of the screen, indicating that the app has been added and no errors were found, as shown in the figure below.

Figure 8-53. *Technical catalog updated successfully*

Similarly, add other apps as discussed above as per your requirements.

CHAPTER 8   SAP FIORI LAUNCHPAD APP MANAGER

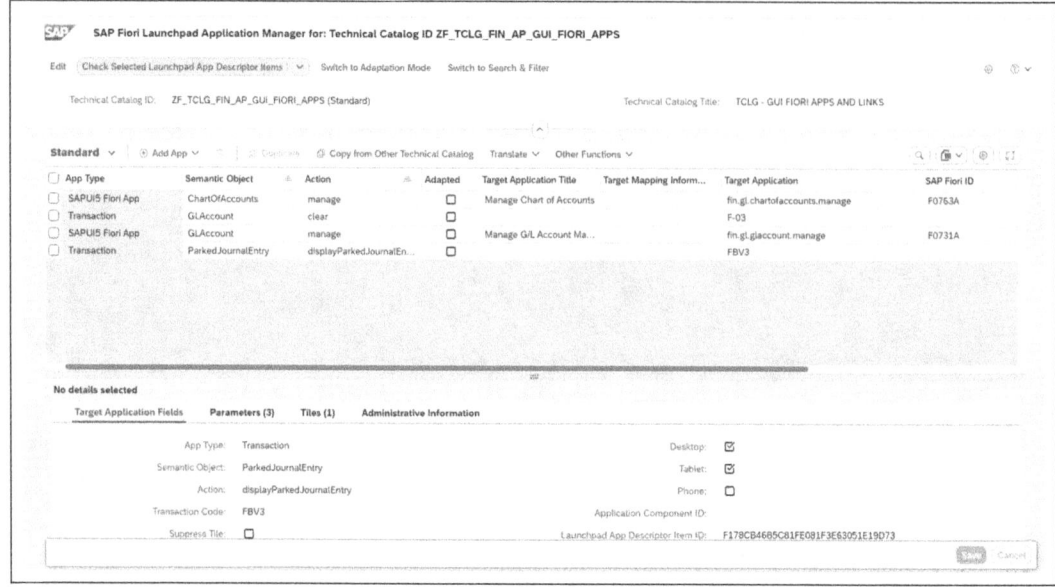

Figure 8-54. *Details of all the apps added to the technical catalog*

Save your changes by clicking the icon **Save**.

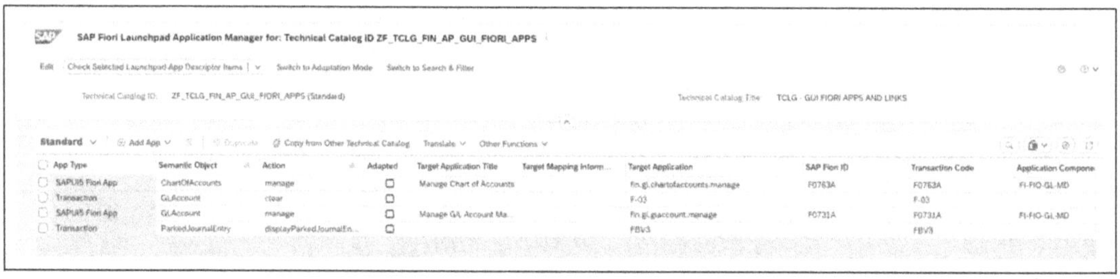

Figure 8-55. *All apps added to the technical catalog*

The custom technical catalog has been created with four apps, as shown in the figure above. The figure below shows the results of returning to the home page and searching for the technical catalog just created.

CHAPTER 8   SAP FIORI LAUNCHPAD APP MANAGER

Figure 8-56. Technical catalog created

> **Note**   A technical catalog is only used as a **reference catalog**.
>
> In **Chapter 12**, a custom catalog example will be recreated using **semantic objects and semantic actions (custom tiles)**.

8.5 Remove Apps from the Technical Catalog

To remove an app from the custom technical catalog, select the app to be removed as shown in the figure below. For example, we are removing FBV3 from the catalog.

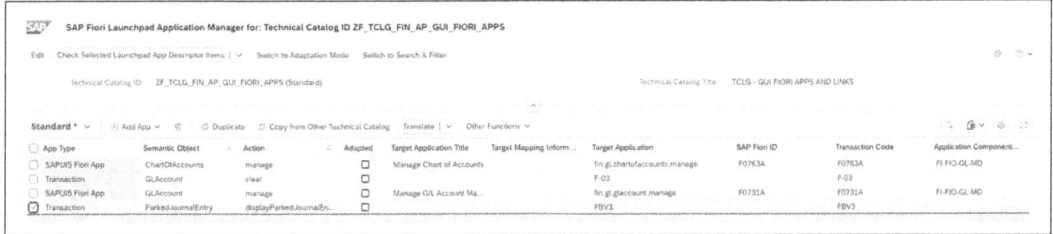

Figure 8-57. App selected for removal

> **Note**   This tool allows you to select multiple apps to remove simultaneously.

393

Select the delete icon 🗑, and a new box window opens, **Select Transport Request**, as shown in the figure below, to remove the app from the custom technical catalog.

Figure 8-58. *App removal transport request*

Click OK, and the app is removed, as shown below.

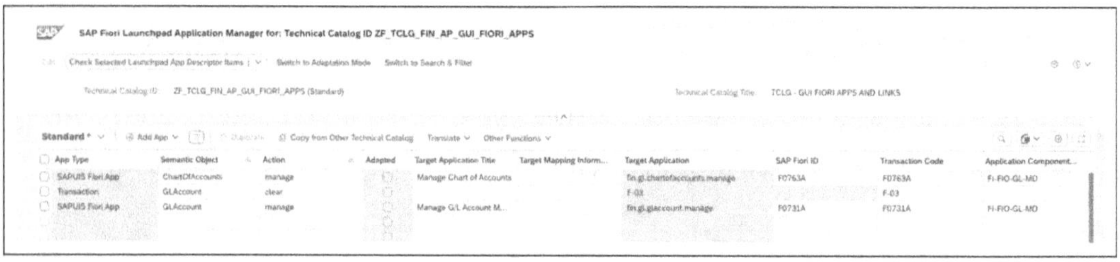

Figure 8-59. *App removed*

Save the changes by clicking the Save icon Save. The app has been removed from the technical catalog, as shown in the figure below.

CHAPTER 8 SAP FIORI LAUNCHPAD APP MANAGER

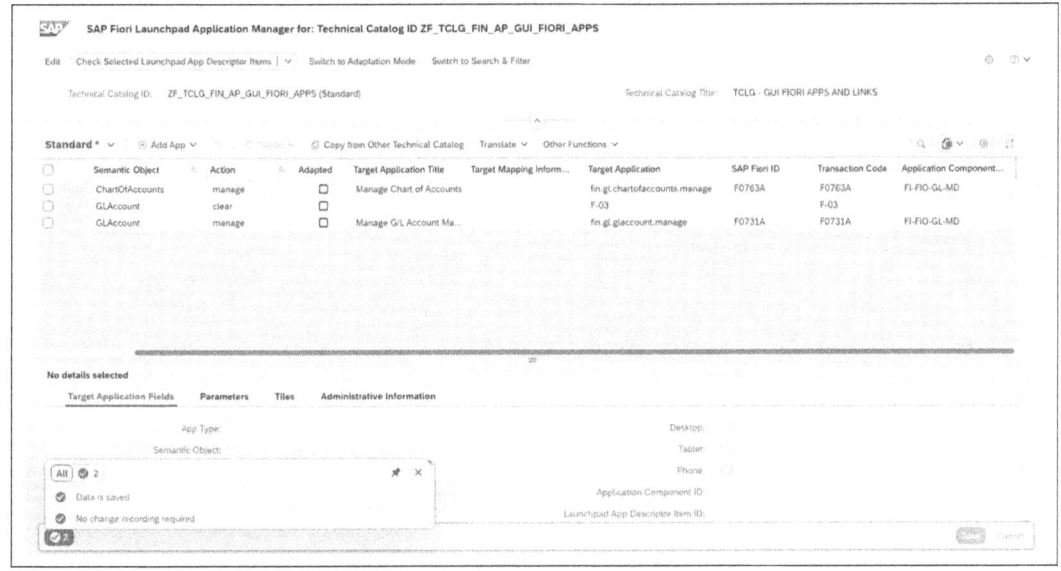

Figure 8-60. *App removed from the technical catalog*

The above figure displays the message **Data is saved**.

8.6 Delete the Technical Catalog

To delete a technical catalog, go back to the home screen and search for the technical catalog you want to delete. As shown in the figure below, we will delete a temporary technical catalog created earlier.

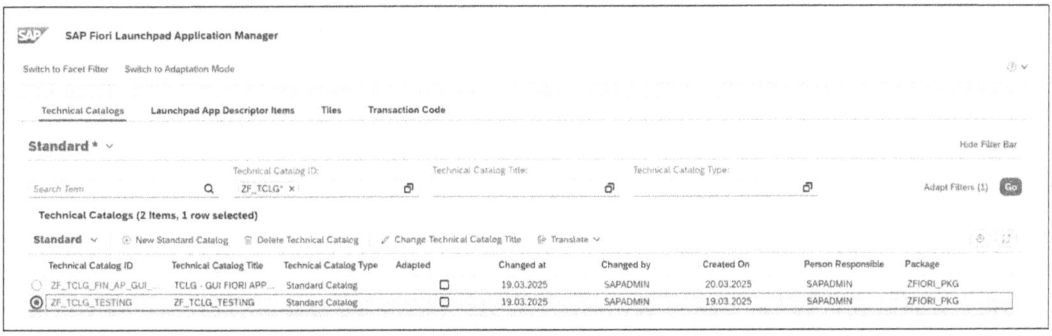

Figure 8-61. *Technical catalog to be removed*

395

CHAPTER 8   SAP FIORI LAUNCHPAD APP MANAGER

Select the icon 🗑 Delete Technical Catalog , and a new window box called **Delete Technical Catalog** opens where we need to add the **transport request**, as shown in figure below.

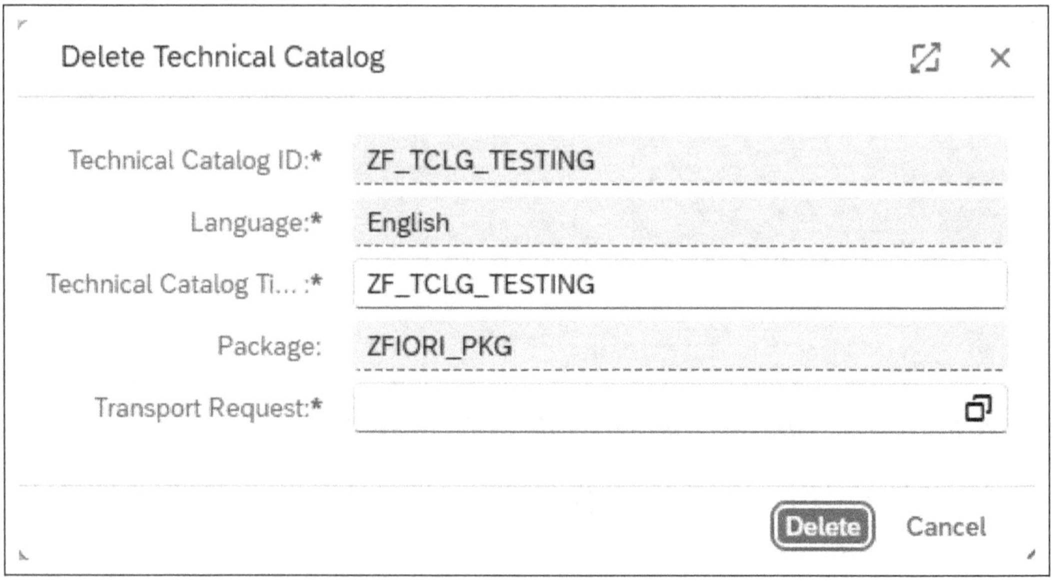

```
┌─────────────────────────────────────────────────────────┐
│  Delete Technical Catalog                        ⤢   ×  │
│                                                         │
│      Technical Catalog ID:*   ZF_TCLG_TESTING           │
│              Language:*       English                   │
│      Technical Catalog Ti... :* ZF_TCLG_TESTING         │
│              Package:         ZFIORI_PKG                │
│      Transport Request:*      _____      ⧉   │
│                                                         │
│                                      [ Delete ]  Cancel │
└─────────────────────────────────────────────────────────┘
```

Figure 8-62. Technical catalog deletion transport request

Enter the details of the transport request as shown in the figure below.

CHAPTER 8   SAP FIORI LAUNCHPAD APP MANAGER

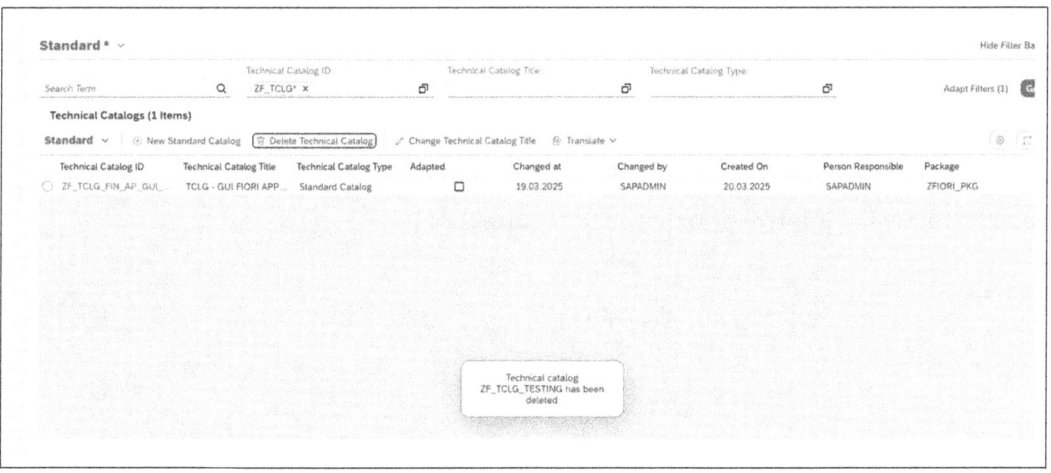

Figure 8-63. Transport request information added

Select the icon Delete **Delete**.

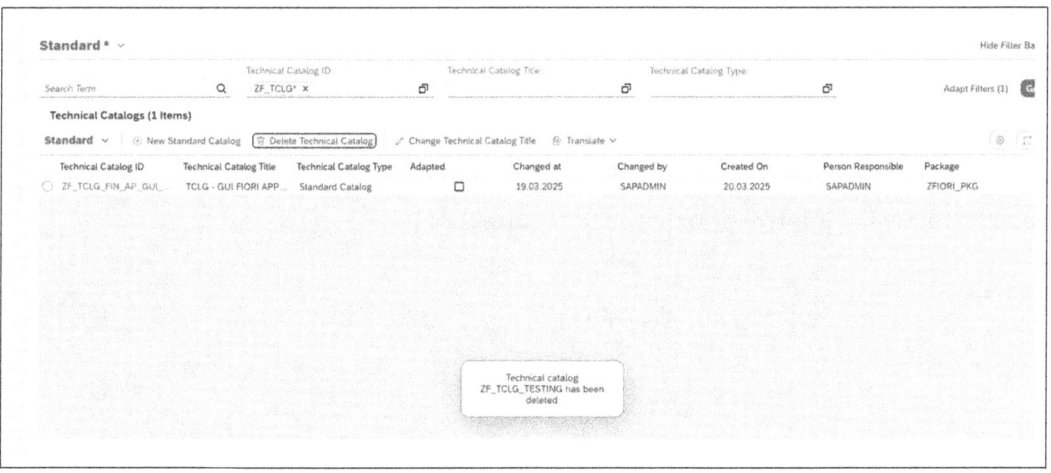

Figure 8-64. Message displaying the technical catalog has been deleted

While deleting a message box opens with a message Technical Catalog ZF_TCLG has been removed, as displayed in the figure above. The final screen with the technical catalog removed is displayed in the figure below.

397

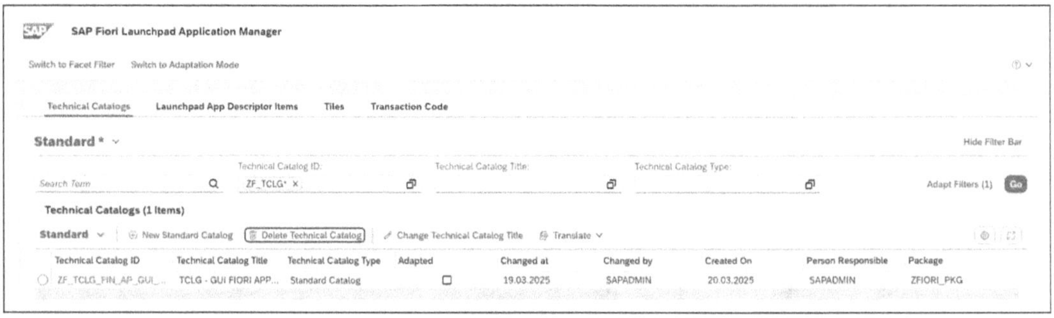

Figure 8-65. Updated technical catalog screen

8.7 Validate the Technical Catalog

Validating and testing the contents of the custom technical catalog is crucial. This can be achieved by creating a test user ID, assigning the technical catalog, and verifying that the applications function correctly.

An SAP Fiori technical catalog is not intended for end users but is primarily designed for system administrators and developers. This catalog contains detailed technical configurations, role setups, and back-end integrations that are specifically unnecessary for end user operations. Instead, end users can access business catalogs tailored to their specific roles. This approach ensures a simplified, relevant, and secure user experience without overwhelming users with technical details.

Assign the test user the technical catalog and the admin user roles; the test user will view the following information on the SAP Launchpad.

CHAPTER 8   SAP FIORI LAUNCHPAD APP MANAGER

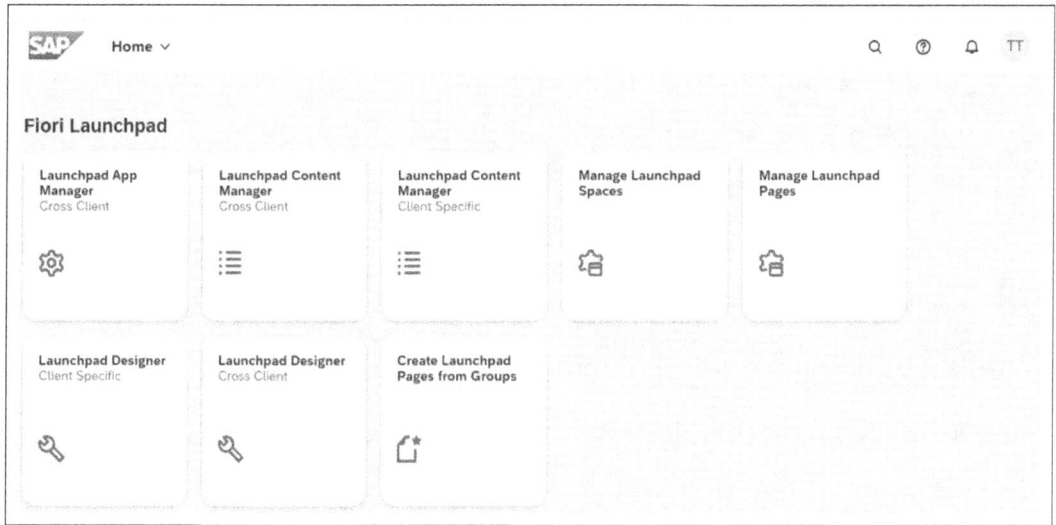

Figure 8-66. Admin user SAP Launchpad initial screen

Under the **User Menu** TT , select **App Finder**, and this will list the three apps assigned to the technical catalog, as shown in the figure below.

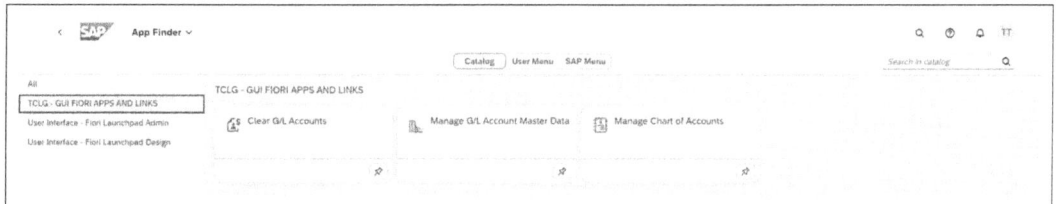

Figure 8-67. Admin user with the technical catalog and three apps assigned

The admin user will see the three apps assigned to the custom technical catalog.

8.8 Verification of the Technical Catalog in the Launchpad Content Manager

Once created, the custom technical catalog can be used to create a business catalog using the transaction /UI2/FLPM_CUST (FLP Content Manager (Client Specific)). This transaction can visualize the technical catalog created in the above sections. Executing and searching for the technical catalog displays details, as shown in the figure below.

399

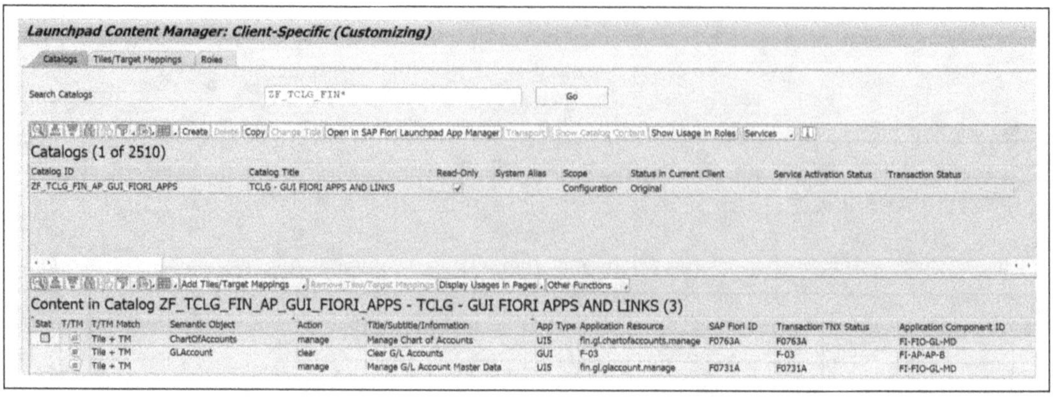

CHAPTER 8　SAP FIORI LAUNCHPAD APP MANAGER

Figure 8-68. *Technical catalog details seen via transaction /UI2/FLPCM_CUST*

> **Note** The transaction **/UI2/FLPCM_CUST** is used to create a **custom business catalog**, which we discuss in detail in Chapter 9. Business catalogs are assigned to the role, which is then assigned to the end user.

The above figure confirms that the technical catalog is visible and has three apps assigned to it. Within this transaction **/UI2/FLPCM_CUST**, the admin can perform the following activities:

- Create

- Copy

- Open in SAP Fiori Launchpad App Manager

- Show Usage in Roles

- Services

- Display Usages in Pages

- Other Functions

Selecting the option Show Usage in Roles `Show Usage in Roles` will display which **roles** the technical catalog is part of, as shown in the figure below.

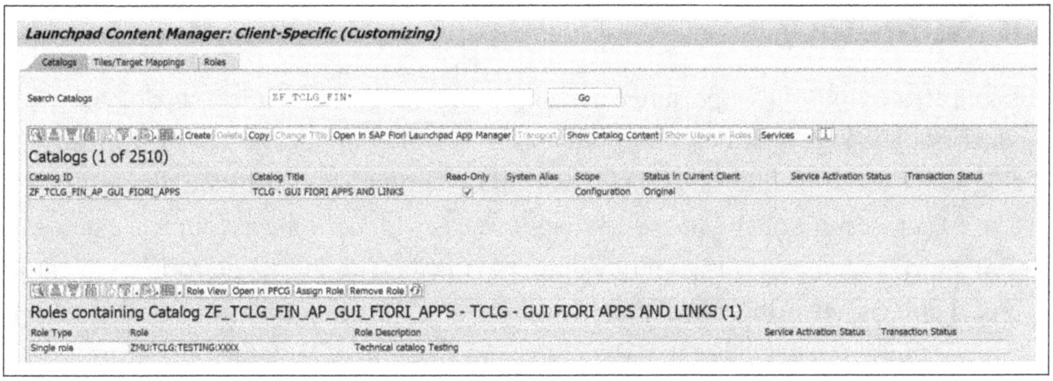

CHAPTER 8   SAP FIORI LAUNCHPAD APP MANAGER

Figure 8-69. Displaying a role name with the technical catalog

The custom technical catalog created is only used as a **reference catalog**, displays Read-Only, and has a checkbox selected.

You can verify if the new technical catalog is accessible using transaction **/UI2/FLPD_CUST** through the previous method.

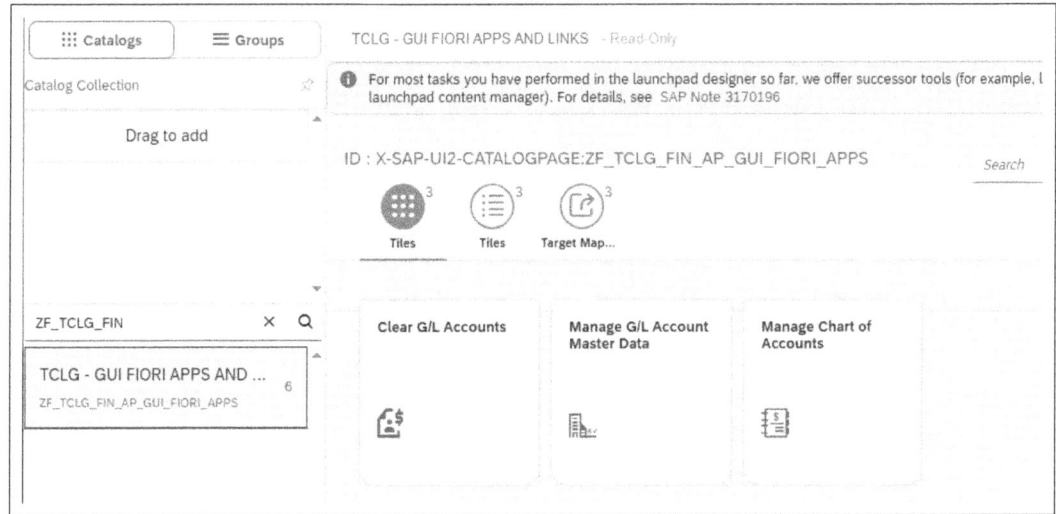

Figure 8-70. Technical catalog in /UI2/FLPD_CUST

The figure above shows that the custom technical catalog is accessible using the transaction code **/UI2/FLPD_CUST**.

8.9 Summary

This chapter outlines the importance of creating an SAP Fiori technical catalog to organize and manage technical components for SAP Fiori applications. A technical catalog stores essential building blocks, like target mappings, application references, and tiles, used across multiple business catalogs. It starts with defining a technical catalog in the SAP Fiori Launchpad Designer or Content Manager. This allows developers to group technical objects, ensuring consistency and reducing redundancy. A technical catalog is carefully maintained to ensure that the correct application parameters, configurations, and services are associated with each tile or target mapping. This setup allows for efficient management and updates propagating to related business catalogs. An SAP Fiori technical catalog simplifies application management, supporting the smooth operation of the SAP Fiori Launchpad.

CHAPTER 9

SAP Fiori Launchpad Content Manager

*The SAP Fiori Launchpad Content Manager (/**UI2/FLPM_CUST**) is a tool designed to simplify the management of business catalogs in the SAP Fiori Launchpad. It allows administrators to create new business catalogs and analyze, modify, and adapt them by copying existing ones, customizing them to meet specific business needs, and checking app assignments, dependencies, and missing configurations. This transaction helps optimize Fiori content by enabling mass adjustments, ensuring proper role-based access, and troubleshooting misconfigured or missing apps. It is beneficial in SAP S/4HANA implementations for maintaining a structured and efficient Fiori Launchpad experience.*

9.1 Introduction

The **SAP Fiori Launchpad Content Manager** tool helps you manage business catalogs in the SAP Fiori Launchpad more easily. It enables you to explore, create, and modify catalogs by copying existing ones and customizing them to meet your business needs. This tool manages SAP Fiori apps and ensures business users can find and access them efficiently. It creates a business catalog containing apps that can be assigned to a business role, which is then assigned to the end user to perform activities.

There are two ways to create a **business catalog**:

- Transaction code **/UI2/FLPD_CUST** – Launchpad Designer (Client Specific)

- Transaction code **/UI2/FLPCM_CUST** – FLP Content Manager (Client Specific)

For configuration that affects the entire system across the landscape, there are two ways to create a **business catalog**:

- Transaction code **/UI2/FLPD_CONF**
- Transaction code **/UI2/FLPCM_CONF**

This chapter discusses creating a new **custom business catalog** using the transaction **/UI2/FLPM_CUST**. **Appendix B** explains how to create a business catalog using the transaction code **/UI2/FLPD_CUST**.

Note The transaction code **/UI2/FLPD_CUST** has been deprecated since SAP's release of S/4HANA 2020. You can still create a business catalog using this transaction. For further details, refer to **Appendix B**.

Fiori developers or administrators primarily use the SAP Fiori transaction code **/UI2/FLPM_CUST** to customize the SAP Fiori Launchpad. Through this transaction, administrators can manage and tailor the Launchpad experience to meet specific business needs, such as defining which catalogs, groups, pages, or tiles are available to different user roles. It allows you to review **groups, spaces, and pages in the catalog, as well as roles** and other aspects related to the content displayed in the Launchpad.

Overall, **/UI2/FLPM_CUST** is a powerful tool for ensuring the SAP Fiori Launchpad is optimized and aligned with the organization's requirements, enhancing user experience and efficiency.

9.1.1 Key Features

The main key features of the transaction **/UI2/FLPM_CUST** are as follows:

- **Exploring Content:** Administrators can explore all available catalogs to identify specific tiles or target mappings, enabling them to find relevant applications that help users access the right tools effectively.

- **Creating Custom Catalogs:** Administrators can create custom catalogs by copying existing SAP-delivered catalogs. This allows them to include only the apps needed for specific business roles.

- **Managing Catalogs:** Administrators can simultaneously add or remove tiles and target mappings and rename or delete catalogs that are no longer needed. Grouping related tiles makes it easier for users to find the desired apps.

- **Checking Role Assignments:** Administrators can view and change role assignments for catalogs. This helps ensure that the right users have access to the correct apps.

- **Identifying Issues/Errors:** The tool checks problems with tiles, target mappings, or catalog loading. This helps keep the Launchpad setup clean and efficient.

- **Saving and Assigning:** Once the administrator tailors the catalog, it can be saved and assigned to the appropriate roles via the SAP Role Maintenance transaction **PFCG**. This ensures that only authorized users can access the custom catalog.

- **Testing and Validation:** Administrators evaluate the catalog before final deployment to ensure all tiles and target mappings function correctly as intended.

Thus, using the FLP Content Manager enables organizations to create customized catalogs tailored to specific roles, meeting their requirements. This improvement boosts productivity and enhances the user experience in the SAP Fiori Launchpad.

9.2 FLP Content Manager Details

The transaction code **/UI2/FLPCM_CUST** is the same as the app **SAP Fiori FLP Content Manager (Client Specific)**, which can be accessed from the SAP Fiori Launchpad to create a business catalog, as shown in the figure below. The SAP S/4HANA 2020 release introduced an innovative approach to creating a business catalog displayed in the Fiori Launchpad.

CHAPTER 9　SAP FIORI LAUNCHPAD CONTENT MANAGER

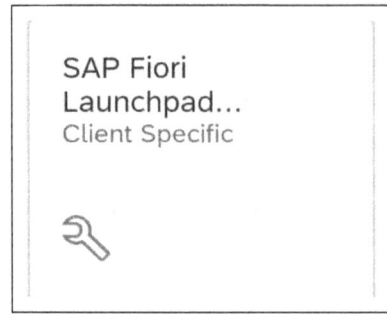

Figure 9-1. *SAP Fiori Launchpad Manager app for administrators*

Execute the transaction code **/UI2/FLPCM_CUST** or click the app in the above figure to open the **Launchpad Content Manager: Client-Specific (Customizing)** window, as shown below.

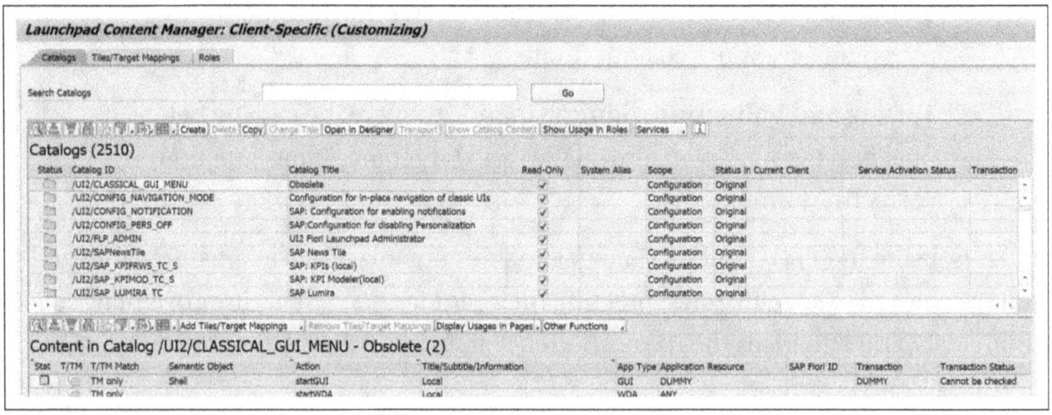

Figure 9-2. *Transaction /UI2/FLPCM_CUST initial screen when executed*

The screen displayed above is identical whether you access it through the transaction or the app in the SAP Fiori Launchpad. It shows the number of catalogs (technical, business, and custom) available in the system. The Launchpad Content Manager screen, as shown in the above figure, has three primary tab categories, which, when selected, provide access to different functionalities that can be performed. The tabs are

- Catalogs
- Tiles/Target Mappings
- Roles

406

The **Catalogs** tab provides activities such as creating, copying, and deleting a business catalog and supports using a technical catalog. Under the **Tiles/Target Mappings** tab, the value **Tile + TM** is displayed for selection at the bottom of the screen. The **Roles** tab gives the desired information related to a business catalog's functionality. As a best practice, SAP recommends **copying SAP catalogs into custom ones** rather than editing **SAP-delivered** content directly. These three tabs and their various sub-tabs are explained below.

9.2.1 Catalogs

The initial screen appears when the transaction **/UI2/FLPCM_CUST** is executed, as shown in the figure above. The tab **Catalogs** is selected by **default.** The Catalogs tab displays all available technical, business, and custom catalogs, including their contents, such as apps, target mappings, and roles. It allows you to copy a technical/business catalog or reference it for a new custom business catalog. Administrators can review, manage, and adjust these catalogs for different user roles. The administrator can also copy a technical or business catalog to a custom business catalog or reference the same catalog under the organization naming space. This transaction enables the conduct of mass administrative tasks. An administrator can copy a technical catalog to a business catalog or reference the same one.

The sub-tabs that appear under the tab **Catalogs** are as follows:

> **Create:** Use the **Create** tab to create custom versions of a business catalog. You can search for and include tiles and targeting mappings in the custom catalog per your business requirements.
>
> **Delete:** This tab deletes custom Launchpad content, such as catalogs created in the Customizing layer. It permanently removes content no longer needed, helping you efficiently clean up and manage your catalog. It **does not delete SAP-delivered (standard) content**; only custom content created in the Customizing scope is deleted.
>
> **Copy:** The **Copy** tab lets you copy standard SAP Launchpad content, including catalogs, into a custom namespace. This will allow you to create a custom version to change or modify. Use the Copy tab to make these editable custom copies of a catalog.

This approach aligns with SAP's recommendation to extend standard content rather than changing it. This also allows you to copy a technical catalog into a business catalog by employing the concepts of soft and deep copy, which are editable.

Change Title: The **Change Title** tab allows you to rename custom catalogs, groups, spaces, or pages. You can modify the display title to make it more meaningful or user-friendly without altering the technical ID or content. This feature enables you to enhance the names of custom Launchpad items, such as catalogs, while maintaining their technical structure.

Open in Designer: The **Open in Designer** tab lets you quickly access the SAP Fiori Launchpad Designer (**/UI2/FLPD_CUST**) directly from the Content Manager for the selected catalog, group, or space/page. This feature also offers a shortcut for editing Launchpad content, including adding and removing tiles and target mappings, using the Fiori Launchpad Designer tool.

Transport: The **Transport** tab lets you assign custom catalogs to a transport request. You use the Transport tab to move custom Fiori content from one system to another, like from development to QA or production, by including it in a Customizing transport request.

Show Catalog Content: The **Show Catalog Content** tab lets you view the details of a selected catalog, including all the tiles and target mappings it contains. You can also view the apps (tiles) and navigation targets in the catalog, which helps you understand their structure and purpose. This tab does not allow you to change the content.

Show Usage in Roles: The **Show Usage in Roles** tab lets you see which PFCG roles utilize a selected catalog, group, space, or page. You can find out which roles have specific Launchpad content. This helps you manage role assignments and understand how content is used throughout the system.

Services: The **Services** tab allows you to verify if the necessary OData services and ICF nodes for Fiori apps in your catalogs are activated. This tab helps you confirm and activate services such as **OData** and **ICF**, ensuring your Launchpad apps function correctly. If the service radio button is red, you can maintain both services within the tab by directing you to the transaction /**IWFND/MAINT_SERVICE** and **SICF**. All services should be green so that they work correctly.

Add Tiles/Target Mappings: The **Add Tiles/Target Mappings** tab allows you to add specific apps (tiles) and their navigation targets from a technical catalog to a custom business catalog. You can use this tab to create custom catalogs that deliver content tailored to specific business roles by selecting the necessary apps from SAP's official technical catalogs. You can also add apps directly to the business catalog without referring to the technical catalog. This tab has two sub-tabs:

- **Add Tiles/Target Mappings:** The **Add Tiles/Target Mappings** option enables you to select specific tiles and their corresponding target mappings from a technical catalog for your custom business catalog. This feature allows you to personalize business catalogs by selecting only the necessary apps. You can also quickly add apps by searching for them directly. As a result, users will only see what is needed in the Fiori Launchpad.

- **Add Selected Tiles/TMs to Other Catalogs:** The **Add Selected Tiles/TMs to Other Catalogs** option allows you to copy chosen tiles and target mappings from one catalog to a different custom catalog. This feature enables you to reuse apps across different business catalogs by allowing you to copy content to another catalog without manually recreating it.

Remove Tiles/Target Mappings: The **Remove Tiles/Target Mappings** tab lets you delete specific tiles and target mappings from a custom business catalog. Use this tab to clean up or adjust your custom catalogs by removing apps (tiles) and their associated navigation targets you no longer need.

Display Usages in Pages: The **Display Usages in Pages** tab shows where catalog tiles are used in different pages of the Fiori Launchpad. This tab helps you see which pages have specific tiles, making it easier to manage and analyze the arrangement of apps in the Launchpad.

Other Functions: The **Other Functions** tab provides access to additional tools for managing your Fiori Launchpad content. These tools help you analyze, repair, or manage technical issues that go beyond basic actions, such as creating, copying, or deleting items. This tab provides access to additional utilities such as

- Checking technical catalogs
- Repairing broken references
- Analyzing app descriptors
- Mass Maintenance functions

9.2.2 Tiles/Target Mappings

A Fiori tile catalog can include two components and be seen as **Tile + TM**:

- **Tiles (T):** Tiles are the visual elements of apps, as seen on the Fiori Launchpad screen, including title, subtitle, information, icon, and the semantic object and action for intent-based navigation.
- **Target Mappings (TM):** This defines the target application (Fiori app, transaction, or Web Dynpro application) that is launched for a given intent and device type. The navigation intent (semantic object and action) can be triggered by clicking a tile or a link.

Note The connection between the **tile** and the **target mapping** is made via **intent**. If no target mapping matches the semantic object, the action, and the device type for a tile, then the tile will not be displayed on the Fiori Launchpad.

The tab **Tiles/Target Mappings** has the following sub-tabs:

Add Reference to Catalog: The **Add Reference to Catalog** tab allows you to link to an existing tile or target mapping from another catalog, rather than creating a copy. By creating references, this option helps you reuse tiles and target mappings in other custom catalogs. This way, you maintain consistency and lower maintenance efforts across catalogs.

Show Usage in Catalogs: The **Show Usage in Catalogs** tab allows you to view where a specific tile or target mapping is used across different catalogs. This feature helps you track a tile or target mapping across various catalogs, making it easier to analyze how they depend on each other and manage Launchpad content effectively.

Show Usage in Roles: The **Show Usage in Roles** tab allows you to check which PFCG roles include a selected tile or target mapping through assigned catalogs. This feature helps you identify which user roles can access a specific app (tile or target mapping), facilitating effective access control and content management.

Services: The **Services** tab allows you to check the necessary OData services and ICF nodes for the selected tile or target mapping. This ensures that all required back-end services are active and available, allowing the app to run smoothly on the Fiori Launchpad.

Catalog View: The **Catalog View** tab enables you to adjust the layout, grouping all tiles and target mappings by their respective catalogs. This feature makes it easier to analyze and manage content in the Launchpad, simplifying maintenance at the catalog level.

Remove: The **Remove** tab lets you delete selected tiles or mappings from a custom catalog. This feature helps you clean up your catalog by removing tiles or mappings you no longer need, keeping your Fiori Launchpad experience organized and relevant.

Open in Designer: The **Open in Designer** option allows you to launch the Fiori Launchpad Designer for the selected catalog quickly. This makes it easy to edit the catalog's contents, such as tiles and target mappings, and provides detailed configuration options.

9.2.3 Roles

The **Roles tab** has the following sub-tabs:

Copy Role: The **Copy Role** tab allows you to duplicate an existing PFCG role. This includes all assigned catalogs, groups, and spaces/pages. This feature enables the creation of similar roles for different users or departments, thereby maintaining consistency across roles.

Open in PFCG: The **Open in PFCG** tab lets you access a selected role directly in the PFCG (Role Maintenance) transaction. This shortcut allows you to modify the role, adjust authorizations, add catalogs or groups, and assign users as needed.

Show Catalogs: The **Show Catalogs** tab allows you to view all catalogs associated with a selected PFCG role. This helps you quickly identify which catalogs and apps are included, making it easier for users to manage Fiori app access.

Show Groups: The **Show Groups** tab allows you to view all **Fiori groups** associated with the selected **PFCG role**. This helps you find the visible tile groups on the Fiori Launchpad for that role.

Show Spaces: The **Show Spaces** tab allows you to view all **spaces** associated with the selected **PFCG role**. This helps you understand the Fiori Launchpad layout and how the apps are organized for that role.

Show Tiles/Target Mappings: The **Show Tiles/Target Mappings** tab provides a comprehensive overview of all the tiles and target mappings associated with a specific role within its catalogs. This feature lets you understand which applications and navigation targets users can access in the Fiori Launchpad.

Services: The **Services** tab enables you to verify the essential OData services and ICF nodes for the selected tile or target mapping. This ensures that all necessary back-end services are active and available, allowing the app to run smoothly on the Fiori Launchpad.

Catalog View: The **Catalog View** tab allows you to switch between viewing by role and viewing by catalog. This feature displays which roles are associated with each catalog. It makes analyzing how catalogs are used easier and helps manage access to Fiori applications based on roles. From a catalog-focused perspective, you can understand how catalogs connect to roles.

Open in Designer: The **Open in Designer** tab lets you quickly access the Fiori Launchpad Designer for the selected catalog. This feature simplifies editing catalog contents, including tiles and target mappings, and offers detailed configuration options.

Add Catalog: The **Add Catalog** tab enables you to assign a business catalog to a PFCG role, allowing users to access specific Fiori apps in their Fiori Launchpad.

Remove Catalog: The **Remove Catalog** tab allows you to delete a business catalog assignment from a PFCG role, revoking access to specific Fiori apps and streamlining app visibility for users.

9.2.4 Technical Catalog Reference Details and Copy

Firstly, search for the technical catalog **ZF_TCLG_FIN_AP_GUI_FIORI_APPS**, which was created earlier in **Chapter 8**. This catalog will be used as a reference. Execute the transaction code **/UI2/FLPCM_CUST** and, in the field Search Catalogs, use the term **ZF_TCLG_FIN*** as shown in the figure below, and click the **Go** [Go] option.

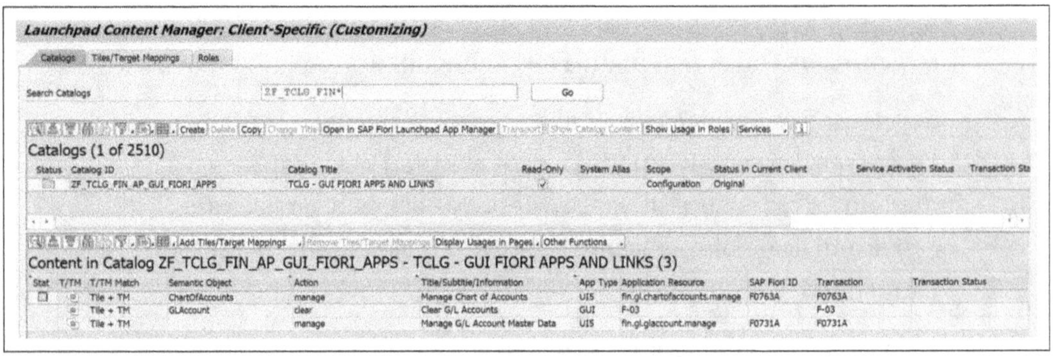

CHAPTER 9 SAP FIORI LAUNCHPAD CONTENT MANAGER

Figure 9-3. The technical catalog created earlier is displayed

The previously created technical catalog can be viewed as shown in the figure above.

Note The technical catalog is set to read-only. Additionally, a new tab called **Open in SAP Fiori Launchpad App Manager** is available. This tab offers quick access to the transaction **/UI2/FLPAM**. You can manage apps, catalogs, and target mappings with the App Manager.

This technical catalog can be copied to a **business catalog** by selecting the tab **Copy** `Copy`, as shown in the figure above. A new window box titled **Copy Catalog** appears to copy the catalog as shown below.

Figure 9-4. Copy the technical catalog with complete details

The system prompts you to enter the name of the custom business catalog to be created. Here, we will create a deep copy of the technical catalog in the business catalog

414

CHAPTER 9 SAP FIORI LAUNCHPAD CONTENT MANAGER

by updating the information required in the above figure and using the proper naming convention per the organization's standards.

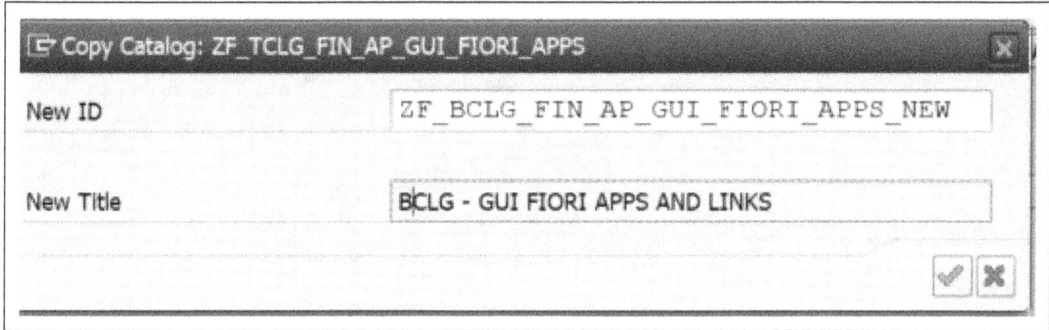

Figure 9-5. Business catalog information updated

Note Make sure the new title for the business catalog is no more than **40 characters**.

Click the continue icon , and the system will prompt for Customizing transport requests. Use the transport created earlier using the **Own Requests** option or create a new one by clicking the **create** icon. For our purposes, we are using the transport created earlier, as shown in the figure below.

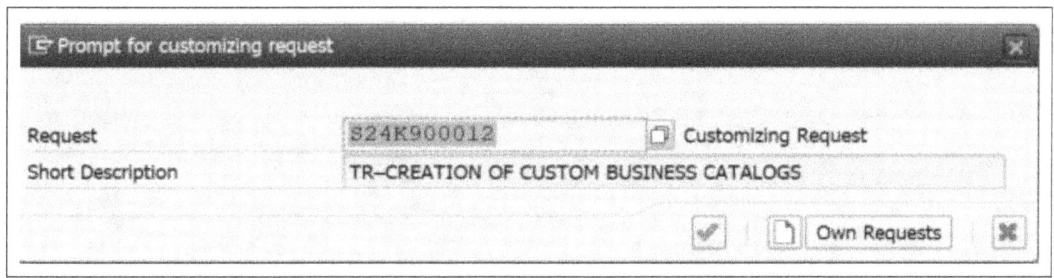

Figure 9-6. Business catalog added to the Customizing transport

Click the **continue** icon , and the business catalog is created with three apps as shown in the figure below.

415

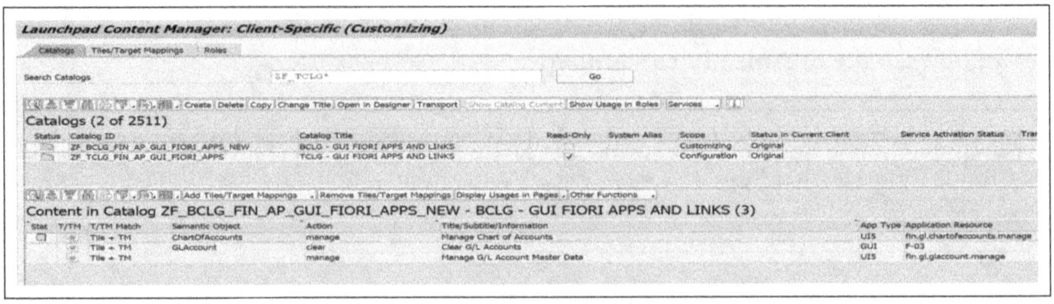

CHAPTER 9   SAP FIORI LAUNCHPAD CONTENT MANAGER

Figure 9-7. Custom business catalog created

> **Note**   BCLG represents the **business catalog**.

A message at the bottom of the screen indicates that the **technical catalog "ZF_BCLG_FIN_AP_GUI_FIORI_APPS"** has been **copied** to a **business catalog**, as shown in the figure above. This business catalog can be edited, modified, and updated as desired. You can also assign the business catalog to a role. The following section will discuss in detail how to create a custom business catalog.

9.3 Creating a Custom Business Catalog

Execute the transaction **/UI2/FLPCM_CUST**, and the **Launchpad Content Manager: Client-Specific (Customizing)** window opens, as shown in the figure below.

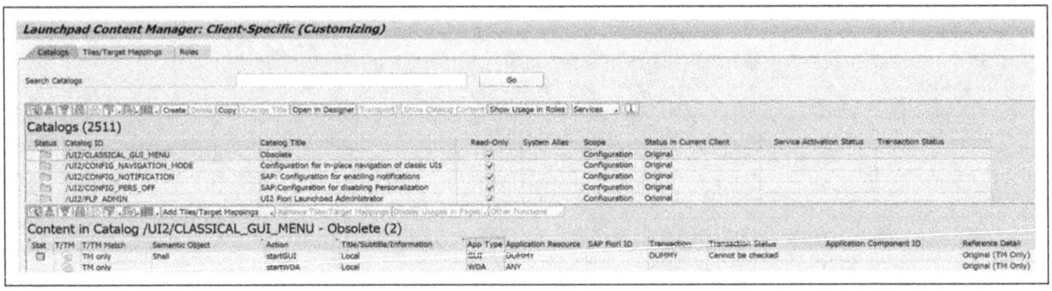

Figure 9-8. Initial screen for transaction /UI2/FLPCM_CUST

To create a new business catalog, select **Create** `Create`, and a new window opens, as shown in the figure below.

CHAPTER 9   SAP FIORI LAUNCHPAD CONTENT MANAGER

Figure 9-9. Create Catalog window

Before proceeding, you must determine the catalog details, required apps, and naming convention for roles, spaces, and pages. Ensure that you have these details available before creating a business catalog. Enter the following information in the Create Catalog window, as shown in the figure below:

- **New ID:** ZF_BCLG_FIN_AR_INVS_CRMEMOS
- **New Title:** BCLG:FIN:AR – Invoices & Credit Memos

Figure 9-10. New business catalog to be created with information added

To proceed further, click the **continue** icon  . The system will prompt you to enter the transport request details in the **Prompt for customizing request** window shown in the figure below.

417

CHAPTER 9　SAP FIORI LAUNCHPAD CONTENT MANAGER

Figure 9-11. Business catalog with Customizing transport request updated

After entering the transport details, to proceed further, click the **continue** icon. The **business catalog** is created as shown in the figure below.

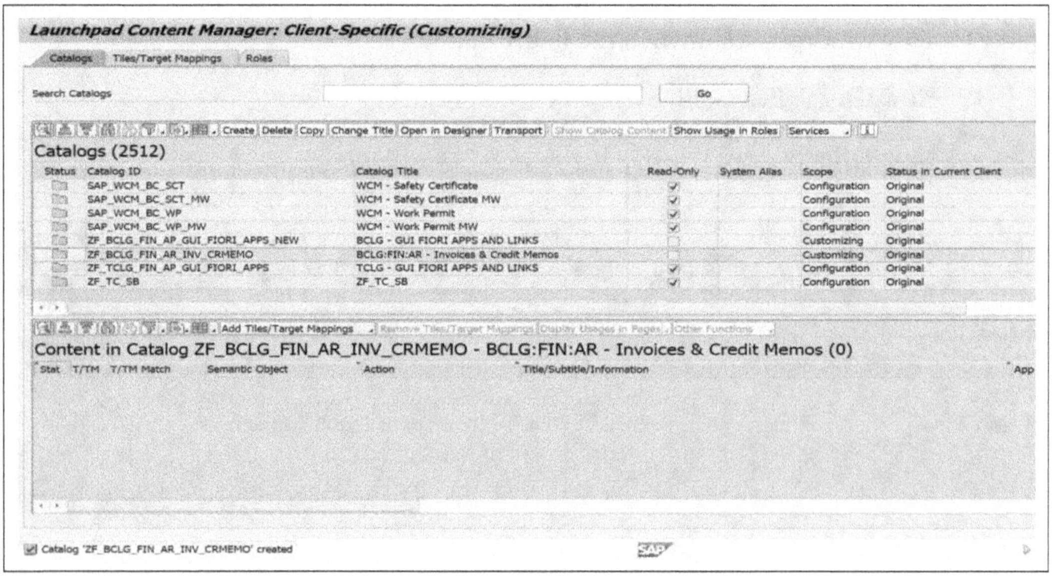

Figure 9-12. Business catalog created

A new message appears at the bottom of the screen as shown in the above figure, indicating that the **catalog "ZF_BCLG_FIN_AR_INV_CRMEMO"** has been created. The custom business catalog is now ready to be updated with any necessary applications. Now, enter the business catalog name in the **Search Catalogs** field and click **Go** as shown in the figure below.

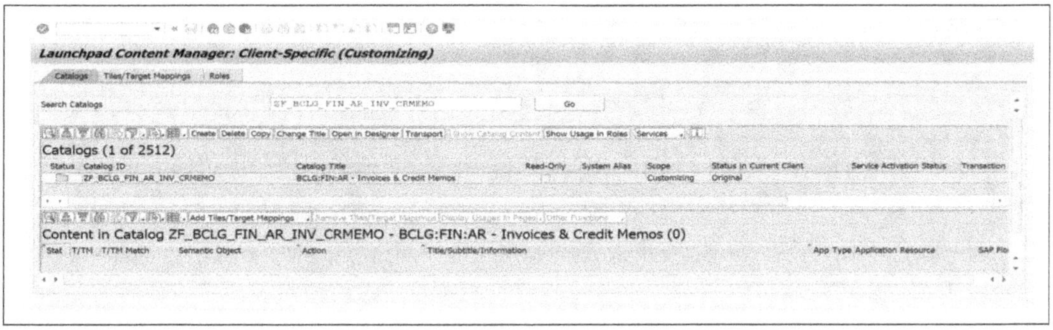

CHAPTER 9   SAP FIORI LAUNCHPAD CONTENT MANAGER

Figure 9-13. Window displaying the business catalog

The FLP Content Manager screen is split into two parts. The top half displays the business catalog name, and the bottom part allows us to update the business catalog with apps/tiles.

To add apps/tiles, select the tab **Add Tiles/Target Mappings** `Add Tiles/Target Mappings` in the above figure and then select the option **Add Tiles/TMs to Selected Catalog** (`Add Tiles/TMs to Selected Catalog`) as shown in the figure below.

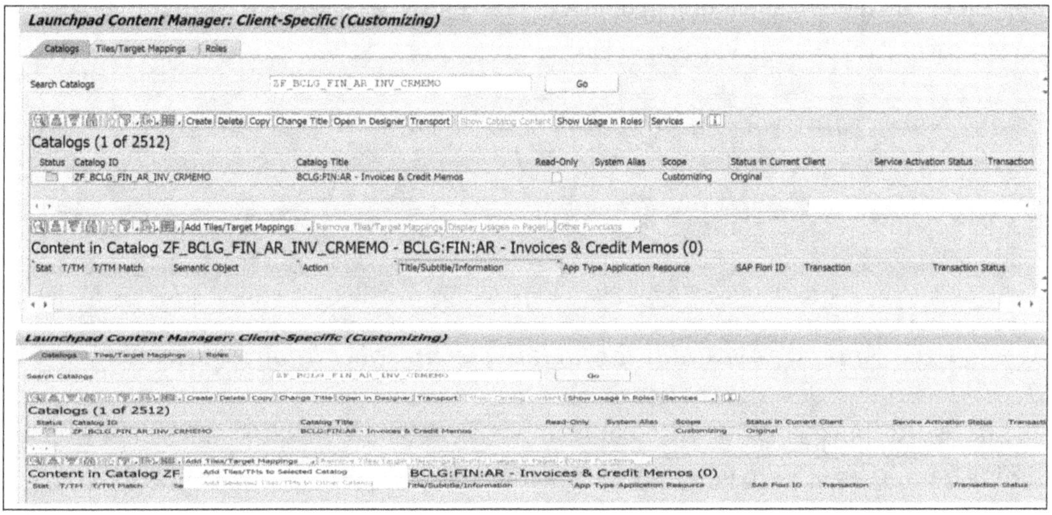

Figure 9-14. Option to add tiles/target mappings to the custom business catalog

When you select the **Add Tiles/TMs to Selected Catalog** option in the figure above, a new window opens for selecting **apps/tiles**, as shown in the figure below.

419

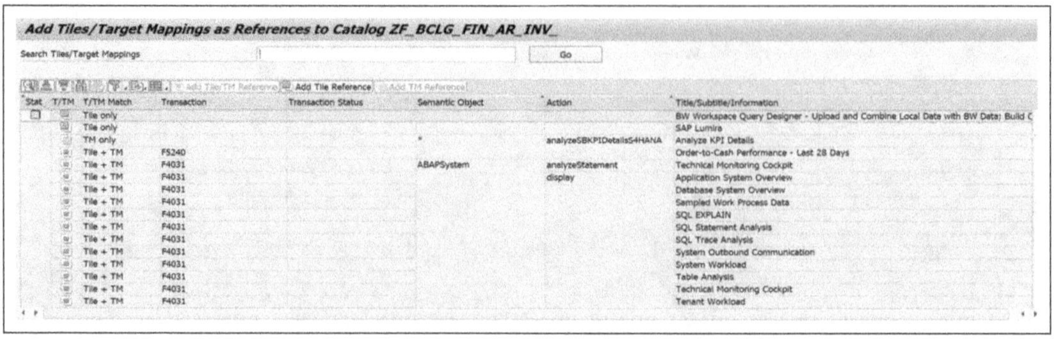

CHAPTER 9 SAP FIORI LAUNCHPAD CONTENT MANAGER

Figure 9-15. Window to add apps/tiles to the custom business catalog

In the above figure, in the field **Search Tiles/Target Mappings**, we can search for a technical or business catalog to reference an app or tile or enter Fiori/GUI apps directly.

9.3.1 Search Apps Based on a Technical Catalog

We can search for our technical catalog created in **Chapter 8**, which lists all the available apps. Enter the technical catalog details **ZF_TCLG_FIN*** as shown in the figure below, and to proceed further, click the icon **Go**   Go   .

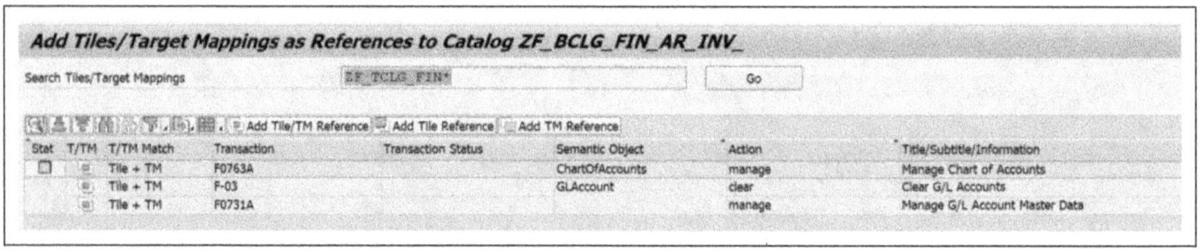

Figure 9-16. Apps are available through the technical catalog for selection

The figure above displays the technical catalog and its associated apps/tiles, which administrators can refer to when reviewing the business catalog. As illustrated in the figure above, these apps are available if needed. However, we will not utilize any of these apps when creating this new business catalog. The process for adding items from this catalog is the same as selecting an app, which will be explained in the next section.

420

The above figure gives you three tabs for updating apps/tiles, and they are

- Add Tile/TM Reference
- Add Tile Reference
- Add TM Reference

Add Tile/TM References

The **Add Tile/TM Reference** tab allows you to copy the visual tile and its associated target mapping from another catalog. This is the most common and reliable method for reusing app content, ensuring that appearance and functionality are preserved.

Additionally, use **Add Tile/TM Reference** to replicate both the tile and the logic for opening the app. The app will then appear on the Launchpad and function correctly when clicked.

Add Tile Reference

The **Add Tile Reference** tab allows you to copy a tile from another catalog without its target mapping. This means the tile may appear on the Launchpad, but it will not function correctly unless the target mapping is added separately. It is rarely used and can lead to navigation issues if not managed carefully.

When you add the tile, it will appear on the Launchpad. However, clicking it might do nothing or show an error if the **TM** is unavailable.

Add TM Reference

The **Add TM Reference** tab allows you to reference only the target mapping of an app without adding a tile to the Launchpad. This is particularly useful when you want the app to function in the background, such as when accessed through smart links or related apps, without displaying it as a tile. It is commonly used in back-end support scenarios or when another app indirectly launches this functionality.

The app will not appear on the Launchpad, but you can still open it using a smart link, a related app, or another tile. For instance, if you are in the **Manage Suppliers app**, which is added to the business catalog, and then click a smart link to **Manage Purchase Orders**, it will work because the TM is available.

9.3.2 Search Apps Based on an App/Tile

We will be adding a mixture of Fiori and GUI apps. To search for any app, such as **FB70**, to be added, enter the details in the **Search Tiles/Target Mappings** field, as shown in the figure below, and click **Go**.

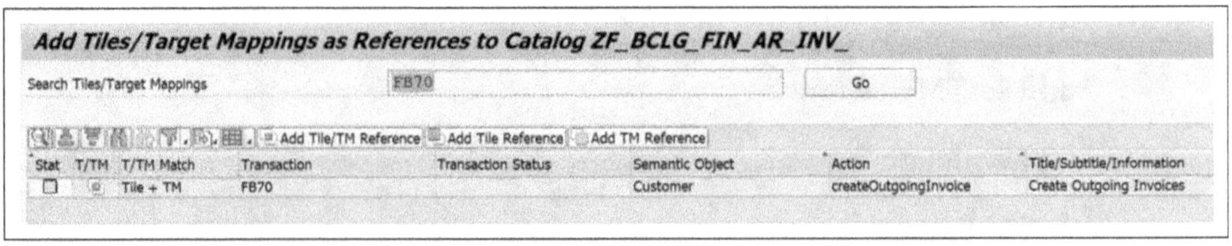

CHAPTER 9   SAP FIORI LAUNCHPAD CONTENT MANAGER

Figure 9-17.   Searching for the app FB70

The figure above shows the app for **FB70**, along with the associated **Tile + TM**, the correct semantic object and action, and the tile information.

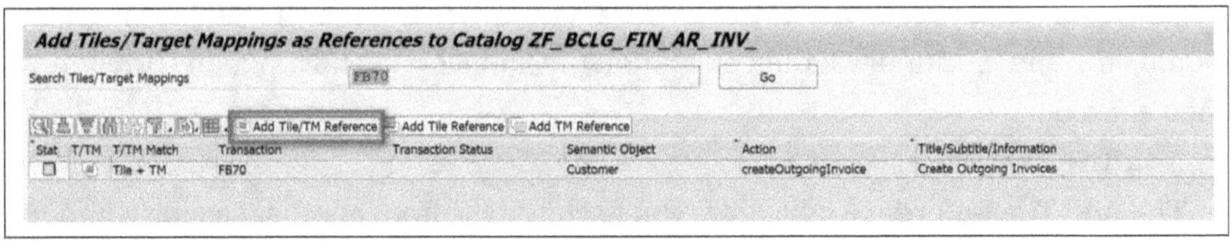

Figure 9-18.   Select the tab Add Tile/TM Reference

To include the chosen Fiori app in the custom business catalog, please select the corresponding option **Add Tile/TM Reference** Add Tile/TM Reference , as shown in the figure above. The app/tile was added to the custom business catalog, as shown in the figure below.

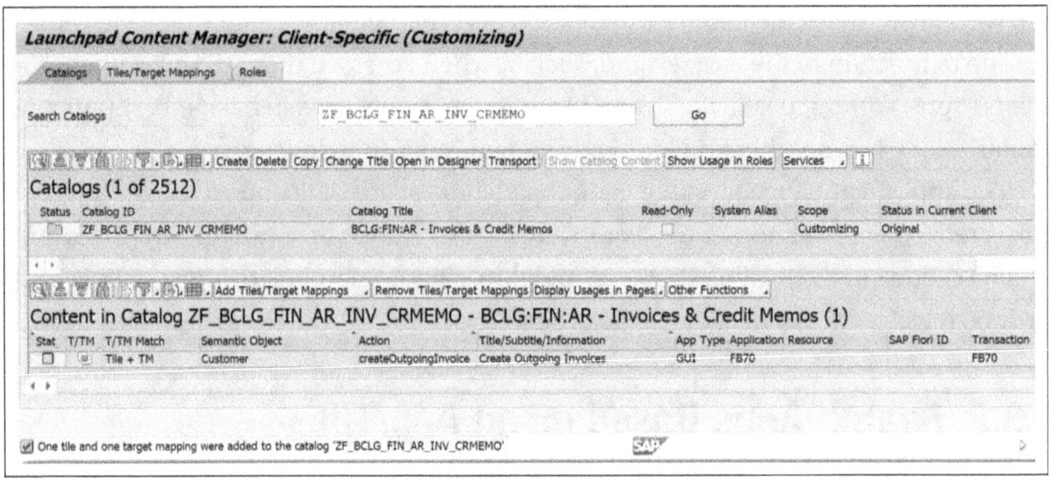

Figure 9-19.   App/tile added to the business catalog

CHAPTER 9 SAP FIORI LAUNCHPAD CONTENT MANAGER

The above figure shows that the app/tile has been added to the business catalog. A new message appears at the bottom of the screen, **One tile and one target mapping were added to the catalog 'ZF_BCLG_FIN_AR_INV_CRMEMO'**.

Note The app/tile is added automatically and saved.

When adding the app **FB03**, we must choose the correct **Tile + TM** from the options shown in the figure below.

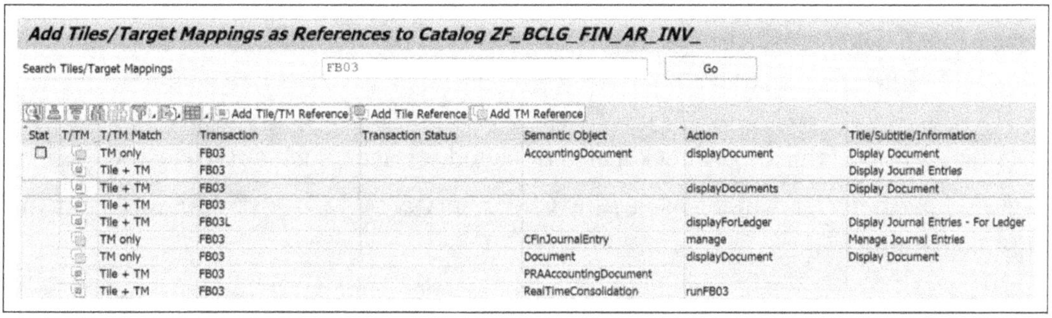

Figure 9-20. App FB03 selected with correct semantic object and action

Based on the above steps, add all the remaining apps and tiles to the business catalog, as shown in the figure below.

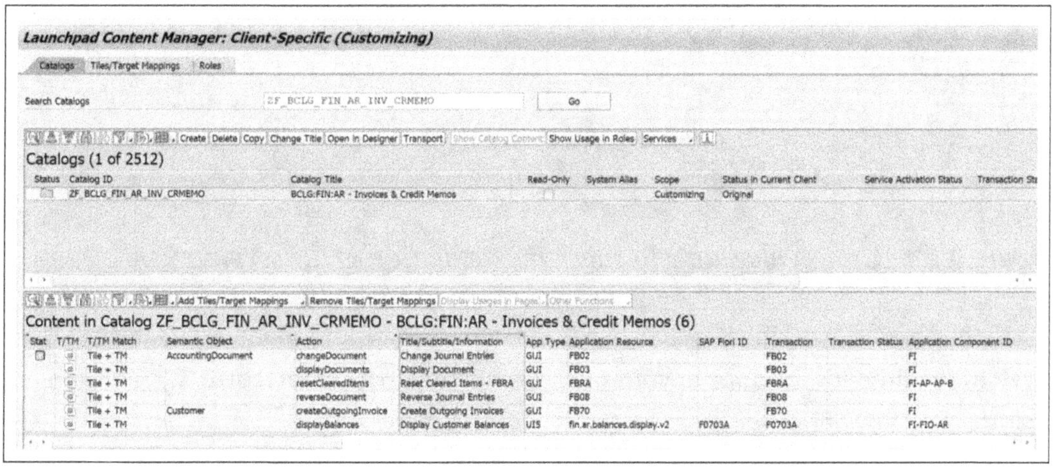

Figure 9-21. All apps/tiles added to the business catalog

423

CHAPTER 9   SAP FIORI LAUNCHPAD CONTENT MANAGER

To proceed further, click the tab Transport `Transport`. The system prompts for transport, as shown in the figure below.

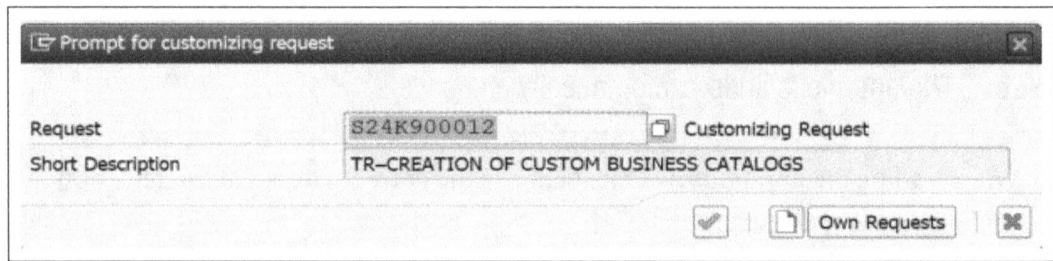

Figure 9-22. Business catalog objects are put into the Customizing transport request

After adding all the apps, check if all associated services, such as OData and SICF services, have been activated by selecting Check Services `Check Services` and using the pull-down menu.

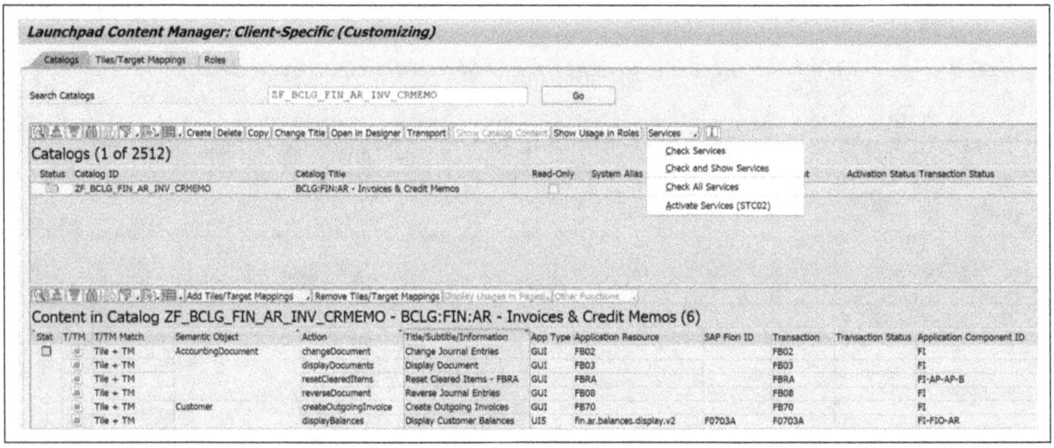

Figure 9-23. Option available to check the activation of the services

In the above figure, the **Services** tab is used to validate and manage OData and ICF services required for the apps in your business catalog to function correctly. This tab includes four key options:

- Check Services
- Check and Show Services

CHAPTER 9   SAP FIORI LAUNCHPAD CONTENT MANAGER

- Check All Services
- Activate Services (STC02)

Check Services ensures that the OData services linked to your catalog's tiles and target mappings are active and correctly assigned. It only checks the services connected to the current catalog and shows whether they are active.

Check and Show Services does the same check as mentioned before and lists the services. This provides a clearer view of which services are active or inactive and the system alias to which they belong.

Check All Services goes beyond just checking the current catalog. It also checks services in all other referenced catalogs, including those linked through **Add Tile/TM Reference** or **Add TM Reference**. This ensures that all connected content has its services verified.

The **Activate Services (STC02)** tool helps you enable any currently missing or inactive OData services. It utilizes the **SAP_GATEWAY_ACTIVATE_ODATA_SERV** task list to activate. This tool saves you time by automating the activation of multiple services, so you do not have to do it one by one using the transaction **/IWFND/MAINT_SERVICE**.

Select **Services ➤ Check and Show Services**.

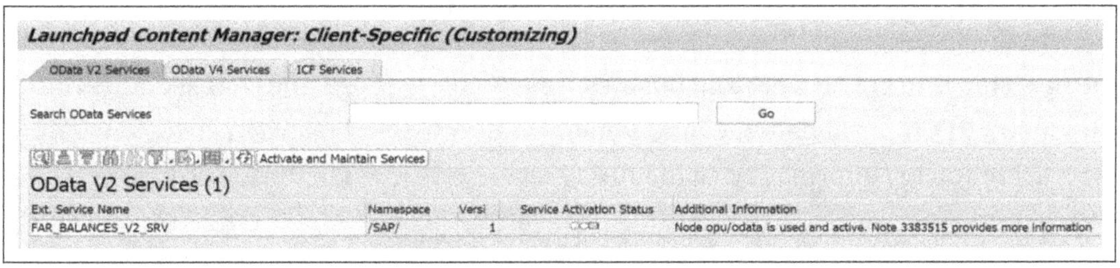

Figure 9-24. OData services within the business catalog with green status

The data indicates that **the OData services** for the custom business catalog are fully functional, marked as **green**, and activated under the **Service Activation Status** header. If any OData services appear as **red**, fix and activate them by selecting the tab **Activate and Maintain Services** Activate and Maintain Services, which will take you to the transaction code **/IWFND/MAINT_SERVICE**. The process of activating is discussed in **Appendix A**, "**Configuration of OData and SICF Services**." Now, select the tab **ICF Services**, as shown in the figure below, which displays that the status is green and the app should work correctly.

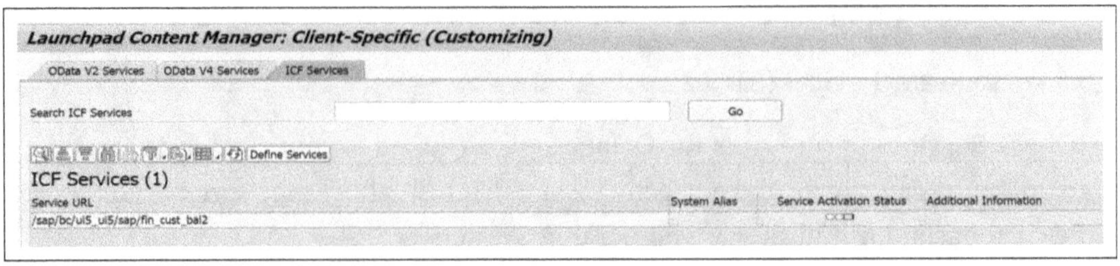

CHAPTER 9   SAP FIORI LAUNCHPAD CONTENT MANAGER

Figure 9-25. *ICF services within the business catalog with status green*

If any ICF services appear **red**, fix and activate them by selecting the **Define Services** tab Define Services, which will take you to the transaction code **SICF**. The process of activating is discussed in **Appendix A**, "**Configuration of OData and SICF Services**."

Note   The **services** are only displayed for **Fiori apps**, not **GUI apps**.

The next step is to create a role to verify the business catalog's functionality and then evaluate the role to confirm that the apps function correctly.

9.3.3 Create a Business Role (PFCG)

The next step is to create a custom business role (CBR) (master role) by executing the transaction **PFCG** to validate the functionality of the custom business catalog created. Enter the following information in the PFCG screen as shown in the figure below:

- **Role:** ZMU_TSK_FIN_AR_INVS_CRMOS:XXXX
- **Description:** FIN: AR – Invoices and Credit Memos

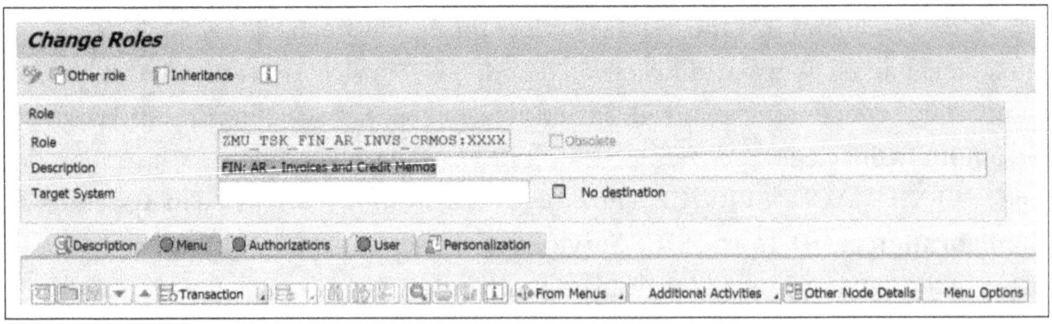

Figure 9-26. *PFCG screen to create a role*

CHAPTER 9 SAP FIORI LAUNCHPAD CONTENT MANAGER

Provide the **role name** and **description**, and then **save** the role. Click **Menu ➤ Transaction ➤ SAP Fiori Launchpad ➤ Launchpad Catalog** as shown in the figure below to add the custom business catalog.

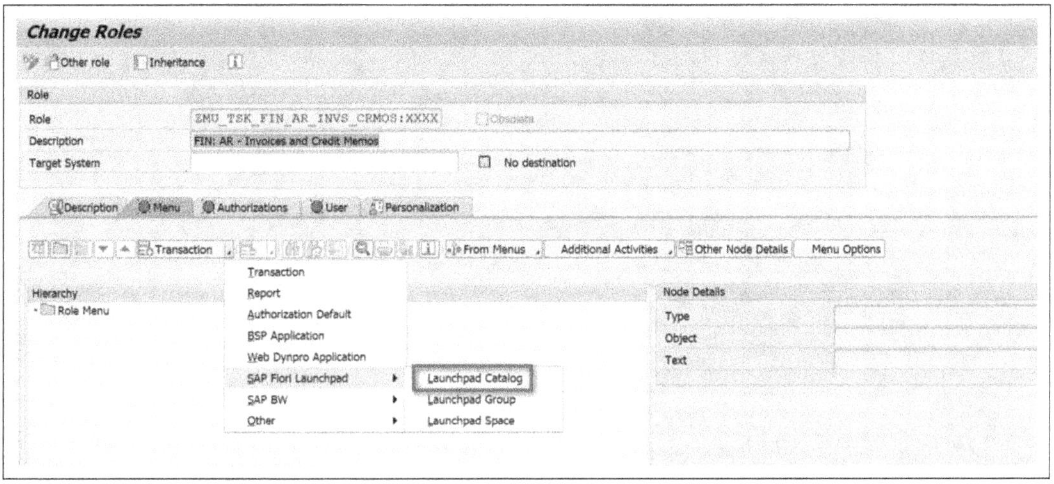

Figure 9-27. Screen to select the Launchpad Catalog option

Once the Launchpad Catalog option is selected, a new window titled **Assign SAP Fiori Launchpad Catalog** will appear. You can enter custom business catalog details in this window, as shown in the figure below.

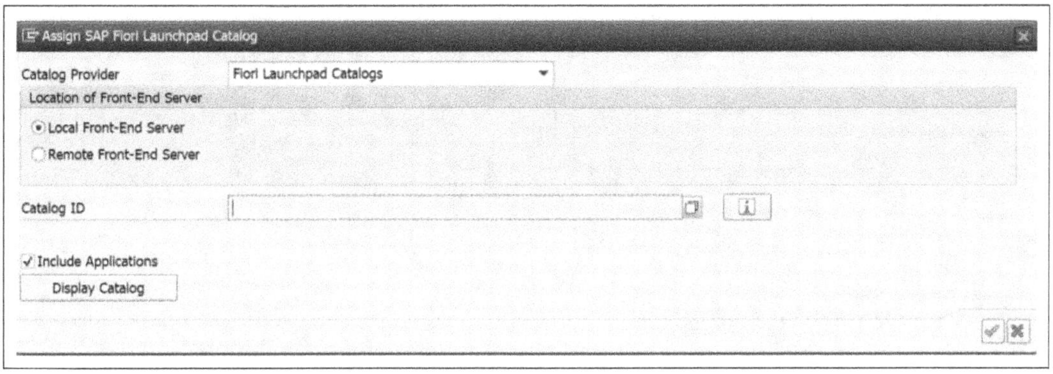

Figure 9-28. Initial screen to enter custom business catalog details

To search for and select the custom business catalog, always use the search icon , as shown in the figure below.

427

CHAPTER 9   SAP FIORI LAUNCHPAD CONTENT MANAGER

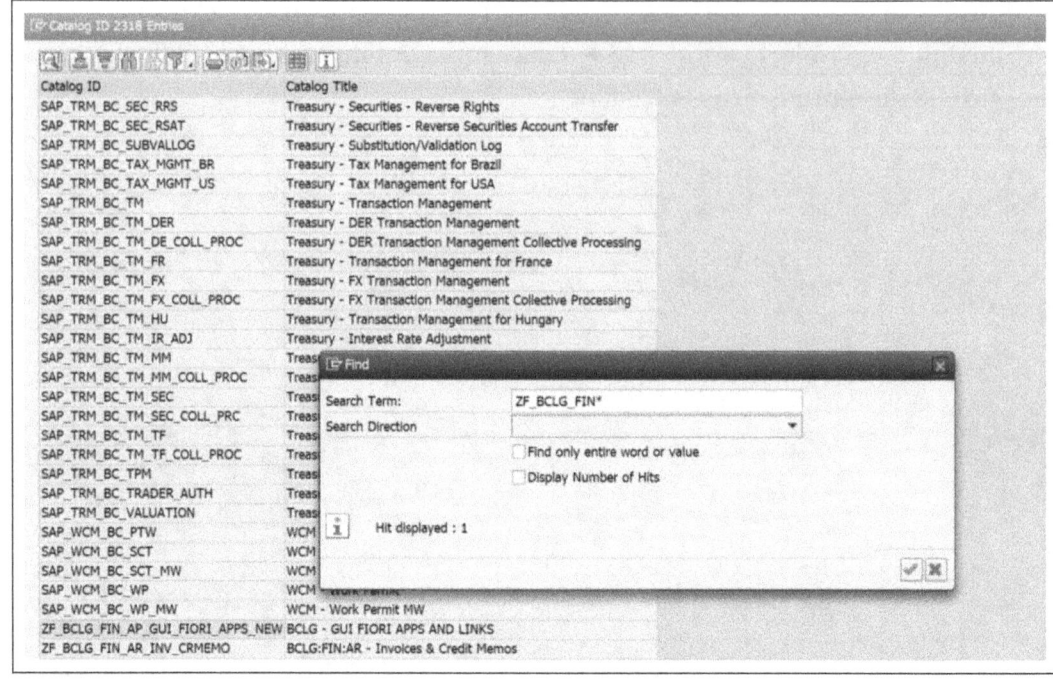

Figure 9-29. *Window to search for the custom business catalog*

As illustrated in the figure below, select the custom business catalog in the Assign SAP Fiori Launchpad Catalog window.

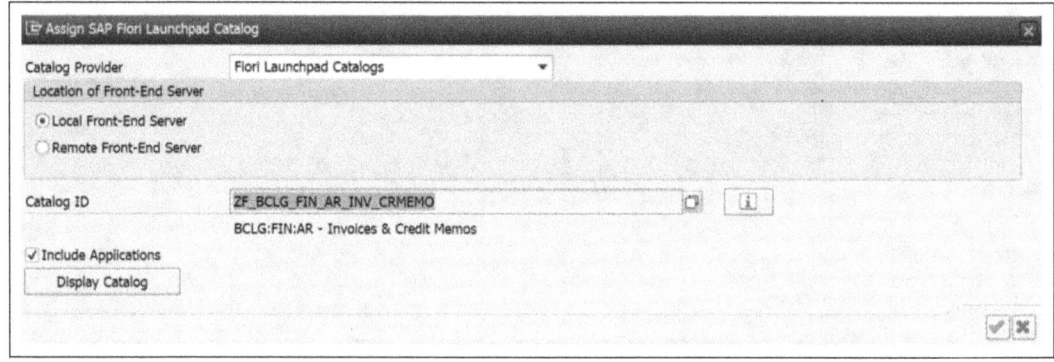

Figure 9-30. *Custom business catalog selected for the business role*

Here, you can use the tab **Display Catalog** to display all apps within the business catalog. This option will direct you by opening another window and displaying the catalog content in the transaction **/UI2/FLPCM_CUST**.

428

CHAPTER 9 SAP FIORI LAUNCHPAD CONTENT MANAGER

Once the business catalog is selected, click Continue to proceed. This will add the business catalog to the role, as shown in the figure below.

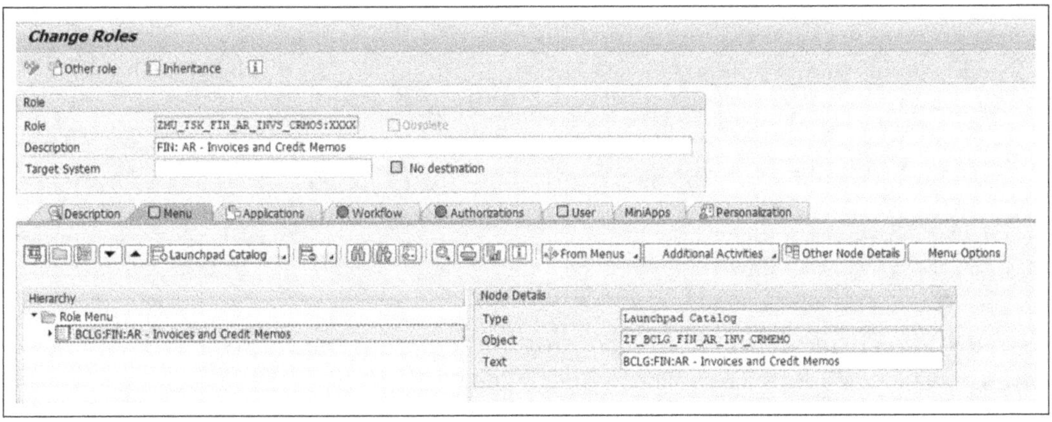

Figure 9-31. *Business catalog added to the role*

> **Note** Prior to entering the catalog selected for the role, we have two options available called **Display Catalog** and **Include Applications**. The option Display Catalog [Display Catalog] will display all apps within the business catalog. This option will direct you by opening another window and displaying the catalog content in the transaction **/UI2/FLPCM_CUST**.

If the **Include Applications** [✓ Include Applications] option is selected, it will bring all the apps included in the business catalog, as shown in the figure below. If the **Include Applications** option is **deselected**, the business catalog will include no underlying app information. The relevant IWSG/IWSV components then must be added manually.

Expanding the catalog will display the added content of the business catalog, as shown in the figure below.

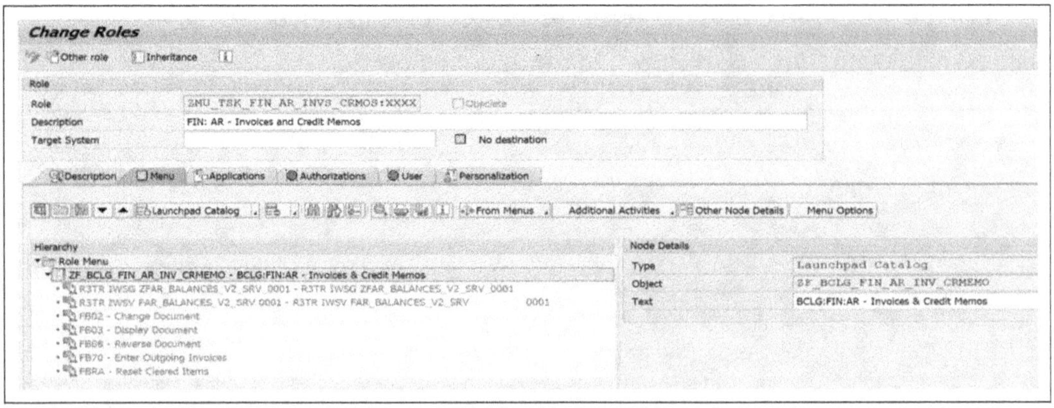

CHAPTER 9   SAP FIORI LAUNCHPAD CONTENT MANAGER

Figure 9-32. Displays the custom catalog content with the IWSG/IWSV component

The **PFCG business role** now includes all components related to **IWSG/IWSV**, and all authorization fields will automatically update based on the settings maintained in transaction **SU24**. Enter the organizational values per your requirements, as illustrated in the figure below.

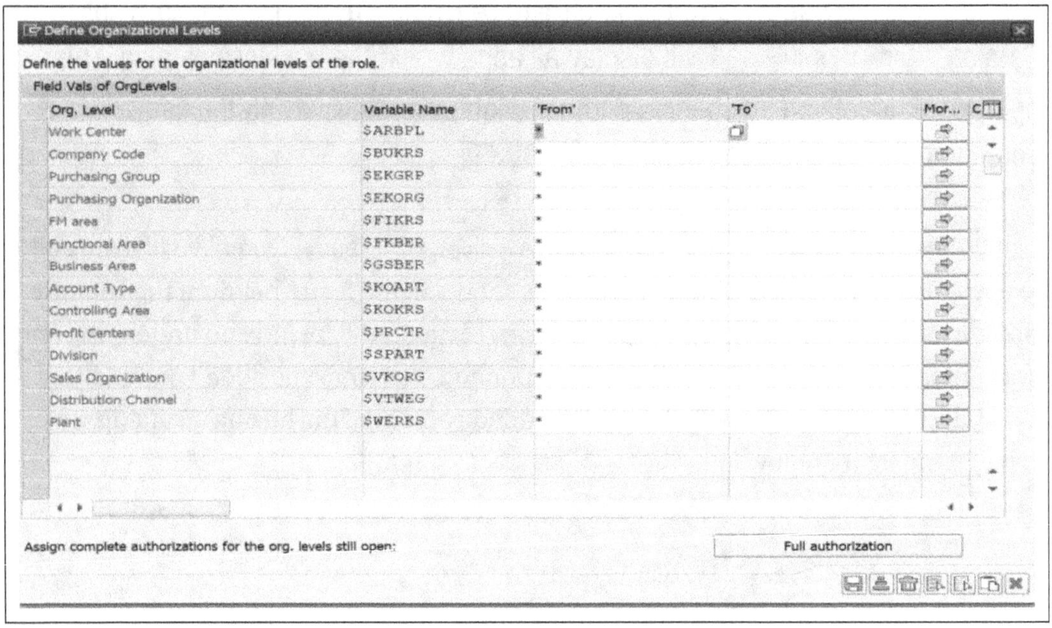

Figure 9-33. Business catalog organizational values updated

CHAPTER 9   SAP FIORI LAUNCHPAD CONTENT MANAGER

Save the organization values by clicking 💾. A message **Org. levels were saved** ☑ Org. levels were saved will appear at the bottom of the screen, as shown in the figure below.

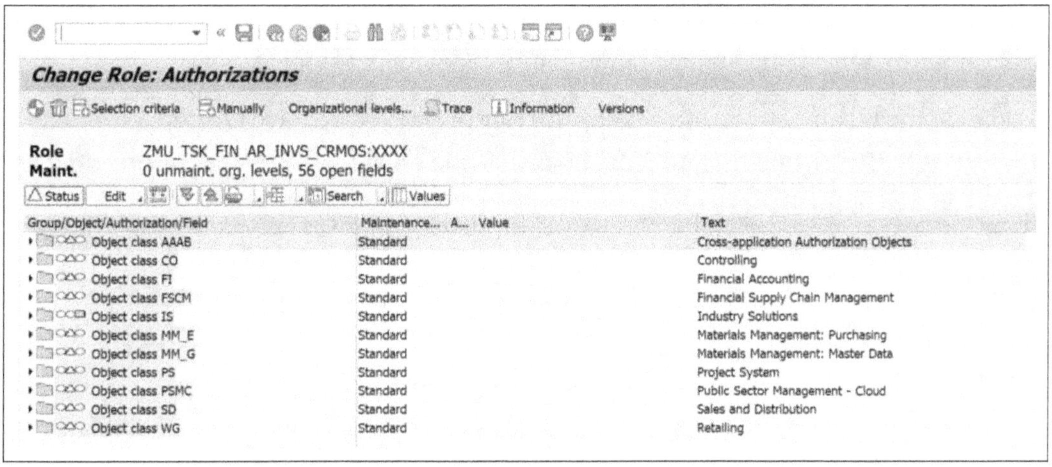

Figure 9-34. Business roles with unmaintained authorization objects

Maintain authorizations in open fields in the authorization objects and generate the role.

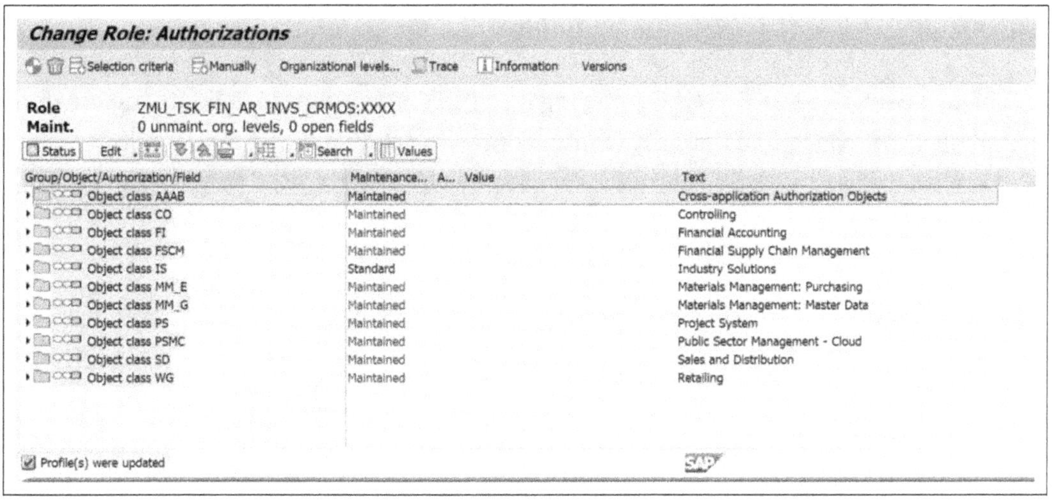

Figure 9-35. Custom business role generated and profile created

431

CHAPTER 9   SAP FIORI LAUNCHPAD CONTENT MANAGER

A new message appears at the bottom of the screen, **Profile(s) were updated** ✓ Profile(s) were updated, as shown in the figure above. This role can now be assigned to a test user ID to validate and test the roles and their associated apps.

9.4 Validation, Testing, and Verification

To validate the business role and catalog, for our purposes, we have created a **test user ID**, **TESTRLE_BCLG**, and assigned the business role created and the common end user roles, as shown in the figure below.

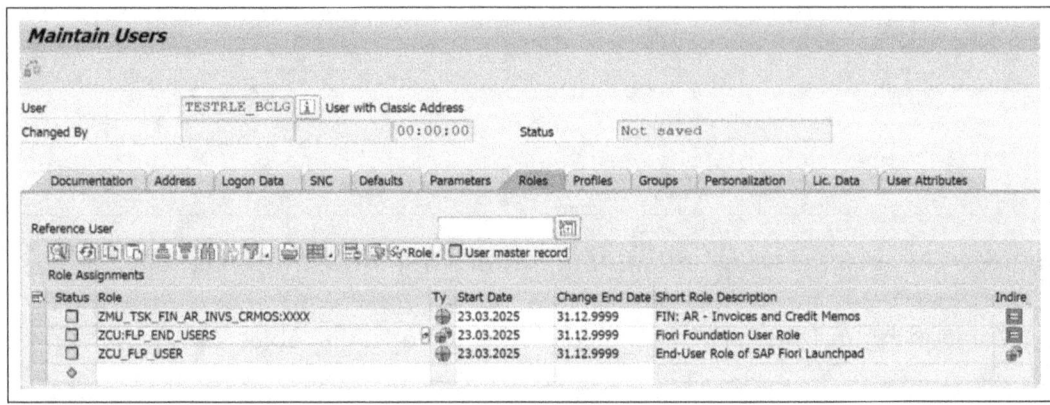

Figure 9-36.   Test user ID created with roles

The test user **TESTRLE_BCLG** must log into the Fiori system to validate the created custom business role and catalog. A window opens, as shown in the figure below.

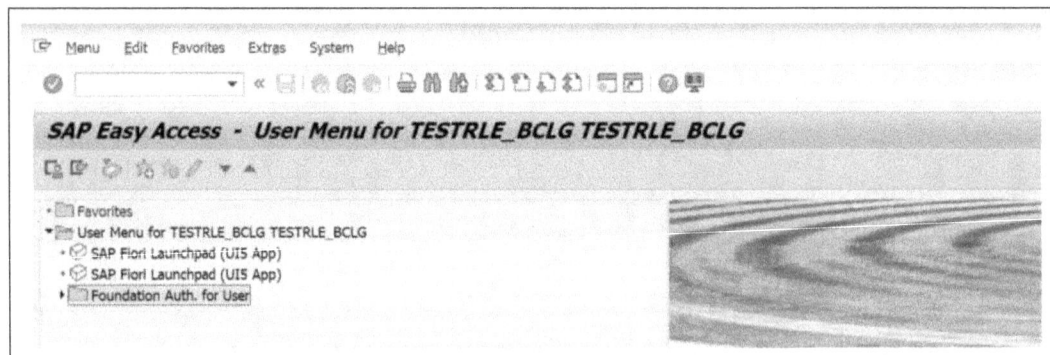

Figure 9-37.   Test user login into the Fiori system

CHAPTER 9 SAP FIORI LAUNCHPAD CONTENT MANAGER

The transaction **F0000 – SAP Fiori Launchpad (UI5 App)** must be selected from the above figure, and the system directs the user to the **Fiori Launchpad** screen, as shown in the figure below.

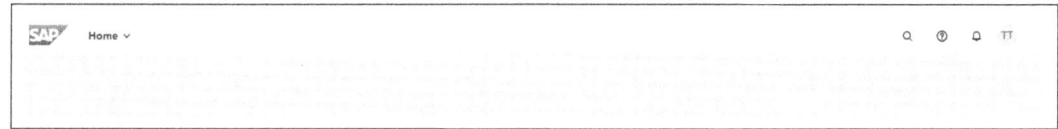

Figure 9-38. Test user Fiori Launchpad screen, which is blank

The above figure displays **no apps** on the SAP Fiori Launchpad home page, as we have not created any **spaces**, **pages**, or **groups**. To visualize the apps in the test user ID buffer, select the User Menu ᵀᵀ and choose **App Finder**, as shown in the figure below.

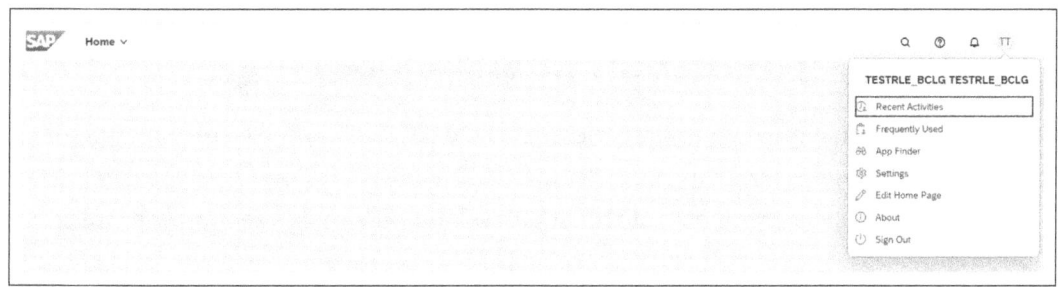

Figure 9-39. App Finder option

Once the **App Finder** option is selected, the business catalog and its associated apps/tiles are displayed as shown in the figure below.

Figure 9-40. Business catalog and apps/tiles available under the test user ID

433

Chapter 9 SAP Fiori Launchpad Content Manager

Note The custom business catalog description is displayed on the left-hand side, as shown in the figure above.

To check if the apps will work correctly, click the tiles to execute each app and see if it executes without errors.

Note The test user should verify the app's functionality during testing. Functional or business users must perform in-depth testing to validate and ensure functionality before moving the role across the system landscape.

9.5 Updating a Custom Business Catalog

The business team may ask to update the role as part of the administrator functionality. This involves adding or removing apps within the business catalog. Once the catalog is updated, the associated business role must be updated too. In this section, we will cover this scenario.

Now, using the transaction **/UI2/FLPCM_CUST**, open the custom business catalog created earlier. It is called **ZF_BCLG_FIN_AR_INV_CRMEMO** and contains six apps, as shown in the figure below.

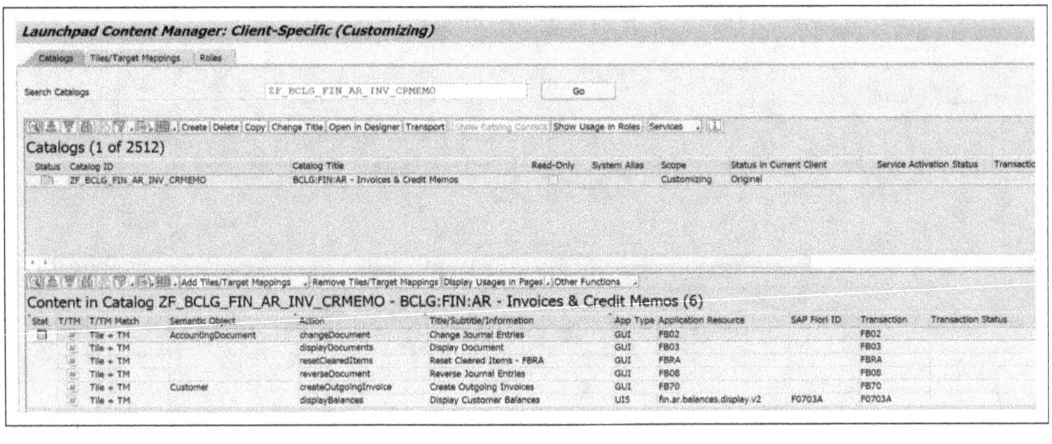

Figure 9-41. List of apps assigned to the custom business catalog

434

CHAPTER 9   SAP FIORI LAUNCHPAD CONTENT MANAGER

Here, we add and remove a few apps to and from the business catalog as listed below:

- **Apps to Be Deleted:** FB03, F0703A
- **Apps to Be Added:** F1060A, F2389, F0859, and F2640

To remove the apps, hold down the **CTRL key** and select both apps, as shown in the figure below. You can also remove the apps individually.

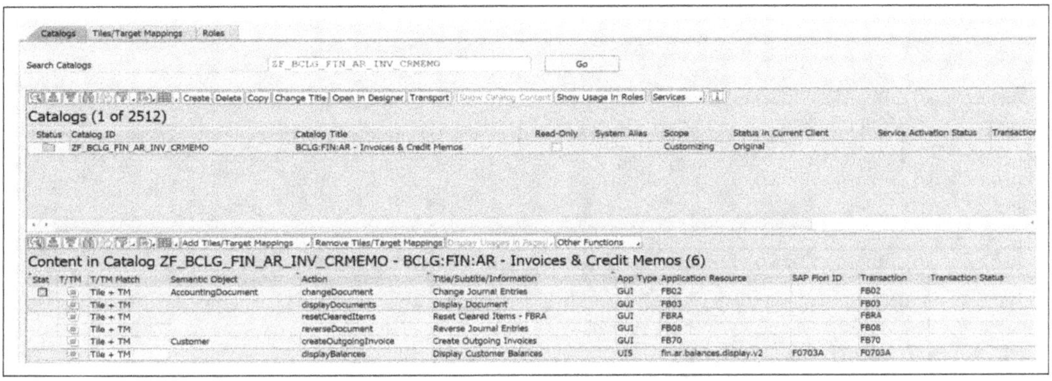

Figure 9-42. Apps selected for removal from the custom business catalog

Once the apps are selected, as shown in the figure above, select the tab **Remove Tiles/Target Mappings** Remove Tiles/Target Mappings, and a new window **Remove References from Catalog** opens, as shown in the figure below.

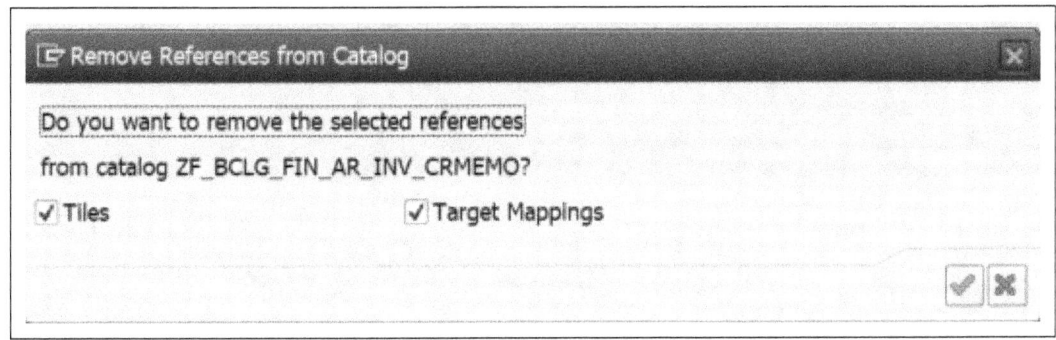

Figure 9-43. Confirmation of apps' removal from the custom business catalog

To proceed further, click the **continue** icon  . The apps are removed, and the custom business catalog is updated. The system also displays a message at the bottom of

CHAPTER 9   SAP FIORI LAUNCHPAD CONTENT MANAGER

the screen, **2 tiles and 2 target mappings were removed from the catalog 'ZF_BCLG_FIN_AR_INV_CRMEMO'**.

The next step is adding the desired apps to the custom business catalog using **Add Tiles/Target Mappings** `Add Tiles/Target Mappings` followed by **Add Tiles/TMs to Selected Catalog**. Then follow the procedure discussed in the above section for adding apps to the custom business catalog.

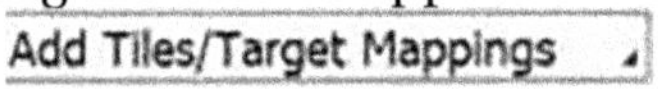

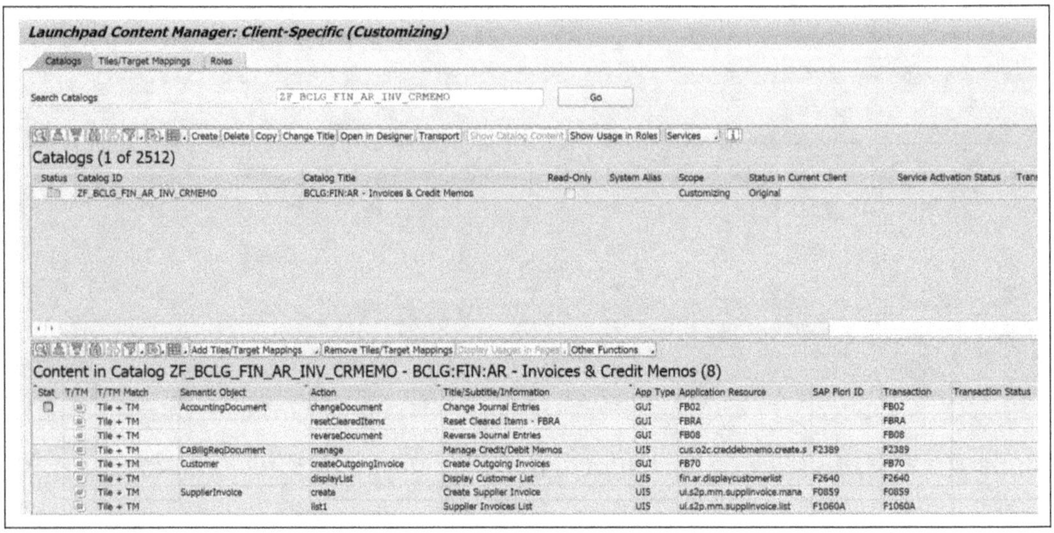

Figure 9-44. Apps added to the custom business catalog

The highlighted rows are the apps added to the custom business catalog, which now consists of **eight** apps. Add the custom business catalog changes to Customizing transport requests, as shown in the figure below.

Figure 9-45. Changes to the custom business catalog added to Customizing transport requests

CHAPTER 9　SAP FIORI LAUNCHPAD CONTENT MANAGER

To proceed further, click the **continue** icon . Return to the initial screen of transaction **PFCG** (Role Maintenance). To update the custom business role, enter the role name **ZMU_TSK_FIN_AR_INVS_CRMOS:XXXX**, and then navigate to the **Utilities** option in the top menu bar, as shown in the figure below.

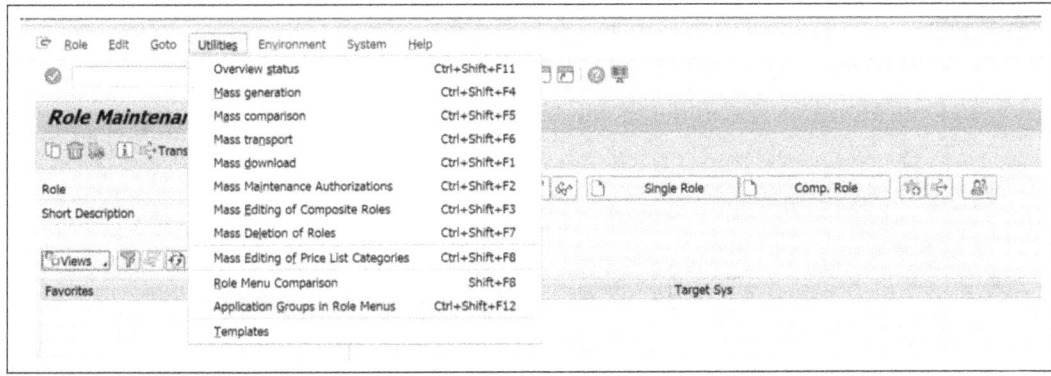

Figure 9-46. Business role update using Utilities, followed by Application Groups in Role Menus

Now select **Application Groups in Role Menus** under the menu **Utilities**, and a new window titled **Update of Application Group in Role Menu** appears, as shown in the figure below.

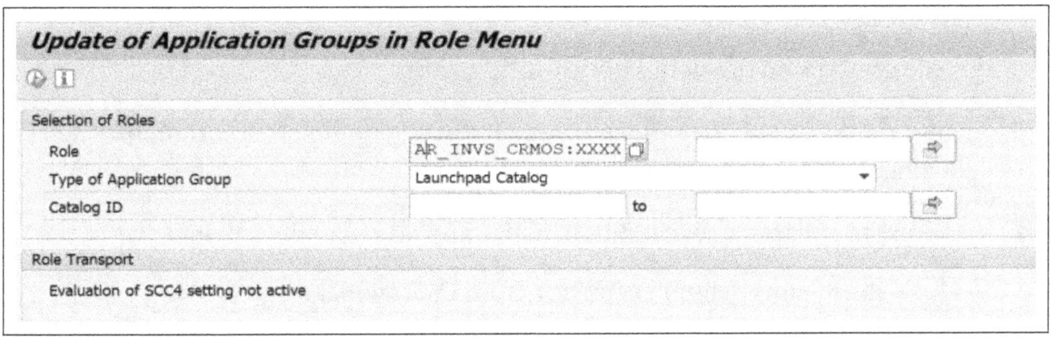

Figure 9-47. Update of Application Groups in Role Menu

437

CHAPTER 9   SAP FIORI LAUNCHPAD CONTENT MANAGER

Note   When we access the transaction **PFCG**, the role is automatically entered, as shown in the figure above. If needed, you can update multiple roles.

You can also use transaction code **PFCGUPDATEROLEMENU** to update the role menu with catalog changes.

To proceed, click the execute icon 🕒 and the window titled **Update of Application Group in Role Menu** will be updated, as shown in the figure below.

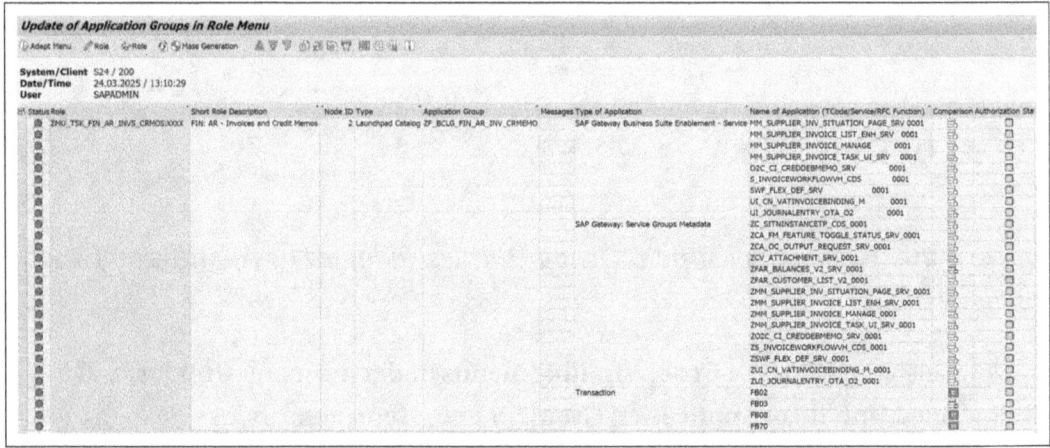

Figure 9-48. *The business role and the custom business catalog get updated*

Here, the symbols on the right signify the following:

- 🗐 : This symbol means no change for the app or line item within the catalog.

- 🗐 : This means a new addition, a new app added to the catalog.

- 🗐 : This means deletion of an app from the catalog.

You can select all the applications by selecting the **select all** icon 🗐 , as shown in the figure below.

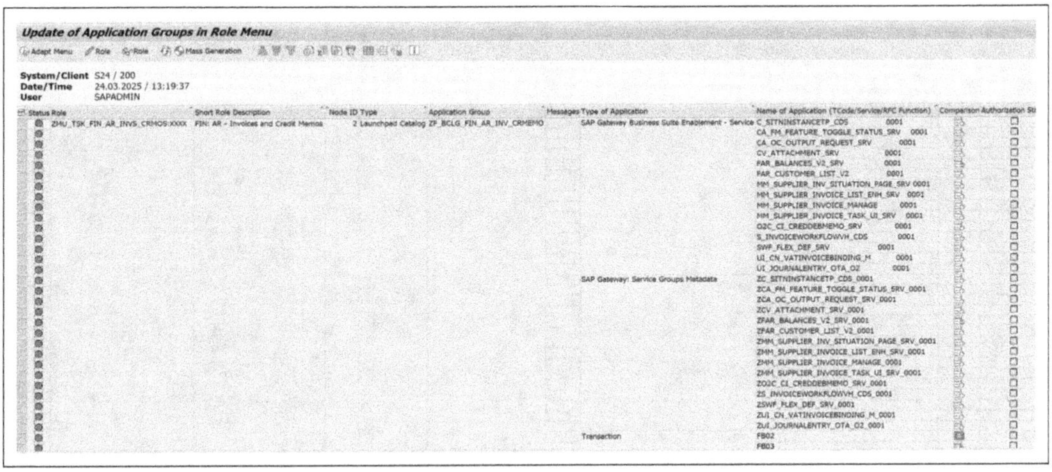

CHAPTER 9   SAP FIORI LAUNCHPAD CONTENT MANAGER

Figure 9-49. All applications selected

Select Adapt Menu to update the role. A new window box titled **Update of Application Groups in Role Menu** appears, asking to execute the menu changes, as shown in the figure below.

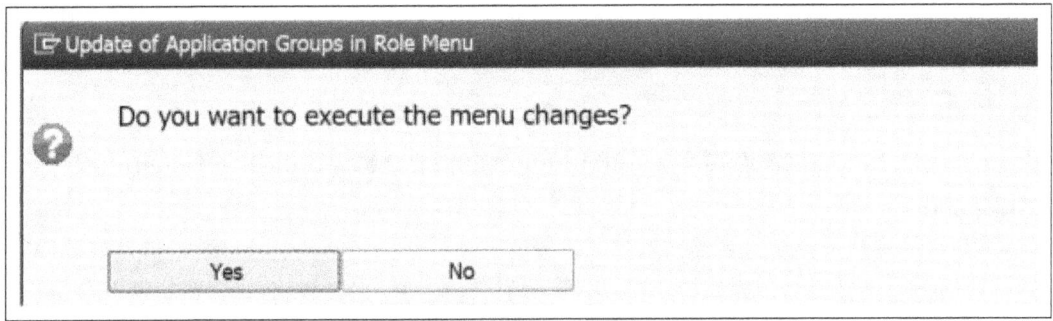

Figure 9-50. Confirmation of Update of Application Groups in Role Menu

To proceed, click **Yes**. The role status will be updated, and a message will appear at the bottom of the screen stating **Data saved**, as shown in the figure below.

439

CHAPTER 9　SAP FIORI LAUNCHPAD CONTENT MANAGER

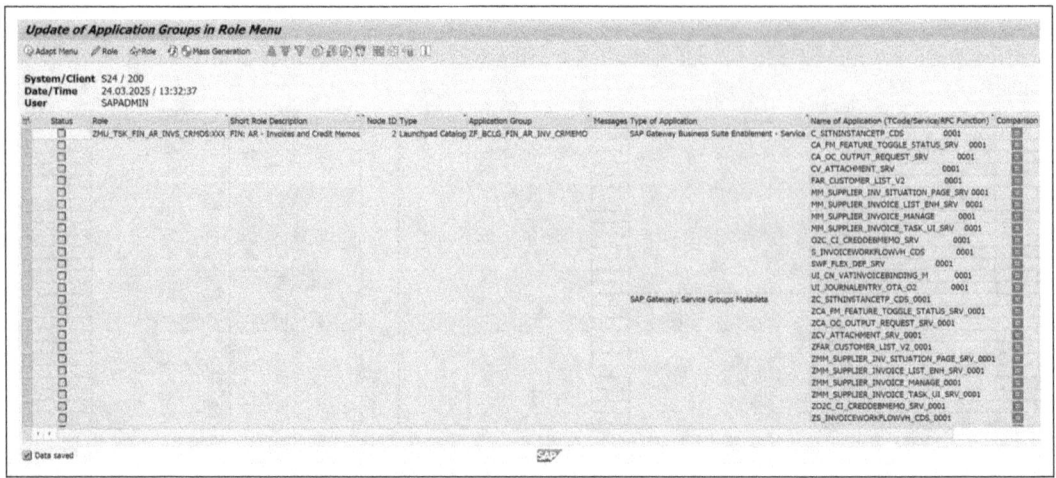

Figure 9-51. *Role updated with status in green*

The above figure illustrates that the role has been updated with a **green** status. This process will not directly trigger the necessary changes in the role. To update the changes within the role, select the menu option **Role** *Role*, and the system will take you to the transaction **PFCG** screen to maintain org value and authorization and to generate the role as shown in the figure below.

Note　These modifications must be made within the **PFCG** (Profile Generator) transaction.

CHAPTER 9 SAP FIORI LAUNCHPAD CONTENT MANAGER

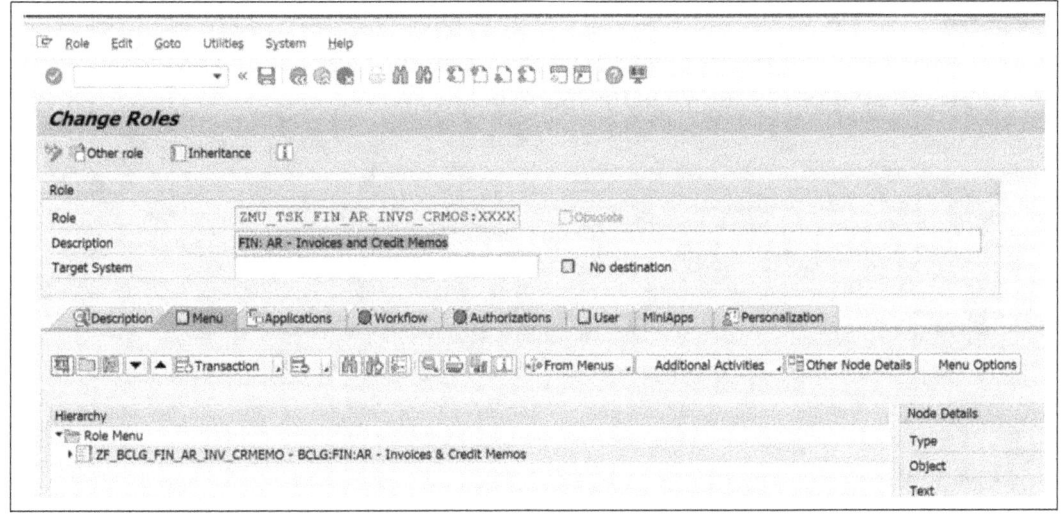

Figure 9-52. *Transaction PFCG showing the business role and custom business catalog*

Expanding the catalog displays all the apps with relevant **IWSG/IWSV** components, as shown in the figure below.

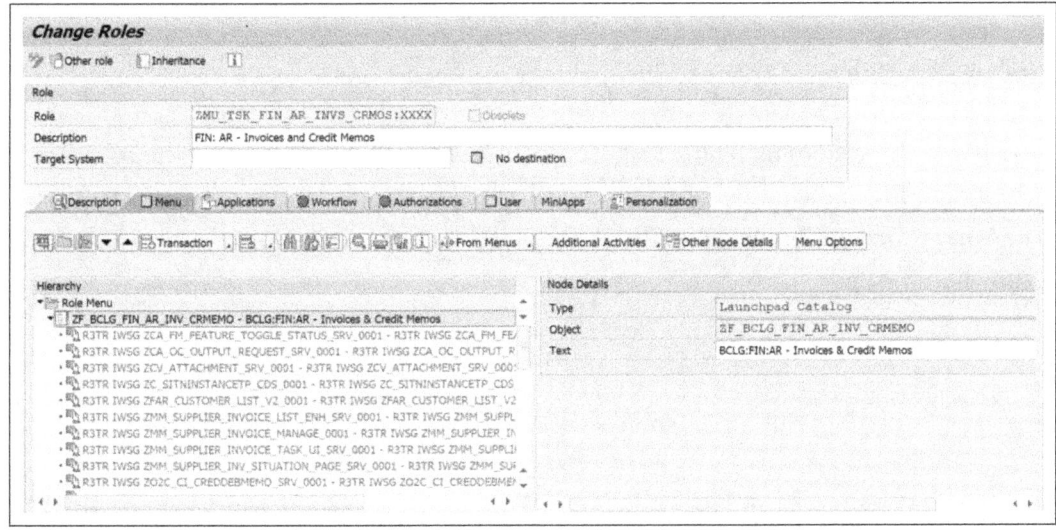

Figure 9-53. *Updated business role*

Maintain the **authorizations** as required and **generate** the role using the icon.

CHAPTER 9 SAP FIORI LAUNCHPAD CONTENT MANAGER

After generating the role, the role content is shown in the figure below, with all authorization objects in **green** status. A message stating **Profile (s) were updated** is also displayed at the bottom as shown in the figure below.

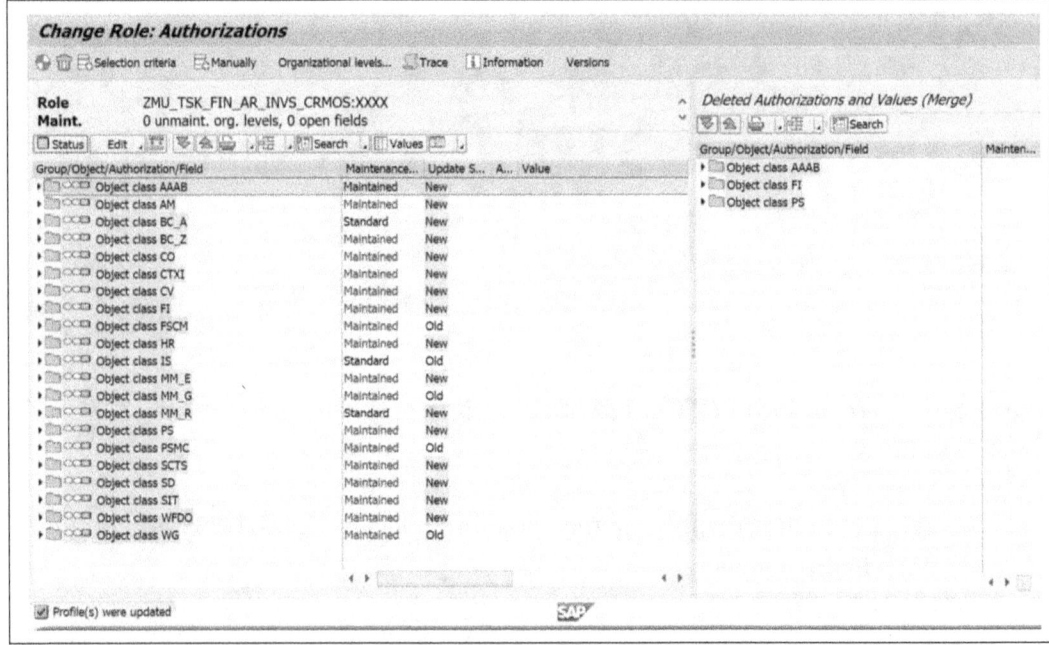

Figure 9-54. *Business role profile updated and generated*

Log into the system using the test user ID created earlier to verify that the role has been updated with the added and removed apps. Execute transaction **/UI2/FLP**. Then go to **App Finder** under the **User Menu** option to display the catalog and associated app, as shown in the figure below.

CHAPTER 9   SAP FIORI LAUNCHPAD CONTENT MANAGER

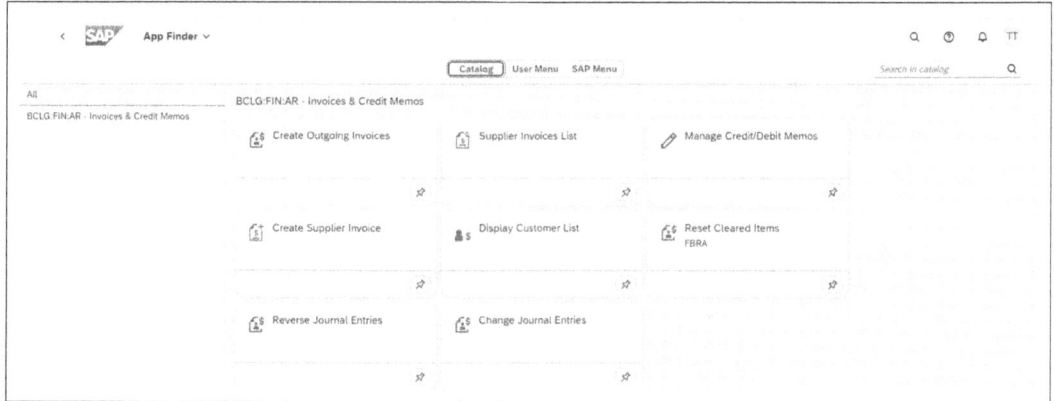

Figure 9-55. *All eight apps are visible to the test user within the Fiori Launchpad.*

The test user can visualize all **eight apps** that are part of the custom business catalog, and all apps work correctly.

9.6 FLP Content Manager Other Functionality

The SAP Fiori Launchpad Content Manager is a powerful, user-friendly, and helpful tool for managing Fiori catalogs, groups, and pages in a centralized location. It simplifies assigning apps to user roles and ensures users have proper access. With its straightforward layout and real-time checks, administrators can efficiently maintain Fiori content without advanced technical skills, making it essential for managing apps and user roles in SAP S/4HANA.

Some of the main features are discussed below.

9.6.1 Catalogs Tab Options

The **Catalogs** tab in the SAP Fiori Launchpad Content Manager enables administrators to manage all available Fiori catalogs within the system. It displays essential details like the assigned tiles, target mappings, and related technical catalogs. This tab is crucial in customizing and maintaining business catalogs assigned to user roles. It also enables administrators to identify inconsistencies, copy or create new catalogs, and enhance app provisioning, making it easier for users to provide the right apps efficiently.

443

CHAPTER 9   SAP FIORI LAUNCHPAD CONTENT MANAGER

Copy

In the Catalogs tab, you can search and select the catalog that you want to copy. After choosing the catalog, click the **Copy** button. The system will open a window box titled **Copy Catalog** to copy the custom business catalog, as shown in the figure below.

Figure 9-56. *Copy option*

Enter the new catalog and description, as shown in the figure below.

Figure 9-57. *Copy the custom business catalog to a new catalog*

To proceed further, click the **continue** icon , and the system will prompt you for transport. Once the transport is assigned, the new custom business catalog is created, and a message is displayed, **Catalog 'ZF_BCLG_FIN_AR_INV_CRMEMO' copied**. The content of the catalog is displayed in the lower section of the screen, as shown in the figure below.

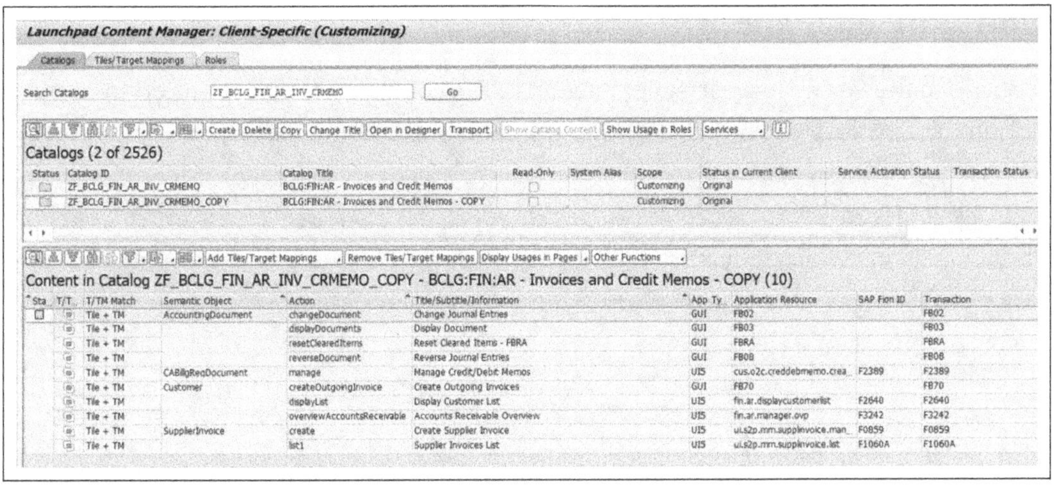

CHAPTER 9 SAP FIORI LAUNCHPAD CONTENT MANAGER

Figure 9-58. New custom business catalog created

Show Usage in Roles

The tab **Show Usage in Roles** will display the roles that contain the custom business catalog, as shown in the figure below.

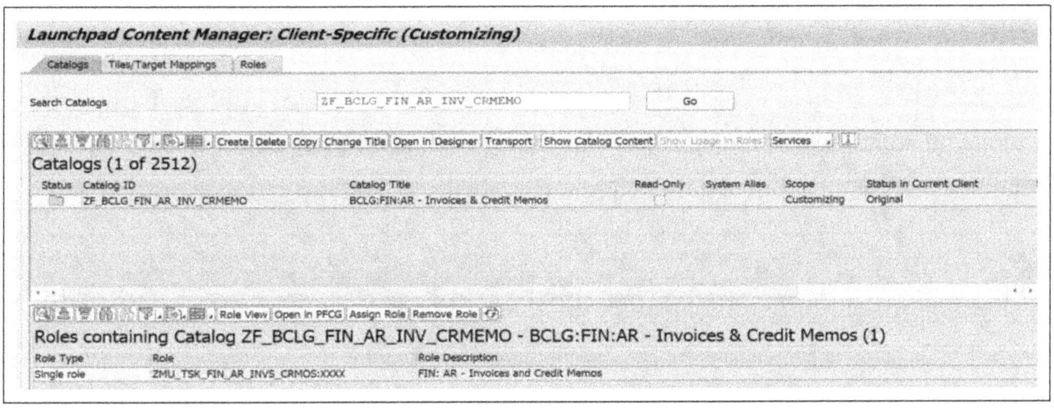

Figure 9-59. Show Usage in Roles

The figure above displays the **roles** assigned to the custom business catalog at the bottom of the screen, along with their **role description** and **role type**.

445

CHAPTER 9 SAP FIORI LAUNCHPAD CONTENT MANAGER

Show Catalog Content

If you are in the Show Usage in Roles section of the catalog, you can see its content by clicking the button Show Catalog Content, as shown in the figure below.

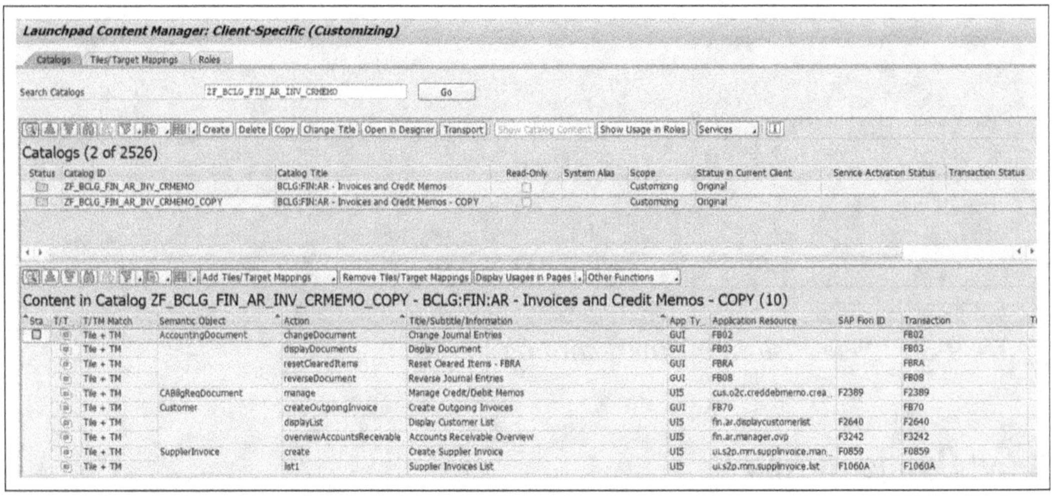

Figure 9-60. Content of the custom business catalog displayed

Delete

The tab Delete, when selected, opens a window box titled **Delete Catalog**, listing the catalog chosen to be deleted, as shown in the figure below. Click the **continue** icon to delete the catalog.

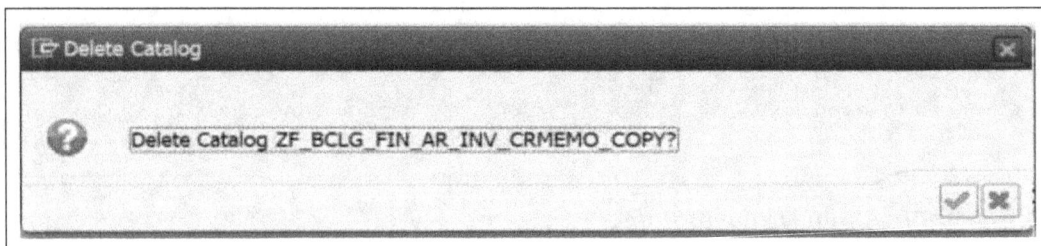

Figure 9-61. Delete option

CHAPTER 9   SAP FIORI LAUNCHPAD CONTENT MANAGER

Change Title

The tab Change Title, when selected, opens a window box titled **Change Title of Catalog**, listing the catalog chosen to be updated as shown in the figure below. Click the **continue** icon after changing the description.

Figure 9-62.   Change Title option

Open in Designer

When you select the option **Open in Designer** Open In Designer, it will open the selected catalog in the Fiori Launchpad Designer (**UI2/FLPD_CUST**), as shown in the figure below.

Figure 9-63.   Open in Designer screen

Services: Check and Show Services

This tab Services followed by **Check and Show Services**, when selected, will direct the system to service tabs as shown in the figure below.

447

CHAPTER 9   SAP FIORI LAUNCHPAD CONTENT MANAGER

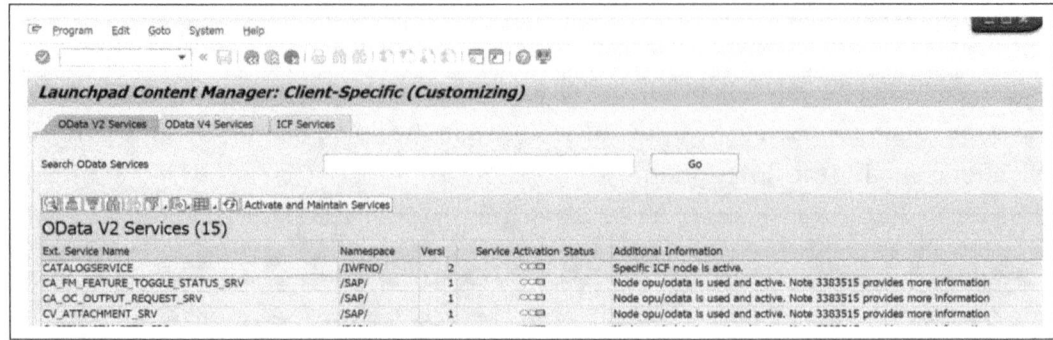

Figure 9-64. *Services ➤ Check and Show Services*

When **Services** is selected, the option **Activate Services (STC02)** will open the task list **SAP_FIORI_FCM_CATLOG_ACTIVATION**, as shown in the figure below.

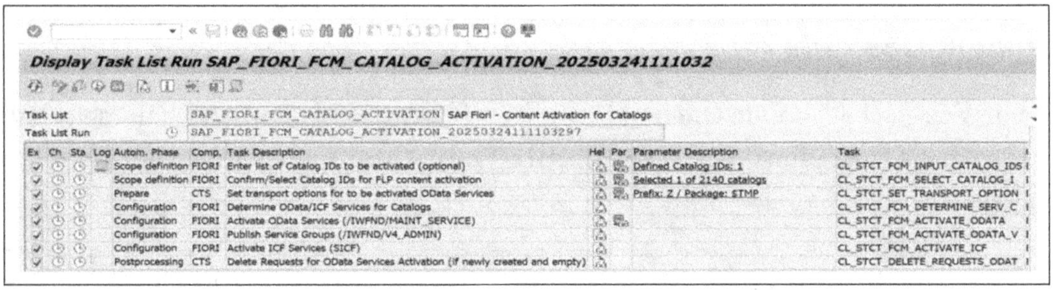

Figure 9-65. *Activate Services (STC02)*

Role View

This tab Role View will take you to the **Roles tab**, which gives further options for role management, as shown in the figure below.

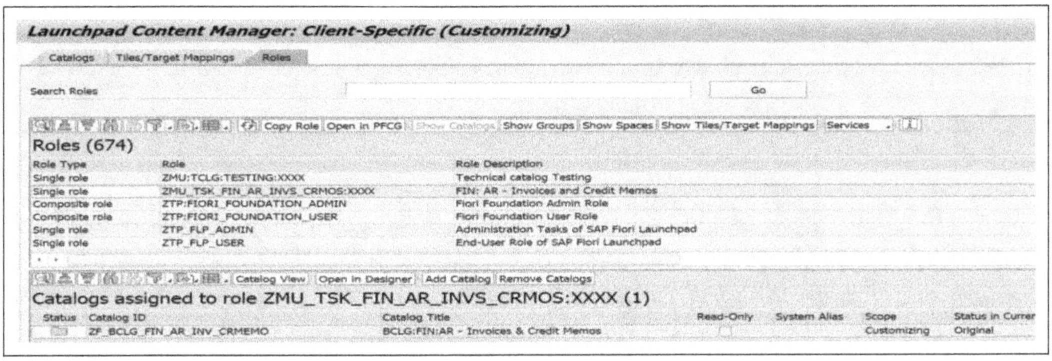

CHAPTER 9   SAP FIORI LAUNCHPAD CONTENT MANAGER

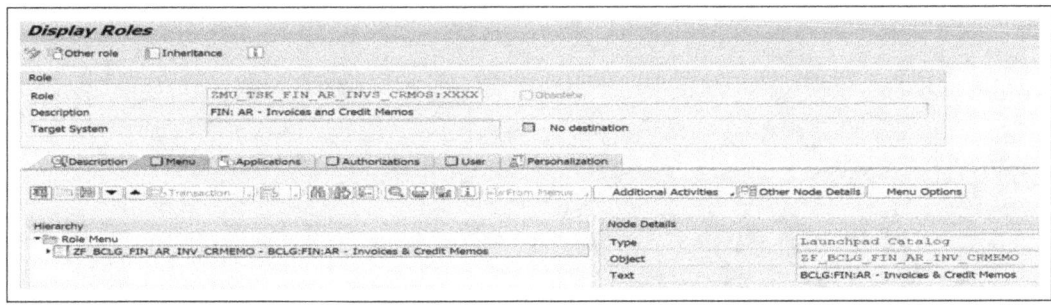

Figure 9-66. Role View option

Open in PFCG

The tab Open in PFCG will take you directly to the transaction **PFCG** for role maintenance, as shown in the figure below.

Figure 9-67. Open in PFCG option

Assign Role

The tab Assign Role allows you to assign the custom business catalog or any other business catalog to a role, in this case, **ZMU_TEST**, via the window box titled **Assign Role to Catalog**, as shown in the figure below.

449

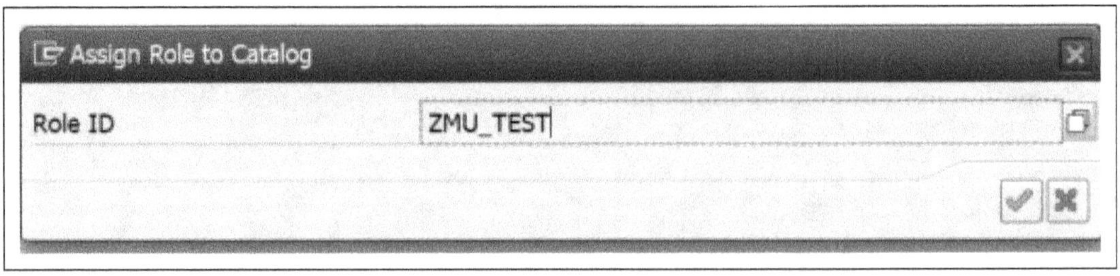

CHAPTER 9 SAP FIORI LAUNCHPAD CONTENT MANAGER

Figure 9-68. Assign Role to Catalog window box

To proceed, click the **continue** icon, and the role gets assigned to the custom business catalog, as shown in the figure below.

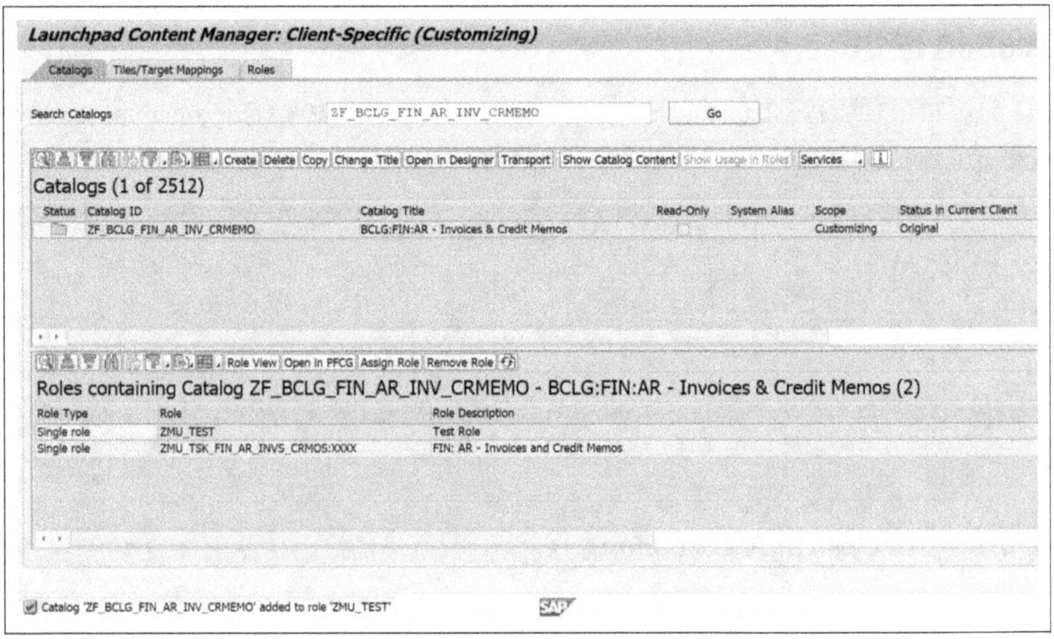

Figure 9-69. The custom business catalog has been assigned to the role

---

Note The role should already exist in the system.

The role was updated with the custom business catalog while being checked in **PFCG**, as shown in the figure below.

CHAPTER 9 SAP FIORI LAUNCHPAD CONTENT MANAGER

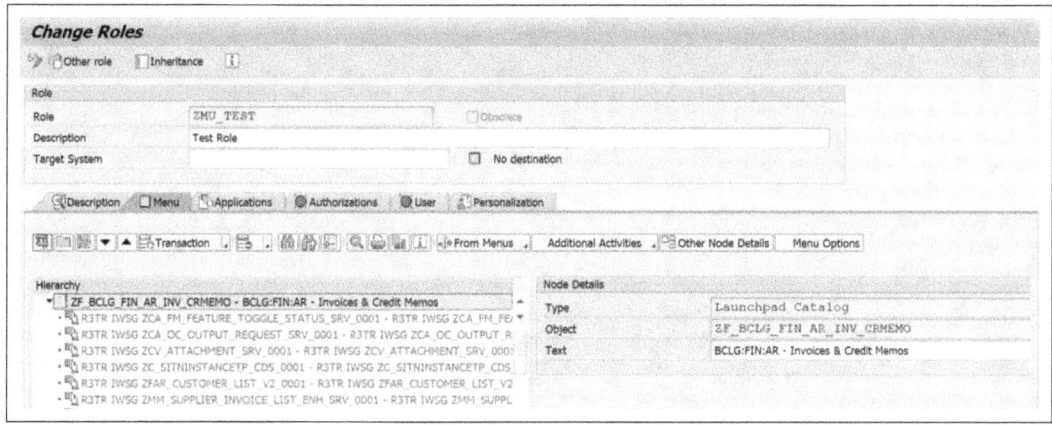

***Figure 9-70.** Role updated through the Assign Role to Catalog option*

Remove Role

This **Remove Role** tab opens a **Remove Role Assignment** window box and removes the custom business catalog assignment, as shown in the figure below.

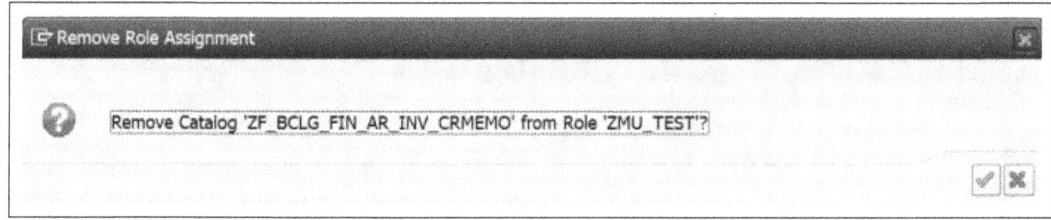

***Figure 9-71.** Remove Role option*

To proceed, click the **continue** icon ✓. The custom business catalog assignment for the role will be removed, as shown in the figure below. A message appears at the bottom of the screen, **Catalog 'ZF_BCLG_FIN_AR_INV_CREMO' removed from role 'ZMU_TEST'**.

451

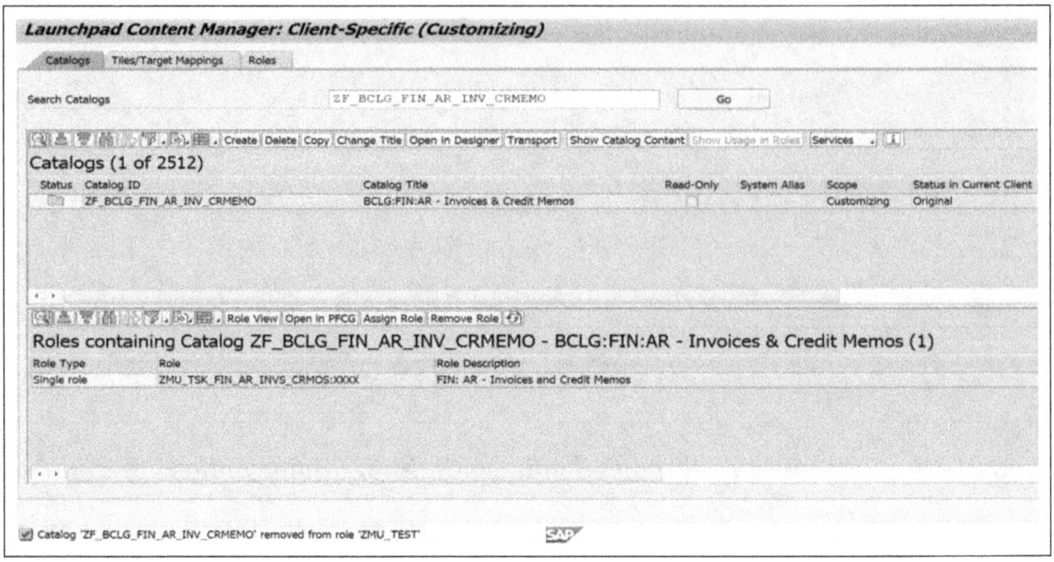

CHAPTER 9   SAP FIORI LAUNCHPAD CONTENT MANAGER

Figure 9-72. *Custom business catalog removed from the role*

Verify in **PFCG** whether the catalog has been removed from the role. The Menu tab is red as the role has no business catalog assigned, as shown in the figure below.

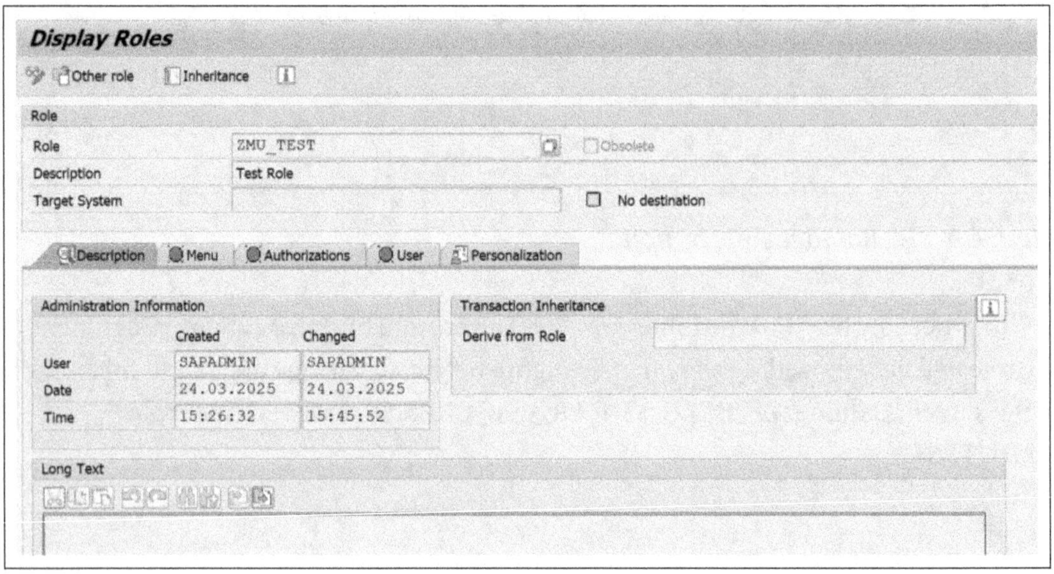

Figure 9-73. *Custom business catalog removed from the role – verification*

CHAPTER 9   SAP FIORI LAUNCHPAD CONTENT MANAGER

Note   Display Usages in Pageswill be covered later.

9.6.2 Tiles/Target Mappings Tab Options

The Tiles/Target Mappings tab in the SAP Fiori Launchpad Content Manager provides a clear view of all tiles and their corresponding target mappings. It helps administrators see how each tile, the app's entry point, connects to a specific action or intent, such as launching a transaction, a URL, or a Fiori app. This tab is essential for checking tile-to-app connections, finding missing mappings, and reusing or adapting existing content when creating custom catalogs. It makes sure users can access apps smoothly from the Fiori Launchpad. Entering the **app ID F2389** displays the **Tile + TM** of apps and the custom business catalogs they are assigned to, as shown in the figure below.

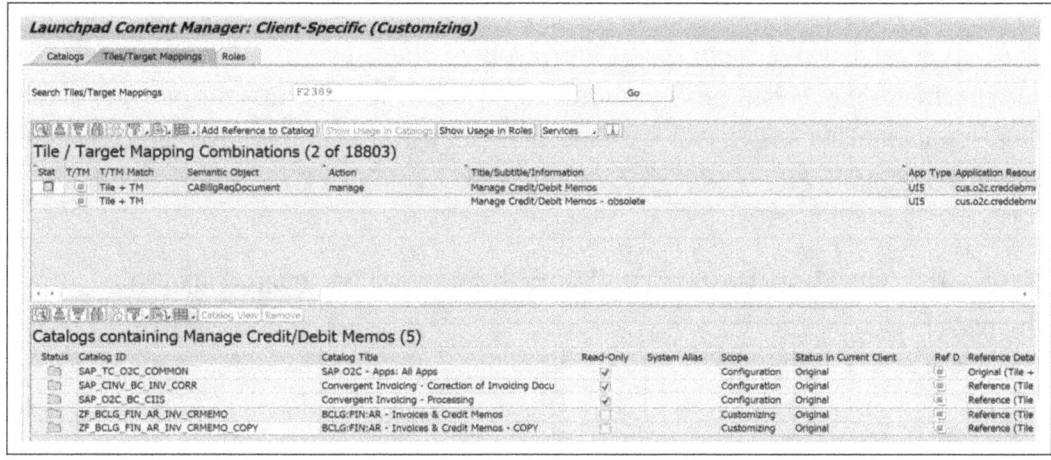

Figure 9-74.   Display Tile + TM of Fiori app

Add Reference to Catalog

When selected, the tab Add Reference to Catalog directs you to window titled Add Tiles/Target Mappings as References, as shown in the figure below.

453

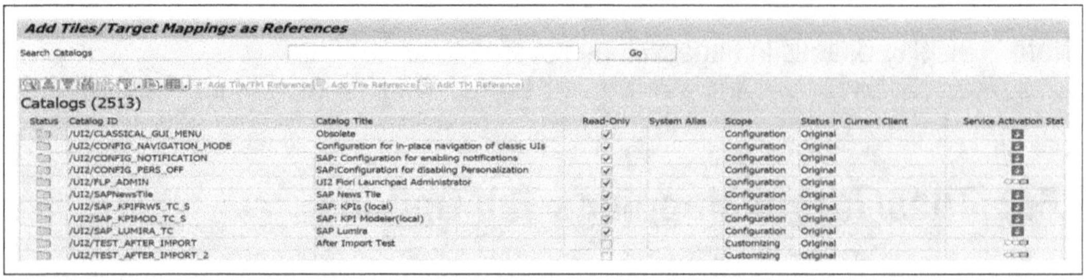

Figure 9-75. Add Reference to Catalog

9.6.3 Roles Tab Options

The **Roles** tab in the SAP Fiori Launchpad Content Manager helps administrators manage the connection between Fiori catalogs, groups, spaces/pages, and the PFCG roles assigned to users. It identifies which roles contain specific Fiori content and helps identify issues, such as missing tiles or target mappings in roles. This tab is essential for ensuring users have the proper access and layout on the Launchpad based on their roles. It also facilitates the resolution of authorization issues and enhances the delivery of role-based applications in SAP S/4HANA. Most of the Roles tab sections have been covered and are self-explanatory.

Note The tabs **Show Groups** and **Show Spaces** will be covered later in the book.

Show Tiles/Target Mappings

Enter the role name in the **Search Roles** option, and then click **Go**. The role content will be listed, as shown in the figure below.

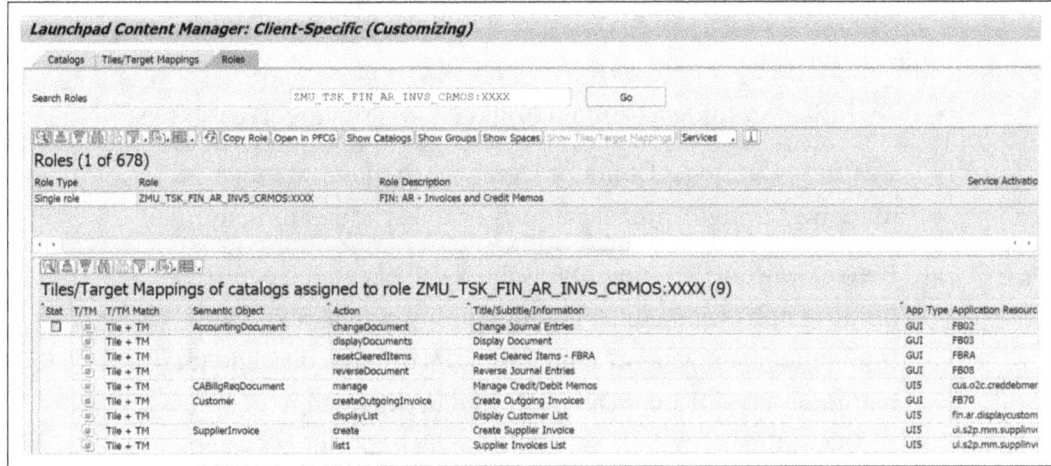

Figure 9-76. *Role with Show Tiles/Target Mappings selected*

9.7 Recommendation

If you want to adapt the content delivered by SAP, use the SAP business catalogs as a starting point. We recommend the following.

9.7.1 SAP-Delivered Catalogs

Here are a few recommendations on how to use SAP-delivered business catalogs:

- Do not change SAP catalogs. Instead, copy SAP business catalogs and use them as the starting point for creating your business catalogs.

  - This will ensure a consistent set of SAP Fiori apps that support app-to-app navigation by including the relevant target mappings. This is not necessarily true when you select only a set of single apps from the technical catalogs.

  - **Exception:** Some apps (mainly SAP GUI for HTML apps) are not contained in any business catalog and are only delivered as part of the technical catalogs. In these cases, you must select a single app (tile/target mapping) from the technical catalog and add it as a reference to your custom business catalog.

- Create separate catalogs for the provisioning and usage of tiles and target mappings:
  - **Technical Catalogs:** Contain original tiles and target mappings.
  - **Business Catalogs:** Contain references to tiles and target mappings from technical catalogs or those added directly.
  - **Reuse Content:** This facilitates the reuse of catalog content because one original tile/target mapping can be referenced from other catalogs. Any changes to the original tiles and target mappings are automatically reflected in the reference (unless the configuration of the reference tile/target mapping was changed).
- Create and change your catalogs in the following scopes:
  - **Technical Catalogs**: Configuration scope allows you to reuse the tiles and target mappings created in the technical catalogs for all clients.
  - **Business Catalogs**: Customizing scope allows you to manage business catalogs for a selected client.
  - Do not modify catalogs created in the Configuration scope while working in the Customizing scope, as this may result in outdated catalogs.
  - Use the following tools to create and change your catalogs:
  - **Technical Catalogs**: Launchpad Designer or Mass Maintenance tool
  - **Business Catalogs**: Launchpad Content Manager

9.7.2 Spaces and Pages

The SAP Fiori Launchpad offers two options for structuring the home page layout: a group-based home page and spaces and pages. The Launchpad home page is the central part of the Launchpad, organizing the content. This page allows users to access all applications relevant to their business case, whether SAP Fiori or classic.

A space is a unit that contains one or more pages and is assigned to the user based on their work profile or user role. Users may see several spaces in their Launchpad displayed in the navigation bar. If more than one page is available, a dropdown menu appears below the corresponding space, allowing the user to navigate to a specific page. If there is only one page in a space, the user is directed to that page when they click the space. You maintain spaces and pages in the Manage Launchpad Spaces and Manage Launchpad Pages applications.

9.7.3 Business Group

Groups in the SAP Fiori Launchpad are predefined structures for organizing the entry page. Each group is a subset of apps assigned to one or more catalogs. The apps displayed on a user's entry page depend on the catalogs and groups assigned to the user's roles. If a group contains apps not assigned to the user by catalogs, those apps will not appear on the user's entry page. If enabled, users can customize the entry page by adding or removing apps to pre-delivered or self-defined groups.

You can use the Launchpad Designer to manage catalogs and groups. SAP provides technical catalogs that contain apps for each application area. Furthermore, SAP provides business catalogs and groups as a sample collection of apps relevant to a specific business role. As an administrator, you can create role-specific business catalogs and groups using the technical catalogs as a repository.

9.8 Summary

In this chapter, we explored the creation of business catalogs through two distinct methods: copying an existing catalog or creating a new one from scratch. We also covered establishing both business catalogs and roles within the SAP system. It is essential to understand that SAP business catalogs reference tiles and target mappings from technical catalogs. This connection ensures that changes to the original tile or target mapping in the technical catalog are automatically reflected in the associated business catalog. Consequently, for both the "Copy" and "Create" options, updating the business role accordingly is imperative to reflect these changes.

CHAPTER 10

Introduction to SAP Fiori Spaces and Pages

SAP Fiori **spaces and pages** offer a modern approach to organizing and displaying apps on the Fiori Launchpad. Instead of a long list of tiles, content is grouped into **spaces** and, within them, the **pages** (such as dashboards with tiles and sections). Spaces and pages maintain the order of the apps as they are added. This makes the Launchpad cleaner, more role-based, and easier to navigate. Each page can contain multiple sections, and each section holds tiles, also known as apps. Spaces and pages are maintained using the **Launchpad App Manager** or **Launchpad Content Manager**, and they are assigned to users via PFCG roles. This new layout is more user-friendly and better aligned with how users work.

10.1 Introduction

In this chapter, we will discuss the concepts of spaces and pages and illustrate them with an example. Before the introduction of SAP S/4HANA 2005 Cloud and SAP S/4HANA 2020, business roles were managed using the **Fiori groups** concept. This method assigns tiles or apps to a custom Fiori group based on the functional requirements. However, this approach had its challenges. For example, a user with a specific business role would access apps through the Fiori Launchpad, where a single home page displays all groups in the top navigation bar, followed by the apps. This setup often resulted in a cluttered and disorganized user experience, a problem that must be addressed. SAP introduced a new concept, **spaces and pages**, to replace the **Fiori groups** concept within SAP Fiori. This transition has overcome the challenges that end users faced with the Fiori groups and provided a better, user-friendly experience alternative. The advantages of this new concept are manifold, offering a more organized and user-friendly experience. The user-friendly nature of **spaces and pages** ensures a smooth and comfortable transition for all users, making them feel at ease and confident about the change.

SAP introduced **spaces and pages** as an alternative to the Fiori groups concept in SAP Fiori, starting with **S/4HANA 2005 Cloud** and **SAP S/4HANA 2020**. This new concept offers a more robust and reliable option, addressing end user issues with the old method to provide a streamlined and efficient user experience. The reliability of this new concept ensures a secure and stable transition for all users, instilling confidence in the future of SAP Fiori.

10.1.1 Challenges/Drawbacks with the Groups Concept

The challenges with the old groups concept are as follows:

- The Fiori groups concept causes issues as user-assigned tiles appear randomly on a single page in the Fiori Launchpad, leading to a disorganized appearance. This becomes especially problematic when tiles come from different plugin systems (ECC, BUSINESS ROLE, HR, and CRM), making it difficult to discern their origin.

- Fiori groups do not guarantee the order in which tiles are added and appear on the home page. Apps are added randomly.

- The Launchpad appears cluttered with numerous tiles assigned to the user, resulting in a less user-friendly Fiori experience and longer load times. By reducing the number of tiles assigned to the user, we can significantly improve the Fiori experience and reduce load times.

- The user must scroll through numerous apps on the Fiori Launchpad App Finder to find the relevant one, which is a tedious and time-consuming process.

- System performance can be affected when end users have access to numerous groups and tiles, which can impact the loading of tiles in the Fiori Launchpad.

- When designing security groups, adding tiles from any catalog removes the hierarchy, making it challenging to identify the catalog to which each tile belongs within the role.

CHAPTER 10 INTRODUCTION TO SAP FIORI SPACES AND PAGES

To address the challenges faced by the Fiori groups concept and enhance the user experience, SAP has introduced a new concept called spaces and pages, which was introduced with **SAP S/4HANA 2020**. The **Fiori groups** concept is currently **deprecated** and will be removed in the future. However, it is still available and will be supported for more releases. Users now have the option to choose between the **Fiori groups** and **spaces and pages** to be displayed in the Fiori Launchpad, accessible through the **Settings option**. SAP has also begun providing standard spaces and pages within the SAP-delivered roles (such as **SAP_BR***), including catalogs and groups, as depicted in the screenshot below.

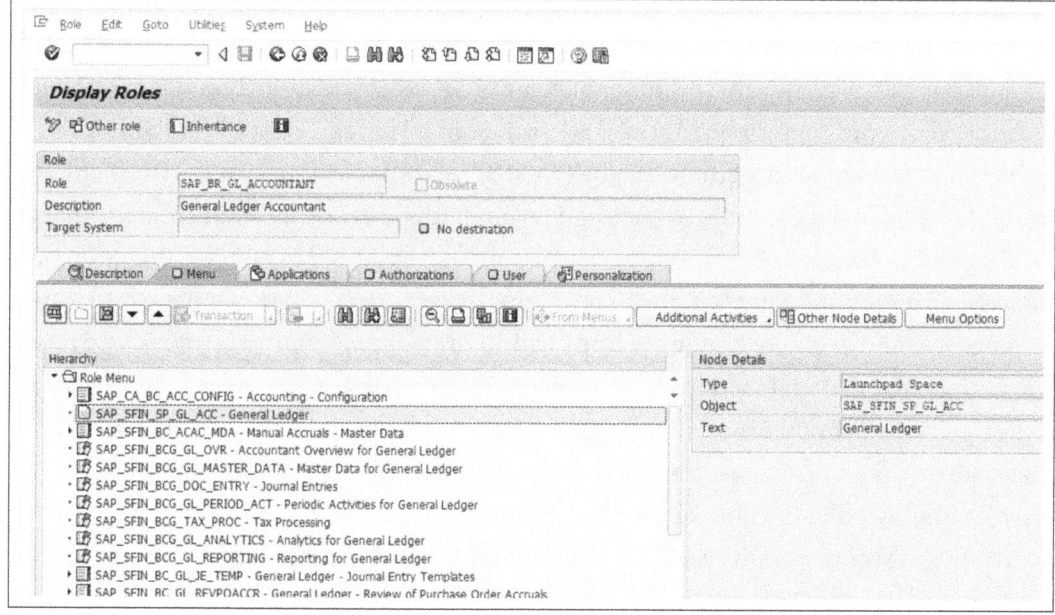

Figure 10-1. *SAP-delivered custom SAP_BR* business role with catalogs, spaces, pages, and groups*

In the above role, both **spaces** (🗂) and **pages** (📄) appear along with the **catalogs** (📁).

Notes SAP plans to **deprecate** the **Fiori groups** concept in upcoming releases, so it is recommended to transition to **spaces and pages** as soon as possible.

10.2 Definition of Spaces, Pages, Sections, and Tiles

Below, we define some of the **SAP Fiori business objects** that will be used as part of building **spaces and pages**.

10.2.1 Spaces and Pages

Spaces and pages was a new concept that was introduced in the **SAP S/4HANA 2020** release, serving as an alternative to or replacement for the Fiori groups concept (at least for now).

Starting with SAP S/4HANA Cloud 2008 and SAP S/4HANA (On-Premise), SAP has introduced two new apps to create **spaces and pages: Manage Launchpad Spaces (F4834)** and **Manage Launchpad Pages (F4512)**. The **spaces** mode offers tremendous flexibility when using the Fiori Launchpad layout to display apps. When created, **spaces** are assigned to **business roles**. **Pages**, when built, are assigned to **spaces**. **Pages** contain sections, and each section contains tiles or apps. A **section** is a part of a **page** and is used to categorize and arrange the tiles or apps within the **page**. Therefore, **spaces and pages** will show all relevant data within a single page. In short, **pages** are technically identical to **groups,** which contain tiles or apps. **Spaces** are assigned to **business roles**, while **pages** are assigned to **spaces**. **Pages** contain **sections**, and **sections** contain **tiles** or **apps**. This allows all relevant data to be shown on a single **Fiori Launchpad page**.

When the security team creates a new custom business role (**CBR**), it includes **catalogs and spaces**. Tiles and apps can be directly a part of a page. If there are too many tiles or apps, they can be divided into **multiple sections** to improve the layout and user experience. Only the tiles or apps associated with a **page** will be displayed when the **page** is selected. As they appear on the SAP Fiori Launchpad home page, **spaces and pages** are shown in the figure below.

CHAPTER 10   INTRODUCTION TO SAP FIORI SPACES AND PAGES

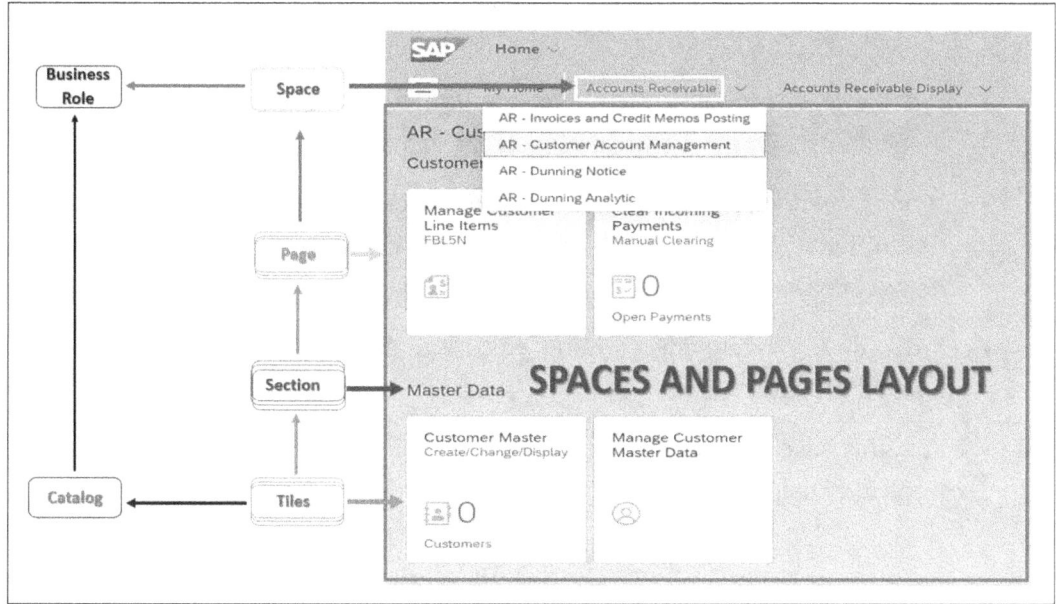

Figure 10-2. *Spaces and pages layout displayed on the SAP Fiori Launchpad home page*

Note   A business role must include at least one **space**; depending on business or design requirements, it can consist of multiple spaces. Furthermore, spaces and pages ensure the order of tiles or apps as developed.

Spaces

A **space** in the Fiori Launchpad is a **container** appearing in the top-level navigation bar, containing predefined sets of apps for end users. It consists of pages and sections associated with tiles or apps, providing flexibility and role-based access for custom content. Thus, **spaces** offer tremendous flexibility and options for developing content structures by providing several role-based pages for end users to access their custom Fiori Launchpad content, rather than relying solely on one home page with groups.

Note   SAP-delivered spaces cannot be changed; they can only be copied. **Spaces** created should have a **space title** and **description**, which are mandatory.

463

CHAPTER 10   INTRODUCTION TO SAP FIORI SPACES AND PAGES

Advantages of Using the Spaces Concept

- When a space is assigned to a role, it automatically inherits the associated catalog structure assigned to the role.

- When launched, it displays all available spaces along with a description. You can switch between custom created and SAP delivered, a selection option in the navigation bar.

- SAP only allows copying, creating, editing, and deleting custom-created spaces.

- You now have the option to duplicate SAP-delivered space templates into your custom namespace template. They cannot be deleted.

- Enables easy addition or removal of pages and allows users to define the order of tiles or apps on the Launchpad via the pull-down menu within the workspace area.

- Provides the option for users to set specific pages as visible or hidden within a space.

- **Spaces** enable users to organize their work environment into **logical groups**, making accessing and managing different tasks easier. Each **space** can contain a set of related **pages**, providing a clean and organized interface that helps users focus on their work without distractions.

- Users can **personalize** their **spaces** according to their roles and needs, ensuring the most relevant information and applications are readily available. This customization improves user satisfaction and productivity.

- Users can quickly navigate between work areas without searching for a cluttered menu by grouping related **pages** and apps into **spaces**. This reduces the time spent navigating and increases efficiency.

- **Spaces** can be configured to align with specific organizational roles, providing users with tailored access to the necessary tools and information. This ensures that each user has a focused and relevant work environment.

- **Spaces** are designed around tasks, allowing users to organize their work into specific focus areas. This helps minimize context switching and interruptions, improving concentration and increasing productivity.

- With all relevant **pages** and apps grouped within a **space**, users can quickly access the tools they need to complete their tasks, reducing delays and improving workflow efficiency.

- **Spaces** help standardize the user experience across different roles and departments, ensuring everyone has a consistent and intuitive interface. This reduces the learning curve, making it easier to onboard new users.

- IT and application administrators can centrally manage **spaces**, ensuring consistency in how different roles access and utilize the SAP Fiori environment. This centralized approach simplifies management and reduces the risk of errors.

- **Spaces** support a modular approach to application design, allowing organizations to add new **spaces** as needed. This scalability ensures that the Fiori environment can grow with the organization's needs without becoming unwieldy.

- **Spaces** can be configured to meet the specific needs of different business units or teams, providing a flexible framework that adapts to various organizational requirements.

- Organizations can create **spaces** dedicated to specific teams or projects, providing a shared environment where team members can access the tools and information they need to collaborate effectively. This fosters better communication and collaboration across the organization.

- **Spaces** can be designed to facilitate shared access to critical resources, making it easier for teams to work together on everyday tasks and objectives.

- Segmenting the user interface into distinct **spaces** prevents users from being overwhelmed by excessive options. This helps maintain focus and reduces the cognitive load, allowing users to work more efficiently.

- Spaces allow users to stay within the context of their current task or workflow, reducing the need to switch between apps or pages. This streamlined workflow enhances efficiency and minimizes distractions.

- Administrators can allocate resources more efficiently by assigning specific **spaces** to different user roles or departments. This focused approach ensures effective resource utilization and user access to necessary tools.

- By limiting the number of active **spaces and pages**, organizations can optimize the performance of their SAP Fiori environment, ensuring that users experience fast and responsive applications.

- **Spaces** allow for better control over access to sensitive information and applications. By organizing content into specific **spaces**, administrators can apply role-based access controls more effectively, ensuring that users only see the information they are authorized to access.

- **Spaces** can be configured to support compliance with industry regulations by ensuring users can access the appropriate data and tools for their specific roles. This helps organizations maintain compliance while providing a secure and controlled environment.

- Users can be empowered to create and manage their **spaces**, allowing them to tailor their work environment to their needs. This self-service capability reduces dependency on IT support and enhances user satisfaction.

- **Spaces** provide a clear and organized view of all available tools and resources, offering users better visibility in their work environment and enabling them to make informed decisions.

Conclusion

Thus, utilizing **spaces** in SAP Fiori offers numerous benefits, resulting in a more organized, efficient, and user-friendly environment. By providing a structured and customizable interface, spaces help organizations enhance productivity, streamline workflows, and ensure users have the tools and information for success.

Pages

A **page** is a part of a **space** containing Fiori tiles or apps grouped into multiple **sections**. When assigned to a role, it is displayed from a pull-down menu in the space description within the Fiori Launchpad, located at the top of the workspace, as a tab next to the Home tab.

Pages are created and managed using the SAP **Maintain Launchpad Pages** app. Only administrators or security users can access this app to create pages.

The app manages pages, including editing, copying, or deleting existing pages (tiles and apps included). Pages and spaces have a many-to-many relation, with a page being assigned to multiple spaces and a space being able to contain multiple pages. From a security standpoint, the business role contains spaces and catalogs.

SAP allows groups and spaces to coexist, meaning the end user can use either **spaces** or **groups.**

- **Pages** can be managed independently of any roles.
- When working in tiles or apps, you can directly add any additional catalogs and tiles from those catalogs to your pages.
- You can only add apps from an associated business catalog.
- You can only add apps (tiles/cards) to pages from the business catalogs assigned to the user's roles. These catalogs must be part of a technical catalog or a business catalog included in the role assigned to the user**.**
- Allows for creating a page layout independently of spaces and then adding spaces and pages, along with role maintenance.

Note The **page** description appears as a header.

- A business role with fewer tiles or apps may use one page per **space**.
- Business roles with multiple apps may use multiple **pages per space**.
- **Pages** consist of **sections**, which can be used to structure the content further.
- End users can personalize the **Fiori Launchpad layout** by creating a new **section** to add tiles/apps, realigning the order of sections, changing the order of pages, etc.
- For faster loading, minimize the number of **pages** per **space**, preferably limited to **five to seven**.

Advantages of Pages

SAP Fiori's use of pages brings several advantages that enhance the overall user experience and efficiency of the applications built on this design paradigm. Here are the key benefits of having pages in SAP Fiori:

- It enables apps to be organized clearly and in a structured manner. Each page can be dedicated to a specific set of related tasks or data, reducing clutter and making it easier for users to find what they need.
- Pages can be tailored to show only the most relevant information and actions based on the user's role and task, improving focus and reducing cognitive load.
- Pages provide a consistent layout and interaction pattern across different Fiori apps, which helps users quickly become familiar with new applications and reduces the learning curve.
- Pages are designed to be responsive, meaning they adapt to various screen sizes and devices, ensuring a seamless experience regardless of whether the user is on a desktop, tablet, or smartphone.
- Pages make navigating an app easier by breaking down complex processes into manageable steps or sections. Users can move

between different pages as they progress through tasks, which improves efficiency and user satisfaction.

- Each **page** can be customized to suit specific user roles or business needs. This flexibility enables the creation of role-based pages that display only the most relevant information and actions, thereby streamlining workflows.

- Developers can update or modify individual **pages** without impacting the entire application, making it easier to roll out changes or improvements incrementally.

- **Pages** can be designed to load content as needed rather than all at once, which can significantly improve performance, especially in data-intensive applications. This ensures that the user interface remains responsive, even when handling large datasets.

- **Pages** can be optimized to handle data more efficiently, with each **page** focusing on a specific set of data or transactions, reducing the load on the system and improving overall performance.

- **Pages** enable a modular approach to application design. New **pages** can be added to an existing application, allowing for easy scaling as the business grows or requirements evolve.

- The **page** design in SAP Fiori supports the reuse of UI components across different **pages** and applications, promoting consistency and reducing development time.

- **Pages** are ideal for managing complex workflows that involve multiple steps or stages. With dedicated pages, users can be guided through each step of the process, ensuring that all necessary actions are completed correctly.

- **Pages** can be organized around specific tasks, making it easy for users to focus on the task without being distracted by unrelated information. **Pages** work seamlessly with other SAP Fiori components, such as smart controls, list reports, and analytical tables, allowing for the creation of robust, integrated applications that meet diverse business needs.

Conclusion

In summary, **pages** in SAP Fiori provide a structured, user-friendly, scalable framework for presenting information and guiding users through tasks. They enhance the overall user experience by making applications more intuitive, efficient, and responsive to the needs of different user roles and business processes.

10.2.2 Sections

A **section** is a substructure or subfolder within a **page** that displays further content or segregates apps. A page contains one or more **sections**, which can contain tiles or apps. **Sections** allow users to visualize the content of a space. For optimal system performance, it is recommended that each section be limited to **2–5 tiles** and a maximum of **25 apps** within the **space.**

Advantages of Sections

SAP Fiori introduces the concept of **sections** within pages, which provides several advantages in terms of usability, design, and data organization. Here are some of the key benefits:

- **Sections** allow for the logical grouping of related information within a page, making it easier for users to find and focus on specific data without being overwhelmed.

- By breaking down the content into **sections**, the **page** becomes more modular, making it easier to manage and update specific parts without affecting the entire **page**.

- Users can intuitively navigate the content as **sections** create a clear structure. This leads to better user engagement as they can quickly find relevant information.

- **Sections** can be made collapsible, allowing users to reduce distractions and concentrate on the parts most relevant to their tasks.

- **Sections** help ensure content is displayed responsively, adapting well to various screen sizes. This is particularly important for users accessing SAP Fiori applications on mobile devices.

- With **sections**, the layout remains consistent across different devices, improving the overall usability and user satisfaction.

- **Sections** can be tailored or personalized to meet the needs of different users or roles. For example, users in other departments may access different sections based on their needs.

- Developers can easily add, remove, or rearrange **sections** (using the drag-and-drop method), offering flexibility in customizing the user interface to match business requirements.

- In some cases, **sections** can be loaded asynchronously, meaning that not all content must be loaded simultaneously. This can improve page load times and performance, particularly in data-heavy applications.

- **Sections** can be designed only to retrieve data when needed, reducing unnecessary data calls and improving application efficiency.

- As the application grows, **sections** make it easier to scale the user interface. New sections can be added without disrupting the existing content, ensuring a smooth and scalable design process.

Conclusion

Thus, by leveraging **sections** in SAP Fiori pages, organizations can create more organized, user-friendly, and scalable applications that enhance users' overall experience and improve productivity.

10.2.3 Links

What is a **link**? A **link** is a crucial component of a space for visualization. It allows users to quickly access business applications and complete tasks, displaying the URL, Web Dynpro, etc.

Advantages of Links

In SAP Fiori, the integration of **links** within spaces and pages offers several advantages that enhance navigation, user experience, and overall application efficiency. Here are the key benefits:

- **Links** within spaces and pages allow users to move effortlessly between different sections, apps, or related content. This cross-navigation capability enables users to access relevant information or tasks without needing to exit the current context, thereby enhancing workflow efficiency.

- Users can be directed directly to a specific section, form, or detail page through **links**, enabling precise navigation without unnecessary steps. This is particularly useful in large applications with multiple

- **Links** can be contextually placed within a page of a space, offering users direct access to related tasks or data. For example, links within a customer overview page can direct users to their order history, contact details, or payment status, making the user experience more intuitive and streamlined.

- Using **links** lets users quickly move between tasks or information without significant disruption, keeping them focused and productive.

- **Links** provide users with quick access to related data or actions directly from the current page or space. For example, a **link** on a sales order page might direct the user to inventory details or shipment tracking, ensuring that all relevant information is easily accessible.

- By **linking** additional resources or details, you can keep the primary page or space uncluttered, allowing users to access detailed information only when needed.

- **Links** can be customized by user roles, ensuring that each user sees relevant links tailored to their tasks, thereby enhancing the overall experience.

- **Links** can be dynamically generated based on the content or context of the page, providing users with the most relevant navigation options at any given time.

- As applications grow, **links** within spaces and pages enable the quick addition of new features or sections without disrupting the existing structure. This makes it easier to scale the application over time.

- Centralizing navigation through **links** simplifies maintaining and updating the application. Changes to linked content or navigation paths can be managed centrally, reducing the need for extensive updates across the application.

- **Links** can guide users through the most efficient paths to complete tasks, reducing the time spent navigating the application and improving overall performance.

- Instead of loading all related content on a single page, **links** allow users to load additional content only when needed, which can improve page load times and responsiveness.

- **Links** within spaces and pages can connect users to external systems, documents, or web resources, extending the functionality of the Fiori application beyond its native capabilities. This integration is crucial for organizations that rely on multiple systems or require external data access.

- **Links** can seamlessly connect different Fiori apps, allowing users to transition between them as part of a broader workflow without switching apps or manually re-entering the data.

- **Links** empower users to navigate the application based on their needs and tasks, providing a level of self-service that reduces dependency on predefined navigation paths.

- **Links** can also guide users to resources, tutorials, or documentation directly within the application, aiding user education and reducing the learning curve.

- **Links** can be reused across different spaces and pages, ensuring consistency in navigation implementation and reducing development time.

CHAPTER 10   INTRODUCTION TO SAP FIORI SPACES AND PAGES

Conclusion

In summary, utilizing links within SAP Fiori spaces and pages offers a powerful mechanism for enhancing navigation, user experience, and application efficiency. Links play a crucial role in making SAP Fiori applications more user-friendly, flexible, and scalable by providing quick access to related content, facilitating seamless cross-application navigation, and supporting dynamic, context-aware user interactions.

10.3 Schematic of Spaces and Pages

The schematic of the above concept of spaces and pages is displayed in the figure below.

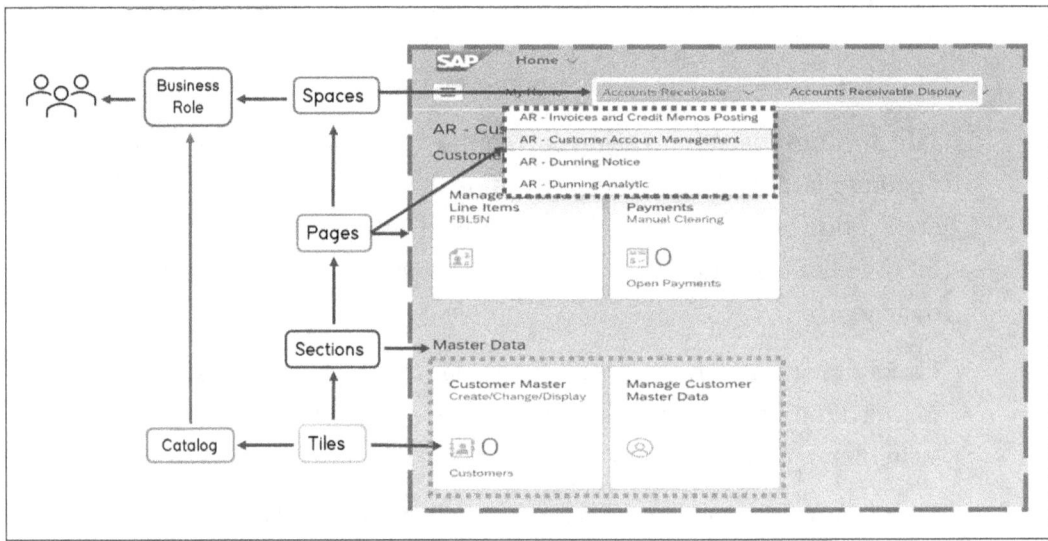

Figure 10-3. Schematic showing the relationship between users, groups with spaces, pages, and section layout

SAP now has three new apps for creating spaces and pages:

- **Manage Launchpad Spaces (F4834):** Create and manage spaces.
- **Manage Launchpad Pages (F4512):** Create and edit page content.
- **Launchpad Pages from Groups (/UI2/FDM_GTP):** Create pages based on existing business groups.

Within the **spaces and pages** schematic, the **space and page** appear as shown in the figure below.

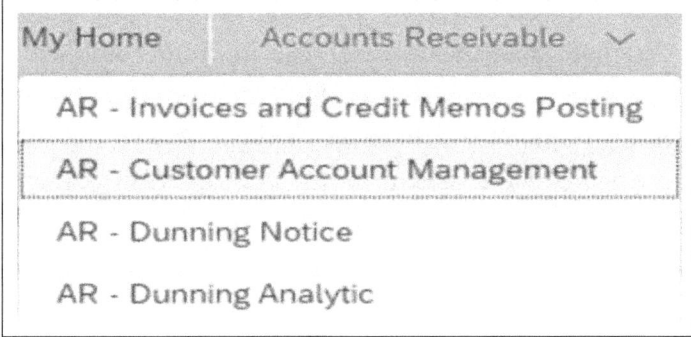

Figure 10-4. Spaces and pages as seen in the SAP Fiori Launchpad

10.4 Prerequisites to Implement Spaces and Pages

To activate or implement the SAP Fiori Launchpad with spaces and pages, a few OData services need to be activated as a prerequisite, which are as follows.

10.4.1 Mandatory OData Service Activation

The four OData services below must be activated to implement spaces and pages. Activation of the OData services can be done in two ways:

- Via a task list
- Manually

Using a Task List

The OData services can be activated simultaneously and automatically by executing the SAP-delivered task list **SAP_FIORI_FOUNDATION_S4 (Using T-Code: STC01)** and selecting the task **"Activate and Configure FLP for Space and Pages"** as it is not chosen in the task list by default.

- FDM_PAGE_REPOSITORY_CUST_SRV
- FDM_SPACE_REPOSITORY_CUST_SRV
- FDM_PAGE_RUNTIME_SRV
- FDM_TRANSPORT_SRV

In the task list, select only the **Activate and Configure FLP for Spaces and Pages** task that must be executed. Once the task list is executed and completed, a message will be displayed at the bottom of the screen: **Created FLP Property: SPACES_ENABLE_USER = True.** It will also generate the necessary **transport** if the desired options are selected. Refer to the figure below: use the transaction **/UI2/FLP_CUS_CONF** (client specific) to view the information that is maintained.

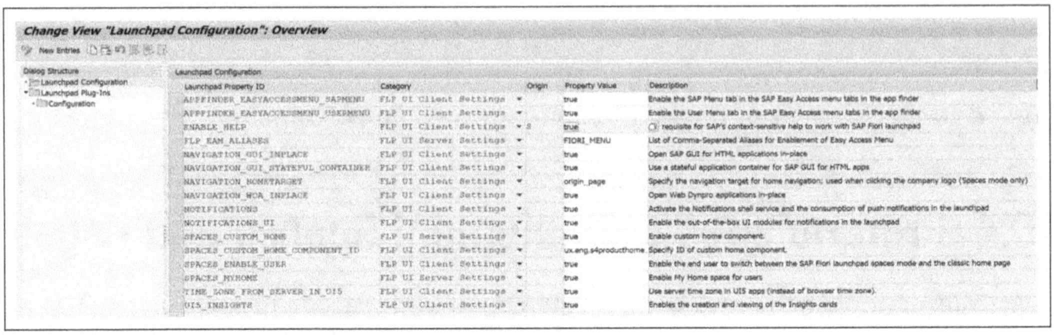

Launchpad Property ID	Category	Origin	Property Value	Description
APPFINDER_EASYACCESSMENU_SAPMENU	FLP UI Client Settings		true	Enable the SAP Menu tab in the SAP Easy Access menu tabs in the app finder
APPFINDER_EASYACCESSMENU_USERMENU	FLP UI Client Settings		true	Enable the User Menu tab in the SAP Easy Access menu tabs in the app finder
ENABLE_HELP	FLP UI Client Settings	S	true	requisite for SAP's context-sensitive help to work with SAP Fiori launchpad
FLP_EAM_ALIASES	FLP UI Server Settings		FIORI_MENU	List of Comma-Separated Aliases for Enablement of Easy Access Menu
NAVIGATION_GUI_INPLACE	FLP UI Client Settings		true	Open SAP GUI for HTML applications in-place
NAVIGATION_GUI_STATEFUL_CONTAINER	FLP UI Client Settings		true	Use a stateful application container for SAP GUI for HTML apps
NAVIGATION_HOMETARGET	FLP UI Client Settings		origin_page	Specify the navigation target for home navigation; used when clicking the company logo (Spaces mode only)
NAVIGATION_WDA_INPLACE	FLP UI Client Settings		true	Open Web Dynpro applications in-place
NOTIFICATIONS	FLP UI Client Settings		true	Activate the Notifications shell service and the consumption of push notifications in the launchpad
NOTIFICATIONS_UI	FLP UI Client Settings		true	Enable the out-of-the-box UI modules for notifications in the launchpad
SPACES_CUSTOM_HOME	FLP UI Server Settings		true	Enable custom home component.
SPACES_CUSTOM_HOME_COMPONENT_ID	FLP UI Client Settings		ux.eng.s4producthome	Specify ID of custom home component.
SPACES_ENABLE_USER	FLP UI Client Settings		true	Enable the end user to switch between the SAP Fiori launchpad spaces mode and the classic home page
SPACES_MYHOME	FLP UI Server Settings		true	Enable My Home space for users
TIME_ZONE_FROM_SERVER_IN_UI5	FLP UI Client Settings		true	Use server time zone in UI5 apps (instead of browser time zone).
UI5_INSIGHTS	FLP UI Client Settings		true	Enables the creation and viewing of the Insights cards

Figure 10-5. *Setting enabled for spaces and pages using transaction /UI2/FLP_CUS_CONF*

Transaction **/UI2/FLP_ SYS_CONF** (cross-client) can be used to configure parameters for cross-client purposes.

Note If the **SPACES** parameter is set to **true**, it will be the default for all users, and the classic home page will not be shown by default.

Activate Manually

If the above-listed OData services were not activated earlier using the task list, then the same can also be activated manually using transaction **/IWFND/MAINT_SERVICES** (Activate and Maintain Services).

Assignment of Roles

Users who create or manage **spaces and pages** should be assigned the role **SAP_FLP_ADMIN** or a copy of the role (recommended) to give access to the apps **Manage Launchpad Spaces** and **Manage Launchpad Pages**.

CHAPTER 10   INTRODUCTION TO SAP FIORI SPACES AND PAGES

Display Spaces and Pages on the Fiori Launchpad

To display any tile on the Fiori Launchpad using spaces and pages, the following prerequisites must be met:

- Custom business catalog
- Custom business role
- Page that needs to be assigned to a space
- The space to be assigned to the same business role
- Access to transaction **/UI2/FLP**

10.5 Setup of the Spaces Setting in the User Menu

If the end user wants the flexibility of using the groups or spaces concept, then specific parameters must be enabled. The **Use Spaces** selection box gives the end user the option to toggle between **groups and spaces**. Currently, SAP does not restrict the use of Fiori groups or spaces.

Another important aspect regarding **spaces and pages** is the setting of parameters **SPACES** and **SPACES_ENABLE_USER** according to your requirements, using the transactions for the Launchpad configuration parameters:

- Transaction **/UI2/FLP_ SYS_CONF** (cross-client)
- Transaction **/UI2/FLP_CUS_CONF** (client specific)

Executing the transaction **/UI2/FLP_CUS_CONF** will display a box titled **Information** displaying **Caution: The table is cross-client**, as shown in the figure below.

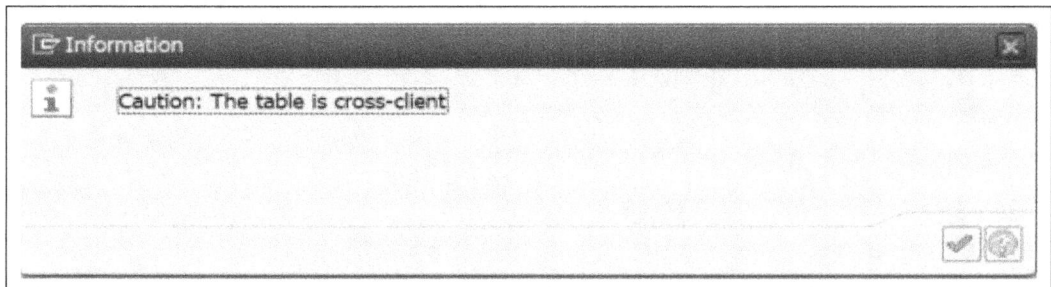

Figure 10-6. *Information: cross-client table*

Click the **continue** icon, and the window titled **Change View "Launchpad Configuration": Overview** will appear, where you can adjust the spaces and pages parameters, as shown in the figure below.

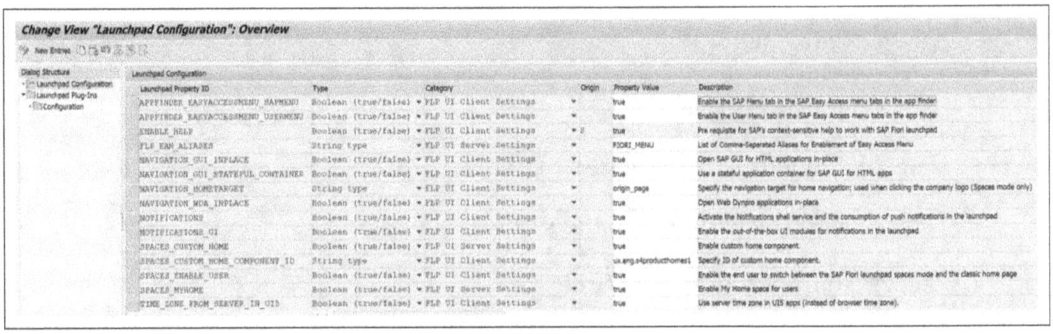

Figure 10-7. Launchpad Configuration option to maintain spaces and pages parameters

If the SPACES parameter is valid, it will be set as the default for all users, and the classic home page (Fiori groups) will not be shown as a default. Furthermore, end users can enable **spaces** by setting the **SPACES_ENABLE_USER** parameter to **true** through the Settings menu in the User Menu, as shown below.

Users can **switch** between the **SAP Fiori Launchpad home page** and **Launchpad spaces** using the **User Menu**. To do this, navigate to **Settings**, and then select **Spaces and Pages**. Activate by selecting the **Use Spaces** option to switch to **Launchpad spaces**. To return to the SAP Fiori Launchpad home page, deactivate the **Use Spaces** option, and the system will switch back to the **Launchpad groups** option. In both cases, the Launchpad will reload.

CHAPTER 10   INTRODUCTION TO SAP FIORI SPACES AND PAGES

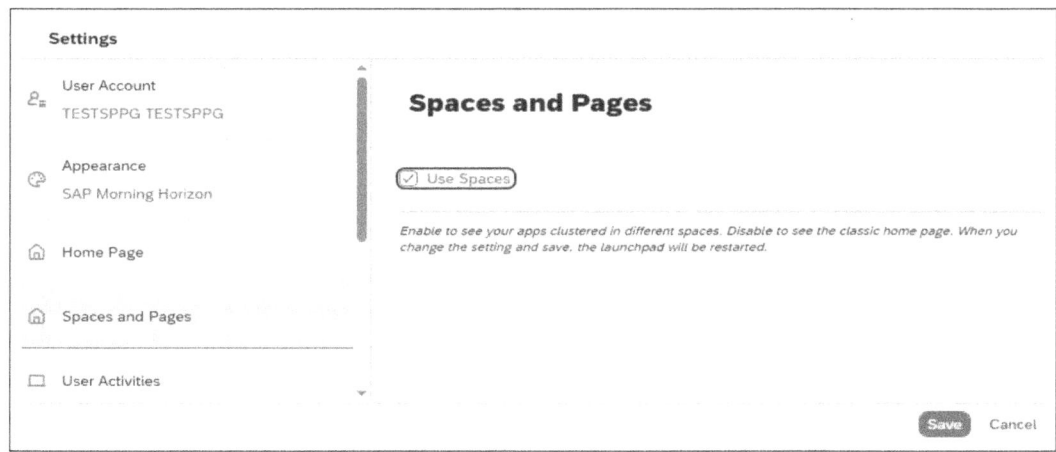

Figure 10-8. *Spaces setting in the User Menu*

Note   If the **User Spaces** box is **not selected** within the **Settings** window, the user will switch from **spaces** to **groups**, as shown in the figure below.

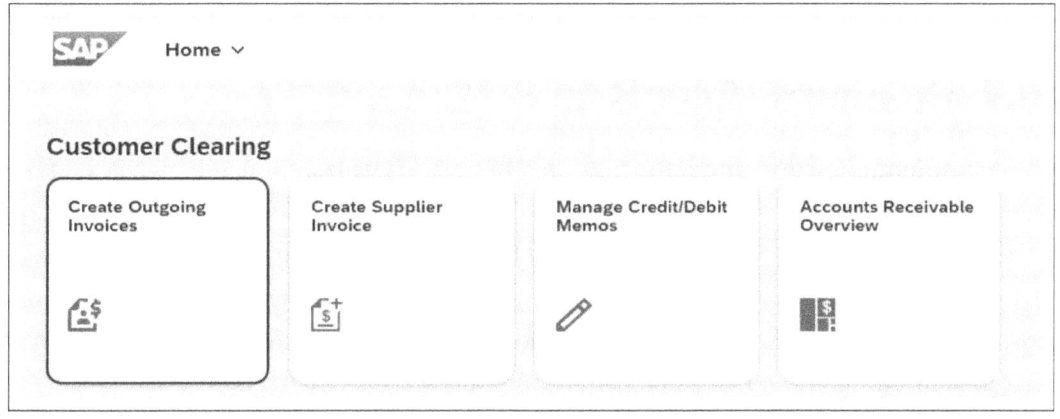

Figure 10-9. *Test user has now switched from spaces to groups in the Fiori Launchpad*

Note   To enforce using **spaces**, set the parameter **SPACES = TRUE**. Users will not be able to switch to groups. Users will not see the Spaces and Pages option in Settings.

479

10.6 Creating New Roles

Follow the steps below to create a new role from a security standpoint. However, before implementing this, the naming convention and design strategy should be predefined for roles, catalogs, spaces, pages, and sections. The figure below describes an overview of creating a **business role.**

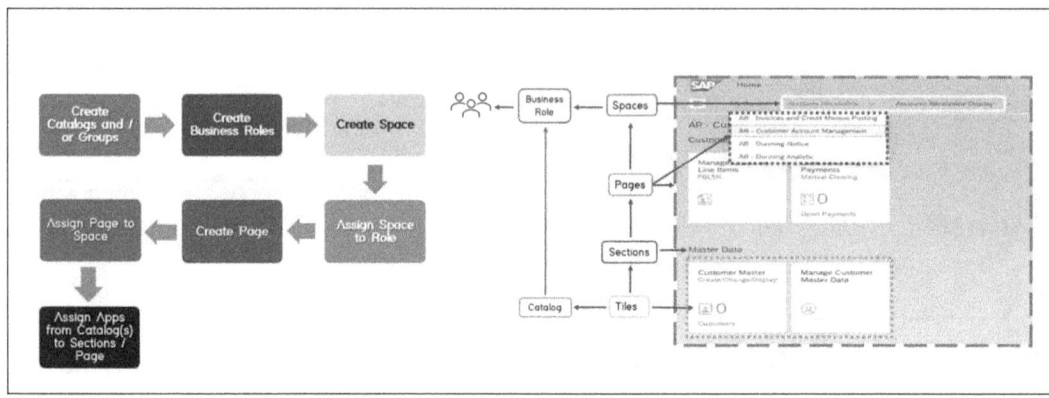

Figure 10-10. Workflow process to create business roles and assign spaces and pages

10.7 Business Objects to Be Created

It is recommended to document the mapping of business roles, catalogs, spaces, pages, and sections using applications such as **Excel** to outline the required information before creating and developing the system. This will help give a basic idea of how the layout of the Launchpad will look for the business users. The sample format used in this guide is shown in the figure below. The tile or app information was taken from the SAP Fiori Apps Reference Library for S/4HANA 2023 FPS02 to construct this matrix.

Role Name - ID	Catalog Name - ID	SPACE - ID	PAGES - ID	Section	Tile/APP	Apps	Semantic Object	Semantic Action	Groups
ZMU_TSK_FIN_AR_INVS_CRMOS:XXXX	ZF_BCLG_FIN_AR_INV_CRMEMO	ZF_SP_FIN_AR	ZF_PG_1_FIN_AR						**ZF_GRP_FIN_AR_INVOICE**
FIN: AR - Invoices and Credit Memos	BCLG:FIN:AR - Invoices & Credit Memos	Account Receivable	AR - Invoices and Credit Memos Posting	Invoices and Credit Memos Posting	Create Outgoing Invoices	F870	Customer	createOutgoingInvoice	AR - Invoice & Credit Memos Posting
					Supplier Invoices List	F1060A	CABillgReqDocument	manage	
					Manage Credit/Debit Memos	F2389	CABillgReqDocument	manage	
				Document Reversal & Reset	Reset Cleared Items	FBRA	AccountingDocument	resetClearedItems	
					Reverse Journal Entries	FB08	AccountingDocument	reverseDocument	
				Document Change & Display	Change Journal Entries	FB02	AccountingDocument	changeDocument	
					Display Document	FB03	AccountingDocument	displayDocument	
				Customer Details	Display Customer List	F2640	Customer	displayList	
					Create Supplier Invoices	F0859	SupplierInvoice	createOutgoingInvoice	
				Overview	Accounts Receivable Overview	F3242	Customer	overviewAccountsReceivable	
ZMU_TSK_FIN_AR_CST_ACTCLG:XXXX	ZF_BCLG_FIN_AR_CS_ACCT_CLG	**ZF_SP_FIN_AR**	ZF_PG_2_FIN_AR						**ZF_GRP_FIN_AR_CUSTOMER**
FIN: AR - Customer Clearing	BCLG:FIN:AR - Customer Clearing	Account Receivable	AR - Customer Account Management	Customer Analysis	Manage Customer Line Item	FBL3N	Customer	manageLineItems	AR - Customer Account
					Clear Incoming Payments	F0773	Customer	clearOpenItems	
				Master Data	Customer Master - Create/Change/Display / Customers	F0850A	Customer	manage	
					Manage Customer Master Data		Customer	manage	
ZMU_TSK_FIN_AR_DUNNG_NOTC:XXXX	ZF_BCLG_FIN_AR_DUNNG_NOTICE	**ZF_SP_FIN_AR_DUNNG**	ZF_PG_1_FIN_AR_DUNNG						**ZF_GRP_FIN_AR_DUNNG**
FIN: AR - Dunning Notice	BCLG:FIN:AR - Dunning Notice	Account Receivable - Dunning	AR - Dunning Notice	Notice	Maintain Dunning Notices	F3678	CADunningNotice	maintain	AR - Dunning Notice
				Run	CreateDunning Notices	F150	CustomerCollections	createDunning	
				Proposal	My Dunning Proposals	F2435	DunningRun	manage	
ZMU_TSK_FIN_AR_DUNNG_ALYT:XXXX	ZF_BCLG_FIN_AR_DUNNG_ANALYTIC	**ZF_SP_FIN_AR_DUNNG**	ZF_PG_2_FIN_AR_DUNGG						**ZF_GRP_FIN_AR_DUNNG_ALY**
FIN: AR - Dunning Analytic	BCLG:FIN:AR - Dunning Analytic	Account Receivable - Dunning	AR - Dunning Analytic	Analytics	Dunning Level Distribution	F1742	DunningLevelDistribution KPI	analyzeSBKPIDunningLevelDistribution	AR - Dunning Analytic
					Analyze Dunning Locks	F1655A	CAOperationalLock	analyzeDunningLocks_new	
					Analyze Dunning Volume	F2122A	CADunningRun	analyzeDunningVolume_new	
					Analyze Dunning Success	F2123A	CADunningRun	analyzeDunningSuccess_new	
				History	Display Dunning History	F2328	Customer	displayDunningHistory	

Figure 10-11. *Sample Excel file with business object details*

Note All **custom business catalogs** and **roles** should be created before creating **spaces and pages**, including **package** and **transport requests**.

To create spaces and pages, we will develop **six** custom business catalogs and roles to illustrate the concept, along with the three spaces. Once all the roles have been created, they must be updated and regenerated before being assigned to the end user.

10.8 Create Spaces and Pages

Spaces and pages were introduced in SAP HANA S/4HANA Cloud 2008 or On-Premise in S/4HANA 2020 via two new apps: **Manage Launchpad Spaces** and **Manage Launchpad Pages**. As discussed, a **space** can have multiple **pages**, and a **page** can have multiple **sections** with numerous **tiles** or **apps**.

Note An administrator needs access to SAP role **SAP_FLP_ADMIN** to create **spaces and pages**.

- **Spaces** are assigned to **custom business roles**.
- **Pages** are displayed in the central area of the Fiori Launchpad screen.
- **Pages** are assigned to **users** via **spaces**.

CHAPTER 10　INTRODUCTION TO SAP FIORI SPACES AND PAGES

- **Pages** contain **sections**, and **sections** contain **tiles or apps**.
- **Tiles or apps** are assigned to **pages**.
- A **page** can be assigned to multiple **spaces**, and a **space** can contain more than one **page**.
- The relation between spaces and pages would be a many-to-many relation.
- Regardless of whether we follow business **groups**, **spaces**, or **pages**, the **business catalogs** and **roles** are **mandatory** and always required. **Note:** The custom business catalog is created using transactions **/UI2/FLPCM_CUST** and **/UI2/FLPD_CUST**.

As discussed in the preceding sections, the **spaces and pages** concept enables users to create spaces and provides them multiple pages to access their SAP Fiori Launchpad content. Users can access various spaces, and each space can have one or more pages, including sections, tiles, apps, and links. Furthermore, **spaces and pages are not enabled by default.** To proceed further, the administrator needs to go to the Fiori Launchpad, as shown in the figure below.

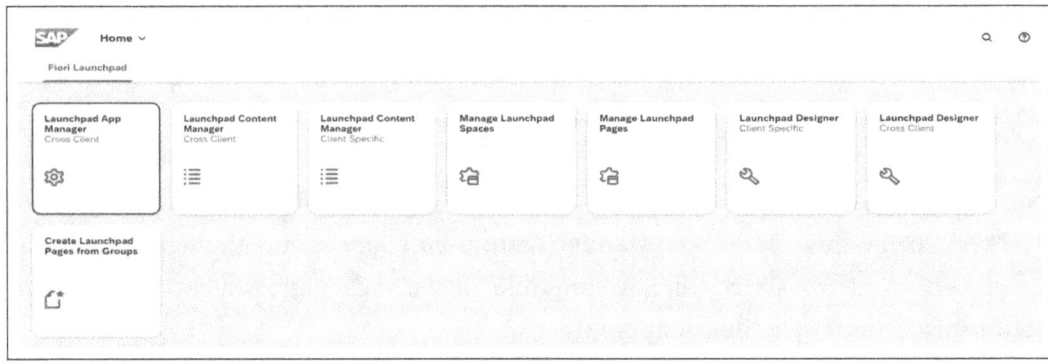

Figure 10-12. Admin user SAP Fiori Launchpad home page

10.8.1　Create a Space

To create a new **space**, open the **Manage Launchpad Spaces** tile. This launches the **Manage Launchpad Spaces screen**, where the administrator can create a **space**, as shown in the figure below.

CHAPTER 10 INTRODUCTION TO SAP FIORI SPACES AND PAGES

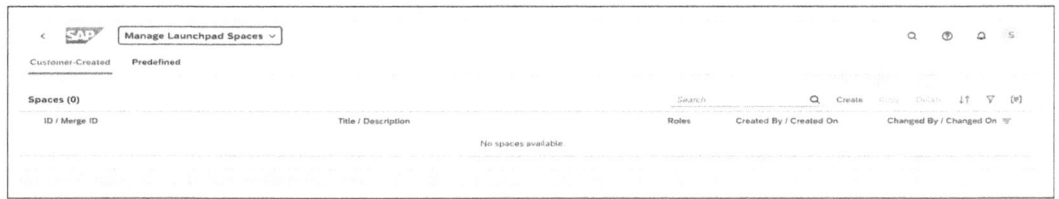

Figure 10-13. *Manage Launchpad Spaces input screen*

Currently, the system's **Spaces** section is empty, and no spaces are maintained, as indicated in the figure above as **Spaces (0)**. To create a new **space**, select **Create** at the top-right corner, which opens a box titled **Create Space**, as shown in the figure below.

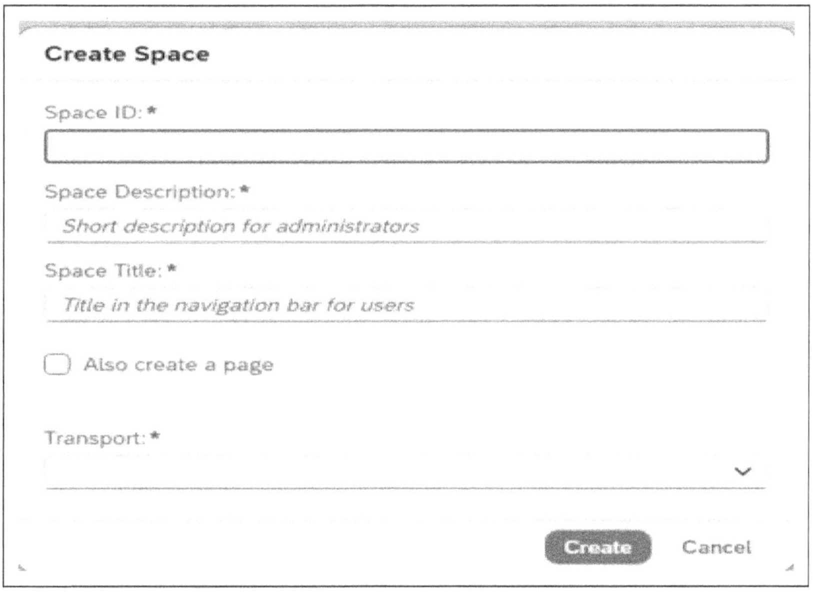

Figure 10-14. *Create Space initial input screen*

The **Create Space** box opens, allowing you to create **spaces and pages** simultaneously. For our purposes, we will create a space only for now and a page separately. Enter the following mandatory information in the above box **Create Space**:

- **Space ID**: ZF_SP_FIN_AR
- **Space Description**: Account Receivable
- **Space Title**: Account Receivable
- **Transport**: S24K900065

483

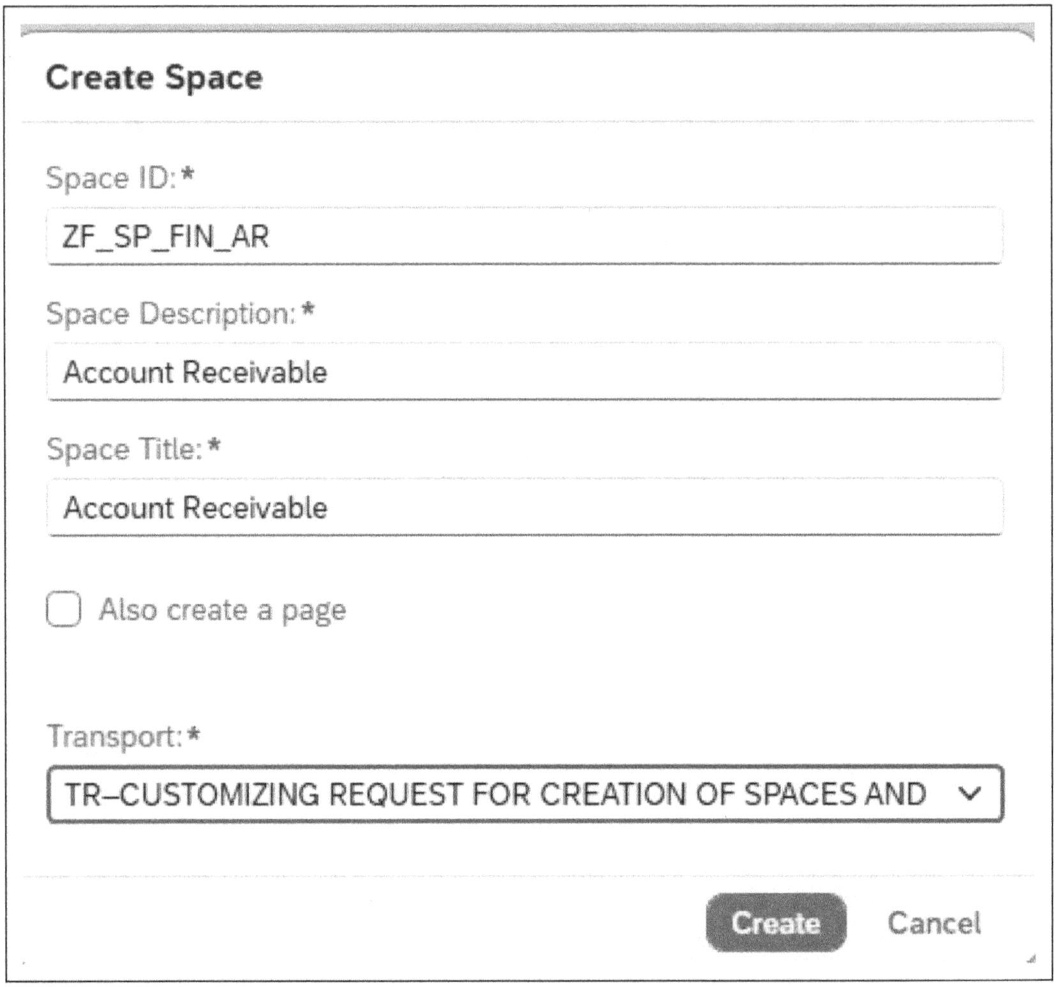

CHAPTER 10 INTRODUCTION TO SAP FIORI SPACES AND PAGES

Create Space

Space ID: *
ZF_SP_FIN_AR

Space Description: *
Account Receivable

Space Title: *
Account Receivable

☐ Also create a page

Transport: *
TR–CUSTOMIZING REQUEST FOR CREATION OF SPACES AND ▼

[Create]   Cancel

Figure 10-15. Space information updated

Note Enter a meaningful description and title. In this example, **Space Description** will appear as **Account Receivable** on the SAP Fiori Launchpad screen navigation bar.

To proceed further, click Create [Create], to create a new **space**.

CHAPTER 10   INTRODUCTION TO SAP FIORI SPACES AND PAGES

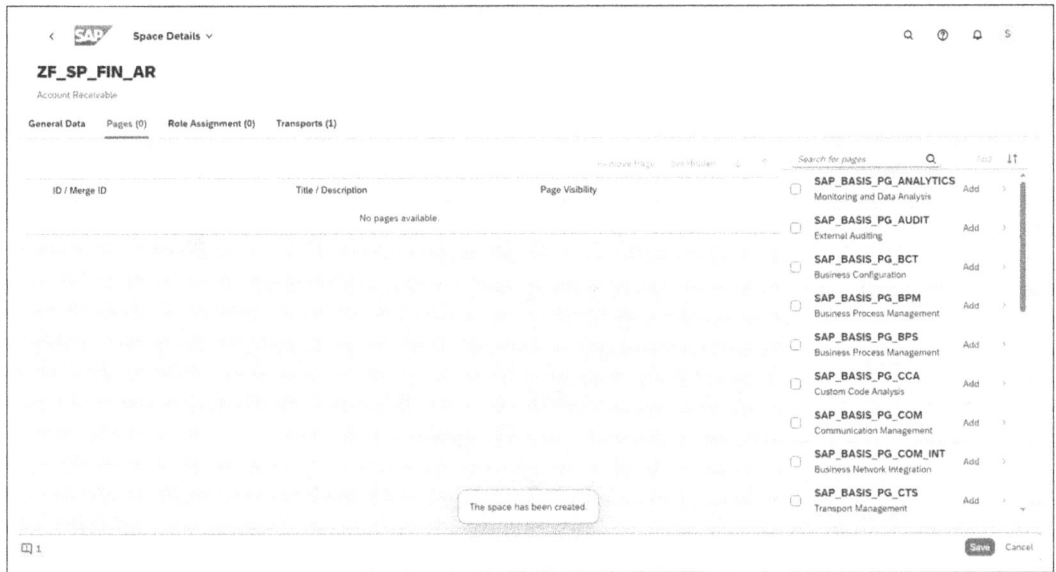

Figure 10-16. The space has been created

The space has been created, and a message box is displayed at the bottom of the screen, as shown in the figure above. Click **Save** at the bottom of the screen to save the **space.** The following figure displays the created **space**.

Figure 10-17. Empty space created with no data

Again, a message is displayed in a box, **Your changes have been saved**, as shown in the figure above. An empty space is created with no data.

485

CHAPTER 10   INTRODUCTION TO SAP FIORI SPACES AND PAGES

The Space Details window as shown in the above figure has four tabs in the navigation bar:

- **General Data:** Displays details of created **spaces**
- **Pages:** Displays details of created and associated **pages**
- **Role Assignment:** Displays details of the role assigned to the **space**
- **Transport:** Displays associated **transport** details for the **space**

The next step is to assign the **space** to a business role. Go back to the initial screen of transaction /**UI2/FLP.** Then, launch the **Manage Launchpad Spaces** app, and you will find the space that was created, as shown in the figure below.

Figure 10-18. *Manage Launchpad Spaces window displaying the recently created space*

The above figure displays the recently created **space** called **ZF_SP_FIN_AR**. Select the space and click the **pencil icon** on the right of the screen, which displays options within the **space** created, as shown in the figure below.

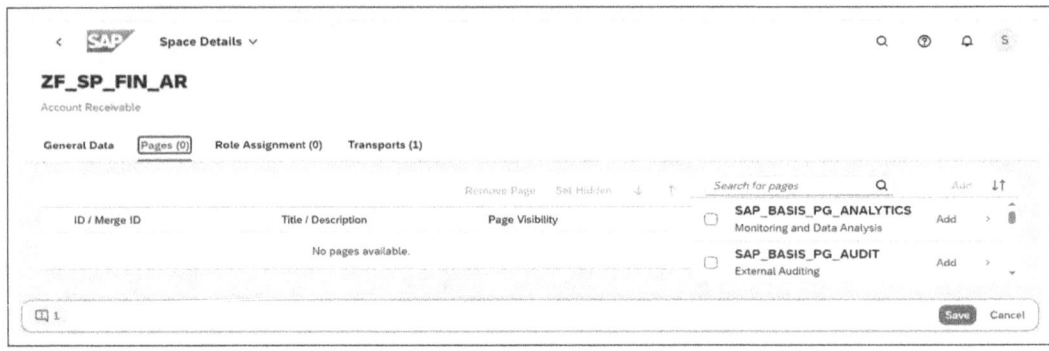

Figure 10-19. *Space Details window displayed*

486

CHAPTER 10   INTRODUCTION TO SAP FIORI SPACES AND PAGES

At the top of the screen in the figure above, it displays **Pages (0), Role Assignment (0),** and **Transports (1)**. This implies that the **space** has been created without any pages or roles assigned. The space has been assigned only to a transport.

The next step is to assign the **space** to a **custom business role**. The assignment can be done in two ways using the following transactions:

- **PFCG**
- **/UI2/FLPCM_CUST**

Transaction: PFCG

Note   As creating roles is outside the scope of this book, we are using an existing role for our purposes.

Execute the transaction **PFCG,** then enter the business role name, and then select **Menu ▶ Transaction ▶ SAP Fiori Launchpad ▶ Launchpad Space**, as shown in the figure below.

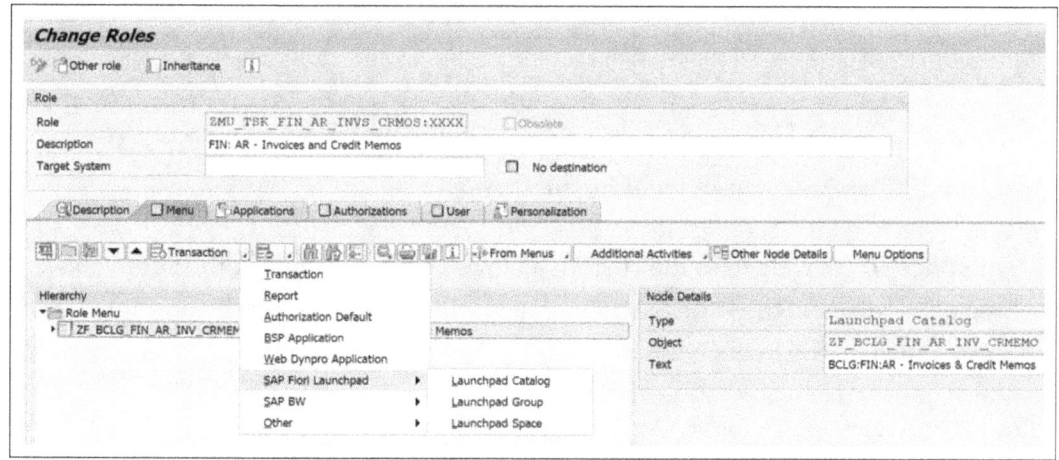

Figure 10-20. Option to assign a Launchpad space to a business role

Selecting the Launchpad Space option will open a box titled **Assign SAP Fiori Launchpad Space**. Enter the **space ID**, **ZF_SP_FIN_AR,** created earlier, as shown in the figure below.

CHAPTER 10　INTRODUCTION TO SAP FIORI SPACES AND PAGES

Figure 10-21. Assign SAP Fiori Launchpad Space

Click the **continue** icon, and a message is displayed at the bottom of the screen, **Entry Created**▬▬▬▬, as shown in the figure below.

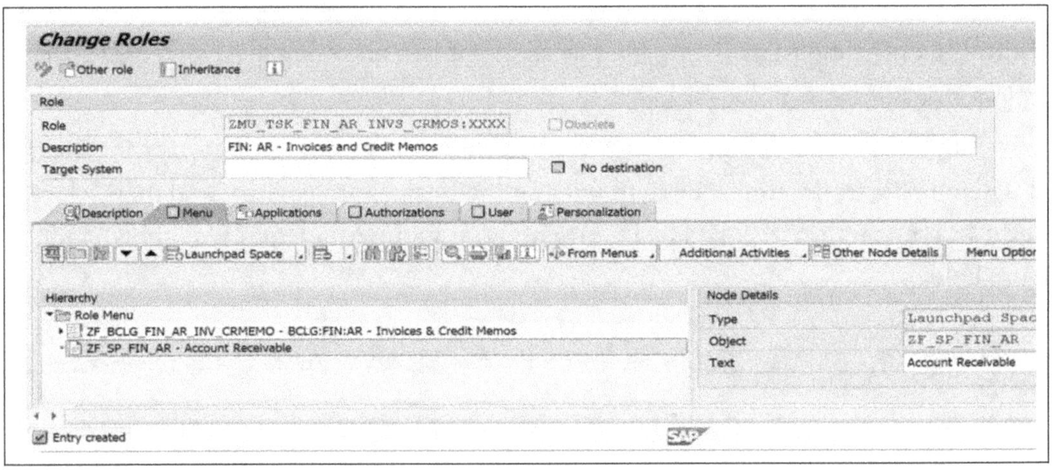

Figure 10-22. Space assigned to a business role

The **space ID** gets added to the custom business role, as shown in the figure above. Now, **save** the role, and the **Data Saved** message will be displayed at the bottom of the screen, as shown in the figure below.

488

CHAPTER 10　INTRODUCTION TO SAP FIORI SPACES AND PAGES

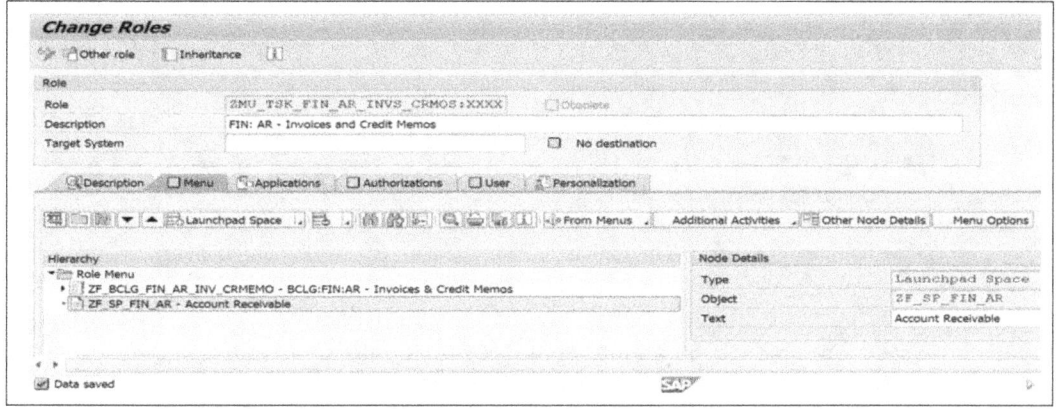

Figure 10-23. *Business role saved along with the space ID*

The above figure illustrates that the **space ID** has been added to the custom business role. The custom business role now includes the **SAP Fiori space**, serving as a container for **pages** and apps. Users with this role will see the **space and its pages** in their Fiori Launchpad, provided they are correctly assigned. This structure organizes apps visually (**Space ➤ Page ➤ Sections ➤ Apps**) forr a more streamlined experience than a flat list of tiles.

Note Since a **space ID** is simply a **container** that does not create any **authorization**, the **role** does not need to be **generated**.

Transaction: /UI2/FLPCM_CUST

The second method of assigning a space to a business role is by using transaction **/UI2/FLPCM_CUST.**

Execute the transaction /UI2/FLPCM_CUST, then enter the **business role name** in the **Search Roles** field, and click **Go**, as shown in the figure below.

489

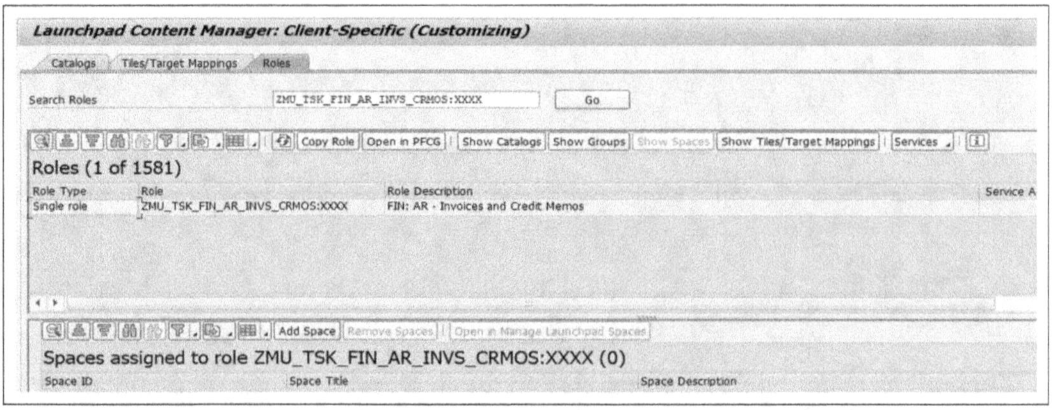

CHAPTER 10   INTRODUCTION TO SAP FIORI SPACES AND PAGES

Figure 10-24. Transaction /UI2/FLPCM_CUST displaying the custom business role and associated business catalog details

Reviewing the above figure, it is evident that the business role has no assigned space, as indicated by the display of **Spaces assigned to role ZMU_TSK_FIN_AR_INVS_CRMOS:XXXX (0)**. Select the tab Show Spaces Show Spaces. A new **Add Space** Add Space tab appears. By selecting the **Add Space** tab, a box titled **Add Space to Role** appears, as shown in the figure below.

Figure 10-25. Add Space to Role option

Enter the **space ID** directly or search for the ID from the search option, as shown in the figure below.

CHAPTER 10 INTRODUCTION TO SAP FIORI SPACES AND PAGES

Figure 10-26. *Add the space ID to the role*

The above figure displays the added **space ID**. Click the **continue** icon, and the **space** is added to the role, as indicated by the message displayed at the bottom of the screen, **Space 'ZF_SP_FIN_AR' added to role 'ZMU_TSK_FIN_AR_INVS_CRMOS:XXXX'**, as shown in the figure below. The figure also indicates that the role has one space assigned to it.

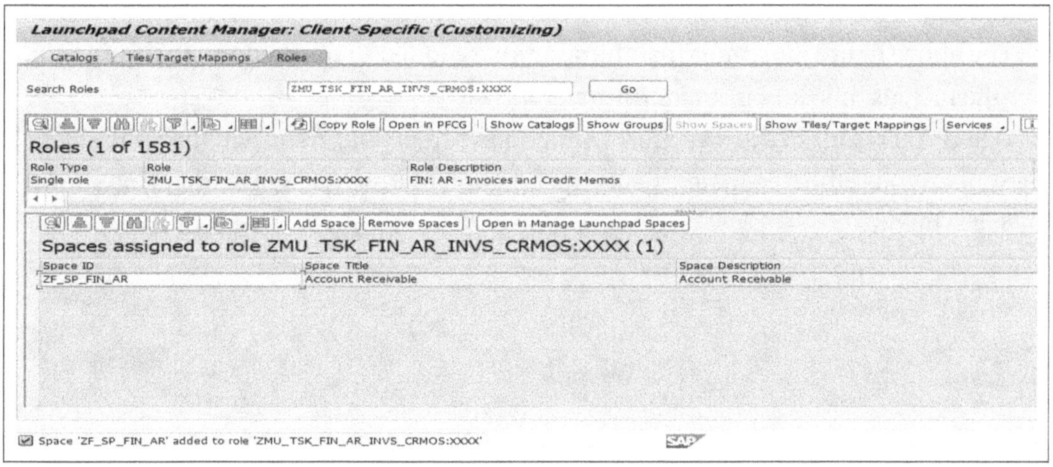

Figure 10-27. *Space added to the custom business role*

Verify that the **space** has been added in transaction **PFCG** and the **space ID** has been assigned to the **role**, as shown in the figure below.

491

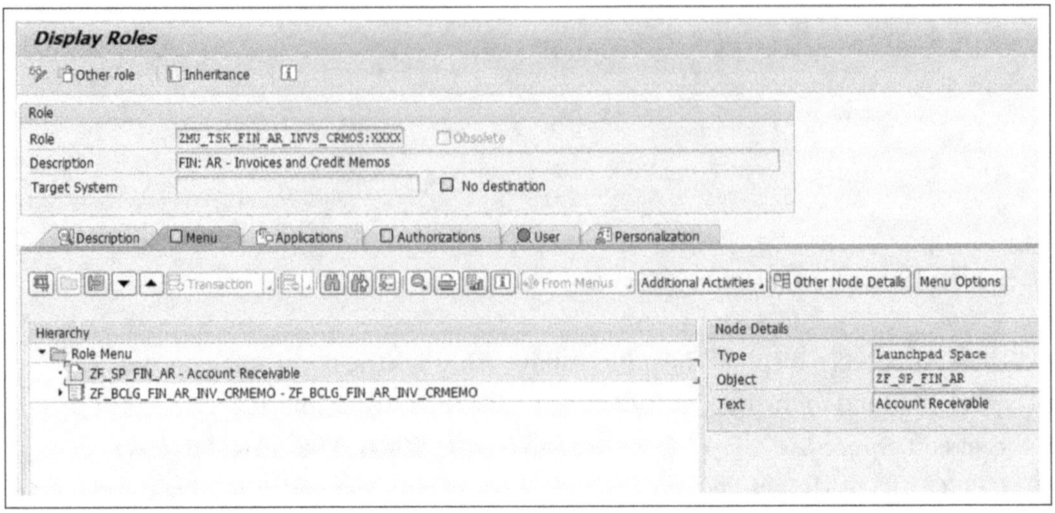

CHAPTER 10   INTRODUCTION TO SAP FIORI SPACES AND PAGES

Figure 10-28. Custom business role updated with the space

The above figure illustrates that the **space** was added to the **custom business role**. Save the role, as this does not require generating it.

When you return to the SAP Fiori Launchpad screen and refresh it, the Space Details page reloads, and the role assignments are updated to **Role Assignment (1)**, as shown in the figure below.

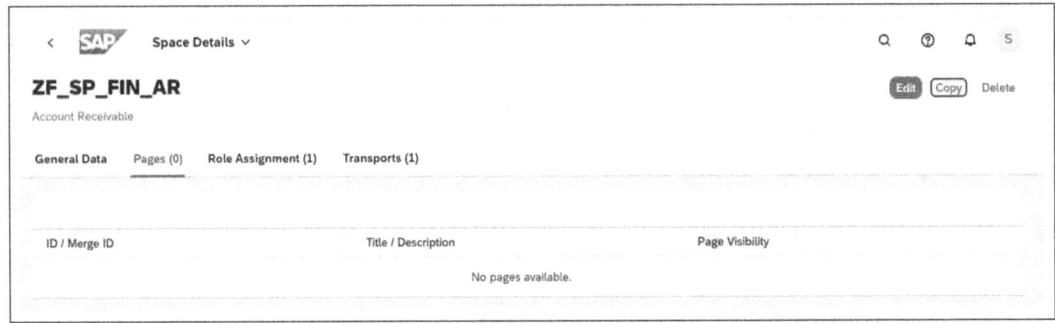

Figure 10-29. Space Details page updated with role assignment

492

CHAPTER 10 INTRODUCTION TO SAP FIORI SPACES AND PAGES

The figure above shows that the **role assignment** has been updated and no **pages** have been maintained as none were created. Selecting the **Role Assignment (1)** tab displays the custom business role name assigned to the **space**, as shown in the figure below.

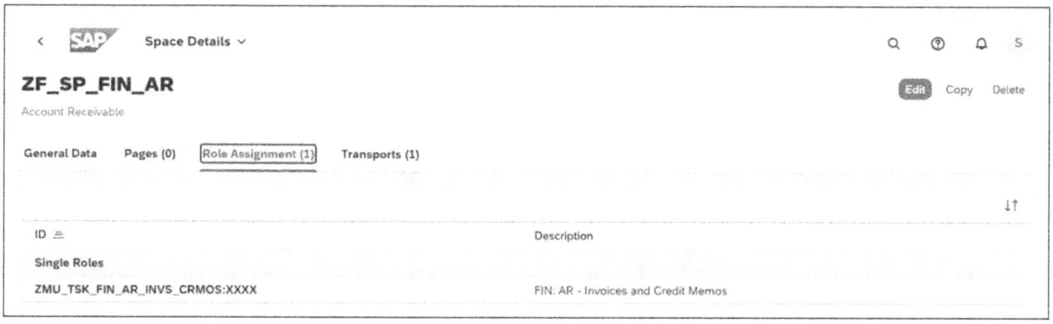

Figure 10-30. Role assigned to the space

The **General Data** tab displays the **space ID** information, which can be updated, if necessary, as shown in the figure below.

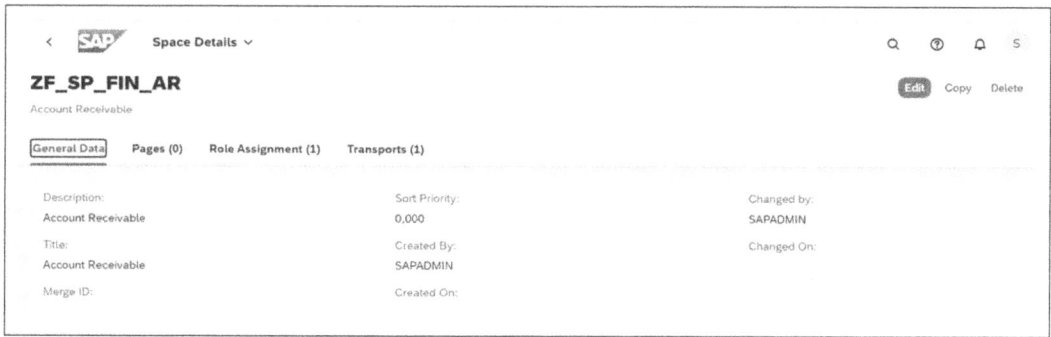

Figure 10-31. General Data tab within the space

In the **General Data** tab, update the Description and Title from **Account Receivable** to **Accounts Receivable** and **save** the changes. A message box appears, stating **Your changes have been saved**, as shown in the figure below.

493

CHAPTER 10 INTRODUCTION TO SAP FIORI SPACES AND PAGES

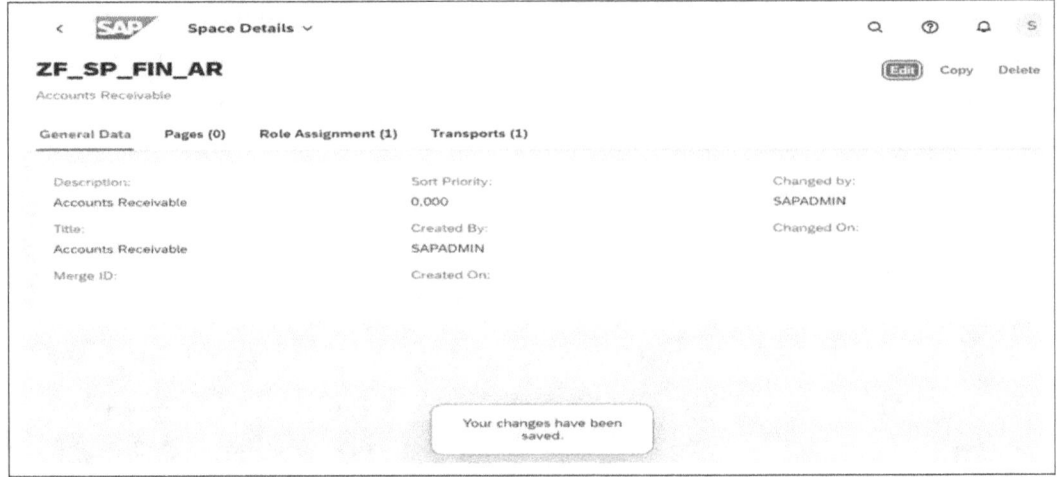

Figure 10-32. *Space changes for Description and Title*

The updated space details are shown in the figure below.

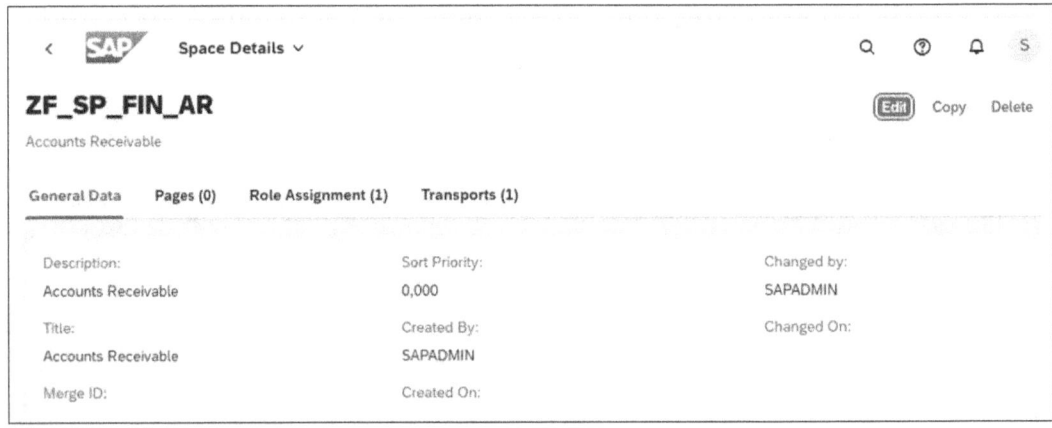

Figure 10-33. *Space details updated*

Note Similarly, update the **descriptions** of the other spaces created.

CHAPTER 10   INTRODUCTION TO SAP FIORI SPACES AND PAGES

In the above figure, we observe that no **page** has been added to the **space ID**, as it displays **Page(0)**, as shown in the figure below.

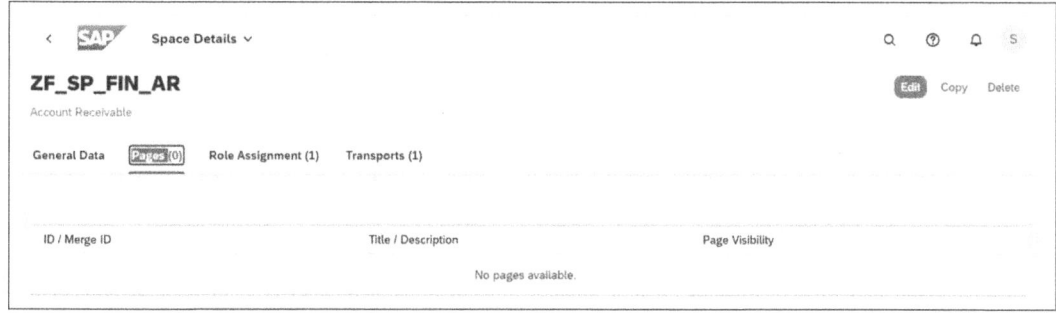

Figure 10-34. No page assigned to the space

10.8.2 Create a Page

To create a new **page**, open the **Manage Launchpad Pages** app from the Fiori Launchpad screen, as shown in the figure below.

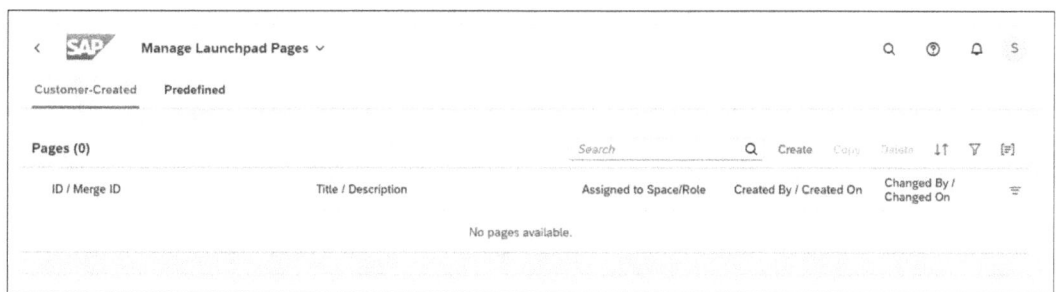

Figure 10-35. Page maintenance input screen

Select **Create** from the right-hand corner of the screen to create a new **page**. A new box titled **Create Page** opens, where we enter **page** information, as shown in the figure below.

495

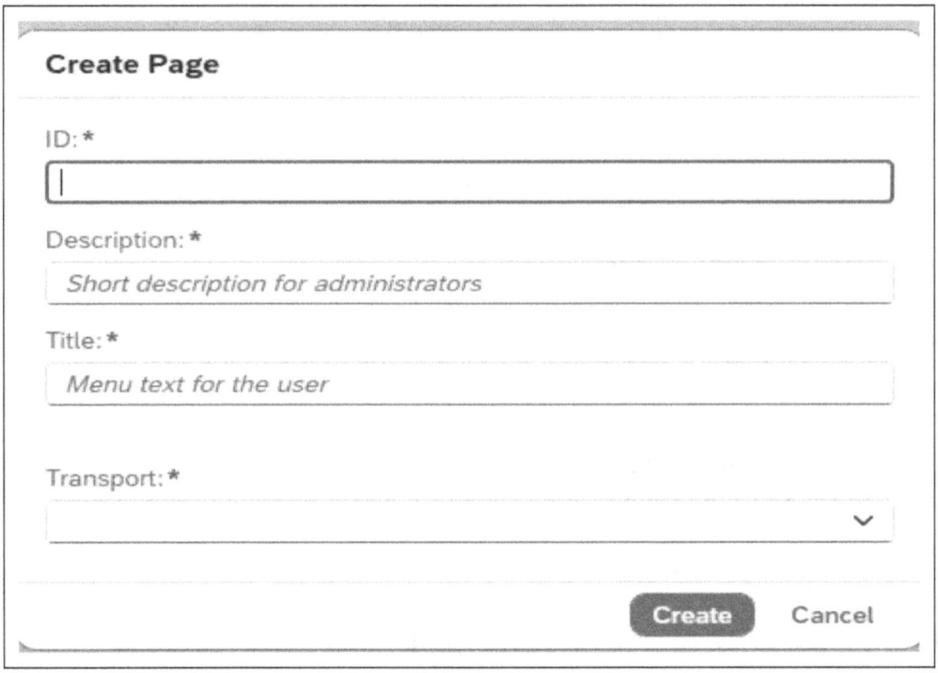

CHAPTER 10 INTRODUCTION TO SAP FIORI SPACES AND PAGES

Figure 10-36. Create Page box to enter page details

For our example, we will enter the following information, as shown in the figure below:

- **ID:** ZF_PG_1_ FIN_AR
- **Description:** AR - Invoices and Credit Memos Posting
- **Title:** AR - Invoices and Credit Memos Posting
- **Transport:** S24K00065

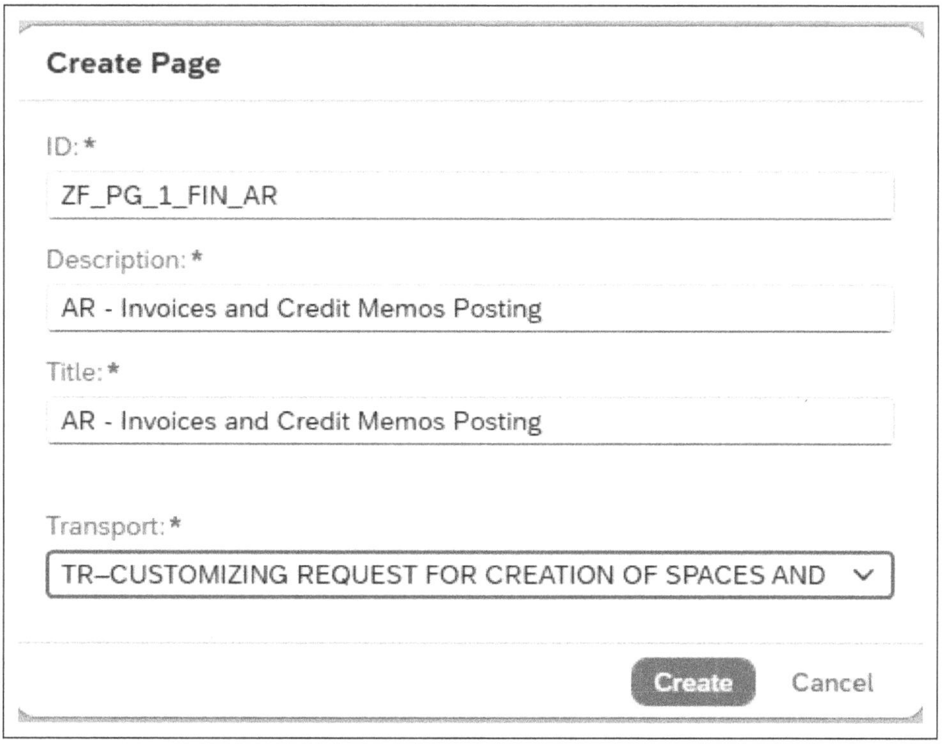

CHAPTER 10　INTRODUCTION TO SAP FIORI SPACES AND PAGES

Figure 10-37. Information of the page to be created added

To proceed further, click Create [Create], to create a new **page**.

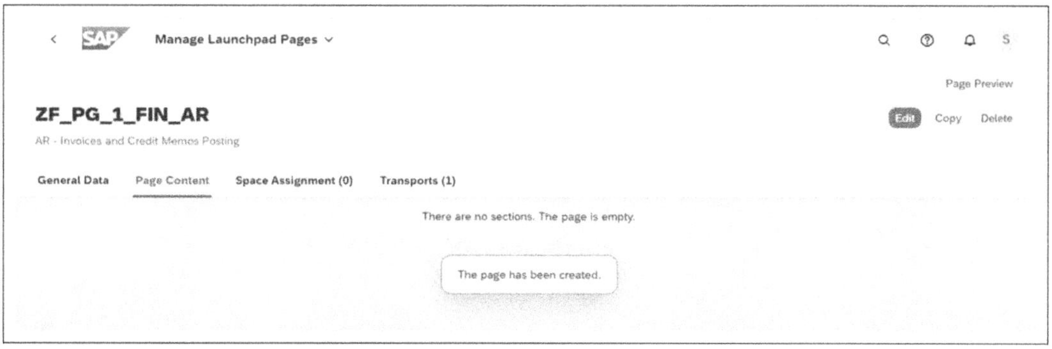

Figure 10-38. A custom page has been created

A message stating **The page has been created** is shown in the figure above. Within the page, **Page Content** is empty, and **Space Assignment (0)** indicates the page has no spaces assigned, as depicted in the figure below.

497

CHAPTER 10   INTRODUCTION TO SAP FIORI SPACES AND PAGES

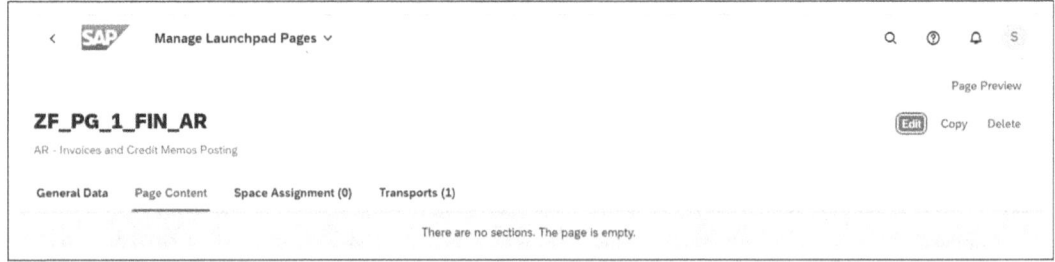

Figure 10-39. *Page created with empty Page Content and no spaces assigned*

The **page** created needs to be linked to the **space**, and this is accomplished by launching the **Manage Launchpad Spaces app**. The **Manage Launchpad Spaces** screen will then open, as shown in the figure below.

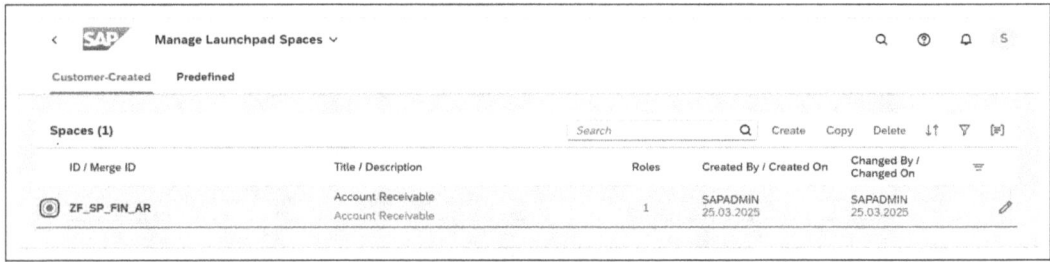

Figure 10-40. *Manage Launchpad Spaces opens from within Manage Launchpad Pages*

The system displays only one **space**, as only one **space** has been created. Now select the radio button of the **space** called **ZF_SP_FIN_AR** and click the **pencil icon** to edit, which opens the option **Page (0)** to assign the **page** to the **space**, as shown in the figure below.

CHAPTER 10   INTRODUCTION TO SAP FIORI SPACES AND PAGES

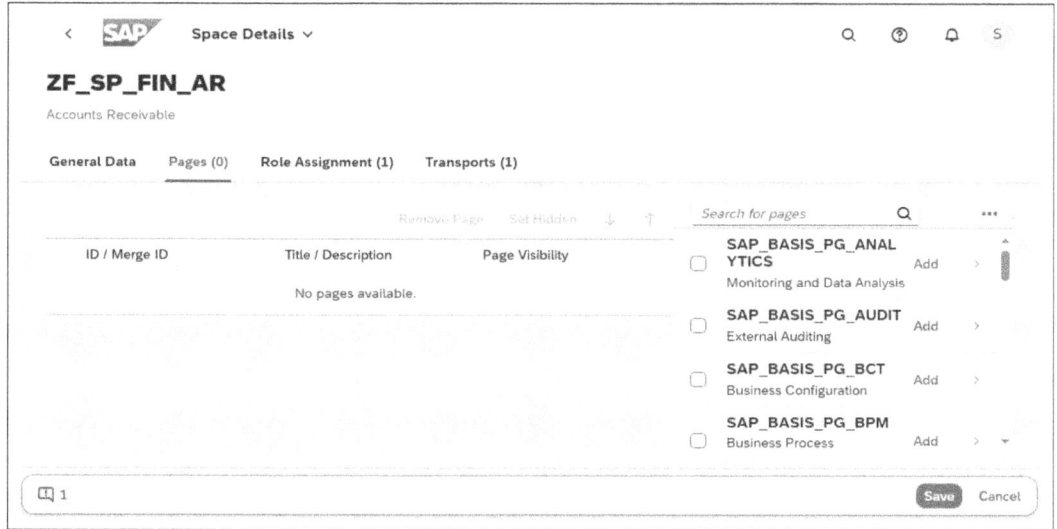

Figure 10-41.   Input screen to assign the page to the space

Note   The issue symbol ⊡1, when selected, opens a box stating **This space has no visible pages**, as shown in the figure below.

499

CHAPTER 10   INTRODUCTION TO SAP FIORI SPACES AND PAGES

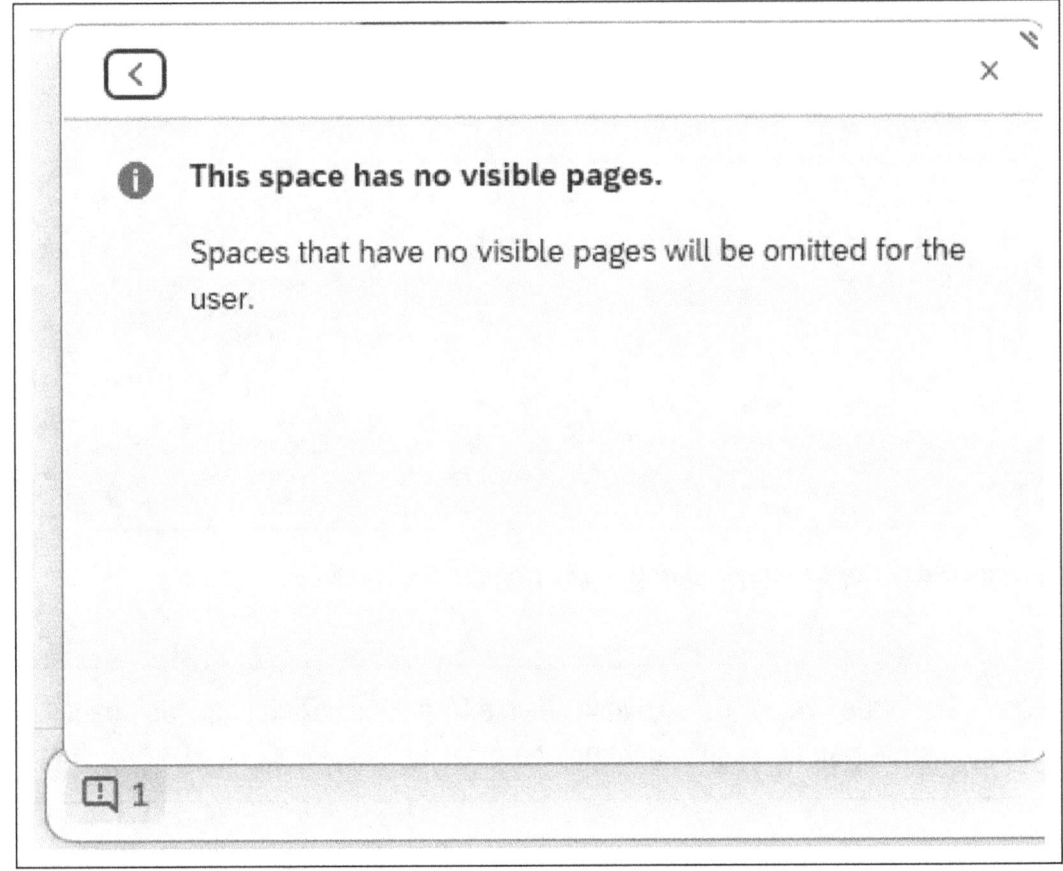

Figure 10-42. Issue encountered - no page visible in the space

The above screen displays **SAP-delivered pages** for searching. Now, search for your page using **Search for pages** by entering the information **ZF_PG**, and the **page** is displayed with the **page ID ZF_PG_1_AR** found. **Select** the **page** as shown in the figure below.

CHAPTER 10   INTRODUCTION TO SAP FIORI SPACES AND PAGES

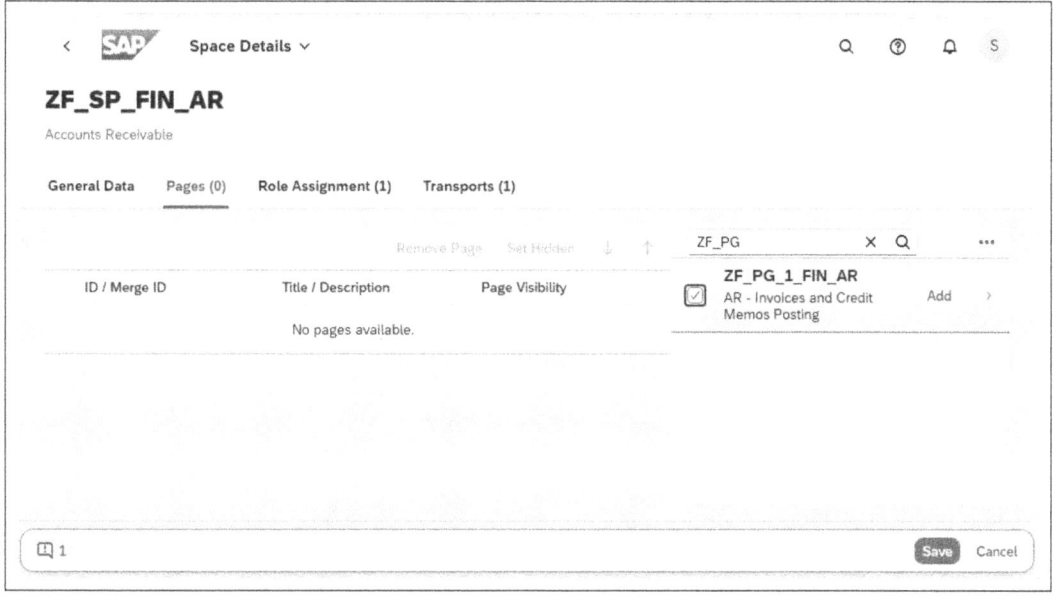

Figure 10-43.   Page ID selected

To add or link the **page** to the **space**, select the **Add** option in the top-right corner of the screen. A message box will appear stating **Page added,** as shown in the figure below.

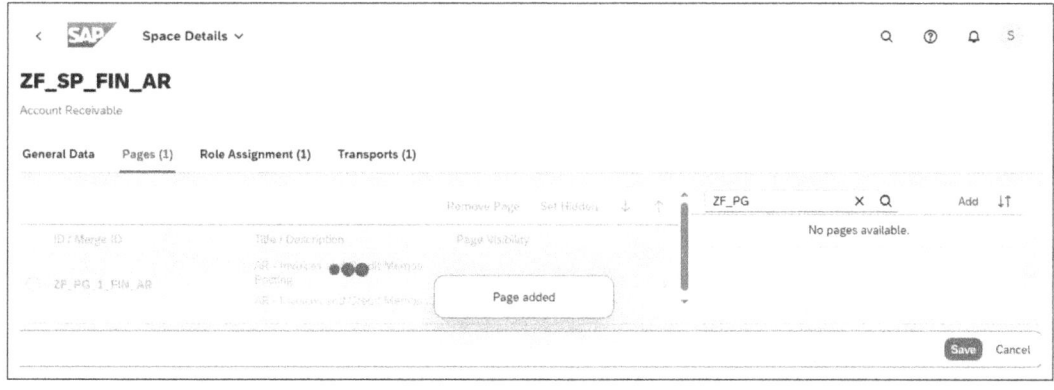

Figure 10-44.   Page added to the space

501

CHAPTER 10 INTRODUCTION TO SAP FIORI SPACES AND PAGES

The **page** is added and updated in the **space**, as shown in the figure below.

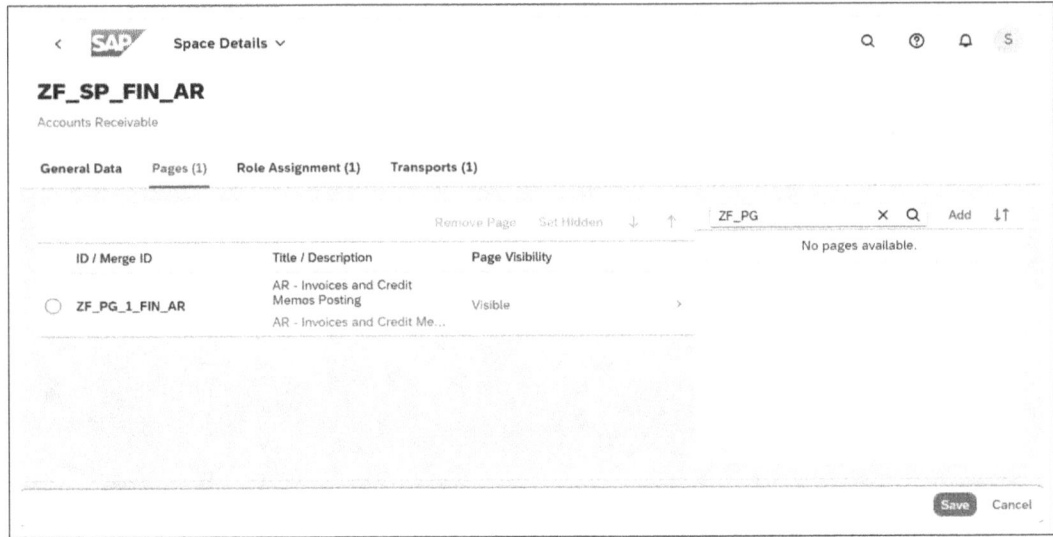

Figure 10-45. *Page is added and updated in the space*

To save your changes, click **Save** at the bottom of the screen. A message box will appear, stating **Your changes have been saved**, as shown in the figure below.

Note You can hide a page by selecting the page and clicking the **Set Hidden** option.

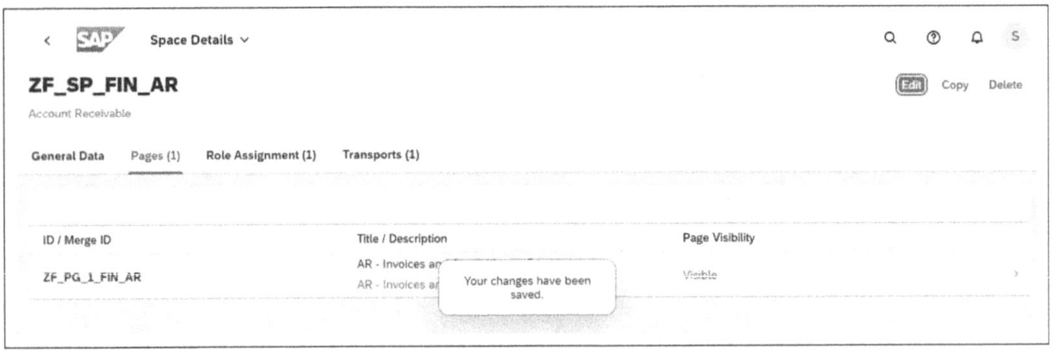

Figure 10-46. *Page has been saved to the space*

502

CHAPTER 10 INTRODUCTION TO SAP FIORI SPACES AND PAGES

The **space** is updated with the **page**, and the tab at the top displays **Page (1)**, as shown in the figure below.

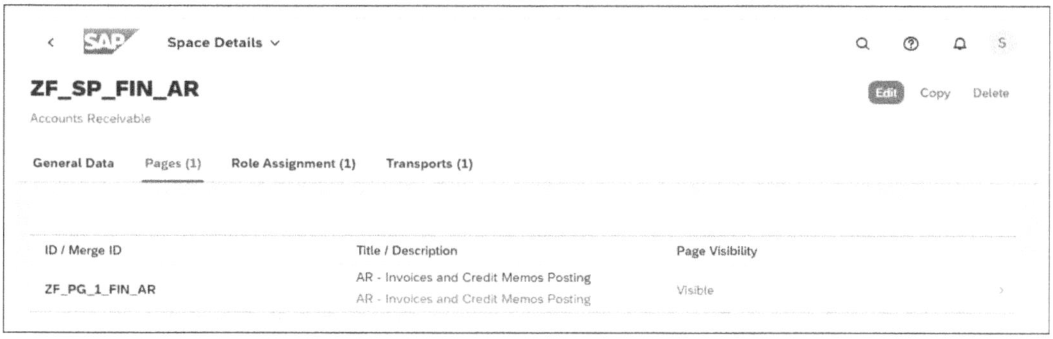

Figure 10-47. Space updated with the page

The above figure indicates that the **page** has been assigned the **space** and is **visible**. Now, go back to the Manage Launchpad Pages app, which displays the **page** recently created and saved, as shown in the figure below.

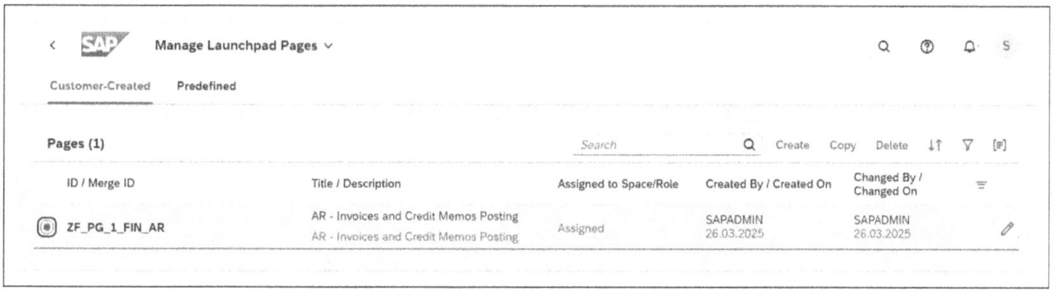

Figure 10-48. Page displayed in the Manage Launchpad Pages app

The above figure displays that the **page** has been **assigned** under the column heading named **Assigned to Space/Role**. To make changes, select the radio button for the page and click the **pencil icon**. This will open the **custom business catalog**, displaying all the apps that can be assigned to the page, as shown in the figure below.

503

CHAPTER 10 INTRODUCTION TO SAP FIORI SPACES AND PAGES

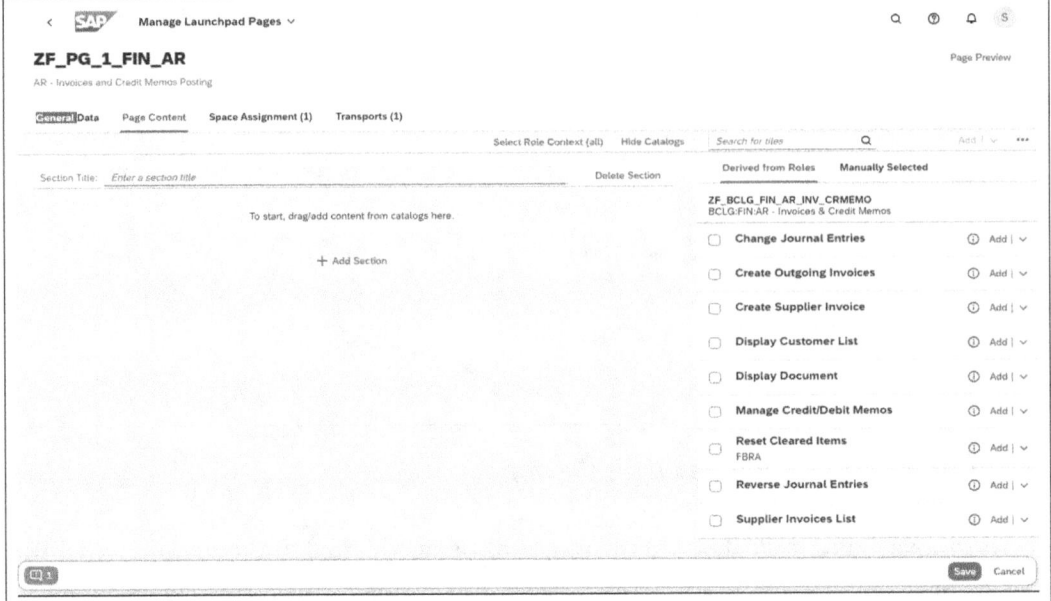

Figure 10-49. Window to assign apps to the page

The system pulls all the apps maintained in the custom business catalog and displays them on the right-hand panel. The tiles or apps displayed on the right-hand side of the screen can be added to the **page** via a **section**. You can select tiles or apps from a set of catalogs based on the business role(s) for which this page was created.

> **Note** This app fully adheres to the principle of what you see is what you get (**WYSIWYG**). Not all apps are assigned to the user. Users can search for apps in the **App Finder**, followed by the business catalog, and then search for specific tiles or apps.

SAP recommends the following best practices for assigning apps to a section. Update **pages** with apps as per SAP best practices as follows:

- Do not use the same title for both the space and the page, as the same title may confuse other users. All **page** and **space** titles must be unique from each other.

- A **page** should not have more than **25 apps**.

- A page should have **two to five sections**.

- A **section** should have **three to eight apps**.

CHAPTER 10   INTRODUCTION TO SAP FIORI SPACES AND PAGES

Note   It is also recommended to review all existing **spaces** and **pages** provided in the SAP business role, starting with those based on **SAP_BR***, to understand their functionality.

10.8.3 Create Sections

The next step is to create **sections**. For our example, we will create the following sections:

- Overview
- Invoice and Credit Memos Posting
- Document Reversal & Reset
- Document Change & Display
- Customer Details

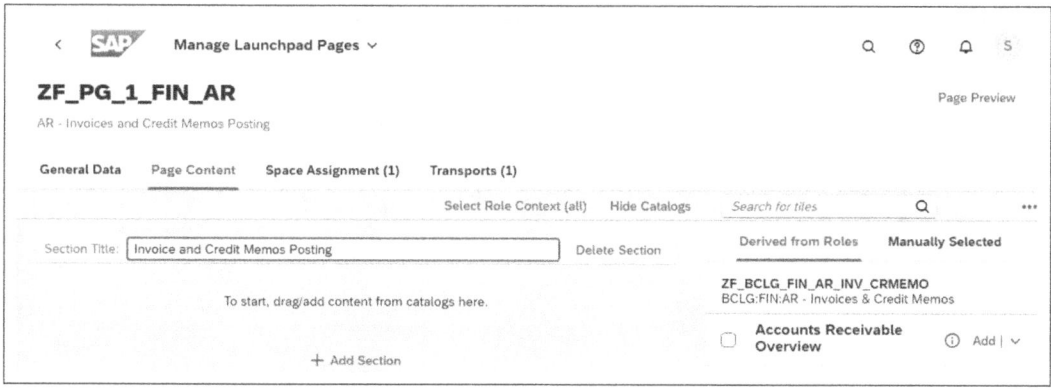

Figure 10-50.   First section title added to the page

To add another **section**, click the option labeled **+ Add Section**, and then enter the title of the new section, as shown in the figure below.

505

CHAPTER 10   INTRODUCTION TO SAP FIORI SPACES AND PAGES

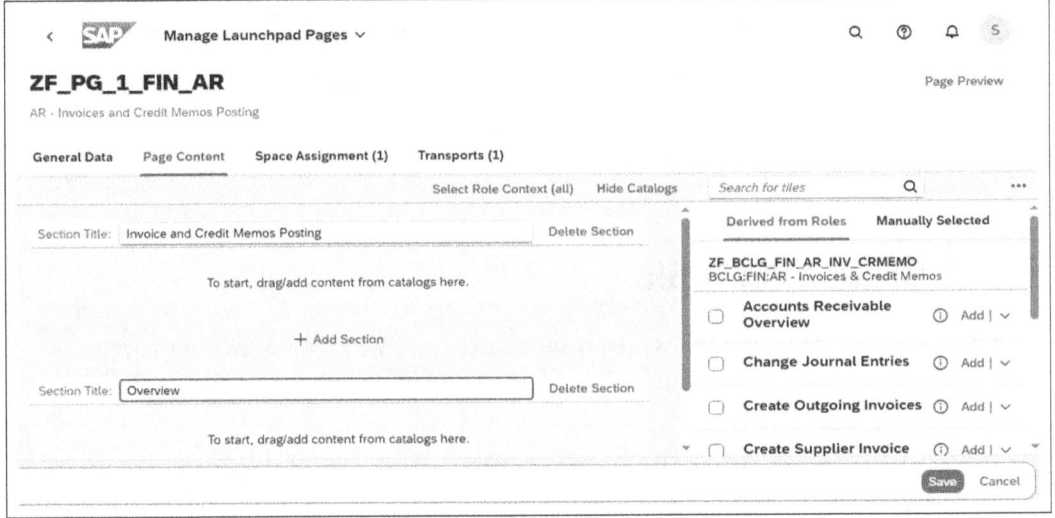

Figure 10-51. Second section title added to the page

You can change the order of sections by selecting a section and dragging it up or down. In this case, drag the **Overview** section to the top of the page. The updated section order is shown in the figure below.

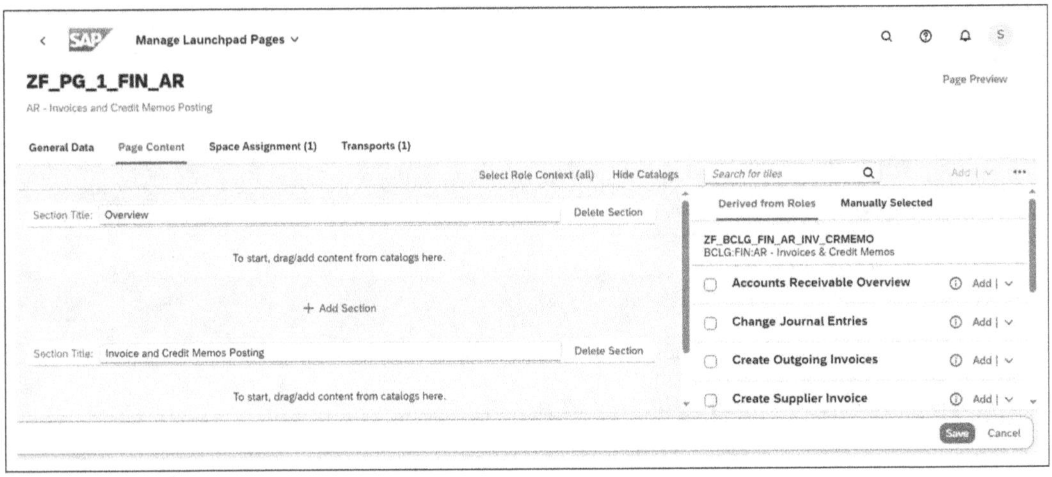

Figure 10-52. Section order changed

The figure above illustrates the change in the order of the sections and displays it accordingly. By creating the new **sections** and saving the changes, a box will appear with a message stating **Your changes have been saved**, as illustrated in the figure below.

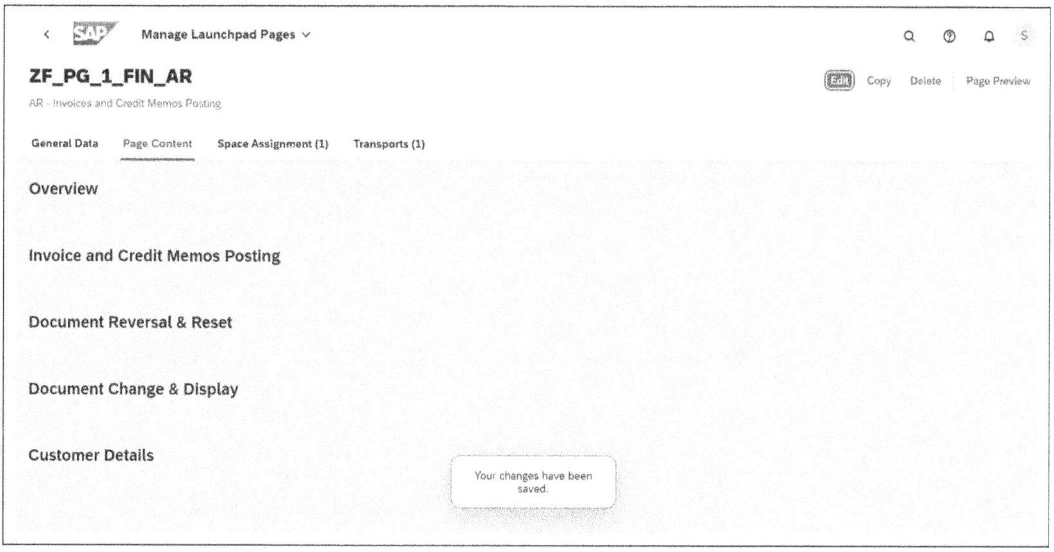

Figure 10-53. A couple of sections created and saved

> **Note** Use the option **Delete Section** for deleting a **section**, if needed.

To add apps to the **Overview** section, click the **Edit** tab. This will direct you to the screen below, where you can add apps.

CHAPTER 10   INTRODUCTION TO SAP FIORI SPACES AND PAGES

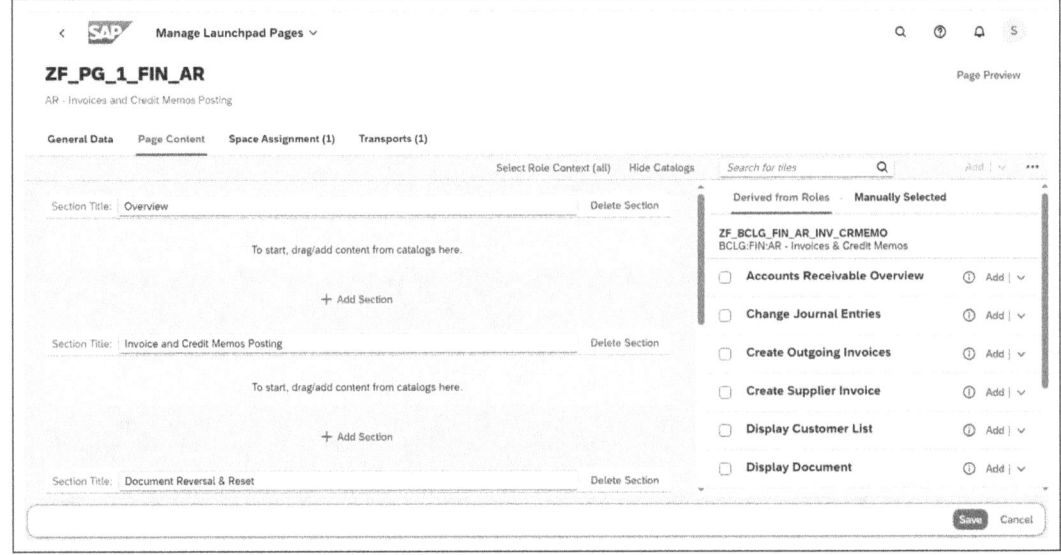

Figure 10-54. Window to add apps to the section within the page

To add an app to the **section**, select the app and then click the down arrowhead next to the **Add** option, as shown in the figure below.

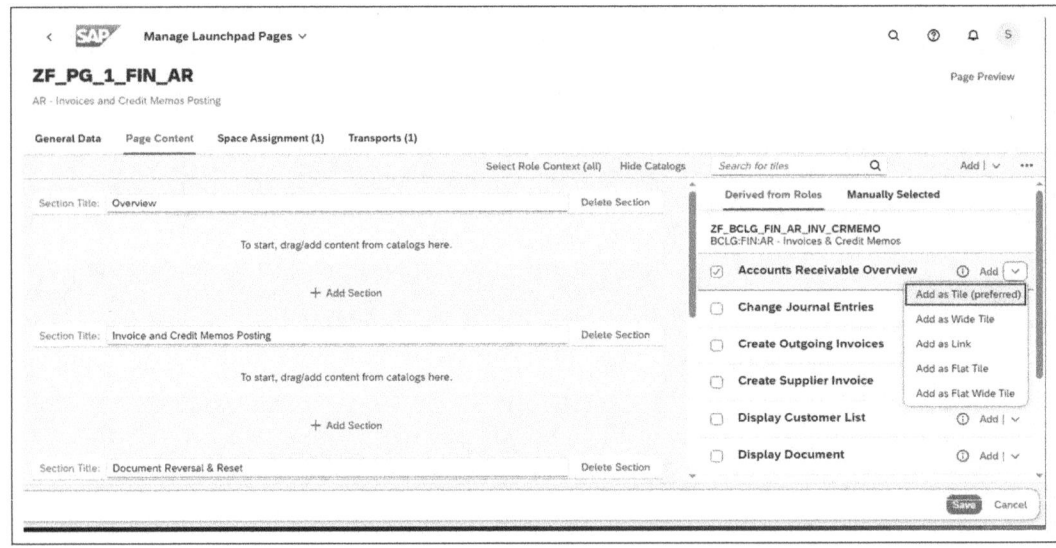

Figure 10-55. Various format options are available to add apps

CHAPTER 10   INTRODUCTION TO SAP FIORI SPACES AND PAGES

There are **five** options available for adding an **app** to the **section**, as listed below and illustrated in the figure above:

- Add as Tile (preferred)
- Add as Wide Tile
- Add as Link
- Add as Flat Tile
- Add as Flat Wide Tile

You can also use the **drag-and-drop method** to add the app. In this case, hover over the section title, Overview, and drop it. The app will be added as shown in the figure below.

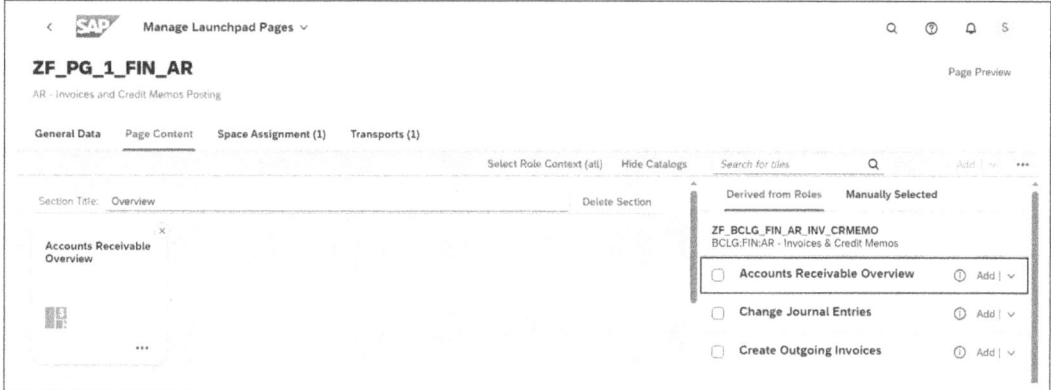

Figure 10-56. *App added to the section by the drag-and-drop method*

The tile or app was added to the section in the format called **Tile (preferred)**, as shown in the figure. Selecting the **three dots** ⋯ on the app displayed provides Visualization Option, which determines how tiles appear on the Fiori Launchpad, as shown in the figure below.

509

CHAPTER 10   INTRODUCTION TO SAP FIORI SPACES AND PAGES

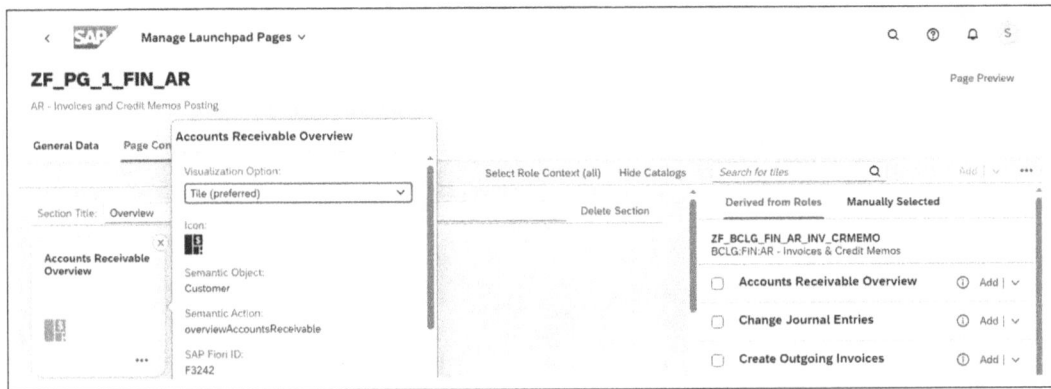

Figure 10-57.   Three dots option available for app visualization

In the above figure, expanding **Visualization Option** allows you to select a different option for viewing the tiles or apps, as shown in the figure below.

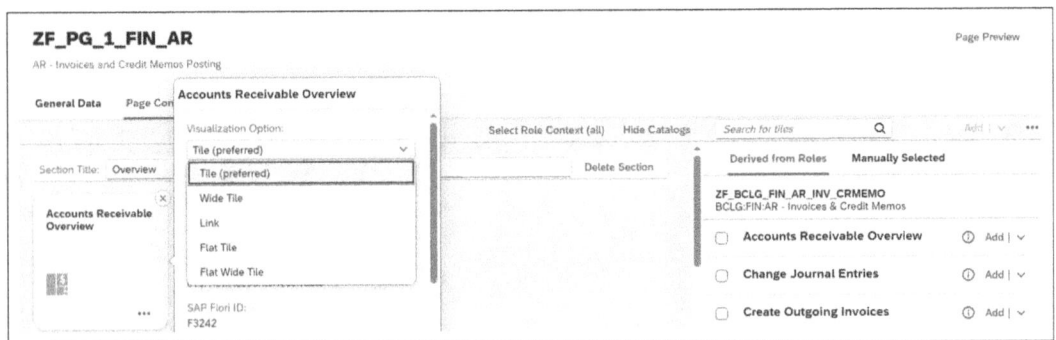

Figure 10-58.   Displays tile visualization format options available

In the figure above, select your preferred format from **Visualization Option**. The tiles or apps will then be added to the section in the chosen format. For this example, select the **Wide Tile** option. As a result, the tiles or apps displayed as **Tile (preferred)** will be replaced, updated, and shown in the selected format, as illustrated in the figure below. The figure below illustrates how the tiles or apps will appear on the Fiori Launchpad for the end user.

510

CHAPTER 10　INTRODUCTION TO SAP FIORI SPACES AND PAGES

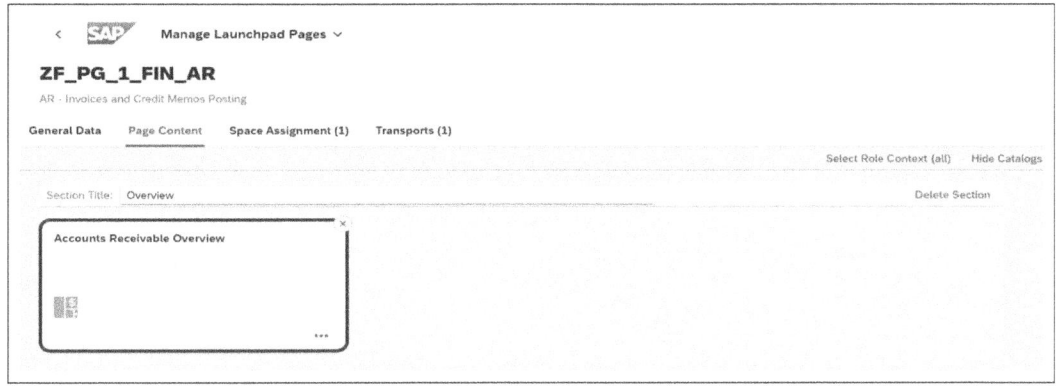

Figure 10-59. *App displayed as Wide Tile*

Select the Flat Wide Tile format option from the pull-down menu to add tiles or apps to the same section or a different section. Once selected, a box titled **Add to Section** will open, listing various section options to insert the app. Select the Invoice and Credit Memos Posting section and click **Add** to insert the app within the **section**. The app is then added, in the format **Flat Wide Tile.** A message appears at the bottom of the screen, stating **Tile added**, as shown in the figure below.

Figure 10-60. *New tile in a new tile format added*

The figure below displays the **five formats** available for viewing tiles or apps on the SAP Fiori Launchpad home page.

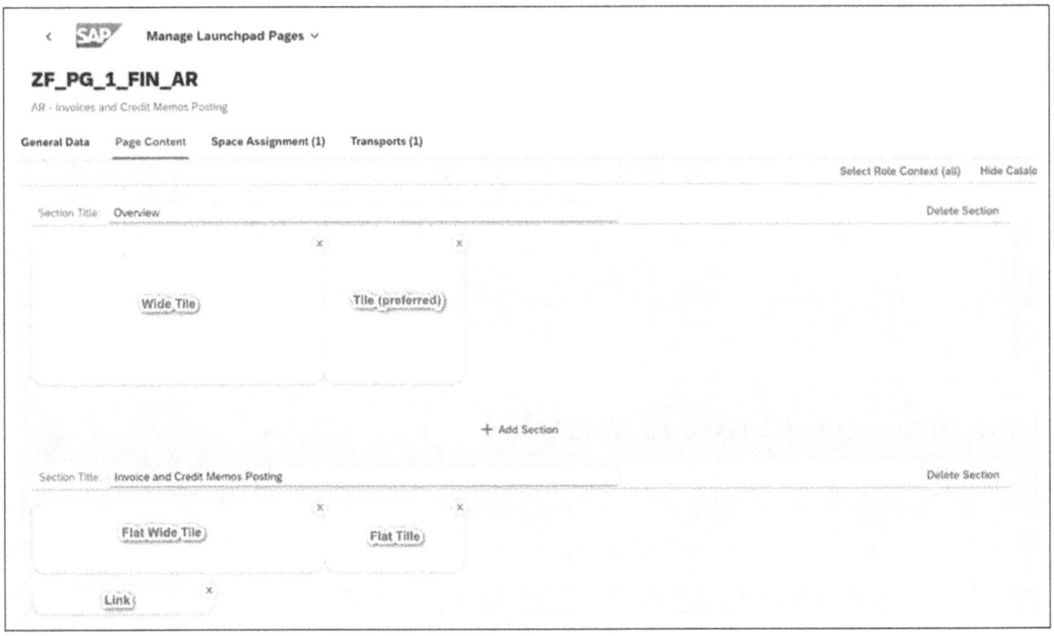

CHAPTER 10 INTRODUCTION TO SAP FIORI SPACES AND PAGES

Figure 10-61. Five app visualization format options are available, as seen by the end user

---

Note You can select multiple tiles or apps and assign them to a section in one go by selecting Add | ∨ ••• in the top right-hand corner of the screen and then selecting the desired **section**.

- Tiles can be moved between **sections** by using the **drag-and-drop** method.

- You can rearrange entire sections by using the **drag-and-drop** method in the order preferred.

- You can also change the order of tiles or apps as to how the apps appear within a **section**.

- You can also find detailed information on **tiles**.

- You can reuse the **pages** in multiple **spaces**, which provides flexibility.

- **Same spaces can be used for multiple roles, hence providing more flexibility.**

CHAPTER 10 INTRODUCTION TO SAP FIORI SPACES AND PAGES

Now add all the tiles or apps into the desired **section** and **save** the changes. A message is displayed stating **Your Changes have been saved** at the bottom of the screen, as shown in the figure below.

Figure 10-62. Page changes saved

The final section layout updated with the correct apps and tiles is shown in the figure below.

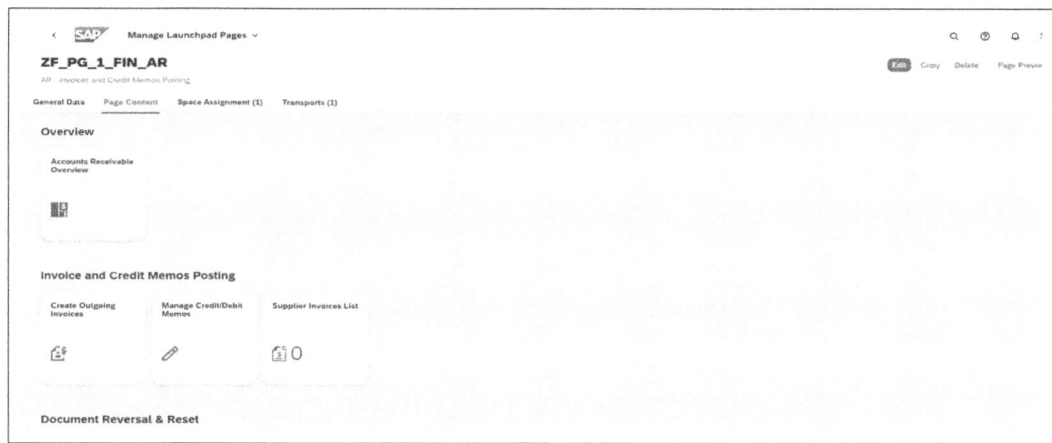

Figure 10-63. Final page output screen

513

Select the **Page Preview** option in the top-right corner to view how the **page** will appear on the SAP Fiori Launchpad home page, as shown in the figure below.

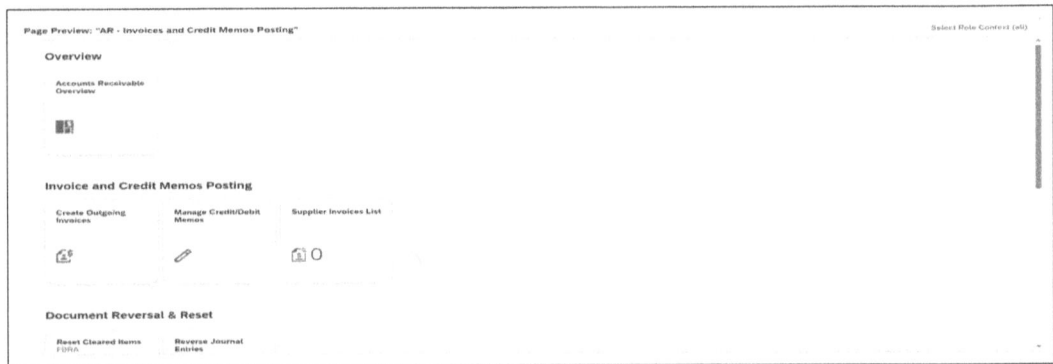

Figure 10-64. *Page Preview as to how the page will appear on the SAP Fiori Launchpad home page*

10.8.4 Testing and Validation

We will use test user ID **TESTSPPG** with the following roles assigned, as shown in the figure below, to test and validate the space and page created earlier.

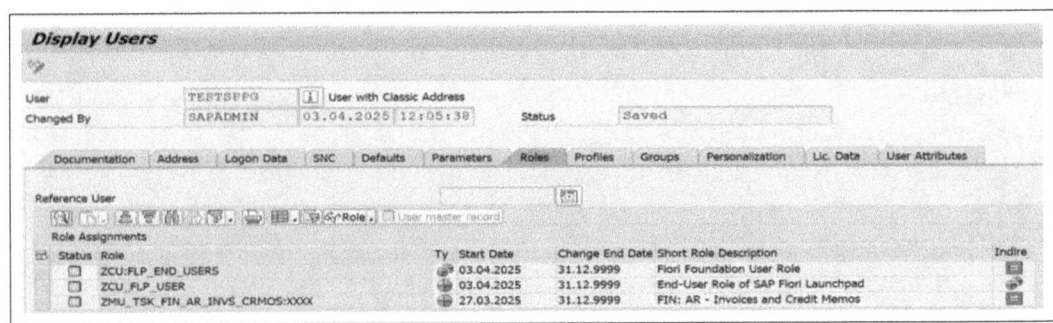

Figure 10-65. *Test user ID with roles assigned*

The test user logs into the **SAP Fiori Launchpad home page**, which displays the **content** along with **spaces** and **pages**, as shown in the figure below.

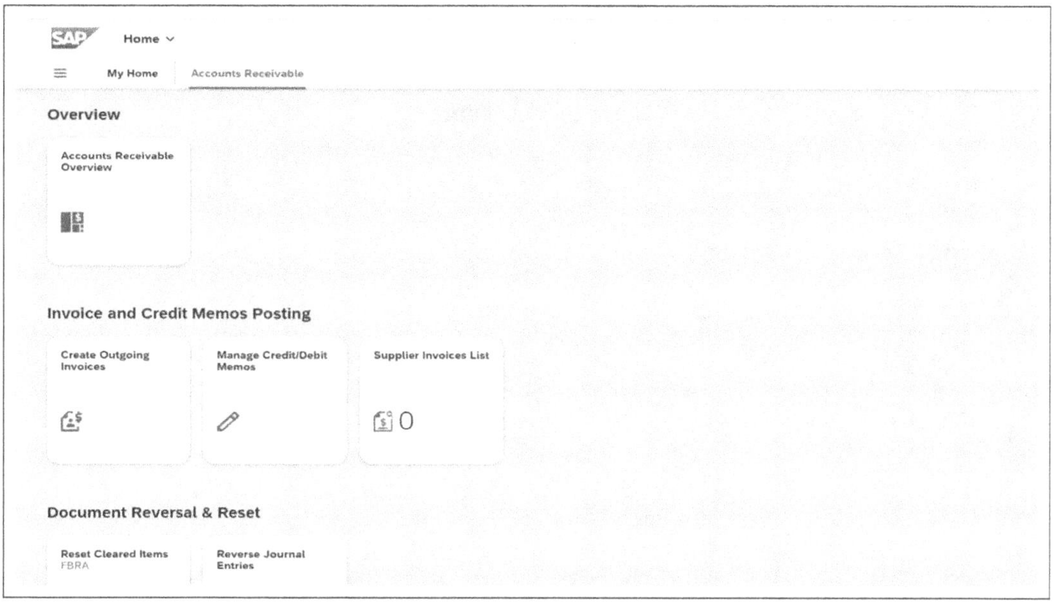

CHAPTER 10   INTRODUCTION TO SAP FIORI SPACES AND PAGES

Figure 10-66. *Test user Fiori Launchpad with spaces and pages displayed*

In the figure above, the **space** is **flat** as it contains only one **page** and has no **pull-down** option available. To enable this feature, we need to create an additional **page** and link it to the **space**.

Furthermore, if the **Spaces and Pages** option does not appear on the SAP Fiori Launchpad, click the **User Menu**, followed by **Settings**, which opens the **Settings** window. Then, select the **Spaces and Pages** option, check **Use Spaces**, and **save** the changes. This will enable **Spaces and Pages** to be displayed on the SAP Fiori Launchpad home page, as shown in the figure below.

515

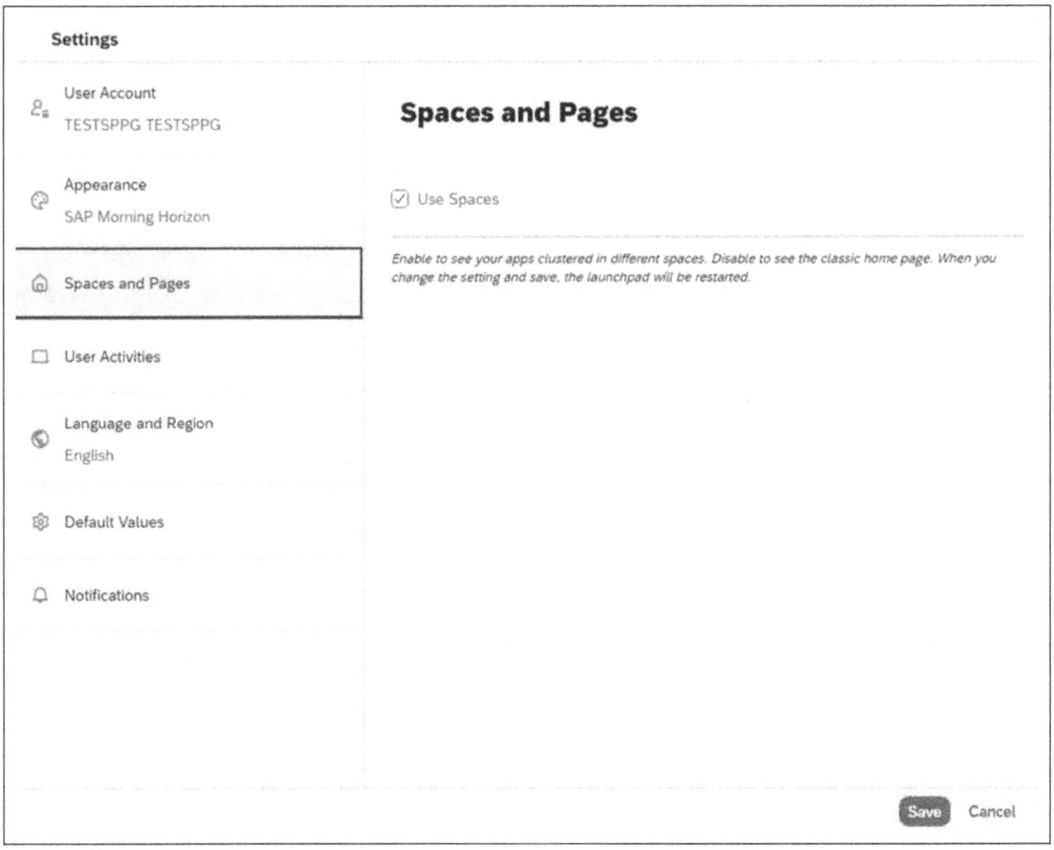

CHAPTER 10   INTRODUCTION TO SAP FIORI SPACES AND PAGES

Figure 10-67. Spaces and Pages enabled

Spaces and pages generally define the **layout** and user experience in the SAP Fiori Launchpad. By assigning the same **space** to **multiple roles**, you ensure that users across different roles can access the same layout or set of **pages**, based on their specific business needs.

Sometimes, if the landing page does not display an app, it does not mean the user has no app assigned. Use the **App Finder** option under the **User Menu** to locate the **apps**, as shown in the figure below.

CHAPTER 10   INTRODUCTION TO SAP FIORI SPACES AND PAGES

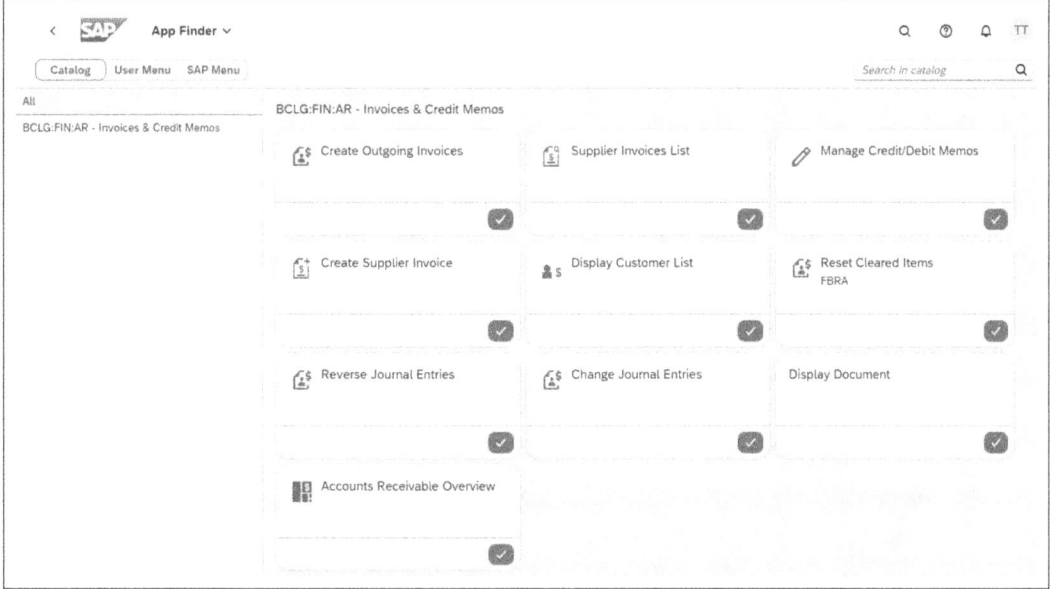

Figure 10-68. Business catalog description displayed on the left panel, along with apps assigned

---

Note   The custom business catalog information is always displayed on the left-hand side as the business catalog description, as shown in the figure above.

10.8.5 Create an Additional Page

So far, we have added only one **page** to the **space** and visualized the output on the SAP Fiori landing page. Currently, the space is displayed as a **flat** option without a dropdown menu to select other pages. This is because multiple **pages** do not exist within the **space** for this feature to be enabled. To address this, we will create an additional **page** with various sections and tiles or apps, which will be discussed in this section.

To create the additional page, we will follow the data shown in the **Excel file** in the above section. The process of making the **page** has been previously described using the Manage **Launchpad Pages** app. Once created, **Manage Launchpad Pages** gets updated with **two pages**, as illustrated in the figure below.

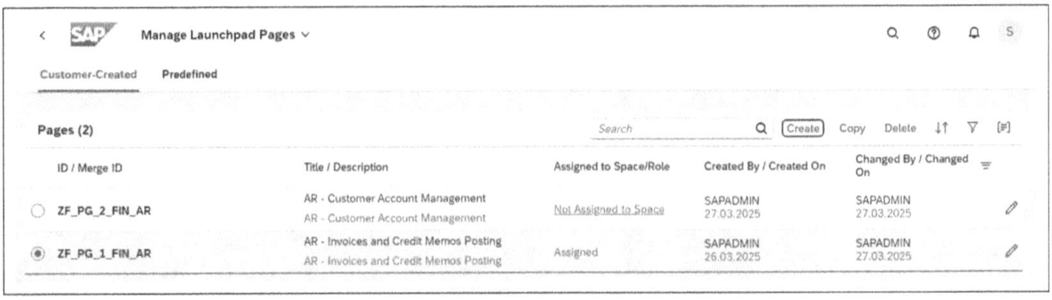

CHAPTER 10   INTRODUCTION TO SAP FIORI SPACES AND PAGES

Figure 10-69. Additional page created

A new, empty page was created, as displayed in the above figure, which also shows that the **page** has been **Not Assigned to Space** under the column heading **Assigned to Space/Role**. The new **page, ZF_PG_2_FIN_AR,** must now be assigned to the **space** using the **Manage Launchpad Spaces app**. Once executed, the **Manage Launchpad Spaces** workspace opens, displaying the space, as shown in the figure below.

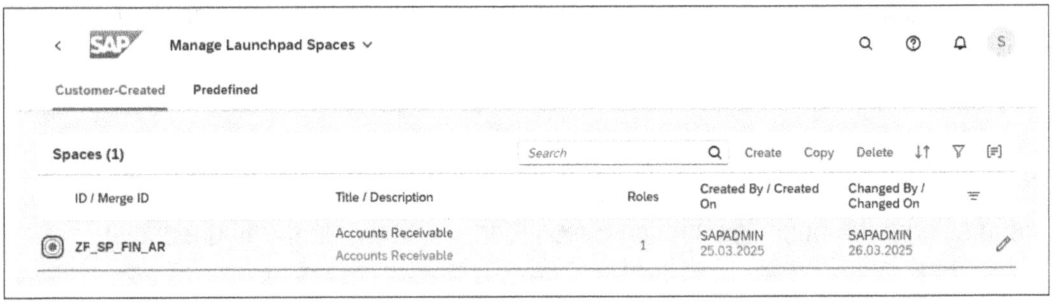

Figure 10-70. Manage Launchpad Spaces workspace displaying only the space

To add a new **page**, first select the **space**. Then, click the **pencil icon** to edit the **space**. This will open the **Space Details** window where you can search for the **page** and assign it to the **space**, as shown in the figure below.

CHAPTER 10   INTRODUCTION TO SAP FIORI SPACES AND PAGES

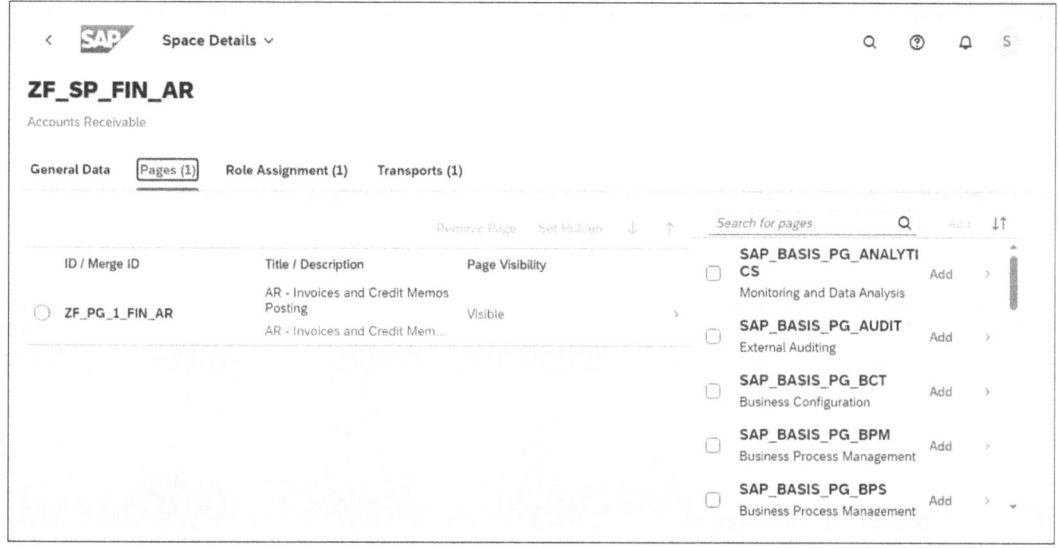

Figure 10-71. Space Details window

The above figure displays the **pages** available on the right-hand side of the screen, as well as the **page** assigned to the **space**. Currently, only **one page** has been assigned to the space. Search for the page **ZF_PG_2**, and the new **page** created is found and displayed along with the page description, as shown in the figure below.

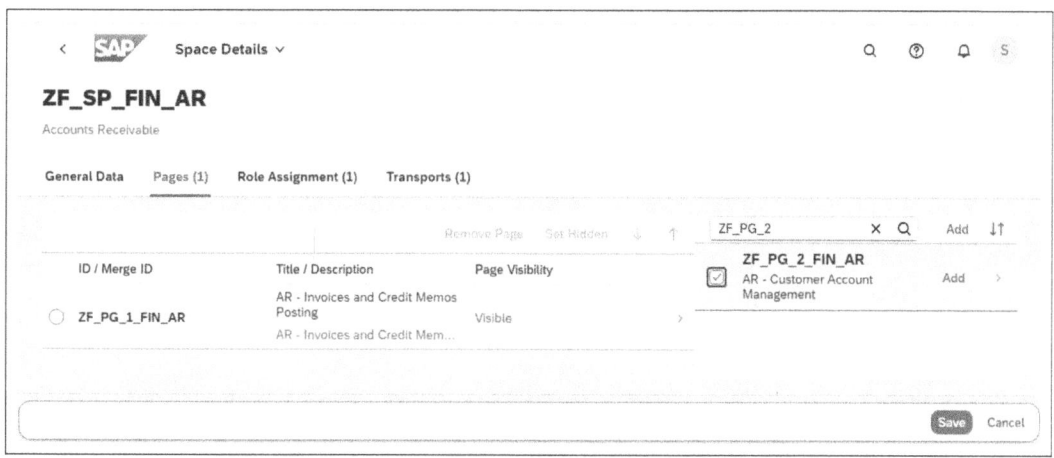

Figure 10-72. Created page found

Now, select the highlighted page **ZF_PG_2_FIN_AR** and select **Add** to assign this **page** to the **space**, as shown in the figure above. This action will assign the **page** to the

519

space, and a message is displayed on the screen stating **Page added**, as shown in the figure below.

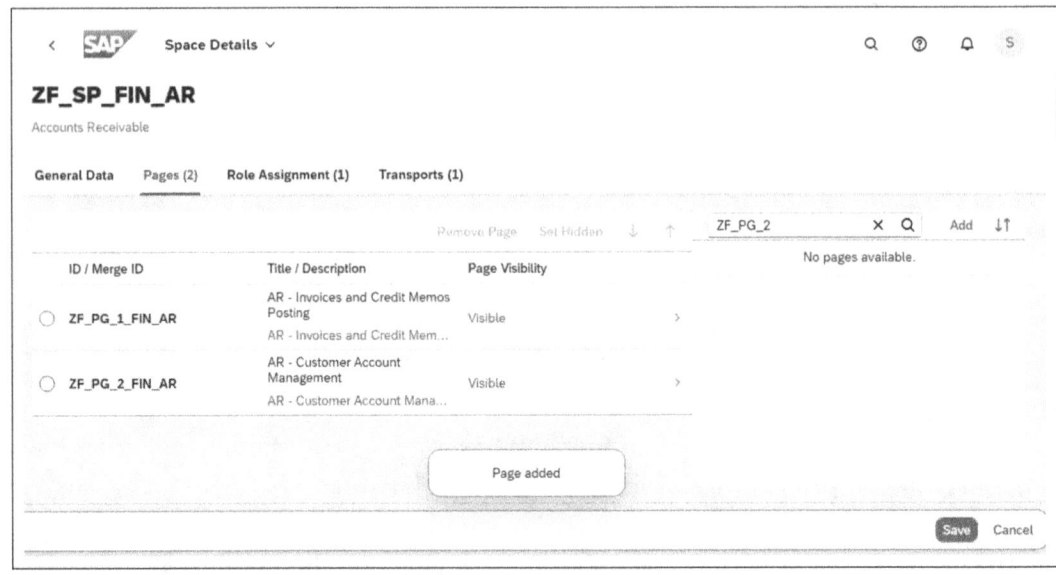

Figure 10-73. New page added to the space

Save the changes by clicking **Save**, and a message is displayed on the screen stating **Your changes have been saved**, as shown in the figure below.

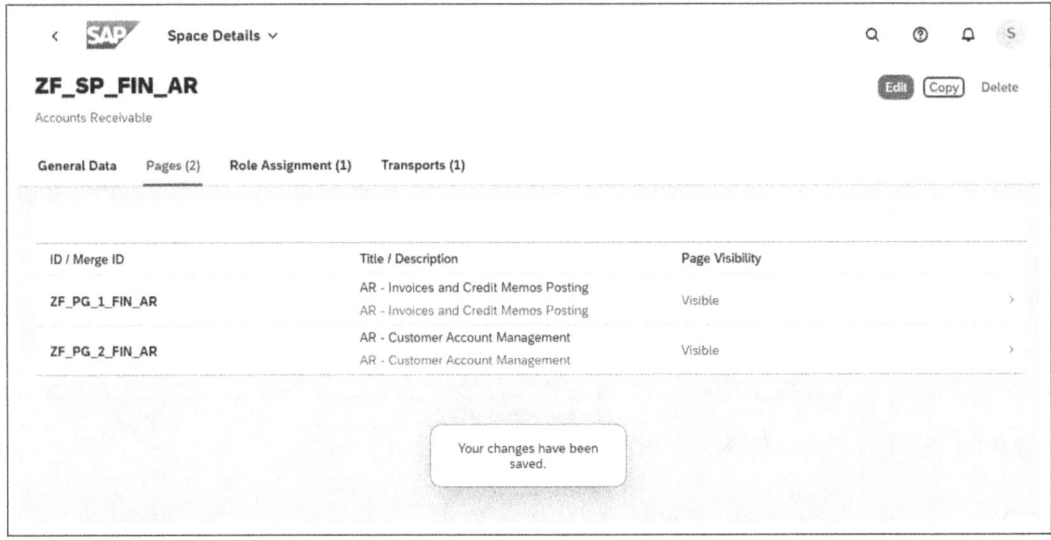

Figure 10-74. Space has been updated with a new page

CHAPTER 10   INTRODUCTION TO SAP FIORI SPACES AND PAGES

Once the **space** is **saved**, it will display that **two pages**, including the new **page**, are part of it, as shown in the figure above.

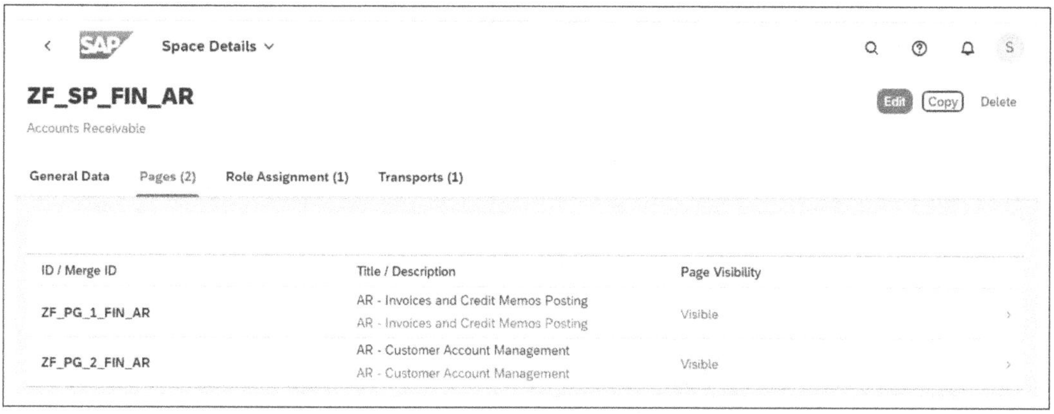

Figure 10-75.   Space Details window displays two pages assigned

The above figure now displays **Pages (2)** indicating two pages added to the **space**, and they are

- ZF_PG_1_ FIN_AR
- ZF_PG_2_ FIN_AR

Note   The **Space Details** window has been updated to display **Pages (2)**, **Role Assignment (1)**, and **Transports (1)**, indicating that the new **page** is automatically added to the role to which the **space** has been assigned and becomes part of the **transport** assigned earlier to the space.

In our example, we created a separate business catalog (**ZF_BCLG_FIN_AR_CS_ACCT_CLG**) and assigned the same space (**ZF_SP_FIN_AR**) that was created earlier to it, and the new page (**ZF_PG_2_FIN_AR**) was created based on this business catalog. The space is already assigned to the role **ZMU_TSK_FIN_AR_INVS_CRMOS:XXXX**.

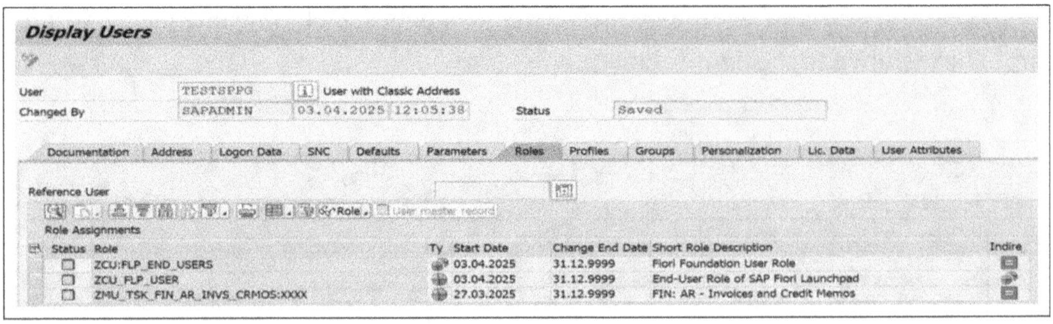

CHAPTER 10   INTRODUCTION TO SAP FIORI SPACES AND PAGES

Figure 10-76. Space assigned to the role using transaction PFCG

The next step involves updating the **page** with its associated business objects using the Manage Launchpad Pages app, which now displays **two pages**, as shown in the figure below.

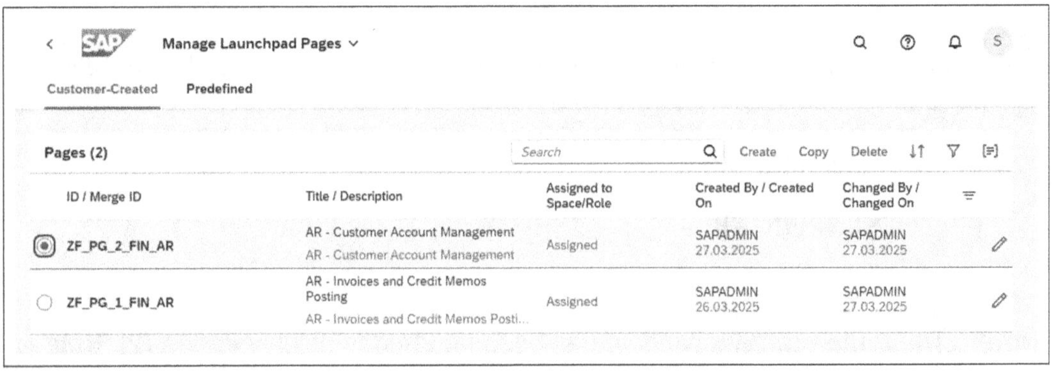

Figure 10-77. Manage Launchpad Pages workspace displaying two pages

Next, select the **page** and use the pencil icon to edit, which opens the Page Content tab to create sections and assign tiles or apps, as shown in the figure below.

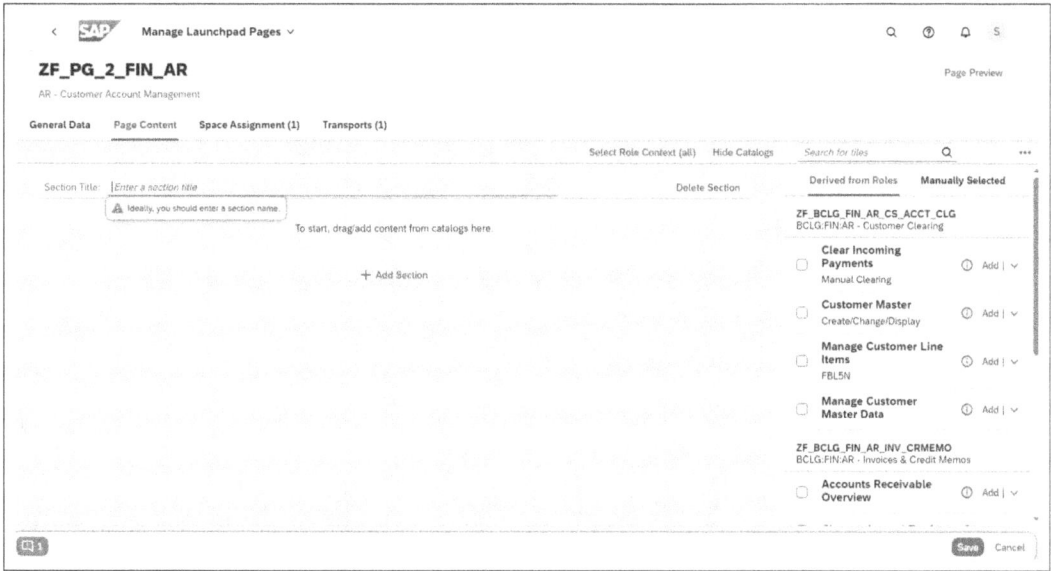

Figure 10-78. Page Content

The figure above illustrates the Page Content tab, which displays the business catalog associated with the **page** and the related tiles or apps it contains. It also displays the other custom business catalog that was created. Once updated and saved, the final Page Content will appear as shown in the figure below. It will also display a message **Your changes have been saved**.

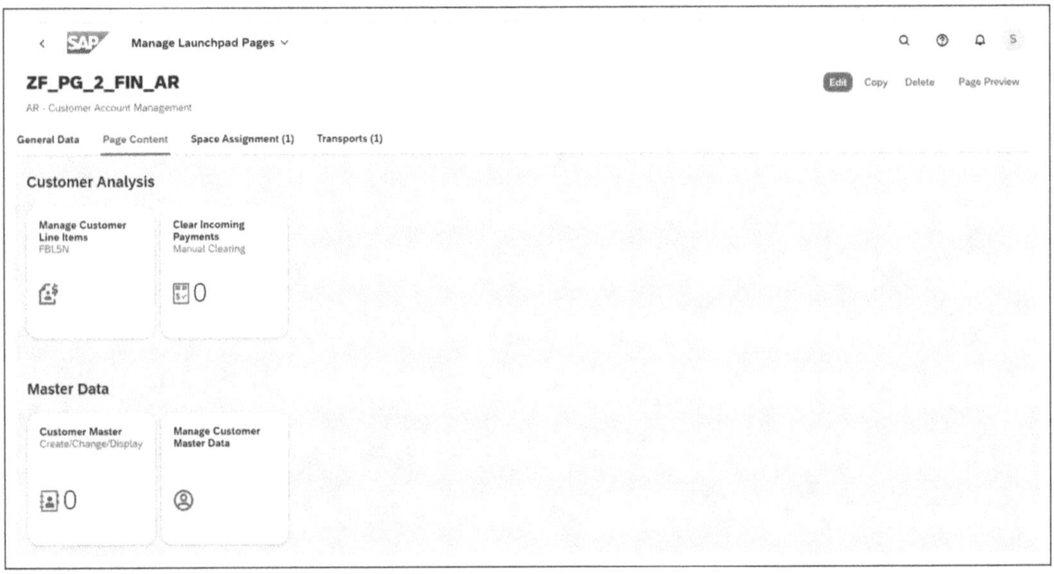

CHAPTER 10   INTRODUCTION TO SAP FIORI SPACES AND PAGES

Figure 10-79. New page updated with sections and tiles

Once saved, the final output of the **page** tiles or apps will appear on the Managed Launched Pages home page as shown in the figure above. Now, select the **Page Preview** option, and it will open the **page** and display how the page will appear on the SAP Fiori Launchpad home page, as shown in the figure below.

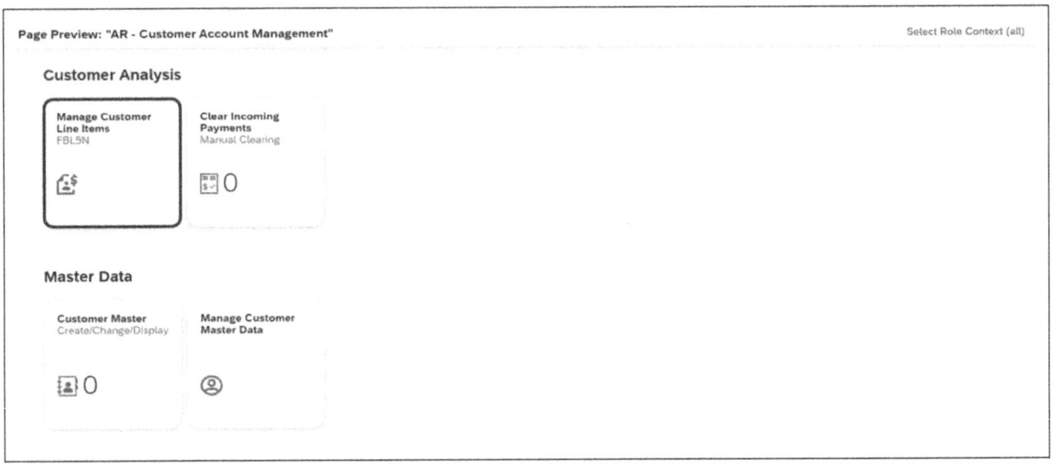

Figure 10-80. Page Preview displaying how the page will appear in the SAP Fiori Launchpad

CHAPTER 10 INTRODUCTION TO SAP FIORI SPACES AND PAGES

10.8.6 Testing and Validation

The next step is to verify whether the test user can access the space and the two pages associated with the space via the pull-down option, which is enabled. The test user's Fiori Launchpad page displays the **space** with the **pull-down option** activated and the descriptions of the two associated pages, as shown in the figure below.

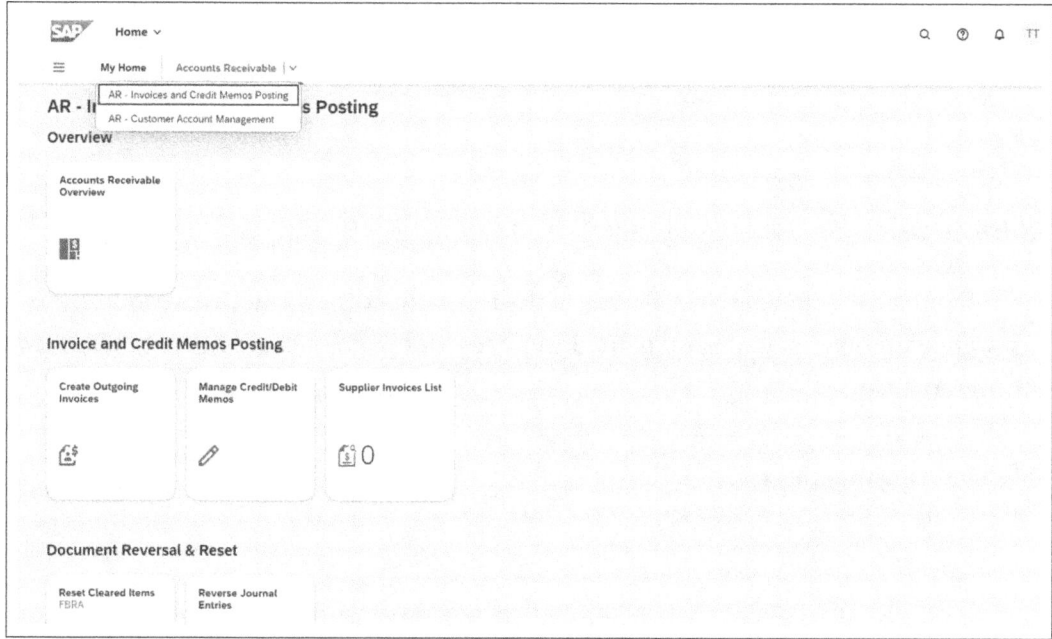

Figure 10-81. Test user SAP Fiori Launchpad landing workspace

10.9 Create a Space with a Page

The previous section explained the concept of creating spaces and pages as separate business objects. Additionally, SAP allows the creation of spaces and pages **simultaneously** in a single operation. Using this method, we will create a new space and pages, which will involve creating a new **space** assigned to **two different roles**. Each **space** will contain multiple **pages**. It is assumed that the roles and their respective business catalogs, associated tiles, and apps have already been created using an **Excel input sheet**.

525

CHAPTER 10   INTRODUCTION TO SAP FIORI SPACES AND PAGES

10.9.1 Create a New Space

To create a new **space and page simultaneously**, open the Manage Launchpad Spaces app. This action will open the Manage Launchpad Spaces landing page, displaying one **space**, as shown in the figure below.

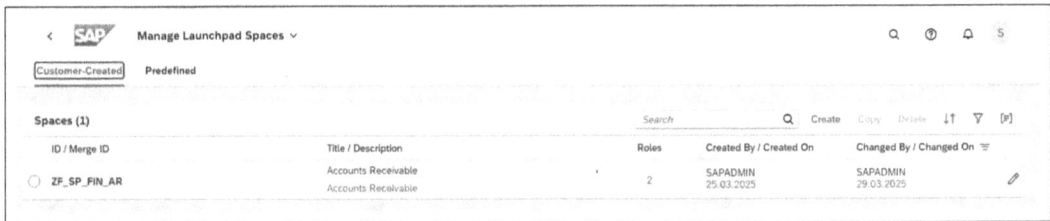

Figure 10-82. Manage Launchpad Spaces app screen display

To create a new **space**, select **Create** at the top-right corner. The **Create Space** box opens, allowing you to create and generate **spaces and pages** simultaneously, as shown in the figure below.

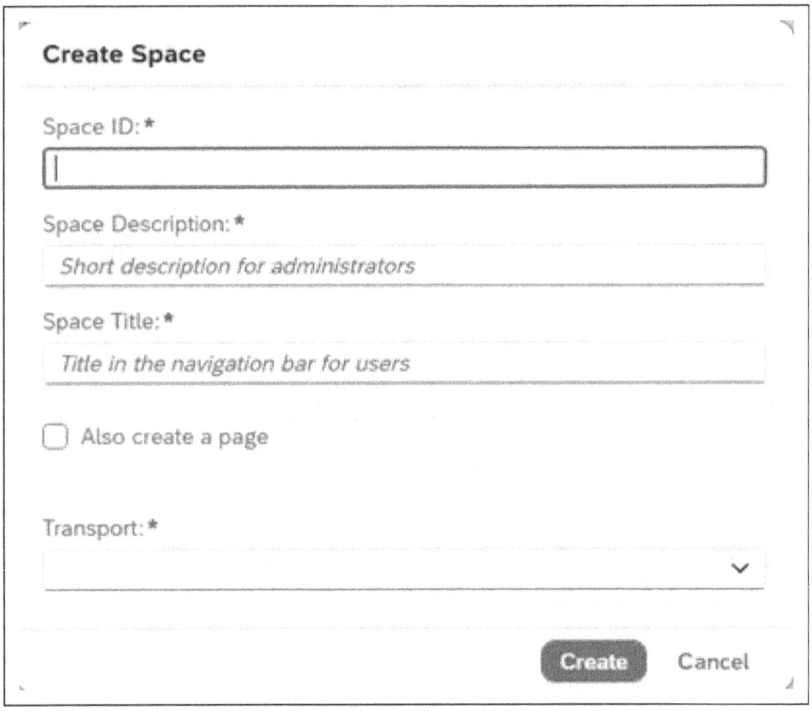

Figure 10-83. Create Space input screen for entering information

CHAPTER 10　INTRODUCTION TO SAP FIORI SPACES AND PAGES

Currently, the Create Space screen displays only input fields for creating a space, but it contains an option with a checkbox: **Also create a page**.

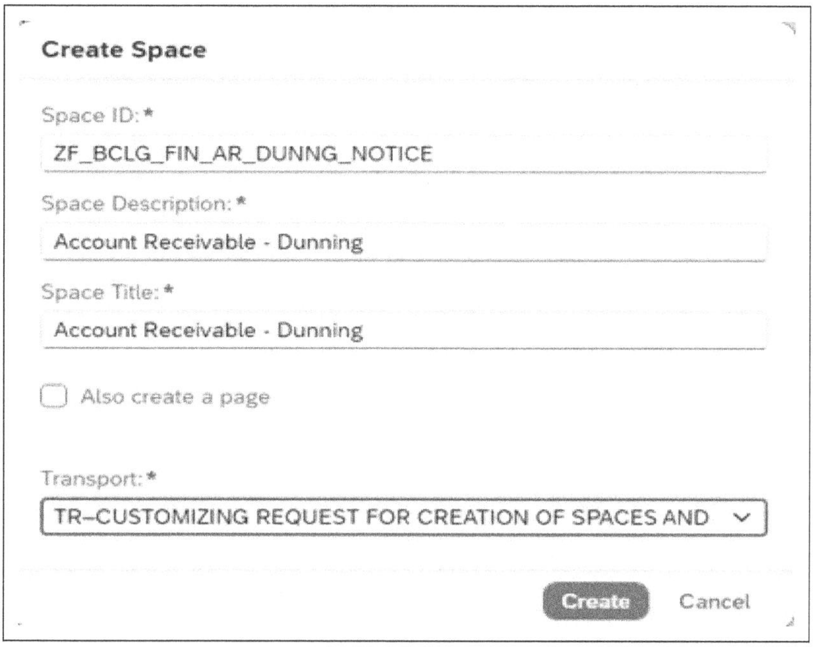

Figure 10-84. Updated details of the new space to be created

After entering the information for creating the new **space**, select the checkbox **Also create a page**. This will bring in initial input details for the **page** to be created, as shown in the figure below.

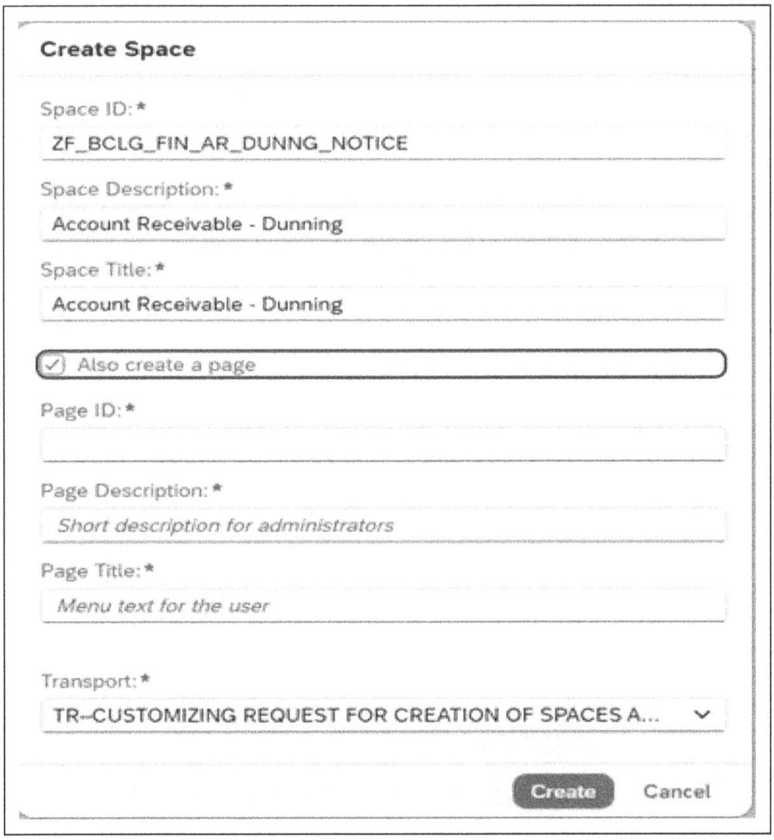

CHAPTER 10　INTRODUCTION TO SAP FIORI SPACES AND PAGES

Figure 10-85. Page input details open within Create Space

Enter the information related to the page to be created. The final Create Space box will appear as shown in the figure below.

CHAPTER 10 INTRODUCTION TO SAP FIORI SPACES AND PAGES

Figure 10-86. Space and page information updated

Enter the page information as shown in the figure above. The final Create Space box appears as shown in the figure above. To create a **space** and **page** simultaneously, click Create `Create`. A message is displayed in a box, **The space has been created**, as shown in the figure below.

Figure 10-87. New space has been created

The system created the **space and page**. The **space** created is displayed at the top, and the **page** created is displayed below the navigation panel with **Page Visibility** set to **Visible**, as shown in the figure below.

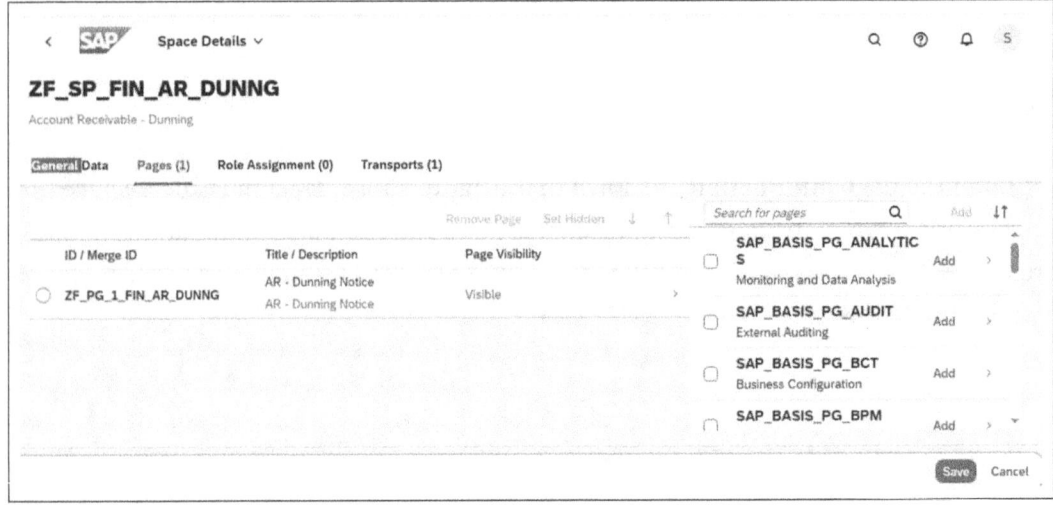

Figure 10-88. Both new space and page were created

The above figure displays the new **space and page** that were created. To proceed, click **Save**. A message is displayed in a box at the bottom of the screen stating **Your changes have been saved**, as shown in the figure below.

CHAPTER 10 INTRODUCTION TO SAP FIORI SPACES AND PAGES

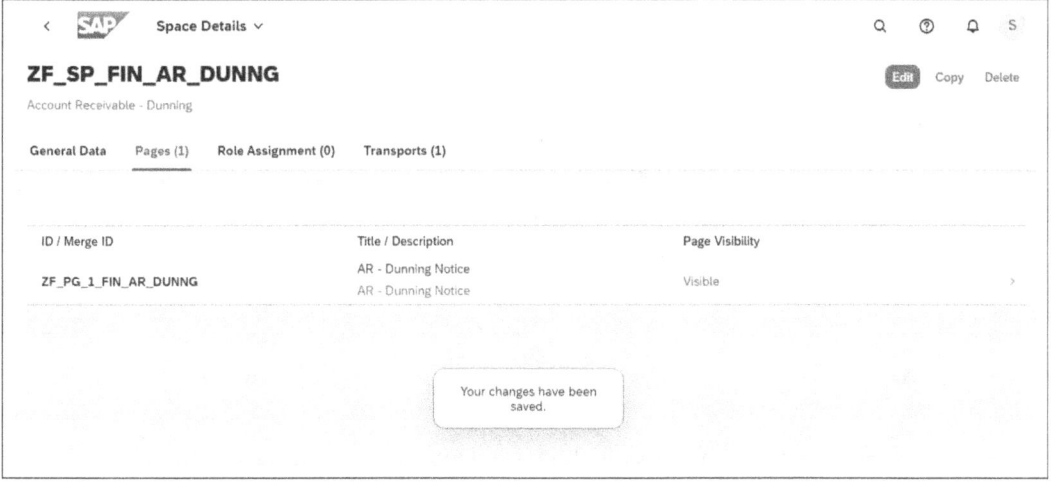

Figure 10-89. Space and page created saved

Once saved, the figure below displays that the **space ZF_SP_FIN_AR_DUNNG** and the subsequent **page ZF_PG_1FIN_AP_DUNNG** have been created and saved.

Figure 10-90. Final output screen of new space and associated page created

Now go back to the home page of Manage Launchpad Spaces, which now **displays two spaces**, as shown in the figure below.

531

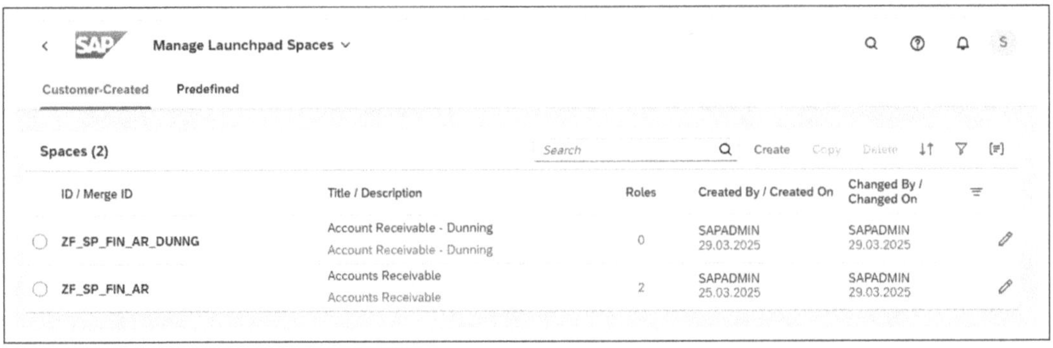

CHAPTER 10 INTRODUCTION TO SAP FIORI SPACES AND PAGES

Figure 10-91. *Manage Launchpad Spaces app displays two spaces*

The figure above shows that no role has been assigned to **space ZF_SP_FIN_AR_DUNNG**. Assigning the **space** to roles using transaction **PFCG** will update the space role assignment, as illustrated in the figure below.

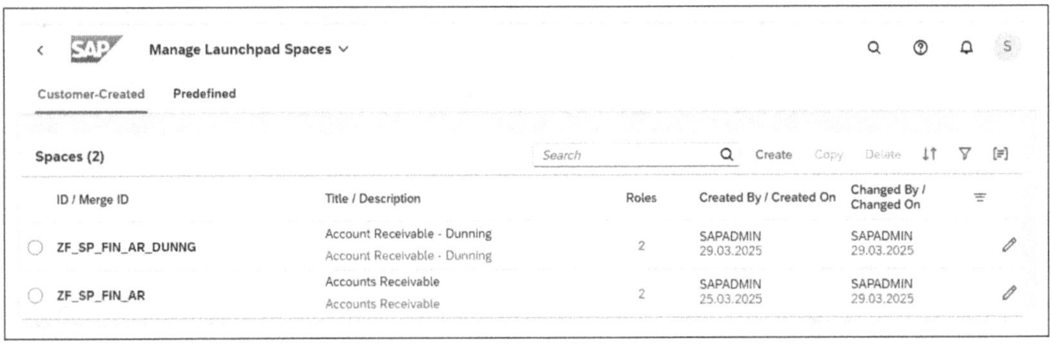

Figure 10-92. *Roles assigned to the space*

The above **space ZF_SP_FIN_AR_DUNNG** now has **two roles** assigned. To create another **page**, open the Manage Launchpad Pages app, which displays all **three** pages created as shown in the figure below.

CHAPTER 10 INTRODUCTION TO SAP FIORI SPACES AND PAGES

10.9.2 Create and Add Another Page

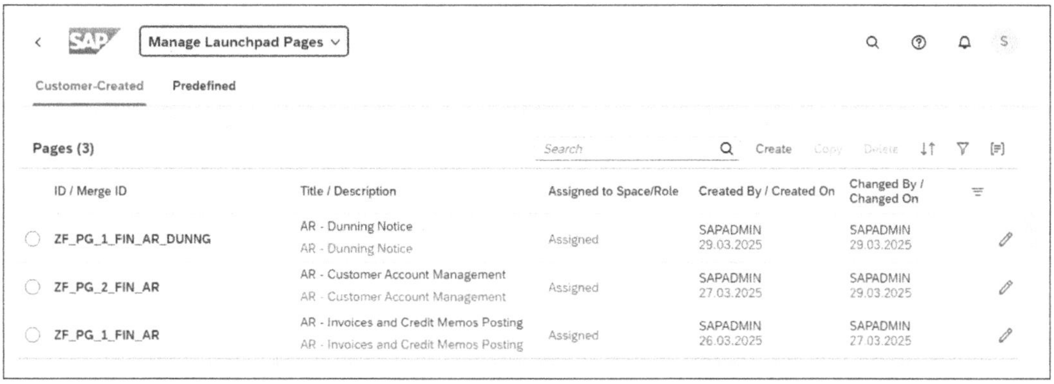

Figure 10-93. *Manage Launchpad Pages app displaying three pages*

Creating another **page** and the Manage Launchpad Pages workspace now has **four** pages, as shown in the figure below.

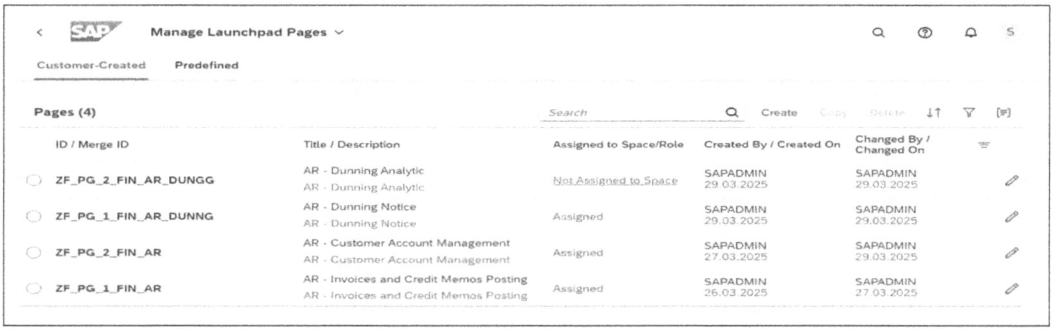

Figure 10-94. *Manage Launchpad Pages app displaying four pages*

The page added shows **Not Assigned to Space** under the **Assigned to Space/Role** column, as shown in the figure above. To assign the space to the page, go to Manage Launchpad Spaces, select the **space**, and then click the **pencil icon**. Search for the respective **page**, as shown in the figure below.

533

CHAPTER 10   INTRODUCTION TO SAP FIORI SPACES AND PAGES

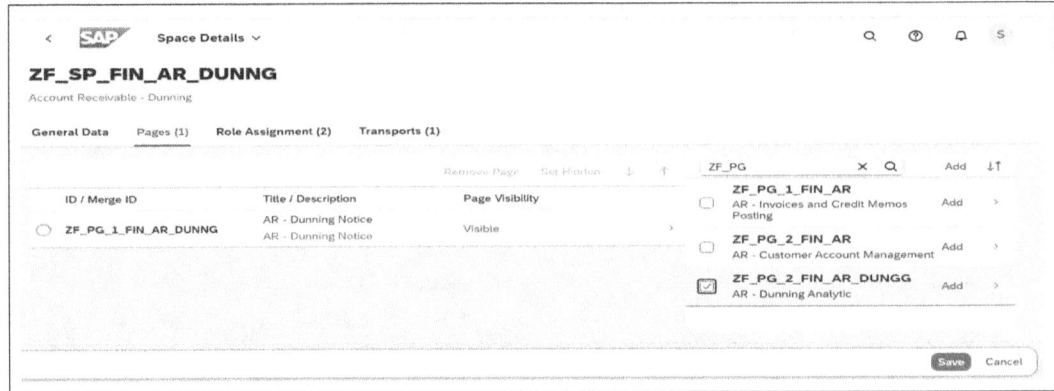

Figure 10-95.   Respected page found and selected to add to the space

Once added, the **space** gets updated with another page, as shown in the figure below.

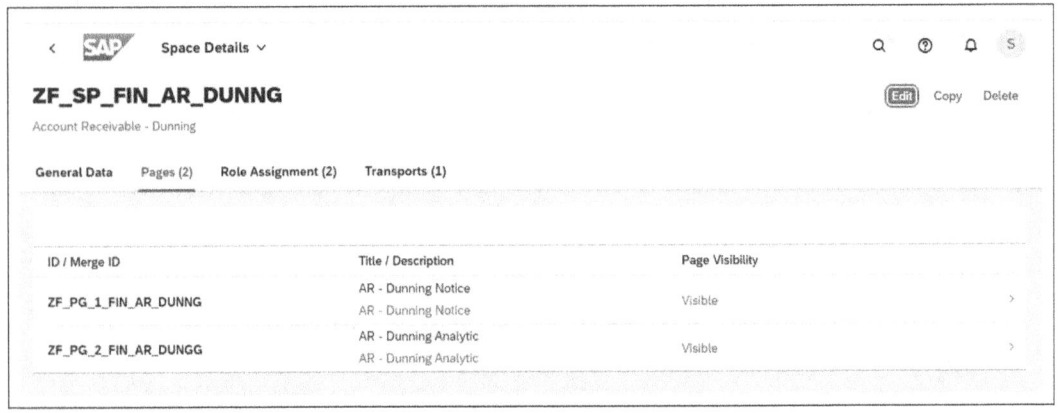

Figure 10-96.   Space Details window displays two pages

The above figure now displays **two pages** added to the **space**. Checking the **Role Assignment (2)** tab displays the roles assigned to the **space**, as shown in the figure below.

534

CHAPTER 10 INTRODUCTION TO SAP FIORI SPACES AND PAGES

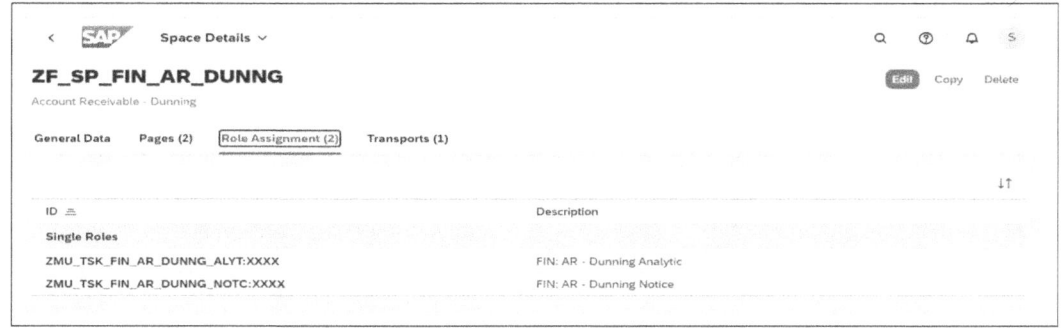

Figure 10-97. Two roles assigned to the new space created

10.9.3 List of Spaces and Pages Created

To illustrate additional features available with the Manage Launchpad Spaces app, we will create another space and pages. The final Manage Launchpad Spaces screen will display three spaces, as shown in the figure below.

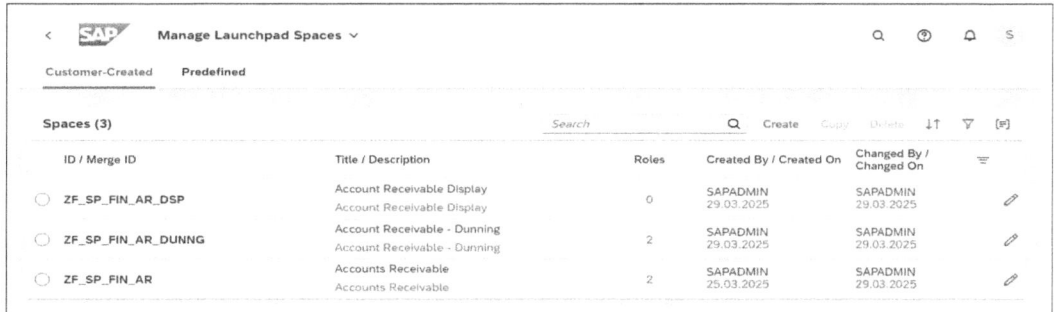

Figure 10-98. Three spaces created within the Manage Launchpad Spaces workspace

The final Manage Launchpad Pages screen will display six pages, as shown in the figure below.

535

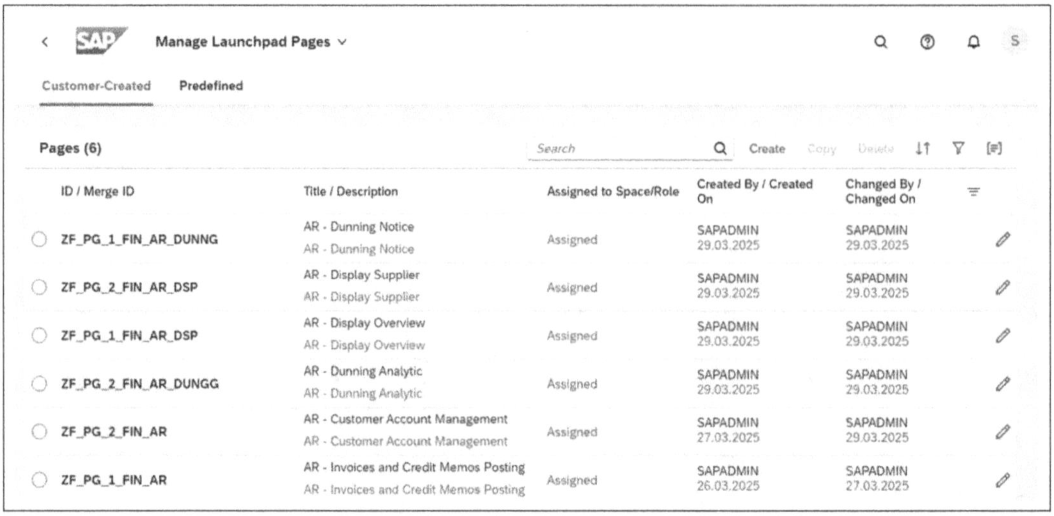

CHAPTER 10   INTRODUCTION TO SAP FIORI SPACES AND PAGES

Figure 10-99. Six pages created within the Manage Launchpad Pages workspace

The new space and page created will automatically be added to the transport. Checking the transport details using transaction **SE09** displays the objects assigned to the transport, as shown in the figure below.

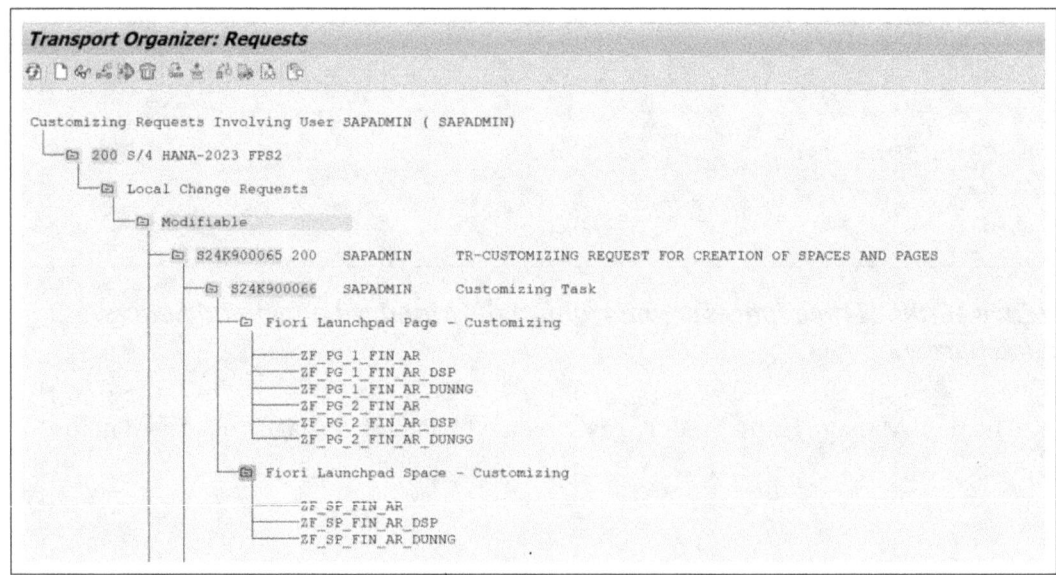

Figure 10-100. Transport generated for business objects created

CHAPTER 10 INTRODUCTION TO SAP FIORI SPACES AND PAGES

10.9.4 Assign Test User ID to the Roles

For our example, we have assigned some other roles containing business catalogs and spaces to our test user ID as shown below.

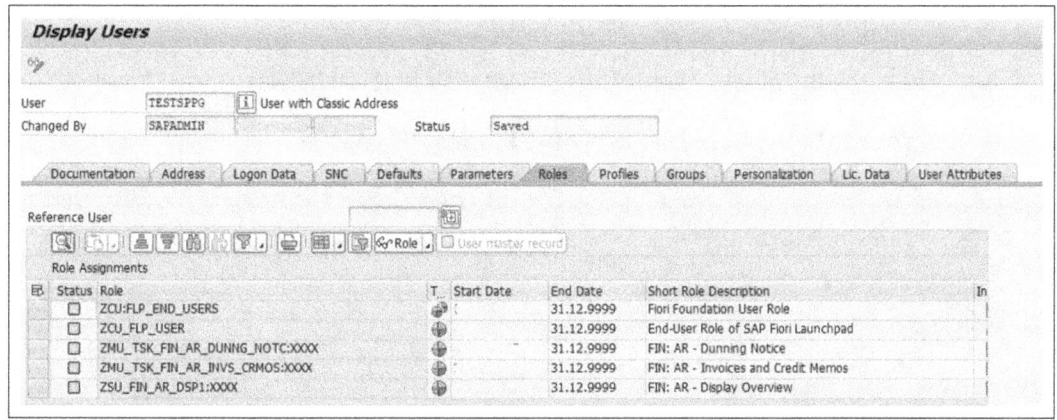

Figure 10-101. Test user role assignments

10.9.5 Testing and Validation

The test user logs into the **SAP Fiori Launchpad**, which displays content along with **spaces** and **pages**, as shown in the figure below.

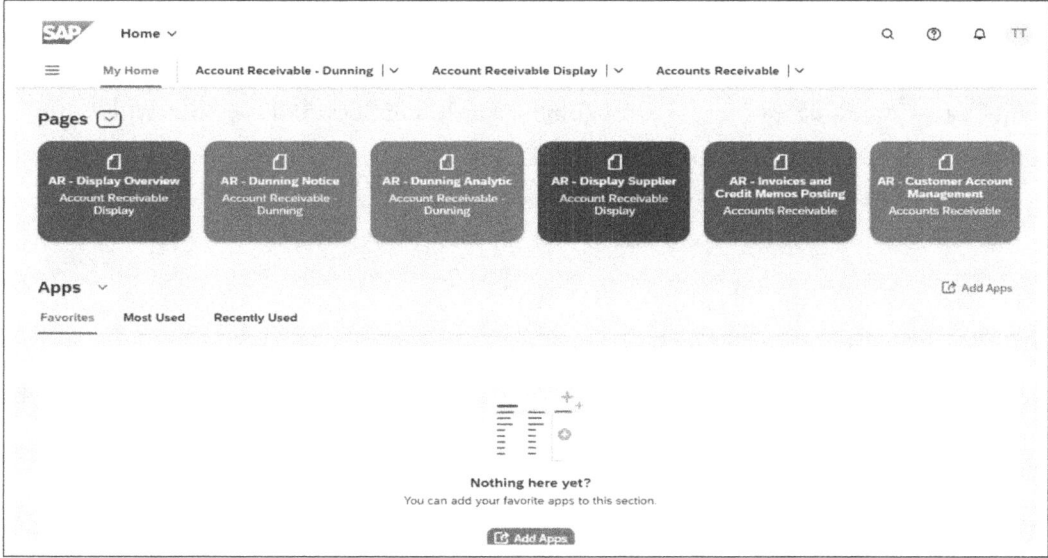

Figure 10-102. Test user ID visualizing three spaces on the SAP Fiori Launchpad

537

CHAPTER 10 INTRODUCTION TO SAP FIORI SPACES AND PAGES

The test user within the SAP Fiori Launchpad landing page visualizes all three **spaces**, as well as the **home page**, as shown in the figure above. However, the **spaces** created are not in the correct order, and they should be in the order in which they were created, which was

- Accounts Receivable (**ZF_SP_FIN_AR**)
- Accounts Receivable Dunning (**ZF_SP_FIN_AR_DUNNG**)
- Accounts Receivable Display (**ZF_SP_FIN_AR_DSP**)

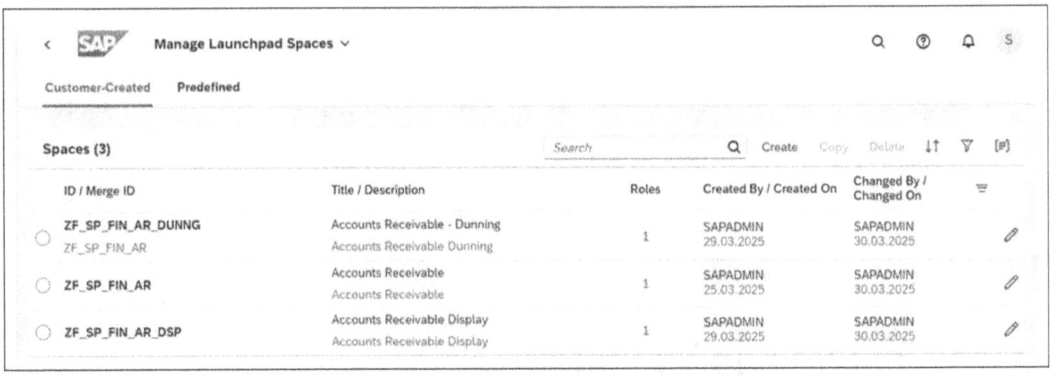

Figure 10-103. Spaces order as they appear in the Manage Launchpad Spaces app

---

Note The spaces are not in order in the above figure; therefore, it needs to be adjusted. The necessary steps are explained in the section below, after which the order of the spaces will be as in the figure below.

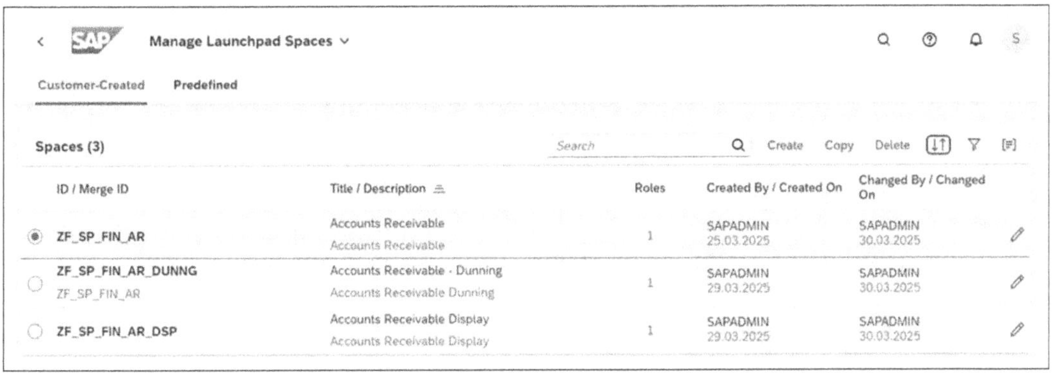

Figure 10-104. *Corrected spaces order as they appear in the Manage Launchpad Spaces app*

10.9.6 Sorting Spaces Order

Sort priority in the Manage Launchpad Spaces app defines the display order of spaces in the SAP Fiori Launchpad. It is a numeric value that determines the sequence in which spaces appear for end users. Sort priority number values are defined as follows:

- **Lower sort values** (e.g., 1, 2, 3) indicate **higher priority**, meaning **spaces** with lower sort priority numbers appear first on the Fiori Launchpad page.

- **Higher sort values (e.g., 50, 99)** indicate **lower priority**, meaning they appear later. In other words, higher numbers correspond to **lower precedence**.

- If multiple **spaces** have the same **sort priority**, they are ordered **alphabetically** by their **technical name**.

- If no **sort priority** is set, spaces are sorted in **ascending order by default**.

CHAPTER 10 INTRODUCTION TO SAP FIORI SPACES AND PAGES

By setting **ZF_PG_2_FIN_AR_DSP** to **99**, it ensures that it appears **after the other two spaces**. You can adjust these values based on additional **spaces** in your system. To control the display order of the spaces in the **SAP Fiori Launchpad in our example**, we will assign the **sort priority** values as follows:

- **ZF_SP_FIN_AR sort priority = 1** (appears first)
- **ZF_SP_FIN_AR_DUNNG sort priority = 2** (appears second)
- **ZF_PG_2_FIN_AR_DSP sort priority = 99** (appears last)

Open the **General Data tab** within the **Space Details window**, select **Edit**, and update the **sort priority of ZF_SP_FIN_AR to 1**. Then, **save**, which displays a message **Your changes have been saved,** as shown in the figure below.

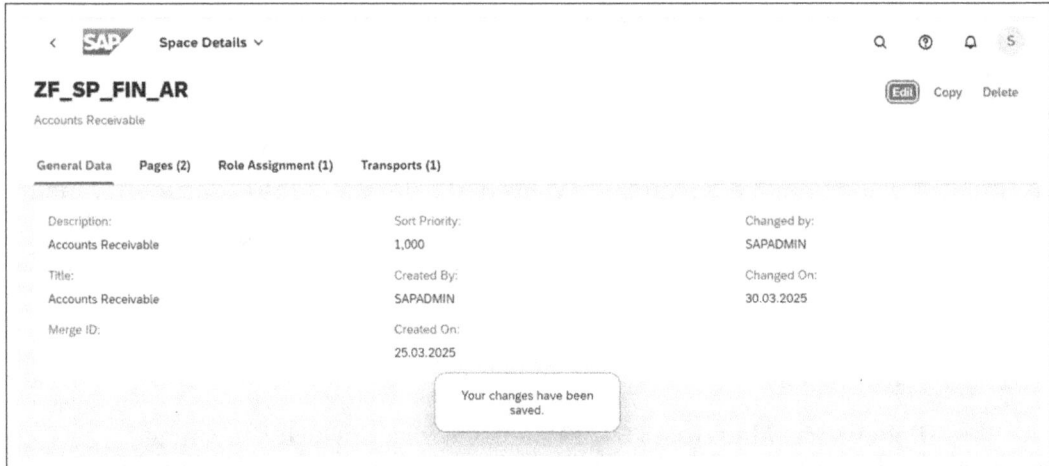

Figure 10-105. Space priority is set to 1 and saved

Once saved, the final screen appears as shown in the figure below.

CHAPTER 10   INTRODUCTION TO SAP FIORI SPACES AND PAGES

Figure 10-106.   The space priority is set to 1

Return to the Manage Launchpad Spaces app page and update the space priority to **99** for **ZF_SP_FIN_AR_DSP**, as shown in the figure below.

Figure 10-107.   The space priority is set to 99 for the lowest priority

Once all the **spaces** are updated, the **Manage Launchpad Spaces** workspace is updated, and the **spaces** appear in the **correct order**, as shown in the figure below.

541

CHAPTER 10   INTRODUCTION TO SAP FIORI SPACES AND PAGES

Figure 10-108. The spaces appear in the correct order

The three **spaces** are displayed correctly in the figure above, and the role assigned to the user includes six pages, which are also shown. Additionally, the description of the space has been corrected and is now accurately displayed on the SAP Fiori Launchpad.

When establishing **priorities**, keep in mind that individual users will only see the **spaces** assigned to their specific user roles, not all available spaces. Therefore, it may not be necessary to assign values for every space or create a strict hierarchy. Instead, it is sufficient to define sort priority values for the most critical and least essential spaces.

When the test user ID logs back into the SAP Fiori Launchpad, the **spaces** appear in the **correct order**, as shown in the figure below.

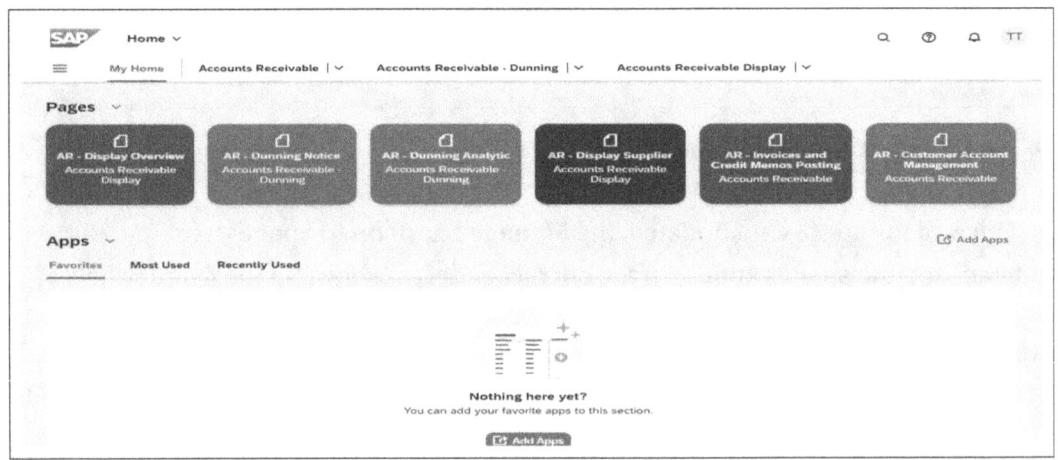

Figure 10-109. Test user ID Launchpad showing spaces in the correct order

CHAPTER 10   INTRODUCTION TO SAP FIORI SPACES AND PAGES

The three **spaces** are displayed correctly in the figure above, and the role assigned to the user includes six pages, which are also shown. Additionally, the description of the space has been corrected and is now accurately displayed on the SAP Fiori Launchpad home page.

> **Note**   Under **My Home**, **six tiles** are displayed in the **Pages** section. Each tile shows descriptions of the space and pages, as illustrated in the figure above. All three spaces have a **pull-down option** for viewing **pages**, as shown in the figure below.

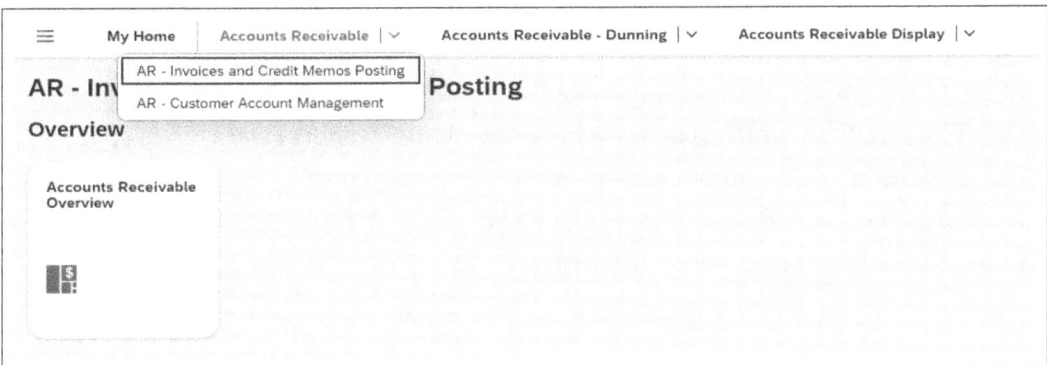

Figure 10-110.   The spaces have a pull-down option

The other two spaces show their respective pages as shown in the figure below.

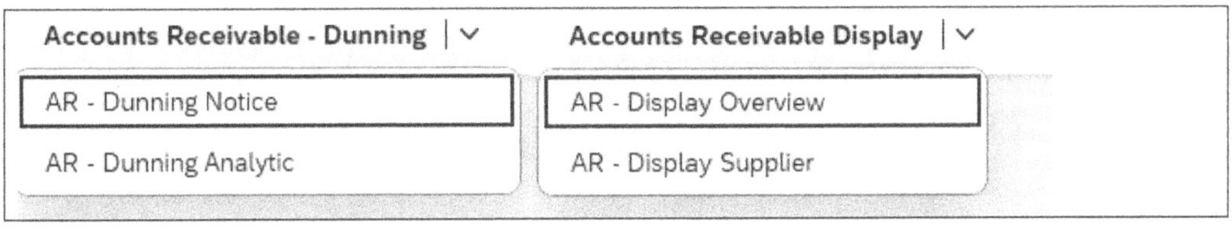

Figure 10-111.   Other spaces with pages created

543

CHAPTER 10   INTRODUCTION TO SAP FIORI SPACES AND PAGES

10.9.7 Merge Spaces

The **Merge ID** information in SAP Fiori Space Details is a unique identifier that combines different **pages** from various roles or sources into a single **space**, enhancing the user experience. It merges two **spaces** into one **space**, with a single **Title** and **Description**. Furthermore, when a user has multiple roles with the same **space ID** but **different pages**, **Merge ID** prevents the creation of various instances of the **same space**, ensuring a consolidated view of all relevant **pages** without **duplication**. This streamlined approach improves navigation and provides users with a seamless interface on the Launchpad.

For example, to merge the **space IDs** using the **Merge ID** option**,** enter the **space ID** of the space that you want to merge in the **Merge ID** field of the space that you want to merge into.

In our example, we are merging space ID **ZF_SP_FIN_AR_DUNNG** with space ID **ZF_SP_FIN_AR**. In order to do that, we have to be in the **General Data** tab of space ZF_SP_FIN_AR_DUNNG and in Edit mode. After that we enter space ID **ZF_SP_FIN_AR** in the Merge ID field and save the settings. A message is displayed stating Your changes have been saved, as shown in the figure below.

Figure 10-112.   Merge ID

Once saved, the final **space ID** is updated with the merged **space ID**, as shown in the figure below.

CHAPTER 10   INTRODUCTION TO SAP FIORI SPACES AND PAGES

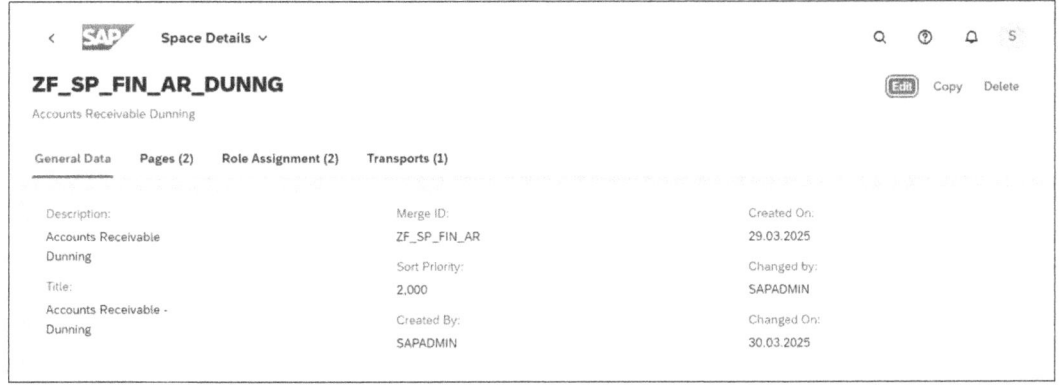

Figure 10-113.   The space ID was updated with the merge ID

When the test user ID logs back into the SAP Fiori Launchpad, the user will view two **spaces** and the **pages merged**, as shown in the figure below.

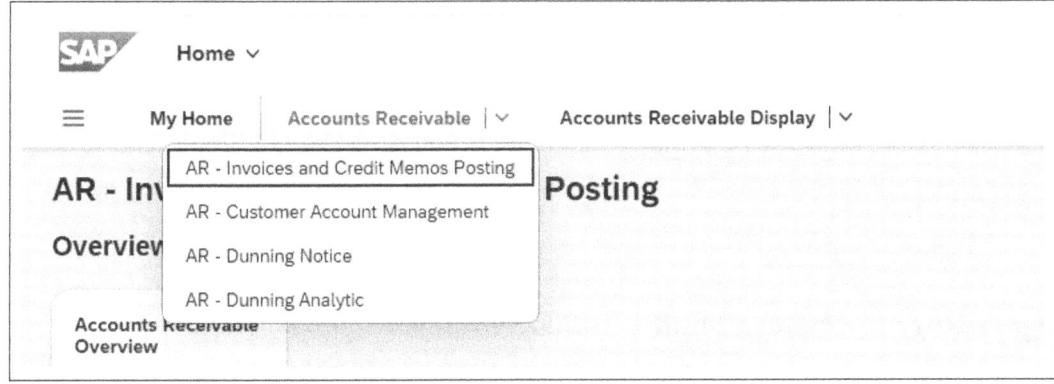

Figure 10-114.   Merged spaces and their associated pages

Note   The pages and tiles, or apps, got merged into one **space**, as shown in the figure above.

545

10.10 Switching Between Spaces and Groups

The role can contain **groups** as well as **spaces**. The concept of creating a **group** will be covered in **Appendix B**. It is assumed that the business groups have already been made. The groups need to be added to the roles for the Launchpad activation using transaction **PFCG**.

We can check if any groups are associated with business catalogs using the transaction **/UI2/FLPCM_CUST**. Enter the role name in the Search **Roles** field and click **Go**. The role has been updated to include its business catalog, as shown in the figure below.

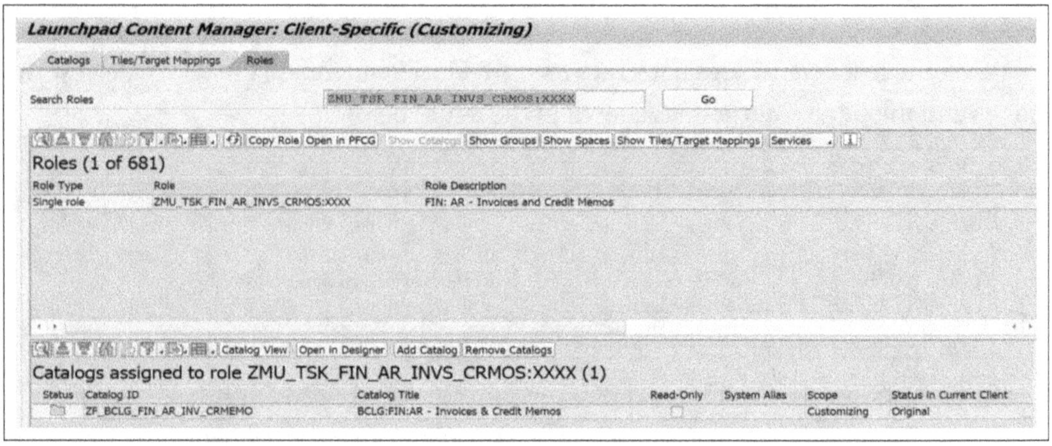

Figure 10-115. Role with business catalog displayed

Select the **Show Groups** 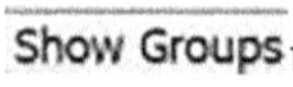 Show Groups tab to display the **group(s)** within the role, as shown in the figure above.

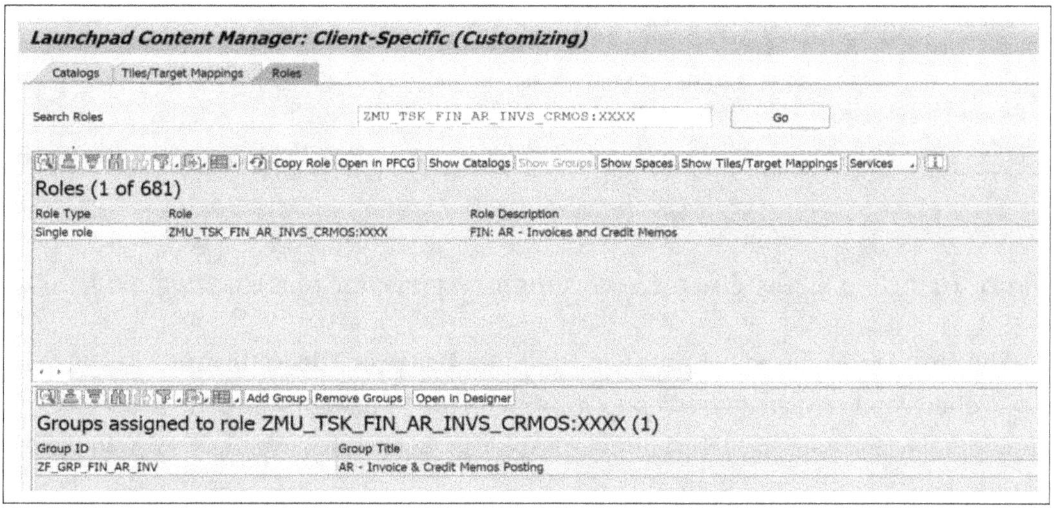

CHAPTER 10   INTRODUCTION TO SAP FIORI SPACES AND PAGES

Figure 10-116. *Group assigned to the role is displayed*

You can also get the group information by searching the business catalog in the **Show Catalog Content** tab as shown in the figure below.

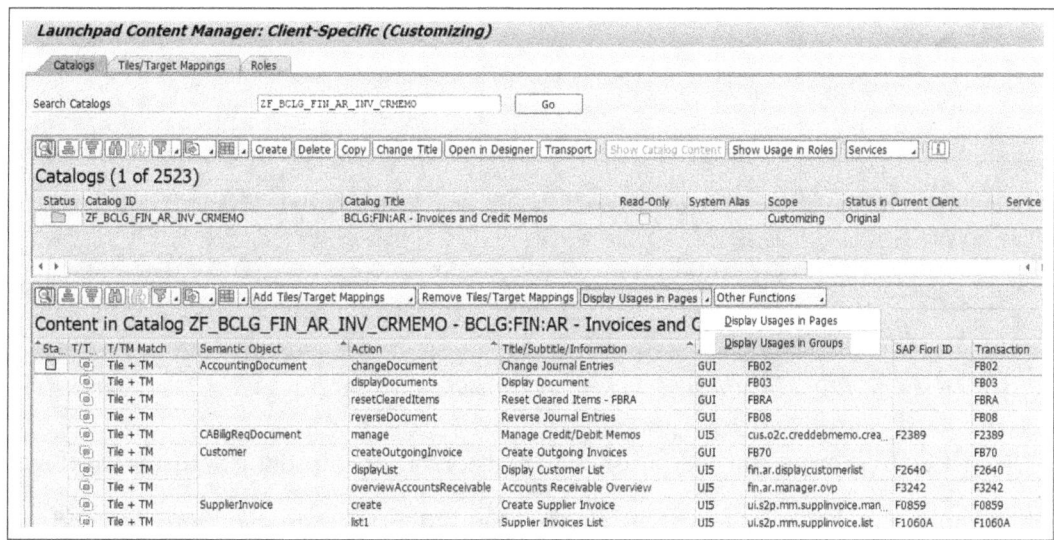

Figure 10-117. *Display Usages in Groups option*

In the above figure, using the pull-down option in the **Display Usages in Pages** tab, click **Display Usages in Groups**. This will display the group(s) associated with the business catalog as shown in the figure below.

547

CHAPTER 10 INTRODUCTION TO SAP FIORI SPACES AND PAGES

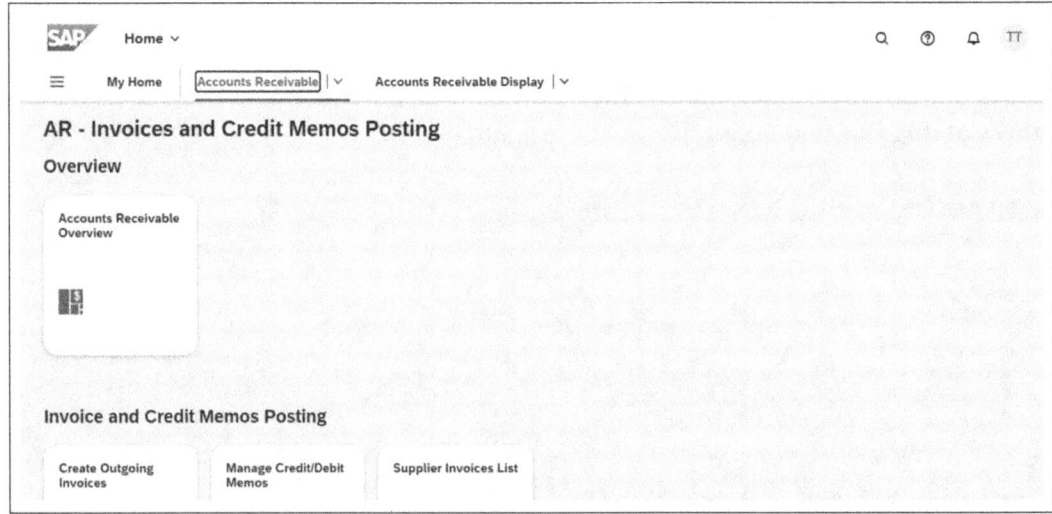

Figure 10-118. Display Usages in Groups for a given business catalog

The group is displayed within a window titled **Usage of Tile in Groups**.

To check and confirm, we will now log in with the test user ID into the SAP Fiori Launchpad home page, and the Launchpad screen will be displayed as shown in the figure below.

Figure 10-119. Fiori Launchpad displays spaces and pages

To switch to **groups**, the user must change the settings within the **Settings** window, which appears in the figure below. Select the User Menu ^{TT} and then **Settings**, and deselect the **Use Spaces** option, as shown in the figure below.

548

CHAPTER 10   INTRODUCTION TO SAP FIORI SPACES AND PAGES

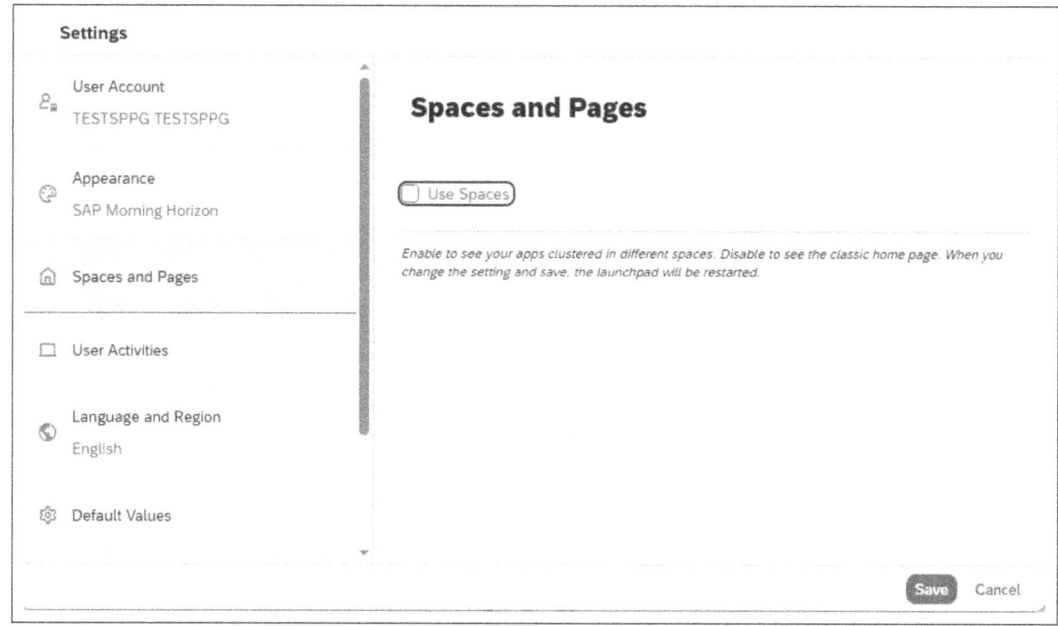

Figure 10-120. *To display groups, deselect Use Spaces*

Save the setting in the above figure, and the user's workspaces switch from **spaces and pages** to groups, as shown in the figure below.

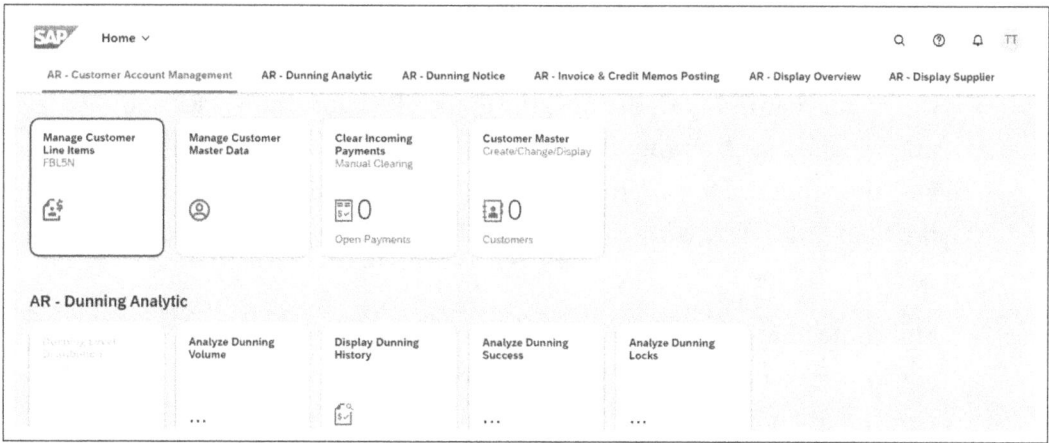

Figure 10-121. *The user can view all the groups and associated apps assigned within the Fiori Launchpad*

549

> **Note** The SAP Fiori Launchpad home page now displays six groups in random order, which cannot be controlled.

10.11 My Home

The SAP Fiori Launchpad is the primary tool for users to access SAP applications, featuring My Home, a personalized landing page that enables users to customize their workspace. This feature helps users work more efficiently by organizing their daily tasks, favorite apps, and key insights in a way that fits their needs. The goal of My Home is to boost productivity by providing a centralized and easy-to-use interface for accessing applications, reports, and widgets.

Key Features

Some of the key features of **My Home** are explained below:

- **My Home** is integrated within spaces and pages, with its content and layout configured by the administrator. Administrators can customize layouts for various user roles.

- Users can choose the **My Home** workspace as their default landing page or select specific spaces or pages.

- Users can view in **My Home** only the apps relevant to their roles and manage tiles, such as apps, links, and widgets, by using the drag-and-drop method to add, remove, rearrange, or organize them. This provides quick access to relevant apps, reducing the number of clicks and search time.

- **My Home** offers the flexibility of custom themes and branding, allowing for a personalized visual experience. It also integrates news feeds and reminders, further enhancing user engagement and convenience.

CHAPTER 10   INTRODUCTION TO SAP FIORI SPACES AND PAGES

10.11.1 Home

The **My Home** tab is where users can manage their frequently used apps. This is divided into three main sections:

- Pages
- Apps
- Insights

The **Home** tab at the top of the Fiori Launchpad screen presents all the **business catalogs** assigned to the user in the left panel. In the right panel, the corresponding **pages, tiles,** or **apps** are displayed, as illustrated in the figure below.

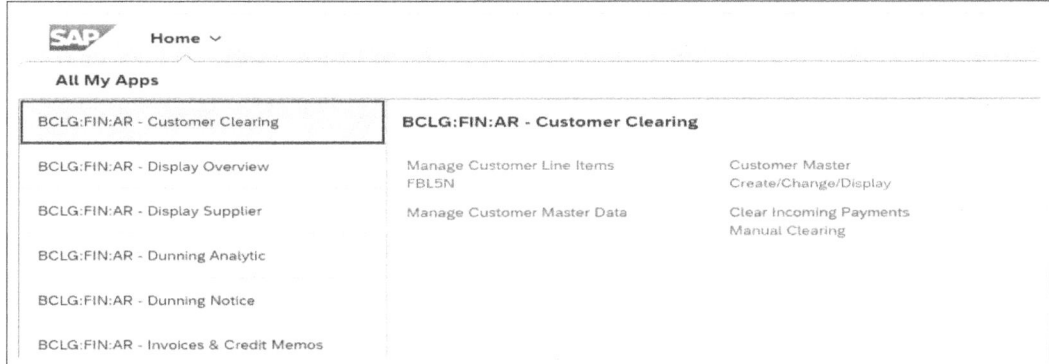

Figure 10-122. *The Home tab displays the business catalogs, pages, and tiles assigned to the test user ID*

10.11.2 Pages

The **Pages** section displays all the **spaces and page IDs** assigned to the user, as shown in the figure below.

CHAPTER 10   INTRODUCTION TO SAP FIORI SPACES AND PAGES

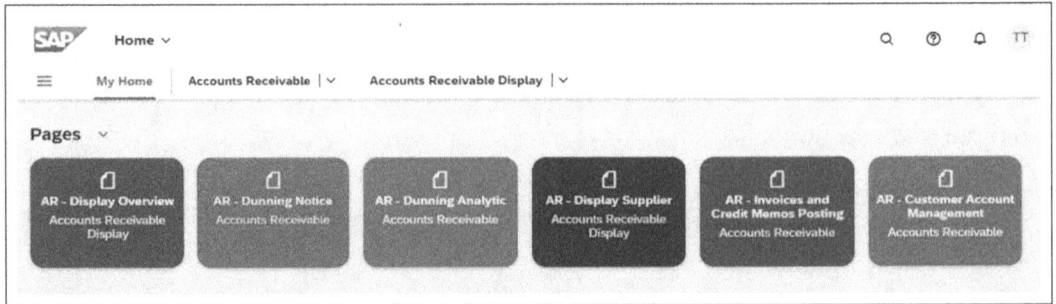

Figure 10-123. Under My Home, the Pages section shows the spaces assigned to the user

The figure above displays the **space/page ID description** in a title format, which is generated based on the **roles** assigned to the user. In this case, the first tile, **AR – Display Overview**, describes both the space and page ID information, as detailed in the figure below.

- **Space Description**: Accounts Receivable Display
- **Page ID Description**: AR – Display Overview

Selecting the **AR – Display Overview** tile takes you directly to the spaces and pages landing workspace, as shown in the figure below.

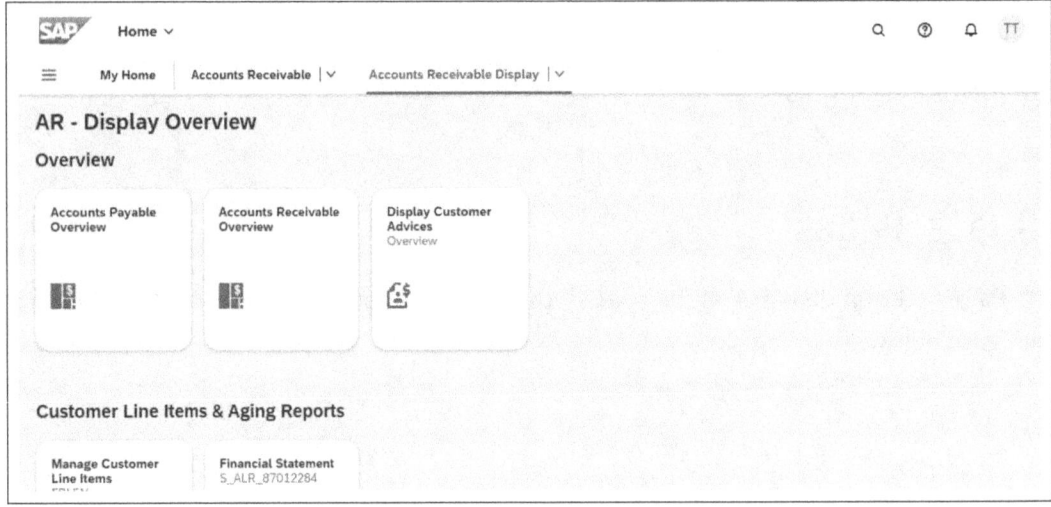

Figure 10-124. Spaces and pages landing workspace

552

CHAPTER 10 INTRODUCTION TO SAP FIORI SPACES AND PAGES

The **Pages** pull-down option provides two extra options, and they are

- Manage Pages
- My Home Settings

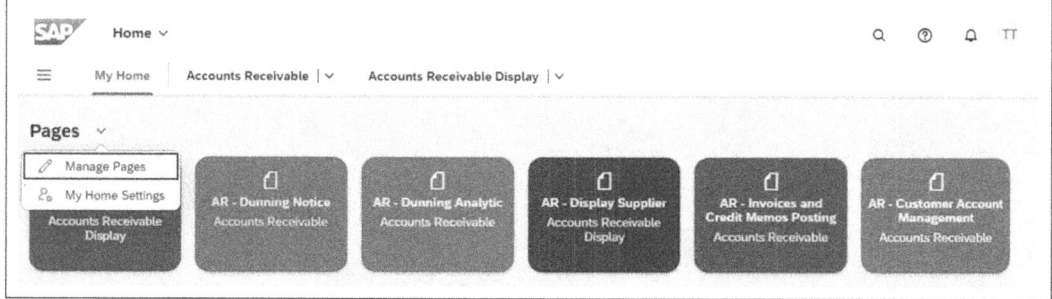

Figure 10-125. Pages: two options displayed

The above figure shows the two options available within the Pages pull-down option.

Manage Pages

The **Manage Pages** option lets users customize the layout of their SAP Fiori **My Home**. Users can add, rename, move, or delete sections to better organize their workspace. This feature helps group apps, links, and widgets based on business functions or personal preferences, creating a more efficient and productive user experience. Selecting the option directs you to the **My Home Settings** window, as shown in the figure below.

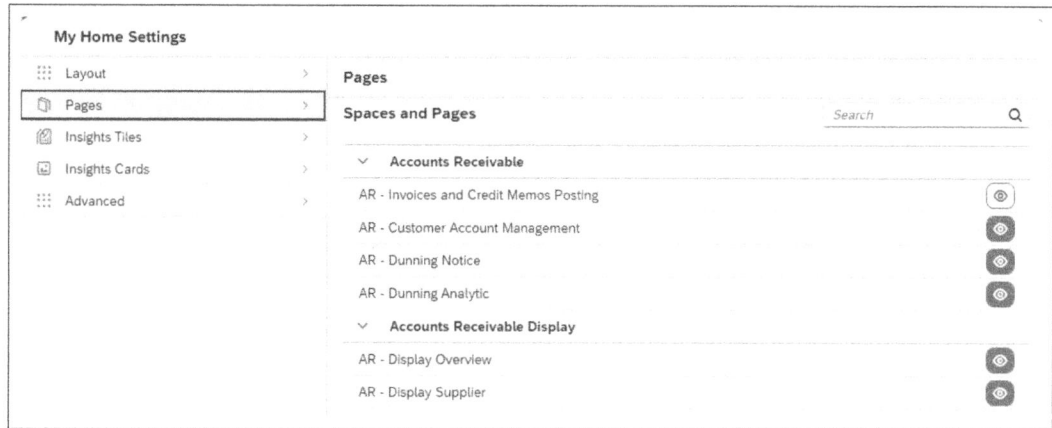

Figure 10-126. Manage Pages with My Home Settings

553

My Home Settings provides five additional options for users to customize as needed, which are listed and explained below:

- Layout
- Pages
- Insights Tiles
- Insights Cards
- Advanced

Layout

The **Layout** option enables users to personalize their **My Home** by organizing the content displayed, as shown in the figure above. You can personalize the layout by turning section visibility on or off and rearranging them using the drag-and-drop method.

Pages

The **Pages** option allows users to manage various pages within their **My Home**. It will enable users to show/hide pages along with tiles by selecting the show option 👁.

Insights Tiles

The **Insights Tiles** feature enables users to add **dynamic tiles** that display real-time information, including KPIs, reports, and alerts, keeping them up to date on critical business metrics without needing to navigate to other applications.

Insights Cards

The **Insights Cards** option gives you a detailed view of business data. Unlike tiles, these cards display key information using visual tools such as graphs, tables, or summaries. This helps you quickly identify and understand key data points. Here, you can select up to ten cards.

Advanced Options

The **Advanced Options** section provides further customization and configuration settings for My Home. Users can choose to enable or disable certain features, adjust default settings, and incorporate external content. This enables a tailored home space experience that aligns with individual preferences and business requirements.

My Home Settings

The **My Home Settings** option allows users to customize their **My Home**. Users can enable or disable My Home, set it as the default page, and adjust personalization options. This helps them personalize their workspace while following company rules. Selecting **My Home Settings** directs you to the same window titled **My Home Settings,** as shown in the figure above.

Manage Pages

The **Manage Pages** option allows users to customize and organize the layout of their SAP Fiori **My Home**. Users can add, rename, move, or delete sections to structure their workspace efficiently. This feature helps in grouping apps, links, and widgets based on business functions or personal preferences, ensuring a streamlined and productive user experience.

My Home Settings

The **My Home Settings** option provides users with configuration controls for their **My Home** experience. It allows users to enable or disable My Home, set it as the default landing page, and manage personalization settings. This ensures that users can tailor their workspace to their needs while maintaining consistency with organizational policies.

10.11.3 Apps

The **Apps** section in the **My Home** tab makes it easy for users to find and manage applications. It shows users apps based on how they use them, so they do not have to search through the entire catalog. Users also have the option of adding apps.

Favorites

The **Favorites** tab shows apps that users have marked as favorites for easy access. This feature helps users keep their most important apps in one place, which saves time when navigating.

Most Used

The **Most Used** tab shows the applications you access most often, based on your activity. It updates automatically to display the tools you use regularly, making them easier to find.

Recently Used

The **Recently Used** tab shows the apps the users have accessed recently. This helps users quickly return to the apps they were using. It is beneficial for picking up tasks without having to search for the app again.

10.11.4 Insights

The **Insights** tab in the **My Home** section provides real-time business data and analytics within My Home. Users can add dynamic tiles that showcase key metrics, such as sales performance, pending approvals, and inventory levels. This feature enables quick visual insights, enhancing decision-making and boosting efficiency.

10.12 High-Level Steps: Create Spaces and Pages

To better understand the concept explained in the previous sections, it can be summarized graphically as shown in the figure below. It is wise to keep this schematic handy when building spaces and pages.

CHAPTER 10 INTRODUCTION TO SAP FIORI SPACES AND PAGES

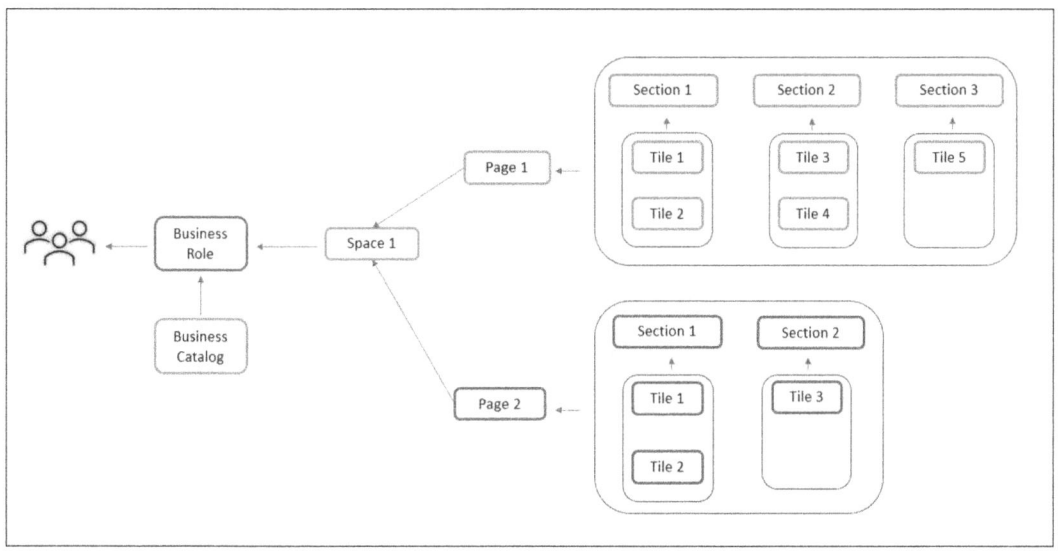

Figure 10-127. Schematic displaying high-level graphical steps to create spaces and pages

The main steps for creating spaces and pages and then assigning them to the user are as follows:

> **Step 1: Enable spaces – to activate spaces and pages, access the User Menu and select Settings.** Under **Spaces and Pages**, select the **Use Spaces** checkbox and then click Save. This will activate the **space-based** layout instead of **groups**. Set the parameters using the transaction **/UI2/FLP_CUS_CONF (client specific).**

PARAMETER	VALUE	DESCRIPTION
SPACES	true	Specify whether users can enable Spaces and Pages: True/False (Default).
SPACES_ENABLE_USER	true	Specify whether users can switch between spaces and the Classic Home Page: True/False (Default).
SPACES_MYHOME	true	Specify whether the My Home space is enabled for users: True (Default)/False

Figure 10-128. Spaces, parameters, values, and descriptions

Step 2: Create a custom business role. Create a role with a description using the transaction **PFCG**. The **role** name should start with either **Z** or **Y** and should not exceed **30 characters**.

Step 3: Create a custom business catalog. Create a **custom business catalog** with a description using the transaction **/UI2/FLPCM_CUST**. The **catalog** name should start with **Z** or **Y** and add **tiles or apps** as required.

Step 4: Assign the business catalog to the role. The custom business catalog can be assigned to the role using the transaction **PFCG**. Once executed insert the catalog into the role using **Menu ➤ Transaction ➤ SAP Fiori Launchpad ➤ Launchpad Catalog**. The business catalog will get all the **IWSG/IWSV** components related to tiles or apps, which are maintained in transaction **SU24**. Maintain authorizations as per your business requirements.

Step 5: Open the SAP Fiori Launchpad home page. Using the transaction **/UI2/FLP** will open the SAP Fiori Launchpad, displaying the **Manage Launchpad Spaces and Manage Launchpad Pages** apps, which will be used to create **spaces** and **pages**.

Step 6: Create a space. Within the SAP Fiori Launchpad, launch the **Manage Launchpad Spaces app**, click the **Create** button, and fill in the necessary details in the pop-up window. The **space ID** name should start with either **Z** or **Y**, along with a corresponding **space description**. It also gives you the option to create a **page** simultaneously. The **space ID** needs to be assigned to the **Customizing transport request**. Clicking **Create**, the space ID is created, and the **Manage Launchpad Spaces** display shows the created space ID.

Step 7: Assign the space to the role. The space can be assigned to the role by using transaction **PFCG** or transaction **/UI2/FLPCM_CUST**. Go to transaction **PFCG**, and insert the Launchpad space into the role via **Menu ➤ Transaction ➤ SAP Fiori Launchpad ➤ Launchpad Space**.

Step 8: Create a page within the space. Within the SAP Fiori Launchpad, launch the **Manage Launchpad Pages** app, click the **Create** button, and fill in the necessary details in the pop-up window. The **page ID** should start with either **Z** or **Y,** along with a corresponding **page description**. The **page ID** needs to be assigned to the **Customizing transport request,** which should have already been created. Clicking **Create**, the **page ID** is created, and the **Manage Launchpad Pages app** display shows the page ID.

Note If the page was already created during the space creation process by selecting the "Also create a page" option, then go to the **page** within **Manage Launchpad Pages** and change the **page ID** visibility to **Visible** if it is currently **hidden**.

Step 9: Link the page to the space. To complete this process, navigate to the **Manage Launchpad Spaces app**. Once you open it, search for the page by entering the **page ID**. The system will display the **page ID**. Select this **page ID** and click **Add**. The **space ID** will be updated with the new **page ID**.

Step 10: Open and edit the page. Open the **page ID** using the **Manage Launchpad Pages app**. The **page** displays the **custom business catalog** assigned to the **page ID.** This **page ID** is linked to a specific custom business role. The related custom business catalog is connected to the **space ID** for that role. It also displays and shows all the **tiles or apps** within the custom business catalog. The **page ID** also shows the **+ Add Section** option, to create a section.

Step 11: Create a section within the page. Sections are part of the page ID. Enter a meaningful name and description for each **section** to add tiles or apps as needed. You can create multiple **sections**, to add the apps.

Step 12: Assign tiles or apps within the sections. Once the **section ID** is created, the Fiori apps (tiles) from the catalog will be displayed in the **page ID**. There are multiple options available to add a tile or an app to the **section**. You can select an app and use the drag-and-drop method to add **tile or app** to the **section**. You can also select the app and click **Add**. Once all the tiles or apps are added, **save** the **page** changes.

Step 13: Page Preview. Once the page is saved, you can also use the **Page Preview** option to view how the **page** will appear and display on the end user's SAP Fiori Launchpad home page.

Step 14: The end user logs into the Launchpad. The user logs into the Launchpad by executing transaction **/UI2/FLP**, which opens the SAP Fiori Launchpad home page, displaying **spaces and pages** with the pull-down option enabled. Clicking the **space ID description** will display the associated **pages'** description.

Step 15: Verify, test, and validate. Once the user is on the SAP Fiori Launchpad home page, they can verify the **layout**, **spaces**, **pages**, **sections,** and **tiles or apps** assigned. The user can then execute any app to check if it works. The functional user will need to perform positive and negative testing.

Note A business role should be part of only **one space**, as both focus on a single business topic.

- A space should consist of **one to five pages**, with each page dedicated to a specific business task.

- A page should consist of **one to five sections**, ordered from insight (top left) to action (bottom right), with tasks.

- A section should consist of **three to seven tiles** or **apps**, ordered in a logical way based on the topic.

- In total, there should not be more than **25 tiles** or **apps** per page to keep it manageable.

CHAPTER 10 INTRODUCTION TO SAP FIORI SPACES AND PAGES

10.13 Report /1BCDWB/DB/UI2/STPGA

The report **/1BCDWB/DB/UI2/STPGAC** in SAP Fiori provides a view of the UI2/STPGAC table, showing relationships between roles, spaces, pages, and catalogs. It helps administrators analyze the structure of Fiori Launchpad content by identifying which pages are linked to each space, including the number of pages per space. Key features include detailing the space–page relationships, assignments, display order, priority, and visibility settings of pages. It also helps troubleshoot issues like missing tiles or blank spaces. This report is executed by using transaction SE38 and entering the table name and using the search criteria for spaces as **ZF_SP***. The output is displayed, as shown in the figure below.

Cl.	Space ID	Page ID	Space-Page Assignment Index	Hidden
200	ZF_SP_FIN_AR	ZF_PG_1_FIN_AR	1	
200	ZF_SP_FIN_AR	ZF_PG_2_FIN_AR	2	
200	ZF_SP_FIN_AR_DSP	ZF_PG_1_FIN_AR_DSP	1	
200	ZF_SP_FIN_AR_DSP	ZF_PG_2_FIN_AR_DSP	2	
200	ZF_SP_FIN_AR_DUNNG	ZF_PG_1_FIN_AR_DUNNG	1	
200	ZF_SP_FIN_AR_DUNNG	ZF_PG_2_FIN_AR_DUNGG	2	

Figure 10-129. List of spaces and pages using table /UI2/STPGAC

10.14 Summary

In this chapter, we discussed spaces and pages within the SAP Fiori Launchpad, exploring their significance in organizing and personalizing the user experience. We explained these concepts clearly and demonstrated the step-by-step process of creating spaces and pages, enabling you to tailor the Launchpad to your specific needs. We also explained how spaces act as macro-level containers for roles, while pages break down tasks into actionable pieces within those roles. This structure ensures clarity, focus, and smooth collaboration in a task-based environment. Furthermore, we compared traditional groups and the more modern spaces and pages, highlighting their distinct features and benefits. The user understands how to leverage spaces and pages to create a user-friendly and efficient Fiori Launchpad environment, enhancing end user productivity and navigation.

CHAPTER 11

Converting SAP Fiori Groups to Pages

The Create Launchpad Pages from Groups app in SAP Fiori helps change existing groups into pages in the spaces and pages system. Its main goal is to make it easier to move from the old groups layout to the newer, more flexible spaces and pages structure. The app automatically creates pages by copying the design and content of chosen groups. The groups will be converted to sections of a page. For each group that you select, a section with the same title and content will be created. This keeps users familiar with the setup while allowing better control, personalization, and layout consistency. This process facilitates a smoother transition, reduces manual work, and enhances the user experience on the SAP Fiori Launchpad.

11.1 Introduction

SAP S/4HANA 2021 FPS01 introduced a new app, **Create Launchpad Pages from Groups**, for creating new **pages** based on existing **Fiori business groups**. Using this app, we can manually convert our **business groups** into **pages**. The **business groups** will be converted to sections of a page. Each selected business group will create a section with the same tiles/apps and content. In a scenario where you have upgraded your S/4HANA Fiori from a lower version and groups have been implemented to a higher version, such as S/4HANA 2023, and would like to move from the groups concept to the spaces and pages concept, the app shown below is helpful for quickly and easily converting business **groups to pages**. These pages can then be associated with spaces.

CHAPTER 11 CONVERTING SAP FIORI GROUPS TO PAGES

Spaces and Pages: New App to Create Pages From Existing Groups

The app **Create Launchpad Pages from Groups** allows you to create new pages based on existing groups. The groups will be converted to the sections of the page. For each group that you select, a section with the same title and content will be created.

Technical Details

Type	New
Functional Localization	Not applicable
Scope Item	Not applicable
Application Component	CA-FLP-ABA-DT (**SAP Fiori Launchpad (ABAP Content Admin Tools)**)
Available As Of	ABAP Platform 2021 FPS01

Figure 11-1. New app to create pages from existing groups

11.1.1 Background

SAP has introduced new features that make it easier to create **spaces and pages** and migrate from **groups** to the spaces and pages concept. In S/4HANA 2021 FPS01, SAP provided a handy feature to check which **apps exist in which business groups**, through **content manager transactions** (**/UI2/FLPM_CUST**). This option will be helpful when migrating from the **business groups** concept to the **pages** concept.

Executing the transaction **/UI2/FLPCM_CUST** and searching for custom business catalogs will give a list of catalogs created. In our example, we are searching for catalogs starting with **ZF_BCLG***, as shown in the figure below.

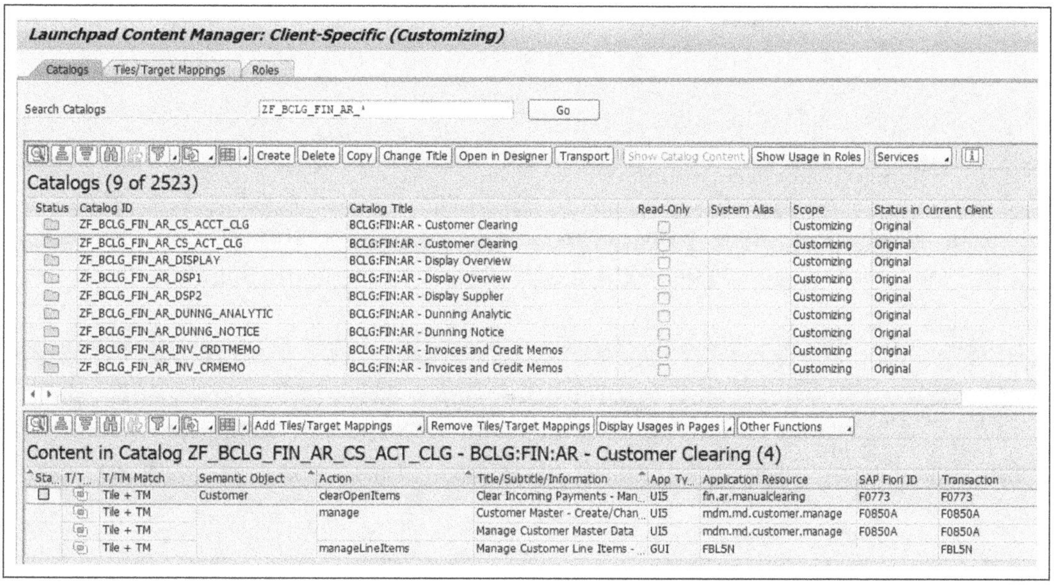

CHAPTER 11 CONVERTING SAP FIORI GROUPS TO PAGES

Figure 11-2. Displaying all the custom business catalogs and content of the selected catalog

The figure above shows all the custom business catalogs created. When you select any catalog, its contents and number of titles are displayed in the bottom panel. Clicking the **Display Usages in Pages** tab opens a new window titled **Usages in Pages**, which presents the output as illustrated in the figure below.

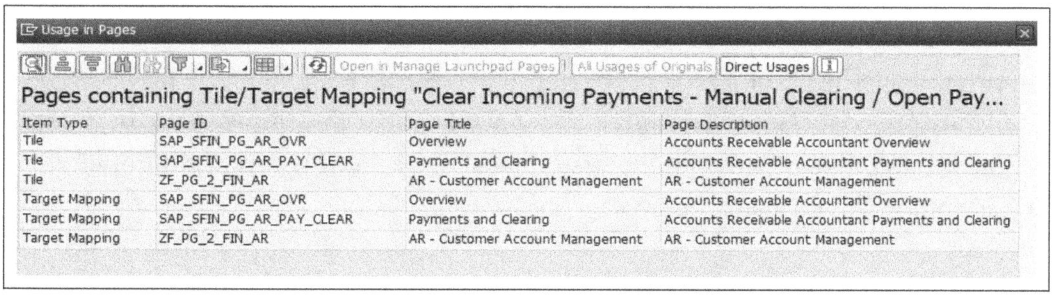

Figure 11-3. Displaying content of the tab Display Usages in Pages

The above figure gives the output for **Display Usages in Pages** for a given business catalog. This tab displays where a selected **page** is used, including the **spaces** and **roles** that reference it. It helps administrators and developers understand connections and the potential impacts of changes or deletions, ensuring safe updates and facilitating impact analysis during Launchpad cleanups or redesigns. Furthermore, the **Display Usages in Pages** tab has a pull-down menu that displays two options, as listed below:

- Display Usages in Pages
- Display Usages in Groups

Similarly, selecting **Display Usages in Groups** from the pull-down menu opens a new window titled **Usage of Tile in Groups,** as shown in the figure below.

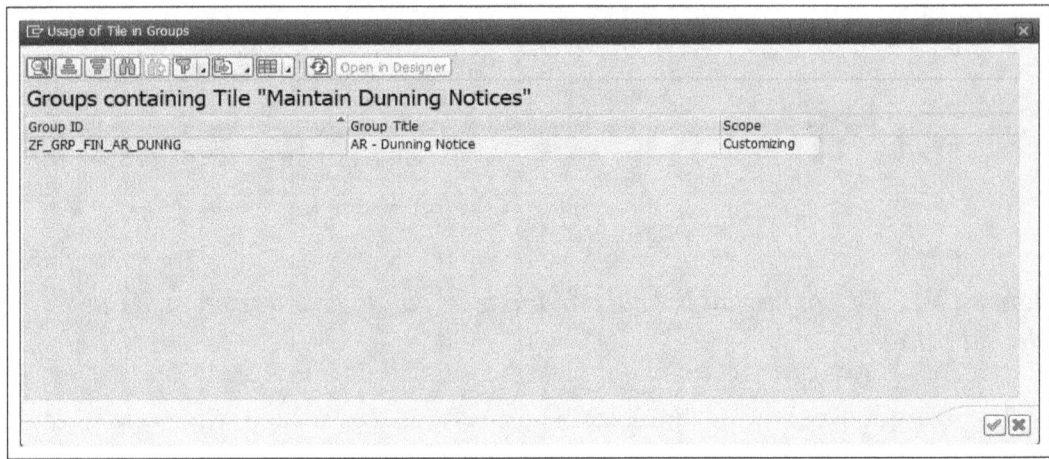

Figure 11-4. *Displaying content of the option Display Usages in Groups*

The above figure displays the output for the **Display Usages in Groups** option for a given business catalog, indicating whether the selected **tile** is part of a Fiori Launchpad group. It provides the **group ID** and **group title** for a given **tile** and where it is used.

In the upper panel for a selected business catalog, selecting **Show Usage in Roles** also helps determine which roles the custom business catalog is part of. This opens the output as shown in the figure below.

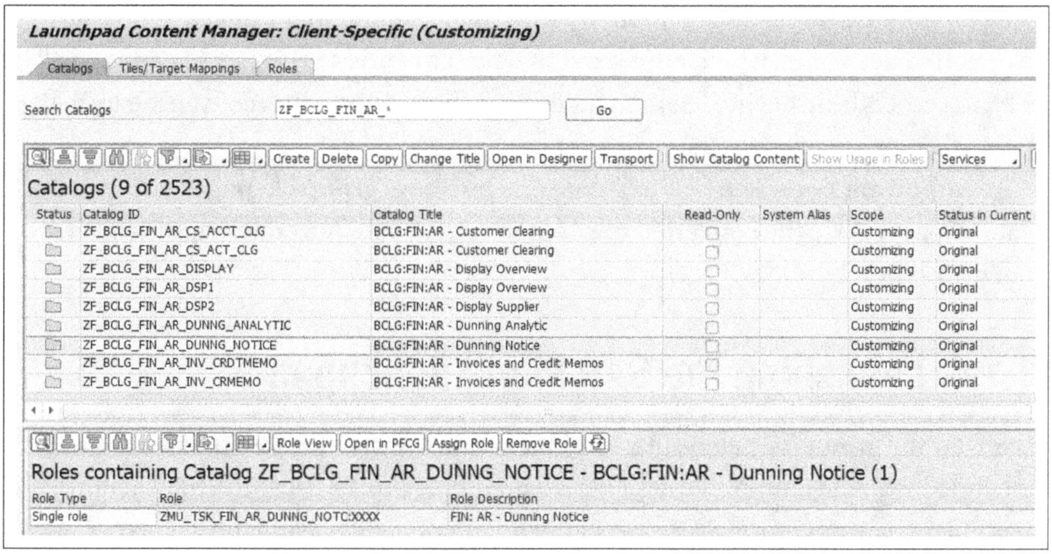

Figure 11-5. Displaying content of the tab Show Usage in Roles

The figure above displays the output of the **Show Usage in Roles** tab. It lists the business roles (**PFCG**) associated with the business catalog. The details include the type, role name, and description. It also lists the number of roles to which the business catalog is assigned.

11.1.2 Prerequisite

A Customizing transport request must be created in transaction **SE09** or **SE10** to transport the pages created across the platform, which is referred to as **converting groups to pages**.

Furthermore, the **groups** should exist in the system before converting them to **pages**. **Appendix B** explains the process of creating a **business group** for a **custom business catalog**. As part of **Chapter 10**, several **groups** were created as examples, and we will use them here.

11.1.3 Process to Convert Existing Groups to Pages

Converting Fiori **business groups** to the **pages** concept is straightforward. You only need to decide on the design aspect of your **page layout**, and this process should be completed before the conversion process.

CHAPTER 11　CONVERTING SAP FIORI GROUPS TO PAGES

As mentioned earlier, the content manager transaction **/UI2/FLPCM_CUST** now has the option to determine which **apps exist in which business groups**. This option will be useful to gather the list of groups associated with the catalog when converting from the **business groups** concept to the **pages** concept.

An important note: The new app converts **business groups** to **pages** but does not create a **Space**. Once the converted **pages** are created, you must manually associate them with **spaces**.

11.1.4 Launching the SAP Fiori Launchpad

To convert the **groups to pages**, the administrator user must log into the Fiori Launchpad with the admin role assigned to their user profile using the transaction **/UI2/FLP**, which opens the SAP Fiori Launchpad home displaying the eight apps, as depicted in the figure below.

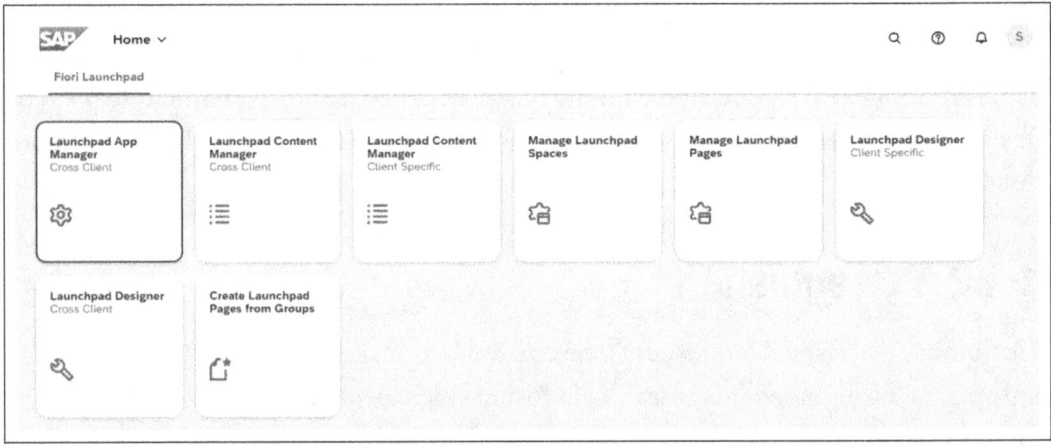

Figure 11-6. SAP Fiori Launchpad home page

11.1.5 Create Launchpad Pages from Groups

Select the **Create Launchpad Pages from Groups** app from the figure above, which opens the **Create Pages from Groups** window, as shown in the figure below.

CHAPTER 11 CONVERTING SAP FIORI GROUPS TO PAGES

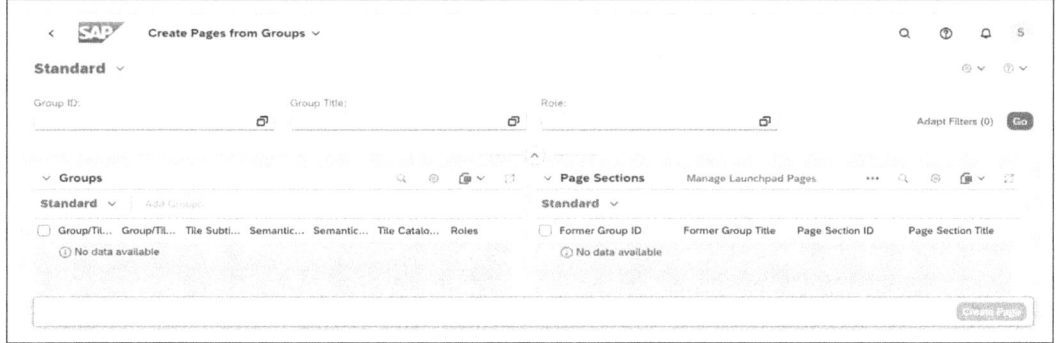

Figure 11-7. *Create Launchpad Pages from Groups app landing page*

You can search for the group using **three** methods, listed below, which are self-explanatory:

- Group ID
- Group Title
- Role

The above figure also shows that the landing page is divided into two panels, mainly:

- Groups
- Pages Sections

In our case, we will use the **Group ID** block and search for **groups** starting with **ZF_GRP_FIN_AR*** and then click **Go** . This will list all the groups related to the search criteria, as shown in the figure below.

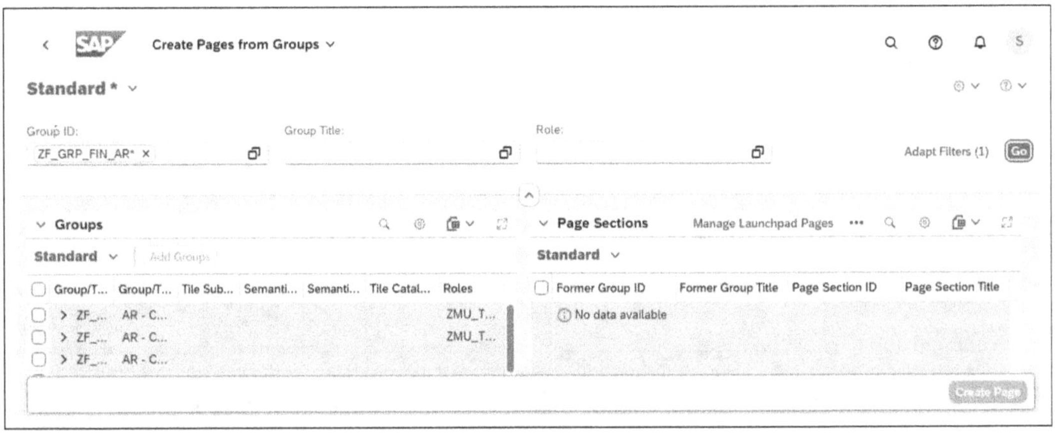

CHAPTER 11 CONVERTING SAP FIORI GROUPS TO PAGES

Figure 11-8. Displaying all groups based on selection criteria

The figure above illustrates all related **groups** based on the selection criteria. The Groups section on the left-hand panel displays all relevant information related to the groups.

By selecting the **settings** option under Groups, a window titled **Settings** opens, allowing you to specify what information is displayed, as shown in the figure below.

Figure 11-9. Settings option available to display the required fields

In the above figure, we will select the checkbox **Allow Horizontal Scrolling** and select the necessary columns to be displayed, as shown in the figure below.

CHAPTER 11   CONVERTING SAP FIORI GROUPS TO PAGES

Figure 11-10. Columns selected

Then, click OK `OK` at the bottom of the screen, as shown in the figure above, and the Create Pages from Groups window updates, as shown in the figure below.

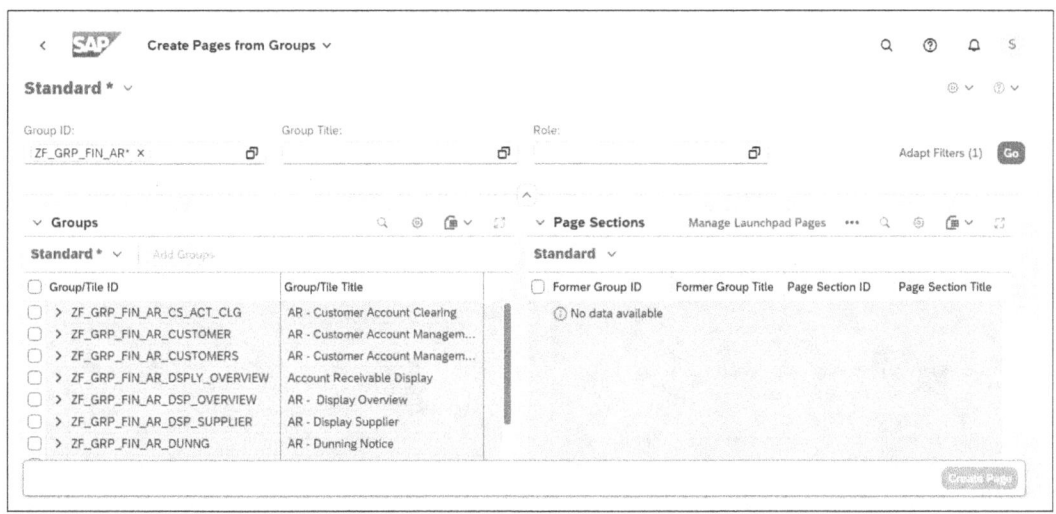

Figure 11-11. Create Pages from Groups window updates with columns selected

In the above figure, expanding the selected **group** by using the symbol ➤ next to the **group/tile ID** displays the available tile IDs and their descriptions, as shown in the figure below.

571

CHAPTER 11   CONVERTING SAP FIORI GROUPS TO PAGES

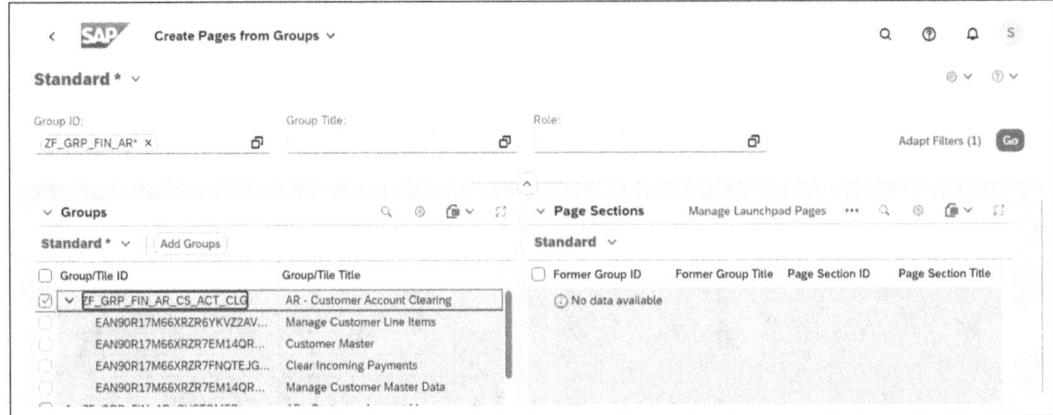

Figure 11-12. Selected group content displayed along with the tile IDs and descriptions

In our example, we will work with the group ID **ZF_GRP_FIN_AR_INVOICE**, as shown in the figure below.

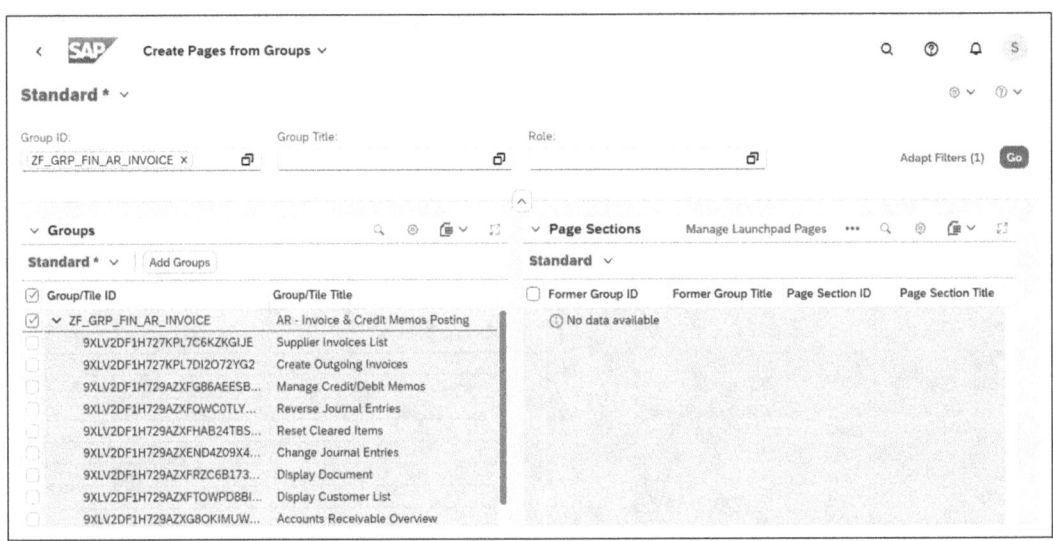

Figure 11-13. Group selected to convert into a page

In the figure above, select the **group**, and then drag and drop it into the **Page Sections** panel, which updates as shown in the figure below.

572

CHAPTER 11   CONVERTING SAP FIORI GROUPS TO PAGES

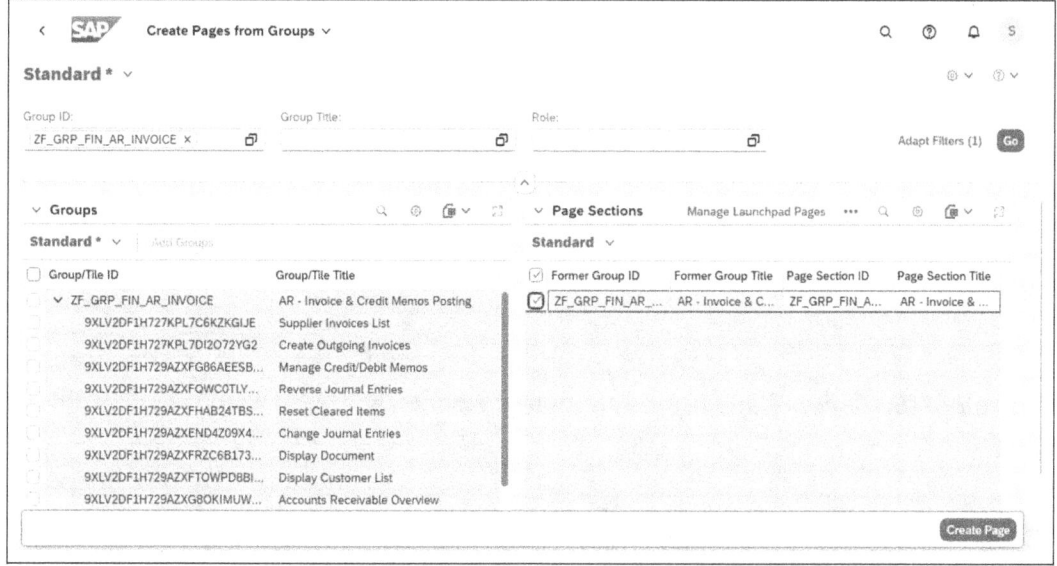

Figure 11-14. *The group moved to Page Sections to create a new page*

The **group** has been moved to **Page Sections,** as shown in the figure above. To create a new **page**, select the **group ID** and click the **Create Page** button at the bottom as shown in the above screen. This action opens a box titled **Create Page**, where you can enter the following necessary information related to the **page** you wish to create, as illustrated in the figure below:

- Page ID
- Page Description
- Page Title
- Request/Task

573

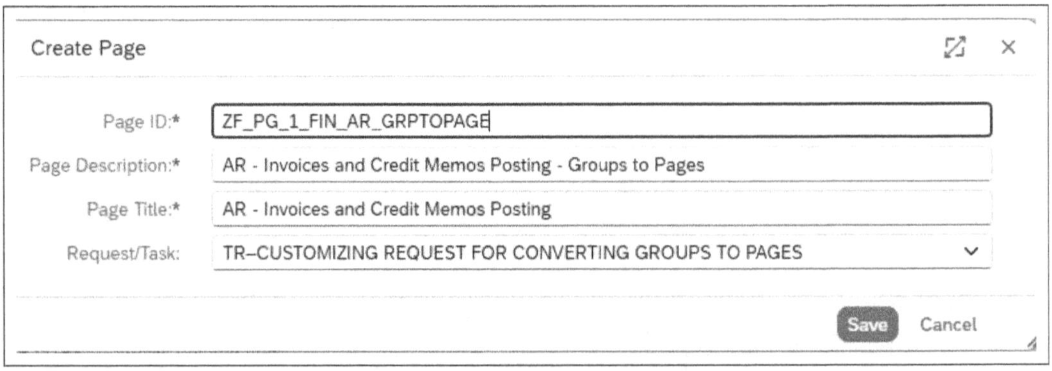

CHAPTER 11   CONVERTING SAP FIORI GROUPS TO PAGES

Figure 11-15. Create Page input screen to add details

> **Note** Sometimes, the **Request/Task** option is grayed out after entering the main information. In this case, **cancel** the request and re-enter the details; **Request/Task** will then become enabled.

In the figure above, once the **page** details are entered, **save** the settings by clicking **Save**, which will create a new **page**, as shown in the figure below.

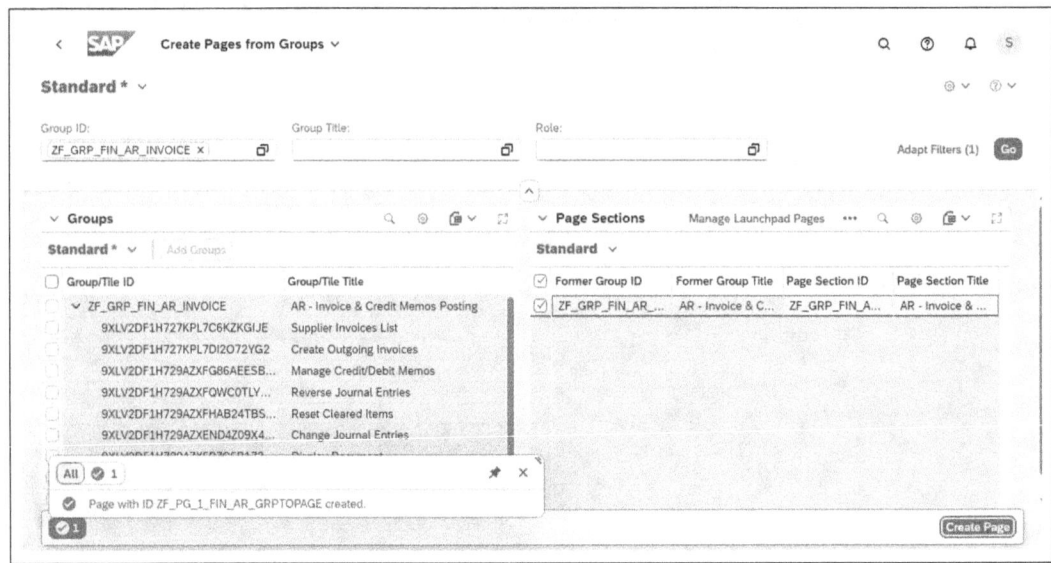

Figure 11-16. Page created successfully

CHAPTER 11 CONVERTING SAP FIORI GROUPS TO PAGES

The page was successfully created, as indicated by the message displayed at the bottom of the above figure: **Page with ID ZF_PG_1_FIN_AR_GRPTOPAGE created.** To verify if the **page** has been created, select the **Manage Launchpad Pages** option in the **Page Sections area**, which will open the Manage Launchpad Pages home page, as shown in the figure below.

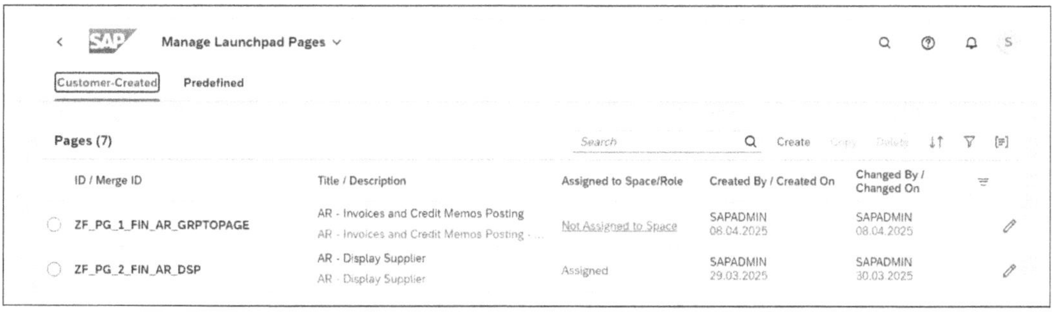

Figure 11-17. Manage Launchpad Pages app displays the new page created

The above figure verifies that the **page** was created successfully within the **Manage Launchpad Pages** app and shows the **page** is **Not Assigned to Space**. Select the pencil icon to open the **Page Content tab**, which displays the new page created along with all the associated tiles, as shown in the figure below.

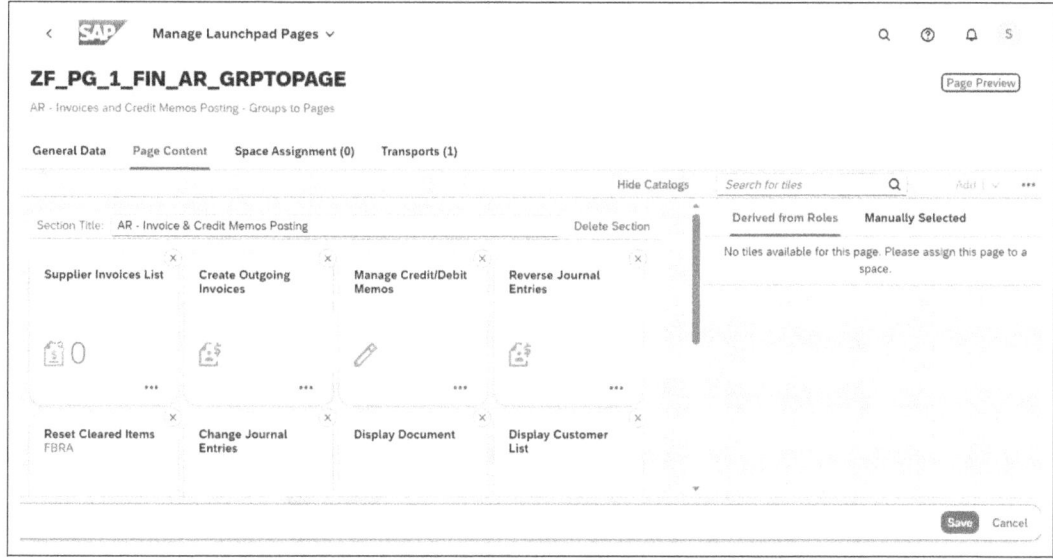

Figure 11-18. New page created with its associated tiles

575

The above figure shows that the new **page** was created and displays the associated tiles that were part of the **group**, which have become available and **visible.** Here, the **group** name is equivalent to the **page** name, and the apps within the **group** become part of a **section**. Within the **Page Content** tab, you can add, delete, and modify pages, sections, apps/tiles as desired. You can also reorder how the apps are displayed on the page by moving them as desired. The **page** is not assigned to a **space**, as indicated by **Space Assignment (0)**, and the **page** is assigned to **one transpor**t, as shown by **Transports (1).** Here, we can create a section and assign tiles to it.

11.1.6 Create a Space

Before proceeding to the next step, we must create a new **space** by launching the **Manage Launchpad Spaces** app and clicking the **Create** option. This will open a **Create Space** window, where a **space** can be created, as shown in the figure below.

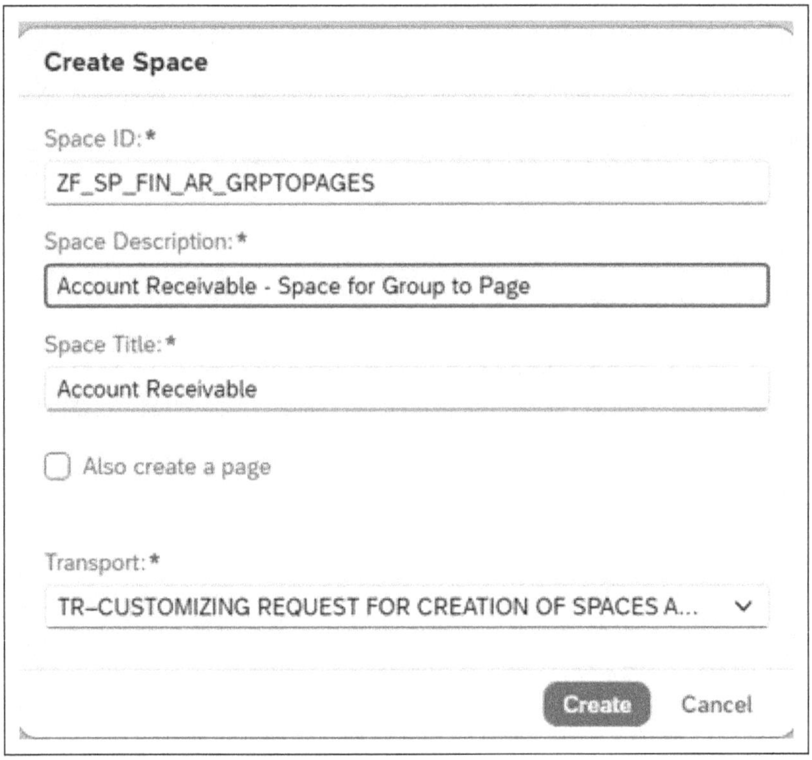

Figure 11-19. Create a new space for assigning the page created by converting the group

In the above figure, enter the desired information and click the **Create** [Create] button to create the **space**. Then search for the **page** and add it to the **space**, as shown in the figure below.

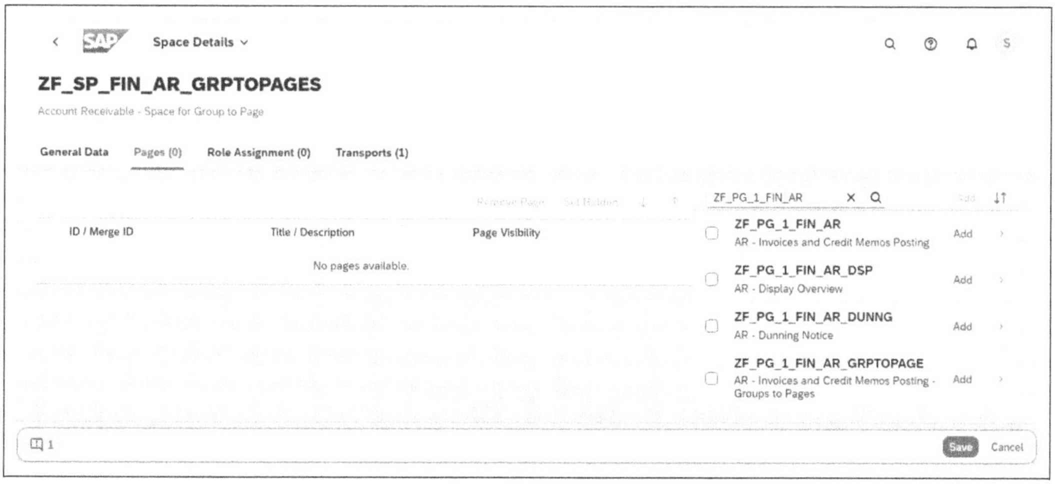

Figure 11-20. New space was created and assigned to the page

The above figure displays that a new **space** was created and assigned to the correct **page**. **Save** the settings for the **space**, and the **Space Details** window is updated, as shown in the figure below.

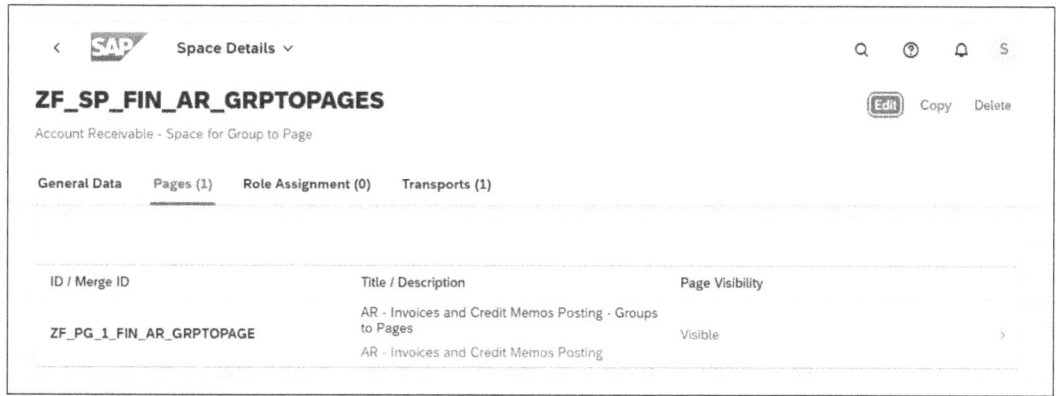

Figure 11-21. Page added to the space

Furthermore, the Manage Launchpad Spaces home page will be updated, as shown in the figure below.

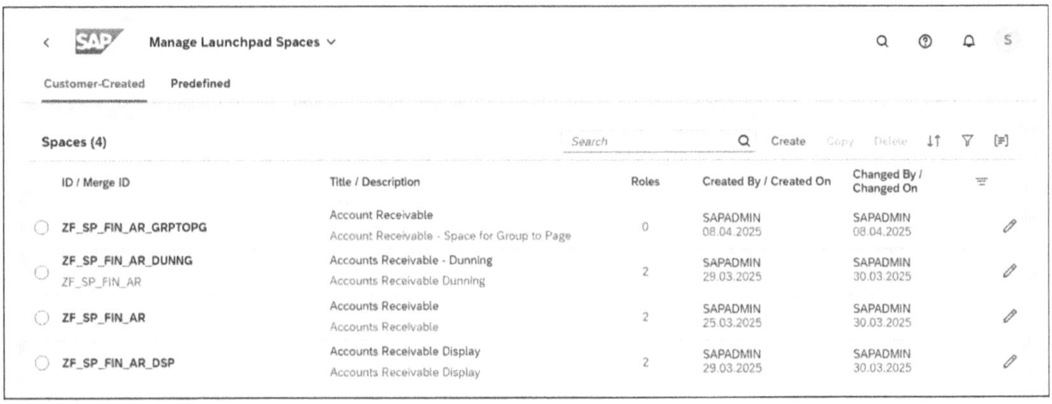

CHAPTER 11   CONVERTING SAP FIORI GROUPS TO PAGES

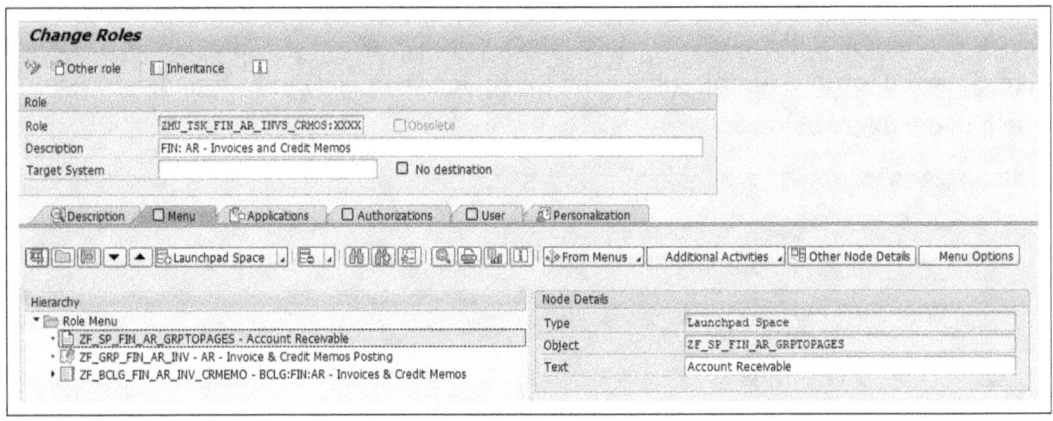

Figure 11-22. Manage Launchpad Spaces home page updated

11.1.7 Assign a Role to a Space

The next step is to assign a **business role** to the **space**. The role also contains the **group**, as shown in the figure below.

Figure 11-23. The business role assigned to the space

The above figure displays the business role, which contains the **custom business catalog**, **space,** and **group**.

CHAPTER 11 CONVERTING SAP FIORI GROUPS TO PAGES

11.1.8 Create Sections

Since the **page** was created earlier, we can create **sections** and distribute the tiles accordingly by launching the **Manage Launchpad Pages** app, as shown in the figure below.

Figure 11-24. Page is assigned to a space/role

The figure above shows that the **page** has been **assigned to a space/role**. Click the **pencil icon** to edit the **page** and create various **sections** as shown in the figure below.

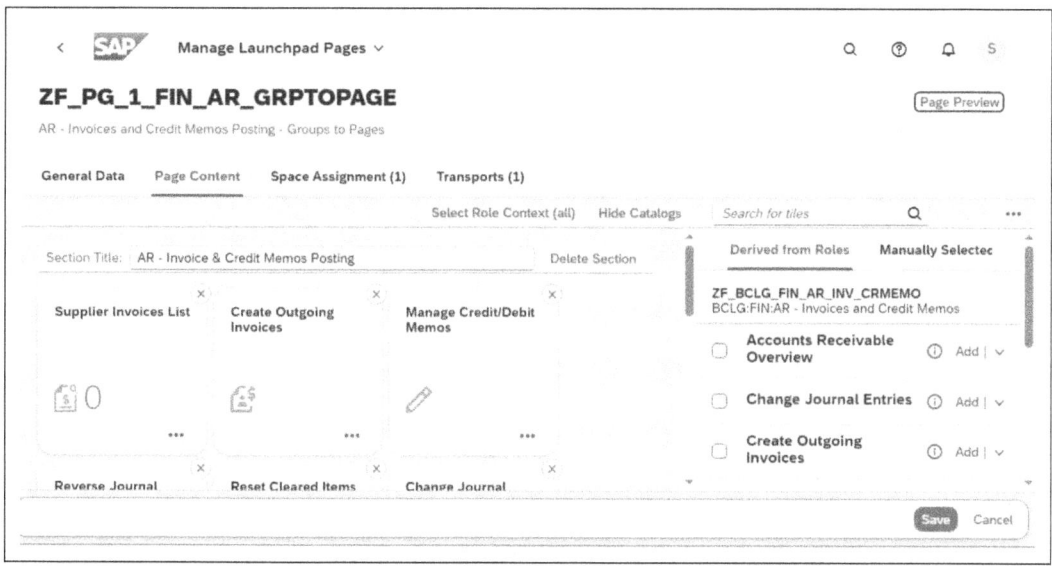

Figure 11-25. Create sections within the page

579

CHAPTER 11   CONVERTING SAP FIORI GROUPS TO PAGES

The above figure also shows the role has an associated **custom business catalog** linked to the **space**.

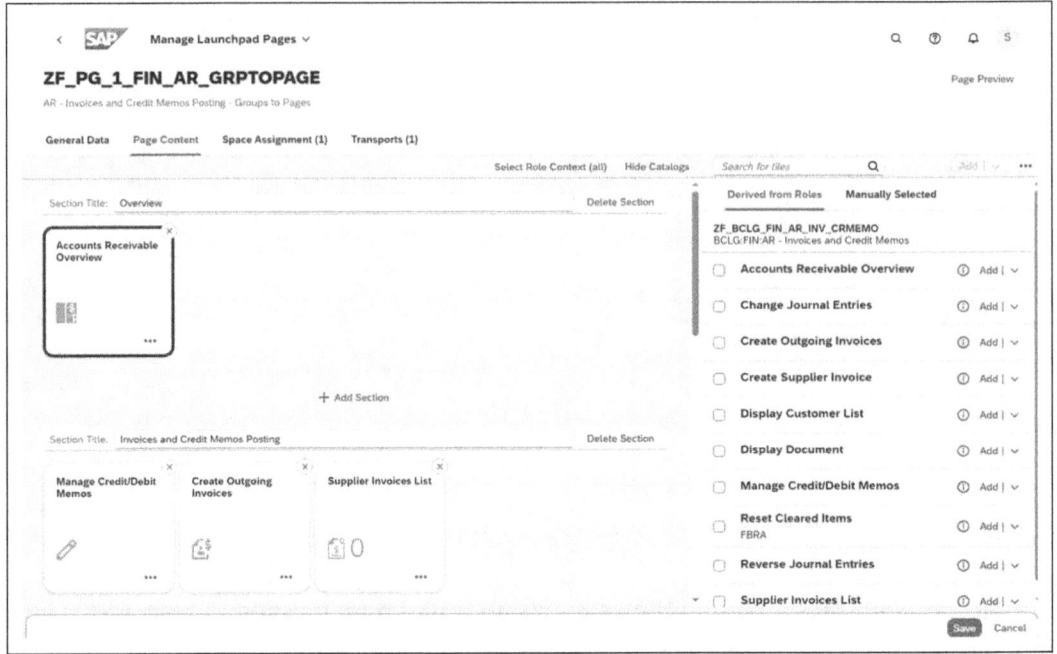

***Figure 11-26.** Sections with tiles assigned within the page*

The figure above shows the **sections** created with the respective tiles arranged. To view how this **page** will appear on the SAP Fiori Launchpad home page, select the option **Page Preview,** and it will display the **page** and the **page content**, as shown in the figure below.

CHAPTER 11 CONVERTING SAP FIORI GROUPS TO PAGES

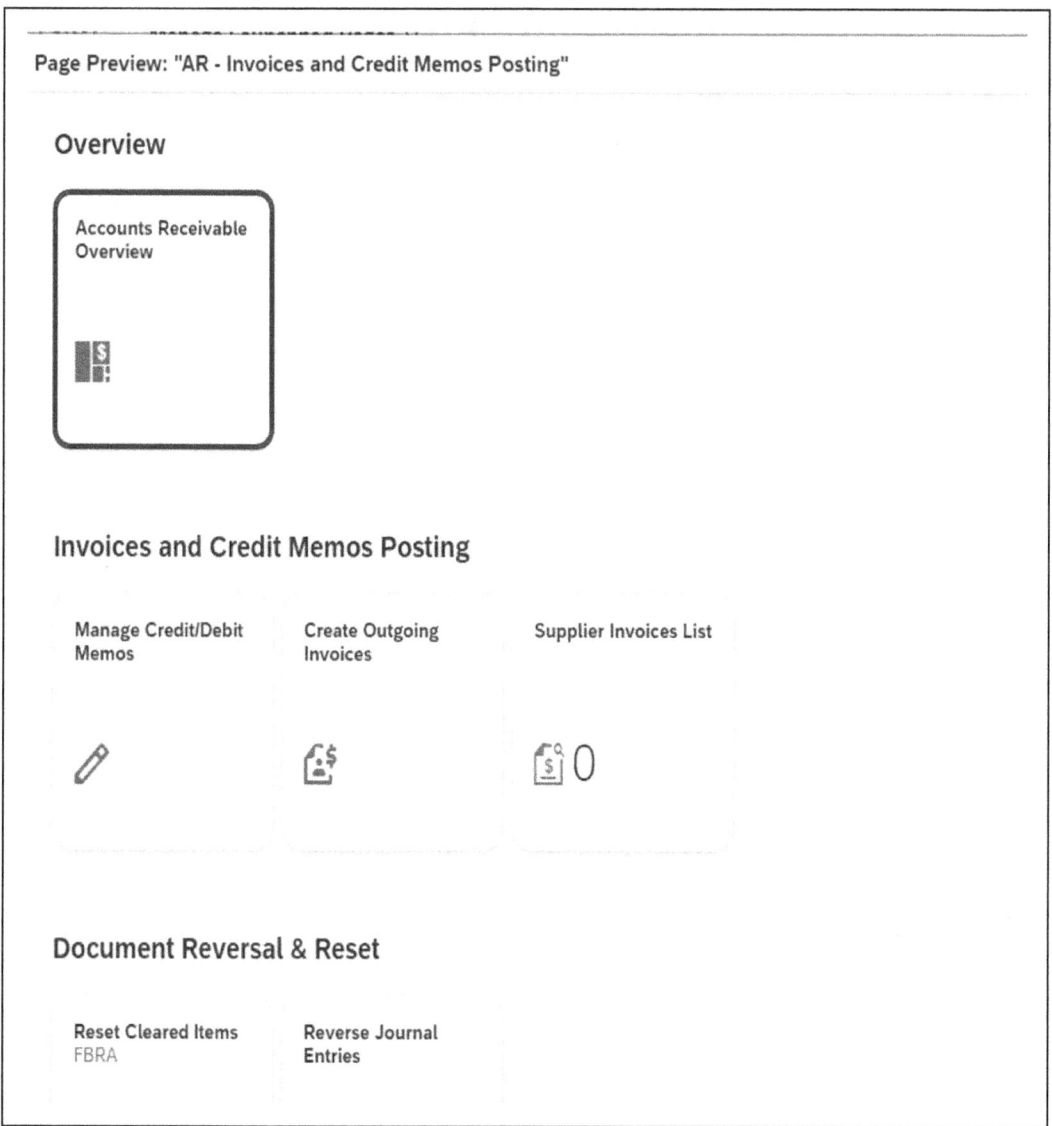

Figure 11-27. *Page Preview as to how the page will appear on the Fiori Launchpad home page*

Once satisfied, save the changes, and the final page screen will appear as shown in the figure above.

CHAPTER 11   CONVERTING SAP FIORI GROUPS TO PAGES

11.1.9 Validation of Group-to-Page Conversion

As part of the testing and validation process, the test user is assigned the following roles, as shown in the figure below.

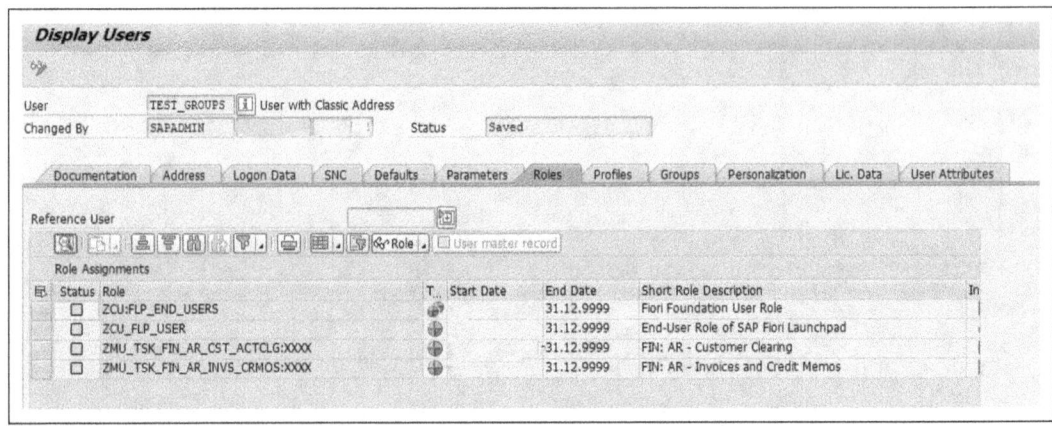

Figure 11-28. Roles assigned to the test user ID

Log in as a test user.

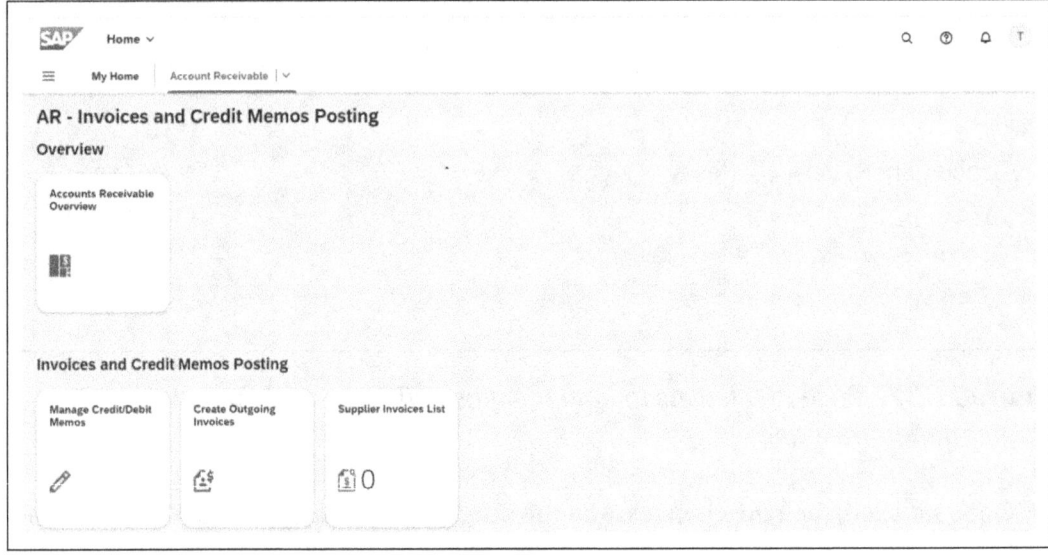

Figure 11-29. Test user content displayed on the SAP Fiori Launchpad home page

582

CHAPTER 11　CONVERTING SAP FIORI GROUPS TO PAGES

The user setting is set to display **spaces and pages** in the above figure, which shows spaces, pages, sections, and tiles. The space contains two pages, as shown in the figure below.

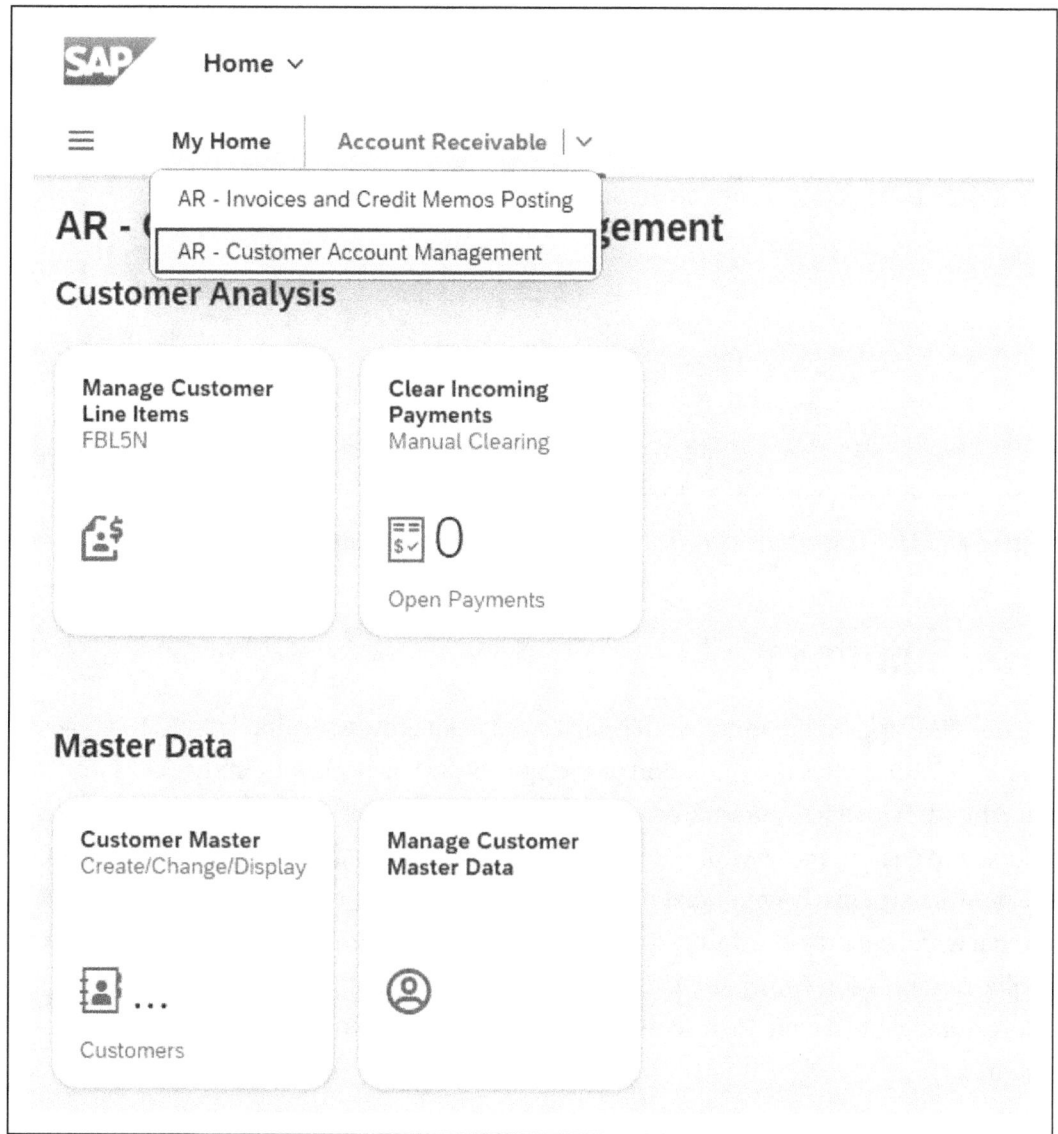

Figure 11-30. *Space and pages displayed on the Launchpad*

Switching back to **groups**, where we need to deselect the **Use Spaces** option, will now display groups with tiles on the SAP Fiori Launchpad home page, as shown in the figure below.

583

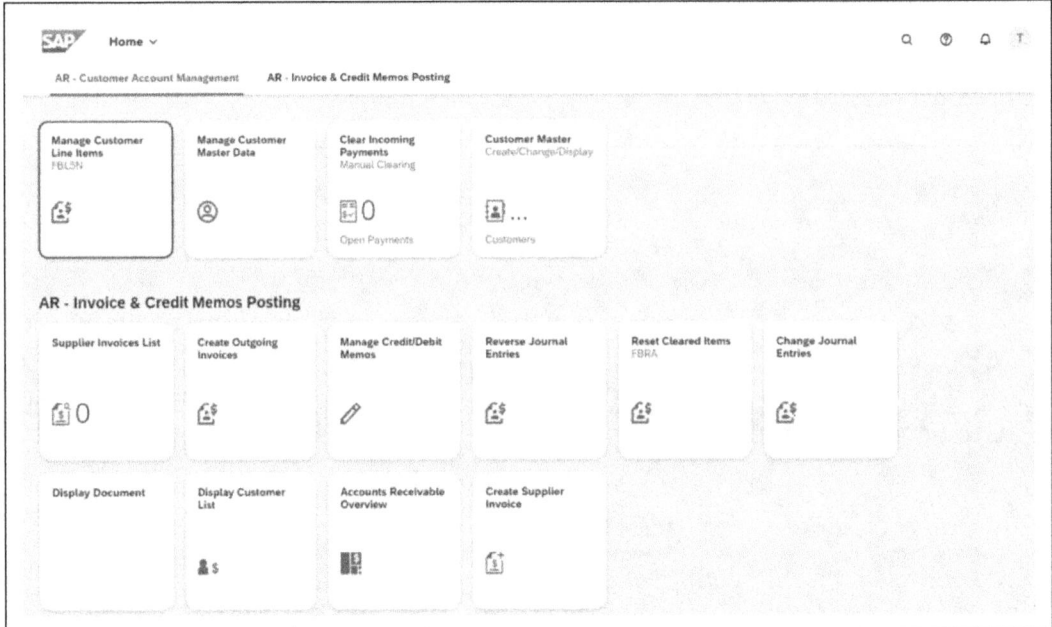

Figure 11-31. *Test user visualizes the group with associated tiles*

11.2 Summary

The new SAP app for creating Launchpad pages from groups, available in S/4HANA 2021 FPS01, simplifies the transition to the spaces and pages layout in the SAP Fiori Launchpad. With a few automated steps, administrators can easily convert existing groups into custom pages while preserving the familiar design and app tiles for users. This tool is particularly beneficial during system upgrades or redesigns, as it reduces manual work, ensures continuity for end users, and promotes the adoption of a more flexible organization within the Launchpad. Remember, assigning a space to a role before linking it to a page for a seamless migration and an enhanced user experience is essential.

CHAPTER 12

Configure Custom SAP Fiori Apps

We utilize custom Fiori apps when standard SAP Fiori apps do not fully address our business requirements or any custom reports must have to be accessed via SAP Fiori. These custom applications allow us to create screens, workflows, and features tailored to our company's operations, making tasks quicker and more user-friendly. The primary benefit of using custom apps is enhanced user experience and increased productivity, as employees receive precisely what they need without unnecessary steps or irrelevant options.

12.1 Introduction

SAP GUI apps are currently available for many SAP standard transaction codes, and with every SAP S/4HANA release, SAP adds newer SAP GUI apps for transaction codes. However, there are still some transaction codes, such as SU53, SU01, SU01D, SUIM, etc., for which no SAP GUI apps are available. So there could be a need to create a custom app for such transaction codes if SAP Fiori becomes the primary interface for accessing SAP.

Another scenario where a custom app could be created is for any custom-developed object, such as custom UI5 applications, custom transaction codes, custom reports, etc. Business users must have access to these transaction codes and programs via the Fiori Launchpad as a tile icon for which no app exists in the SAP Fiori Apps Reference Library.

In this chapter, we will discuss configuring an **SAP transaction** into an **app** in an easy step-by-step process. SAP has announced a new Launchpad App Manager tool that is accessed with transaction code **/UI2/FLPAM** starting from **SAP S/4HANA 2020**. The primary purpose of this tool is to manage all technical catalogs in one place, providing a straightforward and user-friendly experience for managing Launchpad app descriptor items. This is the preferred configuration tool for creating, maintaining, and setting up technical catalogs only. Admin users can access this app using the Fiori Launchpad (/UI2/FLP) with an admin role assigned to their profile.

With the advent of this app, SAP will soon deprecate the **Fiori Launchpad Designer tool**. This new central tool will maintain **tiles and target mapping** (T + TM), a powerful tool that serves as a single entry point for numerous filtering options.

> **Note** This app removes the confusion between the technical and business catalogs.

SAP now recommends using the Fiori **Launchpad App Manager** tool only to explore and maintain **technical catalogs**. This tool can then be referenced to create new custom business catalogs using the Launchpad Content Manager – Client Specific (Customizing) (**/UI2/FLPCM_CUST**). In addition, we will also demonstrate how to create a custom app using the Fiori Launchpad Designer transaction **/UI2/FLPD_CUST**.

In this chapter, we will create tiles for the SAP standard transaction code **SU53** to demonstrate how to create a tile for a standard transaction code without an SAP GUI app.

We will also use the example of a custom transaction, ZPARAM_REP, to demonstrate the creation of a tile for a custom report.

For showing the steps for creating a dynamic tile for a custom SAPUI5 app in a catalog, we will mimic Fiori app ID **F0763A**, which is a SAPUI5 app.

12.2 Create a Custom App for Any SAP Transaction Using /UI2/FLPAM

The transaction **/UI2/FLPAM** (Fiori Launchpad App Manager) helps you to create and manage **static** and **dynamic tiles** in the custom **technical catalogs**. It helps you define **target mappings** and **tile** settings, which are later used in custom business catalogs so they can be displayed on the Launchpad for users.

To create a tile for any transaction code for which there is no SAP GUI app available, or if you want to create a tile for a custom transaction code, we will need to create a semantic object for the transaction code. A semantic object can be created with

CHAPTER 12 CONFIGURE CUSTOM SAP FIORI APPS

transaction **/UI2/SEMOBJ**. We will be using this semantic object to create a tile in the **custom technical catalog** in transaction code /UI2/FLPAM.

You also need to create a custom business catalog, using the transaction **/UI2/FLPCM_CUST**, which will be assigned in a **custom business role** and assigned to the end users.

In this section, we will cover how to create a tile for a given SAP transaction, a custom transaction, and a Fiori app that can be displayed on the Launchpad for the end user as either a static or dynamic tile, using some demo examples.

Note In this section, S/4HANA 2023 FPS02 is used as an embedded system, and the standard technical and business catalog types will be used.

12.2.1 Demo 1: Transaction SU53 – Convert to an App

The SAP transaction **SU53** (Evaluate Authorization Check) helps users check for authorization failures in the SAP system. It is utilized across all modules to analyze why a user could not perform a transaction or activity, and it is used daily by **BASIS** and **security** team members. This transaction shows the last failed authorization check and helps identify missing permissions. As a practice exercise, we will create a custom SAP GUI app for transaction SU53, as no Fiori app exists for this transaction. When you execute **SU53** after encountering an error in **SAP GUI**, the results will be displayed on an output screen, as shown in the figure below.

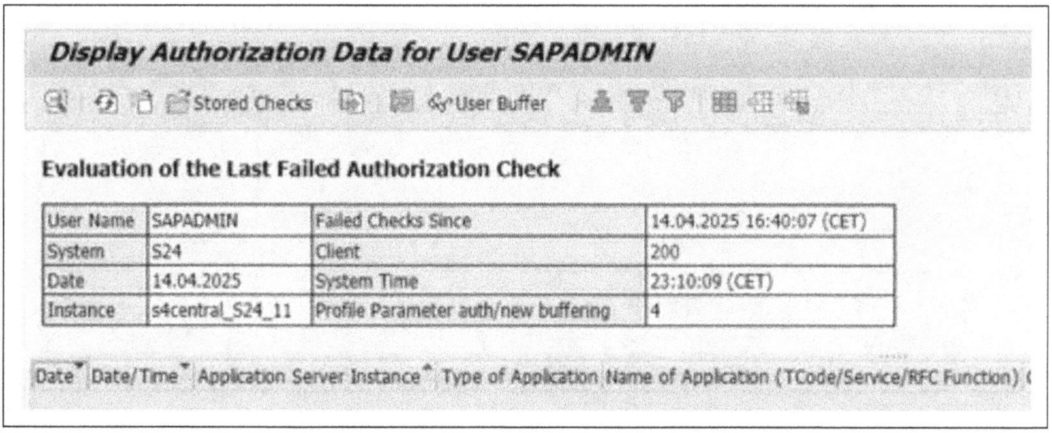

Figure 12-1. Transaction SU53 screenshot in SAP GUI

CHAPTER 12 CONFIGURE CUSTOM SAP FIORI APPS

Verify the Transaction as Marked as SAP GUI for HTML

Open the transaction **SE93**, verify, and check if the transaction **SU53** can be configured for SAP GUI for HTML, which is required to turn the transaction into an app, as shown in the figure below.

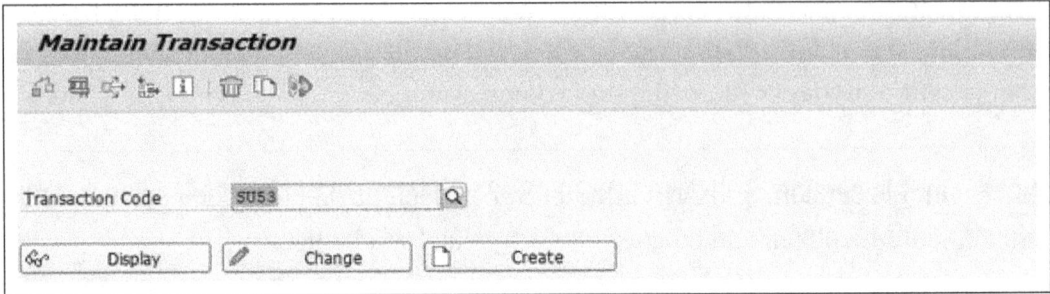

Figure 12-2. *The transaction SE93 initial screen with the transaction SU53*

Next, click the **Display** Display option.

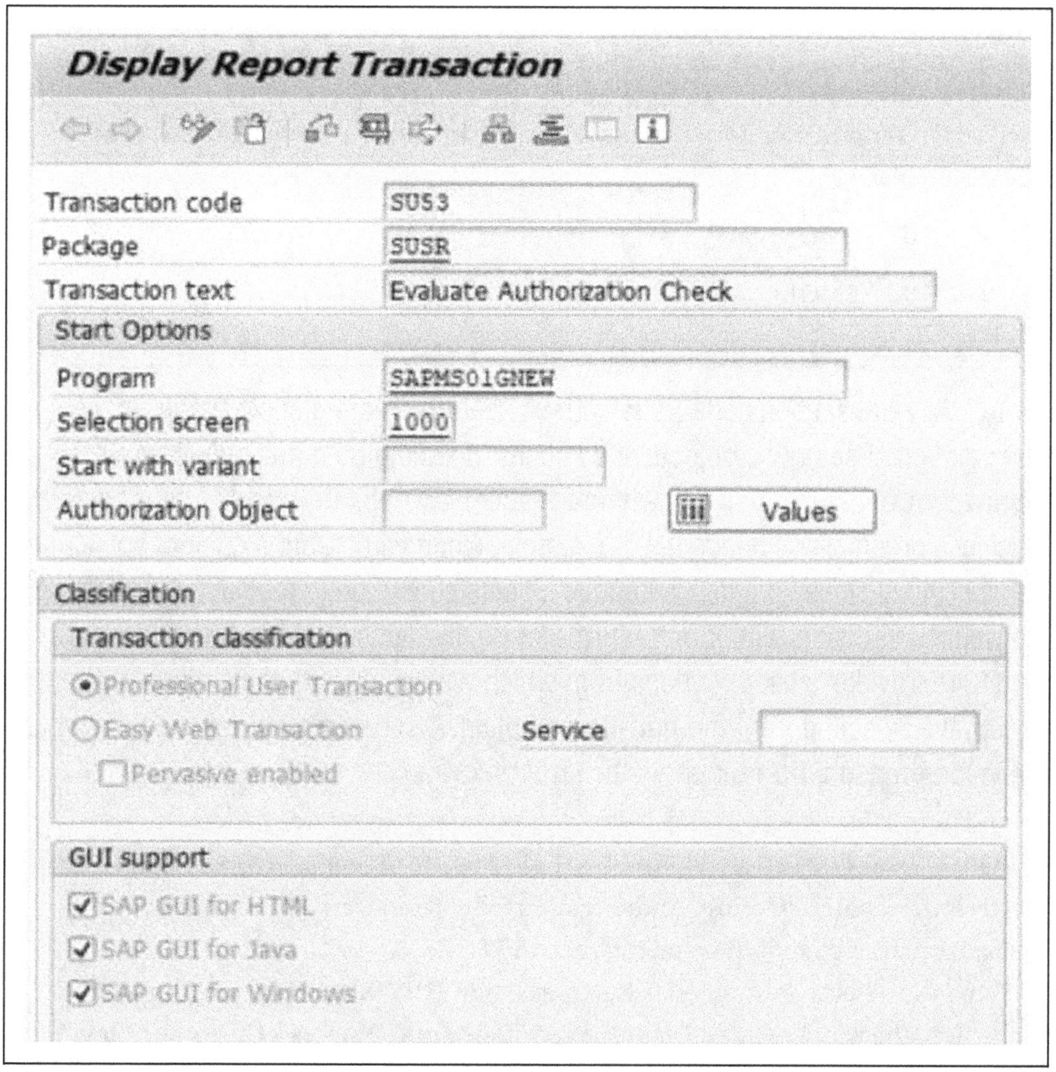

CHAPTER 12 CONFIGURE CUSTOM SAP FIORI APPS

Figure 12-3. Shows that transaction SU53 can be converted to a custom Fiori app

Transaction **SU53** can be converted into a **GUI app** because it is marked as **SAP GUI for HTML**, within the header **GUI support**, as shown in the figure above.

CHAPTER 12   CONFIGURE CUSTOM SAP FIORI APPS

Create a Semantic Object

To create a custom app for a transaction, we need to create an **intent** using a **semantic object** and a **semantic action**. Semantic objects can be created using the transaction codes listed below:

- /UI2/SEMOBJ_SAP
- /UI2/SEMOBJ

Note   Any transaction code for which we need to create a custom app requires the creation of semantic objects and actions. It should be made only if **no SAP equivalent apps** are available within the SAP Fiori Apps Reference Library and the business/organization needs it. For example, when you create a custom application for specific business entities, semantic objects should be in the customer naming convention and start with **Z** or **Y**. Furthermore, the action field is a free-text option, and SAP provides a list of actions from which we can choose the action as desired by always selecting from the **pull-down** option. A **semantic action** should always be in **lowercase with no spaces or underscores**.

Here, a **semantic action** determines the **semantic object's purpose**; it will not directly impact **authorization**. Authorization for custom transaction codes, such as Create, Display, etc., should be maintained in PFCG.

Semantic objects are created using transaction /**UI2/SEMOBJ**. Executing the transaction, the window titled **Display View "Semantic Objects – Customer View": Overview** opens, as shown in the figure below.

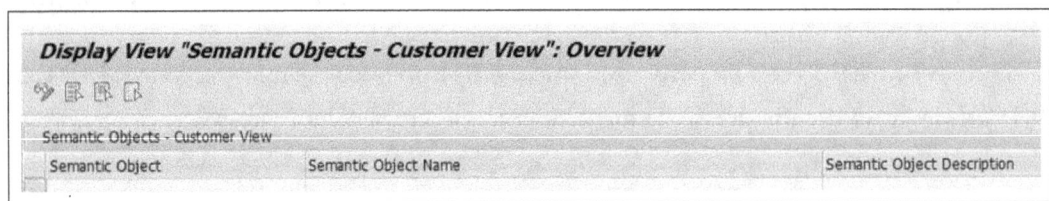

Figure 12-4.   Transaction /UI2/SEMOBJ initial screen

CHAPTER 12 CONFIGURE CUSTOM SAP FIORI APPS

The above figure is empty. This is a new system; no custom semantic objects have been created in this system. Executing the transaction /UI2/SEMOBJ_SAP *displays the SAP-delivered* semantic objects and semantic actions, as shown in the figure below.

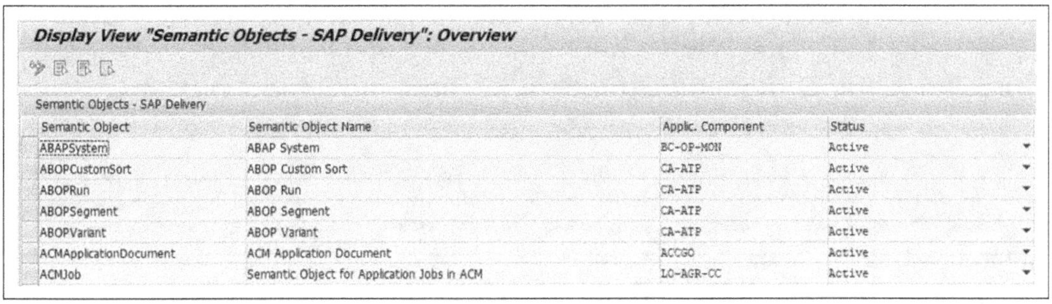

Figure 12-5. Transaction /UI2/SEMOBJ_SAP displaying SAP-delivered objects

To create semantic objects, we will use the table as shown in the figure below to develop and define some of the desired semantic objects.

Figure 12-6. List of semantic objects to be created for custom Fiori apps

From the initial screen of transaction **/UI2/SEMOBJ**, click the **change** icon, and an Information box opens that displays a caution warning that the **table is cross-client**, as shown in the figure below.

591

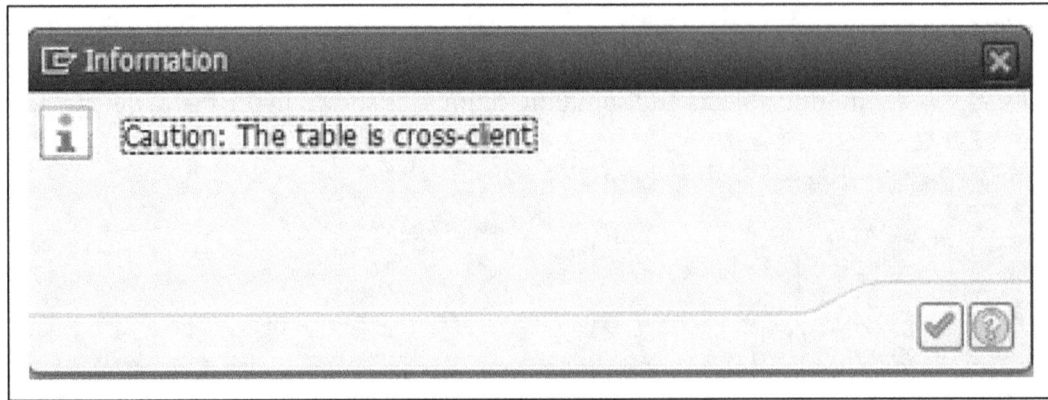

Figure 12-7. Information box stating the table is cross-client

Click the **continue** icon , and then select the option **New Entries** New Entries . This opens the process of adding and creating semantic objects, as shown in the figure below in change mode.

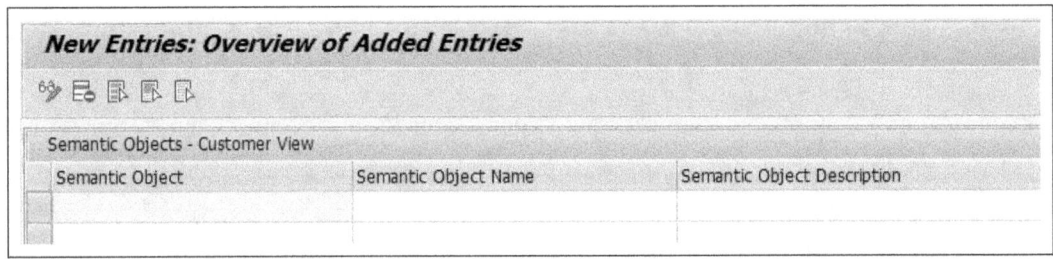

Figure 12-8. Semantic object creation input screen

In the figure above, we must create a unique identifier for the **custom semantic object**. This identifier helps the Fiori Launchpad understand which app to open when a user clicks a tile. This transaction allows you to create multiple **semantic objects** simultaneously. Enter the details of the transaction **SU53** semantic object, as shown in the figure below.

Semantic Object	Semantic Object Name	Semantic Object Description
ZSO_SU53	ZSO_SU53: Displaying Authorization Errors App	Custom Semantic Object for SU53: Display Authorization Errors App

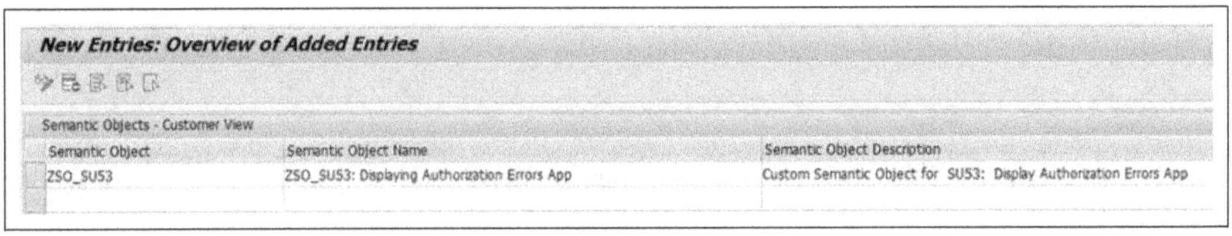

Figure 12-9. Custom semantic object details entered

CHAPTER 12   CONFIGURE CUSTOM SAP FIORI APPS

Click the save icon to save the changes. The system will prompt you to save the changes in a transport. Select a transport if you already have one or create a new one.

Click the **continue** icon, and the **semantic object is created**. A new message is displayed at the bottom of the screen, **Data was saved**, as shown in the figure below.

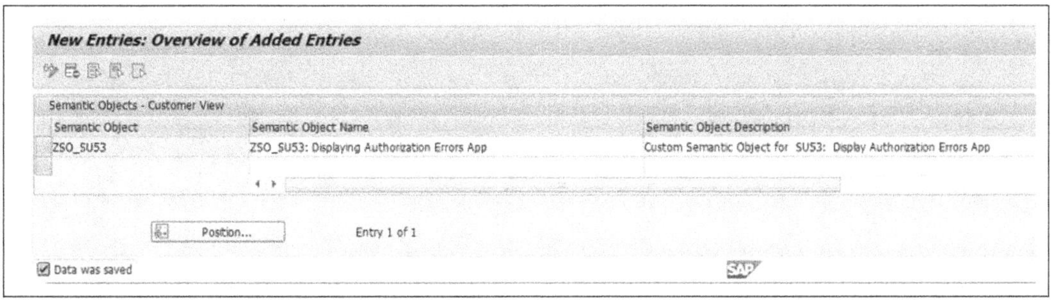

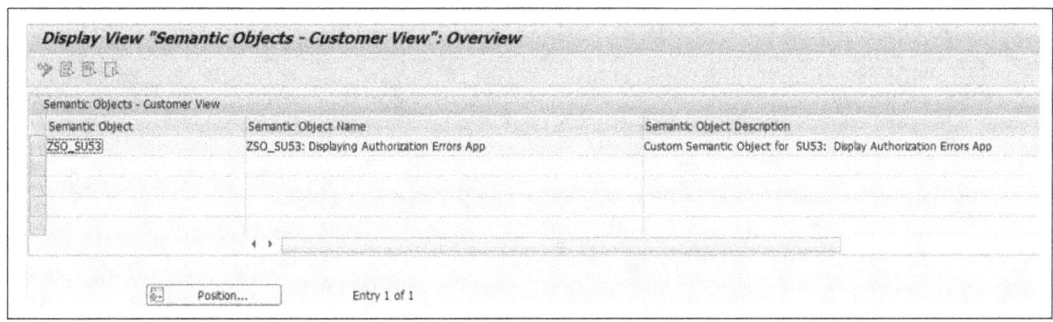

Figure 12-10. Semantic object created and saved

Now click the **go-back** icon and check the screen.

Figure 12-11. Custom semantic object created

Create a New Custom Technical Catalog

To create a new custom technical catalog, use the SAP Fiori Launchpad App Manager transaction **/UI2/FLPAM.**

593

CHAPTER 12 CONFIGURE CUSTOM SAP FIORI APPS

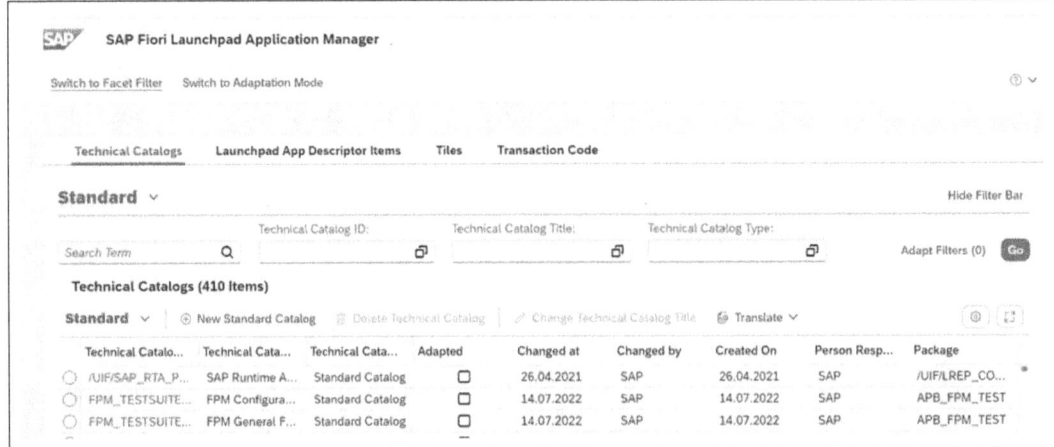

Figure 12-12. *SAP Fiori Launchpad Application Manager /UI2/FLPAM initial screen*

Create a new technical catalog by clicking the **New Standard Catalog** ⊕ New Standard Catalog tab. Enter details as shown in the figure below.

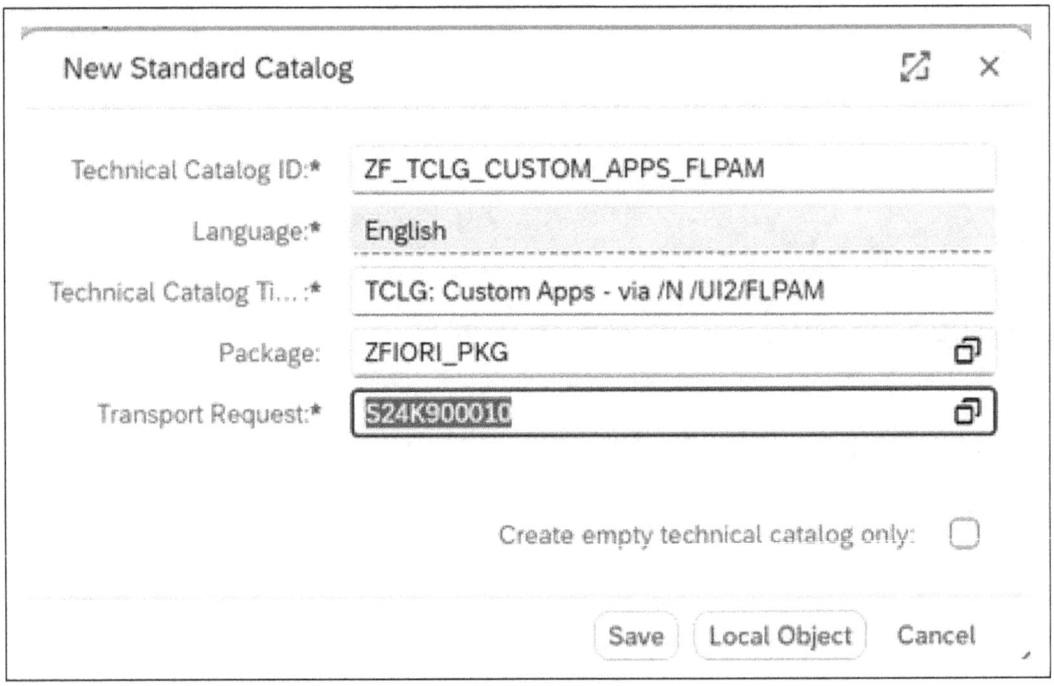

Figure 12-13. *Details of the custom technical catalog to be created*

CHAPTER 12 CONFIGURE CUSTOM SAP FIORI APPS

Click Save `Save` to create the **custom technical catalog**. Search for the technical catalog created as shown in the figure below.

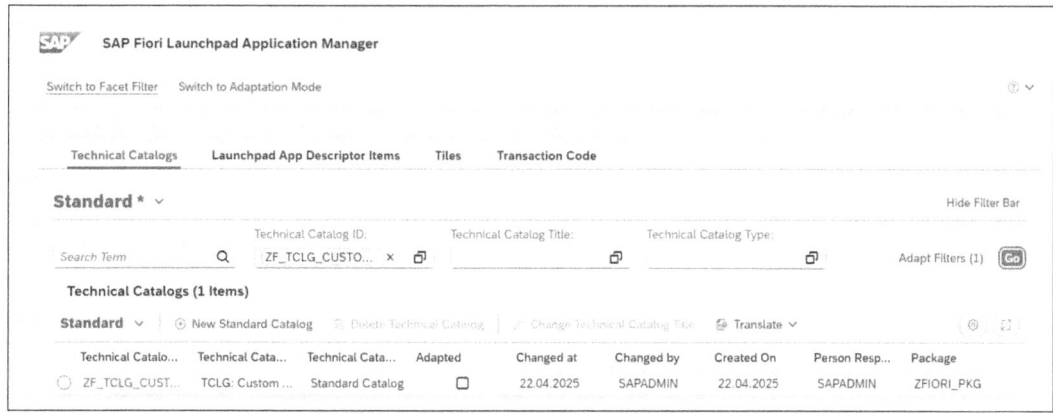

Figure 12-14. Technical catalog found and displayed

Open the technical catalog by selecting and double-clicking it. This opens a new window to enter details of apps to be generated as shown in the figure below.

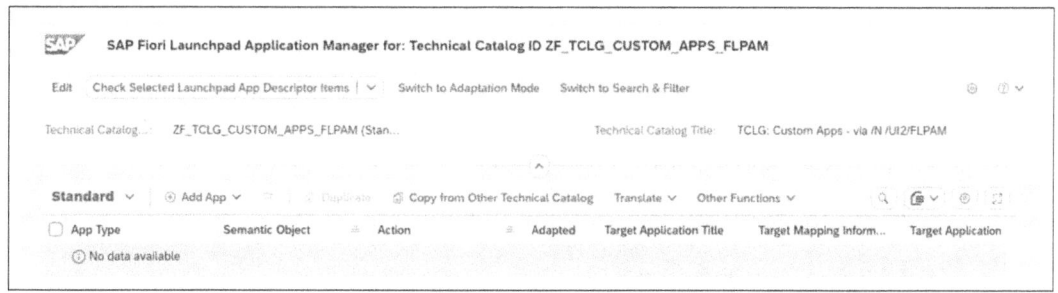

Figure 12-15. Initial screen for adding details of tiles within the custom technical catalog

Next, select the pull-down option **Add App** ⊕ Add App ⌄ , as shown in the figure below.

595

CHAPTER 12 CONFIGURE CUSTOM SAP FIORI APPS

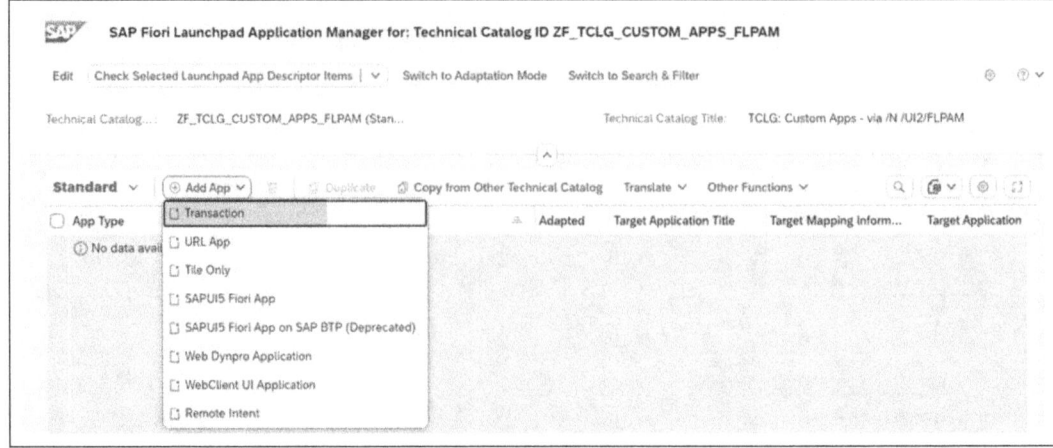

Figure 12-16. Add App options available

Under the **Add App** option, we can add various types of apps to the technical catalog listed below:

- Transaction
- URL App
- Tile Only
- SAPUI5 Fiori App
- SAPUI5 Fiori App on SAP BTP (Deprecated)
- Web Dynpro Application
- WebClient UI Application
- Remote Intent

When you select the Transaction option, the system prompts for a transport. Enter your package name and transport as shown in the figure below.

CHAPTER 12   CONFIGURE CUSTOM SAP FIORI APPS

Figure 12-17. *Package and transport details entered*

To proceed, click **OK**. Under the **App Type** column, the Transaction option selected is displayed, and the row is highlighted in blue, which allows you to enter details, as shown in the figure below.

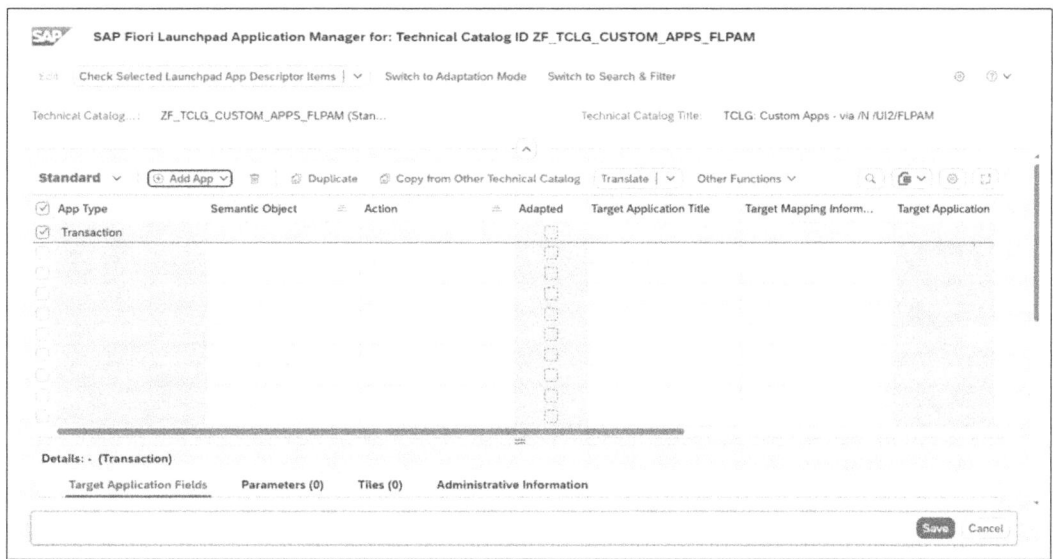

Figure 12-18. *Input screen to enter details of the transaction with the row highlighted*

597

CHAPTER 12   CONFIGURE CUSTOM SAP FIORI APPS

In the above screen, enter the details of the **semantic object** created earlier. As shown in the figure below, it is best to use the search option to find the relevant business object.

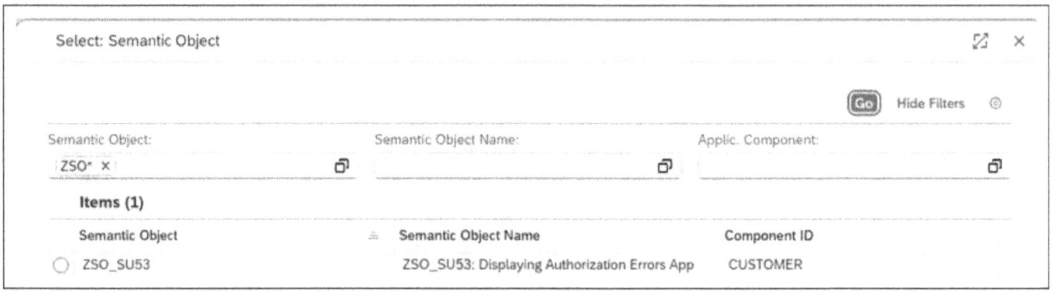

Figure 12-19.   Semantic object selection screen

Select **ZSO_SU53**, and the above screen gets populated, as shown in the figure below.

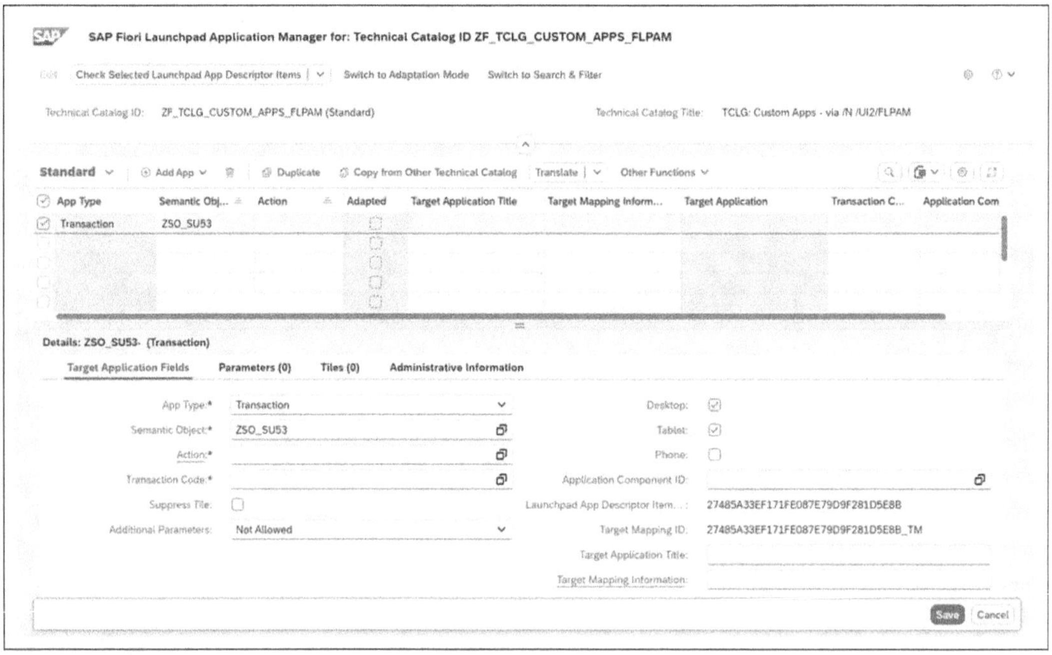

Figure 12-20.   Custom semantic object added

When a field value is updated or added to the top panel, the corresponding field gets automatically populated at the bottom panel, as shown in the figure above.

Next, use the search option in the **Action** header as shown in the figure below.

CHAPTER 12 CONFIGURE CUSTOM SAP FIORI APPS

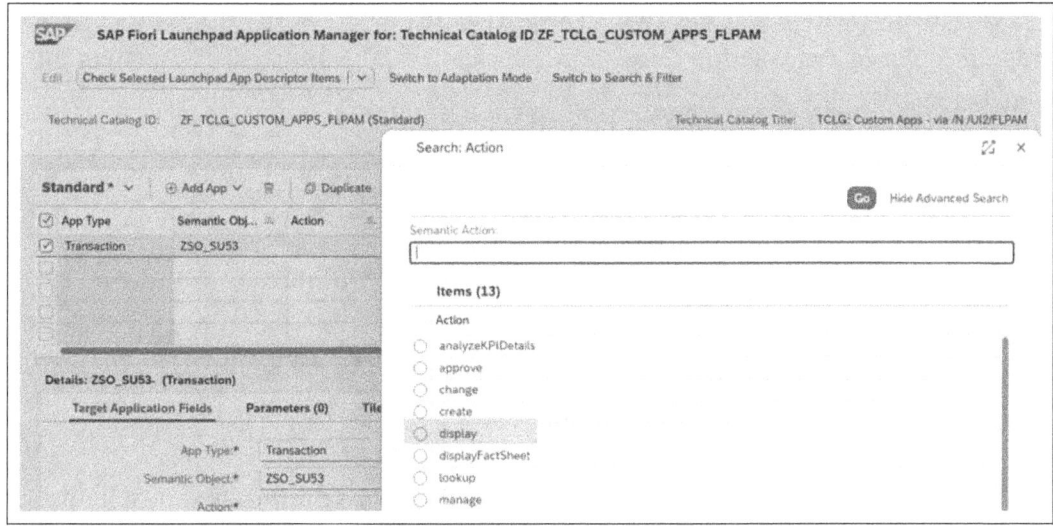

Figure 12-21. *Semantic Action – display selected*

Once **display** under **Semantic Action** is selected, the above screen gets updated, as shown in the figure below.

Figure 12-22. *Semantic action added*

CHAPTER 12 CONFIGURE CUSTOM SAP FIORI APPS

The semantic action was updated, as shown in the figure above. Next, enter **SU53** under the column **Transaction Code**, and the screen will be updated, as shown in the figure below.

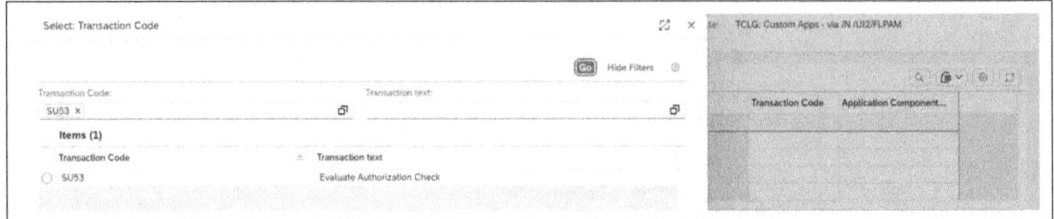

Figure 12-23. *Search for the transaction SU53*

The screen gets populated once the transaction SU53 is selected, as shown in the figure below.

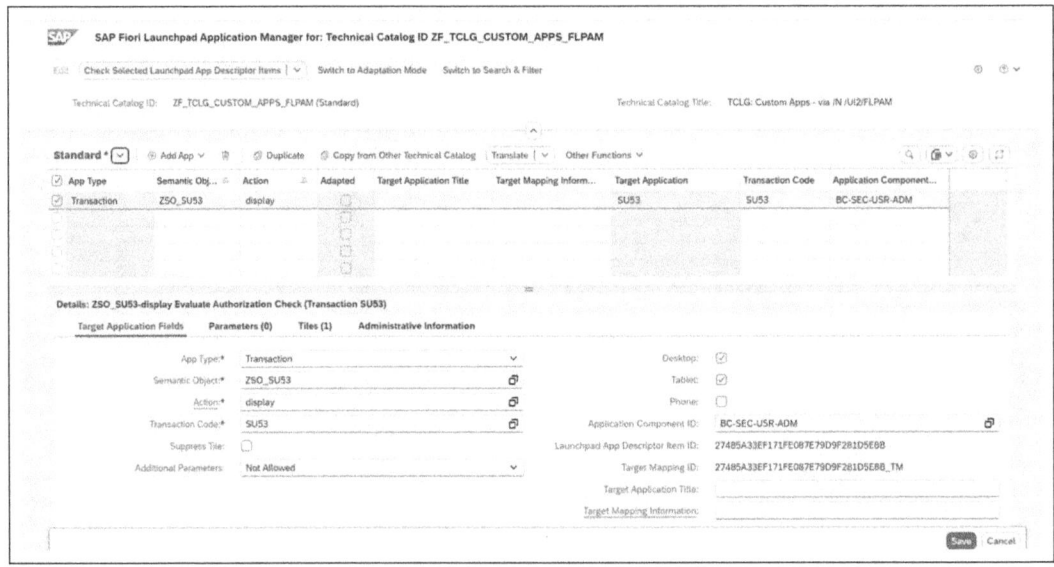

Figure 12-24. *Original transaction SU53 added*

Once SU53 is added under the column **Transaction Code**, many fields are updated automatically in both panels, and they are as follows:

- **Target Application**: SU53
- **Application Component…**: BC-SEC-USR-ADM

CHAPTER 12   CONFIGURE CUSTOM SAP FIORI APPS

Furthermore, the system automatically created a static tile as indicated by **Tiles (1)** shown in the figure below.

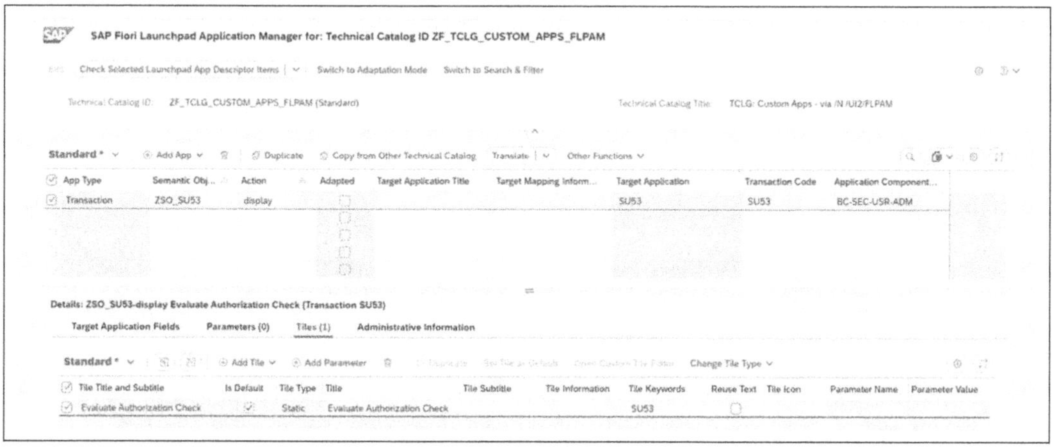

Figure 12-25. Static tile created automatically

You can update some other columns, as shown in the figure below.

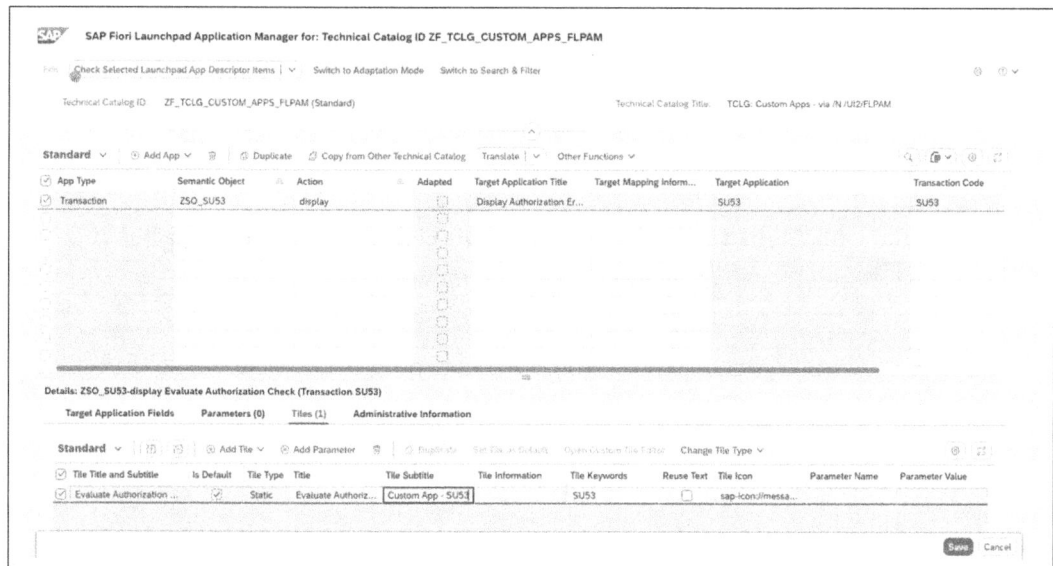

Figure 12-26. Updated static tile information

601

CHAPTER 12   CONFIGURE CUSTOM SAP FIORI APPS

Note The information under Tile Icon was selected from the options shown in the figure below.

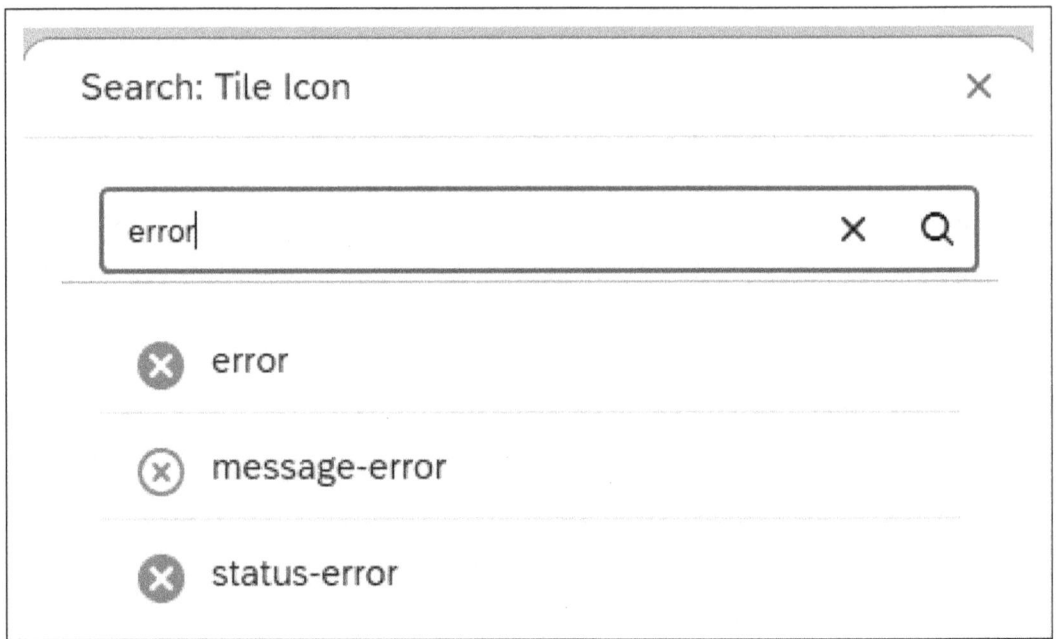

Figure 12-27. Tile Icon options

Now, switch back to the tab **Target Application Fields** in the bottom panel and update some other fields, as shown in the figure below.

CHAPTER 12   CONFIGURE CUSTOM SAP FIORI APPS

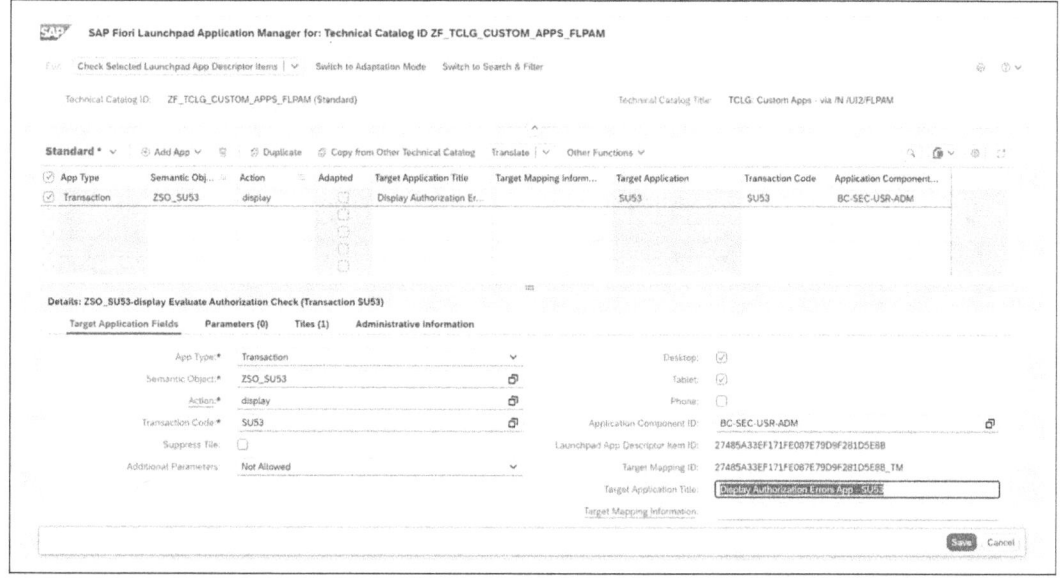

Figure 12-28. *Updated Target Application Fields tab*

In the above figure, the following field was updated:

- **Target Application Title**: Display Authorization Errors App – SU53

Since everything looks fine, save the settings by clicking [Save] at the bottom of the above figure. After saving a message is displayed stating **Data is saved**, as shown in the figure below.

603

CHAPTER 12   CONFIGURE CUSTOM SAP FIORI APPS

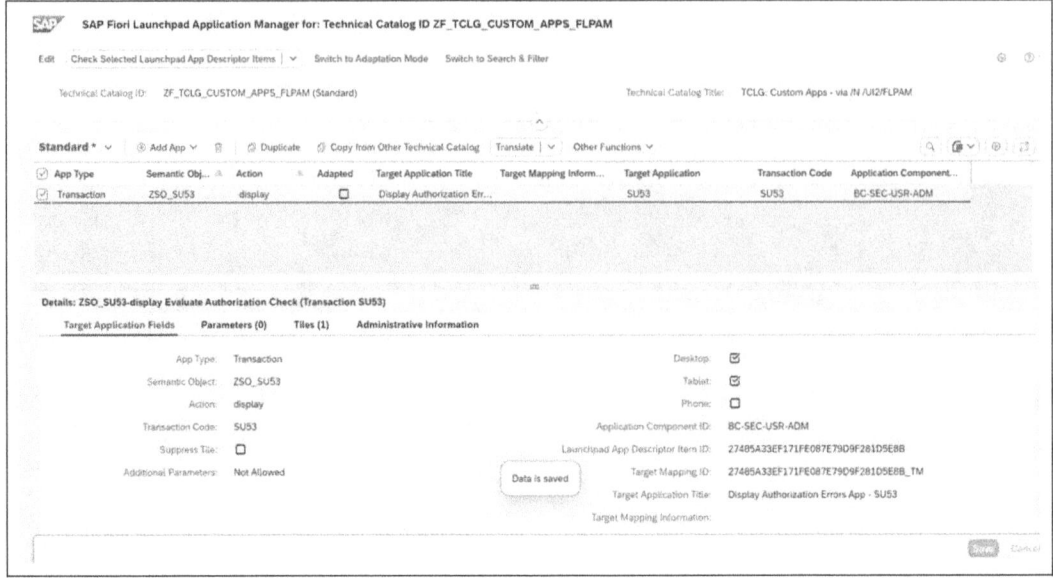

Figure 12-29. *Custom app data is being saved*

This is the minimum amount of information needed to create custom **semantic objects** and **tiles.** More information can be added to the columns as required. The creation of semantic objects and actions can be downloaded into Excel, as shown below in the figure, by clicking **Export**.

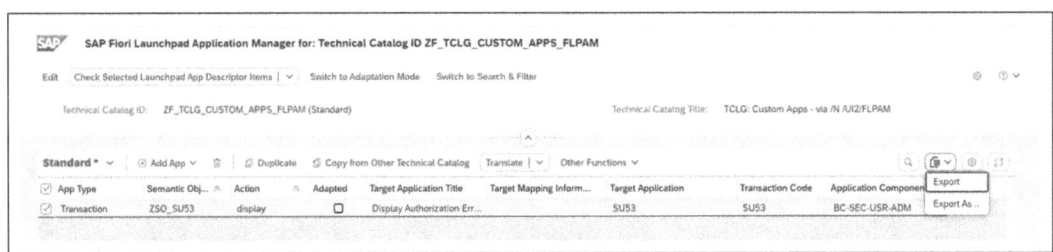

Figure 12-30. *Export option available*

The output file details are shown in the figure below.

604

CHAPTER 12   CONFIGURE CUSTOM SAP FIORI APPS

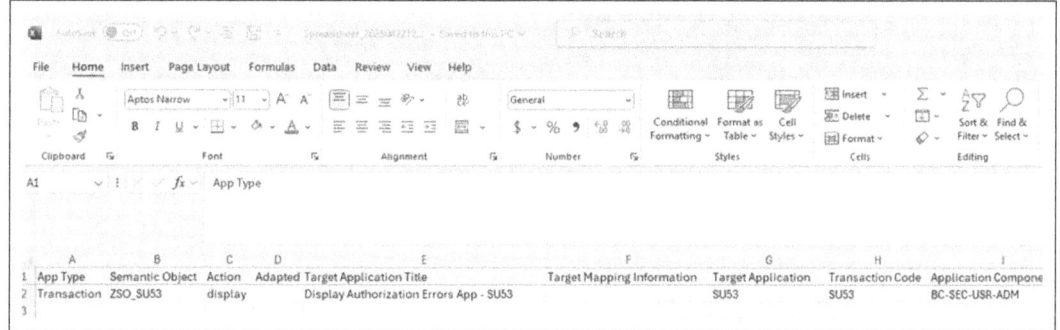

Figure 12-31. Excel shows details of the static tile downloaded

Save the technical Catalog, and the final screen appears, as shown in the figure below.

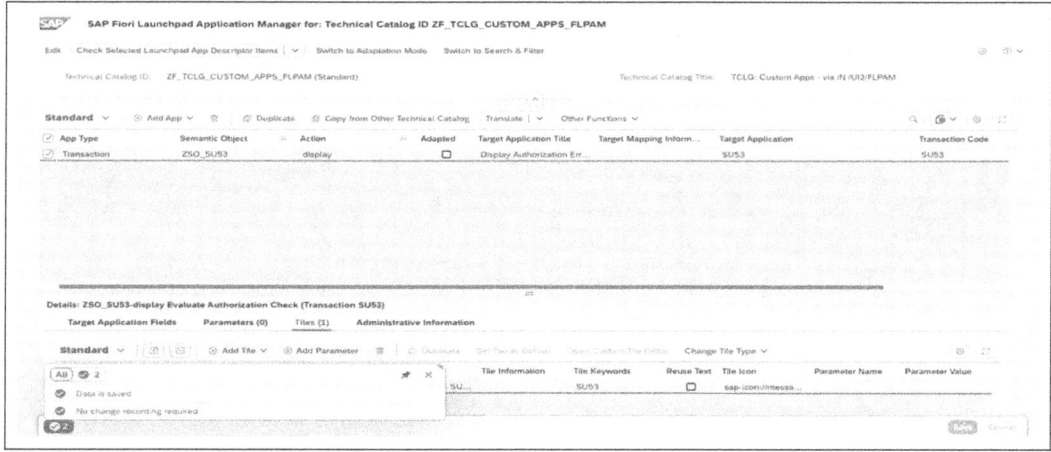

Figure 12-32. Custom technical catalog saved

The above figure displays a message: **Data is saved**.

Create a Custom Business Catalog

After creating the technical catalog, we must create **business catalogs containing custom tiles**. To create a new custom business catalog, use the transaction **/UI2/FLPCM_CUST**. The details of the custom business catalog are as shown in the figure below.

605

CHAPTER 12   CONFIGURE CUSTOM SAP FIORI APPS

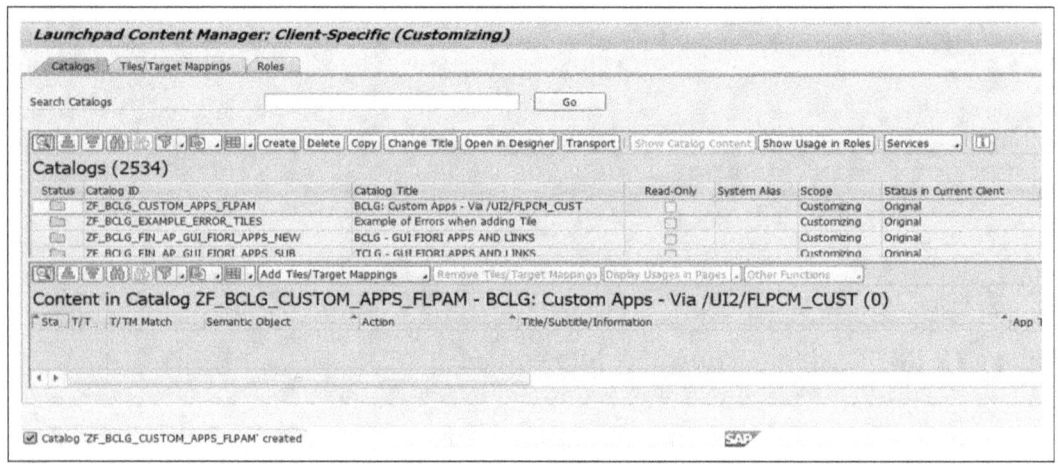

Figure 12-33. Custom business catalog details

Click the **continue** icon . The system will prompt for a transport. Create a transport for the new business catalog.

The custom business catalog will be created and displayed, as shown in the figure below.

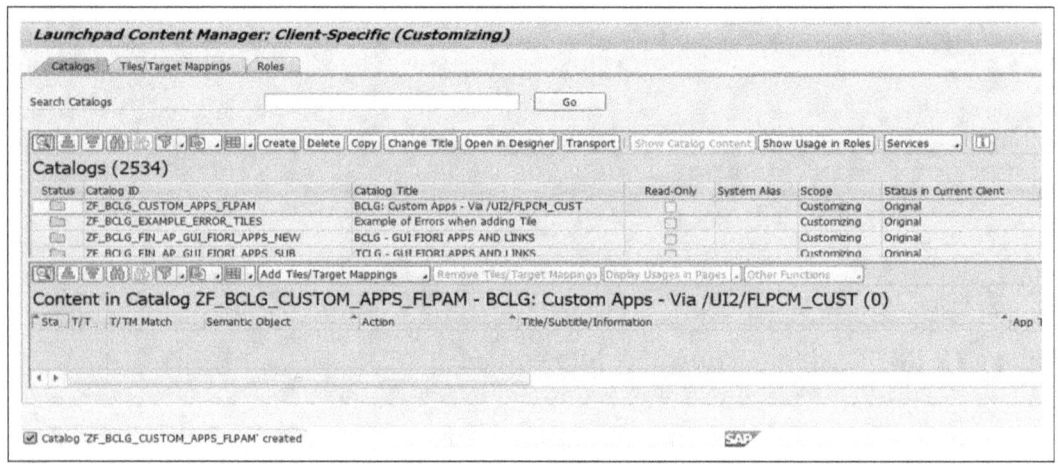

Figure 12-34. Custom business catalog created

Select the business catalog; then, from the bottom panel, click the tab **Add Tiles/Target Mappings**; and add a custom tile.

606

CHAPTER 12 CONFIGURE CUSTOM SAP FIORI APPS

Figure 12-35. *Custom tile selected*

Select **Add Tile/TM Reference**, and the tile is added to the custom business catalog, as shown in the figure below.

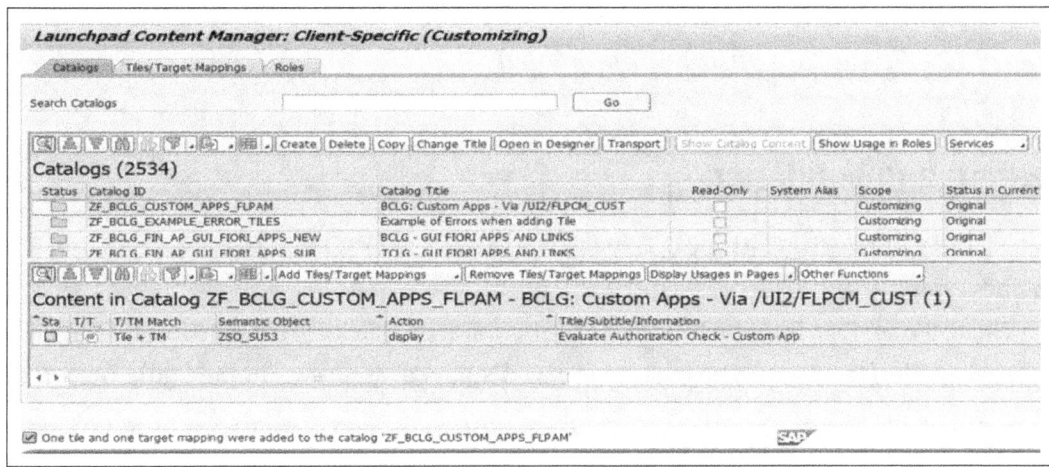

Figure 12-36. *Custom tile added to the custom business catalog*

Create a Custom Role for a Custom Tile

The next step involves creating a custom role using the transaction PFCG and assigning the custom business catalog, as shown in the figure below.

607

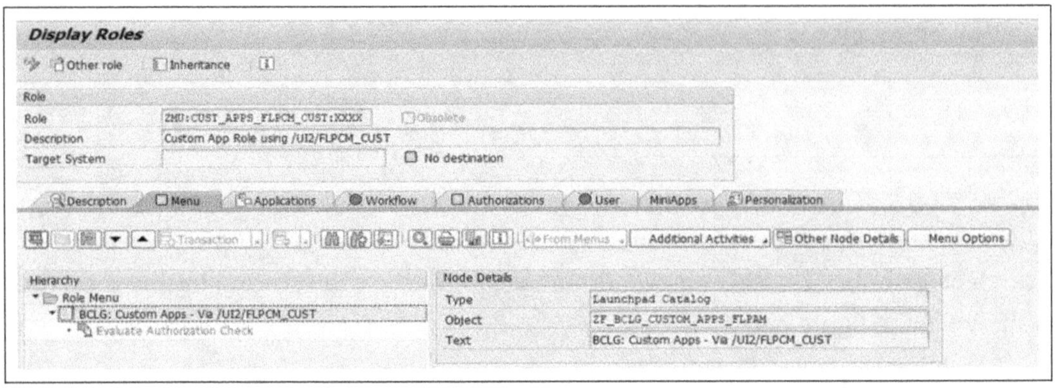

CHAPTER 12   CONFIGURE CUSTOM SAP FIORI APPS

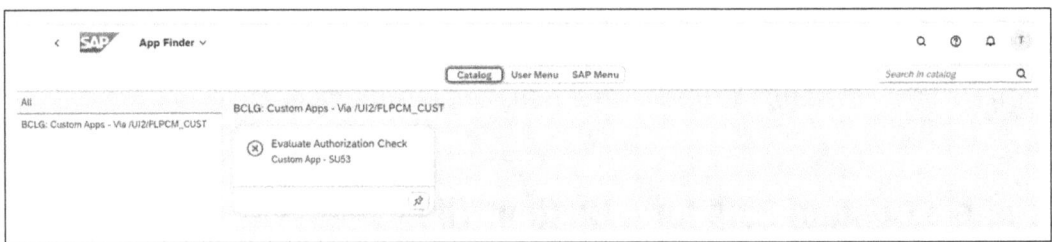

Figure 12-37. Custom business role created

Testing and Validation

To test and validate the tile for SU53, we will use a test user ID that is assigned to the business role.

The test user logs into the SAP Fiori Launchpad and clicks the **User Menu,** followed by the **App Finder** option. The custom app is displayed, as shown in the figure below.

Figure 12-38. Custom app is displayed

The GUI app functions appropriately and displays the same output screen as the SAP transaction **SU53.**

608

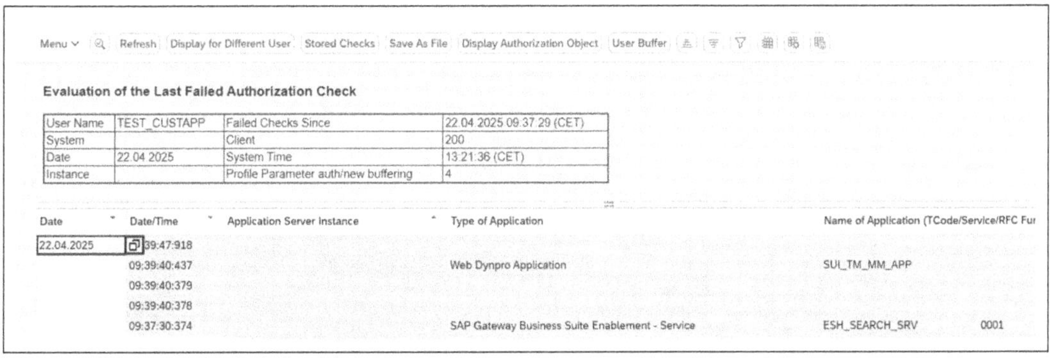

CHAPTER 12 CONFIGURE CUSTOM SAP FIORI APPS

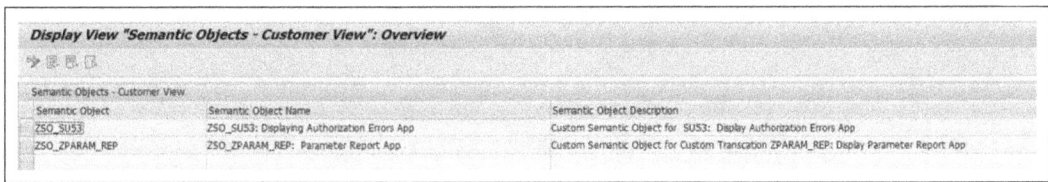

Figure 12-39. *Custom app output screen*

12.2.2 Demo 2: Tile for a Custom Transaction Code

Prerequisite

The custom transaction should have been created. For our example, we have created a custom transaction **ZPARAM_REP** for the report **RSPARAM**.

Create a Semantic Object

Create a new semantic object for the custom transaction using /UI2/SEMOBJ as shown in the figure below.

Figure 12-40. *Semantic object created for the custom transaction*

Update the Existing Technical Catalog

Follow the steps described in our example of SU53 above to create a tile for the custom transaction code.

Once the information is added, the technical catalog final screen will appear as shown in the figure below.

609

CHAPTER 12   CONFIGURE CUSTOM SAP FIORI APPS

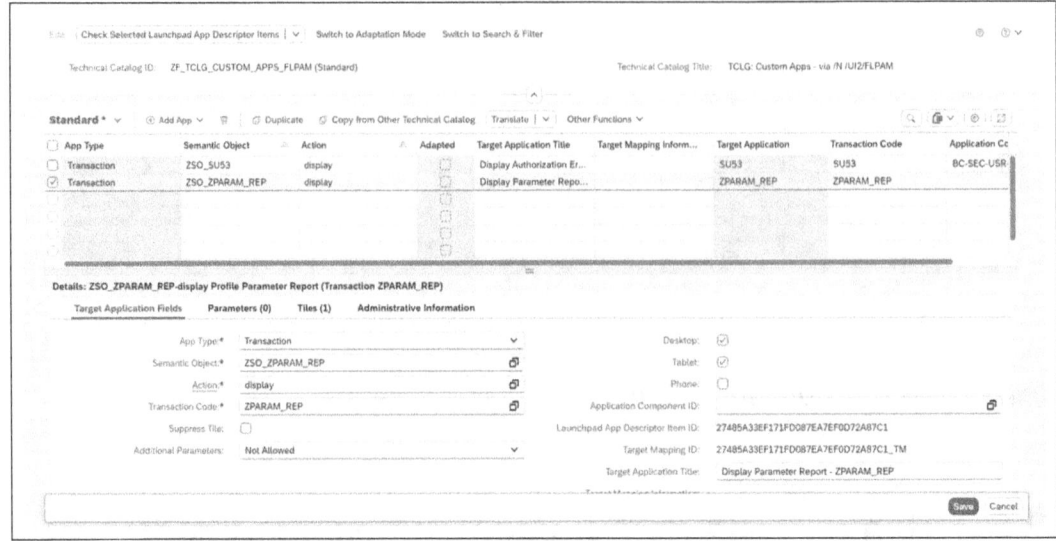

Figure 12-41. *Custom transaction details within the technical catalog*

In this instance, the system also automatically generated a static tile. Static tile details can be updated, as shown in the figure below.

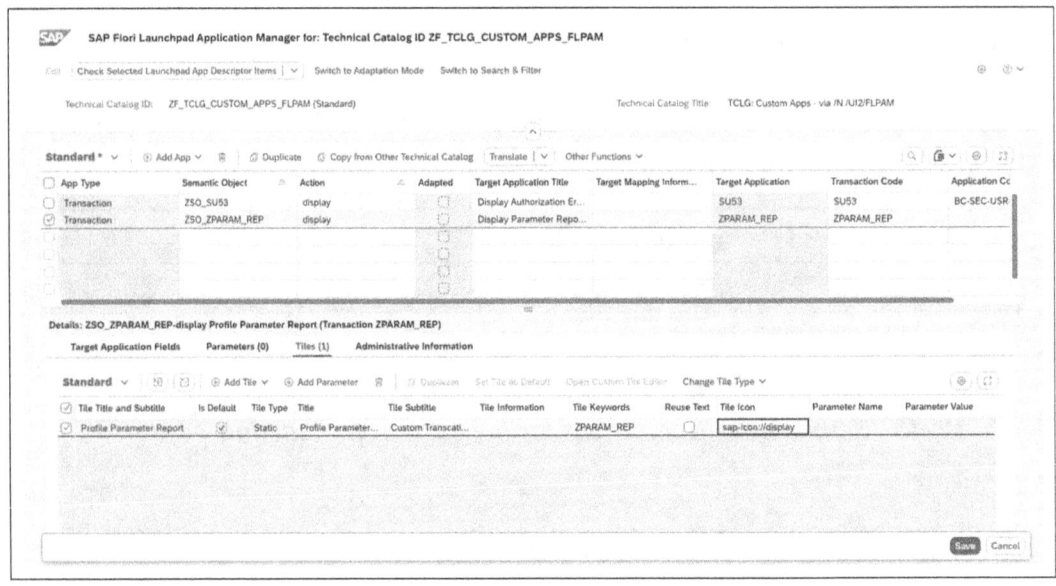

Figure 12-42. *Custom transaction details entered in the technical catalog*

Save the settings.

610

CHAPTER 12   CONFIGURE CUSTOM SAP FIORI APPS

Update the Business Catalog

Follow the steps described earlier to add the tile to the business catalog, as shown in the figure below.

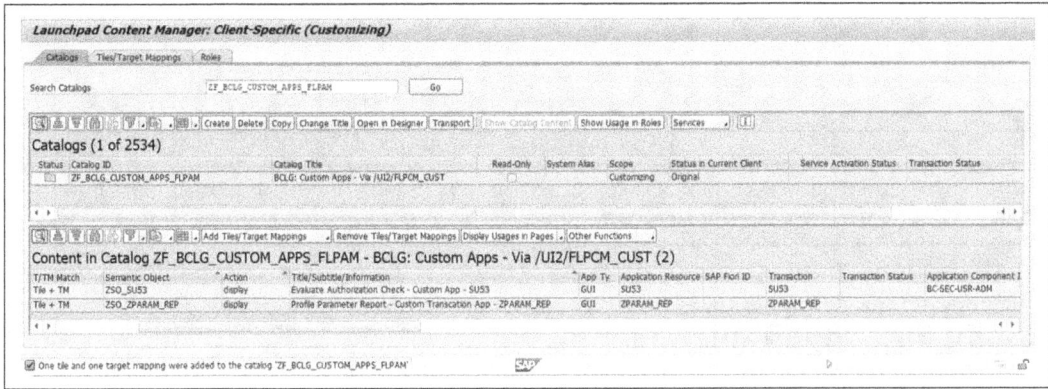

Figure 12-43. *Business catalog updated*

Update the Business Role

The business role needs to be updated in transaction code PFCG by using the option **Utilities** and then **Application Groups in Role Menus,** as shown in the figure below.

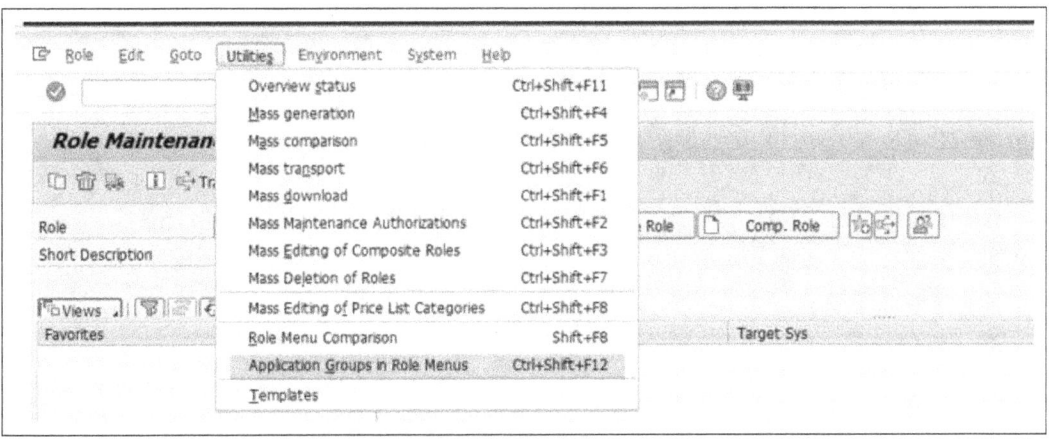

Figure 12-44. *Update the role*

Update and regenerate the role. The business catalog in the role now has two **tiles**, as shown in the figure below.

611

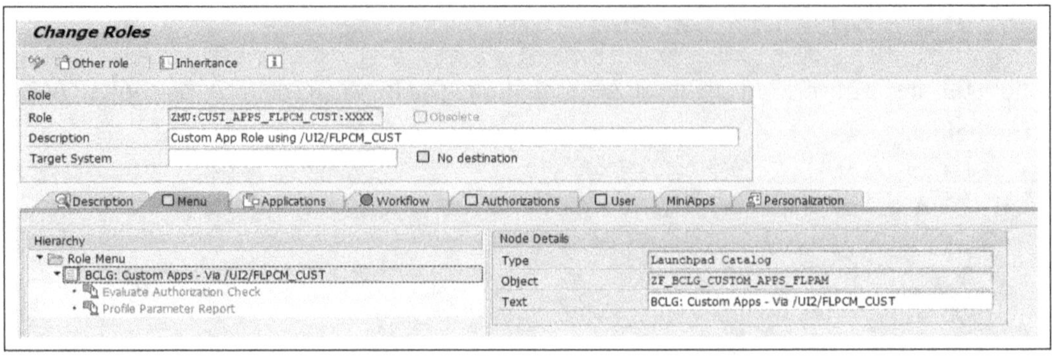

CHAPTER 12 CONFIGURE CUSTOM SAP FIORI APPS

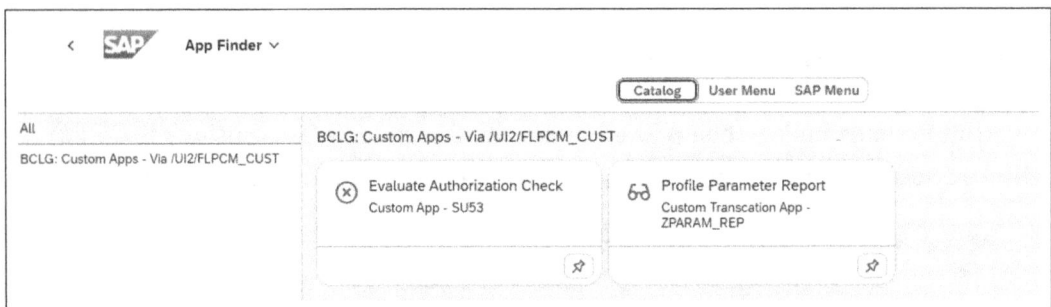

Figure 12-45. Business role update

Testing and Validation

The test user logs into the SAP Fiori Launchpad and clicks the **User Menu,** followed by the **App Finder** option. The custom app is displayed, as shown in the figure below.

Figure 12-46. Custom app is displayed for the custom transaction

Execute the app **ZPARAM_REP**. The output is displayed as shown in the figure below.

612

Figure 12-47. *Custom transaction app output displayed*

12.2.3 Demo 3: Dynamic Tile for a SAPUI5 App

Prerequisite

The developer will create a custom app. We do not have a custom app available, but we will use the **Fiori app F0763A** (Manage Chart of Accounts) to create a dynamic tile.

Create a Semantic Object

The app has the following parameters:

- **Semantic Object**: ChartOfAccounts
- **Semantic Action**: manage
- **Parameter-Value**: (sap-keep-alive = restricted) and (sap-fiori-id = F0763A)

Create a new semantic object for the custom transaction using /UI2/SEMOBJ as shown in the figure below.

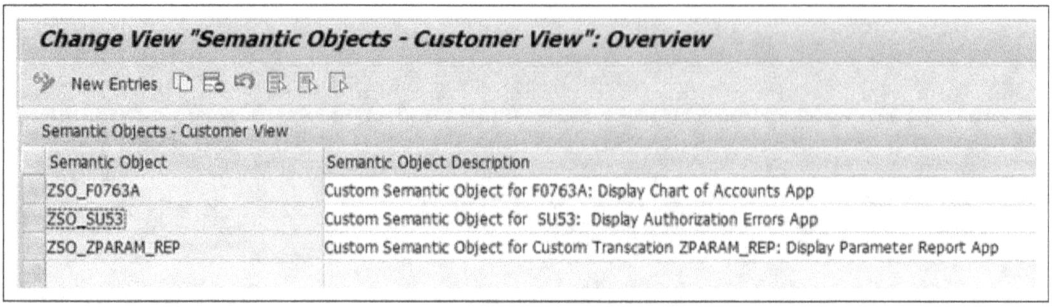

CHAPTER 12　CONFIGURE CUSTOM SAP FIORI APPS

Change View "Semantic Objects - Customer View": Overview	
New Entries 🗋 🖻 ⇌ 🖹 🖺 🖺	
Semantic Objects - Customer View	
Semantic Object	Semantic Object Description
ZSO_F0763A	Custom Semantic Object for F0763A: Display Chart of Accounts App
ZSO_SU53	Custom Semantic Object for SU53: Display Authorization Errors App
ZSO_ZPARAM_REP	Custom Semantic Object for Custom Transcation ZPARAM_REP: Display Parameter Report App

Figure 12-48. *Semantic object created for the custom transaction*

In this case, we will use the same technical catalog created in the above section to add a new tile. The steps to create the custom transaction tile are described above. We will use the SAPUI5 Fiori App option when we add the app, as shown in the figure below.

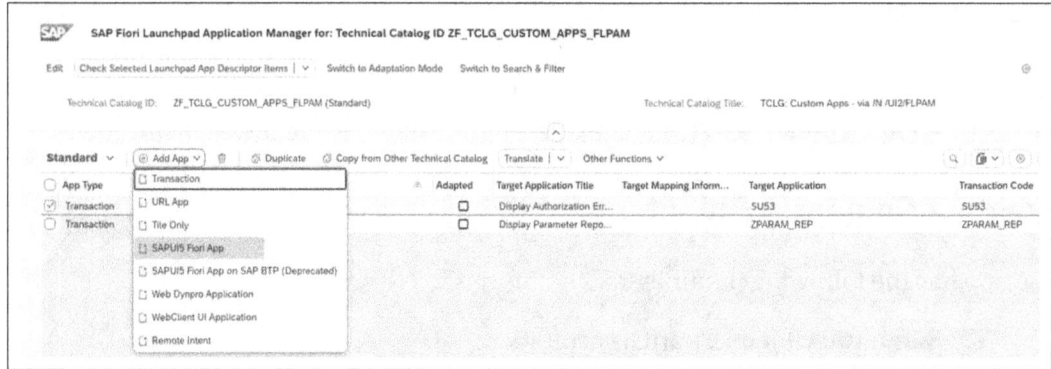

Figure 12-49. *Selecting the SAPUI5 Fiori App option*

The technical catalog screen is updated as shown in the figure below.

CHAPTER 12   CONFIGURE CUSTOM SAP FIORI APPS

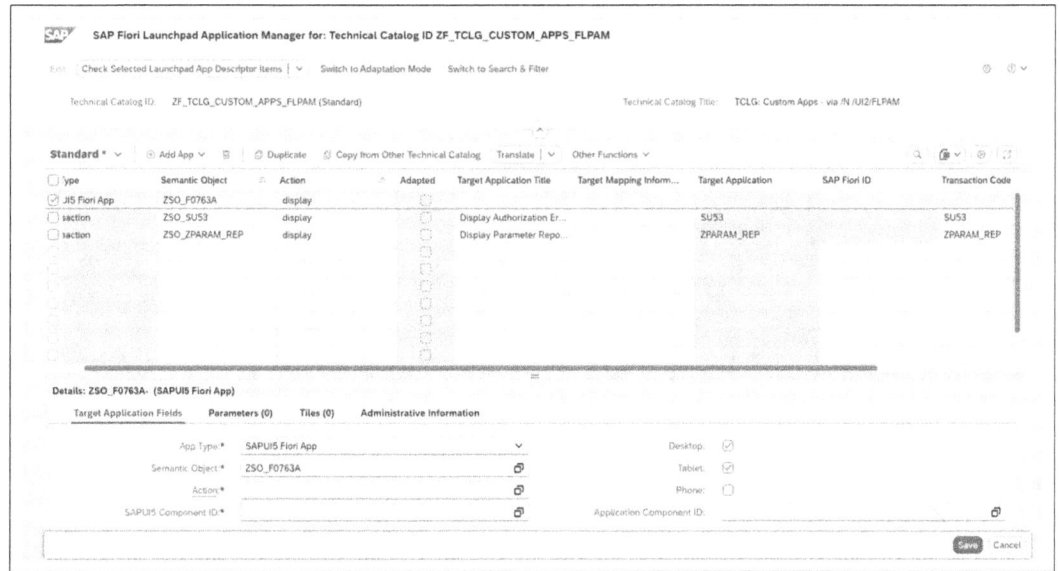

Figure 12-50.   Technical catalog screen updated

The technical catalog has a new column called **SAP Fiori ID**, to which we will add **F0763A**, as well as other information, as shown in the figure below.

CHAPTER 12 CONFIGURE CUSTOM SAP FIORI APPS

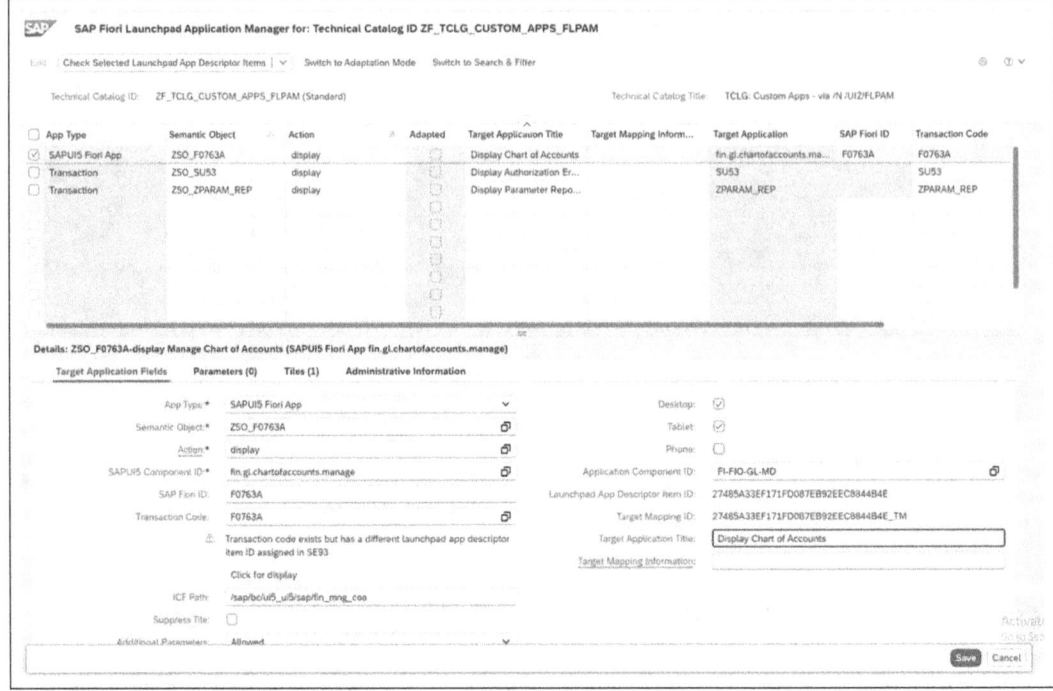

Figure 12-51. *App information updated*

The figure below shows that most of the information for various fields was taken from the transaction **/UI2/FLPD_CUST**. Next, the tab **Tiles (1)** shows that the system created the static tile, as shown in the figure below.

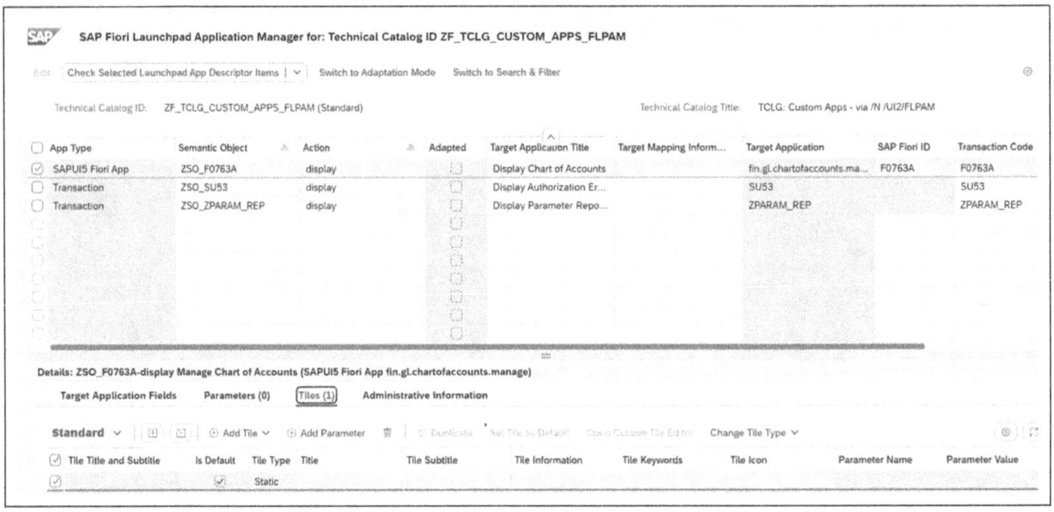

Figure 12-52. *Static tile created*

CHAPTER 12 CONFIGURE CUSTOM SAP FIORI APPS

Select the **Add Tile** option, as shown in the figure below.

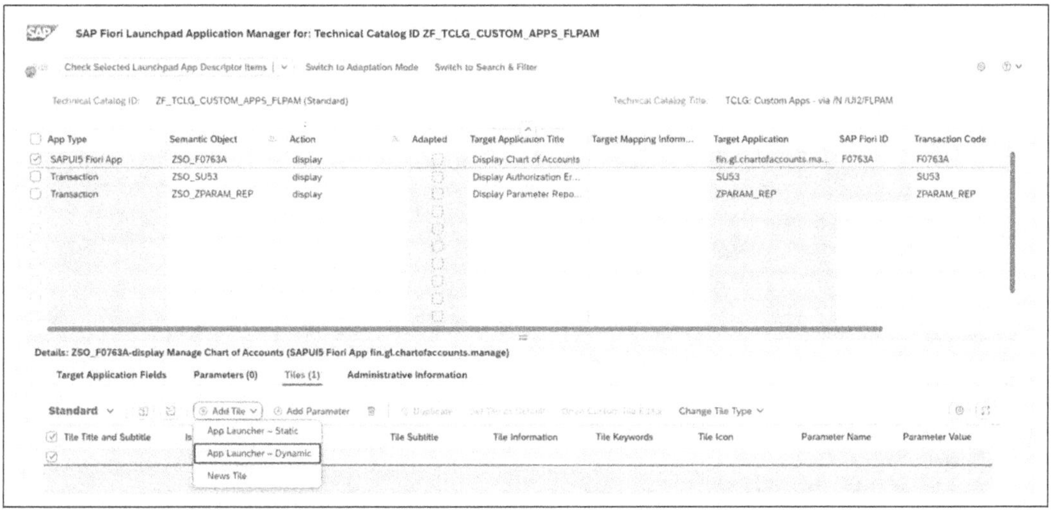

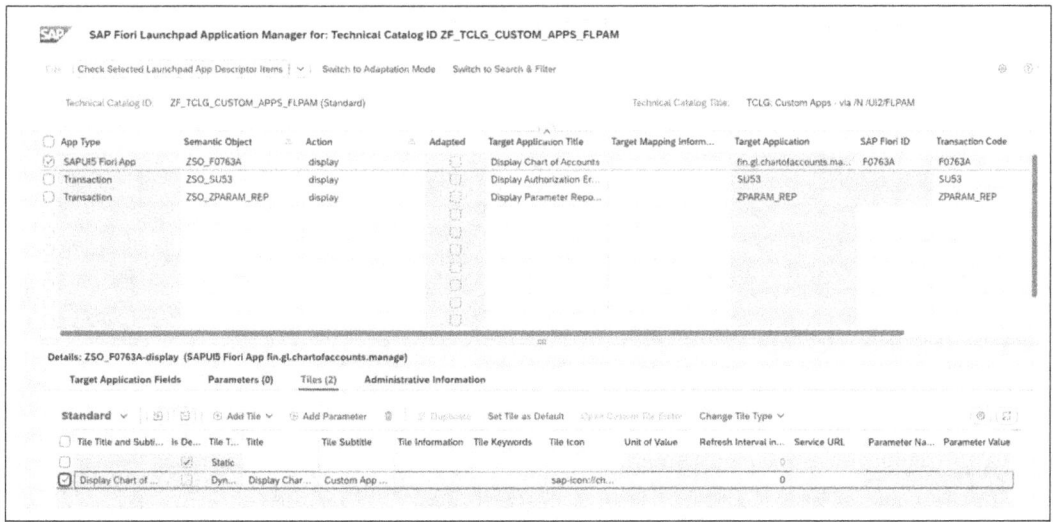

Figure 12-53. *Add Tile option*

Select the **App Launcher – Dynamic** option and fill in the other details, as shown in the figure below.

Figure 12-54. *Dynamic tile added*

Select the row above the dynamic tile row as shown in the figure below.

617

CHAPTER 12   CONFIGURE CUSTOM SAP FIORI APPS

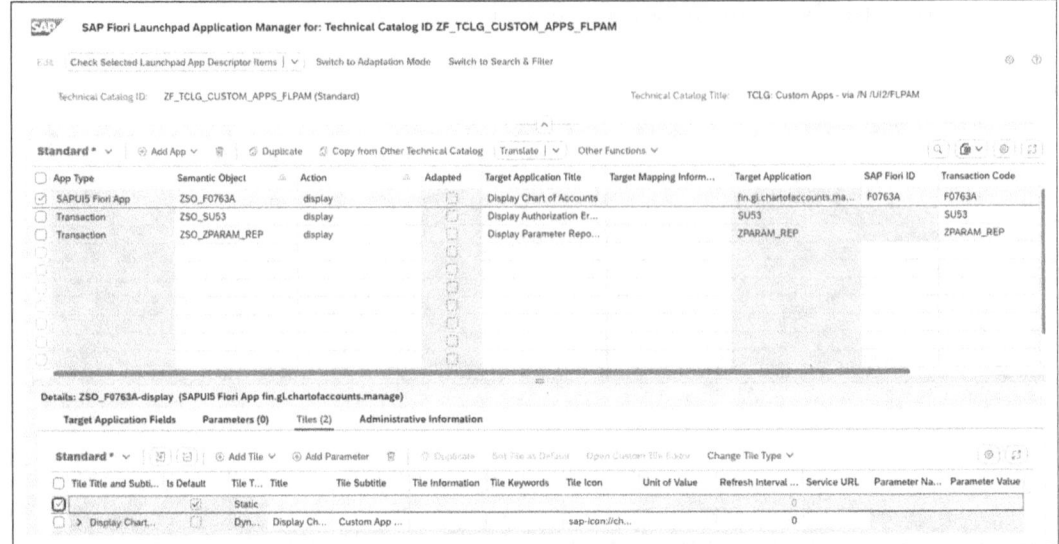

Figure 12-55. *Row with no data selected for deleting*

Use the delete option to delete the row. The row gets deleted, as shown in the figure below.

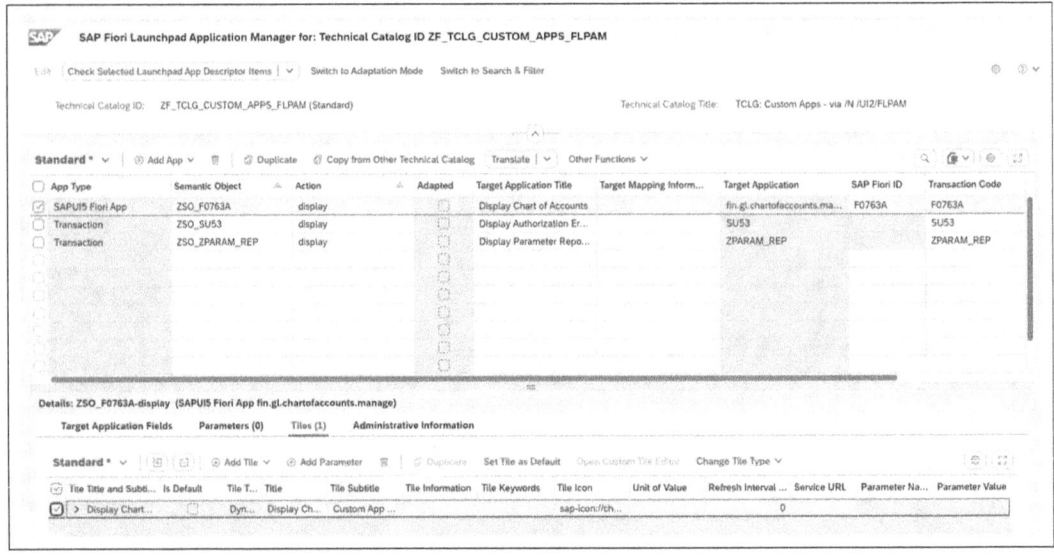

Figure 12-56. *Tile row deleted*

A new option called **Set Tile as Default** will become available. Click it to set the dynamic tile as **the default**, as shown in the figure below.

618

CHAPTER 12 CONFIGURE CUSTOM SAP FIORI APPS

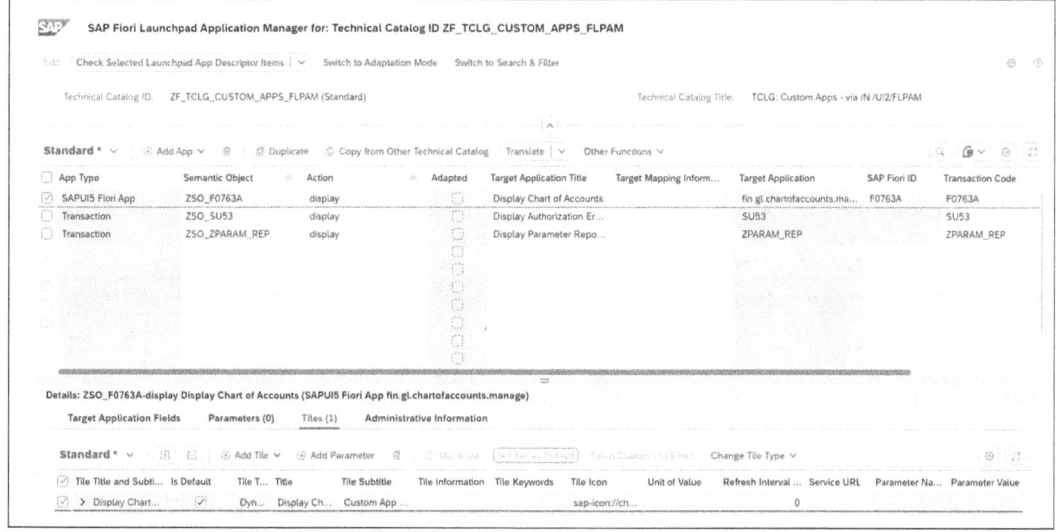

Figure 12-57. *Dynamic tile is now set as the default*

Note Set Tile as Default is now grayed out.

Next, we need to use the tab Add Parameter to enter the values of the dynamic tile.

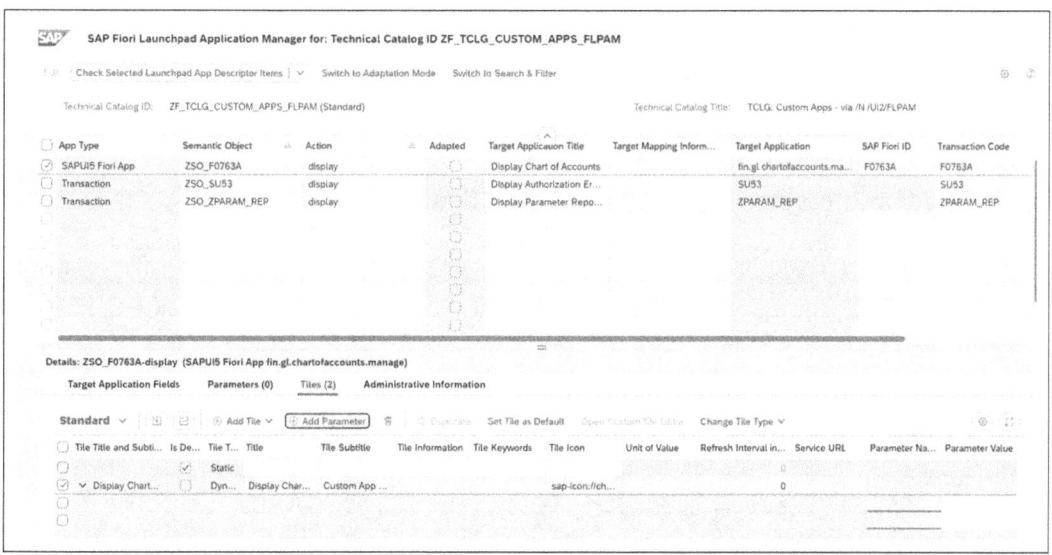

Figure 12-58. *Parameter fields get highlighted to enter the parameter values*

619

CHAPTER 12   CONFIGURE CUSTOM SAP FIORI APPS

Enter the required parameters, as shown in the figure below.

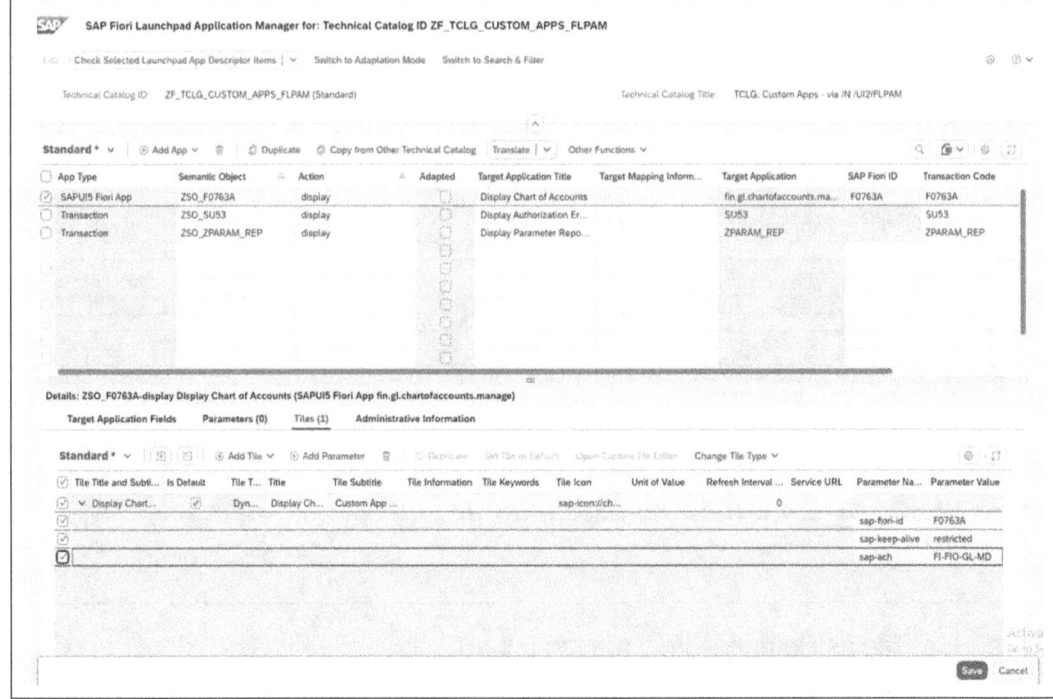

Figure 12-59. *Three related parameters added*

The system will display that the **data has been saved**.

Update the Business Catalog

The updated business catalog is as shown in the figure below.

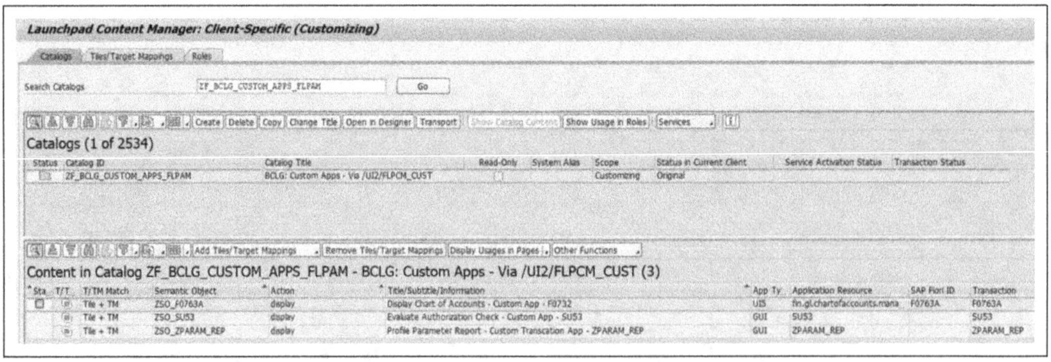

Figure 12-60. *Business catalog updated with the custom dynamic tile*

CHAPTER 12 CONFIGURE CUSTOM SAP FIORI APPS

Update the Business Role

The updated and generated business role is as shown in the figure below.

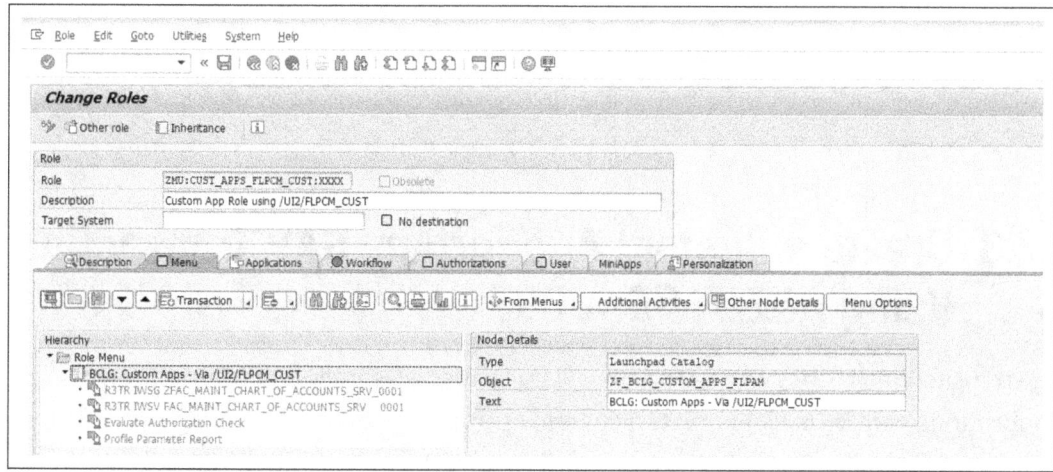

Figure 12-61. Business role updated

Testing and Validation

The test user logs into the SAP Fiori Launchpad and clicks the **User Menu,** followed by the **App Finder** option. The new custom app is displayed, as shown in the figure below.

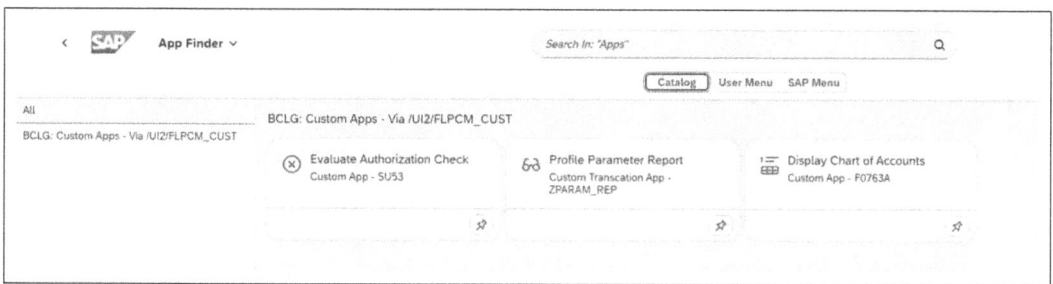

Figure 12-62. The test user can see all three custom apps

Execute the app **Display Chart of Accounts**, and the output is displayed as shown in the figure below.

621

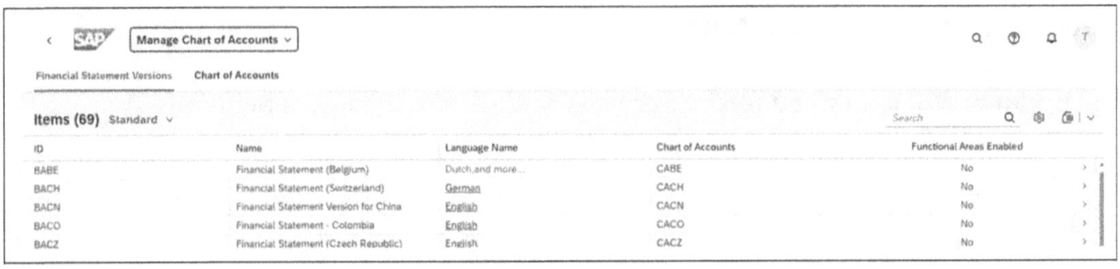

CHAPTER 12 CONFIGURE CUSTOM SAP FIORI APPS

Figure 12-63. *The output of the Display Chart of Accounts app is displayed*

12.3 Create a Custom App for Any SAP Transaction Using /UI2/FLPD_CUST

The transaction **/UI2/FLPD_CUST** (Fiori Launchpad Designer for customer-specific applications) will be used to create a custom app, along with the technical and business catalogs. The process for creating a catalog is explained in Appendix B. Using this transaction, you can make technical and business catalogs. The semantic objects have already been created; we will utilize the same ones.

12.3.1 Demo 4: Custom Transaction ZPARAM_REP – Convert to an App

Prerequisite

For this example, we will use the catalogs and role already created before, and they are as follows:

- **Technical Catalog**: ZF_TCLG_CUSTOM_APPS_FLPD_CUST

- **Technical Catalog Description**: TCLG: Custom Apps – Via /UI2/FLPD_CUST

- **Business Catalog**: ZF_BCLG_CUSTOM_APPS_FLPD_CUST

- **Business Catalog Description**: BCLG: Custom Apps – Via /UI2/FLPD_CUST

- **Business Role**: ZMU:CUST_APPS_FLPD_CUST:XXXX

- **Business Role Description**: Custom App Role using /UI2/FLPCM_CUST

CHAPTER 12   CONFIGURE CUSTOM SAP FIORI APPS

The custom transaction **ZPARAM_REP** will be converted to a custom tile.

Add a Custom Transaction to a Technical Catalog

Open the SAP Fiori Launchpad Designer (Client Specific) transaction **/UI2/FLPD_CUST** and search for the empty technical catalog created earlier, as shown in the figure below.

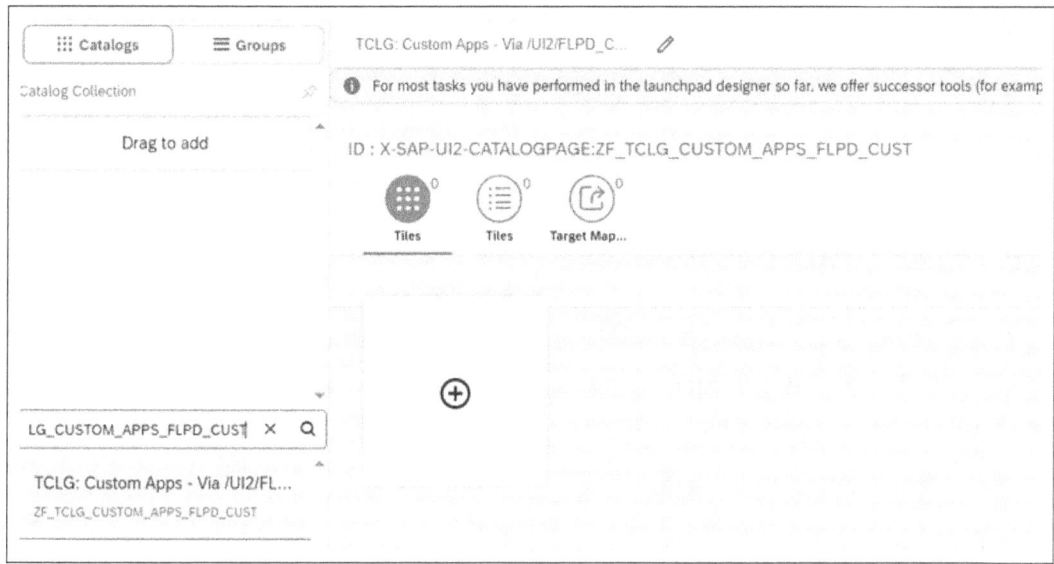

Figure 12-64. Empty custom technical catalog displayed

The first step is to assign a transport, as shown in the figure below.

CHAPTER 12 CONFIGURE CUSTOM SAP FIORI APPS

Figure 12-65. Added to the transport request

The next step is to create a tile by clicking the **+ sign** within an empty shell tile, and it will open a window, titled **Select a tile template**, with three options available to create a tile, as shown in the figure below. These options are

- App Launcher – Dynamic
- News Tile
- App Launcher – Static

Figure 12-66. Select a tile template

CHAPTER 12 CONFIGURE CUSTOM SAP FIORI APPS

In our example, we create a static tile. Selecting App Launcher – Static creates an empty static tile, and a message **Tile App Launcher – Static added successfully** appears at the bottom as shown in the figure below.

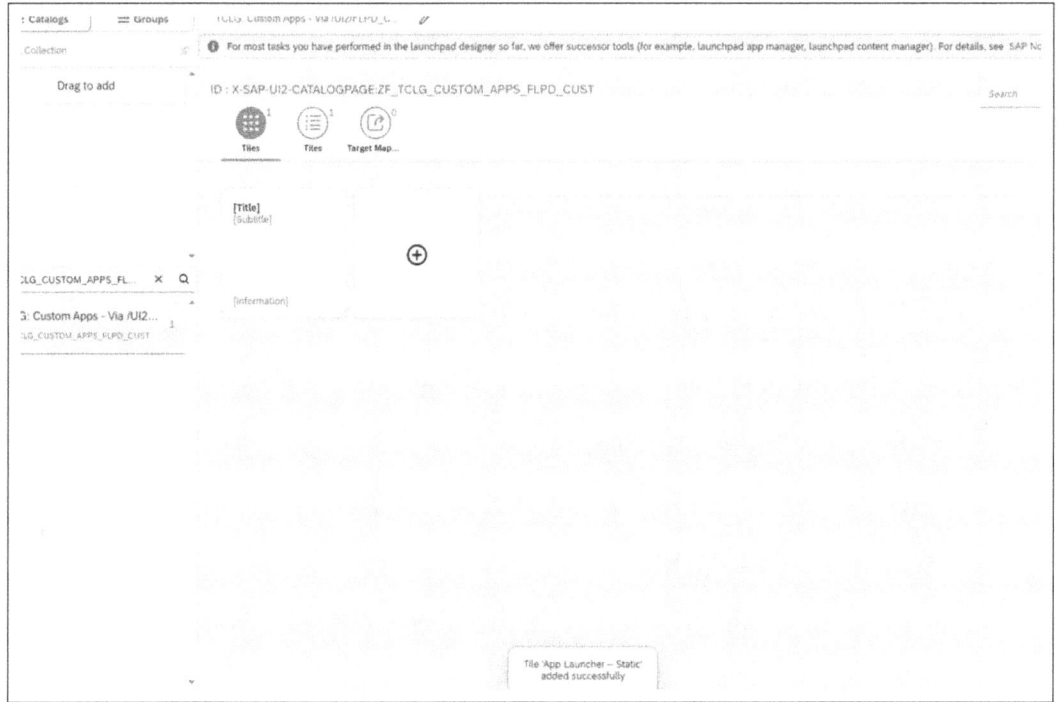

Figure 12-67. *Blank static tile*

Now, click the new tile added, and it opens a new window titled **Configure: 'App Launcher – Static'**, with various empty fields, as shown in the figure below.

625

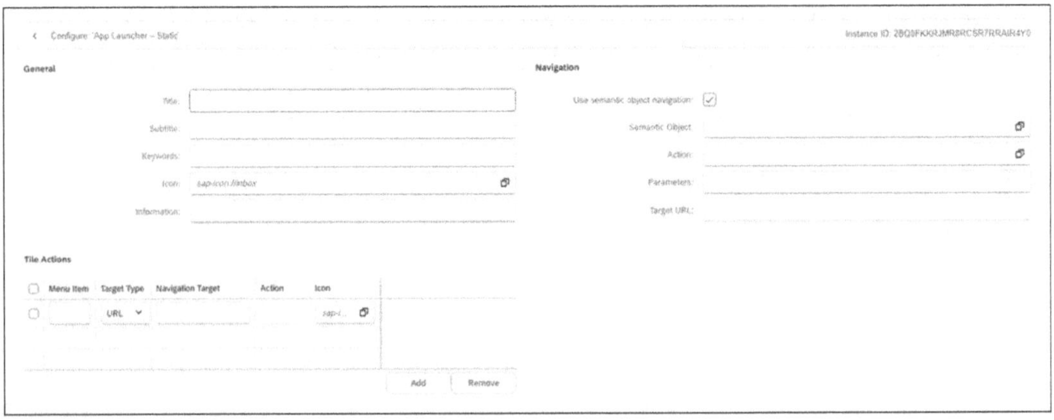

CHAPTER 12   CONFIGURE CUSTOM SAP FIORI APPS

Figure 12-68. Blank static tile and empty fields displayed

Enter the following details for creating the static tile:

- **Title**: System Profile Parameter Report
- **Subtitle**: Custom Transaction App – ZPARAM_REP
- **Keywords**: ZPARAM_REP
- **Icon**: (Choose from the search option and click OK at the bottom.)
- **Information**: Custom ZPARAM_REP App Created
- **Semantic Object**: ZSO_ZPARAM_REP
- **Action**: lookup
- **Target URL**: (Leave it blank.)

CHAPTER 12   CONFIGURE CUSTOM SAP FIORI APPS

Figure 12-69. *Parameter values added*

Also, various options are available for a **semantic action**, as shown in the figure below.

CHAPTER 12   CONFIGURE CUSTOM SAP FIORI APPS

Figure 12-70. Semantic action options available

Once you have entered all the details, click **Save** at the bottom of the screen and the static tile will be added, as shown in the figure below.

CHAPTER 12   CONFIGURE CUSTOM SAP FIORI APPS

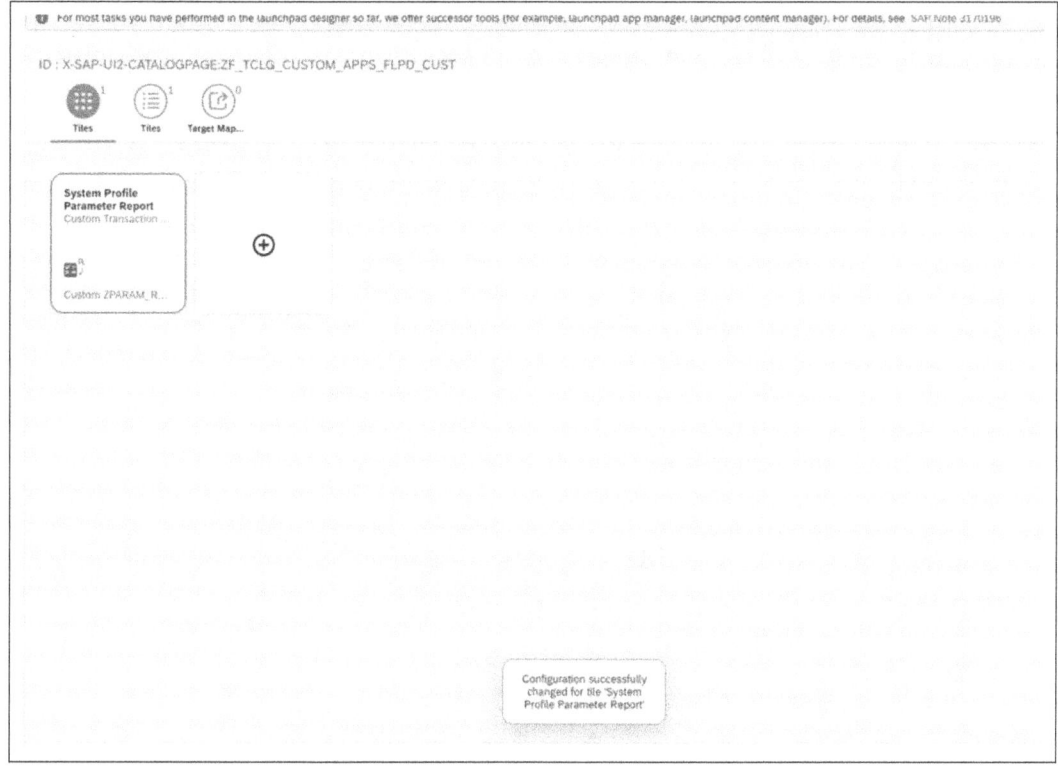

Figure 12-71. *The new custom static tile has been added*

The above figure displays a message stating **Configuration successfully changed for tile 'System Profile Parameter Report'**.

Figure 12-72. *Static tile created with the correct Target URL value*

629

The figure above shows that the **new custom static tile** has been created. When opening the new tile by clicking it, we see that all the parameters created were saved and the **Target URL** field automatically populated with #ZSO_ZPARAM_REP-lookup, as shown in the figure above. Return to the original page, which will display the tile, as shown in the figure below.

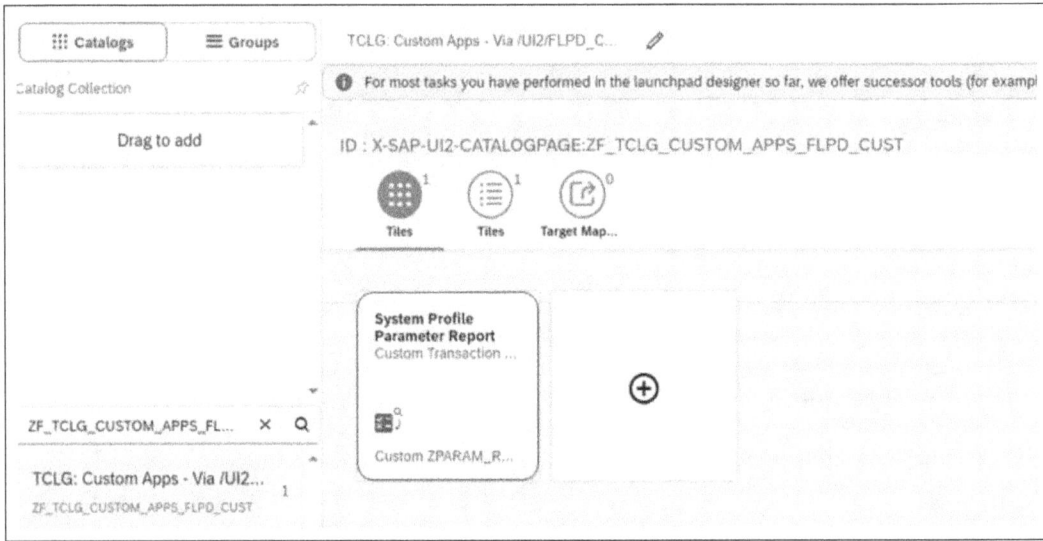

Figure 12-73. Tile with no target mapping

The above figure displays **1 tile** and **0 target mapping**. If you open the tile's tabular format, the output is as shown in the figure below.

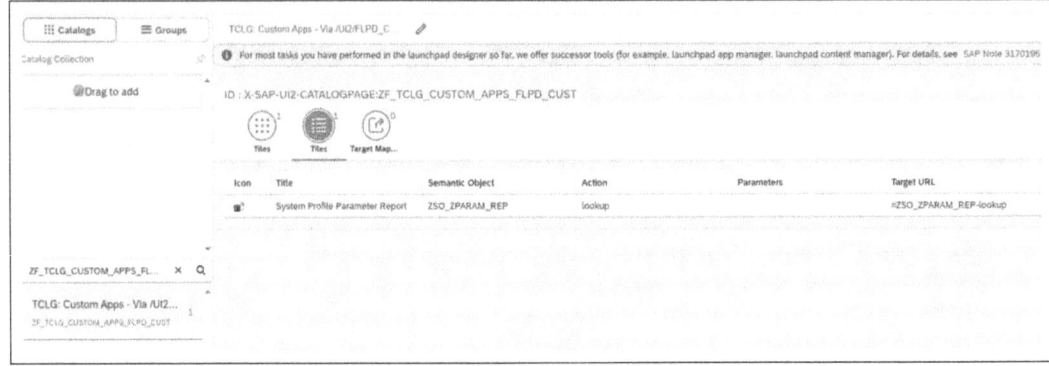

Figure 12-74. Tile data displayed in tabular format

CHAPTER 12 CONFIGURE CUSTOM SAP FIORI APPS

The next step is to create the target mapping for the tile by clicking its icon, as shown in the figure below.

Figure 12-75. Target mapping icon

An empty target mapping page opens, as shown in the figure below.

Figure 12-76. The target mapping page opens with no data

The next step involves creating the matching target mapping for the tile created. Click the Create Target Mapping tab at the bottom of the above figure
 Create Target Mapping . It opens a window titled **Configure: Target Mapping window**, as shown in the figure below.

631

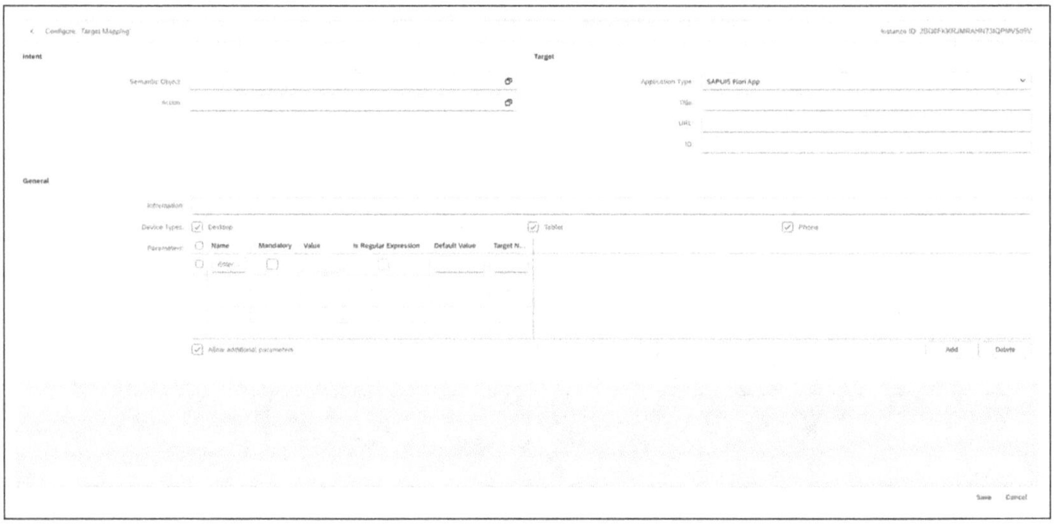

CHAPTER 12   CONFIGURE CUSTOM SAP FIORI APPS

Figure 12-77. Target mapping window to enter field values

Enter the following details in the above figure:

- **Semantic Object**: ZSO_ZPARAM_REP
- **Action**: lookup
- **Application Type**: Transaction (choose from the pull-down option)
- **Title**: System Profile Parameter Report
- **Transaction**: ZPARAM_REP

CHAPTER 12   CONFIGURE CUSTOM SAP FIORI APPS

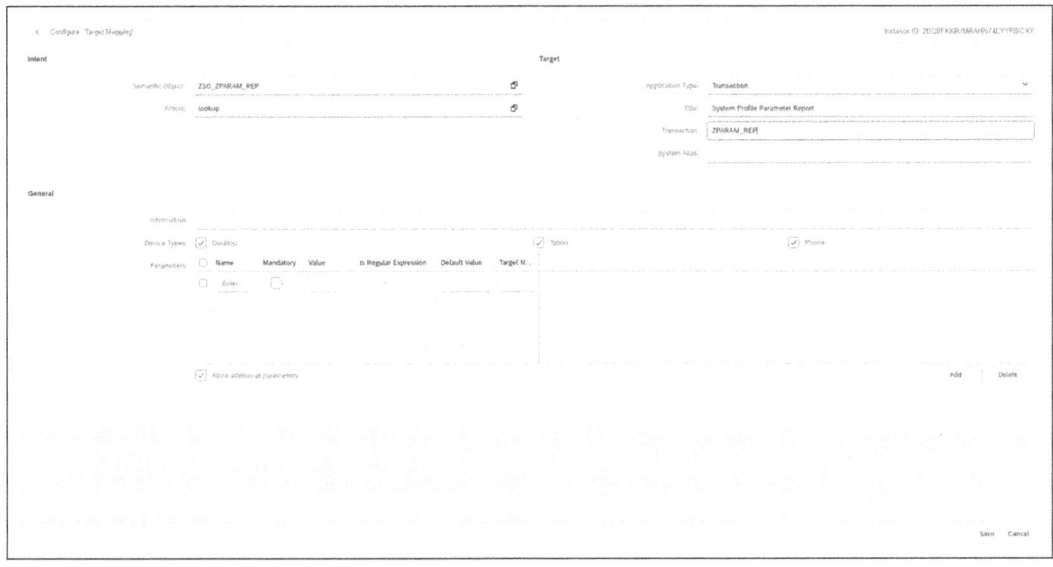

Figure 12-78. Target mapping field values updated

Once you have entered all the details, click **Save** at the bottom of the screen and the target mapping will be added, as shown in the figure below.

Figure 12-79. Target mapping saved

The above figure displays a message stating **Configuration successfully changed for tile 'System Profile Parameter Report'**. The final output is displayed in the figure below.

633

CHAPTER 12   CONFIGURE CUSTOM SAP FIORI APPS

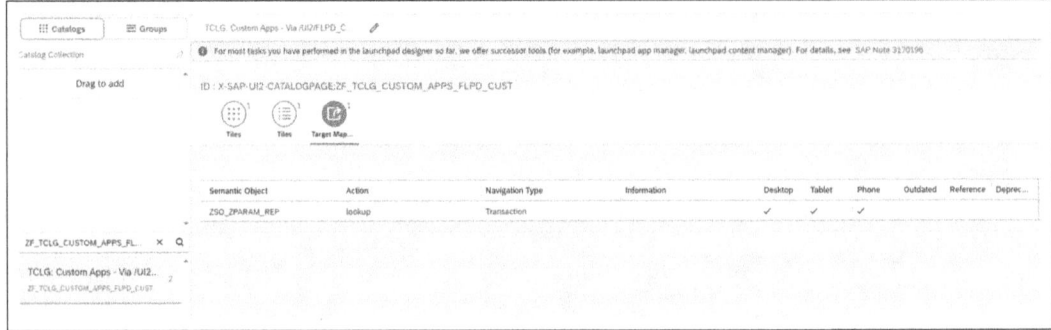

Figure 12-80. *Static tile created with target mapping*

The above figure displays that the static tile was created with target mapping.

Assign a Static Tile to a Business Catalog

The custom tile created using the transaction /UI2/FLPD_CUST must now be assigned to the custom business catalog. As shown in the figure below, you can select the tile to add to the business catalog.

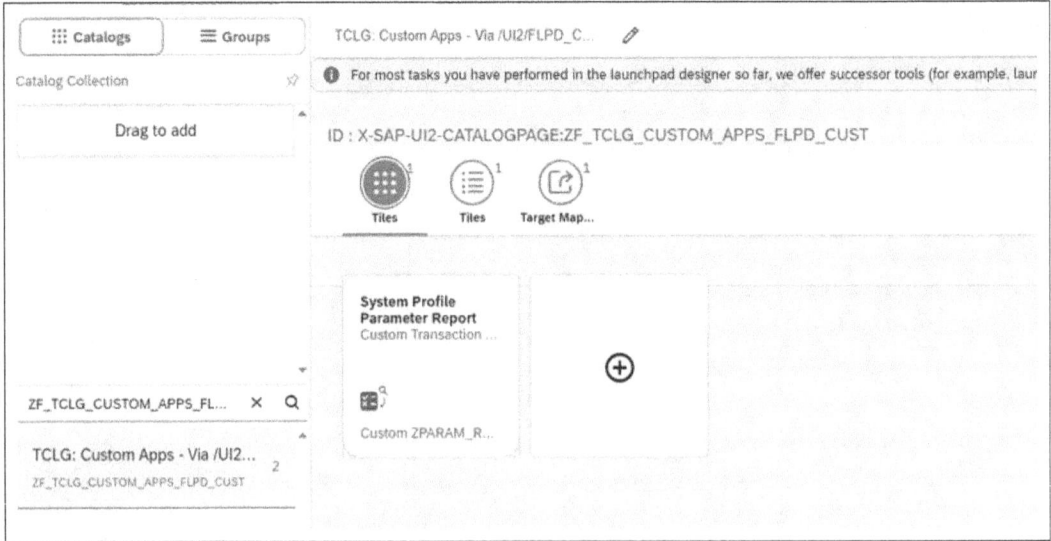

Figure 12-81. *Custom static tile displayed*

Select the System Profile Parameter Report tile and drag and drop it into the **blue Create Reference** box to add the tile, as shown in the figure below.

634

CHAPTER 12 CONFIGURE CUSTOM SAP FIORI APPS

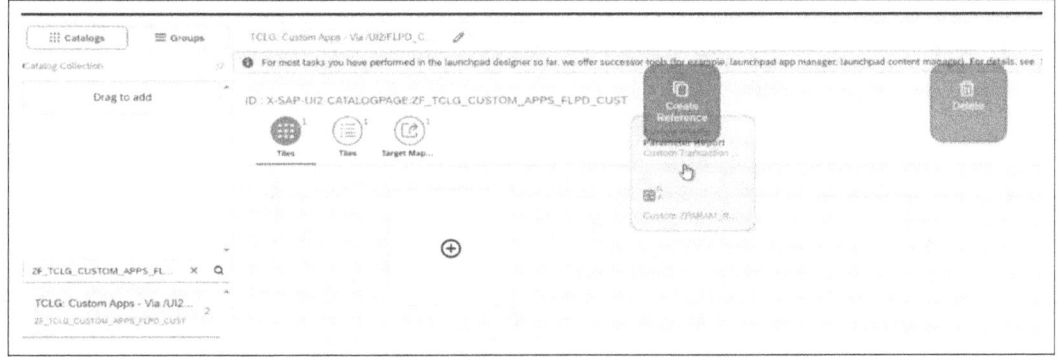

Figure 12-82. *Custom static tile is dragged and dropped into Create Reference*

The system opens a new window asking you to select the business catalog from which you want the tile to be **referenced**. Enter the business catalog ID, as shown in the figure below.

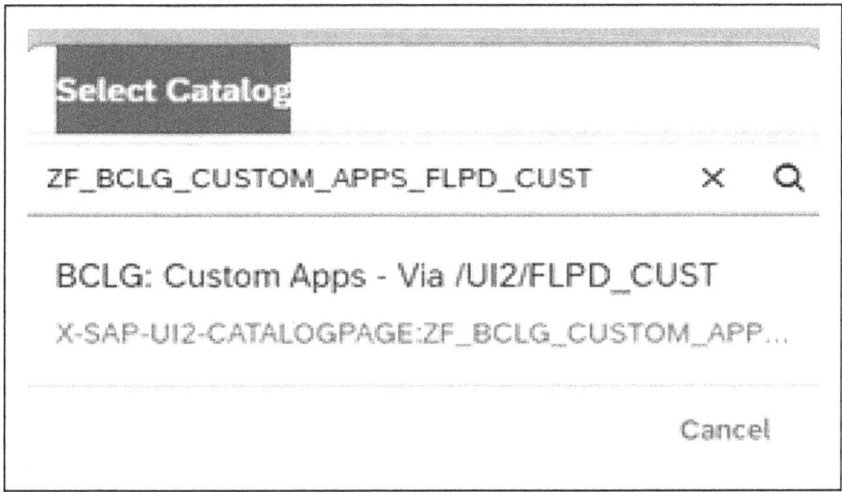

Figure 12-83. *Custom tile being added to the custom business catalog*

To select the target mapping, highlight the entire row, which will turn light blue, as illustrated in the figure below.

635

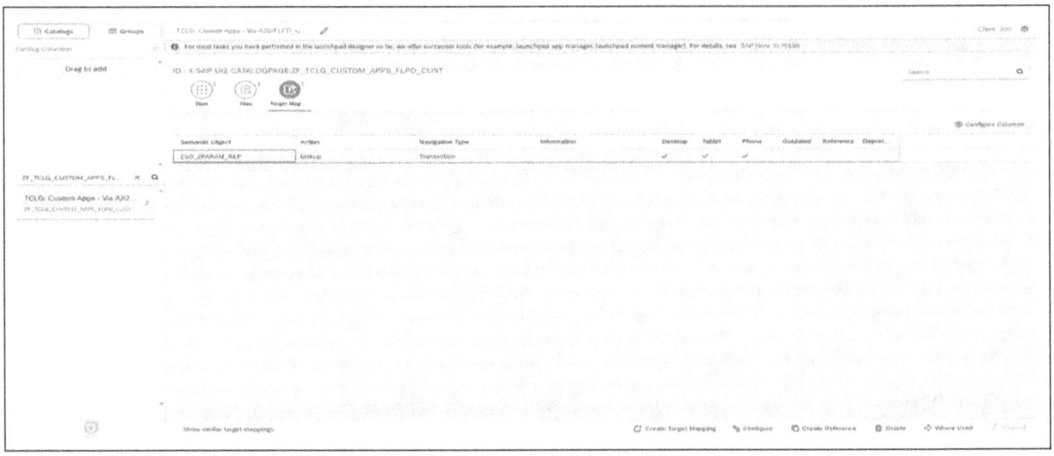

CHAPTER 12 CONFIGURE CUSTOM SAP FIORI APPS

Figure 12-84. Target mapping for the custom tile selected

To add the target mapping to the custom business catalog, select the Create Reference ⬚ Create Reference option at the bottom of the above figure. It will ask you to enter the business catalog ID details. Enter the details, as shown in the figure below.

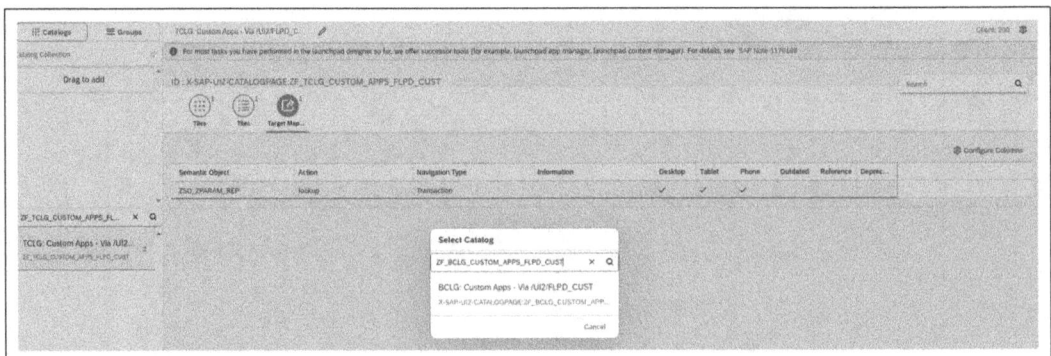

Figure 12-85. The custom business catalog selection screen

Enter the correct custom business catalog ID, as shown in the figure above.

CHAPTER 12 CONFIGURE CUSTOM SAP FIORI APPS

Figure 12-86. Target mapping is being added as a reference to the custom business catalog

After adding the target mapping to the custom business catalog, a message is displayed stating **Reference for 'System Profile Parameter Report' created in the catalog …**, as shown in the figure above.

Figure 12-87. Target mapping of the custom tile is updated within the custom business catalog

In the figure above, the target mapping of the custom tile has been updated within the custom business catalog.

637

CHAPTER 12   CONFIGURE CUSTOM SAP FIORI APPS

Update the Business Catalog and the Role

In the next step, the new custom business catalog created using the transaction /UI2/FLPD_CUST is assigned to the same role created earlier. The role is then generated, and a test user is assigned to it. The updated custom business role, along with the custom business catalog, is displayed, as shown in the figure below.

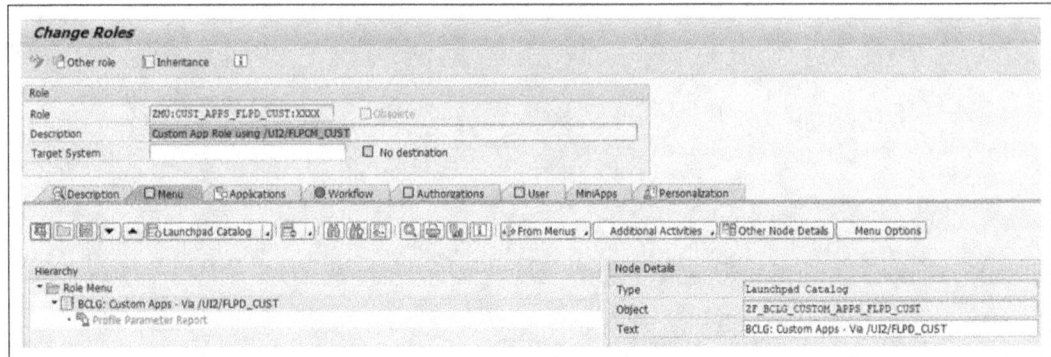

Figure 12-88.   *Updated business role with the custom business catalog*

The above figure also shows that the role has the custom business catalog, which displays the custom tile assigned.

Testing and Validation

The test user logs into the SAP Fiori Launchpad and clicks the **User Menu,** followed by the **App Finder** option. The new custom app is displayed, as shown in the figure below.

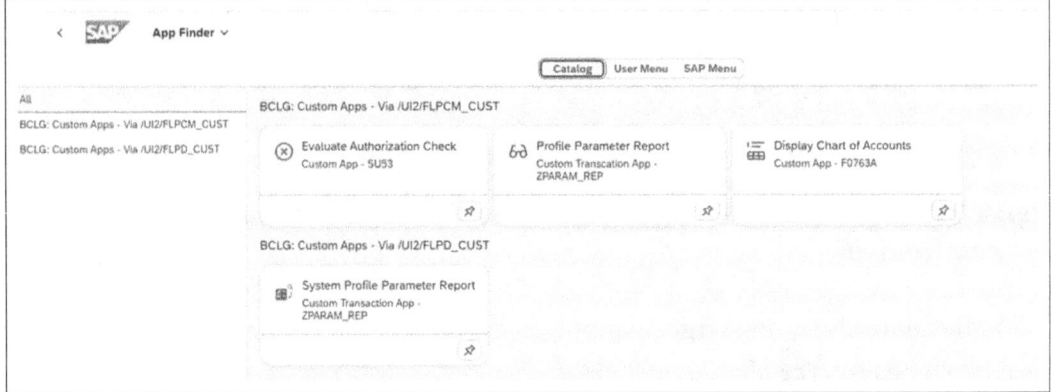

Figure 12-89.   *Test user SAP Fiori Launchpad home page displays the custom tile*

CHAPTER 12 CONFIGURE CUSTOM SAP FIORI APPS

The figure above displays the custom business catalog and the tile assigned to the test user. Selecting the new custom business catalog added on the left panel shows the catalog and tile, as illustrated in the figure below.

Figure 12-90. *Custom business catalog and tile displayed*

In the figure above, the System Profile Parameter Report, when executed, generates the output report shown in Figure 12-90.

12.3.2 Demo 5: Custom App F0763A – Convert to a Dynamic App

Prerequisite

The developer will create a custom app. We do not have a custom app available, but we will use the **Fiori app F0763A** (Manage Chart of Accounts) to create a dynamic tile.

Create a Semantic Object

The developer will create a custom app and provide the semantic object and action. We will use the Fiori app F0763A (Manage Chart of Accounts) to create a dynamic tile for demonstration purposes.

The dynamic app to be created will have the following parameters:

- **Semantic Object**: ChartOfAccounts
- **Semantic Action**: monitor
- **Parameter-Value: (sap-keep-alive = restricted) and (sap-fiori-id = F0763A)**

639

From the **custom technical catalog created** earlier, use the option **App Launcher – Dynamic** to create a new **custom tile**, as shown in the figure below.

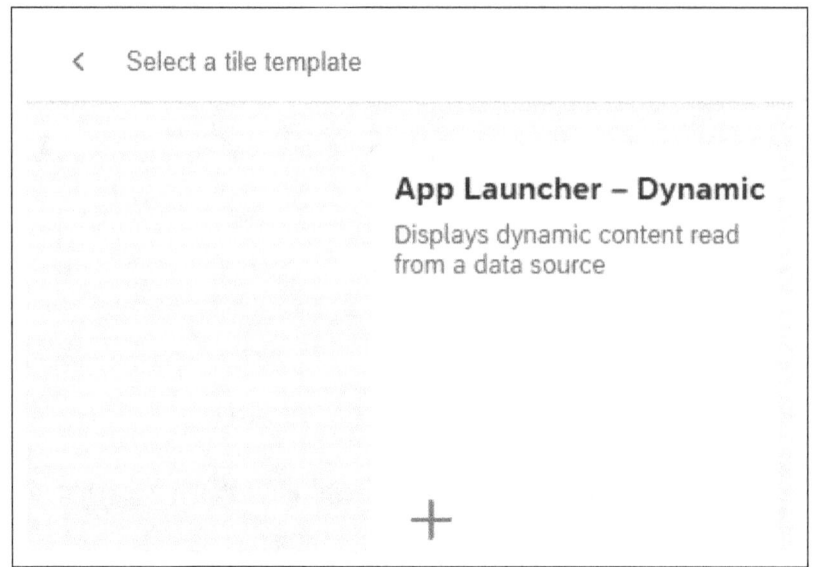

Figure 12-91. The App Launcher – Dynamic option

In the above figure, open the **App Launcher – Dynamic option** by clicking. This will add a dynamic app/tile to the catalog, as shown in the figure below.

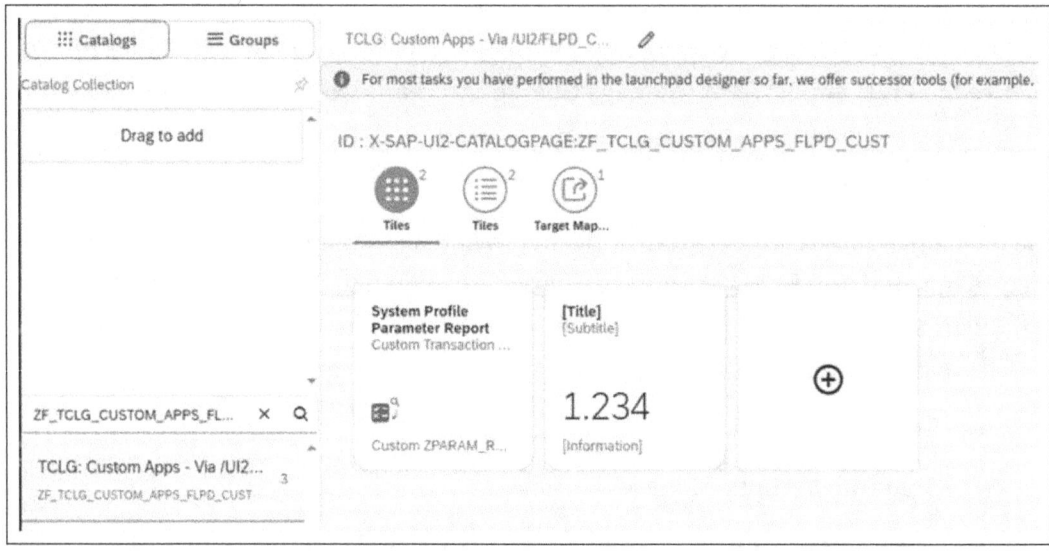

Figure 12-92. Blank dynamic tile added

CHAPTER 12   CONFIGURE CUSTOM SAP FIORI APPS

Opening the **blank dynamic tile** will display a window titled **Configure: "App Launcher – Dynamic'** listing various empty fields to be updated, as shown in the figure below.

Figure 12-93. The blank dynamic tile input screen

In the above figure, enter the following details for the tile to be generated:

- **Title**: Monitor Chart of Accounts
- **Subtitle**: Custom Dynamic App – F0763A
- **Keywords**: Chart of Accounts
- **Icon**: (Choose from the search option and click OK at the bottom.)
- **Information**: Custom Dynamic App – F0763A
- **Semantic Object**: ZSO_F0763A
- **Action**: monitor
- **ID**: fin.gl.chartofaccounts.manage
- **Parameters**: sap-keep-alive = restricted
- **Target URL**: (The system will this field.)

641

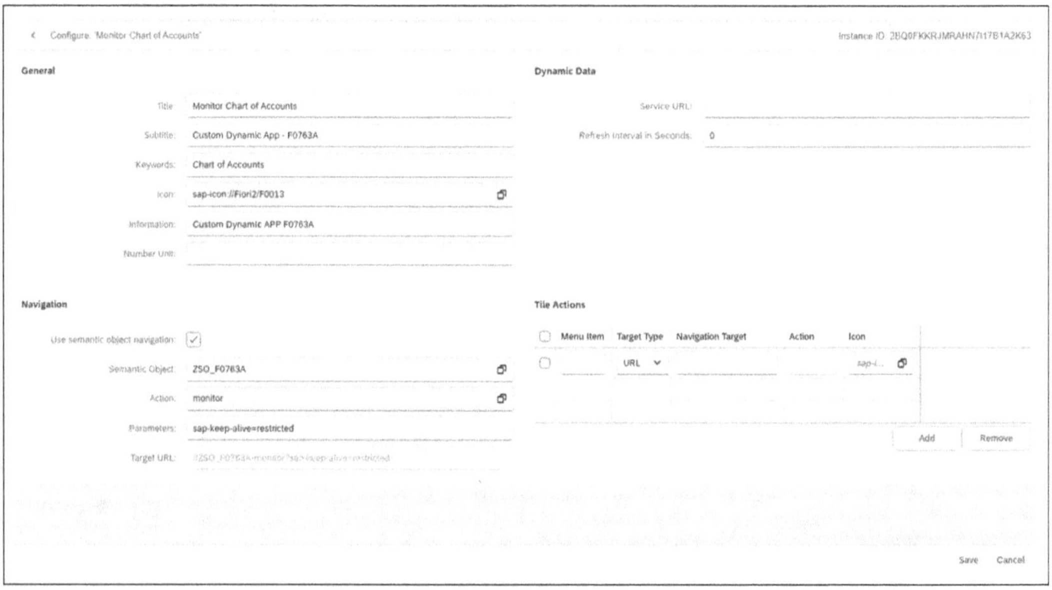

CHAPTER 12   CONFIGURE CUSTOM SAP FIORI APPS

Figure 12-94. Dynamic tile information populated

Once all the field values have been updated, save the changes by clicking the **Save** button at the bottom of the screen. A message will then appear, stating **Configuration successfully changed for tile 'Monitor Chart of Accounts'**, as shown in the figure below.

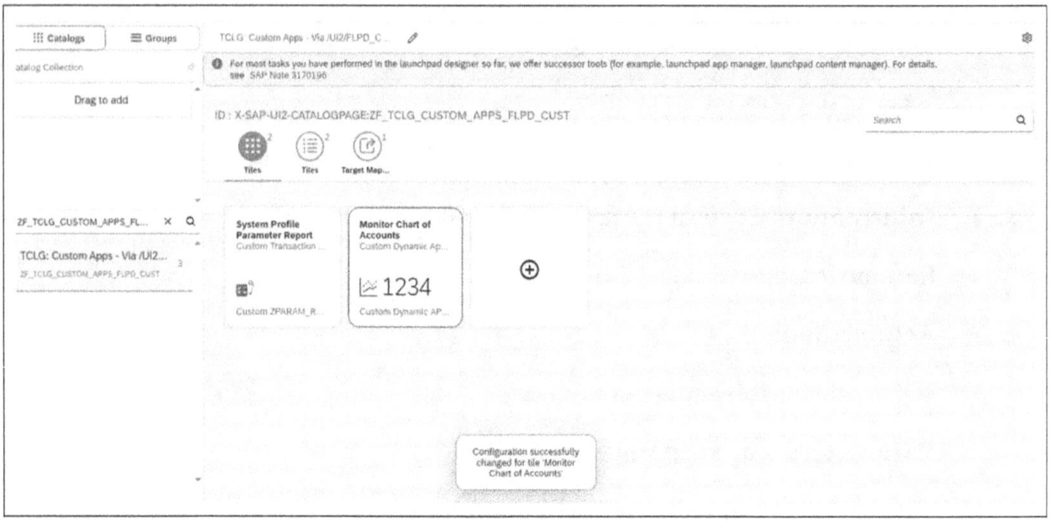

Figure 12-95. Dynamic tile information has been saved

CHAPTER 12 CONFIGURE CUSTOM SAP FIORI APPS

The saved version of the dynamic tile is as shown in the figure below.

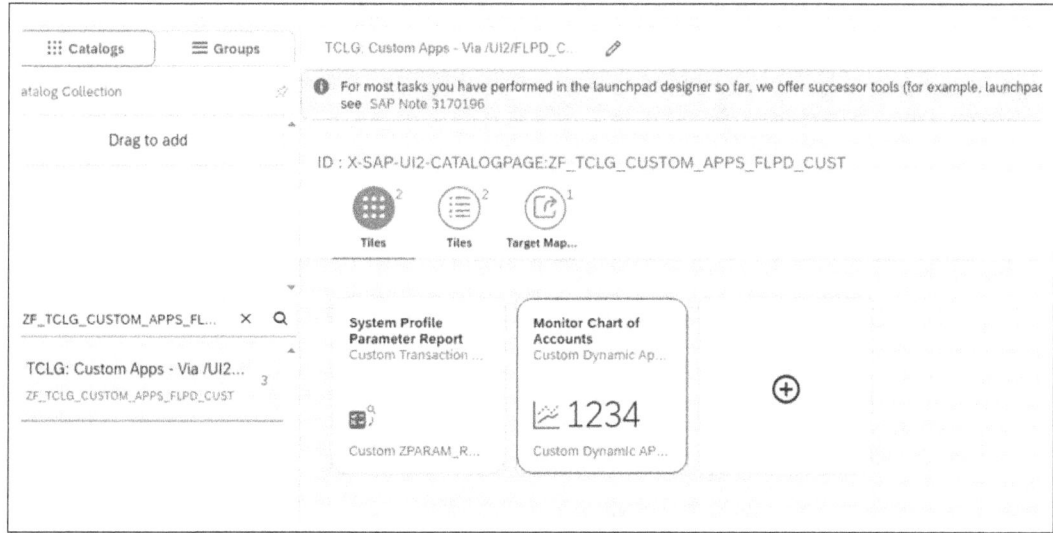

Figure 12-96. Dynamic tile updated with the information

Next, select the tabular format to display the tile information, as shown in the figure below. This system updated most of the other fields per the information added.

Figure 12-97. Dynamic tile displayed in the tabular format

643

CHAPTER 12 CONFIGURE CUSTOM SAP FIORI APPS

The figure above shows that there are currently **two tiles** and **one target mapping**. The next step is to create the **target mapping** by clicking the icon for target mapping, which opens a window titled **Configure: 'Target Mapping'** with various empty field values that need to be updated for the target mapping, as shown in the figure below.

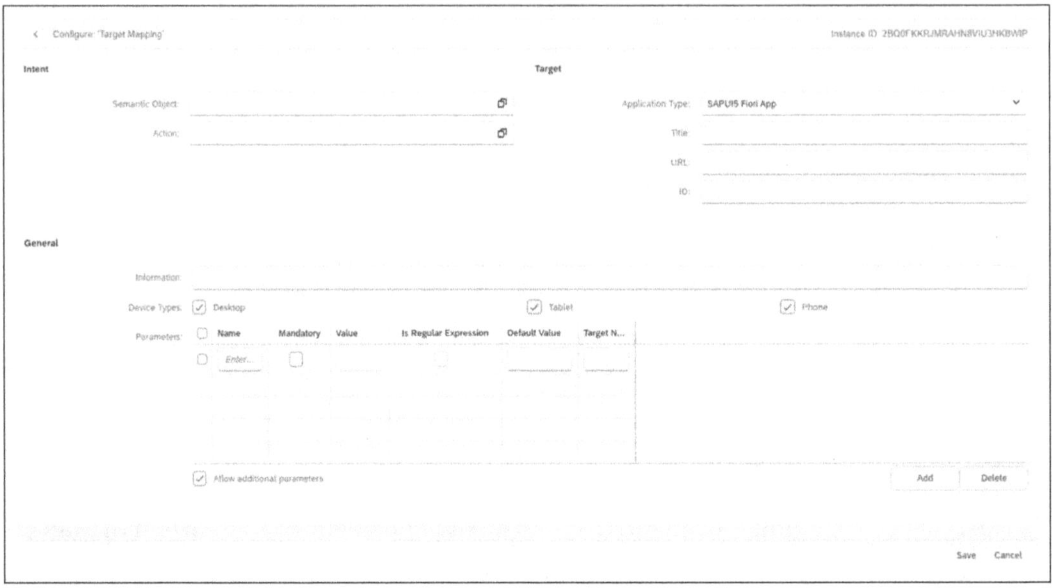

Figure 12-98. Empty target mapping page displayed

Note The system automatically identifies the **application type** as an **SAPUI5 Fiori app** in the above figure.

Now add the values listed below to the figure above. The final input details for target mapping will be shown in the figure below:

- **Semantic Object**: ZSO_F0763A
- **Action**: monitor
- **Application Type**: SAPUI5 Fiori App
- **Title**: Monitor Chart of Accounts
- **URL**: /sap/bc/ui5_ui5/sap/fin_mng_coa
- **ID**: fin.gl.chartofaccounts.manage

CHAPTER 12 CONFIGURE CUSTOM SAP FIORI APPS

- **Parameters**: sap-keep-alive = restricted

    sap-ach = FI-FIO-GL-MD

    sap-fiori-id = F0763A

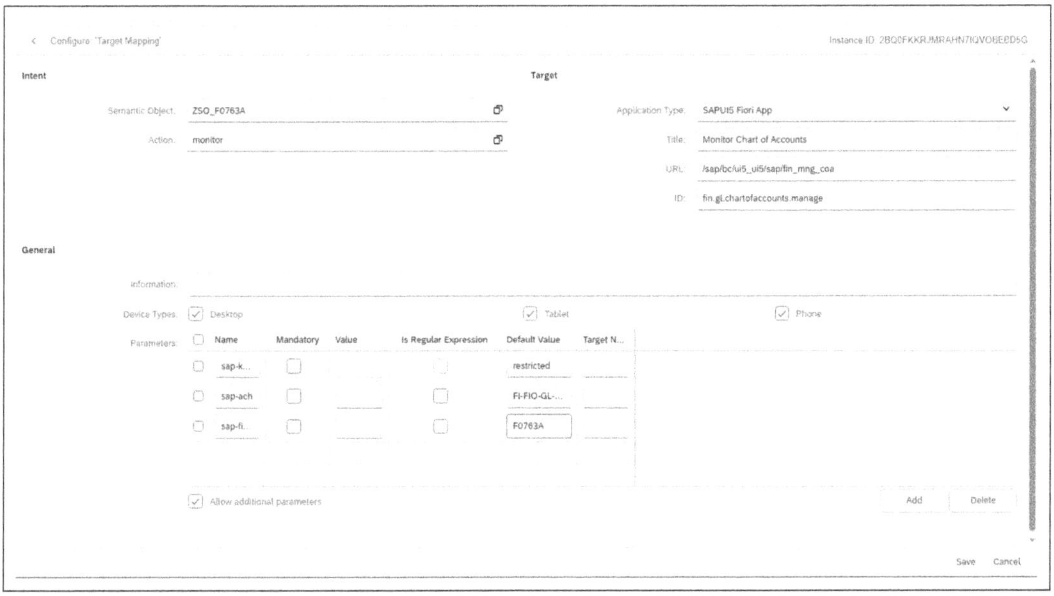

Figure 12-99. Target mapping details entered

Note that you can use the **Add** button to add an **extra parameter**. As shown in the figure above, you can save the settings by clicking the **Save** button at the bottom of the screen.

645

CHAPTER 12   CONFIGURE CUSTOM SAP FIORI APPS

Figure 12-100. The target mapping information has been added to the tile

The figure below shows the target mapping added in tabular format.

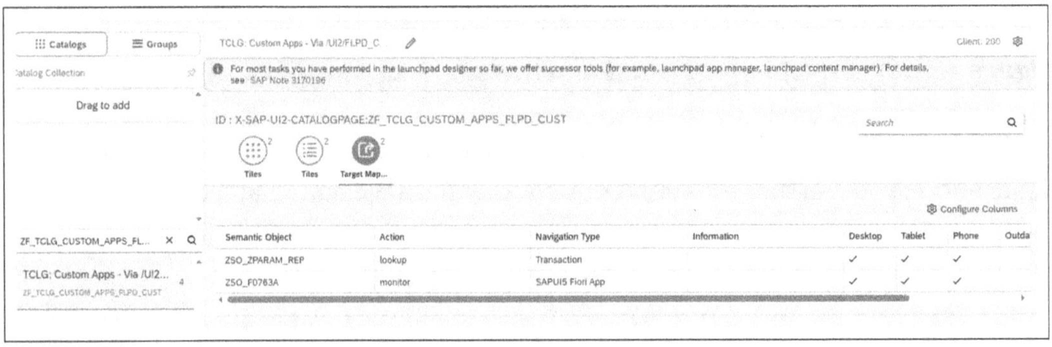

Figure 12-101. Target mapping displayed in tabular format

The figure above shows that the custom technical catalog now has **two tiles** and **two target mappings** assigned.

Update the Custom Business Catalog

As explained earlier, update the business catalog by dragging and dropping the tile and target mapping information. The information will be displayed when you check the business catalog, as shown in the figure below.

CHAPTER 12   CONFIGURE CUSTOM SAP FIORI APPS

Figure 12-102. *The custom business catalog got updated with custom tile information*

Similarly, the custom business catalog was updated with target mapping, as shown in the figure below.

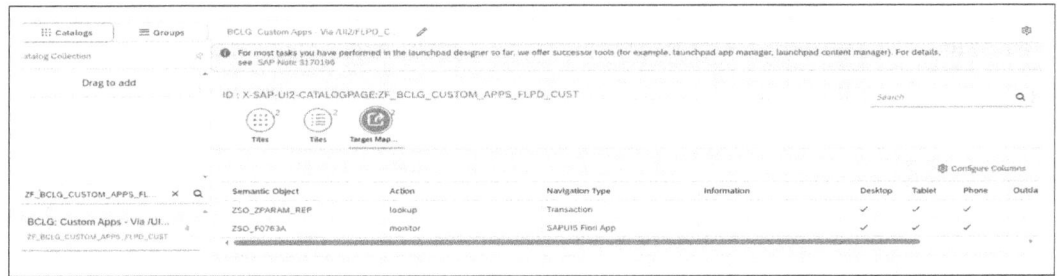

Figure 12-103. *The custom business catalog got updated with custom tile target mapping information*

Update the Business Role

Update the new business role, which has been modified with a new custom tile. Update the authorization and generate it accordingly. The updated role information is displayed in the figure below.

647

CHAPTER 12   CONFIGURE CUSTOM SAP FIORI APPS

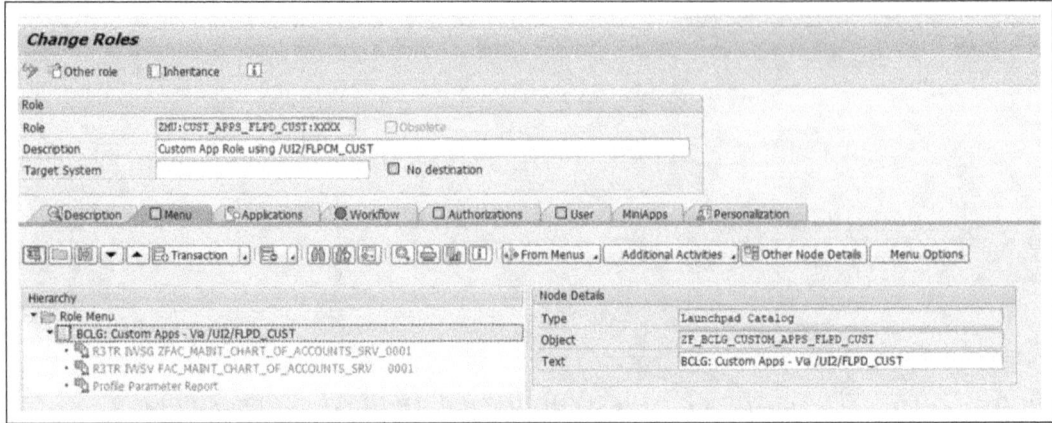

Figure 12-104.   Updated business role displaying both custom tiles

Testing and Validation

The test user logs into the SAP Fiori Launchpad and clicks the **User Menu,** followed by the **App Finder** option. The new custom app is displayed, as shown in the figure below.

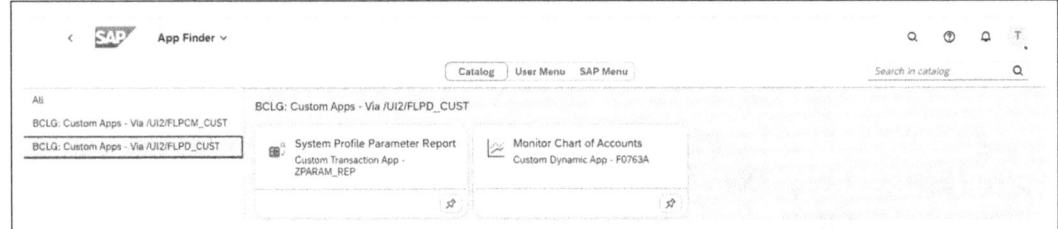

Figure 12-105.   Test user sees both the apps within the custom business catalog

Executing the dynamic app **Monitor Chart of Accounts** displays the output as shown in the figure below.

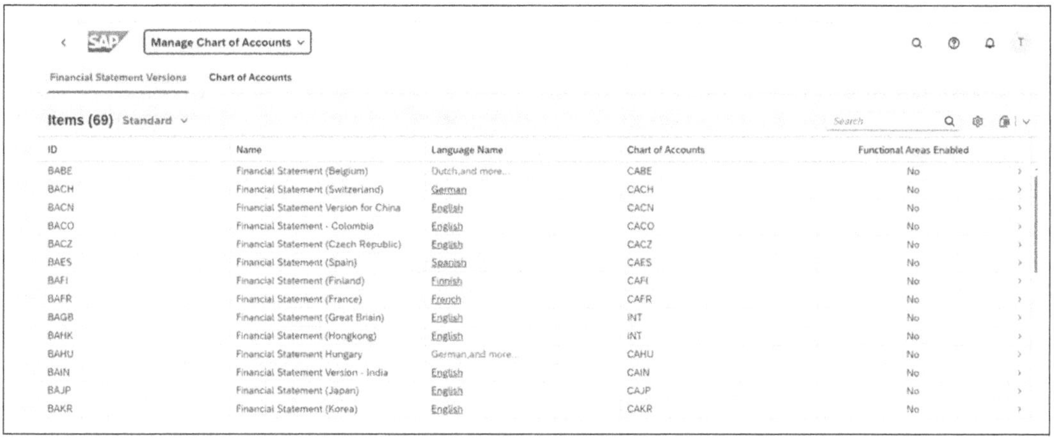

Figure 12-106. Output of dynamic tile Monitor Chart of Accounts

12.4 Summary

This chapter discussed creating custom transaction apps within the SAP Fiori Launchpad, utilizing transaction codes /UI2/FLPAM and /UI2/FLPCM_CUST. It explored step-by-step instructions and practical examples to demonstrate how to seamlessly integrate custom transaction codes into the Fiori environment, providing users with a streamlined and modern experience for accessing these functionalities. Creating custom transaction apps in the SAP Fiori Launchpad involves using the mentioned transaction codes in two key steps. With /UI2/FLPAM (Launchpad App Manager), you can define and register SAP GUI transactions, custom Z transactions, Web Dynpro, or custom-built Fiori apps by assigning a semantic object and action, creating a target mapping, and optionally linking a tile configuration, which makes the app launchable via intent-based navigation. After the app is created, /UI2/FLPCM_CUST (Launchpad Content Manager – Custom) is used to assign it to custom technical catalogs and business catalogs, organizing it for user roles and ensuring visibility in the Fiori Launchpad. This workflow standardizes app accessibility across both standard and custom scenarios, supporting consistency and user-specific tile delivery. Finally, /UI2/FLPD_CUST (Launchpad Designer – Customer Scope) is used to design and maintain tiles, including their appearance, text, parameters, and layout on the Launchpad, ensuring that any SAP or custom app is seamlessly integrated, properly configured, and accessible to end users, allowing them to see all the apps available in the Fiori Launchpad for execution. The user can see all the apps available in the Fiori Launchpad to execute.

CHAPTER 13

SAP Fiori App Support and Troubleshooting

This chapter will explore the typical challenges encountered in SAP Fiori systems and the available troubleshooting mechanisms. We will highlight various tools and transaction codes that can assist users and administrators in effectively analyzing and resolving these issues, ensuring a smoother experience with the platform.

There are different ways to troubleshoot Fiori issues. Some of the mechanisms include browser-based methods and transaction-based options.

Browser-based options include

- App Support
- Browser debug mode

Transaction-based options involve various transactions, such as

- /IWFND/ERROR_LOG
- STAUTHTRACE
- STUSERTRACE
- SU53

Programs and transaction codes are also available to help solve issues related to performance, loading tiles or apps, etc. We will list some examples of these issues at the end of this chapter.

This chapter focuses on configuring, setting up, and troubleshooting the App Support tool in SAP Fiori. This tool helps users and administrators quickly gather technical information and solve issues. First, we will explain step by step how to activate and configure App Support. Following this, we will discuss five common problems that users face in SAP Fiori applications: missing app tiles, incorrect navigation targets, service activation issues, authorization errors, and adaptation inconsistencies. We will show how to diagnose and fix these problems using the App Support tool. By the end of this chapter, you will understand how to use App Support to help resolve issues in SAP Fiori.

13.1 Configuring App Support

App Support helps users easily report issues or request help directly from the app they are using. Configuring App Support in SAP Fiori involves enabling the feature. Enabling App Support is typically set up by activating the associated step in the **task list** or **manually.**

The authorizations for the App Support tool are included in the admin and user foundation roles. Once configured, users can click a help icon within the Fiori app to see technical information like app ID, technical catalog, system aliases, and error logs and contact IT support easily by downloading logs, making troubleshooting faster and smoother without needing back-end access.

13.1.1 Introduction

The Fiori Launchpad App Support plugin is a versatile and user-friendly tool designed to help you quickly identify and resolve issues within the SAP Fiori Launchpad that was introduced with S/4HANA 2020. This plugin offers a centralized platform to manage and monitor all components involved, ensuring optimal performance of the Fiori Launchpad. It is configurable by the BASIS Team and supports various application types, making it an essential resource for maintaining smooth and efficient user experience. This feature supports the following application types:

- SAPUI5 Fiori app
- Transaction codes
- Custom transaction codes
- Web Dynpro application
- Web Client UI application

App Support is available for SAP S/4HANA as part of the SAP_UI component from the following versions:

- SAP_UI 7.54 SP06 in S/4HANA 1909 SP04 or Front-End Server 6.0 SP04

- SAP_UI 7.55 SP02 in S/4HANA 2020 FPS01 or Front-End Server 2020 SP01

This powerful and user-friendly software tool allows you to identify and troubleshoot issues related to Fiori apps directly from the app's user settings. It provides an incredibly user-friendly experience, allowing you to access all the configuration, authorization (**equivalent to Display Authorization Errors App – SU53**), and other error information from the **User Menu** at the top-right corner of every application within the SAP Fiori Launchpad. This gives all the errors in one location. With the App Support tool, you can resolve issues far more quickly and effectively.

Another critical feature of **App Support** is its ability to monitor the application setup in the SAP Fiori Launchpad in **real time**. The tool provides detailed information on the configuration of SAPUI5, Web Dynpro, WebGUI, and Web Content Framework apps. This lets users quickly identify and diagnose configuration issues affecting the currently displayed application. The troubleshooting engine can also suggest solutions to the problem, making it easier for users to resolve an issue quickly and efficiently. Aside from its powerful troubleshooting engine, the tool provides detailed logs and error messages to help you identify the issue's root cause. This includes

- Authorization errors
- Gateway errors
- Runtime errors
- Download logs

Note It allows the admin user to download and see other people's logs, which can then be forwarded.

CHAPTER 13   SAP FIORI APP SUPPORT AND TROUBLESHOOTING

To enable the **in-app** help, you must make it available in the SAP Fiori Launchpad by setting up the underlying framework context. This involves activating OData and SICF services. Once set up, you can see the **help icon** (question mark) in the SAP Fiori Launchpad and at the top of each app that supports in-app help. The App Support option appears under the **User Menu** located at the top-right corner of every application within the SAP Fiori Launchpad, as shown in the figure below.

Figure 13-1. *App Support option within the SAP Fiori Launchpad for troubleshooting*

> **Note** With the App Support tool, different categories of users can do the following:

End users can do the following:

- Check for general configuration errors.
- Check for app-related issues during runtime.
- Download logs and forward them to the admin/security administrators.

An administrator or a security user is also allowed to

- Check, review, and visualize the logs of other users.

13.1.2 Prerequisites

Before configuring App Support (implementation and configuration), the SAP BASIS team at the client site must ensure the following prerequisites are in place:

- SAPUI5 version must be 1.84 or above.
- The authorization logs for the back-end server are only available for systems with **SAP_BASIS NW 7.50** or with a higher **SAP_BASIS** release version. Implement **SAP Note 2871194**.

App Support Set Up Using the Task List

The App Support tool can be set up during the initial configuration of SAP Fiori using the task list **SAP_FIORI_FOUNDATION_S4**.

App Support Set Up Manually

The App Support option can be set up manually too, for which some mandatory services need to be activated and roles updated.

Chapter 13 SAP Fiori App Support and Troubleshooting

Activate SICF Services:

- /default_host/sap/bc/bsp/sap/sui_flp_app_sup
- /default_host/sap/bc/ui5_ui5/sap/sui_flp_app_sup

Activate the SAP Gateway OData Service:

- sui_flp_app_sup_srv

Roles Required:

- **SAP_FLP_ADMIN** is required to see the menu entry in the Launchpad. The **authorization object S_FLP_AS** should have the fields **SUI_ADEUS** as **All** and **Current**.

- **SAP_FLP_USER** is required for the end user to use the tool after it has been configured. The **authorization object S_FLP_AS** should have the field **SUI_ADEUS** as **Current** only.

App Support Authorization Objects:

- To view and **download logs**, you need authorization for object **S_FLP_AS**. In the authorization field **SUI_ADEUS**, you can control if users are allowed to see the logs from other users. The value **Current** restricts you from seeing logs from other users. The value **All** will enable you to see logs from other users.

- Most of the **displayed logs** have their authorization checks. To be able to display the content of these logs, the following authorizations also need to be maintained:

    - ADEFRONTENDERRORLOG
    - ADEFRONTENDRUNTIMELOGS
    - ADELOCALAUTHORIZATIONLOG
    - ADEREMOTEAUTHORIZATIONLOG
    - ADEREMOTEERRORLOG
    - ADEREMOTERUNTIMELOG

CHAPTER 13   SAP FIORI APP SUPPORT AND TROUBLESHOOTING

13.1.3 Steps Required to Activate App Support Automatically

Task List

The task list **SAP_FIOR_FOUNDATION_S4**, when executed, will automatically set up App Support, and its subtask list displays it, as shown in the figure below.

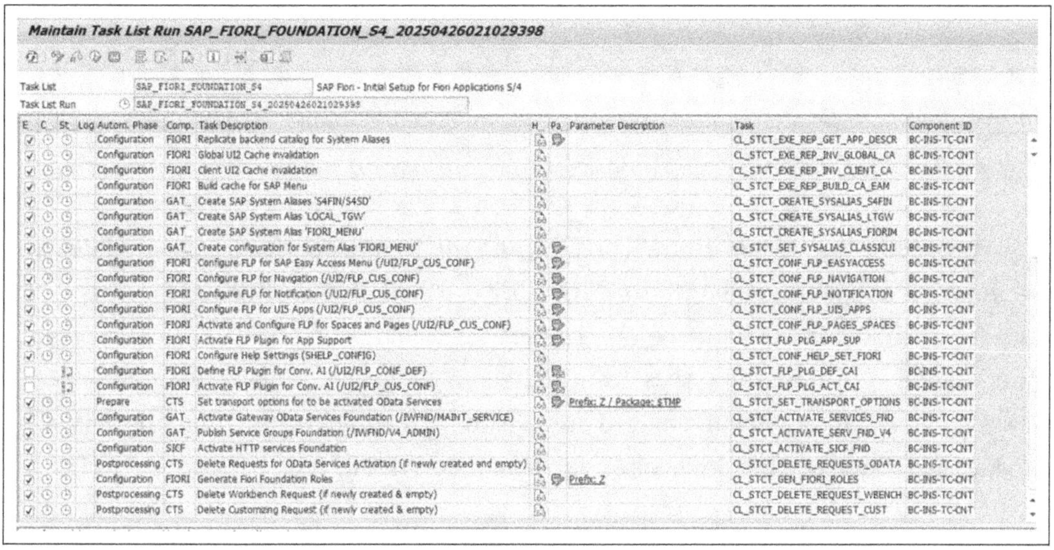

Figure 13-2. Task list showing the subtask that sets up the App Support option

13.1.4 Steps Required to Activate App Support Manually

The manual process is discussed below.

Check and Activate the OData Service

The first step is to verify that the necessary OData service for App Support functionality is up to date. You can do this by executing the transaction **/IWFND/MAINT_SERVICE**. Then search for the OData service **SUI_FLP_APP_SUP_SRV** using the **Filter** tab, as shown in the figure below.

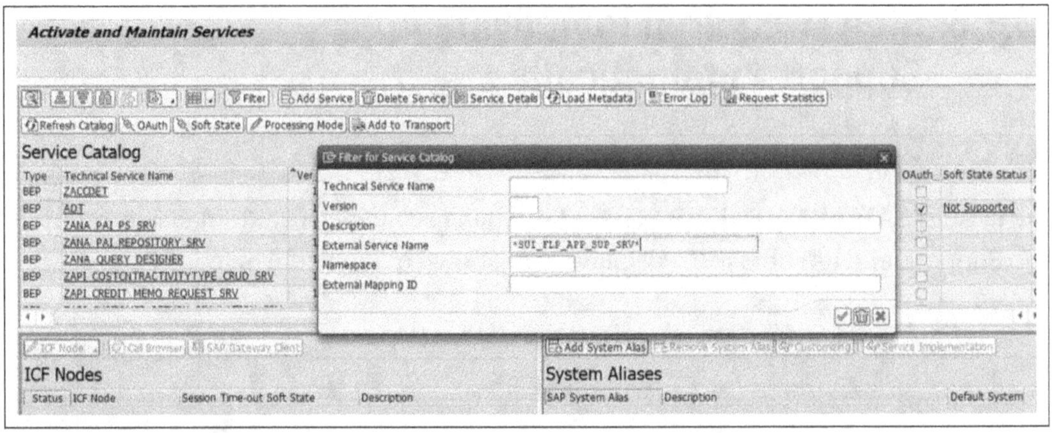

CHAPTER 13 SAP FIORI APP SUPPORT AND TROUBLESHOOTING

Figure 13-3. The OData service needed to be activated for the App Support option

To proceed, click the **continue icon** , and the **OData service** is activated because the prefix **Z** is assigned, appearing as **ZSUI_FLP_APP_SUP_SRV**, needed for **App Support**, as shown in the figure below. The service is activated and can be checked, and under the **ICF Node** tab, the **status** traffic light is **green**. If this is not green, the **OData service** can be activated here. Thus, we do not need to do anything more to activate the **OData service**, as it has already been **activated**.

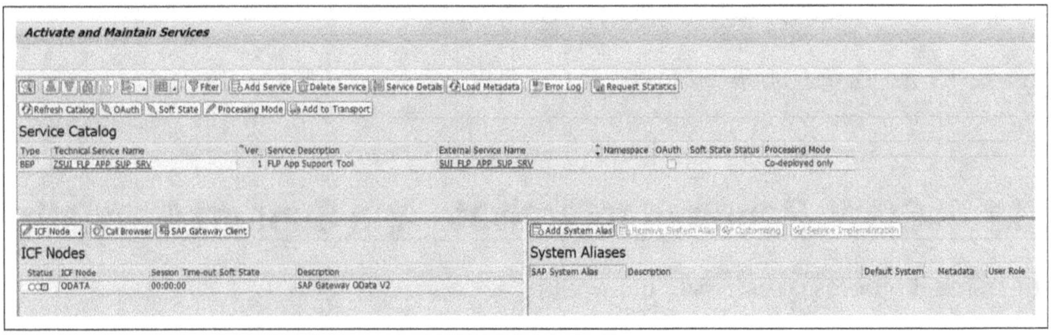

Figure 13-4. The OData service needed for App Support to function is already activated

Note The associated **SICF services** are **automatically enabled** when the **OData service** is **activated**.

658

CHAPTER 13 SAP FIORI APP SUPPORT AND TROUBLESHOOTING

Check the SICF Services

Execute the transaction SICF and check if the SICF service **/default_host/sap/bc/bsp/sap/sui_flp_app_sup** is activated for App Support to function correctly, as shown in the figure below.

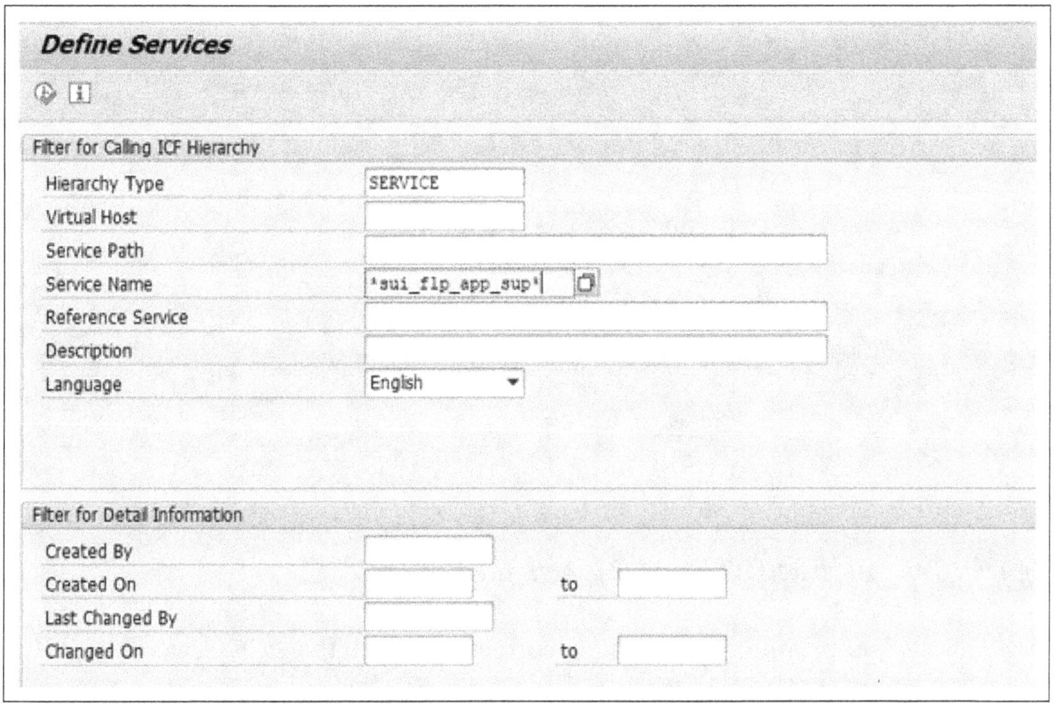

Figure 13-5. Checking for SICF service activation

To proceed, click the **continue icon**. The SICF service is found, and right-clicking shows that it is activated, as the **Activated Service** option is **grayed out**, as shown in the figure below.

659

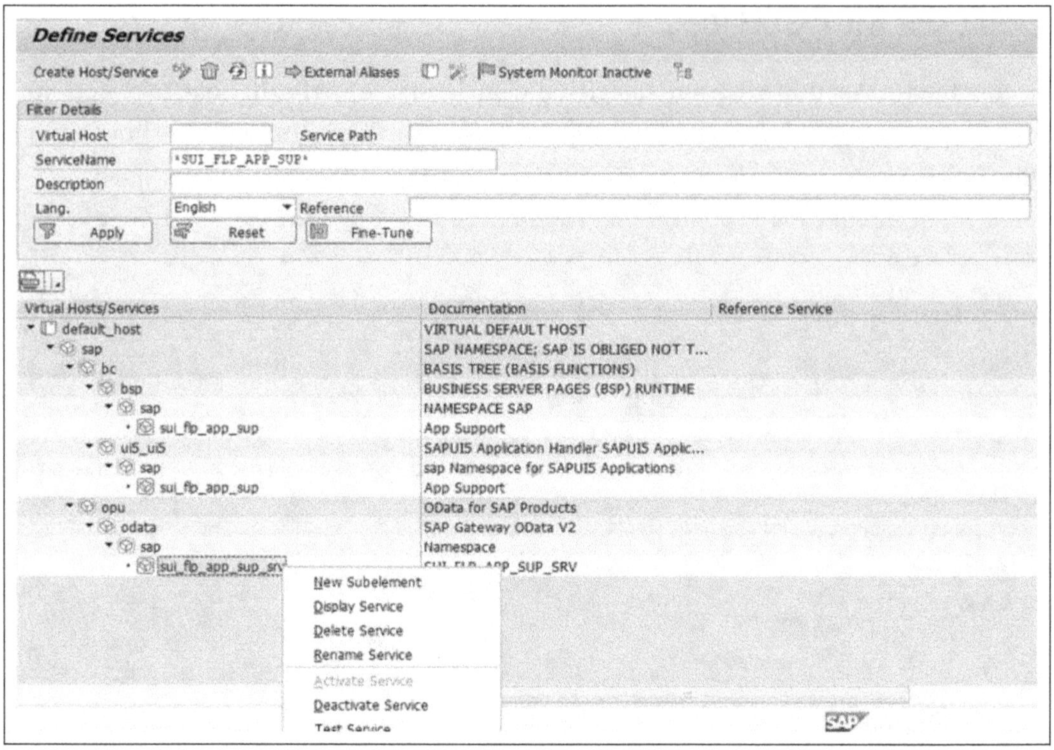

CHAPTER 13 SAP FIORI APP SUPPORT AND TROUBLESHOOTING

Figure 13-6. The listed ICF service is activated

Similarly, for App Support to function correctly, check if the SICF service **/default_host/sap/bc/ui5_ui5/sap/sui_flp_app_sup** is activated. The service is activated, as shown in the figure below.

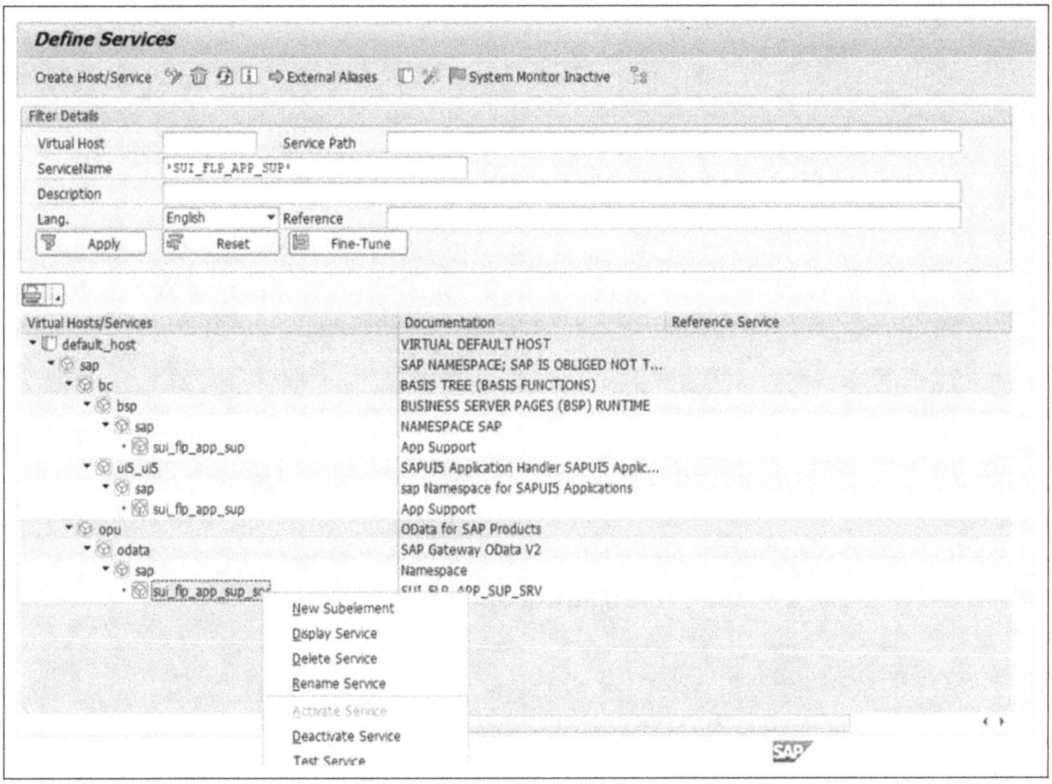

CHAPTER 13 SAP FIORI APP SUPPORT AND TROUBLESHOOTING

Figure 13-7. The other SICF service required is also activated

If the **SICF services** are deactivated, you can activate them here. Since both **SICF services** are already **active**, you do not need to do anything else to activate the **App Support** option, as it is already set up.

Validate the End User Role

Next, we need to validate if the common **FLP user** role assigned to all users has the **authorization object S_FLP_AS** with the **field name** set to **Current**. This is verified and shown in the figure below.

CHAPTER 13   SAP FIORI APP SUPPORT AND TROUBLESHOOTING

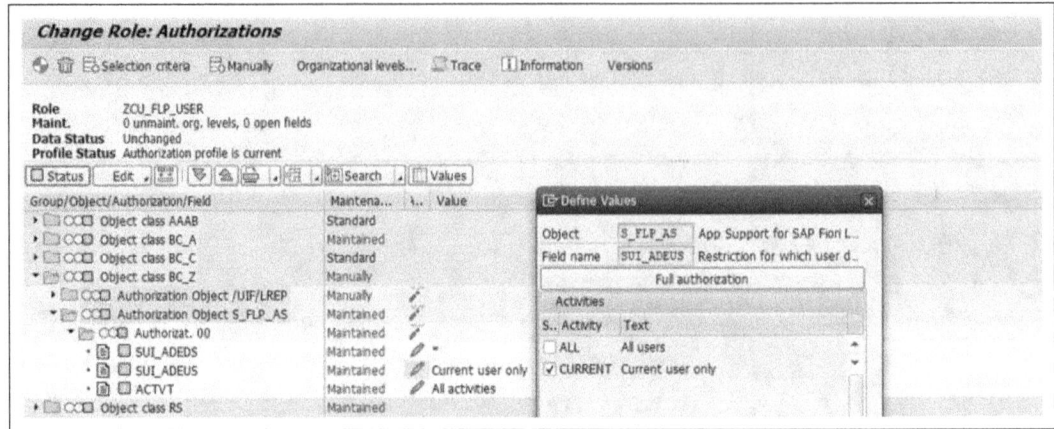

Figure 13-8. End user has the authorization object S_FLP_AS assigned

Additionally, the **ACTVT** is also set to **display and download** for the **FLP user role**, and it is verified, as illustrated in the figure below.

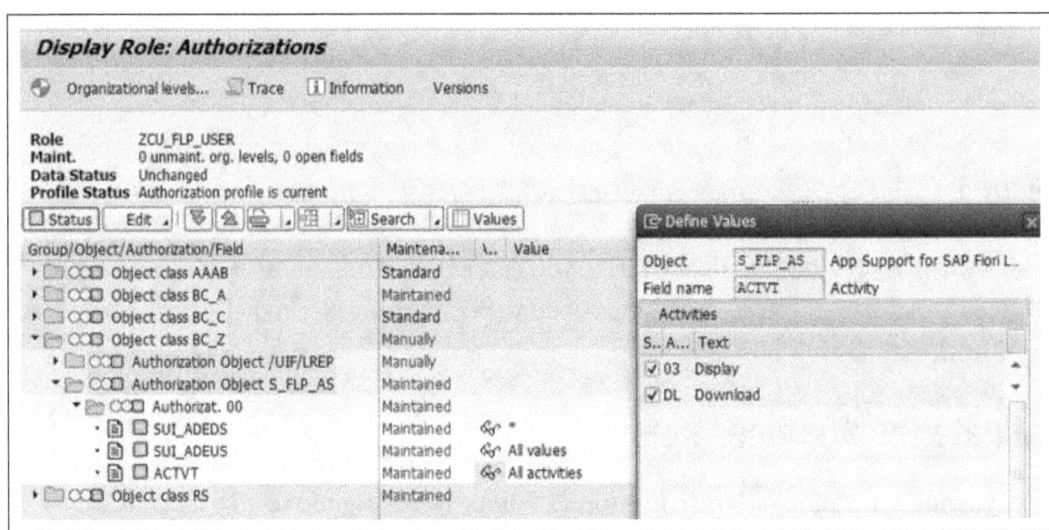

Figure 13-9. ACTVT values are set up correctly for the authorization object for end user roles

The **FLP user** access is set up correctly, so the **App Support** option will appear on the SAP Fiori Launchpad home page.

CHAPTER 13 SAP FIORI APP SUPPORT AND TROUBLESHOOTING

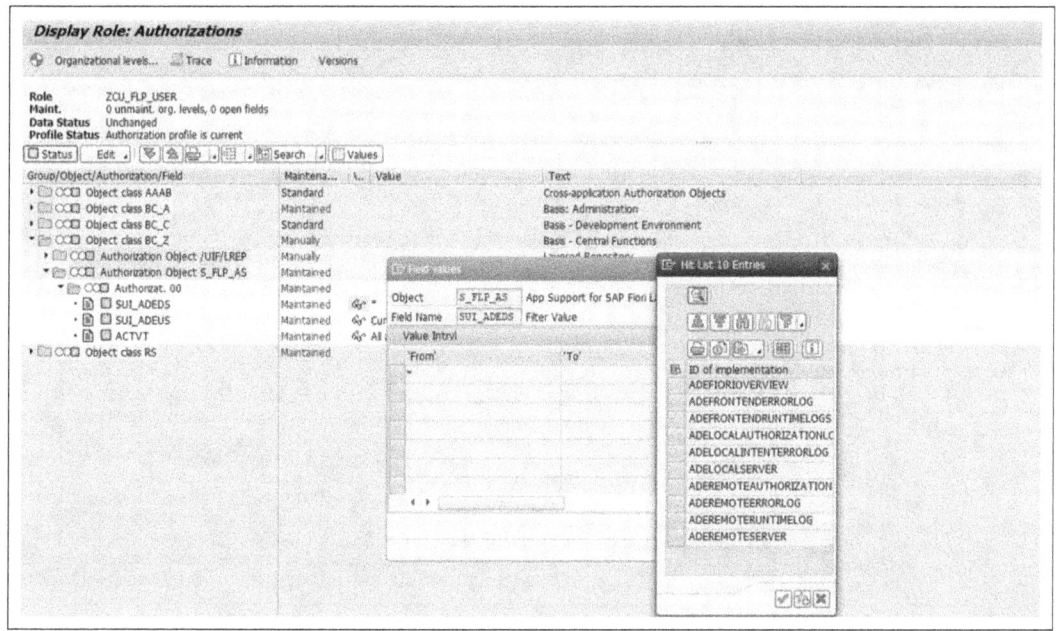

Figure 13-10. *Field name SUI_ADED values*

Validate the Admin User Role

Next, we need to validate if the common **FLP admin user** role assigned to all users has the **authorization object S_FLP_AS** with the **field name** set to **Current**. This is verified and shown in the figure below.

663

CHAPTER 13   SAP FIORI APP SUPPORT AND TROUBLESHOOTING

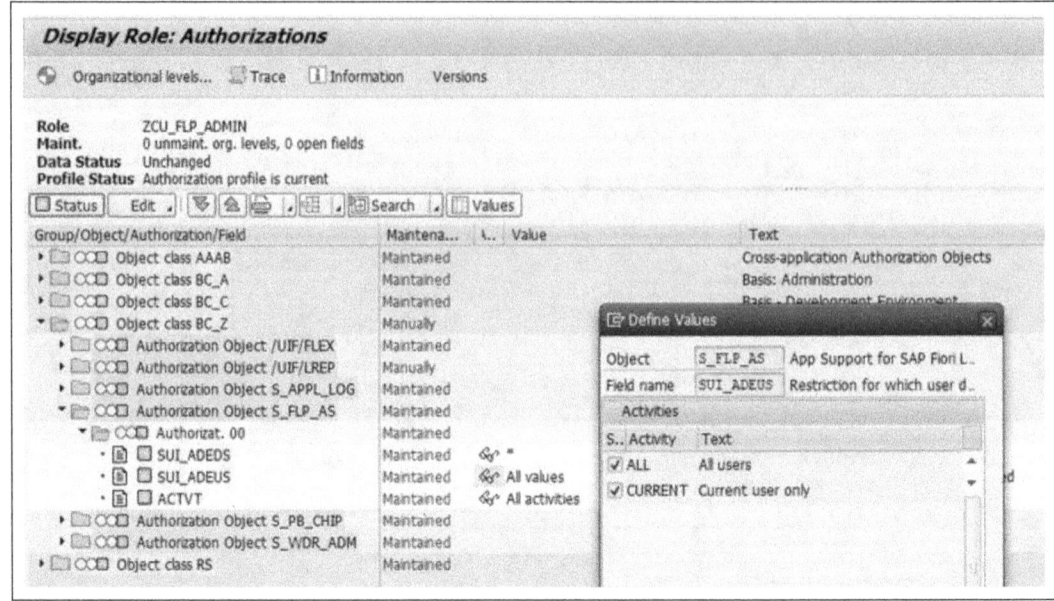

Figure 13-11. The admin user has the authorization object S_FLP_AS assigned

Additionally, the **ACTVT** is also set to **display and download** for the **FLP admin user role**, and it is verified, as illustrated in the figure below.

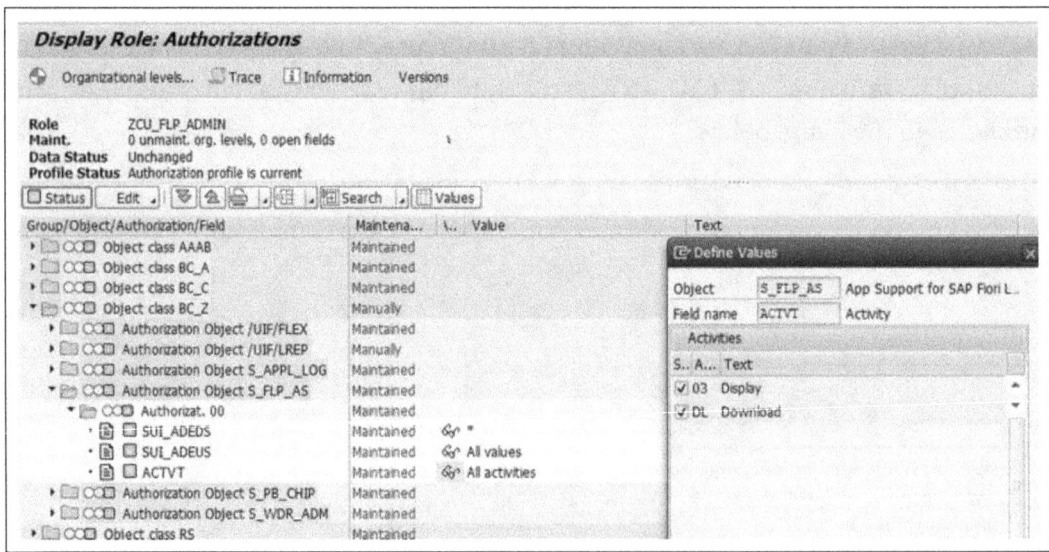

Figure 13-12. ACTVT values are set up correctly for the authorization object for admin user roles

CHAPTER 13 SAP FIORI APP SUPPORT AND TROUBLESHOOTING

The **FLP admin user** access is set up correctly, so the **App Support** option will show on the SAP Fiori Launchpad home page.

13.1.5 Create/Configure the Plugin in Customizing

The plugin can be configured in two ways to make it work:

- Customizing
- Business Catalog

To activate the App Support option, in this scenario, the option **Customizing** will be utilized, which is also a two-step process:

- Configure Plugin
- Activate Plugin

Customizing with Configure Plugin

This Configure Plugin step executes the transaction code **/UI2/FLP_CONF_DEF**, which opens a window titled Information, with a message that it is a cross-client table as shown in the figure below.

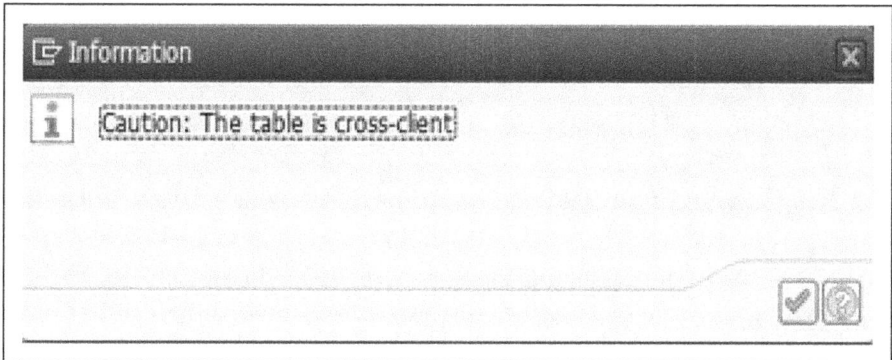

Figure 13-13. Configure Plugin – table is cross-client

To proceed, click the **continue** icon , which displays a message, **Do not make any changes (SAP data)**, as shown in the figure below.

CHAPTER 13 SAP FIORI APP SUPPORT AND TROUBLESHOOTING

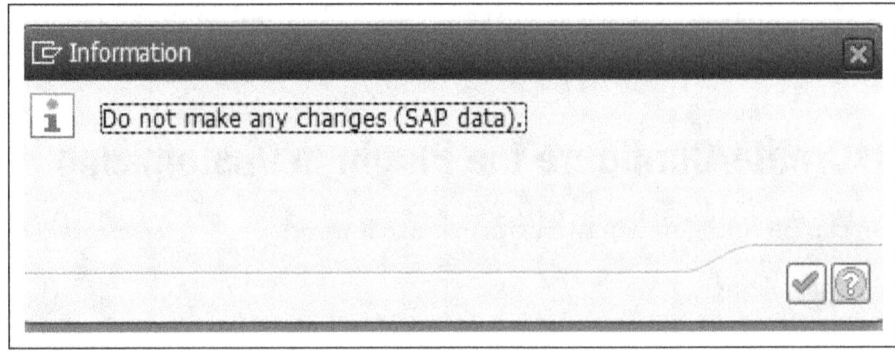

Figure 13-14. Information displaying a message

To proceed, click the continue icon ![], and a window titled **Change View "Define Launchpad Property": Overview** opens, as shown in the figure below.

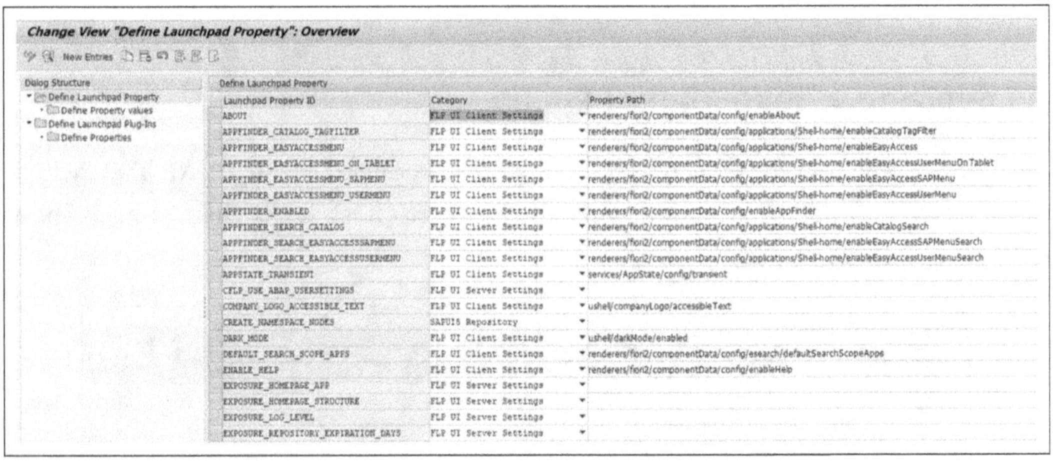

Figure 13-15. Change View "Define Launchpad Property": Overview window

From the left-hand side, under **Dialog Structure,** click the option **Define Launchpad Plug-Ins.**

CHAPTER 13   SAP FIORI APP SUPPORT AND TROUBLESHOOTING

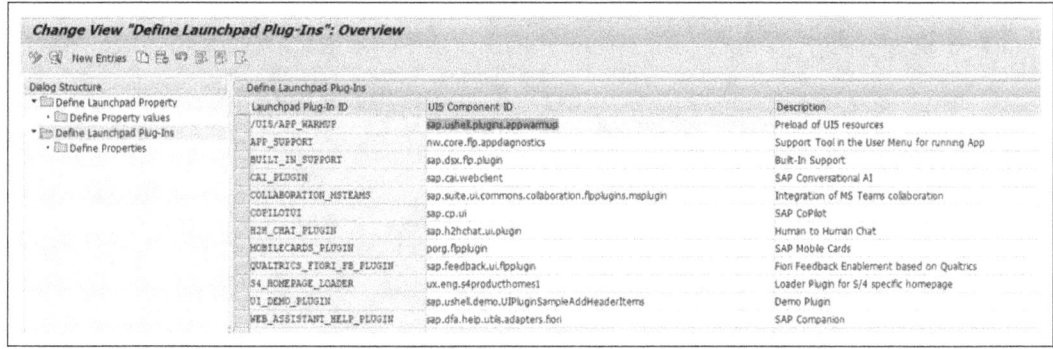

Figure 13-16.   *Define Launchpad Plug-Ins*

Here, we need to define the plugin, which is already done. If it is not done, click the **New Entries** tab in the top menu New Entries, and a window titled **New Entries: Details of Added Entries** opens, as shown in the figure below.

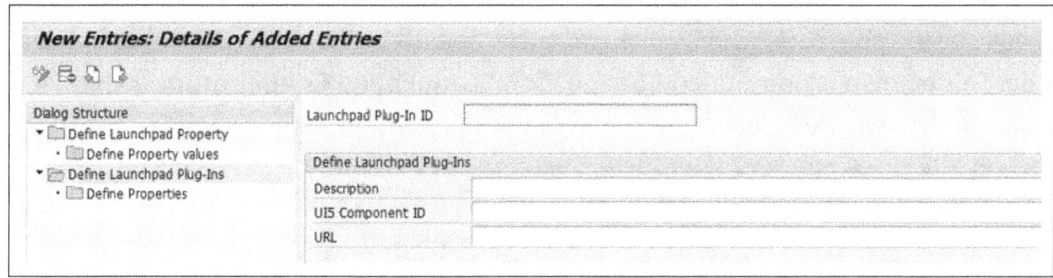

Figure 13-17.   *Window opens to enter App Support details*

In the above figure, maintain the following:

- **Launchpad Plug-In ID**: APP_SUPPORT

- **Description**: APP Support Tool in User Menu for executing Apps

- **UI5 Component ID**: nw.core.flp.appdiagnostics

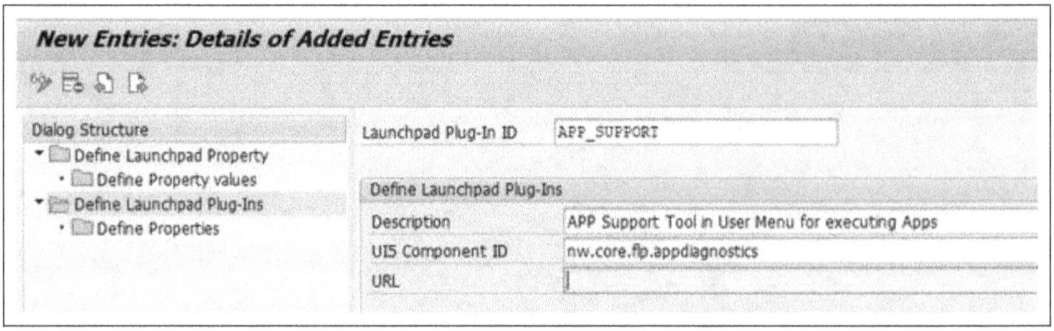

Figure 13-18. App Support plugin details entered

You can save the entries and changes by clicking the top icon. The final screen is as shown in the above figure. Once saved, it will ask for a transport.

Customizing with Activate Plugin

To activate the plugin, use the Launchpad customer **/UI2/FLP_CUS_CONF** transaction code. This opens a window titled **Change View "Launchpad Configuration": Overview**, as shown in the figure below.

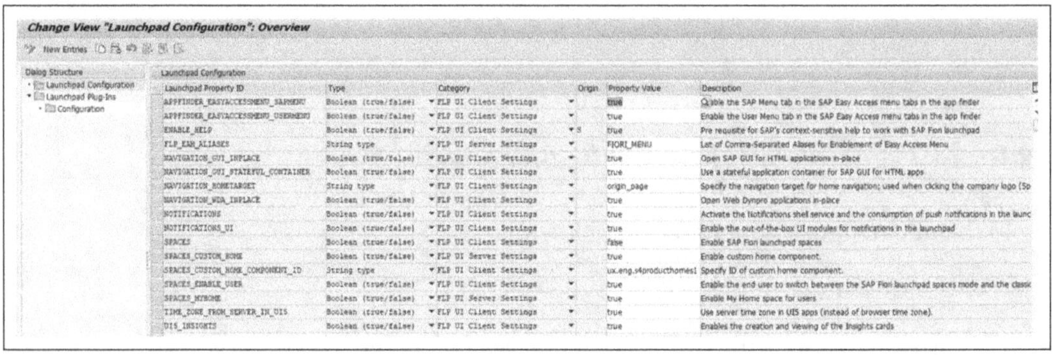

Figure 13-19. Change View "Launchpad Configuration": Overview window

From the left-hand side, under the heading **Dialog Structure,** click the option **Launchpad Plug-Ins**, as shown in the figure below.

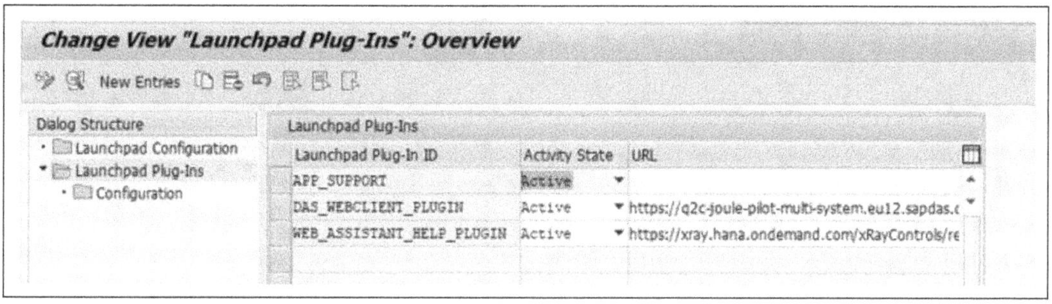

CHAPTER 13 SAP FIORI APP SUPPORT AND TROUBLESHOOTING

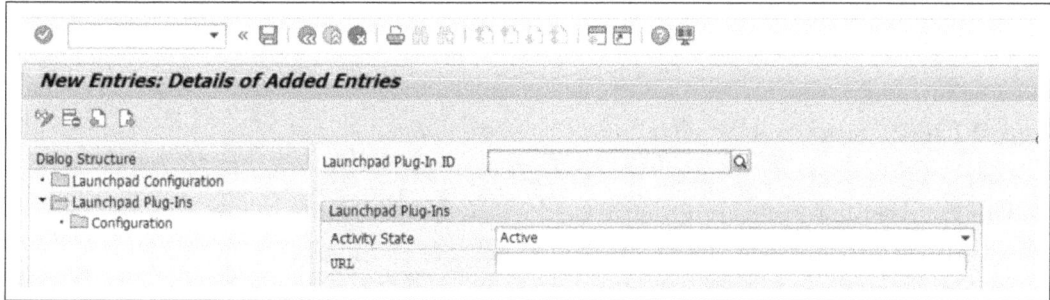

Figure 13-20. Launchpad Plug-Ins option

Here, we need to define the Launchpad plugin, which is already done. If it is not done, click the **New Entries** tab in the top menu New Entries , as shown in the figure below.

Figure 13-21. Window to enter details of the Launchpad plugin

Here, for **Launchpad Plug-In ID,** use the search option and select **APP_ SUPPORT**.

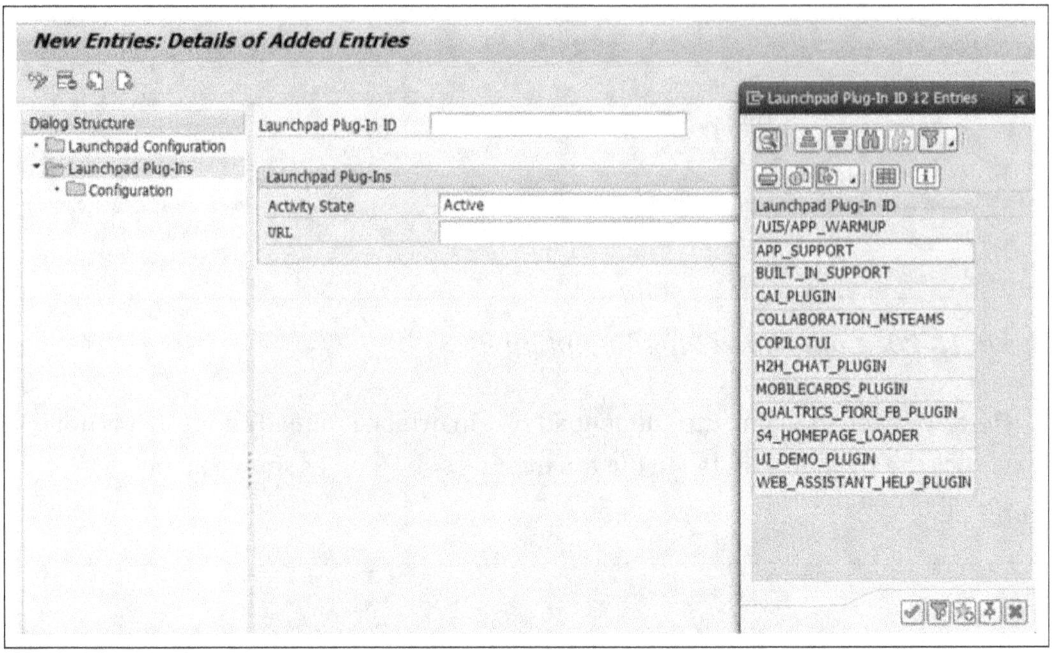

CHAPTER 13   SAP FIORI APP SUPPORT AND TROUBLESHOOTING

Figure 13-22. Option APP_SUPPORT to be selected

Once selected, the screen updates, as illustrated in the figure below.

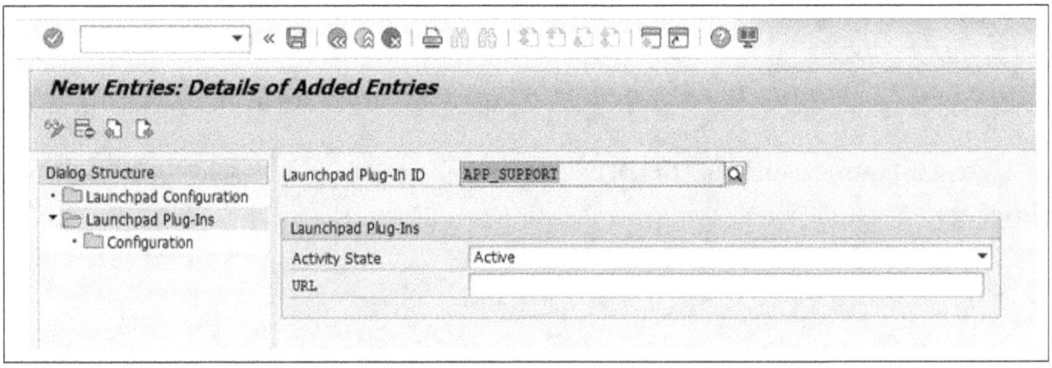

Figure 13-23. Plugin details updated

For **Activity State,** leave as **Active** and save the changes by clicking 💾 in the top menu. Since this is already active, we need to do nothing. If not active, while saving, the system will prompt for a transport.

CHAPTER 13   SAP FIORI APP SUPPORT AND TROUBLESHOOTING

Now that we have verified the steps for configuring the App support tool, in the next few sections, let us see how the App Support tool can be used for troubleshooting authorization issues and a few other methods for resolving other commonly encountered issues in SAP Fiori.

For each scenario, we have created a test user ID and simulated the error.

13.1.6 Authorization Errors

Log into the SAP Fiori Launchpad (/**UI2/FLP**), and then under the **User Menu**, click **App Finder** as shown in the figure below.

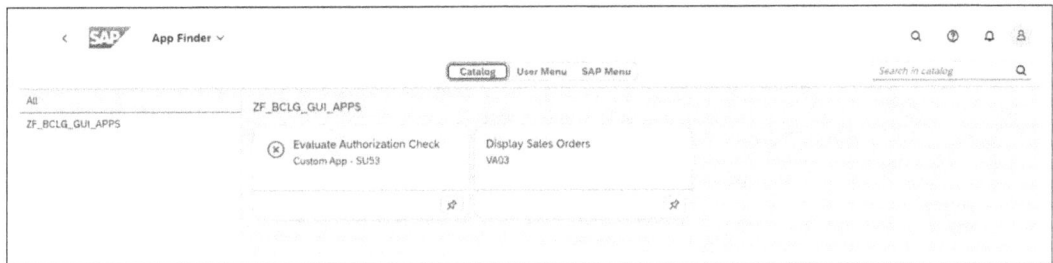

Figure 13-24. *Test user access displayed in the FLP*

Execute the Display Sales Orders app, which opens the Display Sales Documents window, as shown in the figure below.

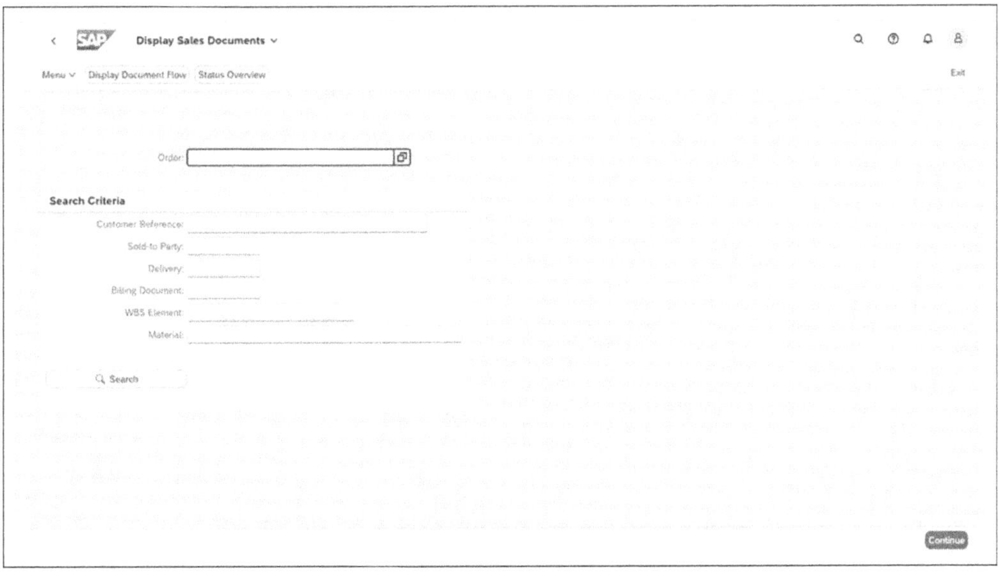

Figure 13-25. *Display Sales Documents window opens*

671

CHAPTER 13 SAP FIORI APP SUPPORT AND TROUBLESHOOTING

A **"No display authorization for document type"** error was encountered when entering details in the **Order** field, as shown in the figure below.

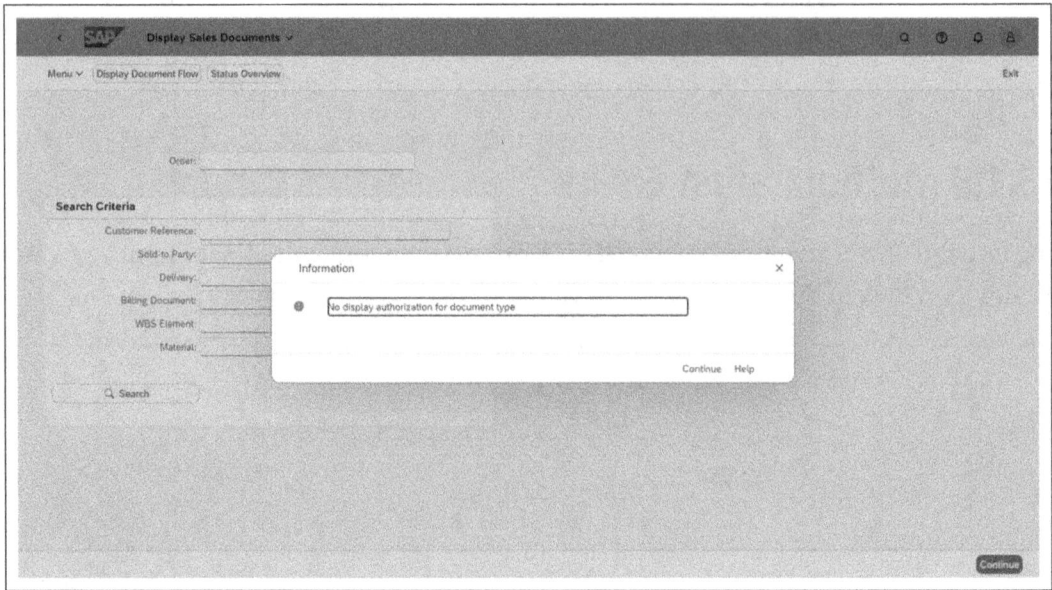

Figure 13-26. *Authorization error encountered*

The above screen displays an error and states that the app needs authorization. Click **Continue** to proceed, which opens a **Sales Document** window for information input, as shown in the figure below.

672

CHAPTER 13 SAP FIORI APP SUPPORT AND TROUBLESHOOTING

Figure 13-27. Sales Document input field parameters

Cancel to proceed. Then go to the **User Menu** tab, and **App Support** becomes available. Select the same, as shown in the figure below.

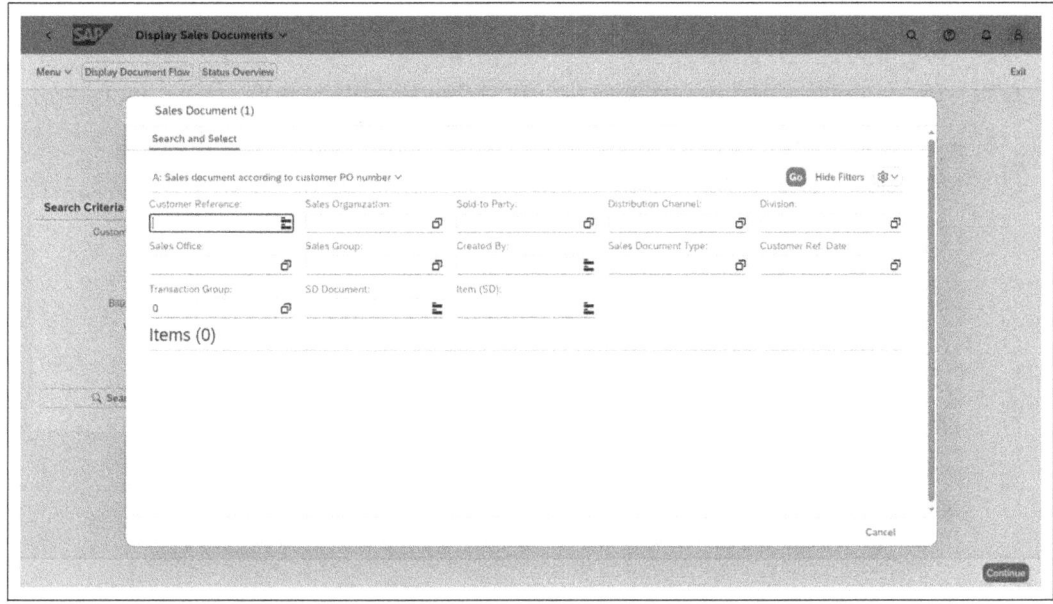

Figure 13-28. App Support option becomes available

CHAPTER 13   SAP FIORI APP SUPPORT AND TROUBLESHOOTING

Note   The above figure indicates that the App Support option under the **User Menu** has been activated and works appropriately. If App Support is not working, an error message will appear, The App Support service cannot be reached, indicating failure, as shown in the figure below.

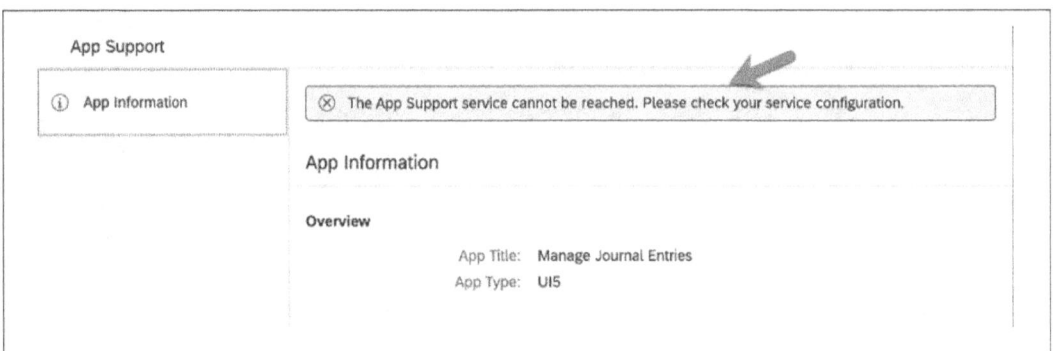

Figure 13-29.   In case App Support is not configured correctly, an error appears

Selecting the **App Support** option will populate the **App Support** window with errors, as shown in the figure below.

CHAPTER 13   SAP FIORI APP SUPPORT AND TROUBLESHOOTING

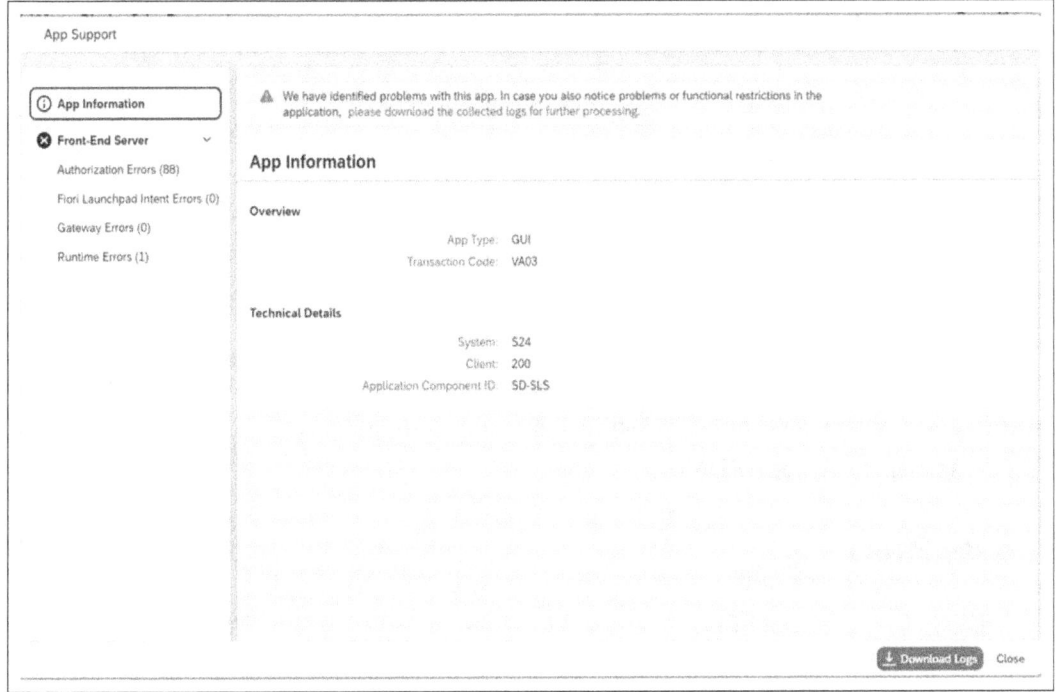

Figure 13-30.   App Support window displaying errors

In the above figure, APP Support displays some options on the left panel as listed below:

- App Information
- Front-End Server
- Authorization Errors
- Gateway Errors
- Runtime Errors

The options on the left panel are defined below.

App Information

The App Information option provides the details of the app executed:

- Front-End Server

675

CHAPTER 13 SAP FIORI APP SUPPORT AND TROUBLESHOOTING

Front-End Server

- Authorization Errors
- Gateway Errors
- Runtime Errors

Authorization Errors

The **Authorization Errors** tab displays missing authorizations, such as specific authorization objects and app field values. Authorization errors are retrieved straight from the transaction Code **SU53.**

Gateway Errors

The **Gateway Errors** tab captures issues related to communication between the Fiori front-end and SAP back-end systems through OData services. Gateway errors are retrieved straight from the transaction **/IWFND/ERROR_LOG** for the embedded deployment.

Runtime Errors

Runtime errors appear in the transaction ST22. This transaction shows ABAP runtime errors, also known as short dumps.

Download Logs

The above screen identifies logs with error messages for the user. Download the log in a structured format, as an Excel workbook, and send it immediately to the next level of support, such as a user admin. To download, click **Download Logs** ↓ **Download Logs** . This file should be shared with the administrator or security personnel.

Click **Authorization Errors** on the left panel to display data as shown in the figure below.

CHAPTER 13 SAP FIORI APP SUPPORT AND TROUBLESHOOTING

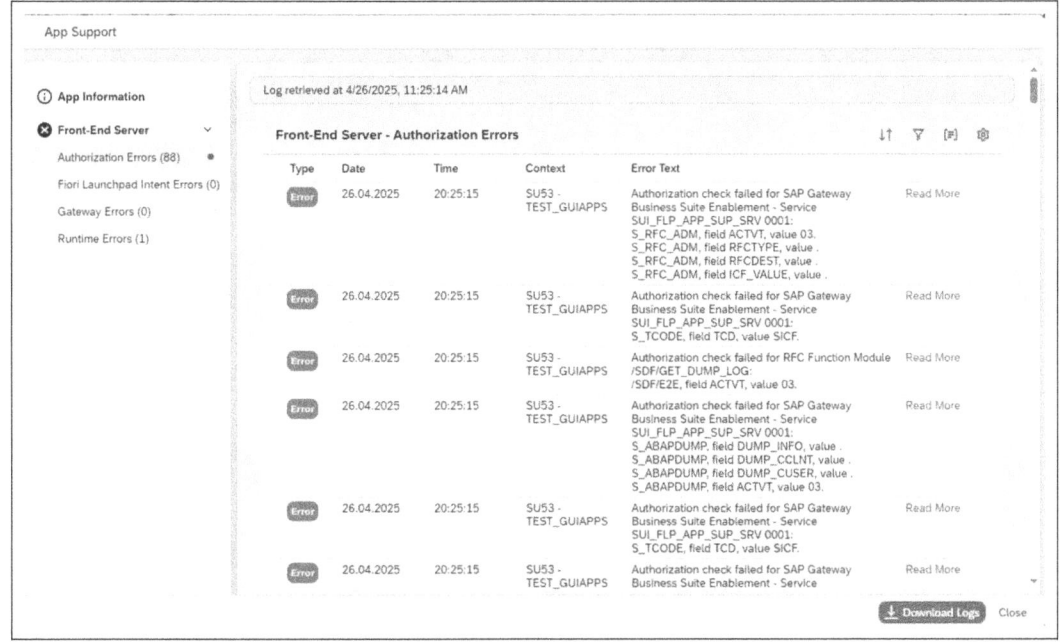

Figure 13-31. *Authorization errors encountered for the app*

The above screen displays many false-positive errors, which should be ignored. Scroll down until you see the exact errors related to authorization displayed as shown in the figure below.

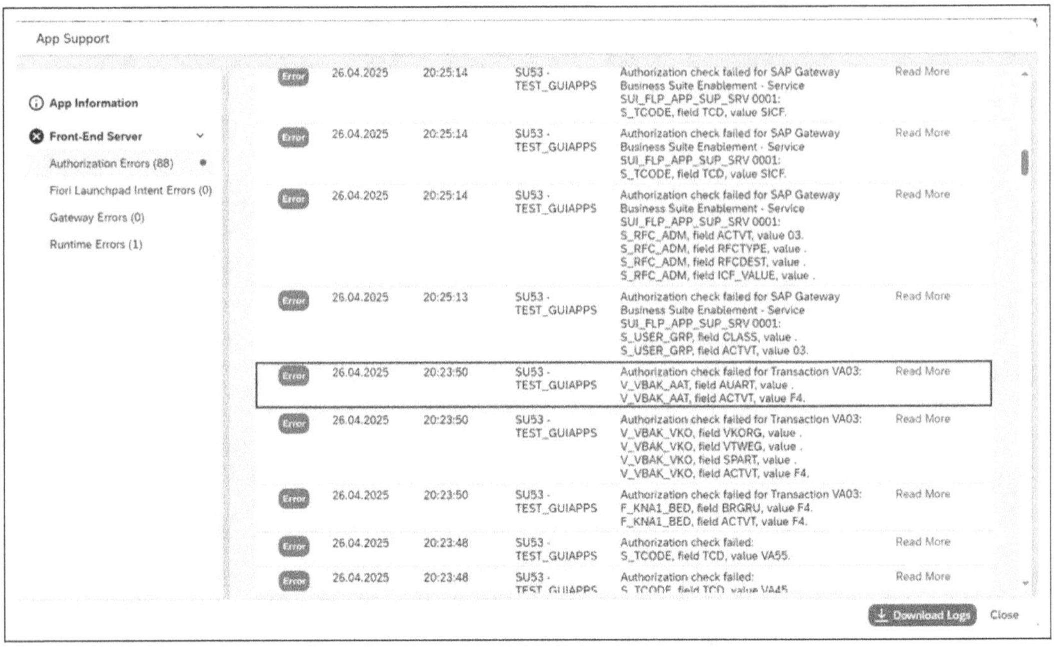

CHAPTER 13   SAP FIORI APP SUPPORT AND TROUBLESHOOTING

Figure 13-32. Authorization errors encountered displayed

The above screen displays the type of authorization errors encountered. It lists the authorization objects and the values missing.

If you are the security admin, ask the end user to download the App Support log by clicking Download Logs ⬇ Download Logs and send the file to you. The log file is downloaded as shown in the figure below.

CHAPTER 13   SAP FIORI APP SUPPORT AND TROUBLESHOOTING

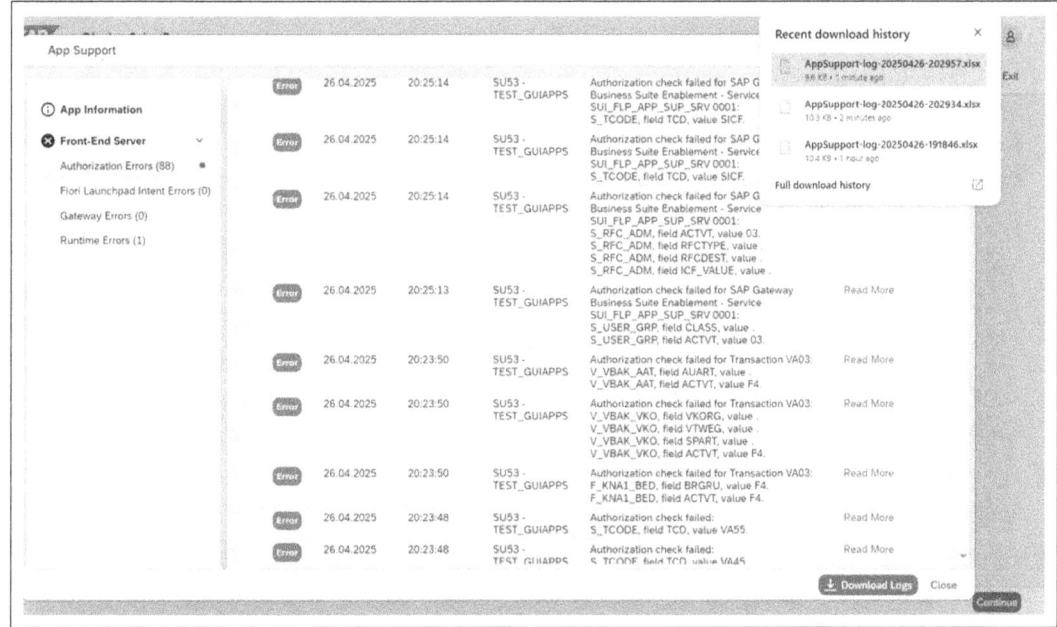

Figure 13-33.   Authorization error log file downloaded

13.1.7 Analyze the Authorization Error File

When the security or admin personnel open the download file to analyze the error, they open the **Excel** file, which displays the data, as shown in the figure below.

679

CHAPTER 13   SAP FIORI APP SUPPORT AND TROUBLESHOOTING

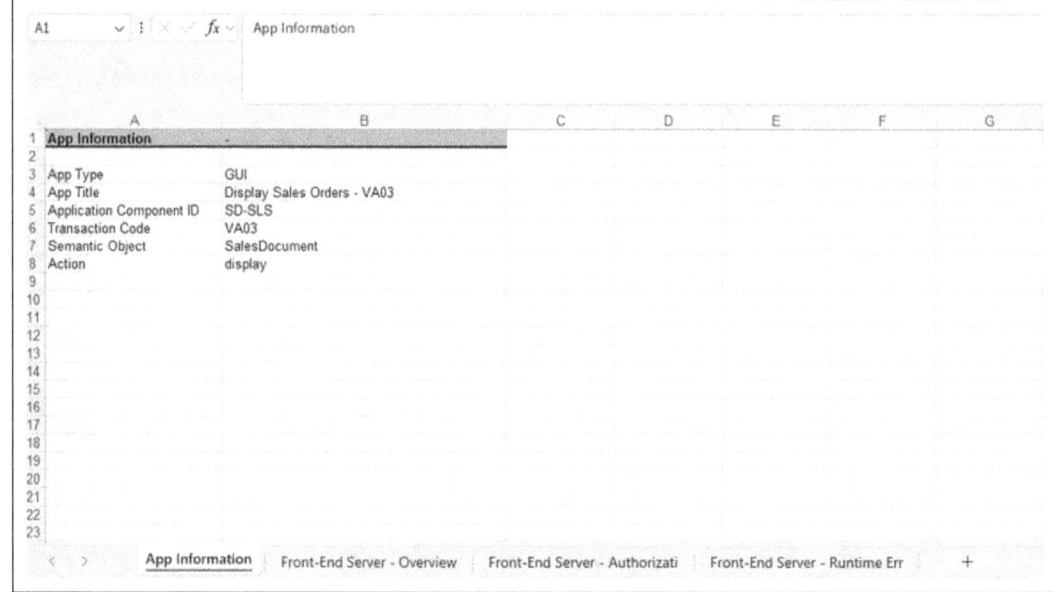

Figure 13-34. *Authorization error log file details*

As displayed in the figure above, there are **four tabs** within the **authorization error file**, which are explained below, along with what they contain:

App Information

Front-End Server – Overview

Front-End Server – Authorization Errors

Front-End Server – Runtime Errors

App Information

The **App Information** tab provides general technical details about the Fiori app you analyze. It shows the following: App Type, App Title, **Application Component** ID, Transaction Code, Semantic Object, and Action, as shown in the figure below.

Front-End Server - Overview

Log ID	Log ID	User Name	Application Type	Context	Icon Message	Date	Time	Error Text
adeLocalServer	adeLocalServer	TEST_GUIAPPS	GUI	System		4/26/2025	11:59:57 PM	S24
adeLocalServer	adeLocalServer	TEST_GUIAPPS	GUI	Client		4/26/2025	11:59:57 PM	200
adeLocalServer	adeLocalServer	TEST_GUIAPPS	GUI	WebGui Service	Error	4/26/2025	11:59:57 PM	WebGui ICF service inactive
adeLocalServer	adeLocalServer	TEST_GUIAPPS	GUI	MIME Repository	Error	4/26/2025	11:59:57 PM	MIME Repository Service inactive
adeLocalServer	adeLocalServer	TEST_GUIAPPS	GUI	RFC Connection	OK	4/26/2025	11:59:57 PM	OK

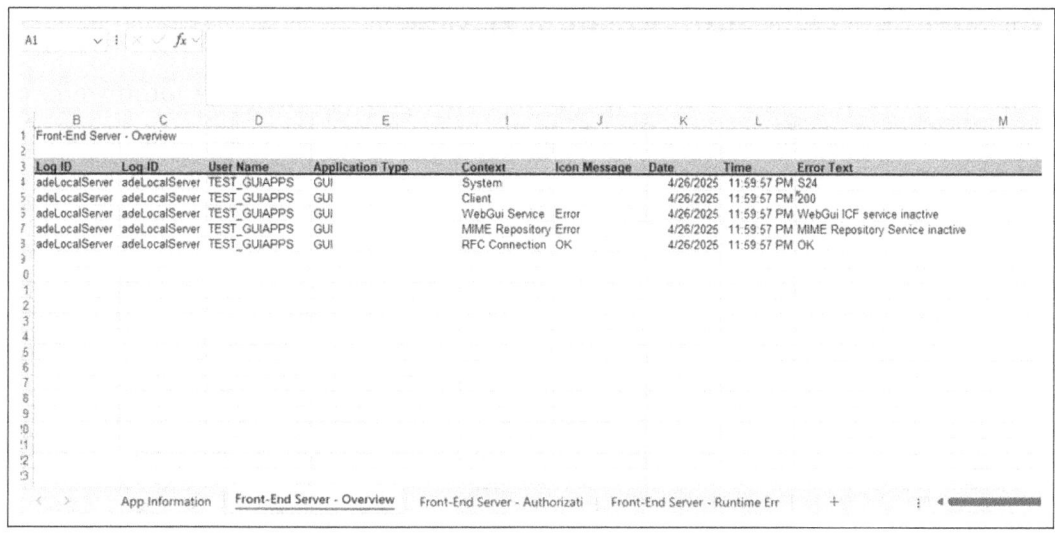

Figure 13-35. *Download log file - tab App Information*

Front-End Server – Overview

The **Front-End Server - Overview tab summarizes the analysis performed on the front-end** (Fiori Launchpad) side, listing gateway errors related to OData and ICF services, as shown in the figure below.

Front-End Server - Overview

Log ID	Log ID	User Name	Application Type	Context	Icon Message	Date	Time	Error Text
adeLocalServer	adeLocalServer	TEST_GUIAPPS	GUI	System		4/26/2025	11:59:57 PM	S24
adeLocalServer	adeLocalServer	TEST_GUIAPPS	GUI	Client		4/26/2025	11:59:57 PM	200
adeLocalServer	adeLocalServer	TEST_GUIAPPS	GUI	WebGui Service	Error	4/26/2025	11:59:57 PM	WebGui ICF service inactive
adeLocalServer	adeLocalServer	TEST_GUIAPPS	GUI	MIME Repository	Error	4/26/2025	11:59:57 PM	MIME Repository Service inactive
adeLocalServer	adeLocalServer	TEST_GUIAPPS	GUI	RFC Connection	OK	4/26/2025	11:59:57 PM	OK

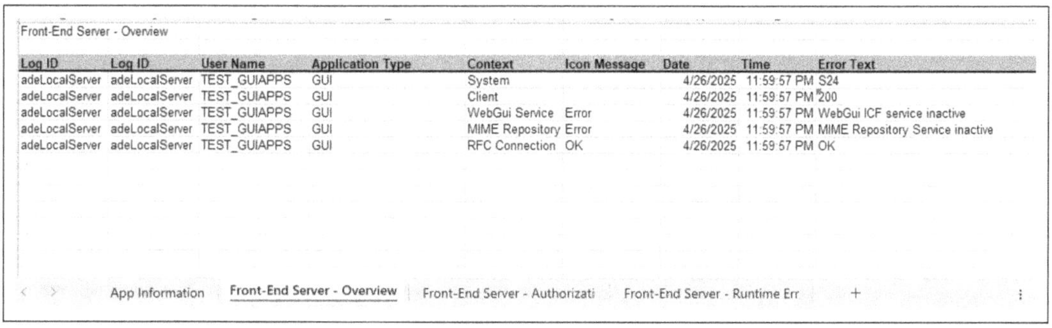

Figure 13-36. *App Support log - Front-End Server - Overview*

CHAPTER 13   SAP FIORI APP SUPPORT AND TROUBLESHOOTING

Front-End Server – Authorization Errors

The **Front-End Server – Authorization Errors** tab shows all the missing authorizations that caused problems while using the app. It lists the authorization objects, field names, and values that were checked and failed, making it easier to spot security gaps.

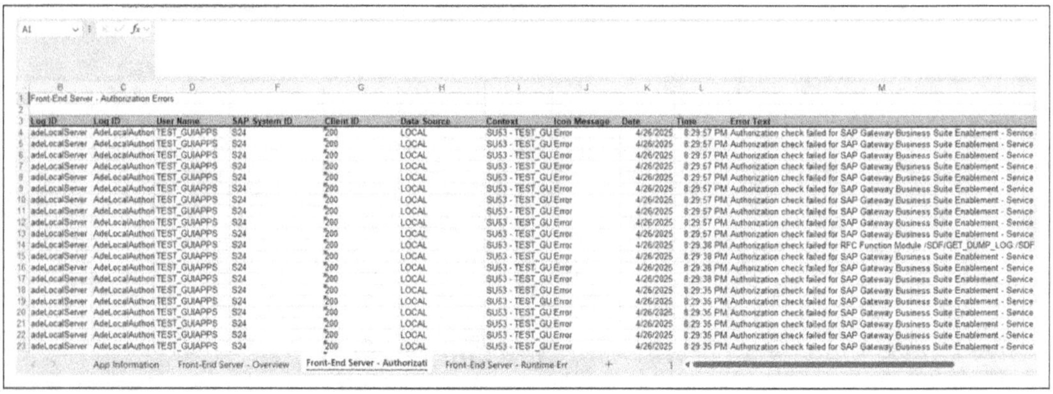

Figure 13-37. *The tab Front-End Server – Authorization Errors*

In the above figure, put the **data filter** on the column called **Error Text** and select only **relevant errors**, as shown in the figure below.

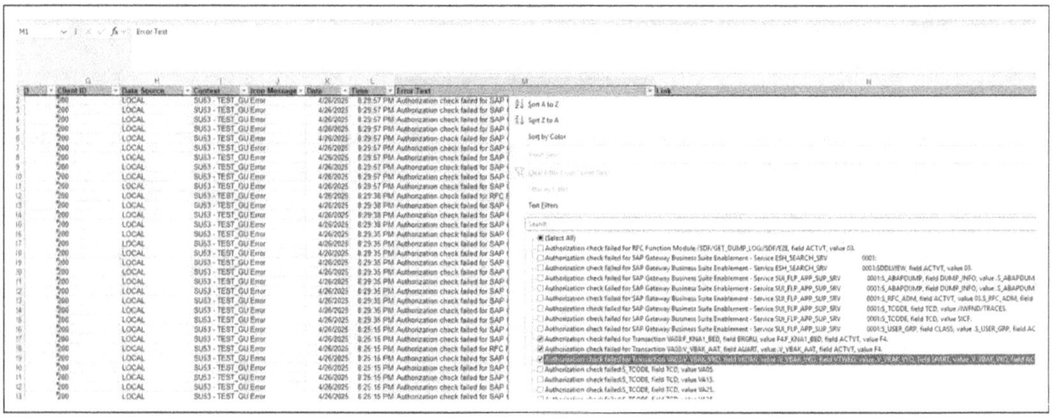

Figure 13-38. *Data filer set on Error Text*

The filter displays all the **authorization errors** encountered with details, as shown in the figure below.

CHAPTER 13   SAP FIORI APP SUPPORT AND TROUBLESHOOTING

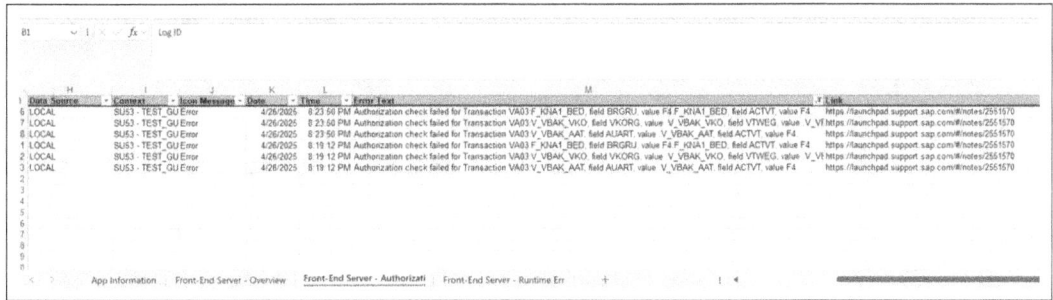

Figure 13-39. Correct authorization errors displayed

Front-End Server – Runtime Errors

The **Front-End Server – Runtime Errors** tab indicates that you are not authorized to use transaction **ST22**.

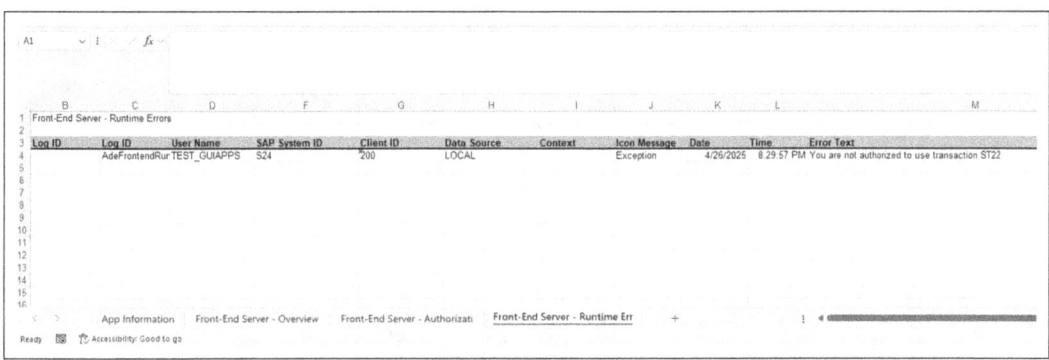

Figure 13-40. Front-End Server – Runtime Errors

13.1.8 Transaction SU53

You can also use the transaction **SU53** on the **ABAP** side on the **SU53 tile** to analyze the authorization and the output, as shown in the figure below.

683

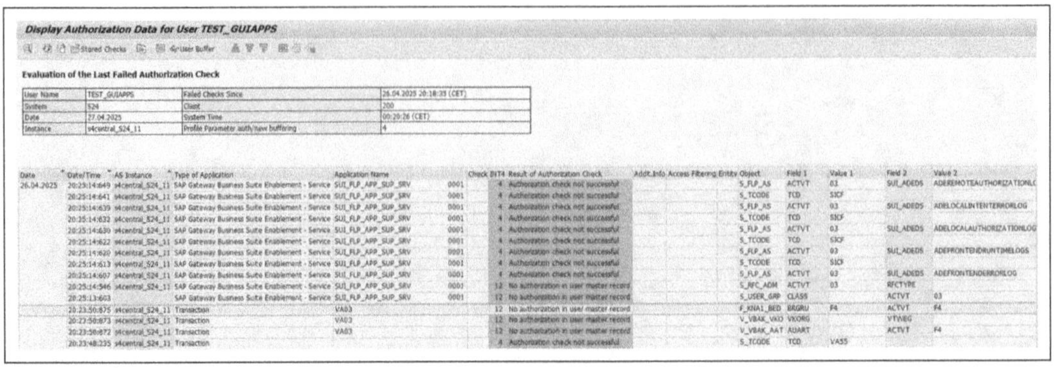

Figure 13-41. Test user ID – SU53 displaying errors

13.1.9 STAUTHTRACE

In SAP, **STAUTHTRACE** is a tool for tracking and recording authorization checks during user activity. It shows which authorization objects are checked, what values are evaluated, and whether access is allowed or denied. This tool provides more detailed information than regular SU53 errors because it records all checks, not just the last one that failed. Use STAUTHTRACE when solving complex authorization problems where SU53 is insufficient. It is also helpful to capture authorization checks during specific app activities or user actions. Set it up before you try to recreate the issue you are looking into, especially when testing Fiori apps or custom **Z** transactions or creating new user roles. This helps ensure you do not miss any hidden authorization needs.

The figure below displays **STAUTHTRACE** set up for the test user ID. Before executing any app, the parameter **auth/auth_user_trace** must be active. Make sure it is set up for **system-wide trace**. Next, set up the trace for the **test user ID**, as shown in the figure below.

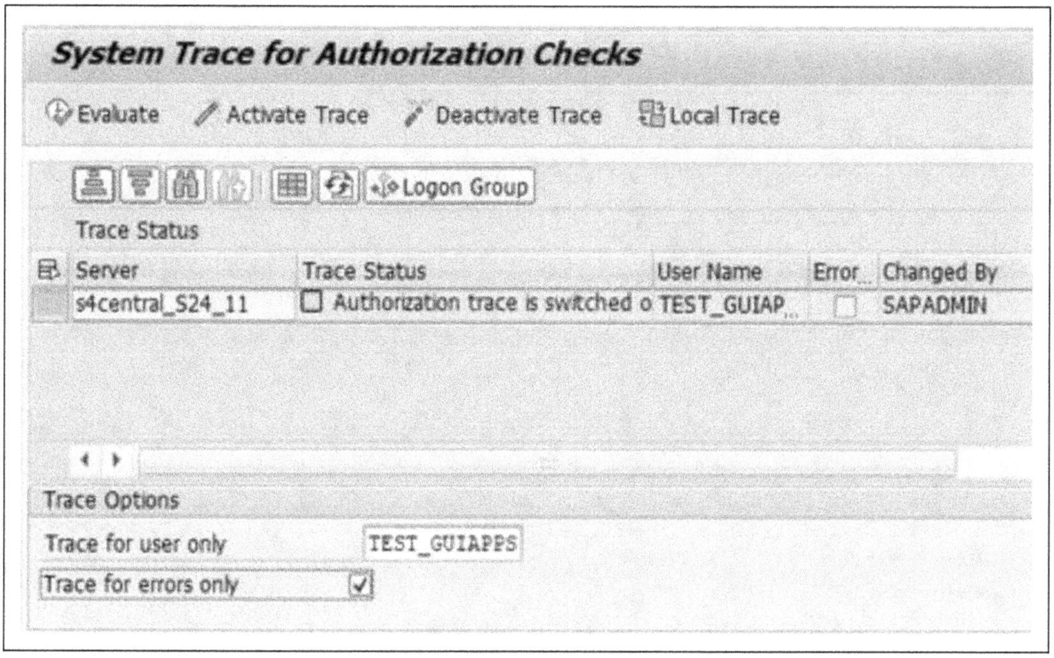

CHAPTER 13 SAP FIORI APP SUPPORT AND TROUBLESHOOTING

Figure 13-42. STAUTHTRACE setup for the user

Select Activate Trace **Activate Trace** to set up STAUTHTRACE for capturing authorization errors. Stop the trace once the user performs the activity by clicking Deactivate Trace **Deactivate Trace**. To evaluate the result, click the option **Evaluate** to set up STAUTHTRACE as shown in the figure below.

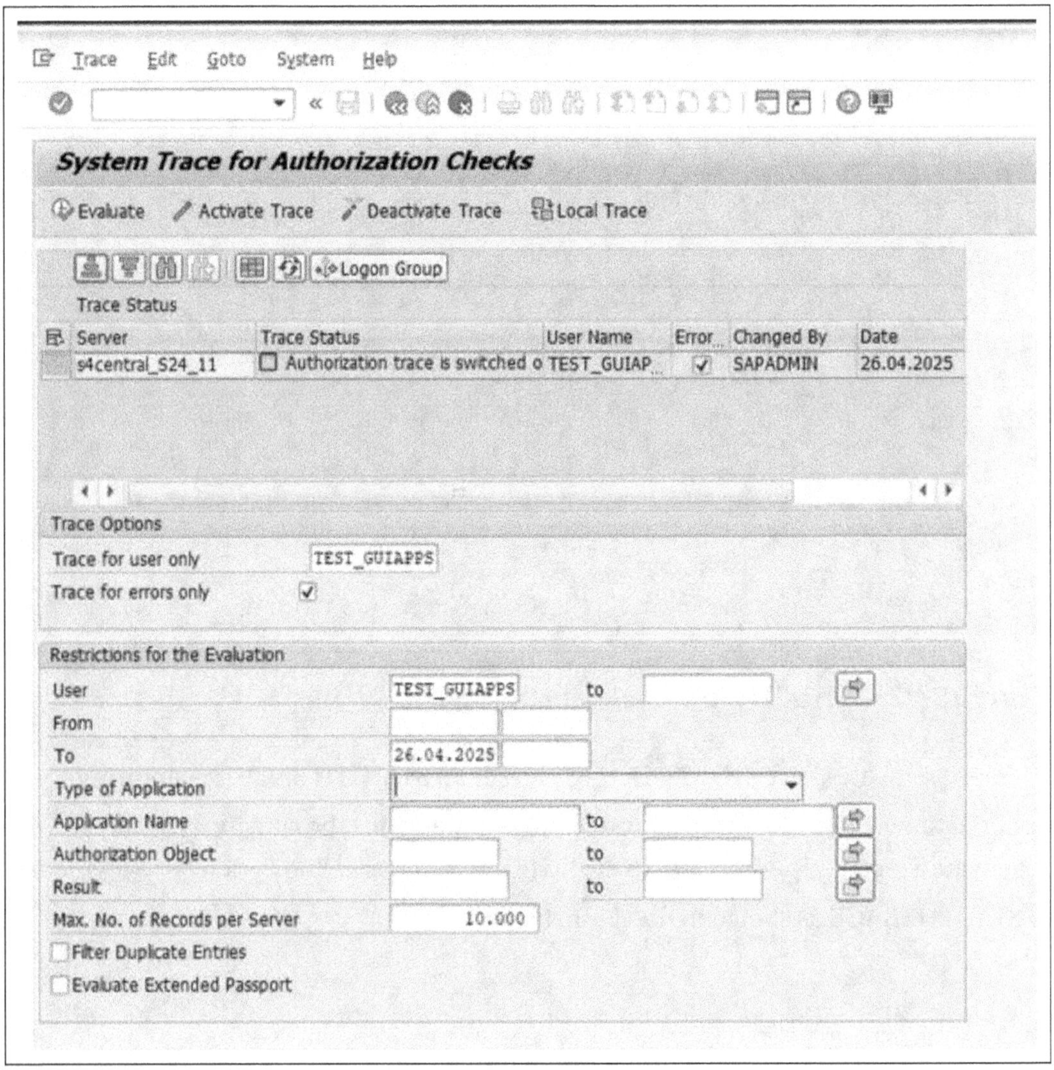

CHAPTER 13   SAP FIORI APP SUPPORT AND TROUBLESHOOTING

Figure 13-43. *STAUTHTRACE evaluation selection screen*

Click Evaluate ⊕ Evaluate and the trace output is displayed, as shown in the figure below.

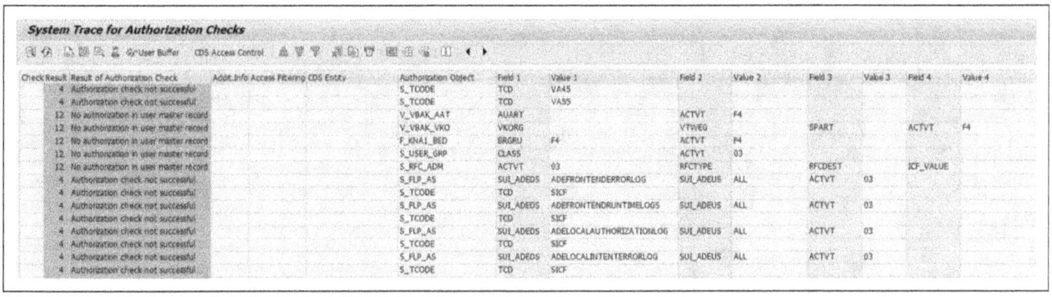

CHAPTER 13   SAP FIORI APP SUPPORT AND TROUBLESHOOTING

Figure 13-44. STAUTHTRACE log

13.1.10 STUSERTRACE

In SAP, the transaction **STUSERTRACE** is used for user-specific authorization tracing. This is particularly useful for analyzing the actual authorizations utilized by users during their routine activities, facilitating the refinement of roles by identifying and removing unnecessary permissions. STUSERTRACE is especially beneficial in scenarios such as role optimization, monitoring background users, and during new implementations.
To activate STUSERTRACE, the system parameter **auth/auth_user_trace** must be set appropriately, and filters can be defined within STUSERTRACE to target specific users or applications, ensuring focused and efficient tracing. You set up filters for up to ten users for tracing at the same time.

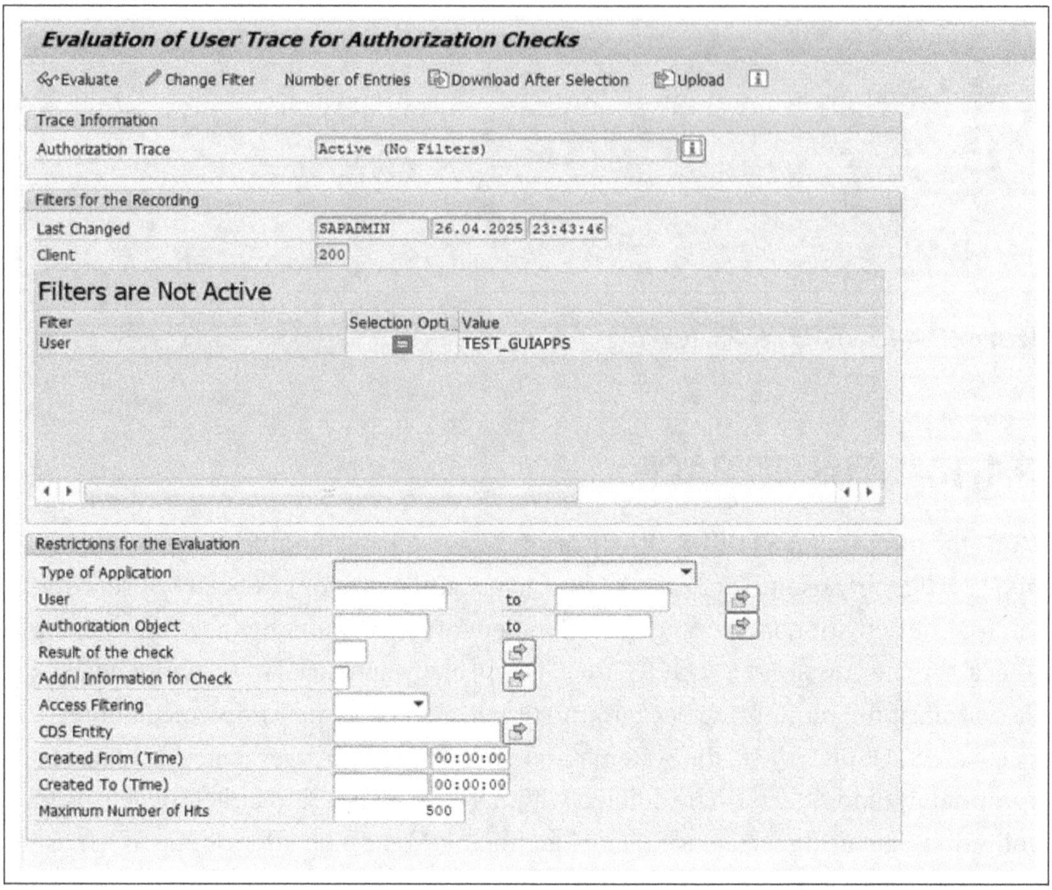

CHAPTER 13　SAP FIORI APP SUPPORT AND TROUBLESHOOTING

Figure 13-45. STUSERTRACE set for the test user ID

Once the user has executed the app and encountered an error, enter the **test user ID** in the **User** field, as shown in the figure below.

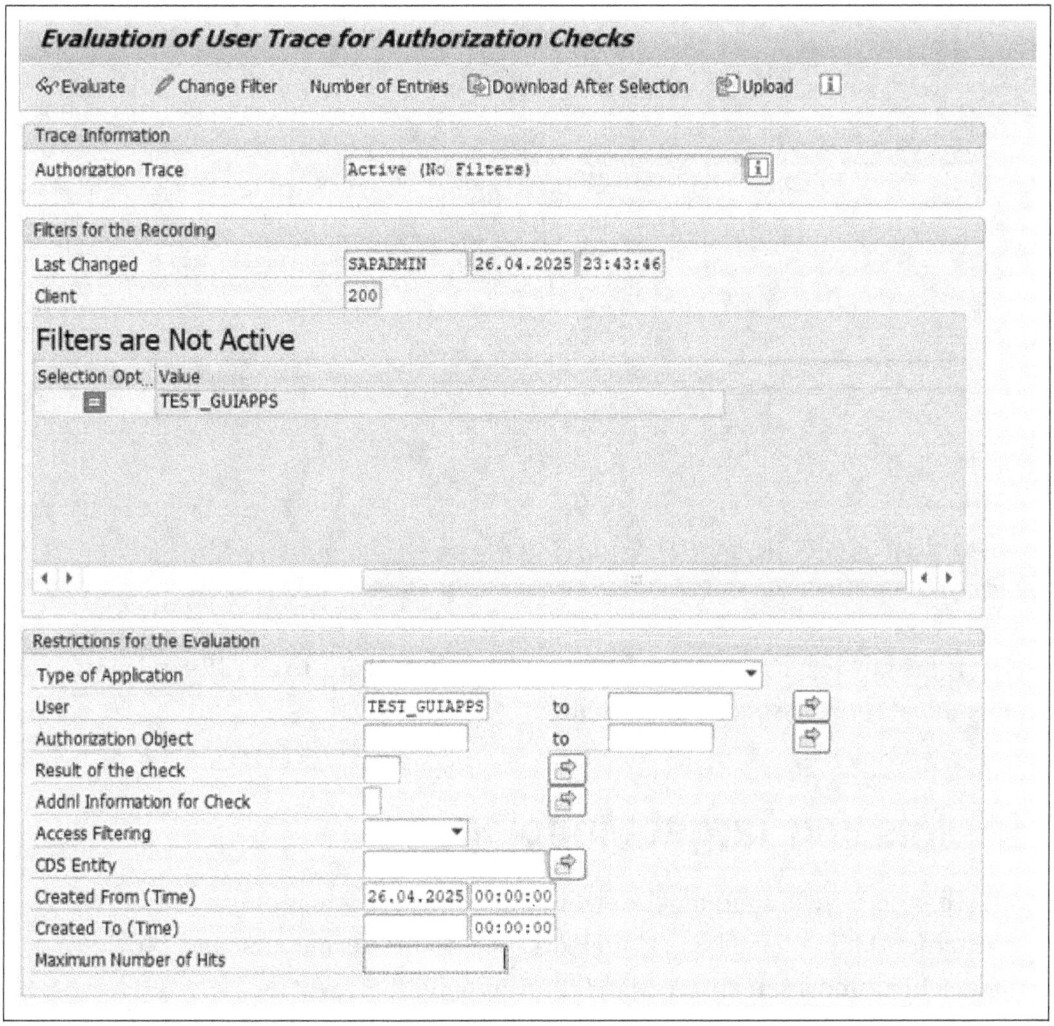

CHAPTER 13 SAP FIORI APP SUPPORT AND TROUBLESHOOTING

Figure 13-46. Updated on the test user ID to assess error issues

Click the **Evaluate** ✧ Evaluate tab to access the encountered errors as displayed in the figure below.

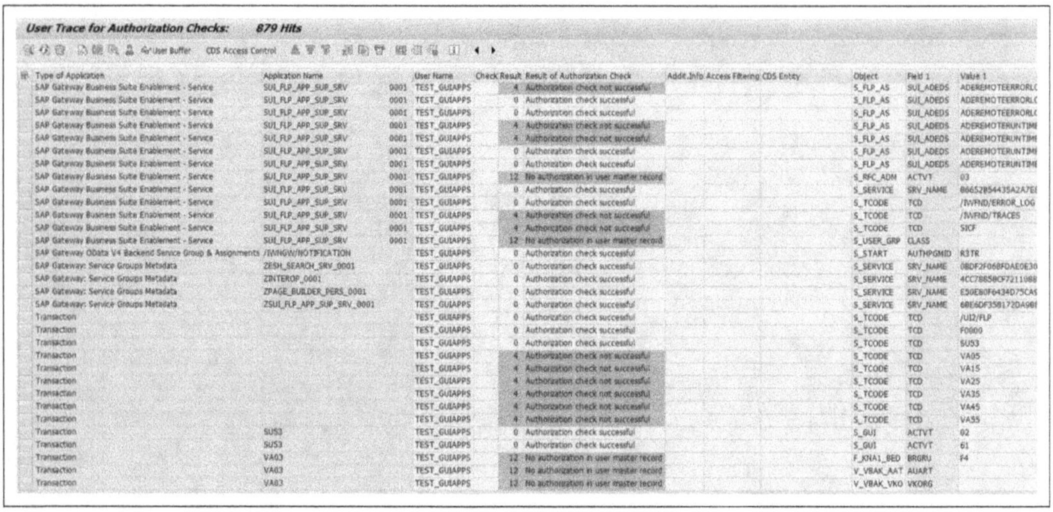

Figure 13-47. STUSERTRACE displaying the errors encountered by the test user ID

In the next two scenarios, we will be simulating errors due to a SICF service issue and another one due to missing target mapping.

13.2 Missing Target Mapping

In this scenario, we will simulate the error for missing target mapping.

Customers build their own custom Fiori apps. So the developers must provide a semantic object and a semantic action for the app too.

In our example, we will use a custom app but without its target mapping.

We have simulated an error for the missing target mapping scenario with a test user ID that encounters an error, as shown in the figure below.

CHAPTER 13 SAP FIORI APP SUPPORT AND TROUBLESHOOTING

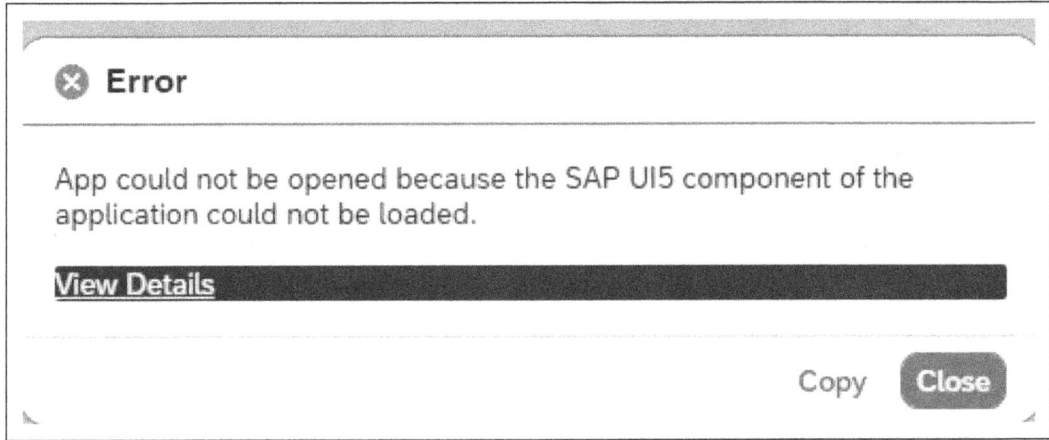

Figure 13-48. Test user ID encounters an error

Opening the **View Details** option displays the details of the error, as shown in the figure below.

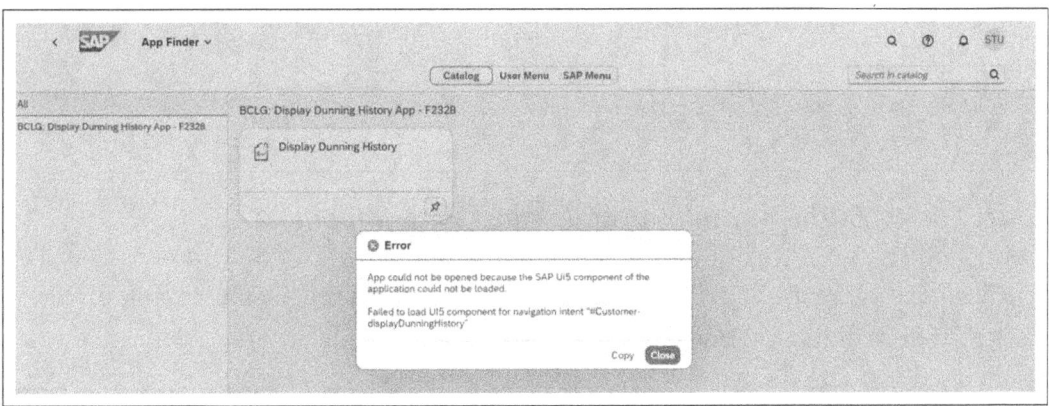

Figure 13-49. Error description in detail

This error shows that **target mapping** is not loading. This could be because of two reasons:

- Target mapping is missing from the catalog.
- SICF services associated with the app have not been activated.

In our example, as you can see from the above figure, there is an error loading the navigation intent (target mapping) **Customer-displayDunningHistory**.

691

CHAPTER 13   SAP FIORI APP SUPPORT AND TROUBLESHOOTING

To resolve the issue, you will identify the associated business catalog that contains the associated app and add the target mapping to it.

13.3 Services Missing

There might be a case where some of the mandatory **OData** and **ICF services** have not been activated.

In our scenario, we are going to use Fiori app F2328 and check for the OData service and SICF service status using the transaction **/UI2/FLPCM_CUST**, and the output is displayed as shown in the figure below.

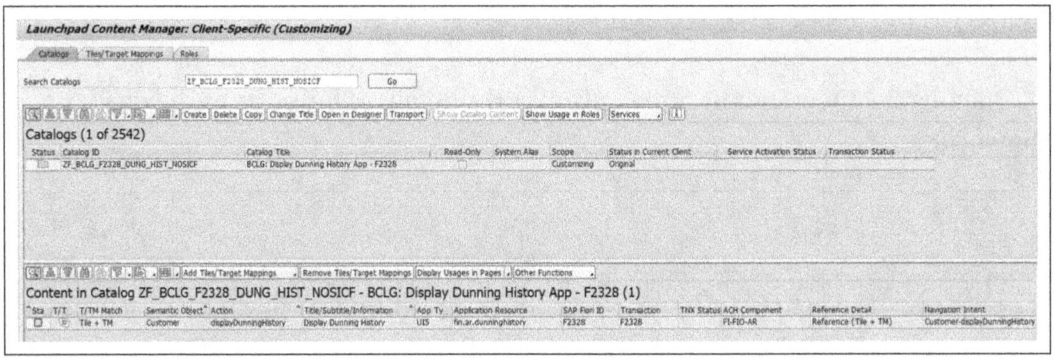

Figure 13-50. Business catalog contains the target mapping

The above figure displays target mapping is available in the business catalog. Now check the **Services** tab, as shown in the figure below.

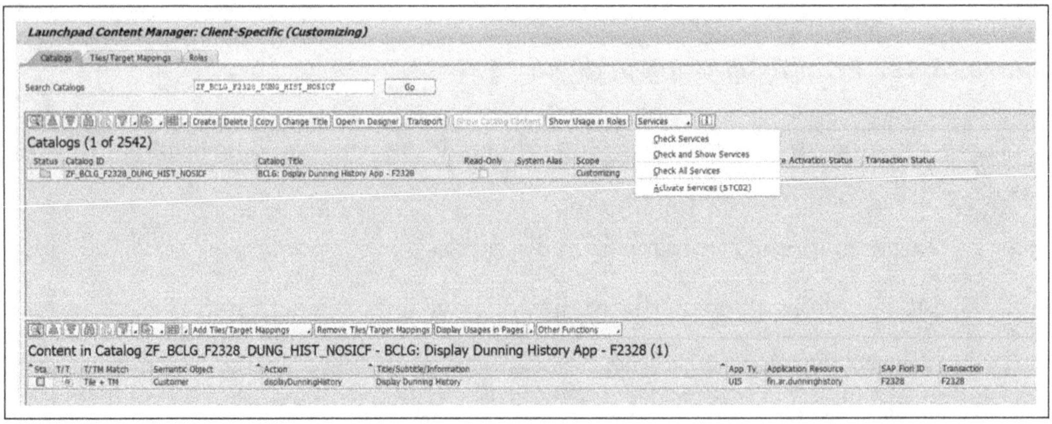

Figure 13-51. Checking the Services tab

CHAPTER 13　SAP FIORI APP SUPPORT AND TROUBLESHOOTING

Selecting the Check Services option in the above figure displays the error with the **service activation status** traffic light as red, as shown in the figure below.

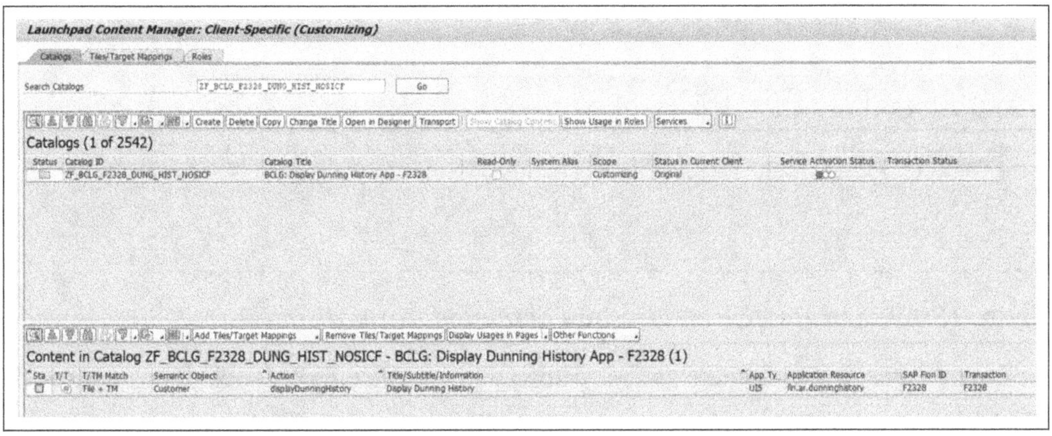

Figure 13-52. *Services are not active within the business catalog*

The above error indicates that some essential services within the business catalog are not active. Select the option **Check and Show Services**, as shown in the figure below.

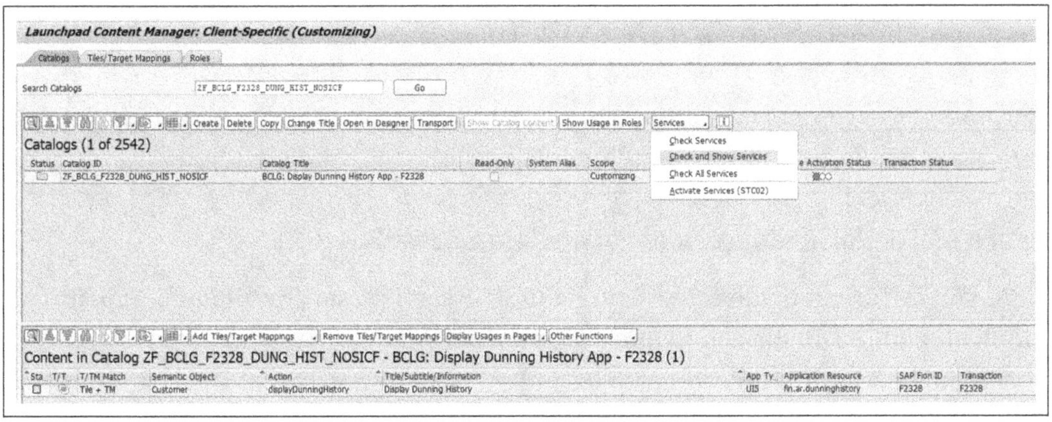

Figure 13-53. *Using the option Check and Show Services*

Selecting the option **Check and Show Services** displays that **OData/ICF services** are not activated, as shown in the figure below.

693

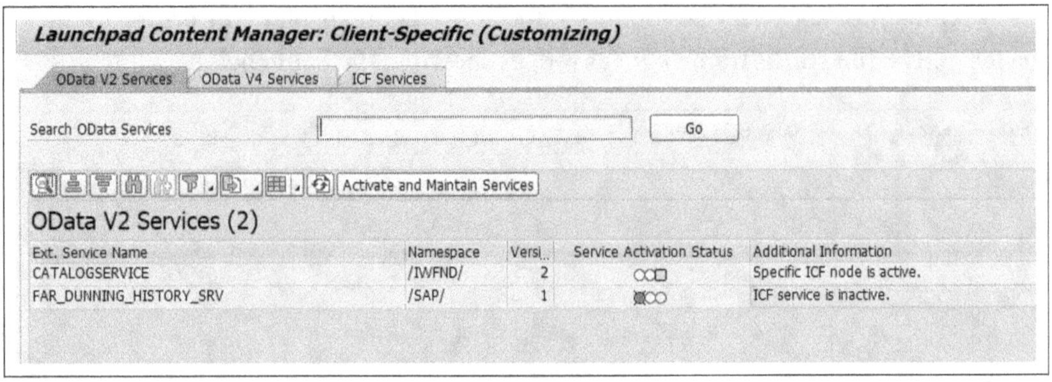

CHAPTER 13   SAP FIORI APP SUPPORT AND TROUBLESHOOTING

Figure 13-54. OData/ICF services not activated status displayed

As you can see from the above figure, the OData service **FAR_DUNNING_HISTORY_SRV** and its associated SICF service are not active.

Click the ICF Services tab and check the status of the SICF service.

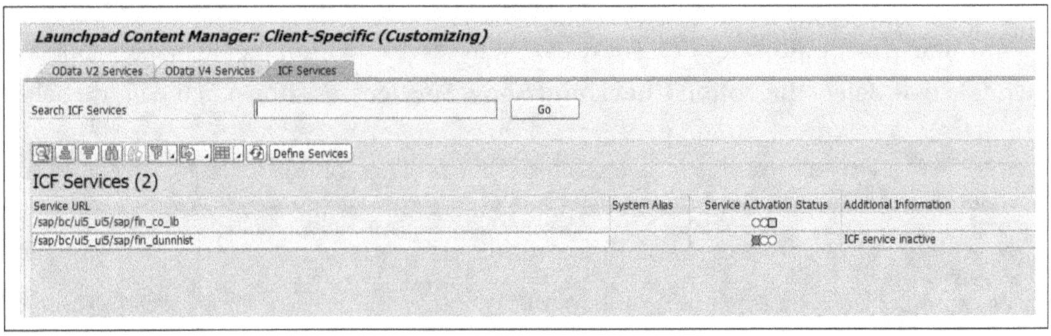

Figure 13-55. SICF service not activated status displayed

As you can see from the above figure, the SICF service **/sap/bc/ui5_ui5/sap/fin_dunnhist** required for the app to function is not active.

We will now log in with a test user ID and execute the app **F2328** and check the App Support log. We will get the following information in the **Front-End Server – Overview** tab of the App Support log.

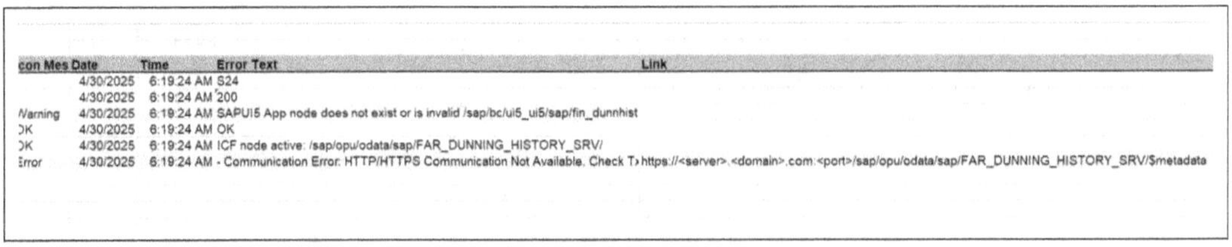

Figure 13-56. Deactivated OData and SICF error information App Support log

CHAPTER 13 SAP FIORI APP SUPPORT AND TROUBLESHOOTING

For the error information related to the OData service, we see an error message for the SICF service:

/sap/opu/odata/sap/FAR_DUNNING_HISTORY_SRV

For the error information related to the SICF service, we see a warning message saying the following:

SAPUI5 App node does not exist or is invalid /sap/bc/ui5_ui5/sap/fin_dunnhist

To resolve this issue, we need to activate the SICF service and OData service.

13.4 Missing Business Catalog

In this scenario, we will discuss the issue of if the business catalog is not assigned but the user is assigned a space or group.

The user might encounter a **blank screen with no app assigned** displayed as shown in the figure below. The user can see the space but does not see any pages or the section with relevant apps from the business role assigned.

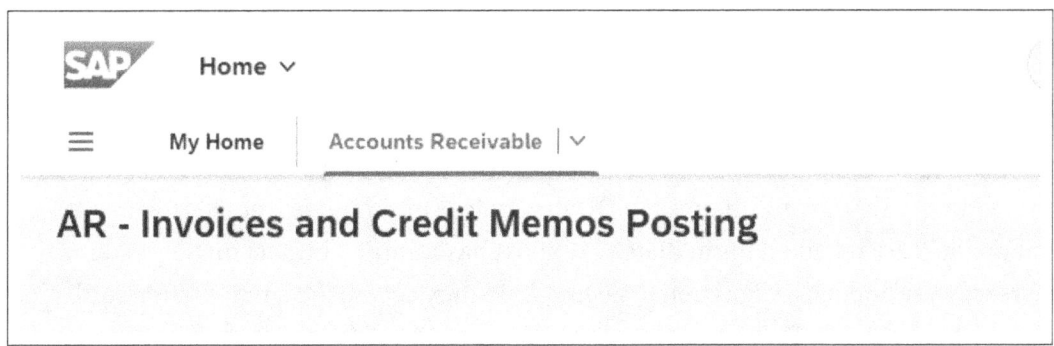

Figure 13-57. *User sees blank screen with no apps assigned*

The blank screen error is due to the business catalog not being assigned to the business role, as shown in the figure below. The role has a space or group assigned, and the same got displayed as shown in the above figure.

Chapter 13   SAP Fiori App Support and Troubleshooting

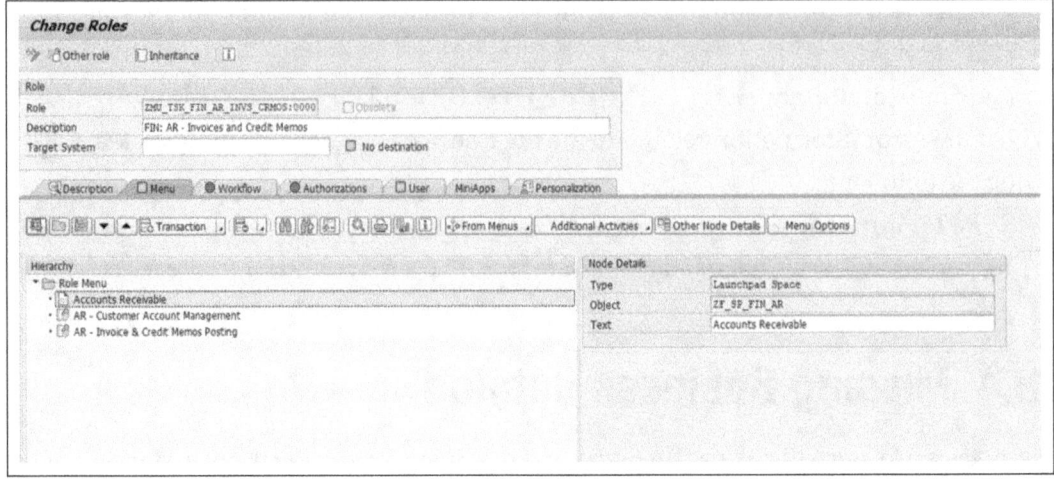

Figure 13-58. *Business role with missing business catalog*

13.5 Clearing Cache

In the Fiori application, a persistence layer utilizes a caching mechanism. For cache-related issues, SAP provides transaction codes to clear the gateway cache, which stores metadata and runtime information for OData services. It's important to run these transactions after making changes to OData services or their data models to ensure that updates are reflected immediately. While it has minimal impact on the system, users may experience a slight delay the first time they access the service, afterward, as the cache rebuilds. Proper authorization is required, and it's best used during deployments, troubleshooting, or system maintenance, ideally in coordination with other administrators in production environments.

Note It is recommended to **always clear the cache** before starting any troubleshooting session.

Clear Metadata Cache:

- Transaction /IWFND/CACHE_CLEANUP on front-end server
- Transaction /IWBEP/CACHE_CLEANUP on back-end server

Synchronize Chip Cache (Front End):

- Run report /UI2/CHIP_SYNCHRONIZE_CACHE.
- Run report /UI2/DELETE_CACHE_AFTER_IMP or /UI2/DELETE_CACHE.

13.6 Reference Lost

In SAP Fiori, a **Reference Lost** error happens when the system cannot find a key object that an app needs, like an OData entity, a missing tile reference, or a UI5 control. This may occur if data is deleted, connections are broken, or components are used before they are ready.

Whenever you have an error that says **Reference Lost** for any of the tiles, then run the program **/UI2/REFERENCE_LOST.** This program should be executed if a relationship or reference is missing between the technical and business catalogs. The program analyzes lost references and recommends corrective actions.

To effectively resolve this issue, it is crucial to confirm that the reference catalogs and tiles are present in the system. Ensuring their existence will pave the way for a smooth resolution.

13.7 OData Services Are Not Active

OData services play a crucial role in data retrieval between the front-end (Fiori Gateway UI) and the back-end system. They serve as a communication bridge that enables SAP Fiori applications to fetch and update data. If an OData service is not active, it can lead to significant issues that negatively impact the functionality of SAP Fiori apps and the overall user experience.

Some of the issues that inactive OData services may cause are

- Error in loading tiles
- **Error 403**
- The factsheet not displayed
- OData call error like **No Service Found for namespace**

To resolve the error, use the task list **SAP_GATEWAY_ACTIVATE_ODATA_SERV** to activate any missing services. The SICF service will be activated as part of this task list. Alternatively, you can manually activate the OData service using transaction **/IWNFD/MAINT_SERVICE**.

13.8 500 Error: Request Failed

A **500 error** in SAP Fiori means there is a problem on the server side. This error happens when the back-end system cannot handle your request.

Common reasons for this include issues with the code, inactive or broken OData services, errors in the application logic, or misconfigured settings. This error may also occur due to the following:

- The SICF service has not been activated.
- Missing authorization in authorization Object S_RFCACL.

To resolve the issue, assign the authorization object to the user.

13.9 Summary

App Support is an essential feature within the SAP Fiori Launchpad in S/4HANA, designed to help users efficiently diagnose and resolve application issues. It provides a structured interface that displays vital information, including App Information, Authorization Errors, Gateway Errors, and Runtime Errors, allowing administrators to check common problems encountered by Fiori applications. By consolidating the information typically accessed through various transaction codes like SU53, STAUTHTRACE, STUSERTRACE, and /IWFND/ERROR_LOG, App Support simplifies troubleshooting for SAP admins, security teams, and end users. The platform showcases a clear list of errors akin to the output from transaction code SU53, eliminating the need for extensive tracking or browser debugging. Users can also download log files in Excel format to share with support teams for further investigation. The App Support plugin in the Fiori Launchpad provides a clear overview of application errors, allowing users to quickly access helpful information and streamline the process of identifying and addressing issues, enhancing the user experience in the S/4HANA environment.

CHAPTER 14

SAP Fiori Upgrade Impact Analysis

The SAP Fiori Upgrade Impact Analysis helps you see how updating SAP S/4HANA or Fiori apps will affect your system. It finds problems like old parts that need fixing and shows what changes are needed for custom and regular apps. The analysis tells you what tests to run to ensure everything works well after the update. Tools like the Fiori Apps Reference Library give you information to help you plan for a smooth update.

14.1 Introduction

This chapter will discuss an SAP tool called the **Fiori Upgrade Impact Analysis** within the **SAP Fiori Apps Reference Library**. This tool helps companies see how an upgrade will change their Fiori apps when they move to a new version of SAP. It shows which apps still work, which will be deprecated, and what new ones are available. This way, businesses can plan their upgrade, avoid problems, and ensure everything goes smoothly. It also helps them understand how the upgrade will affect their current apps and any changes they've made.

14.1.1 Impact Analysis During Upgrade

For impact analysis, a list of transaction codes is required. The upgrade process provides a significant amount of information during the upgrade, which is summarized as follows:

> **Detail Impact Analysis:** After you finish the analysis, you will get a report that shows how your Fiori upgrade will affect you.
>
> **Understand Adaption and Adjustment:** The report shows which apps might need changes or replacements after the upgrade.

Evaluate and Assess Availability: Determine and assess the status of applications in the target release: are they available, deprecated, or obsolete?

Identify and Provide Successors: It determines and chooses possible replacement applications.

Classify and Categorize Results: The analysis results are classified and categorized as follows:

- **Unavailable Apps:** Apps that are obsolete after the upgrade and cannot be used. They need to be replaced by a successor app.
- **Deprecated Apps:** Apps that are still available but are no longer recommended.
- **Available Apps with Successor:** Apps that have a recommended successor.
- **Available Apps:** Apps that remain available.
- **Unknown Apps:** Apps with uncertain status.

14.1.2 Key Features

Compatibility Check: This check determines if the current Fiori applications will work with the new version. It examines whether the existing apps, extensions, and customizations will run smoothly after the upgrade.

Custom Code Analysis: The tool examines your code and extensions to identify issues with the new version. This information helps you determine what changes to make.

UI Changes: This section highlights user interface changes that may affect the system's user experience. It covers changes in design, layout, or functionality.

Configuration Assessment: This process examines current settings and configurations to determine whether they will still work with the new version and whether they need to be changed.

Update Recommendation: This section provides simple tips for fixing problems that arise when you examine things closely. It helps you determine how to solve these problems.

Documentation: C reports that explain what you found in the impact analysis. This is important for planning and talking to everyone involved.

14.1.3 Benefits

Proactive Issue Identification: Organizations can address problems by identifying potential issues before the upgrade.

Reduced Downtime: Understanding how changes affect your system helps you plan better, resulting in shorter wait times and a more straightforward transition.

Better Planning: Identifying potential problems and necessary changes can help create a better upgrade plan and timeline.

Enhanced User Experience: Learning about changes to the user interface (UI) before they happen helps you prepare. This way, users will have the same experience after the upgrade.

14.1.4 How to Use the Tool

Prepare Your Environment: You can access your current SAP Fiori system and the necessary upgrade documents.

Run the Tool: Run the Impact Analysis tool on your current system setup. Depending on your SAP system, this tool may be in the SAP Solution Manager or as a separate tool.

Review Results: Look at the tool's results and recommendations. Focus on any urgent issues or changes that need to be made.

Plan Your Upgrade: Create a detailed upgrade plan that fixes any identified issues and includes recommendations based on the analysis.

Execute and Monitor: Upgrade your system as planned and watch for unexpected problems.

14.2 Prerequisite

To execute the SAP Fiori Upgrade Impact Analysis tool, ensure the system is upgraded to SAP S/4HANA 1909 or higher, as the tool is supported from this release onward. The SAP Fiori Apps Reference Library should be accessible, and the relevant back-end and front-end components must be configured and aligned with the target system version. Ensure you have administrative authorizations (e.g., **SAP_UI2_ADMIN**) and that OData services required for the analysis are active and functioning. Additionally, the client used for the analysis must be correctly configured with valid system aliases for the respective Fiori apps. Follow the steps below once the upgrade plan is created and in place.

14.2.1 Prepare Your System

Document your SAP Fiori 3.0 system with custom apps, extensions, and configurations. Ensure accessibility to the Upgrade Impact Analysis tool within the SAP Fiori Apps Reference Library through SAP Solution Manager or another portal.

14.2.2 Run the Impact Analysis Tool

Initially, set up the tool with your system details, including the current SAP Fiori 3.0 version and the target SAP Fiori 4.0/5.0 version. Then, the tool will collect data from your system, which includes your installed apps, customizations, and configurations.

14.2.3 Analyze Results

The tool checks your custom Fiori apps to see if they work with SAP Fiori 4.0/5.0 and identifies issues. Some apps are not fully compatible due to changes in APIs. The custom code that uses outdated APIs needs updates. Some UI elements have been redesigned, which may change how users experience the app. Finally, some configuration settings might need adjustments because the parameters have changed.

14.2.4 Review Recommendations

It is important to update your custom applications to use the new APIs in SAP Fiori versions 4.0/5.0. To do this, revise your code by replacing old functions with newer ones. Test the updated user interface elements to make sure the user experience is consistent. Finally, adjust your settings based on the guidelines in the SAP Fiori 4.0/5.0 documentation.

14.2.5 Plan the Upgrade

To address the identified issues, we need to create a clear plan that includes timelines for code updates, user interface changes, and configuration adjustments. We should also assign team members specific tasks based on the tool's recommendations, ensuring that each job is handled efficiently and on time.

14.2.6 Execute and Monitor

Follow your upgrade plan to transition from SAP Fiori 3.0 to SAP Fiori 4.0/5.0 and conduct thorough post-upgrade testing to ensure that all issues are resolved and the system functions as expected.

14.2.7 Document and Communicate

We will create an Impact Analysis report that explains the results of our analysis and outlines the steps needed to fix any issues we find. After that, we will share the report and action plan with the relevant stakeholders to ensure they understand the changes and any potential effects these changes may have.

14.2.8 Outcome

After utilizing the tool and implementing the updates, your SAP Fiori landscape successfully transitions from SAP version 3.0 to 4.0/5.0.

14.2.9 Check and Verify

Custom apps work well with the new tools; everything feels the same for users. Then adjust any changes needed. The upgrade happens smoothly without bothering the business too much.

14.3 Upgrade Process Steps

The SAP Fiori Upgrade Impact Analysis tool helps plan and carry out an upgrade effectively. This reduces the chance of unexpected problems and maximizes the advantages of the new version. Below is a simple step-by-step guide, with an example, on using the SAP Fiori Upgrade Impact Analysis tool. In this case, we will consider upgrading from SAP Fiori 3.0 to SAP Fiori 4.0/5.0.

14.3.1 Preparation

Write down all your unique apps and settings in your SAP Fiori 3.0 system. Save a backup to keep your information safe. Check if you can find the SAP Fiori Upgrade tool in SAP Solution Manager or as a separate app. Log in with your username and password to access the systems you need.

14.3.2 Configure the Tool

Provide details about your current SAP Fiori 3.0 environment and mention that you are upgrading to SAP Fiori 4.0/5.0. Connect the tool to your SAP Fiori 3.0 system to gather data. Then, connect it to an SAP Fiori 4.0/5.0 system or check SAP documentation for updates to the new version.

14.3.3 Run the Impact Analysis

The data collection starts by scanning your SAP Fiori 3.0 system to identify installed applications, custom code, and settings. For example, it might find apps with outdated APIs that are not supported in SAP Fiori 4.0/5.0 and that some custom code relies on changed or removed functions. The tool also points out UI changes, like redesigned components, that could affect how users interact with the app. Finally, it notes that the new version's configuration parameters have changed.

14.3.4 Analyze and Plan Remediation

To update your custom apps, first replace any outdated APIs. Next, refactor your code to fit the new methods and change your UI components to match the latest design guidelines. Also, change your configuration settings to fit the new parameters in SAP Fiori 4.0. Create a clear plan that lists tasks and their timelines for these updates. Assign team members to handle specific tasks, such as developers for code updates and designers for UI changes.

14.3.5 Execute the Upgrade

To upgrade from SAP Fiori 3.0 to SAP Fiori 4.0/5.0, follow the standard procedures outlined in SAP's upgrade guides. This includes updating custom code and extensions, adjusting any custom UI components, and applying new configurations based on your analysis.

14.3.6 Post-upgrade Testing

Test all applications, like custom and standard Fiori apps, to make sure they work properly. Ensure the new design does not interfere with user tasks. If you find any problems, like the "Customer Invoice Extension" not working right, fix the bugs and change the code as needed.

14.3.7 Documentation and Communication

After upgrading, write a report that summarizes the changes made. Include updates to the API, modifications to the user interface, and adjustments to the configuration. Also, share your testing results. Then, send this report to the relevant stakeholders. This will inform project managers, end users, and support teams about the upgrade and any important changes they need to know.

14.4 Execute the Upgrade Process

To run the SAP Impact Analysis tool, we need to do the following.

CHAPTER 14   SAP FIORI UPGRADE IMPACT ANALYSIS

14.4.1 Generate an Input Data File

If we need to download all the existing apps within the system to understand the impact of upgrading to a new S/4HANA 2023 FPS02 from S/4HANA 2020, we can do so using the transaction code **/UI2/FLPCA**.

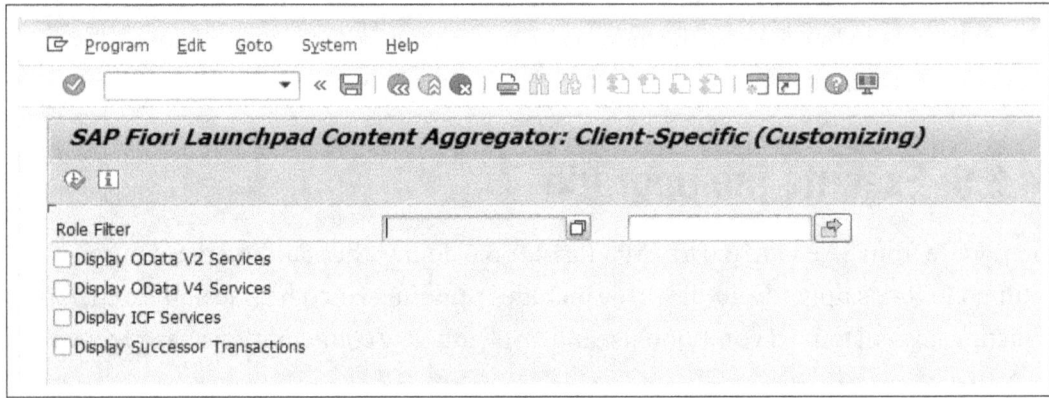

Figure 14-1.   Transaction code /UI2/FLPCA input screen

Note   Ensure you have the latest version of the SAP Fiori Apps Reference Library as a reference.

Below is the list of apps obtained from the **S/4HANA 2020** system for which we need to run the Fiori Upgrade Impact Analysis. The file **FIORIAPPS2020.csv** has been saved in ***.csv** format, as shown in the figure below.

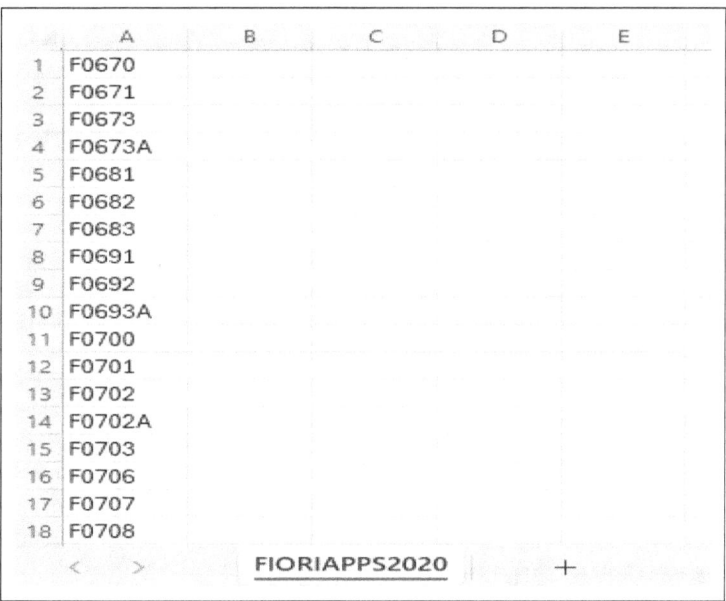

Figure 14-2. SAP Fiori Apps Reference Library data for S/4HANA 2020

Note If Fiori was implemented in an older version, this tool is handy for checking the impact and availability of Fiori apps in 2023. It will list apps that are still available, deprecated, or made obsolete. It will also provide any successor apps that SAP has recommended for any of the apps implemented earlier.

14.4.2 Run the Impact Analysis Tool

To initiate the Fiori Upgrade Impact Analysis tool, navigate to the **SAP Fiori Apps Reference Library** and select the **Run SAP Fiori Upgrade Impact Analysis** tab **Run SAP Fiori Upgrade Impact Analysis**. As shown in the figure below, a new window opens to enter details and input files.

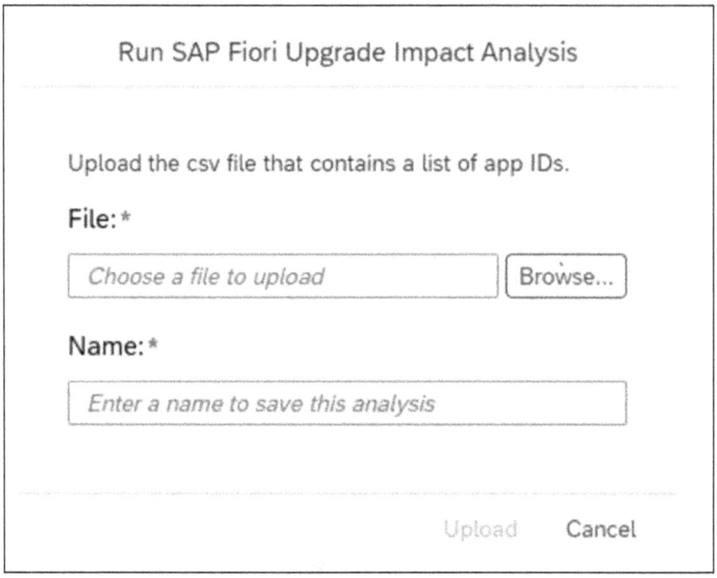

CHAPTER 14 SAP FIORI UPGRADE IMPACT ANALYSIS

Figure 14-3. Run SAP Fiori Upgrade Impact Analysis input box

Note To execute this analysis, an **S user ID** and **password** are required along with the app list. Input the necessary information as depicted in the figure below:

- **File:** FIORIAPPS2020
- **Name:** FIORI UPGRADE ANALYSIS 2020 TO 2023 FSP02

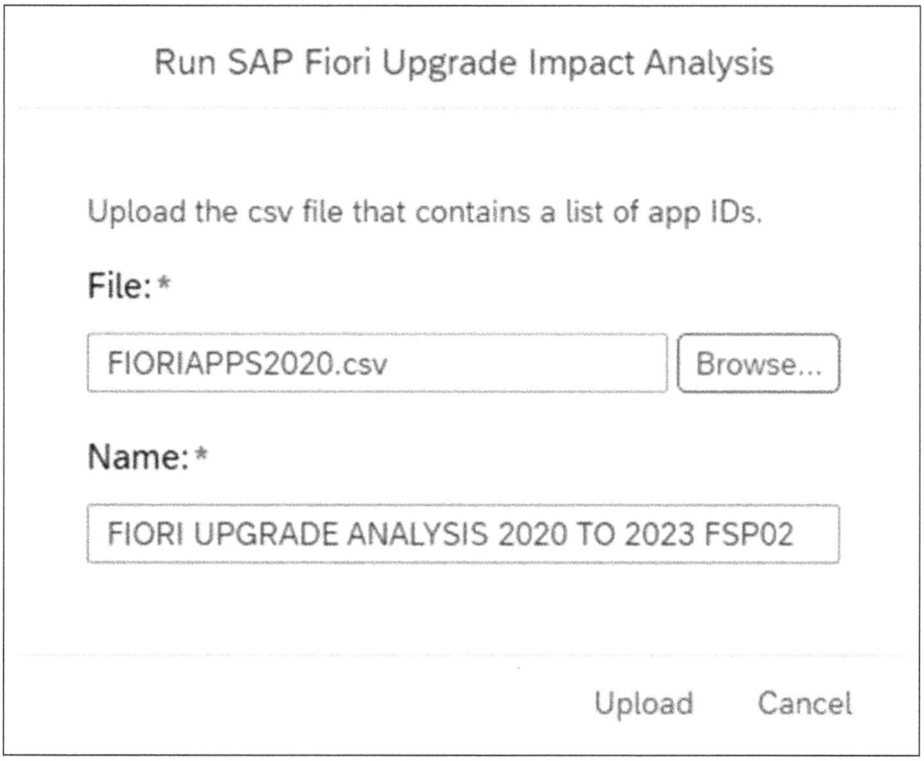

CHAPTER 14 SAP FIORI UPGRADE IMPACT ANALYSIS

Figure 14-4. Load the file and enter the analysis file name

Next, choose the **Upload** option, and the subsequent screen illustrated in the figure below will appear.

CHAPTER 14 SAP FIORI UPGRADE IMPACT ANALYSIS

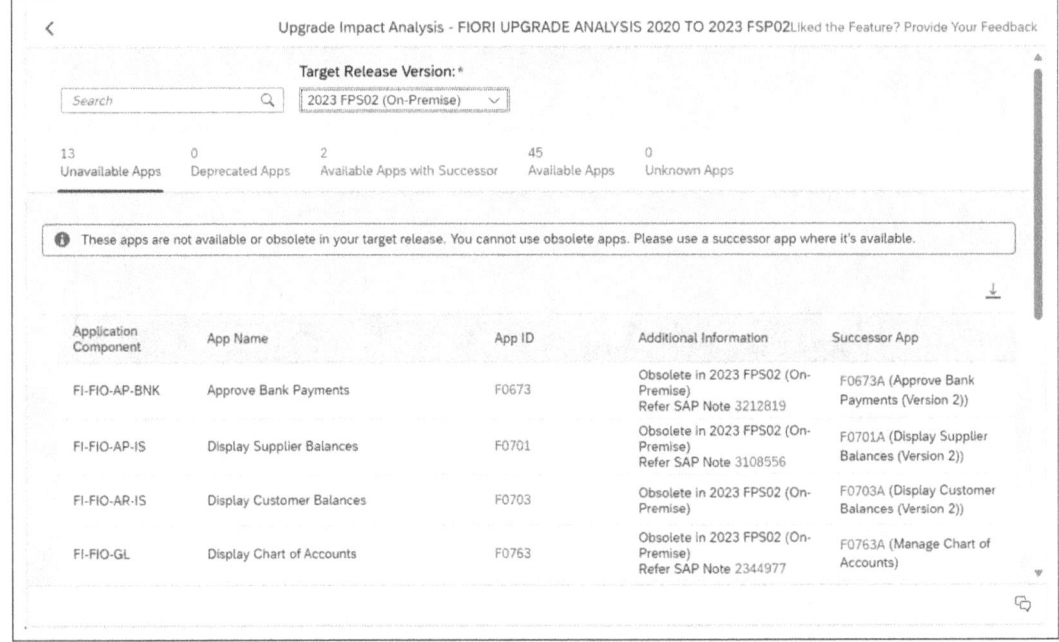

Figure 14-5. Impact Analysis results

14.4.3 Results

The results screen, shown in the figure above, presents five options to view rules, each accompanied by a numerical value. It provides an updated list of the current app statuses, categorized into the following tabs:

- Unavailable Apps (13)
- Deprecated Apps (0)
- Available Apps with Successor (2)
- Available Apps (45)
- Unknown Apps (0)

The output for each section can be downloaded in CSV format by clicking the download icon .

14.4.4 Analyze Results

The uploaded list yields the following results.

Unavailable Apps

The screenshot below displays a list of apps that will be unavailable in 2023. In our case, **13 apps** are unavailable.

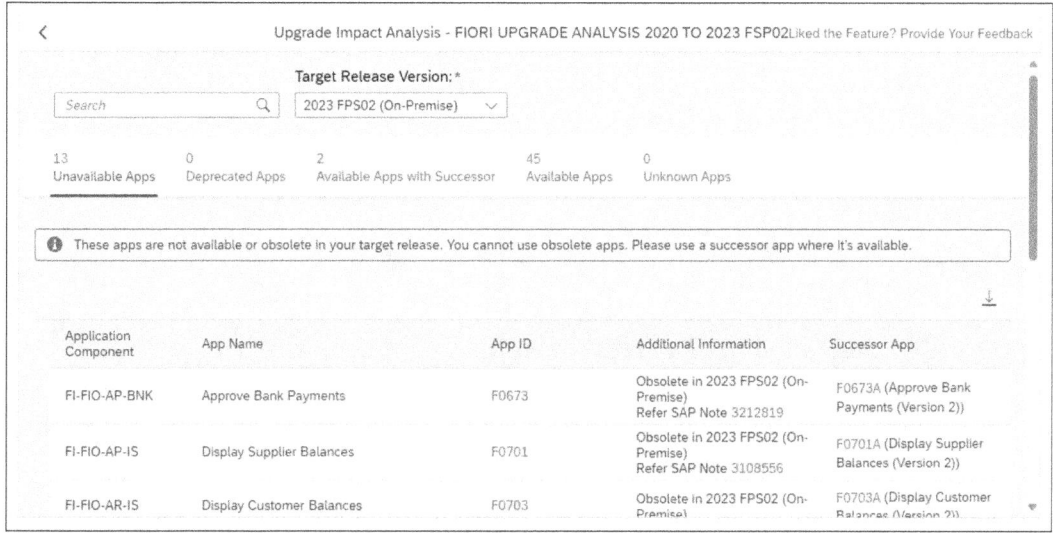

Figure 14-6. *Screenshot showing Unavailable Apps*

When the SAP Fiori Upgrade Impact Analysis tool lists applications as **unknown apps**, it means it cannot recognize them within the upgraded SAP system. This may occur if the apps are custom-developed and not part of the standard catalog, use non-standard configurations, or come from a previous SAP Fiori version or third-party solutions that the tool does not fully recognize.

You must check unknown applications to ensure they work with the new version of the system. Although they may seem to work fine, it's essential to verify their status, including technical settings and dependencies. Also, look for any updates or patches to ensure they function correctly.

Organizations should check if their apps work with the newest SAP technology. They can test essential apps in a safe space first. This helps find problems before they upgrade and shows if they need to change anything.

CHAPTER 14   SAP FIORI UPGRADE IMPACT ANALYSIS

Deprecated Apps

This tab shows that no existing apps in S/4HANA 2020 have been deprecated in S/4HANA 2023 FXP02.

If the SAP Fiori Upgrade Impact Analysis tool shows **0 deprecated apps**, all Fiori apps are good to use with the new SAP version. This is great because it means the apps are up to date and safe.

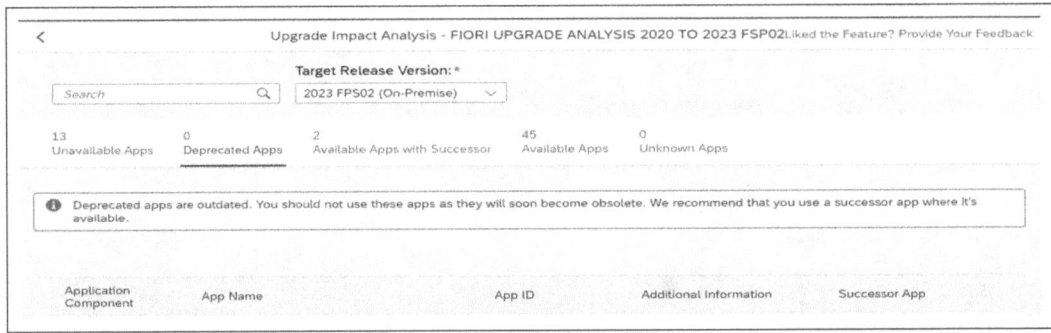

Figure 14-7.   *Data showing Deprecated Apps*

This result assures organizations that their existing Fiori apps will continue working as expected after the upgrade without immediate replacements. SAP has not removed any applications in the new release, allowing focus on upgrading aspects like unavailable or incompatible apps and adopting new features.

It is essential to monitor future SAP updates because new deprecated apps might emerge later. Regularly checking SAP's guidance will help ensure that Fiori apps work well and remain compatible in the long run.

Available Apps with Successor

This tab shows that **two apps have successor apps**, as shown in the figure below.

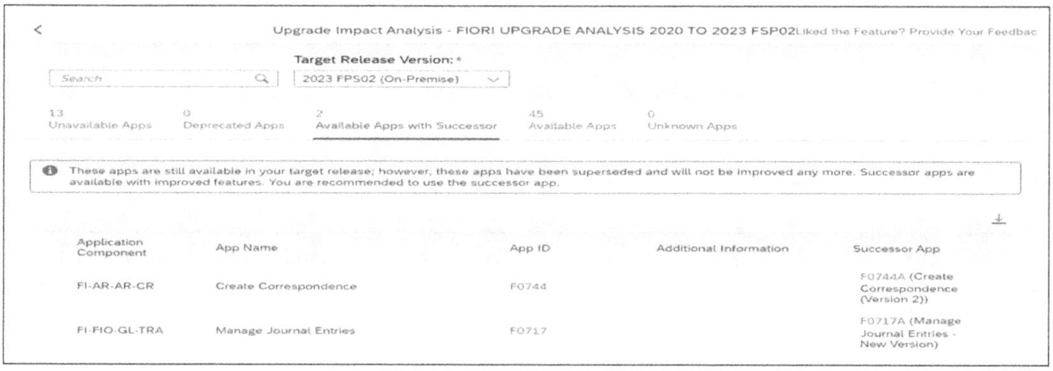

CHAPTER 14 SAP FIORI UPGRADE IMPACT ANALYSIS

Figure 14-8. *Data showing Available Apps with Successor*

When the SAP Fiori Upgrade Impact Analysis tool lists **two available apps with a successor**, it means the applications remain functional and supported in the upgraded version. However, SAP recommends newer alternatives that improve user experience, performance, and compatibility with other components. The **successor** refers to these enhanced versions.

The organization should prepare to switch to new SAP apps soon because the old ones will no longer be supported. The latest apps are better, and we keep getting updates. People should take their time to learn the new apps and make small changes if needed. Using these new tools helps prevent issues and keeps everyone informed about the latest technology.

Available Apps

Forty-five apps remain available, as shown in the figure below, and require no adjustments during the upgrade.

713

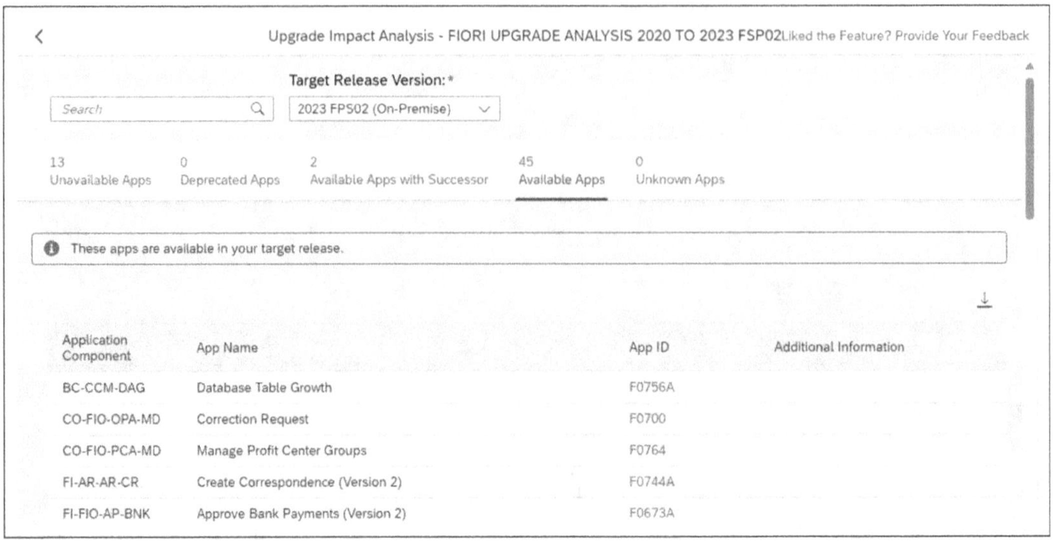

CHAPTER 14   SAP FIORI UPGRADE IMPACT ANALYSIS

Figure 14-9. Data showing Available Apps

The SAP Fiori Upgrade Impact Analysis tool shows 45 available apps that are fully compatible with the new system and do not need significant updates. This means users can expect a smooth experience and that business operations will not be interrupted. Monitoring these apps for future changes is essential by regularly checking the SAP Fiori Apps Reference Library. Testing these apps in a sandbox environment can help avoid problems during upgrades. Overall, these 45 apps help maintain stability for business processes after the upgrade.

Unknown Apps

No apps have an **Unknown Apps** status, as shown in the figure below.

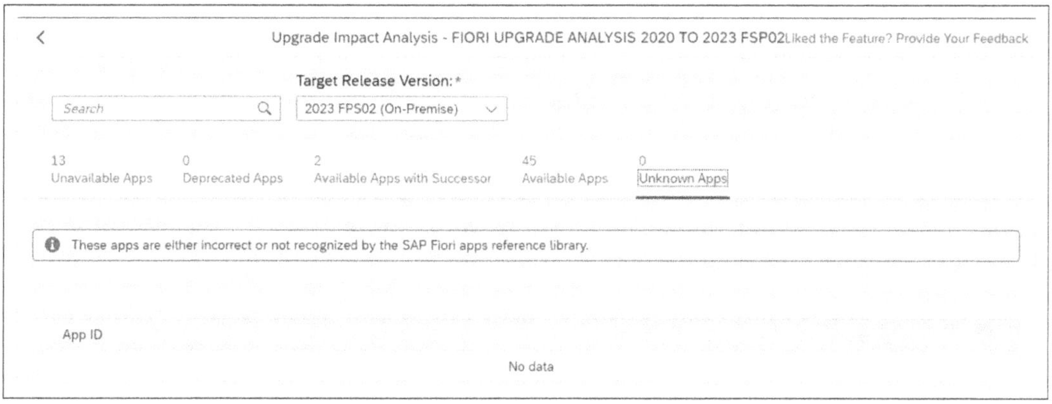

CHAPTER 14 SAP FIORI UPGRADE IMPACT ANALYSIS

Figure 14-10. Data showing Unknown Apps

The SAP Fiori Upgrade Impact Analysis tool lists **unknown apps** when it cannot identify specific applications. This may be due to custom development, non-standard configurations, apps from previous versions, or third-party solutions.

Unknown applications should be investigated for compatibility with the new system. Verify their status, check configurations, and look for updates to ensure proper functionality. The organization should assess unknown custom apps for compatibility with SAP technologies. If essential, test in a sandbox to identify upgrade issues and provide appropriate integration or replacement.

Following these steps, you used the **SAP Fiori Upgrade Impact Analysis** tool to ensure a smooth upgrade. This approach helps keep your business processes running with minimal disruption.

Important Note You can download the generated output and share it with the functional team. This will help in discussing future role updates. This list is particularly pertinent in scenarios where Fiori apps have been deployed (1909–2023). The report proves valuable when upgrading to newer versions. However, in the context of **Greenfield implementations**, this analysis is **unnecessary**. For fresh implementations, leverage the **SAP Fiori App Recommendations** tool during the transition from ECC to S/4HANA.

715

14.5 Summary

The SAP Fiori Upgrade Impact Analysis tool helps companies check what happens when they upgrade their SAP Fiori apps. It advises what changes to make and what to watch out for. The tool tells users if their current system is ready for the upgrade and shows if any parts need to be changed. It helps make upgrades more manageable and smoother.

14.6 References

SAP Fiori Apps Reference Library

CHAPTER 15

SAP Fiori Adapt UI

15.1 Introduction

The **Adapt UI** feature in SAP Fiori, also known as the **Key User Adaptation** feature, allows users with specific roles (typically key users) to modify the interface of SAP Fiori applications without needing to write code or engage in complex development processes. This feature is a part of SAPUI5 and is designed to make the SAP Fiori apps more flexible and customizable to meet specific business needs. SAP S/4HANA comes with over 500 ready-to-use apps delivered out of the box. These apps make sorting and working with many SAP business objects easy.

SAP Fiori's Adapt UI feature is a robust and versatile tool that allows users to customize the interface of SAP Fiori applications without needing deep technical expertise. This tool empowers users to modify Fiori apps' appearance, layout, and functionality to better align with specific business requirements or personal preferences. With **Adapt UI**, users can adjust field positioning, hide or display elements, change labels, and add new fields to enhance usability. These customizations can be saved as **app variants**, which can be used individually or shared across the organization to ensure consistency and efficiency.

The **Adapt UI** feature allows business users and administrators to easily customize the interface of SAP Fiori applications within a test environment. Users can experiment with configurations and save changes like app variants, ensuring consistency across sessions and sharing options with others in the organization. This feature significantly improves user experience by providing control over the interface, aligning it with specific roles and workflows.

CHAPTER 15   SAP FIORI ADAPT UI

Adapt UI enables organizations to tailor their SAP environments without altering the core program code. This helps maintain stability while still allowing for updates and support from SAP. This leads to a more efficient user experience that boosts productivity and adapts to changing business needs.

15.1.1 Main Features

UI Customization:

- **Add or Remove UI Elements:** Users can add new fields, buttons, or other elements to the interface or remove unnecessary ones. This is particularly useful when adapting an application to fit the specific needs of a business role or process.
- **Combine or Split Elements:** Users can combine fields to save space on the UI or split them back into separate fields as needed.

Modes of Adaptation:

- **Adaptation Mode:** This is the primary mode where users can interact with UI controls to make changes, such as adding, removing, combining, or splitting elements.
- **Navigation Mode:** This mode allows users to navigate the application to different views or dialogs without leaving the Adaptation session. It is essential to make changes that depend on the application's navigation.
- **Visualization Mode:** This mode provides an overview of all the changes made during the Adaptation process. It helps users review and manage their modifications.

15.1.2 UI Adaptation Features

The **Adapt UI** editor mode option allows you to try the following:

- Adding new fields
- Adding new groups
- Adding sections to an object page

- Renaming fields and groups
- Moving fields, groups, and object page sections
- Cutting and pasting fields and groups
- Combining fields
- Splitting combined fields
- Deleting fields, groups, and object page sections
- Undoing and redoing changes

15.1.3 Advantages of App Variants

In SAP Fiori, an app variant is a personalized version of a standard SAP Fiori application that can be customized to meet specific business needs or user preferences without modifying the original application code. This allows users and organizations to tailor the SAP Fiori experience to suit their workflows better while still maintaining the integrity and supportability of the standard SAP application. App variant features are as follows:

Personalization and Customization:

- **User-Specific Adjustments:** Users can create app variants to adjust the user interface (UI) layout, filter settings, and other personal preferences. These adjustments can then be saved as a variant, allowing users to quickly switch between views that suit their specific needs quickly.

- **Custom Fields and Layouts:** In some cases, app variants allow the inclusion of custom fields or different layouts, offering a more tailored experience without the need for extensive custom development.

15.1.4 Steps to Create an App Variant

- **Open the App:** Open the SAP Fiori app for which you want to create a variant.

- **Adjust Settings:** You can modify the app's filters, layout, or other settings according to your needs.

- **Save as a Variant:** Save these settings as a new variant once the desired adjustments are made. You can usually do this via the **Save As** option within the app's menu.

- **Name and Share:** Name the variant appropriately, and if needed, choose to share it with other users or set it as a default.

- **Switch Between Variants:** Users can switch between different variants as needed, often from a dropdown menu within the app.

15.1.5 Use Adapt UI

The UI Adaptation mode can be accessed via the **Adapt UI button** in the **User Menu** for the running app. This displays a new **header bar** with actions around RTA. When in Adaptation mode, you can edit all UI elements, such as fields, groups of fields, or sections, which are **highlighted** when you hover the mouse pointer over them or select them.

SAP Fiori provides three main types of apps: transactional apps, analytical apps, and factsheet apps. App variants are customized versions of existing apps created by making UI adjustments through the **Adapt UI** feature. These variants store specific **view settings**, such as **filters**, layout configurations, or control parameters, tailored to meet user needs.

To create an **app variant**, you start by adapting the UI in a test system, where you make the necessary changes. Once the adjustments are complete, save these UI changes as an app variant. After saving, you generate the target mappings and create a tile for the app variant, which integrates it into the SAP Fiori system. The next step involves adding the app variant to your SAP Fiori Launchpad home page, making it easily accessible. You can then open the app variant in UI Adaptation mode if further refinements are needed. Finally, you publish the app variant, making it available in the SAP Fiori environment. This process allows you to create tailored app variants that better align with specific user roles or business processes, enhancing the overall user experience.

Adapt UI is a feature like the transaction variant concept in ECC, which allows the creation of a display version for any particular app.

15.2 Set Up Adapt UI

Adapt UI is adapting your existing apps with some manipulated screens and functionalities. For example, users can create, change, display, or delete bank accounts within these apps. One way of restricting access would be to run a trace, determine what objects are being called in the back end, and then manage the authorizations within those authorization objects.

Upon logging into the app, users may come across certain buttons that are not intended for their use. Clicking these buttons will result in an authorization error, causing confusion and generating unnecessary tickets and emails. To prevent this, these buttons must be hidden from the app if you wish to provide users with display access only for the managed type of apps. This is especially important if you only want to give the users display access to the managed type of apps. Adapt UI helps to utilize the hiding icon and button feature for end users using only the display option.

Adapt UI in SAP Fiori allows the key user (administrator/developer) to create an app variant of the managed app. This key user must be authorized to execute the Adapt UI option in your development environment and have access to the security role **SAP_UI_FLEX_KEY_USER**. For our case, we created a custom role by copying and naming it as **ZSU:SAP_UI_FLEX_KEY_USER** and assigning it to the **admin user**, as shown in the figure below.

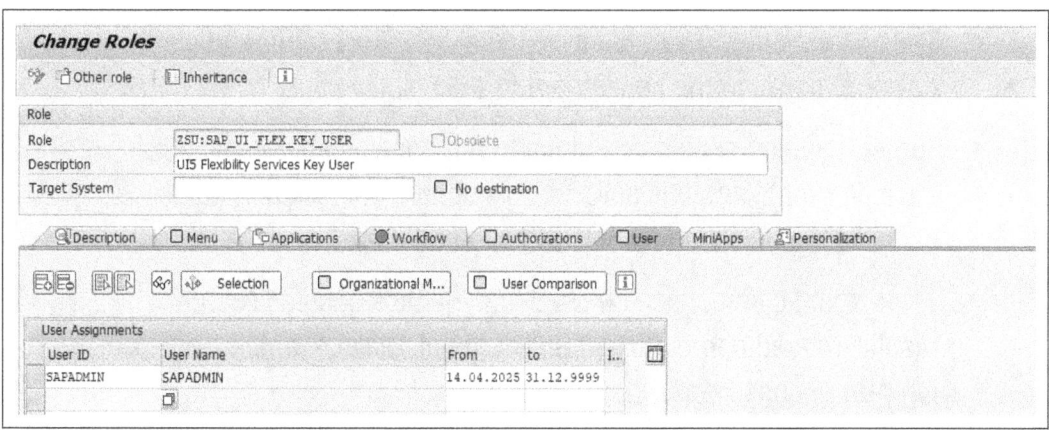

Figure 15-1. Role assigned to the admin user to work with Adapt UI

Note Some key users should be authorized to create a display version of the app, which comes from the role **SAP_UI_FLEX_KEY_USER**. Everything else in the app remains the same. The admin or developer should have this role in their profile.

When the **key user** enters the app in UI Adaptation mode, they can remove the action buttons, rename them, move them, and create new options. They can also rearrange the button or label as desired. They can also cut, paste, drag, and drop buttons. Once completed, what is desired and saved is like an app variant in a transport request, and the system will generate an **app ID**. This app ID can be used to create a tile with a display version of the app and should be added under Target Application. So Adapt UI allows you to manipulate, update, or change the app screen look and feel at runtime.

Therefore, when you create a tile for the display version of the app, everything else will be the same. It will generate the target application while using the Adapt UI steps. **The semantic object should be the same as the original app, but the semantic action must differ.** For example, in the original app, if the semantic action was manageMasterData, then you can use the semantic action displayMasterData. Furthermore, the app name, for example, Display Bank Accounts, can be changed.

Note A semantic action should always start with a lowercase.

- The app variant ID must be added to a new **Fiori technical catalog** to assign the app variant to the display user.

- Target mapping should be unique to the apps as an original but have different semantic actions. This should be assigned to the same semantic object so that you can find it easily.

- The semantic object can be used in dynamics such as search results, related app buttons, intelligent link dialogs, and other jump-to options in analytics.

- In Adapt UI, the option to hide is not available.

- All Adapt UI objects are transported from the development.

CHAPTER 15   SAP FIORI ADAPT UI

15.2.1 Creation of an App Variant Using Adapt UI

For our scenario to create an Adapt UI app variant, we are using SAP Fiori app **F1366A**, **Manage Bank Accounts (BankAccount-manageMasterData)**, as an example.

Access the **UI Adaptation mode** via the **Adapt UI button** in the **User Menu** for the running app. Edit all UI elements, such as fields, groups of fields, or sections, which get highlighted when you hover over or select them.

To do this, the key user should have access to the app via a **business catalog** to create a variant. Initially, create a **business catalog with the app you want to use to make an app variant.** The custom business catalog is designed with two apps, as shown in the figure below.

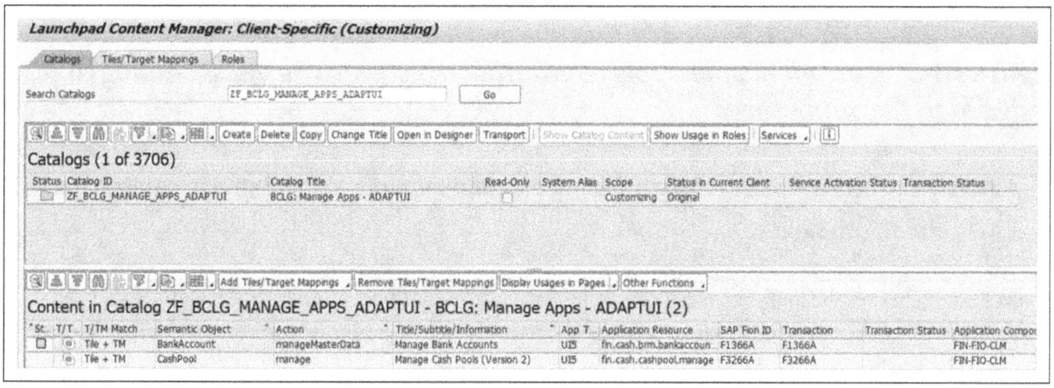

Figure 15-2. Custom business catalog created for Adapt UI

The above figure displays the created custom business catalog **ZF_BCLG_MANAGE_APPS_ADAPTUI**. Then, we confirmed that all the **OData** and **SICF** services were activated. It was then assigned to a custom business role named **ZMU:MANAGE_APPS_ADAPTUI:XXXX** and then to the admin user, as shown in the figure below.

CHAPTER 15   SAP FIORI ADAPT UI

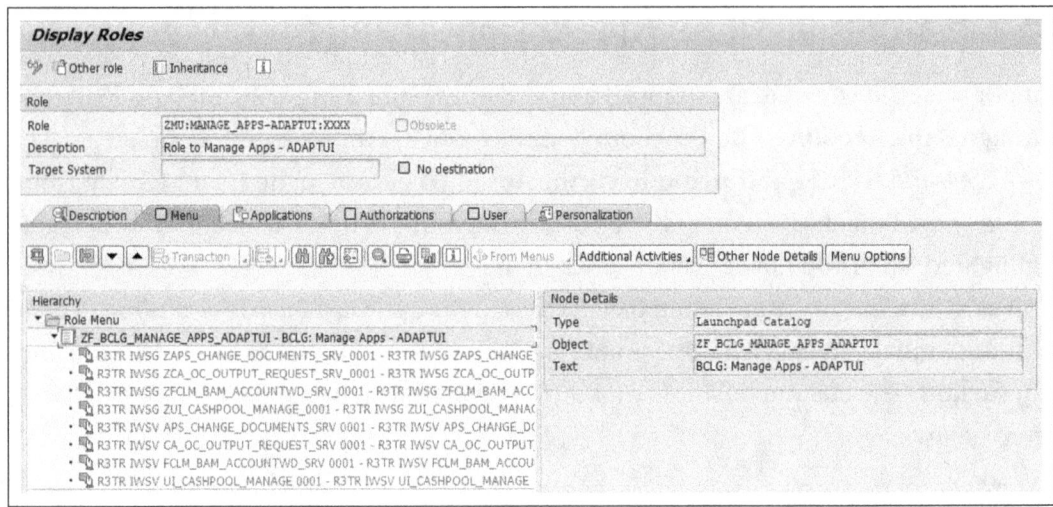

Figure 15-3. Custom business role containing the custom business catalog and assigned to the admin user

Check, on the SAP Fiori Launchpad home page, the custom business catalog, as shown in the figure below.

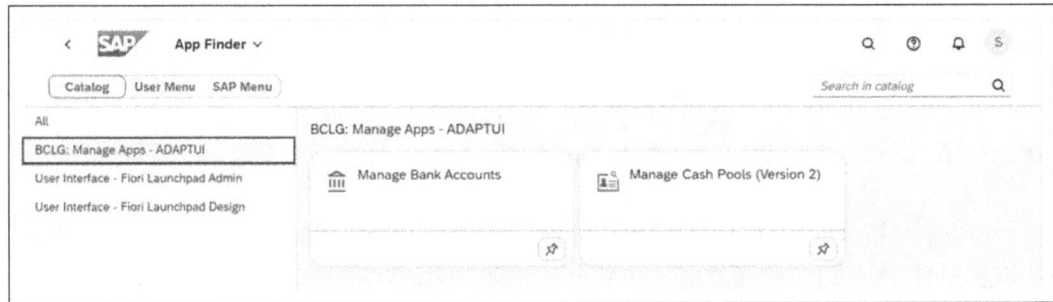

Figure 15-4. App Finder displaying the custom business catalog

You can find the Manage Bank Accounts information within the **User Menu** on the **SAP Fiori Launchpad home page** by selecting **App Finder**, as shown in the figure above. Open the tab, and the app's attributes are displayed, as shown in the figure below.

724

CHAPTER 15   SAP FIORI ADAPT UI

Figure 15-5. *Manage Bank Accounts app's attributes opened*

The figure above does not currently display data. Select the **Go** tab; the output will be displayed as shown in the figure below.

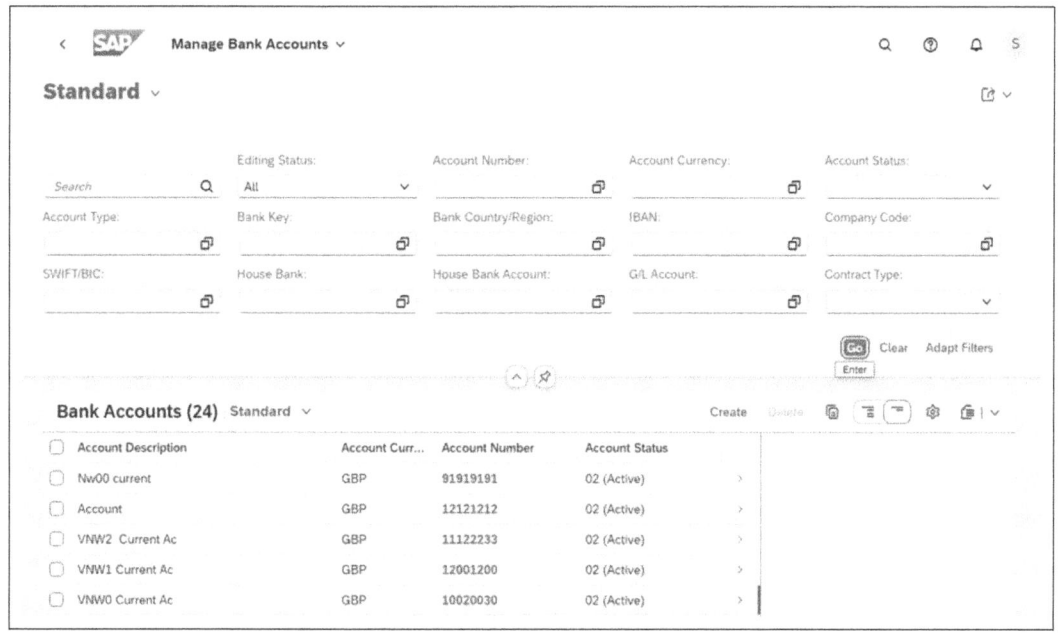

Figure 15-6. *Manage Bank Accounts app details are displayed*

CHAPTER 15   SAP FIORI ADAPT UI

The User Menu also displays the Adapt UI option available for use, as shown in the figure below.

Note As a **key user** (administrator) in the selected app F1366A, you can access the **Adapt UI** feature within the **User Menu** on the **SAP Fiori Launchpad home page**.

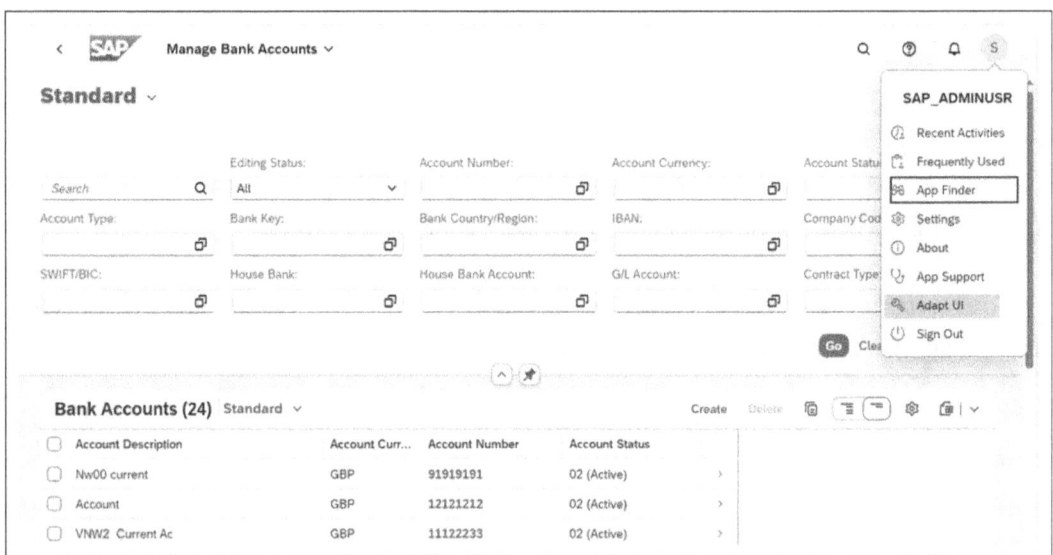

Figure 15-7. The User Menu displaying the Adapt UI option is available for use

As shown above, select the Adapt UI feature under the User Menu option button. The **UI Adaptation page** opens, as shown in the figure below.

CHAPTER 15   SAP FIORI ADAPT UI

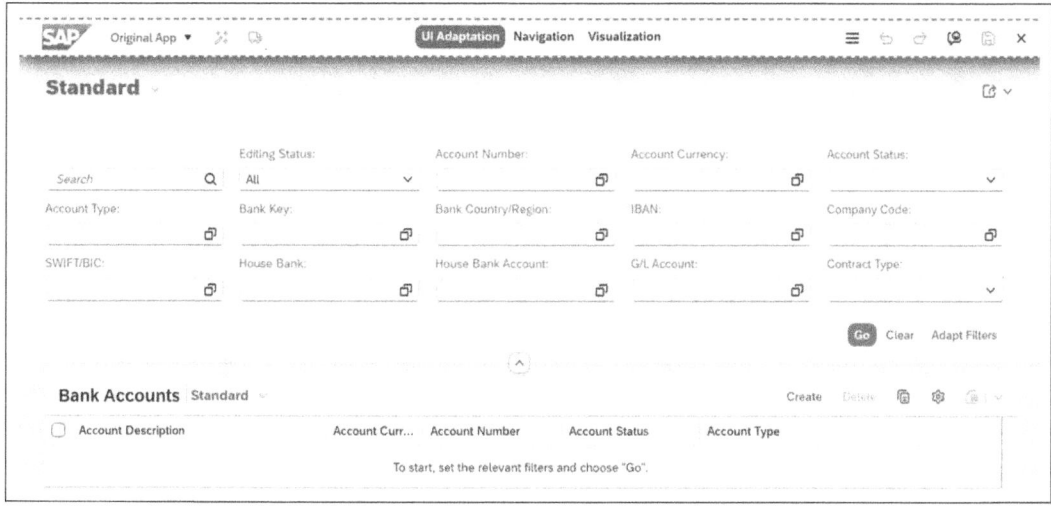

Figure 15-8. *The UI Adaptation work zone screen appears*

In the above figure, we observe that the screen layout has changed, and we can see what we want to change, for example, we need to remove the tabs **Create**, **Delete**, etc., plus add a few blocks. The **Adapt UI** screen of SAP Fiori has three tabs at the top of the screen: **UI Adaptation**, **Navigation**, and **Visualization**. Each tab has a specific purpose for customizing the user interface of Fiori apps:

> The **UI Adaptation tab** allows you to change or modify the app's layout by adding or removing fields, buttons, or blocks. You can also hide or show interface elements based on user roles or preferences.
>
> The **Navigation tab** lets you set up how navigation works. You can decide how buttons or links will direct users to other apps or locations. Here, you can define the semantic objects and actions.
>
> The **Visualization tab** allows you to customize how the app tile looks in the Fiori Launchpad. You can change the title, subtitle, icon, and information. Adjust these details to make things more transparent for users.

In the above mode, users can make desired changes but have **display-only access**, meaning they cannot update data. Options on the right side include Create, Edit, Copy, Delete, Import, Export, Download Template, and View Import History, though some may be grayed out and inaccessible.

CHAPTER 15 SAP FIORI ADAPT UI

The admin can now make changes to the screen as desired. Right-click Create to open a box, as shown in the figure below.

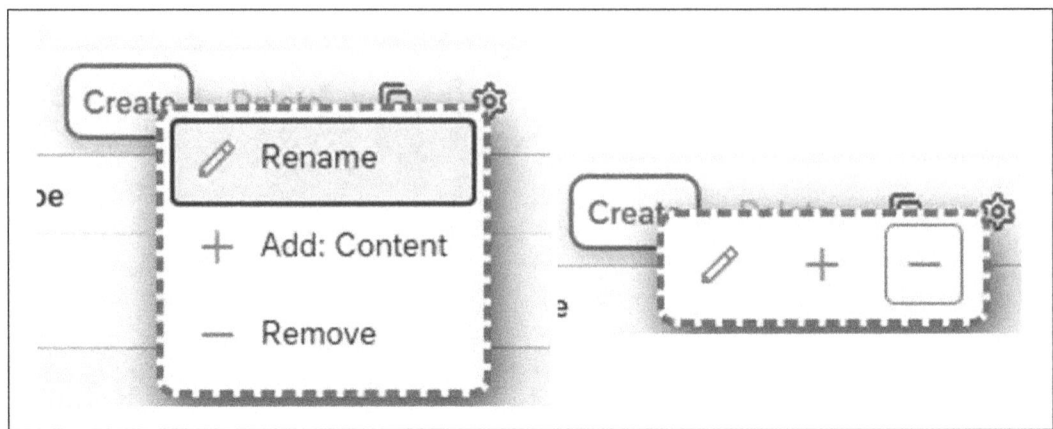

Figure 15-9. *Create options available*

The symbols in the above figure represent the following, and they are sometimes displayed as shown in the figure above. In the Adapt UI screen of SAP Fiori, you can customize the app interface in the **Create** section. There are three options available: Rename, Add: Content, and Remove.

> ✏ **Rename**: Lets you **change labels or text** on the screen.
>
> **+ Add: Content:** This option allows you to insert new UI elements, such as buttons, input fields, or blocks, but only if the app supports such additions.
>
> **– Remove**: Used to **hide or delete elements** (like buttons, fields, or blocks) from the user interface that are not needed for specific users or roles.

Right-click the Create button and then select **Add: Content**, which opens a window titled **Available Content: Content**, as shown in the figure below.

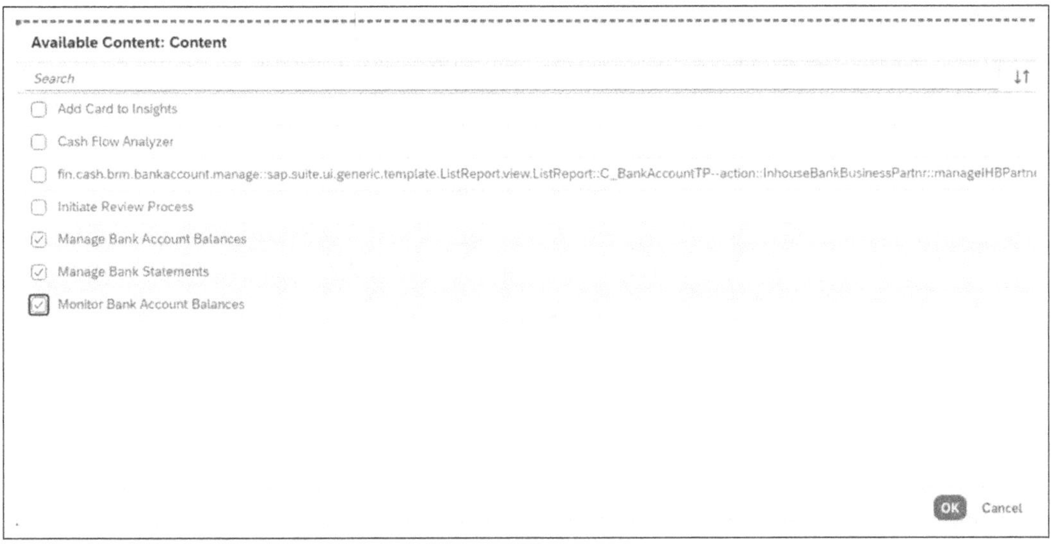

CHAPTER 15 SAP FIORI ADAPT UI

Figure 15-10. Available content that can be added to the screen

In the above figure, we selected three options and chose **OK**. The three new tabs are added to the UI Adaptation screen, which gets updated, as shown in the figure below.

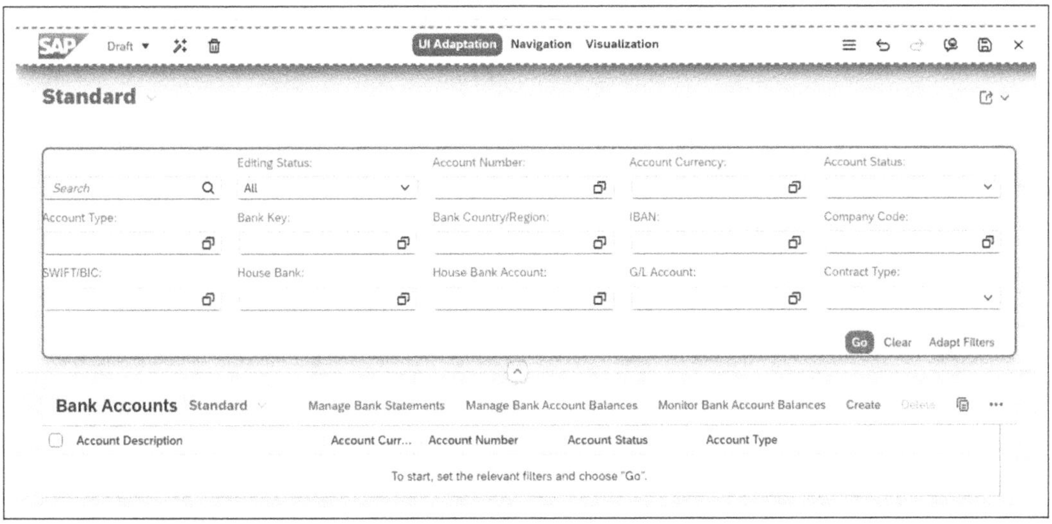

Figure 15-11. Three tabs added to the UI Adaptation screen

729

CHAPTER 15   SAP FIORI ADAPT UI

Since this will be a **display app**, we will remove the **Create** tab and two of the tabs we added by clicking the **Remove** option, as shown in the figure below.

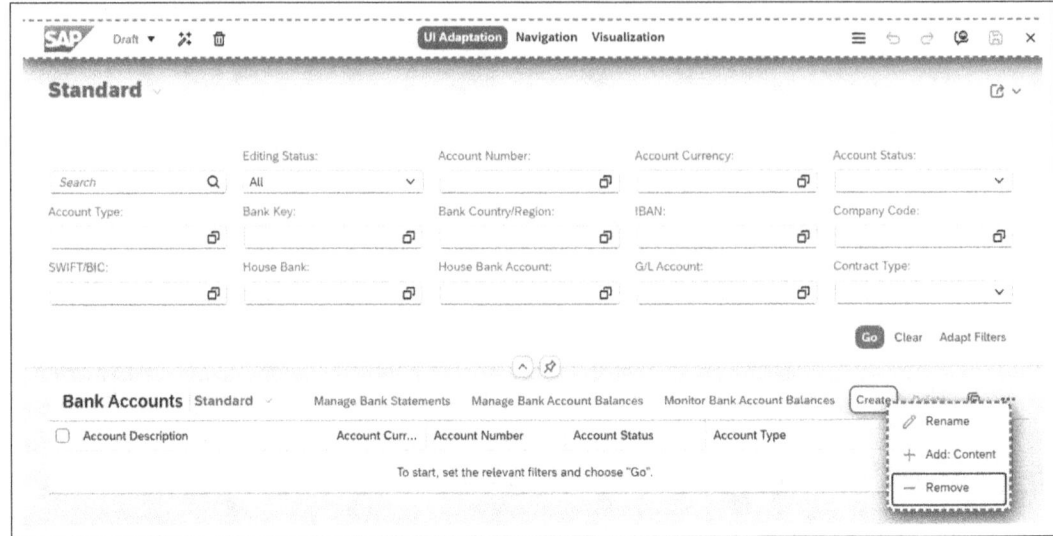

Figure 15-12. *Utilizing the Remove option to remove three tabs*

We will also remove the Delete tab, and the updated screen will appear as shown in the figure below.

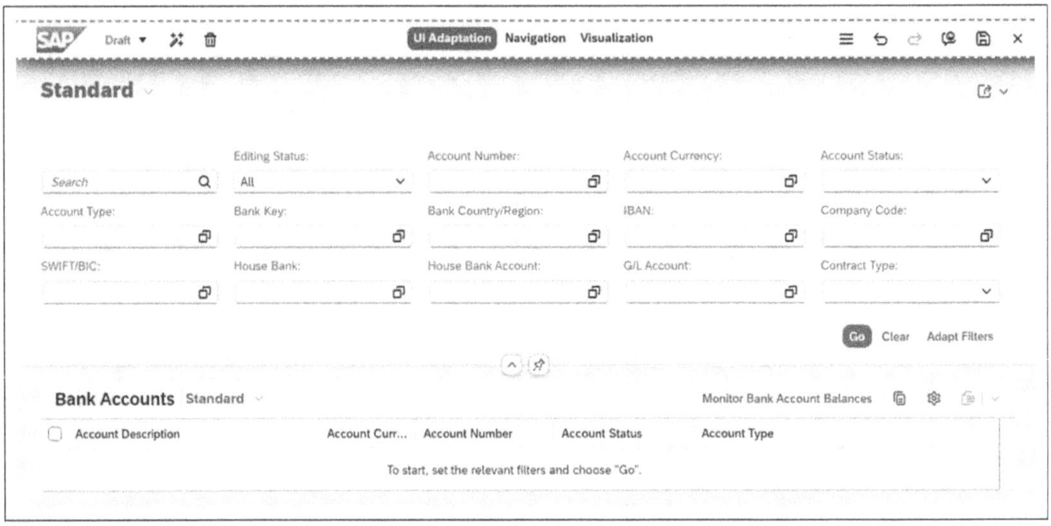

Figure 15-13. *Delete tab removed*

CHAPTER 15   SAP FIORI ADAPT UI

In the above figure, we change the tab **Monitor Bank Account Balances** to **Display Bank Account Balance** by using the option **Rename**, and the screen will update as shown in the figure below.

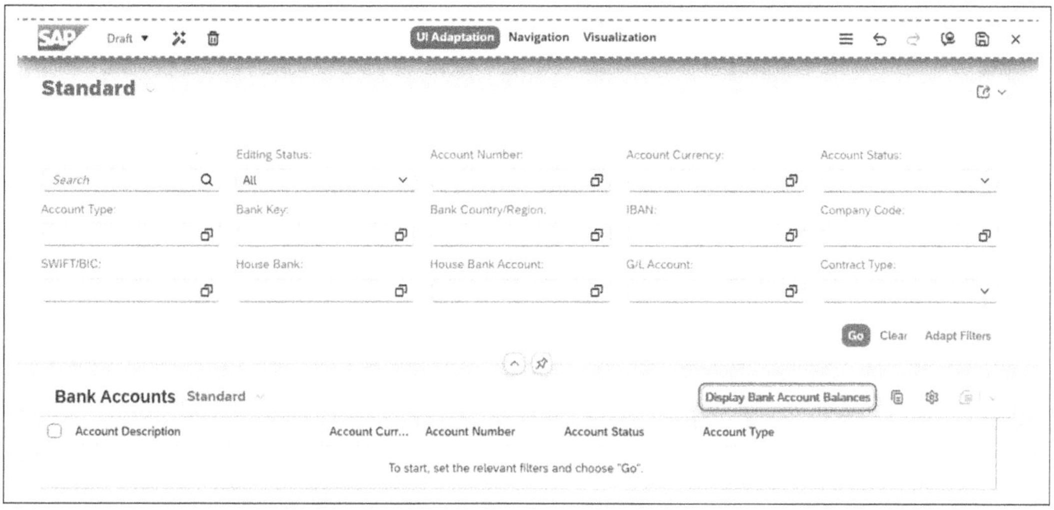

Figure 15-14. *Renamed the tab*

Therefore, you can configure the screen's look and feel with UI Adaptation mode. You can remove an action button, add one, and rename buttons per your requirements. There are apps where you can move the tab, button, or block up and down as desired.

You can add a block or tab at the top of the screen by right-clicking the bar, displaying the options as shown in the figure below.

731

CHAPTER 15   SAP FIORI ADAPT UI

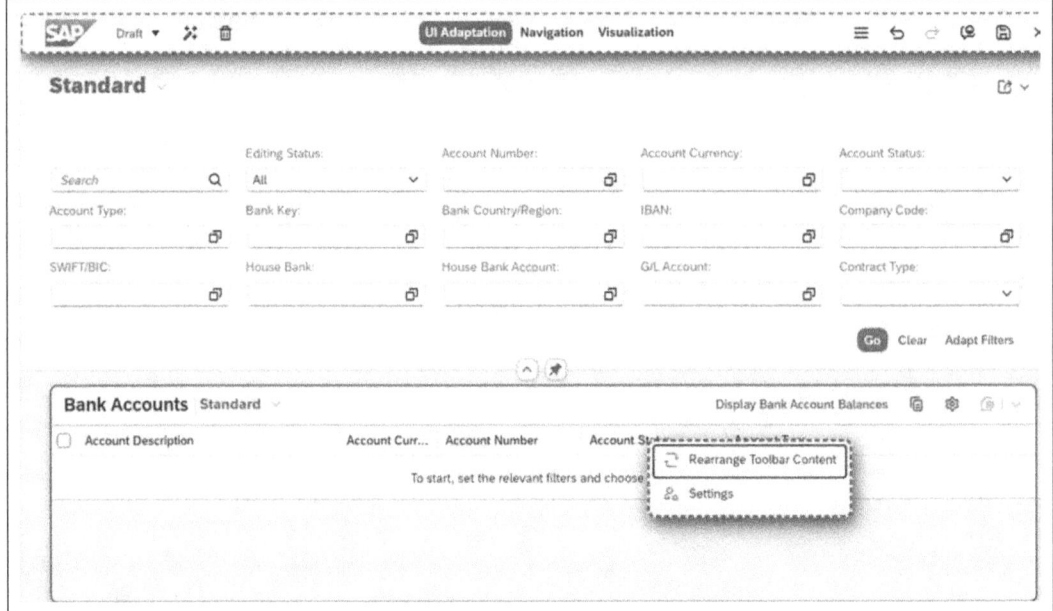

Figure 15-15. Rearrange Toolbar Content option

In the above figure, we can rearrange the toolbar information displayed in a different order, as shown in the figure below.

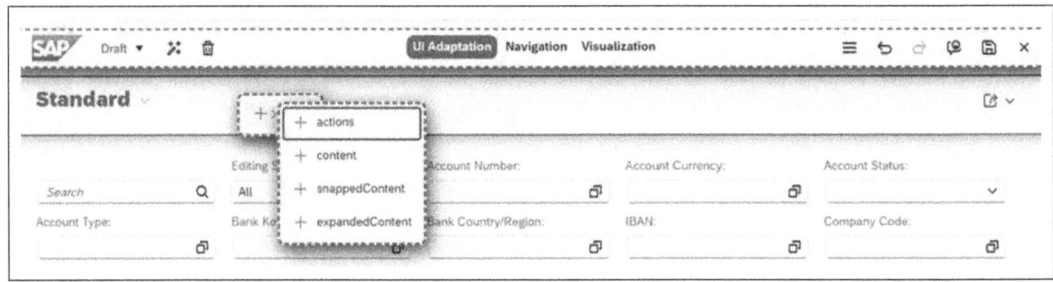

Figure 15-16. Option to add a content field

When the **content** option is selected, another window appears showing options to choose from, as shown in the figure below.

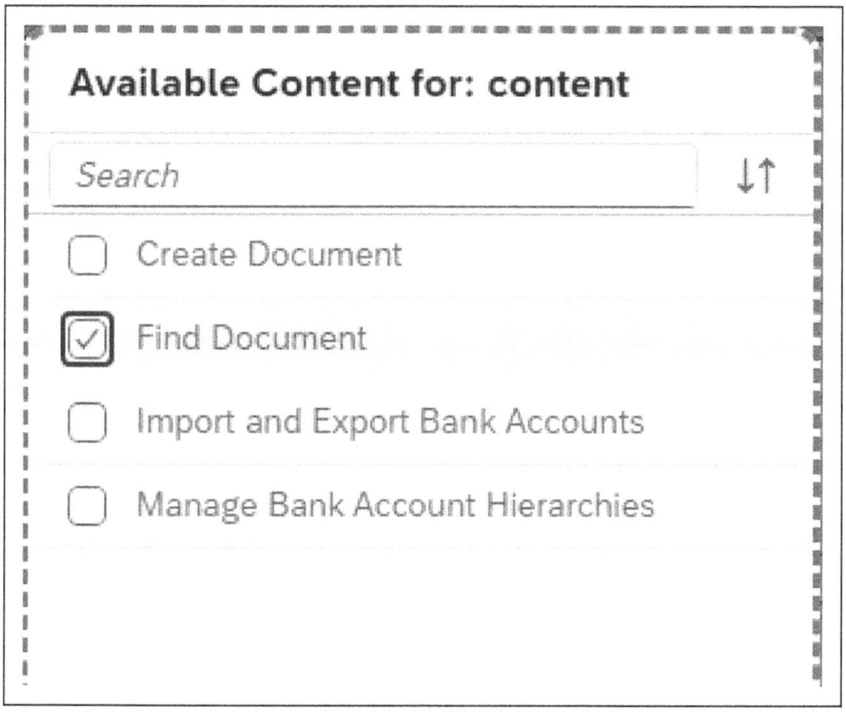

CHAPTER 15 SAP FIORI ADAPT UI

Available Content for: content

Search ↓↑

☐ Create Document
☑ Find Document
☐ Import and Export Bank Accounts
☐ Manage Bank Account Hierarchies

Figure 15-17. Check the Find Document box

In the above screen, selecting **Find Document** will put the block on the top bar, as shown in the figure below.

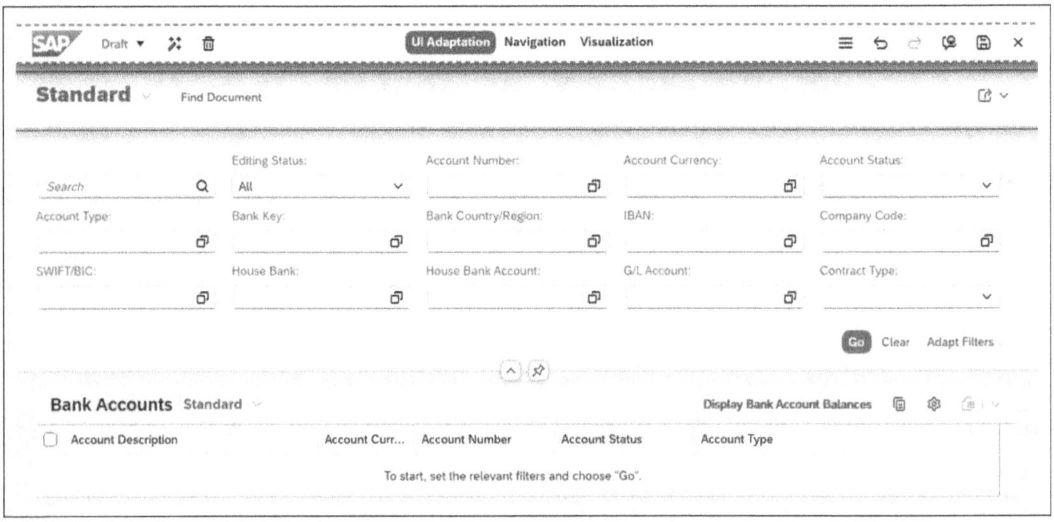

CHAPTER 15   SAP FIORI ADAPT UI

Figure 15-18. Block or tab added on the top

As shown in the figure below, you can move the block by dragging and dropping it.

Figure 15-19. Block Find Document moved to the right side

Click **Adapt Filters** to open the **Adapt Filters** window, which allows you to add more filters, as shown in the figure below.

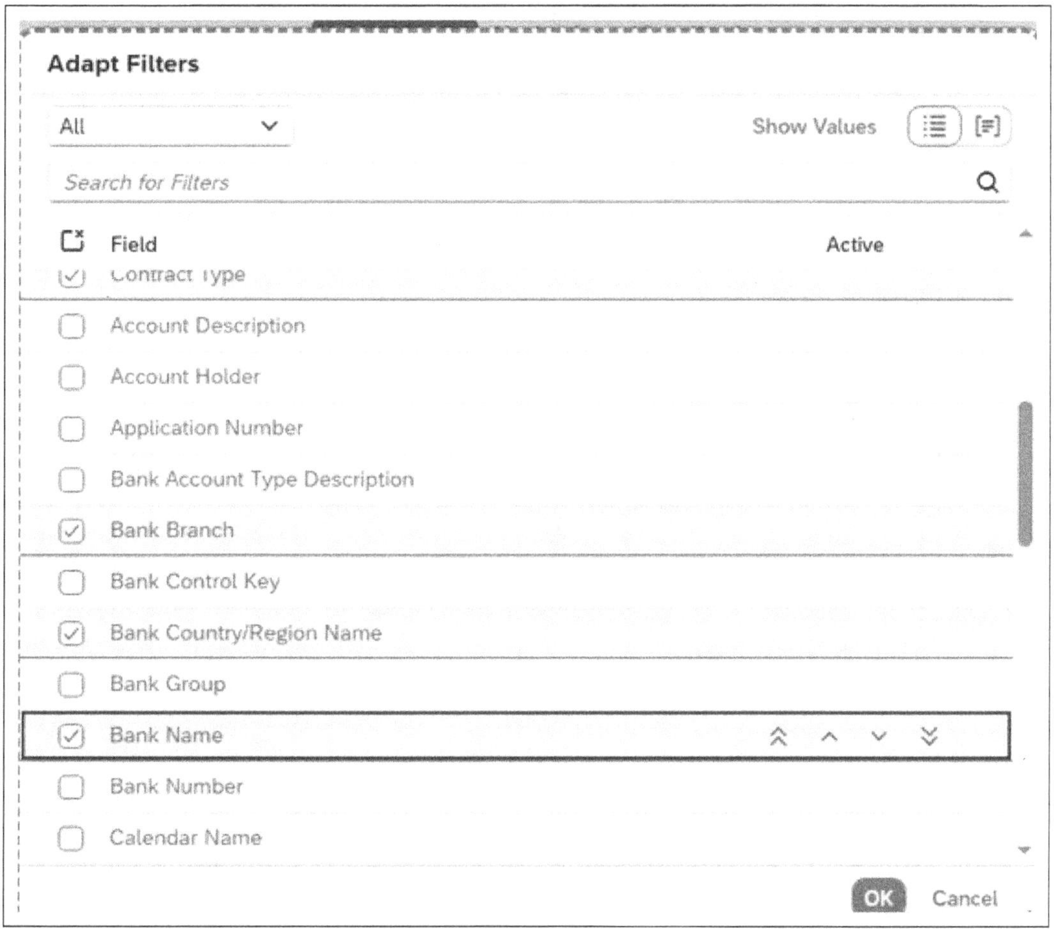

CHAPTER 15   SAP FIORI ADAPT UI

```
Adapt Filters

All  ⌄                                          Show Values  [≡]  [≡]

Search for Filters                                                Q

☐×  Field                                                Active
[✓]  Contract Type
☐    Account Description
☐    Account Holder
☐    Application Number
☐    Bank Account Type Description
[✓]  Bank Branch
☐    Bank Control Key
[✓]  Bank Country/Region Name
☐    Bank Group
[✓]  Bank Name                              ⌇  ⋀  ⋁  ⋎
☐    Bank Number
☐    Calendar Name

                                                   OK   Cancel
```

Figure 15-20. *Adapt Filters with four options selected and to be added*

As shown below, the four chosen fields in the figure above must be saved before any changes. Click **OK,** and a **Warning box** opens, as shown in the figure below.

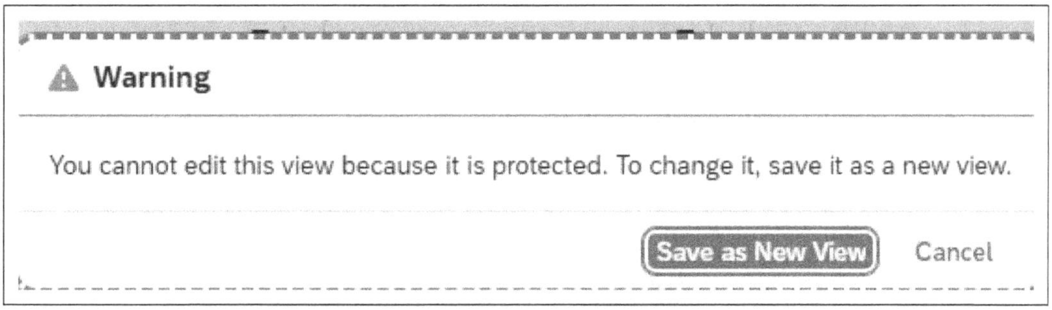

```
⚠ Warning

You cannot edit this view because it is protected. To change it, save it as a new view.

                                    Save as New View   Cancel
```

Figure 15-21. *Warning box opens*

735

CHAPTER 15　SAP FIORI ADAPT UI

The Warning box displays a message stating **You cannot edit this view because it is protected.** It forces you to save the changes to a new view by selecting the **Save as New View** `Save as New View` tab, as shown in the figure above. The **Save View** new window opens, as shown in the figure below.

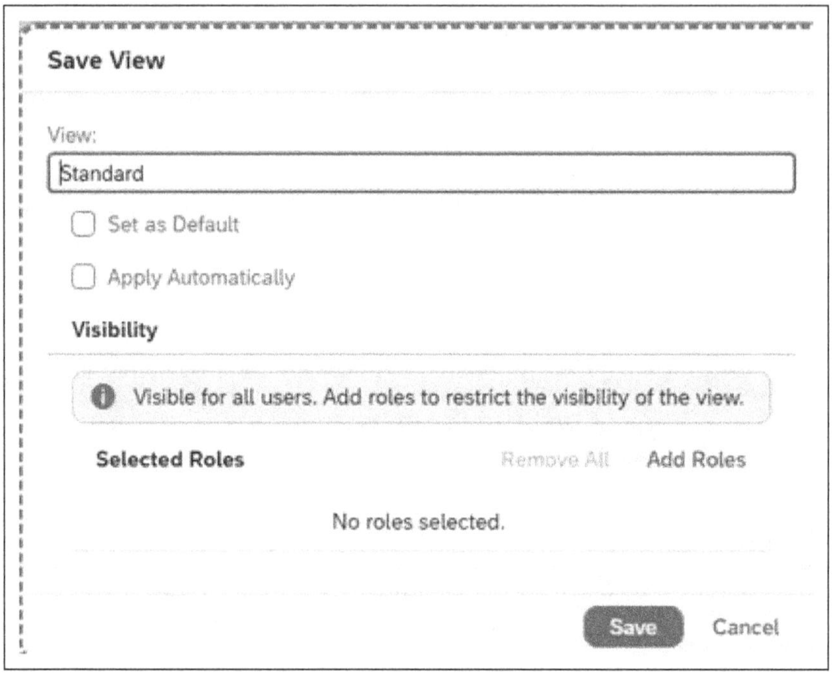

Figure 15-22. Save View window opens

In the above figure, change the **View name** from **Standard** to **Monitor Bank Accounts.**

Select the option **Set as Default**, as shown in the figure below.

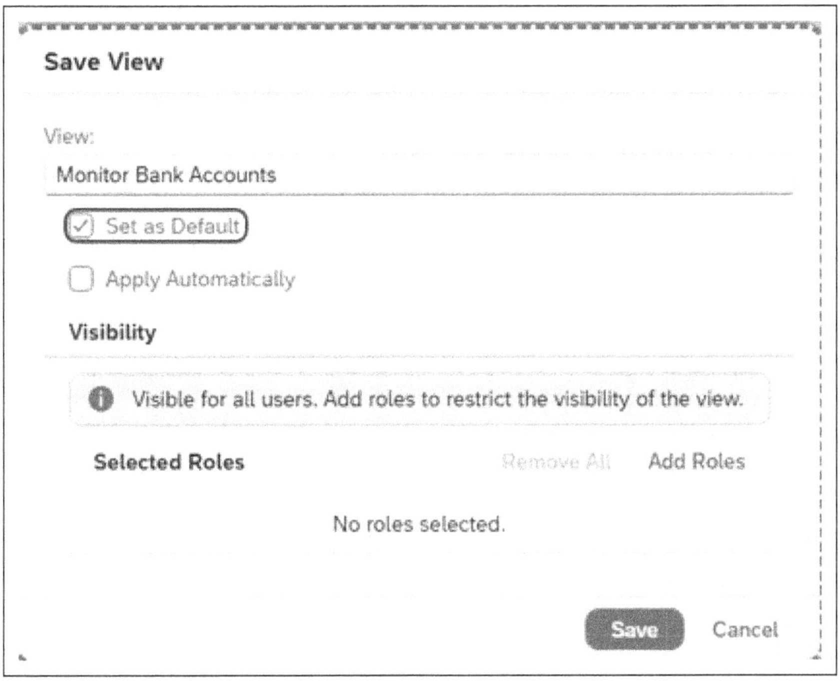

CHAPTER 15   SAP FIORI ADAPT UI

Figure 15-23. Save View details entered

Select **Save** to initiate saving the view, and the screen will be updated, as shown in the figure below.

Figure 15-24. The view name changed

The heading **Standard** was updated to Monitor Bank Accounts, as shown in the figure above. In **SAP Fiori Adapt UI**, the **"Save View"** feature allows you to **save your UI changes** as a **view variant** that can be reused or assigned to specific users/roles. Here is how it works and what each sub-option means:

Save View – Functionality

- It captures the UI adaptations (like hidden fields, renamed labels, reordered elements) and saves them under a custom view name. This lets users switch between the default view and customized ones based on their needs.

Set as Default

- You can set this saved view as the default layout for all users, unless a different view is selected, but only one view can be marked as the default at a time.

Apply Automatically

- When enabled, the view is automatically applied without requiring users to manually select it, making it useful for enforcing a standard layout for specific roles or all users.

Add Roles

- This allows you to assign a view to specific PFCG roles, ensuring that only users with those roles can access the adapted view for a tailored UI experience.

In the above figure, enter the **View name** as **Updated**, select the option **Set as Default**, and save the settings by clicking **Save**.

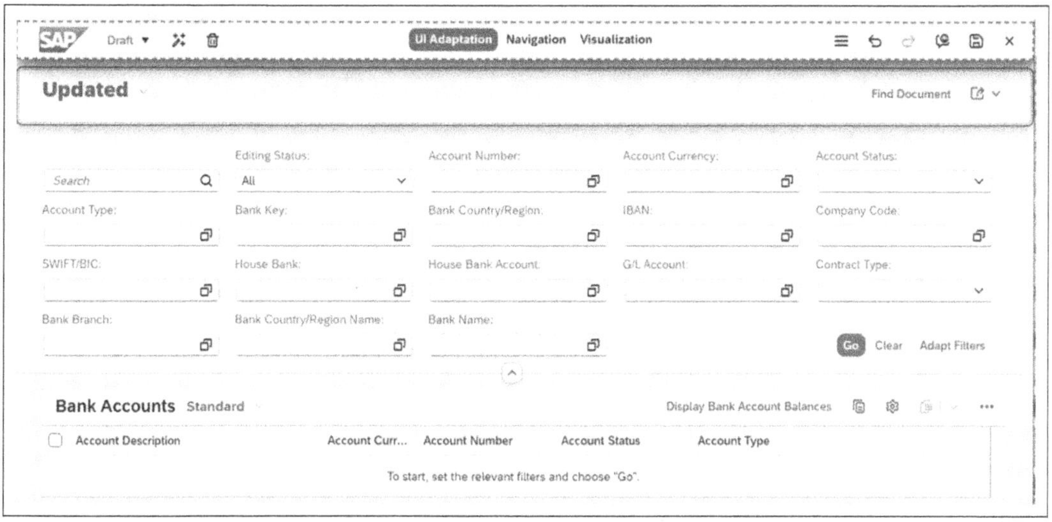

CHAPTER 15 SAP FIORI ADAPT UI

Figure 15-25. New view Updated is displayed

The next step is to activate the changes, which will activate and save the view. Select the **activate** option, and the **Activate New Version** box opens, as shown in the figure below.

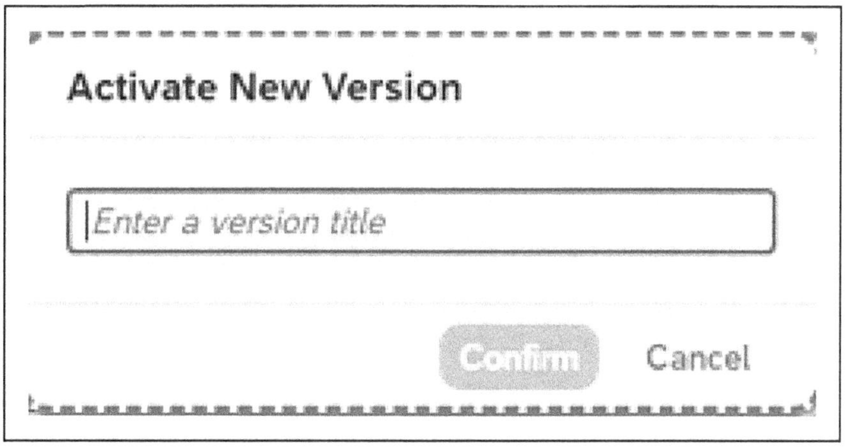

Figure 15-26. Activate New Version window

739

In the above, we need to enter a version title. Here we will enter Monitor Bank Accounts – Ver #1, as shown in the figure below.

Figure 15-27. Version title entered

The system asks you to confirm to activate the view. In the above figure, click the **Confirm**  tab. The version name is updated and appears at the screen's top-left corner, as shown in the figure below. It also displays a message Version was saved.

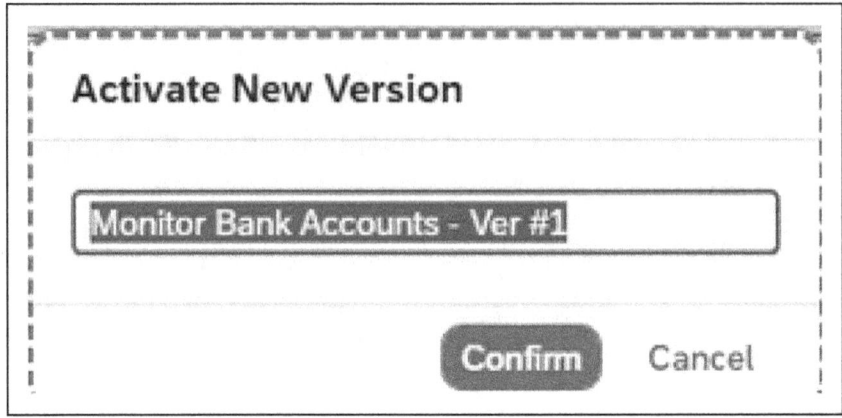

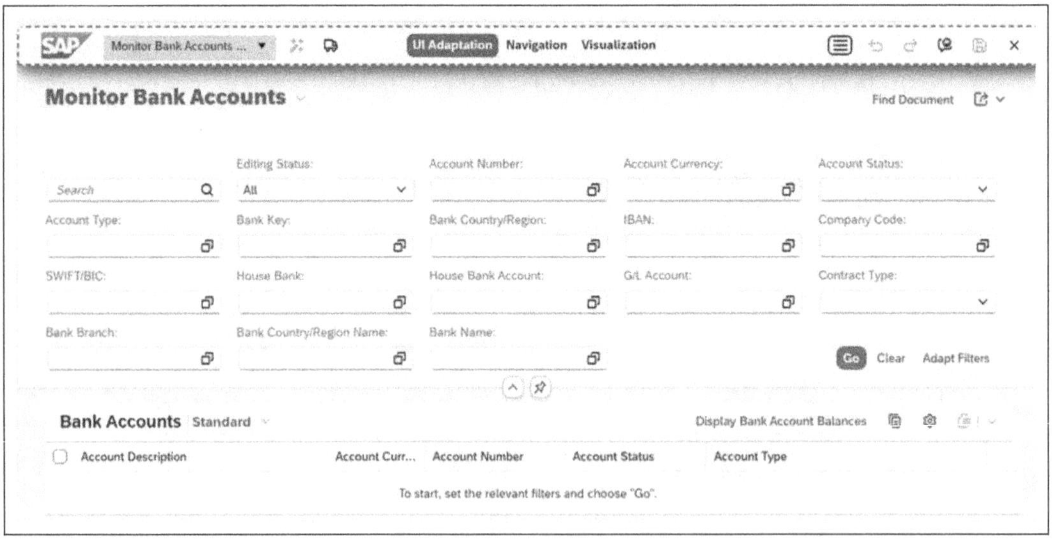

Figure 15-28. The view version is updated

CHAPTER 15 SAP FIORI ADAPT UI

Once all the activity is completed, select the option on the right-hand side of the top menu, the **App Variants** option, and then the **Save As** option, as shown in the figure below.

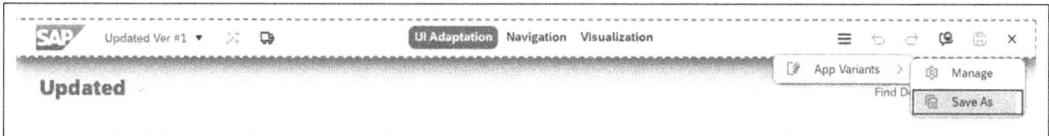

Figure 15-29. *Save the App Variants option*

Selecting the **Save As option** opens the **Save as New App Variant** window to create a **variant**, as shown in the figure below.

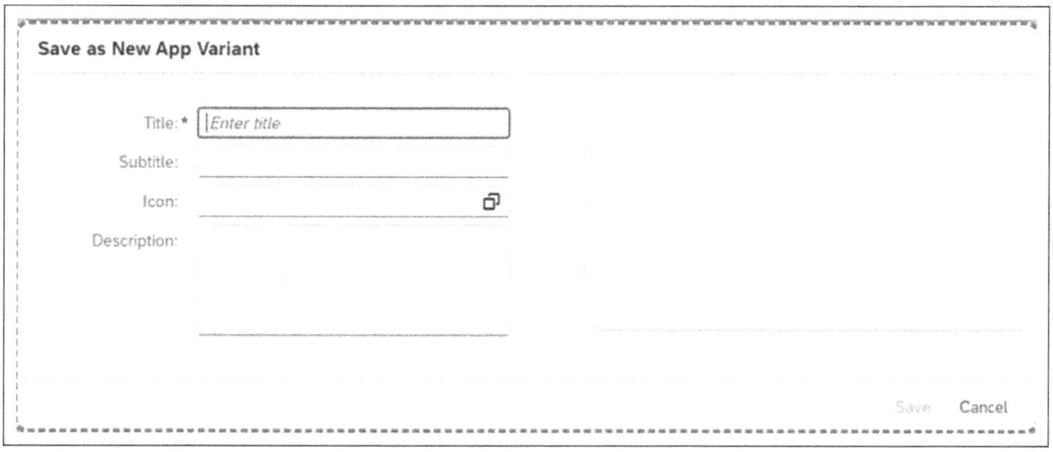

Figure 15-30. *Save as New App Variant dialog box*

In the above figure, enter the following information:

- **Title**: Monitor Bank Accounts
- **Subtitle**: Banks
- **Icon**: Any (select from the list)
- **Description**: Manage Bank Accounts App modified and converted to Monitor Bank Accounts

741

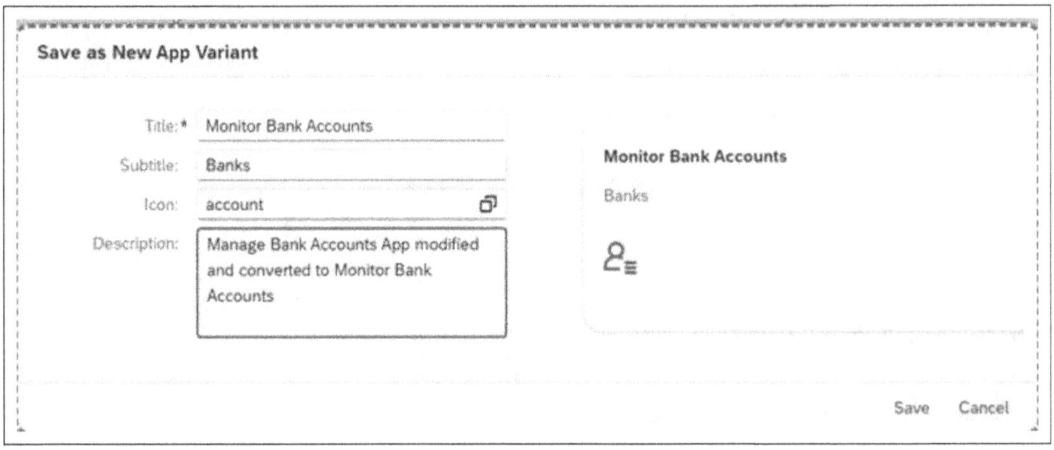

CHAPTER 15   SAP FIORI ADAPT UI

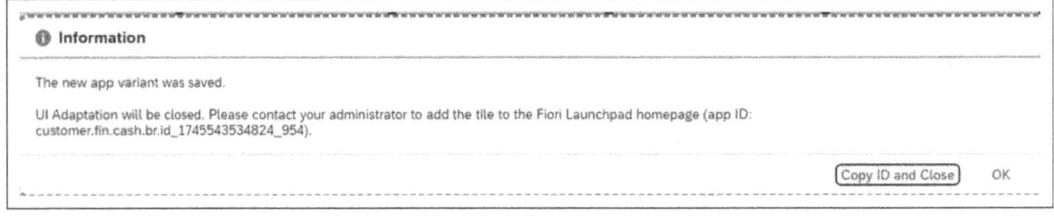

Figure 15-31. *New app variant – tile information added*

The title is mandatory in the above figure. You can choose an icon from the list by selecting the search option, as shown in the figure above.

Note   The box on the right updates simultaneously when you enter information. It will appear as a tile for the end user.

Click the option Save, and an **Information** window opens, as shown in the figure below.

Figure 15-32. *Information window*

The above figure displays the message that the new app variant was saved. To proceed, select the **Copy ID and Close** [Copy ID and Close] tab. The ID copied is as follows: **customer.fin.cash.br.id_1745543534824_954**.

The tile will be added to the **My Home** section of the SAP Fiori Launchpad home page, as shown in the figure below.

742

CHAPTER 15   SAP FIORI ADAPT UI

Figure 15-33. *New tile Monitor Bank Accounts created*

Execute the app to check if it works. The app is executed, and the output is displayed, as shown in the figure below.

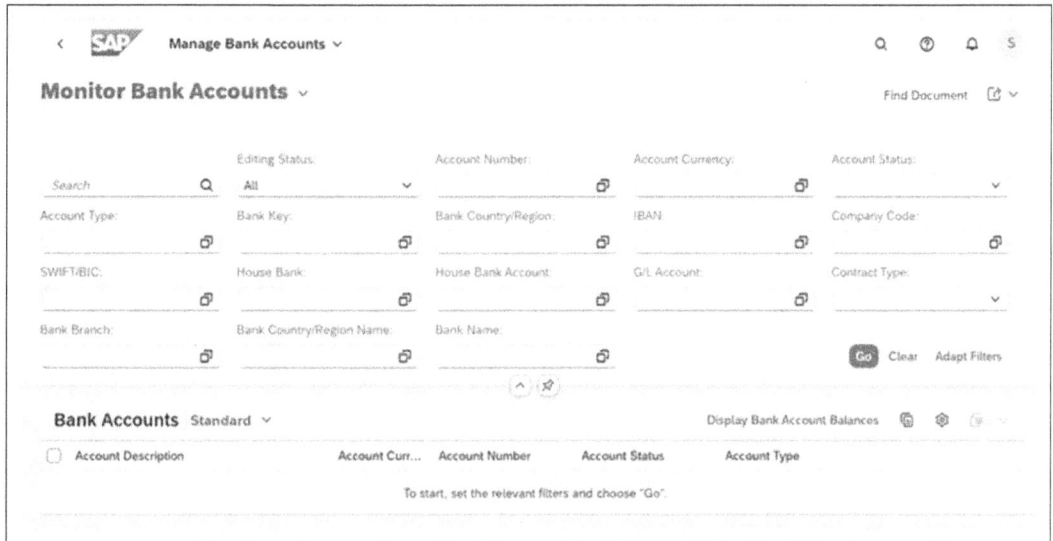

Figure 15-34. *New app variant displayed with update for Fiori app F1366A*

In the figure above, after creating and saving an app variant, the variant appears as a **new app** that closely resembles the **original app F1366A**, but with all the changes applied. It is important to note that the **Delete** button is not displayed as expected, and some fields have been added.

The **ID copied** detailed **customer.fin.cash.br.id_1745543534824_954**, which will be used to create a tile. Thus, this new variant will generate a display tile in the target application.

743

CHAPTER 15 SAP FIORI ADAPT UI

You can check if the variant was saved by clicking the ≡ **app variants option** and then **Manage.** This will open a window titled **Overview of App Variants**, as shown in the figure below.

Overview of App Variants			
App Type	Title	Description	
Original App Currently Adapting	Manage Bank Accounts Manage Bank Accounts	Manage Bank Accounts	Actions ∨
App Variant	Monitor Bank Accounts Banks	Manage Bank Accounts App modified and converted to Monitor Bank Accounts	Actions ∨

Figure 15-35. *The app variant created and saved is displayed*

The above figure confirms that the **app variant** was created and saved. It also shows the original app and will list all the other variants created for the original app within the system. It also provides an **Actions** tab that shows three options when selected, as shown in the figure below.

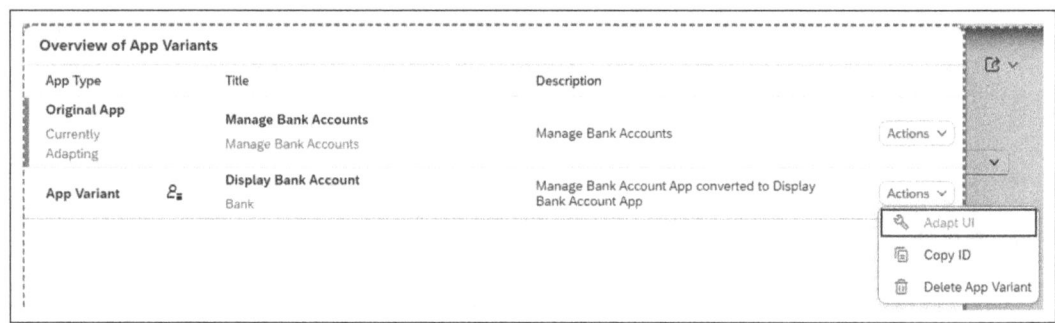

Figure 15-36. *Actions that can be performed on the variant*

The actions that can be performed on the Adapt UI variant are

- **Copy ID**: Allows copying of the ID generated
- **Delete App Variant**: Allows you to delete the app variant

The next step in this process is to create a new technical catalog using **/UI2/FLPAM** or **/UI2/FLPCAT** and generate a catalog called **ZF_TCLG_MANAGE_APPS_ ADAPTUI**. Executing transaction **/UI2/FLPCAT** opens a new window titled **SAP Fiori Technical Launchpad Catalogs** to create **a technical catalog**, as shown in the figure below.

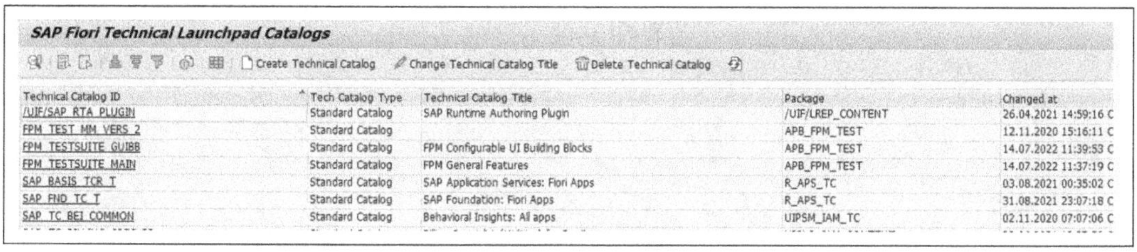

CHAPTER 15   SAP FIORI ADAPT UI

Figure 15-37. Transaction /UI2/FLPCAT initial screen

Select the **Create Technical Catalog** tab, which opens a window titled **Technical Catalog Title**, as shown in the figure below. Enter the following information in the figure below:

- **Technical Catalog ID**: ZF_TCLG_MONIT_BANK _APP_ADAPTUI
- **Catalog Type**: CAT
- **Tech. Catalog Type**: TCGL:FIN:BK – Monitor Bank Act -ADAPTUI
- **Package**: ZFIORI_PKG

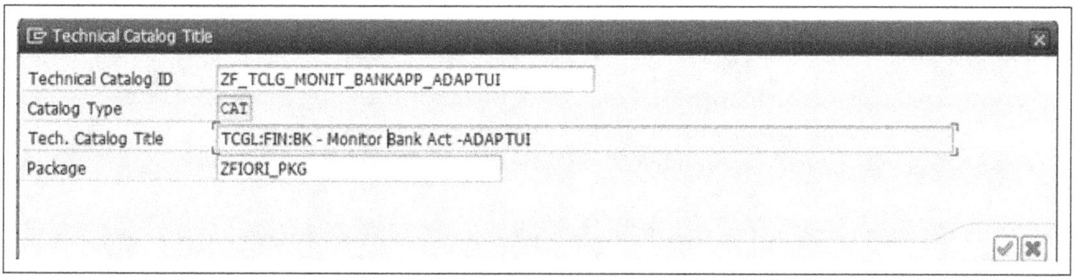

Figure 15-38. New technical catalog details

Click the continue icon and add the transport created earlier. Use the filter option to find the technical catalog created, which is displayed in the figure below.

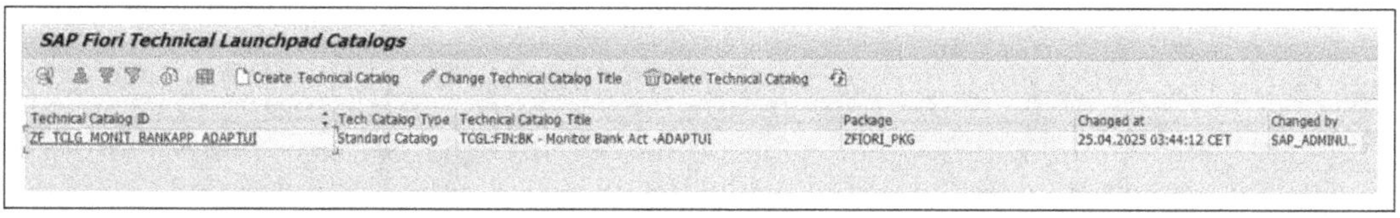

Figure 15-39. Technical catalog created

CHAPTER 15   SAP FIORI ADAPT UI

Double-clicking the technical catalog name opens a portal window to work on the catalog, as shown in the figure below.

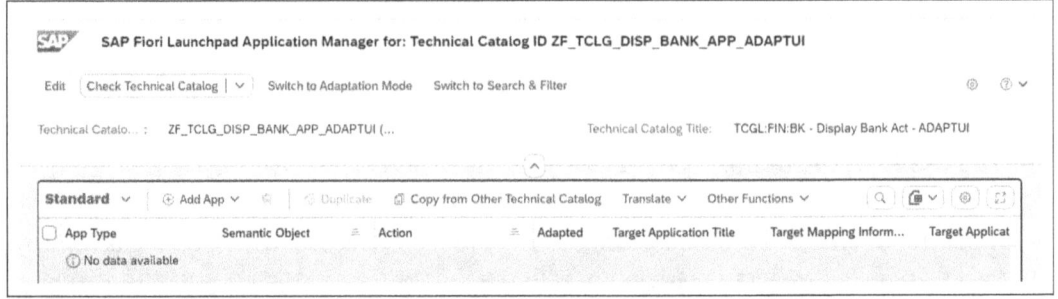

Figure 15-40. Blank technical catalog opens

The above figure displays a blank technical catalog. Under the **Add App** option, select the **SAPUI5 Fiori App** option, and it will ask for transport details. Once transport details are added, click **Continue** to proceed.

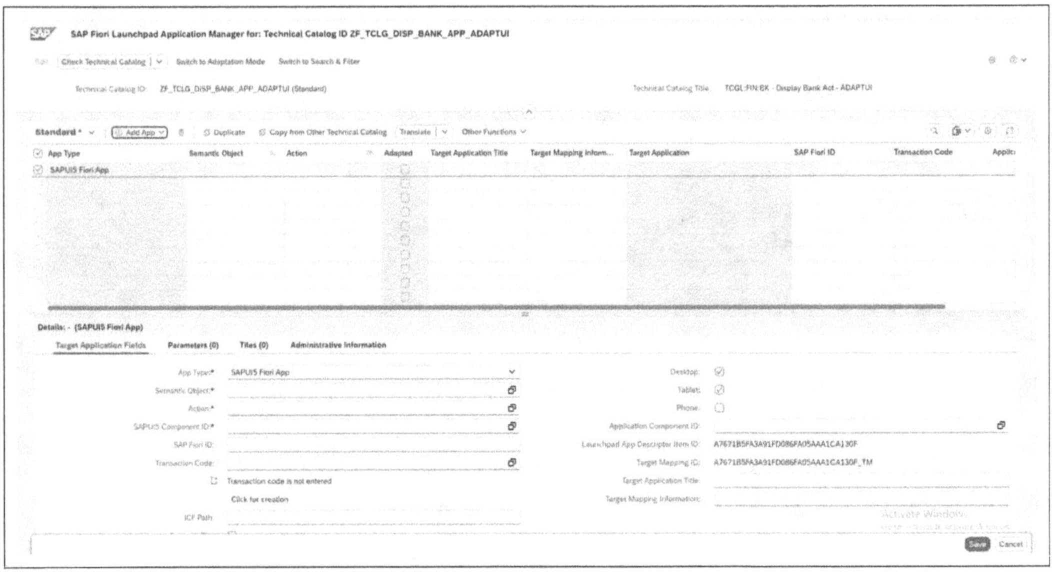

Figure 15-41. Details to enter for the SAPUI5 Fiori app

746

In the original SAP Fiori app shown in the figure above, after creating and saving an **app variant,** the variant appears as a **new app** that closely resembles the **original app F1366A** but includes your applied changes. It is important to note that the **Delete** button is not displayed as expected because it was removed, and several other fields have been added.

Note the Manage Bank Accounts (BankAccount-manageMasterData) app had a **semantic object** named **BankAccount**, which we add**,** and for a **semantic action**, we use monitor. Other information is entered as shown in the figure below.

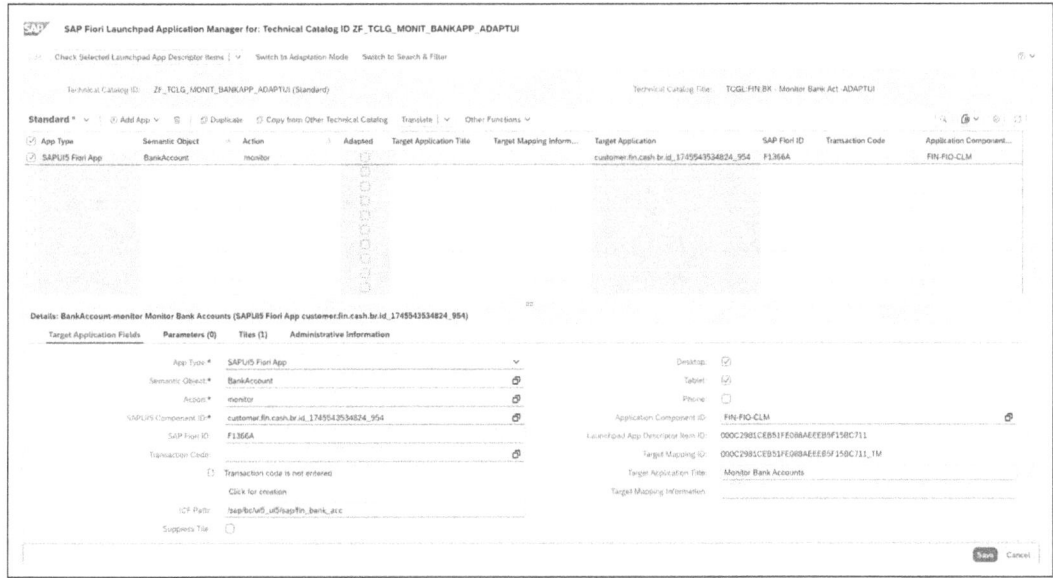

Figure 15-42. New display tile information added

Note You must enter the customer ID created earlier in the SAPUI5 Component ID field.

The system also created the tile. Open the option Tiles (1), which displays all the information related to the new tile called **Monitor Bank Accounts**, as shown in the figure below.

CHAPTER 15   SAP FIORI ADAPT UI

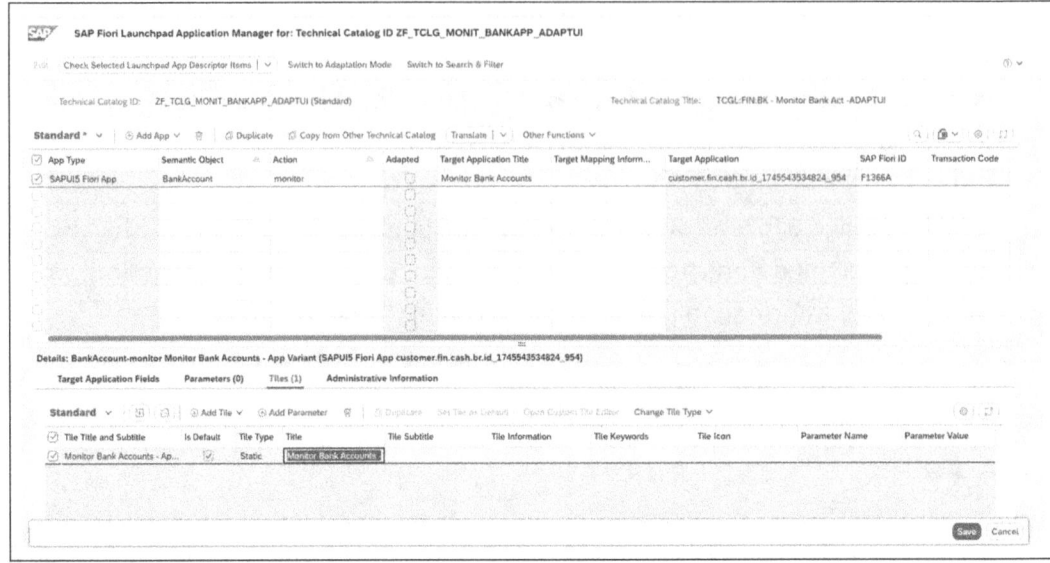

Figure 15-43.   System created a static tile automatically

The above figure shows that the system created the static tile automatically. Everything looks fine here. Click **Save** to save the settings. A message is displayed at the bottom of the screen stating **Data is saved**, as shown in the figure below.

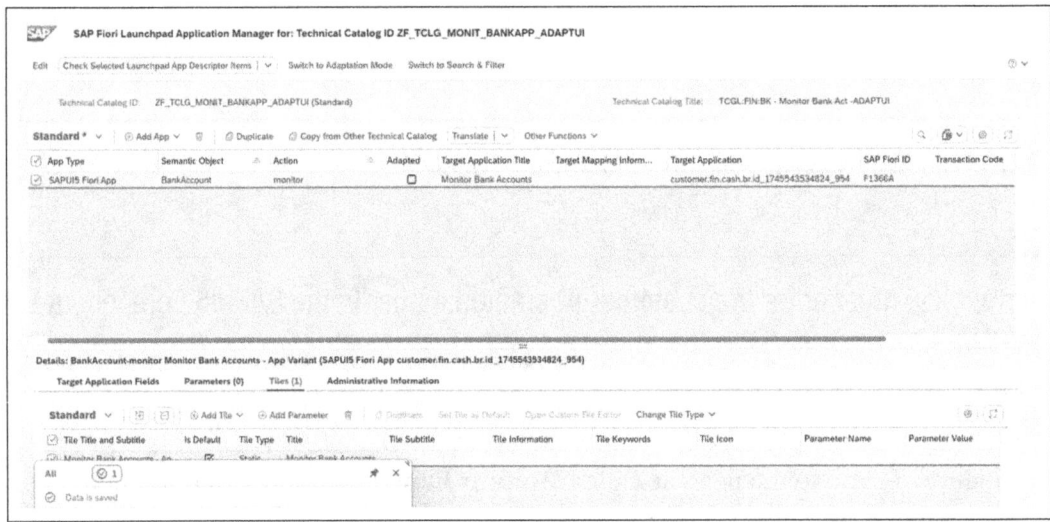

Figure 15-44.   Tile data saved

CHAPTER 15 SAP FIORI ADAPT UI

15.2.2 Create a New Business Catalog

The new business catalog was created, as shown in the figure below.

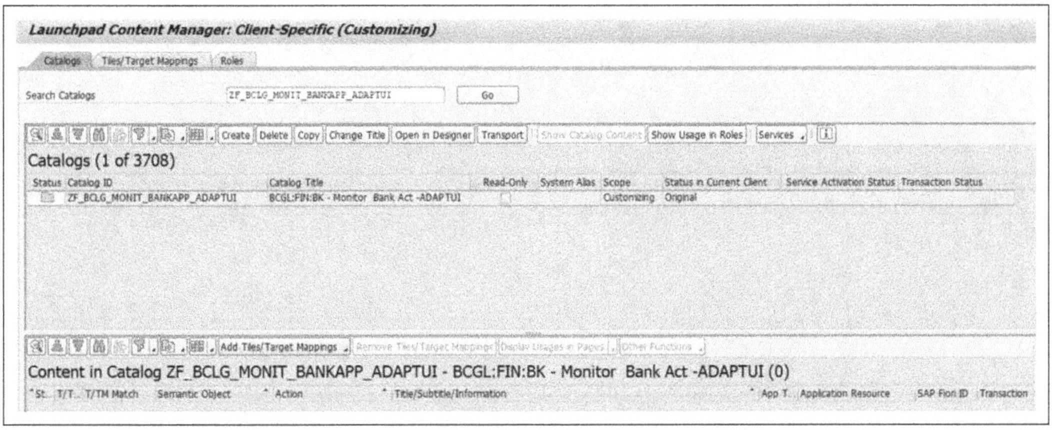

Figure 15-45. Custom business catalog created

Now, we need to add the tile by clicking the tab Add Tiles/Target Mapping. We will search for the app variant tile based on the technical catalog created earlier, as shown in the figure below.

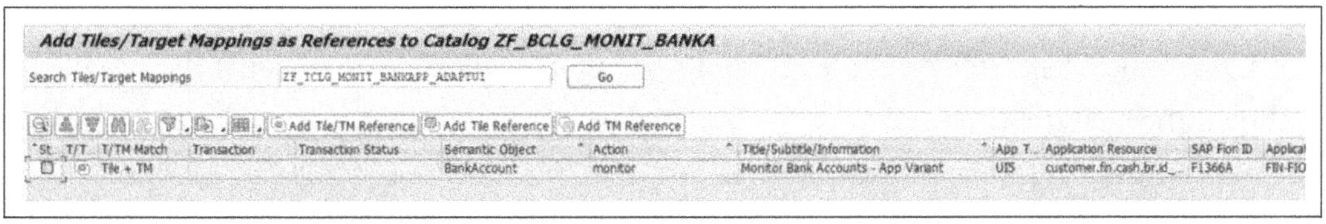

Figure 15-46. App variant tile found and referenced via the technical catalog

Once the app variant is added to the business catalog, it is updated, as shown in the figure below.

749

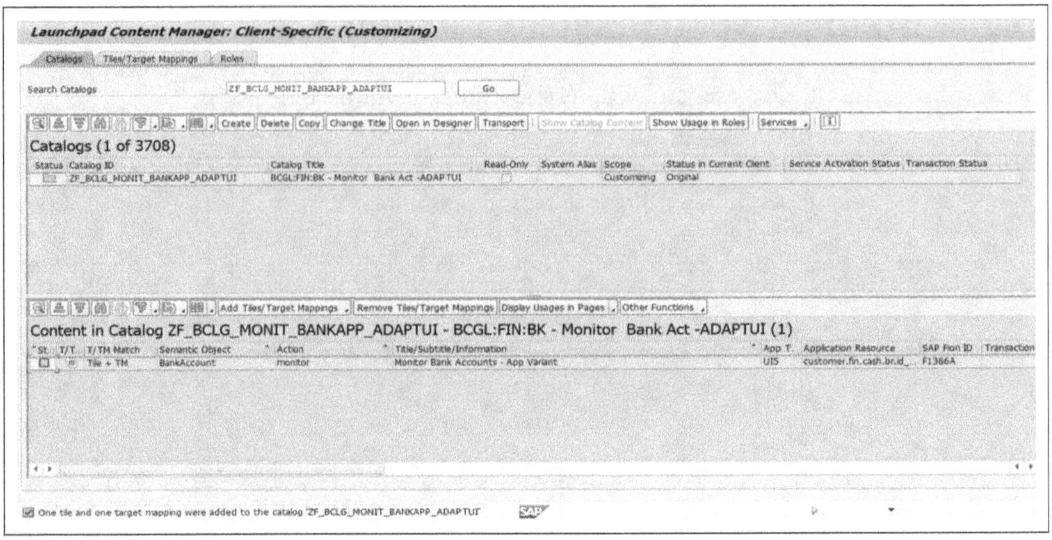

CHAPTER 15   SAP FIORI ADAPT UI

Figure 15-47.   App variant tile added to the custom business catalog

15.2.3 Create a Business Role and Assign the Catalog

The new custom business catalog that has been created needs to be added to the business role, and the authorization should be generated and then assigned to the test user ID. The business role created will be used to test the new **app variant tile** created, as shown in the figure below.

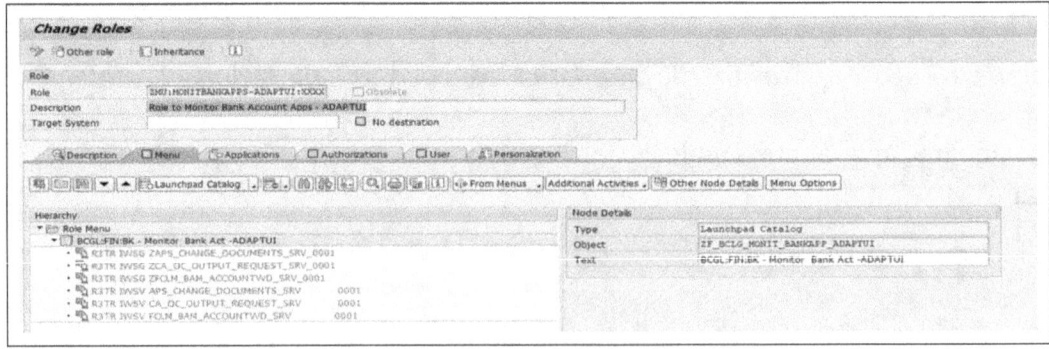

Figure 15-48.   The role created for testing and the created custom business catalog assigned and generated

15.2.4 Testing and Validation

The test user logs into the SAP Fiori Launchpad and clicks the **User Menu,** followed by the **App Finder** option, to locate the custom business catalog. The new custom app is displayed, as shown in the figure below.

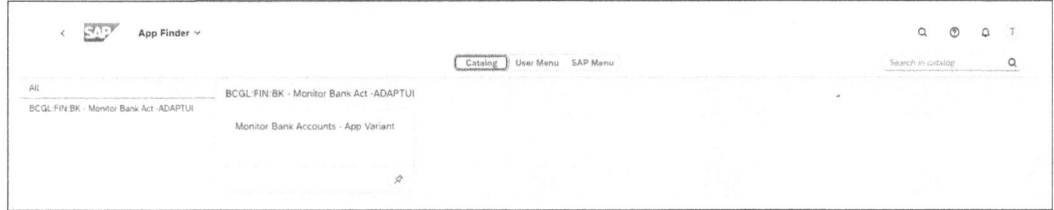

Figure 15-49. The test user ID can visualize the app variant tile

In the above figure, the test user ID can visualize the tile within the custom business catalog. The output is displayed when the user executes the **Monitor Bank Accounts – App Variant** app, as shown in the figure below.

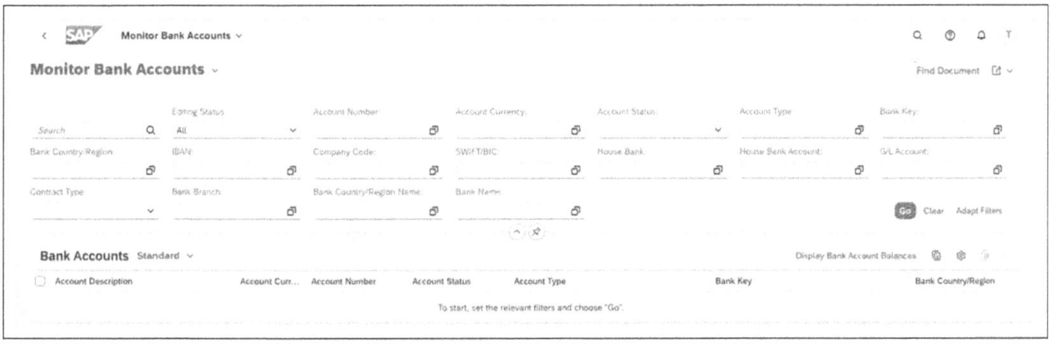

Figure 15-50. The app variant tile successfully executed

The app variant tile was executed successfully, as shown in the figure above. Enter a few parameters as shown in the figure below and click **Go** to run the app.

CHAPTER 15   SAP FIORI ADAPT UI

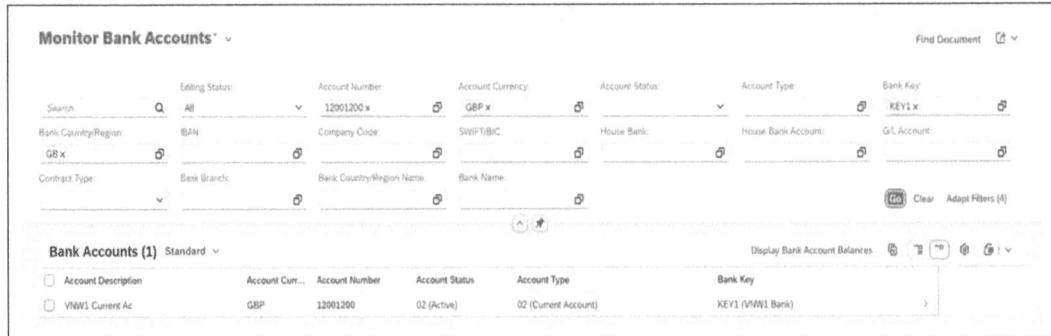

Figure 15-51. Bank account information displayed

The figure above displays the bank account information for a given account number.

15.2.5 Transport

Once everything looks fine, the same **app variant** can be **transported** by selecting the **Adapt UI** option for it and selecting the **truck symbol**.

15.2.6 Conclusion

Thus, a Manage Bank Accounts app was successfully converted into a Monitor Bank Accounts app using Adapt UI.

15.3 Summary

SAP Fiori's Adapt UI feature enables key users to modify the interface of Fiori apps without coding, allowing customization to fit specific business processes and needs. These changes are implemented in real time and impact all users, ensuring a consistent experience across the organization. This capability enhances user engagement and productivity and encourages the adoption of Fiori apps by making them more relevant and efficient. Similarly, SAP Fiori app variants provide a powerful way for organizations to tailor standard Fiori applications to meet unique business requirements. These variants improve user experience and productivity while maintaining the integrity of the underlying system. By allowing applications to adapt to users instead of the other way around, Fiori app variants ensure that SAP Fiori effectively supports your business goals.

CHAPTER 16

SAP Fiori Reports

SAP Fiori provides various modern, user-friendly reporting tools to enhance decision-making across business functions. With features like Smart Business KPIs, analytical list pages, and overview pages, users can access real-time insights, interactive reports, and multidimensional analyses directly from the Fiori Launchpad. These role-based reports are tailored to meet specific business needs, allowing users to easily visualize data through charts and tables and personalize, filter, and export reports for deeper analysis. Additionally, administrators benefit from specialized reports that monitor system health, user adoption, performance, and security, enabling proactive issue resolution and optimization for a smooth SAP Fiori experience.

16.1 Introduction

SAP Fiori provides a comprehensive suite of built-in transaction codes and reports that improve reporting, monitoring, and troubleshooting of applications and user access. SAP Fiori makes reporting easy by offering tools and transactions that help users monitor, analyze, and manage apps and roles. For instance, **/UI2/FLPCA** (Fiori Launchpad Content Aggregator) provides a detailed view of which catalogs and apps are assigned to users based on their roles, making it easier to troubleshoot missing tiles. **/UI2/RSP_LIST** displays a list of all available Fiori apps, their technical IDs, and their status in the system. **/UI2/FLIA** (Fiori Launchpad Inactive Apps) helps identify inactive or broken tiles due to missing OData or ICF services. **/UI2/FLT** allows administrators to analyze which tiles are visible to specific users and from which catalogs, making role troubleshooting more efficient. Similarly, **/UI2/FLC** (Fiori Launchpad Catalogs) provides a detailed view of catalog contents and where each app is used. You can use the classic transaction tool SUIM to generate reports on roles, users, and authorizations for broader authorization checks. Additionally, the report **/UI2/FLP_ADMIN_UI** gives a central dashboard for technical analysis, helping identify performance bottlenecks, failed apps, and UI-related issues, along with helping in troubleshooting and analyzing Fiori Launchpad issues.

CHAPTER 16   SAP FIORI REPORTS

SAP Fiori provides modern reporting features with embedded analytics. Users can access interactive reports and key performance indicators (KPIs) directly from the Launchpad. With tools like Smart Business KPIs and analytical list pages, users can easily visualize data, customize reports, and make better decisions with real-time insights.

Thus, SAP Fiori's various reporting tools are crucial for administrators, security, and support teams, as they enhance the practicality and effectiveness of monitoring. These tools simplify tracking key elements such as app availability, user access, and overall performance. By leveraging these tools, teams can ensure optimal application functioning, promptly address issues, and improve user satisfaction, contributing to a more efficient and well-managed system environment.

Note   SAP has many other transactions and reports for analysis and reporting, which are beyond the scope of this book.

We will use the previously created role, **ZMU_TSK_FIN_AR_INVS_CRMOS:XXXX**, to demonstrate how various transactions and reports display data. The role includes spaces and pages, groups, and custom business catalogs with associated tiles. The two custom business catalogs assigned are listed below:

- ZF_BCLG_FIN_AR_INV_CRMEMO
- ZF_BCLG_FIN_AR_CS_ACCT_CLG

16.2 Transaction: /UI2/FLPCA

16.2.1 Introduction

This section will cover the report published using the transaction code **/UI2/FLPCA,** also called the **Launchpad Content Aggregator**. This transaction helps you analyze Launchpad content, including catalogs, tiles, target mappings, and roles. This tool is helpful in troubleshooting problems and ensuring everything is set up correctly. This tool prints reports that can be downloaded in various formats for further analysis. This section of the SAP Fiori report will also provide step-by-step instructions on generating a **Fiori Role Test Matrix**, an essential tool for capturing positive and negative testing for any given roles, including the SAP-delivered **SAP_BR*** roles within an organization in either the sandbox or the **development** environments. The **Test Matrix** will list associated role names, role descriptions, and associated attributes, empowering the functional team with the responsibility to decide which apps are needed or not during the initial stage of development.

16.2.2 Prerequisite

- The BASIS team has activated the required **OData services** and **ICF services**.

- If using the SAP-delivered business role (SAP_BR*), it must be activated using transaction code **STC01** through task list **SAP_FIORI_FCM_CONTENT_ACTIVATION** and generated successfully. These roles must be copied into the customer naming convention methodology.

- Make sure all the associated **OData** and **SICF** services for the given role are **registered** and **activated**.

- Check that the apps have respective IWSG/IWSV components in the role menu tab and that authorization has been generated.

Note This transaction gives and generates a report for single roles only and not the derived roles.

16.2.3 Using Transaction /UI2/FLPCA

To generate the report and download roles and their respective attributes in **SAP GUI**, we can use the transaction **/UI2/FLPCA**, which stands for **Launchpad Content Aggregator**. Once the transaction is executed, a window opens titled **SAP Fiori Launchpad Content Aggregator: Client-Specific (Customizing),** as shown in the figure below.

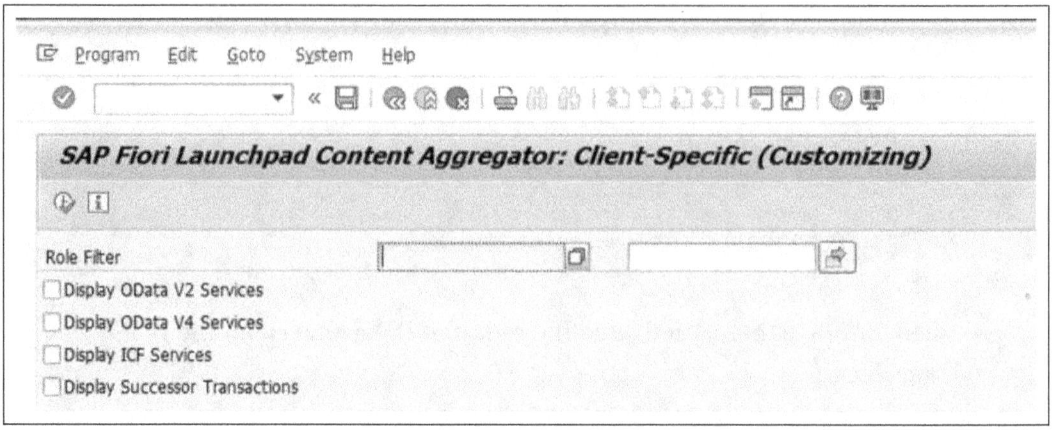

CHAPTER 16 SAP FIORI REPORTS

Figure 16-1. Transaction code /UI2/FLPCA initial input screen

In the above figure, the transaction allows filtering the roles via the **Role Filter** option. Here you can choose single or multiple roles. It also lists four options to select from to display data, and they are listed as follows:

- Display OData V2 Services
- Display OData V4 Services
- Display ICF Services
- Display Successor Transactions

In the above figure, we have an option, **Display Successor Transactions**, for selection. Selecting this option allows Fiori administrators or security administrators to view transactions or apps that succeed any particular existing implemented Fiori app. This feature helps manage Fiori app content, showing how applications evolve. Administrators can understand the relationship between legacy and updated applications by displaying successor transactions, ensuring a smooth user transition. It supports troubleshooting, helps maintain continuity, and facilitates user training on new functionalities, optimizing user experience during transitions to newer applications. It is invaluable during the upgrade. Furthermore, all other options to select have been defined and discussed in previous chapters.

The transaction displays the role's contents in a tabular format, including OData services, ICF services, SAP Fiori app IDs, and other related information. It helps administrators identify which content is assigned to their business roles and what is available in the App Finder, ensuring they can see all apps and tiles linked to their specific roles.

CHAPTER 16   SAP FIORI REPORTS

16.2.4 Execute the Transaction

In the **Role Filter** option of the transaction above, enter the role name and select the first three options, as shown in the figure below.

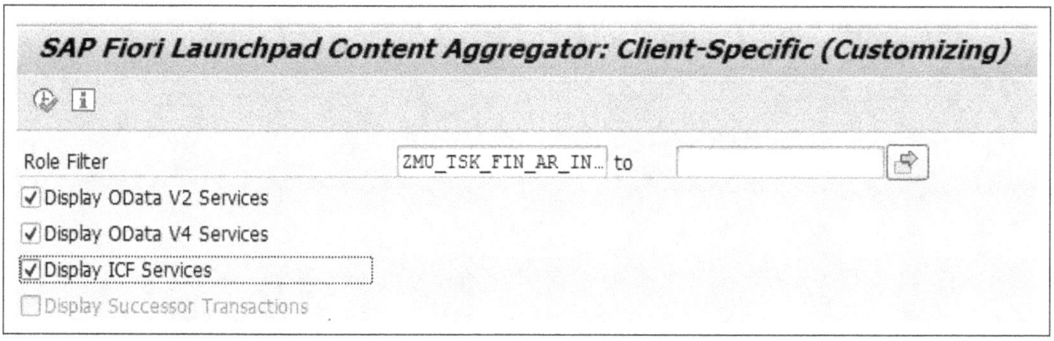

Figure 16-2. Business role information entered with three options selected

When selecting the first three options, the fourth option, **Display Successor Transactions,** is grayed out and cannot be selected, as shown in the figure above.

> **Note**   We can also input multiple roles for report generation.

To proceed, click the **execute** icon and wait a few minutes for the output/report to be generated, which is displayed, as shown in the figure below. The report is very lengthy and has many columns of information. The output screen displays desired roles and their attributes. Scroll right for more attributes. The output has been split into eight screens to display data as shown in the figures below.

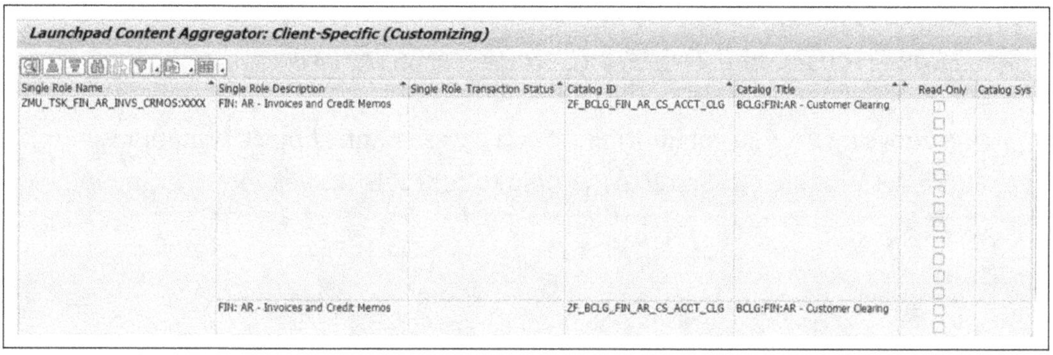

Figure 16-3. Transaction /UI2/FLPCA output screen 1 of 8

CHAPTER 16   SAP FIORI REPORTS

In the above figure, you get information such as the role name, role description, catalog ID, and catalog title.

Scroll to the right to continue to see more information.

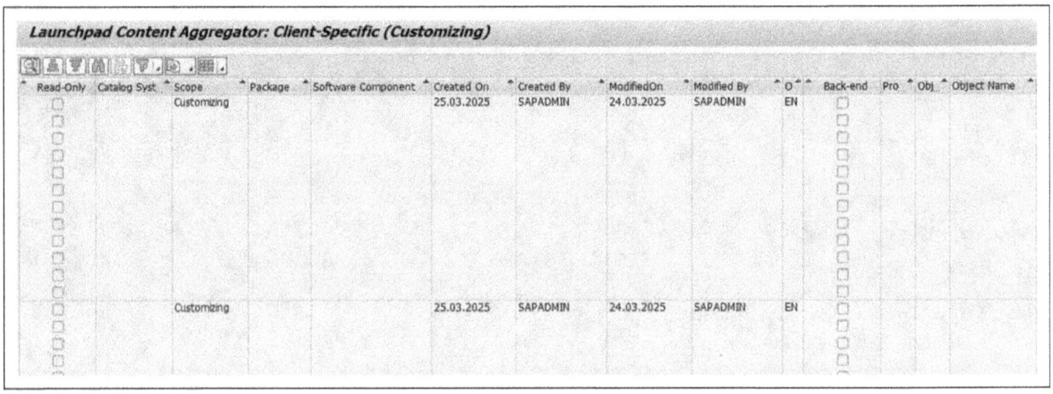

Figure 16-4. Transaction /UI2/FLPCA output screen 2 of 8

In the above figure, you get information such as creation date, modified date, etc. Scroll to the right to continue to see more information.

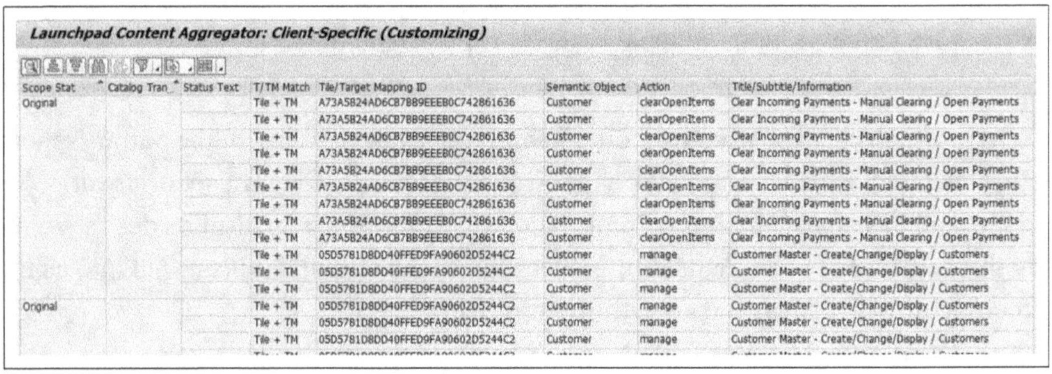

Figure 16-5. Transaction /UI2/FLPCA output screen 3 of 8

In the above figure, you get information such as semantic object, semantic action, tile/subtitle description, etc. Scroll to the right to continue to see more information.

App Ty.	Application Resource	Target Mapping System Alias	SAP Fiori ID	Transaction	TNX Status	Application Component ID	Intent	Tile Semantic Parameters	TM Parameters
UI5	fin.ar.manualclearing		F0773	F0773		FI-FIO-AR	Customer-cle...		(Customer=%%UserDefault
UI5	fin.ar.manualclearing		F0773	F0773		FI-FIO-AR	Customer-cle...		(Customer=%%UserDefault
UI5	fin.ar.manualclearing		F0773	F0773		FI-FIO-AR	Customer-cle...		(Customer=%%UserDefault
UI5	fin.ar.manualclearing		F0773	F0773		FI-FIO-AR	Customer-cle...		(Customer=%%UserDefault
UI5	fin.ar.manualclearing		F0773	F0773		FI-FIO-AR	Customer-cle...		(Customer=%%UserDefault
UI5	fin.ar.manualclearing		F0773	F0773		FI-FIO-AR	Customer-cle...		(Customer=%%UserDefault
UI5	fin.ar.manualclearing		F0773	F0773		FI-FIO-AR	Customer-cle...		(Customer=%%UserDefault
UI5	fin.ar.manualclearing		F0773	F0773		FI-FIO-AR	Customer-cle...		(Customer=%%UserDefault
UI5	mdm.md.customer.manage		F0850A	F0850A		LO-MD-FIO-CM	Customer-ma...		(BusinessPartner=>Business
UI5	mdm.md.customer.manage		F0850A	F0850A		LO-MD-FIO-CM	Customer-ma...		(BusinessPartner=>Business
UI5	mdm.md.customer.manage		F0850A	F0850A		LO-MD-FIO-CM	Customer-ma...		(BusinessPartner=>Business
UI5	mdm.md.customer.manage		F0850A	F0850A		LO-MD-FIO-CM	Customer-ma...		(BusinessPartner=>Business
UI5	mdm.md.customer.manage		F0850A	F0850A		LO-MD-FIO-CM	Customer-ma...		(BusinessPartner=>Business

Figure 16-6. *Transaction /UI2/FLPCA output screen 4 of 8*

In the above figure, you get information such as SAP Fiori ID, transaction code, intent, etc. Scroll to the right to continue to see more information.

Original Tile ID	Original Tile Catalog ID	Tile	Tile Cat.	Tile Launchpad App Descriptor Item ID	Tile Type	Tile Title	Tile Subtitle	Tile Keywords	Info
0002TPL8V25EQSOMT1CD4OOQ9	SAP_TC_FIN_FO_COMMON		CAT	42010AEE2A7C1EEAA884BF9549818EDE	DYNAMIC	Clear Incomin...	Manual Clearing		Open Payme...
0002TPL8V25EQSOMT1CD4OOQ9	SAP_TC_FIN_FO_COMMON		CAT	42010AEE2A7C1EEAA884BF9549818EDE	DYNAMIC	Clear Incomin...	Manual Clearing		Open Payme...
0002TPL8V25EQSOMT1CD4OOQ9	SAP_TC_FIN_FO_COMMON		CAT	42010AEE2A7C1EEAA884BF9549818EDE	DYNAMIC	Clear Incomin...	Manual Clearing		Open Payme...
0002TPL8V25EQSOMT1CD4OOQ9	SAP_TC_FIN_FO_COMMON		CAT	42010AEE2A7C1EEAA884BF9549818EDE	DYNAMIC	Clear Incomin...	Manual Clearing		Open Payme...
0002TPL8V25EQSOMT1CD4OOQ9	SAP_TC_FIN_FO_COMMON		CAT	42010AEE2A7C1EEAA884BF9549818EDE	DYNAMIC	Clear Incomin...	Manual Clearing		Open Payme...
0002TPL8V25EQSOMT1CD4OOQ9	SAP_TC_FIN_FO_COMMON		CAT	42010AEE2A7C1EEAA884BF9549818EDE	DYNAMIC	Clear Incomin...	Manual Clearing		Open Payme...
0002TPL8V25EQSOMT1CD4OOQ9	SAP_TC_FIN_FO_COMMON		CAT	42010AEE2A7C1EEAA884BF9549818EDE	DYNAMIC	Clear Incomin...	Manual Clearing		Open Payme...
0002TPL8V25EQSOMT1CD4OOQ9	SAP_TC_FIN_FO_COMMON		CAT	42010AEE2A7C1EEAA884BF9549818EDE	DYNAMIC	Clear Incomin...	Manual Clearing		Open Payme...
0002TPL8V25GKOVGQNEWW8CED	SAP_TC_CMD_BP_COMMON		CAT	42010AEE2A7C1EEAA8877864EEE70F11	DYNAMIC	Customer Mas...	Create/Chang...	Customer, Ma...	Customers
0002TPL8V25GKOVGQNEWW8CED	SAP_TC_CMD_BP_COMMON		CAT	42010AEE2A7C1EEAA8877864EEE70F11	DYNAMIC	Customer Mas...	Create/Chang...	Customer, Ma...	Customers
0002TPL8V25GKOVGQNEWW8CED	SAP_TC_CMD_BP_COMMON		CAT	42010AEE2A7C1EEAA8877864EEE70F11	DYNAMIC	Customer Mas...	Create/Chang...	Customer, Ma...	Customers

Figure 16-7. *Transaction /UI2/FLPCA output screen 5 of 8*

In the above figure, you get information such as original catalog ID, tile type, tile title, title subtitle, keywords in the tile, etc. Scroll to the right to continue to see more information.

Tile Icon URL	Original Target Mapping ID	Original Target Mapping Catalog ID	TM	TM Cat.	TM Launchpad App Descriptor Item ID	TM Title	TM Information	Desktop	Tablet
sap-icon://Fio...	0002TPL8V25EQSOXODV5UDBVC	SAP_TC_FIN_FO_COMMON		CAT	42010AEE2A7C1EEAA884BF9549818EDE	Clear Incomin...	F0773	✓	✓
sap-icon://Fio...	0002TPL8V25EQSOXODV5UDBVC	SAP_TC_FIN_FO_COMMON		CAT	42010AEE2A7C1EEAA884BF9549818EDE	Clear Incomin...	F0773	✓	✓
sap-icon://Fio...	0002TPL8V25EQSOXODV5UDBVC	SAP_TC_FIN_FO_COMMON		CAT	42010AEE2A7C1EEAA884BF9549818EDE	Clear Incomin...	F0773	✓	✓
sap-icon://Fio...	0002TPL8V25EQSOXODV5UDBVC	SAP_TC_FIN_FO_COMMON		CAT	42010AEE2A7C1EEAA884BF9549818EDE	Clear Incomin...	F0773	✓	✓
sap-icon://Fio...	0002TPL8V25EQSOXODV5UDBVC	SAP_TC_FIN_FO_COMMON		CAT	42010AEE2A7C1EEAA884BF9549818EDE	Clear Incomin...	F0773	✓	✓
sap-icon://Fio...	0002TPL8V25EQSOXODV5UDBVC	SAP_TC_FIN_FO_COMMON		CAT	42010AEE2A7C1EEAA884BF9549818EDE	Clear Incomin...	F0773	✓	✓
sap-icon://Fio...	0002TPL8V25EQSOXODV5UDBVC	SAP_TC_FIN_FO_COMMON		CAT	42010AEE2A7C1EEAA884BF9549818EDE	Clear Incomin...	F0773	✓	✓
sap-icon://Fio...	0002TPL8V25EQSOXODV5UDBVC	SAP_TC_FIN_FO_COMMON		CAT	42010AEE2A7C1EEAA884BF9549818EDE	Clear Incomin...	F0773	✓	✓
sap-icon://Fio...	0002TPL8V25GKOVLC7BXB46A6	SAP_TC_CMD_BP_COMMON		CAT	42010AEE2A7C1EEAA8877864EEE70F11	Customer Mas...		✓	✓
sap-icon://Fio...	0002TPL8V25GKOVLC7BXB46A6	SAP_TC_CMD_BP_COMMON		CAT	42010AEE2A7C1EEAA8877864EEE70F11	Customer Mas...		✓	✓
sap-icon://Fio...	0002TPL8V25GKOVLC7BXB46A6	SAP_TC_CMD_BP_COMMON		CAT	42010AEE2A7C1EEAA8877864EEE70F11	Customer Mas...		✓	✓

Figure 16-8. *Transaction /UI2/FLPCA output screen 6 of 8*

CHAPTER 16   SAP FIORI REPORTS

In the above figure, you get information such as original target mapping catalog ID, target mapping title, TM information, etc. Scroll to the right to continue to see more information.

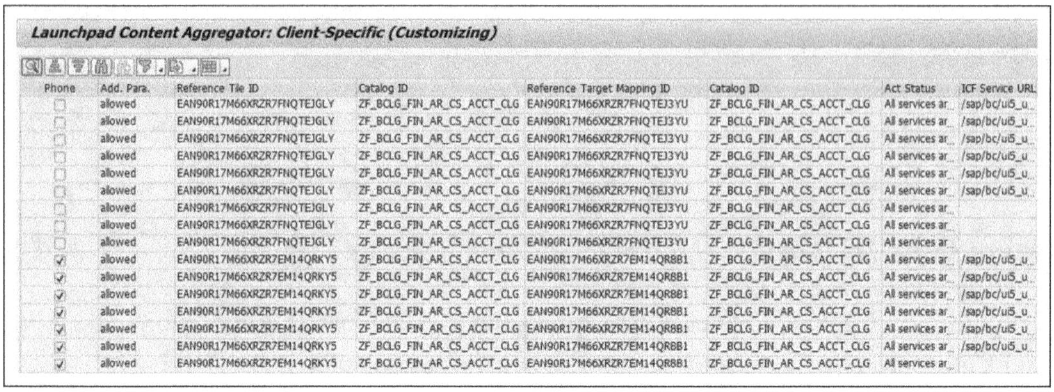

Figure 16-9.   *Transaction /UI2/FLPCA output screen 7 of 8*

In the above figure, you get information such as custom catalog ID in the role, activation status of the services of the app, ICF services associated with the App, etc. Scroll to the right to continue to see more information.

Figure 16-10.   *Transaction /UI2/FLPCA output screen 8 of 8*

In the above figure, you get information such as OData service name, OData service activation status, etc.

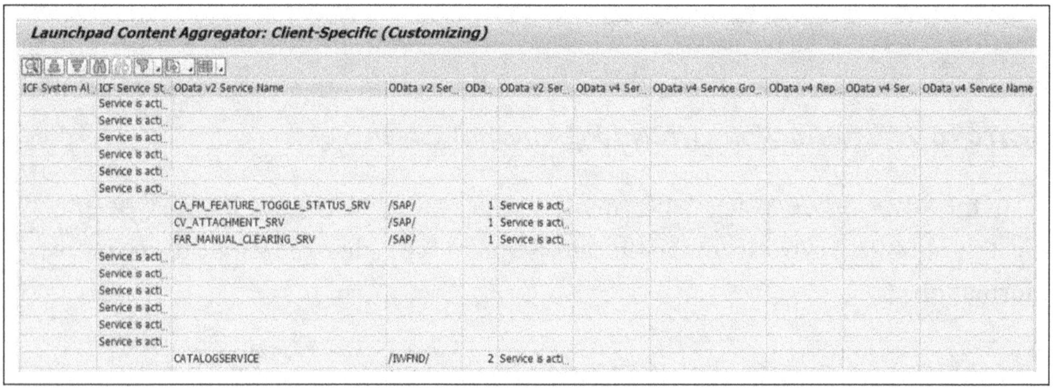

Since visualizing the data is very cumbersome, you can export this output to an **Excel spreadshee**t by clicking the first row, and a box will open as shown in the figure below.

760

CHAPTER 16 SAP FIORI REPORTS

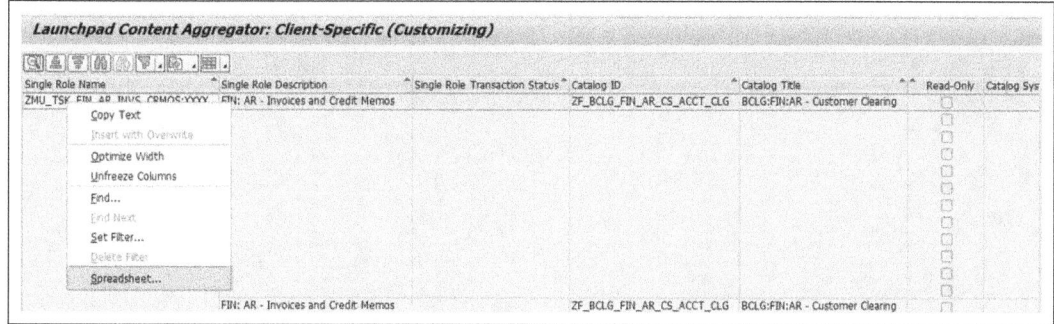

Figure 16-11. Exporting the output of the transaction /UI2/FLPCA into a spreadsheet

Select the **Spreadsheet** option in the above figure and save the file on the computer. In our example, ee save the file by specifying its file name as **EXPORT_WITH_3 SERVICES**, as shown in the figure below.

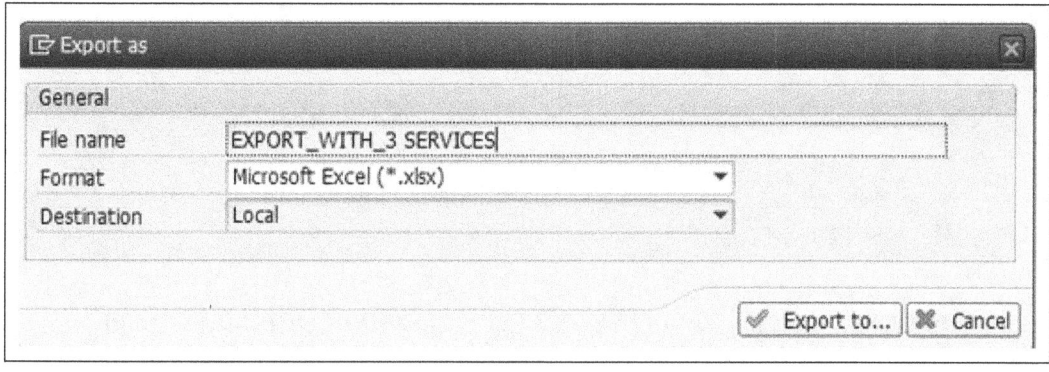

Figure 16-12. Exporting the file with the file name

Click the **Export to** ✓ Export to... tab to download, as shown in the figure above.

Once downloaded, you can open the **Excel** file to display the various columns of data, as shown in the figure below.

761

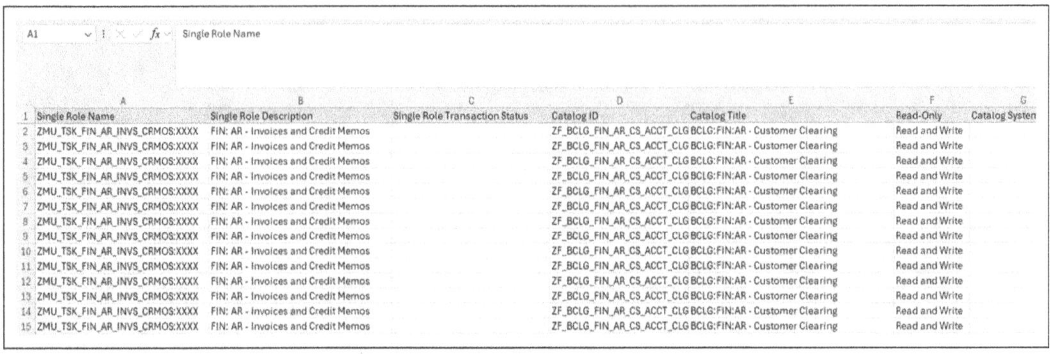

CHAPTER 16   SAP FIORI REPORTS

Figure 16-13. The transaction /UI2/FLPCA output displayed in Excel

Next, select the fourth option, **Display Successor Transactions,** as shown in the figure below.

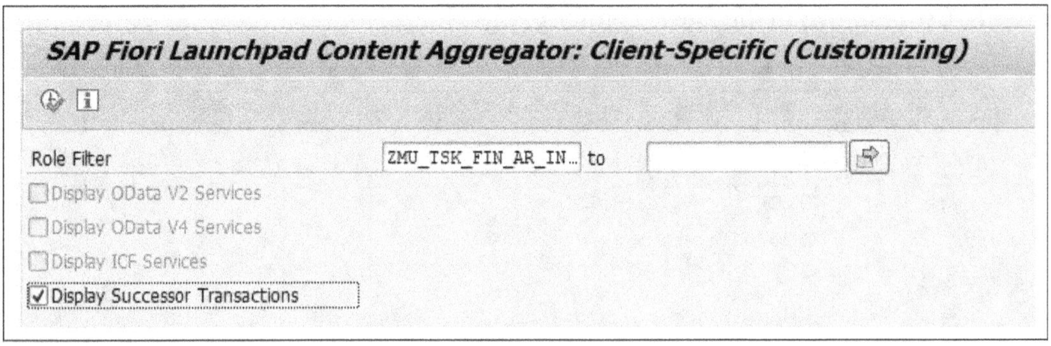

Figure 16-14. The transaction /UI2/FLPCA with option Display Successor Transactions

Once the **Display Successor Transactions** option is selected, the three listed service options are **grayed out**, as shown in the figure **above**. Click the **execute** icon to display the output.

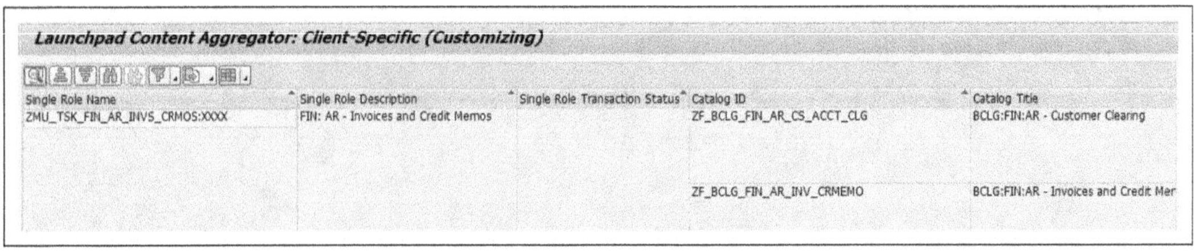

Figure 16-15. The Transaction /UI2/FLPCA with option Display Successor Transactions output screen 1 of 2

CHAPTER 16 SAP FIORI REPORTS

Scroll to the right of the above screen to check the **Successor Transaction** column data, which is empty in this case, as shown in the figure below. Since the column is empty, this indicates that, in our role, there are **no tiles with a new successor app**.

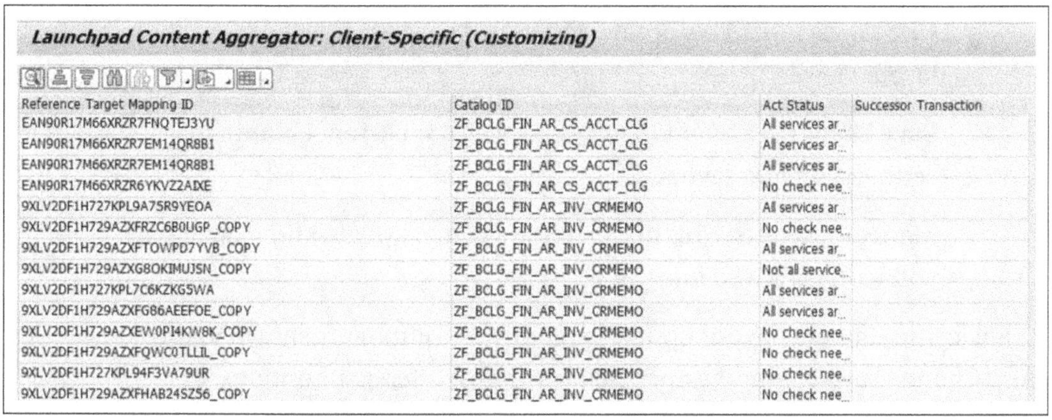

Figure 16-16. The transaction /UI2/FLPCA with option Display Successor Transactions output screen 2 of 2

Note Since we are working with a new S/4HANA 2023 FPS02 directly, we do not have any data in the Successor Transaction column. However, if you are upgrading from a lower S/4HANA Fiori version to a higher version of S/4HANA Fiori such as S/4HANA 2023, this report will suggest the successor apps in the column.

SAP offers various options to customize the order of columns, the type of data to export, and the layout. To do this, select the pull-down menu and click the **Change Layout option** to open the **Change Layout** window, as shown in the figure below.

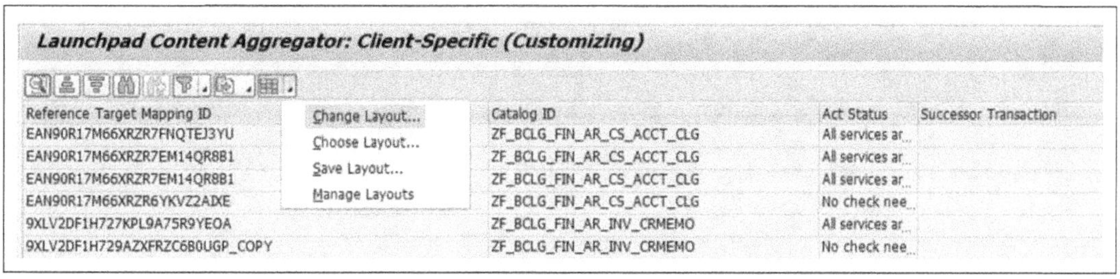

Figure 16-17. Selecting the option Change Layout

SAP has provided four options for layout, and they are as listed below:

Change Layout: This option allows you to adjust which columns are shown and in what order.

Choose Layout: This option allows you to select a saved layout view.

Save Layout: This option lets you save your current column settings as a new layout.

Manage Layouts: This option allows you to update and manage your current Saved layouts.

Select the **Change Layout** option to modify the output. As shown in the figure below, a new Change Layout window opens. This window offers four options:

Displayed Columns: This option allows you to show or hide specific columns.

Sort Order: This option allows you to arrange data based on selected columns.

Filter: This option allows you to display only rows that meet certain conditions.

Display. This option allows you to apply and view the selected layout settings.

CHAPTER 16 SAP FIORI REPORTS

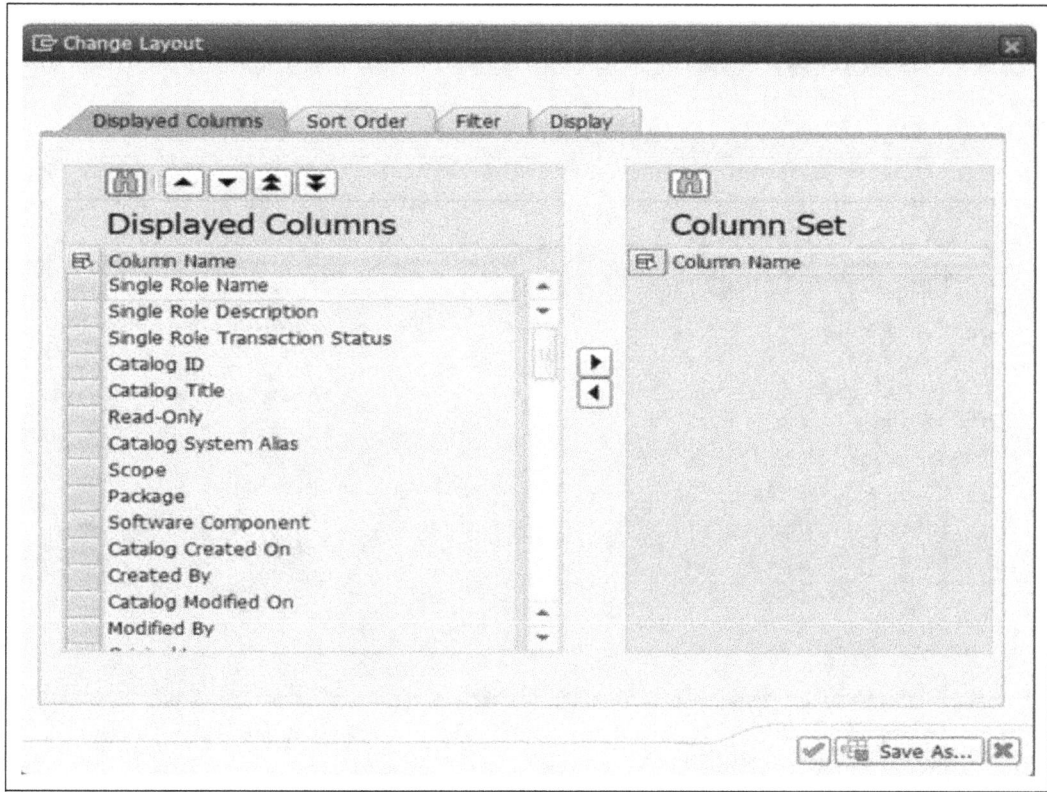

Figure 16-18. *Change Layout screen for selection of data to be displayed*

Furthermore, the Displayed Columns tab in **Change Layout** box has two options: **Displayed Columns** and **Column Set**. The former shows the selected output, while the latter does not. As shown below, use the arrows to arrange the columns for the final layout. We must rearrange the Column Name section to set up the Displayed Columns. Click the icon 🗒 under **Displayed Columns** to select the entire section, as shown in the figure below.

765

CHAPTER 16　SAP FIORI REPORTS

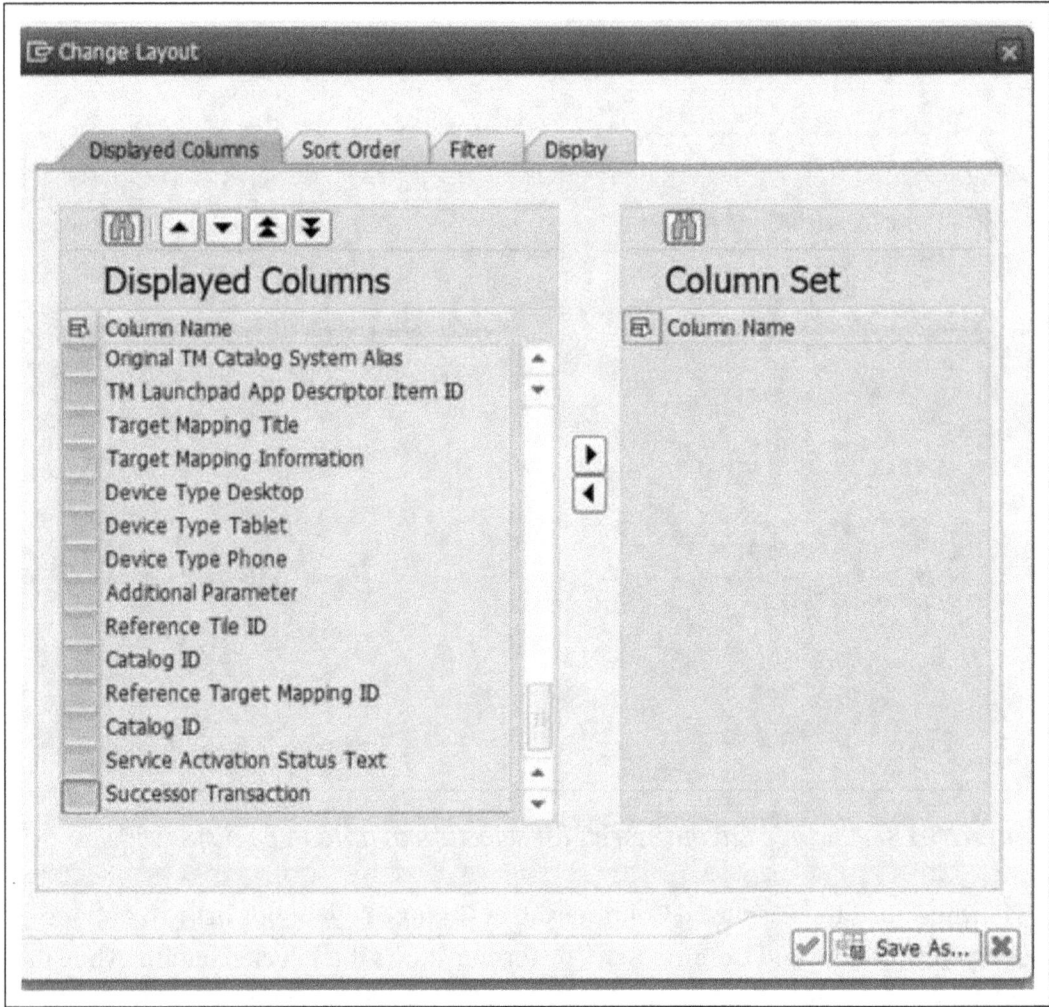

Figure 16-19. *Selected all fields within Display Columns*

Initially, move everything to **Column Set** by clicking the right arrow , as shown in the figure below.

CHAPTER 16 ■ SAP FIORI REPORTS

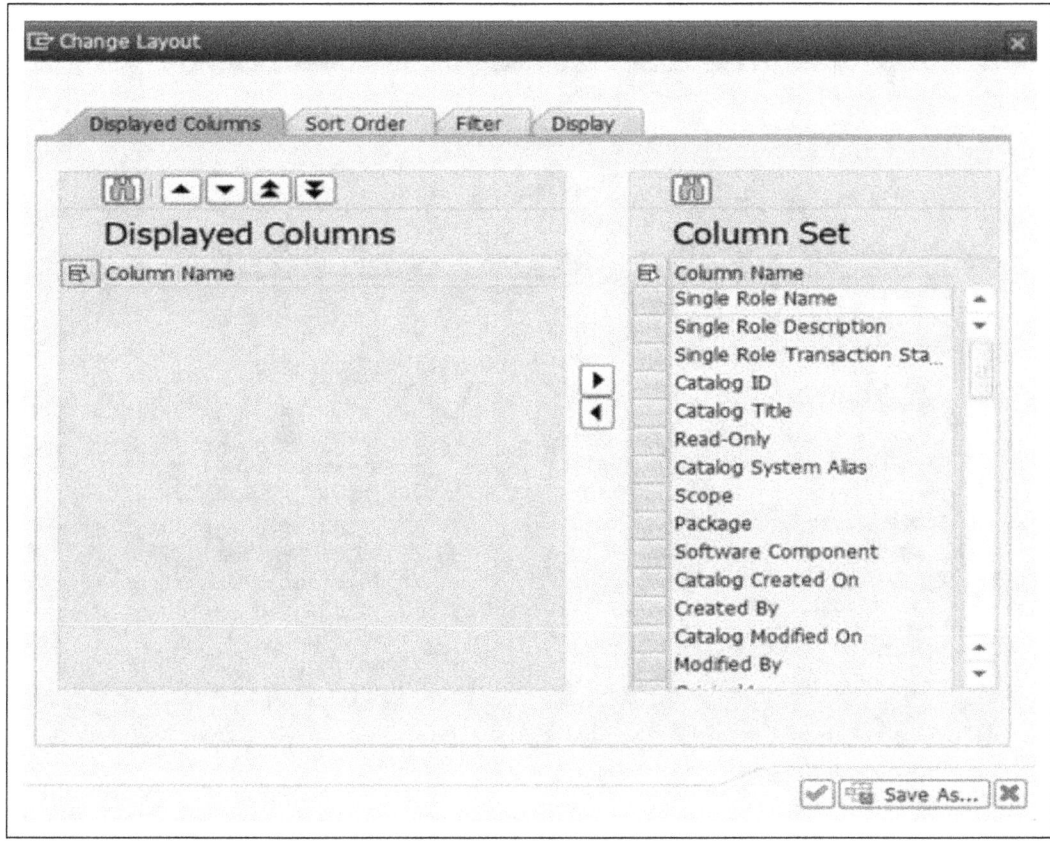

Figure 16-20. *All data fields moved to Column Set*

Use the left arrow to select and move data from **Column Set** to **Display Columns**, as shown in the figure below.

Figure 16-21. *Final Change Layout screen selection for data output*

After selecting the desired columns, click the icon ⌷ Save As... **Save As** to save the layout for future use, as shown in the figure below.

CHAPTER 16 SAP FIORI REPORTS

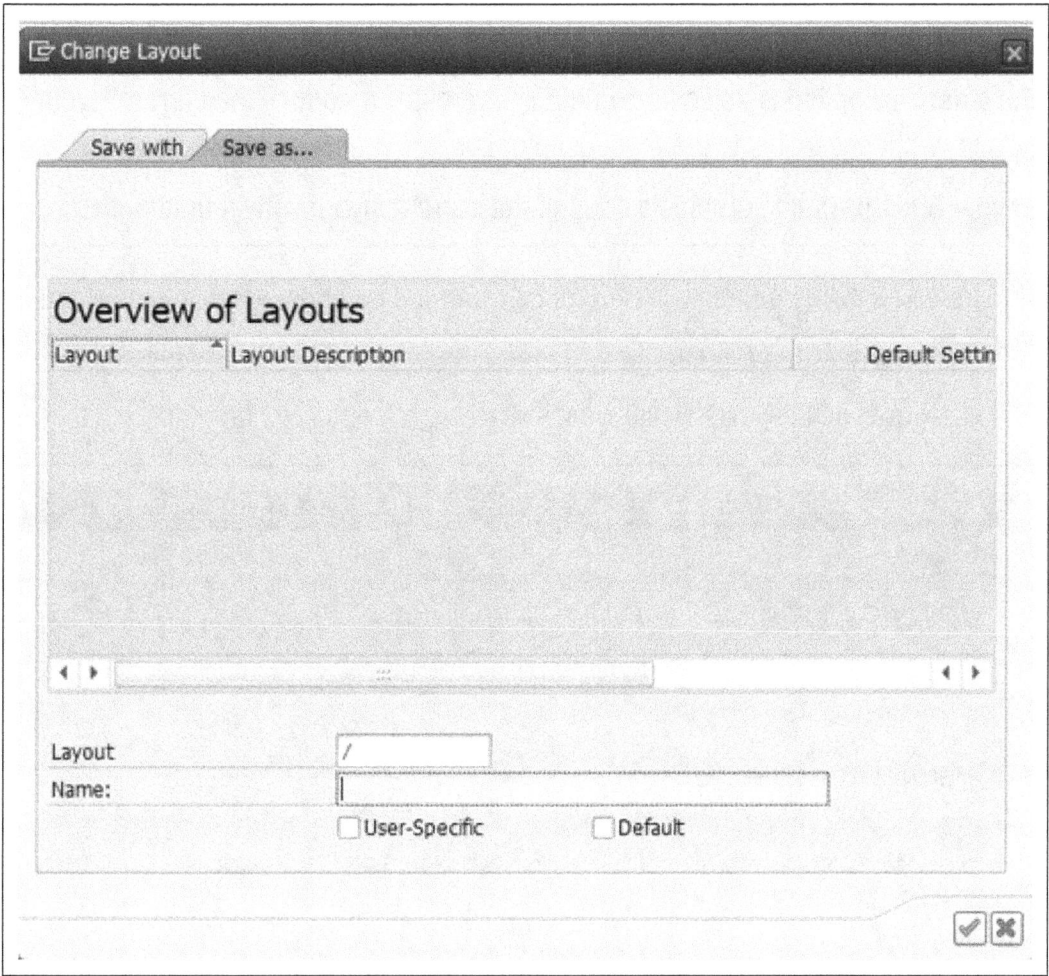

Figure 16-22. *The Change Layout screen Save as option*

In the **Change Layout** window, the tab **Save as** has two options to select at the bottom of the screen, and they are

- User-Specific
- Default

User-Specific: This option saves the layout only for the user who created it, so only you can see it.

Default: The default layout will be visible and applies to all users if you have permission.

769

CHAPTER 16 SAP FIORI REPORTS

Note   The **above screen** also has two tabs as listed below:

Save as: This option is selected by default. It creates a copy of the current layout with your changes. This is the most used option.

Save with: This option creates a copy of the current layout with your changes.

In the above figure, select the User-Specific box and enter the following information:

- **Layout**: ROLE_LAYOUT
- **Name**: ROLE LAYOUT INFORMATION

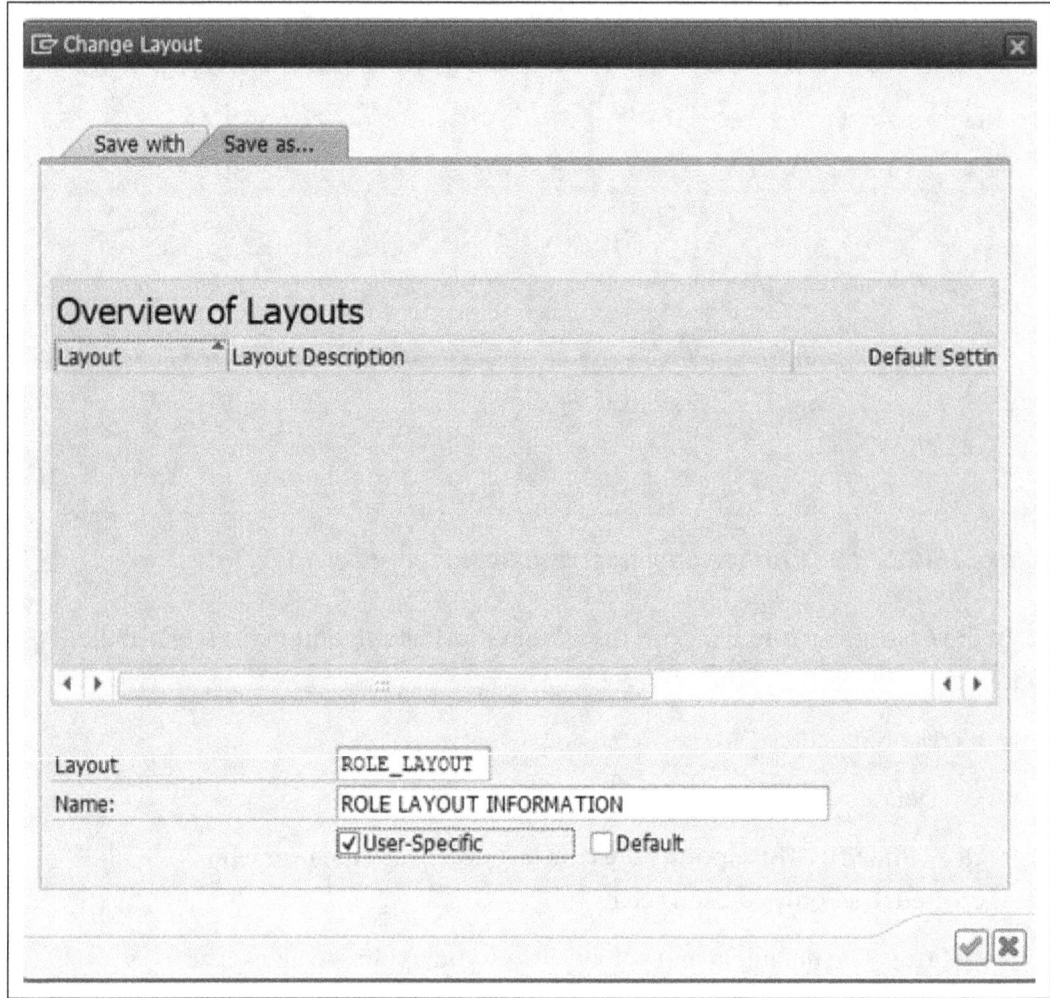

Figure 16-23. Change Layout information added

770

In the above figure, check the box for User-Specific (custom implementation) and then click the **continue** icon. This action will save the layout in the **Launchpad Content Aggregator** window, with a message at the bottom **Layout saved.** The **Current Layout** window has also been updated, as shown in the figure below.

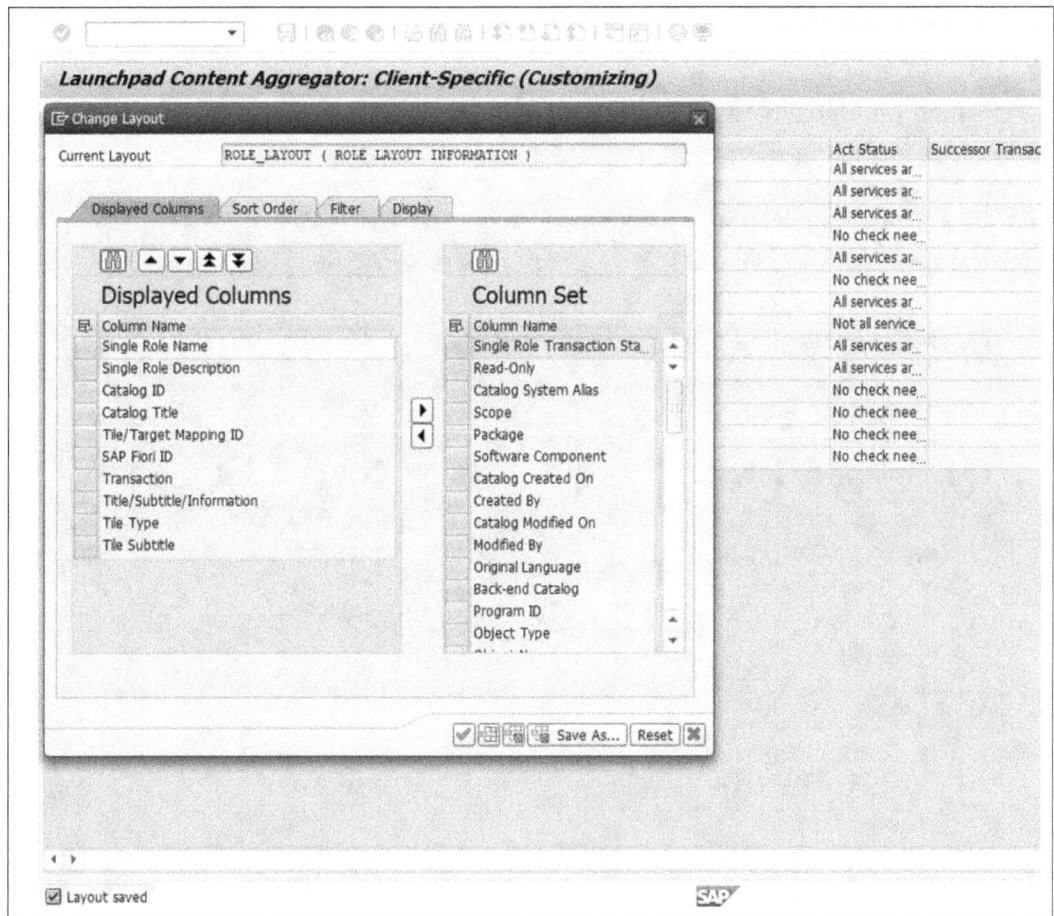

Figure 16-24. Layout saved

The above figure shows that the layout has been saved and can be used later. You can use this saved layout to create more test matrices later.

Note

- This saved layout will only be visible to the user who saves it.
- If the layout is saved with the prefix /, it becomes available for other users.

The final **Change Layout** screen is shown in the figure below.

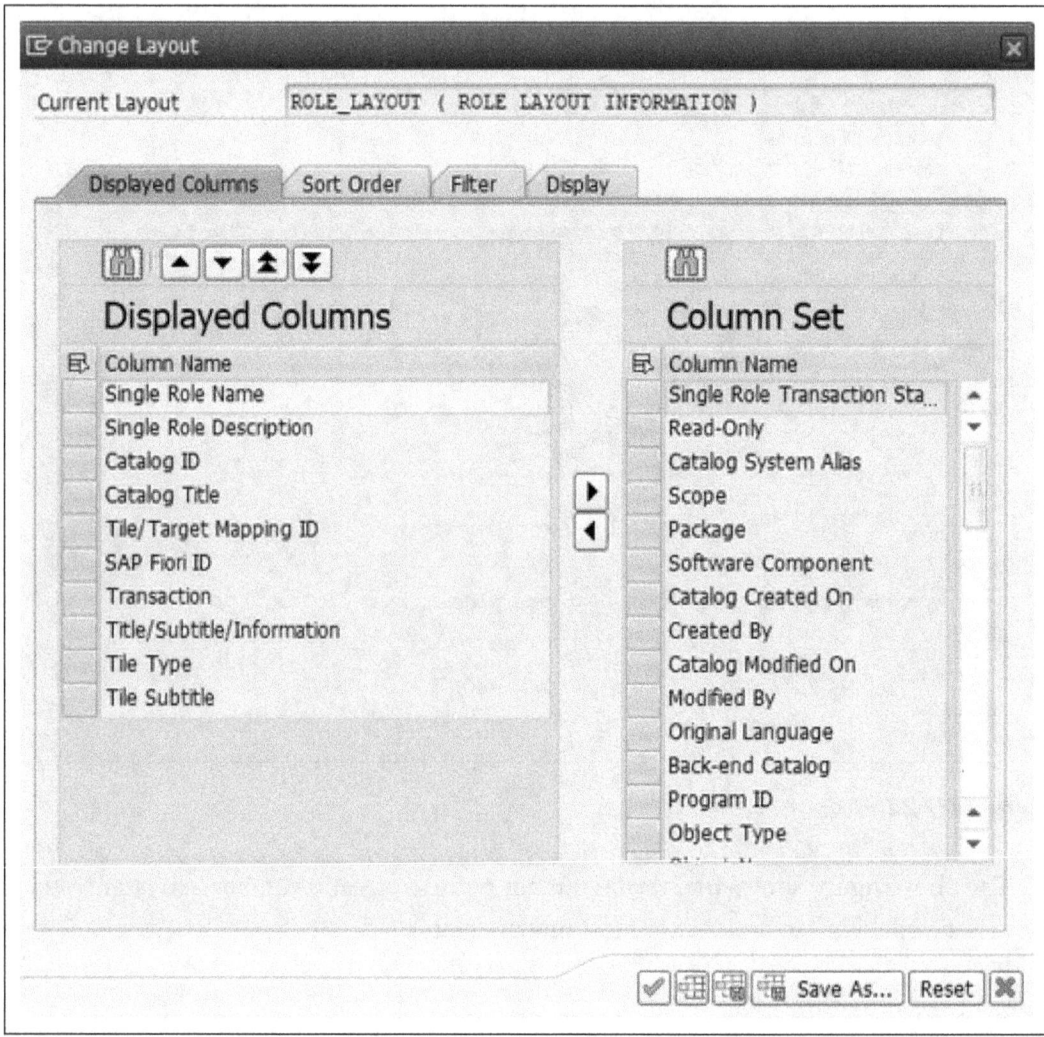

Figure 16-25. Final Change Layout screen

CHAPTER 16 SAP FIORI REPORTS

To proceed further, click the **continue** icon . The output screen updates and displays data based on our selection criteria.

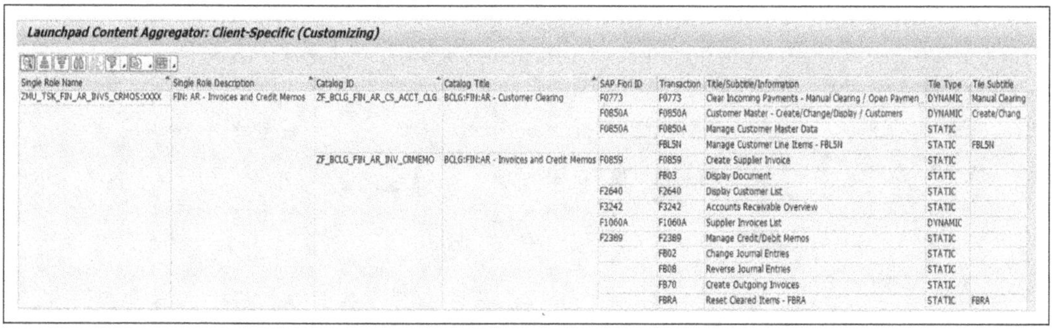

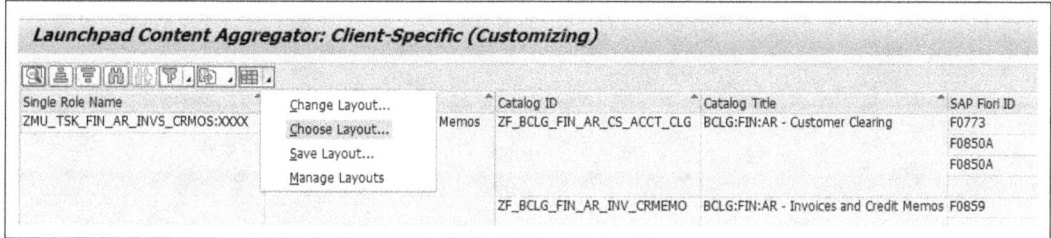

Figure 16-26. Changed Layout data displayed

The above figure displays the data we selected and saved in the layout. To narrow the needed data further or add another field, go back to the pull-down menu, and select **Choose Layout**, as shown below.

Figure 16-27. Choose Layout option selected

Selecting the **Choose Layout** option pops up the following screen.

773

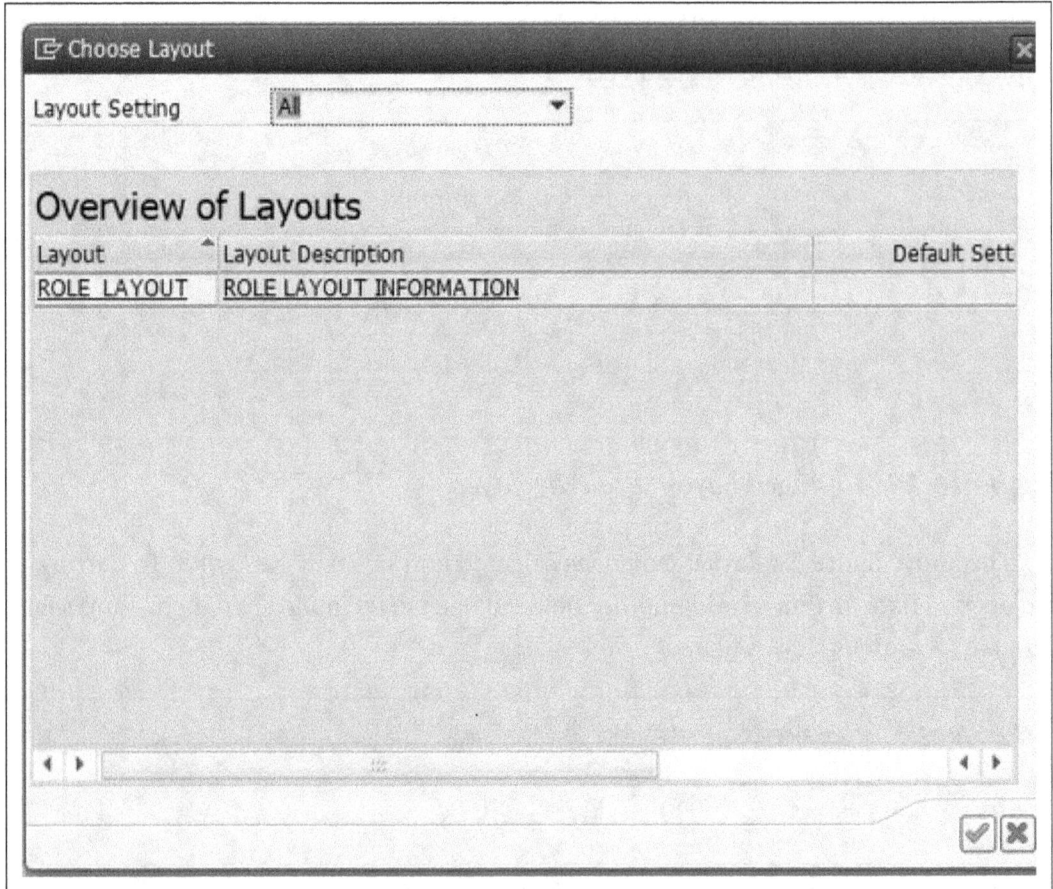

Figure 16-28. *Choose Layout option*

Click the continue icon, and the data saved under Role Layout will be displayed, as shown in the figure below. A message stating **Layout applied** will also be displayed at the bottom of the screen.

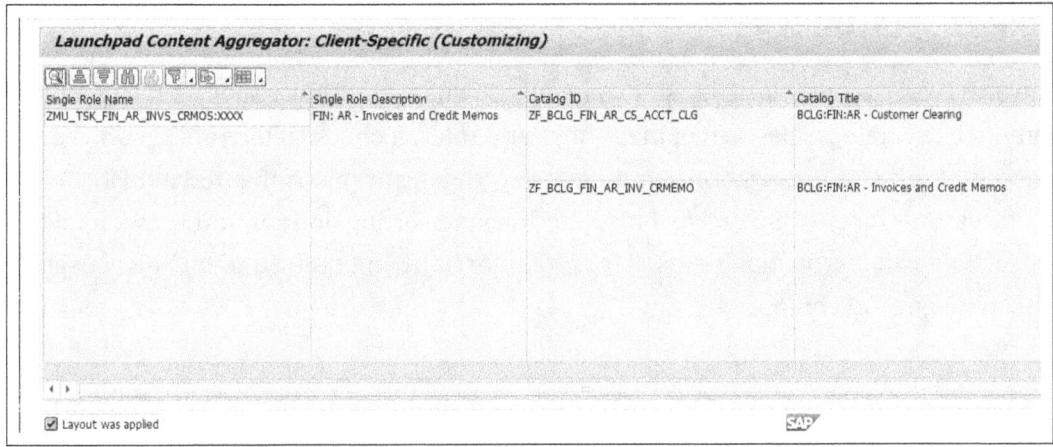

Figure 16-29. *ROLE_LAYOUT applied*

Export the data into Excel.

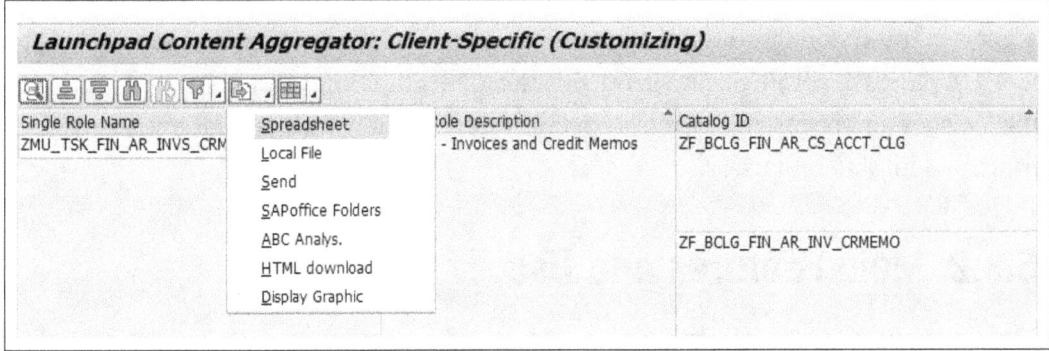

Figure 16-30. *Data to be exported to a spreadsheet*

Select the option Spreadsheet in the above figure. The Excel output is displayed in the figure below.

	Single Role Name	Single Role Description	Catalog ID	Catalog Title	SAP Fiori ID	Transaction	Title/Subtitle/Information	Tile Type	Tile Subtitle	Tile / Target Mapping
2	ZMU_TSK_FIN_AR_INVS_CRMOS:XX	FIN: AR - Invoices and Credit Memos	ZF_BCLG_FIN_AR_CS_ACCT_CLG	BCLG:FIN:AR - Customer Clearing	F0773	F0773	Clear Incoming Payments - Manual Clearing / Open Payments	DYNAMIC	Manual Clearing	Tile + TM
3	ZMU_TSK_FIN_AR_INVS_CRMOS:XX	FIN: AR - Invoices and Credit Memos	ZF_BCLG_FIN_AR_CS_ACCT_CLG	BCLG:FIN:AR - Customer Clearing	F0850A	F0850A	Customer Master - Create/Change/Display / Customers	DYNAMIC	Create/Change/Display	Tile + TM
4	ZMU_TSK_FIN_AR_INVS_CRMOS:XX	FIN: AR - Invoices and Credit Memos	ZF_BCLG_FIN_AR_CS_ACCT_CLG	BCLG:FIN:AR - Customer Clearing	F0850A	F0850A	Manage Customer Master Data	STATIC		Tile + TM
5	ZMU_TSK_FIN_AR_INVS_CRMOS:XX	FIN: AR - Invoices and Credit Memos	ZF_BCLG_FIN_AR_CS_ACCT_CLG	BCLG:FIN:AR - Customer Clearing		FBL5N	Manage Customer Line Items - FBL5N	STATIC	FBL5N	Tile + TM
6	ZMU_TSK_FIN_AR_INVS_CRMOS:XX	FIN: AR - Invoices and Credit Memos	ZF_BCLG_FIN_AR_INV_CRMEMC	BCLG:FIN:AR - Invoices and Credit Memos	F0859	F0859	Create Supplier Invoice	STATIC		Tile + TM
7	ZMU_TSK_FIN_AR_INVS_CRMOS:XX	FIN: AR - Invoices and Credit Memos	ZF_BCLG_FIN_AR_INV_CRMEMC	BCLG:FIN:AR - Invoices and Credit Memos		FB03	Display Document	STATIC		Tile + TM
8	ZMU_TSK_FIN_AR_INVS_CRMOS:XX	FIN: AR - Invoices and Credit Memos	ZF_BCLG_FIN_AR_INV_CRMEMC	BCLG:FIN:AR - Invoices and Credit Memos	F2640	F2640	Display Customer List	STATIC		Tile + TM
9	ZMU_TSK_FIN_AR_INVS_CRMOS:XX	FIN: AR - Invoices and Credit Memos	ZF_BCLG_FIN_AR_INV_CRMEMC	BCLG:FIN:AR - Invoices and Credit Memos	F3242	F3242	Accounts Receivable Overview	STATIC		Tile + TM
10	ZMU_TSK_FIN_AR_INVS_CRMOS:XX	FIN: AR - Invoices and Credit Memos	ZF_BCLG_FIN_AR_INV_CRMEMC	BCLG:FIN:AR - Invoices and Credit Memos	F1060A	F1060A	Supplier Invoices List	DYNAMIC		Tile + TM
11	ZMU_TSK_FIN_AR_INVS_CRMOS:XX	FIN: AR - Invoices and Credit Memos	ZF_BCLG_FIN_AR_INV_CRMEMC	BCLG:FIN:AR - Invoices and Credit Memos	F2389	F2389	Manage Credit/Debit Memos	STATIC		Tile + TM
12	ZMU_TSK_FIN_AR_INVS_CRMOS:XX	FIN: AR - Invoices and Credit Memos	ZF_BCLG_FIN_AR_INV_CRMEMC	BCLG:FIN:AR - Invoices and Credit Memos		FB02	Change Journal Entries	STATIC		Tile + TM
13	ZMU_TSK_FIN_AR_INVS_CRMOS:XX	FIN: AR - Invoices and Credit Memos	ZF_BCLG_FIN_AR_INV_CRMEMC	BCLG:FIN:AR - Invoices and Credit Memos		FB08	Reverse Journal Entries	STATIC		Tile + TM
14	ZMU_TSK_FIN_AR_INVS_CRMOS:XX	FIN: AR - Invoices and Credit Memos	ZF_BCLG_FIN_AR_INV_CRMEMC	BCLG:FIN:AR - Invoices and Credit Memos		FB70	Create Outgoing Invoices	STATIC		Tile + TM
15	ZMU_TSK_FIN_AR_INVS_CRMOS:XX	FIN: AR - Invoices and Credit Memos	ZF_BCLG_FIN_AR_INV_CRMEMC	BCLG:FIN:AR - Invoices and Credit Memos		FBRA	Reset Cleared Items - FBRA	STATIC	FBRA	Tile + TM

Figure 16-31. *Data output displayed*

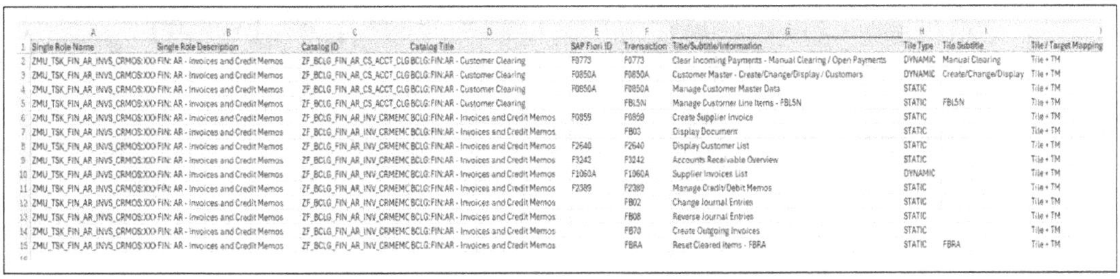

16.2.5 Summary

The SAP Fiori transaction /UI2/FLPCA helps you analyze and fix issues with Launchpad content like catalogs, tiles, target mappings, and roles. It checks if tiles are set up correctly, verifies authorizations, and finds any missing or misconfigured items. The tool offers features for customizing layouts, filtering, and sorting options and shows related transactions and navigation paths. It is helpful for both functional and technical users who manage Fiori content.

16.3 Transaction Code: /UI2/RSP_LIST

16.3.1 Introduction

This section explains a report created with the transaction **/UI2/RSP_LIST**. Since SAP S/4HANA 2021, the transaction lists **all available SAP Fiori roles, spaces, and pages** assigned in the system. Its output contains details such as the **role name**, associated **space ID**, **page ID**, **catalogs**, and **group assignments**, helping administrators verify which spaces and pages are linked to specific roles and how they appear in the Launchpad for different users.

16.3.2 Main Features and Use

The main features are as follows:

- **Overview of Spaces and Pages**: This document lists all the spaces and pages set up in the system. It helps administrators manage the layout and structure of the Launchpad.

- **Content Review and Analysis**: You can review the content of spaces and pages, including the apps and tiles assigned to them, to ensure they match user roles and business needs.

- **Troubleshooting and Issue Resolution**: The transaction helps find problems with spaces and pages, like missing assignments or wrong settings.

- **Improved Efficiency:** It improves the user experience by keeping spaces and pages organized and relevant to users' needs.

CHAPTER 16 SAP FIORI REPORTS

16.3.3 Demo Examples

Execute the transaction, and the following screen opens, as shown in the figure below. Here, you enter the role name. This report can also be exported to a spreadsheet.

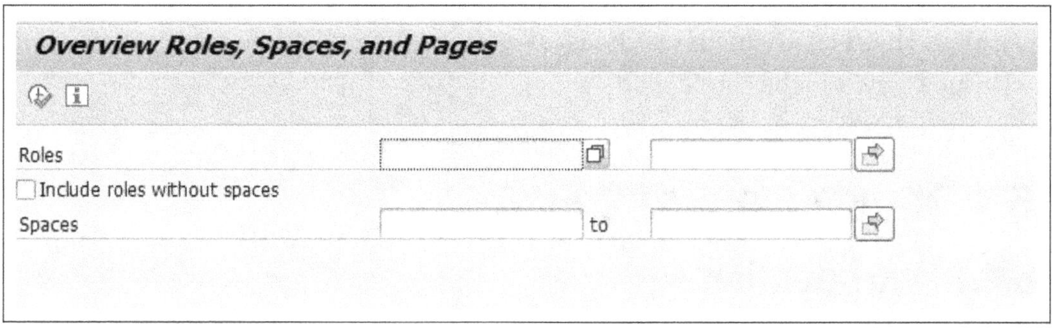

Figure 16-32. Transaction /UI2/RSP_LIST input screen

Enter the role name as shown in the figure below.

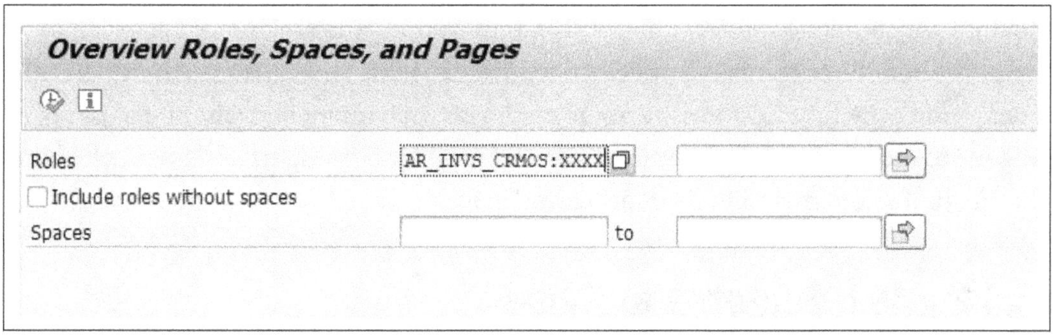

Figure 16-33. Entered the role name

Click the execute icon.

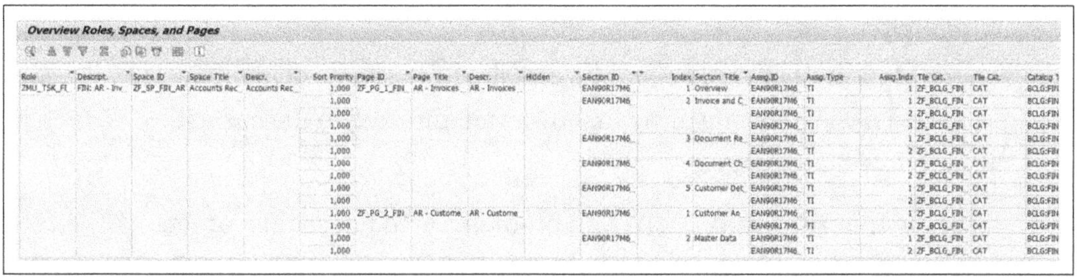

Figure 16-34. Transaction /UI2/RSP_LIST output

777

16.3.4 Summary

The SAP Fiori transaction /UI2/RSP_LIST gives a quick view of how roles connect to spaces and pages in the Fiori Launchpad. It shows which roles are linked to which spaces and pages. This helps administrators set up the Launchpad correctly and improve navigation. This tool also helps check that role-based content is delivered properly and fixes display issues in the Launchpad.

16.4 Transaction: /UI2/FLIA

16.4.1 Introduction

This section guides the use of the report accessible through transaction **/UI2/FLIA – Fiori Launchpad Intent Analysis**. This report lets you view the intents (**semantic object–semantic action**) assigned to a user within the SAP Fiori Launchpad. It displays all intents linked to a user, along with the corresponding authorization roles and their assignments. You can utilize this report to verify the assignment of specific intents to users, filtering results by device type. Access this tool via transaction /UI2/FLIA to determine which **PFCG** roles are associated with each intent and whether a user is assigned to those roles. This transaction is beneficial for developers and administrators who customize and maintain the Fiori Launchpad.

16.4.2 Main Features and Use

The main features are as follows:

- **Navigation Intent Analysis**: Examines navigation intents in the Fiori Launchpad to verify proper configuration of semantic objects and actions.

- **Validation Checks:** The tool verifies the consistency of intent-based navigation, ensuring that users are directed to the correct applications or pages.

- **Issue Identification**: Helps find problems with navigation targets, such as missing or incorrect settings within the Launchpad Designer.

- **Enhancements for User Experience:** Administrators can refine navigation for a smoother experience across the Launchpad by analyzing intents.

16.4.3 Demo Examples

To start, execute the transaction code, and the landing page will appear as shown in the figure below.

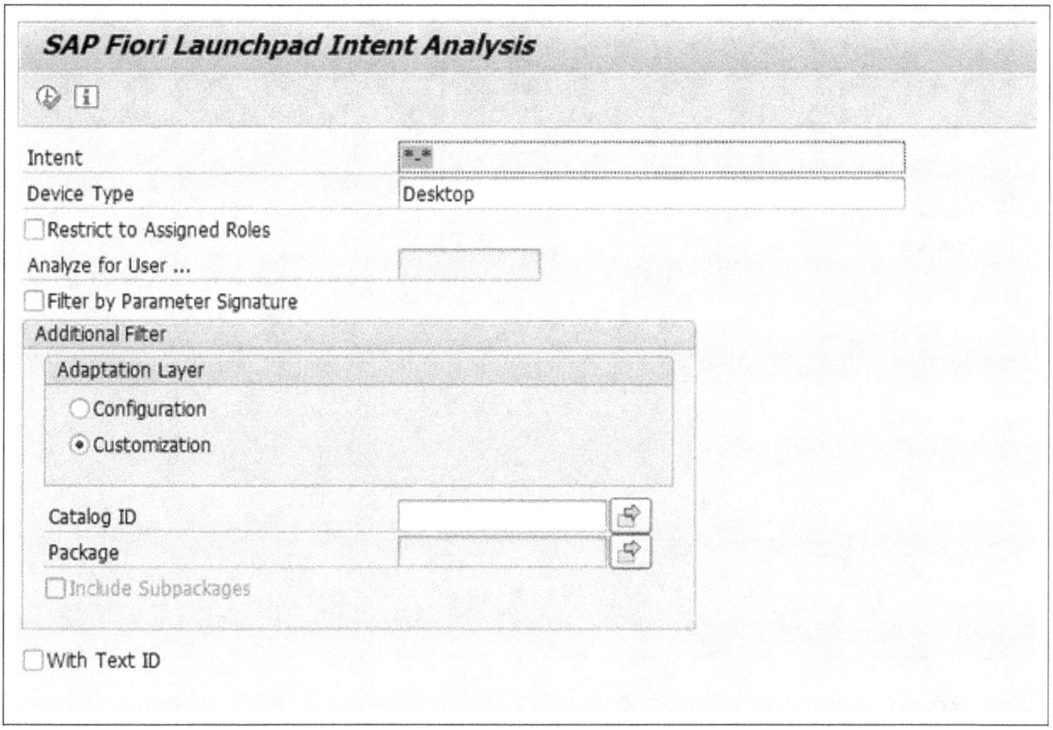

Figure 16-35. Transaction /UI2/FLIA input screen

In the figure above, several options are available. We can filter the content for analysis in multiple ways:

> **Intent**: Here, a combination of a semantic object and an action needs to be passed, separated by a **"-"**. The **intent** of the Fiori app F0850A would be **Customer-manage**.

CHAPTER 16 SAP FIORI REPORTS

Device Type: This filtering feature allows you to filter the content based on the device type defined in the configuration, such as desktop, phone, or tablet.

In the below figure, select the option **Restrict to Assigned Roles** and enter the **TESTSPPG** as a user.

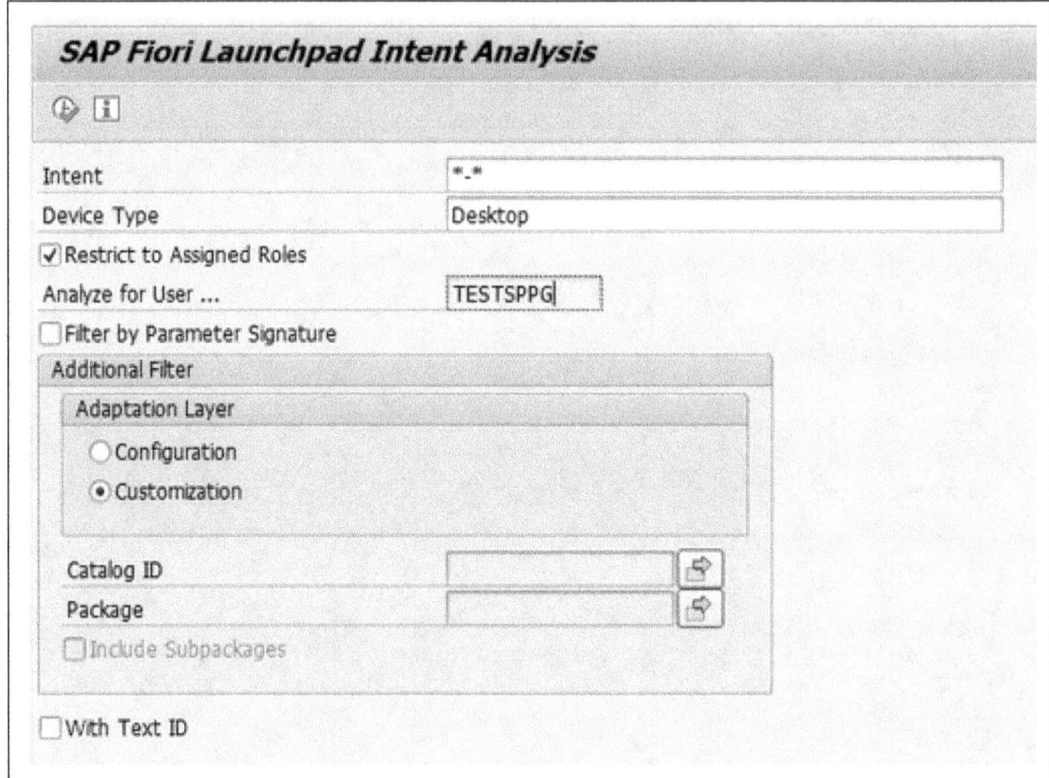

Figure 16-36. Information added

Click the execute icon , and the output is displayed below.

CHAPTER 16   SAP FIORI REPORTS

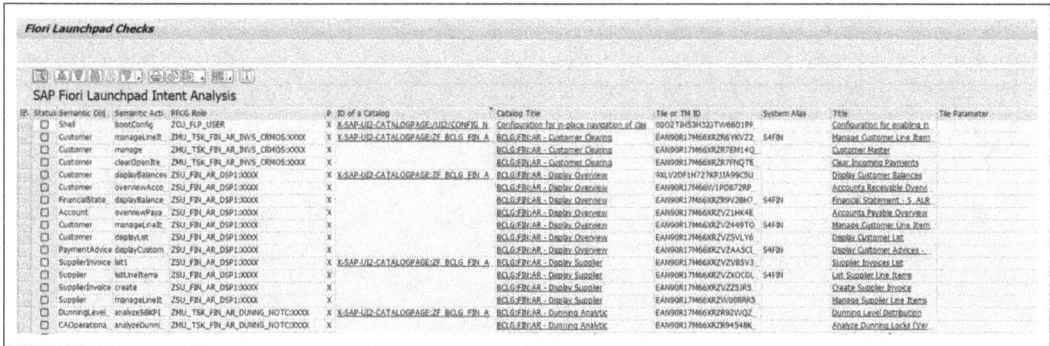

Figure 16-37. *SAP Fiori Launchpad Intent Analysis output*

You can also use the **Additional Filter** option with **Adaptation Layer** as **Customization** and enter **Catalog ID** as shown in the figure below.

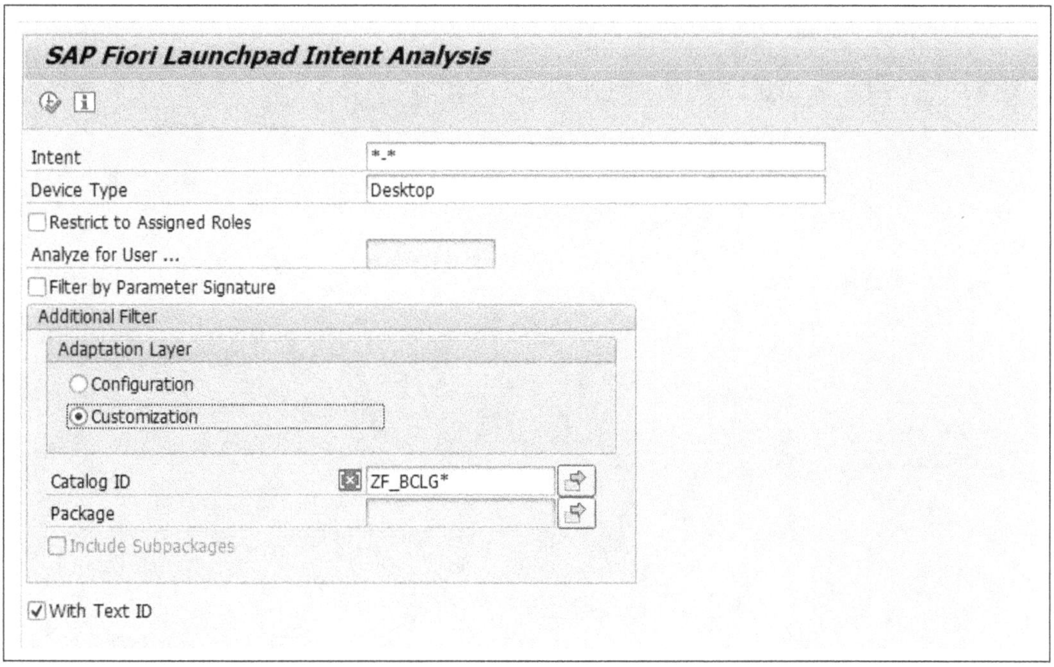

Figure 16-38. *Search based on all business catalogs created*

781

CHAPTER 16   SAP FIORI REPORTS

Executed, the following output appears, as shown in the figure below.

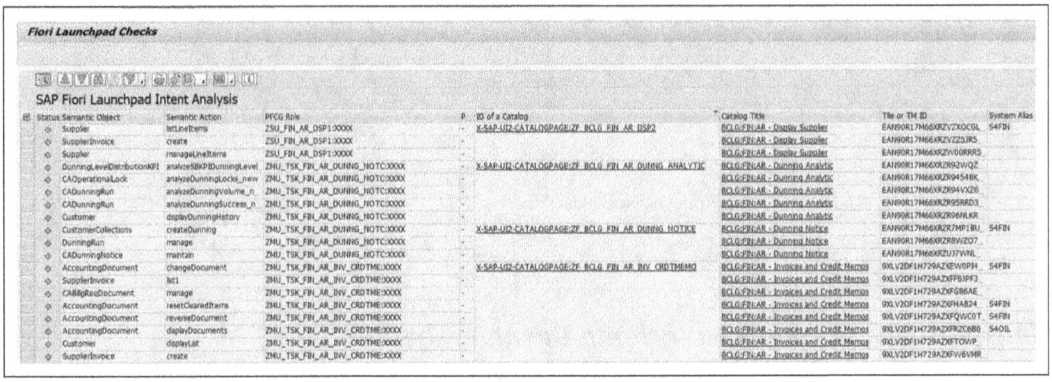

Figure 16-39. Business catalog output details

Select the **Configuration** option and specify **Package**, as shown in the figure below.

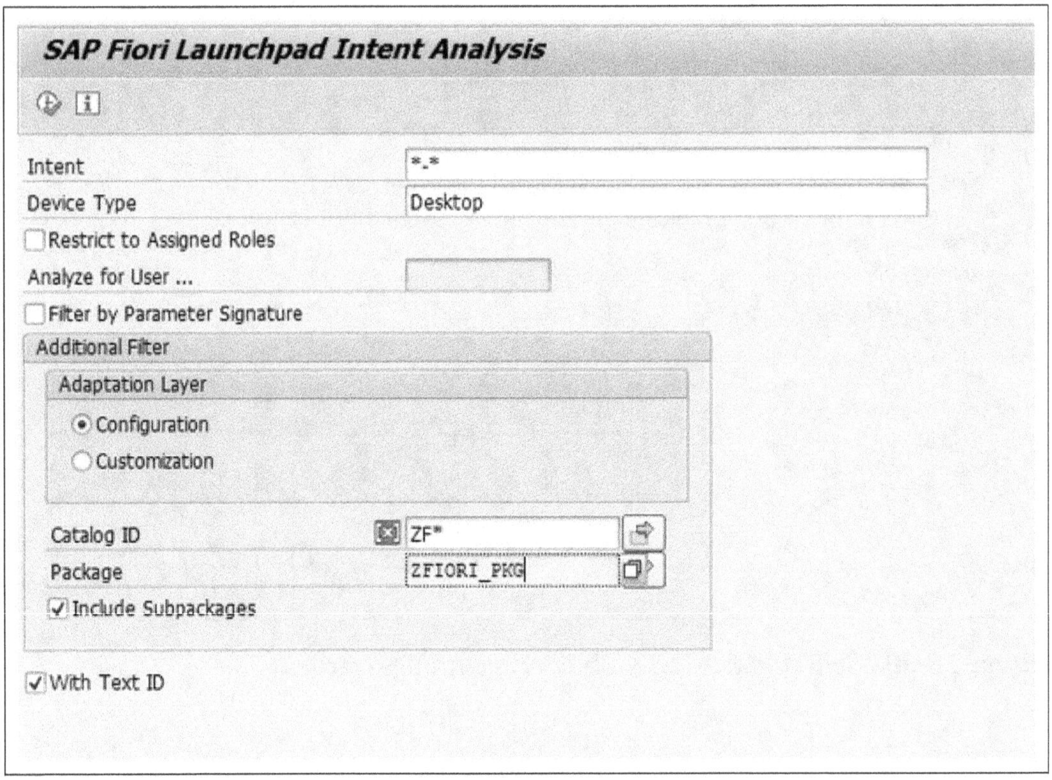

Figure 16-40. Configuration option selected

CHAPTER 16 SAP FIORI REPORTS

Execute and the output displays only the technical catalogs created in the system, as shown in the figure below.

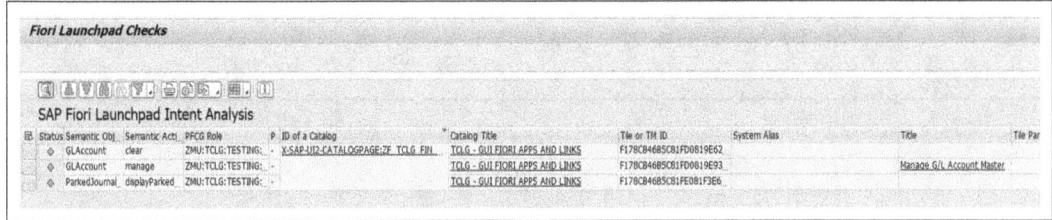

Figure 16-41. *The Configuration option output is displayed*

If an **error** is encountered, it will be highlighted in **red** and found in the **Message** column by scrolling to the right, which is **INFO** in this case, as shown in the figure below.

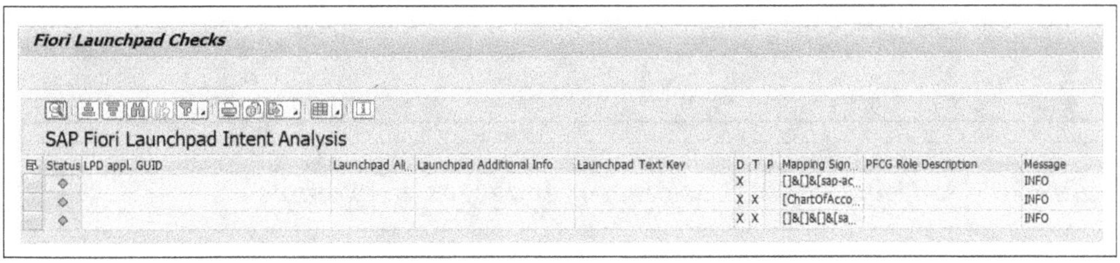

Figure 16-42. *Message column information*

In this situation, the error indicates an invalid semantic object. This could suggest that the incorrect semantic object is maintained either in the tile or target mapping in the transaction **/UI2/SEMOBJ**.

Let's use **Intent** (**Customer-manage**) as an example, as shown in the figure below.

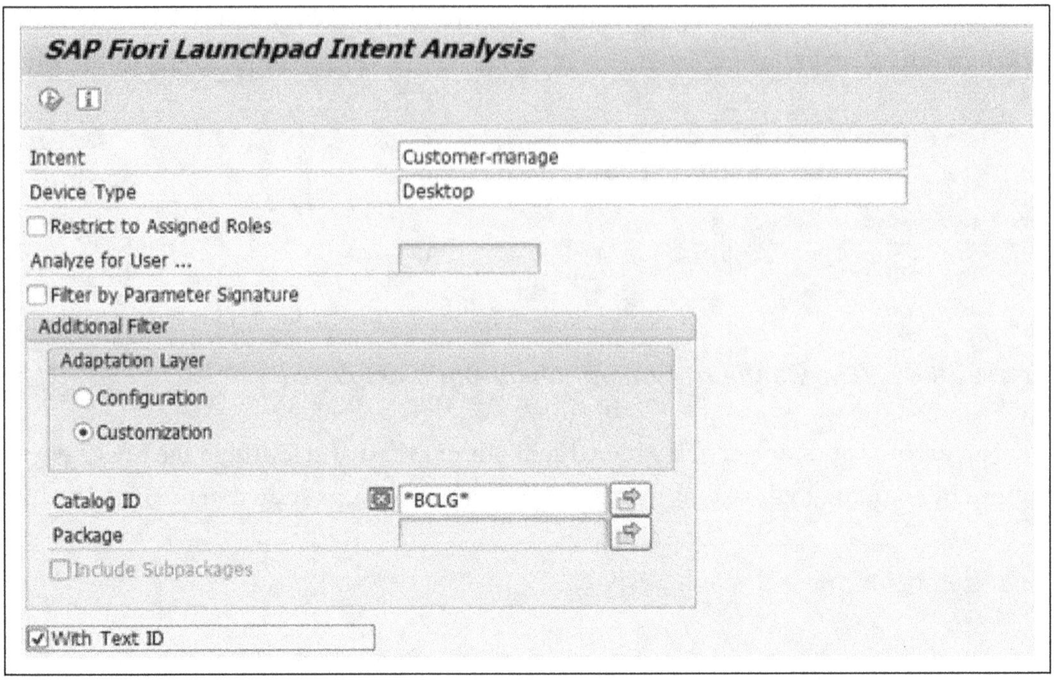

Figure 16-43. *Using Intent (Customer-manage) as an example*

Execute, and the output generated is displayed, as shown in the figure below.

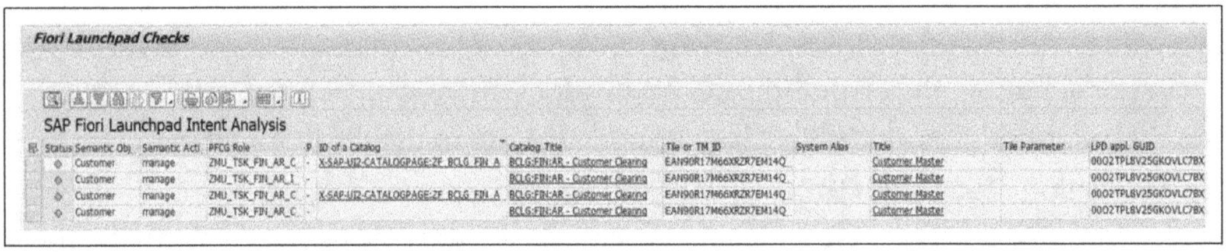

Figure 16-44. *The intent output is displayed*

> **Note** All the output displayed can be downloaded into an Excel file for analysis.

16.4.4 Summary

The transaction code **/UI2/FLIA** in SAP Fiori analyzes and monitors the Fiori Launchpad performance. It provides insights into the usage of different tiles, helps identify issues with app loading times, and monitors the overall user experience. This tool is essential for administrators looking to optimize Fiori applications, as it offers valuable analytics on usage patterns, bottlenecks, and areas for improvement within the Launchpad environment.

16.5 Transaction: /UI2/FLT

16.5.1 Introduction

This section will cover the report published using the transaction **/UI2/FLT – Fiori Launchpad Texts** tool. This tool analyzes texts used in Fiori Launchpad and fixes related issues. This tool is especially helpful for administrators and developers to manage and correct labels, names, and UI text entries utilized throughout the Fiori Launchpad.

16.5.2 Main Features and Use

This tool provides features like

- **Search Business Objects:** The transaction helps identify text strings used in catalogs, groups, and tiles in the Launchpad, which are part of the business content defined in the Fiori Launchpad Designer.

- **Translation Keys:** This tool helps you find technical keys for translation. It allows you to customize or localize texts easily. For example, you can identify translation keys for group names or titles.

- **Text Retrieval:** The tool can help you find texts from back-end systems, such as application titles or WebGUI texts.

- **Text Definition:** To identify the text in the translation system, navigate to the object in the Fiori Launchpad Designer and locate the text ID and configuration ID.

- **Text Management:** This is particularly useful when customizing the user interface to reflect the organization's terminology, language, or branding.

- **Multi-language Support:** The transaction code allows managing texts in multiple languages. This is critical for organizations that operate in different regions with users who speak other languages. Administrators can maintain language-specific texts to ensure a consistent user experience across all users.

- **Standardization:** Through /UI2/FLT, you can ensure that the texts displayed in the Fiori Launchpad are consistent with the organization's guidelines. This includes aligning tile names with business processes and making the interface more intuitive for users.

- **Troubleshooting and Issue Resolution:** If text is not displaying correctly, you can use /UI2/FLT to find the problem. This tool helps identify whether the issue is due to a missing translation or an incorrect configuration.

- **Improving User Experience:** Well-maintained and descriptive texts help users easily identify the purpose of each tile or group, thereby improving navigation and overall user experience within the Fiori Launchpad.

- **Practical Example:** If a company decides to rebrand or introduce new terminology for its processes, an administrator could use transaction/**UI2/FLT** to update all the relevant text elements in the Fiori Launchpad to reflect these changes. For instance, if a tile previously labeled "**Purchase Orders**" needs to be changed to "**Procurement Requests**," this transaction would be used to update the title and description accordingly.

16.5.3 Demo Examples

Execute transaction /**UI2/FLT**; the landing screen will be as shown in the figure below.

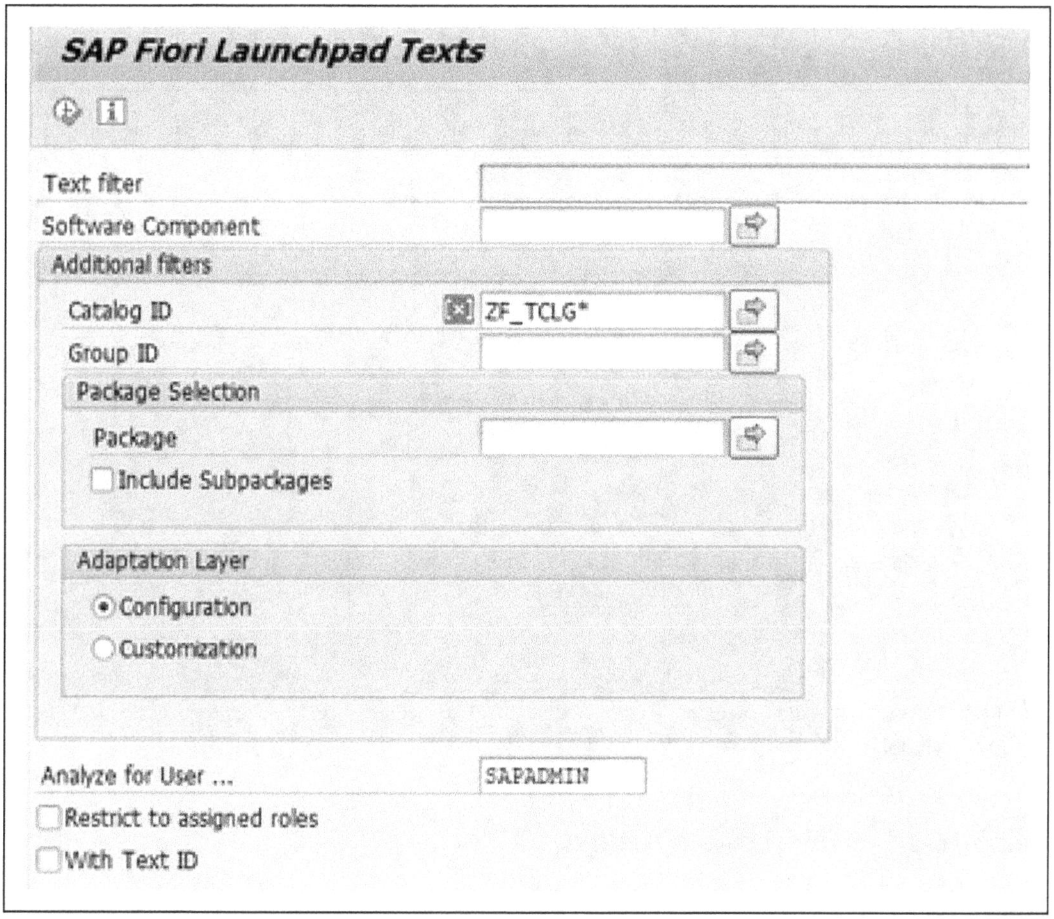

CHAPTER 16 SAP FIORI REPORTS

Figure 16-45. *Transaction /UI2/FLT input screen*

The screen resembles the initial display of the Fiori Intent Analysis report, but there are a couple of notable changes. Instead of the Intent field, we now have a **Text filter** field and another field labeled **Software Component**.

In the screen as shown in the figure below, we will check the **SAP Fiori Launchpad Texts** with **Catalog ID** as **ZF_TCLG***.

787

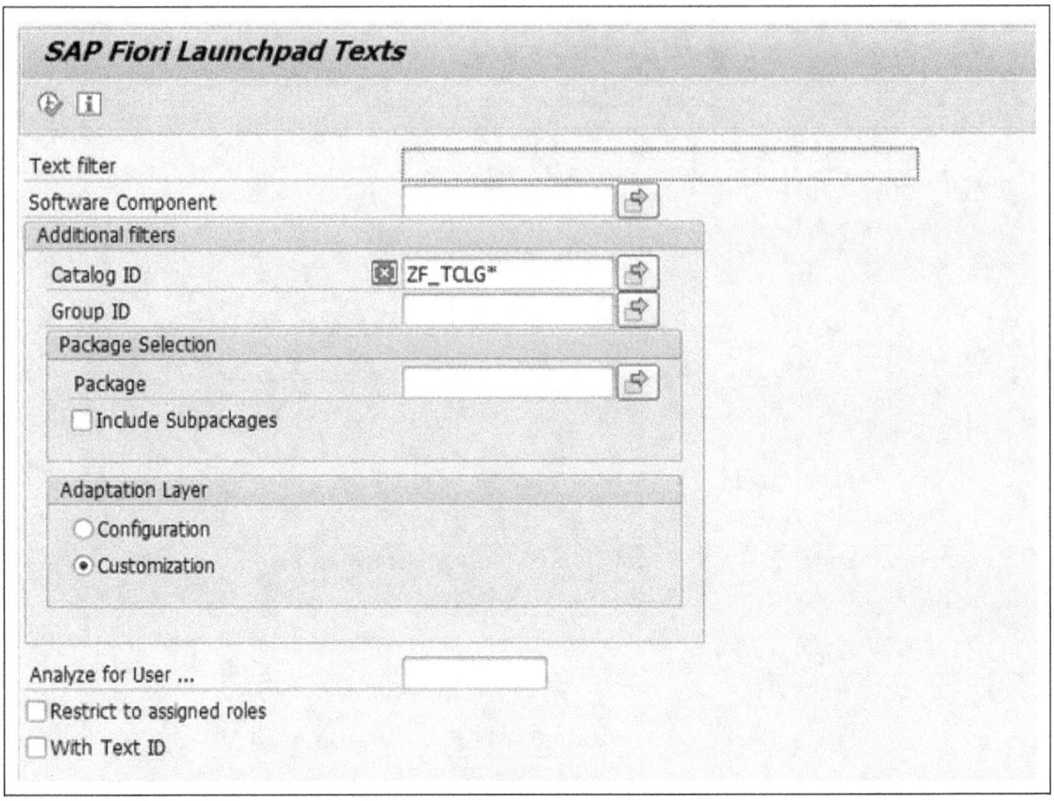

CHAPTER 16　SAP FIORI REPORTS

Figure 16-46. Search based on catalog ID

The output is as shown in the figure below.

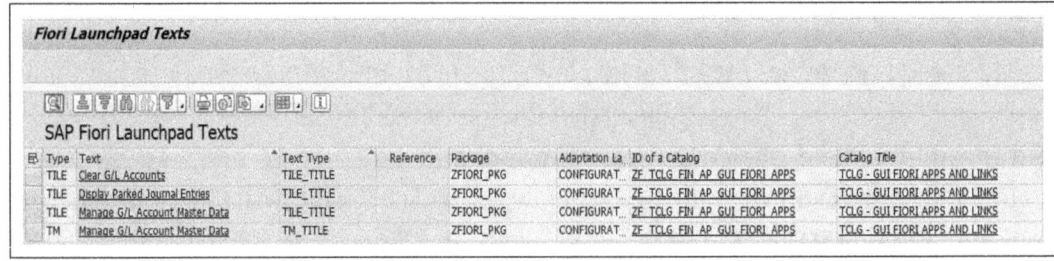

Figure 16-47. Output of search based on catalog ID

Selecting the tile **Clear G/L Accounts** gives the following information, as shown in the figure below.

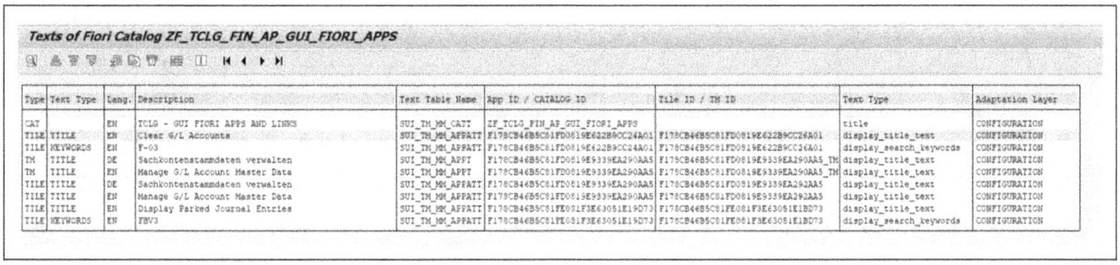

Texts of Fiori Catalog ZF_TCLG_FIN_AP_GUI_FIORI_APPS

Type	Text Type	Lang.	Description	Text Table Name	App ID / CATALOG ID	Tile ID / TM ID	Text Type	Adaptation Layer
CAT		EN	TCLG - GUI FIORI APPS AND LINKS	SUI_TM_MM_CATT	ZF_TCLG_FIN_AP_GUI_FIORI_APPS		title	CONFIGURATION
TILE	TITLE	EN	Clear G/L Accounts	SUI_TM_MM_APPATT	F178CB46B5C81FD0819E622B9CC24A01	F178CB46B5C81FD0819E622B9CC26A01	display_title_text	CONFIGURATION
TILE	KEYWORDS	EN	F-03	SUI_TM_MM_APPATT	F178CB46B5C81FD0819E622B9CC24A01	F178CB46B5C81FD0819E622B9CC26A01	display_search_keywords	CONFIGURATION
TM	TITLE	DE	Sachkontenstammdaten verwalten	SUI_TM_MM_APPT	F178CB46B5C81FD0819E9339EA290AA5	F178CB46B5C81FD0819E9339EA290AA5_TM	display_title_text	CONFIGURATION
TM	TITLE	EN	Manage G/L Account Master Data	SUI_TM_MM_APPT	F178CB46B5C81FD0819E9339EA290AA5	F178CB46B5C81FD0819E9339EA290AA5_TM	display_title_text	CONFIGURATION
TILE	TITLE	DE	Sachkontenstammdaten verwalten	SUI_TM_MM_APPATT	F178CB46B5C81FD0819E9339EA290AA5	F178CB46B5C81FD0819E9339EA292AA5	display_title_text	CONFIGURATION
TILE	TITLE	EN	Manage G/L Account Master Data	SUI_TM_MM_APPATT	F178CB46B5C81FD0819E9339EA290AA5	F178CB46B5C81FD0819E9339EA292AA5	display_title_text	CONFIGURATION
TILE	TITLE	EN	Display Parked Journal Entries	SUI_TM_MM_APPATT	F178CB46B5C81FE081F3E63051E19D73	F178CB46B5C81FE081F3E63051E1BD73	display_title_text	CONFIGURATION
TILE	KEYWORDS	EN	FBV3	SUI_TM_MM_APPATT	F178CB46B5C81FE081F3E63051E19D73	F178CB46B5C81FE081F3E63051E1BD73	display_search_keywords	CONFIGURATION

Figure 16-48. *Selected tile information*

In the screen as shown in the figure below, we will check the **SAP Fiori Launchpad Texts** for the user **TESTSPG** and select the box **Restrict to assigned roles**.

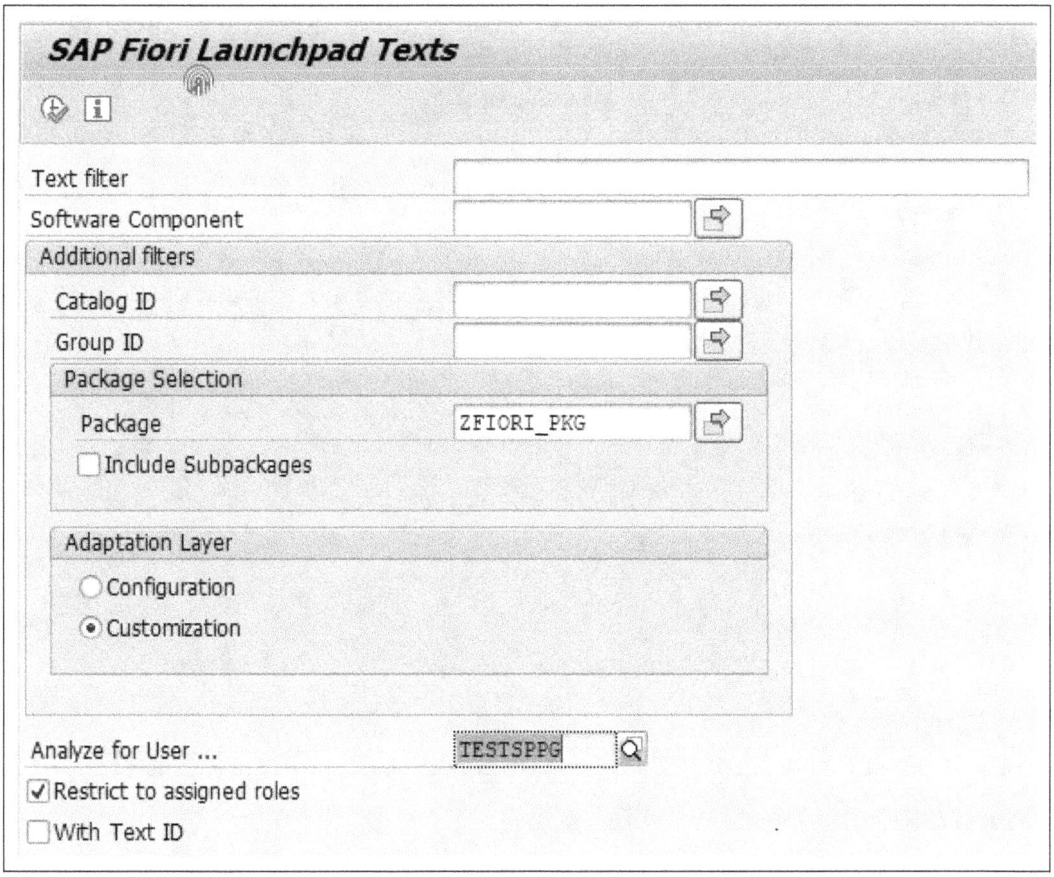

Figure 16-49. *Condition criteria entered*

The output is displayed in the figure below.

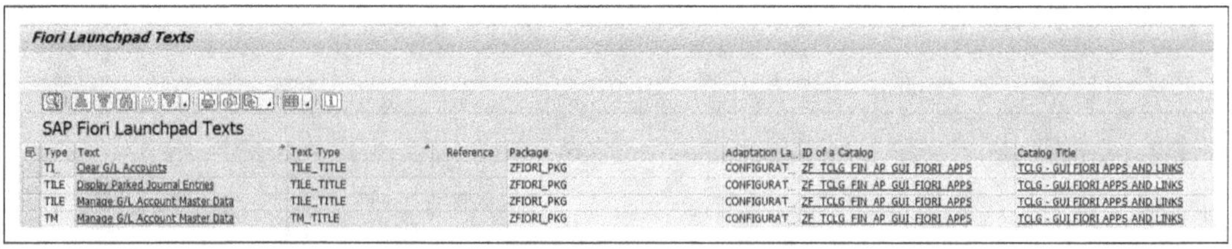

Figure 16-50. User TESTSPG output

Enter the filter criteria and execute the report to analyze the text content. In this case, search for the text **Clear G/L Accounts** and look for it in the roles assigned to the user.

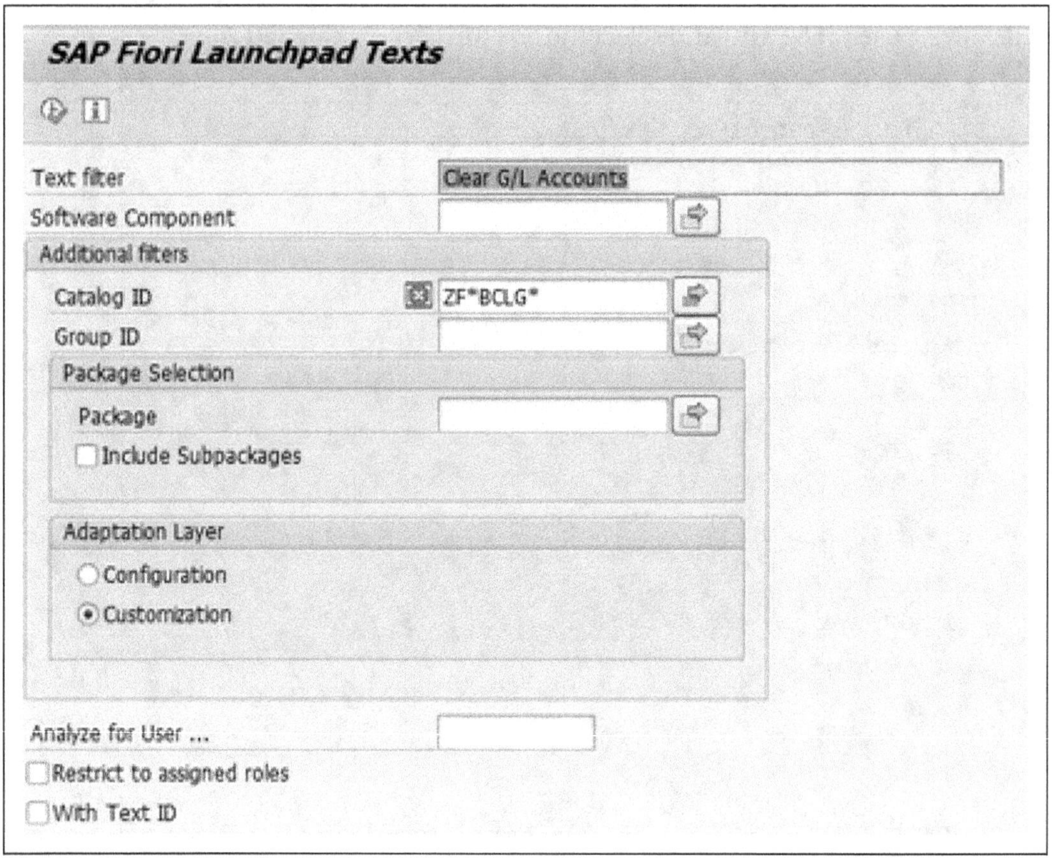

Figure 16-51. Text filter search option

The output is displayed as shown in the figure below. The apps are available within the custom business catalog.

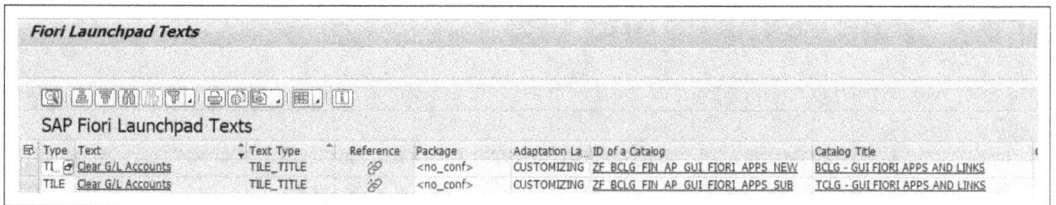

Figure 16-52. Displaying the apps within the custom business catalog

16.5.4 Summary

The Fiori transaction /UI2/FLT is used for the Fiori Launchpad Texts configuration. It allows administrators to manage and maintain the texts displayed in the Fiori Launchpad, such as tile names, descriptions, and other related text elements. The transaction is advantageous when customizing the user interface to better align with the organization's terminology or language preferences. This T-code is essential for tailoring the Fiori Launchpad to meet specific business needs, enhancing the overall user experience.

16.6 Transaction: /UI2/FLC

16.6.1 Introduction

The Fiori Launchpad Checks tool, accessed via transaction **/UI2/FLC – Fiori Launchpad Checks**, allows administrators to manage various settings for the SAP Fiori Launchpad, including system aliases and client-dependent settings. This tool enables users to configure various settings, including system aliases and client-specific configurations, ensuring a tailored and efficient environment. One of its key features is the ability to verify consistency between SAP-delivered standard content and any customized adaptations, which minimizes errors and enhances reliability within the Fiori Launchpad. Administrators and developers can utilize different filters, such as catalog ID, group ID, and user roles, to analyze specific elements like catalogs and user roles, making it easier to perform detailed checks and adjustments. Overall, the Fiori Launchpad Checks tool is vital for maintaining an error-free Fiori Launchpad, providing both oversight and flexibility in managing the platform's diverse functionalities.

16.6.2 Main Features and Use

This tool provides features like

- **System Aliases:** Define and manage system aliases required for accessing back-end systems through the Launchpad.

- **Client Settings:** You can configure client-specific settings for the Fiori Launchpad, such as theming, UI personalization, and role assignments.

- **Feature Management:** Enable or turn off specific features within the Fiori Launchpad environment.

- **Theme Configuration:** Define and assign themes to ensure consistent branding across the Fiori Launchpad.

- **Tile Catalogs and Groups:** Manage catalogs and groups that organize the tiles visible to users based on their roles and tasks.

- **Content Integrity Verification:** This check identifies issues in the setup of catalogs, groups, tiles, and target mappings, such as missing software components or invalid semantic objects.

- **Error Reporting:** Offers detailed error messages and warnings to help administrators identify and fix issues easily.

- **Role-Based Analysis:** Evaluates content assigned to specific roles or users, ensuring the Launchpad meets their requirements.

- **Configuration and Customization Options:** Checks content at client-independent (configuration) and client-dependent (customization) levels.

- **Troubleshooting Assistance:** Essential for resolving problems with Launchpad content, like missing assignments or broken references.

16.6.3 Demo Examples

Utilizing the transaction **/UI2/FLC** (Fiori Launchpad Checks) in SAP systems allows you to customize and tailor the Fiori Launchpad according to your organization's requirements. This transaction provides administrators or security personnel with a centralized interface to manage various aspects of the Fiori Launchpad. It is crucial to have the authorization to perform tasks in /UI2/FLC because this powerful tool can impact the entire Fiori Launchpad. Using this transaction, you can manage the following Fiori components:

- **Catalogs:** Define and manage catalogs that contain groups, apps, and tiles.

- **Groups:** Create and organize groups of Fiori apps for end users.

- **Roles:** Assign roles to user groups to control access to specific catalogs and groups.

- **Tiles:** Customize and configure each Fiori tile from the catalog within its respective groups for a tailored experience.

- **Launchpad Configuration:** Enhance and adjust the visual appeal and functionality of the Fiori Launchpad.

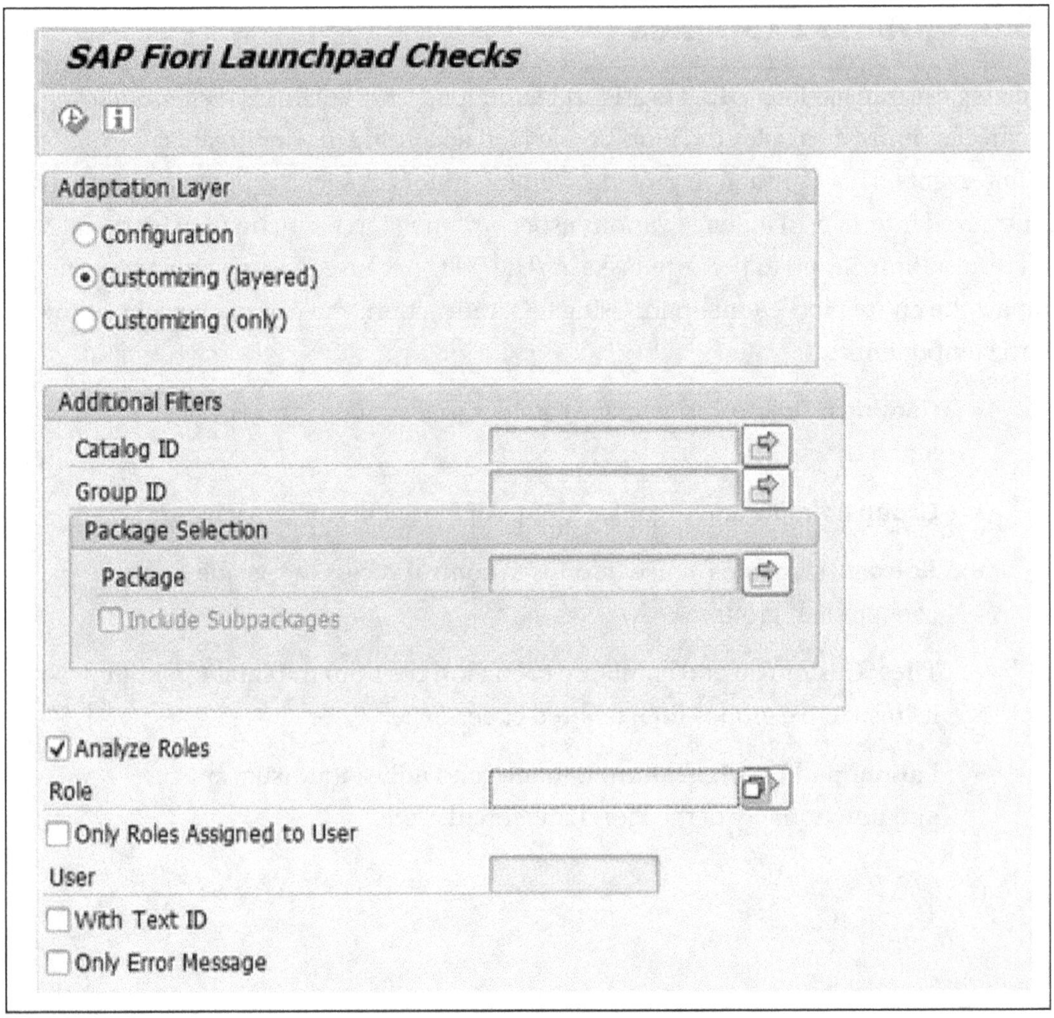

Figure 16-53. The transaction /UI2/FLC initial screen

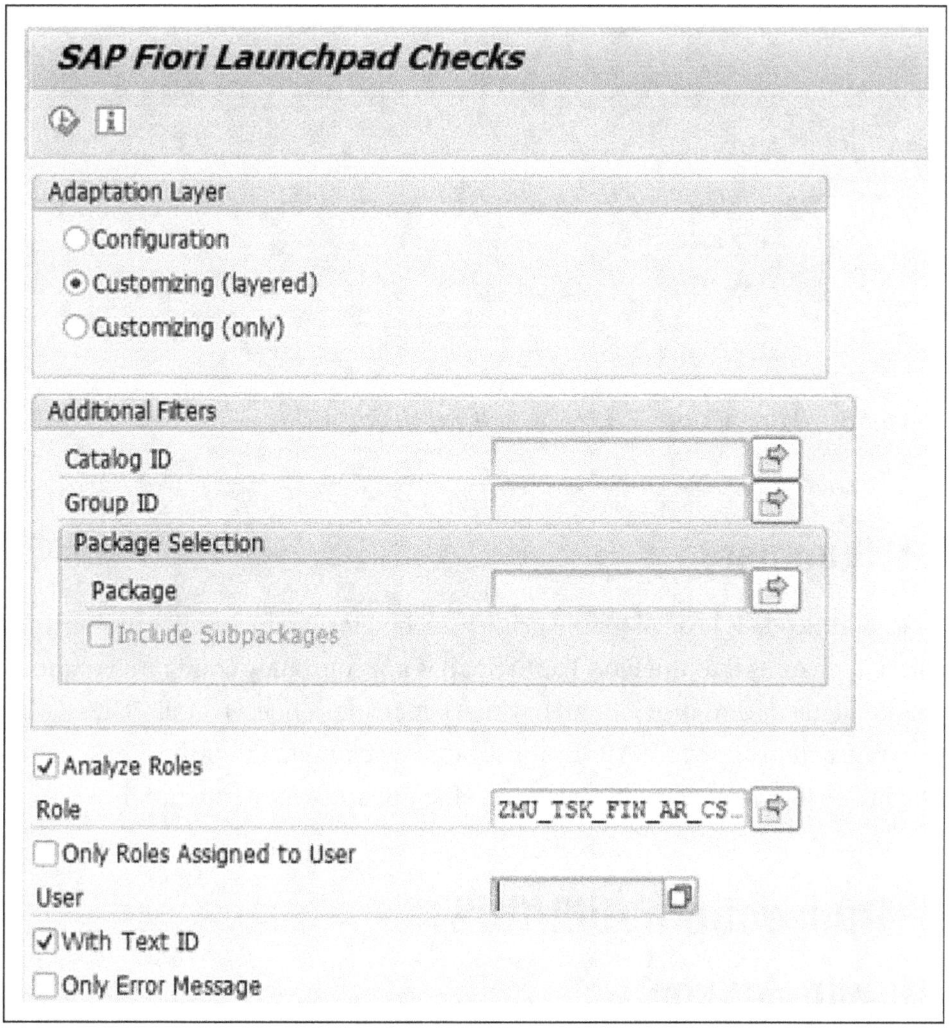

CHAPTER 16 SAP FIORI REPORTS

Figure 16-54. Checks for a role selected

Execute and the output is displayed, as shown in the figure below.

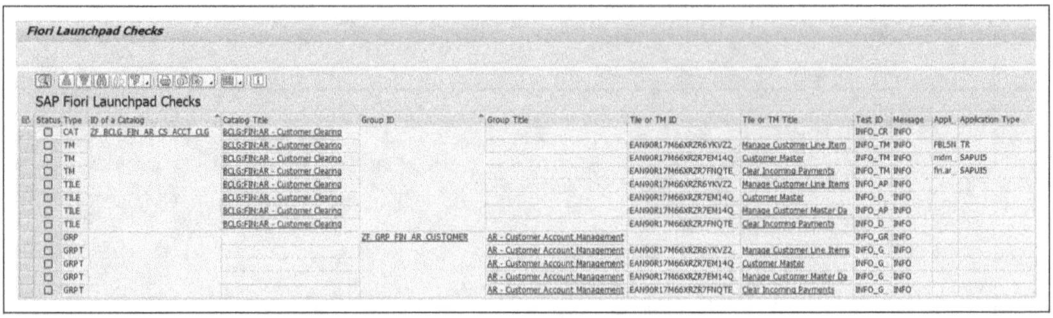

Figure 16-55. Transaction /UI2/FLC output displayed

16.6.4 Summary

This transaction code is crucial for ensuring that the Fiori Launchpad is properly configured. It ensures that the Fiori Launchpad is appropriately configured to meet organizational needs and provides an optimal user experience. Overall, /UI2/FLC is an essential transaction code for SAP administrators who aim to tailor the Fiori Launchpad to fit specific business needs while ensuring efficient and secure operation.

16.7 Transaction: /UI2/CUST

16.7.1 Introduction

This section will cover the report published using the transaction code /UI2/CUST. The transaction code **/UI2/CUST** in SAP Fiori launches the Fiori Launchpad customizing tool, which allows administrators and developers to customize various aspects of the Fiori Launchpad. This tool is an SPRO-type transaction for customizing and configuring SAP Fiori, which is primarily used by administrators and developers who are responsible for customizing the Fiori Launchpad.

16.7.2 Main Features and Use

The main features are outlined as follows:

- **Tile Catalogs and Groups:** You can create, edit, and delete catalogs and groups that organize the tiles that appear on the Fiori Launchpad.

- **Define Spaces and pages:** You can manage spaces and pages within the Fiori Launchpad.

- **Define and Assign Groups:** Create and maintain groups of tiles and assign them to users or roles.

- **Target Mappings:** Set up target mappings to determine user interactions with a tile, including specifying the navigation target, such as opening a specific app or screen. Update or modify as business requirements change.

- **Configure Tile Properties:** Customize the appearance and behavior of tiles, such as their size, title, and target mapping.

- **Adjust Launchpad Layout:** Modify the layout of the Fiori Launchpad to suit your organization's workflows better.

- **Roles and Authorizations:** Manage roles and authorizations related to Fiori Launchpad access and tile visibility.

- **Theme Selection:** Customize the theme and branding settings for the Fiori Launchpad.

- **Navigation and Search:** Configure navigation targets and search settings for tiles and applications.

- **User Interface Settings:** Adjust settings related to the user interface, such as layout and personalization options.

- **Catalog Assignment:** Assign catalogs to users or user groups to control which tiles they can see and access on their Fiori Launchpad.

Note The transaction **/UI2/CUST** can be used to access only the UI-relevant parts of the IMG.

16.7.3 Demo Examples

Executing the transaction displays the output, as shown in the figure below.

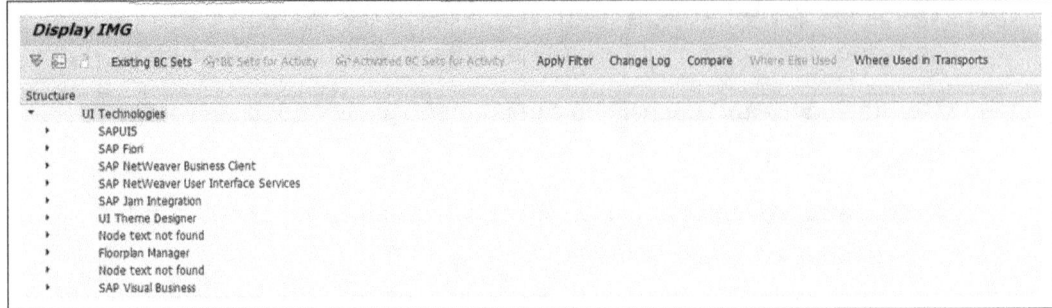

Figure 16-56. *The transaction /UI2/CUST initial screen*

As seen in the above figure, this transaction organizes all **SPRO** configurations in a tree format within the implementation guide, consolidating everything in one simple location.

Accessing the transaction in your SAP system typically opens a web-based interface where you can perform these customizations using a user-friendly interface provided by the SAP Fiori Launchpad Designer.

It is worth noting that the exact features and options available in the transaction /**UI2/CUST** can vary depending on your SAP Fiori version and your system's specific configuration.

16.7.4 Summary

In this section, we summarized that by using transaction/UI2/CUST, you could effectively tailor the Fiori Launchpad to meet specific business needs, ensuring that users have quick and easy access to the tools and information they need.

16.8 Transaction: SUIM

16.8.1 Introduction

The transaction **SUIM** is essential for managing user authorizations and roles in an SAP system.

16.8.2 Main Features and Use

The lists below outline some of its key features:

User Analysis:

- **Users by Complex Selection Criteria:** Search for users based on various criteria, such as user attributes, assigned roles, profiles, and authorization values. This allows for targeted user searches based on specific requirements.

- **User Comparison:** Compare two or more users to identify differences in their authorizations, roles, and profiles. This helps ensure consistency and identify potential security risks.

- **User Information List:** Generate detailed lists of users, including their attributes, roles, profiles, and authorization values. These lists can be exported for further analysis or documentation.

Role Analysis:

- **Roles by Complex Selection Criteria:** Search for roles based on various criteria, such as role name, description, assigned transactions, and authorization objects. This helps find suitable roles for users or identify roles that need to be adjusted.

- **Role Comparison:** Compare two or more roles to identify differences in their assigned transactions, authorization objects, and values. This aids in understanding the relationships between roles and ensuring proper segregation of duties.

- **Role Information List:** Generate lists of roles, including their assigned transactions, authorization objects, and values. These lists can be used for documentation or further analysis.

Authorization Analysis:

- **Authorizations by Complex Selection Criteria:** Search for authorization objects and values based on various criteria, such as object name, field values, and assigned roles. This helps understand the authorization structure and identify potential conflicts or gaps.

- **Authorization Comparison:** Compare authorizations between users or roles to identify inconsistencies or potential security risks.

- **Authorization Change Documents:** Track changes made to authorizations, roles, and profiles over time. This is crucial for audit and compliance purposes.

Benefits:

- **Enhanced Security:** Helps identify and mitigate security risks by analyzing user access and authorizations

- **Improved Compliance:** Facilitates audit and compliance processes by tracking changes and generating reports

- **Efficient Troubleshooting:** Assists in troubleshooting authorization issues by offering detailed analytical capabilities

Other Features:

- **Profile Analysis:** Analyze profiles to identify assigned authorization objects and values.

- **Transaction Analysis:** Search for transactions and view their associated authorization objects.

- **Reporting:** Generate various reports on users, roles, authorizations, and profiles.

16.8.3 Demo Examples

This section will focus solely on the options available under the **Roles tab**. As illustrated in the figure below, other features available with the transaction **SUIM** will not be covered as they are beyond the scope of this book.

Executing the transaction **SUIM** opens a User Information System window, as shown in the figure below.

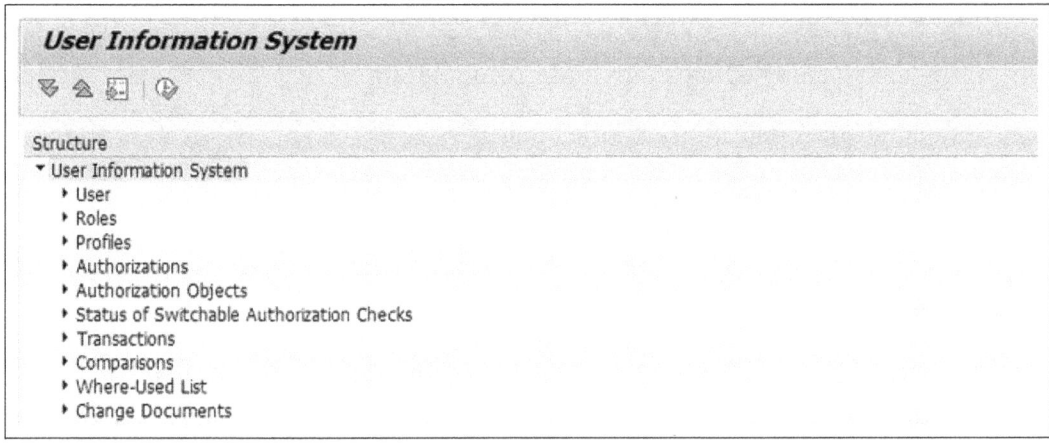

Figure 16-57. *Transaction SUIM initial screen*

This section will cover only the options available under the **Roles** tab. Expanding the tab Roles displays the options available under this tab, as shown in the figure below.

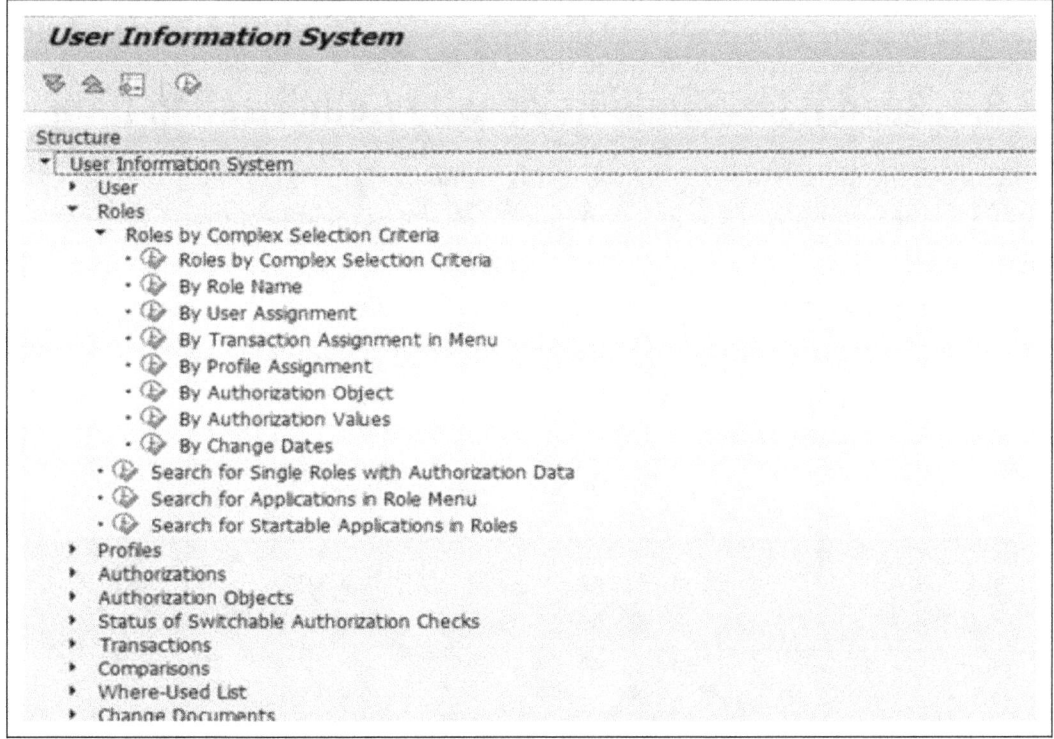

Figure 16-58. *Transaction SUIM – Roles tab available options*

801

From the above figure, we will focus on three options available as listed below:

- Search for Single Roles with Authorization Data
- Search for Applications in Role Menu
- Search For Startable Application in Roles

Important Note

- We will check the output using the role **ZMU_TSK_FIN_AR_CST_ACTCLG:XXXX**.
- **IWSG** refers to the **service group** metadata (used for grouping multiple OData services).
- **IWSV** refers to the **individual OData service versions** (what is called and consumed by Fiori apps).

16.8.4 Search for Single Roles with Authorization Data

In SAP Fiori, the **Search for Single Roles with Authorization Data** feature in transaction SUIM helps security administrators find specific roles that include authorization objects, such as **S_TCODE** and **S_SERVICE**, along with their associated field values. This tool analyzes access to sensitive transactions, identifies potential security risks, and ensures policy compliance. It also aids in troubleshooting by pinpointing roles that may inadvertently grant excessive or insufficient access, making it useful during audits and optimizing role management.

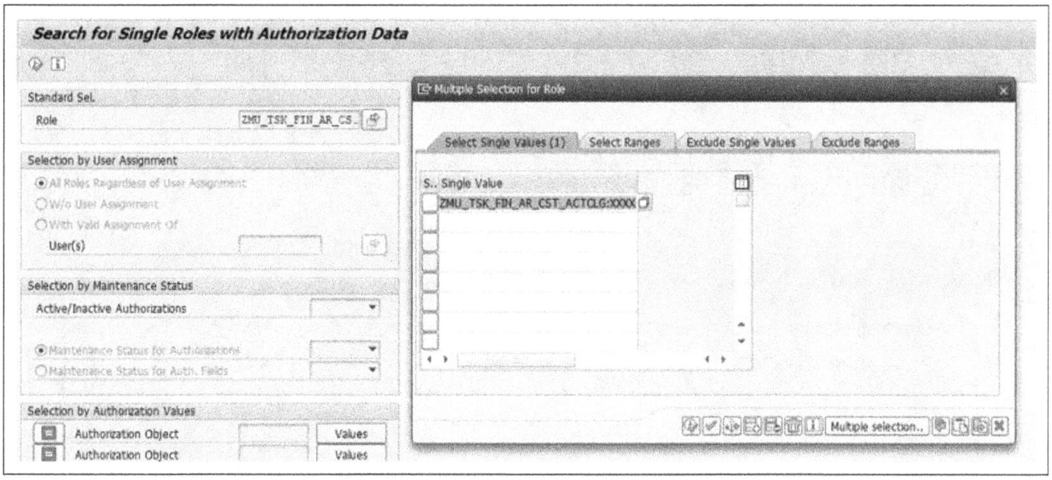

CHAPTER 16　SAP FIORI REPORTS

Figure 16-59. Role attribute added

Executing it by entering the role name displays the columns Object, Authorization, Field name, Maintenance Status, From Value, To Value, Active/Inactive, and Prof. Status, as shown in the figure below.

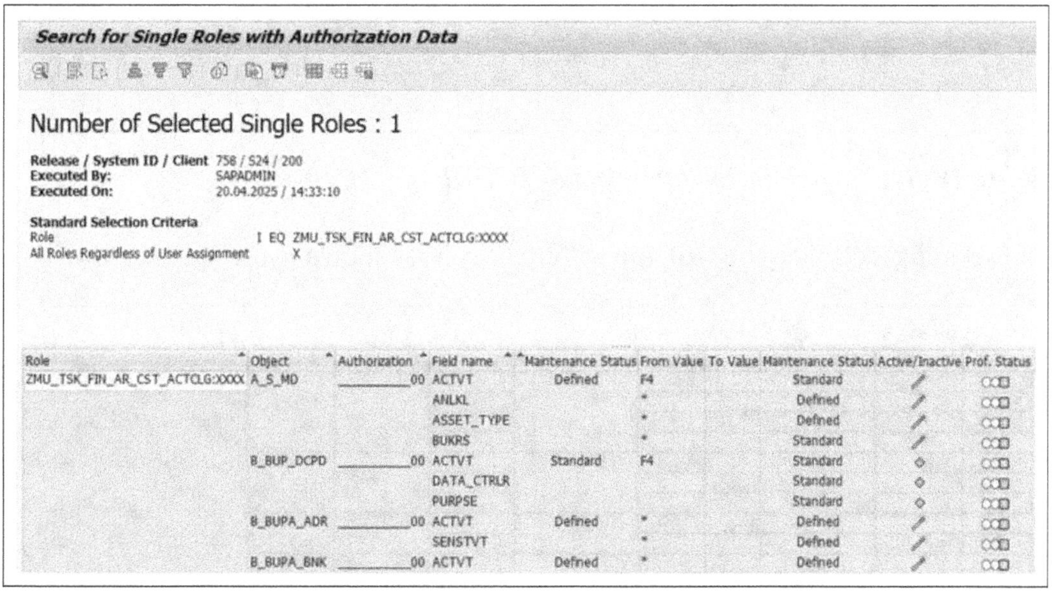

Figure 16-60. Output displaying authorization and value within the role

Next, the Authorization Object filter is set as **S_TCODE** as a search criterion, as shown in the figure below.

803

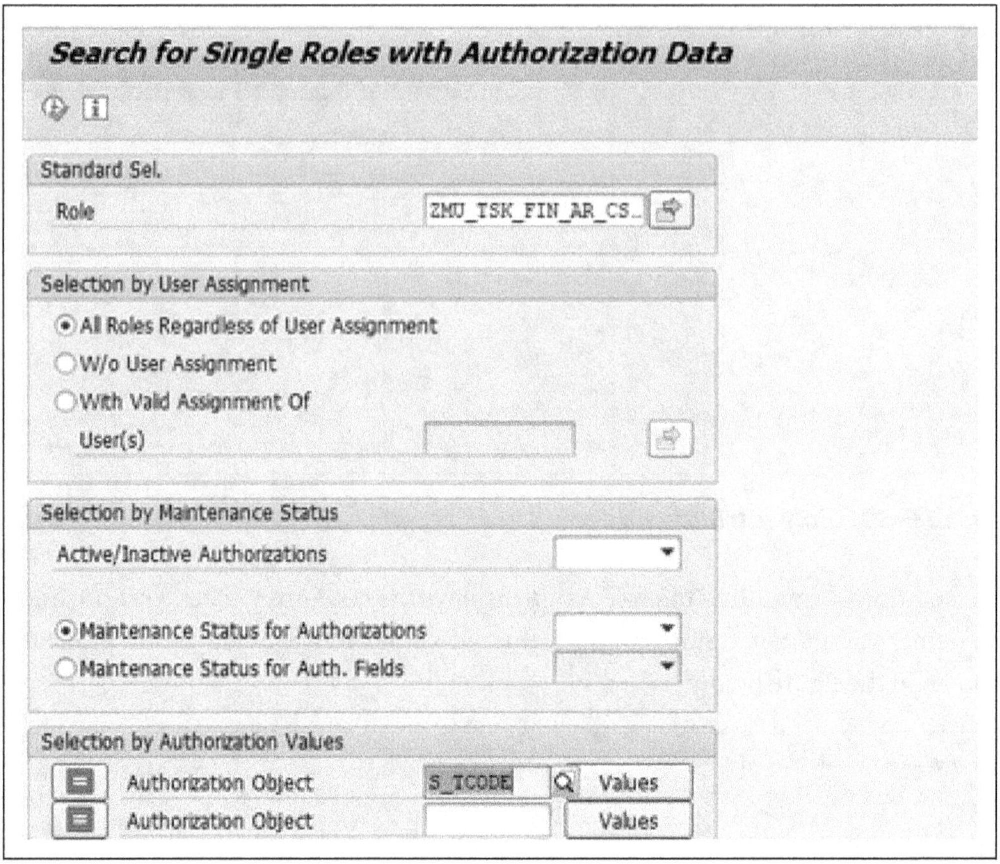

CHAPTER 16   SAP FIORI REPORTS

Figure 16-61. Search based on object S_TCODE

Executing it displays the **GUI app** within the role, as shown in the figure below.

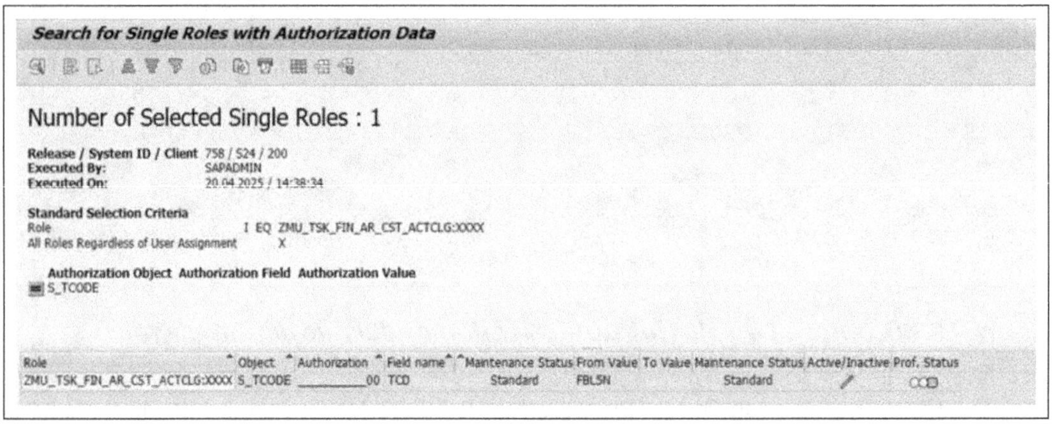

Figure 16-62. Output displayed based on the authorization object S_TCODE

CHAPTER 16 SAP FIORI REPORTS

Next, set **Authorization Object** as **S_SERVICE** within the **role**, as shown in the figure below.

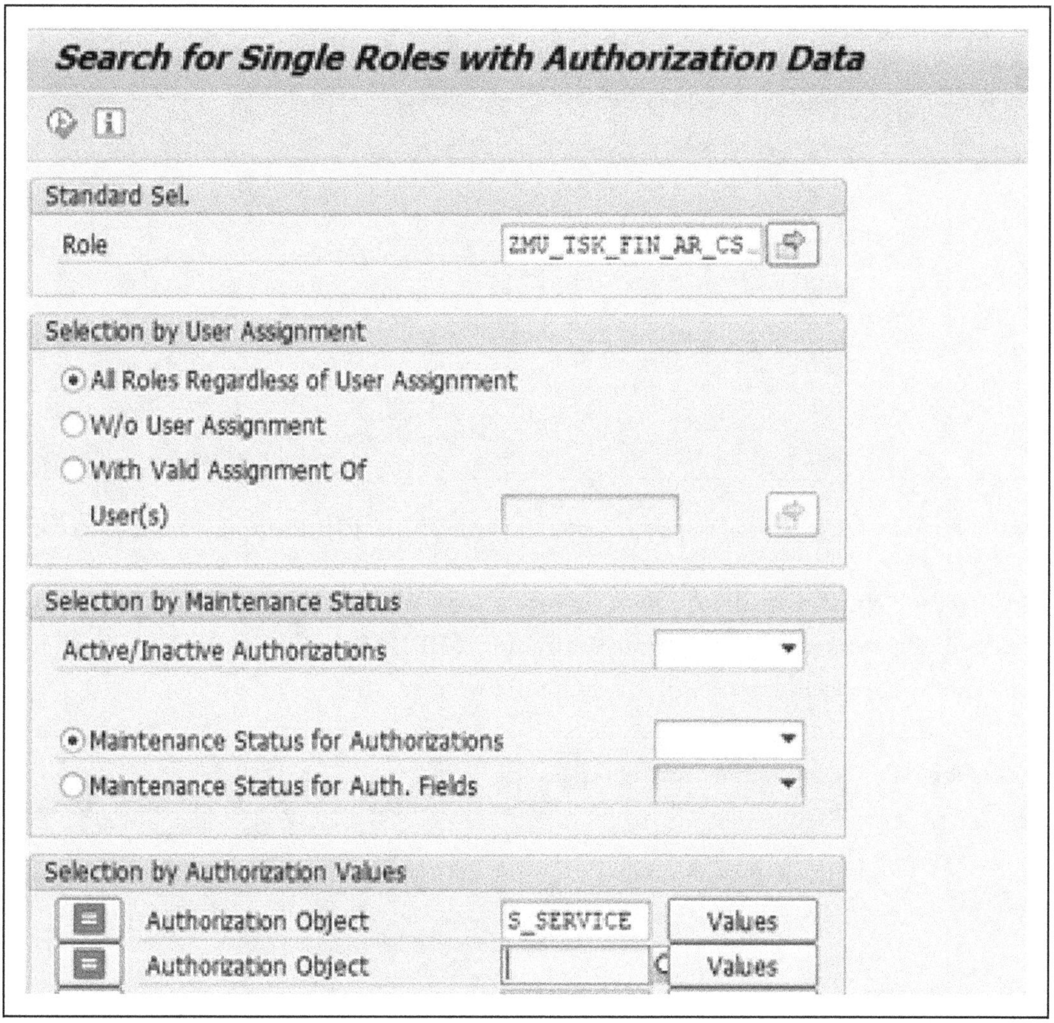

Figure 16-63. Search based on object S_SERVICE

Executing the above search criteria displays the **S_SERVICE** object data, **SRV_NAME** under **Field name** and, under **From value**, the **hash key ID** associated with the services within the role, as shown in the figure below.

805

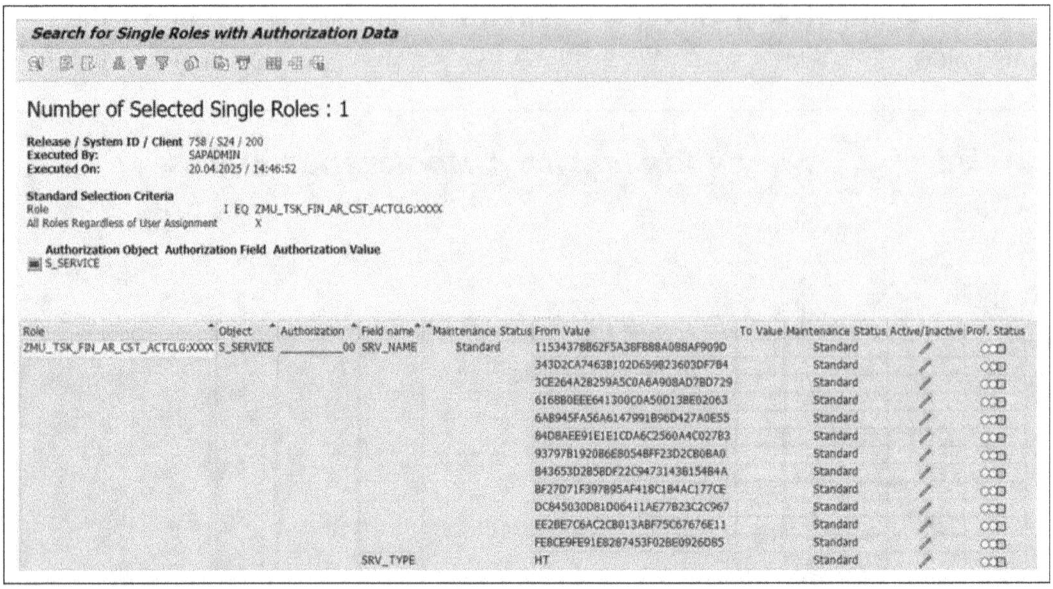

CHAPTER 16 SAP FIORI REPORTS

Figure 16-64. Output displayed based on the authorization object S_SERVICE

Copy the **From Value** data, which serves as the **hash key ID** data of the OData services of the apps in the role, and use it in the **USOBHASH table** under **Name** using transaction **SE16**, as illustrated in the figure below.

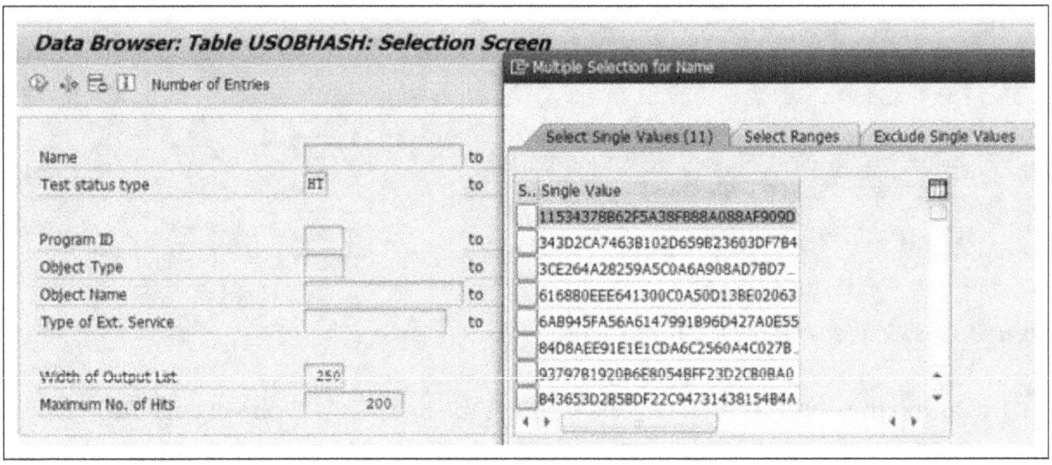

Figure 16-65. USOBHASH table with hash key IDs inserted

In the above figure, ensure the **Test status type** is set to **HT (hash value for TADIR object)**, and then execute. The output displays the **OData services** available within the role and the associated **IWSG/IWSV components**, as shown in the figure below.

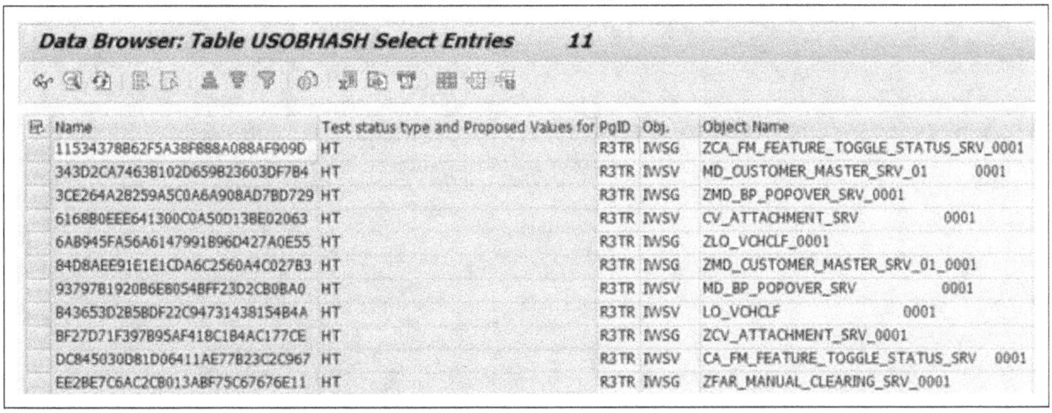

Data Browser: Table USOBHASH Select Entries 11

Name	Test status type and Proposed Values for	PgID	Obj.	Object Name
11534378B62F5A38F888A088AF909D	HT	R3TR	IWSG	ZCA_FM_FEATURE_TOGGLE_STATUS_SRV_0001
343D2CA74638102D659823603DF7B4	HT	R3TR	IWSV	MD_CUSTOMER_MASTER_SRV_01 0001
3CE264A28259A5C0A6A908AD7BD729	HT	R3TR	IWSG	ZMD_BP_POPOVER_SRV_0001
616B80EEE641300C0A50D13BE02063	HT	R3TR	IWSV	CV_ATTACHMENT_SRV 0001
6AB945FA56A6147991B96D427A0E55	HT	R3TR	IWSG	ZLO_VCHCLF_0001
84D8AEE91E1E1CDA6C2560A4C027B3	HT	R3TR	IWSG	ZMD_CUSTOMER_MASTER_SRV_01_0001
937978192086E8054BFF23D2CB0BA0	HT	R3TR	IWSV	MD_BP_POPOVER_SRV 0001
B43653D2B5BDF22C94731438154B4A	HT	R3TR	IWSV	LO_VCHCLF 0001
BF27D71F397B95AF418C1B4AC177CE	HT	R3TR	IWSG	ZCV_ATTACHMENT_SRV_0001
DC845030D81D06411AE77B23C2C967	HT	R3TR	IWSV	CA_FM_FEATURE_TOGGLE_STATUS_SRV 0001
EE2BE7C6AC2CB013ABF75C67676E11	HT	R3TR	IWSG	ZFAR_MANUAL_CLEARING_SRV_0001

***Figure 16-66.** The output displays the OData services available within the role*

16.8.5 Search for Applications in Role Menu

In SAP Fiori, the **Search for Applications in Role Menu** function within transaction SUIM allows users to identify which roles include specific applications, such as transaction codes and Fiori apps. This feature is valuable for administrators to analyze role design, verify application assignments, and confirm if an application is included in existing roles. It also aids in role cleanup, migration projects, and system upgrades by providing essential insights into role-to-application mapping for accurate **access management**.

Executing **Search for Applications in Role Menu** opens a new window, as shown in the figure below.

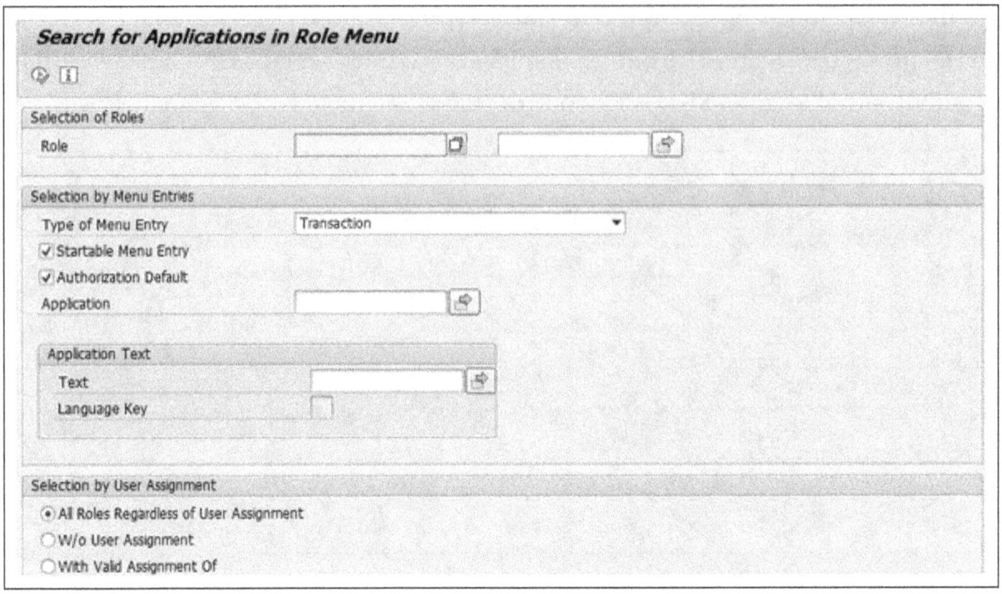

CHAPTER 16   SAP FIORI REPORTS

Figure 16-67. Roles tab, Search for Applications in Role Menu option

In the above figure, under **Type of Menu Entry**, a few options are available. Expanding the same lists the entries available, as shown in the figure below.

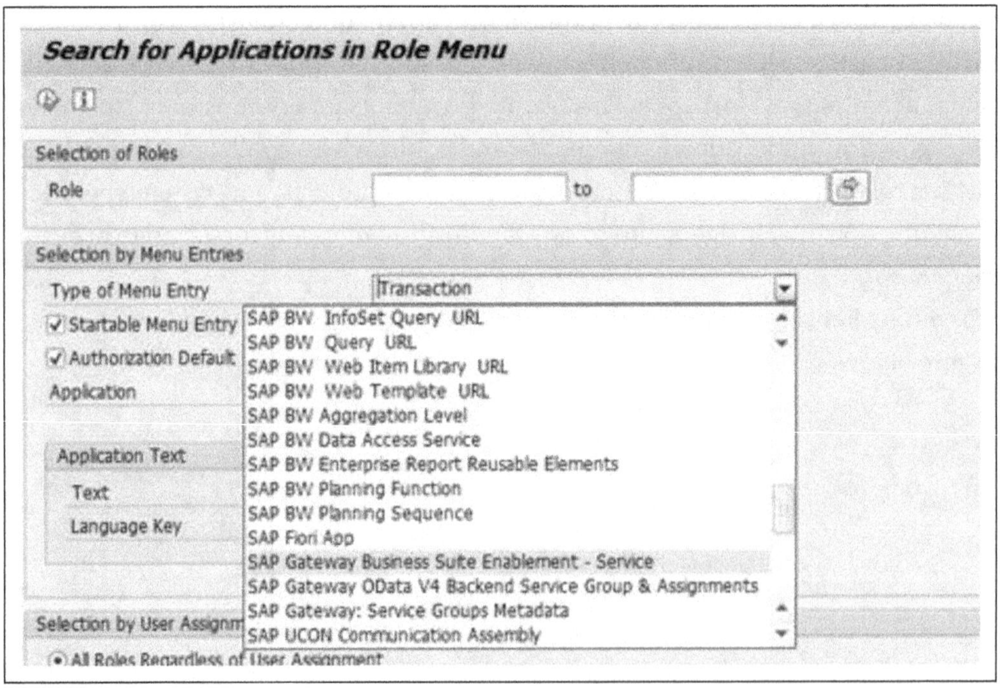

Figure 16-68. Type of Menu Entry available with the role

CHAPTER 16 SAP FIORI REPORTS

The options available in the system to search for are as follows, as shown in the figure above:

- SAP Gateway Business Suite Enablement – Service
- SAP Gateway: Service Groups Metadata
- Launchpad Catalog
- Launchpad Group
- Launchpad Space

> **Note** The above-listed options will be discussed using the role.

SAP Gateway Business Suite Enablement – Service

In SUIM, selecting **SAP Gateway Business Suite Enablement – Service** for a role shows the OData services linked to that role through the authorization object **S_SERVICE**. These services are essential for SAP Fiori applications, enabling them to fetch and display data. The display includes the **technical service name** and related **IWSG components**, indicating service definitions and active versions. This information helps security administrators ensure that the right services are in place so that Fiori apps work correctly. It also helps them fix access problems caused by missing service authorizations. Additionally, it supports compliance by clearly showing which services are provided for optimal access. The SAP Gateway Business Suite Enablement – Service option is shown in the figure below as a search criterion.

809

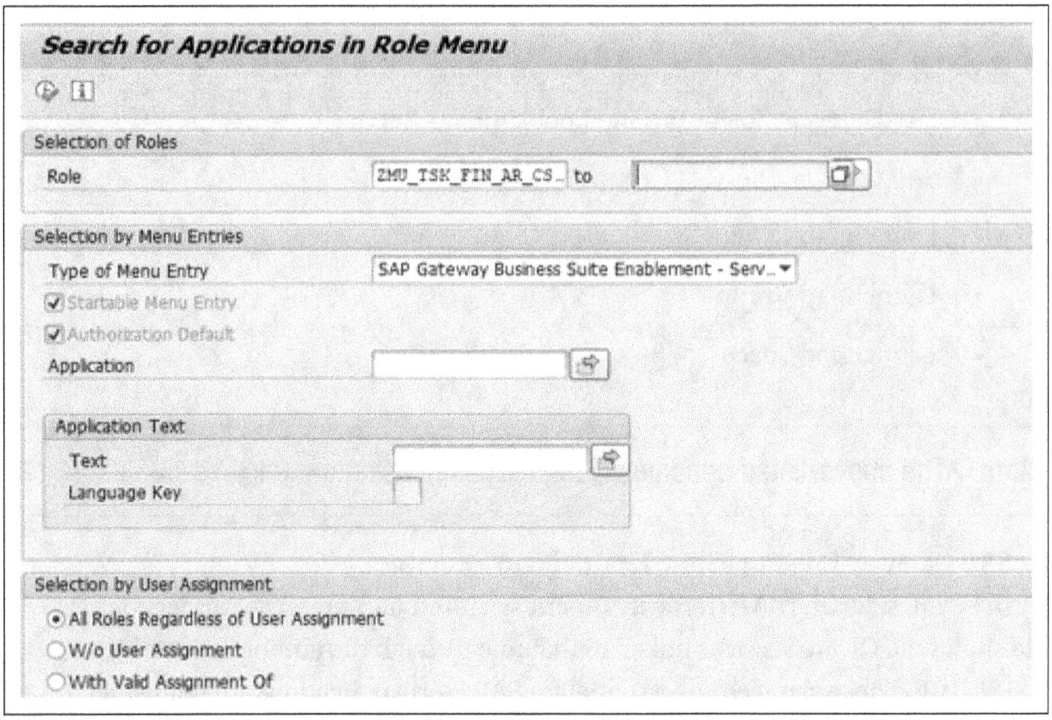

CHAPTER 16   SAP FIORI REPORTS

Figure 16-69. Using the search option SAP Gateway Business Suite Enablement – Service

Using the **execute** icon, in the above figure, displays the **SAP Gateway Business Suite Enablement – Service** output, which is the **IWSV components** within the **role**, as shown in the figure below.

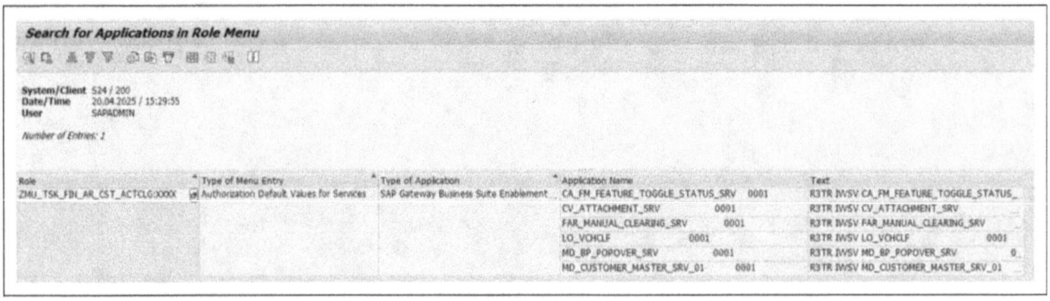

Figure 16-70. IWSV components of OData services within the role displayed

CHAPTER 16 SAP FIORI REPORTS

SAP Gateway: Service Groups Metadata

In **SUIM**, selecting **SAP Gateway: Service Groups Metadata** for a role shows the OData services linked to that role through the authorization object **S_SERVICE**. These services are essential for SAP Fiori applications, enabling them to fetch and display data. The display includes the **technical service name** and related **IWSG components**, indicating service definitions and active versions. This information helps security administrators ensure that the right services are in place so that Fiori apps work correctly. The option **SAP Gateway: Service Groups Metadata** is shown in the figure below as a search criterion.

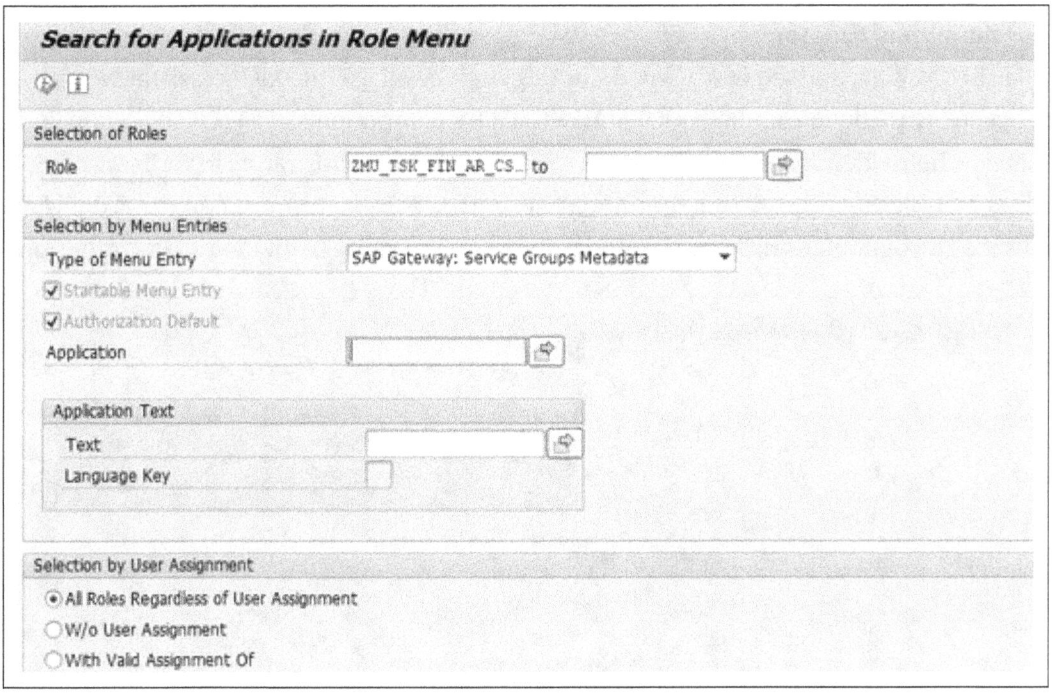

Figure 16-71. Using the search option SAP Gateway: Service Groups Metadata

Using the **execute** icon, in the above figure, displays the **SAP Gateway: Service Groups Metadata** output, which is the **IWSG components** within the **role**, as shown in the figure below.

811

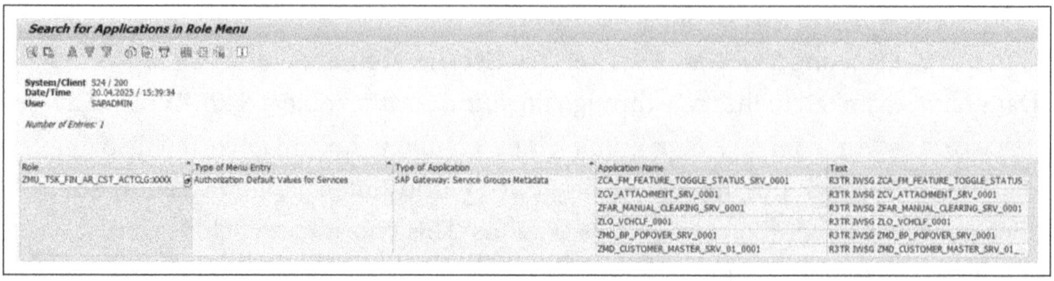

CHAPTER 16   SAP FIORI REPORTS

Figure 16-72. The output IWSV components of OData services within the role are displayed

Launchpad Catalog

In **SUIM**, selecting the **Launchpad Catalog** option will list the business catalog associated with the role and the related **IWSG/IWSV** components of the OData services. This view helps identify catalogs linked to roles, assisting administrators in verifying app access, troubleshooting missing tiles, and ensuring the correct business content is delivered to users. The option **Launchpad Catalog** is shown in the figure below as a search criterion.

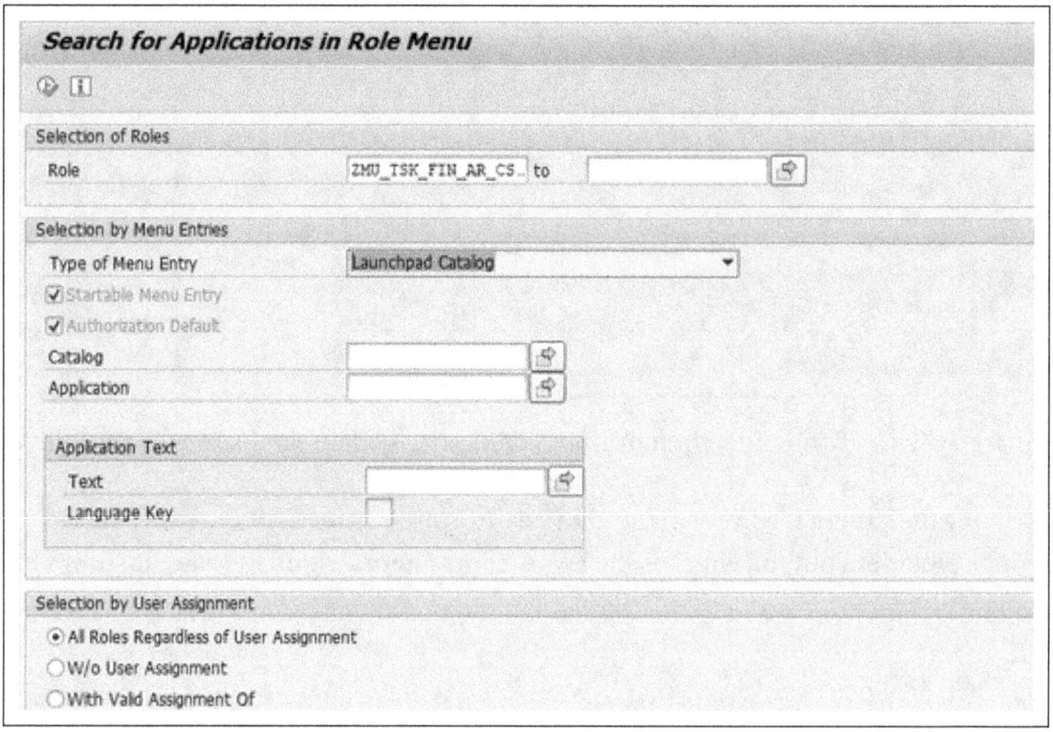

Figure 16-73. Using the search option Launchpad Catalog

CHAPTER 16 SAP FIORI REPORTS

Using the **execute** icon, in the above figure, displays the **Launchpad Catalog** output, which is the **IWSG/IWSV components** and the associated **Launchpad catalog** within the **role**, as shown in the figure below.

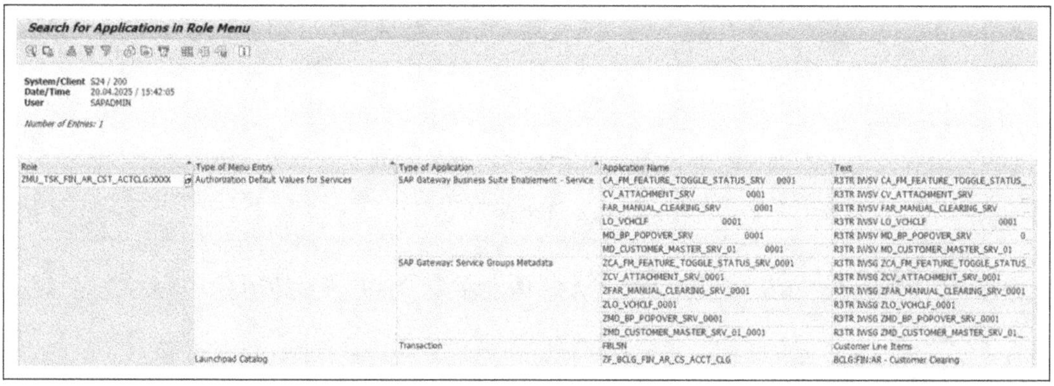

Figure 16-74. The output display of Launchpad Catalog – associated OData service IWSG/IWSV components within the role

Launchpad Group

In **SUIM**, selecting the **Launchpad Group** option will list the business group associated with the **role.** This view helps identify groups linked to roles, assisting administrators in ensuring that the correct business content is delivered to users. The option **Launchpad Group** is shown in the figure below as a search criterion.

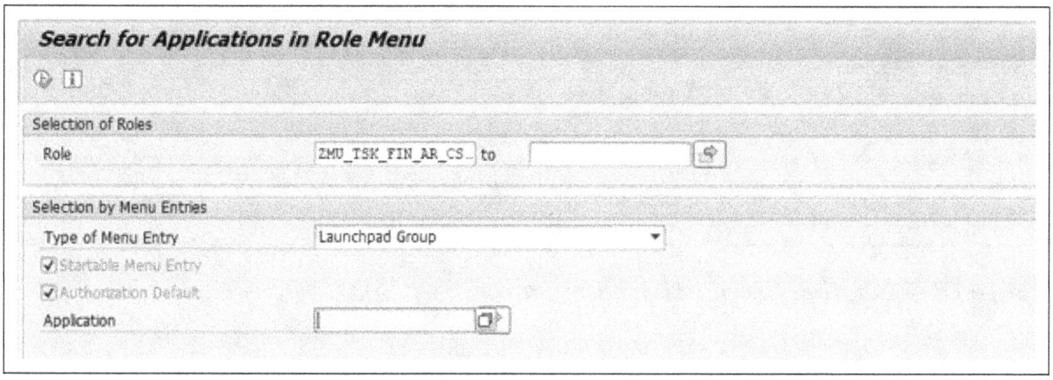

Figure 16-75. Using the search option Launchpad Group

813

Using the **execute** icon, in the above figure, displays the **Launchpad Group** output, which is the group details within the **role**, as shown in the figure below.

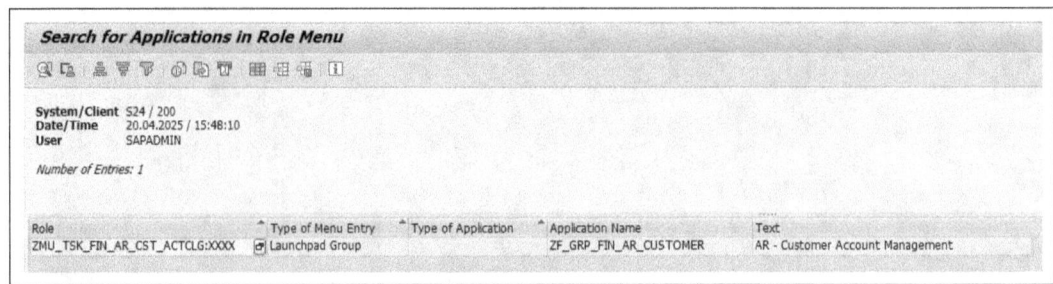

Figure 16-76. *The output display of Launchpad Group – details*

Launchpad Space

In **SUIM**, the **Launchpad Space** option lists the **Launchpad spaces** associated with each role. This view helps identify the spaces linked to roles, assisting administrators in ensuring that the correct business content is delivered to users. The option **Launchpad Space** is shown in the figure below as a search criterion.

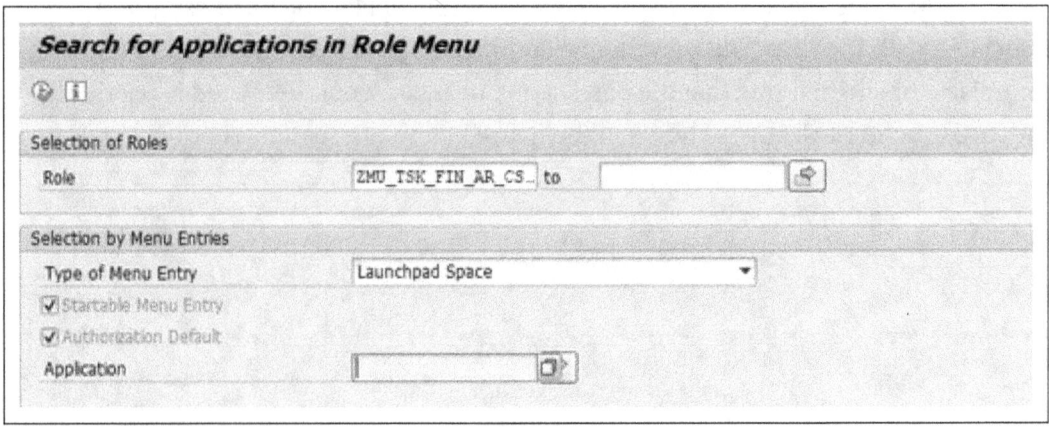

Figure 16-77. *Using the search option Launchpad Space*

Using the **execute** icon, in the above figure, displays the **Launchpad Space** output, which is the space details within the **role**, as shown in the figure below.

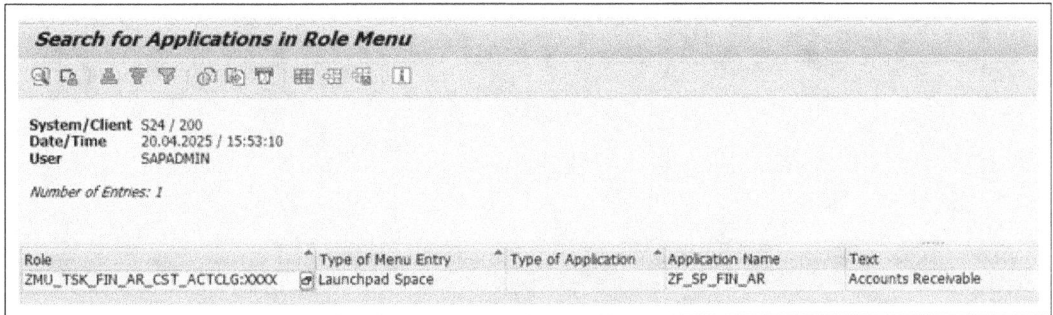

Figure 16-78. The output display of Launchpad Space – details

16.8.6 Search for Startable Application in Roles

In **SUIM**, the **Search for Startable Applications in Roles** function helps administrators find which Fiori applications users can launch from the Fiori Launchpad. This function is useful for confirming if a specific app can be accessed through an assigned role or for cleaning up and optimizing roles. **Under Application Type**, there are only two search options available:

- SAP Gateway Business Suite Enablement – Service
- SAP Gateway: Service Groups Metadata

SAP Gateway: Service Groups Metadata

The **SAP Gateway: Service Groups Metadata** option is shown in the figure below as a search criterion.

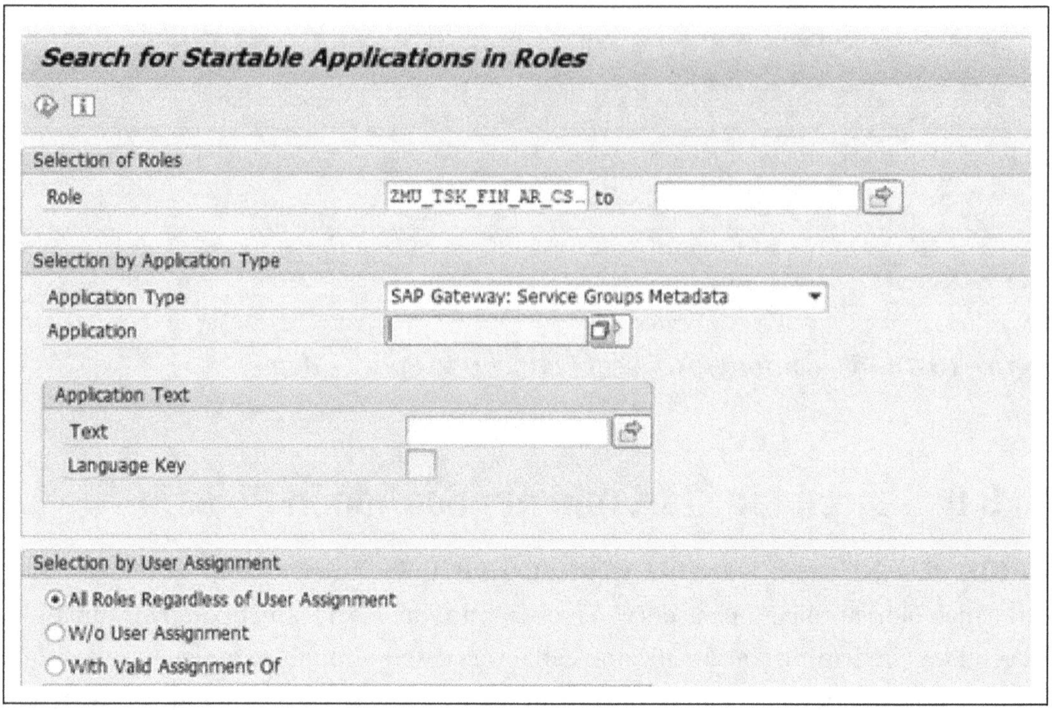

CHAPTER 16   SAP FIORI REPORTS

Figure 16-79. Using the search option SAP Gateway: Service Groups Metadata

Using the **execute** icon, in the above figure, displays the **SAP Gateway: Service Groups Metadata** output, which is the **IWSG components** within the **role**, as shown in the figure below.

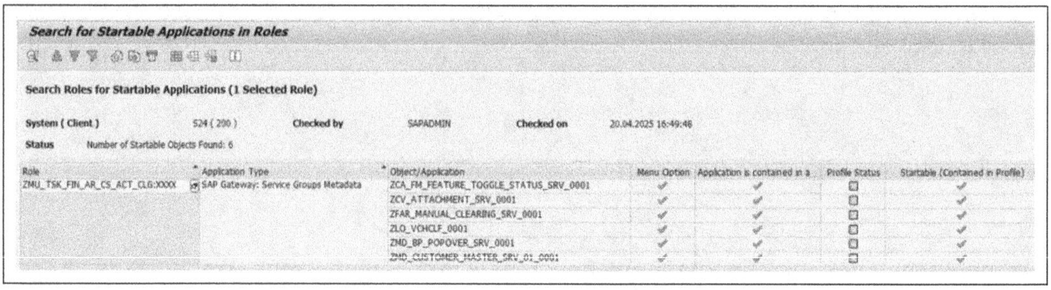

Figure 16-80. The output displays the IWSV components of the OData services

SAP Gateway Business Suite Enablement – Service

The **SAP Gateway Business Suite Enablement – Service** option is shown in the figure below as a search criterion.

816

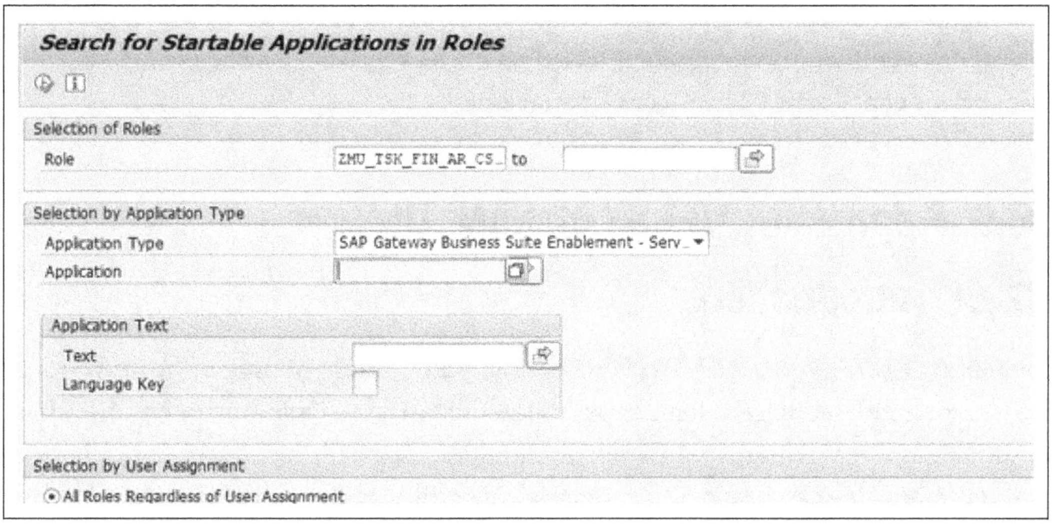

CHAPTER 16 SAP FIORI REPORTS

Figure 16-81. Using the search option SAP Gateway Business Suite Enablement – Service

Using the **execute** icon , in the above figure, displays the **SAP Gateway Business Suite Enablement – Service** output, which is the **IWSV components** within the **role**, as shown in the figure below.

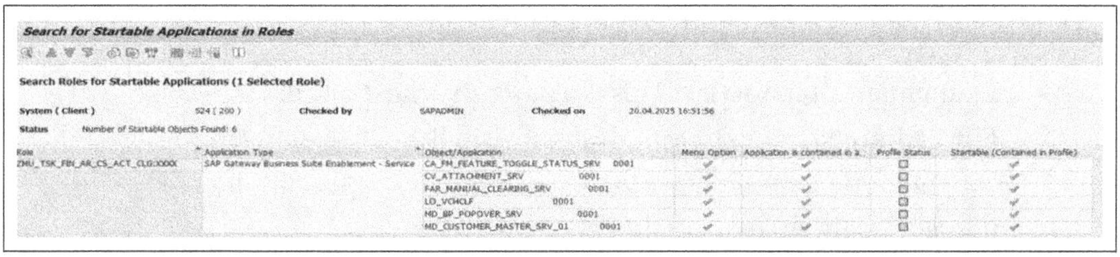

Figure 16-82. The output displays the IWSG components of the OData services

16.8.7 Summary

SUIM (User Information System) is a key tool for managing security in SAP Fiori, requiring the right permissions and a solid understanding of SAP security to prevent unauthorized access. It allows administrators to analyze roles, users, and authorizations, providing insights into Fiori-specific elements like Launchpad catalogs and OData services. This functionality is crucial for ensuring that users have appropriate access to

817

Fiori apps and back-end services. Additionally, SUIM aids in resolving access issues, conducting audits, and creating roles based on the least privilege principle, making it essential for effective SAP Fiori access management.

16.9 Report /UI2/FLP_ADMIN_UI

16.9.1 Introduction

The report **/UI2/FLP_ADMIN_UI (Fiori Launchpad Content Manager – Admin UI)** in SAP Fiori helps launch the Launchpad Content Manager in administrator mode. It is a central tool where administrators can do multiple tasks. This tool provides a central place for managing catalogs, groups, spaces, pages, tiles, and target mappings. It makes it easier for admins to create, edit, or delete content elements and check role assignments all in one spot. This is especially helpful for fixing visibility issues, simplifying content maintenance, and supporting large operations, which makes managing the Fiori landscape more efficient and user-friendly.

16.9.2 Main Features and Use

The list below outlines some of its key features:

- **Launchpad Diagnostics:** This is a **go-to diagnostic tool** for **Fiori administrators** to troubleshoot visibility, navigation, and configuration issues related to the Launchpad – especially after upgrades, role changes, or app deployments.

- **Centralized Admin Options**: The Launchpad home page lists all the options for administrators to navigate directly to various tasks from this page.

16.9.3 Demo Examples

This report can be executed by using transaction **SE38**. Under the program box, enter **/UI2/FLP_ADMIN_UI**. This will open a **UI2 Fiori Admin UI window**, as shown in the figure below.

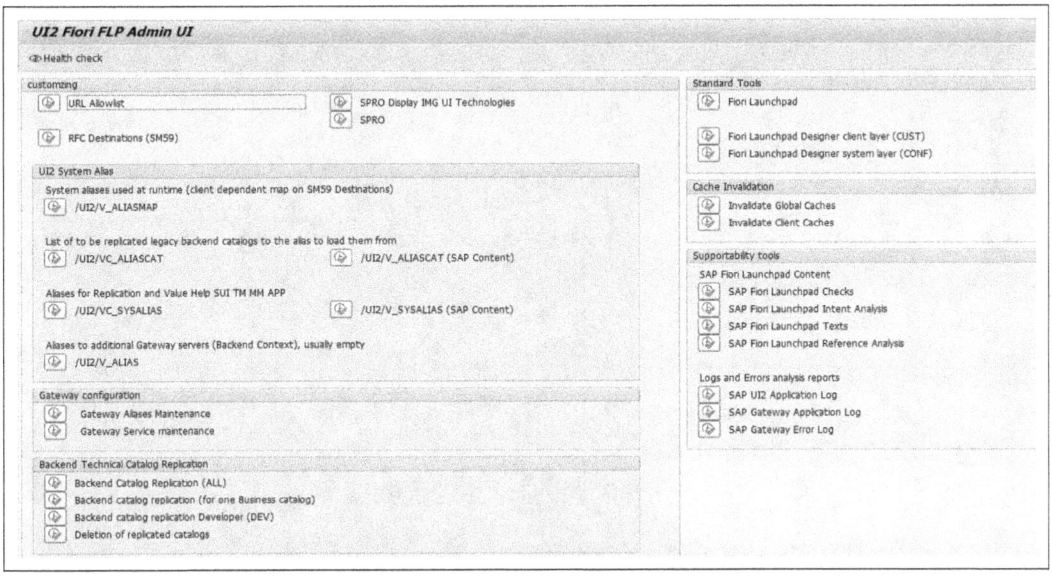

CHAPTER 16   SAP FIORI REPORTS

Figure 16-83. *Program /UI2/FLP_ADMIN_UI initial screen*

In the above figure, selecting any option will take you directly to that option. All the main reports are available under **Standard Tools,** followed by **Supportability tools**, as shown in the figure below.

819

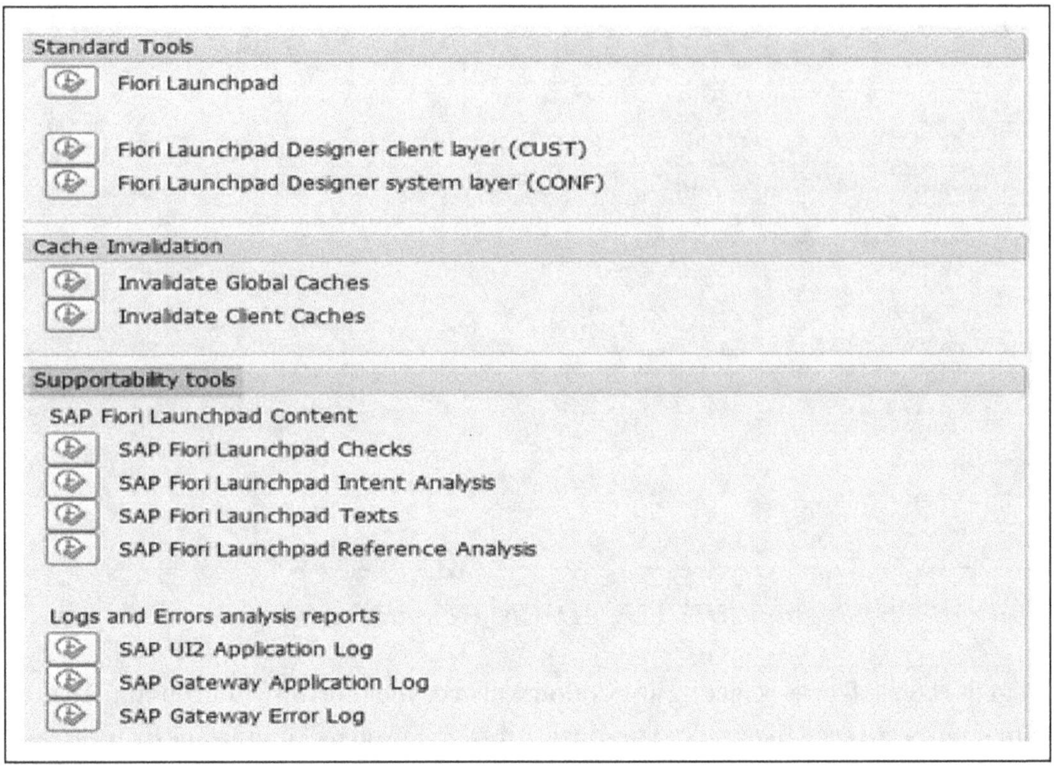

Figure 16-84. *Tools available within the report*

16.10 Report RSUSR_START_APPL

The **RSUSR_START_APPL** report checks PFCG transaction roles for Startable applications. The report RSUSR_START_APPL in SAP can be found in Fiori through **SAP GUI**. It acts as a central access point for user and authorization management tools. This report allows security administrators to quickly reach essential transactions such as SUIM, PFCG, and other reports about roles, profiles, and audits. It simplifies managing user access and authorizations, making it easier for administrators to handle everyday security tasks in the SAP environment. This tool helps administrators make sure that user roles are set up correctly and that applications are easy for users to access.

16.10.1 Main Features and Use

The main features are outlined below:

- **Check User Permissions:** This checks if user roles have all necessary start permissions for applications, focusing on key authorization objects like S_TCODE, S_SERVICE, S_RFC, and S_START.

- **Find Application Locks:** This report searches for locks on applications in transactions such as SM01_DEV and SM01_CUS.

- **Review Role and Data:** It examines the role menu, authorization data, and current profile data to identify applications that can be started.

- **Analyze User Assignments:** You can narrow the search by user roles, focusing on roles with valid user assignments or those without any assignments.

16.10.2 Demo Examples

This report is executed using transaction **SE38**. Once executed, enter the information in the **Role** field as **Z*U*FIN_AR***, and for **Application Type**, select **SAP Gateway Business Suite Enablement – Service**, as shown in the figure below.

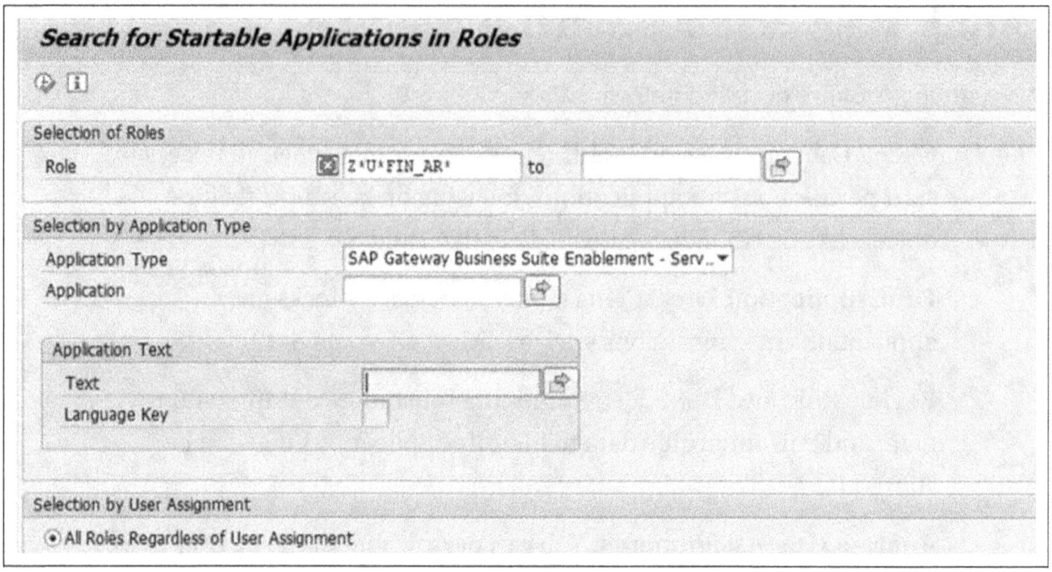

CHAPTER 16   SAP FIORI REPORTS

Figure 16-85. *Enter information in the initial screen of the report RSUSR_START_APPL*

Click the execute icon to display the output, as shown in the figure below.

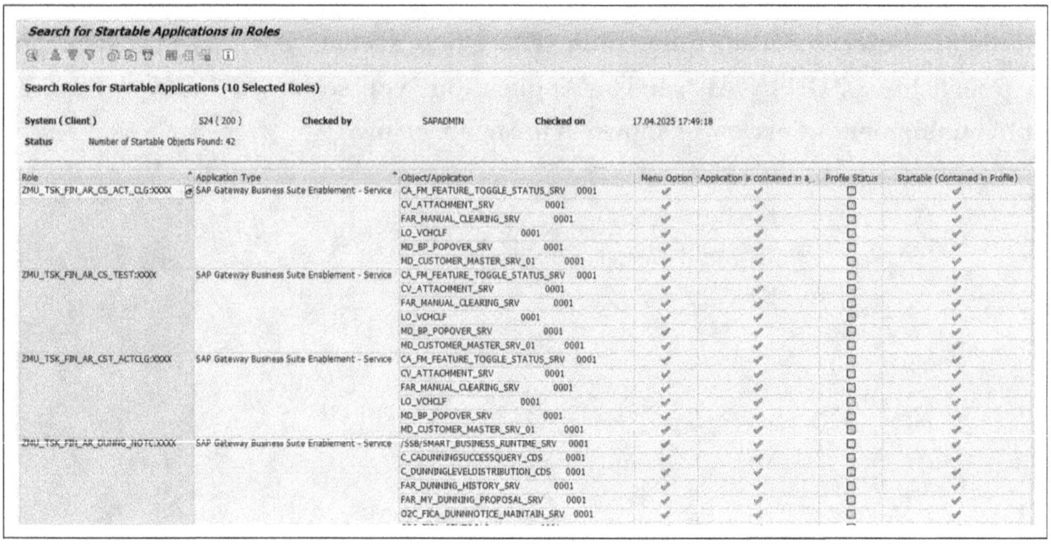

Figure 16-86. *The report RSUSR_START_APPL output*

822

CHAPTER 16 SAP FIORI REPORTS

The above figure displays the role name, application type, and other information. It also shows the profile status, which is green.

Furthermore, by selecting Transaction under Application Type, we can find a Startable application within a role as shown in the figure below.

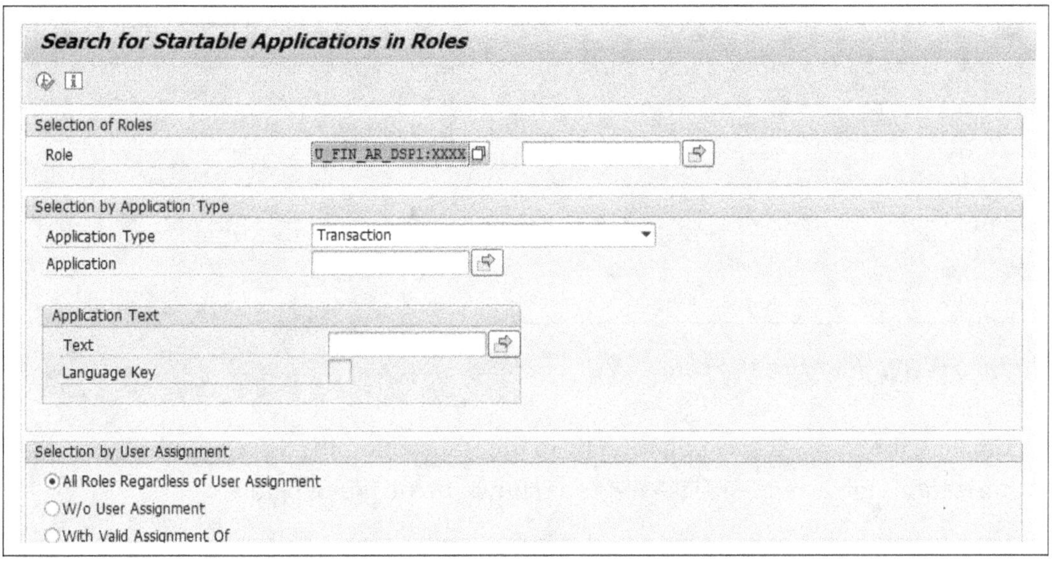

Figure 16-87. Selecting Transaction under Application Type

The output is displayed, as shown in the figure below.

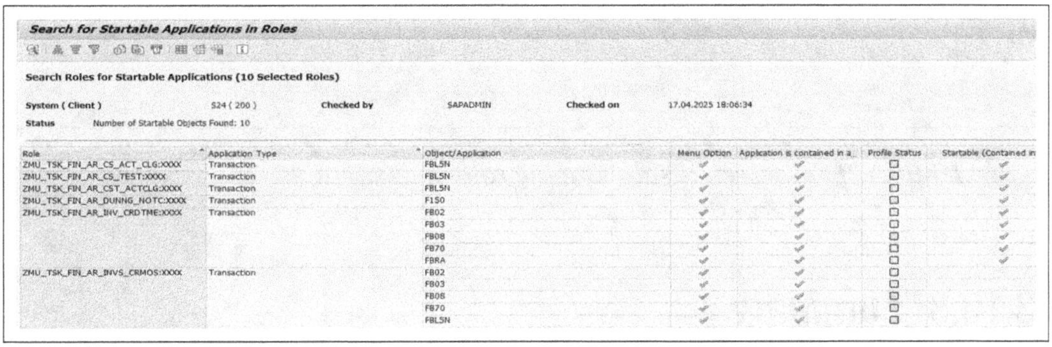

Figure 16-88. Startable transaction within the role displayed

823

CHAPTER 16   SAP FIORI REPORTS

Note   If the profile status shows red 🔴, it means that the role has not been generated as shown in the figure below.

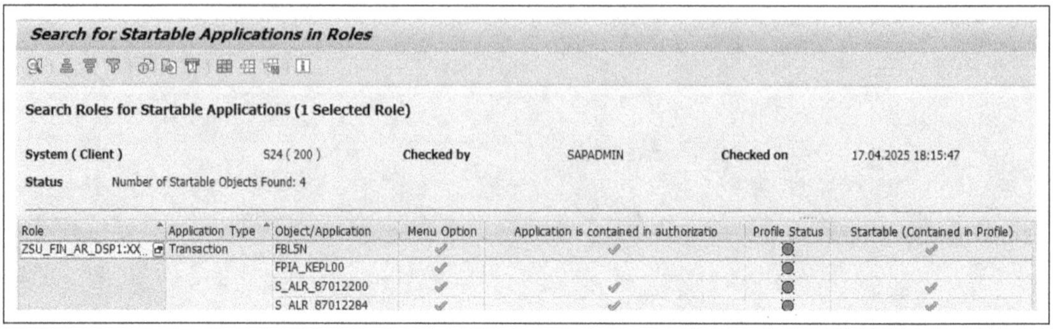

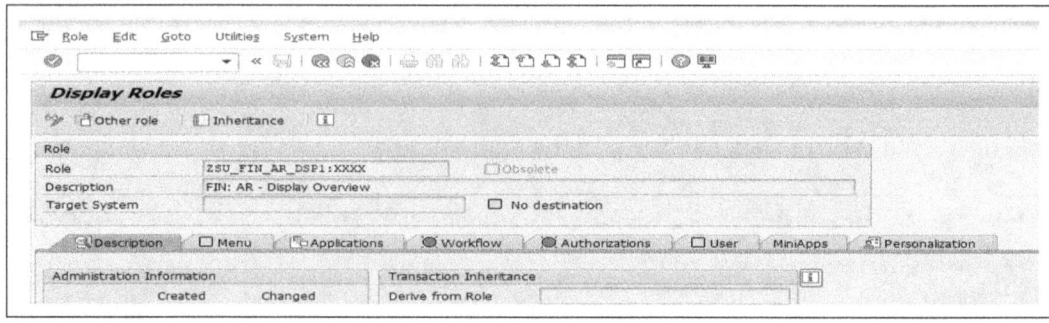

Figure 16-89. *Error in the role*

Clicking the role will take you directly to the transaction PFCG, where the Authorizations tab is red 🔴 Authorizations, as shown in the figure below.

Figure 16-90. *PFCG screen displaying the role not generated*

16.10.3 Summary

This report serves as a comprehensive navigation hub for administrators and security personnel. It enables quick access to essential transactions and presents data in a clear tabular format.

16.11 Table USOBHASH

16.11.1 Introduction

The **USOBHASH** table in SAP (including systems supporting SAP Fiori) is a technical table that stores hash values of a specific node within a service hierarchy of Fiori apps.

This table is crucial for SAP Fiori authorization, particularly for maintaining a detailed level of authorization control.

The authorization object S_SERVICE contains hash values stored in the SRV_NAME field. These hash values are populated when an application is added to the catalog or when IWSV and IWSG components are included in the role.

16.11.2 Demo Examples

In the role as shown in the figure below, you can see the **hash key IDs** in authorization object S_SERVICE.

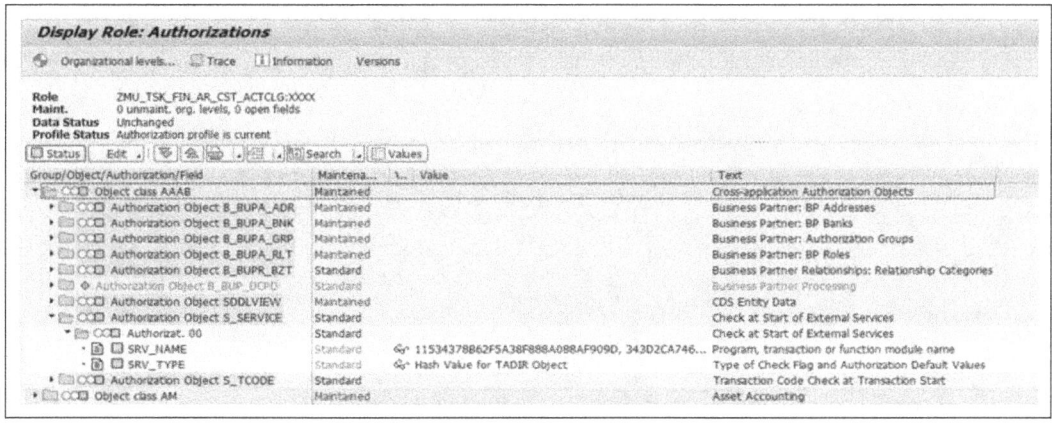

Figure 16-91. Hask keys displayed within the role

To check the list of OData services and their hash key available in the system, go to transaction SE16 and specify the table **USOBHASH** and then enter the key.

CHAPTER 16 SAP FIORI REPORTS

A window will open, as shown in the figure below.

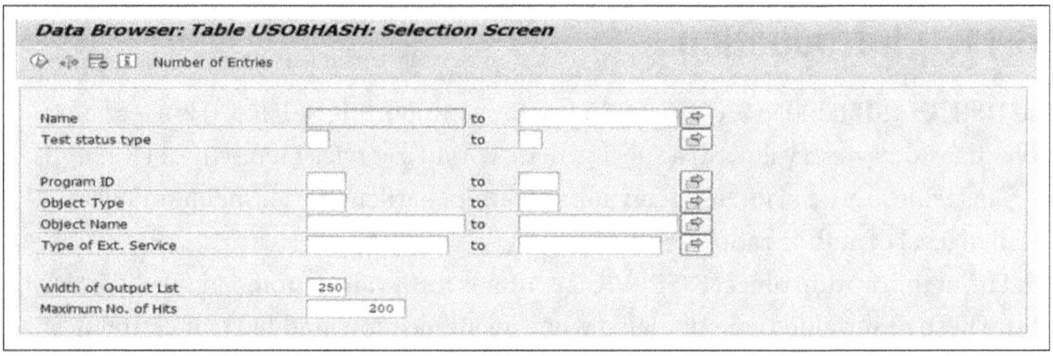

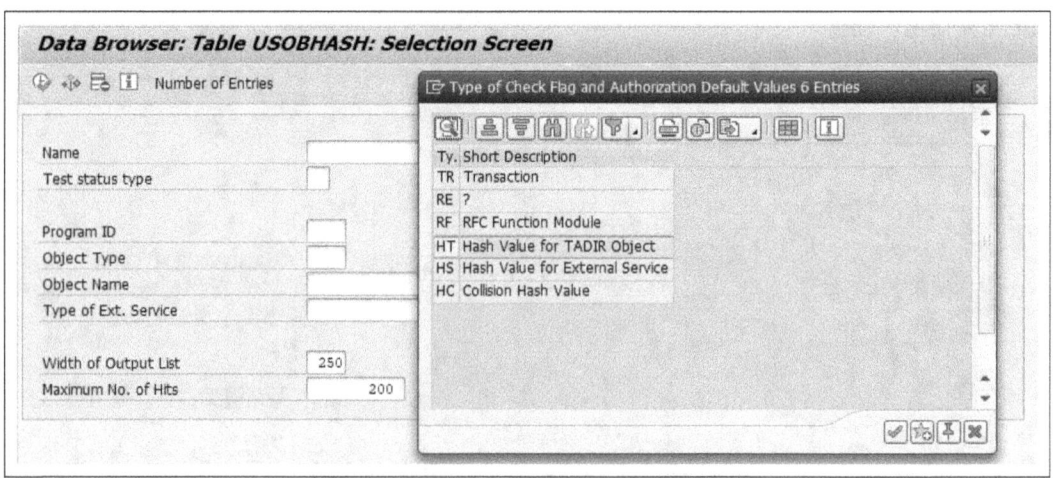

Figure 16-92. *Table USOBHASH initial screen*

Enter or search for the value **HT** in the **Test status type** field as shown in the figure below.

Figure 16-93. *HT entered for Test status type*

For **Object ID**, add **IWSG** and **IWSV** as shown in the figure below.

826

CHAPTER 16 SAP FIORI REPORTS

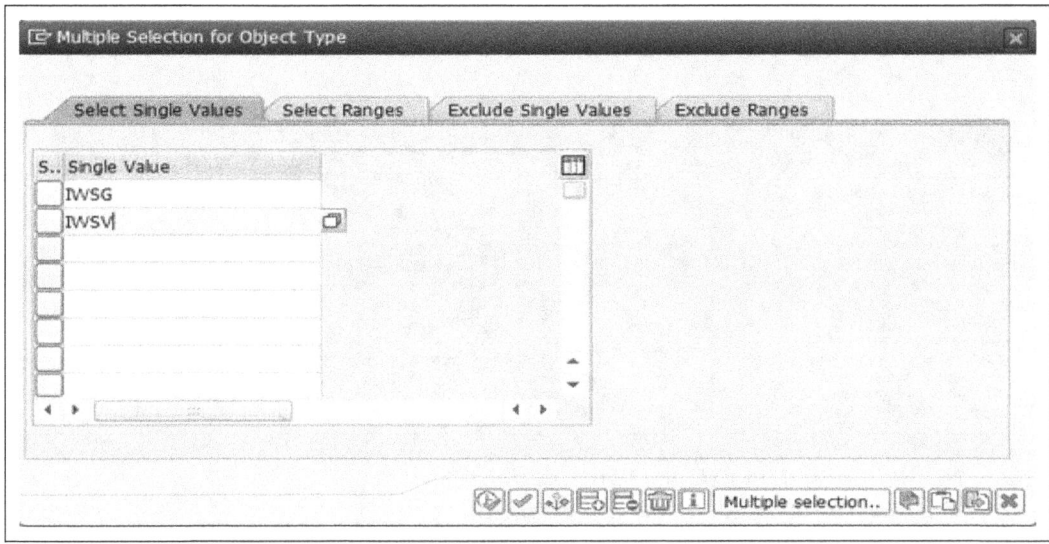

Figure 16-94. Object IDs entered as IWSG and IWSV

Click execute, and the above screen will be updated, as shown in the figure below.

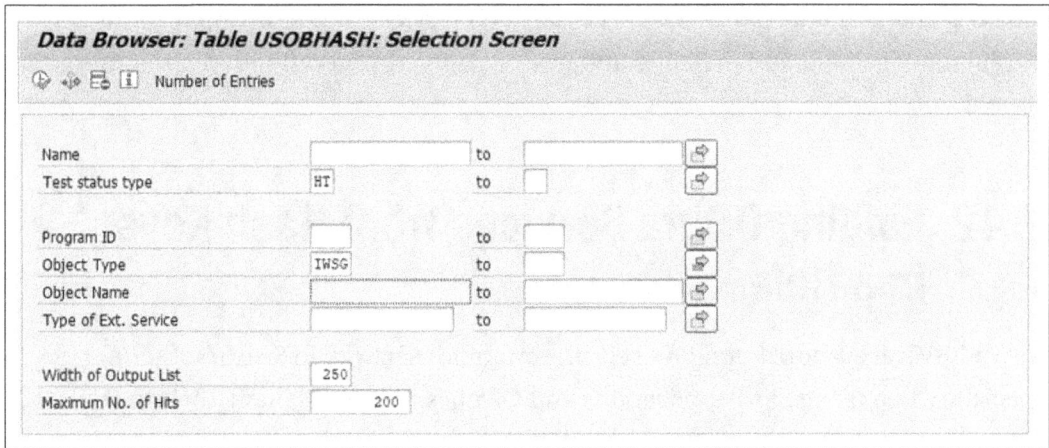

Figure 16-95. Table USOBHASH with the field values updated

Using the **execute** icon , in the above figure, displays the hash key and IWSG/IWSV components of OData services, as shown in the figure below.

827

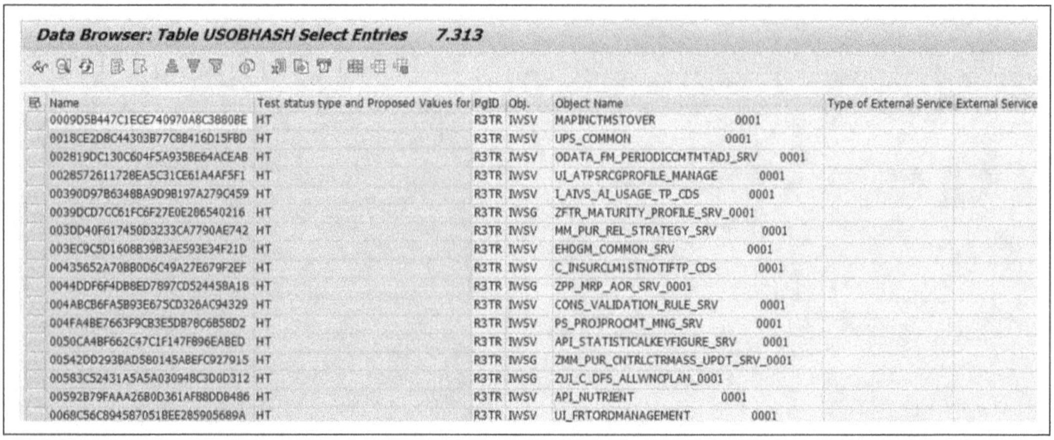

Data Browser: Table USOBHASH Select Entries 7.313

Name	Test status type and Proposed Values for	PgID	Obj.	Object Name	Type of External Service	External Service
0009D5B447C1ECE740970A8C3880BE	HT	R3TR	IWSV	MAPINCTMSTOVER 0001		
0018CE2D8C44303B77C8B416D15FBD	HT	R3TR	IWSV	UPS_COMMON 0001		
002819DC130C604F5A935BE64ACEAB	HT	R3TR	IWSV	ODATA_FM_PERIODICCMTMTADJ_SRV 0001		
002857261172BEA5C31CE61A4AF5F1	HT	R3TR	IWSV	UI_ATPSRCGPROFILE_MANAGE 0001		
00390D97B6348BA9D9B197A279C459	HT	R3TR	IWSV	I_AIVS_AI_USAGE_TP_CDS 0001		
0039DCD7CC61FC6F27E0E286540216	HT	R3TR	IWSG	ZFTR_MATURITY_PROFILE_SRV_0001		
003DD40F617450D3233CA7790AE742	HT	R3TR	IWSV	MM_PUR_REL_STRATEGY_SRV 0001		
003EC9C5D1608B39B3AE593E34F21D	HT	R3TR	IWSV	EHDGM_COMMON_SRV 0001		
00435652A70BB0D6C49A27E679F2EF	HT	R3TR	IWSV	C_INSURCLM1STNOTIFTP_CDS 0001		
0044DDF6F4DB8ED7897CD524458A18	HT	R3TR	IWSG	ZPP_MRP_AOR_SRV_0001		
004ABCB6FA5B93E675CD326AC94329	HT	R3TR	IWSV	CONS_VALIDATION_RULE_SRV 0001		
004FA4BE7663F9CB3E5DB78C6B58D2	HT	R3TR	IWSV	PS_PROJPROCMT_MNG_SRV 0001		
0050CA4BF662C47C1F147F896EABED	HT	R3TR	IWSV	API_STATISTICALKEYFIGURE_SRV 0001		
00542DD293BAD580145ABEFC927915	HT	R3TR	IWSG	ZMM_PUR_CNTRLCTRMASS_UPDT_SRV_0001		
00583C52431A5A5A030948C3D0D312	HT	R3TR	IWSG	ZUI_C_DFS_ALLWNCPLAN_0001		
00592B79FAAA2680D361AFB8DDB486	HT	R3TR	IWSV	API_NUTRIENT 0001		
0068C56C894587051BEE285905689A	HT	R3TR	IWSV	UI_FRTORDMANAGEMENT 0001		

Figure 16-96. *Table USOBHASH output details*

16.11.3 Summary

The USOBHASH table is a critical component of the S/4HANA authorization framework. It enables fine-grained control over access to web services and Fiori applications. Its efficient management and dynamic updates help ensure that only authorized users can access them.

16.12 Finding OData Services from Hash Keys in a Role

The S_SERVICE authorization object is important for security in SAP S/4HANA, especially when using Fiori applications and OData services. Its main job is to control who can access these services. It ensures users can only perform certain actions on services they are authorized to use, like reading, creating, updating, or deleting. Security administrators use this to check the integrity of SU24, improve performance, and resolve authorization issues. While it is not often edited, it serves as a useful reference for understanding changes in transaction security proposals.

16.12.1 Main Features and Use

- **Fiori App Security:** Fiori apps depend on OData services to exchange data with the back end. The S_SERVICE object is essential because it decides which apps a user can access and how much they can interact with the app's data.

- **Web Service Control:** This object controls access to Fiori apps and various web services in S/4HANA. It prevents unauthorized users from accessing sensitive data and functions available through these services.

- **Granular Access Control:** S_SERVICE allows administrators to control who can access specific data within a service. They can clearly define what actions a user can take on each data element.

- **Simplified Authorization Management:** S_SERVICE makes managing user access for Fiori and web services much easier. Instead of dealing with many complicated authorization objects in the traditional SAP GUI, S_SERVICE allows us to control who can access different services more simply.

16.12.2 Demo Examples

Finding the Hash Key IDs from the Role

Go to **SE16**, search for table **AGR_1251**, and hit the Enter key to get to the screen shown in the figure below.

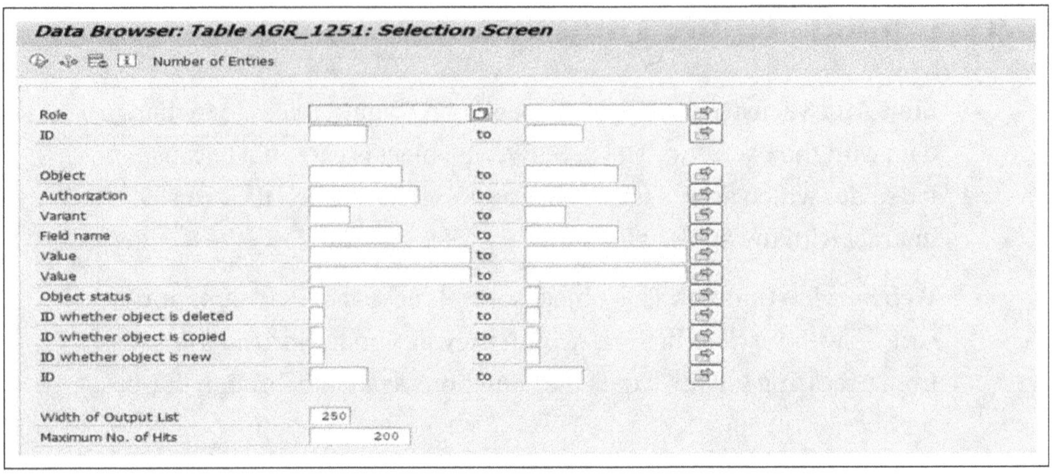

CHAPTER 16 ■ SAP FIORI REPORTS

Figure 16-97. Table AGR_1251 initial screen

Enter the role name **ZMU_TSK_FIN_AR_CST_ACTCLG:XXXX** and the object **S_SERVICE** as shown in the figure below.

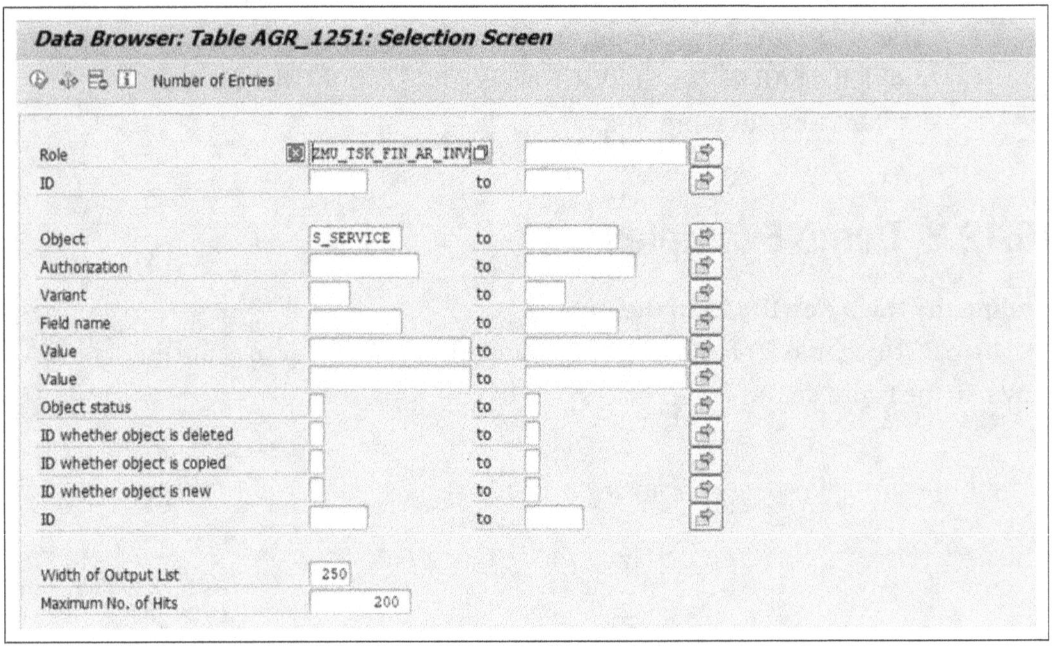

Figure 16-98. Table AGR_1251 with updated field values

Click the execute icon ⊕; the output is displayed in the figure below.

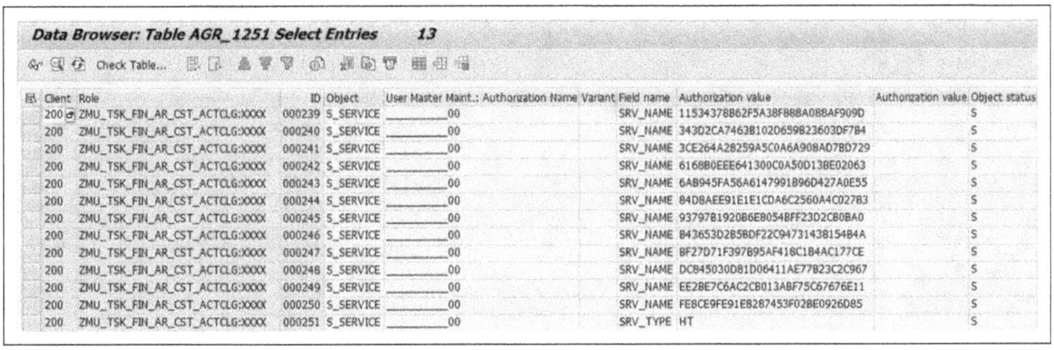

CHAPTER 16 SAP FIORI REPORTS

Figure 16-99. Hash key IDs within the role

The above figure displays the **hash keys** of the OData services within the role in the **Authorization value** column.

You can use these **hash key IDs** in the table **USOBHASH** to find the OData services within the role. The updated **USOBHASH** within **SE16** is as shown below.

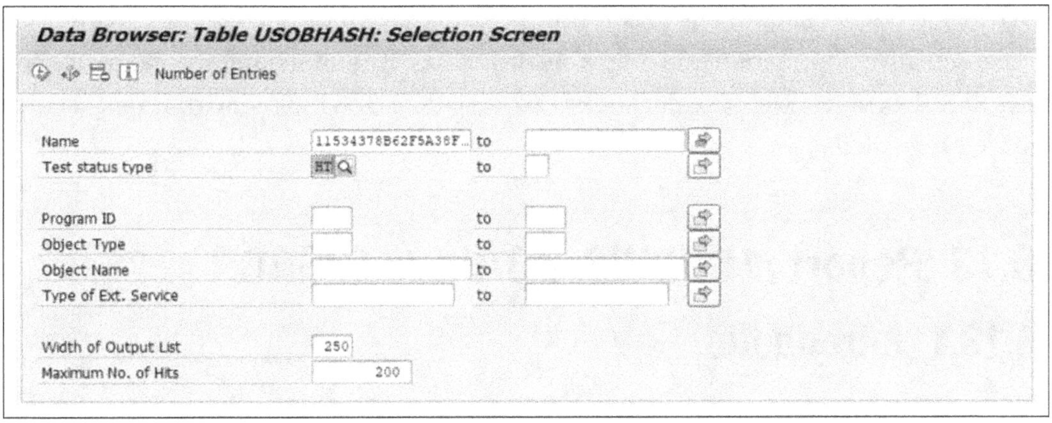

Figure 16-100. Table USOBHASH with hash key ID entered

Click the **execute** icon, and the output displays the OData service with the hash key, as shown in the figure below.

831

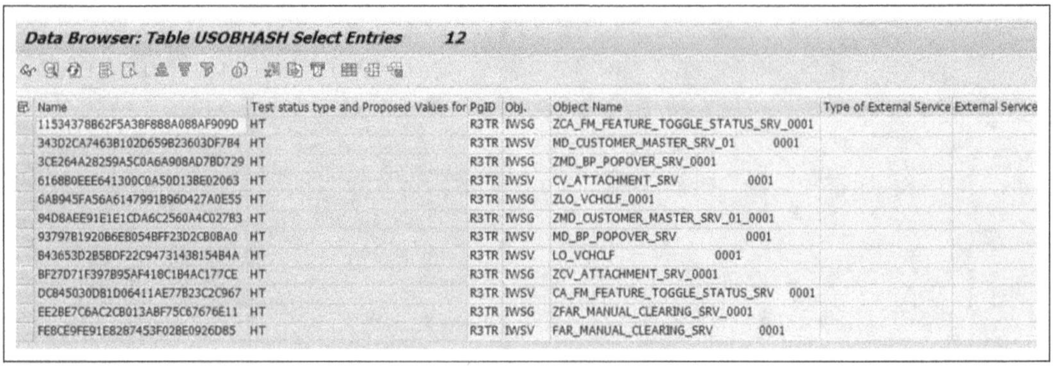

Name	Test status type and Proposed Values for	PgID	Obj.	Object Name	Type of External Service	External Service
11534378B62F5A38F888A088AF909D	HT	R3TR	IWSG	ZCA_FM_FEATURE_TOGGLE_STATUS_SRV_0001		
343D2CA7463B102D659B23603DF7B4	HT	R3TR	IWSV	MD_CUSTOMER_MASTER_SRV_01 0001		
3CE264A28259A5C0A6A908AD7BD729	HT	R3TR	IWSG	ZMD_BP_POPOVER_SRV_0001		
6168B0EEE641300C0A50D13BE02063	HT	R3TR	IWSV	CV_ATTACHMENT_SRV 0001		
6AB945FA56A6147991B960427A0E55	HT	R3TR	IWSG	ZLO_VCHCLF_0001		
84D8AEE91E1E1CDA6C2560A4C027B3	HT	R3TR	IWSG	ZMD_CUSTOMER_MASTER_SRV_01_0001		
93797B1920B6E8054BFF23D2CB08A0	HT	R3TR	IWSV	MD_BP_POPOVER_SRV 0001		
B43653D2B58DF22C94731438154B4A	HT	R3TR	IWSV	LO_VCHCLF 0001		
BF27D71F397B95AF418C1B4AC177CE	HT	R3TR	IWSG	ZCV_ATTACHMENT_SRV_0001		
DC845030D81D06411AE77B23C2C967	HT	R3TR	IWSV	CA_FM_FEATURE_TOGGLE_STATUS_SRV 0001		
EE2BE7C6AC2CB013ABF75C67676E11	HT	R3TR	IWSG	ZFAR_MANUAL_CLEARING_SRV_0001		
FE8CE9FE91E8287453F028E0926D85	HT	R3TR	IWSV	FAR_MANUAL_CLEARING_SRV 0001		

Figure 16-101. *The output of OData services is displayed*

16.12.3 Summary

The **S_SERVICE** object is crucial for securing Fiori applications and web services in S/4HANA. It offers a simple way to control who can access data and features, helping to protect sensitive information and follow security rules. By understanding and managing the S_SERVICE object well, organizations can keep their S/4HANA environment secure and well-regulated.

16.13 Report /1BCDWB/DB/UI2/STPGAC

16.13.1 Introduction

The report **/1BCDWB/DB/UI2/STPGAC** in SAP Fiori is a system-generated data browser view of the **UI2/STPGAC** table, which holds information about the relationship between roles, spaces, pages, and catalogs. It is primarily used to view and analyze **back-end data** related to Fiori Launchpad content structure. This report helps administrators check the relationship between spaces and pages and defines the number of pages within each space. This helps Fiori administrators understand how the user interface is organized for users.

16.13.2 Main Features and Use

The main features of this report are

- **Relation Between Spaces and Pages:** This report establishes the relationship between spaces and pages. It also lists how many pages within a space.

- **Space-Page Assignment Index:** This outlines the assignments of pages to spaces, their display order and priority, and the visibility settings, including default and hidden options.

- **Troubleshooting:** This section provides troubleshooting options for any missing tiles or pages, particularly when users encounter a blank space but are unable to locate any linked items.

16.13.3 Demo Examples

This report is executed by using transaction SE38 and entering the table name. It then opens a window to search for spaces **ZF_SP***, as shown in the figure below.

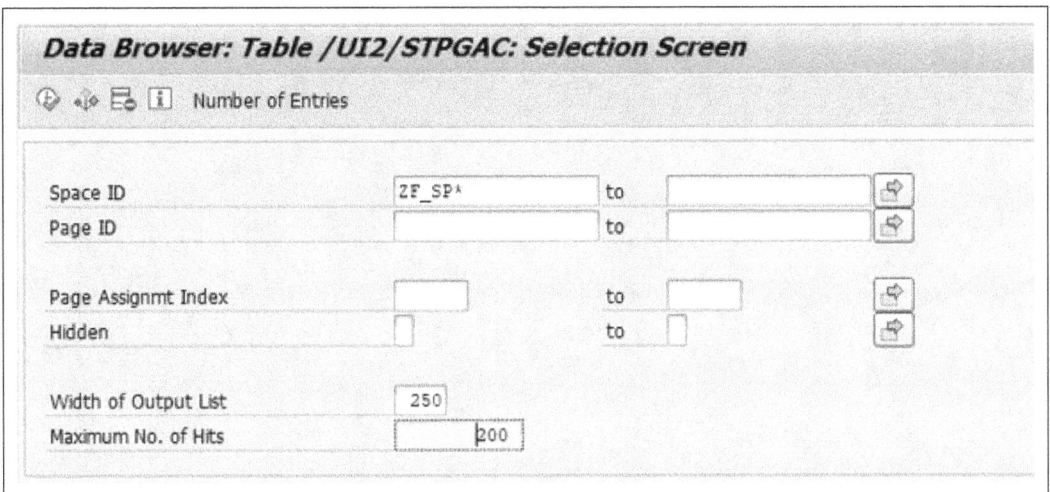

Figure 16-102. Table /UI2/STPGAC

The output is displayed in the figure below.

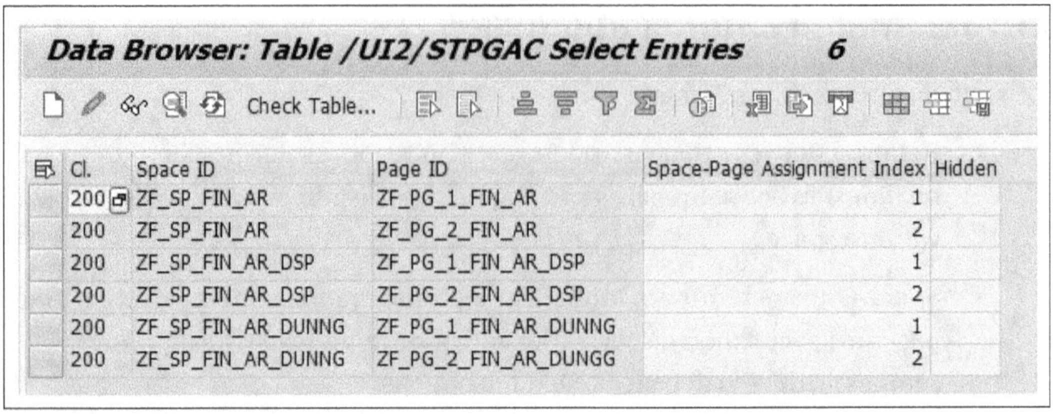

CHAPTER 16 SAP FIORI REPORTS

Cl.	Space ID	Page ID	Space-Page Assignment Index	Hidden
200	ZF_SP_FIN_AR	ZF_PG_1_FIN_AR	1	
200	ZF_SP_FIN_AR	ZF_PG_2_FIN_AR	2	
200	ZF_SP_FIN_AR_DSP	ZF_PG_1_FIN_AR_DSP	1	
200	ZF_SP_FIN_AR_DSP	ZF_PG_2_FIN_AR_DSP	2	
200	ZF_SP_FIN_AR_DUNNG	ZF_PG_1_FIN_AR_DUNNG	1	
200	ZF_SP_FIN_AR_DUNNG	ZF_PG_2_FIN_AR_DUNGG	2	

Figure 16-103. Table /UI2/STPGAC output with spaces and pages displayed

16.13.4 Summary

This tool is highly beneficial during implementation. It allows for quickly identifying relationships between spaces and pages, streamlining the process and enhancing efficiency.

Index

A

Access management, 807
Adaptive design principle, 3
Adapt UI
    activate new version, 739
    adapt filters, 734, 735
    admin user, 721
    app finder, 724
    app variant, 719, 720, 741, 743, 744
    attributes, 724, 725
    bank accounts app details, 725
    blank technical catalog, 746
    block find document, 734
    business role and assign catalog, 750
    business users and administrators, 717
    content, 728, 729
    content field, 732
    creation, 728
    custom business catalog, 723, 724
    defined, 717
    delete tab, 730
    display-only access, 727
    editor mode option, 718
    elements, 723
    features, 717, 718
    find document box, 733
    information window, 742
    logging, 721
    monitor bank accounts, 743
    new business catalog, 749
    new view updated, 738, 739
    organizations, 718
    rearrange toolbar content, 732
    remove option, 730
    rename tab, 731
    SAPUI5 Fiori app, 746
    save view details, 736, 737
    static tile system, 748
    sub-option, 738
    tabs, 729, 734
    target application, 722
    technical catalog details, 745
    testing and validation, 751, 752
    tile information, 747
    transaction /N/UI2/FLPCAT, 745
    transport, 752
    usage, 720
    user interface, 727
    user menu, 726
    version title, 740
    view name changed, 737
    view version, 740
    warning box, 735
    work zone screen, 727
Aggregate function, 64, 65
AGR_TCODES, 73, 74
Analytical apps, 20, 319–322
App Finder, 433
App recommendations analysis report
    business processes and system landscape, 11
    criteria, 59
    data selection, 112, 113
    detail and list views, 106–108

INDEX

App recommendations analysis report (*cont.*)
- determine apps, 63
- explore, 63, 64
- factors, 62
- front-end and back-end system profiles, 81–85
- HANA DB system profiles, 85
- log in, 87
  - create new analysis screen, 89
  - defining analysis, 101–103
  - results and analysis, 104, 105
  - type of analysis, 87–89
  - update system profile, 94–101
  - usage profile, 89–94
- operate and update, 65
- output data, 113, 114
- plan phase, 64
- prerequisites, 65, 66
- relevance score, 109–111
- report lists, 59
- results, 111–118
- set up and configuration, 64
- system readiness status, 108
- usage profile
  - file name, 75
  - GRC, 76–80
  - manual option, 75
  - SE16 and AGR_TCODES, 73–75
  - transaction code ST03/ST03N, 67–72

App support tool
- application types, 652
- authorization errors, 671–683
- automatically set up, 657
- clearing cache, 696, 697
- defined, 652
- features, 653
- 500 error, 698
- manual process
  - admin user, 663–665
  - end user, 661, 662
  - OData service, 657, 658
  - SICF service, 659–661
- missing business catalog, 695
- missing target mapping, 690–692
- OData services, 697, 698
- plugin, 665–671
- prerequisites
  - client site, 655
  - manual set up, 655, 656
  - task list, 655
- problems, 651
- reference lost, 697
- services missing, 692–695
- STAUTHTRACE, 684, 686
- STUSERTRACE, 687–690
- SU53, 683, 684
- troubleshooting, 653, 654
- versions, 653

App variants
- actions, 744
- advantages, 719
- creation, 719, 720, 744
- customizations, 717
- features, 719
- saving, 741
- tile information, 742

Authorization errors, 676
- app information, 675, 680, 681
- data filer set, 682
- displaying errors, 675
- download logs, 676, 678, 679
- encountered, 672

front-end server, 676, 681, 682
input field parameters, 673
log file details, 680
options, 675
user access, 671

B

Back-end server (BES), 1, 8, 12, 99, 100, 137
Bluefield implementation
    benefits, 129, 130
    challenges, 130
    characteristics, 128
    considerations, 128, 130
    defined, 127
    migration approach, 127
    reviewing, 130
    steps, 128, 129
Brownfield implementation
    approach, 123
    benefits, 125
    challenges, 126
    characteristics, 124
    considerations, 124, 126
    reviewing, 126
    S/4HANA, 123
    steps, 124, 125
Browser-based methods, 651
Business catalog (BC), 23, 42, 316, 340, 341, 403, 415–419, 517, 521, 605–607, 611, 620, 634–638, 646, 647, 695, 696
Business client, 18, 19
Business groups, 563, 564, 567, 568
Business roles (BR), 24, 25, 44
Business technology platform (BTP), 10

C

Caching mechanism, 696
Catalogs
    adding reference, 453
    business roles, 341
    change title, 447
    content, 446
    copy, 444
    default, 407
    defined, 22, 339
    delete, 446
    function, 336
    groups, 23, 24
    GUI, 337
    intents, 345
    open in designer, 447
    PFCG, 449
    procurement manager, 336
    recommendations, 346
    remove role, 451, 452
    role assignment, 449–451
    role view, 448, 449
    SAP-delivered, 455, 456
    SAP Fiori Launchpad, 337–339
    security and compliance, 336
    services, 447, 448
    show usage in roles, 445
    sub-tabs, 407–410
    target mapping, 342–344
    technical objects, 347
    tile, 342
    transaction codes, 336
    types, 23
    user-centric approach, 335
Central hub deployment, 142, 153, 171, 172, 352
    administrators, 138

INDEX

Central hub deployment (*cont.*)
    advantages, 138, 139, 141, 145, 151
    authentication, 137
    back-end server, 137
    components requirement, 139
    configuration, 156, 157
    defined, 137
    description, 145
    disadvantages, 141, 146, 151
    environments, 138
    features, 150, 151
    front-end server, 137
    gateway, 137, 145
    implementation, 138
    schematic, 140
    system alias, 154
Coherent design system, 4
Configuration, SAP Fiori
    embedded deployment, 166, 168
    logon and logoff screens
        configuration changes, 298
        confirmation box, 296, 297
        default host, 294
        end user, 291, 292
        ICF service, 293
        page tab, 295
        security alerts/legal notices, 291
        showing path, 294
        URL details, 295, 296
        user redirected, 298, 299
        workbench request transport, 297
    logon screen with company
        logo, 300–306
    manual method
        deployment, 170, 171
        execution, 174, 175
        ICF services, 173
        OData V2 services, 173
        OData V4 services, 173
        prerequisites, 169, 170
        SPRO transaction code,
            168, 169
        task lists, 172, 173
    prerequisites, 166, 167
    SAP_ESH_INITIAL_SETUP_WRK_
        CLIENT, 195–209
    SAP_FIORI_CONTENT_
        ACTIVATION, 248–279
    SAP_FIORI_FCM_CONTENT_
        ACTIVATION, 279–290
    SAP_FIORI_FOUNDATION_
        S4, 213–238
    SAP_GATEWAY_ACTIVATE_ODATA_
        SERV, 242–248
    SAP_GW_FIORI_ERP_ONE_CLNT_
        SETUP, 176–194
    setup, 165
    STC02 transaction code, 167
    /UI2/FLP_HEALTH_CHECKS, 238–241
    /UIF/SCHEDULE_LREP_JOB, 209–213
Converting groups to pages, 567
Custom apps, 21, 330, 331
    custom-developed object, 585
    Fiori Launchpad Designer
        tool, 586
    SAP transaction, 585
    SAPUI5, 613–621
    technical catalogs, 586
    transaction code, 585, 609–612
    /UI2/FLPAM, 586–621
    /UI2/FLPD_CUST, 622–648
Custom business role (CBR), 462, 489–492
Custom transaction code
    business catalog, 611
    business role, 611, 612
    prerequisite, 609

semantic object, 609
technical catalog, 609, 610
testing and validation, 612

D

Data migration, 63
Deep copy, 348–350
Deployment
    architecture, 132–136
    central hub, 137–141
    gateway, 144–146
    SAP NetWeaver Gateway, 142, 143
    S/4HANA schematic, 153
Deprecated apps, 712

E

Embedded deployment, 142, 153, 166, 170, 171, 176, 213, 352
    advantages, 136, 144
    authorizations, 133
    components, 133–135
    configuration, 155
    defined, 132
    description, 144
    disadvantages, 136, 144
    features, 134
    gateway, 144
    schematics, 135
    security mechanisms, 132
    system alias, 154
    task lists, 168
Embedded system, 81, 82, 84
Enterprise resource planning (ERP), 1
Enterprise search (ESH), 195
Extended warehouse management (EWM), 133

F

Facet filter
    adaptation mode, 374
    app type, 367
    attributes, 366, 368
    columns, 370
    criteria, 364
    option, 372, 373
    SAPUI5 Fiori apps, 368
    settings, 369, 370
    sorting and grouping, 371, 372
    spreadsheet export, 373, 374
    switching, 365, 366
    technical catalog ID, 366
Factsheet apps, 20
    databases, 324
    defined, 322
    deployment, 324
    features, 322–324
    HANA database, 322
    manual method, 325, 326
    task list, 326, 327
F0763A custom app
    business catalog, 646
    business role, 647, 648
    dynamic tile, 640–643, 649
    prerequisite, 639
    semantic object, 639–646
    testing and validation, 648
Fiori app F1366A, 743
Fiori launchpad checks (FLC), 791
Fiori launchpad (FLP), 14, 15, 18, 138
Fiori launchpad intent analysis, 778
Fiori launchpad texts (FLT), 785
Fiori role test matrix, 754
FLP Content Manager
    activation services, 424, 425

FLP Content Manager (*cont.*)
    administrators, 404, 406
    application groups, 437
    business catalog, 403, 417
    business role update, 437
    catalogs, 407–410
    confirmation, 435, 439
    creating catalog window, 416, 417
    custom business catalog, 434–436
    custom business role, 431
    customizing transport requests, 424, 436
    features, 404, 405
    functionalities, 406, 443–454
    ICF services, 426
    initial screen, 406
    IWSG/IWSV component, 430
    OData services, 425
    options, 424
    organizational values, 430
    PFCG, 426–432, 441
    recommendations, 455–457
    removal apps, 435
    roles, 412, 413
    screen parts, 419
    search apps, 421–426
    semantic object and action, 423
    symbols, 438
    technical catalog, 413–416, 420, 421
    test user, 443
    tiles/target mappings, 410–412
    transport details, 418
    /UI2/FLPCM_CUST transaction code, 416
    unmaintained authorization objects, 431
    updated business role, 441, 442
    validation, testing and verification, 432–434
Front-end server (FES), 1, 8, 12, 97–99, 137

G

Gateway, 12, 143, 170
    active window, 149, 150
    business suite enablement service, 809, 810, 816
    deployment, 144–146
    service groups metadata, 811, 815, 816
    task list, 146, 147
    transaction code, 147–149
    verification, 193, 194
    See also SAP NetWeaver Gateway
Gateway errors, 676
Governance, risk and compliance (GRC)
    action usage, 78–80
    GRACACTUSAGE table, 76–78
GRACACTUSAGE, 76–78
Graphical user interface (GUI), 1, 328–330, 337
Greenfield implementation
    advantage, 119, 122
    approach, 120
    challenges, 122
    characteristics, 120
    considerations, 120, 122
    reviewing, 123
    steps, 121
Groups, 23, 24
    advantages, 459
    business catalog, 341, 546
    challenges, 460
    deprecation, 461

deselection, 549
display usages, 547, 548, 566
functional requirements, 459
methods, 569
page sections, 572, 573
PFCG, 546
predefined structures, 457
pre-delivered/self-defined, 457
role assignment, 547
search criteria, 569
selection criteria, 570
tile IDs and descriptions, 571, 572
window updates, 571
GUI apps, 21

H

HANA DB system profiles, 85, 101
Hask keys, 825
Hybrid implementation approach, 127

I, J

Impact analysis, upgrade, 60
    benefits, 701
    defined, 699
    execution
        available apps, 713, 714
        deprecated apps, 712
        input data file, 706
        loading file, 709
        results, 710
        running tool, 707, 708
        S/4HANA 2020, 706, 707
        successor apps, 712, 713
        unavailable apps, 711
        unknown apps, 714, 715

    features, 700, 701
    prerequisite
        checking and verification, 704
        documentation and
            communication, 703
        execute and monitor, 703
        outcome, 703
        planning, 703
        prepare your system, 702
        recommendations, 703
        results, 702
        running tool, 702
        target system, 702
    process steps
        analyze and plan
            remediation, 705
        documentation and
            communication, 705
        execution, 705
        preparation, 704
        running, 704
        testing, 705
        tool configuration, 704
    steps, 699
    usage, 701, 702
Intent, 25, 345
Intent-based navigation, 344
Internet communication
    framework (ICF), 26, 173, 258
Internet communication manager (ICM),
    169, 183, 258

K

Key performance indicators (KPIs), 7, 15,
    20, 319, 320, 754
Key user adaptation, 717

L

Launchpad catalog, 812, 813
Launchpad content aggregator, 754, 755, 771
Launchpad group, 813, 814
Launchpad space, 814, 815
Lighthouse scenarios, 11
Links, 471–474
Logical groups, 464
Logon screen with company logo
  backup, 303
  branding and theming, 300
  clients/tenants, 300
  custom logo, 306
  images, 302, 304
  initial screen, 300
  modifications, 300
  replacement image selection, 305
  SE80 transaction code, 301

M

Mass maintenance tool, 348
My Home
  advanced options, 555
  apps, 555, 556
  features, 550
  goals, 550
  insights, 556
  insights cards, 554
  insights tiles, 554
  layout, 554
  pages, 554
  sections, 551
  settings, 553–555
  space/page ID description, 552

N

NetWeaver business client (NWBC), 78

O

OData services, 12, 26, 143, 186, 225, 226, 242, 245, 262, 475–477, 657, 658, 696–698, 807, 810, 812, 832
Open Data Protocol (OData), 26, 257

P, Q

Pages, 24, 576
  adding another pages, 533, 534
  additional, 517–524
  advantages, 468, 469
  assign apps, 504
  background, 564–567
  best practices, 504
  business catalogs, 564, 565
  business groups, 563
  content, 523
  conversion, 582, 583
  converting existing groups, 567, 568
  creating launchpad from groups, 568–576
  creating sections, 579–581
  creation, 495, 496, 564
  custom, 497
  defined, 467
  display usages, 565
  empty content, 498
  high-level steps, 556–560
  Id selection, 500, 501
  information, 496, 497
  input screen, 499
  issues, 500
  layout, 456, 463, 516, 567
  maintenance, 495

manage launchpad spaces, 498, 503
prerequisites, 475-477, 567
preview, 524
pull-down option, 553
roles, 467
SAP Fiori Launchpad, 475, 568
schematic, 474
testing and validation, 525
updation, 502, 503, 524
user experience, 470
workspace, 522, 552
See also Spaces
Personalization, 16-18
Plugin configuration
  change view, 668
  cross-client, 665
  display information, 665, 666
  launchpad property, 666
  new entries, 667
  screen updates, 670
  steps, 665

R

Readiness, 61, 62, 104, 111
Readiness check 2.0, 11
Reference lost, 697
Relevance, 61, 62, 104, 111
  score, 109-111
Remote function calls (RFCs), 8, 13
Reporting, 754
  /1BCDWB/DB/UI2/STPGAC,
    561, 832-834
  concepts, 753
  custom business catalogs, 754
  OData services, 828-832
  RSUSR_START_APPL, 820-824
  technical analysis, 753

tools, 754
USOBHASH table, 825-828
See also Transaction code
RSUSR_START_APPL report
  application type, 823
  concept, 820
  error role, 824
  features, 821
  initial screen, 822
  output, 822
  PFCG screen, 824
  startable transaction, 823
Runtime errors, 676, 683

S

SAP_ESH_INITIAL_SETUP_WRK_CLIENT
  background job completed, 207
  background mode, 205, 206
  client configuration, 197, 204
  connectors, 198-204
  consistency check, 208, 209
  consolidation task, 204
  enterprise search, 195
  execution, 196, 197
  features, 195, 196
  final status, 204, 205
  ICF services, 197
  SAPAPPLH model, 199, 202
  SAPScript replication, 204
  software components, 203
  subtask list, 197
  system consistency, 196
SAP Fiori, 8
See also S/4HANA
  app recommendations (*see* App
    recommendations
    analysis report)

INDEX

SAP Fiori (*cont.*)
  business suite, 8
  clients, 18, 19
  defined, 1
  design principles, 2–4
  features, 4–7
  prerequisites, 11–13
  user experience, 1, 2
SAP Fiori apps
  advantages, 333
  analytical apps, 319–322
  architecture, 308
  characteristics, 307
  comparison, 331, 332
  custom, 330, 331
  defined, 19, 307
  disadvantages, 333
  examples, 22
  factsheet apps, 322–327
  GUI, 328–330
  implementation, 308
  transactional apps, 309–319
  types, 19–21, 309
SAP Fiori Apps Reference Library
  accessing, 32
  aggregate option, 54
  apps list, 33
  attributes, 34
  benefits, 31, 32
  browser-based user interface, 29
  budget and finance, 46
  business catalog, 42
  business role, 46, 47
  column display settings, 48
  concept, 30
  configuration, 40, 41
  corrected apps, 56
  current version, unavailable apps, 55
  details, 30, 31
  downloaded details, 51, 57
  downloading window selection, 57
  exploration, 33–37
  extended apps selection, 41, 42
  features, 31, 32
  filtered data displayed, 59
  implementation information, 39
  information, 61, 62
  information, tabular format, 38
  initial screen, 10, 30, 86
  installation, 39, 40
  line of business, 45, 46
  listing total of 15,121 apps, 53
  list view
    categories, 49
    desired output, 49, 50
    vs. detail view, 48
    downloaded details, 51
  object symbols, 44
  overview, 29
  post incoming payments, 47
  product features, 38, 39
  related apps, 42, 43
  relevance and readiness, 61
  removed downloading, unavailable apps, 55
  required app details, 56
  review app details, 49
  search apps, 45
  search filters and grouping options, 10
  select all apps, 52, 53
  selected and downloaded screen, 53
  selection screen, 52
  tools, 59, 60
  transaction app F3893, 36, 37
  transaction codes, 58
  transaction code VA01, 34, 35

INDEX

usage, 32, 33
variants, 36
verification, 43
window's details, 50
SAP_FIORI_CONTENT_ACTIVATION
    App Finder, 274, 275
    authorization, 252, 253, 270, 271
    business roles, 248, 250–253
    check relevant services, 254, 255
    completed task, 266
    content, 254
    development issues, 249
    entered list, business roles, 261
    FLP content activation, 261, 262
    foreground mode, 267, 268
    ICF services, 258, 259
    insert user IDs, 278
    multiple business roles, 276, 277
    OData services, 262
    OData V2 services, 255, 256
    OData V4 services, 257
    PFCG, 249
    pre-configured roles, 249
    prefix, 263, 264
    prerequisite, 250
    rapid activation, 248
    resources, 278
    sandbox/development system, 250
    spaces and pages, 273
    STC01 transaction code, 260, 261
    test user ID, 264–266
    tiles, 274
    user assignment, 268
    user logged in, 272, 273
    validation, 272
    verification, 269–272
SAP_FIORI_FCM_CONTENT_
    ACTIVATION
    authorization, 280, 281
    business role generated, 288
    custom business role, 282
    execution, 284–286
    FLP content activation, 282, 283
    GUI script, 279
    input screen, 282
    prerequisite, 280, 281
    production environments, 279
    role-naming convention, 279
    single role, 283
    STC01 transaction code, 281
    testing access, 289
    test user, 288–290
    update role menu (PFCG), 283
    validation, 287, 288
SAP_FIORI_FOUNDATION_S4
    activation status, 234, 235
    app support, 238
    background job, 233, 234
    background mode, 229–232
    breakpoint error, 232
    completed task and subtask list, 228, 229
    customizing request, 216, 228
    delete breakpoint option, 233
    dependency, 214
    FLP long texts, 219
    FLP plugin, 223, 224
    foundation roles, 226–228, 235, 236
    generic roles, 213
    help settings, 224
    HTTP services, 216, 226
    navigation, 222
    notification, 222
    OData services, 225, 226
    page cache synchronization, 219
    rapid activation, 214

INDEX

SAP_FIORI_FOUNDATION_S4 (*cont.*)
    SAP menu, 220, 221
    service groups, 226
    SICF services, 217, 218
    spaces and pages, 223, 237
    status mode, 231
    STC01 transaction code, 215, 216
    subtask list, 216
    system alias, 219–221
    UI2 cache invalidation, 220
    UI5 apps, 223
    URL working, 237
    workbench request, 216, 228
SAP 4th Generation, 1
SAP_GATEWAY_ACTIVATE_ODATA_SERV
    co-deployment, 243, 244
    description, 242
    final screen, 246
    foreground mode, 246
    input screen, 243
    OData services, 242, 245–247
    prerequisites, 242
    TADIR table, 244, 245
SAP_GW_FIORI_ERP_ONE_CLNT_SETUP
    adding launchpad/launchpad designer transactions, 185
    batch queries, 181
    cache buster, 183
    catalog types, 185
    customizing requests, 180, 186
    embedded deployments, 176
    execution, task listing, 187–191
    features, 176, 177
    Fiori Content Manager, 185
    gateway activation, 180
    gateway OData services, 181, 182
    HTTP allowlist, 184
    HTTP services, 180, 182, 183, 186
    metadata cache, 181
    OData metadata cache, 181
    OData services, 186
    parameters, 187
    processing mode, 186
    profile parameter, HTTPS, 183
    SAPUI5 app, 184
    SAP web dispatcher, 180
    scheduled job, SAPUI5 app, 184
    settings, 176
    single-client environment, 176
    STC01 transaction code, 178, 179
    steps, 177
    system alias, 181, 184
    /UI2/V_ALIASMAP table, 192
    /UI2/VC_SYSALIAS table, 191, 192
    verification, 191–194
    workbench request, 179, 185
SAP landscape transformation (SLT), 130
SAP NetWeaver, 11
SAP NetWeaver Gateway, 153
    defined, 142
    features, 143
    interfaces, 142
SAPUI5 app
    business catalog, 620
    business role, 621
    dynamic tile, 617, 619
    parameter fields, 619
    prerequisite, 613
    semantic object, 613–620
    static tile, 616
    technical catalog, 614, 615
    testing and validation, 621
SAPUI5 Fiori app, 746
Sections
    adding apps, 508
    advantages, 470, 471

INDEX

creation, 505
defined, 470
drag-and-drop method, 509
final output, 513
first title, 505
format options, 508, 509
order changed, 506
page changes, 513
preview, 514
second title, 506
visualization, 509, 510, 512
wide tile, 510, 511
Self-service tool, 30, 61
Service information and configuration framework (SICF), 26
S/4HANA
defined, 1
deployment, 8, 153
features, 8, 9
integration, 4
S/4HANA 2005 Cloud, 460
S/4HANA 2020, 356, 460
Single sign-on (SSO), 15, 169
SNP Bluefield, 130
Soft copy, 350–352
Software as a service (SaaS), 7
Software development kits (SDKs), 6
Sort priority number values, 539–543
Spaces, 24
admin user, 482
advantages, 464–466
assignment, 487, 576, 578
assign user ID, 537
business objects, 480, 481
business role, 462, 488, 489
creating new roles, 480
creation, 526, 576, 577
cross-client, 477
defined, 463
details, 486, 519
empty with no data, 485
final output, 531
and groups, 546–549
information, 483, 484, 526
input details, 528
input screen, 483
merge, 544, 545
navigation bar, 486
OData services
  assignment roles, 476
  launchpad, 477
  manual activation, 476
  task list, 475, 476
order, 538, 539
and page information, 529
pages layout, 463
page visibility, 530
parameters, 478
PFCG, 487–489
priority, 540–542
role assignment, 532, 537
and roles, 565
SAP Fiori Launchpad, 475
schematic, 474
SE09 transaction code, 536
sorting, 539–543
testing and validation, 514–516, 537, 538
/UI2/FLPCM_CUST, 489–495
updated details, 527
user menu, 477–479
utilization, 467
work profile, 456
workspace, 535, 536
STAUTHTRACE, 684–687

847

INDEX

ST03/ST03N transaction code
    CSV format, 72
    downloaded data information, 71
    download option, 70
    filtered data, 71
    filtered data generated file, 72
    month option, 67, 68
    profile option, 68
    spreadsheet, 69
    standard profile, 68, 69
    usage data, 70
    workload monitor, 67
STUSERTRACE, 687–690
SUIM transaction code
    benefits, 800
    defined, 798
    features
        authorization analysis, 799
        role analysis, 799
        user analysis, 799
    initial screen, 801
    options, 802
    role menu, 807–814
    roles tab, 801
    single roles with authorization data, 802–807
    startable applications, 815–817
SU53 transaction code
    authorization failures, 587
    business catalog, 605–607
    cross-client, 592
    custom role, 607, 608
    export option, 604
    GUI, 588, 589
    package and transport details, 597
    SAP-delivered objects, 591
    SAP GUI, 587
    semantic action, 599
    semantic objects, 590–593, 598
    static tile, 601, 605
    target application fields, 602, 603
    technical catalog, 593–605
    testing and validation, 608
    tile icon, 602
System alias, 219
    backend catalog, 219
    best practices, 157
    central hub deployment, 154, 156, 157
    concept, 154
    embedded deployment, 154
    Fiori Launchpad, 184
    FIORI_MENU, 221
    local, 181
    LOCAL_TGW, 220, 221
    S4FIN and S4SD, 220
    tables, 159–162
    transaction codes, 158
System readiness status report, 104, 105, 108

T

Target mapping, 421, 453, 630, 636, 690–692
    application types, 343
    authorization and role mapping, 344
    business catalog, 637
    configuration, 644
    configuration data, 315
    custom tile, 636
    defined, 25, 26, 342, 410, 453
    device-specific settings, 344
    empty page, 644
    field values, 632, 633
    icon, 631
    ID, 344

INDEX

intent-based navigation, 344
page, 631
parameters, 343
semantic action, 343
semantic object, 343
static tile, 634
sub-tabs, 411, 412
tabular format, 646
tile settings, 586, 630
Technical catalog (TC), 23, 339, 340, 413–416, 420, 421, 586, 593–605, 609, 610, 614, 615, 623–634, 744, 745, 749
    acceptable warning, 382
    columns, 358
    complete details, 380
    copy, 384
    creation, 376, 377
    data selection, 360
    delete, 395–397
    description details, 378
    elements, 348
    example, 376
    FBV3 app, 390, 391
    filter, 359
    final screen, 389
    Fiori app F0731A, 387
    GUI app, 386, 387
    initial screen, 377
    input screen, 382
    Launchpad App Descriptor Items, 361–363
    messages, 385
    naming convention, 375, 376
    package, 378, 379
    prerequisite, 352
    remove apps, 393–395
    search, 380, 381, 384
    settings, 357, 358
    sorting and grouping, 358, 359
    standard, 381
    tiles, 363
    transaction code, 352, 363, 364
    transport information, 383
    types, 383
    updation, 390–392
    validation, 398, 399
    verification, 399–401
    warning message, 388
Tiles, 342, 363
    administrators, 453
    custom, 605
    groups, 566
    insights, 554
    pages, 524
    preferred format, 509
    role content, 454, 455
    sections, 580
    semantic objects, 604
    and target mapping, 25
    types, 25
Transactional apps, 20
    categories, 311
    configuration, 313, 314
    defined, 309
    extensibility, 318
    F4700, 311
    features, 310
    implementation, 310, 311
    installation, 312, 313
    product features, 311
    SAP Fiori Launchpad, 314–317
    SAP notes, 312
    support, 318, 319
    technical configuration, 314
Transaction-based methods, 651

INDEX

Transaction code
   /IWFND/IWF_ACTIVATE, 149
   /IWFND/MAINT_SERVICE, 154
   /IWFND/ROUTING, 158
   MM_APP, 352, 353
   PFCG, 43
   SE16, 73
   SM30, 159
   SPRO, 147-149
   ST03/ST03N, 67-72
   SUIM, 798-818
   /UI2/CUST, 796-798
   /UI2/FLC, 791-796
   /UI2/FLIA, 778-785
   /UI2/FLP_ADMIN_UI, 818, 819
   /UI2/FLPAM, 353-364
   /UI2/FLPCA, 754-776
   /UI2/FLT, 785-791
   /UI2/GW_SYS_ALIAS, 158
   /UI2/ROUTING, 158
   /UI2/RSP_LIST, 776-778
   /UI2/V_SYSALIAS, 154
   VA01, 34-36
Transportation management (TM), 133

U, V, W, X, Y

/UI2/CUST transaction code
   features, 797
   initial screen, 798
   SPRO-type, 796, 798
   web-based interface, 798
/UI2/FLC transaction code
   check role selection, 795
   components, 793
   features, 791, 792
   filters, 791
   initial screen, 794
   output displayed, 796
   system aliases and client-dependent settings, 791
/UI2/FLIA transaction code
   adding information, 780
   business catalogs, 781, 782
   configuration, 782, 783
   content analysis, 779
   features, 778, 779
   input screen, 779
   intents, 778, 779, 784
   lauchpad intent analysis, 781
   message column, 783
   PFCG, 778
/UI2/FLP_ADMIN_UI transaction code, 818, 819
/UI2/FLPCA transaction code
   administrators, 756
   business role information, 757
   change layout option, 763-765, 768-773
   choose layout option, 773, 774
   data fields, 767
   defined, 754
   display columns, 766
   display successor transactions, 762, 763
   execution, 757-775
   exported spreadsheet, 775
   exporting, 761
   initial input screen, 756
   output screen, 757-760
   prerequisite, 755
   role filter, 756
   ROLE_LAYOUT applied, 775
   tabular format, 756

INDEX

test matrix, 755
/UI2/FLPCM_CUST transaction code, 489–495
/UI2/FLP_HEALTH_CHECKS, 238–241
/UI2/FLPM_CUST transaction code, 404
/UI2/FLT transaction code
    catalog ID, 787, 788
    concepts, 785
    condition criteria, 789
    custom business catalog, 790, 791
    features, 785, 786
    input screen, 787
    text filter search option, 790
    tile information, 789
    user TESTSPG output, 790
/UI2/RSP_LIST transaction code
    concepts, 776
    entered role name, 777
    features, 776
    input screen, 777
    output, 777
/UIF/SCHEDULE_LREP_JOB, 209–213
User information system, 817
USOBHASH table, 825–828

Z

ZPARAM_REP transaction
    business catalog, 634–638
    prerequisite, 622
    semantic action, 627, 628
    static tile, 625, 626, 629
    technical catalog, 623–634
    testing and validation, 638, 639
    tile template, 624
    transport request, 624

GPSR Compliance

The European Union's (EU) General Product Safety Regulation (GPSR) is a set of rules that requires consumer products to be safe and our obligations to ensure this.

If you have any concerns about our products, you can contact us on

ProductSafety@springernature.com

In case Publisher is established outside the EU, the EU authorized representative is:

Springer Nature Customer Service Center GmbH
Europaplatz 3
69115 Heidelberg, Germany

www.ingramcontent.com/pod-product-compliance
Lightning Source LLC
LaVergne TN
LVHW080308260326
834688LV00038B/1010